Intervention and Reflection
BASIC ISSUES IN MEDICAL ETHICS
Fifth Edition

Intervention and Reflection
BASIC ISSUES IN MEDICAL ETHICS
Fifth Edition

Ronald Munson

University of Missouri–St. Louis

With the Assistance of
Christopher A. Hoffman

Wadsworth Publishing Company
I⊤P™ An International Thomson Publishing Company

Belmont • Albany • Bonn • Boston • Cincinnati • Detroit • London • Madrid • Melbourne
Mexico City • New York • Paris • San Francisco • Singapore • Tokyo • Toronto • Washington

Philosophy Editor: Tammy Goldfeld

Editorial Assistant: Kelly Zavislak

Production: Cecile Joyner/The Cooper Company

Print Buyer: Barbara Britton

Permissions Editor: Robert Kauser

Interior Designers: Katie Michels and John Edeen

Copy Editor: Lura Harrison

Cover Design: Craig Hansen

Compositor: G&S Typesetters

Printer: Quebecor Printing/Fairfield

*This text is printed on
acid-free recycled paper.*

For more information, contact Wadsworth Publishing Company:

Wadsworth Publishing Company
10 Davis Drive
Belmont, California 94002, USA

International Thomson Publishing Europe
Berkshire House 168-173
High Holborn
London, WC1V 7AA, England

Thomas Nelson Australia
102 Dodds Street
South Melbourne 3205
Victoria, Australia

Nelson Canada
1120 Birchmount Road
Scarborough, Ontario
Canada M1K 5G4

International Thomson Editores
Campos Eliseos 385, Piso 7
Col. Polanco
11560 México D.F. México

International Thomson Publishing GmbH
Königswinterer Strasse 418
53227 Bonn, Germany

International Thomson Publishing Asia
221 Henderson Road
#05-10 Henderson Building
Singapore 0315

International Thomson Publishing Japan
Hirakawacho Kyowa Building, 3F
2-2-1 Hirakawacho
Chiyoda-ku, Tokyo 102, Japan

Library of Congress Cataloging-in-Publication Data

Intervention and reflection : basic issues in medical ethics /
  [selected by] Ronald Munson ; with the assistance of Christopher A. Hoffman. — 5th ed.
     p.   cm.
  Includes bibliographical references.
  ISBN 0-534-25488-8
  1. Medical ethics.   I. Munson, Ronald, 1939– .   II. Hoffman, Christopher A.
  [DNLM: 1. Ethics, Medical—collected works.   2. Ethics, Medical—problems.   W 50 I618 1995]
R724.I57 1995
174'.2—dc20
DNLM/DLC
for Library of Congress   95-15103

To Miriam
"Giver of bright rings"

Ronald Munson is Professor of the Philosophy of Science and Medicine at the University of Missouri–St. Louis. He received his Ph.D. from Columbia University and was a Postdoctoral Fellow in Biology at Harvard University. He has been a Visiting Professor at the University of California, San Diego, and the Harvard Medical School.

His books include *Reasoning in Medicine* (with Daniel Albert and Michael Resnik), *The Way of Words*, and *The Elements of Reasoning* (with David Conway). He is the author of *Fan Mail* and *Night Vision*.

CONTENTS

PREFACE

In shaping the fifth edition of this book, I have tried to capture both the intellectual excitement and the great seriousness that surround the field of medical ethics. In particular, I've done my best to convey these aspects to students new to the field.

In the introductory materials, the choice of topics, and by other means, I have attempted to familiarize readers with the issues and make them active participants in the enterprise. Whether someone is an undergraduate or graduate student, a nursing or medical student, with or without training in ethics, I think she or he will find this a useful and engaging book.

The Topics and Readings

The topics presented here are all fundamental ones in medical ethics. They reflect the range and variety of the problems we now confront and involve the basic ethical and social issues that have excited most concern. But more than this, the problems are so profoundly serious that they lead people to turn hopefully to philosophical consideration in search of satisfactory resolutions.

The reading selections present current thinking about the topics and show that such consideration can be worthwhile. All are readable and nontechnical, and several reveal medical ethics at its very best. Although philosophers are strongly represented in the readings, the authors also include jurists, scientists, social critics, journalists, and practicing physicians. The moral problems of medicine always have scientific, social, legal, and economic aspects, and to deal with them sensibly, we need the knowledge and perceptions of people from a variety of disciplines.

I have also opted for diversity in another way, by trying to see to it that opposing viewpoints are presented for major topics. Part of the intellectual excitement of medical ethics is generated by the searing controversies surrounding its issues, and to ignore these conflicts would be misleading. Even worse, it would deny students the opportunity of dealing directly with proposals and arguments incompatible with their own views.

The Introduction: Ethical Theories and Moral Principles

For some readers, the most important feature of the book may be the two-part general introduction. In the first part, I briefly sketch the basics of five major ethical theories and indicate how they might be used to answer particular moral questions in medicine. The main purpose is to give students without a background in ethics the information they need to understand and evaluate the arguments in the readings. In the second part, with this same end in view, I present and illustrate several major moral principles. The principles are ones endorsed by virtually all ethical theories, even though I don't try to demonstrate how the principles follow from particular theories.

The two parts of the general introduction complement one another, but they are self-contained and may be read separately. The aim of each (and of both) is to help prepare readers for independent inquiry in medical ethics.

Case Presentations, Social Contexts, Chapter Introductions, and Decision Scenarios

Each chapter after the general introduction is like a sandwich with several layers. Each opens with the Case Presentations and Social Contexts. Chapter Introductions are next, followed by the Readings. At the end are the Decision Scenarios. A brief explanation of these components will give a sense of how they work together.

The Case Presentations are based upon (or closely parallel) actual events or situations. They are intended to provide a focus for discussion and to illustrate how genuine moral problems arise in ordinary life. Some of the cases (like Kimberly Bergalis's and Nancy Cruzan's) are well known, while others are obscure. I think the cases may also remind us that in dealing with medical ethics we are not engaged in some purely intellectual abstract game.

The Social Contexts provide information relevant to understanding the current social, political, or biomedical situation in which issues are being debated. (They differ from Case Presentations in offering a broader view of a problem.) In my opinion, if we hope to raise the level of public discussion of an issue and genuinely inform the life of our society, it is essential to consider the social facts as well as the scientific and medical ones.

In the chapter Introductions, I discuss moral problems that occur in actual medical practice and research and present whatever factual information is needed to understand how they arise. I also suggest ways the five moral theories might be used to resolve some of the problems. These suggestions are offered only as starting points in the search for a satisfactory answer.

Several Decision Scenarios appear at the end of each chapter. These are brief, dramatic presentations of situations in which moral questions are crucial—in which ethical or social-policy decisions have to be made. The scenarios are followed by questions asking the reader to decide what the problems are and how they might be dealt with by a particular moral theory or by principles argued for in the Readings. Thus, the Decision Scenarios are really exercises in medical ethics that can direct and structure class discussion.

After the final chapter, the Notes and References section lists sources for materials used in the Decision Scenarios, as well as in the Cases, Contexts, and Introductions.

Finally, at the end of the book is an extensive bibliography arranged to correspond to the chapter divisions. Hence, anyone wanting to do further reading on a topic should have no trouble locating appropriate works.

Compensating for Limitations

An inherent limitation of a book of this sort is the impossibility of including selections dealing with all the major issues in an area. I have tried to compensate for this by raising and discussing in the chapter Introductions, Case Presentations, and Social Contexts more issues than are dealt with in the selections. I hope this will give readers a better sense of the scope and variety of questions in a complex area, even if little can be done to address them in a thorough way.

I also have tried to provide enough relevant medical, scientific, and social information to make it possible for both students and instructors to go beyond the scope of the text. No one need feel confined to the selections or to the problems specifically identified, and readers will be able to raise many serious issues that are not explicitly mentioned.

One way to touch on a larger number of issues is by using short excerpts for the Readings. Because of an increase in the number of issues in medical ethics, as well as ever-increasing literatures, in this edition I have used more shortened versions of articles and chapters than in past editions. I have also sometimes dropped the notes and references of an article, but for the most part, I have done this only when the notes were not discursive and the references were general. When omissions are made, this is clearly indicated.

The Current Edition

Changes in social circumstances, the legal environment, and scientific understanding often have an impact on moral issues in medicine. This edition attempts to present some of the recent major changes and explore the moral issues they raise.

A few examples that are newly discussed in this edition provide a sample:

• Medicine's great success in preserving the lives of babies that are extremely premature raises questions about whether such efforts are always justified.

• Dr. Jack Kevorkian has forced society to debate the merits of physician-assisted suicide, and the 1994 Oregon assisted-suicide law has broadened the debate.

• Participants in radiation experiments conducted during the Cold War may not have been properly informed of the risks.

• Evidence that ZDV taken during pregnancy can significantly reduce the number of newborns who become infected with the HIV virus from HIV-positive mothers gives a practical urgency to the issue of mandatory, un-blinded testing of pregnant women.

- The Human Genome Project is opening up the possibility of testing for a variety of genetic diseases, but should anyone agree to be tested for an unpreventable and incurable disease?

- Motherhood after menopause is now a technological reality, but should it be permitted?

- Cloning makes it possible for identical twins to be born years apart or for several unrelated women to have a genetically identical child, but do we want to live in a society that allows such possibilities to be realized?

Another notable addition to this edition is a thorough discussion of the issues involved in reforming the medical-care system. The Canadian system is presented in some detail, as is the employer-mandated system that has been so successful in Hawaii. Considered also are some of the quick fixes for some of the more egregious problems associated with access to health care.

Other striking changes represented in this new edition include new or expanded discussions of:

- RU-486 and the start of clinical trials in the United States

- the increasingly violent conflicts over abortion

- consent and randomized clinical trials

- new regulations of surrogate pregnancy

- whether ova donors are being exploited

- advances in gene therapy

- genetic discrimination

- buying and selling organs for transplant

- whether alcoholics should be rejected as transplant candidates

- rationing health care in Oregon

Chapter Introductions have been revised in dozens of ways to take into account changes in policies, statistics, and relevant scientific or medical information. Furthermore, a number of Cases, Contexts, and Scenarios have been added or revised to bring them up to date. Finally, the Bibliography has been thoroughly revised and a large number of recent items added.

Teaching Possibilities

I've used this book to teach medical ethics, and I've also had many discussions and some correspondence with others who have chosen it as a text. Perhaps it would be appropriate to close my comments on this book by offering a few suggestions about its use in class.

Topic Organization.   There is a logic in the organization of the book. Roughly, the first topics presented (abortion, euthanasia, and so on) involve making individual moral decisions, while the later topics (genetic screening, distributing resources, and so on) require decisions about social goals and policies. But, of course, virtually all of the issues in medical ethics overlap and intertwine. (Abortion is a good example of this.)

For this reason, it seemed to me sensible to arrange the topics and write the Introductions in a way that would make each chapter more or less independent of the others. Thus, the structure of the book does not have to be followed in teaching. Particular moral problems, social policy issues, or legal issues might all be used as an organizing principle. For example, someone wanting to teach a policy-oriented course might start with the last two chapters (on health-care policies), then go on to discuss regulating reproductive technology, protecting privacy in AIDS testing, and dealing with demands for physician-assisted suicide. It is possible to organize a course in this way without being faced with text or selections that presuppose familiarity with preceding chapters. Indeed, the chapters may be read in any order.

Chapter Organization.   In each chapter, I've placed the Case Presentations and Contexts before the Introduction, because I believe cases provide students with concrete examples that let them appreciate how particular moral issues arise. However, anyone who believes it is better to discuss cases after ethical issues and principles have been presented may want to ask students to read a Case Presentation after the introductory text or the philosophical materials.

The cases are written to stand alone, even when they are explicitly discussed in the selections. For example, it makes as much pedagogical sense to assign the Karen Quinlan Case Presentation after reading the Supreme Court decision on the case as to reverse that order.

Social Contexts also appear before Introductions, and much of what I've said about Case Presentations also applies to them. Some may wish their students to have some basic information about the social and political aspects of an issue like organ transplants before dealing with philosophical claims about just distribution. However, others may choose to focus exclusively on the philosophical issues and ignore the public aspects of the debate, on the grounds that students should make their own connections. The text is compatible with either approach.

I have provided more Cases and Contexts than some instructors may want to assign. This gives them the flexibility to decide which issues they want to emphasize within a particular chapter.

Using the Decision Scenarios.   Finally, the Decision Scenarios naturally lend themselves to being considered after the Readings, because then students can be expected to answer many of the questions. However, another strategy with something to recommend it is to ask students to read the scenarios before the selections. The cases and the questions about them can then serve as guides in reading, as flags marking notable issues.

Also, although time rarely permits it, if the scenarios are sometimes discussed both before and after the selections are read, students are given a chance to see the ways in which their own views change. They are also often in a better position to defend their initial views with relevant arguments.

Finally, the Decision Scenarios offer a rich source for paper topics. Either one or more questions can be selected and assigned or an instructor may refer to the scenario but provide a new question.

I have tried to be helpful without being too intrusive. Anyone who teaches medical ethics wants enough flexibility to arrange a course in the way she or he sees fit. I have tried to offer that flexibility, while at the same time supplying students with the kind of information and support they need.

This book, with its introductory materials and other appurtenances, is more ambitious than any similar work currently available. I've been pleased by responses from my colleagues to the earlier editions. Even their criticisms were tempered by a sympathetic understanding of the difficulty of producing a book of this scope that attempts to do so many things.

Thanks to the help of many people who took the trouble to write to me, I was able to correct errors in this edition that I missed in the last. I am under no illusion that the book has achieved perfection, and I would still appreciate comments or suggestions from those who use the book and discover ways it can be improved.

I owe so many intellectual debts I must declare bankruptcy, and this means that those who invested their help in this project have to settle for an acknowledgment that is less than they are rightly owed. My greatest debt on behalf of this book is to those authors who allowed their work to be printed here. (I particularly thank Laura M. Purdy for allowing me to use a revised version of her influential paper.) I hope they will find no grounds for objecting to the way I have dealt with them. That Chris Hoffman's name appears with mine on the title page is an indication of how grateful I am to him for his hard work in tracking down elusive articles, his sharp philosophical insights, and his keen judgments. The book is better because of him.

I am also grateful to the reviewers for their criticisms and recommendations: Craig Burgdoff, Syracuse University; Bernard Gendreau, Xavier University; Douglas Long, University of North Carolina at Chapel Hill; Bonnie Steinbock, State University of New York at Albany; and Brad Wilson, University of Pittsburgh.

Tammy Goldfeld, Wadsworth's philosophy editor, has shown as steady a faith in this book as her predecessor. I appreciate her encouragement and enthusiasm.

Miriam Grove Munson listened to my complaints with unfailing kindness and supplied much needed encouragement. Rebecca Grove Munson reminded me that there is more to life than the making of books.

I have not always listened to those who have taken the trouble to warn and advise me, and this is reason enough for me to claim the errors here as my own.

Ronald Munson
University of Missouri–St. Louis, 1995

Intervention and Reflection
BASIC ISSUES IN MEDICAL ETHICS
Fifth Edition

MORAL PRINCIPLES, ETHICAL THEORIES, AND MEDICAL DECISIONS: AN INTRODUCTION

"He's stopped breathing, Doctor," the nurse said. She sounded calm and not at all hysterical. By the time Dr. Sarah Cunningham had reached Mr. Sabatini's bedside, the nurse was already providing mouth-to-mouth resuscitation. But Mr. Sabatini still had the purplish blue color of cyanosis, caused by a lack of oxygen in his blood.

Dr. Cunningham knew that, if he was to survive, Mr. Sabatini would have to be given oxygen fast and placed on a respirator. But should she order this done?

Mr. Sabatini was an old man, almost ninety. So far as anyone knew, he was alone in the world and would hardly be missed when he died. His health was poor. He had congestive heart disease and was dying slowly and painfully from intestinal cancer.

Wouldn't it be a kindness to Mr. Sabatini to allow him this quick and painless death? Why condemn him to lingering on for a few extra hours or weeks?

The decision that Sarah Cunningham faces is a moral one. She has to decide whether she should take the steps that might prolong Mr. Sabatini's life or not take them and accept the consequence that he will almost surely die within minutes. She knows the medical procedures that can be employed, but she has to decide whether she should employ them.

This kind of case rivets our attention because of its immediacy and drama. But there are many other situations that arise in the context of medical practice and research that present problems that require moral decisions. Some are equal in drama to the problem facing Dr. Cunningham, while others are not

so dramatic but are of at least equal seriousness. There are far too many to catalogue, but consider this sample: Is it right for a woman to have an abortion for any reason? Should children with serious birth defects be put to death? Do people have a right to die? Does everyone have a right to medical care? Should physicians ever lie to their patients? Should people suffering from a genetic disease be allowed to have children? Can parents agree to allow their children to be used as experimental subjects?

Most of us have little tolerance for questions like these. They seem so cold and abstract. Our attitude changes, however, when we find ourselves in a position in which *we* are the decision makers. It changes, too, when we are in a position in which we must advise those who make the decisions. Or when we are on the receiving end of the decision.

But whether we view the problems abstractly or concretely, we are inclined to ask the same question: Are there any rules, standards, or principles that we can use as guides when we are faced with moral decisions? If there are, then Dr. Cunningham need not be wholly unprepared to decide whether she should order steps taken to save Mr. Sabatini. Nor need we be unprepared to decide issues like those in the questions above.

The branch of philosophy concerned with principles that allow us to make decisions about what is right and wrong is called *ethics* or *moral philosophy*. *Medical ethics* is specifically concerned with moral principles and decisions in the context of medical practice, policy, and research. Moral difficulties connected with medicine are so complex and important that they require special attention.

Medical ethics gives them this attention, but it remains a part of the discipline of ethics. Thus, if we are to answer our question as to whether there are any rules or principles to use when making moral decisions in the medical context, we must turn to general ethical theories and to a consideration of moral principles that have been proposed to hold in all contexts of human action.

In the first major part of this chapter, we will discuss five major ethical theories that have been put forward by philosophers. Each of these theories represents an attempt to supply basic principles that we can rely on in making moral decisions. We'll consider these theories and examine how they might be applied to moral issues in the medical context. We will discuss the reasons that have been offered to persuade us to accept each theory, but we will also point out some of the difficulties that each theory presents.

In the second major part of the chapter, we will examine and illustrate several moral principles that are of special relevance to medical research and practice. These principles are frequently appealed to in discussions of practical ethical problems and are sufficiently uncontroversial as to be endorsed in a general way by any of the ethical theories mentioned in the first section.

The two sections are not dependent on one another, and it is possible to profit from either without reading the other. (The price for this independence is a small amount of repetition.) Nevertheless, reading both is recommended. The discussions and arguments presented in the selections that make up the majority of this book can most easily be followed by someone who has at least some familiarity with basic moral theories. At the same time, some points in discussions turn upon questions about the applicability of certain familiar moral principles. Being acquainted with those principles makes it easier to understand and evaluate such discussions.

PART I. BASIC ETHICAL THEORIES

Ethical theories attempt to articulate and justify principles that can be employed as guides for making moral decisions and as standards for the evaluation of actions and policies. In effect, such theories define what it means to act morally, and in doing so they stipulate in a general fashion the duties or obligations that fall upon us.

Ethical theories also offer a means to explain and justify actions. If our actions are guided by a particular theory, then we can explain them by demonstrating that the principles of the theory required us to act as we did. In such cases, the explanation also constitutes a justification. We justify our actions by showing that, according to the theory, we had an obligation to do what we did. (In some cases, we may justify our actions by showing that the theory *permitted* our actions—that is, didn't require them, but didn't rule them out as wrong.)

Advocates of a particular ethical theory present what they consider to be good reasons and relevant evidence in its support. Their general aim is to show that the theory is one that any reasonable individual would find persuasive or would endorse as correct. Accordingly, appeals to religion, faith, or nonnatural factors are not considered to be either necessary or legitimate to justify the theory. Rational persuasion alone is regarded as the basis of justification.

In this section, we will briefly consider four general ethical theories and one theory of justice that has an essential ethical component. In each case, we will begin by examining the basic principles of the theory and the grounds offered for its acceptance. We will then explore some of the possibilities of applying the theory to problems that arise within the medical context. Finally, we will mention some of the practical consequences and conceptual difficulties that raise questions about the theory's adequacy or correctness.

UTILITARIANISM

The ethical theory known as utilitarianism was given its most influential formulation in the nineteenth century by the British philosophers Jeremy Bentham (1748–1832) and John Stuart Mill (1806–1873). Bentham and Mill did not produce identical theories, but both their versions have come to be spoken of as "classical utilitarianism." Subsequent elaborations and qualifications of utilitarianism are inevitably based on the formulations of Bentham and Mill, so their theories are worth careful examination.

The Principle of Utility

The foundation of utilitarianism is a single apparently simple principle. Mill calls it the "principle of utility" and states it this way: *"Actions are right in proportion as they tend to promote happiness, wrong as they tend to produce the reverse of happiness."*

The principle focuses attention on the *consequences* of actions, rather than upon some feature of the actions themselves. The "utility" or "usefulness" of an action is determined by the extent to which it produces happiness. Thus, no action is *in itself* right or wrong. Nor is an action right or wrong by virtue of the actor's hopes, intentions, or past actions. Consequences alone are important. Breaking a promise, lying, causing pain, or even killing a person may, under certain circumstances, be the right action to take. Under other circumstances, the action might be wrong.

We need not think of the principle as applying to just one action that we are considering. It supplies the basis for a kind of cost-benefit analysis to employ in a situation in which several lines of action are possible. Using the principle, we are supposed to consider the possible results of each of the actions. Then we are to choose the one that produces the most benefit (happiness) at the least cost (unhappiness). The action we take may produce some unhappiness, but it is a balance of happiness over unhappiness that the principle tells us to seek.

Suppose, for example, that a woman in a large hospital is near death: she is in a coma, an EEG shows only minimal brain function, and a respirator is required to keep her breathing. Another patient has just been brought to the hospital from the scene of an automobile accident. His kidneys have been severely damaged, and he is in need of an immediate transplant. There is a good tissue match with the woman's kidneys. Is it right to hasten her death by removing a kidney?

The principle of utility would probably consider the removal justified. The woman is virtually dead, while the man has a good chance of surviving. It is true that the woman's life is threatened even more by the surgery. It may, in fact, kill her. But, on balance, the kidney transplant seems likely to produce more happiness than unhappiness. In fact, it seems better than the alternative of doing nothing. For in that case both patients are likely to die.

The principle of utility is also called the "greatest happiness principle" by Bentham and Mill. The reason for this name is clear when the principle is stated in this way: *Those actions are right that produce the greatest happiness for the greatest number of people.* This alternative formulation makes it obvious that in deciding how to act it is not just my happiness or the happiness of a particular person or group that must be considered. According to utilitarianism, every person is to count just as much as any other person. That is, when we are considering how we should act, everyone's interest must be considered. The right action, then, will be the one that produces the most happiness for the largest number of people.

Mill is particularly anxious that utilitarianism not be construed as no more than a sophisticated justification for crude self-interest. He stresses that in making a moral decision we must look at the situation in an objective way. We must, he says, be a "benevolent spectator" and then act in a way that will bring about the best results for all concerned. This view is summarized in a famous passage:

> The happiness which forms the utilitarian standard of what is right in conduct, is not the agent's own happiness, but that of all concerned. As between his own happiness and that of others, utilitarianism requires him to be as strictly impartial as a disinterested and benevolent spectator. In the golden rule of Jesus of Nazareth, we read the complete spirit of the ethics of utility. To do as you would be done by, and to love your neighbor as yourself, constitute the ideal perfection of utilitarian morality.

The key concept in both formulations of the principle of utility is "happiness." Bentham simply identifies happiness with pleasure—pleasure of any kind. The aim of ethics, then, is to increase the amount of pleasure in the world to the greatest possible extent. To facilitate this, Bentham recommends the use of a "calculus of pleasure and pain," in which characteristics of pleasure such as intensity, duration, and number of people affected are measured and assigned numerical values. To determine which of several possible actions is the right one, we need only determine which one receives the highest numerical score. Unfortunately, Bentham does not tell us what units to use nor how to make the measurements.

Mill also identifies happiness with pleasure, but he differs from Bentham in a major respect. Unlike Bentham, he insists that some pleasures are "higher" than others. Thus, pleasures of the intellect are superior to, say, purely sensual pleasures. This difference in the concept of pleasure can become significant in a medical context. For example, in the choice of using limited resources to save the life of a lathe operator or of an art historian, Mill's view might assign more value to the life of the art historian. That person, Mill might say, is capable of "higher pleasures" than the lathe operator. (Of course other factors would be relevant here for Mill.)

Both Mill and Bentham regard happiness as an intrinsic good. That is, it is something good in itself or for its own sake. Actions, by contrast, are good only to the extent to which they tend to promote happiness. Therefore, they are only instrumentally good. Since utilitarianism determines the rightness of actions in terms of their tendency to promote the greatest happiness for the greatest number, it is considered to be a *teleological* ethical theory. ("Teleological" comes from the Greek word "telos," which means "end" or "goal.") A teleological ethical theory judges the rightness of an action in terms of an external goal or purpose—"general happiness" or utility for utilitarianism. However, utilitarianism is also a *consequentialist* theory, for the outcomes or consequences of actions are the only considerations relevant to determining their moral rightness. Not all teleological theories are consequentialist.

Some more recent formulations of utilitarianism have rejected the notion that happiness, no matter how defined, is the sole intrinsic good that actions or policies must promote. Critics of the classical view have argued that the list of things we recognize as valuable in themselves should be increased to include ones such as knowledge, beauty, love, friendship, liberty, and health. According to this *pluralistic* view, in applying the principle of utility we must consider the entire range of intrinsic goods that an action is likely to promote. Thus, the right action is the one that can be expected to produce the greatest sum of intrinsic goods. In most of the following discussion, we will speak of the greatest happiness or benefit, but it is easy enough to see how the same points can be made from a pluralistic perspective.

Act and Rule Utilitarianism

All utilitarians accept the principle of utility as the standard for determining the rightness of actions. But they divide into two groups over the matter of the application of the principle.

Act utilitarianism holds that the principle should be applied to particular acts in particular circumstances. *Rule utilitarianism* maintains that the principle should be used to test rules, which can in turn be used to decide the rightness of particular acts. Let's consider each of these views and see how it works in practice.

Act utilitarianism holds that an act is right if, and only if, no other act could have been performed that would produce a higher utility. Suppose that a child is born with severe impairments. The child has an open spine, severe brain damage, and dysfunctional kidneys. What should be done? (We will leave open the question of who should decide.)

The act utilitarian holds that we must attempt to determine the consequences of the various actions that are open to us. We should consider, for example, these possibilities: (1) give the child only the ordinary treatment that would be given to a normal child, (2) give the child special treatment for its problems, (3) give the child no treatment—allow it to die, (4) put the child to death in a painless way.

According to act utilitarianism, we must explore the potential results of each of these possibilities. We must realize, for example, that when such a child is given only ordinary treatment it will be worse off, if it survives, than if it had been given special treatment. Also, a child left alone and allowed to die is also likely to suffer more pain than one killed by a lethal injection. Furthermore, a child treated aggressively will have to undergo numerous surgical procedures of limited effectiveness. We must also consider the family of the child and judge the emotional and financial effects that each of the possible actions will have on them. Then, too, we must take into account such matters as the "quality of life" of a child with severe brain damage and multiple defects, the effect on physicians and nurses in killing the child or allowing it to die, and the financial costs to society in providing long-term care.

After these considerations, we should then choose the action that has the greatest utility. We should act in the way that will produce the most benefit for all concerned. Which of the possibilities we select will depend on the precise features of the situation: how impaired the child is, how good its chances are for living an acceptable life, the character and financial status of the family, and so on. The great strength of act utilitarianism is that it invites us to deal with each case as unique. When the circumstances of another case are different, we might, without being inconsistent, choose another of the possible actions.

Act utilitarianism shows a sensitivity to specific cases, but it is not free from difficulties. Some philosophers have pointed out that there is no way that we can be sure that we have made the right choice of actions. We are sure to be ignorant of much relevant information. Besides, we can't know with much certainty what the results of our actions will really be. There is no way to be sure, for example, that even a severely impaired infant will not recover enough to live a better life than we predict.

The act utilitarian can reply that acting morally doesn't mean being omniscient. We need to make a reasonable effort to get relevant information, and we can usually predict the probable consequences of our actions. Acting morally doesn't require any more than this.

Another objection to act utilitarianism is more serious. According to the doctrine, we are obligated to keep a promise only if keeping it will produce more utility than some other action. If some other action will produce the same utility, then keeping the promise is permissible but not obligatory. Suppose that a surgeon promises a patient that only he will perform an operation, then allows a well-qualified resident to perform part of it.

Suppose that all goes well and the patient never discovers that the promise was not kept. The outcome for the patient is exactly the same as if the surgeon had kept the promise. From the point of view of act utilitarianism, there is nothing wrong with the surgeon's failure to keep it. Yet critics charge that there is something wrong, that in making the promise the surgeon took on an obligation. Act utilitarianism is unable to account for obligations engendered by such actions as promising and pledging, critics say, for such actions involve something other than consequences.

A third objection to act utilitarianism arises in situations in which virtually everyone must follow the same rules in order to achieve a high level of utility, but even greater utility can be achieved if a few people do not follow the rules. Consider the relationship between physicians and the Medicaid program. The program pays physicians for services provided to those poor enough to qualify for the program. The program would collapse if nearly all physicians were not honest in billing Medicaid for their services. Not only would many poor people suffer, but physicians themselves would lose a source of income.

Suppose that a particular physician believes that the requirements to qualify for Medicaid are too restrictive and that many who urgently need medical care cannot afford it. As an act utilitarian, he reasons that it is right for him to get money to open a free clinic under the program. He intends to bill for services he does not provide, then use that money to treat those not covered by Medicaid. His claims will be small compared to the entire Medicaid budget, so it is unlikely that anyone who qualifies for Medicaid will go without treatment. Since he will tell no one what he is doing, others are not likely to be influenced by his example and make false claims for similar or less worthy purposes. The money he is paid will bring substantial benefit to those in need of health care. Thus, he concludes, by violating the rules of the program, his actions will produce greater utility than would be produced by following the rules.

The physician's action would be morally right, according to act utilitarianism. Yet, critics say, we expect an action that is morally right to be one that is right for everyone in similar circumstances. If every physician in the Medicaid program acted in this way, however, the program would be destroyed and thus produce no utility at all. Furthermore, according to critics, the physician's action produces unfairness. While it is true that the patients he treats at his free clinic gain a benefit they would not otherwise have, similar patients must go without treatment. The Medicaid policy, whatever its flaws, is at least prima facie fair in providing benefits to all who meet its requirements. Once again, then, according to critics, more seems to be involved in judging the moral worth of an action than can be accounted for by act utilitarianism.

In connection with such objections, some critics have gone so far as to claim that it is impossible to see how a society in which everyone were an act utilitarian could function. We could not count on promises being kept nor take for granted that people were telling us the truth. Social policies would be no more than general guides to action, and we could never be sure that people would regard themselves as obligated to adhere to their provisions. Decisions made by individuals about each individual action would not obviously lead to the promotion of the highest degree of utility. Indeed, some critics say, such a society might collapse, for communication among individuals would be difficult, if not impossible, social cohesion would be weakened, and general policies and regulations would have very uncertain effects.

The critics are not necessarily right, of course, and defenders of act utilitarianism have made substantial efforts to answer the criticisms we have presented. Some have denied that the theory has those implications and argued that some of our generally accepted moral perceptions should be changed.

In connection with this last point, Carl Wellman provides an insight into the sort of conflict between moral feelings and rational judgment that the acceptance of act utilitarianism can produce. Concerning euthanasia, Wellman writes:

> Try as I may, I honestly cannot discover great hidden disutilities in the act of killing an elderly person suffering greatly from an incurable illness, provided that certain safeguards like a written medical opinion by at least two doctors and a request by the patient are preserved. In this case I cannot find any way to reconcile my theory with my moral judgment. What I do in this case is to hold fast to act-utilitarianism and distrust my moral sense. I claim that my condemnation of such acts is an irrational disapproval, a condemnation that will change upon further reasoning about the act. . . . That I feel wrongness is clear, but I cannot state to myself any rational justification for my feeling. Hence, I discount this particular judgment as irrational.

Rule utilitarianism maintains that an action is right if it conforms to a rule of conduct that has been validated by the principle of utility as one that will produce at least as much utility as any other rule applicable to the situation. A rule like "Provide only ordinary care for severely brain-damaged newborns with multiple impairments," if it were established, would allow us to decide about the course of action to follow in situations like that of our earlier example.

The rule utilitarian is not concerned with assessing the utility of individual actions, but of particular rules. In practice, then, we do not have to go through the calculations involved in determining in each case whether a specific action will increase utility. All that we have to establish is that following a certain rule will, in general, result in a situation in which utility is maximized. Once rules are established, they can be relied on to determine whether a particular action is right.

The basic idea behind rule utilitarianism is that having a set of rules that are always observed produces the greatest social utility. Having everyone follow the same rule in each case of the same kind yields more utility for everybody in the long run. An act utilitarian can agree that having rules may produce more social utility than not having them. But the act utilitarian insists that the rules be regarded as no more than general guides to action, as "rules of thumb." Thus, for act utilitarianism it is perfectly legitimate to violate a rule if doing so will maximize utility in that instance. By contrast, the rule utilitarian holds that rules must generally be followed, even though following them may produce less net utility (more unhappiness than happiness) in a particular case.

Rule utilitarianism can endorse rules like "Keep your promises." Thus, unlike act utilitarianism, it can account for the general sense that in making promises we are placing ourselves under an obligation that cannot be set aside for the sake of increasing utility. If "Keep your promises," is accepted as a rule, then the surgeon who fails to perform all of an operation himself, when he has promised his patient he would do so, has not done the right thing, even if the patient never learns the truth.

Rule utilitarians recognize that circumstances can arise in which it would be disastrous to follow a general rule, even when it is true that *in general* greater happiness would result from following the rule all the time. Clearly we should not keep a promise to meet someone for lunch when we have to choose between keeping the promise and rushing a heart-attack victim to the hospital. It is consistent with the theory to formulate rules that include appropriate escape clauses. For example, "Keep your promises, unless breaking them is required to save a life" and "Keep your promises, unless keeping them would lead to a disastrous result unforeseen at the time the promise was made" are rules that a rule utilitarian might regard as more likely to lead to greater utility than "Always keep your promises no matter what the consequences may be." What a rule utilitarian cannot endorse is a rule like "Keep your promises, except when breaking a promise would produce more utility." This would, in effect, transform the rule utilitarian into an act utilitarian.

Of course, rule utilitarians are not committed to endorsing general rules only. It is compatible with the view to offer quite specific rules, and in fact there is no constraint on just how specific a rule may be. A rule utilitarian might, for example, establish a rule like "If an infant is born with an open spine, severe brain damage, and dysfunctional kidneys, then the infant should receive no life-sustaining treatment."

The possibility of formulating a large number of rules and establishing them separately opens this basic version of rule utilitarianism to two objections. First, some rules are likely to conflict when they are applicable to the same case, and basic rule utilitarianism offers no way to resolve such conflicts. What should a physician do when faced both with a rule like that above and with another that directs him to "Provide life-sustaining care to all who require it"? Rules which, when considered individually, pass the test of promoting utility, may when taken together express contradictory demands. A further objection to basic rule utilitarianism is that establishing rules to cover many different circumstances and situations results in such an abundance of rules that employing the rules to make moral decisions becomes virtually impossible in practice.

Partly because of such difficulties, rule utilitarians have taken the approach of establishing the utility of a *set* of rules or an entire moral code. The set can include rules for resolving possible conflicts, and an effort can be made to keep the rules few and simple to minimize the practical difficulty of employing them. Once again, as with individual actions or rules, the principle of utility is employed to determine which set of rules, out of the various sets considered, ought to be accepted.

In this more sophisticated form, rule utilitarianism can be characterized as the theory that an action is right when it conforms to a set of rules that has been determined to produce at least as much overall utility as any other set. It is possible to accept the present forms of social and economic institutions, such as private property and a market economy, as constraints, then argue for the set of rules that will yield the most utility under those conditions. However, it is also possible to be more radical and argue for a particular set of rules that would lead to the greatest possible utility, quite apart from present social forms. Indeed, such a set of rules might be proposed and defended in an effort to bring about changes in present society that are needed to increase the overall level of utility. Utilitarianism, whether act or rule, is not restricted to being a theory about individual moral obligation. It is also a social and political theory.

We have already seen that rule utilitarianism, unlike act utilitarianism, makes possible the sort of obligation we associate with making a promise. But how might rule utilitarianism deal with the case of the physician who files false Medicaid claims to raise money to operate a free clinic? An obvious answer, although certainly not the only one possible, is that any set of rules likely to be adopted by a rule utilitarian will contain at least one rule making fraud morally wrong. Without a rule forbidding fraud, no social program that requires the cooperation of its participants is likely to achieve its aim. Such a rule protects the program from miscalculations of utility that individuals may make for self-serving reasons, keeps the program focused on its goal, and prevents it from becoming fragmented. Even if some few individuals commit fraud, the rule against it is crucial in discouraging as many as possible. Otherwise, as we pointed out earlier, such a program would collapse. By requiring that the program operate as it was designed, rule utilitarian also preserves prima facie fairness, because only those who qualify receive benefits.

The most telling objection to rule utilitarianism, according to some philosophers, is that it is inconsistent. The justification of a set of moral rules is that the rules maximize utility. If rules are to maximize utility, then it seems obvious that they may require that an act produce more utility than any other possible act in a particular situation. Otherwise, the maximum amount of utility would not result. But if the rules satisfy this demand, then they will justify exactly the same actions as act utilitarianism. Thus the rules will consider it right to break promises, make fraudulent claims, and so on. When rule utilitarianism moves to block these possibilities by requiring that rules produce only the most utility overall, it becomes inconsistent: the set of rules is said to maximize utility, but the rules will require actions that do not maximize utility. Thus, rule utilitarianism seems both to accept and reject the principle of utility as the ultimate moral standard.

Preference Utilitarianism

Some philosophers have called into question the idea of using happiness or any other intrinsic value (knowledge or health, for example) as a criterion of the rightness of an action. The notion of an intrinsic value, they have argued, is too imprecise to be used as a practical guide. Furthermore, it is not at all clear that people share the same values, and even if they do, they are not committed to them to the same degree. Someone may value knowledge more than health, while someone else may value physical pleasure over knowledge or health. As a result, there can be no clear-cut procedure for determining what action is likely to produce the best outcome for an individual or group.

The attempt to develop explicit techniques (such as those of decision theory) to help resolve questions about choosing the best action or policy has led some thinkers to replace considerations of intrinsic value with considerations of actual preferences. What someone wants, desires, or prefers can be determined, in principle, in any objective way by consulting the person directly. In addition, people are often able to do more than merely express a preference. Sometimes they can rank their preferences from that which is "most desired" to that which is "least desired."

Such a ranking is of special importance in situations involving risk, for people can be asked to decide how much risk they are willing to take to attempt to realize a given preference. A young woman with a hip injury who is otherwise in good health may be willing to accept the risk of surgery to increase her chances of being restored to many years of active life. By contrast, an elderly woman in frail health may prefer to avoid surgery and accept the limitations that the injury imposes on her physical activities. For the elderly woman, not only are the risks of surgery greater because of her poor health, but even if the surgery is successful, she will have fewer years to benefit from it.

By contrast, the older woman may place such a premium on physical activity that she is willing to take the risk of surgery to improve her chances of securing even a few more years of it. Only she can say what is important to her and how willing she is to take the risk required to secure it.

These considerations about personal preferences can also be raised about social preferences. Statistical information about what people desire and what they are willing to forgo to see their desires satisfied becomes relevant to institutional and legislative deliberations about what policies to adopt. For example, a crucial question facing our own society is whether we are willing to provide everyone with at least a basic minimum of health care, even if this requires increasing taxes or reducing our support for other social goods, such as education and defense.

Employing the satisfaction of preferences as the criterion of the rightness of an action or policy makes it possible to measure some of the relevant factors in some situations. The life expectancy of infants with particular impairments at birth can be estimated by statistics; a given surgical procedure has a certain success rate and a certain mortality rate. Similarly, a particular social policy has a certain financial cost, and if implemented, the policy is likely to mean the loss of other possible benefits and opportunities.

Ideally, information of this kind should allow a rational decision maker to calculate the best course of action for an individual or group. The best action will be the one that best combines the satisfaction of preferences with other conditions (financial costs and risks, for example) that are at least minimally acceptable. To use the jargon of the theorists, the best action is the one that maximizes the utilities of the person or group.

A utilitarianism that employs preferences has the advantage of suggesting more explicit methods of analysis and rules for decision making than the classical formulation. It also has the potential for being more sensitive to the expressed desires of individuals. However, preference utilitarianism is not free from specific difficulties.

Most prominent is the problem posed by preferences that we would generally regard as unacceptable. What are we to say about those who prefer mass murder, child abuse, or torturing animals? Obviously, subjective preferences cannot be treated equally, and we must have a way to distinguish acceptable from unacceptable ones. Whether this can be done by relying on the principle of utility alone is doubtful. In the view of some commentators, some other moral principle (or principles) is needed. (See the discussion of justice immediately following.)

Difficulties

Classical utilitarianism is open to a variety of objectives. We shall concentrate on only one, however, for it seems to reveal a fatal flaw in the structure of the entire theory. This most serious of all objections is that the principle of utility appears to justify the imposition of great suffering on a few people for the benefit of many people.

Certain kinds of human experimentation forcefully illustrate this possibility. Suppose that an investigator is concerned with acquiring a better understanding of brain functions. He could learn a great deal by systematically destroying the brain of one person and carefully noting the results. Such a study would offer many more opportunities for increasing our knowledge of the brain than those studies that use as subjects people who have damage to their brains in accidental ways. We may suppose that the experimenter chooses as his subject a person without education or training, without family or friends, who cannot be regarded as making much of a contribution to society. The subject will die from the experiment, but it is not unreasonable to suppose that the knowledge of the human brain gained from the experiment will improve the lives of countless numbers of people.

The principle of utility seems to make such experiments legitimate because the outcome is a greater amount of good than harm. One or a few have suffered immensely, but the many have profited to an extent that far outweighs that suffering.

Clearly what is missing from utilitarianism is the concept of *justice*. It cannot be right to increase the general happiness at the expense of one person or group. There must be some way of distributing happiness and unhappiness and avoiding exploitation.

Mill was aware that utilitarianism needs a principle of justice, but most contemporary philosophers do not believe that such a principle can be derived from the principle of utility. In their opinion, utilitarianism as an ethical theory suffers severely from this defect. Yet some philosophers, while acknowledging the defect, have still held that utilitarianism is the best substantive moral theory available.

KANT'S ETHICS

For utilitarianism, the rightness of an action depends upon its consequences. In stark contrast to this view is the ethical theory formulated by the German philosopher Immanuel Kant (1724–1804) in his book *Fundamental Principles of the Metaphysics of Morals*. For Kant, the consequences of an action are morally irrelevant. Rather, an action is right when it is in accordance with a rule that satisfies a principle he calls the "categorical imperative." Since this is the basic principle of Kant's ethics, we can begin our discussion with it.

The Categorical Imperative

If you decide to have an abortion and go through with it, it is possible to view your action as involving a rule. You can be thought of as endorsing a rule to the effect "Whenever I am in circumstances like these, then I shall have an abortion." Kant calls such a rule a "maxim." In his view, all reasoned and considered actions can be regarded as involving maxims.

The maxims in such cases are personal or subjective, but they can be thought of as being candidates for moral rules. If they pass the test imposed by the categorical imperative, then we can say that such actions are right. Furthermore, in passing the test, the maxims cease to be merely personal and subjective. They gain the status of objective rules of morality that hold for everyone.

Kant formulates the categorical imperative in this way: Act only on that maxim which you can will to be a universal law. Kant calls the principle "categorical" to distinguish it from "hypothetical" imperatives. These tell us what to do if we want to bring about certain consequences—such as happiness. A categorical imperative prescribes what we ought to do without reference to any consequences. The principle is an "imperative" because it is a command.

The test imposed on maxims by the categorical imperative is one of generalization or "universalizability." The central idea of the test is that a moral maxim is one that can be generalized to apply to all cases of the same kind. That is, you must be willing to see your rule adopted as a maxim by everyone who is in a situation similar to yours. You must be willing to see your maxim universalized, even though it may turn out on some other occasion to work to your disadvantage.

For a maxim to satisfy the categorical imperative it is not necessary that we be agreeable in some psychological sense to see it made into a universal law. Rather, the test is one that requires us to avoid inconsistency or conflict in what we will as a universal rule.

Suppose, for example, that I am a physician and I tell a patient that he has a serious illness, although I know that he doesn't. This may be to my immediate advantage, for the treatment and the supposed cure will increase my income and reputation. The maxim of my action might be phrased as, "Whenever I have a healthy patient, I shall lie to him and say that he has an illness."

Now suppose that I try to generalize my maxim. In doing so, I will discover that I am willing the existence of a practice that has contradictory properties. If "Whenever any physician has a healthy patient, he shall lie to him and say he has an illness" is made a universal law, then every patient will be told that he has an illness. Trust in the diagnostic pronouncements of physicians will be destroyed, while my scheme depends on my patients' trusting me and accepting the truth of my lying diagnosis.

It is as if I were saying, "Let there be a rule of truth telling such that people can assume that others are telling them the truth, but let there also be a rule that physicians may lie to their patients when it is in the interest of the physician to do so." In willing both rules, I am willing something contradictory. Thus, I can will my action in a particular case, but I can't will that my action be universal without generating a logical conflict.

Kant claims that such considerations show that it is always wrong to lie. Lying produces a contradiction in what we will. On one hand, we will that people believe what we say—that they accept our assurances and promises. On the other hand, we will that people be free to give false assurances and make false promises. Lying thus produces a self-defeating situation, for, when the maxim involved is generalized, the very framework required for lying collapses.

Similarly, consider the egoist who seeks only his self-interest and so makes "Never show love or compassion for others" the maxim of his actions. When universalized, this maxim results in the same kind of self-defeating situation that lying does. Since the egoist will sometimes find himself in need of love and compassion, if he wills the maxim of his action to be a universal law, then he will be depriving himself of something that is in his self-interest. Thus, in willing the abolition of love and compassion out of self-interest, he creates a logical contradiction in what he wills.

Another Formulation

According to Kant, there is only one categorical imperative, but it can be stated in three different ways. Each is intended to reveal a different aspect of the principle. The second formulation, the only other we shall consider, can be stated in this way: Always act so as to treat humanity, either yourself or others, always as an end and never as only a means.

This version illustrates Kant's notion that every rational creature has a worth in itself. This worth is not conferred by being born into a society with a certain political structure, nor even by belonging to a certain biological species. The worth is inherent in the sheer possession of rationality. Rational creatures possess what Kant calls an "autonomous, self-legislating will." That is, they are able to consider the consequences of their actions, make

rules for themselves, and direct their actions by those self-imposed rules. Thus, rationality confers upon everyone an intrinsic worth and dignity.

This formulation of the categorical imperative perhaps rules out some of the standards that are sometimes used to determine who is selected to receive certain medical resources (such as kidney machines) when the demand is greater than the supply. Standards that make a person's education, accomplishments, or social position relevant seem contrary to this version of the categorical imperative. They violate the basic notion that each person has an inherent worth equal to that of any other person. Unlike dogs or horses, people cannot be judged on "show points."

For Kant, all of morality has its ultimate source in rationality. The categorical imperative, in any formulation, is an expression of rationality, and it is the principle that would be followed in practice by any purely rational being. Moral rules are not mere arbitrary conventions or subjective standards. They are objective truths that have their source in the rational nature of human beings.

Duty

Utilitarianism identifies the good with happiness or pleasure and makes the production of happiness the supreme principle of morality. But for Kant happiness is at best a conditional or qualified good. In his view, there is only one thing that can be said to be good in itself: a good will.

Will is what directs our actions and guides our conduct. But what makes a will a "good will"? Kant's answer is that a will becomes good when it acts purely for the sake of duty.

We act for the sake of duty (or from duty) when we act on maxims that satisfy the categorical imperative. This means, then, that it is the motive force behind our actions—the character of our will—that determines their moral character. Morality does not rest on results—such as the production of happiness—but neither does it rest on our feelings, impulses, or inclinations. An action is right, for Kant, only when it is done for the sake of duty.

Suppose that I decide to donate one of my kidneys for transplanting. If my hope is to gain approval or praise or even if I am moved by pity and a genuine wish to reduce suffering, and this is the only consideration behind my action, then, although I have done the morally right thing, my action has no inner moral worth. By contrast, if I make the donation because I perceive it is my duty to do so, then my action is not only right, but has moral worth. In the first case, I may have acted *in accordance with duty* (done the same thing as duty would have required), but I did not act *from duty*.

This view of duty and its connection with morality captures attitudes we frequently express. Consider a nurse who gives special care to a severely ill patient. Suppose you learned that the nurse was providing such extraordinary care only because he hoped that the patient or her family would reward him with a special bonus. Knowing this, you would be unlikely to say that the nurse was acting in a morally outstanding way. We might even think the nurse was being greedy or cynical, and we would say that he was doing the right thing for the wrong reasons.

Kant distinguishes between two types of duties: perfect and imperfect. (The distinction corresponds to the two ways in which maxims can be self-defeating when tested by the categorical imperative.) A *perfect* duty is one we must always observe, while an *imperfect* duty is one that we must observe only on some occasions. I have a perfect duty not to injure another person, but I have only an imperfect duty to show love and compassion. I must sometimes show it, but when I show it and which people I select to receive it are entirely up to me.

My duties determine what others can legitimately claim from me as a right. Some

rights can be claimed as perfect rights, while others cannot. Everyone can demand of me that I do him or her no injury. But no one can tell me that I must make him or her the recipient of my love and compassion. In deciding how to discharge my imperfect duties, I am free to follow my emotions and inclinations.

For utilitarianism, an action is right when it produces something that is intrinsically valuable (happiness). Because actions are judged by their contributions to achieving a goal, utilitarianism is a teleological theory. By contrast, Kant's ethics holds that an action has features in itself that make it right or in accordance with duty. These features are distinct from the action's consequences. Such a theory is called "deontological," a term derived from the Greek word for "duty" or "obligation."

Kant's Ethics in the Medical Context

Four years of Kant's ethics are of particular importance in dealing with issues in medical treatment and research:

1. No matter what the consequences may be, it is always wrong to lie.

2. We must always treat people (including ourselves) as ends and not as means only.

3. An action is right when it satisfies the categorical imperative.

4. Perfect and imperfect duties give a basis for claims that certain rights should be recognized.

We can present only two brief examples of how these features can be instrumental in resolving ethical issues, but these are suggestive of other possibilities.

Our first application of Kant's ethics bears on medical research. The task of medical investigators would be easier if they did not have to tell patients that they were going to be made part of a research program. Patients would then become subjects without even knowing it, and more often than not the risk of them would be negligible. Even though no overt lying would be involved, on Kantian principles this procedure would be wrong. It would require treating people as a means only and not as an end.

Likewise, it would never be right for an experimenter to deceive a potential experimental subject. If an experimenter told a patient, "We would like to use this new drug on you because it might help you" and this were not really so, the experimenter would be performing a wrong action. Lying is always wrong.

Nor could the experimenter justify this deception by telling himself that the research is of such importance that it is legitimate to lie to the patient. On Kant's principles, good results never make an action morally right. Thus, a patient must give voluntary and informed consent to become a subject of medical experimentation. Otherwise, he or she is being deprived of autonomy and treated as a means only.

We may volunteer because we expect the research to bring direct benefits to us. But we may also volunteer even though no direct personal benefits can be expected. We may see participation in the research as an occasion for fulfilling an imperfect duty to improve human welfare.

But, just as Kant's principles place restrictions on the researcher, they place limits on us as potential subjects. We have a duty to treat ourselves as ends and act so as to preserve our dignity and worth as humans. Therefore, it would not be right for us to volunteer for an experiment that threatened our lives or threatened to destroy our ability to function as autonomous rational beings without first satisfying ourselves that the experiment was legitimate and necessary.

Our second application of Kant's ethics in a medical context bears on the relationship between people as patients and those who accept responsibility for caring for them. A

physician, for example, has only an imperfect duty to accept me as a patient. He has a duty to make use of his skills and talents to treat the sick, but I cannot legitimately insist on being the beneficiary. How he discharges his duty is his decision.

If, however, I am accepted as a patient, then I can make some legitimate claims. I can demand that nothing be done to cause me pointless harm, because it is never right to injure a person. Furthermore, I can demand that I never be lied to or deceived. Suppose, for example, I am given a placebo (a harmless but inactive substance) and told that it is a powerful and effective medication. Or suppose that a biopsy shows that I have an inoperable form of cancer, but my physician tells me, "There's nothing seriously wrong with you." In both cases, the physician may suppose that he is deceiving me "for my own good": the placebo may be psychologically effective and make me feel better, and the lie about cancer may save me from useless worry. Yet, by being deceived, I am being denied the dignity inherent in my status as a rational being. Lying is wrong in general, and in such cases as these it also deprives me of my autonomy, of my power to make decisions and form my own opinions. As a result, such deception dehumanizes me.

As an autonomous rational being, a person is entitled to control over his or her own body. This means that medical procedures can be performed on me only with my permission. It would be wrong, for example, for my physician to have me held down and injected with a drug that I explicitly refused. It would be wrong even if the medication were needed for my "own good." I may voluntarily put myself under the care of a physician and submit to all that I am asked to, but the decision belongs to me alone.

In exercising control over my body, however, I also have a duty to myself. Suppose, for example, that I refuse to allow surgery to be performed on me, although I have been told it is necessary to preserve my life. Since I have a duty to preserve my life, as does every person, my refusal is morally unjustifiable. Even here, however, it is not legitimate for others to force me to "do my duty." In fact, in Kantian ethics it is impossible to force another to do his or her duty because it is not the action but the maxim involved that determines whether or not one's duty has been done.

It is obvious even from our sketchy examples that Kantian ethics is a fruitful source of principles and ideas for working out some of the specific moral difficulties of medical experimentation and practice. The absolute requirements imposed by the categorical imperative can be a source of strength and even of comfort. By contrast, utilitarianism requires us to weigh alternative courses of actions by anticipating their consequences and deciding whether what we are considering doing can be justified by those results. Kant's ethics saves us from this kind of doubt and indecision; we know we must never lie, no matter what good may come of it. Furthermore, the lack of a principle of justice that is the most severe defect of utilitarianism is met by Kant's categorical imperative. When every person is to be treated as an end and never as only a means, the possibility of legitimately exploiting some for the benefit of others is wholly eliminated.

Difficulties

Kant's ethical theory is complex and controversial. It has problems of a theoretical sort that manifest themselves in practice and lead us to doubt whether the absolute rules determined by the categorical imperative can always provide a straightforward solution to our moral difficulties. We will limit ourselves to discussing just three problems.

First, Kant's principles may produce resolutions to cases in which there is a conflict of duties that seems intuitively wrong. I have a duty to keep my promises, and I also have a duty to help those in need. Suppose, then, that I am a physician and I have promised a

colleague to attend a staff conference. Right before the conference starts, I am talking with a patient who lapses into an insulin coma. If I get involved in treating the patient, I'll have to break my promise to attend the conference. What should I do?

The answer is obvious: I should treat the patient. Our moral intuition tells us this. But, for Kant, keeping promises is a perfect duty, while helping others is an imperfect one. This suggests, then, that according to Kantian principles I should abandon my patient and rush off to keep my appointment. Something is apparently wrong with a view that holds that a promise should never be broken—even when the promise concerns a relatively trivial matter and the consequences of keeping it are disastrous.

Another difficulty with the categorical imperative arises because we are free to choose how we formulate a maxim for testing. In all likelihood none of us would approve a maxim such as "Lie when it is convenient for you." But what about one like "Lie when telling the truth is likely to cause harm to another"? We would be more inclined to make this a universal law. Now consider the maxim "Whenever a physician has good reason to believe that a patient's life will be seriously threatened if he is told the truth about his condition, then the physician should lie." Virtually everyone would be willing to see this made into a universal law.

Yet these three maxims could apply to the same situation. Since Kant does not tell us how to formulate our maxims, it is clear that we can act virtually any way we choose if we are willing to describe the situation in detail. We might be willing to have everyone act just as we are inclined to act whenever they find themselves in *exactly* this kind of situation. The categorical imperative, then, does not seem to solve our moral problems quite so neatly as it first appears to.

A final problem arises from Kant's notion that we have duties to rational beings or persons. Ordinarily, we have little difficulty with this commitment to persons, yet there are circumstances, particularly in the medical context, in which serious problems arise. Consider, for example, a fetus developing in its mother's womb. Is the fetus to be considered a person? The way this question is answered makes all the difference in deciding about the rightness or wrongness of abortion.

A similar difficulty is present when we consider how we are to deal with an infant with serious birth defects. Is it our duty to care for this infant and do all we can to see that it lives? If the infant is not a person, then perhaps we do not owe him the sort of treatment it would be our duty to provide a similarly afflicted adult. It's clear from these two cases that the notion of a person as an autonomous rational being is both too restrictive and arbitrary. It begs important moral questions.

Another difficulty connected with Kant's concept of a rational person is the notion of an "autonomous self-regulating will." Under what conditions can we assume that an individual possesses such a will? Does a child, a mentally retarded person, or someone in prison? Without such a will, in Kant's view, such an individual cannot legitimately consent to be the subject of an experiment or even give permission for necessary medical treatment. This notion is very much in need of development before Kant's principles can be relied on to resolve ethical questions in medicine.

The difficulties that we have discussed require serious consideration. This does not mean, of course, that they cannot be resolved or that because of them Kant's theory is worthless. As with utilitarianism, there are some philosophers who believe the theory is the best available, despite its shortcomings. That it captures many of our intuitive beliefs about what is right (not to lie, to treat people with dignity, to act benevolently) and supplies us with a test for determining our duties (the categorical imperative) recommends it strongly as an ethical theory.

ROSS'S ETHICS

The English philosopher W. D. Ross (b. 1877) presented an ethical theory in his book *The Right and the Good* that can be seen as an attempt to incorporate aspects of utilitarianism and aspects of Kantianism. Ross rejected the utilitarian notion that an action is made right by its consequences alone, but he was also troubled by Kant's absolute rules. He saw not only that such rules fail to show sensitivity to the complexities of actual situations, but also that they sometimes conflict with one another. Like Kant, Ross is a deontologist, but with an important difference. Ross believes it is necessary to consider consequences in making a moral choice, even though he believes that it is not the results of an action taken alone that make it right.

Moral Properties and Rules

For Ross there is an unbridgeable distinction between moral and nonmoral properties. There are only two moral properties—rightness and goodness—and these cannot be replaced by, or explained in terms of, other properties. Thus, to say that an action is "right" is not at all the same as saying that it "causes pleasure" or "increases happiness," as utilitarianism claims.

At the same time, however, Ross does not deny that there is a connection between moral properties and nonmoral ones. What he denies is the possibility of establishing an identity between them. Thus, it may be right to relieve the suffering of someone, but right is not identical with relieving suffering. (More exactly put, the rightness of the action is not identical with the action's being a case of relieving suffering.)

Ross also makes clear that we must often know many nonmoral facts about a situation before we can legitimately make a moral judgment. If I see a physician injecting someone, I cannot say whether she is acting rightly without determining what she is injecting, why she is doing it, and so on. Thus, rightness is a property that depends partly on the nonmoral properties that characterize a situation. I cannot determine whether the physician is doing the right thing or the wrong thing until I determine what the nonmoral properties are.

Ross believes that there are cases in which we have no genuine doubt about whether the property of rightness or goodness is present. The world abounds with examples of cruelty, lying, and selfishness, and in these cases we are immediately aware of the absence of rightness or goodness. But the world also abounds with examples of compassion, reliability, and generosity in which rightness and goodness are clearly present. Ross claims that our experience with such cases puts us in a position to come to know rightness and goodness with the same degree of certainty as when we grasp the mathematical truth that a triangle has three angles.

Furthermore, according to Ross, our experience of many individual cases puts us in a position to recognize the validity of a general statement like "It is wrong to cause needless pain." We come to see such rules in much the same way that we come to recognize the letter A after having seen it written or printed in a variety of handwritings or typefaces.

Thus, our moral intuitions can supply us with moral rules of a general kind. But Ross refuses to acknowledge these rules as absolute. For him they can serve only as guides to assist us in deciding what we should do. Ultimately, in any particular case we must rely not only on the rules, but also on reason and our understanding of the situation.

Thus, even with rules, we may not recognize what the right thing to do is in a given situation. We recognize, he suggests, that there is always *some* right thing to do, but what it is may be far from obvious. In fact, doubt about what is the right way of acting may arise just because we have rules to guide us. We become aware of the fact that there are several possible courses of action, and all of them seem to be right.

Consider the problem of whether to lie to a terminally ill patient about her condition. Let us suppose that, if we lie to her, we can avoid causing her at least some useless anguish. But then aren't we violating her trust in us to act morally and to speak the truth?

In such cases, we seem to have a conflict in our duties. It is because of such familiar kinds of conflicts that Ross rejects the possibility of discovering absolute, invariant moral rules like "Always tell the truth" and "Always eliminate needless suffering." In cases like the one above, we cannot hold that both rules are absolute without contradicting ourselves. Ross says that we have to recognize that every rule has exceptions and must in some situations be overridden.

Actual Duties and Prima Facie Duties

If rules like "Always tell the truth" cannot be absolute, then what status can they have? When our rules come into conflict in particular situations, how are we to decide which rule applies? Ross answers this question by making use of a distinction between what is actually right and what is prima facie right. Since we have a duty to do what is right, this distinction can be expressed as one between *actual duty* and *prima facie duty.*

An actual duty is simply what my real duty is in a situation. It is the action that, out of the various possibilities, I ought to perform. More often than not, however, I may not know what my actual duty is. In fact, for Ross, the whole problem of ethics might be said to be the problem of knowing what my actual duty is in any given situation.

"Prima facie" literally means "at first sight," but Ross uses the phrase to mean something like "other things being equal." Accordingly, a prima facie duty is one that dictates what I should do when other relevant factors in a situation are not considered. If I promised to meet you for lunch, then I have a prima facie duty to meet you. But suppose I am a physician and, just as I am about to leave for an appointment, the patient I am with suffers cardiac arrest. In such circumstances, according to Ross's view, I should break my promise and render aid to the patient. My prima facie duty to keep my promise doesn't make that fact obligatory. It constitutes a moral reason for meeting you, but there is also a moral reason for not meeting you. I also have a prima facie duty to aid my patient, and this is a reason that outweighs the first one. Thus, aiding the patient is both a prima facie duty and, in this situation, my actual duty.

The notion of a prima facie duty permits Ross to offer a set of moral rules stated in such a way that they are both universal and free from exceptions. For Ross, for example, lying is always wrong, but it is wrong prima facie. It may be that in a particular situation my actual duty requires that I lie. Even though what I have done is prima facie wrong, it is the morally right thing to do if some other prima facie duty that requires lying in the case is more stringent than the prima facie duty to tell the truth. (Perhaps only by lying am I able to prevent a terrorist from blowing up an airplane.) I must be able to explain and justify my failure to tell the truth, and it is of course possible that I may not be able to do so. It may be that I was confused and misunderstood the situation or failed to consider other alternatives. I may have been wrong to believe that my actual duty required me to lie. However, even if I was correct in my belief, that I lied is still prima facie wrong. It is this fact (and for Ross it is a fact) that requires me to explain and justify my action.

We have considered only a few simple examples of prima facie duties, but Ross is more thorough and systematic than our examples might suggest. He offers a list of duties that he considers binding on all moral agents. Here they are in summary form:

1.   Duties of Fidelity: telling the truth, keeping actual and implicit promises, and not representing fiction as history.

2.   Duties of Reparation: righting the wrongs we have done to others.

3.   Duties of Gratitude: recognizing the services others have done for us.

4.   Duties of Justice: preventing a distribution of pleasure or happiness that is not in keeping with the merit of the people involved.

5.   Duties of Beneficence: helping to better the condition of other beings with respect to virtue, intelligence, or pleasure.

6.   Duties of Self-Improvement: bettering ourselves with respect to virtue or intelligence.

7.   Duties of Nonmaleficence: avoiding or preventing an injury to others.

Ross doesn't claim that this is a complete list of the prima facie duties that we recognize. However, he does believe that the duties on the list are all ones that we acknowledge and are willing to accept as legitimate and binding without argument. He believes that if we simply reflect on these prima facie duties we will see that they may be truly asserted. As he puts the matter:

> I . . . am claiming that we *know* them to be true. To me it seems as self-evident as anything could be, that to make a promise, for instance, is to create a moral claim on us in someone else. Many readers will perhaps say that they do *not* know this to be true. If so I certainly cannot prove it to them. I can only ask them to reflect again, in the hope that they will ultimately agree that they also know it to be true.

Notice that Ross explicitly rejects the possibility of providing us with reasons or arguments to convince us to accept his list of prima facie duties. We are merely invited to reflect on certain kinds of cases, like keeping promises, and Ross is convinced that this reflection will bring us to accept his claim that these are true duties. Ross, like other intuitionists, tries to get us to agree with his moral perceptions in much the same way as we might try to get people to agree with us about our color perceptions. We might, for example, show a paint sample to a friend and say, "Don't you think that looks blue? It does to me. Think about it for a minute."

We introduced the distinction between actual and prima facie duties to deal with those situations in which duties seem to conflict. The problem, as we can now state it, is this: What are we to do in a situation in which we recognize more than one prima facie duty and it is not possible for us to act in a way that will fulfill them? We know, of course, that we should act in a way that satisfies our actual duty. But that is just our problem. What, after all, is our actual duty when our prima facie duties are in conflict?

Ross offers us two principles to deal with cases of conflicting duty. The first principle is designed to handle situations in which just two prima facie duties are in conflict: *That act is one's duty which is in accord with the more stringent prima facie obligation.*

The second principle is intended to deal with cases in which several prima facie duties are in conflict: *That act is one's duty which has the greatest balance of prima facie rightness over prima facie wrongness.*

Unfortunately, both these principles present problems in application. Ross does not tell us how we are to determine when an obligation is "more stringent" than another. Nor does he give us a rule for determining the "balance" of prima facie rightness over wrongness. Ultimately, according to Ross, we must simply rely upon our perceptions of the situation. There is no automatic or mechanical procedure that can be followed. If we learn the facts in the case, consider the consequences of our possible actions, and reflect on our prima facie duties, we should be able to arrive at a conclusion as to the best course of action—in Ross's view something that we as moral agents must and can do.

To return to specific cases, perhaps there is no direct way to answer the abstract ques-tion, Is the duty not to lie to a patient "more stringent" than the duty not to cause needless suffering? So much depends on the character and condition of the individual patient that an abstract determination of our duty based on "balance" or "stringency" is useless. However, knowing the patient, we should be able to perceive what the right course of action is.

Ross further believes that there are situations in which there are no particular difficulties about resolving the conflict between prima facie duties. For example, most of us would agree that, if we can save someone from serious injury by lying, then we have more of an obligation to save someone from injury than we do to tell the truth.

Ross's Ethics in the Medical Context

Ross's moral rules are not absolute in the sense that Kant's are; consequently, as with utilitarianism, it is not possible to say what someone's duty would be in an actual concrete situation. We can discuss in general, however, the advantages that Ross's theory brings to medical-moral issues. We shall mention only two for illustration.

First and most important is Ross's list of prima facie duties. The list of duties can serve an important function in the moral education of physicians, researchers, and other medical personnel. The list encourages each person responsible for patient care to reflect on the prima facie obligations that he or she has toward those people and to set aside one of those obligations only when morally certain that another obligation takes precedence.

The specific duties imposed in a prima facie way are numerous and can be expressed in terms relevant to the medical context: do not injure patients; do not distribute scarce resources in a way that fails to recognize individual worth; do not lie to patients; show patients kindness and understanding; educate patients in ways useful to them; do not hold out false hopes to patients, and so on.

Second, like utilitarianism, Ross's ethics encourages us to show sensitivity to the unique features of situations before acting. Like Kant's ethics, however, Ross's also insists that we look at the world from a particular moral perspective. In arriving at decisions about what is right, we must learn the facts of the case and explore the possible consequences of our actions. Ultimately, however, we must guide our actions by what is right, rather than by what is useful, or by what will produce happiness, or anything of the kind.

Since for Ross actions are not always justified in terms of their results, we cannot say unequivocally "It's right to trick this person into becoming a research subject because the experiment may benefit thousands." Yet, we cannot say that it is always wrong for a researcher to trick a person into volunteering. An action is right or wrong regardless of what we think about it, but in a particular case circumstances might justify an experimenter in allowing some other duty to take precedence over the duty of fidelity.

Fundamentally, then, Ross's ethics offers us the possibility of gaining the advantages of utilitarianism without ignoring the fact that there seem to be duties with an undeniable moral force behind them that cannot be accounted for by utilitarianism. Ross's ethics accommodates not only our intuition that certain actions should be performed just because they are right but also our inclination to pay attention to the results of actions and not just the motives behind them.

Difficulties

The advantages Ross's ethics offers over both utilitarianism and Kantianism are offset by some serious difficulties. To begin with, it seems false that we all grasp the same principles. We are well aware that people's beliefs about what is right and about what their duties are result from the kind of education and experience that they have had. The ability to perceive what is good or right does not appear to be universally shared. Ross does say that the principles are the convictions of "the moral consciousness of the best people." In any ordinary sense of "best," there is reason to say that such people don't always agree on moral principles. If "best" means "morally best," then Ross is close to being circular: the best people are those who acknowledge the same prima facie obligations, and those who recognize the same prima facie obligations are the best people.

Some have objected that Ross's list of prima facie duties seems incomplete. For example, Ross does not explicitly say that we have a prima facie obligation not to steal, but most people would hold that if we have any prima facie duties at all, the duty not to steal must surely be counted among them. Of course, it is possible to say that stealing is covered by some other obligation—the duty of fidelity, perhaps, since stealing may violate a trust. Nevertheless, from a theory based on intuition, the omission of such duties leaves Ross's list peculiarly incomplete.

Further, some critics have claimed that it is not clear that there is always even a prima facie obligation to do some of the things Ross lists. Suppose that I promise to lie about a friend's physical condition so that he can continue to collect insurance payments. Some would say that I have no obligation at all to keep such an unwise promise. In such a case, there would be no conflict of duties, because I don't have even a prima facie duty to keep such a promise.

Finally, Ross's theory, some have charged, seems to be false to the facts of moral disagreements. When we disagree with someone about an ethical matter, we consider reasons for and against some position. Sometimes the discussion results in agreement. But according to Ross's view this should not be possible. Although we may discuss circumstances and consequences and agree about the prima facie duties involved, ultimately I arrive at my judgment about the duty that is most stringent or has the greatest degree of prima facie rightness and you arrive at yours. At this point, it seems, there can be no further discussion, even though the two judgments are incompatible. Thus, a choice between the two judgments about what act should be performed becomes arbitrary.

Few contemporary philosophers would be willing to endorse Ross's ethical theory without serious qualifications. The need for a special kind of moral perception (or "intuition") marks the theory as unacceptable for most philosophers. Yet many would acknowledge that the theory has great value in illuminating such aspects of our moral experience as reaching decisions when we feel the pull of conflicting obligations. Furthermore, at least some would acknowledge Ross's prima facie duties as constituting an adequate set of moral principles.

RAWLS'S THEORY OF JUSTICE

In 1971 the Harvard philosopher John Rawls published a book called *A Theory of Justice*. The work continues to attract a considerable amount of attention and has been described by some as the most important book in moral and social philosophy of this century.

One commentator, R. P. Wolfe, points out that Rawls attempts to develop a theory that combines the strengths of utilitarianism with those of the deontological position of Kant and Ross, while avoiding the weaknesses of each view. Utilitarianism claims outright that happiness is fundamental and suggests a direct procedure for answering ethical-social questions. But it is flawed by its lack of a principle of justice. Kant and Ross make rightness a fundamental moral notion and stress the ultimate dignity of human beings. Yet neither provides a workable method for solving problems of social morality. Clearly, Rawls's theory promises much if it can succeed in uniting the two ethical traditions we have discussed.

The Original Position and the Principles of Justice

For Rawls the central task of government is to preserve and promote the liberty and welfare of individuals. Thus, principles of justice are needed to serve as standards for designing and evaluating social institutions and practices. They provide a way of resolving conflicts among the competing claims that individuals make and a means of protecting the legitimate interests of individuals. In a sense, the principles of justice constitute a blueprint for the development of a just society.

But how are we to formulate principles of justice? Rawls makes use of a hypothetical device he calls "the original position." Imagine a group of people like those who make up our society. These people display the ordinary range of intelligence, talents, ambitions, convictions, and social and economic advantages. They include both sexes and members of various racial and ethnic groups.

Furthermore, suppose that this group is placed behind what Rawls calls "a veil of ignorance." Assume that each person is made ignorant of his or her sex, race, natural endowments, social position, economic condition, and so on. Furthermore, assume that these people are capable of cooperating with one another, that they follow the principles of rational decision making, and that they are capable of a sense of justice and will adhere to principles they agree to adopt. Finally, assume that they all desire what Rawls calls "primary goods": the rights, opportunities, powers, wealth, and such that are both worth possessing in themselves and are necessary to securing the more specific goods an individual may want.

Rawls argues that the principles of justice chosen by such a group will be just if the conditions under which they are selected and the procedures for agreeing on them are fair. The original position, with its veil of ignorance, characterizes a state in which alternative notions of justice can be discussed freely by all. Since the ignorance of the participants means that individuals cannot gain advantage for themselves by choosing principles that favor their own circumstances, the eventual choices of the participants will be fair. Since the participants are assumed to be rational, they will be persuaded by the same reasons and arguments. These features of the original position lead Rawls to characterize his view as "justice as fairness."

We might imagine at first that some people in the original position would gamble and argue for principles that would introduce gross inequalities in their society. For example, some might argue for slavery. If these people should turn out to be masters after the veil of ignorance is stripped away, they would gain immensely. But if they turn out to be slaves, then they would lose immensely. However, since the veil of ignorance keeps them from knowing their actual positions in society, it would not be rational for them to endorse a principle that might condemn them to the bottom of the social order.

Given the uncertainties of the original situation, there is a better strategy that these rational people would choose. In the economic discipline known as game theory, this strategy is called "maximin." When we choose in uncertain situations, this strategy directs us to select from the alternatives the one whose worst possible outcome is better than the worst possible outcome of the other alternatives. (If you don't know whether you're going to be a slave, you shouldn't approve a set of principles that permits slavery when you have other options.)

Acting in accordance with this strategy, Rawls argues that people in the original position would agree on the following two principles of justice:

1. Each person is to have an equal right to the most extensive total system of equal basic liberties compatible with a similar system of liberty for all.

2. Social and economic inequalities are to be arranged so that they are both: (a) to the greatest benefit of the least advantaged . . . , and (b) attached to offices and positions open to all under conditions of fair equality of opportunity.

For Rawls, these two principles are taken to govern the distribution of all social goods: liberty, property, wealth, and social privilege. The first principle has priority. It guarantees a system of equal liberty for all. Furthermore, because of its priority, it explicitly prohibits the bartering away of liberty for social or economic benefits. (For example, a society cannot withhold the right to vote from its members on the grounds that voting rights damage the economy.)

The second principle governs the distribution of social goods other than liberty. Although society could organize itself in a way that would eliminate differences in wealth and abolish the advantages that attach to different social positions, Rawls argues that those in the original position would not choose this form of egalitarianism. Instead, they would opt for the second principle of justice. This means that in a just society differences in wealth and social position can be tolerated only when they can be shown to benefit everyone and to benefit, in particular, those who have the fewest advantages. A just society is not one in which everyone is equal, but one in which inequalities must be demonstrated to be legitimate. Furthermore, there must be a genuine opportunity for acquiring membership in a group that enjoys special benefits. Those not qualified to enter medical schools because of past discrimination in education, for example, can claim a right for special preparation to qualify them. (Of course in a Rawlsian society there would be no discrimination to be compensated for.)

Rawls argues that these two principles are required to establish a just society. Furthermore, in distributing liberty and social goods, the principles guarantee the worth and self-respect of the individual. People are free to pursue their own conception of the good and fashion their own lives. Ultimately, the only constraints placed on them as members of society are those expressed in the principles of justice.

Yet Rawls also acknowledges that those in the original position would recognize that we have duties both to ourselves and to others. They would, for example, want to take measures to see that their interests are protected if they should meet with disabling accidents, become seriously mentally disturbed, and so on. Thus, Rawls approves a form of paternalism: others should act for us when we are unable to act for ourselves. When our preferences are known to them, those acting for us should attempt to follow what we would wish. Otherwise, they should act for us as they would act for themselves if they were viewing our situation from the standpoint of the original position. Paternalism is thus a duty to ourselves that would be recognized by those in the original position.

Rawls is also aware of the need for principles that bind and guide individuals as moral decision makers. He claims that those in the original position would reach agreement on principles for such notions as fairness in our dealings with others, fidelity, respect for persons, and beneficence. From these principles we gain some of our obligations to one another.

But, Rawls claims, there are also "natural duties" that would be recognized by those in the original position. Among those Rawls mentions are (1) the duty of justice—supporting and complying with just institutions, (2) the duty of helping others in need or jeopardy, (3) the duty not to harm or injure another, (4) the duty to keep our promises.

For the most part, these are duties that hold between or among people. They are only some of the duties that would be offered by those in the original position as unconditional duties. Thus, Rawls in effect endorses virtu-

ally the same duties as those that Ross presents as prima facie duties. Rawls realizes that the problem of conflicts of duty was left unsolved by Ross and so perceives the need for assigning priorities to duties—ranking them as higher and lower. Rawls believes that a full system of principles worked out from the original position would include rules for ranking duties. Rawls's primary concern, however, is with justice in social institutions, and he does not attempt to establish any rules for ranking.

Rawls's Theory of Justice in the Medical Context

Rawls's "natural duties" are virtually the same as Ross's prima facie duties. Consequently, most of what we said earlier about prima facie duties and moral decision making applies to Rawls.

Rawls endorses the legitimacy of paternalism, although he does not attempt to specify detailed principles to justify individual cases. He does tell us that we should consider the preferences of others when they are known to us and when we are in a situation in which we must act for them because they are unable to act for themselves. For example, suppose we know that a person approves of electroconvulsive therapy (shock treatments, or ECT) for the treatment of severe depression. If that person should become so depressed as to be unable to reach a decision about his own treatment, then we would be justified in seeing to it that he received ECT.

To take a similar case, suppose that you are a surgeon and have a patient who has expressed to you her wish to avoid numerous operations that may prolong her life six months or so but will be unable to restore her to health. If in operating you learned that she has a form of uterine cancer that had spread through her lower extremities and if in your best judgment nothing could be done to restore her to health, then it would be your duty to her to allow her to die as she chooses. Repeated operations would be contrary to her concept of her own good.

The most important question in exploring Rawls's theory is how the two principles of justice might apply to the social institutions and practices of medical care and research. Most obviously, Rawls's principles repair utilitarianism's flaw with respect to human experimentation. It would never be right, in Rawls's view, to exploit one group of people or even one person for the benefit of others. Thus, experiments in which people are forced to be subjects or are tricked into participating are ruled out. They involve a violation of basic liberties of individuals and of the absolute respect for persons that the principles of justice require.

A person has a right to decide what risks she is willing to take with her own life and health. Thus, voluntary consent is required before someone can legitimately become a research subject. However, society might decide to reward research volunteers with money, honors, or social privileges to encourage participation in research. Provided that the overall structure of society already conforms to the two principles of justice, this is a perfectly legitimate practice so long as it brings benefits (ideally) to everyone and the possibility of gaining the rewards of participation is open to all.

Regarding the allocation of social resources in the training of medical personnel (physicians, nurses, therapists, and so on), one may conclude that such investments are justified only if the withdrawal of the support would work to the disadvantage of those already most disadvantaged. Public money may be spent in the form of scholarships and institutional grants to educate personnel, who may then derive great social and economic benefits from their education. But for Rawls the inequality that is produced is not necessarily unjust. Society can invest its resources in this way if it brings benefits to those most in need of them.

The implication of this position seems to be that everyone is entitled to health care. First, it could be argued that health is among the "primary goods" that Rawls's principles are designed to protect and promote. After all, without health an individual is hardly in a position to pursue other more specific goods, and those in the original position might be imagined to be aware of this and to endorse only those principles of justice that would require providing at least basic health care to those in the society. Furthermore, it could be argued that the inequalities of the health-care system can be justified only if those in most need can benefit from them. Since this is not obviously the case with the present system, Rawls's principles seem to call for a reform that would provide health care to those who are unable to pay.

However, it is important to point out that it is not at all obvious that a demand to reform our health-care system follows from Rawls's position. For one thing, it is not clear that Rawls's principles are intended to be directly applied to our society as it is. Our society includes among its members people with serious disabilities and ones with both acute and chronic diseases. If Rawls's principles are intended to apply only to people with normal physical and psychological abilities and needs, as he sometimes suggests, then it is not clear that those who are ill can be regarded as appropriate candidates. If they are considered appropriate, then the results may be unacceptable. The principles of justice may require that we devote vast amounts of social resources to making only marginal improvements in the lives of those who are ill.

Furthermore, Rawls does not explicitly mention the promotion of health as one of the primary goods. It may seem reasonable to include it among them, giving the significance of health as a condition for additional pursuits, but this is a point that requires support. (Norman Daniels is one who has argued for considering health a primary good.) This seems the most promising position to take if Rawls's principles are to be used as a basis for evaluating our current health policies and practices.

It seems reasonable to hold that Rawls's principles, particularly the second, can be used to restrict access to certain kinds of health care. In general, individuals may spend their money in any way they wish to seek their notions of what is good. Thus, if someone wants cosmetic surgery to change the shape of his chin and has the money to pay a surgeon, then he may have it done. But if medical facilities or personnel should become overburdened and unable to provide needed care for the most seriously afflicted, then the society would be obligated to forbid cosmetic surgery. By doing this it would then increase the net access to needed health care by all members of society. By doing this it would then increase the net access to needed health care by all members of society. The rich who desired cosmetic surgery would not be permitted to exploit the poor who needed basic health care.

These are just a few of the possible implications that Rawls's theory has for medical research and practice. It seems likely that more and more applications of the theory will be worked out in detail in the future.

Difficulties

Rawls's theory is currently the subject of much discussion in philosophy. The debate is often highly technical, and a great number of objections have been raised. At present, however, there are no objections that would be acknowledged as legitimate by all critics. Rather than attempt to summarize the debate, we shall simply point to two aspects of Rawls's theory that have been acknowledged as difficulties.

One criticism concerns the original position and its veil of ignorance. Rawls does not permit those in the original position to know anything of their own purposes, plans, or interests—of their conception of the good. They do not know whether they prefer tennis to Tennyson, pleasures of mind over pleasures of the body. They are allowed to consider only those goods—self-respect, wealth, social position—that Rawls puts before them. Thus, critics have said, Rawls has excluded morally relevant knowledge. It is impossible to see how people could agree on principles to regulate their lives when they are so ignorant of their desires and purposes. Rawls seems to have biased the original position in his favor, and this calls into question his claim that the original position is a fair and reasonable way of arriving at principles of justice.

A second criticism focuses on whether Rawls's theory is really as different from utilitarianism as it appears to be. Rawls's theory may well permit inequalities of treatment under certain conditions in the same way that the principle of utility permits them. The principles of justice that were stated earlier apply, Rawls says, only when liberty can be effectively established and maintained. Rawls is very unclear about when a situation may be regarded as one of this kind. When it is not, his principles of justice are ones of a "general conception." Under this conception, liberties of individuals can be restricted, provided that the restrictions are for the benefit of all. It is possible to imagine, then, circumstances in which we might force individuals to become experimental subjects both for their own benefit and for that of others. We might, for example, require that all cigarette smokers participate in experiments intended to acquire knowledge about lung and heart damage. Since everyone would benefit, directly or indirectly, from such knowledge, forcing their participation would be legitimate. Thus, under the general conception of justice, the difference between Rawls's principles and the principle of utility may, in practice, become vanishingly small.

NATURAL LAW ETHICS AND MORAL THEOLOGY

The general view that the rightness of actions is something determined by nature itself, rather than by the laws and customs of societies or the preferences of individuals, is called "natural law theory." Moral principles are thus regarded as objective truths that can be discovered in the nature of things by reason and reflection. The basic idea of the theory was expressed succinctly by the Roman philosopher Cicero (103–43 B.C.). "Law is the highest reason, implanted in Nature, which commands what ought to be done and forbids the opposite. This reason, when firmly fixed and fully developed in the human mind, is Law."

The natural law theory originated in classical Greek and Roman philosophy and has immensely influenced the development of moral and political theories. Indeed, all the ethical theories we have discussed are indebted to the natural law tradition. The reliance upon reason as a means of settling upon or establishing ethical principles and the emphasis on the need to reckon with the natural abilities and inclinations of human nature are just two of the threads that are woven into the theories that we have discussed.

Purposes, Reason, and the Moral Law as Interpreted by Roman Catholicism

The natural law theory of Roman Catholicism was given its most influential formulation in the thirteenth century by St. Thomas Aquinas (1225–1274). Contemporary versions of the theory are mostly elaborations and interpretations of Aquinas's basic statement. Thus, an understanding of Aquinas's views is important for grasping the philosophical principles that underlie the Roman Catholic position on such issues as abortion.

Aquinas was writing at a time in which a great number of the texts of Aristotle (384–322 B.C.) were becoming available in the West, and Aquinas's philosophical theories incorporated many of Aristotle's principles. A fundamental notion borrowed by Aquinas is the

view that the universe is organized in a teleological way. That is, the universe is structured in such a way that each thing in it has a goal or purpose. Thus, when conditions are right, a tadpole will develop into a frog. In its growth and change, the tadpole is following "the law of its nature." It is achieving its goal.

Humans have a material nature, just as a tadpole does, and in their own growth and development they too follow a law of their material nature. But Aquinas also stresses that humans possess a trait that no other creature does—reason. Thus, the full development of human potentialities—the fulfillment of human purpose—requires that we follow the direction of the law of reason, as well as being subjected to the laws of material human nature.

The development of reason is one of our ends as human beings, but we also rely upon reason to determine what our ends are and how we can achieve them. It is this function of reason that leads Aquinas to identify reason as the source of the moral law. Reason is practical in its operation, for it directs our actions so that we can bring about certain results. In giving us directions, reason imposes an obligation on us, the obligation to bring about the results that it specifies. But Aquinas says that reason cannot arbitrarily set goals for us. Reason directs us toward our good as the goal of our action, and what that good is, is discoverable within our nature. Thus reason recognizes the basic principle "Good is to be done and evil avoided."

But this principle is purely formal, or empty of content. To make it a practical principle we must consider what the human good is. According to Aquinas, the human good is that which is suitable or proper to human nature. It is what is "built into" human nature in the way that, in a sense, a frog is already "built into" a tadpole. Thus, the good is that to which we are directed by our natural inclinations as both physical and rational creatures.

Like other creatures, we have a natural inclination to preserve our lives; consequently, reason imposes on us an obligation to care for our health, not to kill ourselves, and not to put ourselves in positions in which we might be killed. We realize through reason that others have a rational nature like ours, and we see that we are bound to treat them with the same dignity and respect that we accord ourselves. Furthermore, when we see that humans require a society to make their full development possible, we realize that we have an obligation to support laws and practices that make society possible.

Thus, for example, as we have a natural inclination to propagate our species (viewed as a "natural" good), reason places on us an obligation not to thwart or pervert this inclination. As a consequence, to fulfill this obligation within society, reason supports the institution of marriage.

Reason also finds in our nature grounds for procedural principles. For example, because everyone has an inclination to preserve his life and well-being, no one should be forced to testify against himself. Similarly, because all individuals are self-interested, no one should be permitted to be a judge in his own case.

Physical inclinations, under the direction of reason, point us toward our natural good. But, according to Aquinas, reason itself can also be a source of inclinations. For example, Aquinas says that reason is the source of our natural inclination to seek the truth, particularly the truth about the existence and nature of God.

Just from the few examples we have considered, it should be clear how Aquinas believed it was possible to discover in human nature natural goods. Relying upon these as goals or purposes to be achieved, reason would then work out the practical way of achieving them. Thus, through the subtle application of reason, it should be possible to establish a body of moral principles and rules. These are the doctrines of natural law.

Because natural law is founded on human nature, which is regarded as unchangeable,

Aquinas regards natural law itself as unchangeable. Moreover, it is seen as the same for all people, at all times, and in all societies. Even those without knowledge of God can, through the operation of reason, recognize their natural obligations.

For Aquinas and for Roman Catholicism, this view of natural law is just one aspect of a broader theological framework. The teleological organization of the universe is attributed to the planning of a creator—goals or purposes are ordained by God. Furthermore, although natural law is discoverable in the universe, its ultimate source is divine wisdom and God's eternal law. Everyone who is rational is capable of grasping natural law. But because passions and irrational inclinations may corrupt human nature and because some people lack the abilities or time to work out the demands of natural law, God also chose to reveal our duties to us in explicit ways. The major source of revelation, of course, is taken to be the Biblical scriptures.

Natural law, scriptural revelation, the interpretation of the scriptures by the Church, Church tradition, and the teachings of the Church are regarded in Roman Catholicism as the sources of moral ideals and principles. By guiding one's life by them, one can develop the rational and moral part of one's nature and move towards the goal of achieving the sort of perfection that is suitable for humans.

This general moral-theological point of view is the source for particular Roman Catholic doctrines that have special relevance to medicine. We shall consider just two of the most important principles.

The Principle of Double Effect. A particular kind of moral conflict arises when the performance of an action will produce both good and bad effects. On the basis of the good effect, it seems it is our duty to perform the action; but on the basis of the bad effect, it seems our duty not to perform it.

Let's assume that the death of a fetus is in itself a bad effect and consider a case like the following: A woman who is three months pregnant is found to have a cancerous uterus. If the woman's life is to be saved, the uterus must be removed at once. But if the uterus is removed, then the life of the unborn child will be lost. Should the operation be performed?

The principle of double effect is intended to help in the resolution of these kinds of conflicts. The principle holds that such an action should be performed only if the intention is to bring about the good effect and the bad effect will be an unintended or indirect consequence. More specifically, four conditions must be satisfied:

1.   The action itself must be morally indifferent or morally good.

2.   The bad effect must not be the means by which the good effect is achieved.

3.   The motive must be the achievement of the good effect only.

4.   The good effect must be at least equivalent in importance to the bad effect.

Are these conditions satisfied in the case that we mentioned? The operation itself, if this is considered to be the action, is at least morally indifferent. That is, in itself it is neither good nor bad. That takes care of the first condition. If the mother's life is to be saved, it will not be *by means of* killing the fetus. It will be by means of removing the cancerous uterus. Thus, the second condition is met. The motive of the surgeon, we may suppose, is not the death of the fetus but saving the life of the woman. If so, then the third condition is satisfied. Finally, since two lives are at stake, the good effect (saving the life of the woman) is at least equal to the bad effect (the death of the fetus). The fourth condition is thus met. Under ordinary conditions, then, these conditions would be considered satisfied and such an operation would be morally justified.

The principle of double effect is most often mentioned in a medical context in cases of abortion. But, in fact, it has a much wider range of application in medical ethics. It bears on cases of contraception, sterilization, organ transplants, and the use of extraordinary measures to maintain life.

The Principle of Totality.   The principle of totality can be expressed in this way: An individual has a right to dispose of his organs or to destroy their capacity to function only to the extent that the general well-being of the whole body demands it. Thus, it is clear that we have a natural obligation to preserve our lives, but, by the Roman Catholic view, we also have a duty to preserve the integrity of our bodies. This duty is based on the belief that each of our organs was designed by God to play a role in maintaining the functional integrity of our bodies, that each has a place in the divine plan. As we are the custodians of our bodies, not their owners, it is our duty to care for them as a trust.

The principle of totality has implications for a great number of medical procedures. Strictly speaking, even cosmetic surgery is morally right only when it is required to maintain or assure the normal functioning of the rest of the body. More important, procedures that are typically employed for contraceptive purposes—vasectomies and tubal ligations—are ruled out. After all, such procedures involve "mutilation" and the destruction of the capacity of the organs of reproduction to function properly. The principle of totality thus also forbids the sterilization of the mentally retarded.

As an ethical theory, natural law theory is sometimes described as teleological. In endorsing the principle "Good is to be done and evil avoided," the theory identifies a goal with respect to which the rightness of an action is to be judged. As the principle of double effect illustrates, the intention of the individual who acts is crucial to determining whether the goal is sought. In a sense, the intention of the action, what the individual wills, defines the action. Thus, "performing an abortion" and "saving a woman's life" are not necessarily the same action, even in those instances in which their external features are the same. Unlike utilitarianism, which is also a teleological theory, natural law theory is not consequentialist: the outcome of an action is not the sole feature to consider in determining the moral character of the action.

Applications of Roman Catholic Moral-Theological Viewpoints in the Medical Context

Roman Catholic ethicists and moral theologians have written on numerous aspects of medical ethics and developed a body of widely accepted doctrine. We shall consider only four topics.

First, the application of the principle of double effect and the principle of totality have definite consequences in the area of medical experimentation. Since we hold our bodies in trust, we are responsible for assessing the degree of risk present in an experiment in which we are asked to be a subject. Thus, we need to be fully informed of the nature of the experiment and the risks that it holds for us. If after obtaining this knowledge we decide to give our consent, it must be given freely and not as the result of deception or coercion.

Because human experimentation carries with it the possibility of injury and death, the principle of double effect and its four strictures apply. If scientific evidence indicates that a sick person may benefit from participating in an experiment, then the experiment is morally justifiable. If, however, the evidence indicates that the chances of helping that person are slight and he or she may die or be gravely injured, then the experiment is not justified. In general, the likelihood of a person's benefiting from the experiment must exceed the danger of that person's suffering greater losses.

A person who is incurably ill may volunteer to be an experimental subject, even though she or he cannot reasonably expect personal gain in the form of improved health.

The good that is hoped for is good for others, in the form of increased medical knowledge. Even here, however, there are constraints imposed by the principle of double effect. There must be no likelihood that the experiment will seriously injure, and the probable value of the knowledge expected to result must balance the risk run by the patient. Not even the incurably ill can be made subjects of trivial experiments.

The good sought by healthy volunteers is also the good of others. The same restrictions mentioned in connection with the incurably ill apply to experimenting on healthy people. Additionally, the principle of totality places constraints on what a person may volunteer to do with his or her body. No healthy person may submit to an experiment that involves the probability of serious injury, impaired health, mutilation, or death.

A second medical topic addressed by Roman Catholic theologians is whether "ordinary" or "extraordinary" measures are to be taken in the preservation of human life. While it is believed that natural law and divine law impose on us a moral obligation to preserve our lives, Catholic moralists have interpreted this obligation as requiring that we rely upon only ordinary means. In the medical profession, the phrase "ordinary means" is used to refer to medical procedures that are standard or orthodox, in contrast with those that are untried or experimental. But from the viewpoint of Catholic ethics, "ordinary" used in the medical context applies to "all medicines, treatments, and operations which offer a reasonable hope of benefit for the patient and which can be obtained and used without excessive expense, pain, or other inconvenience." Thus, by contrast, extraordinary means are those that offer the patient no reasonable hope or whose use causes serious hardship for the patient or others.

Medical measures that would save the life of a patient but subject her to years of pain or would produce in her severe physical or mental incapacities are considered extraordinary.

A patient or her family are under no obligation to choose them, and physicians are under a positive obligation not to encourage their choice.

The third medical topic for consideration is euthanasia. In the Roman Catholic ethical view, euthanasia in any form is considered immoral. It is presumed to be a direct violation of God's dominion over creation and the human obligation to preserve life. The Ethical Directives for Catholic Hospitals is explicit on the matter of taking a life:

> The direct killing of any innocent person, even at his own request, is always morally wrong. Any procedure whose sole immediate effect is the death of a human being is a direct killing. . . . Euthanasia ("mercy killing") in all its forms is forbidden. . . . The failure to supply the ordinary means of preserving life is equivalent to euthanasia.

According to this view, It is wrong to allow babies suffering from serious birth defects to die. If they can be saved by ordinary means, there is an obligation to do so. It is also wrong to act to terminate the lives of those hopelessly ill, either by taking steps to bring about their deaths or by failing to take steps to maintain their lives by ordinary means.

It is never permissible to hasten the death of a person as a direct intention. It is, however, permissible to administer drugs that alleviate pain. The principle of double effect suggests that giving such drugs is a morally justifiable action even though the drugs may indirectly hasten the death of a person.

Last, we may inquire how Roman Catholicism views abortion. According to the Roman Catholic view, from the moment of conception the conceptus (later, the fetus) is considered to be a person with all the rights of a person. For this reason, direct abortion at any stage of pregnancy is regarded as morally wrong. Abortion is "direct" when it results from a procedure "whose sole immediate effect is the termination of pregnancy." This means that what is generally referred to as therapeutic abortion, in which an abortion is performed to safeguard the life or health of the woman, is considered wrong. For example, a woman with serious heart disease who becomes pregnant cannot morally justify an abortion on the grounds that the pregnancy is a serious threat to her life. Even when the ultimate aim is to save the life of the woman, direct abortion is wrong.

We have already seen, however, that the principle of double effect permits the performance of an action that may result in the death of an unborn child if the action satisfies the four criteria for applying the principle. Thus, *indirect* abortion is considered to be morally permissible. That is, the abortion must be the outcome of some action (for example, removal of a cancerous uterus) that is performed for the direct and total purpose of treating a pathological condition affecting the woman. The end sought in direct abortion is the destruction of life, but the end sought in indirect abortion is the preservation of life.

Difficulties

Our discussion has centered on the natural law theory of ethics as it has been interpreted in Roman Catholic theology. Thus, there are two possible types of difficulties: those associated with natural law ethics in its own right and those associated with its incorporation into theology. The theological difficulties go beyond the scope of our aims and interests. We shall restrict ourselves to considering the basic difficulty that faces natural law theory as formulated by Aquinas. Since it is this formulation that has been used in Roman Catholic moral theology, we shall be raising a problem for it in an indirect way.

The fundamental difficulty with Aquinas's argument for natural law is caused by the assumption, borrowed from Aristotle, that the universe is organized in a teleological fashion. (This is the assumption that every kind of thing has a goal or purpose.) This assumption is essential to Aquinas's ethical theory, for he identifies the good of a thing with its natural mode of operation. Without the assumption, we are faced with the great diversity and moral indifference of nature. Inclinations, even when shared by all humans, are no more than inclinations. There are no grounds for considering them "goods," and they have no moral status. The universe is bereft of natural values.

Yet, there are many reasons to consider this assumption false. Physics surrendered the notion of a teleological organization in the world as long ago as the seventeenth century—the rejection of Aristotle's physics also entailed the rejection of Aristotle's teleological view of the world. This left biology as the major source of arguments in favor of teleology. But contemporary evolutionary theory shows that the apparent purposive character of evolutionary change can be accounted for by the operation of natural selection on random mutations. Also, the development and growth of organisms can be explained by the presence of genetic information that controls the processes. The tadpole develops into a frog because evolution has produced a genetic program that directs the sequence of complicated chemical changes. Thus, there seems to be no adequate grounds for asserting that the teleological organization of nature is anything more than apparent.

Science and "reason alone" do not support teleology. It can be endorsed only if one is willing to assume that any apparent teleological organization is the product of a divine plan. Yet, because all apparent teleology can be explained in nonteleological ways, this assumption seems neither necessary nor legitimate.

Without its foundation of teleology, Aquinas's theory of natural law ethics seems to collapse. This is not to say, of course, that some other natural law theory, one not requiring the assumption of teleology, might not be persuasively defended.

PART II. MAJOR MORAL PRINCIPLES

Making moral decisions is always a difficult and stressful task. Abstract discussions of issues never quite capture the feelings of uncertainty and self-doubt we characteristically experience when called upon to decide what ought to be done or to judge whether someone did the right thing. There are no mechanical processes or algorithms we can apply in a situation of moral doubt. There are no computer programs to supply us with the proper decision when given the relevant data.

In a very real sense, we are on our own when it comes to making ethical decisions. This does not mean that we are without resources and must decide blindly or even naively. When we have the luxury of time, when the need to make a decision is not pressing, then we may attempt to work out an answer to a moral question by relying upon a general ethical theory like those discussed earlier. However, in ordinary life we rarely have the opportunity or time to engage in an elaborate process of reasoning and analysis.

A more practical approach is to employ moral principles that have been derived from and justified by a moral theory. A principle such as "Avoid causing needless harm" can serve as a more direct guide to action and decision making than, say, Kant's categorical imperative. With such a principle in mind, we realize that, if we are acting as a physician, then we have a duty to use our knowledge and skills to protect our patients from injury. For example, we should not expose a patient to the needless risk of a diagnostic test that does not promise to yield useful information.

In this section, we will present and illustrate five moral principles. All are ones of special relevance to dealing with the ethical issues presented by decisions concerning medical care. The principles have their limitations. For one thing, they are in no sense complete. Moral issues arise, even in the context of medicine, for which they can supply no direct guidance. In other situations, the principles themselves may come into conflict and point toward incompatible solutions. (How can we both avoid causing harm and allow a terminally ill patient to die?) The principles themselves indicate no way such conflicts can be resolved, for, even taken together, they do not constitute a coherent moral theory. To resolve conflicts, it may be necessary to employ the more basic principles of such a theory.

It is fair to say that each of the five basic moral theories we have discussed endorses the legitimacy of these principles. Not all would formulate them in the same way, and not all would give them the same moral weight. Nevertheless, each theory would accept them as expressing appropriate guidelines for moral decision making.

Indeed, the best way to think about the principles is as guidelines. They are in no way rules that can be applied automatically. Rather, they express standards to be consulted in attempting to arrive at a justified decision. As such, they provide a basis for evaluating actions or policies as well as for making individual moral decisions. They help guarantee that our decisions are made in accordance with principles and not according to our whims or prejudices. By following them we are more likely to reach decisions that are reasoned, consistent, and applicable to similar cases.

THE PRINCIPLE OF NONMALEFICENCE

"Above all, do no harm" is perhaps the most famous and most quoted of all moral maxims in medicine. It captures in a succinct way what is universally considered to be an overriding duty of anyone who undertakes the care of a patient. We believe that in treating a patient a physician should not by carelessness, malice, inadvertence, or avoidable ignorance do anything that will cause injury to the patient.

The maxim is one expression of what is sometimes called in ethics the principle of nonmaleficence. The principle can be formulated in various ways, but here is one relatively noncontroversial way of stating it: *We ought to act in ways that do not cause needless harm or injury to others.* Stated in a positive fashion, the principle tells us that we have a duty to avoid maleficence, that is to avoid harming or injuring other people.

In the most obvious case, we violate the principle of nonmaleficence when we intentionally do something we know will cause someone harm. For example, suppose that a surgeon during the course of an operation deliberately severs a muscle, knowing that by doing so he will cripple the patient. The surgeon is guilty of maleficence and is morally (as well as legally) blameworthy for his action.

The principle may also be violated when no malice or intention to do harm is involved. A nurse who carelessly gives a patient the wrong medication and causes the patient to suffer irreversible brain damage may have had no intention of causing the patient any injury. However, the nurse was negligent in his actions and failed to exercise due care in discharging his responsibilities. His actions resulted in an avoidable injury to his patient. Hence, he failed to meet his obligation of nonmaleficence.

The duty imposed by the principle of nonmaleficence is not a demand to accomplish the impossible. We realize that we cannot reasonably expect perfection in the practice of medicine. We know that the results of treatments are often uncertain and may cause more harm than good. We know that the knowledge we have of diseases is only partial and that decisions about diagnosis and therapy typically involve the exercise of judgment, with no guarantee of correctness. We know there is an uncertainty built into the very nature of things and that our power to control the outcome of natural processes is limited. Consequently, we realize that we cannot hold physicians and other health professionals accountable for every instance of death and injury involving patients under their care.

Nevertheless, we can demand that physicians and others live up to reasonable standards of performance. In the conduct of their professions, we can expect them to be cautious and diligent, patient and thoughtful. We can expect them to pay attention to what they are doing and to deliberate about whether a particular procedure should be done. In addition, we can expect them to possess the knowledge and skills relevant to the proper discharge of their duties.

These features and others like them make up the standards of performance that define what we have a right to expect from physicians and other health professionals. In the language of the law, these are the standards of "due care," and it is by reference to them that we evaluate the medical care given to patients. Failure to meet the standards opens practitioners (physicians, nurses, dentists, therapists) to the charge of moral or legal maleficence.

In our society, we have attempted to guarantee that at least some of the due-care standards are met by relying upon such measures as degree programs, licensing laws, certifying boards, and hospital credentials committees. Such an approach offers a way of seeing to it that physicians and others have acquired at least a minimum level of knowledge, skill, and experience before undertaking the responsibilities attached to their roles. The approach also encourages such values as diligence, prudence, and caution, but there is of course no way of guaranteeing that in a particular case a physician will exhibit those virtues. Haste, carelessness, and inattention are always possible, and the potential that a patient will suffer an injury from them is always present.

The standards of due care are connected in some respects with such factual matters as the current state of medical knowledge and training and the immediate circumstances in which a physician provides care. For example, in the 1920s and 1930s, it was not at all unusual for a general practitioner to perform relatively complicated surgery. This was particularly true of someone practicing in a rural area. In performing surgery, he would be acting in a reasonable and expected fashion and could not be legitimately charged with violating the principle of nonmaleficence.

However, the change in medicine from that earlier time to the present has also altered our beliefs about what is reasonable and expected. Today a general practitioner who has had no special training and is not board certified and yet performs surgery on his patients may be legitimately criticized for maleficence. The standards of due care in surgery are now higher and more exacting than they once were, and the general practitioner who undertakes to perform most forms of surgery causes his patients to undergo an unusual and unnecessary risk literally at his hands. Their interest would be better served if their surgery were performed by a trained and qualified surgeon.

Such a case also illustrates that no actual harm or injury must occur for someone to be acting in violation of the principle of nonmaleficence. The general practitioner performing surgery may not cause any injury to his patients, but he puts them in a position in which the possibility of harm to them is greater than it needs to be. It is in this respect that he is not exercising due care in his treatment and so can be charged with maleficence. He has subjected his patients to *unnecessary* risk, risk greater than they would be subject to in the hands of a trained surgeon.

It is important to stress that the principle of nonmaleficence does not require that a physician subject a patient to no risks at all. Virtually every form of diagnostic testing and medical treatment involves some degree of risk to the patient, and to provide medical care at all, a physician must often act in ways that involve a possible injury to the patient. For example, a physician who takes a thorough medical history and performs a physical examination, then treats a patient with an antibiotic for bacterial infection cannot be held morally responsible if the patient suffers a severe drug reaction. That such a thing might happen is a possibility that cannot be foreseen in an individual case.

Similarly, a serious medical problem may justify subjecting the patient to a serious risk. (Gaining the consent of the patient is an obvious consideration, however.) A life-threatening condition, such as an occluded right coronary artery, may warrant coronary-bypass surgery, with all its attendant dangers.

In effect, the principle of nonmaleficence tells us to avoid needless risk and, when risk is an inevitable aspect of an appropriate diagnostic test or treatment, to minimize the risk as much as is reasonably possible. A physician who orders a lumbar puncture for a patient who complains of occasional headaches is acting inappropriately, given the nature of the complaint, and is subjecting his patient to needless risk. By contrast, a physician who orders such a test after examining a patient who has severe and recurring headaches, a fever, pain and stiffness in his neck, and additional key clinical signs is acting appropriately. The risk to the patient from the lumbar puncture is the same in both cases, but the risk is warranted in the second case and not in the first. A failure to act with due care violates the principle of nonmaleficence, even if no harm results, whereas acting with due care does not violate the principle, even if harm does result.

THE PRINCIPLE OF BENEFICENCE

"As to diseases, make a habit of two things—to help or at least to do no harm." This directive from the Hippocratic writings stresses that the physician has two duties. The second of them ("at least to do no harm") we discussed in connection with the principle of nonmaleficence. The first of them ("to help") we will consider here in connection with the principle of beneficence.

Like the previous principle, the principle of beneficence can be stated in various and different ways. Here is one formulation: *We should act in ways that promote the welfare of other people.* That is, we should help other people when we are able to do so.

Some philosophers have expressed doubt that we have an actual duty to help others. We certainly have a duty not to harm other people, but it has seemed to some that there are no grounds for saying that we have a duty to promote their welfare. We would deserve praise if we did, but we would not deserve blame if we did not. From this point of view, being beneficent is beyond the scope of duty.

We need not consider whether this view is correct in general. For our purposes, it is enough to realize that the nature of the relationship between a physician and a patient does impose the duty of acting in the patient's welfare. That is, the duty of beneficence is inherent in the role of physician. A physician who was not acting for the sake of the patient's good would, in a very real sense, not be acting as a physician.

That we recognize this as a duty appropriate to the physician's role is seen most clearly in cases in which the physician is also a researcher and his patient is also an experimental subject. In such instances, there is a possibility of a role conflict, for the researcher's aim of acquiring knowledge is not always compatible with the physician's aim of helping the patient. (See Chapter 5 for a discussion of this problem.)

The duty required by the principle of beneficence is inherent in the role not only of physicians but of all health professionals. Nurses, therapists, clinical psychologists, social workers, and others accept the duty of promoting the welfare of their patients or clients as an appropriate part of their responsibilities. We expect nurses and others to do good for us, and it is this expectation that leads us to designate them as belonging to what are often called "the helping professions."

The extent to which beneficence is required as a duty for physicians and others is not a matter easily resolved. In practice, we recognize that there are limits to what can be expected from even those who have chosen to make a career of helping others. We do not expect physicians to sacrifice completely their self-interest and welfare on behalf of their patients. We do not think their duty demands that they be totally selfless. If some do, we may praise them as secular saints or moral heroes, but that is because they go beyond the demands of duty. At the same time, we would have little good to say of a physician who always put her interest above that of her patients, who never made a personal sacrifice to serve their interests.

Just as there are standards of due care that explicitly and implicitly define what we consider to be right conduct in protecting patients from harm, so there seem to be implicit standards of beneficence. We obviously expect physicians to help patients by providing them with appropriate treatment. More than this, we expect physicians to be prepared to make *reasonable* sacrifices for the sake of their patients. Even in the age of "health-care terms," a single physician assumes responsibility for a particular patient when the patient is hospitalized or treated for a serious illness. It is this physician who is expected to make the crucial medical decisions, and we expect him or her to realize that discharging that responsibility may involve an interruption of private plans and activities. A surgeon who is informed that her postoperative patient has started to bleed can be expected to cancel her plan to attend a concert. Doing so is a reasonable duty imposed by the principle of beneficence. If she failed to discharge the duty, in the absence of mitigating circumstances, she would become the object of disapproval by her patient and by her medical colleagues.

It would be very difficult to spell out exactly what duties are required by the principle of beneficence. Even if we limited ourselves to the medical context, there are so many ways of promoting someone's welfare and so many different circumstances to consider that it would be virtually impossible to provide anything like a catalogue of appropriate actions. However, such a catalogue is hardly necessary. Most people most often have a sense of what is reasonable and what is not, and it is this sense that we rely on in making judgments about whether physicians and others are fulfilling the duty of beneficence in their actions.

The principles of nonmaleficence and beneficence impose social duties also. In the most general terms, we look to society to take measures to promote the health and safety of its citizens. The great advances made in public health during the nineteenth century were made because the society recognized a responsibility to attempt to prevent the spread of disease. Water treatment plants, immunization programs, and quarantine restrictions were all in recognition of society's duty of nonmaleficence.

These and similar programs have been continued and augmented, and our society has also recognized a duty of beneficence in connection with health care. The Medicaid program for the poor and Medicare for the elderly are major efforts to see to at least some of the health needs of a large segment of the population. Prenatal programs for expectant mothers and public clinics are among the other social responses we have made to promote the health of citizens.

Less obvious than programs that provide direct medical care are ones that support medical research and basic science. Directly or indirectly, such programs contribute to meeting the health needs of our society. Much basic research is relevant to acquiring an understanding of the processes involved in both health and disease, and much medical research is specifically aimed at the development of effective diagnostic and therapeutic measures.

In principle, social beneficence has no limits, but in practice it must. Social resources like tax revenues are in restricted supply, and the society must decide how they are to be spent. Housing and food for the poor, education, defense, the arts, and the humanities are just some of the areas demanding support in the name of social beneficence. Medical care is just one among many claimants, and we must decide as a society what proportion of our social resources we want to commit to medical care. Are we prepared to guarantee to all whatever medical care they need? Are we willing to endorse only a basic level of care? Do we want to say that what is available to some (the rich or well-insured) must be available to all (the poor and uninsured)? Just how beneficent we wish to be—and can afford to be—is a matter still under discussion (see Chapter 9).

THE PRINCIPLE OF UTILITY

The principle of utility can be formulated in this way: *We should act in such a way as to bring about the greatest benefit and the least harm.* As we discussed earlier, the principle is the very foundation of the moral theory of utilitarianism. However, the principle need not be regarded as unique to utilitarianism. It can be thought of as one moral principle among others that present us with a prima facie duty, and as such it need not be regarded as always taking precedence over others. In particular, we would never think it was justified to deprive someone of a right, even if by doing so we could bring benefit to many others.

We need not repeat the discussion of the principle of utility presented earlier, but it may be useful to consider here how the principle relates to the principles of nonmaleficence and beneficence. When we consider the problem of distributing social resources, it becomes clear that acting in accordance with the principles of nonmaleficence and beneficence usually involves tradeoffs. To use our earlier example, as a society we are concerned with providing for the health-care needs of our citizens. To accomplish this end, we support various programs—Medicare, Medicaid, hospital-building programs, medical research, and so on.

However, there are limits to what we can do. Medical care is not the only concern of our society. We are interested in protecting people from harm and in promoting their interests, but there are many forms of harm and many kinds of interest to be promoted. With finite resources at our disposal, the more money we spend on health care, the less we can spend on education, the arts, the humanities, and so on.

Even if we decided to spend more money on health care than we are currently spending, there would come a point at which we would receive only a marginal return for our money. General health would eventually reach such a level that it would be difficult to raise it still higher. To save even one additional life, we would have to spend a vast sum of money. By contrast, at the start of a health-care program, relatively little money can make a relatively big difference. Furthermore, money spent for marginal improvements would be directed away from other needs that had become even more crucial because of underfunding. Thus, we could not spend all our resources on health care without ignoring other social needs.

The aim of social planning is to balance the competing needs of the society. Taken alone, the principles of nonmaleficence and beneficence are of no help in resolving the conflicts among social needs. The principle of utility must come into play to establish and rank needs and to serve as a guide for determining to what extent it is possible to satisfy one social need in comparison with others. In effect, the principle imposes a social duty on us all to use our resources to do as much good as possible. That is, we must do the most good *overall,* even when this means we are not able to meet all needs in a particular area.

The application of the principle of utility is not limited to large-scale social issues, such as how to divide our resources among medical care, defense, education, and so on. We may also rely on the principle when we are deliberating about the choice of alternative means of accomplishing an aim. For example, we might decide to institute a mandatory screening program to detect infants with PKU but decide against a program to detect those with Tay-Sachs. PKU can often be treated successfully if discovered early enough, whereas early detection of Tay-Sachs makes little or no difference in the outcome of the disease. Furthermore, PKU is distributed in the general population, whereas Tay-Sachs occurs mostly in a special segment of the population. In general, then, the additional money spent on screening for Tay-Sachs would not be justified by the results. The money could do more good, produce more benefits, were it spent some other way.

The principle of utility is also relevant to making decisions about the diagnosis and treatment of individuals. For example, as we mentioned earlier, no diagnostic test can be justified if it causes the patient more risk than the information likely to be gained is worth. Invasive procedures are associated with a certain rate of injury and death (morbidity and mortality). It would make no sense to subject a patient to a kidney biopsy if the findings were not likely to affect the course of treatment or if the risk from the biopsy were greater than the risk of the suspected disease itself.

Attempts are well underway in medicine to employ the formal theories of decision analysis to assist physicians in determining whether a particular mode of diagnosis, therapy, or surgery can be justified in individual cases. Underlying the details of formal analysis is the principle of utility, which directs us to act in a way that will bring about the greatest benefit and the least harm.

PRINCIPLES OF DISTRIBUTIVE JUSTICE

We expect (and can demand) to be treated justly in our dealings with other people and with institutions. If our insurance policy covers up to thirty days of hospitalization, then we expect a claim against the policy for that amount of time to be honored. If we arrive in an emergency room with a broken arm before the arrival of someone else with a broken arm, we expect to be attended to before that person.

We do not always expect that being treated justly will work to our direct advantage. Although we would prefer to keep all the money we earn, we realize that we must pay our share of taxes. If a profusely bleeding person arrives in the emergency room after we do, we recognize that he is in need of immediate treatment and should be attended to before we are.

Justice has at least two major aspects. Seeing to it that people receive that to which they are entitled, that their rights are recognized and protected, falls under the general heading of *noncomparative justice.* By contrast, *comparative justice* is concerned with the application of laws and rules and with the distribution of burdens and benefits.

The concern of comparative justice that is most significant to the medical context is *distributive justice.* As the name suggests, distributive justice concerns the distribution of such social benefits and burdens as medical services, welfare payments, public offices, taxes, and military service. In general, the distribution of income has been the focus of recent discussions of distributive justice. In medical ethics, the focus has been the distribution of health care. Is everyone in the society entitled to receive health-care benefits, whether or not she or he can pay for them? If so, then is everyone entitled to the same amount of health care? (See Chapter 9 for a discussion of this issue.)

Philosophical theories of justice attempt to resolve questions of distributive justice by providing a detailed account of the features of individuals and society that will justify our making distinctions in the ways we distribute benefits and burdens. If some people are to be rich and others poor, if some are to rule and others serve, then there must be some rational and moral basis for such distinctions. We look to theories of justice to provide us with such a basis. (See the earlier discussion of John Rawls's theory for an outstanding recent example.)

Theories of justice differ significantly, but at the core of all theories is the basic principle that "Similar cases ought to be treated in similar ways." The principle expresses the notion that justice involves fairness of treatment. For example, it is manifestly unfair to award two different grades to two people who score the same on a multiple-choice exam. If two cases are the same, then it is arbitrary or irrational to treat them differently. To justify different treatment, we would have to show that in some relevant respect the cases are also dissimilar.

This fairness principle is known as the *formal* principle of justice. It is called "formal" because, like a sentence with blanks, it must be filled in with information. Specifically, we must be told what factors or features are to be considered *relevant* in deciding whether or not two cases are similar. If two cases differ in *relevant* respects, we may be justified in treating them differently. We may do so without being either irrational or arbitrary.

Theories of distributive justice present us with *substantive* (or *material*) principles of justice. The theories present us with arguments to show why certain features or factors should be considered relevant in deciding whether cases are similar. The substantive principles can then be referred to in determining whether particular laws, practices, or public policies can be considered just. Further, the substantive principles can be employed as guidelines for framing laws and policies and for developing a just society.

Arguments in favor of particular theories of justice are too lengthy to present here. However, it is useful to consider briefly four substantive principles that have been offered by various theorists as ones worthy of acceptance. To a considerable extent, differences among these principles help explain present disagreements in our society about the ways in which such social "goods" as income, education, and health care should be distributed. Although the principles themselves direct the distribution of burdens (taxation, public service, and so on) as well as benefits, we will focus on benefits. The basic question answered by each principle is, "Who is entitled to what proportion of society's goods?"

The Principle of Equality

According to the principle of equality, all benefits and burdens are to be distributed equally. Everyone is entitled to the same size slice of the pie, and everyone must bear an equal part of the social load. The principle, strictly interpreted, requires a radical egalitariansim—everyone is to be treated the same in all respects.

The principle is most plausible for a society above the margin of production. When there is enough to go around but not much more, then it is manifestly unfair for some to have more than they need and for others to have less than they need. When a society is more affluent, the principle may lose some of its persuasiveness. When greater efforts by a few produce more goods than the efforts of the ordinary person, it may be unfair not to recognize the accomplishments of a few by greater rewards. Rawls's theory remains an egalitarian one, while providing a way to resolve this apparent conflict. According to Rawls, any departure from equality is arbitrary, unless it can be shown that the inequality will work out to *everyone's* advantage.

The Principle of Need

The principle of need is an extension of the egalitarian principle of equal distribution. If goods are parceled out according to individual need, those who have greater needs will receive a greater share. However, the outcome will be one of equality. Since the basic needs of everyone will be met, everyone will end up at the same level. The treatment of individuals will be equal, in this respect, even though the proportion of goods they receive will not be.

What is to count as a need is a significant question that cannot be answered by a principle of distribution alone. Obviously, basic biological needs (food, clothing, shelter) must be included, but what about psychological or intellectual needs? The difficulty of resolving the question of needs is seen in the fact that—even in our affluent society, the richest in the history of the world—we are still debating the question of whether health care should be available to all.

The Principle of Contribution

According to the principle of contribution, everyone should get back that proportion of social goods that is the result of his or her productive labor. If two people work to grow potatoes and the first works twice as long or twice as hard as the second, then the first should be entitled to twice as large a share of the harvest.

The difficulty with this principle in an industrialized, capitalistic society is that contributions to production can take forms other than time and labor. Some people risk their money in investments needed to make production possible, and others contribute crucial ideas or inventions. How are comparisons to be made? Furthermore, in highly industrialized societies it is the functioning of the entire system, rather than the work of any particular individual, that creates the goods to be distributed. A single individual's claim on the outcome of the whole system may be very small.

Nonetheless, it is individuals who make the system work, so it does seem just that individuals should benefit from their contributions. If it is true that it is the system of social organization itself that is most responsible for creating the goods, then this is an argument for supporting the system through taxation and other means. If individual contributions count for relatively little (although for something), there may be no real grounds for attempting to distinguish among them in distributing social benefits.

The Principle of Effort

According to the principle of effort, the degree of effort made by the individual should determine the proportion of goods received by the individual. Thus, the file clerk who works just as hard as the president of a company should receive the same proportion of social goods as the president. Those who are lazy and refuse to exert themselves will receive proportionally less than those who work hard.

The advantage of the principle is that it captures our sense of what is fair—that those who do their best should be similarly rewarded, while those who do less than their best should be less well rewarded. The principle assumes that people have equal opportunities to do their best and that if they do not it is their own fault. One difficulty with this assumption is that, even if the society presents equal opportunities, nature does not. Some people are born with handicaps or meet with accidents, and their misfortunes may make it difficult for them to want to do their best, even when they are given the opportunity.

Each principle has its shortcomings, but this does not mean that adjustments cannot be made to correct their weaknesses. A complete theory of justice need not be limited in the number of principles that it accepts, and it is doubtful that any theory can be shown to be both fair and plausible if it restricts itself to only one principle. While all theories require adjustment, theories fall into types in accordance with the principles they emphasize. For example, Marxist theories select need as basic, while libertarian theories stress personal contribution as the grounds for distribution. Utilitarian theories employ that combination of principles that promises to maximize both private and public interests.

Joel Feinberg, to whom the preceding discussion is indebted, may be mentioned as an example of a careful theorist who recommends the adoption of a combination of principles. Feinberg sees the principle of equality based on needs as the basic determination of distributive justice. After basic needs have been satisfied, the principles of contribution and effort should be given the most weight.

According to Feinberg, when there is an economic abundance, then the claim to "minimally decent conditions" can reasonably be made for every person in the society. To have one's basic needs satisfied under such conditions amounts to a fundamental right. However, when everyone's basic needs are taken care of and society produces a surplus of goods, then considerations of contribution and effort become relevant. Those who contribute most to the increase of goods or those who work the hardest to produce it (or some combination) can legitimately lay claim to a greater share.

The principles of justice we have discussed may seem at first to be intolerably abstract and so irrelevant to the practical business of society. However, it is important to keep in mind that it is by referring to such principles that we criticize our society and its laws and practices. The claim that society is failing to meet some basic need of all of its citizens and that this is unfair or unjust is a powerful charge. It can be a call to action in the service of justice. If the claim can be demonstrated, it has more than rhetorical power. It imposes upon us all an obligation to eliminate the source of the injustice.

Similarly, in framing laws and formulating policies, we expect those who occupy the offices of power and influence to make their decisions in accordance with principles. Prominent among these must be principles of justice. It may be impossible in the conduct of daily business to apply any principle directly or exclusively, for we can hardly remake our society overnight. Yet if we are committed to a just society, then the principles of justice can at least serve as guidelines when policy decisions are made. They remind us that it is not always fair for the race to go to the swift.

THE PRINCIPLE OF AUTONOMY

The principle of autonomy can be stated this way: *Rational individuals should be permitted to be self-determining.* According to this formulation, we act autonomously when our actions are the result of our own choices and decisions. Thus, autonomy and self-determination are equivalent.

Autonomy is associated with the status we ascribe to rational beings as persons in the morally relevant sense. We are committed to the notion that persons are by their very nature uniquely qualified to decide what is in their own best interest. This is because, to use Kant's terms, they are ends in themselves, not means to some other end. As such, they have an inherent worth, and it is the duty of others to respect that worth and avoid treating them as though they were just ordinary parts of the world to be manipulated according to the will of someone else. A recognition of autonomy is a recognition of that inherent worth, and a violation of autonomy is a violation of our concept of what it is to be a person. To deny someone autonomy is to treat her or him as something less than a person.

This view of the nature of autonomy and its connection with our recognition of what is involved in being a person is shared by several significant moral theories. At the core of each theory is the concept of the rational individual as a moral agent who, along with other moral agents, possesses an unconditional worth. Moral responsibility itself is based on the assumption that such agents are free to determine their own actions and pursue their own aims.

Autonomy is significant not only because it is a condition for moral responsibility, but because it is through the exercise of autonomy that individuals shape their lives. We might not approve of what people do with their lives. It is sad to see talent wasted and opportunities for personal development rejected. Nevertheless, as we sometimes say, "It's *his* life." We recognize that people are entitled to attempt to make their lives what they want them to be and that it would be wrong for us to take control of their lives and dictate their actions, even if we could. We recognize that a person must walk to heaven or hell by his own freely chosen path.

Simply put, to act autonomously is to decide for one's self what to do. Of course, decisions are never made outside of a context, and the world and the people in it exert influence, impose constraints, and restrict opportunities. It is useful to call attention to three interrelated aspects of autonomy in order to get a better understanding of the ways in which autonomy can be exercised, denied, and restricted. We will look at autonomy in the contexts of actions, options, and decision making.

Autonomy and Actions

Consider the following situations:

A police officer shoves a demonstrator off the sidewalk during an abortion protest.

An attendant in a psychiatric ward warns a patient to stay in bed or be strapped down.

A corrections officer warns a prison inmate that if he does not donate blood he will not be allowed out of his cell to eat dinner.

A state law requires that anyone admitted to a hospital be screened for the AIDS antibody.

In each of these situations, either actual force, the threat of force, or potential penalties are employed to direct the actions of an individual toward some end. All involve some form of coercion, and the coercion is used to restrict the freedom of individuals to act as they might choose.

Under such circumstances, the individual ceases to be the agent who initiates the action as a result of his or her choice. The individual's initiative is set aside, wholly or partially, in favor of someone else's.

Autonomy is violated in such cases even if the individual intends to act in the way that is imposed or demanded. Perhaps the prison inmate would have donated blood anyway, and surely some people would have wanted to be screened for AIDS. However, the use of coercion makes the wishes or intentions of the individual partly or totally irrelevant to whether the act is performed.

Autonomy as the initiation of action through one's own intention and choice can clearly be restricted to a greater or lesser degree. Someone who is physically forced to become a subject in a medical experiment, as in a Nazi concentration camp, is totally deprived of autonomy. The same is true of someone tricked into becoming a subject without knowing it. In the infamous Tuskegee syphilis studies, some participants were led to believe they were receiving appropriate medical treatment, when in fact they were part of a control group in the experiment. The situation is somewhat different for someone who agrees to become a subject in order to receive needed medical care. Such a person is acting under strong coercion, but the loss of autonomy is not complete. It is at least possible to refuse to participate, even if the cost of doing so may be extremely high.

In situations more typical than those above, autonomy may be compromised, rather than denied. For example, someone who is by nature nonassertive or someone who is poor and uneducated may find it very difficult to preserve his power of self-determination when he becomes a patient in a hospital. Medical authority, represented by physicians and the hospital staff, may be so intimidating to such a person that he does not feel free to exercise his autonomy. In such a case, although no one may be deliberately attempting to infringe on the patient's autonomy, social and psychological factors may constitute a force so coercive that the patient feels he has no choice but to do what he is told.

Autonomy and Options

Autonomy involves more than freedom from duress in making decisions. There must be genuine possibilities to decide among. A forced option is no option at all, and anyone who is in the position of having to take what she can get can hardly be regarded as self-determining or as exercising free choice.

In our society, economic and social conditions frequently limit the options available in medical care. As a rule, the poor simply do not have the same choices available to them as the rich. Someone properly insured or financially well off who might be helped by a heart transplant can decide whether or not to undergo the risk of having one. That is an option not generally available to someone who is uninsured and poor.

Similarly, a woman who depends on Medicaid and lives in a state in which Medicaid funds cannot be used to pay for abortions may not have the option of having an abortion. Her choice is not a genuine one, for she lacks the means to implement it. The situation is quite different for a middle-class woman faced with the same question. She may decide against having an abortion, but whatever she decides, the choice is real. She is autonomous in a way that the poor woman is not.

Those who believe that one of the goals of our society is to promote and protect the autonomy of individuals have frequently argued that we must do more to offer all individuals the same range of health-care options. If we do not, they have suggested, then our society cannot be one in which everyone has an equal degree of autonomy. In a very real sense, those who are rich will have greater freedom of action than those who are poor.

Autonomy and Decision Making

More is involved in decision making than merely saying yes or no. In particular, relevant information is an essential condition for genuine decision making. We are exercising our autonomy in the fullest sense only when we are making *informed* decisions.

It is pointless to have options if we are not aware of them, and we can hardly be said to be directing the course of our lives if our decisions must be made in ignorance of information that is available and relevant to our choices. These are the reasons that lying and other forms of deception are so destructive of autonomy. If someone with a progressive and ordinarily fatal disease is not told about it by her physician, then she is in no position to decide how to shape what remains of her life. The lack of a crucial piece of information—that she is dying—is likely to lead her to make decisions different from the ones she would make were she in possession of the information.

Information is the key to protecting and preserving autonomy in most medical situations. A patient who is not informed of alternative forms of treatment and their associated risks is denied the opportunity to make his own wishes and values count for something in his own life. For example, someone with coronary artery disease who is not told of the relative merits of medical treatment with drugs but is told only that he is a candidate for coronary-artery bypass surgery, is in no position to decide what risks he wishes to take and what ordeals he is prepared to undergo. A physician who does not supply the patient with the information the patient needs is restricting the patient's autonomy. The principle of autonomy requires *informed* consent, for consent alone does not involve genuine self-determination.

Making decisions for "the good" of others (paternalism), without consulting their wishes, deprives them of their status as autonomous agents. For example, some people at the final stages of a terminal illness might prefer to be allowed to die without heroic intervention, while others might prefer to prolong their lives as long as medical skills and technological powers make possible. If a physician or family undertakes to make a decision in this matter on behalf of the patient, then no matter what their motive, they are denying to the patient the power of self-determination.

Because autonomy is so bound up with informed consent and decision making, special problems arise in the case of those unable to give consent and make decisions. Patients who are comatose, severely brain-damaged, psychotic, or seriously mentally impaired are not capable of making decisions on their own behalf. The nature of their condition has already deprived them of their autonomy. Of course this does not mean that they have no status as moral persons or that they have no interests. It falls to others to see that their interests are served.

The situation is similar for those, such as infants and young children, who are incapable of understanding. Any consent that is given must be given by others. But what are the limits of consent that can be legitimately given for some other person? Consenting to needed medical care seems legitimate, but what about rejecting needed medical care? What about consenting to becoming a subject in a research program? These questions are as crucial as they are difficult to resolve.

Restrictions on Autonomy

Autonomy is not an absolute or unconditional value. We would regard it as absurd for someone to claim that he was justified in committing a murder because he was only exercising his power of self-determination. Such a defense would be morally ludicrous.

However, we do value autonomy and recognize a general duty to respect it and even to promote its exercise. We demand compelling reasons to justify restricting the power of individuals to make their own choices and direct their own lives.

We will briefly examine four principles that are frequently appealed to in justifying restrictions on autonomy. The principles have been discussed most in the context of social and legal theory, for it is through laws and penalties that a society most directly regulates the conduct of its citizens. However, the principles can also be appealed to justify policies and practices of institutions (such as hospitals) and the actions of individuals that affect other people.

Appealing to a principle can provide, at best, only a prima facie justification. Even if a principle can be shown to apply to a particular case in which freedom of action is restricted, we may value the lost freedom more than what is gained by restricting it. Reasons suggested by the principle may not be adequately persuasive. Furthermore, the principles themselves are frequently the subjects of controversy, and, with the exception of the harm principle, it is doubtful that any of the principles would be universally endorsed by philosophers and legal theorists.

The Harm Principle.   According to the harm principle, we may restrict the freedom of people to act if the restriction is necessary to prevent harm to others. In the most obvious case, we may take action to prevent violence like rape, robbery, killing, or assault. We may act to protect someone who is in apparent risk of harm from the action of someone else. The risk of harm need not be the result of the intention to harm. Thus, we might take steps to see that a surgeon whose skills and judgment have been impaired through drug use is not permitted to operate. The risk that he poses to his patients warrants the effort to keep him from acting as he wishes.

The harm principle may also be used to justify laws that exert coercive force and so restrict freedom of action. Laws against homicide and assault are clear examples, but the principle extends also to the regulation of institutions and practices. People may be robbed at the point of a pen, as well as at the point of a knife, and the harm produced by fraud may be as great as that produced by outright theft. Careless or deceptive medical practitioners may cause direct harm to their patients, and laws that regulate the standards of medical practice restrict the freedom of practitioners for the protection of patients.

The Principle of Paternalism. In its weak version, the principle of paternalism is no more than the harm principle applied to the individual himself. According to the principle, we are justified in restricting someone's freedom to act if doing so is necessary to prevent him from harming himself. Thus, we might force an alcoholic into a treatment program and justify our action by claiming that we did so to prevent him from continuing to harm himself by his drinking.

In its strong version, the principle of paternalism justifies restricting someone's autonomy if by doing so we can benefit her. In such a case, our concern is not only with preventing the person from harming herself, but also with promoting her good in a positive way. The principle might be appealed to even in cases in which our actions go against the other's known wishes. For example, a physician might decide to treat a patient with a placebo (an inactive drug), even if she has asked to be told the truth about her medical

condition and her therapy. He might attempt to justify his action by claiming that if the patient knew she was receiving a placebo, then the placebo would be less likely to be effective. Since taking the placebo while believing that it is an active drug makes her feel better, the physician may claim that by deceiving her he is doing something to help her.

Paternalism may be expressed in laws and public policies, as well as in private actions. Some have suggested the drug laws as a prime example of governmental paternalism. By making certain drugs illegal and inaccessible and by placing other drugs under the control of physicians, the laws aim to protect people from themselves. Self-medication is virtually eliminated, and the so-called recreational use of drugs is prohibited. The price for such laws is a restriction on individual autonomy. Some have argued that the price is too high and that the most the government should do is warn and educate the individual about the consequences of using certain drugs.

The Principle of Legal Moralism. The principle of legal moralism holds that a legitimate function of the law is to enforce morality by turning the immoral into the illegal. Hence, the restrictions placed on actions by the law are justified by the presumed fact that the actions are immoral and so ought not to be performed.

To a considerable extent, laws express the values of a society and the society's judgments about what is morally right. In our society, homicide and theft are recognized as crimes, and those who commit them are guilty of legal, as well as moral, wrongdoing. Society attempts to prevent such crimes and to punish offenders.

The degree to which the law should embody moral judgments is a hard question. It is particularly difficult to answer in a pluralistic society like ours, in which there may be sharp differences of opinion about the moral legitimacy of some actions. Until quite recently, for example, materials considered obscene could not be freely purchased, birth-control literature could not be freely distributed nor contraceptives legally prescribed in some states, and the conditions of divorce were generally stringent and punitive. Even now many states outlaw homosexual solicitation and acts, and prostitution is generally illegal. The foundation for such laws is the belief by many that the practices proscribed are morally wrong.

The current heated debate over abortion reflects, in some of its aspects, the conflict between those who favor strong legal moralism and those who oppose it. Many who consider abortion morally wrong would also like to see it made illegal once more. Others, even though they may oppose abortion, believe that it is a private moral matter and that the attempt to regulate it by law is an unwarranted intrusion of state power.

The Welfare Principle. The welfare principle holds that it is justifiable to restrict individual autonomy if doing so will result in providing benefits to others. Those who endorse this principle are not inclined to think that it demands a serious self-sacrifice for the welfare of others. Rather, in their view, an ideal application of the principle would be the case in which we give up just a little autonomy to bring about a great deal of benefit to others.

For example, transplant organs are in short supply at the moment because their availability depends mostly on their being freely donated. The situation could be dramatically changed by a law requiring that organs from the recently dead be salvaged and made available for use as transplants.

Such a law would end the present system of voluntary donation, and by doing so it would restrict our freedom to decide what is to be done with our bodies after death. However, it would be easy to argue that the tremendous value that others might gain from such a law easily outweighs the slight restriction on autonomy that it would involve.

These four principles are not the only ones that offer grounds for abridging the autonomy of individuals, but they are the most relevant to decision making and policy planning in medicine. It is important to keep in mind that merely appealing to a principle is not enough to warrant a limit on autonomy. A principle points in the direction of an argument, but it is no substitute for one. The high value we place on autonomy gives its preservation a high priority, and compelling considerations are required to justify compromising it. In the view of some philosophers, who endorse the position taken by Mill, only the harm principle can serve as grounds for legitimately restricting autonomy. Other theorists find persuasive reasons to do so in other principles.

PART III. RETROSPECT

The two major tasks of this chapter have been to provide information about several important ethical theories and to formulate and illustrate several generally accepted moral principles. One aim in performing these tasks was to make it easier to follow the arguments and discussions in the selections that make up the major part of this book.

Another and ultimately more serious aim has been to call attention to ethical theories and principles you may wish to consider adopting. From this standpoint, the problems and issues presented in the selections can be considered test cases for the theories and principles. You may find that some of the theories that we have discussed are inadequate to deal with certain moral issues in the medical context, although they may seem satisfactory in more common or simpler cases. Or you may discover that certain commonly accepted moral principles lead to contradictory results or to conclusions that you find difficult to accept. Other theories or principles may appear to give definite and persuasive answers to medical-moral problems, but you may find that they rest on assumptions that it does not appear reasonable to accept. Such a dialectical process of claims and criticism is slow and frustrating. Yet it offers the best hope of settling on theories and principles that we can accept with confidence and employ without misgivings.

During the last ten years, a great amount of effort has been expended addressing the moral problems of medical practice and research. Without question, progress has been made in developing a better understanding of a number of issues and securing agreement about how they are to be dealt with. Nevertheless, a large number of moral issues in medicine remain unsettled or even unexplored. Even in the absence of moral consensus on these issues, the demands of practical decision making generate a force that presses us for immediate solutions.

In such a situation, we cannot afford to try to settle all doubts about moral principles in an abstract way and only then apply them to problems in medicine. The dialectical process must be made practical. Formulating and testing theories and principles must go on at the same time as we are actually making moral decisions. We must do our best to discover the principles of aerodynamics while staying aloft.

To a considerable extent, that is what this book is about. Positions are taken and defended by the authors. But they, too, are aware that they are participating in a search for a satisfactory resolution to the problems they discuss, and few, if any, would regard their solutions as beyond criticism. Medical ethics is still an area in which there are more legitimate questions than there are satisfactory answers, but the answers that we do have are better supported and better reasoned than those available even ten years ago.

PART I

TERMINATION ⬚

CHAPTER 1

ABORTION ⬚

SOCIAL CONTEXT: THE CONTINUING STRUGGLE OVER ABORTION

The Background: *Roe* v. *Wade*

Norma McCorvey of Dallas was unmarried, poor, and pregnant. She wished to have an abortion, but under Texas law, abortion was a criminal offense, except when required to save the woman's life. California law was less restrictive, and McCorvey believed she could get an abortion there, but she lacked money for travel and expenses. Unwillingly, she bowed to legal and economic necessity and carried the fetus to term. She then gave up the newborn child for adoption.

When McCorvey was later approached by a public interest attorney and asked if she would agree to be the plaintiff in a class-action suit against Henry Wade, the district attorney of Dallas County, challenging the constitutionality of the Texas abortion law, she readily consented. Federal courts ruled that the Texas statute was void, but Wade appealed to the Supreme Court.

Because McCorvey wished her identity to be protected by a pseudonym, the 1973 Supreme Court decision in the case was titled *Roe* v. *Wade*. In a 7-to-2 decision, written by Justice Harry A. Blackmun, the court found the Texas law unconstitutional. In doing so, the court effectively decriminalized abortion,

for abortion laws in most other states differed little from the Texas statute.

The *Roe* decision did not require that abortion be unregulated, but it placed limits on the restrictions states could impose. According to the ruling, during the first twelve weeks (the first trimester) of pregnancy, states cannot restrict a woman's decision about abortion. During the second trimester, states may restrict abortion to protect the health of the woman. In the final trimester, because the fetus may be considered viable, states may limit abortions to those necessary to preserve the health of the woman.

After the *Roe* decision, abortions became easily obtainable by most women who wanted them. Yet the decision also triggered a firestorm of controversy between proponents of relatively unregulated choice ("prochoice" advocates) and opponents of so-called abortion on demand ("prolife" or "right-to-life" advocates) that shows no sign of dying down. While those who favor making abortion a matter of individual decision were pleased by the *Roe* decision, those morally opposed to abortion were not.

Many, if not most, who believe abortion is morally wrong also think it should be illegal, except in very special cases. Within the limits of regulation imposed by the *Roe* decision, opponents of abortion have taken various legal measures to attempt to slow or halt its practice. They have become politically active and have often succeeded in getting laws passed that impose requirements on abortion that make it difficult to get one. As this has happened, advocates of personal choice have often charged that the laws are unconstitutional and have filed suits that have frequently ended up before the Supreme Court.

Supreme Court Decisions after *Roe*

The conflict over abortion has been expressed, in part, in a continuing series of legal skirmishes that have produced a number of Supreme Court decisions seeking to define abortion rights and limits. To get some sense of the way in which laws, regulations, and practices have changed since the *Roe* decision in 1973, it is instructive to review a few Court decisions briefly and consider in more detail the two that have most influenced the direction of public policy on abortion.

Roe v. *Bolton* (1973).   The Court rejected the requirement that abortions had to be performed in hospitals, thus opening the way for abortion clinics.

Planned Parenthood v. *Danforth* (1976). The Missouri law requiring a husband's consent for an abortion was struck down. Also, parents of minor, unmarried girls were found not to have an absolute veto over their daughter's decision to have an abortion.

Maher v. *Roe* (1977).   The Court decided that states do not have a constitutional obligation to pay for abortions for the poor. Hence, the Court left it up to states to decide whether they wished to include funding for abortion as part of their contribution to the Medicaid program.

Harris v. *McRae* (1980).   The Court upheld the Hyde Amendment, the federal law banning the use of federal Medicaid funds to pay for abortions. Hence, those wanting an

abortion and unable to pay for it would have to depend on money from other sources. (States, however, have no constitutional obligation to provide money for abortions.)

City of Akron v. *Akron Center for Reproductive Health* (1983).   The Court struck down a law requiring that women wanting an abortion receive counseling that includes the statement that "the unborn child is a human life from the moment of conception," then wait at least twenty-four hours before reaffirming their decision.

Webster v. *Reproductive Health Services* (1989).   The Missouri law in the *Webster* case is similar to those the Supreme Court had previously held to be void. However, the law was carefully crafted by prolife advocates to avoid the specific difficulties that had led the Court to reject them.

The preamble of the law asserts that "life begins at conception," but at issue in the court dispute were three provisions of the law restricting abortion.

1.   Public employees, including physicians and nurses, are forbidden to perform an abortion, except when necessary to save a woman's life.

2.   Public hospitals, clinics, or other tax-supported facilities cannot be used to perform abortions not necessary to save a woman's life, even if no public funds are involved.

3.   Physicians are required to perform tests to determine the viability of a fetus, if they have reason to believe the woman has been pregnant for at least twenty weeks.

On July 3, 1989, the Supreme Court in a 5-to-4 decision upheld the constitutionality of the law. Chief Justice William Rehnquist, writing the majority opinion, held that the Court did not have to rule against the claim that life begins at conception, for such language is only an expression of a permissible value judgment. Furthermore, "Nothing in the Constitution requires States to enter or remain in the business of performing abortions. Nor . . . do private physicians and their patients have some kind of constitutional right of access to public facilities for the performance of abortions."

So far as viability is concerned, Rehnquist saw a problem, not with the Missouri law, but with *Roe* v. *Wade*'s "rigid trimester analysis of the course of a pregnancy." That is, he found the law more sensitive to the issue of viability than the trimester rule, which holds that the state can regulate abortion in the second trimester to protect a woman's health and regulate it more stringently, down to prohibiting it, in the last trimester. Furthermore, "the key elements" of *Roe* v. *Wade* are "not found in the text of the Constitution or in any place else one would expect to find a constitutional principle."

Justice Harry A. Blackmun, the author of the majority opinion in *Roe* v. *Wade*, wrote the dissenting opinion in *Webster*. He made clear that he regarded the Court's decision as an outright attack on *Roe*. Rehnquist, he argued, failed to consider the case for viability on appropriate grounds—namely, the right to privacy or autonomy, on which *Roe* was decided. Instead, he misread the Missouri law in a way that seemed to conflict with the trimester structure established in *Roe* to balance the state's interest in maternal health and potential life against the right to privacy.

The hope of abortion opponents was that the Court would use the *Webster* case to overturn *Roe* v. *Wade*. The Court stopped short of doing that, but the *Webster* decision made it clear that the Court was willing to approve restrictions on abortion of a sort that it had held unconstitutional until then. Various new state and local regulations were formulated and passed into law.

***Planned Parenthood* v. *Casey* (1992).** The Pennsylvania Abortion Control Act was one of those pieces of legislation framed with the intention of making abortions more difficult to secure. It included the following restrictions:

1. A physician must inform a woman seeking an abortion about the procedure and its risks, the stage of the pregnancy, and the alternative of carrying the fetus to term.

2. The woman must wait at least twenty-four hours after receiving this information before having an abortion.

3. A girl under the age of eighteen must secure the informed consent of at least one parent before having an abortion, and a parent must accompany the girl to counseling. Alternatively, consent may be sought from a court.

4. A married woman must (except under certain circumstances) sign a statement that she has notified her husband of her intention to have an abortion.

The 5-to-4 Court ruling upheld most sections of the Pennsylvania law, but it rejected the provision requiring a married woman to notify her husband of her intention to have an abortion.

However, in the view of some observers, the most important outcome of the *Casey* decision was that it reaffirmed what it called the "essence" of the constitutional right to an abortion, while also introducing a new legal standard for testing the constitutional legitimacy of regulations governing abortions. The Court considered the provisions of the Pennsylvania law in terms of whether they had the purpose or result of imposing an "undue burden" on a woman seeking an abortion. In the Court's definition, a burden is "undue" if it places a "substantial obstacle in the path of a woman seeking an abortion before the fetus attains viability." Only the spousal notification requirement, in the Court's view, imposed such a burden.

The undue-burden standard makes it clear that, in the opinion of the Court, laws that attempt to prohibit abortions outright or those that attempt to reduce the frequency of abortions by making them extraordinarily difficult to obtain are unconstitutional.

In its decision, the Court explicitly endorsed *Roe* v. *Wade* as having established "a rule of law and a component of liberty that we cannot renounce." The majority opinion held that *Roe* has acquired a "rare precedential force" and could be repudiated only "at the cost of both profound and unnecessary damage to the Court's legitimacy and to the nation's commitment to the rule of law."

Until the *Webster* decision, abortion was considered a fundamental right that could not be restricted, except to serve a compelling state interest. This meant that during the first two trimesters of pregnancy, almost all restrictions were considered unconstitutional. After *Webster*, it seemed to many that the way was open for more and heavier regulation of abortion. However, although the "undue-burden" standard introduced in *Casey* will permit considerable regulation during this period, it will not allow opponents of abortion to regulate the practice so heavily as to make it virtually unavailable.

The Court decisions discussed here, as well as a number of others, have had at their core the basic issue of the principle of privacy (or autonomy) with respect to abortion that was enunciated in *Roe* v. *Wade*.

Abortion opponents have repeatedly urged the Supreme Court to restrict the principle of privacy (autonomy) with respect to abortion and to declare abortion unacceptable in all but the most narrow of circumstances. Advocates of personal choice in abortion have just as strongly urged the recognition and strengthening of the privacy principle and have fought against the imposition of regulations that would restrict it. In *Casey*, the most sweeping recent decision, the Court continued to attempt to balance a woman's right of privacy with the state's interest in the protection of prenatal life.

Abortion Protests, Violence, and Intimidation

Three women and two men parade the sidewalk in front of the redbrick building that houses the Women's Clinic. They carry placards that read "Abortion = Murder," "Babies Are People," and "God is Prolife." One of the men carries a glass jar containing the remains of a twenty-week-old fetus.

"They're killing babies in there!" one of the men yells at a woman going into the building. "What if your mother had had an abortion?" another picketer shouts. The woman glances at the group, then pointedly ignores them.

The demonstrators walk their posts three days a week, the days abortions are performed in the clinic. Those willing to stop to talk to them they attempt to convince of the immorality of abortion. Women who admit to being pregnant and considering abortion are subjected to great verbal pressure. Sometimes tempers flare into open anger and fights break out. Patients of the clinic complain that they are being harassed. The protesters claim they are only exercising their freedom of speech and speaking out against a practice that is as wrong as any other form of murder.

The scene could be almost anyplace in the United States during the last few years. The tone of the abortion debate has become angry as some people, convinced of abortion's immorality, have adopted an activist stance. Frustration at failing to make abortion illegal has encouraged some of its opponents to discourage or halt its practice by more direct means.

The first shocking event during a protest occurred on March 10, 1993 in Pensacola, Florida. At a demonstration by Rescue America, an extremist antiabortion group, outside the Pensacola Women's Medical Services clinic, Dr. David Gunn was killed by a man who came out of the crowd and shot him three times. Dr. Gunn regularly traveled throughout Florida, Alabama, and Georgia performing abortions. Arrested and charged with Dr. Gunn's murder was Michael F. Griffin, a fundamentalist Christian who had recently become active in antiabortion protests.

Death returned to Pensacola seventeen months later. On July 29, 1994, Dr. John B. Britton, the physician who took over Dr. Gunn's role, and James H. Barrett, a retired Air Force Lieutenant Colonel acting as his bodyguard, were shot to death outside the Pensacola Ladies Center. Colonel Barrett and his wife, June, were volunteer escorts at the clinic, and they had picked up Dr. Britton at the airport for his scheduled weekly visit. The three were sitting in the Barrett's pickup truck outside the clinic when a man armed with a 12-gauge shotgun walked up to an open window and shot Dr. Britton and Colonel Barrett in the head. Mrs. Barrett was shot in the arm.

Paul J. Hill, a forty-year-old former Presbyterian minister, was arrested and charged with two counts of first-degree murder and one count of attempted murder. Hill was already well known to the local police for having been involved in protest incidents at the clinic. At the time of the shooting, he was due to face trial on a disorderly conduct charge for having shouted, "Oh, Mommy, Mommy, don't kill me" through a clinic window.

Hill was also known for advocating the view that violence against those who perform abortions is justifiable. On the television program "Nightline," Hill stated: "We're saying that 30 million children have died, and sometimes you have to use force, as the police use force, to stop a murderer. Sometimes you have to use force to stop people from killing innocent children."

A few days after the shooting of Dr. Gunn, Hill had appeared on "Donahue" with Gunn's son and offered the view that the shooting of Gunn by Michael Griffin was a justifiable act. He repeated this view on "Sonya Live."

The organization founded by Hill, Defensive Action, is one of several recent groups that endorse the view that if violence is employed to put an end to abortion, it may be justifiable. The most radical leaders view the killing of so-called abortion doctors as cases of justifiable homicide. Hill's group circulated a petition asserting that, "Whatever force is necessary to defend the life of a born child is legitimate to defend the life of an unborn child."

Harassment of Providers and Patients. While the deaths of Gunn, Britton, and Barrett are viewed by most abortion opponents as isolated incidents that are the work of mentally disturbed people, physicians and others associated with abortion clinics have a different view. They see the killings as the culmination of more than a decade of harassment. Threatening letters and phone calls, blocking access of patients to facilities, fire bombings, vandalism, and drive-by shootings have all increased. By some estimates, in the last fifteen years, over a hundred clinics have been destroyed by arson and over a thousand acts of violence against abortion providers have been documented.

Physicians who regularly perform abortions and personnel at clinics admit to feeling frightened by the possibility of violence. Before Dr. Gunn was killed, "Wanted" posters with his picture were circulated and protesters carried signs that said "David Gunn Murders Babies." Some physicians have had protesters follow them home, picket their houses, and harass their families with phone calls. Some have been shot at, and many others have received death threats. Fear has become a constant companion for most.

The tactics have taken their toll. Clinics have closed; hospitals are often unwilling or legally unable to offer abortions to patients; and many physicians have given up performing the procedure. Furthermore, the procedure is such a focus of controversy and strife that some medical schools no longer teach their students to perform it. As a result of this variety of factors, the percentage of women who have no access to abortion is increasing.

Abortion continues to be legally permissible, but its availability is not guaranteed.

In addition to the harassment of abortion providers, pressure on those seeking abortions has increased. Women attempting to gain access to clinics have had their way physically blocked by mobs of protesters or have been subjected to threats, taunts, and psychological pressure in the attempt to discourage them from having an abortion.

Organized Antiabortion Groups. The pressures on abortion providers and patients is partly the result of the emergence of groups organized for the purpose of discouraging abortions. One of these groups, the Lambs of God, is an association of deeply religious Roman Catholics who travel from city to city to do all they can, short of using violence, to discourage abortion. They mount twenty-four hour prayer vigils at the homes of physicians who perform abortions, then block their driveways so they cannot get to work. At abortion clinics, they blockade doors and run up to patients, reciting the Hail Mary or crying, "Mommy, please don't kill me." The Lambs even go so far as to offer to pay women to change their minds. Many Lambs have left their families and given up conventional life to devote themselves to the cause of preventing abortions. For them, opposing abortion is a religious vocation.

The most militant of the abortion-protest groups is Operation Rescue. It was founded by Randall Terry in 1987 and became known nationally in 1991 when it blockaded a clinic in Wichita, Kansas, for forty-six days. Over two thousand people were arrested, and the judge issuing an order to protesters to permit access to the clinic received numerous death threats. Operation Rescue promotes the use of "wanted" posters, picketing physicians' homes, harassing their children and neighbors, and blocking access to abortion services.

Operation Rescue sees its mission as stopping abortion wherever it takes place, so it sends members to various towns and cities. Buffalo and Minneapolis also have been scenes of intensive efforts. The organization also sees part of its role as the training of its members in techniques effective in discouraging or preventing women from getting abortions. However, many moderate opponents of abortion have rejected the tactics of Operation Rescue and dissociated themselves from the organization.

Protective Measures. Legal steps have recently been taken with the aim of protecting the rights of those seeking abortion, while also preserving the First Amendment rights of those protesting abortion. In 1993, Judge Robert McGregor of Florida Circuit Court issued an injunction to protect access to the clinic operated by the Aware Woman Center for Choice in Melbourne, Florida. Demonstrators from Operation Rescue and several related organizations were made subject to the injunction. The order imposed a 300-foot protected zone around the clinic, forbade the display of signs with slogans and images of fetuses that could be seen from inside the clinic, and barred demonstrators from making excessive noise.

In a 6-to-3 ruling written by Justice Rehnquist in the case of *Madsen* v. *Women's Health Center* (June 1994), the Supreme Court upheld the basic provisions of the injunction. The Court approved an approximately thirty-six-foot buffer zone to keep protesters away from the clinic's entrance and parking lot and off a public right-of-way. The buffer zone "burdens no more speech than necessary to accomplish the government's interest," Justice Rehnquist wrote. The Court also upheld a ban on excessive noise during the clinic's hours of operation "to insure the health and well-being of patients at the clinic."

The Court rejected the 300-foot buffer zone within which protesters could not approach clinic patients or employees. It also rejected a similar zone around the homes of the clinic's physicians and staff members. However, the Court indicated that a smaller zone or additional limits on demonstrations around residences would be constitutionally acceptable. Finally, the Court overturned restrictions on signs and images that might be seen from inside the clinic.

Although the Florida case was a local one, it is considered important as an indicator of how the Supreme Court is likely to react to challenges to the Freedom of Access to Clinic Entrances Act that was recently passed by Congress and signed into law by President Clinton. The act is designed to provide federal remedies, including criminal penalties, to restrict violent protests at abortion clinics. Some observers believe that the Florida ruling indicates that the Court is prepared to support the law in the interest of insuring the well-being of patients and providing for public order and safety.

New Policies and the Continuing Struggle

Among the first official acts of President Clinton after taking office was to sign five memoranda to reverse many of the abortion restrictions developed by Republican administrations during the previous twelve years. Among the changes were:

1. restoring congressionally appropriated U.S. financing to the United Nations and other international family planning programs that provide abortion counseling or abortions as part of their work.

2. permitting abortions to be performed in military hospitals, if the women pay for them. (Congress, by the Hyde Amendment, has forbidden the spending of federal funds for abortion.)

3. permitting the use of tissue from aborted fetuses to be used for research purposes. (See Chapter 9, Social Context: Fetal-Cell Implants.)

4. ordering federal regulators to review the safety and effectiveness of RU-486, the so-called abortion pill. (See in this chapter, Social Context: RU-486.)

By taking these steps, President Clinton symbolically indicated a change in governmental attitude toward abortion. He also indicated that he would continue to attempt to persuade Congress to lift Medicaid restrictions on abortion so that it will be available to women who cannot pay for it and who live in states that do not include abortion as part of the state program. Controversy has already arisen over a change in the Hyde Amendment that now requires states to fund abortion through Medicaid for indigent women in cases of incest or rape. The federal requirement is in conflict with the laws of states like Arkansas that forbid spending state funds to pay for abortion, unless it is to save the woman's life.

President Clinton's actions were regarded with approval and relief by those who see abortion decisions as properly matters of individual autonomy. Those generally opposed to abortion reacted with anger and dismay.

The battle over abortion is certain to continue in the courts, streets, media, and classrooms. The issues are of great social importance, yet highly personal and explosively emotional. The best hope for a resolution continues to rest with the condemnation of violence and an emphasis on the traditional strategies of verbal persuasion, rational argument, and the appeal to basic moral principles.

On November 2, 1994, Paul J. Hill was found guilty of two counts of first-degree murder by a Florida jury. Hill chose to represent himself and to present no defense. Judge Frank Bell had ruled at the beginning of the trial that he would not accept a defense of justifiable homicide.

On December 6, after the penalty phase of the trial, Hill was sentenced to die in the electric chair. In passing sentence, Judge Bell described how Hill had stalked his victims, shot them, then took a few moments to examine his work before dropping his shotgun and walking away. "The defendant was looking at what he had accomplished with pride and satisfaction," Judge Bell said.

CASE PRESENTATION
The Ordeal of Alice Wilson

Late in the afternoon on a September day, twelve-year-old Alice Wilson (as we will call her) was walking the eight blocks home from the public school she attended. She liked the walk, for the south St. Louis neighborhood she lived in was a generally pleasant place. Large, turn-of-the-century brick houses predominated, and the streets were lined with leafy sycamore trees.

But, like many urban areas, the neighborhood showed signs of decay. Several houses were abandoned, their windows boarded up with unpainted plywood. The streets were littered, and once well-tended front lawns were often hardly more than scraggly patches of weeds.

At the corner of Grand and Hervy, Alice left the well-traveled sidewalk through the business district and crossed the street to Shaw Park.

Alice stayed on the main asphalt path leading across the park and passed by the first picnic area. Then, just beyond that area, she was attacked by three teenage males. They were older and larger than Alice, and she had never seen them before. One grabbed her from behind and put his hand over her mouth so she couldn't scream. Another said they would kill her if she didn't keep quiet. They dragged her off the path and into a place surrounded by bushes. Then all three of them raped her.

Afterward the boys ran from the park, leaving Alice crying on the ground. She eventually recovered enough to dress herself and walk the rest of the way home. When her mother came home from work, Alice told her what had happened. Because Alice seemed to be basically unhurt, except for being frightened and distraught, Mrs. Wilson decided that Alice didn't need medical attention. Alice's father was dead, so Mrs. Wilson was responsible for making decisions about her welfare.

Alice went back to school and resumed her normal life. But not long thereafter she developed a high fever and vaginal pains and discharges. Mrs. Wilson was sufficiently alarmed to take her daughter to the clinic of nearby South General Hospital.

After a physical examination and laboratory tests, Dr. Charles Kranski, a resident at South General working at the clinic, first talked with Alice, then presented the results to Mrs. Wilson. He explained that Alice was in generally good health, but the chances were quite high that she had been infected with gonorrhea as result of the sexual assault. It would be necessary to wait for a culture to grow to be certain; meanwhile, Alice would be treated with a course of penicillin.

The most troubling news, however, was that Alice was pregnant from the rape. That would be an unfortunate thing to happen to any rape victim, but in Alice's case it was particularly terrible. Dr. Kranski explained that, although Alice was old enough to conceive a child, she was not really old enough to have one. She was simply not sufficiently developed physiologically to undergo pregnancy. She might well have a spontaneous abortion (a miscarriage), but, if she did not, the chances were very good that attempting to have the child might kill her.

Dr. Kranski told Mrs. Wilson that he had discussed Alice's case with two obstetricians and that they both agreed with him that the only reasonable course of action was for Alice to have an abortion as soon as possible. In fact, Dr. Kranski said, as soon as the venereal disease was controlled, he would like to schedule Alice for an abortion for therapeutic reasons. He had already explained the situation to Alice, he said, and she agreed to the abortion. But because she was still a minor, it was necessary to have Mrs. Wilson's consent before the operation could be performed.

To Dr. Kranski's surprise, Mrs. Wilson told him that she would not give her consent. "I belong to the Church of the Spiritual Life," she said. "We follow the commandment 'Thou shalt not kill.'"

Thinking that she had not understood the implications of Alice's pregnancy, Dr. Kranski again explained that Alice would probably die unless she had an abortion. Because of Alice's youth and small size, he said, the developing fetus would severely compress her internal organs and perhaps rupture them. If that happened, she would probably bleed to death. Even if that did not happen, she might suffer irreversible liver or kidney damage.

Mrs. Wilson remained totally unmoved. "God will save my daughter's life, if He wants it saved," she said. "And God will abort the child she's carrying, if He wants it aborted."

Dr. Kranski gave up his attempt to secure Mrs. Wilson's approval for the abortion. Later, he explained the situation to the director of the clinic, Dr. Saul Mendlovitz. Dr. Mendlovitz took up the matter with the legal staff of South General Hospital, and it was decided to seek a court order permitting the abortion.

The appropriate legal steps were taken, and after a court hearing at which Mrs. Wilson was represented by a state-appointed attorney, South General Hospital was granted permission to take necessary medical steps to save the life of Alice Wilson. No appeal was filed.

Despite her mother's continued personal opposition, Alice Wilson underwent an abortion.

SOCIAL CONTEXT: THE CONFLICT OVER RU-486— "THE ABORTION PILL"

Sandra Crane, as we'll call her, decided she had missed her period. She was thirty-one years old, and ordinarily her menstrual cycle was as regular as the calendar. Since she was now a week overdue, she felt sure she was pregnant.

The feeling was familiar. She had two children already, six-year-old Jennifer and two-year-old Thomas. She and her husband had decided they weren't going to have any more. They had discussed the matter, and she resolved that if she became pregnant, she would seek medical help to end her pregnancy.

The next morning Sandra Crane consulted her gynecologist, and a day later she received a phone call informing her that she was pregnant. She explained that she wanted the pregnancy ended as soon as possible, and was told to return to the clinic to pick up a 600-milligram dosage of the drug RU-486.

She took the RU-486 that evening, then two days later, as directed, she returned to the clinic and took a 400-milligram dosage of prostaglandins. Later, she began to experience cramping and bleeding, but soon the uterine lining was expelled. She felt some discomfort, but the process differed little from an unusually heavy menstrual period.

After a day of rest, she felt almost her usual self again. A week later, she returned to the clinic for an examination to make sure the abortion was complete.

RU-486 or mifepristone was developed by the French endocrinologist Etienne-Émile Baulieu. The drug works by blocking the action of progesterone, the hormone that prepares the uterine wall for the implantation of the fertilized egg. The dose of prostaglandins then induces uterine contractions that expel the sloughed-off lining, including the zygote. To be most effective, the drug must be taken during the first five to seven weeks of pregnancy. Physicians urge that the drug be taken as early as possible, but some researchers suggest that its use might be extended even to the tenth week of pregnancy.

If RU-486 is taken early in pregnancy, it blocks the action of progesterone, and as a result, a fertilized egg will not be able to follow its usual course of implanting itself in the uterine wall. Hence, the drug has the possibility of serving as a "morning-after pill" for preventing pregnancy, even after fertilization. In the view of some population researchers, this action of the drug may be even more important than its power to induce an abortion chemically.

In initial testing, 100 women volunteers less than a month pregnant were given RU-486. Of these, 85% aborted within four days, without reporting the pain or psychological difficulties that can accompany surgical abortion. The later use of prostaglandin injections in conjunction with the drug increased the speed of the process. An oral dose of prostaglandins later replaced the injection. Women tolerated this better, and the price was significantly lower.

Additional clinical trials in France and the use of the drug by more than 150,000 women have shown it to be safe and 95.5% effective. With the use of the oral prostaglandins, the effectiveness rises to 96.9%. Some women bleed excessively and a proportion do not abort as expected (about 3%, according to a French study) and require surgical intervention. For these reasons, the drug is intended for use only under close medical supervision. All in all, however, the evidence suggests that the use of the drug is safer and cheaper than surgical abortion.

Recent studies of RU-486 indicate that it may be of value in preventing endometriosis (a major cause of infertility) and fibroid tumors, which often require a hysterectomy. Thus, the drug may have a role in aiding women in getting pregnant, as well preventing or ending pregnancies. Other studies suggest that the drug may help prevent breast cancer and Cushing's syndrome (a metabolic disorder).

The Conflict

The drug was developed in 1980 by the pharmaceutical company Roussel-Uclaf and approved for use in France in September 1988. A month later, in response to a boycott of the company's products by abortion opponents, Roussel took the drug off the market.

This provoked public protests, and Health Minister Claude Evin notified the company that if it did not release the drug the government, which owned 36.25% of the company, would permanently transfer the patent to another company. "From the moment the governmental approval of the drug was granted, RU-486 became the moral property of women,

not just the property of the drug company," Evin said. Two days later the company resumed marketing the drug.

Roussel licensed the drug for use in China, Sweden, and Britain. Initial plans to market the drug in the United States have been delayed, if not abandoned, because of opposition from right-to-life groups. Since opponents of abortion generally consider RU-486 as no more than a biochemical means for producing an abortion, they oppose its use. According to the president of the National Right-to-Life Coalition, RU-486 represents "chemical warfare against an entire class of innocent humans."

In accord with this view, the National Right-to-Life Coalition (NRL) and other groups opposed to abortion have informed drug companies that they will boycott all of a company's products if it tries to market an abortion-inducing drug. "Our basic position is that death drugs designed to kill unborn babies have no place in America," the NRL education director said.

Baulieu, the drug's developer, charges that fears of such reprisals have kept RU-486 from being distributed worldwide. Indeed, the fear of boycotts of Roussel and Hoechst, the German pharmaceutical company that is its majority stockholder, led the company to decide against applying for approval to sell the drug in the United States. No U.S. drug company has applied to the Food and Drug Administration (FDA) for approval out of fear of the response of the prolife movement.

Baulieu also charges that Roussel should not have put approval of the drug for international use in the hands of the World Health Organization (WHO). The WHO, he claims, has delayed its approval because it is so financially dependent on the United States that a reprisal in the form of a withdrawal of U.S. funds would severely cripple its operations.

"I believe the key to the future of RU-486 lies in the United States," Baulieu said at a news conference. He said that because of the drug's simplicity, it could dramatically reduce the number of illegal abortions and related maternal deaths throughout the world. "How can we ignore that 500 women a day die as a result of badly executed abortions?" he asked. "At present, things are so bad in the Third World that anything that improves the situation is welcome. I think it is our moral duty to act."

Louise B. Tyrer of Planned Parenthood similarly characterized the lack of availability of the drug, calling it "discriminatory to women" and "a threat to their safety and health." In her view and in the opinion of prochoice advocates, "Women should have a choice between medical and surgical abortion."

President Clinton made it clear that his administration favored a quick approval by the FDA of RU-486. In addition, various legislative bills have been framed attempting to find a way around the pharmaceutical patent held by Roussel. Abortion Rights Mobilization announced in 1993 that it had obtained a chemical equivalent of RU-486 from China and that it would conduct clinical trials with the drug and submit them to the FDA.

In April 1993, the situation changed when Roussel-Uclaf agreed to license the drug and the technology used to make it to the Population Council, a New York-based nonprofit research organization. The council agreed to find a manufacturer, establish a clinical trial, and then apply to the FDA to license the drug for use in the United States.

Trials Begin. In October 1994, clinical trials of RU-486 finally began. Women at the participating clinics will be offered the drug until 2,100 women have used it. The trials are expected to be completed by 1995, and the drug is expected to be available to physicians throughout the country by 1996.

The accessibility of RU-486 to women who wish to take advantage of it is likely to reduce considerably the number of surgical abortions. However, it is not likely to put an end to the debate over abortion.

CASE RETROSPECTIVE

When Abortion Was Illegal: Mrs. Sherri Finkbine and the Thalidomide Tragedy

Background Note: The following case concerns an event that took place before the U.S. Supreme Court decision in Roe v. Wade *was handed down in 1973. That decision had the effect of legalizing abortion in the United States. Before the decision, most state laws permitted abortion only for the purpose of saving the life of the mother. The case presented here illustrates the kinds of problems faced by many women who sought an abortion for other reasons.*

In 1962 Mrs. Sherri Finkbine was the mother of four normal children and was pregnant. Her health was good, but she was having some trouble sleeping. Rather than talking with her doctor, she simply took some of the tranquilizers that her husband had brought back from a trip to Europe. The tranquilizers were widely used there, and, like aspirin, they could simply be bought over the counter.

Subsequently, Mrs. Finkbine read an article that told of the great increase in the number of deformed children being born in Europe. Some of

the children's arms and legs failed to develop or developed only in malformed ways; other children were blind and deaf or had seriously defective internal organs. The birth defects had been traced to the use in pregnancy of a supposedly harmless and widely used tranquilizer. Its active ingredient was thalidomide.

Mrs. Finkbine was worried enough to ask her doctor to find out if the pills she had been taking contained thalidomide. They did. When he learned this, her doctor told her "The odds are so against you that I am recommending termination of pregnancy." He explained that getting approval for an abortion should not be difficult. She had good medical reasons, and all she had to do was explain them to the three-member medical board of Phoenix.

Mrs. Finkbine agreed with her doctor's advice. But then she began to think that maybe it was her duty to inform other women who may have been taking thalidomide about its disastrous consequences. She called a local newspaper and told her story to the editor. He agreed not to use her name, but on a front page, bordered in black, he used the headline "BABY-DEFORMING DRUG MAY COST WOMAN HER CHILD HERE."

The story was picked up by the wire services, and it was not long before Mrs. Finkbine's identity became known. The medical board had already approved her request for an abortion, but because of the great publicity her case received they canceled their approval. The State of Arizona abortion statute legally sanctioned abortion only when it was required to save the life of the mother. The board was afraid that their decision might be challenged in court and that the decision could not stand up to the challenge.

Mrs. Finkbine became the object of a great outpouring of antiabortion feelings. *Il Osservatore Romano,* the official Vatican newspaper, condemned Mrs. Finkbine and her husband as murderers. Although she received some letters of support, others were abusive. One writer said: "I hope someone takes the other four children and strangles them, because it is all the same thing." Another wrote from the perspective of the fetus: "Mommy, please dear Mommy, let me live. Please, please, I want to live. Let me love you, let me see the light of day, let me smell a rose, let me sing a song, let me look into your face, let me say Mommy."

Although Mrs. Finkbine tried to obtain a legal abortion outside her own state, she was unable to do so. Eventually, she went to Sweden. After a rigorous investigation by a medical board, Mrs. Finkbine was given an abortion in a Swedish hospital.

Mrs. Finkbine saw her own problem as solved at last. But she continued to have sympathy with those thousands of potential parents of thalidomide children who lacked the money to follow the course of action she had been forced to take by abortion laws she considered to be restrictive and inhumane.

INTRODUCTION

Less than two decades ago, most Americans considered abortion a crime so disgusting that it was rarely mentioned in public. Back-alley abortionists with dirty hands and unclean instruments were real enough, but they were also the villains of cautionary tales to warn women against being tempted into the crime. Abortion was the dramatic stuff of novels and movies portraying "girls in trouble" or women pushed to the brink. To choose to have an abortion was to choose to be degraded.

The Supreme Court decision in *Roe* v. *Wade* changed all that in 1973. The decision had the effect of legalizing abortion, and since then abortion has gained acceptance from a majority of the population. Yet controversy over the legitimacy of abortion continues to flare. Indeed, no other topic in medical ethics has attracted more attention or so polarized public opinion. The reason is understandable. In the abortion question, major moral, legal, and social issues are intertwined to form a problem of great subtlety and complexity.

Before focusing on some of the specific issues raised by abortion, we would do well to have in hand some of the relevant factual information about human developmental biology and the techniques of abortion.

HUMAN DEVELOPMENT AND ABORTION

Fertilization occurs when an ovum is penetrated by a sperm cell and the nuclei of the two unite to form a single cell containing forty-six chromosomes. This normally occurs in the Fallopian tube (or oviduct), a narrow tube leading from the ovary into the uterus (womb). The fertilized ovum—zygote, or conceptus—continues its passage down the Fallopian tube, and during its two- to three-day passage it undergoes a number of cell divisions that increase its size. (Rarely, the zygote does not descend but continues to develop in the Fallopian tube. Because the tube is so small, the pregnancy usually has to be terminated surgically.) After reaching the uterus, a pear-shaped organ, the zygote floats free in the intrauterine fluid. Here it develops into a blastocyst, a ball of cells surrounding a fluid-filled cavity.

By the end of the second week, the blastocyst becomes embedded in the wall of the uterus. At this point and until the end of the eighth week, it is known as an embryo. During the fourth and fifth weeks, organ systems begin to develop, and the external features take on a definitely human shape.

During the eighth week, brain activity usually becomes detectable. At this time, the embryo comes to be known as a fetus.

Birth generally occurs about nine months after fertilization. It is customary to divide this time into three three-month periods, or trimesters. At present, pregnancy cannot be diagnosed with certainty by ordinary methods until ten to fourteen days after a woman has missed her menstrual period.

Abortion is the termination of pregnancy. It can occur because of internal biochemical factors or as a result of physical injury to the woman. Terminations from such causes are usually referred to as "spontaneous abortions," but they are also commonly called miscarriages.

Abortion can also be a deliberate process resulting from human intervention. The methods used in contemporary medicine depend to a great extent on the stage of the pregnancy. The earliest intervention involves the use of drugs (like RU-486) to prevent the embedding of the blastocyst in the uterine wall. Subsequent intervention during the first trimester (up to about twelve weeks) commonly employs one of two techniques. The first of the two is uterine or vacuum aspiration. The cervix, the narrow outer opening of the uterus, is dilated (widened) by instruments. Then a small tube is inserted into the uterus, and its contents are emptied by suction. The second commonly used procedure is dilation and curettage. The cervix is dilated and its contents are gently scraped out by the use of a curette, a spoon-shaped surgical instrument.

After sixteen weeks, when the fetus is too large to make the other methods practical, the most common abortion technique is saline injection. The fluid in the membrane sac (amnion) surrounding the fetus is withdrawn through a hollow needle and replaced by a solution of salt and water. This induces a miscarriage.

Another second method, hysterotomy, is a surgical procedure in which the fetus is removed from the uterus through an incision. The procedure is the same as that known as Caesarean section and is rarely performed for the purpose of abortion.

These facts about pregnancy and abortion put us in a position to discuss some of the moral problems connected with them. We shall not be able to untangle the skein of issues wrapped around the abortion question. We shall only attempt to state a few of the more serious ones and to indicate the lines of argument that have been offered to support positions taken with respect to them. Afterward we will sketch out some possible responses that might be offered on the basis of the ethical theories we considered in the introductory chapter. Finally, we will present summary statements of the views taken by the authors of the selections that make up the bulk of this chapter.

THE STATUS OF THE FETUS

It is absolutely crucial for the application of the principles of any moral theory that we have a settled opinion about the objects and subjects of morality. Although principles are generally stated with respect to rational individuals, every theory recognizes that there are people who in fact cannot be considered rational agents. For example, mental and physical incapacities may diminish or destroy rationality. But ethical theories generally recognize that we still have duties to people who are so incapacitated.

The basic problem that this raises is: Who or what is to be considered a person? Are there characteristics that we can point to and say that it is by virtue of possessing these characteristics that an individual must be considered a person and thus accorded moral treatment?

The abortion issue raises this question most particularly with regard to the fetus. (We will use the term "fetus," for the moment, to refer to the developing organism at any stage.) Just what is the status of the fetus in the world? We must find a satisfactory answer to this question, some writers have suggested, before we can resolve the general moral problem of abortion.

Let's consider the possible consequences of answering the question one way or the other. First, if a fetus is a person, then it has a serious claim to life. We must assert the claim on its behalf, for, like an unconscious person, the fetus is unable to do so. The claim of the fetus as a person must be given weight and respect in deliberating about any action that would terminate its life. Perhaps only circumstances as extreme as a threat to the life of the mother would justify abortion.

Assuming that the fetus is a person, then an abortion would be a case of killing and not something to be undertaken without reasons sufficient to override the fetus's claim to life. In effect, only conditions of the same sort as would justify our killing an adult person (for example, self-defense) would justify our killing a fetus. Thus, the moral burden in every case would be to demonstrate that abortion is not a case of wrongful killing.

By contrast, if a fetus is not a person in a morally relevant sense, the abortion need not be considered a case of killing equivalent to the killing of an adult. In one view, it might be said that an abortion is not essentially different from an appendectomy. According to this way of thinking, a fetus is no more than a complicated clump of organic material, and its removal involves no serious moral difficulty.

In another view, it could be argued that, even though the fetus is not a person, it is a *potential* person, and thus is a significant and morally relevant property. The fetus's very potentiality makes it unique and distinguishes it from a diseased appendix or a cyst or any other kind of organic material. Thus, because

the fetus can become a person, abortion does present a moral problem. A fetus can be destroyed only for serious reasons. Thus, preventing a person from coming into existence must be justified to an extent comparable to the justification required for killing a person. (Some have suggested that the justification does not have to be identical because the fetus is only a potential person. The justification we might present for killing a person would thus serve only as a guide for those that might justify abortion.)

So far we have used the word "fetus," and this usage tends to obscure the fact that human development is a process with many stages. Perhaps it is only in the later stages of development that the entity becomes a person. But exactly when might this happen?

The difference between a fertilized ovum and a fully developed baby just a few minutes before birth are considerable. The ovum and the blastocyst seem just so much tissue. But the embryo and the fetus present more serious claims to being persons. Should abortion be allowed until the fetus becomes visibly human, or until the fetus shows heartbeat and brain waves, or until the fetus can live outside the uterus (becomes viable)?

The process of development is continuous, and so far it has proved impossible to find differences between stages that can be generally accepted as morally relevant. Some writers on abortion have suggested that it is useless to look for such differences, because any place where the line is drawn will be arbitrary. Others have claimed that it is possible to draw the line by relying on criteria that can be rationally defended. A few have even argued that a reasonable set of criteria for determining who shall be considered a person might even deny the status to infants.

PREGNANCY, ABORTION, AND THE RIGHTS OF WOMEN

Pregnancy and fetal development are normal biological processes, and most women who choose to have a child carry it to term without unusual difficulties. However, it is important to keep in mind that even a normal pregnancy involves changes and stresses that are uniquely burdensome. Once the process of fetal growth is initiated, a woman's entire physiology is altered by the new demands placed on it and by the biochemical changes taking place within her body. For example, metabolic rate increases, the thyroid gland grows larger, the heart pumps more blood to meet fetal needs, and a great variety of hormonal changes take place. The growing fetus physically displaces the woman's internal organs and alters the size and shape of her body.

As a result of such changes, the pregnant woman may suffer a variety of ailments. More common ones include severe nausea and vomiting ("morning sickness"), muscle cramps, abdominal pain, anemia, tiredness, and headaches. For many women such complaints are relatively mild or infrequent, while for others they are severe or constant. Nausea and vomiting can lead to dehydration and malnutrition so serious as to be life-threatening. Women who suffer from diseases like diabetes are apt to face special health problems as a result of pregnancy.

Partly because of hormonal changes, women are also more likely to experience psychological difficulties when pregnant, such as emotional lability (mood swings), severe depression, and acute anxiety. Such conditions are often accompanied by quite realistic concerns about the loss of freedom associated with becoming a parent, compromised job status, loss of sexual attractiveness due to the change in body shape, and the pains and risks of childbirth.

The woman who intends to carry a child to term is also likely to have to alter her behavior in many ways. She may have to curtail the time she spends working, take a leave of absence, or even quit her job. Any career plans she has are likely to suffer. She may be unable to participate in social activities to the extent she previously did, and give up some entirely. In addition, if she recognizes an obligation to the developing fetus and is well informed, she may have to alter her diet, stop smoking, and strictly limit the amount of alcohol she consumes.

In summary, the physical and emotional price paid by a woman for a full-term pregnancy is high. Even a normal pregnancy, one that proceeds without any special difficulties, exacts a toll of discomfort, stress, restricted activity, and worry.

Women who wish to have a child are generally willing to undergo the rigors of pregnancy to satisfy this desire. But is it a woman's duty to nurture and carry to term an unwanted child? Pregnancies resulting from rape and incest are the kinds of dramatic cases frequently mentioned to emphasize the seriousness of the burden imposed on women. But the question is also important when the conditions surrounding the pregnancy are more ordinary.

Suppose that a woman becomes pregnant unintentionally and decides that having a child will be harmful to her career or her way of life. Or suppose that she simply does not wish to subject herself to the pains of pregnancy. Does a woman have a moral duty to see to it that the developing child comes to be born?

A number of writers have taken the position that women have an exclusive right to control their own reproductive function. In their view, such a right is based upon the generally recognized right to control what is done to our bodies. Since pregnancy is something that involves a woman's body, the woman concerned may legitimately decide whether to continue the pregnancy or terminate it. The decision is hers alone, and social or legal policies that restrict the free exercise of her right are unjustifiable.

Essentially the same point is sometimes phrased by saying that women own their bodies. Because their bodies are their own "property," women alone have the right to decide whether to become pregnant and, if pregnant unintentionally, whether to have an abortion.

Critics have pointed out that this general line of argument, taken alone, does not support the strong conclusion that women should be free from all constraints in making abortion decisions. Even granting that women's bodies are their own property, we nevertheless recognize restrictions on exercising property rights. We have no right to shoot trespassers, and we cannot endanger our neighbors by burning down our house. Similarly, if any legitimate moral claims can be made on behalf of the fetus, then the right of women to decide whether to have an abortion may not be unrestricted.

Some philosophers (Judith J. Thomson, for example) have taken the view that, although women are entitled to control their bodies and make abortion decisions, the decision to have an abortion must be supported by weighty reasons. They have suggested that, even if we grant that a fetus is a person, its claim to life cannot be given unconditional precedence over the woman's claim to control her own life. She is entitled to autonomy and the right to arrange her life in accordance with her own concept of the good. It would be wrong for her to destroy the fetus for a trivial reason, but legitimate and adequate reasons for taking the life of the fetus might be offered.

Others, by contrast, have argued that when a woman becomes pregnant she assumes an obligation for the life of the fetus. It is, after all, completely dependent on her for its continued existence. She has no more right to take its life in order to seek her own best interest than she has to murder someone whose death may bring benefits to her.

THERAPEUTIC ABORTION

Abortion is sometimes required to save the life of the mother or in order to provide her with medical treatment that may correct some life-threatening condition. Abortion performed for such a purpose is ordinarily regarded as a case of self-defense. For this reason, it is almost universally considered to be morally unobjectionable. (Strictly speaking, the Roman Catholic view condemns abortion in all of its forms. It does approve of providing medical treatment for the mother, even if this results in the death of the fetus, but the death of the fetus must never be intended.)

If the principle of preserving the life and health of the mother justifies abortion, then what conditions fall under that principle? If a woman has cancer of the uterus and her life can be saved only by an operation that will result in the death of the fetus, then this clearly falls under the principle. But what about psychological conditions? Is a woman's mental health relevant to deciding whether an abortion is justified? What if a psychiatrist believes that a woman cannot face the physical rigors of pregnancy or bear the psychological stresses that go with it without developing severe psychiatric symptoms? Would such a judgment justify an abortion? Or is the matter of psychological health irrelevant to the abortion issue?

Consider, too, the welfare of the fetus. Suppose that prenatal tests or other reliable means indicate that the developing child suffers from serious abnormalities. (This was the case of the "thalidomide babies.") Is abortion for the purpose of preventing the birth of such children justifiable?

It might be argued that it is not, that an impaired fetus has as much right to its life as an impaired person. We do not, after all, consider it legitimate to kill people who become seriously injured or suffer from diseases that render them helpless. Rather, we care for them and work to improve their lives—at least we ought to.

Someone might argue, however, that abortion in such cases is not only justifiable, but a duty. (See, for example, the article by H. T. Engelhardt in Chapter 2.) It is our duty to kill the fetus to spare the person that it will become a life of unhappiness and suffering. We might even be said to be acknowledging the dignity of the fetus by doing what it might do for itself if it could—what any rational creature would do. Destroying such a fetus would spare future pain to the individual and his or her family and save society from an enormous expense. Thus, we have not only the justification to kill such a fetus, but also the positive obligation to do so.

In this chapter, we will not deal explicitly with the issues that are raised by attempting to decide whether it is justifiable to terminate the life of an impaired fetus. Because such issues are directly connected with prenatal genetic diagnosis and treatment, we will discuss them more fully in Chapter 7. Nonetheless, in considering the general question of the legitimacy of abortion, it is important to keep such special considerations in mind.

ABORTION AND THE LAW

Abortion in our society has been a legal issue as well as a moral issue. Until the Supreme Court decision in *Roe* v. *Wade,* nontherapeutic abortion was illegal in virtually all states. The *Webster* decision (see the earlier Social Context) is a recent indication that the Court is willing to accept more state restrictions than previously, but even so abortions are far from being illegal. Yet there are groups lobbying strongly for a constitutional amendment that would protect a fetus's "right to life" and prohibit elective abortion.

The rightness or wrongness of abortion is a moral matter, one whose issues can be resolved only by appealing to a moral theory. Different theories may yield incompatible answers, and even individuals who accept the same theory may arrive at different conclusions.

Such a state of affairs raises the question of whether the moral convictions or conclusions of some people should be embodied in laws that govern the lives of all people in the society. The question can be put succinctly: Should the moral beliefs of some people serve as the basis for laws that will impose those beliefs on everyone?

There is no straightforward way of answering this general question. To some extent, which moral beliefs are at issue is a relevant consideration. So too are the political prin-

ciples that we are willing to accept as basic to our society. Every ethical theory recognizes that there is a scope of action that must be left to individuals as moral agents acting freely on the basis of their own understanding and perceptions. Laws requiring the expression of benevolence or gratitude, for example, seem peculiarly inappropriate.

Yet, one of the major aims of a government is to protect the rights of its citizens. Consequently, a society must have just laws that recognize and enforce those rights. In a very real way, then, the moral theory that we hold and the conclusions arrived at on the basis of it will determine whether we believe that certain types of laws are justified. They are justified when they protect the rights recognized in our moral theories—when political rights reflect moral rights. (See the Introduction to Chapter 10 for a fuller discussion of moral rights and their relation to political rights.)

An ethical theory that accords the status of a person to a fetus is likely to claim also that the laws of the society should recognize the rights of the fetus. A theory that does not grant the fetus this position is not likely to regard laws forbidding abortion as justifiable.

ETHICAL THEORIES AND ABORTION

Theories like those of Mill, Kant, Ross, and Rawls attribute to individuals autonomy or self-direction. An individual is entitled to control his or her own life, and it seems reasonable to extend this principle to apply to one's own body. If so, then a woman should have the right to determine whether or not she wishes to have a child. If she is pregnant with an unwanted child, then, no matter how she came to be pregnant, she might legitimately decide on an abortion. Utilitarianism also suggests this answer on consequential grounds. In the absence of other considerations, if it seems likely that having a child will produce more unhappiness than an abortion would, then an abortion would be justifiable.

If the fetus is considered to be a person, however, the situation is different for some theories. The Roman Catholic view holds that the fetus is an innocent person and that direct abortion is never justifiable. Even if the pregnancy is due to rape, the fetus cannot be held at fault and made to suffer through its death. Even though she may not wish to have the child, the mother has a duty to preserve the life of the fetus.

For deontological theories like those of Kant and Ross, the situation becomes more complicated. If the fetus is a person, then it has an inherent dignity and worth. It is an innocent life which cannot be destroyed except for the weightiest moral reasons. Those reasons may include the interests and wishes of the woman, but deontological theories provide no clear answer as to how those are to be weighed.

For utilitarianism, by contrast, even if the fetus is considered a person, the principle of utility may still justify an abortion. Killing a person is not, for utilitarianism, inherently wrong. (Yet it is compatible with rule utilitarianism to argue that permitting elective abortion as a matter of policy would produce more unhappiness than forbidding abortion altogether. Thus, utilitarianism does not offer a definite answer to the abortion issue.)

As we have already seen, both utilitarianism and deontological theories can be used to justify therapeutic abortion. When the mother's life or health is at stake, then the situation may be construed as one of self-defense. Both Kant and Ross recognize that we each have a right to protect ourselves, even if it means taking the life of another person. For utilitarianism, preserving one's life is justifiable, for being alive is a necessary condition for all forms of happiness.

We have also indicated that abortion "for the sake of the fetus" can be justified by both utilitarianism and deontological theories. If by killing the fetus we can spare it a life of suffering, minimize the sufferings of its family, and preserve the resources of the society, then abortion is legitimate on utilitarian grounds. In the terms of Kant and Ross, destroying the fetus might be a way of recognizing its dignity. If we assume that it is a person, then by sparing it a life of indignity and pain we are treating it in the way that a rational being would want to be treated.

The legitimacy of laws forbidding abortion is an issue that utilitarianism would resolve by considering their effects. If such laws promote the general happiness of the society, then they are justifiable. Otherwise, they are not. In general, Kant, Ross, Rawls, and natural law theory recognize intrinsic human worth and regard as legitimate laws protecting that worth, even if those holding this view are only a minority of the society. Thus, laws discriminating against blacks and women, for example, would be considered unjust on the basis of these theories. Laws enforcing equality, by contrast, would be considered just.

But what about fetuses? The Roman Catholic interpretation of natural law would regard the case as exactly the same. As full human persons, they are entitled to have their rights protected by law. Those who fail to recognize this are guilty of moral failure, and laws permitting abortion are the moral equivalent of laws permitting murder.

For Kant and other deontologists, the matter is less clear. As long as there is substantial doubt about the status of the fetus, it is not certain that it is legitimate to demand that the rights of fetuses be recognized and protected by law. It is clear that the issue of whether or not the fetus is considered a person is most often taken as the crucial one in the abortion controversy.

ABORTION TRENDS

The social problems of abortion show no signs of being resolved, but the number of abortions has declined since 1979. At present about 1.5 million abortions are performed every year in the United States. But the percentage of pregnancies ending in abortion has dropped, and so has the number of abortions per 1,000 women of traditional (15 to 44) child-bearing age.

About 27.5% of pregnancies currently end in abortion. The previous high was 30%. The number of abortions per 1,000 reproductive-age women is about 26. This is down from the old high of 29 per 1,000.

The reasons for this change are matters of speculation. One factor is probably the greater availability and effectiveness of contraception. As fewer unwanted conceptions occur, abortions might be expected to go down. A second factor is that a greater social acceptance of unmarried women with children and single-parent families may have taken some of the pressure off women to have abortions. Data show that the number of births to unmarried women increased more than 20% between 1988 and 1991. Births to unmarried women increased by more than 200,000, while abortion declined by about 60,000. As new data become available, they are expected to show a continuation of this trend throughout the 1990s.

A third factor may be that access to abortion has become more restricted for many women. The number of abortion providers has become steadily smaller, and most services are concentrated in urban areas. Also, securing an abortion has become increasingly difficult for many women. The angry tone of the debate is perceived by some as threatening, and picketers and protesters at abortion clinics many discourage many pregnant women from attempting to secure their services.

In 1977 the Supreme Court ruled that states are under no obligation to fund elective abortions for the poor under the Medicaid program, and in 1980 the Court held that the federal government is not required to fund abortions of any kind. Medicaid is presently both a state and federally funded program. Some fourteen states, accounting for 75% of the women eligible for Medicaid, chose to continue to finance elective abortions with state funds. In those states, nearly 98% of the women seeking an abortion obtained one. In

---

Views on Abortion

A woman should be able to get an abortion no matter what the reason:	47%
Abortion should only be legal in certain circumstances, such as rape, incest, or saving the life of the mother:	39%
Abortion should be illegal in all circumstances:	12%
A woman should have to wait twenty-four hours before having an abortion:	Favor 74%; Oppose 22%
Minors should get parental consent before having an abortion:	Favor 69%; Oppose 26%
RU-486 should be available in the United States:	Favor 55%; Oppose 40%

Reprinted with permission from a *Time*/CNN Poll by Yankelovich Partners (May 18–19, 1994).

---

states providing no funding, about 20% of women wanting abortions were forced to continue their pregnancies. Those securing abortions either obtained money from private sources to pay for legal abortions or (in 4% of the cases) had illegal ones.

Opponents of abortion have generally approved the Supreme Court decisions regarding abortion payments. By contrast, those who support elective abortion point out that the result of the decisions is to deny to some women an opportunity open to others. Women with financial means will have no difficulty obtaining abortions, whereas those without money will have either to bear children they don't want or to take their chances with back-alley abortionists whose services they can afford.

A new and pressing public policy issue about abortion concerns whether a federal national health plan should pay for abortion services without restriction. Advocates of abortion rights argue that abortion is a necessary part of basic reproductive health care. If every American is to have the same access to health care that is open to any other American, then abortion services must be part of the package.

Yet, should those who consider abortion a form of murder have to pay through taxes for an operation that commits it? This is just one of the moral dilemmas that must be worked out before the issue of the place of abortion in society can be resolved.

An Almost Absolute Value in History

John T. Noonan, Jr.

John T. Noonan argues that at the moment of fertilization a developing human being becomes a person. Noonan reviews some distinctions used by abortion proponents who maintain that personhood is achieved at a later stage development (viability, experience, and social visibility) and concludes that they are all illegitimate. Noonan argues that conception is the decisive moment of humanization, because it is then that the new being receives a genetic code from its parents.

The basic principle that should govern our attitude toward the fetus, Noonan claims, is a theological and humanistic one: Do not injure your fellow man without a sufficient reason. Thus, abortion is never right except to save the mother's life. Abortion is immoral because it "violates the rational humanistic tenet of the equality of human lives."

The most fundamental question involved in the long history of thought on abortion is: How do you determine the humanity of a being? To phrase the question that way is to put in comprehensive humanistic terms what the theologians either dealt with as an explicitly theological question under the heading of "ensoulment" or dealt with implicitly in their treatment of abortion. The Christian position as it originated did not depend on a narrow theological or philosophical concept. It had no relation to theories of infant baptism. It appealed to no special theory of instantaneous ensoulment. It took the world's view on ensoulment as that view changed from Aristotle to Zacchia. There was, indeed, theological influence affecting the theory of ensoulment finally adopted, and, of course, ensoulment itself was a theological concept, so that the position was always explained in theological terms. But the theological notion of ensoulment could easily be translated into humanistic language by substituting "hu-

man" for "rational soul"; the problem of knowing when a man is a man is common to theology and humanism.

If one steps outside the specific categories used by the theologians, the answer they gave can be analyzed as a refusal to discriminate among human beings on the basis of their varying potentialities. Once conceived, the being was recognized as man because he had man's potential. The criterion for humanity, thus, was simple and all-embracing: if you are conceived by human parents, you are human.

The strength of this position may be tested by a review of some of the other distinctions offered in the contemporary controversy over legalizing abortion. Perhaps the most popular distinction is in terms of viability. Before an age of so many months, the fetus is not viable, that is, it cannot be removed from the mother's womb and live apart from her. To that extent, the life of the fetus is absolutely dependent on the life of the mother. This dependence is made the basis of denying recognition to its humanity.

There are difficulties with this distinction. One is that the perfection of artificial incubation may make the fetus viable at any time: it may be removed and artificially sustained. Experiments with animals already show that such a procedure is possible. This hypothetical extreme case relates to an actual difficulty: there is considerable elasticity to the idea of viability. Mere length of life is not an exact measure. The viability of the fetus depends on the extent of its anatomical and functional development. The weight and length of the fetus are better guides to the state of its development than age, but weight and length vary. Moreover, different racial groups have different ages at which their fetuses are viable. Some evidence, for example, suggests that Negro fetuses mature more quickly than white fetuses. If viability is the norm, the standard would vary with race and with many individual circumstances.

The most important objection to this approach is that dependence is not ended by viability. The fetus is still absolutely dependent on someone's care in order to continue existence; indeed a child of one or three or even five years of age is absolutely dependent on another's care for existence; uncared for, the older fetus or the younger child will die as surely as the early fetus detached from the mother. The unsubstantial lessening in dependence at viability does not seem to signify any special acquisition of humanity.

A second distinction has been attempted in terms of experience. A being who has had experience, has lived and suffered, who possesses memories, is more human than one who has not. Humanity depends on formation by experience. The fetus is thus "unformed" in the most basic human sense.

This distinction is not serviceable for the embryo which is already experiencing and reacting. The embryo is responsive to touch after eight weeks and at least at that point is experiencing. At an earlier stage the zygote is certainly alive and responding to its environment. The distinction may also be challenged by the rare case where aphasia has erased adult memory: has it erased humanity? More fundamentally, this distinction leaves even the older fetus or the younger child to be treated as a unformed inhuman thing. Finally, it is not clear why experience as such confers humanity. It could be argued that certain central experiences such as loving or learning are necessary to make a man hu-

man. But then human beings who have failed to love or to learn might be excluded from the class called man. . . .

Finally, a distinction is sought in social visibility. The fetus is not socially perceived as human. It cannot communicate with others. Thus, both subjectively and objectively, it is not a member of society. As moral rules are rules for the behavior of members of society to each other, they cannot be made for behavior toward what is not yet a member. Excluded from the society of men, the fetus is excluded from the humanity of men.

By force of the argument from the consequences, this distinction is to be rejected. It is more subtle than that founded on an appeal to physical sensation, but it is equally dangerous in its implications. If humanity depends on social recognition, individuals or whole groups may be dehumanized by being denied any status in their society. Such a fate is fictionally portrayed in *1984* and has actually been the lot of many men in many societies. In the Roman empire, for example, condemnation to slavery meant the practical denial of most human rights; in the Chinese Communist world, landlords have been classified as enemies of the people and so treated and nonpersons by the state. Humanity does not depend on social recognition, though often the failure of society to recognize the prisoner, the alien, the heterodox as human has led to the destruction of human beings. Anyone conceived by a man and a woman is human. Recognition of this condition by society follows a real event in the objective order, however imperfect and halting the recognition. Any attempt to limit humanity to exclude some group runs the risk of furnishing authority and precedent for excluding other groups in the name of the consciousness or perception of the controlling group in the society.

A philosopher may reject the appeal to the humanity of the fetus because he views "humanity" as a secular view of the soul and because he doubts the existence of anything real and objective which can be identified as humanity. One answer to such a philosopher is to ask how he reasons about moral questions without supposing that there is a sense in which he and the others of whom he speaks are human. Whatever group is taken as the society which determines who may be killed is thereby taken as human. A second answer is to ask if he does not believe that there is a right and wrong way of deciding moral questions. If there is such a difference, experience may be appealed to: to decide who is human on the basis of the sentiment of a given society has led to consequences which rational men would characterize as monstrous.

The rejection of the attempted distinctions based on viability and visibility, experience and feeling, may be buttressed by the following considerations: Moral judgments often rest on distinctions, but if the distinctions are not to appear arbitrary *fiat*, they should relate to some real difference in probabilities. There is a kind of continuity in all life, but the earlier stages of the elements of human life possess tiny probabilities of development. Consider for example, the spermatozoa in any normal ejaculate: There are about 200,000,000 in any single ejaculate, of which one has a chance of developing into a zygote. Consider the oocytes which may become ova: there are 100,000 to 1,000,000 oocytes in a female infant, of which a maximum of 390 are ovulated. But once spermatozoa and ovum meet and the conceptus is formed, such studies as have been made show that roughly in only 20 percent of the cases will spontaneous abortion occur. In other words, the chances are about 4 out of 5 that this new being will develop. At this stage in the life of the being there is a sharp shift in probabilities, an immense jump in potentialities. To make a distinction between the rights of spermatozoa and the rights of the fertilized ovum is to respond to an enormous shift in possibilities. For about twenty days after conception the egg may split to form twins or combine with another egg to form a chimera, but the probability of either event happening is very small.

It may be asked, What does a change in biological probabilities have to do with establishing humanity? The argument from probabilities is not aimed at establishing humanity but at establishing an objective discontinuity which may be taken into account in moral discourse. As life itself is a matter of probabilities, as most moral reasoning is an estimate of probabilities, so it seems in accord with the structure of reality and the nature of moral thought to found a moral judgment on the change in probabilities at conception. The appeal to probabilities is the most commonsensical of arguments, to a greater or smaller degree all of us base our actions on probabilities, and in morals, as in law, prudence and negligence are often measured by the account one has taken of the probabilities. If the chance is 200,000,000 to 1 that the movement in the bushes into which you shoot is a man's, I doubt if many

persons would hold you careless in shooting; but if the chances are 4 out of 5 that the movement is a human being's, few would acquit you of blame. Would the argument be different if only one out of ten children conceived came to term? Of course this argument would be different. This argument is an appeal to probabilities that actually exist, not to any and all state of affairs which may be imagined.

The probabilities as they do exist do not show the humanity of the embryo in the sense of a demonstration in logic any more than the probabilities of the movement in the bush being a man demonstrate beyond all doubt that the being is a man. The appeal is a "buttressing" consideration, showing the plausibility of the standard adopted. The argument focuses on the decisional factor in any moral judgment and assumes that part of the business of a moralist is drawing lines. One evidence of the nonarbitrary character of the line drawn is the difference of probabilities on either side of it. If a spermatozoon is destroyed, one destroys a being which had a chance of far less than 1 in 200 million of developing into a reasoning being, possessed of the genetic code, a heart and other organs, and capable of pain. If a fetus is destroyed, one destroys a being already possessed of the genetic code, organs, and sensitivity to pain, and one which had an 80 percent chance of developing further into a baby outside the womb who, in time, would reason.

The positive argument for conception as the decisive moment of humanization is that at conception the new being receives the genetic code. It is this genetic information which determines his characteristics, which is the biological carrier of the possibility of human wisdom, which makes him a self-evolving being. A being with a human genetic code is man.

This review of current controversy over the humanity of the fetus emphasizes what a fundamental question the theologians resolved in asserting the inviolability of the fetus. To regard the fetus as possessed of equal rights with other humans was not, however, to decide every case where abortion might be employed. It did decide the case where the argument was that the fetus should be aborted for its own good. To say a being was human was to say it had a destiny to decide for itself which could not be taken from it by another man's decision. But human beings with equal rights often come in conflict with each other, and some decision must be made as whose claims are to prevail. Cases of conflict involving the fetus are different only in two respects: the total inability of the fetus to speak for itself and the fact that the right of the fetus regularly at stake is the right to life itself.

The approach taken by the theologians to these conflicts was articulated in terms of "direct" and "indirect." Again, to look at what they were doing from outside their categories, they may be said to have been drawing lines or "balancing values." "Direct" and "indirect" are spatial metaphors; "line-drawing" is another. "To weigh" or "to balance" values is a metaphor of a more complicated mathematical sort hinting at the process which goes on in moral judgments. All the metaphors suggest that, in the moral judgments made, comparisons were necessary, that no value completely controlled. The principle of double effect was no doctrine fallen from heaven, but a method of analysis appropriate where two relative values were being compared. In Catholic moral theology, as it developed, life even of the innocent was not taken as an absolute. Judgments of acts affecting life issued from a process of weighing. In the weighing, the fetus was always given a value greater than zero, always a value separate and independent from its parents. This valuation was crucial and fundamental in all Christian thought on the subject and marked it off from any approach which considered that only the parents' interests needed to be considered.

Even with the fetus weighed as human, one interest could be weighed as equal or superior: that of the mother in her own life. The casuists between 1450 and 1895 were willing to weigh this interest as superior. Since 1895, that interest was given decisive weight only in the two special cases of the cancerous uterus and the ectopic pregnancy. In both of these cases the fetus itself had little chance of survival even if the abortion were not performed. As the balance was once struck in favor of the mother whenever her life was endangered, it could be so struck again. The balance reached between 1895 and 1930 attempted prudentially and pastorally to forestall a multitude of exceptions for interests less than life.

The perception of the humanity of the fetus and the weighing of fetal rights against other human rights constituted the work of the moral analysts. But what spirit animated their abstract judgments? For the Christian community it was the injunction of Scripture to love your neighbor as yourself. The fetus as human was a neighbor; his life had parity with one's own. The commandment gave life to what otherwise would have been only rational calculation.

The commandment could be put in humanistic as well as theological terms: Do not injure your fellow man without reason. In these terms, once the humanity of the fetus is perceived, abortion is never right except in self-defense. When life must be taken to save life, reason alone cannot say that a mother must prefer a child's life to her own. With this exception, now of great rarity, abortion violates the rational humanist tenet of the equality of human lives.

For Christians the commandment to love had received a special imprint in that the exemplar proposed of love was the love of the Lord for his disciples. In the light given by this example, self-sacrifice carried to the point of death seemed in the extreme situations not without meaning. In the less extreme cases, preference for one's own interests to the life of another seemed to express cruelty or selfishness irreconcilable with the demands of love.

A Defense of Abortion [1]

Judith Jarvis Thomson

Judith Jarvis Thomson, in this very influential article, avoids the problem of determining when the fetus becomes a person. For the sake of argument only, she grants the conservative view that the fetus is a person from the moment of conception. She points out, however, that the conservative argument using this claim as a premise actually involves an additional unstated premise. The argument typically runs: The fetus is an innocent person; therefore, killing a fetus is always wrong. The argument requires that we assume that killing an innocent person is always wrong. But, Thomson claims, killing an innocent person is sometimes allowable. This is most clearly so when self-defense requires it.

Using several moral analogies, Thomson attempts to show that a fetus's right to life does not consist in the right not to be killed, but in the right not to be killed unjustly. The fetus's claim to life is not an absolute one which must always be granted unconditional precedence over the interests of its mother. Thus, abortion is not always permissible, but neither is it always impermissible. When the reasons for having an abortion are trivial, then abortion is not legitimate. When the reasons are serious and involve the health or welfare of the woman, then abortion is justifiable.

Most opposition to abortion relies on the premise that the fetus is a human being, a person, from the moment of conception. The premise is argued for, but, as I think, not well. Take, for example, the most common argument. We are asked to notice that the development of a human being from conception through birth into childhood is continuous; then it is said that to draw a line, to choose a point in this development and say "before this point the thing is not a person, after this point it is a person" is to make an arbitrary choice, a choice for which in the nature of things no good reason can be given. It is concluded that the fetus is, or anyway that we had better say it is, a person from the moment of conception. But this conclusion does not follow. Similar things might be said about the development of an acorn into an oak trees, and it does not follow that acorns are oak trees, or that we had better say they are. Arguments of this form are sometimes called "slippery slope arguments"—the phrase is perhaps self-explanatory—and it is dismaying that opponents of abortion rely on them so heavily and uncritically.

I am inclined to agree, however, that the prospects for "drawing a line" in the development of the fetus look dim. I am inclined to think also that we shall probably have to agree that the fetus has already become a human person well before birth. Indeed, it comes as a surprise when one first learns how early in its life it begins to acquire human characteristics. By the tenth week, for example, it already has a face, arms and legs, fingers and toes; it has internal organs, and brain activity is de-

tectable.[2] On the other hand, I think that the premise is false, that the fetus is not a person from the moment of conception. A newly fertilized ovum, a newly implanted clump of cells, is no more a person than an acorn is an oak tree. But I shall not discuss any of this. For it seems to me to be of great interest to ask what happens if, for the sake of argument, we allow the premise. How, precisely, are we supposed to get from there to the conclusion that abortion is morally impermissible? Opponents of abortion commonly spend most of their time establishing that the fetus is a person, and hardly any time explaining the step from there to the impermissibility of abortion. Perhaps they think the step too simple and obvious to require much comment. Or perhaps instead they are simply being economical in argument. Many of those who defend abortion rely on the premise that the fetus is not a person, but only a bit of tissue that will become a person at birth; and why pay out more arguments than you have to? Whatever the explanation, I suggest that the step they take is neither easy nor obvious, that it calls for closer examination than it is commonly given, and that when we do give it this closer examination we shall feel inclined to reject it.

I propose, then, that we grant that the fetus is a person from the moment of conception. How does the argument go from here? Something like this, I take it. Every person has a right to life. So the fetus has a right to life. No doubt the mother has a right to decide what shall happen in and to her body; everyone would grant that. But surely a person's right to life is stronger and more stringent than the

Judith Jarvis Thomson, "A Defense of Abortion," *Philosophy & Public Affairs*, Vol. 1, no. 1 (Fall 1971).

mother's right to decide what happens in and to her body, and so outweighs it. So the fetus may not be killed; an abortion may not be performed.

It sounds plausible. But now let me ask you to imagine this. You wake up in the morning and find yourself back to back in bed with an unconscious violinist. A famous unconscious violinist. He has been found to have a fatal kidney ailment, and the Society of Music Lovers has canvassed all the available medical records and found that you alone have the right blood type to help. They have therefore kidnapped you, and last night the violinist's circulatory system was plugged into yours, so that your kidneys can be used to extract poisons from his blood as well as your own. The director of the hospital now tells you, "Look, we're sorry the Society of Music Lovers did this to you—we would never have permitted it if we had known. But still, they did it, and the violinist is now plugged into you. To unplug you would be to kill him. But never mind, it's only for nine months. By then he will have recovered from his ailment, and can safely be unplugged from you." Is it morally incumbent on you to accede to this situation? No doubt it would be very nice of you if you did, a great kindness. But do you *have* to accede to it? What if it were not nine months, but nine years? Or longer still? What if the director of the hospital says, "Tough luck, I agree, but now you've got to stay in bed, with the violinist plugged into you, for the rest of your life. Because remember this. All persons have a right to life, and violinists are persons. Granted you have a right to decide what happens in and to your body, but a person's right to life outweighs your right to decide what happens in and to your body. So you cannot ever be unplugged from him." I imagine you would regard this as outrageous, which suggests that something really is wrong with that plausible-sounding argument I mentioned a moment ago.

In this case, of course, you were kidnapped; you didn't volunteer for the operation that plugged the violinist into your kidneys. Can those who oppose abortion on the ground I mentioned make an exception for a pregnancy due to rape? Certainly. They can say that persons have a right to life only if they didn't come into existence because of rape; or they can say that all persons have a right to life, but that some have less of a right to life than others, in particular, that those who came into existence because of rape have less. But these statements have a rather unpleasant sound. Surely the question of

whether you have a right to life at all, or how much of it you have, shouldn't turn on the question of whether or not you are a product of a rape. And in fact the people who oppose abortion on the ground I mentioned do not make this distinction, and hence do not make an exception in case of rape.

Nor do they make an exception for a case in which the mother has to spend the nine months of her pregnancy in bed. They would agree that would be a great pity, and hard on the mother; but all the same, all persons have a right to life, the fetus is a person, and so on. I suspect, in fact, that they would not make an exception for a case in which, miraculously enough, the pregnancy went on for nine years, or even the rest of the mother's life.

Some won't even make an exception for a case in which continuation of the pregnancy is likely to shorten the mother's life; they regard abortion as impermissible even to save the mother's life. Such cases are nowadays very rare, and many opponents of abortion do not accept this extreme view. All the same, it is a good place to begin: a number of points of interest come out in respect to it.

1.

Let us call the view that abortion is impermissible even to save the mother's life "the extreme view." I want to suggest first that it does not issue from the argument I mentioned earlier without the addition of some fairly powerful premises. Suppose a woman has become pregnant, and now learns that she has a cardiac condition such that she will die if she carries the baby to term. What may be done for her? The fetus, being a person, has a right to life, but as the mother is a person too, so has she a right to life. Presumably they have an equal right to life. How is it supposed to come out that an abortion may not be performed? If mother and child have an equal right to life, shouldn't we perhaps flip a coin? Or should we add to the mother's right to life her right to decide what happens in and to her body, which everybody seems to be ready to grant—the sum of her rights now outweighing the fetus's right to life?

The most familiar argument here is the following. We are told that performing the abortion would be directly killing[3] the child, whereas doing nothing would not be killing the mother, but only letting her die. Moreover, in killing the child, one would be killing an innocent person, for the child has committed no crime, and is not aiming at his mother's death. And then there are a variety of ways in which this might be continued. (1) But as directly killing an innocent person is always and absolutely impermissible, an abortion may not be performed. Or, (2) as directly killing an innocent person is murder, and murder is always and absolutely impermissible, an abortion may not be performed.[4] Or, (3) as one's duty to refrain from directly killing an innocent person is more stringent than one's duty to keep a person from dying, an abortion may not be performed. Or, (4) if one's only options are directly killing an innocent person or letting a person die, one must prefer letting the person die, and thus an abortion may not be performed.[5]

Some people seem to have thought that these are not further premises which must be added if the conclusion is to be reached, but that they follow from the very fact that an innocent person has a right to life.[6] But this seems to me to be a mistake, and perhaps the simplest way to show this is to bring out that while we must certainly grant that innocent persons have a right to life, the theses in (1) through (4) are all false. Take (2), for example. If directly killing an innocent person is murder, and thus is impermissible, then the mother's directly killing the innocent person inside her is murder, and thus is impermissible. But it cannot seriously be thought to be murder if the mother performs an abortion on herself to save her life. It cannot seriously be said that she *must* refrain, that she *must* sit passively by and wait for her death. Let us look again at the case of you and the violinist. There you are, in bed with the violinist, and the director of the hospital says to you, "It's all most distressing, and I deeply sympathize, but you see this is putting an additional strain on your kidneys, and you'll be dead within the month. But you *have* to stay where you are all the same. Because unplugging you would be directly killing an innocent violinist, and that's murder, and that's impermissible." If anything in the world is true, it is that you do not commit murder, you do not do what is impermissible, if you reach around to your back and unplug yourself from that violinist to save your life.

The main focus of attention in writings on abortion has been on what a third party may or may not do in answer to a request from a woman for an abortion. This is in a way understandable. Things being as they are, there isn't much a woman can safely do to abort herself. So the question asked is what a third party may do, and what the mother may do, if it is mentioned at all, is deduced, almost as an afterthought, from what it is concluded that third parties may do. But it seems to me that to treat the matter in this way is to refuse to grant to the mother that very status of person which is so firmly insisted on for the fetus. For we cannot simply read off what a person may do from what a third party may do. Suppose you find yourself trapped in a tiny house with a growing child. I mean a very tiny house, and a rapidly growing child—you are already up against the wall of the house and in a few minutes you'll be crushed to death. The child on the other hand won't be crushed to death; if nothing is done to stop him from growing he'll be hurt, but in the end he'll simply burst open the house and walk out a free man. Now I could well understand it if a bystander were to say, "There's nothing we can do for you. We cannot choose between your life and his, we cannot be the ones to decide who is to live, we cannot intervene." But it cannot be concluded that you too can do nothing, that you cannot attack it to save your life. However innocent the child may be, you do not have to wait passively while it crushes you to death. Perhaps a pregnant woman is vaguely felt to have the status of house, to which we don't allow the right of self-defense. But if the woman houses the child, it should be remembered that she is a person who houses it.

I should perhaps stop to say explicitly that I am not claiming that people have a right to do anything whatever to save their lives. I think, rather, that there are drastic limits to the right of self-defense. If someone threatens you with death unless you torture someone else to death, I think you have not the right, even to save your life, to do so. But the case under consideration here is very different. In our case there are only two people involved, one whose life is threatened, and one who threatens it. Both are innocent: the one who is threatened is not threatened because of any fault, the one who threatens does not threaten because of any fault. For this reason we may feel that we bystanders cannot intervene. But the person threatened can.

In sum, a woman surely can defend her life against the threat to it posed by the unborn child, even if doing so involves its death. And this shows not merely that the theses in (1) through (4) are false; it shows also that the extreme view of abortion is false, and so we need not canvass any other possible ways of arriving at it from the argument I mentioned at the outset.

2.

The extreme view could of course be weakened to say that while abortion is permissible to save the mother's life, it may not be performed by a third party, but only by the mother herself. But this cannot be right either. For what we have to keep in mind is that the mother and the unborn child are not like two tenants in a small house which has, by an unfortunate mistake, been rented to both: the mother *owns* the house. The fact that she does adds to the offensiveness of deducing that the mother can do nothing from the supposition that third parties can do nothing. But it does more than this: it casts a bright light on the supposition that third parties can do nothing. Certainly it lets us see that a third party who says "I cannot choose between you" is fooling himself if he thinks this is impartiality. If Jones has found and fastened on a certain coat, which he needs to keep him from freezing, but which Smith also needs to keep him from freezing, then it is not impartiality that says "I cannot choose between you" when Smith owns the coat. Women have said again and again "This body is *my* body!" and they have reason to feel angry, reason to feel that it has been like shouting into the wind. Smith, after all, is hardly likely to bless us if we say to him, "Of course it's your coat, anybody would grant that it is. But no one may choose between you and Jones who is to have it."

We should really ask what it is that says "no one may choose" in the face of the fact that the body that houses the child is the mother's body. It may be simply a failure to appreciate this fact. But it may be something more interesting, namely the sense that one has a right to refuse to lay hands on people, even where it would be just and fair to do so, even where justice seems to require that somebody do so. Thus justice might call for somebody to get Smith's coat back from Jones, and yet you have a right to refuse to be the one to lay hands on Jones, a right to refuse to do physical violence to him. This, I think, must be granted. But then what should be said is not "no one may choose," but only

"I cannot choose," and indeed not even this, but "*I* will not *act*," leaving it open that somebody else can or should, and in particular that anyone in a position of authority, with the job of securing people's rights, both can and should. So this is no difficulty. I have not been arguing that any given third party must accede to the mother's request that he perform an abortion to save her life, but only that he may.

I suppose that in some views of human life the mother's body is only on loan to her, the loan not being one which gives her any prior claim to it. One who held this view might well think it impartiality to say "I cannot choose." But I shall simply ignore this possibility. My own view is that if a human being has any just, prior claim to anything at all, he has a just, prior claim to his own body. And perhaps this needn't be argued for here anyway, since, as I mentioned, the arguments against abortion we are looking at do grant that the woman has a right to decide what happens in and to her body.

But although they do grant it, I have tried to show that they do not take seriously what is done in granting it. I suggest the same thing will reappear even more clearly when we turn away from cases in which the mother's life is at stake, and attend, as I propose we now do, to the vastly more common cases in which a woman wants an abortion for some less weighty reason than preserving her own life.

3.

Where the mother's life is not at stake, the argument I mentioned at the outset seems to have a much stronger pull. "Everyone has a right to life, so the unborn person has a right to life." And isn't the child's right to life weightier than anything other than the mother's own right to life, which she might put forward as ground for an abortion?

This argument treats the right to life as if it were unproblematic. It is not, and this seems to me to be precisely the source of the mistake.

For we should now, at long last, ask what it comes to, to have a right to life. In some views having a right to life includes having a right to be given at least the bare minimum one needs for continued life. But suppose that what in fact *is* the bare minimum a man needs for continued life is something he has no right at all to be given? If I am sick unto death, and the only thing that will save my life is the touch of Henry Fonda's cool hand on my fevered brow, then all the same, I have no right to be given the touch of Henry Fonda's cool hand on my fevered brow. It would be frightfully nice of him to fly in from the West Coast to provide it. It would be less nice, though no doubt well meant, if my friends flew out to the West Coast and carried Henry Fonda back with them. But I have no right at all against anybody that he should do this for me. Or again, to return to the story I told earlier, the fact that for continued life the violinist needs the continued use of your kidneys does not establish that he has a right to be given the continued use of your kidneys. He certainly has no right against you that *you* should give him continued use of your kidneys. For nobody has any right to use your kidneys unless you give him this right—if you do allow him to go on using your kidneys, this is a kindness on your part, and not something he can claim from you as his due. Nor has he any right against anybody else that *they* should give him continued use of your kidneys. Certainly he had no right against the Society of Music Lovers that they should plug him into you in the first place. And if you now start to unplug yourself, having learned that you will otherwise have to spend nine years in bed with him, there is nobody in the world who must try to prevent you, in order to see to it that he is given something he has a right to be given.

Some people are rather stricter about the right to life. In their view, it does not include the right to be given anything, but amounts to, and only to, the right not to be killed by anybody. But here a related difficulty arises. If everybody is to refrain from killing that violinist, then everybody must refrain from doing a great many different sorts of things. Everybody must refrain from slitting his throat, everybody must refrain from shooting him—and everybody must refrain from unplugging you from him. But does he have a right against everybody that they shall refrain from unplugging you from him? To refrain from doing this is to allow him to continue to use your kidneys. It could be argued that he has a right against us that *we* should allow him to continue to use your kidneys. That is, while he had no right against us that we should give him the use of your kidneys, it might be argued that he anyway has a right against us that we shall not now intervene and deprive him of the use of your kidneys. I shall come back to third-party interventions later. But certainly the violinist has no

right against you that *you* shall allow him to continue to use your kidneys. As I said, if you do allow him to use them, it is a kindness on your part, and not something you owe him.

The difficulty I point to here is not peculiar to the right of life. It reappears in connection with all the other natural rights, and it is something which an adequate account of rights must deal with. For present purposes it is enough just to draw attention to it. But I would stress that I am not arguing that people do not have a right to life—quite to the contrary, it seems to me that the primary control we must place on the acceptability of an account of rights is that it should turn out in that account to be a truth that all persons have a right to life. I am arguing only that having a right to life does not guarantee having either a right to be given the use of or a right to be allowed continued use of another person's body—even if one needs it for life itself. So the right to life will not serve the opponents of abortion in the very simple and clear way in which they seem to have thought it would.

4.

There is another way to bring out the difficulty. In the most ordinary sort of case, to deprive someone of what he has a right to is to treat him unjustly. Suppose a boy and his small brother are jointly given a box of chocolates for Christmas. If the older boy takes the box and refuses to give his brother any of the chocolates, he is unjust to him, for the brother has been given a right to half of them. But suppose that, having learned that otherwise it means nine years in bed with that violinist, you unplug yourself from him. You surely are not being unjust to him, for you gave him no right to use your kidneys, and no one else can have given him any such right. But we have to notice that in unplugging yourself, you are killing him; and violinists, like everybody else, have a right to life, and thus in the view we were considering just now, the right not to be killed. So here you do what he supposedly has a right you shall not do, but you do not act unjustly to him in doing it.

The emendation which may be made at this point is this: the right to life consists not in the right not to be killed, but rather in the right not to be killed unjustly. This runs a risk of circularity, but never mind: it would enable us to square the fact that the violinist has a right to life with the fact that you do not act unjustly toward him in unplugging yourself, thereby killing him. For if you do not kill him unjustly, you do not violate his right to life, and so it is no wonder you do him no injustice.

But if this emendation is accepted, the gap in the argument against abortion stares us plainly in the face: it is by no means enough to show that the fetus is a person, and to remind us that all persons have a right to life—we need to be shown also that killing the fetus violates its right to life, i.e., that abortion is unjust killing. And is it?

I suppose we may take it as a datum that in a case of pregnancy due to rape the mother has not given the unborn person a right to the use of her body for food and shelter. Indeed, in what pregnancy could it be supposed that the mother has given the unborn person such a right? It is not as if there were unborn persons drifting about the world, to whom a woman who wants a child says "I invite you in."

But it might be argued that there are other ways one can have acquired a right to the use of another person's body than by having been invited to use it by that person. Suppose a woman voluntarily indulges in intercourse, knowing of the chance it will issue in pregnancy, and then she does become pregnant; is she not in part responsible for the presence, in fact the very existence, of the unborn person inside? No doubt she did not invite it in. But doesn't her partial responsibility for its being there itself give it a right to the use of her body?[7] If so, then her aborting it would be more like the boys taking away the chocolates, and less like your unplugging yourself from the violinist—doing so would be depriving it of what it does have a right to, and thus would be doing it an injustice.

And then, too, it might be asked whether or not she can kill it even to save her own life: If she voluntarily called it into existence, how can she now kill it, even in self-defense?

The first thing to be said about this is that it is something new. Opponents of abortion have been so concerned to make out the independence of the fetus, in order to establish that it has a right to life, just as its mother does, that they have tended to overlook the possible support they might gain from making out that the fetus is *dependent* on the mother, in order to establish that she has a special kind of responsibility for it, a responsibility that gives it rights against her which are not possessed by any independent person—such as an ailing violinist who is a stranger to her.

On the other hand, this argument would give the unborn person a right to its mother's body only if her pregnancy resulted from a voluntary act, undertaken in full knowledge of the chance a pregnancy might result from it. It would leave out entirely the unborn person whose existence is due to rape. Pending the availability of some further argument, then, we would be left with the conclusion that unborn persons whose existence is due to rape have no right to the use of their mothers' bodies, and thus that aborting them is not depriving them of anything they have a right to and hence is not unjust killing.

And we should also notice that it is not at all plain that this argument really does go even as far as it purports to. For there are cases and cases, and the details make a difference. If the room is stuffy, and I therefore open a window to air it, and a burglar climbs in, it would be absurd to say, "Ah, now he can stay, she's given him a right to the use of her house—for she is partially responsible for his presence there, having voluntarily done what enabled him to get in, in full knowledge that there are such things as burglars, and that burglars burgle." It would be still more absurd to say this if I had had bars installed outside my windows, precisely to prevent burglars from getting in, and a burglar got in only because of a defect in the bars. It remains equally absurd if we imagine it is not a burglar who climbs in, but an innocent person who blunders or falls in. Again, suppose it were like this: people-seeds drift about in the air like pollen, and if you open your windows, one may drift in and take root in your carpets or upholstery. You don't want children, so you fix up your windows with fine mesh screens, the very best you can buy. As can happen, however, and on very, very rare occasions does happen, one of the screens is defective, and a seed drifts in and takes root. Does the person-plant who now develops have a right to the use of your house? Surely not—despite the fact that you voluntarily opened your windows, you knowingly kept carpets and upholstered furniture, and you knew that screens were sometimes defective. Someone may argue that you are responsible for its rooting, that it does have a right to your house, because after all you could have lived out your life with bare floors and furniture, or with sealed windows and doors. But this won't do—for by the same token anyone can avoid a pregnancy due to rape by having a hysterectomy, or anyway by never leaving home without a (reliable!) army.

It seems to me that the argument we are looking at can establish at most that there are *some* cases in which the unborn person has a right to the use of its mother's body, and therefore *some* cases in which abortion is unjust killing. There is room for much discussion and argument as to precisely which, if any. But I think we should sidestep this issue and leave it open, for at any rate the argument certainly does not establish that all abortion is unjust killing.

5.

There is room for yet another argument here, however. We surely must all grant that there may be cases in which it would be morally indecent to detach a person from your body at the cost of his life. Suppose you learn that what the violinist needs is not nine years of your life, but only one hour: all you need do to save his life is to spend one hour in that bed with him. Suppose also that letting him use your kidneys for that one hour would not affect your health in the slightest. Admittedly you were kidnapped. Admittedly you did not give anyone permission to plug him into you. Nevertheless it seems to me plain you *ought* to allow him to use your kidneys for that hour—it would be indecent to refuse.

Again, suppose pregnancy lasted only an hour, and constituted no threat to life or health. And suppose that a woman becomes pregnant as a result of rape. Admittedly she did not voluntarily do anything to bring about the existence of a child. Admittedly she did nothing at all which would give the unborn person a right to the use of her body. All the same it might well be said, as in the newly amended violinist story, that she *ought* to allow it to remain for that hour—that it would be indecent of her to refuse.

Now some people are inclined to use the term "right" in such a way that it follows from the fact that you ought to allow a person to use your body for the hour he needs, that he has a right to use your body for the hour he needs, even though he has not been given that right by any person or act. They may say that it follows also that if you refuse, you act unjustly toward him. This use of the term is perhaps so common that it cannot be called wrong; nevertheless it seems to me to be an unfortunate loosening of what we would do better to keep a tight rein on. Suppose that box of chocolates I mentioned earlier had not been given to both boys jointly, but was given only to the older boy. There he sits, stolidly eating his way through the box, his small brother watching enviously. Here we are likely to say, "You ought not to be so mean. You ought to give your brother some of those chocolates." My own view is that it just does not follow from the truth of this that the brother has any right to any of the chocolates. If the boy refuses to give his brother any, he is greedy, stingy, callous—but not unjust. I suppose that the people I have in mind will say it does follow that the brother has a right to some of the chocolates, and thus that the boy does act unjustly if he refuses to give his brother any. But the effect of saying this is to obscure what we should keep distinct, namely the difference between the boy's refusal in this case and the boy's refusal in the earlier case, in which the box was given to both boys jointly, and in which the small brother thus had what was from any point of view clear title to half.

A further objection to so using the term "right" that from the fact that A ought to do a thing for B, it follows that B has a right against A that A do it for him, is that it is going to make the question of whether or not a man has a right to a thing turn on how easy it is to provide him with it; and this seems not merely unfortunate, but morally unacceptable. Take the case of Henry Fonda again. I said earlier that I had no right to the touch of his cool hand on my fevered brow, even though I needed it to save my life. I said it would be frightfully nice of him to fly in from the West Coast to provide me with it, but that I had no right against him that he should do so. But suppose he isn't on the West Coast. Suppose he has only to walk across the room, place a hand briefly on my brow—and lo, my life is saved. Then surely he ought to do it, it would be indecent to refuse. Is it to be said, "Ah, well, it follows that in this case she has a right to the touch of his hand on her brow, and so it would be an injustice in him to refuse"? So that I have a right to it when it is easy for him to provide it, though no right when it's hard? It's rather a shocking idea that anyone's rights should fade away and disappear as it gets harder and harder to accord them to him.

So my own view is that even though you ought to let the violinist use your kidneys for the one hour he needs, we should not conclude that he has a right to do so—we should say that if you refuse, you are, like the boy who owns all the chocolates and will give none away, self-centered and callous, indecent in fact, but not unjust. And similarly, that even supposing a case in which a woman pregnant due to rape ought to allow the unborn person to use her body for the hour he needs, we should not conclude that he has a right to do so; we should conclude that she is self-centered, callous, indecent, but not unjust, if she refuses. The complaints are no less grave; they are just different. However, there is no need to insist on this point. If anyone does wish to deduce "he has a right" from "you ought," then all the same he must surely grant that there are cases in which it is not morally required of you that you allow that violinist to use your kidneys, and in which he does not have a right to use them, and in which you do not do him an injustice if you refuse. And so also for mother and unborn child. Except in such cases as the unborn person has a right to demand it—and we were leaving open the possibility that there may be such cases—nobody is morally *required* to make large sacrifices, of health, of all other interests and concerns, of all other duties and commitments, for nine years, or even for nine months, in order to keep another person alive.

6.

We have in fact to distinguish between two kinds of Samaritan: the Good Samaritan and what we might call the Minimally Decent Samaritan. The story of the Good Samaritan, you will remember, goes like this:

> A certain man went down from Jerusalem to Jericho, and fell among thieves, which stripped him of his raiment, and wounded him, and departed, leaving him half dead.
>
> And by chance there came down a certain priest that way: and when he saw him, he passed by on the other side.
>
> And likewise a Levite, when he was at the place, came and looked on him, and passed by on the other side.
>
> But a certain Samaritan, as he journeyed, came where he was; and when he saw him he had compassion on him.
>
> And went to him, and bound up his wounds, pouring in oil and wine, and set him on his own beast, and brought him to an inn, and took care of him.
>
> And on the morrow, when he departed, he took out two pence, and gave them to the host, and said unto him, "Take care of him; and whatsoever thou spendest more, when I come again, I will repay thee." (Luke 10:30–35)

The Good Samaritan went out of his way, at some cost to himself, to help one in need of it. We are not told what the options were, that is, whether or not the priest and the Levite could have helped by doing less than the Good Samaritan did, but assuming they could have, then the fact they did nothing at all shows they were not even Minimally Decent Samaritans, not because they were not Samaritans, but because they were not even minimally decent.

These things are a matter of degree, of course, but there is a difference, and it comes out perhaps most clearly in the story of Kitty Genovese, who, as you will remember, was murdered while thirty-eight people watched or listened, and did nothing at all to help her. A Good Samaritan would have rushed out to give direct assistance against the murderer. Or perhaps we had better allow that it would have been a Splendid Samaritan who did this, on the ground that it would have involved a risk of death for himself. But the thirty-eight not only did not do this, they did not even trouble to pick up a phone to call the police. Minimally Decent Samaritanism would call for doing at least that, and their not having done it was monstrous.

After telling the story of the Good Samaritan, Jesus said, "Go, and do thou likewise." Perhaps he meant that we are morally required to act as the Good Samaritan did. Perhaps he was urging people to do more than is morally required of them. At all events it seems plain that it was not morally required of any of the thirty-eight that he rush out to give direct assistance at the risk of his own life, and that it is not morally required of anyone that he give long stretches of his life—nine years or nine months—to sustaining the life of a person who has no special right (we were leaving open the possibility of this) to demand it.

Indeed, with one rather striking class of exceptions, no one in any country in the world is *legally* required to do anywhere near as much as this for anyone else. The class of exceptions is obvious.

My main concern here is not the state of the law in respect to abortion, but it is worth drawing attention to the fact that in no state in this country is any man compelled by law to be even a Minimally Decent Samaritan to any person; there is no law under which charges could be brought against the thirty-eight who stood by while Kitty Genovese died. By contrast, in most states in this country women are compelled by law to be not merely Minimally Decent Samaritans, but Good Samaritans to unborn persons inside them. This doesn't by itself settle anything one way or the other, because it may well be argued that there should be laws in this country—as there are in many European countries—compelling at least Minimally Decent Samaritanism.[8] But it does show that there is a gross injustice in the existing state of the law. And it shows also that the groups currently working against liberalization of abortion laws, in fact working toward having it declared unconstitutional for a state to permit abortion, had better start working for the adoption of Good Samaritan laws generally, or earn the charge that they are acting in bad faith.

I should think, myself, that Minimally Decent Samaritan laws would be one thing, Good Samaritan laws quite another, and in fact highly improper. But we are not here concerned with the law. What we should ask is not whether anybody should be compelled by law to be a Good Samaritan, but whether we must accede to a situation in which somebody is being compelled—by nature, perhaps—to be a Good Samaritan. We have, in other words, to look now at third-party interventions. I have been arguing that no person is morally required to make large sacrifices to sustain the life of another who has no right to demand them, and this even where the sacrifices do not include life itself; we are not morally required to be Good Samaritans or anyway Very Good Samaritans to one another. But what if a man cannot extricate himself from such a situation? What if he appeals to us to extricate him? It seems to me plain that there are cases in which we can, cases in which a good Samaritan would extricate him. There you are, you were kidnapped, and nine years in bed with that violinist lie ahead of you. You have your own life to lead. You are sorry, but you simply cannot see giving up so much of your life to the sustaining of his. You cannot extricate yourself, and ask us to do so. I should have thought that—in light of his having no

right to the use of your body—it was obvious that we do not have to accede to your being forced to give up so much. We can do what you ask. There is no injustice to the violinist in our doing so.

7.

Following the lead of the opponents of abortion, I have throughout been speaking of the fetus merely as a person, and what I have been asking is whether or not the argument we began with, which proceeds only from the fetus's being a person, really does establish its conclusion. I have argued that it does not.

But of course there are arguments and arguments, and it may be said that I have simply fastened on the wrong one. It may be said that what is important is not merely the fact that the fetus is a person, but that it is a person for whom the woman has a special kind of responsibility issuing from the fact that she is its mother. And it might be argued that all my analogies are therefore irrelevant—for you do not have that special kind of responsibility for that violinist, Henry Fonda does not have that special kind of responsibility for me. And our attention might be drawn to the fact that men and women both *are* compelled by law to provide support for their children.

I have in effect dealt (briefly) with this argument in section 4 above; but a (still briefer) recapitulation now may be in order. Surely we do not have any such "special responsibility" for a person unless we have assumed it, explicitly or implicitly. If a set of parents do not try to prevent pregnancy, do not obtain an abortion, but rather take it home with them, then they have assumed responsibility for it, they have given it rights, and they cannot *now* withdraw support from it at the cost of its life because they now find it difficult to go on providing for it. But if they have taken all reasonable precautions against having a child, they do not simply by virtue of their biological relationship to the child who comes into existence have a special responsibility for it. They may wish to assume responsibility for it, or they may not wish to. And I am suggesting that if assuming responsibility for it would require large sacrifices, then they may refuse. A Good Samaritan would not refuse—or anyway, a Splendid Samaritan, if the sacrifices that had to made were enormous. But then so would a Good Samaritan assume responsibility for that violinist; so would Henry Fonda, if he is a Good Samaritan, fly in from the West Coast and assume responsibility for me.

8.

My argument will be found unsatisfactory on two counts by many of those who want to regard abortion as morally permissible. First, while I do argue that abortion is not impermissible, I do not argue that it is always permissible. There may well be cases in which carrying the child to term requires only Minimally Decent Samaritanism of the mother, and this is a standard we must not fall below. I am inclined to think it a merit of my account precisely that it does *not* give a general yes or a general no. It allows for and supports our sense that, for example, a sick and desperately frightened fourteen-year-old schoolgirl, pregnant due to rape, may *of course* choose abortion, and that any law which rules this out is an insane law. And it also allows for and supports our sense that in other cases resort to abortion is even positively indecent. It would be indecent in the woman to request an abortion, and indecent in a doctor to perform it, if she is in her seventh month, and wants the abortion just to avoid the nuisance of postponing a trip abroad. The very fact that the arguments I have been drawing attention to treat all cases of abortion, or even all cases of abortion in which the mother's life is not at stake, as morally on a par ought to have made them suspect at the outset.

Second, while I am arguing for the permissibility of abortion in some cases, I am not arguing for the right to secure the death of the unborn child. It is easy to confuse these two things in that up to a certain point in the life of the fetus it is not able to survive outside the mother's body; hence removing it from her body guarantees its death. But they are importantly different. I have argued that you are not morally required to spend nine months in bed, sustaining the life of that violinist; but to say this is by no means to say that if, when you unplug yourself, there is a miracle and he survives, you then have a right to turn round and slit his throat. You may detach yourself even if this costs him his life; you have no right to be guaranteed his death, by some other means, if unplugging yourself does not kill him. There are some people who will feel dissatisfied by this feature of my argument. A woman may be utterly devastated by the thought of a child,

a bit of herself, put out for adoption and never seen or heard of again. She may therefore want not merely that the child be detached from her, but more, that it die. Some opponents of abortion are inclined to regard this as beneath contempt—thereby showing insensitivity to what is surely a powerful source of despair. All the same, I agree that the desire for the child's death is not one which anybody may gratify, should it turn out to be possible to detach the child alive.

At this place, however, it should be remembered that we have only been pretending throughout that the fetus is a human being from the moment of conception. A very early abortion is surely not the killing of a person, and so is not dealt with by anything I have said here.

Notes

1. I am very much indebted to James Thomson for discussion, criticism, and many helpful suggestions.

2. Daniel Callahan, *Abortion: Law, Choice and Morality* (New York, 1970), p. 373. This book gives a fascinating survey of the available information on abortion. The Jewish tradition is surveyed in David M. Feldman, *Birth Control in Jewish Law* (New York, 1968). Part 5, the Catholic tradition in John T. Noonan, Jr., "An Almost Absolute Value in History," in *The Morality of Abortion,* ed. John T. Noonan, Jr. (Cambridge, Mass., 1970).

3. The term "direct" in the arguments I refer to is a technical one. Roughly, what is meant by "direct killing" is either killing as an end in itself, or killing as a means to some end, for example, the end of saving someone else's life. See note 6, below, for an example of its use.

4. Cf. *Encyclical Letter of Pope Pius XI on Christian Marriage,* St. Paul Editions (Boston, n.d.), p. 32: "However much we may pity the mother whose health and even life is gravely imperiled in the performance of the duty allotted to her by nature, nevertheless what could ever be a sufficient reason for excusing in any way the direct murder of the innocent? This is precisely what we are dealing with here." Noonan (*The Morality of Abortion,* p. 43) reads this as follows: "What cause can ever avail to excuse in any way the direct killing of the innocent? For it is a question of that."

5. The thesis in (4) is in an interesting way weaker than those in (1), (2), and (3): they rule out abortion even in cases in which both mother *and* child will die if the abortion is not performed. By contrast, one who held the view expressed in (4) could consistently say that one needn't prefer letting two persons die to killing one.

6. Cf. the following passage from Pius XII, *Address to the Italian Catholic Society of Midwives:* "The baby in the maternal breast has the right to life immediately from God.—Hence there is no man, no human authority, no science, no medical, eugenic, social, economic or moral 'indication' which can establish or grant a valid juridical ground for a direct deliberate disposition of an innocent human life, that is a disposition which looks to its destruction either as an end or as a means to another end perhaps in itself not illicit.—The baby, still not born, is a man in the same degree and for the same reason as the mother" (quoted in Noonan, *The Morality of Abortion,* p. 45).

7.   The need for a discussion of this argument was brought home to me by members of the Society for Ethical and Legal Philosophy, to whom this paper was originally presented.

8.   For a discussion of the difficulties involved, and a survey of the European experience with such laws, see *The Good Samaritan and the Law,* ed. James M. Ratcliffe (New York, 1966).

On the Moral and Legal Status of Abortion

Mary Anne Warren

Mary Anne Warren takes an even stronger position than Thomson (see preceding article), arguing that a woman's right to have an abortion is unrestricted. She attempts to show that there is no adequate basis for holding that the fetus has "a significant right to life" and that, whatever right can be appropriately granted to the fetus, it can never override a woman's right to protect her own interest and well-being. Accordingly, laws that restrict access to abortion are an unjustified violation of a woman's rights.

Warren is critical of both Noonan (see earlier article) and Thomson. Noonan, she claims, fails to demonstrate that whatever is genetically human (the fetus) is also morally human (a person). Thomson, Warren argues, is mistaken in believing that it is possible both to grant that the fetus is a person and to produce a satisfactory defense of the right to obtain an abortion. Contrary to Thomson's aim, her central argument supports the right to abortion only in cases in which the woman is in no way responsible for her pregnancy.

Like Noonan, Warren conceives the basic issue in abortion to be the question of what properties something must possess to be a person in the moral sense. She offers five traits she believes anyone would accept as central and argues that the fetus, at all stages of development, possesses none of them. Since the fetus is not a person, it is not entitled to the full range of moral rights. That the fetus has the potential to become a person may give it a prima facie right to life, but the rights of an actual person always outweigh those of a potential person.

We will be concerned with both the moral status of abortion, which for our purposes we may define as the act which a woman performs in voluntarily terminating, or allowing another person to terminate, her pregnancy, and the legal status which is appropriate for this act. I will argue that, while it is not possible to produce a satisfactory defense of a woman's right to obtain an abortion without showing that a fetus is not a human being, in the morally relevant sense of that term, we ought not to conclude that the difficulties involved in determining whether or not a fetus is human make it impossible to produce any satisfactory solution to the problem of the moral status of abortion. For it is possible to show that, on the basis of intuitions which we may expect even the opponents of abortion to share, a fetus is not a person, and hence not the sort of entity to which it is proper to ascribe full moral rights.

Of course, while some philosophers would deny the possibility of any such proof,[1] others will deny that there is any need for it, since the moral permissibility of abortion appears to them to be too obvious to require proof. But the inadequacy of this attitude should be evident from the fact that

Reprinted with permission from *The Monist*, LaSalle, Illinois 61301, Vol. 57, no. 1.

both the friends and the foes of abortion consider their position to be morally self-evident. Because pro-abortionists have never adequately come to grips with the conceptual issues surrounding abortion, most if not all, of the arguments which they advance in opposition to laws restricting access to abortion fail to refute or even weaken the traditional antiabortion argument, i.e., that a fetus is a human being, and therefore abortion is murder.

These arguments are typically of one of two sorts. Either they point to the terrible side effects of the restrictive laws, e.g., the deaths due to illegal abortions, and the fact that it is poor women who suffer the most as a result of these laws, or else they state that to deny a woman access to abortion is to deprive her of her right to control her own body. Unfortunately, however, the fact that restricting access to abortion has tragic side effects does not, in itself, show that the restrictions are unjustified, since murder is wrong regardless of the consequences of prohibiting it; and the appeal to the right to control one's body, which is generally construed as a property right, is at best a rather feeble argument for the permissibility of abortion. Mere ownership does not give me the right to kill innocent people whom I find on my property, and indeed I am apt to be held responsible if such people injure themselves while on my property. It is equally unclear that I have any moral right to expel an innocent person from my property when I know that doing so will result in his death. . . .

. . . John Noonan is correct in saying that "the fundamental question in the long history of abortion is, How do you determine the humanity of a being?"[2] He summarizes his own antiabortion argument, which is a version of the official position of the Catholic Church, as follows:

> . . . it is wrong to kill humans, however poor, weak, defenseless, and lacking in opportunity to develop their potential they may be. It is therefore morally wrong to kill Biafrans. Similarly, it is morally wrong to kill embryos.[3]

Noonan bases his claim that fetuses are human upon what he calls the theologians' criterion of humanity: that whoever is conceived of human beings is human. But although he argues at length for the appropriateness of this criterion, he never questions the assumption that if a fetus is human then abortion is wrong for exactly the same reason that murder is wrong.

Judith Thomson is, in fact, the only writer I am aware of who has seriously questioned this assumption; she has argued that, even if we grant the antiabortionist his claim that a fetus is a human being, with the same right to life as any other human being, we can still demonstrate that, in at least some and perhaps most cases, a woman is under no moral obligation to complete an unwanted pregnancy.[4] Her argument is worth examining, since if it holds up it may enable us to establish the moral permissibility of abortion without becoming involved in problems about what entitles an entity to be considered human, and accorded full moral rights. To be able to do this would be a great gain in the power and simplicity of the proabortion position, since, although I will argue that these problems can be solved at least as decisively as can any other moral problem, we should certainly be pleased to be able to avoid having to solve them as part of the justification of abortion.

On the other hand, even if Thomson's argument does not hold up, her insight, i.e., that it requires argument to show that if fetuses are human then abortion is properly classified as murder, is an extremely valuable one. The assumption she attacks is particularly invidious, for it amounts to the decision that it is appropriate, in deciding the moral status of abortion, to leave the rights of the pregnant woman out of consideration entirely, except possibly when her life is threatened. Obviously, this will not do; determining what moral rights, if any, a fetus possesses is only the first step in determining the moral status of abortion. Step two, which is at least equally essential, is finding a just solution to the conflict between whatever rights the fetus may have, and the rights of the woman who is unwillingly pregnant. While the historical error has been to pay far too little attention to the second step, Ms. Thomson's suggestion is that if we look at the second step first we may find that a woman has a right to obtain an abortion *regardless* of what rights the fetus has.

Our own inquiry will also have two stages. In Section I, we will consider whether or not it is possible to establish that abortion is morally permissible even on the assumption that a fetus is an entity with a full-fledged right to life. I will argue that in fact this cannot be established, at least not with the conclusiveness which is essential to our hopes of convincing those who are skeptical about the morality of abortion, and that we therefore cannot avoid dealing with the question of whether or not a fetus really does have the same right to life as a (more fully developed) human being.

In Section II, I will propose an answer to this question, namely, that a fetus cannot be considered a member of the moral community, the set of beings with full and equal moral rights, for the simple reason that it is not a person, and that it is personhood, and not genetic humanity, i.e., humanity as defined by Noonan, which is the basis for membership in this community. I will argue that a fetus, whatever its stage of development, satisfies none of the basic criteria of personhood, and is not even enough *like* a person to be accorded even some of the same rights on the basis of this resemblance. Nor, as we will see, is a fetus's *potential* personhood a threat to the morality of abortion, since, whatever the rights of potential people may be, they are invariably overridden in any conflict with the moral rights of actual people.

I

We turn now to Professor Thomson's case for the claim that even if a fetus has full moral rights, abortion is still morally permissible, at least sometimes, and for some reasons other than to save the woman's life. Her argument is based upon a clever, but I think faulty, analogy. She asked us to picture ourselves waking up one day, in bed with a famous violinist. Imagine that you have been kidnapped, and your bloodstream hooked up to that of the violinist, who happens to have an ailment which will certainly kill him unless he is permitted to share your kidneys for a period of nine months. No one else can save him, since you alone have the right type of blood. He will be unconscious all that time, and you will have to stay in bed with him, but after the nine months are over he may be unplugged, completely cured, that is provided that you have cooperated.

Now then, she continues, what are your obligations in this situation? The antiabortionist, if he is consistent, will have to say that you are obligated to stay in bed with the violinist: for all people have a right to life, and violinists are people, and therefore it would be murder for you to disconnect yourself from him and let him die.[5] But this is outrageous, and so there must be something wrong with the same argument when it is applied to abortion. It would certainly be commendable of you to agree to

save the violinist, but it is absurd to suggest that your refusal to do so would be murder. His right to life does not obligate you to do whatever is required to keep him alive; nor does it justify anyone else in forcing you to do so. A law which required you to stay in bed with the violinist would clearly be an unjust law, since it is no proper function of the law to force unwilling people to make huge sacrifices for the sake of other people toward whom they have no such prior obligation.

Thomson concludes that, if this analogy is an apt one, then we can grant the antiabortionist his claim that a fetus is a human being, and still hold that it is at least sometimes the case that a pregnant woman has the right to refuse to be a Good Samaritan towards the fetus, i.e., to obtain an abortion. For there is a great gap between the claim that x has a right to life, and the claim that y is obligated to do whatever is necessary to keep x alive, let alone that he ought to be forced to do so. It is y's duty to keep x alive only if he has somehow contracted a *special* obligation to do so; and a woman who is unwillingly pregnant, e.g., who was raped, has done nothing which obligates her to make the enormous sacrifice which is necessary to preserve the conceptus.

This argument is initially quite plausible, and in the extreme case of pregnancy due to rape it is probably conclusive. Difficulties arise, however, when we try to specify more exactly the range of cases in which abortion is clearly justifiable even on the assumption that the fetus is human. Professor Thomson considers it a virtue of her argument that it does not enable us to conclude that abortion is *always* permissible. It would, she says, be "indecent" for a woman in her seventh month to obtain an abortion just to avoid having to postpone a trip to Europe. On the other hand, her argument enables us to see that "a sick and desperately frightened schoolgirl pregnant due to rape may *of course* choose abortion, and that any law which rules this out is an insane law" (p. 65). So far, so good; but what are we to say about the woman who becomes pregnant not through rape but as a result of her own carelessness, or because of contraceptive failure, or who gets pregnant intentionally and then changes her mind about wanting a child? With respect to such cases, the violinist analogy is of much less use to the defender of the woman's right to obtain an abortion.

Indeed, the choice of a pregnancy due to rape, as an example of a case in which abortion is permissible even if a fetus is considered a human being, is extremely significant; for it is only in the case of pregnancy due to rape that the woman's situation is adequately analogous to the violinist case for our intuitions about the latter to transfer convincingly. The crucial difference between a pregnancy due to rape and the normal case of an unwanted pregnancy is that in the normal case we cannot claim that the woman is in no way responsible for her predicament; she could have remained chaste, or taken her pills more faithfully, or abstained on dangerous days, and so on. If on the other hand, you are kidnapped by strangers, and hooked up to a strange violinist, then you are free of any shred of responsibility for the situation, on the basis of which it would be argued that you are obligated to keep the violinist alive. Only when her pregnancy is due to rape is a woman clearly just as nonresponsible.[6]

Consequently, there is room for the antiabortionist to argue that in the normal case of unwanted pregnancy a woman has, by her own actions, assumed responsibility for the fetus. For if x behaves in a way which he could have avoided, and which he knows involves, let us say, a 1 percent chance of bringing into existence a human being, with a right to life, and does so knowing that if this should happen then that human being will perish unless x does certain things to keep him alive, then it is by no means clear that when it does happen x is free of any obligation to what he knew in advance would be required to keep that human being alive.

The plausibility of such an argument is enough to show that the Thomson analogy can provide a clear and persuasive defense of a woman's right to obtain an abortion only with respect to those cases in which the woman is in no way responsible for her pregnancy, e.g., where it is due to rape. In all other cases, we would almost certainly conclude that it was necessary to look carefully at the particular circumstances in order to determine the extent of the woman's responsibility, and hence the extent of her obligation. This is an extremely unsatisfactory outcome, from the viewpoint of the opponents of restrictive abortion laws, most of whom are convinced that a woman has a right to obtain an abortion regardless of how and why she got pregnant.

Of course a supporter of the violinist analogy might point out that it is absurd to suggest that forgetting her pill one day might be sufficient to obligate a woman to complete an unwanted pregnancy. And indeed it *is* absurd to suggest this. As we will

see, the moral right to obtain an abortion is not in the least dependent upon the extent to which the woman is responsible for her pregnancy. But unfortunately, once we allow the assumption that a fetus has full moral rights, we cannot avoid taking this absurd suggestion seriously. Perhaps we can make this point more clear by altering the violinist story just enough to make it more analogous to a normal unwanted pregnancy and less to a pregnancy due to rape, and then seeing whether it is still obvious that you are not obligated to stay in bed with the fellow.

Suppose, then, that violinists are peculiarly prone to the sort of illness the only cure for which is the use of someone else's bloodstream for nine months, and that because of this there has been formed a society of music lovers who agree that whenever a violinist is stricken they will draw lots and the loser will, by some means, be made the one and only person capable of saving him. Now then, would you be obligated to cooperate in curing the violinist if you had voluntarily joined this society, knowing the possible consequences, and then your name had been drawn and you had been kidnapped? Admittedly, you did not promise ahead of time that you would, but you did deliberately place yourself in a position in which it might happen that a human life would be lost if you did not. Surely this is at least a prima facie reason for supposing that you have an obligation to stay in bed with the violinist. Suppose that you had gotten your name drawn deliberately; surely *that* would be quite a strong reason for thinking that you had such an obligation.

It might be suggested that there is one important disanalogy between the modified violinist case and the case of an unwanted pregnancy, which makes the woman's responsibility significantly less, namely, the fact that the fetus *comes into existence* as the result of the woman's actions. This fact might give her a right to refuse to keep it alive, whereas she would not have had this right had it existed previously, independently, and then as a result of her actions become dependent upon her for its survival.

My own intuition, however, is that x has no more right to bring into existence, either deliberately or as a foreseeable result of actions he could have avoided, a being with full moral rights (y), and then refuse to do what he knew beforehand would be required to keep that being alive, than he has to enter into an agreement with an existing person, whereby he may be called upon to save that person's life, and then refuse to do so when so called upon. Thus *x*'s responsibility for *y*'s existence does not seem to lessen his obligation to keep *y* alive, if he is also responsible for *y*'s being in a situation in which only he can save him.

Whether or not this intuition is entirely correct, it brings us back once again to the conclusion that once we allow the assumption that a fetus has full moral rights it becomes an extremely complex and difficult question whether and when abortion is justifiable. Thus the Thomson analogy cannot help us produce a clear and persuasive proof of the moral permissibility of abortion. Nor will the opponents of the restrictive laws thank us for anything less; for their conviction (for the most part) is that abortion is obviously *not* a morally serious and extremely unfortunate, even though sometimes justified act, comparable to killing in self-defense or to letting the violinist die, but rather is closer to being a morally neutral act, like cutting one's hair.

The basis of this conviction, I believe, is the realization that a fetus is not a person, and thus does not have a full-fledged right to life. Perhaps the reason why this claim has been so inadequately defended is that it seems self-evident to those who accept it. And so it is, insofar as it follows from what I take to be perfectly obvious claims about the nature of personhood, and about the proper grounds for ascribing moral rights, claims which ought, indeed, to be obvious to both the friends and foes of abortion. Nevertheless, it is worth examining these claims, and showing how they demonstrate the moral innocuousness of abortion, since this apparently has not been adequately done before.

II

The question which we must answer in order to produce a satisfactory solution to the problem of the moral status of abortion is this: How are we to define the moral community, the set of beings with full and equal moral rights, such that we can decide whether a human fetus is a member of this community or not? What sort of entity, exactly, has the inalienable rights to life, liberty, and the pursuit of happiness? Jefferson attributed these rights to all *men*, and it may or may not be fair to suggest that he intended to attribute them *only* to men. Perhaps he

ought to have attributed them to all human beings. If so, then we arrive, first, at Noonan's problem of defining what makes a being human, and, second, at the equally vital question which Noonan does not consider, namely, What reason is there for identifying the moral community with the set of all human beings, in whatever way we have chosen to define that term?

1. On the Definition of "Human"

One reason why this vital second question is so frequently overlooked in the debate over the moral status of abortion is that the term "human" has two distinct, but not often distinguished, senses. This fact results in a slide of meaning, which serves to conceal the fallaciousness of the traditional argument that since (1) it is wrong to kill innocent human beings, and (2) fetuses are innocent human beings, then (3) it is wrong to kill fetuses. For if "human" is used in the same sense in both (1) and (2) then, whichever of the two senses is meant, one of these premises is question-begging. And if it is used in two different senses then of course the conclusion doesn't follow.

Thus, (1) is a self-evident moral truth,[7] and avoids begging the question about abortion, only if "human being" is used to mean something like "a full-fledged member of the moral community." (It may or may not also be meant to refer exclusively to members of the species *Homo sapiens*.) We may call this the *moral* sense of "human." It is not to be confused with what we will call the *genetic* sense; i.e., the sense in which *any* member of the species is a human being, and no member of any other species could be. If (1) is acceptable only if the moral sense is intended, (2) is non-question-begging only if what is intended is the genetic sense.

In "Deciding Who is Human," Noonan argues for the classification of fetuses with human beings by pointing to the presence of the full genetic code, and the potential capacity for rational thought (p. 135). It is clear that what he needs to show, for his version of the traditional argument to be valid, is that fetuses are human in the moral sense, the sense in which it is analytically true that all human beings have full moral rights. But, in the absence of any argument showing that whatever is genetically human is also morally human, and he gives none, nothing more than genetic humanity can be demonstrated by the presence of the human genetic code. And, as we will see, the *potential* capacity for rational thought can at most show that an entity has the potential for *becoming* human in the moral sense.

2. Defining the Moral Community

Can it be established that genetic humanity is sufficient for moral humanity? I think that there are very good reasons for not defining the moral community in this way. I would like to suggest an alternative way of defining the moral community, which I will argue for only to the extent of explaining why it is, or should be, self-evident. The suggestion is simply that the moral community consists of all and *only* people, rather than all and only human beings;[8] and probably the best way of demonstrating its self-evidence is by considering the concept of personhood, to see what sorts of entity are and are not persons, and what the decision that a being is or is not a person implies about its moral rights.

What characteristics entitle an entity to be considered a person? This is obviously not the place to attempt a complete analysis of the concept of personhood, but we do not need such a fully adequate analysis just to determine whether and why a fetus is or isn't a person. All we need is a rough and approximate list of the most basic criteria of personhood, and some idea of which, or how many, of these an entity must satisfy in order to properly be considered a person.

In searching for such criteria, it is useful to look beyond the set of people with whom we are acquainted, and ask how we would decide whether a totally alien being was a person or not. (For we have no right to assume that genetic humanity is necessary for personhood.) Imagine a space traveler who lands on an unknown planet and encounters a race of beings utterly unlike any he has ever seen or heard of. If he wants to be sure of behaving morally toward these beings, he has to somehow decide whether they are people, and hence have full moral rights, or whether they are the sort of thing which he need not feel guilty about treating as, for example, a source of food.

How should he go about making this decision? If he has some anthropological background, he might look for such things as religion, art, and the manufacturing of tools, weapons, or shelters, since these factors have been used to distinguish our human from our prehuman ancestors, in what seems

to be closer to the moral than the genetic sense of "human." And no doubt he would be right to consider the presence of such factors as good evidence that the alien beings were people, and morally human. It would, however, be overly anthropocentric of him to take the absence of these things as adequate evidence that they were not, since we can imagine people who have progressed beyond, or evolved without ever developing, these cultural characteristics.

I suggest that the traits which are most central to the concept of personhood, or humanity in the moral sense, are, very roughly, the following:

1. consciousness (of objects and events external and/or internal to the being), and in particular the capacity to feel pain;

2. reasoning (the *developed* capacity to solve new and relatively complex problems);

3. self-motivated activity (activity which is relatively independent of either genetic or direct external control);

4. the capacity to communicate, by whatever means, messages of an indefinite variety of types, that is, not just with an indefinite number of possible contents, but on indefinitely many possible topics;

5. the presence of self-concepts, and self-awareness, either individual or racial, or both.

Admittedly, there are apt to be a great many problems involved in formulating precise definitions of these criteria, let alone in developing universally valid behavioral criteria for deciding when they apply. But I will assume that both we and our explorer know approximately what (1)–(5) mean, and that he is also able to determine whether or not they apply. How, then, should he use his findings to decide whether or not the alien beings are people? We needn't suppose that an entity must have *all* of these attributes to be properly considered a person; (1) and (2) alone may well be sufficient for personhood, and quite probably (1)–(3) are sufficient. Neither do we need to insist that any one of these criteria is necessary for personhood, although once again (1) and (2) look like fairly good candidates for necessary conditions, as does (3), if "activity" is construed so as to include the activity of reasoning.

All we need to claim, to demonstrate that a fetus is not a person, is that any being which satisfies *none* of (1)–(5) is certainly not a person. I consider this claim to be so obvious that I think anyone who denied it, and claimed that a being which satisfied none of (1)–(5) was a person all the same, would thereby demonstrate that he had no notion at all of what a person is—perhaps because he had confused the concept of a person with that of genetic humanity. If the opponents of abortion were to deny the appropriateness of these five criteria, I do not know what further arguments would convince them. We would probably have to admit that our conceptual schemes were indeed irreconcilably different, and that our dispute could not be settled objectively.

I do not expect this to happen, however, since I think that the concept of a person is one which is very nearly universal (to people), and that it is common to both proabortionists and antiabortionists, even though neither group has fully realized the relevance of this concept to the resolution of their dispute. Furthermore, I think that on reflection even the antiabortionists ought to agree not only that (1)–(5) are central to the concept of personhood, but also that it is a part of this concept that all and only people have full moral rights. The concept of a person is in part a moral concept; once we have admitted that *x* is a person we have recognized, even if we have not agreed to respect, *x*'s right to be treated as a member of the moral community. It is true that the claim that *x* is a *human being* is more commonly voiced as part of an appeal to treat *x* decently than is the claim that *x* is a person, but this is either because "human being" is here used in the sense which implies personhood, or because the genetic and moral senses of "human" have been confused.

Now if (1)–(5) are indeed the primary criteria of personhood, then it is clear that genetic humanity is neither necessary nor sufficient for establishing that an entity is a person. Some human beings are not people, and there may well be people who are not human beings. A man or woman whose consciousness has been permanently obliterated but who remains alive is a human being which is no longer a person; defective human beings, with no appreciable mental capacity, are not and presumably never will be people; and a fetus is a human being which is not yet a person, and which therefore cannot coherently be said to have full moral rights. Citizens of the next century should be prepared to recognize highly advanced, self-aware robots or computers, should such be developed, and intelligent inhabitants of other worlds, should such be found, as people in the fullest sense, and to respect their moral rights. But to ascribe full moral rights to an entity which is not a person is as absurd as to ascribe moral obligations and responsibilities to such an entity.

3. Fetal Development and the Right to Life

Two problems arise in the application of these suggestions for the definition of the moral community to the determination of the precise moral status of a human fetus. Given that the paradigm example of a person is a normal adult being, then (1) How like this paradigm, in particular how far advanced since conception, does a human being need to be before it begins to have a right to life by virtue, not of being fully a person as of yet, but of being *like* a person? and (2) To what extent, if any, does the fact that a fetus has the *potential* for becoming a person endow it with some of the same rights? Each of these questions requires some comment.

In answering the first question, we need not attempt a detailed consideration of the moral rights of organisms which are not developed enough, aware enough, intelligent enough, etc., to be considered people, but which resemble people in some respects. It does seem reasonable to suggest that the more like a person, in the relevant respects, a being is, the stronger is the case for regarding it as having a right to life, and indeed the stronger its right to life is. Thus we ought to take seriously the suggestion that, insofar as "the human individual develops biologically in a continuous fashion . . . the rights of a human person might develop in the same way."[9] But we must keep in mind that the attributes which are relevant in determining whether or not an entity is enough like a person to be regarded as having some of the same moral rights are no different from those which are relevant to determining whether or not it is fully a person—i.e., are no different from (1)–(5)—and that being genetically human, or having recognizably human facial and other physical features, or detectable brain activity, or the capacity to survive outside the uterus, are simply not among these relevant attributes.

Thus it is clear that even though a seven- or eight-month fetus has features which makes it apt to arouse in us almost the same powerful protective instinct as is commonly aroused by a small infant, nevertheless it is not significantly more personlike than is a very small embryo. It is *somewhat* more personlike; it can apparently feel and respond to pain, and it may even have a rudimentary form of consciousness, insofar as its brain is quite active. Nevertheless, it seems safe to say that it is not fully conscious, in the way that an infant of a few months is, and that it cannot reason, or communicate messages of indefinitely many sorts, does not engage in self-motivated activity, and has no self-awareness. Thus, in the *relevant* respects, a fetus, even a fully developed one, is considerably less personlike than is the average mature mammal, indeed the average fish. And I think that a rational person must conclude that if the right to life of a fetus is to be based upon its resemblance to a person, then it cannot be said to have any more right to life than, let us say, a newborn guppy (which also seems to be capable of feeling pain), and that a right of that magnitude could never override a woman's right to obtain an abortion, at any stage of her pregnancy.

There may, of course, be other arguments in favor of placing legal limits upon the stage of pregnancy in which an abortion may be performed. Given the relative safety of the new techniques of artificially inducing labor during the third trimester, the danger to the woman's life or health is no longer such an argument. Neither is the fact that people tend to respond to the thought of abortion in the later stages of pregnancy with emotional repulsion, since mere emotional responses cannot take the place of moral reasoning in determining what ought to be permitted. Nor, finally, is the frequently heard argument that legalizing abortion, especially late in the pregnancy, may erode the level of respect for human life, leading, perhaps, to an increase in unjustified euthanasia and other crimes. For this threat, if it is a threat, can be better met by educating people to the kinds of moral distinctions which we are making here than by limiting access to abortion (which limitation may, in its disregard for the rights of women, be just as damaging to the level of respect for human rights).

Thus, since the fact that even a fully developed fetus is not personlike enough to have any significant right to life on the basis of its personlikeness shows that no legal restrictions upon the stage of pregnancy in which an abortion may be performed can be justified on the grounds that we should protect the rights of the older fetus; and since there is no other apparent justification for such restrictions, we may conclude that they are entirely unjustified. Whether or not it would be *indecent* (whatever that means) for a woman in her seventh month to obtain an abortion just to avoid having to postpone a trip to Europe, it would not, in itself, be *immoral,* and therefore it ought to be permitted.

4. Potential Personhood and the Right to Life

We have seen that a fetus does not resemble a person in any way which can support the claim that it has even some of the same rights. But what about its *potential,* the fact that if nurtured and allowed to develop naturally it will very probably become a person? Doesn't that alone give it at least some right to life? It is hard to deny that the fact that an entity is a potential person is a strong prima facie reason for not destroying it; but we need not conclude from this that a potential person has a right to life, by virtue of that potential. It may be that our feeling that it is better, other things being equal, not to destroy a potential person is better explained by the fact that potential people are still (felt to be) an invaluable resource, not to be lightly squandered. Surely, if every speck of dust were a potential person, we would be much less apt to conclude that every potential person has a right to become actual.

Still, we do not need to insist that a potential person has no right to life whatever. There may well be something immoral, and not just imprudent, about wantonly destroying potential people, when doing so isn't necessary to protect anyone's rights. But even if a potential person does have some prima facie right to life, such a right could not possibly outweigh the right of a woman to obtain an abortion, since the rights of any actual person invariably outweigh those of any potential person, whenever the two conflict. Since this may not be immediately obvious in the case of a human fetus, let us look at another case.

Suppose that our space explorer falls into the hands of an alien culture, whose scientists decide to create a few hundred thousand or more human beings, by breaking his body into its component cells, and using these to create fully developed human beings, with, of course, his genetic code. We may imagine that each of these newly created men will have all of the original man's abilities, skills, knowledge, and so on, and also have an individual self-concept, in short that each of them will be a bona fide (though hardly unique) person. Imagine that the whole project will take only seconds, and that its chances of success are extremely high, and that our explorer knows all of this, and also knows that these people will be treated fairly. I maintain that in such a situation he would have every right to escape if he could, and thus to deprive all of these potential people of their potential lives; for his right to life outweighs all of theirs together, in spite of the fact that they are all genetically human, all innocent, and all have a very high probability of becoming people very soon, if only he refrains from acting.

Indeed, I think he would have a right to escape even if it were not his life which the alien scientists planned to take, but only a year of his freedom, or, indeed, only a day. Nor would he be obligated to stay if he had gotten captured (thus bringing all these people-potentials into existence) because of his own carelessness, or even if he had done so deliberately, knowing the consequences. Regardless of how he got captured, he is not morally obligated to remain in captivity for *any* period of time for the sake of permitting any number of potential people to come into actuality, so great is the margin by which one actual person's right to liberty outweighs whatever right to life even a hundred thousand potential people have. And it seems reasonable to conclude that the rights of a woman will outweigh by a similar margin whatever right to life a fetus may have by virtue of its potential personhood.

Thus, neither a fetus's resemblance to a person, nor its potential for becoming a person provides any basis whatever for the claim that it has any significant right to life. Consequently, a woman's right to protect her health, happiness, freedom, and even her life,[10] by terminating an unwanted pregnancy, will always override whatever right to life it may be appropriate to ascribe to a fetus, even a fully developed one. And thus, in the absence of any overwhelming social need for every possible child, the laws which restrict the right to obtain an abortion, or limit the period of pregnancy during which an abortion may be performed, are a wholly unjustified violation of a woman's most basic moral and constitutional rights.[11]

Notes

1. For example, Roger Wertheimer, who in "Understanding the Abortion Argument" (*Philosophy and Public Affairs,* 1, No. I [Fall, 1971], 67–95), argues that the problem of the moral status of abortion is insoluble, in that the dispute over the status of the fetus is not a question of fact at all, but only a question of how one responds to the facts.

2. John Noonan, "Abortion and the Catholic Church: A Summary History," *Natural Law Forum,* 12 (1967), 125.

3. John Noonan, "Deciding Who Is Human," *Natural Law Forum,* 13 (1968), 134.

4. "A Defense of Abortion."

5. Judith Thomson, "A Defense of Abortion," *Philosophy and Public Affairs,* 1, No. 1 (Fall, 1971), 47–66.

6. We may safely ignore the fact that she might have avoided getting raped, e.g., by carrying a gun, since by similar means you might likewise have avoided getting kidnapped, and in neither case does the victim's failure to take all possible precautions against a highly unlikely event (as opposed to reasonable precautions against a rather likely event) mean that he is morally responsible for what happens.

7. Of course, the principle that it is (always) wrong to kill innocent human beings is in need of many other modifications, e.g., that it may be permissible to do so to save a greater number of other innocent human beings, but we may safely ignore these complications here.

8. From here on, we will use "human" to mean genetically human, since the moral sense seems closely connected to, and perhaps derived from, the assumption that genetic humanity is sufficient for membership in the moral community.

9. Thomas L. Hayes, "A Biological View," *Commonweal, 85* (March 17, 1967), 677–78; quoted by Daniel Callahan, in *Abortion, Law, Choice, and Morality* (London: Macmillan & Co., 1970).

10. That is, insofar as the death rate, for the woman, is higher for childbirth than for early abortion.

11. My thanks to the following people, who were kind enough to read and criticize an earlier version of this paper: Herbert Gold, Gene Glass, Anne Lauterbach, Judith Thomson, Mary Mothersill, and Timothy Binkley.

Why Abortion Is Immoral

Don Marquis

Don Marquis offers what he considers to be an essentially new argument to establish the basic wrongness of abortion. The reason murder is wrong, according to Marquis, is that it deprives a person of the value of his or her future. Because a fetus, if not aborted, can be assumed to have a future like ours that is also of value, abortion, like any other kind of killing, can be justified only by the most compelling reasons. Contraception, by contrast, is not wrong, because there is no identifiable individual to be deprived of a future.

The view that abortion is, with rare exceptions, seriously immoral has received little support in the recent philosophical literature. No doubt most philosophers affiliated with secular institutions of higher education believe that the anti-abortion position is either a symptom of irrational religious dogma or a conclusion generated by seriously confused philosophical argument. The purpose of this essay is to undermine this general belief. This essay sets out an argument that purports to show, as well as any argument in ethics can show, that abortion is, except possibly in rare cases, seriously immoral, that it is in the same moral category as killing an innocent adult human being. . . .

. . . [A] necessary condition of resolving the abortion controversy is a more theoretical account of the wrongness of killing. After all, if we merely believe, but do not understand, why killing adult human beings such as ourselves is wrong, how could we conceivably show that abortion is either immoral or permissible?

II

In order to develop such an account, we can start from the following unproblematic assumption concerning our own case: it is wrong to kill *us*. Why is it wrong? Some answers can be easily eliminated. It might be said that what makes killing us wrong is that a killing brutalizes the one who kills. But the brutalization consists of being inured to the performance of an act that is hideously immoral; hence, the brutalization does not explain the immorality. It might be said that what makes killing us wrong is the great loss others would experience due to our absence. Although such hubris is understandable, such an explanation does not account for the wrongness of killing hermits, or those whose lives are relatively independent and whose friends find it easy to make new friends.

A more obvious answer is better. What primarily makes killing wrong is neither its effect on the murderer nor its effect on the victim's friends and relatives, but its effect on the victim. The loss of one's life is one of the greatest losses one can suffer. The loss of one's life deprives one of all the experiences, activities, projects, and enjoyments that would otherwise have constituted one's future. Therefore, killing someone is wrong, primarily because the killing inflicts (one of) the greatest possible losses on the victim. To describe this as the loss of life can be misleading, however. The change in my biological state does not by itself make killing me wrong. The effect of the loss of my biological life is the loss to me of all those activities, projects, experiences, and enjoyments which would otherwise have constituted my future personal life. These activities, projects, experiences, and enjoyments are either valuable for their own sakes or are means to something else that is valuable for its own sake. Some parts of my future are not valued by me now, but will come to be valued by me as I grow older and as my values and capacities change. When I am killed, I am deprived both of what I now value which would have been part of my future personal life, but also what I would come to value. Therefore, when I die, I am deprived of all of the value of my future. Inflicting this loss on me is ultimately what makes killing me wrong. This being the case, it would seem that what makes killing *any* adult human being prima facie seriously wrong is the loss of his or her future. . . .

The claim that what makes killing wrong is the loss of the victim's future is directly supported by two considerations. In the first place, this theory explains why we regard killing as one of the worst of crimes. Killing is especially wrong, because it deprives the victim of more than perhaps any other crime. In the second place, people with AIDS or

Reprinted with permission of the author and the publisher from Don Marquis, "Why Abortion Is Immoral," *The Journal of Philosophy*, Vol. 86, no. 4, (April 1989), pp. 183, 189–198, 201–202. (Notes omitted.)

cancer who know they are dying believe, of course, that dying is a very bad thing for them. They believe that the loss of a future to them that they would otherwise have experienced is what makes their premature death a very bad thing for them. A better theory of the wrongness of killing would require a different natural property associated with killing which better fits with the attitudes of the dying. What could it be?

The view that what makes killing wrong is the loss to the victim of the value of the victim's future gains additional support when some of its implications are examined. In the first place, it is incompatible with the view that it is wrong to kill only beings who are biologically human. It is possible that there exists a different species from another planet whose members have a future like ours. Since having a future like that is what makes killing someone wrong, this theory entails that it would be wrong to kill members of such a species. Hence, this theory is opposed to the claim that only life that is biologically human has great moral worth, a claim which many anti-abortionists have seemed to adopt. This opposition, which this theory has in common with personhood theories, seems to be a merit of the theory.

In the second place, the claim that the loss of one's future is the wrong-making feature of one's being killed entails the possibility that the futures of some actual nonhuman mammals on our own planet are sufficiently like ours that it is seriously wrong to kill them also. Whether some animals do have the same right to life as human beings depends on adding to the account of the wrongness of killing some additional account of just what it is about my future or the futures of other adult human beings which makes it wrong to kill us. No such additional account will be offered in this essay. Undoubtedly, the provision of such an account would be a very difficult matter. Undoubtedly, any such account would be quite controversial. Hence, it surely should not reflect badly on this sketch of an elementary theory of the wrongness of killing that it is indeterminate with respect to some very difficult issues regarding animal rights.

In the third place, the claim that the loss of one's future is the wrong-making feature of one's being killed does not entail, as sanctity of human life theories do, that active euthanasia is wrong. Persons who are severely and incurably ill, who face a future of pain and despair, and who wish to die will not have suffered a loss if they are killed. It is, strictly speaking, the value of a human's future which makes killing wrong in this theory. This being so, killing does not necessarily wrong some persons who are sick and dying. Of course, there may be other reasons for a prohibition of active euthanasia, but that is another matter. Sanctity-of-human-life theories seem to hold that active euthanasia is seriously wrong even in an individual case where there seems to be good reason for it independently of public policy considerations. This consequence is most implausible, and it is a plus for the claim that the loss of a future of value is what makes killing wrong that it does not share this consequence.

In the fourth place, the account of the wrongness of killing defended in this essay does straightforwardly entail that it is prima facie seriously wrong to kill children and infants, for we do presume that they have futures of value. Since we do believe that it is wrong to kill defenseless little babies, it is important that a theory of the wrongness of killing easily account for this. Personhood theories of the wrongness of killing, on the other hand, cannot straightforwardly account for the wrongness of killing infants and young children. Hence, such theories must add special ad hoc accounts of the wrongness of killing the young. The plausibility of such ad hoc theories seems to be a function of how desperately one wants such theories to work. The claim that the primary wrong-making feature of a killing is the loss to the victim of the value of its future accounts for the wrongness of killing young children and infants directly; it makes the wrongness of such acts as obvious as we actually think it is. This is a further merit of this theory. Accordingly, it seems that this value of a future-like-ours theory of the wrongness of killing shares strengths of both sanctity-of-life and personhood accounts while avoiding weaknesses of both. In addition, it meshes with a central intuition concerning what makes killing wrong.

The claim that the primary wrong-making feature of a killing is the loss to the victim of the value of its future has obvious consequences for the ethics of abortion. The future of a standard fetus includes a set of experiences, projects, activities, and such which are identical with the futures of adult human beings and are identical with the futures of young children. Since the reason that is sufficient to explain why it is wrong to kill human beings after the time of birth is a reason that also applies to fetuses, it follows that abortion is prima facie seriously morally wrong.

This argument does not rely on the invalid inference that, since it is wrong to kill persons, it is wrong to kill potential persons also. The category that is morally central to this analysis is the category of having a valuable future like ours; it is not the category of personhood. The argument to the conclusion that abortion is prima facie seriously morally wrong proceeded independently of the notion of person or potential person or any equivalent. . . .

Of course, this value of a future-like-ours argument, if sound, shows only that abortion is prima facie wrong, not that it is wrong in any and all circumstances. Since the loss of the future to a standard fetus, if killed, is, however, at least as great a loss as the loss of the future to a standard adult human being who is killed, abortion, like ordinary killing, could be justified only by the most compelling reasons. The loss of one's life is almost the greatest misfortune that can happen to one. Presumably abortion could be justified in some circumstances, only if the loss consequent on failing to abort would be at least as great. Accordingly, morally permissible abortions will be rare indeed unless, perhaps, they occur so early in pregnancy that a fetus is not yet definitely an individual. Hence, this argument should be taken as showing that abortion is presumptively very seriously wrong, where the presumption is very strong—as strong as the presumption that killing another adult human being is wrong.

III

How complete an account of the wrongness of killing does the value of a future-like-ours account have to be in order that the wrongness of abortion is a consequence? This account does not have to be an account of the necessary conditions for the wrongness of killing. Some persons in nursing homes may lack valuable human futures, yet it may be wrong to kill them for other reasons. Furthermore, this account does not obviously have to be the sole reason killing is wrong where the victim did have a valuable future. This analysis claims only that, for any killing where the victim did have a valuable future like ours, having that future by itself is sufficient to create the strong presumption that the killing is seriously wrong.

One way to overturn the value of a future-like-ours argument would be to find some account of the wrongness of killing which is at least as intelligible and which has different implications for the ethics of abortion. Two rival accounts possess at least some degree of plausibility. One account is based on the obvious fact that people value the experience of living and wish for that valuable experience to continue. Therefore, it might be said, what makes killing wrong is the discontinuation of that experience for the victim. Let us call this the *discontinuation account.* Another rival account is based upon the obvious fact that people strongly desire to continue to live. This suggests that what makes killing us so wrong is that it interferes with the fulfillment of a strong and fundamental desire, the fulfillment of which is necessary for the fulfillment of any other desires we might have. Let us call this the *desire account.*

Consider first the desire account as a rival account of the ethics of killing which would provide the basis for rejecting the anti-abortion position. Such an account will have to be stronger than the value of a future-like-ours account of the wrongness of abortion if it is to do the job expected of it. To entail the wrongness of abortion, the value of a future-like-ours account has only to provide a sufficient, but not a necessary, condition for the wrongness of killing. The desire account, on the other hand, must provide us also with a necessary condition for the wrongness of killing in order to generate a pro-choice conclusion on abortion. The reason for this is that presumably the argument from the desire account moves from the claim that what makes killing wrong is interference with a very strong desire to the claim that abortion is not wrong because the fetus lacks a strong desire to live. Obviously, this inference fails if someone's having the desire to live is not a necessary condition of its being wrong to kill that individual.

One problem with the desire account is that we do regard it as seriously wrong to kill persons who have little desire to live or who have no desire to live or, indeed, have a desire not to live. We believe it is seriously wrong to kill the unconscious, the sleeping, those who are tired of life, and those who are suicidal. The value-of-a-human-future account renders standard morality intelligible in these cases;

these cases appear to be incompatible with the desire account.

The desire account is subject to a deeper difficulty. We desire life, because we value the goods of this life. The goodness of life is not secondary to our desire for it. If this were not so, the pain of one's own premature death could be done away with merely by an appropriate alteration in the configuration of one's desires. This is absurd. Hence, it would seem that it is the loss of the goods of one's future, not the interference with the fulfillment of a strong desire to live, which accounts ultimately for the wrongness of killing. . . .

The discontinuation account looks more promising as an account of the wrongness of killing. It seems just as intelligible as the value of a future-like-ours account, but it does not justify an anti-abortion position. Obviously, if it is the continuation of one's activities, experiences, and projects, the loss of which makes killing wrong, then it is not wrong to kill fetuses for that reason, for fetuses do not have experiences, activities, and projects to be continued or discontinued. Accordingly, the discontinuation account does not have the anti-abortion consequences that the value of a future-like-ours account has. Yet, it seems as intelligible as the value of a future-like-ours account, for when we think of what would be wrong with our being killed, it does seem as if it is the discontinuation of what makes our lives worthwhile which makes killing us wrong.

Is the discontinuation account just as good an account as the value of a future-like-ours account? The discontinuation account will not be adequate at all, if it does not refer to the *value* of the experience that may be discontinued. One does not want the discontinuation account to make it wrong to kill a patient who begs for death and who is in severe pain that cannot be relieved short of killing. (I leave open the question of whether it is wrong for other reasons.) Accordingly, the discontinuation account must be more than a bare discontinuation account. It must make some reference to the positive value of the patient's experience. But, by the same token, the value of a future-like-ours account cannot be a bare future account either. Just having a future surely does not itself rule out killing the above patient. This account must make some reference to the value of the patient's future experience and projects also. Hence, both accounts involve the value of experiences, projects, and activities. So far we still have symmetry between the accounts.

The symmetry fades, however, when we focus on the time period of the value of the experiences, etc., which has moral consequences. Although both accounts leave open the possibility that the patient in our example may be killed, this possibility is left open only in virtue of the utterly bleak future for the patient. It makes no difference whether the patient's immediate past contains intolerable pain, or consists of being in a coma (which we can imagine is a situation of indifference), or consists in a life of value. If the patient's future is a future of value, we want our account to make it wrong to kill the patient. If the patient's future is intolerable, whatever his or her immediate past, we want our account to allow killing the patient. Obviously, then, it is the value of that patient's future which is doing the work in rendering the morality of killing the patient intelligible.

This being the case, it seems clear that whether one has immediate past experiences or not does no work in the explanation of what makes killing wrong. The addition the discontinuation account makes to the value of a human future account is otiose. Its addition to the value-of-a-future account plays no role at all in rendering intelligible the wrongness of killing. Therefore, it can be discarded with the discontinuation account of which it is a part.

IV

The analysis of the previous section suggests that alternative general accounts of the wrongness of killing are either inadequate or unsuccessful in getting around the anti-abortion consequences of the value of a future-like-ours argument. A different strategy for avoiding these anti-abortion consequences involves limiting the scope of the value of a future argument. More precisely, the strategy involves arguing that fetuses lack a property that is essential for the value-of-a-future argument (or for any anti-abortion argument) to apply to them.

One move of this sort is based upon the claim that a necessary condition of one's future being valuable is that one values it. Value implies a valuer. Given this one might argue that, since fetuses cannot value their futures, their futures are not valuable to them. Hence, it does not seriously wrong them deliberately to end their lives.

This move fails, however, because of some ambiguities. Let us assume that something cannot be of value unless it is valued by someone. This does not entail that my life is of no value unless it is valued by me. I may think, in a period of despair, that my future is of no worth whatsoever, but I may be wrong because others rightly see value—even great value—in it. Furthermore, my future can be valuable to me even if I do not value it. This is the case when a young person attempts suicide, but is rescued and goes on to significant human achievements. Such young people's futures are ultimately valuable to them, even though such futures do not seem to be valuable to them at the moment of attempted suicide. A fetus's future can be valuable to it in the same way. Accordingly, this attempt to limit the anti-abortion argument fails. . . .

V

In this essay, it has been argued that the correct ethic of the wrongness of killing can be extended to fetal life and used to show that there is a strong presumption that any abortion is morally impermissible. If the ethic of killing adopted here entails, however, that contraception is also seriously immoral, then there would appear to be a difficulty with the analysis of this essay.

But this analysis does not entail that contraception is wrong. Of course, contraception prevents the actualization of a possible future of value. Hence, it follows from the claim that futures of value should be maximized that contraception is prima facie immoral. This obligation to maximize does not exist, however; furthermore, nothing in the ethics of killing in this paper entails that it does. The ethics of killing in this essay would entail that contraception is wrong only if something were denied a human future of value by contraception. Nothing at all is denied such a future by contraception, however.

Candidates for a subject of harm by contraception fall into four categories: (1) some sperm or other, (2) some ovum or other, (3) a sperm and an ovum separately, and (4) a sperm and an ovum together. Assigning the harm to some sperm is utterly arbitrary, for no reason can be given for making a sperm the subject of harm rather than an ovum. Assigning the harm to some ovum is utterly arbitrary, for no reason can be given for making an ovum the subject of harm rather than a sperm. One might attempt to avoid these problems by insisting that contraception deprives both the sperm and the ovum separately of a valuable future like ours. On this alternative, too, many futures are lost. Contraception was supposed to be wrong, because it deprived us of one future of value, not two. One might attempt to avoid this problem by holding that contraception deprives the combination of sperm and ovum of a valuable future like ours. But here the definite article misleads. At the time of contraception, there are hundreds of millions of sperm, one (released) ovum and millions of possible combinations of all of these. There is no actual combination at all. Is the subject of the loss to be a merely possible combination? Which one? This alternative does not yield an actual subject of harm either. Accordingly, the immorality of contraception is not entailed by the loss of a future-like-ours argument simply because there is no nonarbitrarily identifiable subject of the loss in the case of contraception.

VI

The purpose of this essay has been to set out an argument for the serious presumptive wrongness of abortion subject to the assumption that the moral permissibility of abortion stands or falls on the moral status of the fetus. Since a fetus possesses a property, the possession of which in adult human beings is sufficient to make killing an adult human being wrong, abortion is wrong. . . .

Abortion through a Feminist Ethics Lens _____

Susan Sherwin

Susan Sherwin sees the abortion controversy as part of the larger struggle for women's liberation. She argues that the power to control the incidence, timing, and frequency of childbearing is central to the control of most other things in a woman's life. Only the woman herself is in a position to weigh all the relevant factors necessary to determine whether abortion is the best response to the situation.

The fetus is morally significant, but its status is dependent upon its relation to the pregnant woman. Patterns of male sexual dominance mean that women often have little control over their sexual lives, and because women cannot rely on birth control alone to avoid pregnancy, abortion must be available if they are to be genuinely liberated from male dominance.

. . . [M]ost feminists believe that a pregnant woman is in the best position to judge whether abortion is the appropriate response to her circumstances. Since she is usually the only one able to weigh all the relevant factors, most feminists reject attempts to offer any general abstract rules for determining when abortion is morally justified. . . . Although I think that it is possible for a woman to make a mistake in her moral judgment on this matter (i.e., it is possible that a woman may come to believe that she was wrong about her decision to continue or terminate a pregnancy), the intimate nature of this sort of decision makes it unlikely that anyone else is in a position to arrive at a more reliable conclusion; it is, therefore, improper to grant others the authority to interfere in women's decisions to seek abortions.

Feminist analysis regards the effects of unwanted pregnancies on the lives of women individually and collectively as a central element in the moral evaluation of abortion. Even without patriarchy, bearing a child would be a very important event in a woman's life. It involves significant physical, emotional, social, and (usually) economic changes for her. The ability to exert control over the incidence, timing, and frequency of childbearing is often tied to her ability to control most other things she values. Since we live in a patriarchal society, it is especially important to ensure that women have the authority to control their own reproduction. Despite the diversity of opinion among feminists on most other matters, virtually all feminists seem to agree that women must gain full control over their own reproductive lives if they are to free themselves from male dominance. Many perceive the commitment of the political right wing to opposing abortion as part of a general strategy to reassert patriarchal control over women in the

face of significant feminist influence (Petchesky 1980, p. 112).

Women's freedom to choose abortion is also linked with their ability to control their own sexuality. Women's subordinate status often prevents them from refusing men sexual access to their bodies. If women cannot end the unwanted pregnancies that result from male sexual dominance, their sexual vulnerability to particular men can increase, because caring for an(other) infant involves greater financial needs and reduced economic opportunities for women. As a result, pregnancy often forces women to become dependent on men. Since a woman's dependence on a man is assumed to entail that she will remain sexually loyal to him, restriction of abortion serves to channel women's sexuality and further perpetuates the cycle of oppression.

In contrast to most non-feminist accounts, feminist analyses of abortion direct attention to the question of how women get pregnant. Those who reject abortion seem to believe that women can avoid unwanted pregnancies by avoiding sexual intercourse. Such views show little appreciation for the power of sexual politics in a culture that oppresses women. Existing patterns of sexual dominance mean that women often have little control over their sexual lives. They may be subject to rape by strangers, or by their husbands, boyfriends, colleagues, employers, customers, fathers, brothers, uncles, and dates. Often, the sexual coercion is not even recognized as such by the participants, but is the price of continued "good will"—popularity, economic survival, peace, or simple acceptance. Few women have not found themselves in circumstances where they do not feel free to refuse a man's demands for intercourse, either because he is holding a gun to her head or because he threatens to be

Reprinted with permission from Susan Sherwin, "Abortion through a Feminist Ethics Lens," *Dialogue* 30, 1991, pp. 329–331, 334–335, 336, 338–339. (Notes omitted.)

emotionally hurt if she refuses (or both). Women are socialized to be compliant and accommodating, sensitive to the feelings of others, and frightened of physical power; men are socialized to take advantage of every opportunity to engage in sexual intercourse and to use sex to express dominance and power. Under such circumstances, it is difficult to argue that women could simply "choose" to avoid heterosexual activity if they wish to avoid pregnancy. Catherine MacKinnon neatly sums it up: "the logic by which women are supposed to consent to sex [is]: preclude the alternatives, then call the remaining option 'her choice'" (MacKinnon 1989, p. 192).

Nor can women rely on birth control alone to avoid pregnancy. There simply is no form of reversible contraception available that is fully safe and reliable. The pill and the IUD are the most effective means offered, but both involve significant health hazards to women and are quite dangerous for some. No woman should spend the 30 to 40 years of her reproductive life on either form of birth control. Further, both have been associated with subsequent problems of involuntary infertility, so they are far from optimum for women who seek to control the timing of their pregnancies.

The safest form of birth control involves the use of barrier methods (condoms or diaphragms) in combination with spermicidal foams or jelly. But these methods also pose difficulties for women. They may be socially awkward to use: young women are discouraged from preparing for sexual activity that might never happen and are offered instead romantic models of spontaneous passion. (Few films or novels interrupt scenes of seduction for the fetching of contraceptives.) Many women find their male partners unwilling to use barrier methods of contraception and they do not have the power to insist. Further, cost is a limiting factor for many women. Condoms and spermicides are expensive and are not covered under most health care plans. There is only one contraceptive option which offers women safe and fully effective birth control: barrier methods with the back-up option of abortion.

From a feminist perspective, a central moral feature of pregnancy is that it takes place in *women's bodies* and has profound effects on *women's* lives. Gender-neutral accounts of pregnancy are not available; pregnancy is explicitly a condition associated with the female body. Because the need for abortion is experienced only by women, policies about abortion affect women uniquely. Thus, it is important to consider how proposed policies on abortion fit into general patterns of oppression for women. Unlike non-feminist accounts, feminist ethics demands that the effects on the oppression of women be a principal consideration when evaluating abortion policies. . . .

A Feminist View of the Fetus

Because the public debate has been set up as a competition between the rights of women and those of fetuses, feminists have often felt pushed to reject claims of fetal value in order to protect women's claims. Yet, as Addelson (1987) has argued, viewing abortion in this way "tears [it] out of the context of women's lives" (p. 107). There are other accounts of fetal value that are more plausible and less oppressive to women.

On a feminist account, fetal development is examined in the context in which it occurs, within women's bodies rather than in the imagined isolation implicit in many theoretical accounts. Fetuses develop in specific pregnancies which occur in the lives of particular women. They are not individuals housed in generic female wombs, nor are they full persons at risk only because they are small and subject to the whims of women. Their very existence is relational, developing as they do within particular women's bodies, and their principal relationship is to the women who carry them.

On this view, fetuses are morally significant, but their status is relational rather than absolute. Unlike other human beings, fetuses do not have any independent existence; their existence is uniquely tied to the support of a specific other. Most non-feminist commentators have ignored the relational dimension of fetal development and have presumed that the moral status of fetuses could be resolved solely in terms of abstract metaphysical criteria of personhood. They imagine that there is some set of properties (such as genetic heritage, moral agency, self-consciousness, language use, or self-determination) which will entitle all who possess them to be granted the moral status of persons (Warren 1973, Tooley 1972). They seek some particular feature by which we can neatly divide the world into the dichotomy of moral persons (who are to be valued and protected) and others (who are not entitled to the same group privileges); it follows that it is a merely empirical question whether or not fetuses possess the relevant properties.

But this vision misinterprets what is involved in personhood and what it is that is especially valued about persons. Personhood is a social category, not an isolated state. Persons are members of a community; they develop as concrete, discrete, and specific individuals. To be a morally significant category, personhood must involve personality as well as biological integrity. It is not sufficient to consider persons simply as Kantian atoms of rationality; persons are all embodied, conscious beings with particular social histories. . . .

No human, and especially no fetus, can exist apart from relationships; feminist views of what is valuable about persons must reflect the social nature of their existence. Fetal lives can neither be sustained nor destroyed without affecting the women who support them. Because of a fetus's unique physical status—*within* and dependent on a particular woman—the responsibility and privilege of determining its specific social status and value must rest with the woman carrying it. Fetuses are not persons because they have not developed sufficiently in social relationships to be persons in any morally significant sense (i.e., they are not yet second persons). Newborns, although just beginning their development into persons, are immediately subject to social relationships, for they are capable of communication and response in interaction with a variety of other persons. Thus, feminist accounts of abortion stress the importance of protecting women's right to continue as well as to terminate pregnancies as each sees fit.

Feminist Politics and Abortion

. . . Feminist analysis addresses the context as well as the practice of abortion decisions. Thus, feminists also object to the conditions which lead women to abort wanted fetuses because there are not adequate financial and social supports available to care for a child. Because feminist accounts value fetuses that are wanted by the women who carry them, they oppose practices which force women to abort because of poverty or intimidation. Yet, the sorts of social changes necessary if we are to free women from having abortions out of economic necessity are vast; they include changes not only in legal and health-care policy, but also in housing, child care, employment, etc. (Petchesky 1980, p. 112). Nonetheless, feminist ethics defines reproductive freedom as the condition under which women are able to make truly voluntary choices about their reproductive lives, and these many dimensions are implicit in the ideal.

Clearly, feminists are not "pro-abortion," for they are concerned to ensure the safety of each pregnancy to the greatest degree possible; wanted fetuses should not be harmed or lost. Therefore, adequate pre- and postnatal care and nutrition are also important elements of any feminist position on reproductive freedom. Where anti-abortionists direct their energies to trying to prevent women from obtaining abortions, feminists seek to protect the health of wanted fetuses. They recognize that far more could be done to protect and care for fetuses if the state directed its resources at supporting women who continue their pregnancies, rather than draining away resources in order to police women who find that they must interrupt their pregnancies. Caring for the women who carry fetuses is not only a more legitimate policy than is regulating them; it is probably also more effective at ensuring the health and well-being of more fetuses.

Feminist ethics also explores how abortion policies fit within the politics of sexual domination. Most feminists are sensitive to the fact that many men support women's right to abortion out of the belief that women will be more willing sexual partners if they believe they can readily terminate an unwanted pregnancy. Some men coerce their partners into obtaining abortions the women may not want. Feminists understand that many women oppose abortion for this very reason, being unwilling to support a practice that increases women's sexual vulnerability (Luker 1984, p. 209–15). Thus, it is important that feminists develop a coherent analysis of reproductive freedom that includes sexual freedom (as women choose to define it). That requires an analysis of sexual freedom that includes women's right to refuse sex; such a right can only be assured if women have equal power to men and are not subject to domination by virtue of their sex.

In sum, then, feminist ethics demands that moral discussions of abortion be more broadly defined than they have been in most philosophic discussions. Only by reflecting on the meaning of ethical pronouncements on actual women's lives and the connections between judgments on abortion and the conditions of domination and subordination can we come to an adequate understanding of the moral status of abortion in our society. As Rosalind Petchesky (1980) argues, feminist discussion of abortion "must be moved beyond the frame-work of a 'woman's right to choose' and connected to a much broader revolutionary movement that addresses all of the conditions of women's libera-tion" (p. 113).

References

Addelson, Kathryn Pyne. 1987. "Moral Passages." In *Women and Moral Theory.* Edited by Eva Feder Kittay and Diana T. Meyers. Totowa, NJ: Rowman & Littlefield.

Luker, Kristin. 1984. *Abortion and the Politics of Motherhood.* Berke-ley: University of California Press.

MacKinnon, Catherine. 1989. *Toward a Feminist Theory of the State.* Cambridge, MA: Harvard University Press.

Petchesky, Rosalind Pollack. 1980. "Reproductive Freedom: Be-yond 'A Woman's Right to Choose.'" In *Women: Sex and Sexual-ity.* Edited by Catharine R. Stimpson and Ethel Spector Person. Chicago: University of Chicago Press.

Tooley, Michael. 1972. "Abortion and Infanticide." *Philosophy and Public Affairs,* 2, 1 (Fall): 37–65.

Warren, Mary Anne. 1973. "On the Moral and Legal Status of Abortion." *The Monist,* 57: 43–61.

United States Supreme Court Decision in *Roe* v. *Wade*

In *Roe* v. *Wade* the U.S. Supreme Court declared unconstitutional a Texas statute that restricted legal abortions to cases in which the life of the mother was threat-ened. The decision implied that all such state laws regulating abortion were un-constitutional. In effect, then, the decision made abortion legal in the United States.

The decision rested, in part, on the reasoning that a woman has a right to act for her own health and well-being as part of a more general right of privacy. The Court also considered the question of the legitimate limits of state interference to protect a woman's health and to protect the life of a fetus. The Court refused to recognize the fetus as a "person in the full sense" or to grant the right of the state to act on its behalf until the time (around the twenty-eighth week) that it can live outside the mother's body.

The ruling laid down three guidelines for regulating abortion: (1) until the end of the first trimester, the abortion decision is a medical one that must be left to the woman and her physician; (2) after the end of the first trimester, the state may reg-ulate the abortion procedure in ways reasonably related to maternal health; (3) af-ter the fetus is viable, the state may regulate or even prohibit abortion, except where it is necessary to preserve the life or health of the mother. (See *Social Con-text: The Continuing Struggle over Abortion* at the beginning of this chapter, for back-ground information.)

Three reasons have been advanced to explain historically the enactment of criminal abortion laws in the 19th century and to justify their continued existence.

It has been argued occasionally that these laws were the product of a Victorian social concern to discourage illicit sexual conduct. Texas, however, does not advance this justification in the present case, and it appears that no court or commentator has taken the argument seriously. The appellants and *amici* contend, moreover, that this is not a proper state purpose at all and suggest that, if it were, the Texas statutes are overbroad in protecting it since the law fails to distinguish between married and unwed mothers.

A second reason is concerned with abortion as a medical procedure. When most criminal abor-tion laws were first enacted, the procedure was a

United States Supreme Court, 410 U.S. 113, 93 S. Ct. 705. January 22, 1973.

hazardous one for the woman. This was particularly true prior to the development of antisepsis. Antiseptic techniques, of course, were based on discoveries by Lister, Pasteur, and others first announced in 1867, but were not generally accepted and employed until about the turn of the century. Abortion mortality was high. Even after 1900, and perhaps until as late as the development of antibiotics in the 1940's, standard modern techniques such as dilation and curettage were not nearly so safe as they are today. Thus it has been argued that a State's real concern in enacting a criminal abortion law was to protect the pregnant woman, that is, to restrain her from submitting to a procedure that placed her life in serious jeopardy.

Modern medical techniques have altered this situation. Appellants and various *amici* refer to medical data indicating that abortion in early pregnancy, that is, prior to the end of first trimester, although not without its risk, is now relatively safe. Mortality rates for women undergoing early abortions, where the procedure is legal, appear to be as low as or lower than the rates for normal childbirth. Consequently, any interest of the State in protecting the woman from an inherently hazardous procedure, except when it would be equally dangerous for her to forego it, has largely disappeared. Of course, important state interests in the area of health and medical standards do remain. The state has legitimate interest in seeing to it that abortion, like any other medical procedure, is performed under circumstances that insure maximum safety for the patient. This interest obviously extends at least to the performing physician and his staff, to the facilities involved, to the availability of after-care, and to adequate provision for any complication or emergency that might arise. The prevalence of high mortality rates at illegal "abortion mills" strengthens, rather than weakens, the State's interest in regulating the conditions under which abortions are performed. Moreover, the risk to the woman increases as her pregnancy continues. Thus the State retains a definite interest in protecting the woman's own health and safety when an abortion is proposed at a late stage of pregnancy.

The third reason is the State's interest—some phrase it in terms of duty—in protecting prenatal life. Some of the argument for this justification rests on the theory that a new human life is present from the moment of conception. The State's interest and general obligation to protect life then extends, it is argued, to prenatal life. Only when the life of the pregnant mother herself is at stake, balanced against the life she carries within her, should the interest of the embryo or fetus not prevail. Logically, of course, a legitimate state interest in this area need not stand or fall on acceptance of the belief that life begins at conception or at some point prior to live birth. In assessing the State's interest, recognition may be given to the less rigid claim that as long as at least *potential* life is involved, the State may assert interests beyond the protection of the pregnant woman alone.

Parties challenging state abortion laws have sharply disputed in some courts the contention that a purpose of these laws, when enacted, was to protect prenatal life. Pointing to the absence of legislative history to support the contention, they claim that most state laws were designed solely to protect the woman. Because medical advances have lessened this concern, at least with respect to abortion in early pregnancy, they argue that with respect to such abortions the laws can no longer be justified by any state interest. There is some scholarly support for this view of original purpose. The few state courts called upon to interpret their laws in the late 19th and early 20th centuries did focus on the State's interest in protecting the woman's health rather than in preserving the embryo and fetus. Proponents of this view point out that in many States, including Texas, by statute or judicial interpretation, the pregnant woman herself could not be prosecuted for self-abortion or for cooperating in an abortion performed upon her by another. They claim that adoption of the "quickening" distinction through received common law and state statutes tacitly recognizes the greater health hazards inherent in late abortion and impliedly repudiates the theory that life begins at conception.

It is with these interests, and the weight to be attached to them, that this case is concerned.

The Constitution does not explicitly mention any right of privacy. In a line of decisions, however, going back perhaps as far as *Union Pacific R. Co. v. Botsford*, 141 U.S. 250, 251 (1891), the Court has recognized that a right of personal privacy, or a guarantee of certain areas or zones of privacy, does exist under the Constitution. In varying contexts the Court or individual Justices have indeed found at least the roots of that right in the First Amendment, in the Fourth and Fifth Amendments, in the penumbras of the Bill of Rights, in the Ninth Amendment, or in the concept of liberty guaranteed by the first section of the Fourteenth Amendment. These decisions make it clear that only personal rights that can be deemed "fundamental" or "implicit in the concept of ordered liberty" are included in this guarantee of personal privacy. They also make it clear that the right has some extension to activities relating to marriage, procreation, contraception, family relationships, and child rearing and education.

This right of privacy, whether it be founded in the Fourteenth Amendment's concept of personal liberty and restriction upon state action, as we feel it is, or, as the District Court determined, in the Ninth Amendment's reservation of rights to the people, is broad enough to encompass a woman's decision whether or not to terminate her pregnancy. The detriment that the State would impose upon the pregnant woman by denying this choice altogether is apparent. Specific and direct harm medically diagnosable even in early pregnancy may be involved. Maternity, or additional offspring, may force upon the woman a distressful life and future. Psychological harm may be imminent. Mental and physical health may be taxed by child care. There is also the distress, for all concerned, associated with the unwanted child, and there is the problem of bringing a child into a family already unable, psychologically and otherwise, to care for it. In other cases, as in this one, the additional difficulties and continuing stigma of unwed motherhood may be involved. All these are factors the woman and her responsible physician will consider in consultation.

On the basis of elements such as these, appellants and some *amici* argue that the woman's right is absolute and that she is entitled to terminate her pregnancy at whatever time, in whatever way, and for whatever reason she alone chooses. With these we do not agree. Appellants' arguments that Texas either has no valid interest at all in regulating the abortion decision, or no interest strong enough to support any limitation upon the woman's sole determination, is unpersuasive. The Court's decisions recognizing a right of privacy also acknowledge that some state regulation in areas protected by that right is appropriate. As noted above, a state may

properly assert important interests in safeguarding health, in maintaining medical standards, and in protecting potential life. At some point in pregnancy, these respective interests become sufficiently compelling to sustain regulation of the factors that govern the abortion decision. The privacy right involved, therefore, cannot be said to be absolute. In fact, it is not clear to us that the claim asserted by some *amici* that one has an unlimited right to do with one's body as one pleases bears a close relationship to the right of privacy previously articulated in the Court's decisions. The Court has refused to recognize an unlimited right of this kind in the past.

We therefore conclude that the right of personal privacy includes the abortion decision, but that this right is not unqualified and must be considered against important state interests in regulation.

We note that those federal and state courts that have recently considered abortion law challenges have reached the same conclusion. A majority, in addition to the District Court in the present case, have held state laws unconstitutional, at least in part, because of vagueness or because of overbreadth and abridgement of rights.

Although the results are divided, most of these courts have agreed that the right of privacy, however based, is broad enough to cover the abortion decision; that the right, nonetheless, is not absolute and is subject to some limitations; and that at some point the state interests as to protection of health, medical standards, and prenatal life, become dominant. We agree with this approach.

Where certain "fundamental rights" are involved, the Court has held that regulation limiting these rights may be justified only by a "compelling state interest" . . . and that legislative enactments must be narrowly drawn to express only the legitimate state interests at stake.

In the recent abortion cases courts have recognized these principles. Those striking down state laws have generally scrutinized the State's interest in protecting health and potential life and have concluded that neither interest justified broad limitations on the reasons for which a physician and his pregnant patient might decide that she should have an abortion in the early stages of pregnancy. Courts sustaining state laws have held that the State's determinations to protect health or prenatal life are dominant and constitutionally justifiable.

The District Court held that the appellee failed to meet his burden of demonstrating that the Texas statute's infringement upon Roe's rights was necessary to support a compelling state interest, and that, although the defendant presented "several compelling justifications for state presence in the area of abortions," the statutes outstripped these justifications and swept "far beyond any areas of compelling state interest." Appellant and appellee both contest that holding. Appellant, as has been indicated, claims an absolute right that bars any state imposition of criminal penalties in the area. Appellee argues that the State's determination to recognize and protect prenatal life from and after conception constitutes a compelling state interest. As noted above, we do not agree fully with either formulation.

A. The appellee and certain *amici* argue that the fetus is a "person" within the language and meaning of the Fourteenth Amendment. In support of this they outline at length and in detail the well-known facts of fetal development. If this suggestion of personhood is established, the appellant's case, of course, collapses, for the fetus' right to life is then guaranteed specifically by the Amendment. The appellant conceded as much on reargument. On the other hand, the appellee conceded on reargument that no case could be cited that holds that a fetus is a person within the meaning of the Fourteenth Amendment.

The Constitution does not define "person" in so many words. Section I of the Fourteenth Amendment contains three references to "person." . . .But in nearly all these instances, the use of the word is such that it has application only postnatally. None indicates, with any assurance, that it has any possible prenatal application.

All this, together with our observation, *supra*, that throughout the major portion of the 19th century prevailing legal abortion practices were far freer than they are today, persuades us that the word "person," as used in the Fourteenth Amendment, does not include the unborn. . . .

B. The pregnant woman cannot be isolated in her privacy. She carries an embryo and, later, a fetus, if one accepts the medical definitions of the developing young in the human uterus. See Dorland's Illustrated Medical Dictionary, 478–479, 547 (24th ed. 1965). The situation therefore is inherently different from marital intimacy, or bedroom possession of obscene material, or marriage, or procreation, or education, with which *Eisenstadt, Giswold, Stanley, Loving, Skinner, Pierce,* and *Meyer* were respectively concerned. As we have intimated above, it is reasonable and appropriate for a State to decide that at some point in time another interest, that of health of the mother or that of potential human life, becomes significantly involved. The woman's privacy is no longer sole and any right of privacy she possesses must be measured accordingly.

Texas urges that, apart from the Fourteenth Amendment, life begins at conception and is present throughout pregnancy, and that, therefore, the State has a compelling interest in protecting that life from and after conception. We need not resolve the difficult question of when life begins. When those trained in the respective disciplines of medicine, philosophy, and theology are unable to arrive at any consensus, the judiciary, at this point in the development of man's knowledge, is not in a position to speculate as to the answer.

It should be sufficient to note briefly the wide divergence of thinking on this most sensitive and difficult question. There has always been strong support for the view that life does not begin until live birth. This was the belief of the Stoics. It appears to be the predominant, though not the unanimous, attitude of the Jewish faith. It may be taken to represent also the position of a large segment of the Protestant community, insofar as that can be ascertained; organized groups that have taken a formal position on the abortion issue have generally regarded abortion as a matter for the conscience of the individual and her family. As we have noted, the common law found greater significance in quickening. Physicians and their scientific colleagues have regarded that event with less interest and have tended to focus either upon conception or upon live birth or upon the interim point at which the fetus becomes "viable," that is, potentially able to live outside the mother's womb, albeit with artificial aid. Viability is usually placed at about seven months (28 weeks) but may occur earlier, even at 24 weeks. The Aristotelian theory of "mediate animation," that held sway throughout the Middle Ages and the Renaissance in Europe, continued to be official Roman Catholic dogma until the 19th century, despite opposition to this "ensoulment" theory from those in the Church who would recognize the existence of life from the moment of conception. The latter is now, of course, the official belief of the Catholic Church. As one of the briefs *amicus* discloses, this is a view strongly held by many non-Catholics as well, and by many physicians. Substantial problems for precise definition of this view are posed, however, by new embryological data that purport to indicate that conception is a "process" over time, rather than an event, and by new medical techniques such as menstrual extraction, the "morning-after" pill, implantation of embryos, artificial insemination, and even artificial wombs.

In areas other than criminal abortion the law has been reluctant to endorse any theory that life, as we recognize it, begins before live birth or to accord legal rights to the unborn except in narrowly defined situations and except when the rights are contingent upon live birth. For example, the traditional rule of tort law had denied recovery for prenatal injuries even though the child was born alive. That rule has been changed in almost every jurisdiction. In most States recovery is said to be permitted only if the fetus was viable, or at least quick, when the injuries were sustained, though few courts have squarely so held. In a recent development, generally opposed by the commentators, some States permit the parents of a stillborn child to maintain an action for wrongful death because of prenatal injuries. Such an action, however, would appear to be one to vindicate the parents' interest and is thus consistent with the view that the fetus, at most, represents only the potentiality of life. Similarly, unborn children have been recognized as acquiring rights or interests by way of inheritance or other devolution of property, and have been represented by guardians *ad litem*. Perfection of the interests involved, again, has generally been contingent upon live birth. In short, the unborn have never been recognized in the law as persons in the whole sense.

In view of all this, we do not agree that, by adopting one theory of life, Texas may override the rights of the pregnant woman that are at stake. We repeat, however, that the State does have an important and legitimate interest in preserving and protecting the health of the pregnant woman, whether she be a resident of the State or a nonresident who seeks medical consultation and treatment there, and that it had still *another* important and legitimate interest in protecting the potentiality of human life. These interests are separate and distinct. Each grows in substantiality as the woman approaches

term and, at a point during pregnancy, each becomes "compelling."

With respect to the State's important and legitimate interest in the health of the mother, the "compelling" point, in the light of present medical knowledge, is at approximately the end of the first trimester. This is so because of the now established medical fact . . . that until the end of the first trimester mortality in abortion is less than mortality in normal childbirth. It follows that, from and after this point, a State may regulate the abortion procedure to the extent that the regulation reasonably relates to the preservation and protection of maternal health. Examples of permissible state regulation in this area are requirements as to the qualifications of the person who is to perform the abortion; as to the licensure of that person; as to the facility in which the procedure is to be performed, that is, whether it must be a hospital or may be a clinic or some other place of less-than-hospital status; as to the licensing of the facility; and the like.

This means, on the other hand, that, for the period of pregnancy prior to this "compelling" point, the attending physician, in consultation with his patient, is free to determine, without regulation by the State, that in his medical judgment the patient's pregnancy should be terminated. If that decision is reached, the judgment may be effectuated by an abortion free of interference by the State.

With respect to the State's important and legitimate interest in potential life, the "compelling" point is at viability. This is so because the fetus then presumably has the capability of meaningful life outside the mother's womb. State regulation protective of fetal life after viability thus has both logical and biological justifications. If the State is interested in protecting fetal life after viability, it may go so far as to proscribe abortion during that period except when it is necessary to preserve the life or health of the mother.

Measured against these standards, Art. 1196 of the Texas Penal Code, in restricting legal abortions to those "procured or attempted by medical advice for the purpose of saving the life of the mother," sweeps too broadly. The statute makes no distinction between abortions performed early in pregnancy and those performed later, and it limits to a single reason, "saving" the mother's life, the legal justification for the procedure. The statute, therefore, cannot survive the constitutional attack made upon it here. . . .

To summarize and to repeat:

1. A state criminal abortion statute of the current Texas type, that excepts from criminality only a *life saving* procedure on behalf of the mother, without regard to pregnancy stage and without recognition of the other interests involved, is violative of the Due Process Clause of the Fourteenth Amendment.

   a. For the stage prior to approximately the end of the first trimester, the abortion decision and its effectuation must be left to the medical judgment of the pregnant woman's attending physician.

   b. For the stage subsequent to approximately the end of the first trimester, the State, in promoting its interest in the health of the mother, may, if it chooses, regulate the abortion procedure in ways that are reasonably related to maternal health.

   c. For the stage subsequent to viability the State, in promoting its interest in the potentiality of human life, may, if it chooses, regulate, and even proscribe, abortion except where it is necessary, in appropriate medical judgment, for the preservation of the life or health of the mother.

2. The State may define the term "physician" . . . to mean only a physician currently licensed by the State, and may proscribe any abortion by a person who is not a physician as so defined. . . .

This holding, we feel, is consistent with the relative weights of the respective interests involved, with the lessons and example of medical and legal history, with the lenity of the common law, and with the demands of the profound problems of the present day. The decision leaves the State free to place increasing restrictions on abortion as the period of pregnancy lengthens, so long as those restrictions are tailored to the recognized state interests. The decision vindicates the right of the physician to administer medical treatment according to his professional judgment up to the points where important state interests provide compelling justifications for intervention. Up to those points the abortion decision in all its aspects is inherently, and primarily, a medical decision, and basic responsibility for it must rest with the physician. If an individual practitioner abuses the privilege of exercising proper medical judgment, the usual remedies, judicial and intra-professional, are available. . . .

Decision Scenario 1 ••

Ruth Perkins is twenty-four years old, and her husband, Carl Freedon, is four years older. Both are employed, Ruth as an executive for Laporte Gas Transmission and Carl as a systems analyst at a St. Louis bank. Their combined income is over $140,000 a year.

Perkins and Freedon live up to their income. They have an eleven-room house with a tennis court in a high-priced suburb, they both dress well, and Carl is a modest collector of sports cars (three MG-TDs). Both like to travel, and they try to get out of the country at least twice a year—Europe for a month in the summer and Mexico or the Caribbean for a couple of weeks during the winter.

Perkins and Freedon have no children. They agreed when they were married that children would not be a part of their plan for life together. They were distressed when Ruth became pregnant and at first refused to face the problem. They worried about it for several months, considering arguments for and against abortion. At last they decided that Ruth should have an abortion.

"I don't see why I have to go through with this interview," Ruth said to the woman at the Morton Hospital Counseling Center.

"It's required of all who request an abortion," the counselor explained. "We think it's better for a person to be sure what she is doing so she won't regret it later."

"My husband and I are certain," Ruth said. "A child doesn't fit in at all with our life-style. We go out a lot, and we like to do things. A child would just get in the way."

"A child can offer many pleasures," the woman said.

"I don't doubt it. If some want them, that's fine with me. We don't. Besides, we both have careers that we're devoted to. I'm not about to quit my job to take care of a child, and the same is true of my husband."

"How long have you been pregnant?"

Ruth looked embarrassed. "Almost six months," she said. "Carl and I weren't sure what we wanted to do at first. It took a while for us to get used to the idea."

"You don't think you waited too long?"

"That's stupid," Ruth said. She could hardly keep her voice under control. "I didn't mean that personally. But Carl and I have a right to live our lives the way we want. So far as we are concerned a six-month fetus is not a person. If we want to get rid of it, that's our business."

"Would you feel the same if it were a child already born?"

"I might," Ruth said. "I mean, a baby doesn't have much personality or anything, does it?"

"I take it you're certain you want the abortion."

"Absolutely. My husband and I think it's the right thing for us. If others think we're wrong . . . well, it's their right to think what they please."

1. How might Warren's arguments be used to support Perkins's position?

2. Could someone who accepts Thomson's arguments consider abortion justified in this case?

3. Do you believe Perkins is right about a six-month fetus not being a person? If not, why not?

4. What position might Sherwin take on Perkins's decision to have an abortion in this case?

Decision Scenario 2 ....

It happened after a concert. Sixteen-year-old Mary Pluski had gone with three of her friends to hear Bruce Springsteen at Chicago's Blanton Auditorium. After the concert, in a crowd estimated at 11,000, Mary became separated from the other three girls. She decided that the best thing to do was to meet them at the car.

But when she got to the eight-story parking building, Mary realized she wasn't sure what level they had parked on. She thought it might be somewhere in the middle so she started looking on the fourth floor. While she was walking down the aisles of cars, two men in their early twenties, one white and the other black, stopped her and asked if she was having some kind of trouble.

Mary explained the situation to them, and one of the men suggested that they get his car and drive around inside the parking building. Mary hesitated, but both seemed so polite and genuinely concerned to help that she decided to go with them.

Once they were in the car, however, the situation changed. They drove out of the building and toward the South Side. Mary pleaded with them to let her out of the car, but they refused. They threatened her with violence if she called for help or tried to escape from the car. Then, some seven miles from the auditorium, the driver stopped the car in a dark area behind a vacant building. Mary was then raped by both men.

Mary was treated at Allenworth Hospital and released into the custody of her parents. She filed a complaint with the police, but her troubles were not yet over. Two weeks after she missed her menstrual period, tests showed that Mary was pregnant.

"How do you feel about having this child?" asked Sarah Ruben, the Pluski family physician.

"I hate the idea," Mary said. "I feel guilty about it, though. I mean, it's not the child's fault."

"Let me ask a delicate question," said Dr. Ruben. "I know from what you've told me before that you and your boyfriend have been having sex. Can you be sure this pregnancy is not really the result of that?"

Mary shook her head. "Not really. I use my diaphragm, but I know it doesn't give a hundred percent guarantee."

"That's right. Now, does it make any difference to you who the father might be, so far as a decision about terminating the pregnancy is concerned?"

"If I were sure that it was Bob, I guess the problem would be even harder," Mary said.

"There are some tests we can use to give us that information," Dr. Ruben said. "But that would mean waiting for the embryo to develop into a fetus. It would be easier and safer to terminate the pregnancy now."

Mary started crying. "I don't want a child," she said. "I don't want any child. I don't care who's the father. It was forced on me, and I want to get rid of it."

"I'll make the arrangements," said Dr. Ruben.

1. *What reasons would Sherwin offer in defense of Mary Pluski's right to have an abortion?*

2. *Would Noonan consider abortion immoral in this case?*

3. *Suppose the fetus is a person; would the maxim in this case satisfy the categorical imperative?*

4. *Does Mary's uncertainty about the father add any special moral difficulties?*

5. *Would Marquis consider abortion immoral in this case?*

Decision Scenario 3 ●●●

"I don't want no more children," Mrs. Hinson said. "I've already got five, and I can't look after them the way they should be looked after. My husband's been gone three years. I don't know where he is, but I know he ain't coming back."

After two years as a psychiatric social worker, David Rossum found Mrs. Hinson's situation familiar. He looked around the small living room. It was clean but crowded with broken second-hand furniture. Cheap dime-store metal frames lined the top of the television set. Children smiled in the blurry color snapshots.

"You're sure you're pregnant?" Rossum asked.

"The doctor at the clinic told me so," Mrs. Hinson said. "He gave me a paper to prove it. But I'm already on welfare and the ADC. I can't do right by my children if I have another one to take care of."

"And you can't count on the father of this child to help you?"

"I can't count on him for nothing," said Mrs. Hinson. "I don't even see him anymore."

"So what do you want to do?" Rossum asked. He knew the answer, but the main part of his job was just listening.

"I want an abortion. That's what I want. But the people at the clinic, they told me I'd have to talk to you people first. If you won't say it's okay they won't do it, because there won't be nobody to pay for it."

"That's right," Rossum said. "You've got to have an authorization from our agency for any kind of special medical procedure of a nonemergency kind."

1. *Suppose that you are David Rossum. On what grounds would you authorize (or refuse to authorize) Mrs. Hinson's request? If you were opposed to all abortions on moral grounds, ought you to allow this to influence your decision?*

2. *Does the reasoning in* Roe v. Wade *apply in this case?*

3. *Do Rawls's principles of justice suggest a legitimate social policy to cover such cases?*

4. *Does the principle of utility suggest a policy?*

5. *If the fetus is a person, are there sufficient reasons for considering abortion here a case of justified killing?*

Decision Scenario 4 ●●

Clare Macwurter was twenty-two years old chronologically, but mentally she remained a child. As a result of her mother's prolonged and difficult labor, Clare had been deprived of an adequate blood-oxygen supply during her birth. The consequence was that she suffered irreversible brain damage.

Clare enjoyed life and was generally a happy person. She couldn't read, but she liked listening to music and watching television, although she could rarely understand the stories. She was physically attractive and, with the help of her parents, she could care for herself.

Clare was also interested in sex. When she was seventeen, she and a fellow student at the special school they attended had been caught having intercourse. Clare's parents had been told about the incident, but after Clare left the school the following year, they took no special precautions to ensure that Clare would not become sexually involved with anyone. After all, she stayed at home with her mother every day, and, besides, it was a matter they didn't much like to think about.

The Macwurters were both surprised and upset when Clare became pregnant. At first they couldn't imagine how it could have happened. Then they recalled that on several occasions Clare had been sent to stay at the house of Mr. Macwurter's brother and his wife while Mrs. Macwurter went shopping.

John Macwurter at first denied that he had had anything to do with Clare's pregnancy. But during the course of a long and painful conversation with his brother, he admitted that he had had sexual relations with Clare.

"I wasn't wholly to blame," John Macwurter said. "I mean, I know I shouldn't have done it. But still, she was interested in it too. I didn't really rape her. Nothing like that."

The Macwurters were at a loss about what they should do. The physician they consulted told them that Clare would probably have a perfectly normal baby. But of course Clare couldn't really take care of herself, much less a baby. She was simply unfit to be a mother. Mrs. Macwurter, for her part, was not eager to assume the additional responsibilities of caring for another child. Mr. Macwurter would be eligible to retire in four more years, and the couple had been looking forward to selling their house and moving back to the small town in Oklahoma where they had first met and then married. The money they had managed to save, plus insurance and a sale of their property, would permit them to place Clare in a long-term care facility after their deaths. Being responsible for another child would both ruin their plans and jeopardize Clare's future well-being.

"I never thought I would say such a thing," Mrs. Macwurter told her husband, "but I think we should arrange for Clare to have an abortion."

"That's killing," Mr. Macwurter said.

"I'm not so sure it is. I don't really know. But even if it is, I think it's the best thing to do."

Mrs. Macwurter made the arrangements with Clare's physician for an abortion to be performed. When Mr. Macwurter asked his brother to pay for the operation, John Macwurter refused. He explained that he was opposed to abortion and so it would not be right for him to provide money to be used in that way.

1. Could Thomson's defense of abortion be employed here to show that the proposed abortion is permissible?

2. Why would Noonan oppose abortion here? What alternatives might he recommend? What if it were likely that the baby would be defective? Would this alter the situation for Noonan?

3. Do the traits Warren lists as central to the concept of personhood require that we think of Clare Macwurter as not being a person in a morally relevant sense?

Decision Scenario 5 ••

Daniel Bocker was worried. The message his secretary had taken merely said "Go to see Dr. Tai at 3:30 today." He hadn't been asked if 3:30 was convenient for him, and he hadn't been given a reason for coming in.

Mr. Bocker knew it would have to do with his wife, Mary. She had been suffering a lot of pain during her pregnancy, and the preceding week she had been examined by a specialist that Dr. Tai, her gynecologist, had sent her to see. The specialist had performed a thorough examination and taken blood, tissue, and urine samples, but he had told Mary nothing.

"Thank you for coming in," Dr. Tai said. "I want to talk to you before I talk to your wife, because I need your help."

"The tests showed something bad, didn't they?" Mr. Bocker said. "Something is wrong with the baby."

"The baby is fine, but there is something wrong with your wife, something very seriously wrong. She has what we call uterine neoplasia."

"Is that cancer?"

"Yes it is," said Dr. Tai. "But I don't want either of you to panic about it. It's not at a very advanced stage, and at the moment it's localized. If an operation is performed very soon, then she has a good chance to make a full recovery. The standard figures show about 80% success."

"But what about the baby?"

"The pregnancy will have to be terminated," Dr. Tai said. "And I should tell you that your wife will not be able to have children after the operation."

Mr. Bocker sat quietly for a moment. He had always wanted children; for him a family without children was not a family at all. He and Mary had talked about having at least three, and the one she was pregnant with now was the first.

"Is it possible to save the baby?" he asked Dr. Tai.

"Mrs. Bocker is only in her fourth month; there is no chance the child could survive outside her body."

"But what if she didn't have the operation? Would the baby be normal?"

"Probably so, but the longer we wait to perform the operation, the worse your wife's chances become. I don't want to seem to tell you what to do, but my advice is for your wife to have an abortion and to undergo the operation as soon as it is reasonably possible."

"But she might recover, even if she had the child and then had the operation, mightn't she?"

"It's possible, but her chances of recovery are much less. I don't know what the exact figures would be, but she would be running a terrible risk."

Mr. Bocker understood what Dr. Tai was saying, but he also understood what he wanted.

"I'm not going to encourage Mary to have an abortion," he said. "I want her to have a child, and I think she wants that, too."

"What if she wants to have a better chance to live? I think the decision is really hers. After all, it's her life that is at stake."

"But it's not just her decision," Mr. Bocker said. "It's a family decision, hers and mine. I'm not going to agree to an abortion, even if she does want one. I'm going to try to get her to take the extra risk and have the child before she has the operation."

"I think that's the cruelest, most immoral thing I've ever heard," Dr. Tai said.

1. *Would the doctrine of double effect justify taking steps to treat Mrs. Bocker's illness, even at the cost of terminating her pregnancy?*

2. *Would both Noonan and Thomson see the situation as one in which considerations of self-defense are relevant?*

3. *It is sometimes said that the father of a child also has a right to decide whether an abortion is to be performed. Would Daniel Bocker be justified in urging his wife to take the risk of having the child?*

4. *Does the categorical imperative have any relevance in determining whether an abortion is morally right in this case?*

Decision Scenario 6 ••

Mrs. Lois Bishop (as we will call her) learned that she was carrying twins at the same time that she learned one of the twins had Down syndrome.

"There's no question in my mind," she said. "I want to have an abortion. I had the tests done in the first place to do what I could to guarantee that I would have a normal, healthy child. I knew from the first that there was a possibility that I would have to have an abortion, so I'm prepared for it."

Her obstetrician, Dr. George Savano, nodded. "I understand that," he said. "You are certainly within your rights to ask for an abortion, and I can arrange for you to have one. But there is another possibility, an experimental one, that you might want to consider as an option."

The possibility consisted of the destruction of the abnormally developing fetus. In the end, it was the possibility that Mrs. Bishop chose. A long, thin needle was inserted through Mrs. Bishop's abdomen and guided into the heart of the fetus. A solution was then injected directly into the fetal heart.

Although there was a risk that Mrs. Bishop would have a miscarriage, she did not. The surviving twin continued to develop normally, and Mrs. Bishop had an uneventful delivery. The child, a boy, is now over five years old.

Dr. Savano was criticized by some physicians as "misusing medicine," but he rejects such charges. Mrs. Bishop also has no regrets, for if the procedure had not been performed, she would have been forced to abort both twins.

1. What sort of utilitarian argument might be offered to justify Dr. Savano's experimental procedure in this case?

2. Would Marquis consider the destruction of the fetus with Down syndrome immoral? After all, it *may be argued that persons with Down syndrome do not have "a future like ours."*

3. The procedure leads to the death of a developing fetus, so one might say that it is morally equivalent to abortion. Are there any morally relevant factors that distinguish this case from more ordinary cases involving abortion?

Decision Scenario 7 ••

Helen and John Kent waited nervously in the small consulting room while Laurie Stent, their Genetic Counselor, went to tell Dr. Charles Blatz that they had arrived to talk to him.

"I regret that I have some bad news for you," Dr. Blatz told them. "The karyotyping that we do after amniocentesis shows a chromosomal abnormality."

He looked at them, and Helen felt she could hardly breathe. "What is it?" she asked.

"It's a condition known as Trisomy-21, and it produces a birth defect we call Down syndrome. You may have heard of it under the old name of mongolism."

"Oh, God," John said. "How bad is it?"

"Such children are always mentally retarded, " Dr. Blatz said. "Some are severely retarded and others just twenty or so points below average. They have some minor physical deformities, and they sometimes have heart damage. They typically don't live beyond their thirties, but by and large they seem happy and have good dispositions."

Helen and John looked at each other with great sadness. "What do you think we should do?" Helen asked. "Should I have an abortion, and then we could try again?"

"I don't know," John said. "I really don't know. You've had a hard time being pregnant these last five months, and you'd have to go through that again. Besides, there's no guarantee this wouldn't happen again."

"But this won't be the normal baby we wanted," Helen said. "Maybe in the long run we'll be even unhappier than we are now."

1. Explain the nature of the conflict between the positions taken by Noonan and Warren that arises in this case.

2. If one accepts Thomson's view, what factors are relevant to deciding whether an abortion is justifiable in this instance?

CHAPTER 2

TREATING OR TERMINATING: ⬚
THE PROBLEM OF IMPAIRED INFANTS

SOCIAL CONTEXT: THE DILEMMA OF EXTREME PREMATURITY

When Jan Anderson went into labor, she was twenty-three weeks pregnant—seventeen weeks short of the normal forty-week pregnancy. "They told me I had a beautiful baby boy," she said.

But her son, Aaron, weighed only a little more than 750 grams (about 1½ pounds), and when she finally saw him, he was in the neonatal intensive-care unit. He was attached to a battery of monitors, IV lines, and a respirator. Surrounding him were people checking his heart and respiration rates, monitoring his blood gases, siphoning the mucus from his mouth and underdeveloped lungs, and injecting a variety of medications needed to keep his condition stable.

"It was pretty scary," Ms. Anderson, a single woman, told reporter Gina Kolata.

Aaron spent four months in the hospital before Ms. Anderson was allowed to take him home. Aaron's life was preserved, but despite all the treatment he received, he was left with permanent disabilities. By age two, he was quadriplegic and virtually blind, had cerebral palsy, and was perhaps mentally impaired.

Every year at least 287,000 babies are born at least six weeks prematurely, and about 45,000 of them weigh less than 1600 grams (about 3½ pounds). Thanks to the development of new procedures and new drugs for treating premature infants, almost 85% live long enough to leave the hospital (though many must return), and about 20% have no lasting major physical or mental impairment.

However, the more premature an infant and the lower the birth weight, the more likely it is that the infant will die soon after birth or be severely physically and mentally impaired. About half of premature infants in the 500- to 750-gram (1- to 1½-pound) range fail to survive. From 25% to 33% of babies under 750 grams have irreversible neurological damage. The figure rises to between 40% to 50% for those with a birth weight between 500 and 600 grams. About 5% to 10% of these very-low-birth-weight babies will have cerebral palsy, and a similar percentage will have IQs below seventy, where one hundred is average.

Premature babies have not spent enough time in the uterus, and as a result, they are physiologically underdeveloped. The more premature the infant, the more underdeveloped it is. Birth weight, generally, is an index of developmental prematurity. Extremely premature neonates are "fetal infants" that have spent hardly more than half of the forty-week gestation period in their mother's uterus.

Extremely premature infants are liable to life-threatening disorders. Many have problems eating, digesting food, and absorbing nutrients. Their lungs are small and brittle and fill up with secretions, making it impossible for them to breathe normally. They must be put on a mechanical ventilator, and they tend to suffer from respiratory infections.

Poor prenatal development also makes smaller infants prone to cerebral hemorrhages or "brain bleeds" that can result in a variety of devastating consequences. Infants that have had brain bleeds are prone to seizure disorders, blindness, low vision, deafness, mental retardation, and various more subtle mental difficulties that may show up only years later.

At present more than half of the babies in the 500- to 700-gram range survive, but a mere dozen years ago, babies born weighing less than about 700 grams rarely lived. Before the early 1970s, prior to the advent of neonatal intensive-care units (NICUs), a child with a birth weight under 900 grams (about 2 pounds) would not be likely to live for long.

Because of aggressive intervention and the use of new drugs and technology, the survival rates of even the most premature infants have risen steadily over the last two decades. Laboratories can now perform dozens of biochemical tests on a few drops of blood, instead of the full vial testing previously required. Newly developed artificial pulmonary surfactants can increase the breathing capacity of an infant's lungs and shorten the time a respirator is needed.

Most important, a twelve-year study published in 1994 showed great value in the use of corticosteroids to treat pregnant women who are likely to give birth during the period from twenty-four to thirty-four weeks of gestation. The drug stimulates fetal development and speeds up the maturation of the lungs. The steroid therapy may reduce by as much as one-third the amount of time a premature infant must remain in intensive care.

As intervention strategies and technologies have improved, so has the need for them. Babies born prematurely to women who have had no prenatal care and "crack babies" born prematurely to drug-using mothers have placed heavy demands on neonatal intensive care units.

However, the new success in "saving babies" has not come without financial costs. The cost of keeping alive a premature infant runs about $3,000 per day. A very-low-birth-weight neonate may have to remain in inten-sive care for weeks or even months. The most premature infants may run up bills of more than $500,000. Despite having the highest treatment costs, these infants are also the ones least likely to benefit from the care they are given.

Moreover, the cost of the care is most likely to be borne by the taxpayer, for the mothers of the greatest number of very-low-birth-weight babies are often uninsured and unemployed women whose medical care is covered by the federal- and state-funded Medicaid program. Most of these women have received no prenatal care, and many are drug users.

Some critics believe that too much money is being spent on trying to save infants who are not likely to gain significant benefits. According to Michael Rie, a neonatologist at the University of Kentucky, "The hundred highest users of Medicaid dollars in each state are preemies who end up for months on ventilators and end up with cerebral bleeds and extremely lousy outcomes." It costs three times as much to care for an infant under 750 grams as it does to care for a victim of serious burns in a burn unit. It costs 20% more to care for such an infant than it does to pay for heart transplant surgery. Most hospitals spend more money on very young patients than they do on the very old, the group often singled out in discussions of medical costs as consuming a disproportionate amount of health-care funds.

Concern with medical costs led the state of Oregon to formulate criteria for Medicaid spending, with the result that the treatment of very-low-birth-weight infants was given low priority. The criteria take into account both the seriousness of a disorder and the outcome that might be expected if the disorder is treated. (See Chapter 10, *Social Context* for details.) Thus, a life-threatening disease that can be treated with a high degree of success at little cost (such as antibiotic treatment for tuberculosis) is given a high place on the funding list. In contrast, even a serious medical condition, but one with little chance of being improved by treatment, is assigned a low priority. Intensive-care service for newborns under 500 grams was ranked 708 on a list of 709 items.

Not everyone thinks that the Oregon decision can be adequately defended. Indeed, the basic moral question about extremely low-birth-weight infants is whether they ought to be treated. Some neonatologists regard the treatment of all infants as a moral obligation. They resuscitate fully any infant showing the slightest signs of life at delivery, regardless of its gestational age or weight. They believe this is the right course of action, even though they know that surviving infants will be likely to have severe mental and physical impairments.

Other neonatologists view the outcome of extraordinary efforts as likely to be so grim as to make resuscitation an unacceptable option. As one NICU physician states the policy at his hospital for dealing with infants weighing less than 500 grams, "We generally keep them warm and let them expire by themselves. These are not viable babies, and it's crazy to do anything more."

Because of these differences in beliefs about the right way to act, a premature infant may be the object of an all-out medical effort to save his life at one hospital, while at another hospital he might be provided only the care needed to keep him comfortable.

The same divergence of views about withholding treatment is found in the question of discontinuing treatment. Some clinicians say that they would go to court to secure an order, if a parent asked that a respirator sustaining an infant be turned off. Other clinicians view the matter as one concerning the best interest of the child. As one put the point in a hypothetical case, "If a baby survives a major head bleed, we'll tell the parents he'll almost surely be damaged and he's suffering a great deal and we don't think we should do anything more."

Perhaps partly because of the development of neonatal intensive-care units and partly because of a misimpression of federal regulations, there has been an increased tendency for physicians to make the basic decisions about whether a premature infant is treated and the extent and limit of the treatment. Parents sometimes say that they were not even consulted about their child's treatment. Indeed, some report that although they did not want their child treated or wanted treatment discontinued, their wishes were disregarded by physicians, who did whatever they thought best.

This was the experience of Jan Anderson. Believing that the outcome of her premature baby's treatment would not be a good one, she twice asked Aaron's physicians to turn off the ventilator. But no one would even discuss the possibility with her. According to Ms. Anderson, one physician screamed at her, "We're trying to save your child, not kill him."

After four months of hospitalization, Aaron went home, but he was a virtually blind quadriplegic, with cerebral palsy and perhaps a permanent mental impairment. Although Ms. Anderson loves him and takes care of him, she says that if she had been given the opportunity, she would have discontinued her baby's life support when he was born. She also says that if she were pregnant and went into labor again at twenty-three weeks, then "I would make sure there was no discussion about saving the child." In her view, "There is no need for anyone to suffer like this."

Some physicians no doubt believe that it is their duty to preserve the lives of premature infants, no matter what the parents of the child might think. However, it is the parents who typically must bear the financial, family, and emotional burdens that a severely impaired child imposes. The courts have often shared this view and allowed the final decision about treatment to rest with the parents. (See *Case Presentation: Baby Owens* and *Social Context: The Baby Doe Cases* in this chapter.)

Some physicians apparently still guide their conduct by the so-called Baby Doe laws passed in 1985. These federal regulations were initially interpreted to require that all newborns, regardless of their degree of impairment or the likelihood of their survival, receive lifesaving treatment and support. Physicians were threatened with federal prosecution for not following strict guidelines issued by the Surgeon General. However, a series of court decisions stripped away the enforcement provisions of the regulations, and the older practice of making treatment decisions on a case-by-case basis has become acceptable once again.

Insurance companies typically pay the bills for premature infants that receive treatment in neonatal intensive-care units. Hence, physicians do not have to allow financial costs to play a major role in making treatment decisions. This may incline them to ignore the life-long expenses that will have to be borne somehow by the family. Physicians can go on to the next case, but parents must remain with their child, no matter what the child's condition and prospects. Again, since parents must bear the burden, they have a good claim on being included in the decision-making process.

Does an NICU physician have an incentive, other than the best interest of a patient, to initiate or continue treatment of a low-birth-weight infant? One rarely mentioned reason for aggressive treatment is that neonatologists want to explore the limits of the modes of treatment and the technology currently used. By understanding the limits, it may be possible to take steps to extend them so that smaller and smaller premature infants can be kept alive. Hence, some neonatologists, motivated by an interest in research, may not give parents an adequate opportunity to take part in treatment decisions.

In fairness, it should be mentioned that parents do not always want to be included in the decision-making process. Some prefer to turn over to physicians all responsibility involving initiating or withdrawing medical treatment. Furthermore, physicians themselves do not always know when aggressive treatment is appropriate. They must make recommendations and decisions in an environment of crisis about a patient whose condition is in a constant state of change.

Some neonatologists and philosophers argue that hospital ethics committees should play a crucial role in deciding how premature infants should be treated. Such committees, having no vested interest in the outcome of a decision, could weigh the issues more objectively than either the neonatologist or the parents.

SOCIAL CONTEXT: THE BABY DOE CASES

In Bloomington, Indiana, in 1982, a child was born with Down syndrome and esophageal atresia. The parents and the physicians of the infant, who became known as Baby Doe, decided against the surgery that was needed to open the esophagus and allow the baby to be fed. The decision was upheld by the courts, and six days after birth Baby Doe died of starvation and dehydration.

A month later, in May of 1982, the Secretary of Health and Human Services (HHS) notified hospitals that any institution receiving federal funds could not lawfully "withhold from a handicapped infant nutritional sustenance or medical or surgical treatment required to correct a life-threatening condition if (1) the withholding is based on the fact that the infant is handicapped and (2) the handicap does not render treatment or nutritional sustenance contraindicated."

Ten months later, acting under instructions from President Reagan, an additional and more detailed regulation was issued. Hospitals were required to display a poster in neonatal intensive-care units and pediatric wards indicating that "discrimination" against handicapped infants was a violation of federal law. The poster also listed a toll-free, twenty-four-hour "hotline" number for reporting suspected violations. In addition, the regulations authorized representatives of HHS to take "immediate remedial action" to protect infants. Further, hospitals were required to permit HHS investigators access to the hospital and to relevant patient records.

A group of associations, including the American Academy of Pediatrics, brought suit against HHS in an attempt to stop the regulations from becoming legally effective. Judge Gerhard Gesell of the U.S. District Court ruled, in April 1983, that HHS had not followed the proper procedures in putting the regulations into effect and so they were invalid. In particular, the regulations were issued without notifying and consulting with those affected by them, a procedure that is legally required to avoid arbitrary bureaucratic actions. The judge held that, while HHS had considered relevant factors in identifying a problem, it had failed to consider the effects of the use of the hotline number. An "anonymous tipster" could cause "the sudden descent of Baby Doe squads" on hospitals, and "monopolizing physician and nurse time, and making hospital charts and records unavailable during treatment, can hardly be presumed to produce quality care for the infant."

Furthermore, Judge Gesell held, the main purpose of the regulations was apparently to "require physicians treating newborns to take into account wholly medical risk-benefit considerations and to prevent parents from having any influence upon decisions as to whether further medical treatment is desirable." The regulations explored no other ways to prevent "discriminatory medical care." In his conclusion, Judge Gesell held that federal regulations dealing with imperiled newborns should "reflect caution and sensitivity" and that "wide public comment prior to rule-making is essential."

The Department of Health and Human Services responded to the court decision by drafting another regulation (July 5, 1983) that attempted to resolve the procedural objection that invalidated the first. Sixty days was allowed for the filing of written comments. Since the substance of the regulation was virtually the same, the proposal was widely contested, and on January 12, 1984, another set of regulations was published. Although changing some of the more controversial requirements of the original regulations and providing for infant-care advisory committees, the regulations were still the object of controversy and criticism.

Meanwhile, a second Baby Doe case had become the focus of public attention and legal action. On October 11, 1983, an infant who became known as Baby Jane Doe was born in Port Jefferson (Long Island), New York. Baby Jane Doe suffered from meningomyelocele, anencephaly, and hydrocephaly. (See Case Presentation: *Baby Owens* for an explanation of these conditions.) Her parents were told that without surgery the child might be expected to live from two weeks to two years, while with surgery she might survive twenty years. However, she would be severely retarded, epileptic, paralyzed, and likely to have constant urinary and bladder infections.

The parents consulted with neurologists, a Roman Catholic priest, nurses, and social workers. In the end they decided that surgery was not in the best interest of the child and opted, instead, for the use of antibiotics to prevent infection of the exposed spinal nerves. "We love her very much," her mother said, "and that's why we made the decision we did."

Lawrence Washburn, Jr., a lawyer who for a number of years had initiated lawsuits on behalf of the unborn and handicapped, somehow learned that Baby Jane Doe was being denied life-prolonging surgery and entered a petition on her behalf before the New York State Supreme Court. Because Mr. Washburn was not related to the infant and had no personal knowledge of her condition or of her parents' decision, his legal standing in the case was questionable, and the court appointed William E. Weber to represent the interest of Baby Jane Doe. After a hearing, the judge ruled that the infant was in need of surgery to preserve her life and authorized Mr. Weber to consent.

This decision was reversed on appeal. The court held that the parents' decision was in the best interest of the infant. Hence, the state had no basis to intervene. The ruling was then appealed to the New York Court of Appeals and upheld. The court held that the parents' right to privacy was invaded when a person totally unrelated and with no knowledge of the infant's condition and treatment entered into litigation in an attempt to challenge the discharge of parental responsibility. However, the main grounds for allowing the ruling to stand were procedural, for the suit had not followed New York law requiring that the state intervene in the treatment of children only through the family court.

In the cases of both Baby Doe and Baby Jane Doe, the federal government went to court to demand the medical records of the infants. In both cases, the government charged that decisions against treatment represented discrimination against the handicapped. However, the courts consistently rejected the government's demands. In June of 1985, the Supreme Court agreed to hear arguments to decide whether the federal laws that protect the handicapped against discrimination also apply to the treatment of imperiled newborns who are denied life-prolonging treatment.

On May 15, 1985, the third anniversary of the death of Baby Doe, the Department of Health and Human Services' final "Baby Doe" regulation went into effect. The regulation was an implementation of an amendment to the Child Abuse Prevention and Treatment Act that was passed into law in October 1985. The amendment was the result of negotiations among some nineteen groups representing right-to-life advocates, the disabled, the medical professions, and members of Congress.

The regulation extended the term "medical neglect" to cover cases of "withholding of medically indicated treatment from a disabled infant with a life-threatening condition." Such treatment was defined as

> the failure to respond to the infant's life-threatening conditions by providing treatment (including appropriate nutrition, hydration, and medication) which, in the treating physician's (or physicians') reasonable medical judgment, will be most likely to be effective in ameliorating or correcting all such conditions. . . .

Withholding treatment, but not food and water, was not "medical neglect" in three kinds of cases:

1. The infant is chronically and irreversibly comatose.

2. The provision of such treatment would merely prolong dying, not be effective in ameliorating or correcting all of the infant's life-threatening conditions, or otherwise be futile in terms of the survival of the infant.

3. The provision of such treatment would be virtually futile in terms of the survival of the infant, and the treatment itself under such circumstances would be inhumane.

The regulation defined "reasonable medical judgment" as "a medical judgment that would be made by a reasonably prudent physician knowledgeable about the case and the treatment possibilities with respect to the medical conditions involved." State child-protection service agencies were designated as the proper organizations to see to it that infants were not suffering "medical neglect," and, in order to receive any federal funds, such agencies were required to develop a set of procedures to carry out this function.

On June 9, 1986, the Supreme Court, in a 5-to-3 ruling with one abstention, struck down the Baby Doe regulations. The Court held that there was no evidence that hospitals had discriminated against impaired infants or had refused treatments sought by parents. Accordingly, there was no basis for federal intervention.

Justice John Paul Stevens, in the majority opinion, stressed the absence of any law that might serve as a basis for federal intervention. According to Justice Stevens, no federal law requires hospitals to treat impaired infants without parental consent. Nor does the government have the right "to give unsolicited advice either to parents, to hospitals, or to state officials who are faced with difficult treatment decisions concerning handicapped children." Furthermore, state child-protection agencies "may not be conscripted against their will as the foot soldiers in a Federal crusade."

Representatives of hospitals and those directly involved in neonatal care were generally relieved by the Supreme Court decision. In their arguments before the Court, they had claimed that federal "Baby Doe squads arriving within hours after birth" had second-guessed the agonizing decisions made by par-

ents and physicians and that this had "a devastating impact on the parents."

The Court decision once again places the major responsibility for making decisions about withholding life-sustaining treatment from imperiled newborns on families and physicians acting in consultation.

One recommendation made in the Baby Doe regulations may continue to have influence. The regulations encouraged hospitals to establish Infant Care Review Committees, and similar recommendations have been made by the President's Commission for the Study of Ethical Problems in Medicine and by the American Academy of Pediatrics. Exactly how such committees might operate, how they would be composed, and what powers they should have continues to be a matter of discussion and disagreement.

The proper role of government, the power of committees, and the responsibilities of parents are merely some of the problems that form the complex of moral issues associated with imperiled and impaired infants.

CASE PRESENTATION
Baby K

The female child known in court records as Baby K was born in 1993 at Fairfax Hospital in Falls Church, Virginia. She was born with the catastrophic impairment called anencephaly—she lacks all brain structures, with the exception of a rudimentary brain stem.

The standard treatment for anencephalic infants is to make them comfortable, provide them with nourishment, then wait until their organ systems fail and death ensues. Death usually comes within a few days or weeks from respiratory failure, because the brain stem does not function adequately to regulate breathing.

Baby K has been kept alive much longer than most babies with her impairment, primarily because of her mother's insistence that the baby's periodic respiratory crises be treated aggressively, including

the use of a mechanical ventilator to breathe for her. The mother was described in one court document as "acting out of a firm Christian faith that all life should be protected."

Baby K, at the age of sixteen months, does not live at home with her mother but in an extended-care facility so that she can receive the constant attention that she requires. She leaves the nursing home only when she must have respiratory treatment. As of February 1994, she had been admitted to Fairfax Hospital three times for such treatment.

After her second admission, the hospital went to the federal district court to seek a ruling that it would not violate any state or federal law by refusing to provide Baby K with additional treatment. Physicians at the hospital held that further treatment would be futile, and a hospital ethics committee decided that withholding aggressive treatment would be legitimate. Nevertheless, the court ruled that the hospital had to provide the care required to preserve the infant's life.

The hospital appealed the district court ruling to the United States Court of Appeals. The appeal was supported by Baby K's father (who is not married to her mother) and by a court-appointed guardian. However, the court ruled 2-to-1 that the 1986 Federal Emergency Medical Treatment and Active Labor Act required the hospital to provide treatment for Baby K. The court held that, although providing assisted breathing for an anencephalic infant might not be expected to produce a medical benefit, the law as passed by Congress made no exceptions for situations in which the "required treatment would exceed the prevailing standard of medical care."

The appeals court's extension of the Emergency Medical Treatment Act to the Baby K case surprised most observers. The law was passed to keep private hospitals from "dumping" to public facilities patients with emergency problems (including pregnant women in labor) but no money and no health insurance to pay for the cost of their care. (The act is usually referred to as an antidumping law.) However, payment was not an issue in the Baby K case, for her mother was fully insured as a member of the Kaiser Permanente health maintenance organization.

According to the mother's attorney, Ellen J. Flannery, the court simply applied the law in a straightforward manner. "There's no dispute that the appropriate treatment for acute respiratory distress is ventilation," she said during an interview. "The care is not physiologically futile. It will achieve the result required by the mother, and that is to stabilize the baby." The physicians in the case, she claimed, based their decision on judgment about the quality of life such a child might have, and the law does not address such issues.

Others saw the consequences of extending the law as threatening the power of physicians, hospitals, and ethics committees to have a say in decisions about treating infants with profound birth anomalies. Arthur H. Kohrman, head of the American Academy of Pediatrics ethics committee, was quoted as saying that "This is a profoundly important case, because it strips away the ability of physicians to act as moral agents and turns them into instruments of technology. [Anencephalic] babies are born dying, and the issue is not prolonging their death but supporting it in a humane and dignified way."

Robert M. Veatch, head of the Kennedy Institute for Bioethics, testifying on behalf of the mother, expressed the view that courts should not defer their judgment to that of physicians. "These are religious and philosophical judgments on which physicians have no more expertise than parents," he said.

The impact that the extension of the antidumping law to cases of severe birth impairment may have on treatment decisions is not yet obvious. As the appeals court pointed out, Congress made no exceptions with respect to providing care above the accepted standard in cases judged to be futile. The law might be amended by Congress to include exceptions.

If the law is not amended, decisions to provide no more than standard treatment for impaired infants may turn out to have no effect in particular cases. When emergency medical attention is requested by a parent, the Emergency Treatment law may require that an earlier decision about limiting treatment be set aside.

CASE PRESENTATION
Baby Owens: Down Syndrome and Duodenal Atresia

On a chilly December evening in 1976, Dr. Joan Owens pushed through the plateglass doors of Midwestern Medical Center and walked over to the admitting desk. Dr. Owens was a physician in private practice and regularly visited Midwestern to attend to her patients.

But this night was different. Dr. Owens was coming to the hospital to be admitted as a patient.

She was pregnant, and shortly after 9:00 she began having periodic uterine contractions. Dr. Owens recognized them as the beginnings of labor pains. She was sure of this not only because of her medical knowledge but also because the pains followed the same pattern they had before her other three children were born.

While her husband, Phillip, parked the car, Dr. Owens went through the formalities of admission. She was not particularly worried, for the birth of her other children had been quite normal and uneventful. But the pains were coming more frequently now, and she was relieved when she completed the admission process and was taken to her room. Phillip came with her, bringing her small blue suitcase of personal belongings.

At 11:30 that evening, Dr. Owens gave birth to a 4½-pound baby girl. The plastic bracelet fastened around her wrist identified her as Baby Owens and listed her patient number as 23-764-2509.

Dr. Owens was groggy from exhaustion and from the medication she had received. But when the baby was shown to her, she saw at once that it was not normal. The baby's head was misshapen and the skin around her eyes strangely formed. Dr. Owens recognized that her daughter had Down syndrome.

"Clarence," she called to her obstetrician. "Is the baby mongoloid?"

"We'll talk about it after your recovery," Dr. Clarence Ziner said.

"Tell me now," said Dr. Owens. "Examine it!"

Dr. Ziner made a hasty examination of the child. He had already seen that Dr. Owens was right and was doing no more than making doubly certain. A more careful examination would have to be made later.

When Dr. Ziner confirmed Joan Owens's suspicion, she did not hesitate to say what she was thinking. "Get rid of it," she told Dr. Ziner. "I don't want a mongoloid child."

Dr. Ziner tried to be soothing. "Just sleep for a while now," he told her. "We'll talk about it later."

Four hours later, a little after 5:00 in the morning and before it was fully light, Joan Owens woke up. Phillip was with her, and he had more bad news to tell. A more detailed examination had shown that the child's small intestine had failed to develop properly and was closed off in one place—the condition known as duodenal atresia. It could be corrected by a relatively simple surgical procedure, but until surgery was performed the child

could not be fed. Phillip had refused to consent to the operation until he had talked to his wife.

Joan Owens had not changed her mind: she did not want the child. "It wouldn't be fair to the other children to raise them with a mongoloid," she told Phillip. "It would take all of our time, and we wouldn't be able to give David, Sean, and Melinda the love and attention they need."

"I'm willing to do whatever you think best," Phillip said. "But what can we do?"

"Let the child die," Joan said. "If we don't consent to the surgery, the baby will die soon. And that's what we have to let happen."

Phillip put in a call for Dr. Ziner, and, when he arrived in Joan's room, they told him of their decision. He was not pleased with it.

"The surgery has very low risk," he said. "The baby's life can almost certainly be saved. We can't tell how retarded she'll be, but most DS children get along quite well with help from their families. The whole family will grow to love her."

"I know," Joan said. "And I don't want that to happen. I don't want us to center our lives around a defective child. Phillip and I and our other children will be forced to lose out on many of life's pleasures and possibilities."

"We've made up our minds," Phillip said. "We don't want the surgery."

"I'm not sure the matter is as simple as that," Dr. Ziner said. "I'm not sure we can legally just let the baby die. I'll have to talk to the Director and the hospital attorney."

At 6:00 in the morning, Dr. Ziner called Dr. Felix Entraglo, the Director of Midwestern Medical Center, and Isaac Putnam, the head of the center's legal staff. They agreed to meet at 9:00 to talk over the problem presented to them by the Owenses.

They met for two hours. It was Putnam's opinion that the hospital would not be legally liable if Baby Owens were allowed to die because her parents refused to give consent for necessary surgery.

"What about getting a court order requiring surgery?" Dr. Entraglo asked. "That's the sort of thing we do when an infant requires a blood transfusion or immunization and his parents' religious beliefs make them refuse consent."

"This case is not exactly parallel," said Mr. Putnam. "Here we're talking about getting a court to force parents to allow surgery to save the life of a defective infant. The infant will still be defective after the surgery, and I think a court would be reluctant to make a family undergo significant emotional and financial hardships when the parents have seriously deliberated about the matter and decided against surgery."

"But doesn't the child have some claim in this situation?" Dr. Ziner asked.

"That's not clear," said Mr. Putnam. "In general we assume that parents will act for the sake of their child's welfare, and when they are reluctant to do so we look to the courts to act for the child's welfare. But in a situation like this . . . who can say? Is the Owens baby really a person in any legal or moral sense?"

"I think I can understand why a court would hesitate to order surgery," said Dr. Entraglo. "What sort of life would it be for a family when they had been pressured into accepting a child they didn't want? It would turn a family into a cauldron of guilt and resentment mixed in with love and concern. In this case, the lives of five normal people would be profoundly altered for the worse."

"So we just stand by and let the baby die?" asked Dr. Ziner.

"I'm afraid so," Dr. Entraglo said.

It took twelve days for Baby Owens to die. Her lips and throat were moistened with water to lessen her suffering, and in a small disused room set apart from the rooms of patients, she was allowed to starve to death.

Many nurses and physicians thought it was wrong that Baby Owens was forced to die such a lingering death. Some thought it was wrong for her to have to die at all, but such a protracted death seemed needlessly cruel. Yet they were cautioned by Dr. Entraglo that anything done to shorten the baby's life would probably constitute a criminal action. Thus, fear of being charged with a crime kept the staff from administering any medication to Baby Owens.

The burden of caring for the dying baby fell on the nurses in the obstetrics ward. The physicians avoided the child entirely, and it was the nurses who had to see to it that she received her water and was turned in her bed. This was the source of much resentment among the nursing staff, and a few nurses refused to have anything to do with the dying child. Most kept their ministrations to an absolute minimum.

But one nurse, Sara Ann Moberly, was determined to make Baby Owens's last days as comfortable as possible. She held the baby, rocked her, and talked soothingly to her when she cried. Doing all

for the baby that she could do soothed Sara Ann as well.

But even Sara Ann was glad when Baby Owens died. "It was a relief to me," she said. "I almost couldn't bear the frustration of just sitting there day after day and doing nothing that could really help her."

INTRODUCTION

If we could speak of nature in human terms, we would often say that it is cruel and pitiless. Nowhere does it seem more heartless than in the case of babies born into the world with severe physical impairments and deformities. The birth of such a child transforms an occasion of expected joy into one of immense sadness. It forces the child's parents to make a momentous decision at a time they are least prepared to reason clearly: Shall they insist that everything be done to save the child's life? Or shall they request that the child be allowed an easeful death?

Nor can physicians and nurses escape the burden that the birth of such a child delivers. Committed to saving lives, can they condone the death of that child? What shall the physician say to the parents when they turn to him or her for advice? No one involved in the situation can escape the moral agonies that it brings.

To see more clearly what the precise moral issues are in such cases, we need to consider some of the factual details that may be involved in them. We need also to mention other kinds of moral considerations that may be relevant to deciding how an impaired newborn child is to be dealt with by those who have the responsibility to decide.

GENETIC AND CONGENITAL IMPAIRMENTS

The development of a child to the point of birth is an unimaginably complicated process, and there are many ways in which it can go wrong. Two kinds of errors are most frequently responsible for producing impaired children: genetic errors and congenital errors.

1. *Genetic errors.* The program of information that is coded into DNA (the genetic material) may be in some way abnormal because of the occurrence of a mutation. Consequently, when the DNA blueprint is "read" and its instructions followed, the child that develops will be impaired. The defective gene may have been inherited, or it may be due to a new mutation.

2. *Congenital errors.* "Congenital" means only "present at birth," and, since genetic defects have results that are present at birth, the term is misleading. Ordinarily, however, the phrase is used to designate errors that result during the developmental process. The impairment, then, is not in the original blueprint (genes) but results either from genetic damage or from the reading of the blueprint. The manufacture and assembly of the materials that constitute the child's development are affected.

We know that many factors can influence fetal development. Radiation (such as X rays), drugs (such as thalidomide), chemicals (such as mercury), and nutritional deficiencies can all cause changes in an otherwise normal process. Also, biological disease agents, such as certain viruses or spirochetes, may intervene in development. They may alter the machinery of the cells, interfere with the formation of tissues, and defeat the carefully programmed process that leads to a normal child.

Genetic impairments are inherited; they are the outcome of the genetic endowment of the child. A carrier of defective genes who has children can pass on the genes. Congenital impairments are not inherited and cannot be passed on. This point is of great theoretical and practical importance. With proper genetic counseling, individuals belonging to families in which certain diseases "run" can assess the risk that their children might be impaired. Also, some genetic diseases can be diagnosed before birth. A blood test for the presence of the substance alphafetoprotein can indicate the likelihood of neural tube defects characteristic of spina bifida. Ultrasound can be used to confirm or detect these or other developmental anomalies. In a procedure known as amniocentesis, fluid is drawn from the uterus, and cells from the developing embryo are examined for genetic abnormalities. (The newer procedure of chorion sampling takes the cells directly from the fetal membrane.) If abnormalities are present, the woman may decide to have an abortion rather than give birth to an impaired child. A recognition of some kinds of developmental errors can lead to efforts to eliminate the impairments by controlling the factors responsible for them. (For additional information on genetic errors, screening, and attempts to correct their results, see the Introduction in Chapter 7.)

Once the impaired child is born, the medical and moral problems are immediate. Let us consider now some of the defects commonly found in newborn children. Our focus will be on what they are rather than on what caused them, for, as far as the moral issue is concerned in a particular case, how the child came to be impaired is of no importance.

Down Syndrome

This is a genetic disease first identified in 1866 by the English physician J. L. H. Down. Normally, humans have twenty-three pairs of chromosomes, but Down syndrome results from the presence of an extra chromosome. The condition is called Trisomy-21, for, instead of a twenty-first pair of chromosomes, the affected person has a twenty-first *triple.* (Less often, the syndrome is produced when the string of chromosomes gets twisted and chromosome pair number 21 sticks to number 15.)

In ways not wholly understood, the normal process of development is altered by this extra chromosome. The child is born with retardation and various physical abnormalities. Typically, these are relatively minor and include such features as a broad skull, a large tongue, and an upward slant of the eyelids. It is this last feature that led to the name "mongolism" for the condition.

Down syndrome occurs in about one of every 1,000 births. It occurs most frequently in women over the age of thirty-five, although it is not known why this should be so. In 1984 researchers discovered that certain chromosomes sometimes contain an extra copy of a segment known as the "nucleolar organizing region." This abnormality seems linked to Down syndrome, and families in which either parent has the abnormality are twenty times more likely to have an affected child. Researchers hope to use this information to develop a reliable screening test.

There is no cure for Down syndrome—no way to compensate for the abnormality of the development process. Those with the defect generally have an IQ of about 50–80 and usually require the care and help of others. They can be taught easy tasks, and despite their impairment, those with Down syndrome usually seem to be quite happy people.

Spina Bifida

Spina bifida is a general name for birth defects that involve an opening in the spine. In development, the spine of the child fails to fuse properly, and often the open vertebrae permit the membrane covering the spinal cord to protrude to the outside. The membrane sometimes forms a bulging, thin sac that contains spinal fluid and nerve tissue. When nerve tissue is present, the condition is called myelomeningocele. This form of spina bifida is a very severe one.

Complications arising from spina bifida must often be treated surgically. The initial condition, the opening in the spine, must be closed up. In severe cases, the sac is removed

and the nerve tissue inside is placed within the spinal canal. Normal skin is then grafted over the area. The danger of an infection of the meninges (meningitis) is great; thus, treatment with antibiotic drugs is also necessary.

Furthermore, a child with spina bifida is also likely to require orthopedic operations to attempt to correct the deformities of the legs and feet that occur because of muscle weakness and lack of muscular control due to nerve damage. The bones of such children are thin and brittle, and fractures are frequent.

A child born with spina bifida is virtually always paralyzed to some extent. Generally the paralysis is below the waist. Because of the nerve damage, the child will have limited sensation in the lower part of the body. This means that he will have no control over his bladder or bowels. The lack of bladder control may result in infection of the bladder, urinary tract, and kidneys, because the undischarged urine may serve as a breeding place for microorganisms. Surgery may help with the problem of lack of control of the bladder and bowels.

Spina bifida occurs in between one and ten per 1,000 births. For reasons not understood, the rate in white families of low socioeconomic status is three times higher than that in families of higher socioeconomic status. The rate in the black population is less than half of that in the white population. A recent study also shows that women who took multivitamins during pregnancy ran less than half the risk of having an affected child than those who did not, but the significance of this result remains uncertain.

Spina bifida is almost always accompanied by hydrocephaly.

Hydrocephaly

This term literally means "water on the brain." When, for whatever reasons, the flow of fluid through the spinal canal is blocked, the cerebrospinal fluid produced within the brain cannot escape. Pressure buildup from the fluid can cause brain damage, and if it is not released the child will die. Although hydrocephaly is frequently the result of spina bifida, it can have several causes and can develop late in a child's life.

Treatment requires surgically inserting a thin tube, or shunt, to drain the fluid from the skull to the heart or abdomen where it can be absorbed. The operation can save the baby's life, but physical and mental damage is frequent. Placing the shunt and getting it to work properly are difficult tasks that may require many operations. If hydrocephaly accompanies spina bifida (and it almost always does), it is treated first.

Anencephaly

This term means literally "without brain." In this condition, the brain is partially or almost totally absent. The defect is related to spina bifida, for in some forms the bones of the skull are not completely formed and leave an opening through which brain material bulges to the outside.

In some cases, death is a virtual certainty. Other cases can be dealt with in much the same way as is spina bifida. Ordinarily, the individual is so severely retarded that he has minimum control over bodily movements and functions. There is never hope for improvement by any known means.

Esophageal Atresia

In medical terms, an atresia is the closing of a normal opening or canal. The esophagus is the muscular tube that extends from the back of the throat to the stomach. Sometimes the tube forms without an opening, or it does not completely develop so that it does not extend to the stomach. The condition must be corrected by surgery in order for the child to get food into its stomach. The chances of success in such surgery are very high.

Duodenal Atresia

The duodenum is the upper part of the small intestine. Food from the stomach empties into it. When the duodenum is closed off, food cannot pass through and be digested. Surgery can repair this condition and is successful in most cases.

An estimated 6% of all live births, some 200,000 infants a year, require intensive neonatal care. The afflictions that we have singled out for special mention are those that are most often the source of major moral problems. Those correctable by standard surgical procedures present no special moral difficulties. But even they are often involved with other impairments, such as Down syndrome, that make them important factors in moral deliberations.

Problems of Extreme Prematurity

A normal pregnancy lasts approximately forty weeks. Infants born after only twenty-six weeks of growth or less typically fail to live. Those born in the weeks after that time have extremely low birth weights. About half of those weighing from 1 to 1½ pounds fail to survive, and those that do have a multiplicity of problems resulting from the fact that their bodies have simply not had the time to develop adequately to cope with the demands of life outside the uterus.

The undeveloped lungs of premature infants are inefficient and prone to infections. The mechanical ventilation needed to assist their breathing may result in long-term lung damage. Extremely premature infants are subject to cerebral hemorrhages ("brain bleeds") that may lead to seizures, blindness, deafness, retardation, and a variety of less noticeable disabilities.

For a discussion of extremely premature infants and the moral issues they present with respect to withholding or withdrawing treatment, see the Social Context at the front of this chapter.

ETHICAL THEORIES AND THE PROBLEM OF BIRTH IMPAIRMENTS

A great number of serious moral issues are raised by impaired newborns. Should they be given only ordinary care, or should special efforts be made to save their lives? Should they be given no care and allowed to die? Should they be killed in a merciful manner? Who should decide what is in the interest of the child? Might acting in the interest of the child require not acting to save the child's life?

A more basic question that cuts even deeper than these concerns the status of the newborn. It is virtually the same as the question raised in Chapter 1 about the fetus. Namely, are severely impaired newborns persons? It might be argued that some infants are so severely impaired that they should not be considered persons in a relevant moral sense. Not only do they lack the capacity to function, but they lack even the potentiality for ordinary psychological and social development. In this respect, they are worse off than most maturing fetuses.

If this view is accepted, then the principles of our moral theories do not require that we act to preserve the lives of impaired newborns. We might, considering their origin, be disposed to show them some consideration and treat them benevolently—perhaps in the same way we might deal with animals that are in a similarly hopeless condition. We might kill them or allow them to die as a demonstration of our compassion.

One major difficulty with this view is that it is not at all clear which impaired infants could legitimately be considered nonpersons. Birth defects vary widely in severity, and, unless one is prepared to endorse infanticide generally, it is necessary to have defensible criteria for distinguishing among newborns.

Also, one must defend a general concept of a person that would make it reasonable to regard human offspring as occupying a different status.

By contrast, it might be claimed that the fact that a newborn is a human progeny is sufficient to consider it a person. Assuming that this is so, the question becomes, "How ought we to treat a severely impaired infant person?" Just because they are infants, impaired newborns cannot express wishes, make claims, or enter into deliberations. All that is done concerning them must be done by others.

A utilitarian might decide that the social and personal cost (the suffering of the infant, the anguish of the parents and family, the monetary cost to society) of saving the life of such an infant is greater than the social and personal benefits that can be expected. Accordingly, such a child should not be allowed to live, and it should be killed as painlessly as possible to minimize its suffering. Yet a rule utilitarian might claim, on the contrary, that the rule "Save every child where possible" would, in the long run, produce more utility than disutility.

The natural law position of Roman Catholicism is that even the most defective newborn is a human person. Yet this view does not require that extraordinary means be used to save the life of such a child. The suffering of the family, great expense, and the need for multiple operations would be reasons for providing only ordinary care. Ordinary care does not mean that every standard medical procedure that might help should be followed. It means only that the defective newborn should receive care of the same type provided for a normal infant. It would be immoral to kill the child or to cause its death by withholding all care.

If the infant is a person, then Kant would regard it as possessing an inherent dignity and value. But the infant in its condition lacks the capacity to reason and to express its will.

How, then, should we, acting as its agents, treat it? Kant's principles provide no clear-cut answer. The infant does not threaten our own existence, and we have no grounds for killing it. But, it could be argued, we should allow the child to die. We can imaginatively put ourselves in the place of the infant. Although it would be morally wrong to will our own death (which, Kant claimed, would involve a self-defeating maxim), we might express our autonomy and rationality by choosing to refuse treatment that would prolong a painful and hopeless life. If this is so, then we might act in this way on behalf of the defective child. We might allow the child to die. Indeed, it may be our duty to do so. A similar line of argument from Ross's viewpoint might lead us to decide that, although we have a prima facie duty to preserve the child's life, our actual duty is to allow it to die.

Another basic question remains: Who is to make the decision about how an impaired newborn is to be treated? Traditionally, the assumption has been that this is a decision best left to the infant's parents and physicians. Because they can be assumed to have the highest concern for his welfare and the most knowledge about his condition and prospects, they are the ones who should have the primary responsibility for deciding his fate. If there is reason to believe that they are not acting in a responsible manner, then it becomes the responsibility of the courts to guarantee that the interests of the infant are served.

Hardly any responsible person advocates heroic efforts to save the lives of infants who are most severely impaired, and hardly anyone advocates not treating infants with relatively simple and correctable impairments. The difficult cases are those that fall somewhere along the continuum. Advances in medical management and technology can now save the lives of many infants who earlier would have died relatively quickly, and yet we still lack the power to provide those infants with a life that we might judge to be worthwhile. Yet a failure to treat such infants does not invariably result in their deaths, and a failure to provide them with early treatment may mean that they are even more impaired than they would be otherwise.

No one believes that we currently have a satisfactory solution to this dilemma. It is important to keep in mind that it is not a purely intellectual problem. The context in which particular decisions are made is one of doubt and confusion and genuine anguish.

Examination of Arguments in Favor of Withholding Ordinary Medical Care from Defective Infants

John A. Robertson

John A. Robertson defends a conservative natural law position in criticizing two arguments in favor of withholding "necessary but ordinary" medical care from impaired infants. He rejects the claim made by Michael Tooley that infants are not persons and argues that, on the contrary, there is no nonarbitrary consideration that requires us to protect the past realization of conceptual capability but not its potential realization.

The second argument that Robertson considers is one to the effect that we have no obligation to treat defective newborns when the cost of doing so greatly outweighs the benefits (a utilitarian argument). In criticism, Robertson claims that we have no way of judging this. Life itself may be of sufficient worth to an impaired person to offset his or her suffering, and the suffering and cost to society are not sufficient to justify withholding care.

1. Defective Infants Are Not Persons

Children born with congenital malformations may lack human form and the possibility of ordinary, psychosocial development. In many cases mental retardation is or will be so profound, and physical incapacity so great, that the term "persons" or "humanly alive" have odd or questionable meaning when applied to them. In these cases the infant's physical and mental defects are so severe that they will never know anything but a vegetative existence, with no discernible personality, sense of self, or capacity to interact with others. Withholding ordinary medical care in such cases, one may argue, is justified on the ground that these infants are not persons or human beings in the ordinary or legal sense of the term, and therefore do not possess the right of care that persons possess.

Central to this argument is the idea that living products of the human uterus can be classified into offspring that are persons, and those that are not. Conception and birth by human parents does not automatically endow one with personhood and its accompanying rights. Some other characteristic or feature must be present in the organism for personhood to vest, and this the defective infant arguably lacks. Lacking that property, an organism is not a person or deserving to be treated as such.

Before considering what "morally significant features" might distinguish persons from nonpersons, and examining the relevance of such features to the case of the defective infant, we must face an initial objection to this line of inquiry. The objection questions the need for any distinction among human offspring because of

> the monumental misuse of the concept of "humanity" in so many practices of discrimination and atrocity throughout history. Slavery, witch-hunts and wars have all been justified by their perpetrators on the grounds that they held their victims to be less than fully human. The insane and the criminal have for long periods been deprived of the most basic necessities for similar reasons, and been excluded from society. . . .
>
> . . . Even when entered upon with the best of intentions, and in the most guarded manner, the enterprise of basing the protection of human life upon such criteria and definitions is dangerous. To question someone's humanity or personhood is a first step to mistreatment and killing.

Hence, according to this view, human parentage is a necessary and sufficient condition for personhood, whatever the characteristics of the offspring, because qualifying criteria inevitably lead to abuse and untold suffering to beings who are unquestionably human. Moreover, the human species is sufficiently different from other sentient species that assigning its members greater rights on birth alone is not arbitrary.

This objection is indeed powerful. The treatment accorded slaves in the United States, the Nazi denial of personal status to non-Aryans, and countless other incidents, testify that man's inhumanity to man is indeed greatest when a putative nonperson is involved. Arguably, however, a distinction based on gross physical form, profound mental incapacity, and the very existence of personality or selfhood, besides having an empirical basis in the monstrosities and mutations known to have been born to women is a basic and fundamental one. Rather than distinguishing among the particular characteristics that persons might attain through the contingencies of race, culture, and class, it merely separates out those who lack the potential for assuming any personal characteristics beyond breathing and consciousness.

This reply narrows the issue: should such creatures be cared for, protected, or regarded as

Reprinted by permission of the publisher from "Involuntary Euthanasia of Defective Newborns: A Legal Analysis," *Stanford Law Review* 27 (1975): 246–261. Copyright 1975 by the Board of Trustees of the Leland Stanford Junior University. Editor's Note: The footnotes in this essay are too lengthy to be included here.

"ordinary" humans? If such treatment is not warranted, they may be treated as nonpersons. The arguments supporting care in all circumstances are based on the view that all living creatures are sacred, contain a spark of the divine, and should be so regarded. Moreover, identifying those human offspring unworthy of care is a difficult task and will inevitably take a toll on those whose humanity cannot seriously be questioned. At this point the argument becomes metaphysical or religious and immune to resolution by empirical evidence, not unlike the controversy over whether a fetus is a person. It should be noted, however, that recognizing all human offspring as persons, like recognizing the fetus to be a person, does not conclude the treatment issue.

Although this debate can be resolved only by reference to religious or moral beliefs, a procedural solution may reasonably be considered. Since reasonable people can agree that we ordinarily regard human offspring as persons, and further, that defining categories of exclusion is likely to pose special dangers of abuse, a reasonable solution is to presume that all living human offspring are persons. This rule would be subject to exception only if it can be shown beyond a reasonable doubt that certain offspring will never possess the minimal properties that reasonable persons ordinarily associate with human personality. If this burden cannot be satisfied, then the presumption of personhood obtains.

For this purpose I will address only one of the many properties proposed as a necessary condition of personhood—the capacity for having a sense of self—and consider whether its advocates present a cogent account of the nonhuman. Since other accounts may be more convincingly articulated, this discussion will neither exhaust nor conclude the issue. But it will illuminate the strengths and weaknesses of the personhood argument and enable us to evaluate its application to defective infants.

Michael Tooley has recently argued that a human offspring lacking the capacity for a sense of self lacks the rights to life or equal treatment possessed by other persons. In considering the morality of abortion and infanticide, Tooley considers "what properties a thing must possess in order to have a serious right to life," and he concludes that:

[h]aving a right to life presupposes that one is capable of desiring to continue existing as a subject of experiences and other mental states.

This in turn presupposes both that one has the concept of such a continuing entity and that one believes that one is oneself such an entity. So an entity that lacks such a consciousness of itself as a continuing subject of mental states does not have a right to life.

However, this account is at first glance too narrow, for it appears to exclude all those who do not presently have a desire "to continue existing as a subject of experiences and other mental states." The sleeping or unconscious individual, the deranged, the conditioned, and the suicidal do not have such desires, though they might have had them or could have them in the future. Accordingly, Tooley emphasizes the capability of entertaining such desires, rather than their actual existence. But it is difficult to distinguish the capability for such desires in an unconscious, conditioned, or emotionally disturbed person from the capability existing in a fetus or infant. In all cases the capability is a future one; it will arise only if certain events occur, such as normal growth and development in the case of the infant, and removal of the disability in the other cases. The infant, in fact, might realize its capability long before disabled adults recover emotional balance or consciousness.

To meet this objection, Tooley argues that the significance of the capability in question is not solely its future realization (for fetuses and infants will ordinarily realize it), but also its previous existence and exercise. He seems to say that once the conceptual capability has been realized, one's right to desire continued existence permanently vests, even though the present capability for desiring does not exist, and may be lost for substantial periods or permanently. Yet, what nonarbitrary reasons require that we protect the past realization of conceptual capability but not its potential realization in the future? As a reward for its past realization? To mark our reverence and honor for someone who has realized that state? Tooley is silent on this point.

Another difficulty is Tooley's ambiguity concerning the permanently deranged, comatose, or conditioned. Often he phrases his argument in terms of a temporary suspension of the capability of conceptual thought. One wonders what he would say of someone permanently deranged, or with massive brain damage, or in a prolonged coma. If he seriously means that the past existence of a desire for life vests these cases with the right to life, then it is indeed difficult to distinguish the comatose or deranged from the infant profoundly re-tarded at birth. Neither will ever possess the con-ceptual capability to desire to be a continuing sub-ject of experiences. A distinction based on reward or desert seems arbitrary, and protection of life applies equally well in both cases. Would Tooley avoid this problem by holding that the permanently comatose and deranged lose their rights after a cer-tain point because conceptual capacity will never be regained? This would permit killing (or at least withholding of care from) the insane and coma-tose—doubtless an unappealing prospect. More-over, we do not ordinarily think of the insane, and possibly the comatose, as losing personhood before their death. Although their personality or identity may be said to change, presumably for the worse, or become fragmented or minimal, we still regard them as specific persons. If a "self" in some mini-mal sense exists here then the profoundly retarded, who at least is conscious, also may be considered a self, albeit a minimal one. Thus, one may argue that Tooley fails to provide a convincing account of cri-teria distinguishing persons and nonpersons. He both excludes beings we ordinarily think of as per-sons—infants, deranged, conditioned, possibly the comatose—and fails to articulate criteria that con-vincingly distinguish the nonhuman. But, even if we were to accept Tooley's distinction that beings lacking the potential for desire and a sense of self are not persons who are owed the duty to be treated by ordinary medical means, this would not appear to be very helpful in deciding whether to treat the newborn with physical or mental defects. Few infants, it would seem, would fall into this class. First, those suffering from malformations, however gross, that do not affect mental capabili-ties would not fit the class of nonpersons. Second, frequently even the most severe cases of mental re-tardation cannot be reliably determined until a much later period; care thus could not justifiably be withheld in the neonatal period, although this prin-ciple would permit nontreatment at the time when nonpersonality is clearly established. Finally, the only group of defective newborns who would clearly qualify as nonpersons is anencephalics, who altogether lack a brain or those so severely brain-damaged that it is immediately clear that a sense of self or personality can never develop. Mongols, myelomeningoceles, and other defective infants from whom ordinary care is now routinely with-held would not qualify as nonpersons. Thus, even

the most coherent and cogent criteria of humanity are only marginally helpful in the situation of the de-fective infant. We must therefore consider whether treatment can be withheld on grounds other than the claim that such infants are not persons.

2. No Obligation to Treat Exists When the Costs of Maintaining Life Greatly Outweigh the Benefits

If we reject the argument that defective newborns are not persons, the question remains whether circumstances exist in which the conse-quences of treatment as compared with nontreat-ment are so undesirable that the omission of care is justified. As we have seen, the doctrine of necessity permits one to violate the criminal law when essen-tial to prevent the occurrence of a greater evil. The circumstances, however, when the death of a non-consenting person is a lesser evil than his continu-ing life are narrowly circumscribed, and do not in-clude withholding care from defective infants. Yet many parents and physicians deeply committed to the loving care of the newborn think that treating severely defective infants causes more harm than good, thereby justifying the withholding of ordi-nary care. In their view the suffering and dimin-ished quality of the child's life do not justify the so-cial and economic costs of treatment. This claim has a growing commonsense appeal, but it assumes that the utility or quality of one's life can be mea-sured and compared with other lives, and that health resources may legitimately be allocated to produce the greatest personal utility. This argu-ment will now be analyzed from the perspective of the defective patient and others affected by his care.

a. The Quality of the Defective Infant's Life

Comparisons of relative worth among persons, or between persons and other interests, raise moral and methodological issues that make any argument that relies on such comparisons extremely vulner-able. Thus the strongest claim for not treating the defective newborn is that treatment seriously harms the infant's own interests, whatever may be the effects on others. When maintaining his life involves great physical and psychosocial suffering for the patient, a reasonable person might conclude that such a life is not worth living. Presumably the patient, if fully informed and able to communicate, would agree. One then would be morally justified in withholding lifesaving treatment if such action served to advance the best interests of the patient.

Congenital malformations impair development in several ways that lead to the judgment that deformed retarded infants are "a burden to themselves." One is the severe physical pain, much of it resulting from repeated surgery that defective infants will suffer. Defective children also are likely to develop other pathological features, leading to repeated fractures, dislocations, surgery, malfunctions, and other sources of pain. The shunt, for example, inserted to relieve hydrocephalus, a common problem in defective children, often becomes clogged, necessitating frequent surgical interventions.

Pain, however, may be intermittent and manageable with analgesics. Since many infants and adults experience great pain, and many defective infants do not, pain alone, if not totally unmanageable, does not sufficiently show that a life is so worthless that death is preferable. More important are the psychosocial deficits resulting from the child's handicaps. Many defective children never can walk even with prosthesis, never interact with normal children, never appreciate growth, adolescence, or the fulfillment of education and employment, and seldom are even able to care for themselves. In cases of severe retardation, they may be left with a vegetative existence in a crib, incapable of choice or the most minimal response to stimuli. Parents or others may reject them, and much of their time will be spent in hospitals, in surgery, or fighting the many illnesses that beset them. Can it be said that such a life is worth living?

There are two possible responses to the quality-of-life argument. One is to accept its premises but to question the degree of suffering in particular cases, and thus restrict the justification for death to the most extreme cases. The absence of opportunities for schooling, career, and interaction may be the fault of social attitudes and the failings of healthy persons, rather than a necessary result of congenital malformations. Psychosocial suffering occurs because healthy, normal persons reject or refuse to relate to the defective, or hurry them to poorly funded institutions. Most nonambulatory, mentally retarded persons can be trained for satisfying roles. One cannot assume that a nonproductive existence is necessarily unhappy; even social rejection and nonacceptance can be mitigated. Moreover, the psychosocial ills of the handicapped often do not differ in kind from those experienced by many persons. With training and care, growth, development, and a full range of experiences are possible for most people with physical and mental handicaps. Thus, the claim that death is a far better fate than life cannot in most cases be sustained.

This response, however, avoids meeting the quality-of-life argument on its strongest grounds. Even if many defective infants can experience growth, interaction, and most human satisfactions if nurtured, treated, and trained, some infants are so severely retarded or grossly deformed that their response to love and care, in fact their capacity to be conscious, is always minimal. Although mongoloid and nonambulatory spina bifida children may experience an existence we would hesitate to adjudge worse than death, the profoundly retarded, nonambulatory blind, deaf infant who will spend his few years in the back-ward cribs of a state institution is clearly a different matter.

To repudiate the quality-of-life argument, therefore, requires a defense of treatment in even these extreme cases. Such a defense would question the validity of any surrogate or proxy judgments of the worth or quality of life when the wishes of the person in question cannot be ascertained. The essence of the quality-of-life argument is a proxy's judgment that no reasonable person can prefer the pain, suffering, and loneliness of, for example, life in a crib at an IQ level of 20, to an immediate, painless death.

But in what sense can the proxy validly conclude that a person with different wants, needs, and interests, if able to speak, would agree that such a life were worse than death? At the start one must be skeptical of the proxy's claim to objective disinterestedness. If the proxy is also the parent or physician, as has been the case in pediatric euthanasia, the impact of treatment on the proxy's interests, rather than solely on those of the child, may influence his assessment. But even if the proxy were truly neutral and committed only to caring for the child, the problem of egocentricity and knowing another's mind remains. Compared with the situation and life prospects of a "reasonable man," the child's potential quality of life indeed appears dim.

Yet a standard based on healthy, ordinary development may be entirely inappropriate to this situation. One who has never known the pleasures of mental operation, ambulation, and social interaction surely does not suffer from their loss as much as one who has. While one who has known these capacities may prefer death to a life without them, we have no assurance that the handicapped person, with no point of comparison, would agree. Life, and life alone, whatever its limitations, might be of sufficient worth to him.

One should also be hesitant to accept proxy assessments of quality-of-life because the margin of error in such predictions may be very great. For instance, while one expert argues that by a purely clinical assessment he can accurately forecast the minimum degree of future handicap an individual will experience, such forecasting is not infallible, and risks denying care to infants whose disability might otherwise permit a reasonably acceptable quality-of-life. Thus given the problems in ascertaining another's wishes, the proxy's bias to personal or culturally relative interests, and the unreliability of predictive criteria, the quality-of-life argument is open to serious question. Its strongest appeal arises in the case of a grossly deformed, retarded, institutionalized child, or one with incessant unmanageable pain, where continued life is itself torture. But these cases are few, and cast doubt on the utility of any such judgment. Even if the judgment occasionally may be defensible, the potential danger of quality-of-life assessments may be a compelling reason for rejecting this rationale for withholding treatment.

b. The Suffering of Others

In addition to the infant's own suffering, one who argues that the harm of treatment justifies violation of the defective infant's right to life usually relies on the psychological, social, and economic costs of maintaining his existence to family and society. In their view the minimal benefit of treatment to persons incapable of full social and physical development does not justify the burdens that care of the defective infant imposes on parents, siblings, health professionals, and other patients. Matson, a noted pediatric neurosurgeon, states:

> [I]t is the doctor's and the community's responsibility to provide [custodial] care and to minimize suffering, but, at the same time, it

is also their responsibility not to prolong such individual, familial, and community suffering unnecessarily, and not to carry out multiple procedures and prolonged, expensive, acute hospitalization in an infant whose chance for acceptable growth and development is negligible.

Such a frankly utilitarian argument raises problems. It assumes that because of the greatly curtailed orbit of his existence, the costs or suffering of others [are] greater than the benefit of life to the child. This judgment, however, requires a coherent way of measuring and comparing interpersonal utilities, a logical-practical problem that utilitarianism has never surmounted. But even if such comparisons could reliably show a net loss from treatment, the fact remains that the child must sacrifice his life to benefit others. If the life of one individual, however useless, may be sacrificed for the benefit of any person, however useful, or for the benefit of any number of persons, then we have acknowledged the principle that rational utility may justify any outcome. As many philosophers have demonstrated, utilitarianism can always permit the sacrifice of one life for other interests, given the appropriate arrangement of utilities on the balance sheet. In the absence of principled grounds for such a decision, the social equation involved in mandating direct, involuntary euthanasia becomes a difference of degree, not kind, and we reach the point where protection of life depends solely on social judgments of utility.

These objections may well be determinative. But if we temporarily bracket them and examine the extent to which care of the defective infant subjects others to suffering, the claim that inordinate suffering outweighs the infant's interest in life is rarely plausible. In this regard we must examine the impact of caring for defective infants on the family, health professionals, and society-at-large.

The Family. The psychological impact and crisis created by birth of a defective infant is devastating. Not only is the mother denied the normal tension release from the stresses of pregnancy, but both parents feel a crushing blow to their dignity, self-esteem and self-confidence. In a very short time, they feel grief for the loss of the normal expected child, anger at fate, numbness, disgust, waves of helplessness, and disbelief. Most feel personal blame for the defect, or blame their spouse.

Adding to the shock is fear that social position and mobility are permanently endangered. The transformation of a "joyously awaited experience into one of catastrophe and profound psychological threat" often will reactivate unresolved maturational conflicts. The chances for social pathology—divorce, somatic complaints, nervous and mental disorders—increase and hard-won adjustment patterns may be permanently damaged.

The initial reactions of guilt, grief, anger, and loss, however, cannot be the true measure of family suffering caused by care of a defective infant, because these costs are present whether or not the parents choose treatment. Rather, the question is to what degree treatment imposes psychic and other costs greater than would occur if the child were not treated. The claim that care is more costly rests largely on the view that parents and family suffer inordinately from nurturing such a child.

Indeed, if the child is treated and accepted at home, difficult and demanding adjustments must be made. Parents must learn how to care for a disabled child, confront financial and psychological uncertainty, meet the needs of other siblings, and work through their own conflicting feelings. Mothering demands are greater than with a normal child, particularly if medical care and hospitalization are frequently required. Counseling or professional support may be nonexistent or difficult to obtain. Younger siblings may react with hostility and guilt, older with shame and anger. Often the normal feedback of child growth that renders the turmoil of childrearing worthwhile develops more slowly or not at all. Family resources can be depleted (especially if medical care is needed), consumption patterns altered, or standards of living modified. Housing may have to be found closer to a hospital, and plans for further children changed. Finally, the anxieties, guilt, and grief present at birth may threaten to recur or become chronic.

Yet, although we must recognize the burdens and frustrations of raising a defective infant, it does not necessarily follow that these costs require nontreatment, or even institutionalization. Individual and group counseling can substantially alleviate anxiety, guilt, and frustration, and enable parents to cope with underlying conflicts triggered by the birth and the adaptations required. Counseling also can reduce psychological pressures on siblings, who can be taught to recognize and accept their own possibly hostile feelings and the difficult position of their parents. They may even be taught to help their parents care for the child.

The impact of increased financial costs also may vary. In families with high income or adequate health insurance, the financial costs are manageable. In others, state assistance may be available. If severe financial problems arise or pathological adjustments are likely, institutionalization, although undesirable for the child, remains an option. Finally, in many cases, the experience of living through a crisis is a deepening and enriching one, accelerating personality maturation, and giving one a new sensitivity to the needs of spouse, siblings, and others. As one parent of a defective child states: "In the last months I have come closer to people and can understand them more. I have met them more deeply. I did not know there were so many people with troubles in the world."

Thus, while social attitudes regard the handicapped child as an unmitigated disaster, in reality the problem may not be insurmountable, and often may not differ from life's other vicissitudes. Suffering there is, but seldom is it so overwhelming or so imminent that the only alternative is death of the child.

Health Professionals.   Physicians and nurses also suffer when parents give birth to a defective child, although, of course, not to the degree of the parents. To the obstetrician or general practitioner the defective birth may be a blow to his professional identity. He has the difficult task of informing the parents of the defects, explaining their causes, and dealing with the parents' resulting emotional shock. Often he feels guilty for failing to produce a normal baby. In addition, the parents may project anger or hostility on the physician, questioning his professional competence or seeking the services of other doctors. The physician also may feel that his expertise and training are misused when employed to maintain the life of an infant whose chances for a productive existence are so diminished. By neglecting other patients, he may feel that he is prolonging rather than alleviating suffering.

Nurses, too, suffer role strain from care of the defective newborn. Intensive-care-unit nurses may work with only one or two babies at a time. They face the daily ordeals of care—the progress and relapses—and often must deal with anxious parents who are themselves grieving or ambivalent toward the child. The situation may trigger a nurse's own ambivalence about death and mothering, in a context in which she is actively working to keep alive a child whose life prospects seem minimal.

Thus, the effects of care on physicians and nurses are not trivial, and must be intelligently confronted in medical education or in management of a pediatric unit. Yet to state them is to make clear that they can but weigh lightly in the decision of whether to treat a defective newborn. Compared with the situation of the parents, these burdens seem insignificant, are short term, and most likely do not evoke such profound emotions. In any case, these difficulties are hazards of the profession—caring for the sick and dying will always produce strain. Hence, on these grounds alone it is difficult to argue that a defective person may be denied the right to life.

Society.   Care of the defective newborn also imposes societal costs, the utility of which is questioned when the infant's expected quality-of-life is so poor. Medical resources that can be used by infants with a better prognosis, or throughout the health-care system generally, are consumed in providing expensive surgical and intensive-care services to infants who may be severely retarded, never lead active lives, and die in a few months or years. Institutionalization imposes costs on taxpayers and reduces the resources available for those who might better benefit from it, while reducing further the quality of life experienced by the institutionalized defective.

One answer to these concerns is to question the impact of the costs of caring for defective newborns. Precise data showing the costs to taxpayers or the trade-offs with health and other expenditures do not exist. Nor would ceasing to care for the defective necessarily lead to a reallocation within the health budget that would produce net savings in suffering or life; in fact, the released resources might not be reallocated for health at all. In any case, the trade-offs within the health budget may well be small. With advances in prenatal diagnosis of genetic disorders, many deformed infants who would formerly require care will be aborted beforehand. Then, too, it is not clear that the most technical and expensive procedures always constitute the best treatment for certain malformations. When compared with the almost seven percent of the GNP now spent on health, the money in the defense budget, or tax revenues generally, the public resources required to keep defective newborns alive seem marginal, and arguably worth the commitment to life that such expenditures reinforce. Moreover, as the Supreme Court recently recognized, conservation of the taxpayer's purse does not justify serious infringement of fundamental rights. Given legal and ethical norms against sacrificing the lives of nonconsenting others, and the imprecisions in diagnosis and prediction concerning the eventual outcomes of medical care, the social-cost argument does not compel nontreatment of defective newborns.

Ethical Issues in Aiding the Death of Young Children

H. Tristram Engelhardt, Jr.

H. T. Engelhardt contends that children are not persons in the full sense. They must exist in and through their families. Thus, parents, in conference with a physician who provides information, are the appropriate ones to decide whether to treat an impaired newborn when (1) there is not only little likelihood of a full human life, but also the likelihood of suffering if the life is prolonged, or (2) the cost of prolonging the life is very great.

Engelhardt further argues that it is reasonable to speak of a *duty* not to treat an impaired infant when this will only prolong a painful life or would only lead to a painful death. He bases his claim on the legal notion of a "wrongful life." This notion suggests that there are cases in which nonexistence would be better than existence under the conditions in which a person must live. Life can thus be seen as an injury, rather than as a gift.

Euthanasia in the pediatric age group involves a constellation of issues that are materially different from those of adult euthanasia. The difference lies in the somewhat obvious fact that infants and young children are not able to decide about their own futures and thus are not persons in the same sense that normal adults are. While adults usually decide their own fate, others decide on behalf of young children. Although one can argue that euthanasia is or should be a personal right, the sense of such an argument is obscure with respect to children. Young children do not have any personal rights, at least none that they can exercise on their own behalf with regard to the manner of their life and death. As a result, euthanasia of young children raises special questions concerning the standing of the rights of children, the status of parental rights, the obligations of adults to prevent the suffering of children, and the possible effects on society of allowing or expediting the death of seriously defective infants.

What I will refer to as the euthanasia of infants and young children might be termed by others infanticide, while some cases might be termed the withholding of extraordinary life-prolonging treatment. One needs a term that will encompass both death that results from active intervention and death that ensues when one simply ceases further therapy. In using such a term, one must recognize that death is often not directly but only obliquely intended. That is, one often intends only to treat no further, not actually to have death follow, even though one knows death will follow.

Finally, one must realize that deaths as the result of withholding treatment constitute a significant proportion of neonatal deaths. For example, as high as 14 percent of children in one hospital have been identified as dying after a decision was made not to treat further, the presumption being that the children would have lived longer had treatment been offered.

Even popular magazines have presented accounts of parental decisions not to pursue treatment. These decisions often involve a choice between expensive treatment with little chance of achieving a full, normal life for the child and "letting nature take its course," with the child dying as a result of its defects. As this suggests, many of these problems are products of medical progress. Such children in the past would have died. The quandaries are in a sense an embarrassment of riches; now that one *can* treat such defective children, *must* one treat them? And, if one need not treat such defective children, may one expedite their death?

I will here briefly examine some of these issues. First, I will review differences that contrast the euthanasia of adults to euthanasia of children. Second, I will review the issue of the rights of parents and the status of children. Third, I will suggest a new notion, the concept of the "injury of continued existence," and draw out some of its implications with respect to a duty to prevent suffering. Finally, I will outline some important questions that remain unanswered even if the foregoing issues can be settled. In all, I hope more to display the issues involved in a difficult question than to advance a particular set of answers to particular dilemmas.

For the purpose of this paper, I will presume that adult euthanasia can be justified by an appeal to freedom. In the face of imminent death, one is usually choosing between a more painful and more protracted dying and a less painful or less protracted dying, in circumstances where either choice makes little difference with regard to the discharge of social duties and responsibilities. In the case of suicide, we might argue that, in general, social duties (for example, the duty to support one's family) restrain one from taking one's own life. But in the face of imminent death and in the presence of the pain and deterioration of a fatal disease, such duties are usually impossible to discharge and are

This article first appeared in the book *Beneficient Euthanasia,* edited by Marvin Kohl, published by Prometheus Books, Buffalo, N.Y., 1975, and is reprinted by permission. (Notes and references omitted.)

thus rendered moot. One can, for example, picture an extreme case of an adult with a widely disseminated carcinoma, including metastases to the brain, who because of severe pain and debilitation is no longer capable of discharging any social duties. In these and similar circumstances, euthanasia becomes the issue of the right to control one's own body, even to the point of seeking assistance in suicide. Euthanasia is, as such, the issue of assisted suicide, the universalization of a maxim that all persons should be free, *in extremis*, to decide with regard to the circumstances of their death.

Further, the choice of positive euthanasia could be defended as the more rational choice: the choice of a less painful death and the affirmation of the value of a rational life. In so choosing, one would be acting to set limits to one's life in order not to live when pain and physical and mental deterioration make further rational life impossible. The choice to end one's life can be understood as a non-contradictory willing of a smaller set of states of existence for oneself, a set that would not include a painful death. As such, it would not involve a desire to destroy oneself. That is, adult euthanasia can be construed as an affirmation of the rationality and autonomy of the self.

The remarks above focus on the active or positive euthanasia of adults. But they hold as well concerning what is often called passive or negative euthanasia, the refusal of life-prolonging therapy. In such cases, the patient's refusal of life-prolonging therapy is seen to be a right that derives from personal freedom, or at least from a zone of privacy into which there are no good grounds for social intervention.

Again, none of these considerations apply directly to the euthanasia of young children, because they cannot participate in such decisions. Whatever else pediatric, in particular neonatal, euthanasia involves, it surely involves issues different from those of adult euthanasia. Since infants and small children cannot commit suicide, their right to assisted suicide is difficult to pose. The difference between the euthanasia of young children and that of adults resides in the difference between children and adults. The difference, in fact, raises the troublesome question of whether young children are persons, or at least whether they are persons in the sense in which adults are. Answering that question will resolve in part at least the right of others to decide whether a young child should live or die and whether he should receive life-prolonging treatment.

The Status of Children

Adults belong to themselves in the sense that they are rational and free and therefore responsible for their actions. Adults are *sui juris*. Young children, though, are neither self-possessed nor responsible. While adults exist in and for themselves, as self-directive and self-conscious beings, young children, especially newborn infants, exist for their families and those who love them. They are not, nor can they in any sense be, responsible for themselves. If being a person is to be a responsible agent, a bearer of rights and duties, children are not persons in a strict sense. They are, rather, persons in a social sense: others must act on their behalf and bear responsibility for them. They are, as it were, entities defined by their place in social roles (for example, mother-child, family-child) rather than beings that define themselves as persons, that is, in and through themselves. Young children live as persons in and through the care of those who are responsible for them, and those responsible for them exercise the children's rights on their behalf. In this sense children belong to families in ways that most adults do not. They exist in and through their family and society.

Treating young children with respect has, then, a sense different from treating adults with respect. One can respect neither a newborn infant's or very young child's wishes nor its freedom. In fact, a newborn infant or young child is more an entity that is valued highly because it will grow to be a person and because it plays a social role as if it were a person. That is, a small child is treated as if it were a person in social roles such as mother-child and family-child relationships, though strictly speaking the child is in no way capable of claiming or being responsible for the rights imputed to it. All the rights and duties of the child are exercised and "held in trust" by others for a future time and for a person yet to develop.

Medical decisions to treat or not to treat a neonate or small child often turn on the probability and cost of achieving that future status—a developed personal life. The usual practice of letting anencephalic children (who congenitally lack all or most of the brain) die can be understood as a decision based on the absence of the possibility of achieving a personal life. The practice of refusing treatment to at least some children born with meningomyelocele can be justified through a similar, but more utilitarian, calculus. In the case of anencephalic children one might argue that care for them as persons is futile since they will never be persons. In the case of a child with meningomyelocele, one might argue that when the cost of cure would likely be very high and the probable lifestyle open to attainment very truncated, there is not a positive duty to make a large investment of money and suffering. One should note that the cost here must include not only financial costs but also the anxiety and suffering that prolonged and uncertain treatment of the child would cause the parents.

This further raises the issue of the scope of positive duties not only when there is no person present in a strict sense, but when the likelihood of a full human life is also very uncertain. Clinical and parental judgment may and should be guided by the expected lifestyle and the cost (in parental and societal pain and money) of its attainment. The decision about treatment, however, belongs properly to the parents because the child belongs to them in a sense that it does not belong to anyone else, even to itself. The care and raising of the child falls to the parents, and when considerable cost and little prospect of reasonable success are present, the parents may properly decide against life-prolonging treatment.

The physician's role is to present sufficient information in a usable form to the parents to aid them in making a decision. The accent is on the absence of a positive duty to treat in the presence of severe inconvenience (costs) to the parents; treatment that is very costly is not obligatory. What is suggested here is a general notion that there is never a duty to engage in extraordinary treatment and that "extraordinary" can be defined in terms of costs. This argument concerns children (1) whose future quality of life is likely to be seriously compromised and (2) whose present treatment would be very costly. The issue is that of the circumstances under which parents would not be obliged to take on severe burdens on behalf of their children or those circumstances under which society would not be so obliged. The argument should hold as well for those cases where the expected future life would surely be of normal quality, though its attainment would be extremely costly. The fact of little likelihood of success in attaining a normal life

for the child makes decisions to do without treatment more plausible because the hope of success is even more remote and therefore the burden borne by parents or society becomes in that sense more extraordinary. But very high costs themselves could be a sufficient criterion, though in actual cases judgments in that regard would be very difficult when a normal life could be expected.

The decisions in these matters correctly lie in the hands of the parents, because it is primarily in terms of the family that children exist and develop—until children become persons strictly, they are persons in virtue of their social roles. As long as parents do not unjustifiably neglect the humans in those roles so that the value and purpose of that role (that is, child) stands to be eroded (thus endangering other children), society need not intervene. In short, parents may decide for or against the treatment of their severely deformed children.

However, society has a right to intervene and protect children for whom parents refuse care (including treatment) when such care does not constitute a severe burden and when it is likely that the child could be brought to a good quality of life. Obviously, "severe burden" and "good quality of life" will be difficult to define and their meanings will vary, just as it is always difficult to say when grains of sand dropped on a table constitute a heap. At most, though, society need only intervene when the grains clearly do not constitute a heap, that is, when it is clear that the burden is light and the chance of a good quality of life for the child is high. A small child's dependence on his parents is so essential that society need intervene only when the absence of intervention would lead to the role "child" being undermined. Society must value mother-child and family-child relationships and should intervene only in cases where (1) neglect is unreasonable and therefore would undermine respect and care for children, or (2) where societal intervention would prevent children from suffering unnecessary pain.

The Injury of Continued Existence

But there is another viewpoint that must be considered: that of the child or even the person that the child might become. It might be argued that the child has a right not to have its life prolonged. The idea that forcing existence on a child could be wrong is a difficult notion, which, if true, would serve to amplify the foregoing argument. Such an argument would allow the construal of the issue in terms of the perspective of the child, that is, in terms of a duty not to treat in circumstances where treatment would only prolong suffering. In particular, it would at least give a framework for a decision to stop treatment in cases where, though the costs of treatment are not high, the child's existence would be characterized by severe pain and deprivation.

A basis for speaking of continuing existence as an injury to the child is suggested by the proposed legal concept of "wrongful life." A number of suits have been initiated in the United States and in other countries on the grounds that life or existence itself is, under certain circumstances, a tort or injury to the living person. Although thus far all such suits have ultimately failed, some have succeeded in their initial stages. Two examples may be instructive. In each case the ability to receive recompense for the injury (the tort) presupposed the existence of the individual, whose existence was itself the injury. In one case a suit was initiated on behalf of a child against his father alleging that his father's siring him out of wedlock was an injury to the child. In another case a suit on behalf of a child born of an inmate of a state mental hospital impregnated by rape in that institution was brought against the state of New York. The suit was brought on the grounds that being born with such historical antecedents was itself an injury for which recovery was due. Both cases presupposed that nonexistence would have been preferable to the conditions under which the person born was forced to live.

The suits for tort for wrongful life raise the issue not only of when it would be preferable not to have been born but also of when it would be *wrong* to cause a person to be born. This implies that someone should have judged that it would have been preferable for the child never to have had existence, never to have been in the position to judge that the particular circumstances of life were intolerable. Further, it implies that the person's existence under those circumstances should have been prevented and that, not having been prevented, life was not a gift but an injury. The concept of tort for wrongful life raises an issue concerning the responsibility for giving another person existence, namely the notion that giving life is not always necessarily a good and justifiable action. Instead, in certain circumstances, so it has been argued, one may have a

duty *not* to give existence to another person. This concept involves the claim that certain qualities of life have a negative value, making life an injury, not a gift; it involves, in short, a concept of human accountability and responsibility for human life. It contrasts with the notion that life is a gift of God and thus similar to other "acts of God" (that is, events for which no man is accountable). The concept thus signals the fact that humans can now control reproduction and that where rational control is possible humans are accountable. That is, the expansion of human capabilities has resulted in an expansion of human responsibilities such that one must now decide when and under what circumstances persons will come into existence.

The concept of tort for wrongful life is transferable in part to the painfully compromised existence of children who can only have their life prolonged for a short, painful, and marginal existence. The concept suggests that allowing life to be prolonged under such circumstances would itself be an injury of the person whose painful and severely compromised existence would be made to continue. In fact, it suggests that there is a duty not to prolong life if it can be determined to have a substantial negative value for the person involved. Such issues are moot in the case of adults, who can and should decide for themselves. But small children cannot make such a choice. For them it is an issue of justifying prolonging life under circumstances of painful and compromised existence. Or, put differently, such cases indicate the need to develop social canons to allow a decent death for children for whom the only possibility is protracted, painful suffering.

I do not mean to imply that one should develop a new basis for civil damages. In the field of medicine, the need is to recognize an ethical category, a concept of wrongful continuance of existence, not a new legal right. The concept of injury for continuance of existence, the proposed analogue of the concept of tort for wrongful life, presupposes that life can be of a negative value such that the medical maxim *primum non nocere* ("first do no harm") would require not sustaining life.

The idea of responsibility for acts that sustain or prolong life is cardinal to the notion that one should not under certain circumstances further prolong the life of a child. Unlike adults, children cannot decide with regard to euthanasia (positive or negative), and if more than a utilitarian justification is sought, it must be sought in a duty not to inflict life on another person in circumstances where that life would be painful and futile. This position must rest on the facts that (1) medicine now can cause the prolongation of the life of seriously deformed children who in the past would have died young and that (2) it is not clear that life so prolonged is a good for the child. Further, the choice is made not on the basis of costs to the parents or to society but on the basis of the child's suffering and compromised existence.

The difficulty lies in determining what makes life not worth living for a child. Answers could never be clear. It seems reasonable, however, that the life of children with diseases that involve pain and no hope of survival should not be prolonged. In the case of Tay-Sachs disease (a disease marked by a progressive increase in spasticity and dementia usually leading to death at age three or four), one can hardly imagine that the terminal stages of spastic reaction to stimuli and great difficulty in swallowing are at all pleasant to the child (even insofar as it can only minimally perceive its circumstances). If such a child develops aspiration pneumonia and is treated, it can reasonably be said that to prolong its life is to inflict suffering. Other diseases give fairly clear portraits of lives not worth living: for example, Lesch-Nyhan disease, which is marked by mental retardation and compulsive self-mutilation.

The issues are more difficult in the case of children with diseases for whom the prospects for normal intelligence and a fair lifestyle do exist, but where these chances are remote and their realization expensive. Children born with meningomyelocele present this dilemma. Imagine, for example, a child that falls within Lorber's fifth category (an IQ of sixty or less, sometimes blind, subject to fits, and always incontinent). Such a child has little prospect of anything approaching a normal life, and there is a good chance of its dying even with treatment. But such judgments are statistical. And if one does not treat such children, some will still survive and, as John Freeman indicates, be worse off if not treated. In such cases one is in a dilemma. If one always treats, one must justify extending the life of those who will ultimately die anyway and in the process subjecting them to the morbidity of multiple surgical procedures. How remote does the prospect of a good life have to be in order not to be worth great pain and expense? It is probably best to decide, in the absence of a positive duty to treat, on the basis

of the cost and suffering to parents and society. But, as Freeman argues, the prospect of prolonged or even increased suffering raises the issue of active euthanasia.

If the child is not a person strictly, and if death is inevitable and expediting it would diminish the child's pain prior to death, then it would seem to follow that, all else being equal, a decision for active euthanasia would be permissible, even obligatory. The difficulty lies with "all else being equal," for it is doubtful that active euthanasia could be established as a practice without eroding and endangering children generally, since, as John Lorber has pointed out, children cannot speak in their own behalf. Thus although there is no argument in principle against the active euthanasia of small children, there could be an argument against such practices based on questions of prudence. To put it another way, even though one might have a duty to hasten the death of a particular child, one's duty to protect children in general could override that first duty. The issue of active euthanasia turns in the end on whether it would have social consequences that refraining would not, on whether (1) it is possible to establish procedural safeguards for limited active euthanasia and (2) whether such practices would have a significant adverse effect on the treatment of small children in general. But since these are procedural issues dependent on sociological facts, they are not open to an answer within the confines of this article. In any event, the concept of the injury of continued existence provides a basis for the justification of the passive euthanasia of small children—a practice already widespread and somewhat established in our society—beyond the mere absence of a positive duty to treat.

Conclusion

Though the lack of certainty concerning questions such as the prognosis of particular patients and the social consequence of active euthanasia of children prevents a clear answer to all the issues raised by the euthanasia of infants, it would seem that this much can be maintained: (1) Since children are not persons strictly but exist in and through their families, parents are the appropriate ones to decide whether or not to treat a deformed child when (a) there is not only little likelihood of full human life but also great likelihood of suffering if the life is prolonged, or (b) when the cost of prolonging life is very great. Such decisions must be made in consort with a physician who can accurately give estimates of cost and prognosis and who will be able to help the parents with the consequences of their decision. (2) It is reasonable to speak of a duty not to treat a small child when such treatment will only prolong a painful life or would in any event lead to a painful death. Though this does not by any means answer all the questions, it does point out an important fact—that medicine's duty is not always to prolong life doggedly but sometimes is quite the contrary.

Life-and-Death Decisions in the Midst of Uncertainty

Robert F. Weir

Robert F. Weir argues for a position midway between those of Robertson and Engelhardt. He agrees with Robertson that decisions about extremely premature or impaired infants ought not be based on considerations of economic, social, or emotional costs, but he also agrees with Engelhardt that infants are not persons in the full sense. Accordingly, in some cases we may reasonably decide that it is not in the best interest of the infant to be treated.

In Weir's view, neonates not suffering from severe neurological impairments are "potential persons," and as such, they possess basic human rights, including the right not to be killed. However, all infants, including those lacking the potential to become persons in the full sense, are entitled to have their "best interest" considered, and Weir provides eight criteria for determining the best interest of an infant. In accordance with these criteria, an infant's interest may sometimes be served best by withholding treatment and allowing the child to die. Physicians and parents, Weir maintains, ought to make treatment decisions based exclusively on the benefits and burdens of treatment to the infant.

A Neonatal Intensive Care Unit (NICU) is characterized by premature and disabled patients with life-threatening conditions, highly trained medical and nursing specialists, state-of-the-art medical technology, an endless stream of medical consultants, parents grappling with frightening possibilities, and numerous decisions that have to be made in the midst of impenetrable uncertainty. Whether made while looking down at an imperiled baby, in consultation with the baby's parents, or in a conference room near the NICU, many of these decisions are crucial because a baby will continue to live or will die as a consequence of the decisions. . . .

Do Neonates Count as Persons?

. . . To the extent that there is consensus among philosophers on the concept of personhood, that consensus focuses on the intrinsic rather than the extrinsic qualities of persons. Most philosophers agree on at least the core properties or traits of personhood, if not on all of their applications. Joel Feinberg, in his discussion of "commonsense personhood," puts forth the consensus view of personhood as being the possession of three necessary and jointly sufficient properties: consciousness, self-awareness, and at least minimum rationality. Such properties, for him and many others, represent "person-making characteristics."

The possession of personhood, therefore, has to do with neurological development and, at least among human beings, the absence of profound neurological dysfunction or impairment. The answer to the question of whether neonates are to be counted as persons depends on three interrelated factors:

1. How much neurological development is required for personhood;

2. How much neurological impairment is necessary to rule out personhood; and

3. Whether any significance is to be placed on the principle of potentiality as it applies to personhood.

In my judgment, there are three basic positions regarding the personhood of neonates (and other human beings whose personhood may be questioned), and the positions are distinguishable largely because of their handling of the factors of neurological development, neurological impairment, and potential personhood. The first position holds that *all neonates,* whether normal or neurologically impaired, *are nonpersons.* . . .

The second position stands at the other end of a philosophical and political spectrum, and represents a very common view of neonates held by many physicians, nurses, and other people as well. . . .

The third position stands between the other positions, differing from the first position's insufficient claims and the second position's excessive claims regarding the personhood of human newborns. This position, which holds that *most neonates are potential persons,* can be compared with the alternative views on the basis of its four claims:

1. Personhood is a moral category attaching to beings (of any species) with certain characteristics, principally cognitive capacities;

2. Neonates lack the intrinsic qualities that make a human into a person, as do fetuses;

3. Having the potential to become a person through the normal course of development does count, and neonates without severe neurological impairment (and fetuses having exhibited brain activity) have this potential; and

4. All *potential* persons have a *prima facie* claim to the moral benefits of personhood, including the right not to be killed, because they will subsequently acquire an *actual* person's moral and legal right to life.

The last of these positions, in my view, is the correct way of describing the ontological status of neonates. This position is preferable to the neonates-are-not-persons view of some philosophers, because it grants more than a species value to human newborns—and avoids the major weakness of having to allow, in principle, for the indiscriminate termination of an indeterminate number of neonatal lives, whether these lives are cognitively impaired, physically disabled, or normal. The third position is also preferable to the neonates-are-actual-persons view (especially as put forth by several prolife groups), because it takes the philosophical and psychological concept of personhood seriously—and avoids the major weakness of having to say, in principle, that a baby has no more claim to the moral benefits of personhood than an early human embryo does.

What Is the Best Ethical Option for Making Decisions to Initiate, Continue, or Abate Life-Sustaining Treatment?

. . . The options range from very conservative to very liberal, and they differ from one another regarding the substantive and, to a lesser extent, the procedural aspects of making life-and-death decisions for nonautonomous young patients.

The most conservative of these ethical options is the ethical perspective that was enacted into public policy by the Reagan administration through the "Baby Doe" regulations and subsequent Child Abuse regulations. Incensed that one "Baby Doe" (the 1982 Bloomington, Indiana, case) had died who could have lived with surgical intervention and concerned that other disabled infants were unnecessarily being allowed to die in other hospitals, the leaders of the Reagan administration went to great lengths to advocate the ethical perspective held by Surgeon General C. Everett Koop, and many of the administration's prolife supporters.

This ethical position holds that there is one and only one acceptable moral reason for not sustaining an infant's life, namely, the medical futility in a very limited number of cases of trying to do so. According to this ethical perspective, decisions not to sustain a severely disabled infant's life are acceptable only when such an infant is irretrievably dying (or, for some persons holding this position, an infant whose condition is some form of permanent unconsciousness). Therefore, the only cases in which such decisions by physicians or parents are justifiable are those unusual cases in which there is actually no moral decision to make: God, nature, fate, the roll of the genetic "dice," or some force beyond our control prevents medical efforts at sustaining life from working.

The most liberal option is a position that carries significant weight in some philosophical circles, but not, as we have already discussed, among physicians and others who are more oriented toward a practical, empirically based view of reality. This position, in sharp contrast to the first position, is based on the ontological status of the young lives at risk in critical care units rather than on the severity of their medical conditions. Instead of calling for life-sustaining treatment to be administered to all neonates or young children who are not dying (or permanently unconscious), the philosophers holding this position (e.g., Michael Tooley, Mary Anne Warren, and Peter Singer) argue that physicians and parents are obligated only to provide life-sustaining treatment for neonates and young children who count as persons. The catch is, as we have seen, that according to this perspective no neonates meet the criteria for personhood, and no moral weight is placed on the potential they may have to become persons later in the course of their development. An unresolved problem for these philosophers—and one of the reasons that this position will never become public policy—is that of defining the "magic moment" beyond the neonatal period when young children do meet the criteria for personhood and are thus protected from having their lives arbitrarily terminated.

The third position is the first of three positions that reside closer to the middle of the philosophical spectrum than either of the views just discussed. The physicians, philosophers, and other individuals who hold this view do not believe that all nondying neonates should be given life-sustaining treatment, nor do they believe that the lives of neonates can be terminated morally on the basis of a definitional point about personhood. Rather, they are convinced that the most important aspect of decisions not to sustain some infants' lives is the procedural question of who should make these difficult decisions. The correct answer to that question, according to the advocates of this position, is that the appropriate decision maker is the parent or parents of the neonate or young child whose life is threatened by his or her medical condition, even though the current federal regulations do not permit this kind of parental discretion. Since the parents of a disabled infant are the ones who stand to gain or lose the most, depending on what happens to the infant, it is they—instead of the physicians, an ethics committee, or anybody else—who should have the right to make the life-or-death decision in all cases over which there is some disagreement about whether a disabled infant should continue to live with or die in the absence of life-sustaining treatment.

Advocates of a fourth ethical position are convinced that quality-of-life judgments are unavoidable in cases of severe neurological or physiological malformation, in spite of what the federal regulations say to the contrary. All of the responsible parties in cases of serious neonatal abnormalities are morally obligated—and should be legally permitted—to raise important questions about the most likely future ahead of these children if their lives are to be prolonged with medical treatment. Of fundamental importance in such cases is not only the question of whether a given child can be salvaged with the abnormalities he or she has, but also what kind of life he or she is most likely to have with those abnormalities. The most important abnormalities to consider are neurological in nature. If a neurological disorder is sufficiently serious that pediatric neurologists and neonatologists project a life with severe disabilities for the child, virtually all persons holding a quality-of-life position would find the abatement of life-sustaining treatment in such a case to be morally justifiable.

The fifth position is held by individuals who are convinced that life-sustaining treatment should be provided to normal and disabled neonates whenever such treatment is in their best interests, and that life-sustaining treatment should be abated in the care of severely premature or severely disabled neonates (and other young children) whenever such treatment is judged not to be in their best interests.

Persons holding this position tend to be in agreement with quality-of-life advocates whose projections of a given child's future focus *entirely* on that child's likely abilities and disabilities, not on the child's impact on anybody else or ability to attain somebody else's minimal standard of acceptability for personal human life. By contrast, persons having a best-interests position disagree with quality-of-life advocates who tend to compare mentally and physically abnormal children with normal children, emphasize the problems that disabled children cause for their families and society, and try to protect families and society from having to deal with disabled children who cannot meet some arbitrary standard of acceptability. Like all advocates of the quality-of-life position, proponents of the best-interests position hold a view that is more liberal than the current federal regulations.

The best-interests position, in my judgment, is the preferable ethical perspective to take in regard to difficult decisions about initiating, continuing, or abating life-sustaining treatment with any patients having life-threatening medical conditions. Neonatal and other young pediatric patients are no exception. They, like other nonautonomous patients, should receive life-sustaining treatment whenever the decision makers are convinced that the treatments available provide a balance of benefit to burden for the child. Such decisions should focus on the child's medical condition, concern suffering and irremediable handicap rather than projected social worth, and involve comparative judgments about the continuation of the child's injurious existence as opposed to the child's nonexistence.

What Does "Best Interests" Mean When Patients Are Neonates?

Even though widely supported in theory, the best-interests position is not without problems. Some of the advocates of the position admit that the concept of the patient's best interests is inherently vague, especially when the patient is a neonate. Nevertheless, they argue that the concept is helpful in decision making about life-sustaining treatment for neonates, because it focuses the decision-making process on precisely the human lives that ought to be the primary focus of concern.

Some of the critics of the best-interests position, at least as it applies to neonates, think that the conceptual foundation on which it stands is fundamentally flawed. Martin Benjamin argues that neonates simply do not yet possess the cognitive awareness, much less the specific wants and purposes, that are necessary for ascribing to them an interest in continued life. Howard Brody is convinced that any attempt to apply the concept of best interests to infants is bound to fail, because the concept is either incoherent or inadequate as a guide for tough clinical decisions. He argues that, even if infants can intelligibly be said to have interests, such interests would be unknowable by adult decision makers. . . .

. . . One's "interests" consist of relationships, activities, and things in which one has a stake and on which one places value. To have interests (as opposed to sensations or instincts) normally requires as necessary conditions that one be conscious, aware of oneself, and able cognitively to have wants and purposes. In other words, to have interests normally requires that one be a person.

Yet, as Joel Feinberg points out in a discussion of fetal interests, it is plausible to ascribe *future* interests to a "prepersonal fetus." Even though a fetus "presumably has no actual interests," it can correctly be said to have future interests on the assumption that it will at some future point in its normal development (at birth or subsequent to birth) become a person and, thus, the possessor of actual interests. In a similar manner, the law recognizes that fetuses can have "contingent rights," such as the right to property, that will become actual rights the moment the fetus becomes a baby. Any contingent right of a fetus is instantly voided if the fetus dies before birth.

The same kind of reasoning about interests can be used in analyzing the interests that are ascribable to neonates, even by philosophers who claim that all neonates are nonpersons. For even if neonates as nonpersons cannot correctly be said to be the possessors of actual interests, they can be said to have future interests (assuming that they will at some future point become persons) that can be interfered with or damaged by decisions or actions by adults long before these developing human lives become persons. For example, a neonate with myelomeningocele could reasonably be said to have a future interest in physical mobility, but come to realize later in life that a decision by physicians or parents during the neonatal period not to have the lesion surgically corrected had preempted that future interest from being actualized.

An alternative conceptual framework for discussing the interests of neonates was presented earlier, namely the philosophical view that neonates without severe neurological impairments are to be regarded as potential persons. In this framework, an analysis of the interests of neonates does not involve the ascription of future interests to them because they are thought likely to become persons at some "magic moment" in the future, but ascribes future interests to them because they have the potential to become the possessors of interests through the normal course of their development.

The point is a fundamental one. Just as potentiality is an important aspect of the concept of personhood, so potentiality is an important feature of a philosophical understanding of interests (but not of legal rights). Interests change from time to time after one becomes a person, with some interests intensifying over time, others waning, and others appearing as though newly born. For that reason, a discussion of the future interests of any given neonate becomes problematic if one can only project the actual interests that child will have when he or she meets the criteria for personhood at some future point in time. By contrast, the principle of potentiality, as it applies both to the possession of personhood and the possession of interests, permits one reasonably to ascribe to any given neonate the most general and basic kinds of interests that most individuals tend to have as they develop from young children to older children and on through the various phases of personal life. . . .

When applied to neonates, the concept of "best interests" can obviously not refer to the specific wants and purposes any given neonate may have in continued life, much less to the specific wants and purposes that the neonate may have later in life. However, the concept of "best interests" can be used to capture the most fundamental future interest that persons have when they are patients, namely, an interest in not being harmed on balance during the course of medical treatment. For most patients in most clinical situations, this vital interest in not being harmed on balance means that they prefer continued life to death—unless intractable pain and other suffering have made continued life more harmful than the prospect of death. To ascribe this general and basic interest to neonates is to claim that all neonates lacking severe neurological impairment can reasonably be said to have this future interest in not being harmed, an interest that will become actualized as they become persons during the normal course of their development.

. . . [T]he toughest aspect of using the concept of best interests in decision making in NICUs is determining the factors that should be considered in any given case. How can physicians and parents assess the beneficial and detrimental aspects of medical treatment in a case? How can they decide if life-sustaining treatment is in a neonate's best interests or is contrary to those interests?

My suggestion is to regard the patient's-best-interests standard as having eight variables. In neonatal (and other young pediatric) cases, the variables are as follows:

1. Severity of the patient's medical condition;
2. Availability of curative or corrective treatment;
3. Achievability of important medical goals;
4. Presence of serious neurological impairments;
5. Extent of the infant's suffering;
6. Multiplicity of other serious medical problems;
7. Life expectancy of the infant; and
8. Proportionality of treatment-related benefits and burdens to the infant.

The last of these variables is, in many respects, a summation of the preceding variables. For decision makers in such cases, a consideration of the benefits of the treatment (both short-term and long-term) to the patient is the "bottom line" for determining whether life-sustaining treatment or the abatement of life-sustaining treatment is in a particular neonate's best interests. In making this assessment, decision makers arrive at a subjective judgment that includes objective factors, but is not finally reducible to quantifiable information. For to decide in rare clinical situations that treatment is, on balance, harmful to the infant rather than beneficial is to make a moral judgment. . . .

Should Life-Sustaining Treatment for Neonates and Other Young Children Ever Be Abated for Economic Reasons?

Neonatologists and other pediatric specialists place considerable importance on providing good patient care. In terms of the patient's-best-interests position, this emphasis on the medical needs and interests of individual patients is the morally preferable perspective for pediatricians and other physicians to have. According to this view, the needs and interests of each patient related to continued life correctly outweigh any competing interests of parents, siblings, or society. Simply put, no neonate or other young, nonautonomous patient should die merely because their medical and hospital care is expensive, even when the physicians and parents in a given case know that the family's income and insurance cannot over the costs involved in the patient's care.

In the last few years, however, a number of factors have combined to create uncertainty about this basic moral premise for the provision of medical care, especially as it applies to cases of extremely premature or severely disabled neonates. Physicians, hospital administrators, and other concerned persons often question the importance that should be placed on the economic aspects of sustaining the lives of some neonates and other young children, especially when these lives predictably will be characterized by severe mental and physical disabilities. Case discussions in NICUs, PICUs, and specialized chronic care units for young children increasingly have comments and questions by staff physicians, residents, nurses, social workers, and ethicists regarding the costs of the ongoing treatment and who will have to pay for those costs. . . .

. . . [A] factor contributing to uncertainty about the role of economics in neonatal cases pertains to the escalating costs of the care needed by extremely premature or severely disabled newborns. This uncertainty is brought about not only by an awareness of the escalating costs of providing care for these babies, but also by the realization that efforts to provide comparative cost figures for neonatal care have proven less than satisfactory, that the application of diagnosis-related group (DRG) categories has not worked well in NICUs, and that the cost-effectiveness of neonatal care for low-birthweight neonates is still questionable. . . .

Studies published in recent years all document the increasing cost of providing care for disabled neonates and young children in chronic care units. For example, one study from Canada (using 1978 Canadian dollars) found that the costs of intensive care for infants weighing less than 1000 grams averaged $102,500 per survivor. A study from Australia (using 1984 Australian dollars) determined that the total direct cost for level-III, high-dependency care in one hospital was $690 per day. Studies in the United States, varying greatly in methodology,

have found the total cost for selected survivors of neonatal intensive care in a Boston hospital to range from $14,600 to $40,700, for long-term survivors in a Washington, DC, pediatric hospital to be $182,500 for a year, and for extremely low-birthweight survivors of NICUs in six medical centers to range from $72,110 to $524,110, with a mean cost of care per infant of $158,800 for 137 days.

. . . [Another] factor has been the increased recognition that the financial pressures created by expensive neonatal and pediatric treatment can greatly damage and sometimes destroy families. For example, a 1988 Minnesota followup study of disabled infants and their families had a number of disturbing findings: the proportion of families with young children, but lacking health insurance is increasing, 16% of the families in the study pay the entire cost of their health insurance, middle-income families have not qualified for state financial assistance, several of the families have filed for bankruptcy, and at least one family still owes a hospital and physicians over $300,000 for the care of their young child. The report concludes: "Families should not have to lose their homes, mortgage their future, or neglect other children's needs to pay for the care of a chronically ill or disabled child."

A related, but different factor has to do with the long-term costs of providing medical, nursing, and surgical care for severely disabled children who remain in hospitals for months and years. Sometimes called "boarder babies," these children have complicated, chronic medical conditions, are usually dependent on mechanical ventilation and other technological assistance for survival, and frequently come from low-income, single-parent families that simply cannot afford (in terms of money and time) to have the child at home.

If no other institutional home can be arranged (usually because of the cost and technology involved), and if foster parents are not a realistic option, such children may reside for several years in a specialized chronic care unit in the hospital in which they were born. When that happens, the children become living symbols of a "second generation" type of problem brought about by the successes of neonatal intensive care: They are survivors of the NICU, but remain captives of medical technology in an institution that nobody would choose to call home. . . .

Given the uncertainty generated by these variables, what should be done? For two of the ethical positions described earlier, the answer is reasonably simple: revise or ignore the federal regulations, abate life-sustaining treatment more quickly on the basis of (1) parental discretion or (2) projected quality of life for the neonates involved (including the impact of a neonate's later life on others), and thus cut down on the costs in NICUs, to families, and to institutions.

To go that way, for that reason, would be a mistake. The economic aspects of neonatal intensive care would become a dominant factor in decision making by parents and physicians, and many premature and disabled neonates would have their lives cut short to save money. To establish a policy that would encourage parents to make life-and-death decisions in individual cases as a money-saving strategy for themselves (or for physicians to do the same to save money for their hospitals) is not the best policy for addressing the very real problem of escalating costs for neonatal intensive care, especially if that policy is to be guided by the ethical principles of beneficence, nonmaleficence, and justice.

There is, in my judgment, a better alternative. That alternative is a combination of:

1. Continued use of the patient's-best-interests standard in clinical settings, including increased emphasis on the eight variables that comprise the standard;

2. The establishment of a national policy, based on sound clinical evidence, that would restrict the use of neonatal intensive care in terms of infants' birthweights; and

3. The establishment of a national health insurance program that would pay for the catastrophic health-care expenses generated by providing care for extremely premature and severely disabled newborns.

The results of this combined approach would be threefold. A more consistent application of the best-interests standard would result in an increased number of decisions, as difficult as they are, by parents and physicians to discontinue life-sustaining treatment in individual cases. Such decisions would not be made to save money, but would be based on an honest conclusion that the treatment available, although capable of sustaining a neonate's life, is contrary to the infant's best interests.

In addition, the establishment of a national policy that would limit life-sustaining treatment to neonates over a certain birthweight (e.g., 600 grams) would not only cut down on the enormously high costs of caring for extremely low-birthweight infants, but could also be defended, depending on the rationale and details of the policy, as meeting the requirements of justice. Such a policy would surely not solve all of the problems of uncertainty in NICUs, but could provide a measure of greater certainty, if based on a consensus among neonatologists, in establishing a minimum weight limit for neonates who would be given life-sustaining treatment.

Finally, by establishing a national insurance program, the federal government would help pay for the enormous costs that are involved in neonatal intensive care and specialized chronic-care units for young children. For the federal government to mandate that virtually all neonates, unless dying or permanently unconscious, be kept alive, and then to make no serious effort to help parents and institutions pay for that expensive care is unjust. In the absence of such a program, parents and physicians will continue to be faced with the task of making life-and-death decisions for newborns in the midst of great uncertainty—including whether the family will be destroyed financially by costs of the medical care.

Decision Scenario 1 ••

I had been working as a bioethics advisor at University Hospital for three months before I was called in to consult on a pediatrics case. Dr. Savano, the attending obstetrician, asked me to meet with him and Dr. Hinds, one of the staff surgeons, to talk with the father of a newborn girl.

I went to the consulting room with Dr. Savano, and he introduced me and Dr. Hinds to Joel Blake.

From what Dr. Savano had already told me, I knew that Mr. Blake was in his early twenties and worked as a clerk at a discount store called the Bargain Barn. The baby's mother was Hilda Godgeburn, and she and Mr. Blake were not married.

Mr. Blake was very nervous. He knew that the baby had been born just three hours or so before and that Ms. Godgeburn was in very good condition. But Dr. Savano had not told him anything about the baby.

"I'm sorry to have to tell you this," Dr. Savano said. "But the baby was born with severe defects."

"My God," Blake said. "What's the matter?"

"It's a condition called spina bifida," Dr. Savano said. "There's a hole in the baby's back just below the shoulder blades, and some of the nerves from the spine are protruding through it. The baby will have little or no control over her legs, and she won't be able to control her bladder or bowels." Dr. Savano paused to see if Mr. Blake was understanding him. "The legs and feet are also deformed to some extent because of the defective spinal nerves."

Mr. Blake was shaking his head, paying close attention but hardly able to accept what he was being told.

"There's one more thing," Dr. Savano said. "The spinal defect is making the head fill up with liquid from the spinal canal. That's putting pressure on the brain. We can be sure that the brain is already damaged, but if the pressure continues the child will die."

"Is there anything that can be done?" Blake asked. "Anything at all?"

Dr. Savano nodded to Dr. Hinds. "We can do a lot," Dr. Hinds said. "We can drain the fluid from the head, repair the opening in the spine, and later we can operate on the feet and legs."

"Then why aren't you doing it?" Mr. Blake asked. "Do I have to agree to it? If I do, then I agree. Please go ahead."

"It's not that simple," Dr. Hinds said. "You see, we can perform surgery, but that won't turn your baby into a normal child. She will always be paralyzed and mentally retarded. To what extent, we can't say now. Her bodily wastes will have to be drained to the outside by means of artificial devices that we'll have to connect surgically. There will have to be several operations, probably, to get the drain from her head to work properly. A number of operations on her feet will be necessary."

"Oh, God," Mr. Blake said. "Hilda and I can't take it. We don't have enough money for the opera-

tions. And even if we did, we would have to spend the rest of our lives taking care of the child."

"The child could be put into a state institution," Dr. Hinds said.

"That's even worse," Mr. Blake said. "Just handing our problem to somebody else. And what kind of life would she have? A pitiful, miserable life."

None of the rest of us said anything. "You said she would die without the operation to drain her head," Mr. Blake said. "How long would that take?"

"A few hours, perhaps," Dr. Savano said. "But we can't be sure. It may take several days, and conceivably she might not die at all."

"Oh, God," Mr. Blake said again. "I don't want her to suffer. Can she just be put to sleep painlessly?"

Dr. Savano didn't answer the question. He seemed not even to hear it. "We'll have to talk to Ms. Godgeburn also," he said. "And before you make up your mind for good, I want you to talk with the bioethics advisor. You two discuss the matter, and the advisor will perhaps bring out some things you haven't thought about. Dr. Hinds will leave you both together now. Let me know when you've reached your final decision and we'll talk again."

1. *Assume that you are the bioethics advisor in this case. Would you attempt to persuade Mr. Blake that attempts should be made to save the child's life?*

2. *Do you think he is right in asking that the child be painlessly killed? If such killing is not legally permissible, is this relevant to deciding whether the child should be saved if possible? What considerations for and against such an attempt might you mention to help Mr. Blake to reach a decision?*

3. *Are there any arguments in what you have read that seem to you entirely persuasive in such a case?*

4. *What factual considerations (if any) do you consider relevant to resolving the moral issues here?*

5. *Would Robertson, Engelhardt, and Weir all agree that the child should be treated?*

Decision Scenario 2 ••

Brookhaven, as we will call it, is a long-term health-care institution in the Washington metropolitan area. Most of Brookhaven's patients are in resi-

dence there for only a few months; either they succumb to their ailments and die, or they recover sufficiently to return to their homes.

But for some patients death has no immediate likelihood, nor is recovery a possibility. They linger on at Brookhaven, day after day and year after year. Juli Meyers is such a patient, although that is not really her name.

Juli is seventeen and has been in Brookhaven for six years. But before Brookhaven there were other institutions. In fact, Juli has spent most of her life in hospitals and special-care facilities. But Juli does not seem to be aware of any of this.

At Brookhaven she spends her days lying in a bed surrounded with barred metal panels. The bars have been padded with foam rubber. Although most of the time Juli is curled tightly in a fetal position, she sometimes flails around wildly and makes guttural sounds. The padding keeps her from injuring herself.

Juli's body is thin and underdeveloped, with sticklike arms and legs. She is blind and deaf and has no control over her bowels and bladder. She is totally dependent on others to clean her and care for her. She can swallow the food put into her mouth, but she cannot feed herself. She makes no response to the people or events around her.

There is no hope that Juli will walk or talk, laugh or cry, or even show the slightest sign of intelligence or awareness. She is the victim of one of the forms of Schilder's disease. The nerve fibers that make up her central nervous system have mostly degenerated. The cause of the degeneration is not fully known, nor is it known how to halt the process. The condition is irreversible, and Juli will never be better than she is.

At birth Juli seemed perfectly normal and healthy, but at three months she began to lose her sight and hearing. She made the gurgling noises typical of babies less and less frequently. By the end of her first year, she made no sounds at all and was completely blind and deaf. Also, she was losing control of her muscles, and her head lolled on her shoulders, like a doll with a broken neck.

She became highly subject to infections, and more than once she had pneumonia. Once when she was on the critical list, a specialist suggested to her mother that it would be pointless to continue treating her. Even if she recovered from the pneumonia, she would remain hopelessly impaired. Mrs. Meyers angrily rejected the suggestion and insisted that everything possible be done to save Juli's life.

Although not wealthy, the family bore the high cost of hospitalization and treatments. Mrs. Meyers devoted herself almost totally to caring for Juli at home, and the other four children in the family received little of her attention. Eventually, Mrs. Meyers began to suffer from severe depression, and when Juli was eight and a half her parents decided she would have to be placed in an institution. Since then, Juli has changed little. No one expects her to change. Her mother visits her three times a month and brings Juli freshly laundered and ironed clothes.

1. *Would Robertson's arguments support Mrs. Meyers's decision not to allow Juli to die? How might a utilitarian criticize the decision?*

2. *Would treatment for pneumonia in Juli's case be considered "normal medical measures" in the Roman Catholic view?*

3. *Are there any grounds for supposing that Juli is being made to suffer what Engelhardt calls "the injury of continued existence"?*

4. *Would your decision have been the same as Mrs. Meyers's?*

5. *Is it possible to justify using society's limited medical resources to keep Juli alive?*

6. *Evaluate the following argument: Opponents of abortion oppose spending public funds for abortion on the grounds that they (the opponents) are being forced to support murder, which is a serious moral evil. Keeping Juli alive is a serious moral evil. Therefore, no public funds should be used for this purpose.*

Decision Scenario 3 ••

Susan Roth was looking forward to being a mother. She had quit her secretarial job three months before her baby was due so she could spend the time getting everything ready. Her husband, David, was equally enthusiastic, and they spent many hours happily speculating about the way things would be when their baby came. It was their first child.

"I hope they don't mix her up with some other baby," Mrs. Roth said to her husband after delivery. She didn't know yet that there was little chance of confusion. The Roth infant was seriously deformed. Her arms and legs had failed to develop, her skull was misshapen, and her face deformed. Her large intestine emptied through her vagina, and she had no muscular control over her bladder.

When she was told, Mrs. Roth said "We cannot let it live, for her sake and ours." On the day she left the hospital with the child, Mrs. Roth mixed a lethal dose of a tranquilizing drug with the baby's formula and fed it to her. The child died that evening.

Mrs. Roth and her husband were charged with infanticide. During the court proceedings, Mrs. Roth admitted to the killing but said she was satisfied she had done the right thing. "I know I could not let my baby live like that," she said. "If only she had been mentally abnormal, she would not have known her fate. But she had a normal brain. She would have known. Placing her in an in-

stitution might have helped me, but it wouldn't have helped her."

The jury, after deliberating for two hours, found Mrs. Roth and her husband guilty of the charge.

1. Are laws against infanticide unjust?

2. Does the fact that the intelligence of the child is normal support the mother's claim that killing was justifiable? Might normal intelligence make the "injury of continued existence" even greater than subnormal intelligence?

3. Why might Robertson consider the mother's action morally wrong?

4. Would the "best-interest"-of-the-infant standard, as presented by Weir, offer any support for the mother's action?

Decision Scenario 4 ●●

I can't believe God has done this to me, Mike Chovo said to himself. Tears came to his eyes, and his nose started running.

His wife, Carol, handed him a tissue from the box by her bed. "It's all right, Mikey," she said. "We'll make it all right."

Mike wiped his eyes and blew his nose. The yellow tissue struck him as being absurdly cheerful. Given the circumstances, it seemed totally out of place in the hospital room.

"I know," he said. "But it's going to be so hard, so very hard. And it's going to be terrible for Chris and Jan."

"They'll adjust," Carol said. "In some ways it will be good for them to have a brother like Terry. They'll learn somebody doesn't have to be perfect for you to love them."

"Oh, Jesus," Mike said. "Maybe we should have told them not to do anything. He's in such bad shape. The doctors told me they're not sure he has enough of a brain even to learn who we are. I mean, it may be like he's unconscious all of his life."

Mike pulled another tissue out of the box and held it over his eyes. He pressed hard with his fingertips. He wanted Terry to die, but he couldn't tell Carol that. He could barely allow himself to think it. He wished he hadn't given permission for the operation to drain the fluid from Terry's head. But he couldn't oppose Carol at a time like this.

"But we'll love him anyway," Carol said. "We'll take care of him until God calls him away."

"I wonder if we're doing him a favor. I wonder if he's really fit for this world."

"We couldn't just stand by and let him die," Carol said.

"No, I guess we couldn't." Mike hesitated, then went on. "You know, this one operation won't be the end of them. Dr. Flanners told me that it's not unusual to have to operate ten or twelve times in cases like this."

"It's going to be expensive."

"That's right, and I don't know where we're going to get the money."

"We can probably borrow some from my parents. And if we have to, I guess we can get a second mortgage on the house."

"I guess so," Mike admitted.

Carol looked at Mike and smiled at him. After a moment, he smiled back.

1. Would the line of reasoning taken by Robertson tend to support the decision made by Carol Chovo?

2. Might the considerations mentioned by Engelhardt be used to argue that it would have been better for the Chovos to allow their son to die?

3. Does the natural law view require treatment in such a case?

4. *On what grounds might Kantian principles be appealed to in order to justify a decision not to treat Terry Chovo?*

5. *In what ways, if any, are such considerations as the financial status of the Chovos and the likely influence on the other two children of having a wholly dependent and impaired brother relevant to the decision that faced the parents?*

6. *Would the "best-interest" standard discussed by Weir provide grounds for justifying a decision to withhold medical treatment?*

Decision Scenario 5 •••

Irene Towers had been a nurse for almost twelve years; for the last three of those years she had worked in the Neonatal Unit of Halifax County Hospital. It was a job she loved. Even when the infants were ill or required special medical or surgical treatment, she found the job of caring for them immensely rewarding. She knew that without her efforts many of the babies would simply die.

Irene Towers was on duty the night that Siamese twins were born to Corrine Couchers and brought at once to the Neonatal Unit. Even Irene, with all her experience, was distressed to see them. The twin boys were joined at their midsections in a way that made it impossible to separate them surgically. Because of the position of the single liver and the kidneys, not even one twin could be saved at the expense of the life of the other. Moreover, both children were severely deformed, with incompletely developed arms and legs and misshapen heads. As best as the neurologist could determine, both suffered severe brain damage.

The father of the children was Dr. Harold Couchers. Dr. Couchers, a slightly built man in his early thirties, was a specialist in internal medicine with a private practice.

Irene felt sorry for him the night the children were born. When he went into the room with the obstetrician to examine his sons, he had already been told what to expect. He showed no signs of grief as he stood over the slat-sided crib, but the corners of his mouth were drawn tight, and his face was almost unnaturally empty of expression. Most strange for a physician, Irene thought, he merely looked at the children and did not touch them. She was sure that in some obscure way he must be blaming himself for what had happened to them.

Later that evening, Irene saw Dr. Couchers sitting in the small conference room at the end of the hall with Dr. Cara Rosen, Corrine Couchers's obstetrician. They were talking earnestly and quietly when Irene passed the open door. Then, while she was looking over the assignment sheet at the nursing station, the two of them walked up. Dr. Rosen took a chart from the rack behind the desk and made a notation. After returning the chart, she shook hands with Dr. Couchers, and he left.

It was not until the end of her shift that Irene read the chart; Dr. Rosen's note said that the twin boys were to be given neither food nor water. At first Irene couldn't believe the order. But when she asked her supervisor, she was told that the supervisor had telephoned Dr. Rosen and that the obstetrician had confirmed the order.

Irene said nothing to the supervisor or to anyone else, but she made her own decision. She believed it was wrong to let the children die, particularly in such a horrible way. They deserved every chance to fight for their lives, and she was going to help them the way she had helped hundreds of other babies in the unit.

For the next week and a half, Irene saw to it that the children were given water and fed the standard infant formula. She did it all herself, on her own initiative. Although some of the other nurses on the floor saw what she was doing, none of them said anything to her. One even smiled and nodded to her when she saw Irene feeding the children.

Apparently someone else also disapproved of the order to let the twins die. Thirteen days after their birth, an investigator from the state Family Welfare Agency appeared in the neonatal ward. The rumor was that his visit had been prompted by an anonymous telephone call.

Late in the afternoon of the day of that visit, the deformed twins were made temporary wards of the Agency, and the orders on the chart were changed—the twins were now to be given food and water. On the next day, the county prosecutor's office announced publicly that it would conduct an investigation of the situation and decide whether criminal charges should be brought against Dr. Couchers or members of the hospital staff.

Irene was sure that she had done the right thing. Nevertheless, she was glad to be relieved of the responsibility.

1. *Might a utilitarian argument be offered in defense of Dr. Couchers's decision to allow the twins to die?*

2. *What criticism of such an argument might Robertson offer?*

3. *Is there a morally relevant distinction between not treating (and allowing to die) and not providing such minimal needs as food and water (and allowing to die)?*

4. *Does Engelhardt's line of reasoning support the action taken by Irene Towers?*

5. *Did Irene Towers exceed the limits of her responsibility, or did she act in a morally heroic way?*

6. *Federal regulations require that impaired infants be given food and water, even if medical treatment can justifiably be withheld. Are .there any moral grounds for making the distinction between treatment and nutritional support?*

Decision Scenario 6 ··

Dr. Daniel McKay and his wife, Carol, had only a few moments of joy at the birth of their son. They learned almost immediately that the child was severely impaired. Half an hour later, the infant was dead—Dr. McKay, a veterinarian, had slammed him onto the floor of the delivery room.

Mrs. McKay had had problems during pregnancy. An ultrasound test indicated excessive fluid in the uterus, a sign that something might be wrong. Dr. Joaquin Ramos assured the McKays that everything was all right and that the pregnancy should continue. On June 27, 1983, he ordered Mrs. McKay admitted to the Markham, Illinois, hospital so that labor could be induced.

"Don't do any heroic measures," Dr. McKay told Dr. Ramos when Dr. McKay learned that the infant was impaired. Dr. Ramos explained that that was not his choice, for hospital policy required that everything possible be done for babies, even ones like the McKay baby that might not live more than a few months. The child had webbed fingers, heart and lung malfunctions, and missing testicles. It was suspected that the child also had a genetic disorder that might mean kidney malfunctions, mental retardation, and death within months.

Dr. McKay smashed the infant's head against the floor several times, splattering the wall and floor with brain tissue and blood. "Dan, what have you done?" a nurse shouted. Dr. McKay later said that while holding the child he asked himself "Can I accept and love this child, or would it be better off dead?" He had just talked to his wife. "I said to Dan, 'Is it a boy or a girl?' He said it was a little boy.

I said, 'Oh, Dan, we got our boy!' Dan really wasn't saying anything. He had tears in his eyes." She then realized that the baby was not crying and asked her husband to go see what was wrong.

Dr. McKay was charged with murder. Two defense psychiatrists testified that he had been temporarily insane. Two others said that he had succumbed to stress. A prosecution psychiatrist said that he was legally sane but that "he made a decision that he had a moral imperative to do what he did." The jury could not agree whether Dr. McKay was guilty, not guilty, guilty but not mentally ill, or not guilty by reason of insanity. A mistrial was declared, but another trial was scheduled.

1. *How might the hospital policy of "doing everything possible" for all impaired infants be criticized in terms of the "best-interest" standard presented by Weir?*

2. *Would any of the authors here endorse such a policy? If so, on what grounds?*

3. *Would the McKay infant count as a potential person according to Weir? How does the potential personhood of the infant affect the decision whether or not to withhold treatment?*

4. *Might one argue that Dr. McKay's action was morally right, whether or not it was legally justifiable?*

5. *Under what conditions, if any, ought the parents of an impaired infant be allowed to decide how the child is to be treated?*

Decision Scenario 7 ••

On February 8, 1984, Traci Messenger had an emergency Caesarean section at the E. W. Sparrow Hospital in East Lansing, Michigan, and her son, Michael, was delivered after only a twenty-five-week gestation period—fifteen weeks prematurely. Michael weighed 1 pound, 11 ounces, was very likely to have serious brain damage, and was given a 30% to 50% chance of survival.

Before Traci Messenger's surgery, Michael's father, Dr. Gregory Messenger, a dermatologist on the staff of the hospital, had spoken with his wife's physicians and requested that no extraordinary measures be taken to prolong the child's life. However, after the child was born, the neonatologist, Dr. Padmoni Karna insisted that the baby be given respiratory support and diagnostic tests.

About an hour after Michael was delivered, Dr. Messenger went into the child's room and asked the nurses to leave. He then disconnected the life-support system, setting off an alarm. The child died, and the hospital called the police. A short time later, the county prosecutor, Donald E. Martin, charged Dr. Messenger with manslaughter.

Although most states, including Michigan, allow parents to decide to withdraw life support from their ailing child, Mr. Martin said he had decided to prosecute, because Dr. Messenger had not waited for the results of medical tests. "The father appeared to make a unilateral decision to end life for his infant son," Mr. Martin said.

Dr. Messenger's attorney replied that Dr. Messenger had several warnings of severe medical problems during delivery and immediately after birth. Monitoring of the baby suggested that he was not receiving sufficient oxygen and would be severely brain damaged. Blood tests at birth indicated that the baby had a 14% level of oxygen, and as a physician testified at a preliminary hearing, five minutes at a less than 50% level is enough to damage the brain. "The parents made a decision when the outcome was so grim and the prognosis was so bad they indicated 'we do not want this intervention.' I think it was incumbent on hospital personnel to honor their directive, and they didn't do that."

Dr. Karna said that she would have agreed to removing the life support, given the blood-test results, but that Dr. Messenger had acted without consulting her.

1. *Might Michael Messenger be considered likely to suffer "the injury of continued existence"?*

2. *Robertson would claim that the infant should be treated. On what grounds might he support this claim?*

3. *Would the infant be a potential person according to Weir's standards?*

4. *Suppose that after the test results the parents and Dr. Karna disagreed as to whether the infant should be treated. Whose opinion should be decisive?*

5. *Would Weir's criteria for determining the "best interest" of the infant be of help in resolving a conflict between the Messengers and Dr. Karna?*

CHAPTER 3

EUTHANASIA

SOCIAL CONTEXT:
DR. KEVORKIAN AND
PHYSICIAN-ASSISTED SUICIDE

On August 5, 1993, Thomas W. Hyde Jr., a thirty-year-old Michigan construction worker with a wife and a two-year-old daughter, was taken inside a battered white 1968 Volkswagen bus parked behind the apartment building in the Detroit suburb of Royal Oak where sixty-five-year-old retired pathologist Dr. Jack Kevorkian lived.

Dr. Kevorkian fitted a respiratory mask over Mr. Hyde's face and connected the plastic tubing leading from the mask to a short cylinder of carbon monoxide gas. Dr. Kevorkian placed a string in Mr. Hyde's hand. At the opposite end of the string was a paper clip crimping the plastic tubing and shutting off the flow of gas. Mr. Hyde jerked on the string, pulled loose the paper clip, then breathed in the carbon monoxide flowing into the mask. Twenty minutes later, Mr. Hyde was dead.

Mr. Hyde suffered from amyotrophic lateral sclerosis (Lou Gehrig's disease), a degenerative and progressive neurological disorder. Mr. Hyde was paralyzed, unable even to swallow, and without suctioning, he would have choked to death on his own saliva. He reported that he was in great pain, and like hundreds before him, he approached Dr. Kevorkian to help him end his life.

In a videotape made on July 1, 1993, Mr. Hyde said to Dr. Kevorkian, "I want to end this. I want to die." Dr. Kevorkian agreed to help, and Mr. Hyde became the twentieth person since 1990 whom Dr. Kevorkian assisted in committing suicide.

After the death of Mr. Hyde, Dr. Kevorkian was arrested and charged with violating the 1992 Michigan law that had been enacted specifically to stop his activities. The law applies to anyone who knows that another person intends to commit suicide and either "provides the physical means" or "participates in a physical act" by which the suicide is carried out. However, the law explicitly excludes those administering medications or procedures that may cause death, "if the intent is to relieve pain or discomfort."

On May 2, 1994, a jury found that Dr. Kevorkian was innocent of the charge of assisting suicide. As one juror said publicly, "He convinced us he was not a murderer, that he was really trying to help people out." According to another, Dr. Kevorkian had acted to relieve Mr. Hyde's pain, and that is an action allowed by the law.

Several jurors expressed skepticism and resentment at the attempt to legislate behavior falling within such a private sphere. "I don't feel it's our obligation to choose for someone else how much pain and suffering they can go through," one said. "That's between them and their God."

After the decision was made, Dr. Kevorkian reiterated his often-stated position that people have a right to decide when to end their lives. He acted, he said, to protect that right. "I want that option as I get older, and I want it unencumbered, unintimidated, free with my medical colleagues," he said. "So I did it for myself, too, just as any competent adult would want to do."

The Patient Self-Determination Act requires hospitals to inform patients that they have the right to refuse or discontinue treatment and that by living wills and powers of attorney for health care, they can put their decisions into practice. The Supreme Court in the *Cruzan* decision implicitly acknowledges a "right to die," in that it permits the withdrawal of life-sustaining treatment when clear and compelling evidence shows that this reflects the wishes of an individual.

Despite the legal possibility of exercising control over medical care during the last stages of one's life, various barriers stand in the way of actual control:

- Surveys of physicians and health-care workers show that many are not aware of the legal options open to patients or are not willing to respect them. Many in health care are not aware of laws that allow them to withhold or discontinue such care as mechanical ventilation, kidney dialysis, or even feeding tubes. Many believe that once a treatment has been started, it is illegal to discontinue it. Courts have repeatedly upheld the right of individuals to decide that, at a certain point in their treatment, they do not want to be provided with food or water, yet 42% of health-care workers rejected this as an option patients could choose.

- The living wills or powers of attorney made out by patients may have no force because they are not included among the documents constituting a patient's medical chart. In one study, when 71 patients were moved to a nursing home, 25 of them had living wills that were not sent with them. As a result, patients may be forced to accept decisions about their care made by physicians or nurses in accordance with their own values or institutional policies.

- Families may override the wishes expressed by patients in their living wills. Even though the views of the patient take legal precedence over those of a relative, in practice a physician or hospital may do as the relative wishes. Families never sue because of the overtreatment of a patient, but they do because of withholding or discontinuing treatment.

Against this background of practice, it is not surprising that many people still believe that they cannot count on physicians and hospitals to follow their directives. When it comes to dying, most people want to do it quickly and painlessly and not be kept alive beyond the point of hope for a decent life by drugs, machines, and surgery. Some wish to exercise control over their lives to the point of deciding when to end it, but they also realize that they may need help ending it, if they are to exit the way they wish. They would like to have the assistance of a physician, and it is this group that Kevorkian says he wishes to help.

Kevorkian has always insisted that he practices physician-assisted suicide only in accordance with stringent safeguards. "You act only after it is absolutely justifiable," he says. "The patient must be mentally competent, the disease incurable." He maintains that other physicians should determine that a candidate for assisted suicide is incurable and that a psychiatrist should assess the patient's mental state and determine that he or she is competent. In practice, however, Kevorkian himself has not proceeded in this fashion, because other physicians have refused to cooperate with him.

Critics of Kevorkian charge that without the safeguard of a psychiatric evaluation, patients who seek him out to help them kill themselves are likely to be suffering from depression. Hence, they cannot be regarded as having made an informed, rational decision to end their lives.

Other opponents of Kevorkian worry that, if physicians are allowed to play a role in terminating the lives of patients, that role could expand. That is, physicians may begin by assisting those who ask their help, but they may then move on to making their own decisions about who should live or they may be recruited to carry out a government policy identifying those who should be "assisted" in dying. The potential for abuse is so serious that physicians should not be associated in any way with procedures intended to end the lives of patients.

Finally, some critics, though disagreeing with Kevorkian, believe that he has pointed out a major flaw in the health-care system—the medical profession is so committed to preserving life that it has not developed ways of dealing with death in cases in which it is inevitable. Rather than help people kill themselves, critics say, physicians ought to surrender the idea of treatment and concentrate on making those with terminal illnesses pain free so that they may spend their remaining time enjoying the comfort of their families and friends.

Hospitals and other institutions have set up hospices to provide nursing care and support for the dying. So far, however, hospices have not become an accepted part of the medical establishment, and physicians associated with them are given little respect by their colleagues.

The extent of the desire that people have to exercise control over how their lives end is shown by the astonishing popularity of Derek Humphry's best-selling *Final Exit*. The book is a handbook of effective methods for committing suicide or as the subtitle puts it, the book is about "The Practicalities of Self-Deliverance and Assisted Suicide for the Dying." Journalist Betty Rollins's foreword to the book describes the hundreds of letters she received from people who read her book, *Last Wish*, on her mother's suicide because of a terminal illness. The saddest of the letters, she said, were from those who had tried to die, failed in their attempt, and suffered even more as a result. "Until there is a law which would allow physicians to help these people who want a final exit, there is Derek Humphry's book, fittingly named, to guide them."

More than twenty states currently have laws against assisted suicide, but over the last few years people have indicated in various ways that they are not wholly opposed to having physicians help patients end their lives. In California, an effort was made to place a voluntary euthanasia proposal on the November 1988 ballot. The "Humane and Dignified Death Act" would have allowed terminally ill patients to execute a directive authorizing a physician to assist them in dying "by any medical procedure that will terminate the life . . . swiftly, painlessly, and humanely." The proposal was sponsored by Americans Against Human Suffering and the Hemlock Society, organizations favoring making voluntary euthanasia an individual option. The act was opposed by the California Nurses Association and the California Medical Association. The proposal failed to get enough signatures to get on the ballot.

A Washington State initiative that was substantially the same as the one in California received enough support to make it to the ballot. Although the proposal was defeated at the polls, it managed to win 46% of the votes cast. Such a strong showing is evidence that the issue of physician-assisted suicide is not going to go away. (For the Dutch experience with the practice, see the Introduction to this chapter.) Various polls suggest that nearly a majority of the American people favor a policy of voluntary physician-assisted suicide, and in cases less well known than the Kevorkian case, in which physicians have been charged with aiding the death of their patients, they have typically been found not guilty or been given suspended sentences.

Oregon's 1994 "Written Request for Medication to End One's Life in a Humane and Dignified Manner" is the first physician-suicide measure passed by any state. The measure does not permit a physician to play a role in ending a patient's life that is anything like the one played by Dr. Kevorkian. The major accomplishment of the measure is to allow physicians to prescribe lethal drugs for terminally ill patients without risking criminal prosecution.

The law spells out a set of conditions that must be followed by patients and physicians:

1. A primary-care physician and a consulting physician must both agree that the patient has six months or less to live.

2. The patient must make two oral requests (at least forty-eight hours apart) for drugs to use to terminate his or her life.

3. The patient must wait at least fifteen days after the initial oral request, then make a written request to the physician.

4. If either physician thinks the patient has a mental disorder or is suffering from impaired judgment from depression, they must recommend the patient for counseling.

5. The patient can terminate the request at any time during the process.

Under the Oregon law, the physician is not permitted to assist a patient to die by any means more active than prescribing a medication that can cause death and indicating the manner in which it can be used.

The law in Oregon passed by the slight margin of 52% to 48% of the vote. Immediately after it was clear that the law had passed, it was challenged in court.

CASE PRESENTATION
Elizabeth Bouvia's Demand to Starve

On September 3, 1983, Elizabeth Bouvia was admitted, at her own request, to Riverside General Hospital in Riverside, California. She sought admission on the grounds that she was suicidal. She was twenty-six years old, a victim of cerebral palsy, and almost totally paralyzed. She had the partial use of one arm, could speak, and could chew her food if someone fed it to her. In addition to her paralysis, she suffered almost constant pain from arthritis.

Despite the severity of her handicap, Mrs. Bouvia had earned a degree in social work, been married, and lived independently with the assistance of relatives and others. Then matters became particularly difficult for her. She had not been successful in an attempt to have a child, her husband left her, and she lost the state grant that paid for her special transportation needs.

After her admission, Mrs. Bouvia announced to the hospital staff that she wished to starve herself to death. She asked to be provided with hygienic care and pain-killing medicines but no food. She explained that she wanted the hospital to be a place where she would "just be left alone and not bothered by friends or family or anyone else" so that she could "ultimately starve to death" and be free from her "useless body."

Mrs. Bouvia refused to eat the solid food offered to her, and her attending physician declared that, if she did not eat, he would have her declared mentally ill and a danger to herself. She could then be force-fed. She responded by calling local newspapers and asking for legal assistance. The American Civil Liberties Union agreed to provide her an attorney, and Richard Stanley Scott became her legal representative.

Mr. Scott convinced her to allow herself to be fed while he made efforts to secure a court order restraining the hospital from either discharging her or force-feeding her. At the court hearing, Mrs. Bouvia testified as to her reasons for refusing nourishment:

I hate to have someone care for every personal need . . . it's humiliating. It's disgusting, and I choose to no longer do that, no longer to be dependent on someone to take care of me in that manner. . . . I am choosing this course of action due to my physical limitation and disability.

Dr. Donald E. Fisher, head of psychiatry at the hospital, testified that he would force-feed Mrs. Bouvia, even if the court ordered him not to.

On behalf of his client, Mr. Scott argued that her decision to refuse nourishment was "exactly medically and morally analogous to the patient deciding to forgo further kidney dialysis," knowingly accepting death as the consequence.

Judge John H. Hews refused to grant the restraining order. He expressed the view that Mrs. Bouvia was a competent, rational, and sincere person whose decision was based on her physical condition and not upon her recent misfortunes. Nevertheless, allowing her to starve herself to death in the hospital would "have a profound effect" on the staff, other patients, and other handicapped people. Mrs. Bouvia, Judge Hews held, was "not terminal" and might expect to live another fifteen to twenty years. Accordingly, he held that "the established ethics of the medical profession clearly outweigh and overcome her own rights of self-determination," and "forced feeding, however invasive, would be administered for the purpose of saving the life of an otherwise nonterminal patient and should be permitted. There is no other reasonable option." In effect, in Judge Hews's view, Mrs. Bouvia had a right to commit suicide, but she did not have the right to have others assist her.

Mrs. Bouvia later refused to eat, and Judge Hews authorized the hospital to feed her against her will. Her attorney argued that this was an unlawful invasion of her privacy and appealed to the California Supreme Court. The court unanimously refused to grant a hearing on the appeal, thus allowing the lower court ruling to stand.

In February 1986, Mrs. Bouvia was back in court. Through her attorney, she sought an injunction to stop High Desert Hospital of Lancaster, California, where she had become a patient, from using a nasogastric tube to feed her against her wishes. In a public statement, she asserted that she had no intention to attempt to starve herself to death but wished only to receive a liquid diet. The hospital's physicians and lawyers maintained that a liquid diet would be a form of starvation and that the law precluded them from agreeing to her demand. The eventual court decision was again in favor of Mrs. Bouvia, and in April the feeding tube was removed.

However, Mrs. Bouvia eventually decided she would begin to eat voluntarily. The hospital resumed feeding her, and, when her health was considered stable once more, she was released. She announced at that time that she had changed her mind about dying, but in 1987 she again reversed herself. She tried starving herself to death but gave up the effort when she was told it might take several weeks. She felt she could not endure such side effects as the constant vomiting caused by taking pain-killing medications without food. "Starving myself would take too long," she said. "I wish there were a quicker way."

She moved to Los Angeles and for the past several years has lived in a small cell-like room at the Los Angeles County-USC Medical Center. The cost of the room, more than $800 a day, is paid for by MediCal.

Her father and two sisters visit her from out of state a couple of times a year, and various friends visit about once a week. Mostly, though, she just lies in her bed and watches TV. "The thought of being here another ten years, I just can't fathom," she says. "I would rather be dead than lie here."

CASE PRESENTATION
The Death of J. K. Collums

On November 16, 1981, sixty-nine-year-old Woodrow Collums went into the Oak Hills Care Center in the small town of Poteet, Texas, to visit his seventy-two-year-old brother, J. K. Collums. J. K. was a victim of Alzheimer's disease, a poorly understood illness in which the brain undergoes progressive degeneration. J. K. had already reached the point of being unable to care for any of his bodily needs, and he could no longer speak or respond to others. A nasogastric tube fed him the nutrients needed to keep him alive.

"I just stood there and looked at him a few minutes," Woody Collums said about his brother. "He was beyond saying anything to me. So I left and went back to the car, thinking I'd just go on and let the Lord take care of it. But I got to the car, and this gun was in the car."

Mr. Collums decided to shoot his brother and he took the gun back into the room. But once there, he changed his mind. "So I started to leave, and I looked back at him, and I just couldn't go off and leave him like that. I turned around and shot him five times, just as fast as I could shoot him. He never moved. He was the most peaceful-looking guy you've ever seen."

Mr. Collums then checked his brother's pulse to be sure that he was dead. He put the pistol down on a bedside tray and waited for someone to call the police. While waiting, he said to a staff member "I've killed horses, cows, and dogs that were suffering. He's suffered long enough."

Mr. Collums freely admitted shooting his brother, but he refused to acknowledge that he had murdered him. "I feel like he's been dead since he's been in this condition," he said.

A Bexar County, Texas, grand jury indicted Mr. Collums for the shooting of his brother. But even the county prosecutors regarded the action as a clear case of mercy killing. The two brothers had been very close all their lives, and, although J. K. Collums had not signed an actual "living will," which is legal in Texas, he had written a letter to his physician in which he expressed his views about being kept alive by extraordinary means. According to J. K. Collums's wife, Helen, he said that "if they couldn't do something to help his brain, to please put him to sleep forever." The letter was written before the disease had progressed to the point that he was no longer able to reason and communicate.

When asked if she blamed her brother-in-law for his actions, Helen Collums said "Oh, no! God, no, no!" She went on to say "I thank God Jim's out of his misery. I hate to think it had to be done the way it was done, but I understand it. I couldn't ever have shot him. I could have asked for the life sup-

ports to be taken away, because I don't believe in life supports. I just think it's cruelty for someone who's terminally ill, to stuff a tube down his nose from May to November. That's agony and cruelty. People don't know about these things. I just hope it helps somebody else, so they don't have to go through what he went through."

Helen Collums now believes she should not have allowed the stomach tube to be put into place. But, once it had been, other members of the family refused to allow it to be removed. They thought removing it would constitute murder. Besides, it was not clear that the nursing home would agree to its removal. Court decisions allow the removal of support systems that are "extraordinary means" of prolonging life when the patient has "clearly and convincingly" rejected the use of such means beforehand. But is a feeding tube "extraordinary"?

Woodrow Collums received much public sympathy, but not everyone approved of his action. Theresa Brock, the administrator of the Oak Hills Care Center, expressed the opposition view. "None of us knows," she said, "and nobody here can tell you, nobody on this earth can tell you, what Jim was able to feel, or perceive, or think or know, and it's not up to any of us to end somebody's life for them."

Everyone agreed that J. K. Collums could still recognize his wife and could still pucker his lips as if to kiss her. He did just that on the day that he died.

In February of 1982, Woodrow Collums pleaded guilty to a charge of murder. He waived a jury trial, and at a punishment hearing he told Judge Tom Rickhoff about what he had done. Mr. Collums said of his brother "He looked like he was just begging me to get him out of his misery. I regret having to do what I did, but I don't regret doing it. I felt he would have done it himself if he could have."

Mr. Collums's lawyer, Roy Barrera, expressed the hope that the hearing would help people understand the need for euthanasia. "If we can do mercy killings for animals to relieve pain and suffering," he said, "I just can't see where under the proper conditions a human being would be given any less than what we give animals."

Judge Rickhoff was faced with the decision of whether to send Mr. Collums to jail or to put him on probation. On March 4, Judge Rickhoff ruled that Mr. Collums was to be placed on probation for a period of ten years. During that time, he would be required to spend ten hours each week working at homes for the elderly.

SOCIAL CONTEXT: THE CRUZAN CASE: THE SUPREME COURT UPHOLDS A RIGHT TO DIE

In the early morning of January 11, 1983, twenty-five-year-old Nancy Cruzan was driving on a deserted county road in Missouri. The road was icy and the car skidded, then flipped over and crashed. Nancy Cruzan was thrown from the driver's seat and landed face down in a ditch by the side of the road.

An ambulance arrived quickly, but not quickly enough to save her from suffering irreversible brain damage. Nancy Cruzan never regained consciousness, and her physicians eventually concluded that she had entered into what is known medically as a persistent vegetative state, awake but unaware. The higher brain functions responsible for recognition, memory, comprehension, anticipation, and other cognitive functions had all been lost.

Her arms and legs were drawn into a fetal position, her knees against her chest, and her body stiff and contracted. Only loud sounds and painful stimuli evoked responses, but even those were no more than neurological reflexes.

"We've literally cried over Nancy's body, and we've never seen anything," her father, Joe Cruzan, said. "She has no awareness of herself."

Nancy Cruzan was incapable of eating, but her body was sustained by a feeding tube surgically implanted in her stomach. She was a patient at the Missouri Rehabilitation Center, but no one expected her to be rehabilitated. She could only be kept alive.

"If only the ambulance had arrived five minutes earlier—or five minutes later," her father lamented.

The cost of Nancy Cruzan's care was $130,000 a year. The bill was paid by the state. Because she was a legal adult when her accident occurred, her family was not responsible for her medical care. Had she been under twenty-one, the Cruzans would have been responsible for her medical bills, as long as they had any financial resources to pay them.

In 1991 Nancy Cruzan was thirty-two years old. Her physicians estimated that she might live another thirty years. She was like some 10,000 other Americans at any given time. They are lost in a dark, dimensionless limbo that lies between living and dying. Those who love them can think of them only with sadness and despair. Given a choice between lingering in this twilight world and dying, most people find it difficult to imagine that some might choose not to die.

Hope eventually faded for Nancy Cruzan's parents. They faced the fact that she would never recover her awareness, and the time came when they wanted their daughter to die, rather than be kept alive in her hopeless condition. They asked that the feeding tube used to keep Nancy alive be withdrawn. Officials at the Missouri Rehabilitation Center refused, and Joe and Louise Cruzan were forced to go to court.

During the court hearings, the family testified that Nancy would not have wanted to be kept alive in her present condition. Her sister Christy said Nancy had told her that she never wanted to be kept alive "just as a vegetable." A friend also testified that Nancy had said that if she were injured or sick she wouldn't want to continue her life, unless she could live "half-way normally." Family and friends spoke in general terms of Nancy's vigor and her sense of independence.

In July 1988, Charles E. Teel of the Jasper County Circuit Court ruled that artificially prolonging the life of Nancy Cruzan violated her constitutional right. As he wrote, "There is a fundamental right expressed in our Constitution as 'the right to liberty,' which permits an individual to refuse or direct the withholding or withdrawal of artificial death-prolonging procedures when the person has no cognitive brain function."

Missouri Attorney General William Webster said that Judge Teel's interpretation of the Missouri living-will law was much broader than the legislature intended. Acting on behalf of the state, Webster appealed the ruling to the state supreme court.

In November 1988, the Missouri Supreme Court in a 4-to-3 decision overruled the decision of the lower court—Nancy Cruzan's parents would not be allowed to disconnect the feeding tube.

The court focused on the state's living-will statute. The law permits the withdrawing of artificial life-support systems in cases in which individuals are hopelessly ill or injured and there is "clear and convincing evidence" that this is what they would want done. The act specifically forbids the withholding of food and water. Judge Teel's reasoning in the lower court decision was that the surgically implanted tube was an invasive medical treatment that the Missouri law permitted her parents, as guardians, to order withdrawn.

The Missouri Supreme Court held that the evidence as to what Nancy Cruzan would have wanted did not meet the "clear and convincing" standard required by the law. In addition, the evidence did not show that the implanted feeding tube was "heroically invasive" or "burdensome." In the circumstance, then, the state's interest in preserving life should override other considerations.

In the words of the decision, the court found "no principled legal basis" to permit the Cruzans "to choose the death of their ward." In the absence of such a basis, "and in the face of the state's strongly stated policy in favor of life, we choose to err on the side of life, respecting the right of incompetent persons who may wish to live despite a severely diminished quality of life."

The Cruzans' attorney, William Colby, appealed the ruling to the United States Supreme Court. For the first time the Court agreed to hear a case involving "right to die" issues. On June 25, 1990, the Court issued what is considered a landmark ruling. In a 5-to-4 decision, the Court rejected Colby's argument that the Court should reject as unconstitutional the State of Missouri's stringent standard requiring "clear and convincing evidence" as to a comatose patient's wishes. This meant that Nancy Cruzan's parents had lost their case.

Despite the cruel disappointment of the Cruzans, the Court acknowledged for the first time a strong constitutional basis for living wills and for the designation of another person to act as a surrogate in making medical decisions on behalf of another. Unlike the decisions in *Roe v. Wade* and *Quinlan,* which found a right of privacy in the Constitution, the Court decision in *Cruzan* appealed to a Fourteenth Amendment "liberty interest." The interest involves being free to reject unwanted medical treatment. The Court found grounds for this interest in the common-law tradition, according to which, if one person even touches another without consent or legal justification, then battery is committed.

The Court regarded this as the basis for requiring that a patient give informed consent to medical treatment. The "logical corollary" of informed consent, the Court held, is that the patient also possesses the right to withhold consent. A difficulty arises, though, when a patient is in no condition to give consent. The problem becomes one of knowing what the patient's wishes would be.

Rehnquist, in the majority opinion, held that the Constitution permits states to decide on the standard that must be met in determining the wishes of a comatose patient. Hence, Missouri's rigorous standard that requires "clear and convincing proof" of the wishes of the patient was allowed to stand. The Court held that it was legitimate for the state to err on the side of caution, "because an erroneous decision not to terminate treatment results in the maintenance of the status quo," while an erroneous decision to end treatment "is not susceptible of correction."

Justice William Brennan dissented strongly from this line of reasoning. He pointed out that making a mistake about a comatose patient's wishes and continuing treatment also has a serious consequence. Maintaining the status quo "robs a patient of the very qualities protected by the right to avoid unwanted medical treatment."

Justice Stevens, in another dissenting opinion, argued that the Court's focus on how much weight to give previous statements by the patient missed the point. The Court should have focused on the issue of the best interest of the patient. Otherwise, the only people who are eligible to exercise their constitutional right to be free of unwanted medical treatment are those "who had the foresight to make an unambiguous statement of their wishes while competent."

One of the more significant aspects of the decision was that the Court made no distinction between providing nutrition and hydration and other forms of medical treatment. One argument on behalf of the state was that providing food and water was not medical treatment. However, briefs filed by medical associations made it clear that determining the formula required by a person in Nancy Cruzan's condition and regulating her feeding are medically complex procedures. The situation is more comparable to determining the contents of an intravenous drip than to giving someone food and water.

The Missouri living-will statute explicitly forbids the withdrawal of food and water. However, the law was not directly at issue in the Cruzan case, because Nancy Cruzan's accident occurred before the law was passed. The Court's treatment of nutrition and hydration as just another form of medical treatment is expected to serve as a basis for challenging the constitutionality of the Missouri law, as well as laws in several other states containing a similar provision.

The Court decision placed much emphasis on the wishes of the individual in accepting or rejecting medical treatment. In doing so,

it underscored the importance of the living will as a way of indicating our wishes, if something should happen to render us incapable of making them known directly. In some states, though, living wills have a legal force only when the individual has a terminal illness (Nancy Cruzan did not) or when the individual has been quite specific about what treatments are unwanted. (As noted above, in some states a directive rejecting nourishment and hydration is not legally enforceable.) Because of such limitations, some legal observers recommend that individuals sign a durable power of attorney designating someone to make medical decisions for them if they become legally incompetent.

The Court decision left undecided the question of the constitutionality of what is sometimes called assisted suicide. Some state courts have held that, although individuals have a right to die, they do not have a right to the assistance of others in killing themselves. (See the Elizabeth Bouvia Case Presentation.) Some AIDS advocates have been particularly concerned with making it legal for the medical profession to provide people with AIDS who wish it a means of dying quickly at a certain time, rather than lingering and suffering until the end.

What of Nancy Cruzan? The State of Missouri withdrew from the case, and both the family's attorney and the state-appointed guardian filed separate briefs with the Jasper County Circuit Court asking that the implanted feeding tube be removed. A hearing was held to consider both her medical condition and evidence from family and friends about what Nancy Cruzan would wish to be done. On December 14, 1990, Judge Charles Teel ruled that there was evidence to show that her intent, "if mentally able, would be to terminate her nutrition and hydration," and he authorized the request to remove the feeding tube.

Even after the tube was removed, controversy did not end. About twenty-five protesters tried to force their way into Nancy

Cruzan's hospital room to reconnect the feeding tube. "The best we can do is not cooperate with anyone trying to starve an innocent person to death," one of the protest leaders said.

Twelve days after the tube was removed, on December 26, 1990, Nancy Cruzan died. Her parents, sisters, and grandparents were at her bedside. Almost eight years had passed since the accident that destroyed her brain and made the remainder of her life a matter of debate.

"We all feel good that Nancy is free at last," her father said at her graveside.

William Webster, Missouri's Attorney General, urged the state legislature to pass a bill that would alter the existing living-will statute. The new bill would provide a remedy in a case in which a patient has been in a "persistent oblivious state" for thirty-six months, three physicians have agreed there is no hope of recovery, and family members agree that extraordinary measures should be ended.

The bill would also weaken the current standard of proof concerning a patient's wishes from "clear and convincing evidence" to "a preponderance of evidence." According to its usual legal interpretation, this standard requires more evidence for a particular claim than against it.

The *Cruzan* decision, by acknowledging a "right to die" and by finding a basis for it in the Constitution, provides states with new opportunities to resolve the issues surrounding the thousands of cases as sad and tragic as Nancy Cruzan's.

CASE PRESENTATION
Karen Quinlan

At two in the morning on Tuesday, April 14, 1975, Mrs. Julie Quinlan was awakened by a telephone call. When she hung up she was crying. "Karen is very sick," Mrs. Quinlan said to her husband, Joseph. "She's unconscious, and we have to go to Newton Hospital right away."

The Quinlans thought that their twenty-one-year-old adopted daughter might have been in an automobile accident. But the doctor in the intensive care unit told them that wasn't so. Karen was in a critical comatose state of unknown cause and was being given oxygen through a mask taped over her nose and mouth. She had been brought to the hospital by two friends who had been with her at a birthday party. After a few drinks, she had started to pass out, and her friends decided she must be drunk and put her to bed. Then a girl checked on her later in the evening and found that Karen wasn't breathing. Her friends gave her mouth-to-mouth resuscitation and took her to the nearest hospital.

Blood and urine tests showed that Karen had not consumed a dangerous amount of alcohol. They also showed the presence of .6 milligram percent of aspirin and the tranquilizer Valium. Two milligrams would have been toxic, and five lethal. Why Karen stopped breathing was mysterious. But it was during that time that part of her brain died from oxygen depletion.

After Karen had been unconscious for about a week, she was moved to St. Clare's Hospital in nearby Denville, where testing and life-support facilities were better. Dr. Robert J. Morse, a neurologist, and Dr. Arshad Javed, a pulmonary internist, became her physicians. Additional tests were made. Extensive brain damage was confirmed, and several possible causes of the coma were ruled out.

During the early days, the Quinlans were hopeful. Karen's eyes opened and closed, and her mother and her nineteen-year-old sister, Mary Ellen, thought that they detected signs that she recognized them. But Karen's condition began to deteriorate. Her weight gradually dropped from 120 pounds to seventy. Her body began to contract into a rigid fetal position, until her five-foot-two-inch frame was bent into a shape hardly longer than three feet. She was now breathing mechanically, by means of an MA-1 respirator that pumped air through a tube in her throat.

By early July, Karen's physicians and her mother, sister, and brother had come to believe it was hopeless to expect her ever to regain consciousness. Only her father continued to believe it might be possible. But when he told Dr. Morse about some encouraging sign he had noticed, Dr. Morse said to him "Even if God did perform a miracle so that Karen would live, her damage is so extensive she would spend the rest of her life in an institution." Mr. Quinlan then realized that Karen would never again be as he remembered her. He now agreed with Karen's sister: "Karen would never want to be kept alive on machines like this. She would hate this."

The Quinlans' parish priest, Father Thomas Trapasso, had also assured them that the moral doctrines of the Roman Catholic Church did not require the continuation of extraordinary measures to support a hopeless life. Before making his decision, Mr. Quinlan asked the priest "Am I playing God?" Father Thomas said "God has made the decision that Karen is going to die. You're just agreeing with God's decision, that's all."

On July 31, after Karen had been unconscious for three and a half months, the Quinlans gave Drs. Morse and Jared their permission to take Karen off the respirator. The Quinlans signed a letter authorizing the discontinuance of extraordinary procedures and absolving the hospital from all legal liability. "I think you have come to the right decision," Dr. Morse said to Mr. Quinlan.

But the next morning Dr. Morse called Mr. Quinlan. "I have a moral problem about what we agreed on last night," he said. "I feel I have to consult somebody else and see how he feels about it." The next day, Dr. Morse called again. "I find I will not do it," he said. "And I've informed the administrator at the hospital that I will not do it."

The Quinlans were upset and bewildered by the change in Dr. Morse. Later they talked with the hospital attorney and were told by him that, because Karen was over twenty-one, they were no longer her legal guardians. The Quinlans would have to go to court and be appointed to guardianship. After that, the hospital might or might not remove Karen from the respirator.

Mr. Quinlan consulted attorney Paul Armstrong. Because Karen was an adult without income, Mr. Quinlan explained, Medicare was paying the $450 a day it cost to keep her alive. The Quinlans

thus had no financial motive in asking that the respirator be taken away. Mr. Quinlan said that his belief that Karen should be allowed to die rested on his conviction that it was God's will, and it was for this reason that he wanted to be appointed Karen's guardian.

Mr. Armstrong filed a plea with Judge Robert Muir of the New Jersey Superior Court on September 12, 1975. He explicitly requested that Mr. Quinlan be appointed Karen's guardian so that he would have "the express power of authorizing the discontinuance of all extraordinary means of sustaining her life." Later, on October 20, Mr. Armstrong argued the case on three constitutional grounds. First, he claimed that there is an implicit right to privacy guaranteed by the Constitution and that this right permits individuals or others acting for them to terminate the use of extraordinary medical measures, even when death may result. This right holds, Armstrong said, unless there are compelling state interests that set it aside.

Second, Armstrong argued that the First Amendment guarantee of religious freedom extended to the Quinlan case. If the court did not allow them to act in accordance with the doctrines of their church, their religious liberty would be infringed. Finally, Armstrong appealed to the "cruel and unusual punishment" clause of the Eighth Amendment. He claimed that "for the state to require that Karen Quinlan be kept alive, against her will and the will of her family, after the dignity, beauty, promise and meaning of earthly life have vanished, is cruel and unusual punishment."

Karen's mother, sister, and a friend testified that Karen had often talked about not wanting to be kept alive by machines. An expert witness, a neurologist, testified that Karen was in a "chronic vegetative state" and that it was unlikely that she would ever regain consciousness. Doctors testifying for St. Clare's Hospital and Karen's physicians agreed with this. But, they argued, her brain still showed patterns of electrical activity, and she still had a discernible pulse. Thus, she could not be considered dead by legal or medical criteria.

On November 10, Judge Muir ruled against Joseph Quinlan. He praised Mr. Quinlan's character and concern, but he decided that Mr. Quinlan's anguish over his daughter might cloud his judgment about her welfare so he should not be made her guardian. Furthermore, Judge Muir said, because Karen is still medically and legally alive, "the Court should not authorize termination of the respirator. To do so would be homicide and an act of euthanasia."

Mr. Armstrong appealed the decision to the New Jersey Supreme Court. On January 26, 1976, the court convened to hear arguments, and Mr. Armstrong argued substantially as before. But this time the court's ruling was favorable. The court agreed that Mr. Quinlan could assert a right of privacy on Karen's behalf and that whatever he decided for her should be accepted by society. It also set aside any criminal liability for removing the respirator, claiming that if death resulted it would not be homicide and that, even if it were homicide, it would not be unlawful. Finally, the court stated that, if Karen's physicians believed that she would never emerge from her coma, they should consult an ethics committee to be established by St. Clare's Hospital. If the committee accepted their prognosis, then the respirator could be removed. If Karen's present physicians were then unwilling to take her off the respirator, Mr. Quinlan was free to find a physician who would.

Six weeks after the court decision, the respirator still had not been turned off. In fact, another machine, one for controlling body temperature, had been added. Mr. Quinlan met with Morse and Jared and demanded that they remove the respirator. They agreed to "wean" Karen from the machine, and soon she was breathing without mechanical assistance. Dr. Morse and St. Clare's Hospital were determined that Karen would not die while under their care. Although she was moved to a private room, it was next door to the intensive-care unit. They intended to put her back on the respirator at the first sign of breathing difficulty.

Because Karen was still alive, the Quinlans began a long search for a chronic-care hospital. Twenty or more institutions turned them away, and physicians expressed great reluctance to become involved in the case. Finally, Dr. Joseph Fennelly volunteered to treat Karen, and on June 9 she was moved from St. Clare's to the Morris View Nursing Home.

Karen Quinlan continued to breathe. She received high-nutrient feedings and regular doses of antibiotics to ward off infections. During some periods she was more active than at others, making reflexive responses to touch and sound.

On June 11, 1985, at 7:01 in the evening, ten years after she lapsed into a coma, Karen Quinlan finally died. She was thirty-one years old.

INTRODUCTION

Death comes to us all. We hope that when it comes it will be swift and allow us to depart without prolonged suffering, our dignity intact. We also hope that it will not force burdens on our family and friends, making them pay both financially and emotionally by our lingering and hopeless condition.

Such considerations give euthanasia a strong appeal. Should we not be able to snip the thread of life when the weight of suffering and hopelessness grows too heavy to bear? The answer to this question is not so easy as it may seem, for hidden within it are a number of complicated moral issues.

Just what is euthanasia? The word comes from the Greek for "good death," and in English it has come to have the meaning "easy death." But this does very little to help us understand the concept. For consider this: If we give ourselves an easy death, are we committing suicide? If we assist someone else to an easy death (with or without that person's permission), are we committing murder? Anyone who opposed killing (either of oneself or of others) on moral grounds might also consider it necessary to object to euthanasia.

It may be, however, that the answer to both of these questions is no. But if it is, then it is necessary to specify the conditions that distinguish euthanasia from both suicide and murder. Only then would it be possible to argue, without contradiction, that euthanasia is morally acceptable but the other two forms of killing are not. (Someone believing that suicide is morally legitimate would not object to euthanasia carried out by the person herself, but he would still have to deal with the problem posed by the euthanasia/murder issue.)

ACTIVE AND PASSIVE EUTHANASIA

We have talked of euthanasia as though it involved directly taking the life of a person, either one's own life or the life of another.

However, some philosophers distinguish between "active euthanasia" and "passive euthanasia," which in turn rests on a distinction between *killing* and *letting die*. To kill someone (including oneself) is to take a definite action to end his or her life (administering a lethal injection, for example). To allow someone to die, by contrast, is to take no steps to prolong a person's life when those steps seem called for (failing to give an injection of antibiotics, for example). Active euthanasia, then, is direct killing and is an act of commission. Passive euthanasia is an act of omission.

This distinction is used in most contemporary codes of medical ethics (that of the American Medical Association, for example) and is also recognized in the Anglo-American tradition of law. Except in special circumstances, it is illegal to deliberately cause the death of another person. It is not, however, illegal (except in special circumstances) to allow a person to die. Clearly, one might consider active euthanasia morally wrong while recognizing passive euthanasia as morally legitimate.

Some philosophers, however, have argued that the active-passive distinction is morally irrelevant with respect to euthanasia. Both are cases of causing death, and it is the circumstances in which death is caused, not the manner of causing it, that is of moral importance. (This is the claim defended by James Rachels in his essay "Active and Passive Euthanasia," included in this chapter.) Furthermore, the active-passive distinction is not always clear-cut. If a person dies after special life-sustaining equipment has been withdrawn, is this a case of active or passive euthanasia? Or is it a case of euthanasia at all?

VOLUNTARY, INVOLUNTARY, AND NONVOLUNTARY EUTHANASIA

Philosophers and other writers on euthanasia have often thought it important to distinguish between voluntary, involuntary, and nonvoluntary euthanasia. Voluntary euthanasia includes cases in which a person takes his or her own life, either directly or by refusing treatment. But it also includes cases in which a person deputizes another to act in accordance with his wishes. Thus, a person might instruct her family *not* to permit the use of artificial support systems, should she become unconscious, suffer from brain damage, and be unable to speak for herself. Or a person might request that he be given a lethal injection, after suffering third-degree burns over most of his body and being told that he has virtually no hope of recovery. Finally, assisted suicide, in which the individual requests the direct help of someone else in ending his life, falls into this category. (Some may think that one or more of the earlier examples are also cases of assisted suicide. What counts as assisted suicide is both conceptually and legally unclear.) That the individual explicitly consents to death is a necessary feature of voluntary euthanasia.

Involuntary euthanasia consists in ending the life of someone contrary to that person's wish. The person killed not only fails to give consent, but expresses the desire not to be killed. No one arguing in favor of nonvoluntary euthanasia holds that involuntary euthanasia is justifiable. Those who oppose both voluntary and nonvoluntary euthanasia often argue that to permit either runs the risk of opening the way for involuntary euthanasia.

Nonvoluntary euthanasia includes those cases in which the decision about death is not made by the person who is to die. Here the person gives no specific consent or instructions, and the decision is made by family, friends, or physicians. The distinction between voluntary and nonvoluntary euthanasia is not always a clear one. Physicians sometimes assume that people are "asking" to die, even when no explicit request has been made. Also, the wishes and attitudes that people express when they are not in extreme life-threatening medical situations may be too vague for us to be certain that they would choose death when they are in such a situation. Is "I never want to be hooked up to one of those machines" an adequate indication that the person who says this does not want to be put on a respirator should she meet with an accident and fall into a comatose state?

If the distinctions we have made are considered legitimate and relevant, we can distinguish eight cases in which euthanasia becomes a moral decision:

1. Self-administered euthanasia
    a. active
    b. passive

2. Other-administered euthanasia
    a. active and voluntary
    b. active and involuntary
    c. active and nonvoluntary
    d. passive and voluntary
    e. passive and involuntary
    f. passive and nonvoluntary

Even these possibilities do not exhaust the cases that euthanasia presents us with. For example, notice that the voluntary/nonvoluntary distinction does not appear in connection with self-administered euthanasia in our scheme. Yet it might be argued that it should, for a person's decision to end his life (actively or passively) may well not be a wholly voluntary or free decision. People who are severely depressed by their illness and decide to end their lives, for example, might not be thought of as having made a voluntary choice. Hence, one might approve of self-administered voluntary euthanasia, yet think that the nonvoluntary form should not be permitted. It should not be allowed not because it is necessarily morally wrong, but because it would not be a genuine decision by the person. The person might be thought of as suffering from a psychiatric disability. Indeed, the debate about physician-assisted suicide turns, in part, on just this issue.

DEFINING "DEATH"

The advent of new medical technologies, pharmaceutical agents, and modes of treatment raises the question of when we should consider someone dead. Suppose that someone's heartbeat, blood pressure, respiration, and liver and kidney functions can be maintained within the normal range of values by medical intervention. Should we still include this individual among living persons, even though she is in an irreversible coma or a chronic vegetative state?

If we consider the individual to be a living person, we need to decide how she ought to be treated. Should she be allowed to die or be maintained by medical means? This is the kind of question faced by families, physicians, and the courts in the Quinlan and Cruzan cases, and it is one faced every day in dozens of unpublicized, though no less agonizing, cases.

But what if an unconscious individual lacking higher cortical functioning is no longer a living person? Could a physician who disconnected a respirator or failed to give an antibiotic be said to have killed a person? If nutrition and hydration are withheld from a "brain dead" individual or even if the individual is given a lethal injection, is it reasonable to say that this is a case of killing? Perhaps the person died when his brain stopped functioning at a certain level. Or perhaps he died when he lapsed into coma.

A practical question that advances in medicine have made even more pressing is when or whether a comatose individual may be regarded as a source of transplant organs. If the individual remains a living person, it may be morally wrong (at least prima facie) to kill him to obtain organs for transplant. But what if the comatose individual is not really alive? What if he is dead already and no longer a person? Then there seem to be no reasonable grounds for objecting to removing his organs and using them to save the lives of those who need them.

Questions like the ones raised here have prompted various attempts to define the notion of *death*. In the view of many commentators, the traditional notion of death is no longer adequate to serve as a guide to resolving issues about the treatment of individuals who, through disease or accident, have fallen into states in which many of their basic physiological functions can be maintained by medical means, although they remain comatose or lacking in higher-brain function. Until recently, the traditional notion of death has been enshrined in laws defining crimes such as homicide and manslaughter. Given the change in medical technology, actions like removing a respirator, that might once have been regarded as criminal for causing the death of a person, perhaps should now be viewed in a different way. Perhaps a person may be dead already, even though major physiological systems are still functioning.

Four major notions or concepts of death have emerged during the last two decades. We will list each of them, but it is important to keep in mind that there is a difference between specifying the concept of death (or, as it is sometimes put, defining "death") and the criteria for determining that the concept fits in particular cases. This is analogous to defining "the best team" as the one winning the most games, then providing criteria for determining what counts as winning a game.

The following concepts are merely sketched and the criteria for applying them only hinted at.

1. *Traditional.* A person is dead when he is no longer breathing and his heart is not beating. Hence, death may be defined as the permanent cessation of breathing and blood flow. This notion is sometimes known as the "heart-lung criterion" for death.

2. *Whole-brain.* Death is regarded as the irreversible cessation of all brain functions. Essentially, this means that there is no electrical activity in the brain, and even the brain stem is not functioning. Application of the concept depends on the use of electroencephalographic or imaging data.

3. *Higher-brain.* Death is considered to involve the permanent loss of consciousness. Hence, someone in an irreversible

coma would be considered dead, even though the brain stem continued to regulate breathing and heartbeat. Clinical, electroencephalographic, and imaging data are relevant to applying the concept. So, too, are statistics concerning the likelihood of the individual's regaining consciousness.

4. *Personhood.* Death occurs when an individual ceases to be a person. This may mean the loss of features that are essential to personal identity or (in some statements) the loss of what is essential to being a person. Criteria for personal identity or for being a person are typically taken to include a complex of such activities as reasoning, remembering, feeling emotion, possessing a sense of the future, interacting with others, and so on. The criteria for applying this concept have more to do with the way an individual functions than with data about his brain.

The criteria for applying each of these concepts are often complex, and a discussion of them would not be appropriate here. Technology made it necessary to take a fresh look at the traditional notion of death, but technology also provides data that have allowed for the development of new notions. It would be pointless, for example, to talk about brain death without having some means to determine when the concept might be satisfied.

The whole-brain concept of death was proposed by the 1981 Report of the President's Commission for the Study of Ethical Problems in Medicine and included in the Uniform Death Act. As a consequence, state laws employing the traditional concept of death generally have been modified in keeping with the whole-brain concept.

The whole-brain concept has the advantage of being relatively clear-cut in application. However, applying the concept is not without difficulty and controversy. In the view of some, the concept is too restrictive and so fails to resolve some of the difficulties that prompted the need for a new concept. For example, both Karen Quinlan and Nancy Cruzan would have been considered alive by the whole-brain criteria. However, those who favor concepts of death based on the loss of higher-brain function or the loss of person-hood might argue that both cases were ones in which the affected individuals were, in the respective technical senses, dead.

Furthermore, critics charge, the whole-brain concept is not really as straightforward in its application as it might seem. Even when there appears to be complete lack of cognitive functioning and even when basic brain-stem functions appear to have disappeared, a brain may remain electrically active to some degree. Isolated cells or groups of cells continue to be alive, and monitoring of the brain yields data that are open to conflicting interpretations.

However, the higher-brain and person-hood concepts face even greater difficulties. Each must formulate criteria that are accepted as nonarbitrary and as sufficient grounds for deciding that an individual is dead. No one has yet solved either of these problems for either of these concepts. The fact that there can be controversy over whole-brain death indicates how much harder it is to get agreement about when higher-brain functions are lost. Further, securing agreement on criteria for determining when an entity either becomes or ceases to be a person is a conceptual difficulty far from being resolved to the satisfaction of most philosophers. (See the discussion of persons in connection with abortion in Chapter 1, "Status of the Fetus" for more on this topic.)

THE DUTCH EXPERIENCE

In 1993, the Netherlands passed a law establishing specific rules to allow physicians to assist in the suicide of a terminally ill patient or to kill the patient at the patient's explicit request without risking criminal prosecution.

This law gives a new legal status to a practice that has been followed in the Netherlands for more than a decade. Ending a patient's life or assisting in suicide remains illegal, but the law provides physicians with protection from prosecution, if they follow the provisions of the law. The Dutch criminal code previously provides as much as twelve years in prison for anyone who "takes the life of another at his or her explicit and serious request." However, in a 1972 case involving a physician who put her mother to death at the mother's request, a court refused to impose a penalty. Since then and with the reenforcement of a major court decision in 1984, the extralegal practice of voluntary, active, physician-administered euthanasia became established in the Netherlands.

The new law requires that a physician follow a twenty-eight point checklist to avoid prosecution. The safeguards built into the law include the following:

1. *Patient-initiated request.* The request for euthanasia must be made "entirely of the patient's own free will" and not under pressure from others, including family, friends, or physicians. The patient must make the request personally, and relatives cannot make a request on behalf of a patient.

2. *Patient competence.* At the time of the decision, the patient must be in a rational state of mind and able to make informed decisions. Those who suffer from dementia or are in a coma are not candidates for euthanasia.

3. *Informed as to alternatives.* The patient must be informed about alternatives to assisted-suicide or euthanasia. The patient should then be encouraged to discuss them with physicians, family, and advisors.

4. *Enduring decision.* The patient must have a "lasting longing for death." Requests to physicians made on impulse or ones that may be the result of depression cannot be regarded as legitimate.

5. *Unbearable suffering.* "The patient must experience his or her suffering as per-

petual, unbearable, and hopeless." The physician must be able to make the reasonable judgment that the suffering the patient is experiencing is unendurable.

6. *Professional consultation.* The physician must consult with at least one other physician who has had experience in dealing with patients requesting euthanasia or help in dying.

7. *Government report.* The physician must submit a report to the government in which the patient's medical history is presented and the physician declares that all the conditions required for assisting in suicide or performing euthanasia have been observed.

The patient must also sign a witnessed explicit authorization for the act to be carried out. Typically, the physician then injects a barbiturate to induce sleep, combined with curare to produce death.

A study conducted by the Dutch government reported that in 1990 there were 2,300 deaths by voluntary euthanasia and about 400 cases of assisted suicide. These represented some 2% of the total number of deaths in the Netherlands that year. The report also indicated that physicians had reported a total of 9,000 requests for euthanasia. Apparently, a majority of requests were turned down.

An opinion poll conducted in 1993 in the Netherlands showed that 78% of those questioned supported the right of the terminally ill to ask for euthanasia. (A previous poll showed that about 50% of Roman Catholics also favor this.) Ten percent were opposed, and 71% said that physicians who act in accordance with the rules should not have to justify themselves in a court of law.

The new law was not regarded with approval by all Dutch physicians. Karel Gunning, former president of the League of Dutch Physicians, a group opposed to both abortion and euthanasia, claimed that "killing is not part of medicine." The problem, as he sees it, is for society to respond to the challenge presented by dying people. "If people's feelings, their self-respect suffers, the solution is better care, to change our attitude, not agreeing that they should die." About 11% of Dutch physicians report that they will refuse to practice euthanasia.

The Dutch practice and the new law is often mentioned in the United States as an example of what a reasonable euthanasia policy might include. In particular, the practice is offered as a model for providing an option to continuing treatment of individuals suffering from a lingering terminal illness. People with AIDS, for example, have often expressed a wish for a social and legal policy that would permit active, voluntary euthanasia or assisted suicide. These are just the sort of people the Dutch practice has evolved to deal with.

However, the medical-care situation in the United States is different in what may be considered a relevantly important way. Dutch citizens are almost universally participants in health plans that cover their medical costs. Hence, individuals are not under economic pressures to make decisions about ending their lives. They need not worry that they are running out of insurance coverage or may be bankrupting their families by remaining alive.

Furthermore, the Dutch practice does not deal with the type of cases that have caused much concern and controversy in this country. Until recently, the proper treatment of individuals in irreversible comas, as in the Quinlan and Cruzan cases, have been at the focus of dispute. Since the practice in Holland requires that individuals be conscious and intellectually competent, it embodies no principles that could be appealed to for resolving the troublesome issues involved in dealing with those in persistent vegetative states.

Nevertheless, the Dutch experience may still be valuable in showing whether it is possible to have a social policy permitting assisted suicide and voluntary euthanasia without the abuses or corruption of medical power feared by critics.

LIVING WILLS

Like so many issues in medical ethics, euthanasia has traditionally been discussed only in the back rooms of medicine. Often decisions about whether to allow a patient to die are made by physicians acting on their own authority. Such decisions do not represent so much an arrogant claim to godlike wisdom as an acknowledgment of the physician's obligation to do what is best for the patient. Most physicians admit that allowing or helping a patient to die is sometimes the best assistance that can be given. Decisions made in this fashion depend on the beliefs and judgment of particular physicians. Because these may differ from those of the patient concerned, it is quite possible that the physician's decision may not reflect the wishes of the patient.

But covert decisions made by a physician acting alone are becoming practices of the past as euthanasia is discussed more widely and openly. Court cases, such as *Quinlan* and *Cruzan*, have both widened the scope of legally permissible actions and reinforced the notion that an individual has a right to refuse or discontinue life-sustaining medical treatment. Such cases have also made it clear that there are limits to the benefits that can be derived from medicine—that, under some conditions, individuals may be better off if everything that technologically can be done is not done. Increasingly, people want to be sure that they have some say in what happens to them should they fall victim to hopeless injury or illness.

One indication of this interest is that the number of states permitting individuals to sign "living wills" has now increased to more than forty, and it is reasonable to believe that before long every state will have some living-will procedure. The first living-will legislation was the "Natural Death Act," passed by the California legislature on August 30, 1977. The act is generally representative of all such legislation. It permits a competent adult to sign a directive that will authorize physicians to withhold or discontinue "mechanical" or "artificial" life-support equipment if the person is judged to be "terminal" and if "death is imminent."

The strength of living wills is that they allow a person to express in an explicit manner how he or she wishes to be treated before treatment is needed. In this way, the autonomy of the individual is recognized. Even though unconscious or comatose, a person can continue to exert control over his or her life. This, in turn, means that physicians need not and should not be the decisive voice in determining the continuation or use of special medical equipment.

Critics of living-will legislation have claimed that it does not go far enough in protecting autonomy and making death easier (where this is what is wanted). They point out that the directive specified in the California bill and most others would have made no difference in the case of Karen Quinlan. She had not been diagnosed as having a "terminal condition" at least two weeks prior to being put on a respirator, yet this is one of the requirements of the act. Consequently, the directive would have been irrelevant to her condition.

Nor, for that matter, would those people be allowed to die who wish to, if their disease or injury does not involve treatment by "artificial" or "mechanical" means. Thus, a person suffering from throat cancer would simply have to bear the pain and wait for a "natural" death. Finally, at the moment, some states explicitly exclude nutrition and hydration as medical treatments that can be discontinued. The Supreme Court in the *Cruzan* case accepted the notion that the nutrition received by Nancy Cruzan through a feeding tube implanted in her stomach was a form of medical treatment that could be withdrawn. However, the Court did not rule on the Missouri law that forbids withdrawal. Until this law or some other like it is successfully challenged in court, a living will does not necessarily guarantee that such treatment will be discontinued, even when requested.

Limitations of such kinds on living wills have led some writers to recommend that individuals sign a legal instrument known as a durable power of attorney. In such a document, an individual can name someone to act on his behalf should be become legally incompetent to act. Hence, unlike the living will, a durable power of attorney allows a surrogate to exercise control over novel and unanticipated situations. For example, the surrogate may order the discontinuation of artificial feeding, something that a living will might not permit.

The widespread wish to have some control over the end of one's life is reflected in a new federal law that took effect in 1991. The Self-Determination Act is sometimes referred to as a "medical Miranda warning." It requires that hospitals, nursing homes, and other health-care facilities receiving federal funding provide patients at the time of admission with written information about relevant state laws and the rights of citizens under those laws to refuse or discontinue treatment. Patients must also be told about the practices and policies at that particular institution so they can choose a facility willing to abide by their decisions. The institutions must also record whether a patient has provided a written "advance directive" (e.g., a living will or power of attorney for health care) that will take effect should the patient become incapacitated.

Another sign of change is the recent concern with the medical circumstances in which people die. The medical ideal of a "hospital death," one in which the patient's temperature, pulse rate, and respiration are brought within normal limits by medication and machinery, is being severely challenged. This is reflected in the policy reaffirmed in 1988 by the AMA that holds that it may be morally appropriate to withhold "all means of life prolonging medical treatment," including artificial feeding, from patients in irreversible comas.

A new ideal of natural death also seems to be emerging. In this view, the kind of support a dying patient needs is psychological counseling and contact with family and friends, rather than heroic medical efforts. An acceptance of death as a normal end of life and the development of new means of caring for the dying may ease the problem of euthanasia. If those who are hopeless and near death are offered an alternative to either euthanasia or an all-out medical effort to preserve their lives, they may choose that alternative. "Death with dignity" need not always mean choosing a lethal injection.

Public Views on Euthanasia

	Agree	Disagree	Neither
1. If a person has a fatal illness, that person should have the right to have all life-sustaining devices removed, including feeding tubes.	79%	12%	9%
2. If a person is in a coma that cannot be reversed, relatives should be allowed to tell doctors to remove all life-sustaining devices, including feeding tubes.	81%	11%	8%
3. In case of fatal illness, doctors should be allowed to help that person end his or her life.	49%	35%	16%
4. If a person has been diagnosed as having a fatal illness, he or she should be allowed to take his or her own life.	39%	45%	16%

Source: *Parade Magazine* (9 February 1992) mail survey of 3,750 people aged twenty-one or older; 2,203 respondents. Reprinted with permission from *Parade*, copyright © 1992.

ETHICAL THEORIES AND EUTHANASIA

Roman Catholicism explicitly rejects all forms of euthanasia as being against the natural law duty to preserve life. It considers euthanasia as morally identical with either suicide or murder. This position is not so rigid as it may seem, however. As we have already seen in the introductory chapter and in the last chapter, the principle of double effect makes it morally acceptable to give medication for the relief of pain—even if the indirect result of the medication will be to shorten the life of the recipient. The intended result is not the death of the person but the relief of suffering. The difference in intention is thus considered to be a morally significant one. Those not accepting the principle of double effect would be likely to classify the administration of a substance that would relieve pain but would also cause death as a case of euthanasia.

Furthermore, on the Catholic view there is no moral obligation to continue treatment when a person is medically hopeless. It is legitimate to allow people to die as a result of their illness or injury, even though their lives might be lengthened by the use of extraordinary means. Additionally, we may legitimately make the same decisions about ourselves that we make about others who are in no condition to decide. Thus, without intending to kill ourselves, we may choose measures for the relief of pain that may secondarily hasten our end. Or we may refuse extraordinary treatment and let "nature" take its course, let "God's will" determine the outcome. (See the introductory chapter for a fuller discussion of the Roman Catholic position on euthanasia and extraordinary means of sustaining life.)

At first sight, utilitarianism would seem to endorse euthanasia in all of its forms. Whenever suffering is great and the condition of the person is one without legitimate medical hope, then the principle of utility might be invoked to approve putting the person to death.

After all, in such a case we seem to be acting to end suffering and to bring about a state of affairs in which happiness exceeds unhappiness. Thus, whether the person concerned is ourself or another, euthanasia would seem to be a morally right action.

A utilitarian might argue in this way, but this is not the only way in which the principle of utility might be applied. It could be argued, for example, that, since life is a necessary condition for happiness, it is wrong to destroy that condition because, by doing so, the possibility of all future happiness is lost. Furthermore, a rule utilitarian might well argue that a rule like "The taking of a human life is permissible when suffering is intense and the condition of the person permits no legitimate hope" would be open to abuse. Consequently, in the long run the rule would actually work to increase the amount of unhappiness in the world. Obviously, it is not possible to say there is such a thing as "the utilitarian view of euthanasia." The principle of utility supplies a guide for an answer, but it is not itself an answer.

Euthanasia presents a considerable difficulty for Kant's ethics. For Kant, an autonomous rational being has a duty to preserve his or her life. Thus, one cannot rightly refuse needed medical care or commit suicide. Yet our status as autonomous rational beings also endows us with an inherent dignity. If that status is destroyed or severely compromised, as it is when people become comatose, and unknowing because of illness or injury, then it is not certain that we have a duty to maintain our lives under such conditions. It may be more in keeping with our freedom and dignity for us to instruct others either to put us to death or to take no steps to keep us alive should we ever be in such a state. Voluntary euthanasia may be compatible with (if not required by) Kant's ethics.

By a similar line of reasoning, it may be that nonvoluntary euthanasia might be seen as a duty that we have to others. We might argue that by putting to death a comatose and hopeless person we are recognizing the dignity that person possessed in his or her previous state. Also, as we mentioned in the last chapter, it might also be argued that a human being in a vegetative state is not a person in the relevant moral sense. Thus, our ordinary duty to preserve life does not hold.

According to Ross, we have a strong prima facie obligation not to kill a person except in justifiable self-defense—unless we have an even stronger prima facie moral obligation to do something that cannot be done without killing. Since active euthanasia typically requires taking the life of an innocent person, there is a moral presumption against it. However, another of Ross's prima facie obligations is that we keep promises made to others. Accordingly, if someone who is now in an irreversible coma with no hope of recovery has left instructions that in case of such an event's

happening she wishes her life to be ended, then we are under a prima facie obligation to follow her instructions. Thus, in such a case, we may be justified in overriding the presumption against taking an innocent life.

What if there are no such instructions? It could be argued that our prima facie obligation of acting beneficently toward others requires us to attempt to determine what someone's wishes would be from what we know about him as a person. We would then treat him the way that we believe that he would want us to. In the absence of any relevant information, we might make the decision on the basis of how a rational person would want to be treated in similar circumstances. Of course, if anyone has left instructions that his life is to be maintained, if possible, under any circumstances, then we have a prima facie obligation to respect this preference also.

The Wrongfulness of Euthanasia

J. Gay-Williams

J. Gay-Williams defines "euthanasia" as intentionally taking the life of a person who is believed to be suffering from some illness or injury from which recovery cannot reasonably be expected. Gay-Williams rejects passive euthanasia as a *name* for actions that are usually designated by the phrase but seems to approve of the actions themselves. He argues that euthanasia as intentional killing goes against natural law because it violates the natural inclination to preserve life. Furthermore, both self-interest and possible practical consequences of euthanasia provide reasons for rejecting it.

My impression is that euthanasia—the idea, if not the practice—is slowly gaining acceptance within our society. Cynics might attribute this to an increasing tendency to devalue human life, but I do not believe this is the major factor. The acceptance is much more likely to be the result of unthinking sympathy and benevolence. Well-publicized, tragic

stories like that of Karen Quinlan elicit from us deep feelings of compassion. We think to ourselves, "She and her family would be better off if she were dead." It is an easy step from this very human response to the view that if someone (and others) would be better off dead, then it might be all right to kill that person.[1] Although I respect the compassion that leads to this conclusion, I believe the conclusion is wrong. I want to show that euthanasia is wrong. It is inherently wrong, but it is also wrong judged from the standpoints of self-interest and of practical effects.

Before presenting my arguments to support this claim, it would be well to define "euthanasia." An essential aspect of euthanasia is that it involves taking a human life, either one's own or that of another. Also, the person whose life is taken must be someone who is believed to be suffering from some disease or injury from which recovery cannot reasonably be expected. Finally, the action must be deliberate and intentional. Thus, euthanasia is intentionally taking the life of a presumably hopeless person. Whether the life is one's own or that of another, the taking of it is still euthanasia.

It is important to be clear about the deliberate and intentional aspect of the killing. If a hopeless person is given an injection of the wrong drug by mistake and this causes his death, this is wrongful killing but not euthanasia. The killing cannot be the result of accident. Furthermore, if the person is given an injection of a drug that is believed to be necessary to treat his disease or better his condition and the person dies as a result, then this is neither wrongful killing nor euthanasia. The intention was to make the patient well, not kill him. Similarly, when a patient's condition is such that it is not reasonable to hope that any medical procedures or treatments will save his life, a failure to implement the procedures or treatments is not euthanasia. If the person dies, this will be as a result of his injuries or disease and not because of his failure to receive treatment.

The failure to continue treatment after it has been realized that the patient has little chance of benefiting from it has been characterized by some as "passive euthanasia." This phrase is misleading and mistaken.[2] In such cases, the person involved is not killed (the first essential aspect of euthanasia), nor is the death of the person intended by the withholding of additional treatment (the third essential aspect of euthanasia). The aim may be to spare the person additional and unjustifiable pain, to save him from the indignities of hopeless manipulations, and to avoid increasing the financial and emotional burden on his family. When I buy a pencil it is so that I can use it to write, not to contribute to an increase in the gross national product. This may be the unintended consequence of my action,

but it is not the aim of my action. So it is with failing to continue the treatment of a dying person. I intend his death no more than I intend to reduce the GNP by not using medical supplies. His is an unintended dying, and so-called "passive euthanasia" is not euthanasia at all.

1. The Argument from Nature

Every human being has a natural inclination to continue living. Our reflexes and responses fit us to fight attackers, flee wild animals, and dodge out of the way of trucks. In our daily lives we exercise the caution and care necessary to protect ourselves. Our bodies are similarly structured for survival right down to the molecular level. When we are cut, our capillaries seal shut, our blood clots, and fibrogen is produced to start the process of healing the wound. When we are invaded by bacteria, antibodies are produced to fight against the alien organisms, and their remains are swept out of the body by special cells designed for clean-up work.

Euthanasia does violence to this natural goal of survival. It is literally acting against nature because all the processes of nature are bent towards the end of bodily survival. Euthanasia defeats these subtle mechanisms in a way that, in a particular case, disease and injury might not.

It is possible, but not necessary, to make an appeal to revealed religion in this connection.[3] Man as trustee of his body acts against God, its rightful possessor, when he takes his own life. He also violates the commandment to hold life sacred and never to take it without just and compelling cause. But since this appeal will persuade only those who are prepared to accept that religion has access to revealed truths, I shall not employ this line of argument.

It is enough, I believe, to recognize that the organization of the human body and our patterns of behavioral responses make the continuation of life a natural goal. By reason alone, then, we can recognize that euthanasia sets us against our own nature.[4] Furthermore, in doing so, euthanasia does violence to our dignity. Our dignity comes from seeking our ends. When one of our goals is survival, and actions are taken that eliminate that goal, then our natural dignity suffers. Unlike animals, we are conscious through reason of our nature and our ends. Euthanasia involves acting as if this dual nature—inclination towards survival and awareness of this as an end—did not exist. Thus, euthanasia denies our basic human character and requires that we regard ourselves or others as something less than fully human.

2. The Argument from Self-Interest

The above arguments are, I believe, sufficient to show that euthanasia is inherently wrong. But there are reasons for considering it wrong when judged by standards other than reason. Because death is final and irreversible, euthanasia contains within it the possibility that we will work against our own interest if we practice it or allow it to be practiced on us.

Contemporary medicine has high standards of excellence and a proven record of accomplishment, but it does not possess perfect and complete knowledge. A mistaken diagnosis is possible, and so is a mistaken prognosis. Consequently, we may believe that we are dying of a disease when, as a matter of fact, we may not be. We may think that we have no hope of recovery when, as a matter of fact, our chances are quite good. In such circumstances, if euthanasia were permitted, we would die needlessly. Death is final and the chance of error too great to approve the practice of euthanasia.

Also, there is always the possibility that an experimental procedure or a hitherto untried technique will pull us through. We should at least keep this option open, but euthanasia closes it off. Furthermore, spontaneous remission does occur in many cases. For no apparent reason, a patient simply recovers when those all around him, including his physicians, expected him to die. Euthanasia would just guarantee their expectations and leave no room for the "miraculous" recoveries that frequently occur.

Finally, knowing that we can take our life at any time (or ask another to take it) might well incline us to give up too easily. The will to live is strong in all of us, but it can be weakened by pain and suffering and feelings of hopelessness. If during a bad time we allow ourselves to be killed, we never have a chance to reconsider. Recovery from a serious illness requires that we fight for it, and anything that weakens our determination by suggesting that there is an easy way out is ultimately against our own interest. Also, we may be inclined towards euthanasia because of our con-cern for others. If we see our sickness and suffering as an emotional and financial burden on our family, we may feel that to leave our life is to make their lives easier.[5] The very presence of the possibility of euthanasia may keep us from surviving when we might.

3. The Argument from Practical Effects

Doctors and nurses are, for the most part, totally committed to saving lives. A life lost is, for them, almost a personal failure, an insult to their skills and knowledge. Euthanasia as a practice might well alter this. It could have a corrupting influence so that in any case that is severe doctors and nurses might not try hard enough to save the patient. They might decide that the patient would simply be "better off dead" and take the steps necessary to make that come about. This attitude could then carry over to their dealings with patients less seriously ill. The result would be an overall decline in the quality of medical care.

Finally, euthanasia as a policy is a slippery slope. A person apparently hopelessly ill may be allowed to take his own life. Then he may be permitted to deputize others to do it for him should he no longer be able to act. The judgment of others then becomes the ruling factor. Already at this point euthanasia is not personal and voluntary, for others are acting "on behalf of" the patient as they see fit. This may well incline them to act on behalf of other patients who have not authorized them to exercise their judgment. It is only a short step, then, from voluntary euthanasia (self-inflicted or authorized), to directed euthanasia administered to a patient who has given no authorization, to involuntary euthanasia conducted as part of a social policy.[6] Recently many psychiatrists and sociologists have argued that we define as "mental illness" those forms of behavior that we disapprove of.[7] This gives us license then to lock up those who display the behavior. The category of the "hopelessly ill" provides the possibility of even worse abuse. Embedded in a social policy, it would give society or its representatives the authority to eliminate all those who might be considered too "ill" to function normally any longer. The dangers of euthanasia are too great to all to run the risk of approving it in any form. The first slippery step may well lead to a serious and harmful fall.

I hope that I have succeeded in showing why the benevolence that inclines us to give approval of euthanasia is misplaced. Euthanasia is inherently wrong because it violates the nature and dignity of human beings. But even those who are not convinced by this must be persuaded that the potential personal and social dangers inherent in euthanasia are sufficient to forbid our approving it either as a personal practice or as a public policy.

Suffering is surely a terrible thing, and we have a clear duty to comfort those in need and to ease their suffering when we can. But suffering is also a natural part of life with values for the individual and for others that we should not overlook. We may legitimately seek for others and for ourselves an easeful death, as Arthur Dyck has pointed out.[8] Euthanasia, however, is not just an easeful death. It is a wrongful death. Euthanasia is not just dying. It is killing.

Notes

1. For a sophisticated defense of this position see Philippa Foot, "Euthanasia," *Philosophy and Public Affairs,* vol. 6 (1977), pp. 85–112. Foot does not endorse the radical conclusion that euthanasia, voluntary and involuntary, is always right.

2. James Rachels rejects the distinction between active and passive euthanasia as morally irrelevant in his "Active and Passive Euthanasia," *New England Journal of Medicine,* vol. 292, pp. 78–80. But see the criticism by Foot, pp. 100–103.

3. For a defense of this view see J. V. Sullivan, "The Immorality of Euthanasia," in *Beneficent Euthanasia,* ed. Marvin Kohl (Buffalo, N.Y.: Prometheus Books, 1975), pp. 34–44.

4. This point is made by Ray V. McIntyre in "Voluntary Euthanasia: The Ultimate Perversion," *Medical Counterpoint,* vol. 2, pp. 26–29.

5. See McIntyre, p. 28.

6. See Sullivan, "Immorality of Euthanasia," pp. 34–44, for a fuller argument in support of this view.

7. See, for example, Thomas S. Szasz, *The Myth of Mental Illness,* rev. ed. (New York: Harper & Row, 1974).

8. Arthur Dyck, "Beneficent Euthanasia and Benemortasia," Kohl, op. cit., pp. 117–129.

Active and Passive Euthanasia

James Rachels

James Rachels challenges both the use and the moral significance of the distinction between active and passive euthanasia. Since both forms of euthanasia result in the death of a person, Rachels argues that active euthanasia ought to be preferred to passive. It is more humane because it allows suffering to be brought to a speedy end. Furthermore, Rachels claims, the distinction itself can be shown to be morally irrelevant. Is there, he asks, any genuine moral difference between drowning a child and merely watching a child drown and doing nothing to save it?

Finally, Rachels attempts to show that the bare fact that there is a difference between killing and letting die doesn't make active euthanasia wrong. Killing of any kind is right or wrong depending on the intentions and circumstances in which it takes place; if the intentions and circumstances are of a certain kind, then active euthanasia can be morally right.

For these reasons, Rachels suggests that the approval given to the active-passive euthanasia distinction in the Code of Ethics of the American Medical Association is unwise. He encourages physicians to rely upon the distinction only to the extent that they are forced to do so by law but not to give it any significant moral weight. In particular, they should not make use of it when writing new policies or guidelines.

Reprinted by permission from the *New England Journal of Medicine* 292, no. 2 (January 9, 1975): 78–80.

The distinction between active and passive euthanasia is thought to be crucial for medical ethics. The idea is that it is permissible, at least in some cases, to withhold treatment and allow a patient to die, but it is never permissible to take any direct action designed to kill the patient. This doctrine seems to be accepted by most doctors, and it is endorsed in a statement adopted by the House of Delegates of the American Medical Association on December 4, 1973:

> The intentional termination of the life of one human being by another—mercy killing—is contrary to that for which the medical profession stands and is contrary to the policy of the American Medical Association.
>
> The cessation of the employment of extraordinary means to prolong the life of the body when there is irrefutable evidence that biological death is imminent is the decision of the patient and/or his immediate family. The advice and judgment of the physician should be freely available to the patient and/or his immediate family.

However, a strong case can be made against this doctrine. In what follows I will set out some of the relevant arguments, and urge doctors to reconsider their views on this matter.

To begin with a familiar type of situation, a patient who is dying of incurable cancer of the throat is in terrible pain, which can no longer be satisfactorily alleviated. He is certain to die within a few days, even if present treatment is continued, but he does not want to go on living for those days since the pain is unbearable. So he asks the doctor for an end to it, and his family joins in the request.

Suppose the doctor agrees to withhold treatment, as the conventional doctrine says he may. The justification for his doing so is that the patient is in terrible agony, and since he is going to die anyway, it would be wrong to prolong his suffering needlessly. But now notice this. If one simply withholds treatment, it may take the patient longer to die, and so he may suffer more than he would if more direct action were taken and a lethal injection given. This fact provides strong reason for thinking that, once the initial decision not to prolong his agony has been made, active euthanasia is actually preferable to passive euthanasia, rather than the reverse. To say otherwise is to endorse the option that leads to more suffering rather than less, and is contrary to the humanitarian impulse that prompts the decision not to prolong his life in the first place.

Part of my point is that the process of being "allowed to die" can be relatively slow and painful, whereas being given a lethal injection is relatively quick and painless. Let me give a different sort of example. In the United States about one in 600 babies is born with Down syndrome. Most of these babies are otherwise healthy—that is, with only the usual pediatric care, they will proceed to an otherwise normal infancy. Some, however, are born with congenital defects such as intestinal obstructions that require operations if they are to live. Sometimes, the parents and the doctor will decide not to operate, and let the infant die. Anthony Shaw describes what happens then:

> . . . When surgery is denied [the doctor] must try to keep the infant from suffering while natural forces sap the baby's life away. As a surgeon whose natural inclination is to use the scalpel to fight off death, standing by and watching a salvageable baby die is the most emotionally exhausting experience I know. It is easy at a conference, in a theoretical discussion, to decide that such infants should be allowed to die. It is altogether different to stand by in the nursery and watch as dehydration and infection wither a tiny being over hours and days. This is a terrible ordeal for me and the hospital staff—much more so than for the parents who never set foot in the nursery.[1]

I can understand why some people are opposed to all euthanasia, and insist that such infants must be allowed to live. I think I can also understand why other people favor destroying these babies quickly and painlessly. But why should anyone favor letting "dehydration and infection wither a tiny being over hours and days"? The doctrine that says that a baby may be allowed to dehydrate and wither, but may not be given an injection that would end its life without suffering, seems so patently cruel as to require no further refutation. The strong language is not intended to offend, but only to put the point in the clearest possible way.

My second argument is that the conventional doctrine leads to decisions concerning life and death made on irrelevant grounds.

Consider again the case of the infants with Down syndrome who need operations for congenital defects unrelated to the syndrome to live. Sometimes, there is no operation, and the baby dies, but when there is no such defect, the baby lives on. Now, an operation such as that to remove an intestinal obstruction is not prohibitively difficult. The reason why such operations are not performed in these cases is, clearly, that the child has Down syndrome and the parents and doctor judge that because of that fact it is better for the child to die.

But notice that this situation is absurd, no matter what view one takes of the lives and potentials of such babies. If the life of such an infant is worth preserving, what does it matter if it needs a simple operation? Or, if one thinks it better that such a baby should not live on, what difference does it make that it happens to have an unobstructed intestinal tract? In either case, the matter of life and death is being decided on irrelevant grounds. It is the Down syndrome, and not the intestines, that is the issue. The matter should be decided, if at all, on that basis, and not be allowed to depend on the essentially irrelevant question of whether the intestinal tract is blocked.

What makes this situation possible, of course, is the idea that when there is an intestinal blockage, one can "let the baby die," but when there is no such defect there is nothing that can be done, for one must not "kill" it. The fact that this idea leads to such results as deciding life or death on irrelevant grounds is another good reason why the doctrine should be rejected.

One reason why so many people think that there is an important moral difference between active and passive euthanasia is that they think killing someone is morally worse than letting someone die. But is it? Is killing, in itself, worse than letting die? To investigate this issue, two cases may be considered that are exactly alike except that one involves killing whereas the other involves letting someone die. Then, it can be asked whether this difference makes any difference to the moral assessments. It is important that the cases be exactly alike, except for this one difference, since otherwise one cannot be confident that it is this difference and not some other that accounts for any variation in the assessments of the two cases. So, let us consider this pair of cases:

In the first, Smith stands to gain a large inheritance if anything should happen to his six-year-old cousin. One evening while the child is taking his bath, Smith sneaks into the bathroom and drowns the child, and then arranges things so that it will look like an accident.

In the second, Jones also stands to gain if anything should happen to his six-year-old cousin. Like Smith, Jones sneaks in planning to drown the child in his bath. However, just as he enters the bathroom Jones sees the child slip and hit his head, and fall face down in the water. Jones is delighted; he stands by, ready to push the child's head back under if it is necessary, but it is not necessary. With only a little thrashing about, the child drowns all by himself, "accidentally," as Jones watches and does nothing.

Now Smith killed the child, whereas Jones "merely" let the child die. That is the only difference between them. Did either man behave better, from a moral point of view? If the difference between killing and letting die were in itself a morally important matter, one should say that Jones's behavior was less reprehensible than Smith's. But does one really want to say that? I think not. In the first place, both men acted from the same motive, personal gain, and both had exactly the same end in view when they acted. It may be inferred from Smith's conduct that he is a bad man, although that judgment may be withdrawn or modified if certain further facts are learned about him—for example, that he is mentally deranged. But would not the very same thing be inferred about Jones from his conduct? And would not the same further considerations also be relevant to any modification of this judgment? Moreover, suppose Jones pleaded, in his own defense, "After all, I didn't do anything except just stand there and watch the child drown. I didn't kill him; I only let him die." Again, if letting die were in itself less bad than killing, this defense should have at least some weight. But it does not. Such a "defense" can only be regarded as a grotesque perversion of moral reasoning. Morally speaking, it is no defense at all.

Now, it may be pointed out, quite properly, that the cases of euthanasia with which doctors are concerned are not like this at all. They do not involve personal gain or the destruction of normal healthy children. Doctors are concerned only with cases in which the patient's life is of no further use to him, or in which the patient's life has become or will soon become a terrible burden. However, the point is the same in these cases: the bare difference between killing and letting die does not, in itself, make a moral difference. If a doctor lets a patient die, for humane reasons, he is in the same moral position as if he had given the patient a lethal injection for humane reasons. If his decision was wrong—if, for example, the patient's illness was in fact curable—the decision would be equally regrettable no matter which method was used to carry it out.

And if the doctor's decision was the right one, the method used is not in itself important.

The AMA policy statement isolates the crucial issue very well; the crucial issue is "the intentional termination of the life of one human being by another." But after identifying this issue, and forbidding "mercy killing," the statement goes on to deny that the cessation of treatment is the intentional termination of a life. This is where the mistake comes in, for what is the cessation of treatment, in these circumstances, if it is not "the intentional termination of the life of one human being by another"? Of course it is exactly that, and if it were not, there would be no point to it.

Many people will find this judgment hard to accept. One reason, I think, is that it is very easy to conflate the question of whether killing is, in itself, worse than letting die, with the very different question of whether most actual cases of killing are more reprehensible than most actual cases of letting die. Most actual cases of killing are clearly terrible (think, for example, of all the murders reported in the newspapers), and one hears of such cases every day. On the other hand, one hardly ever hears of a case of letting die, except for the actions of doctors who are motivated by humanitarian reasons. So one learns to think of killing in a much worse light than of letting die. But this does not mean that there is something about killing that makes it in itself worse than letting die, for it is not the bare difference between killing and letting die that makes the difference in these cases. Rather, the other factors—the murderer's motive of personal gain, for example, contrasted with the doctor's humanitarian motivation—account for different reactions to the different cases.

I have argued that killing is not in itself any worse than letting die; if my contention is right, it follows that active euthanasia is not any worse than passive euthanasia. What arguments can be given on the other side? The most common, I believe, is the following:

"The important difference between active and passive euthanasia is that, in passive euthanasia, the doctor does not do anything to bring about the patient's death. The doctor does nothing, and the patient dies of whatever ills already afflict him. In active euthanasia, however, the doctor does something to bring about the patient's death: he kills him. The doctor who gives the patient with cancer a lethal injection has himself caused his patient's death; whereas if he merely ceases treatment, the cancer is the cause of the death."

A number of points need to be made here. The first is that it is not exactly correct to say that in passive euthanasia the doctor does nothing, for he does do one thing that is very important: he lets the patient die. "Letting someone die" is certainly different, in some respects, from other types of action—mainly in that it is a kind of action that one may perform by way of not performing certain other actions. For example, one may let a patient die by way of not giving medication, just as one may insult someone by way of not shaking his hand. But for any purpose of moral assessment, it is a type of action nonetheless. The decision to let a patient die is subject to moral appraisal in the same way that a decision to kill him would be subject to moral appraisal: it may be assessed as wise or unwise, compassionate or sadistic, right or wrong. If a doctor deliberately let a patient die who was suffering from a routinely curable illness, the doctor would certainly be to blame for what he had done, just as he would be to blame if he had needlessly killed the patient. Charges against him would then be appropriate. If so, it would be no defense at all for him to insist that he didn't "do anything." He would have done something very serious indeed, for he let his patient die.

Fixing the cause of death may be very important from a legal point of view, for it may determine whether criminal charges are brought against the doctor. But I do not think that this notion can be used to show a moral difference between active and passive euthanasia. The reason why it is considered bad to be the cause of someone's death is that death is regarded as a great evil—and so it is. However, if it has been decided that euthanasia—even passive euthanasia—is desirable in a given case, it has also been decided that in this instance death is no greater an evil than the patient's continued existence. And if this is true, the usual reason for not wanting to be the cause of someone's death simply does not apply.

Finally, doctors may think that all of this is only of academic interest—the sort of thing that philosophers may worry about but that has no practical bearing on their own work. After all, doctors must be concerned about the legal consequences of what they do, and active euthanasia is clearly forbidden by the law. But even so, doctors should also be concerned with the fact that the law is forcing upon them a moral doctrine that may well be indefensible, and has a considerable effect on their practices. Of course, most doctors are not now in the position of being coerced in this matter, for they do not regard themselves as merely going along with what the law requires. Rather, in statements such as the AMA policy statement that I have quoted, they are endorsing this doctrine as a central point of medical ethics. In that statement, active euthanasia is condemned not merely as illegal but as "contrary to that for which the medical profession stands," whereas passive euthanasia is approved. However, the preceding considerations suggest that there is really no moral difference between the two, considered in themselves (there may be important moral differences in some cases in their *consequences*, but, as I pointed out, these differences may make active euthanasia, and not passive euthanasia, the morally preferable option). So, whereas doctors may have to discriminate between active and passive euthanasia to satisfy the law, they should not do any more than that. In particular, they should not give the distinction any added authority and weight by writing it into official statements of medical ethics.

Note

1. A. Shaw, "Doctor, Do We Have a Choice?" *The New York Times Magazine,* January 30, 1972, p. 54.

When Self-Determination Runs Amok

Daniel Callahan

Daniel Callahan argues against any social policy allowing voluntary euthanasia and assisted suicide. He maintains that self-determination and mercy (the two values supporting them) may become separated. When this happens, assisted suicide for any reason and nonvoluntary euthanasia for the incompetent will become acceptable.

Callahan rejects Rachel's claim that the difference between killing and letting die is morally irrelevant. He holds that the difference is fundamental and that the decision to terminate a life requires a judgment about meaning and quality that physicians are not competent to make.

In general, Callahan warns us, we must not allow physicians to move beyond the bounds of promoting health and exercise the power of deciding questions about human happiness and well-being. Permitting them to make such decisions will lead to wide-spread abuse and destroy the integrity of the medical profession.

The euthanasia debate is not just another moral debate, one in a long list of arguments in our pluralistic society. It is profoundly emblematic of three important turning points in Western thought. The first is that of the legitimate conditions under which one person can kill another. The acceptance of voluntary active euthanasia would morally sanction what can only be called "consenting adult killing." By that term I mean the killing of one person by another in the name of their mutual right to be killer and killed if they freely agree to play those roles. This turn flies in the face of a long-standing effort to limit the circumstances under which one person can take the life of another, from efforts to control the free flow of guns and arms, to abolish capital punishment, and to more tightly

Daniel Callahan, "When Self-Determination Runs Amok," *Hastings Center Report* 22 (March/April 1992), pp. 52–55. Reprinted by permission.

control warfare. Euthanasia would add a whole new category of killing to a society that already has too many excuses to indulge itself in that way.

The second turning point lies in the meaning and limits of self-determination. The acceptance of euthanasia would sanction a view of autonomy holding that individuals may, in the name of their own private, idiosyncratic view of the good life, call upon others, including such institutions as medicine, to help them pursue that life, even at the risk of harm to the common good. This works against the idea that the meaning and scope of our own right to lead our own lives must be conditioned by, and be compatible with, the good of the community, which is more than an aggregate of self-directing individuals.

The third turning point is to be found in the claim being made upon medicine: it should be prepared to make its skills available to individuals to help them achieve their private vision of the good life. This puts medicine in the business of promoting the individualistic pursuit of general human happiness and well-being. It would overturn the traditional belief that medicine should limit its domain to promoting and preserving human health, redirecting it instead to the relief of that suffering which stems from life itself, not merely from a sick body.

I believe that, at each of these three turning points, proponents of euthanasia push us in the wrong direction. Arguments in favor of euthanasia fall into four general categories, which I will take up in turn: (1) the moral claim of individual self-determination and well-being; (2) the moral irrelevance of the difference between killing and allowing to die; (3) the supposed paucity of evidence to show likely harmful consequences of legalized euthanasia; and (4) the compatibility of euthanasia and medical practice.

Self-Determination

Central to most arguments for euthanasia is the principle of self-determination. People are presumed to have an interest in deciding for themselves, according to their own beliefs about what makes life good, how they will conduct their lives. That is an important value, but the question in the euthanasia context is, What does it mean and how far should it extend? If it were a question of suicide, where a person takes their own life without assistance from another, that principle might be perti-

nent, at least for debate. But euthanasia is not that limited a matter. The self-determination in that case can only be effected by the moral and physical assistance of another. Euthanasia is thus no longer a matter only of self-determination, but of a mutual, social decision between two people, the one to be killed and the other to do the killing.

How are we to make the moral move from my right of self-determination to some doctor's right to kill me—from *my* right to *his* right? Where does the doctor's moral warrant to kill come from? Ought doctors to be able to kill anyone they want as long as permission is given by competent persons? Is our right to life just like a piece of property, to be given away or alienated if the price (happiness, relief of suffering) is right? And then to be destroyed with our permission once alienated?

In answer to all those questions, I will say this: I have yet to hear a plausible argument why it should be permissible for us to put this kind of power in the hands of another, whether a doctor or anyone else. The idea that we can waive our right to life, and then give to another the power to take that life, requires a justification yet to be provided by anyone.

Slavery was long ago outlawed on the ground that one person should not have the right to own another, even with the other's permission. Why? Because it is a fundamental moral wrong for one person to give over his life and fate to another, whatever the good consequences, and no less a wrong for another person to have that kind of total, final power. Like slavery, dueling was long ago banned on similar grounds: even free, competent individuals should not have the power to kill each other, whatever their motives, whatever the circumstances. Consenting adult killing, like consenting adult slavery or degradation, is a strange route to human dignity.

There is another problem as well. If doctors, once sanctioned to carry out euthanasia, are to be themselves responsible moral agents—not simply hired hands with lethal injections at the ready—then they must have their own *independent* moral grounds to kill those who request such services. What do I mean? As those who favor euthanasia are quick to point out, some people want it because their life has become so burdensome it no longer seems worth living.

The doctor will have a difficulty at this point. The degree and intensity to which people suffer from their diseases and their dying, and whether they find life more of a burden than a benefit, has very little directly to do with the nature or extent of their actual physical condition. Three people can have the same condition, but only one will find the suffering unbearable. People suffer, but suffering is as much a function of the values of individuals as it is of the physical causes of that suffering. Inevitably in that circumstance, the doctor will in effect be treating the patient's values. To be responsible, the doctor would have to share those values. The doctor would have to decide, on her own, whether the patient's life was "no longer worth living."

But how could a doctor possibly know that or make such a judgment? Just because the patient said so? I raise this question because, while in Holland at the euthanasia conference reported by Maurice de Wachter elsewhere in this issue, the doctors present agreed that there is no objective way of measuring or judging the claims of patients that their suffering is unbearable. And if it is difficult to measure suffering, how much more difficult to determine the value of a patient's statement that her life is not worth living?

However one might want to answer such questions, the very need to ask them, to inquire into the physician's responsibility and grounds for medical and moral judgment, points out the social nature of the decision. Euthanasia is not a private matter of self-determination. It is an act that requires two people to make it possible, and a complicit society to make it acceptable.

Killing and Allowing to Die

Against common opinion, the argument is sometimes made that there is no moral difference between stopping life-sustaining treatment and more active forms of killing, such as lethal injection. Instead I would contend that the notion that there is no morally significant difference between omission and commission is just wrong. Consider in its broad implications what the eradication of the distinction implies: that death from disease has been banished, leaving only the actions of physicians in terminating treatment as the cause of death. Biology, which used to bring about death, has apparently been displaced by human agency. Doctors have finally, I suppose, thus genuinely become gods, now doing what nature and the deities once did.

What is the mistake here? It lies in confusing causality and culpability, and in failing to note the way in which human societies have overlaid natural causes with moral rules and interpretations. Causality (by which I mean the direct physical causes of death) and culpability (by which I mean our attribution of moral responsibility to human actions) are confused under three circumstances.

They are confused, first, when the action of a physician in stopping treatment of a patient with an underlying lethal disease is construed as *causing* death. On the contrary, the physician's omission can only bring about death on the condition that the patient's disease will kill him in the absence of treatment. We may hold the physician morally responsible for the death, if we have morally judged such actions wrongful omissions. But it confuses reality and moral judgment to see an omitted action as having the same causal status as one that directly kills. A lethal injection will kill both a healthy person and a sick person. A physician's omitted treatment will have no effect on a healthy person. Turn off the machine on me, a healthy person, and nothing will happen. It will only, in contrast, bring the life of a sick person to an end because of an underlying fatal disease.

Causality and culpability are confused, second, when we fail to note that judgments of moral responsibility and culpability are human constructs. By that I mean that we human beings, after moral reflection, have decided to call some actions right or wrong, and to devise moral rules to deal with them. When physicians could do nothing to stop death, they were not held responsible for it. When, with medical progress, they began to have some power over death—but only its timing and circumstances, not its ultimate inevitability—moral rules were devised to set forth their obligations. Natural causes of death were not thereby banished. They were, instead, overlaid with a medical ethics designed to determine moral culpability in deploying medical power.

To confuse the judgments of this ethics with the physical causes of death—which is the connotation of the word *kill*—is to confuse nature and human action. People will, one way or another, die of some disease; death will have dominion over all of us. To say that a doctor "kills" a patient by allowing this to happen should only be understood as a moral judgment about the licitness of his omission, nothing more. We can, as a fashion of speech only, talk about a doctor *killing* a patient by omitting treatment he should have provided. It is a fashion of speech precisely because it is the underlying disease that brings death when treatment is omitted; that is its cause, not the physician's omission. It is a misuse of the word *killing* to use it when a doctor stops a treatment he believes will no longer benefit the patient—when, that is, he steps aside to allow an eventually inevitable death to occur now rather than later. The only deaths that human beings invented are those that come from direct killing—when, with a lethal injection, we both cause death and are morally responsible for it. In the case of omissions, we do not cause death even if we may be judged morally responsible for it.

This difference between causality and culpability also helps us see why a doctor who has omitted a treatment he should have provided has "killed" that patient while another doctor—performing precisely the same act of omission on another patient in different circumstances—does not kill her, but only allows her to die. The difference is that we have come, by moral convention and conviction, to classify unauthorized or illegitimate omissions as acts of "killing." We call them "killing" in the expanded sense of the term: a culpable action that permits the real cause of death, the underlying disease, to proceed to its lethal conclusion. By contrast, the doctor who, at the patient's request, omits or terminates unwanted treatment does not kill at all. Her underlying disease, not his action, is the physical cause of death; and we have agreed to consider actions of that kind to be morally licit. He thus can truly be said to have "allowed" her to die.

If we fail to maintain the distinction between killing and allowing to die, moreover, there are some disturbing possibilities. The first would be to confirm many physicians in their already too-powerful belief that, when patients die or when physicians stop treatment because of the futility of continuing it, they are somehow both morally and physically responsible for the deaths that follow. That notion needs to be abolished, not strengthened. It needlessly and wrongly burdens the physician, to whom should not be attributed the powers of the gods. The second possibility would be that, in every case where a doctor judges medical treatment no longer effective in prolonging life, a quick and direct killing of the patient would be seen as the next, most reasonable step, on grounds of both humaneness and economics. I do not see how that logic could easily be rejected.

Calculating the Consequences

When concerns about the adverse social consequences of permitting euthanasia are raised, its advocates tend to dismiss them as unfounded and overly speculative. On the contrary, recent data about the Dutch experience suggests that such concerns are right on target. From my own discussions in Holland, and from the articles on that subject in this issue and elsewhere, I believe we can now fully see most of the *likely* consequences of legal euthanasia.

Three consequences seem almost certain, in this or any other country: the inevitability of some abuse of the law; the difficulty of precisely writing, and then enforcing, the law; and the inherent slipperiness of the moral reasons for legalizing euthanasia in the first place.

Why is abuse inevitable? One reason is that almost all laws on delicate, controversial matters are to some extent abused. This happens because not everyone will agree with the law as written and will bend it, or ignore it, if they can get away with it. From explicit admissions to me by Dutch proponents of euthanasia, and from the corroborating information provided by the Remmelink Report and the outside studies of Carlos Gomez and John Keown, I am convinced that in the Netherlands there are a substantial number of cases of nonvoluntary euthanasia, that is, euthanasia undertaken without the explicit permission of the person being killed. The other reason abuse is inevitable is that the law is likely to have a low enforcement priority in the criminal justice system. Like other laws of similar status, unless there is an unrelenting and harsh willingness to pursue abuse, violations will ordinarily be tolerated. The worst thing to me about my experience in Holland was the casual, seemingly indifferent attitude toward abuse. I think that would happen everywhere.

Why would it be hard to precisely write, and then enforce, the law? The Dutch speak about the requirement of "unbearable" suffering, but admit that such a term is just about indefinable, a highly subjective matter admitting of no objective standards. A requirement for outside opinion is nice, but it is easy to find complaisant colleagues. A requirement that a medical condition be "terminal" will run aground on the notorious difficulties of knowing when an illness is actually terminal.

Apart from those technical problems there is a more profound worry. I see no way, even in principle, to write or enforce a meaningful law that can guarantee effective procedural safeguards. The reason is obvious yet almost always overlooked. The euthanasia transaction will ordinarily take place within the boundaries of the private and confidential doctor-patient relationship. No one can possibly know what takes place in that context unless the doctor chooses to reveal it. In Holland, less than 10 percent of the physicians report their acts of euthanasia and do so with almost complete legal impunity. There is no reason why the situation should be any better elsewhere. Doctors will have their own reasons for keeping euthanasia secret, and some patients will have no less a motive for wanting it concealed.

I would mention, finally, that the moral logic of the motives for euthanasia contain within them the ingredients of abuse. The two standard motives for euthanasia and assisted suicide are said to be our right of self-determination, and our claim upon the mercy of others, especially doctors, to relieve our suffering. These two motives are typically spliced together and presented as a single justification. Yet if they are considered independently—and there is no inherent reason why they must be linked—they reveal serious problems. It is said that a competent, adult person should have a right to euthanasia for the relief of suffering. But why must the person be suffering? Does not that stipulation already compromise the principle of self-determination? How can self-determination have any limits? Whatever the person's motives may be, why are they not sufficient?

Consider next the person who is suffering but not competent, who is perhaps demented or mentally retarded. The standard argument would deny euthanasia to that person. But why? If a person is suffering but not competent, then it would seem grossly unfair to deny relief solely on the grounds of incompetence. Are the incompetent less entitled to relief from suffering than the competent? Will it only be affluent, middle-class people, mentally fit and savvy about working the medical system, who can qualify? Do the incompetent suffer less because of their incompetence?

Considered from these angles, there are no good moral reasons to limit euthanasia once the principle of taking life for that purpose has been legitimated. If we really believe in self-determination, then any competent person should have a right to be killed by a doctor for any reason that suits him. If we believe in the relief of suffering, then it seems cruel and capricious to deny it to the incompetent. There is, in short, no reasonable or logical stopping point once the turn has been made down the road to euthanasia, which could soon turn into a convenient and commodious expressway.

Euthanasia and Medical Practice

A fourth kind of argument one often hears both in the Netherlands and in this country is that euthanasia and assisted suicide are perfectly compatible with the aims of medicine. I would note at the very outset that a physician who participates in another person's suicide already abuses medicine. Apart from depression (the main statistical cause of suicide), people commit suicide because they find life empty, oppressive, or meaningless. Their judgment is a judgment about the value of continued life, not only about health (even if they are sick). Are doctors now to be given the right to make judgments about the kinds of life worth living and to give their blessing to suicide for those they judge wanting? What conceivable competence, technical or moral, could doctors claim to play such a role? Are we to medicalize suicide, turning judgments about its worth and value into one more clinical issue? Yes, those are rhetorical questions.

Yet they bring us to the core of the problem of euthanasia and medicine. The great temptation of modern medicine, not always resisted, is to move beyond the promotion and preservation of health into the boundless realm of general human happiness and well-being. The root problem of illness and mortality is both medical and philosophical or religious. "Why must I die?" can be asked as a technical, biological question or as a question about the meaning of life. When medicine tries to respond to the latter, which it is always under pressure to do, it moves beyond its proper role.

It is not medicine's place to lift from us the burden of that suffering which turns on the meaning we assign to the decay of the body and its eventual death. It is not medicine's place to determine when lives are not worth living or when the burden of life is too great to be borne. Doctors have no conceivable way of evaluating such claims on the part of patients, and they should have no right to act in response to them. Medicine should try to relieve human suffering, but only that suffering which is brought on by illness and dying as biological phenomena, not that suffering which comes from anguish or despair at the human condition.

Doctors ought to relieve those forms of suffering that medically accompany serious illness and the threat of death. They should relieve pain, do what they can to allay anxiety and uncertainty, and be a comforting presence. As sensitive human beings, doctors should be prepared to respond to patients who ask why they must die, or die in pain. But here the doctor and the patient are at the same level. The doctor may have no better an answer to those old questions than anyone else; and certainly no special insight from his training as a physician. It would be terrible for physicians to forget this, and to think that in a swift, lethal injection, medi-

cine has found its own answer to the riddle of life. It would be a false answer, given by the wrong people. It would be no less a false answer for patients. They should neither ask medicine to put its own vocation at risk to serve their private interests, nor think that the answer to suffering is to be killed by another. The problem is precisely that, too often in human history, killing has seemed the quick, efficient way to put aside that which burdens us. It rarely helps, and too often simply adds to one evil still another. That is what I believe euthanasia would accomplish. It is self-determination run amok.

Voluntary Active Euthanasia

Dan W. Brock

Dan W. Brock examines the possible results of legalizing voluntary euthanasia and assisted suicide and argues that, with procedural safeguards, the value of promoting self-determination and individual well-being outweighs the likely bad consequences.

Brock denies that physician participation in euthanasia is incompatible with the commitment to healing and that it will undermine the moral center of medicine. He argues that medicine's moral center is found in respecting patients' self-determination and promoting their well-being. He regards voluntary euthanasia as compatible with these values and rejects the notion that euthanasia and assisted suicide would undermine the general respect for life or weaken the prohibition against homicide.

The Central Ethical Argument for Voluntary Active Euthanasia

The central ethical argument for euthanasia is familiar. It is that the very same two fundamental ethical values supporting the consensus on patient's rights to decide about life-sustaining treatment also support the ethical permissibility of euthanasia. These values are individual self-determination or autonomy and individual well-being. By self-determination as it bears on euthanasia, I mean people's interest in making important decisions about their lives for themselves according to their

own values or conceptions of a good life, and in being left free to act on those decisions. Self-determination is valuable because it permits people to form and live in accordance with their own conception of a good life, at least within the bounds of justice and consistent with others doing so as well. In exercising self-determination people take responsibility for their lives and for the kinds of persons they become. A central aspect of human dignity lies in people's capacity to direct their lives in this way. The value of exercising self-determination presupposes some minimum of decisionmaking capacities or competence, which thus limits the scope of eu-

From Dan W. Brock, "Voluntary Active Euthanasia," *Hastings Center Report*, March/April 1992, pp. 11–12, 14–17, 19–21. Reprinted by permission.

thanasia supported by self-determination; it cannot justifiably be administered, for example, in cases of serious dementia or treatable clinical depression.

Does the value of individual self-determination extend to the time and manner of one's death? Most people are very concerned about the nature of the last stage of their lives. This reflects not just a fear of experiencing substantial suffering when dying, but also a desire to retain dignity and control during this last period of life. Death is today increasingly preceded by a long period of significant physical and mental decline, due in part to the technological interventions of modern medicine. Many people adjust to these disabilities and find meaning and value in new activities and ways. Others find the impairments and burdens in the last stage of their lives at some point sufficiently great to make life no longer worth living. For many patients near death, maintaining the quality of one's life, avoiding great suffering, maintaining one's dignity, and insuring that others remember us as we wish them to become of paramount importance and outweigh merely extending one's life. But there is no single, objectively correct answer for everyone as to when, if at all, one's life becomes all things considered a burden and unwanted. If self-determination is a fundamental value, then the great variability among people on this question makes it especially important that individuals control the manner, circumstances, and timing of their dying and death.

The other main value that supports euthanasia is individual well-being. It might seem that individual well-being conflicts with a person's self-determination when the person requests euthanasia. Life itself is commonly taken to be a central good for persons, often valued for its own sake, as well as necessary for pursuit of all other goods within a life. But when a competent patient decides to forgo all further life-sustaining treatment then the patient, either explicitly or implicitly, commonly decides that the best life possible for him or her with treatment is of sufficiently poor quality that it is worse than no further life at all. Life is no longer considered a benefit by the patient, but has now become a burden. The same judgment underlies a request for euthanasia: continued life is seen by the patient as no longer a benefit, but now a burden. Especially in the often severely compromised and debilitated states of many critically ill or dying patients, there is no objective standard, but only the competent patient's judgment of whether continued life is no longer a benefit.

Of course, sometimes there are conditions, such as clinical depression, that call into question whether the patient has made a competent choice, either to forgo life-sustaining treatment or to seek euthanasia, and then the patient's choice need not be evidence that continued life is no longer a benefit for him or her. Just as with decisions about treatment, a determination of incompetence can warrant not honoring the patient's choice; in the case of treatment, we then transfer decisional authority to a surrogate, though in the case of voluntary active euthanasia a determination that the patient is incompetent means that choice is not possible. . . .

Most opponents do not deny that there are some cases in which the values of patient self-determination and well-being support euthanasia. Instead, they commonly offer two kinds of arguments against it that on their view outweigh or override this support. The first kind of argument is that in any individual case where considerations of the patient's self-determination and well-being do support euthanasia, it is nevertheless always ethically wrong or impermissible. The second kind of argument grants that in some individual cases euthanasia may *not* be ethically wrong, but maintains nonetheless that public and legal policy should never permit it. The first kind of argument focuses on features of any individual case of euthanasia, while the second kind focuses on social or legal policy. . . .

Would the Bad Consequences of Euthanasia Outweigh the Good?

The argument against euthanasia at the policy level is stronger than at the level of individual cases, though even here I believe the case is ultimately unpersuasive, or at best indecisive. The policy level is the place where the main issues lie, however, and where moral considerations that might override arguments in favor of euthanasia will be found, if they are found anywhere. It is important to note two kinds of disagreement about the consequences for public policy of permitting euthanasia. First, there is empirical or factual disagreement about what the consequences would be. This disagreement is greatly exacerbated by the lack of firm data on the issue. Second, since on any reasonable assessment there would be both good and bad consequences, there are moral disagreements about the relative importance of different effects. In addition to these two sources of disagreement, there is also

no single, well-specified policy proposal for legalizing euthanasia on which policy assessments can
focus. But without such specification, and especially without explicit procedures for protecting
against well-intentioned misuse and ill-intentioned
abuse, the consequences for policy are largely speculative. Despite these difficulties, a preliminary
account of the main likely good and bad consequences is possible. This should help clarify where
better data or more moral analysis and argument
are needed, as well as where policy safeguards
must be developed.

**Potential Good Consequences of Permitting
Euthanasia.** What are the likely good consequences? First, if euthanasia were permitted it
would be possible to respect the self-determination
of competent patients who want it, but now cannot
get it because of its illegality. We simply do not
know how many such patients and people there
are. In the Netherlands, with a population of about
14.5 million (in 1987), estimates in a recent study
were that about 1,900 cases of voluntary active
euthanasia or physician-assisted suicide occur annually. No straightforward extrapolation to the
United States is possible for many reasons, among
them, that we do not know how many people here
who want euthanasia now get it, despite its illegality. Even with better data on the number of persons who want euthanasia but cannot get it, significant moral disagreement would remain about how
much weight should be given to any instance of
failure to respect a person's self-determination in
this way.

One important factor substantially affecting
the number of persons who would seek euthanasia
is the extent to which an alternative is available.
The widespread acceptance in the law, social policy,
and medical practice of the right of a competent patient to forgo life-sustaining treatment suggests that
the number of competent persons in the United
States who would want euthanasia if it were permitted is probably relatively small.

A second good consequence of making euthanasia legally permissible benefits a much larger
group. Polls have shown that a majority of the
American public believes that people should have a
right to obtain euthanasia if they want it.[1] No doubt
the vast majority of those who support this right to
euthanasia will never in fact come to want euthanasia for themselves. Nevertheless, making it legally

permissible would reassure many people that if
they ever do want euthanasia they would be able to
obtain it. This reassurance would supplement the
broader control over the process of dying given by
the right to decide about life-sustaining treatment.
Having fire insurance on one's house benefits all
who have it, not just those whose houses actually
burn down, by reassuring them that in the unlikely
event of their house burning down, they will receive the money needed to rebuild it. Likewise, the
legalization of euthanasia can be thought of as a
kind of insurance policy against being forced to
endure a protracted dying process that one has
come to find burdensome and unwanted, especially
when there is no life-sustaining treatment to forgo.
The strong concern about losing control of their
care expressed by many people who face serious illness likely to end in death suggests that they give
substantial importance to the legalization of euthanasia as a means of maintaining this control.

A third good consequence of the legalization of
euthanasia concerns patients whose dying is filled
with severe and unrelievable pain or suffering.
When there is a life-sustaining treatment that, if forgone, will lead relatively quickly to death, then doing so can bring an end to these patients' suffering
without recourse to euthanasia. For patients receiving no such treatment, however, euthanasia may be
the only release from their otherwise prolonged
suffering and agony. This argument from mercy
has always been the strongest argument for euthanasia in those cases to which it applies.[2]

The importance of relieving pain and suffering
is less controversial than is the frequency with
which patients are forced to undergo untreatable
agony that only euthanasia could relieve. If we focus first on suffering caused by physical pain, it is
crucial to distinguish pain that *could* be adequately
relieved with modern methods of pain control,
though it in fact is not, from pain that is relievable
only by death.[3] For a variety of reasons, including
some physicians' fear of hastening the patient's
death, as well as the lack of a publicly accessible
means for assessing the amount of the patient's
pain, many patients suffer pain that could be, but is
not, relieved.

Specialists in pain control, as for example the
pain of terminally ill cancer patients, argue that
there are very few patients whose pain could not
be adequately controlled, though sometimes at the
cost of so sedating them that they are effectively un-

able to interact with other people or their environment. Thus, the argument from mercy in cases of physical pain can probably be met in a large majority of cases by providing adequate measures of pain relief. This should be a high priority, whatever our legal policy on euthanasia—the relief of pain and suffering has long been, quite properly, one of the central goals of medicine. Those cases in which pain could be effectively relieved, but in fact is not, should only count significantly in favor of legalizing euthanasia if all reasonable efforts to change pain management techniques have been tried and have failed.

Dying patients often undergo substantial psychological suffering that is not fully or even principally the result of physical pain.[4] The knowledge about how to relieve this suffering is much more limited than in the case of relieving pain, and efforts to do so are probably more often unsuccessful. If the argument from mercy is extended to patients experiencing great and unrelievable psychological suffering, the numbers of patients to which it applies are much greater.

One last good consequence of legalizing euthanasia is that once death has been accepted, it is often more humane to end life quickly and peacefully, when that is what the patient wants. Such a death will often be seen as better than a more prolonged one. People who suffer a sudden and unexpected death, for example by dying quickly or in their sleep from a heart attack or stroke, are often considered lucky to have died in this way. We care about how we die in part because we care about how others remember us, and we hope they will remember us as we were in "good times" with them and not as we might be when disease has robbed us of our dignity as human beings. As with much in the treatment and care of the dying, people's concerns differ in this respect, but for at least some people, euthanasia will be a more humane death than what they have often experienced with other loved ones and might otherwise expect for themselves.

Some opponents of euthanasia challenge how much importance should be given to any of these good consequences of permitting it, or even whether some would be good consequences at all. But more frequently, opponents cite a number of bad consequences that permitting euthanasia would or could produce, and it is to their assessment that I now turn.

Potential Bad Consequences of Permitting Euthanasia. Some of the arguments against permitting euthanasia are aimed specifically against physicians, while others are aimed against anyone being permitted to perform it. I shall first consider one argument of the former sort. Permitting physicians to perform euthanasia, it is said, would be incompatible with their fundamental moral and professional commitment as healers to care for patients and to protect life. Moreover, if euthanasia by physicians became common, patients would come to fear that a medication was intended not to treat or care, but instead to kill, and would thus lose trust in their physicians. This position was forcefully stated in a paper by Willard Gaylin and his colleagues:

> The very soul of medicine is on trial . . . This issue touches medicine at its moral center; if this moral center collapses, if physicians become killers or are even licensed to kill, the profession—and, therewith, each physician—will never again be worthy of trust and respect as healer and comforter and protector of life in all its frailty.

These authors go on to make clear that, while they oppose permitting anyone to perform euthanasia, their special concern is with physicians doing so:

> We call on fellow physicians to say that they will not deliberately kill. We must also say to each of our fellow physicians that we will not tolerate killing of patients and that we shall take disciplinary action against doctors who kill. And we must say to the broader community that if it insists on tolerating or legalizing active euthanasia, it will have to find nonphysicians to do its killing.[5]

If permitting physicians to kill would undermine the very "moral center" of medicine, then almost certainly physicians should not be permitted to perform euthanasia. But how persuasive is this claim? Patients should not fear, as a consequence of permitting *voluntary* active euthanasia, that their physicians will substitute a lethal injection for what patients want and believe is part of their care. If active euthanasia is restricted to cases in which it is truly voluntary, then no patient should fear getting it unless she or he has voluntarily requested it. . . . Patients' trust of their physicians could be increased, not eroded, by knowledge that physicians will provide aid in dying when patients seek it. . . .

. . . In spelling out above what I called the positive argument for voluntary active euthanasia, I suggested that two principal values—respecting patients' self-determination and promoting their well-being—underlie the consensus that competent patients, or the surrogates of incompetent patients, are entitled to refuse any life-sustaining treatment and to choose from among available alternative treatments. It is the commitment to these two values in guiding physicians' actions as healers, comforters, and protectors of their patients' lives that should be at the "moral center" of medicine, and these two values support physicians' administering euthanasia when their patients make competent requests for it.

What should not be at that moral center is a commitment to preserving patients' lives as such, without regard to whether those patients want their lives preserved or judge their preservation a benefit to them. . . .

A second bad consequence that some foresee is that permitting euthanasia would weaken society's commitment to provide optimal care for dying patients. We live at a time in which the control of health care costs has become, and is likely to continue to be, the dominant focus of health care policy. If euthanasia is seen as a cheaper alternative to adequate care and treatment, then we might become less scrupulous about providing sometimes costly support and other services to dying patients. Particularly if our society comes to embrace deeper and more explicit rationing of health care, frail, elderly, and dying patients will need to be strong and effective advocates for their own health care and other needs, although they are hardly in a position to do this. We should do nothing to weaken their ability to obtain adequate care and services.

This second worry is difficult to assess because there is little firm evidence about the likelihood of the feared erosion in the care of dying patients. There are at least two reasons, however, for skepticism about this argument. The first is that the same worry could have been directed at recognizing patients' or surrogates' rights to forgo life-sustaining treatment, yet there is no persuasive evidence that recognizing the right to refuse treatment has caused a serious erosion in the quality of care of dying patients. The second reason for skepticism about this worry is that only a very small proportion of deaths would occur from euthanasia if it were permitted. In the Netherlands, where euthanasia under specified circumstances is permitted by the courts, though not authorized by statute, the best estimate of the proportion of overall deaths that result from it is about 2 percent.[6] Thus, the vast majority of critically ill and dying patients will not request it, and so will still have to be cared for by physicians, families, and others. Permitting euthanasia should not diminish people's commitment and concern to maintain and improve the care of these patients. . . .

The [third] potential bad consequence of permitting euthanasia has been developed by David Velleman and turns on the subtle point that making a new option or choice available to people can sometimes make them worse off, even if once they have the choice they go on to choose what is best for them.[7] Ordinarily, people's continued existence is viewed by them as given, a fixed condition with which they must cope. Making euthanasia available to people as an option denies them the alternative of staying alive by default. If people are offered the option of euthanasia, their continued existence is now a choice for which they can be held responsible and which they can be asked by others to justify. We care, and are right to care, about being able to justify ourselves to others. To the extent that our society is unsympathetic to justifying a severely dependent or impaired existence, a heavy psychological burden of proof may be placed on patients who think their terminal illness or chronic infirmity is not a sufficient reason for dying. Even if they otherwise view their life as worth living, the opinion of others around them that it is not can threaten their reason for living and make euthanasia a rational choice. Thus the existence of the option becomes a subtle pressure to request it.

This argument correctly identifies the reason why offering some patients the option of euthanasia would not benefit them. Velleman takes it not as a reason for opposing all euthanasia, but for restricting it to circumstances where there are "unmistakable and overpowering reasons for persons to want the option of euthanasia," and for denying the option in all other cases. But there are at least three reasons why such restriction may not be warranted. First, polls and other evidence support that most Americans believe euthanasia should be permitted. . . . Thus, many more people seem to want the choice than would be made worse off by getting it. Second, if giving people the option of ending their life really makes them worse off, then we should not only prohibit euthanasia, but also take back from people the right they now have to decide about life-sustaining treatment. The feared harmful effect should already have occurred from securing people's right to refuse life-sustaining treatment, yet there is no evidence of any such widespread harm or any broad public desire to rescind that right. Third, since there is a wide range of conditions in which reasonable people can and do disagree about whether they would want continued life, it is not possible to restrict the permissibility of euthanasia as narrowly as Velleman suggests without thereby denying it to most persons who would want it; to permit it only in cases in which virtually everyone would want it would be to deny it to most who would want it.

A [fourth] potential bad consequence of making euthanasia legally permissible is that it might weaken the general legal prohibition of homicide. This prohibition is so fundamental to civilized society, it is argued, that we should do nothing that erodes it. If most cases of stopping life support are killing, as I have already argued, then the court cases permitting such killing have already in effect weakened this prohibition. However, neither the courts nor most people have seen these cases as killing and so as challenging the prohibition of homicide. The courts have usually grounded patients' or their surrogates' rights to refuse life-sustaining treatment in rights to privacy, liberty, self-determination, or bodily integrity, not in exceptions to homicide laws.

Legal permission for physicians or others to perform euthanasia could not be grounded in patients' rights to decide about medical treatment. Permitting euthanasia would require qualifying, at least in effect, the legal prohibition against homicide, a prohibition that in general does not allow the consent of the victim to justify or excuse the act. Nevertheless, the very same fundamental basis of the right to decide about life-sustaining treatment—respecting a person's self-determination—does support euthanasia as well. Individual self-determination has long been a well-entrenched and fundamental value in the law, and so extending it to euthanasia would not require appeal to novel legal values or principles. That suicide or attempted suicide is no longer a criminal offense in virtually all states indicates an acceptance of individual self-determination in the taking of one's own life analogous to that required for voluntary active euthana-

sia. The legal prohibition (in most states) of assisting in suicide and the refusal in the law to accept the consent of the victim as a possible justification of homicide are both arguably a result of difficulties in the legal process of establishing the consent of the victim after the fact. If procedures can be designed that clearly establish the voluntariness of the person's request for euthanasia, it would under those procedures represent a carefully circumscribed qualification on the legal prohibition of homicide. Nevertheless, some remaining worries about this weakening can be captured in the final potential bad consequence, to which I will now turn.

This final potential bad consequence is the central concern of many opponents of euthanasia and, I believe, is the most serious objection to a legal policy permitting it. According to this "slippery slope" worry, although active euthanasia may be morally permissible in cases in which it is unequivocally voluntary and the patient finds his or her condition unbearable, a legal policy permitting euthanasia would inevitably lead to active euthanasia being performed in many other cases in which it would be morally wrong. To prevent those other wrongful cases of euthanasia we should not permit even morally justified performance of it.

Slippery slope arguments of this form are problematic and difficult to evaluate.[8] From one perspective, they are the last refuge of conservative defenders of the status quo. When all the opponents's objections to the wrongness of euthanasia itself have been met, the opponent then shifts ground and acknowledges both that it is not in itself wrong and that a legal policy which resulted only in its being performed would not be bad. Nevertheless, the opponent maintains, it should still not be permitted because doing so would result in its being performed in other cases in which it is not voluntary and would be wrong. In this argument's most extreme form, permitting euthanasia is the first and fateful step down the slippery slope to Nazism. Once on the slope we will be unable to get off.

Now it cannot be denied that it is *possible* that permitting euthanasia could have these fateful consequences, but that cannot be enough to warrant prohibiting it if it is otherwise justified. A similar *possible* slippery slope worry could have been raised to securing competent patients' rights to decide about life support, but recent history shows such a worry would have been unfounded. It must be relevant how likely it is that we will end with horrendous consequences and an unjustified practice of euthanasia. How *likely* and *widespread* would the abuses and unwarranted extensions of permitting it be? By abuses, I mean the performance of euthanasia that fails to satisfy the conditions required for voluntary active euthanasia, for example, if the patient has been subtly pressured to accept it. By unwarranted extensions of policy, I mean later changes in legal policy to permit not just voluntary euthanasia, but also euthanasia in cases in which, for example, it need not be fully voluntary. Opponents of voluntary euthanasia on slippery slope grounds have not provided the data or evidence necessary to turn their speculative concerns into well-grounded likelihoods.

It is at least clear, however, that both the character and likelihood of abuses of a legal policy permitting euthanasia depend in significant part on the procedures put in place to protect against them. I will not try to detail fully what such procedures might be, but will just give some examples of what they might include:

1. The patient should be provided with all relevant information about his or her medical condition, current prognosis, available alternative treatments, and the prognosis of each.

2. Procedures should ensure that the patient's request for euthanasia is stable or enduring (a brief waiting period could be required) and fully voluntary (an advocate for the patient might be appointed to ensure this).

3. All reasonable alternatives must have been explored for improving the patient's quality of life and relieving any pain or suffering.

4. A psychiatric evaluation should ensure that the patient's request is not the result of a treatable psychological impairment such as depression.[9]

These examples of procedural safeguards are all designed to ensure that the patient's choice is fully informed, voluntary, and competent, and so a true exercise of self-determination. Other proposals for euthanasia would restrict its permissibility further—for example, to the terminally ill—a restriction that cannot be supported by self-determination. Such additional restrictions might, however, be justified by concern for limiting potential harms from abuse. At the same time, it is important not to

impose procedural or substantive safeguards so restrictive as to make euthanasia impermissible or practically infeasible in a wide range of justified cases.

These examples of procedural safeguards make clear that it is possible to substantially reduce, though not to eliminate, the potential for abuse of a policy permitting voluntary active euthanasia. Any legalization of the practice should be accompanied by a well-considered set of procedural safeguards together with an ongoing evaluation of its use. Introducing euthanasia into only a few states could be a form of carefully limited and controlled social experiment that would give us evidence about the benefits and harms of the practice. Even then firm and uncontroversial data may remain elusive, as the continuing controversy over what has taken place in the Netherlands in recent years indicates. . . .[10]

The Role of Physicians

If euthanasia is made legally permissible, should physicians take part in it? Should only physicians be permitted to perform it, as is the case in the Netherlands? In discussing whether euthanasia is incompatible with medicine's commitment to curing, caring for, and comforting patients, I argued that it is not at odds with a proper understanding of the aims of medicine, and so need not undermine patients' trust in their physicians. If that argument is correct, then physicians probably should not be prohibited, either by law or by professional norms, from taking part in a legally permissible practice of euthanasia (nor, of course, should they be compelled to do so if their personal or professional scruples forbid it). Most physicians in the Netherlands appear not to understand euthanasia to be incompatible with their professional commitments.

Sometimes patients who would be able to end their lives on their own nevertheless seek the assistance of physicians. Physician involvement in such cases may have important benefits to patients and others beyond simply assuring the use of effective means. Historically, in the United States suicide has carried a strong negative stigma that many today believe unwarranted. Seeking a physician's assistance, or what can almost seem a physician's blessing, may be a way of trying to remove that stigma and show others that the decision for suicide was made with due seriousness and was justified under the circumstances. The physician's involvement provides a kind of social approval, or more accurately helps counter what would otherwise be unwarranted social disapproval.

There are also at least two reasons for restricting the practice of euthanasia to physicians only. First, physicians would inevitably be involved in some of the important procedural safeguards necessary to a defensible practice, such as seeing to it that the patient is well-informed about his or her condition, prognosis, and possible treatments, and ensuring that all reasonable means have been taken to improve the quality of the patient's life. Second, and probably more important, one necessary protection against abuse of the practice is to limit the persons given authority to perform it, so that they can be held accountable for their exercise of that authority. Physicians, whose training and professional norms give some assurance that they would perform euthanasia responsibly, are an appropriate group of persons to whom the practice may be restricted.

Notes

1. P. Painton and E. Taylor, "Love or Let Die," *Time,* 19 March 1990, pp. 62–71; *Boston Globe*/Harvard University Poll, *Boston Globe,* 3 November 1991.

2. James Rachels, *The End of Life* (Oxford: Oxford University Press, 1986).

3. Marcia Angell, "The Quality of Mercy," *NEJM* 306 (1982): 98–99; M. Donovan, P. Dillon, and L. Mcguire, "Incidence and Characteristics of Pain in a Sample of Medical-Surgical Inpatients," *Pain* 30 (1987): 69–78.

4. Eric Cassell, *The Nature of Suffering and the Goals of Medicine* (New York: Oxford University Press, 1991).

5. Willard Gaylin, Leon R. Kass, Edmund D. Pellegrino, and Mark Siegler, "Doctors Must Not Kill," *JAMA* 259 (1988): 2139–40.

6. Paul J. Van der Maas et al., "Euthanasia and Other Medical Decisions Concerning the End of Life," *Lancet* 338 (1991): 669–74.

7. My formulation of this argument derives from David Velleman's statement of it in his commentary on an earlier version of this paper delivered at the American Philosophical Association Central Division meetings; a similar point was made to me by Elisha Milgram in discussion on another occasion. For more general development of the point see Thomas Schelling, *The Strategy of Conflict* (Cambridge, Mass.: Harvard University Press, 1960); and Gerald Dworkin, "Is More Choice Better Than Less?" in *The Theory and Practice of Autonomy* (Cambridge: Cambridge University Press, 1988).

8. Frederick Schauer, "Slippery Slopes," *Harvard Law Review* 99 (1985): 361–83; Wibren van der Burg, "The Slippery Slope Argument," *Ethics* 102 (October 1991): 42–65.

9. There is evidence that physicians commonly fail to diagnose depression. See Robert I. Misbin, "Physicians Aid in Dying," *NEJM* 325 (1991): 1304–7.

10. Richard Fenigsen, "A Case against Dutch Euthanasia," Special Supplement, *Hastings Center Report* 19, no. 1 (1989): 22–30.

Terminal, but Not Hopeless

Sandol Stoddard

Sandol Stoddard points out that the debate over assisted suicide has ignored "the care, comfort, and dignity" offered to people approaching death by hospices. The debate rests on two false assumptions: that terminally ill people must expect to suffer in ways that make death a welcome alternative and that those who are old, frail, or ill are somehow failures and should depart from life. Hospices, Stoddard claims, provide the sort of care that keeps people from wanting to kill themselves. He ends by warning us that the steps between assisted suicide, homicide, and genocide are short ones.

It is amazing that in all the recent discussion of assisted suicide there has been hardly a reference to hospices as a way of caring for the terminally ill. The American hospice movement has been one of the outstanding expressions in recent years of inventiveness and compassion in combating suffering. At the same time, in hospitals and medical schools, hospice philosophy and expertise are helping to develop more humanely responsible attitudes in the general practice of medicine.

The modern hospice has arisen over the past 25 years to provide care, comfort and dignity to people approaching death. Most hospices in the U.S. today are small, independent nonprofit organizations, though many work in conjunction with local visiting nurse associations, hospitals and medical centers. The interdisciplinary hospice team consists of physicians, nurses, social workers, members of the clergy, therapists of various kinds, nutritionists and specially trained lay volunteers. Family and friends are also part of the team, and continue to receive support during bereavement.

Much of the current suicide controversy seems to be based on a pair of false assumptions. The first is that seriously ill people must expect agonies and humiliations from which death itself is the only merciful release. This is not so. Hospice patients are treated with respect. They are not attached to machines that prolong dying while destroying whatever quality of life remains.

A great deal more can be done today than was possible in the past to relieve the pain of conditions like terminal cancer. Nearly three decades of clinical experience in America and England have made it clear that skilled hospice teamwork can keep patients quite comfortable, physically and emotionally—often in their own homes—throughout the final stage of life. Studies have also shown that these patients do not become addicted to painkillers, nor do they come to require dangerously high doses. In fact, quite the opposite is true: In the supportive hospice setting, levels of pain medication are frequently reduced.

The second false assumption is perhaps less obvious, but more dangerous to society. Privately, too many of us believe that human perfection can be achieved—that if only we can find the correct program, with all the directions on the package, we can be thin, beautiful, bright, popular, healthy, rich and powerful forever. Such a shallow, simplistic view of life may seem innocent enough on the surface. But underneath it is the unspoken, often unconscious conviction that those who are very ill, very old or very frail have not done it right and should not be here among us. This attitude not only fouls our own lives, but presses the loaded gun, or the overdose, into the hands of sufferers.

Thousands of hospice workers in this country today are witness to the fact that people who are comfortable, secure and lovingly cared for *do not want* to commit suicide. They can also tell us that it is a great and often inspiring privilege to be with these individuals as they travel the last miles of the road that lies before us all. In the meantime we need to remember a lesson history has taught us: that it's but a short step that leads from assisted suicide to homicide, to genocide and the ultimate moral abyss.

Must Patients Always Be Given Food and Water? _____

Joanne Lynn and James F. Childress

Lynn and Childress consider whether it is ever permissible to withhold or withdraw food or nutrition from a patient. After rejecting the notion that such an action would be intrinsically wrong, they describe how providing nutrition as a medical treatment differs from ordinary feeding. They then mention three circumstances in which such treatment is not obligatory: when it would be futile, when it could bring no benefit to the patient, and when any benefit brought is outweighed by the burden imposed on the patient. They reject four arguments that hold that nutrition and hydration must be provided: because it is a part of ordinary care, because treatment begun must be continued, because we should not cause death, and because such treatment is symbolically significant.

Many people die from the lack of food or water. For some, this lack is the result of poverty or famine, but for others it is the result of disease, or deliberate decision. In the past, malnutrition and dehydration must have accompanied nearly every death that followed an illness of more than a few days. Most dying patients do not eat much on their own, and nothing could be done for them until the first flexible tubing for instilling food or other liquid into the stomach was developed about a hundred years ago. Even then, the procedure was so scarce, so costly in physician and nursing time, and so poorly tolerated that it was used only for patients who clearly could benefit. With the advent of more reliable and efficient procedures in the past few decades, these conditions can be corrected or ameliorated in nearly every patient who would otherwise be malnourished or dehydrated. In fact, intravenous lines and nasogastric tubes have become common images of hospital care.

Providing adequate nutrition and fluids is a high priority for most patients, both because they suffer directly from inadequacies and because these deficiencies hinder their ability to overcome other diseases. But are there some patients who need not receive these treatments? This question has become a prominent public policy issue in a number of recent cases. In May 1981, in Danville, Illinois, the parents and the physician of newborn conjoined twins with shared abdominal organs decided not to feed these children. Feeding and other treatments were given after court intervention, though a grand jury refused to indict the parents.[1] Later that year, two physicians in Los Angeles discontinued intravenous nutrition to a patient who had severe brain damage after an episode involving loss of oxygen following routine surgery. Murder charges were brought, but the hearing judge dismissed the charges at a preliminary hearing. On appeal, the charges were reinstated and remanded for trial.[2]

In April 1982, a Bloomington, Indiana, infant who had tracheoesophageal fistula and Down Syndrome was not treated or fed, and he died after two courts ruled that the decision was proper but before all appeals could be heard.[3] When the federal government then moved to ensure that such infants would be fed in the future,[4] the Surgeon General, Dr. C. Everett Koop, initially stated that there is never adequate reason to deny nutrition and fluids to a newborn infant.

While these cases were before the public, the nephew of Claire Conroy, an elderly incompetent woman with several serious medical problems, petitioned a New Jersey court for authority to discontinue her nasogastric tube feedings. Although the intermediate appeals court has reversed the ruling,[5] the trial court held that he had this authority since the evidence indicated that the patient would not have wanted such treatment and that its value to her was doubtful.

In all these dramatic cases and in many more that go unnoticed, the decision is made to deliberately withhold food or fluid known to be necessary for the life of the patient. Such decisions are unsettling. There is now widespread consensus that sometimes a patient is best served by not undertaking or continuing certain treatments that would sustain life, especially if these entail substantial suffering.[6] But food and water are so central to an array of human emotions that it is almost impossible to consider them with the same emotional detachment that one might feel toward a respirator or a dialysis machine.

Nevertheless, the question remains: Should it ever be permissible to withhold or withdraw food and nutrition? The answer in any real case should acknowledge the psychological contiguity between feeding and loving and between nutritional satisfaction and emotional satisfaction. Yet this acknowledgment does not resolve the core question.

Some have held that it is intrinsically wrong not to feed another. The philosopher G. E. M. Anscombe contends: "For wilful starvation there can be no excuse. The same can't be said quite without qualification about failing to operate or to adopt some courses of treatment."[7] But the moral issues are more complex than Anscombe's comment suggests. Does correcting nutritional deficiencies always improve patients' well-being? What should be our reflective moral response to withholding or withdrawing nutrition? What moral principles are relevant to our reflections? What medical facts about ways of providing nutrition are relevant? And what policies should be adopted by the society, hospitals, and medical and other health care professionals?

Reprinted by permission of the authors and The Hastings Center from *Hastings Center Report 13* (October 1983), pp. 17–21.

In our effort to find answers to these questions, we will concentrate upon the care of patients who are incompetent to make choices for themselves. Patients who are competent to determine the course of their therapy may refuse any and all interventions proposed by others, as long as their refusals do not seriously harm or impose unfair burdens upon others.[8] A competent patient's decision regarding whether or not to accept the provision of food and water by medical means such as tube feeding or intravenous alimentation is unlikely to raise questions of harm or burden to others.

What then should guide those who must decide about nutrition for a patient who cannot decide? As a start, consider the standard by which other medical decisions are made: one should decide as the incompetent person would have if he or she were competent, when that is possible to determine, and advance that person's interests in a more generalized sense when individual preferences cannot be known.

The Medical Procedures

There is no reason to apply a different standard to feeding and hydration. Surely, when one inserts a feeding tube, or creates a gastrostomy opening, or inserts a needle into a vein, one intends to benefit the patient. Ideally, one should provide what the patient believes to be of benefit, but at least the effect should be beneficial in the opinions of surrogates and caregivers.

Thus, the question becomes, is it ever in the patient's interest to become malnourished and dehydrated, rather than to receive treatment? Posing the question so starkly points to our need to know what is entailed in treating these conditions and what benefits the treatments offer.

The medical interventions that provide food and fluids are of two basic types. First, liquids can be delivered by a tube that is inserted into a functioning gastrointestinal tract, most commonly through the nose and esophagus into the stomach or through a surgical incision in the abdominal wall and directly into the stomach. The liquids used can be specially prepared solutions of nutrients or a blenderized version of an ordinary diet. The nasogastric tube is cheap; it may lead to pneumonia and often annoys the patient and family, sometimes even requiring that the patient be restrained to prevent its removal.

Creating a gastrostomy is usually a simple surgical procedure, and, once the wound is healed, care is very simple. Since it is out of sight, it is aesthetically more acceptable and restraints are needed less often. Also, the gastrostomy creates no additional risk of pneumonia. However, while elimination of a nasogastric tube requires only removing the tube, a gastrostomy is fairly permanent, and can be closed only by surgery.

The second type of medical intervention is intravenous feeding and hydration, which also has two major forms. The ordinary hospital or peripheral IV, in which fluid is delivered directly to the bloodstream through a small needle, is useful only for temporary efforts to improve hydration and electrolyte concentrations. One cannot provide a balanced diet through the veins in the limbs: to do that requires a central line, or a special catheter placed into one of the major veins in the chest. The latter procedure is much more risky and vulnerable to infections and technical errors, and it is much more costly than any of the other procedures. Both forms of intravenous nutrition and hydration commonly require restraining the patient, cause minor infections and other ill effects, and are costly, especially since they ordinarily require the patient to be in a hospital.

None of these procedures, then, is ideal; each entails some distress, some medical limitations, and some costs. When may a procedure be forgone that might improve nutrition and hydration for a given patient? Only when the procedure and the resulting improvement in nutrition and hydration do not offer the patient a net benefit over what he or she would otherwise have faced.

Are there such circumstances? We believe that there are; but they are few and limited to the following three kinds of situations: (1) the procedures that would be required are so unlikely to achieve improved nutritional and fluid levels that they could be correctly considered futile; (2) the improvement in nutritional and fluid balance, though achievable, could be of no benefit to the patient; (3) the burdens of receiving the treatment may outweigh the benefit.

When Food and Water May Be Withheld

Futile Treatment.   Sometimes even providing "food and water" to a patient becomes a monumental task. Consider a patient with a severe clotting deficiency and a nearly total body burn. Gaining access to the central veins is likely to cause hemorrhage or infection, nasogastric tube placement may be quite painful, and there may be no skin to which to suture the stomach for a gastrostomy tube. Or consider a patient with severe congestive heart failure who develops cancer of the stomach with a fistula that delivers food from the stomach to the colon without passing through the intestine and being absorbed. Feeding the patient may be possible, but little is absorbed. Intravenous feeding cannot be tolerated because the fluid would be too much for the weakened heart. Or consider the infant with infarction of all but a short segment of bowel. Again, the infant can be fed, but little if anything is absorbed. Intravenous methods can be used, but only for a short time (weeks or months) until their complications, including thrombosis, hemorrhage, infections, and malnutrition, cause death.

In these circumstances, the patient is going to die soon, no matter what is done. The ineffective efforts to provide nutrition and hydration may directly cause suffering that offers no counterbalancing benefit for the patient. Although the procedures might be tried, especially if the competent patient wanted them or the incompetent patient's surrogate had reason to believe that this incompetent patient would have wanted them, they cannot be considered obligatory. To hold that a patient must be subjected to this predictably futile sort of intervention just because protein balance is negative or the blood serum is concentrated is to lose sight of the moral warrant for medical care and to reduce the patient to an array of measurable variables.

No Possibility of Benefit.   Some patients can be reliably diagnosed to have permanently lost consciousness. This unusual group of patients includes those with anencephaly, persistent vegetative state, and some preterminal comas. In these cases, it is very difficult to discern how any medical intervention can benefit or harm the patient. These patients cannot and never will be able to experience any of the events occurring in the world or in their bodies. When the diagnosis is exceedingly clear, we sustain their lives vigorously mainly for their loved ones and the community at large.

While these considerations probably indicate that continued artificial feeding is best in most cases, there may be some cases in which the family and the caregivers are convinced that artificial feeding is offensive and unreasonable. In such cases,

there seems to be more adequate reason to claim that withholding food and water violates any obligations that these parties or the general society have with regard to permanently unconscious patients. Thus, if the parents of an anencephalic infant or of a patient like Karen Quinlan in a persistent vegetative state feel strongly that no medical procedures should be applied to provide nutrition and hydration, and the caregivers are willing to comply, there should be no barrier in law or public policy to thwart the plan.[9]

Disproportionate Burden.   The most difficult cases are those in which normal nutritional status or fluid balance could be restored, but only with a severe burden for the patient. In these cases, the treatment is futile in a broader sense—the patient will not actually benefit from the improved nutrition and hydration. A patient who is competent can decide the relative merits of the treatment being provided, knowing the probable consequences, and weighing the merits of life under various sets of constrained circumstances. But a surrogate decision maker for a patient who is incompetent to decide will have a difficult task. When the situation is irremediably ambiguous, erring on the side of continued life and improved nutrition and hydration seems the less grievous error. But are there situations that would warrant a determination that this patient, whose nutrition and hydration could surely be improved, is not thereby well served?

Though they are rare, we believe there are such cases. The treatments entailed are not benign. Their effects are far short of ideal. Furthermore, many of the patients most likely to have inadequate food and fluid intake are also likely to suffer the most serious side effect of these therapies.

Patients who are allowed to die without artificial hydration and nutrition may well die more comfortably than patients who receive conventional amounts of intravenous hydration.[10] Terminal pulmonary edema, nausea, and mental confusion are more likely when patients have been treated to maintain fluid and nutrition until close to the time of death.

Thus, those patients whose "need" for artificial nutrition and hydration arises only near the time of death may be harmed by its provision. It is not at all clear that they receive any benefit in having a slightly prolonged life, and it does seem reasonable to allow a surrogate to decide that, for this patient at this time, slight prolongation of life is not warranted if it involves measures that will probably increase the patient's suffering as he or she dies.

Even patients who might live much longer might not be well served by artificial means to provide fluid and food. Such patients might include those with fairly severe dementia for whom the restraints required could be a constant source of fear, discomfort, and struggle. For such a patient, sedation to tolerate the feeding mechanisms might preclude any of the pleasant experiences that might otherwise have been available. Thus, a decision not to intervene, except perhaps briefly to ascertain that there are no treatable causes, might allow such a patient to live out a shorter life with fair freedom of movement and freedom from fear, while a decision to maintain artificial nutrition and hydration might consign the patient to end his or her life in unremitting anguish. If this were the case a surrogate decision-maker would seem to be well justified in refusing the treatment.

Inappropriate Moral Constraints

Four considerations are frequently proposed as moral constraints on foregoing medical feeding and hydration. We find none of these to dictate that artificial nutrition and hydration must always be provided.

The Obligation to Provide "Ordinary" Care. Debates about appropriate treatment are often couched in terms of "ordinary" and "extraordinary" means of treatment. Historically, this distinction emerged in the Roman Catholic tradition to differentiate optional treatment from treatment that was obligatory for medical professionals to offer and for patients to accept.[11] These terms also appear in many secular contexts, such as court decisions and medical codes. The recent debates about ordinary and extraordinary means of treatment have been interminable and often unfruitful, in part because of a lack of clarity about what the terms mean. Do they represent the premises of an argument or the conclusion, and what features of a situation are relevant to the categorization as "ordinary" or "extraordinary"?[12]

Several criteria have been implicit in debates about ordinary and extraordinary means of treatment; some of them may be relevant to determining whether and which treatments are obligatory and which are optional. Treatments have been distinguished according to their simplicity (simple/complex), their naturalness (natural/artificial), their customariness (usual/unusual), their invasiveness (noninvasive/invasive), their chance of success (reasonable chance/futile), their balance of benefits and burdens (proportionate/disproportionate), and their expense (inexpensive/costly). Each set of paired terms or phrases in the parentheses suggests a continuum: as the treatment moves from the first of the paired terms to the second, it is said to become less obligatory and more optional.

However, when these various criteria, widely used in discussions about medical treatment, are carefully examined, most of them are not morally relevant in distinguishing optional from obligatory medical treatments. For example, if a rare, complex, artificial, and invasive treatment offers a patient a reasonable chance of nearly painless cure, then one would have to offer a substantial justification not to provide that treatment to an incompetent patient.

What matters, then, in determining whether to provide a treatment to an incompetent patient is not a prior determination that this treatment is "ordinary" per se, but rather a determination that this treatment is likely to provide this patient benefits that are sufficient to make it worthwhile to endure the burdens that accompany the treatment. To this end, some of the considerations listed above are relevant: whether a treatment is likely to succeed is an obvious example. But such considerations taken in isolation are not conclusive. Rather, the surrogate decision-maker is obliged to assess the desirability to this patient of each of the options presented, including nontreatment. For most people at most times, this assessment would lead to a clear obligation to provide food and fluids.

But sometimes, as we have indicated, providing food and fluids through medical interventions may fail to benefit and may even harm some patients. Then the treatment cannot be said to be obligatory, no matter how usual and simple its provision may be. If "ordinary" and "extraordinary" are used to convey the conclusion about the obligation to treat, providing nutrition and fluids would have become, in these cases, "extraordinary." Since this phrasing is misleading, it is probably better to use "proportionate" and "disproportionate," as the Vatican now suggests,[13] or "obligatory" and "optional."

Obviously, providing nutrition and hydration may sometimes be necessary to keep patients comfortable while they are dying even though it may temporarily prolong their dying. In such cases, food and fluids constitute warranted palliative care. But in other cases, such as a patient in a deep and irreversible coma, nutrition and hydration do not appear to be needed or helpful, except perhaps to comfort the staff and family.[14] And sometimes the interventions needed for nutrition and hydration are so burdensome that they are harmful and best not utilized.

The Obligation to Continue Treatments Once Started.   Once having started a mode of treatment, many caregivers find it very difficult to discontinue it. While this strongly felt difference between the ease of withholding a treatment and the difficulty of withdrawing it provides a psychological explanation of certain actions, it does not justify them. It sometimes even leads to a thoroughly irrational decision process. For example, in caring for a dying, comatose patient, many physicians apparently find it harder to stop a functioning peripheral IV than not to restart one that has infiltrated (that is, has broken through the blood vessel and is leaking fluid into surrounding tissue), especially if the only way to reestablish an IV would be to insert a central line into the heart or to do a cutdown (make an incision to gain access to the deep large blood vessels).[15]

What factors might make withdrawing medical treatment morally worse than withholding it? Withdrawing a treatment seems to be an action, which, when it is likely to end in death, initially seems more serious than an omission that ends in death. However, this view is fraught with errors. Withdrawing is not always an act: failing to put the next infusion into a tube could be correctly described as an omission, for example. Even when withdrawing is an act, it may well be morally correct and even morally obligatory. Discontinuing intravenous lines in a patient now permanently unconscious in accord with that patient's well-informed advance directive would certainly be such a case. Furthermore, the caregiver's obligation to serve the patient's interests through both acts and omissions rules out the exculpation that accompanies omissions in the usual course of social life. An omission that is not warranted by the patient's interests is culpable.

Sometimes initiating a treatment creates expectations in the minds of caregivers, patients, and family that the treatment will be continued indefinitely or until the patient is cured. Such expectations may provide a reason to continue the treatment as a way to keep a promise. However, as with all promises, caregivers could be very careful when initiating a treatment to explain the indications for its discontinuation, and they could modify preconceptions with continuing reevaluation and education during treatment. Though all patients are entitled to expect the continuation of care in the patient's best interests, they are not and should not be entitled to the continuation of a particular mode of care.

Accepting the distinction between withholding and withdrawing medical treatment as morally significant also has a very unfortunate implication: caregivers may become unduly reluctant to begin some treatments precisely because they fear that they will be locked into continuing treatments that are no longer of value to the patient. For example, the physician who had been unwilling to stop the respirator while the infant Andrew Stinson died over several months is reportedly "less eager to attach babies to respirators now."[16] But if it were easier to ignore malnutrition and dehydration and to withhold treatments for these problems than to discontinue the same treatments when they have become especially burdensome and insufficiently beneficial for the patient, then the incentives would be perverse. Once a treatment has been tried, it is often much clearer whether it is of value to the patient, and the decision to stop it can be made more reliably.

The same considerations should apply to starting as to stopping a treatment, and whatever assessment warrants withholding should also warrant withdrawing.

The Obligation to Avoid Being the Unambiguous Cause of Death.   Many physicians will agree with all that we have said and still refuse to allow a choice to forgo food and fluid because such a course seems to be a "death sentence." In this view death seems to be more certain from malnutrition and dehydration than from forgoing other forms of medical therapy. This implies that it is acceptable to act in ways that are likely to cause death, as in not operating on a gangrenous leg, only if there remains a chance that the patient will survive. This is a comforting formulation for caregivers, to be sure, since they can thereby avoid feeling the full weight of the responsibility for the time and manner of a patient's death. However, it is not a persuasive moral argument.

First, in appropriate cases discontinuing certain medical treatments is generally accepted despite the fact that death is as certain as with nonfeeding. Dialysis in a patient without kidney function or transfusions in a patient with severe aplastic anemia are obvious examples. The dying that awaits such patients often is not greatly different from dying of dehydration and malnutrition.

Second, the certainty of a generally undesirable outcome such as death is always relevant to a decision, but it does not foreclose the possibility that this course is better than others available to this patient.[17] Ambiguity and uncertainty are so common in medical decision-making that caregivers are tempted to use them in distancing themselves from direct responsibility. However, caregivers are in fact responsible for the time and manner of death for many patients. Their distaste for this fact should not constrain otherwise morally justified decisions.

The Obligation to Provide Symbolically Significant Treatment. One of the most common arguments for always providing nutrition and hydration is that it symbolizes, expresses, or conveys the essence of care and compassion. Some actions not only aim at goals, they also express values. Such expressive actions should not simply be viewed as means to ends; they should also be viewed in light of what they communicate. From this perspective food and water are not only goods that preserve life and provide comfort; they are also symbols of care and compassion. To withhold or withdraw them—to "starve" a patient—can never express or convey care.

Why is providing food and water a central symbol of care and compassion? Feeding is the first response of the community to the needs of newborns and remains a central mode of nurture and comfort. Eating is associated with social interchange and community, and providing food for someone else is a way to create and maintain bonds of sharing and expressing concern. Furthermore, even the relatively low levels of hunger and thirst that most people have experienced are decidedly uncomfortable, and the common image of severe malnutrition or dehydration is one of unremitting agony. Thus, people are rightly eager to provide food and water. Such provision is essential to minimally tolerable existence and a powerful symbol of our concern for each other.

However, *medical* nutrition and hydration, we have argued, may not always provide net benefits to patients. Medical procedures to provide nutrition and hydration are more similar to other medical procedures than to typical human ways of providing nutrition and hydration, for example, a sip of water. It should be possible to evaluate their benefits and burdens, as we evaluate any other medical procedure. Of course, if family, friends, and caregivers feel that such procedures affirm important values even when they do not benefit the patient, their feelings should not be ignored. We do not contend that there is an obligation to withhold or to withdraw such procedures (unless consideration of the patient's advance directives or current best interest unambiguously dictates that conclusion); we only contend that nutrition and hydration may be forgone in some cases.

The symbolic connection between care and nutrition or hydration adds useful caution to decision making. If decision makers worry over withholding or withdrawing medical nutrition and hydration, they may inquire more seriously into the circumstances that putatively justify their decisions. This is generally salutary for health care decision making. The critical inquiry may well yield the sad but justified conclusion that the patient will be served best by not using medical procedures to provide food and fluids.

A Limited Conclusion

Our conclusion—that patients or their surrogates, in close collaboration with their physicians and other caregivers and with careful assessment of the relevant information, can correctly decide to forgo the provision of medical treatments intended to correct malnutrition and dehydration in some circumstances—is quite limited. Concentrating on incompetent patients, we have argued that in most cases such patients will be best served by providing nutrition and fluids. Thus, there should be a presumption in favor of providing nutrition and fluids as part of the broader presumption to provide means that prolong life. But this presumption may be rebutted in particular cases.

We do not have enough information to be able to determine with clarity and conviction whether withholding or withdrawing nutrition and hydration was justified in the cases that have occasioned public concern, though it seems likely that the Danville and Bloomington babies should have been fed and that Claire Conroy should not.

It is never sufficient to rule out "starvation" categorically. The question is whether the obligation to act in the patient's best interests was discharged by withholding or withdrawing particular medical treatments. All we have claimed is that nutrition and hydration by medical means need not always be provided. Sometimes they may not be in accord with the patient's wishes or interests. Medical nutrition and hydration do not appear to be distinguishable in any morally relevant way from other life-sustaining medical treatments that may on occasion be withheld or withdrawn.

Notes

1. John A. Robertson, "Dilemma in Danville," *Hastings Cent. Rep.* 11: 5–8 (October 1981).

2. T. Rohrlich, "2 Doctors Face Murder Charges in Patient's Death." *L.A. Times,* August 19, 1982. A-1; Jonathan Kirsch, "A Death at Kaiser Hospital." *Calif. Mag.* (1982), 79ff; Magistrate's findings. California v. Barber and Nejdl, No. A 925586, Los Angeles Man. Ct. Cal. (March 9, 1983); Superior Court of California, County of Los Angeles, California v. Barber and Nejdl, No. A0 25586k tentative decision May 5, 1983.

3. *In re* Infant Doe, No. GU 8204-00 (Cir. Ct. Monroe County, Ind., April 12, 1982), *writ of mandamus dismissed sub nom.* State ex rel. Infant Doe v. Baker, No. 482 S140 (Indiana Supreme Ct., May 27, 1982).

4. Office of the Secretary, Department of Health and Human Services, "Nondiscrimination on the Basis of Handicap," *Federal Register* 48 (1983), 9630-32. (Interim final rule modifying 45 C.F.R. #84.61.) See Judge Gerhard Gesell's decision, American Academy of Pediatrics v. Heckler, No. 83–0774, U.S. District Court, D.C., April 24, 1983; and also George J. Annas, "Disconnecting the Baby Doe Hotline," *Hastings Cent. Rep.* 13: 14–16 (June 1983).

5. *In re* Conroy, 190 N.J. Super. 453, 464 A.2d 303 (App. Div. 1983).

6. President's Commission for the Study of Ethical Problems in Medicine and Biomedical and Behavioral Research. *Deciding to Forego Life-Sustaining Treatment.* Washington, D.C.: U.S. Government Printing Office (1982).

7. G. E. M. Anscombe, "Ethical Problems in the Management of Some Severely Handicapped Children: Commentary 2," *J. Med. Ethics* 7: 117–124 (1981).

8. See, e.g., President's Commission for the Study of Ethical Problems in Medicine and Biomedical and Behavioral Research, *Making Health Care Decisions,* Washington, D.C.: U.S. Government Printing Office (1982).

9. President's Commission, *Deciding to Forego,* at 171–196.

10. Joyce V. Zerwekh, "The Dehydration Question," *Nursing 83,* 47–51 (1983) with comments by Judith R. Brown and Marion B. Dolan. See also chapter 3.

11. James J. McCartney, "The Development of the Doctrine of Ordinary and Extraordinary Means of Preserving Life in Catholic Moral Theology before the Karen Quinlan Case," *Linacre Q.* 47: 215 (1980).

12. President's Commission. *Deciding to Forego,* at 82–90. For an argument that fluids and electrolytes can be "extraordinary," see Carson Strong, "Can Fluids and Electrolytes be 'Extraordinary' Treatment?" *J. Med. Ethics* 7: 83–85 (1981).

13. The Sacred Congregation for the Doctrine of the Faith, Declaration on Euthanasia, Vatican City, May 5, 1980.

14. Paul Ramsey, *The Patient as Person,* New Haven: Yale University Press (1970), 128–129; Paul Ramsey, *Ethics at the Edges of Life: Medical and Legal Intersections,* New Haven: Yale University Press (1978), 275; Bernard Towers, "Irreversible Coma and Withdrawal of Life Support: Is It Murder If the IV Line Is Disconnected?" *J. Med. Ethics* 8: 205 (1982).

15. See Kenneth C. Micetich, Patricia H. Steinecker, and David C. Thomasma, "Are Intravenous Fluids Morally Required for a Dying Patient?" *Arch. Intern. Med.* 143: 975–978 (1983), also chapter 4.

16. Robert and Peggy Stinson, *The Long Dying of Baby Andrew,* Boston: Little, Brown and Co. (1983), 355.

17. See chapter 4 [in original volume].

In the Matter of Karen Quinlan, an Alleged Incompetent

The Supreme Court of New Jersey

The 1976 decision of the New Jersey Supreme Court in the case of Karen Quinlan was significant in establishing that a legally based right of privacy permits a patient to decide to refuse medical treatment. The court also held that this right can be exercised by a parent or guardian when the patient herself is in no position to do so. Thus, in the opinion of the court, removal of life-sustaining equipment would not be a case of homicide (or any other kind of wrongful killing), even if the patient should die as a result.

The ruling in the *Quinlan* case has had an enormous impact on decisions about discontinuing extraordinary medical measures. However, the ruling has been generally construed rather narrowly so as to apply only to mentally incompetent patients who are brain-dead, comatose, or in an irreversible coma.

Background Note. The decision of the court was issued on March 31, 1976. It was delivered by Chief Justice Hughes. The following abridgment omits references and case citations.

Constitutional and Legal Issues

I. The Free Exercise of Religion

Simply stated, the right to religious beliefs is absolute but conduct in pursuance thereof is not wholly immune from governmental restraint. So it is that, for the sake of life, courts sometimes (but not always) order blood transfusions for Jehovah's Witnesses (whose religious beliefs abhor such procedure), forbid exposure to death from handling virulent snakes or ingesting poison (interfering with deeply held religious sentiments in such regard), and protect the public health as in the case of compulsory vaccination (over the strongest of religious objections). . . . The Public interest is thus considered paramount, without essential dissolution of respect for religious beliefs.

We think, without further examples, that, ranged against the State's interest in the preservation of life, the impingement of religious belief, much less religious "neurality" as here, does not reflect a constitutional question, in the circumstances at least of the case presently before the Court. Moreover, like the trial court, we do not recognize an independent parental right of religious freedom to support the relief requested.

II. Cruel and Unusual Punishment

Similarly inapplicable to the case before us is the Constitution's Eighth Amendment protection against cruel and unusual punishment which, as held by the trial court, is not relevant to situations other than the imposition of penal sanctions. Historic in nature, it stemmed from punitive excesses in the infliction of criminal penalties. We find no precedent in law which would justify its extension to the correction of social injustice or hardship, such as, for instance, in the case of poverty. The latter often condemns the poor and deprived to horrendous living conditions which could certainly be described in the abstract as "cruel and unusual punishment." Yet the constitutional base of protection from "cruel and unusual punishment" is plainly irrelevant to such societal ills which must be remedied, if at all, under other concepts of constitutional and civil right.

So it is in the case of the unfortunate Karen Quinlan. Neither the State, nor the law, but the accident of fate and nature, has inflicted upon her conditions which though in essence cruel and most unusual, yet do not amount to "punishment" in any constitutional sense.

Neither the judgment of the court below, nor the medical decision which confronted it, nor the law and equity perceptions which impelled its action, nor the whole factual base upon which it was predicated, inflicted "cruel and unusual punishment" in the constitutional sense.

III. The Right of Privacy

It is the issue of the constitutional right of privacy that has given us most concern, in the exceptional circumstances of this case. Here a loving parent, *qua* parent and raising the rights of his incompetent and profoundly damaged daughter, probably irreversibly doomed to no more than a biologically vegetative remnant of life, is before the court. He seeks authorization to abandon specialized technological procedures which can only maintain for a time a body having no potential for resumption or continuance of other than a "vegetative" existence.

We have no doubt, in these unhappy circumstances, that if Karen were herself miraculously lucid for an interval (not altering the existing prognosis of the condition to which she would soon return) and perceptive of her irreversible condition, she could effectively decide upon discontinuance of

From *In the Matter of Karen Quinlan, an Alleged Incompetent.* Supreme Court of New Jersey, 70 N.J. 10, 355 A. 2d 647.

the life-support apparatus, even if it meant the prospect of natural death. To this extent we may distinguish [a case] which concerned a severely injured young woman (Delores Heston), whose life depended on surgery and blood transfusion; and who was in such extreme shock that she was unable to express an informed choice (although the Court apparently considered the case as if the patient's own religious decision to resist transfusion were at stake), but most importantly a patient apparently salvable to long life and vibrant health;—a situation not at all like the present case.

We have no hesitancy in deciding, in the instant diametrically opposite case, that no external compelling interest of the State could compel Karen to endure the unendurable, only to vegetate a few measurable months with no realistic possibility of returning to any semblance of cognitive or sapient life. We perceive no thread of logic distinguishing between such a choice on Karen's part and a similar choice which, under the evidence in this case, could be made by a competent patient terminally ill, riddled by cancer and suffering great pain; such a patient would not be resuscitated or put on a respirator in the example described by Dr. Korein, and *a fortiori* would not be kept *against his will* on a respirator.

Although the Constitution does not explicitly mention a right of privacy, Supreme Court decisions have recognized that a right of personal privacy exists and that certain areas of privacy are guaranteed under the Constitution. The Court has interdicted judicial intrusion into many aspects of personal decision, sometimes basing this restraint upon the conception of a limitation of judicial interest and responsibility, such as with regard to contraception and its relationship to family life and decision.

The Court in *Griswold* found the unwritten constitutional right of privacy to exist in the penumbra of specific guarantees of the Bill of Rights "formed by emanations from those guarantees that help give them life and substance." Presumably this right is broad enough to encompass a patient's decision to decline medical treatment under certain circumstances, in much the same way as it is broad enough to encompass a woman's decision to terminate pregnancy under certain conditions.

The claimed interests of the State in this case are essentially the preservation and sanctity of human life and defense to the right of the physician to administer medical treatment according to his best judgment. In this case the doctors say that removing Karen from the respirator will conflict with their professional judgment. The plaintiff answers that Karen's present treatment serves only a maintenance function; that the respirator cannot cure or improve her condition but at best can only prolong her inevitable slow deterioration and death; and that the interests of the patient, as seen by her surrogate, the guardian, must be evaluated by the court as predominant, even in the face of an option *contra* by the present attending physicians. Plaintiff's distinction is significant. The nature of Karen's care and the realistic chances of her recovery are quite unlike those of the patients discussed in many of the cases where treatments were ordered. In many of those cases the medical procedure required (usually a transfusion) constituted a minimal bodily invasion and the chances of recovery and return to functioning life were very good. We think that the State's interest *contra* weakens and the individual's right to privacy grows as the degree of bodily invasion increases and the prognosis dims. Ultimately there comes a point at which the individual's rights overcome the State interest. It is for that reason that we believe Karen's choice, if she were competent to make it, would be vindicated by the law. Her prognosis is extremely poor—she will never resume cognitive life. And the bodily invasion is very great—she requires 24-hour intensive nursing care, antibiotics, and the assistance of a respirator, a catheter and feeding tube.

Our affirmance of Karen's independent right of choice, however, would ordinarily be based upon her competency to assert it. The sad truth, however, is that she is grossly incompetent and we cannot discern her supposed choice based on the testimony of her previous conversation with friends, where such testimony is without sufficient probative weight. Nevertheless we have concluded that Karen's right of privacy may be asserted on her behalf by her guardian under the peculiar circumstances here present.

If a putative decision by Karen to permit this non-cognitive, vegetative existence to terminate by natural forces is regarded as a valuable incident of her right of privacy, as we believe it to be, then it should not be discarded solely on the basis that her condition prevents her conscious exercise of the choice. The only practical way to prevent destruction of the right is to permit the guardian and family of Karen to render their best judgment, subject to the qualifications hereinafter stated, as to whether she would exercise it in these circumstances. If their conclusion is in the affirmative this decision should be accepted by a society the overwhelming majority of whose members would, we think, in similar circumstances, exercise such a choice in the same way for themselves or for those closest to them. It is for this reason that we determine that Karen's right of privacy may be asserted in her behalf, in this respect, by her guardian and family under the particular circumstances presented by this record. [Sections IV (Medical Factors), V (Alleged Criminal Liability), and VI (Guardianship of the Person) omitted.]

Declaratory Relief

We thus arrive at the formulation of the declaratory relief which we have concluded is appropriate to this case. Some time has passed since Karen's physical and mental condition was described to the Court. At that time her continuing deterioration was plainly projected. Since the record has not been expanded we assume that she is now even more fragile and nearer to death than she was then. Since her present treating physicians may give reconsideration to her present posture in the light of this opinion, and since we are transferring to the plaintiff as guardian the choice of the attending physician and therefore other physicians may be in charge of the case who may take a different view from that of the present attending physicians, we herewith declare the following affirmative relief on behalf of the plaintiff. Upon the concurrence of the guardian and family of Karen, should the responsible attending physicians conclude that there is no reasonable possibility of Karen's ever emerging from her present comatose condition to a cognitive, sapient state and that the life-support apparatus now being administered to Karen should be discontinued, they shall consult with the hospital "Ethics Committee" or like body of the institution in which Karen is then hospitalized. If that consultative body agrees that there is no reasonable possibility of Karen's ever emerging from her present comatose condition to a cognitive, sapient state, the present life-support system may be withdrawn and said action shall be without any civil or criminal liability therefore on the part of any participant, whether guardian, physician, hospital or others. We herewith specifically so hold.

Decision Scenario 1 ....

"Apparently he was inside the tank with an oxygen hose to provide ventilation," Dr. Mangel said. "There was some oil residue on the walls. When Mr. Golenga struck an arc to weld the seam, there was a flash fire."

Mrs. Golenga gripped the hand of her nineteen-year-old son, Cervando. Both had been crying, but now listening was so important that they forced back their tears.

"How badly hurt is he?" Mrs. Golenga asked.

"Very badly," Dr. Mangel said. "Most of his body is covered with severe burns, and his lungs are damaged from breathing in the fire and smoke."

"Will he live?" Cervando asked.

"I have to be honest with you and say that I don't think he will," Dr. Mangel said. "We are giving him plasma and saline solutions to rehydrate him and antibiotics to try to stop infections. But he hasn't got much of a chance."

"The pain, what about the pain?" asked Mrs. Golenga.

"There's only so much we can do."

"There's really no hope?" Cervando asked.

"I wouldn't say that," Dr. Mangel said. "There is always hope. But in this case it is very limited. He might die in a few hours, or he might die tomorrow or the next day."

"Please," Mrs. Golenga said. "Can you help him die? I know he doesn't want to suffer if he has no real hope. He told me often 'If something happens to me, don't let them stick me full of needles and keep me alive. Tell them to put me out of my misery.' Can you do that, Doctor?"

"Are you sure that's what he would want?" Dr. Mangel asked.

"My mother is right," Cervando said. "I've heard my father say that many times. He said he never wanted to just lie around and suffer, being a burden to himself and everyone. We want to do as he wanted us to."

"We could stop treating him," Dr. Mangel said. "Then let nature take its course."

"That sounds terrible," Mrs. Golenga said. "To make a man fight for his life when he has no hope and no help. It is cold and cruel."

"I'm sorry," said Dr. Mangel. "It is all that the law permits me to do."

1. *Would Rachels regard this as the kind of case in which active euthanasia would be morally acceptable? Why would Callahan disagree?*

2. *According to the conservative view of Gay-Williams, is there anything that might be done to*

put an end to Mr. Golenga's life that would also be morally acceptable?

3. *Would the line of reasoning taken by Chief Justice Hughes in the* Quinlan *case make Mrs. Golenga and Cervando the appropriate people to decide whether Mr. Golenga receives additional treatment, is allowed to die, or is killed?*

4. *Would the Court's reasoning in* Cruzan *be likely to lead to the same opinion?*

5. *According to the considerations advanced by Lynn and Childress, would it be morally acceptable for Mr. Golenga's physicians to stop the procedure to rehydrate him?*

Decision Scenario 2

Mr. Jeffry Box was eighty-one years old when he was brought to Doctor's Hospital. His right side was paralyzed, he spoke in a garbled way, and he had trouble understanding even the simplest matters. His only known relative was a sister four years younger, and she lived half a continent away. When a hospital social worker called to tell her about her brother's condition, she was quite uninterested. "I haven't seen him in fifteen years," she said. "I thought he might already be dead. Just do whatever you think best for him. I'm too old to worry about him."

Neurological tests and X-ray studies showed Mr. Box was suffering from a brain hemorrhage caused by a ruptured blood vessel.

"Can you fix it?" asked Dr. Hollins. She was the resident responsible for Mr. Box's primary care. The man she addressed was Dr. Carl Oceana, the staff's only neurosurgeon.

"Sure," said Dr. Oceana. "I can repair the vessel and clean out the mess. But it won't do much good, you know."

"You mean he'll still be paralyzed?"

"That's right. And he'll still be mentally incoherent. After the operation he'll have to be put in a nursing home or some other chronic-care place, because he won't be able to see to his own needs."

"And if you don't operate?" Dr. Hollins asked.

Dr. Oceana shrugged. "He'll be dead by tomorrow. Maybe sooner, depending on how long it takes for the pressure in his skull to build up."

"What would you do?"

"I know what I would want done to me if I were the patient," said Dr. Oceana. "I'd want people to keep their knives out of my head and let me die a nice, peaceful death."

"But we don't know what he would want," Dr. Hollins said. "He's never been our patient before, and the social worker hasn't been able to find any friends who might tell us what he'd want done."

"Let's just put ourselves in his place," said Dr. Oceana. "Let's do unto others what we would want done unto us."

"That means letting Mr. Box die."

"Exactly."

1. *On what grounds might Gay-Williams object to Dr. Oceana's view?*

2. *Would Rachels's principles justify active euthanasia?*

3. *Would the natural law view make the operation discussed a moral mandate?*

4. *How might Callahan assess Dr. Oceana's reasoning?*

5. *Could Justice Stevens's arguments against the majority opinion in* Cruzan *be used to support Oceana's position? (See Social Context: The Cruzan Case.)*

Decision Scenario 3 ••

On April 8, 1984, Mr. William Bartling was admitted to the Glendale Adventist Medical Center in Los Angeles. He was seventy years old and suffered from five ordinarily fatal diseases: emphysema, diffuse arteriosclerosis, coronary arteriosclerosis, an abdominal aneurysm, and inoperable lung cancer. During the performance of a biopsy to diagnose the lung cancer, Mr. Bartling's left lung collapsed. He was placed in the ICU, and a chest tube and mechanical respirator were used to assist his breathing.

Mr. Bartling complained about the pain the respirator caused him, and he repeatedly asked to have it removed. When his physician refused, he pulled out the chest tube himself. This happened so often that eventually Mr. Bartling's hands were tied to the bed to keep him from doing it. He had signed a living will in an attempt to avoid just such a situation.

Although after discussions with Richard S. Scott, Mr. Bartling's attorney, Mr. Bartling's physician and the hospital administration agreed to disconnect the respirator, the hospital's attorney refused to permit it. He argued that, since Mr. Bartling was not terminally ill, brain-dead, or in a persistent vegetative state, the hospital might be open to legal action.

Mr. Scott took the case to Los Angeles Superior Court. He argued that Mr. Bartling was legally competent to make a decision about his welfare and that, although he did not want to die, he understood that disconnecting the respirator might lead to his death. The hospital's attorney took the position that Mr. Bartling was ambivalent on the question of his death. His statements "I don't want to die" and "I don't want to live on the respirator" were taken as inconsistent and so as evidence of ambivalence. Removing the respirator, the attorney argued, would be tantamount to aiding suicide or even committing homicide.

The court refused either to allow the respirator to be removed or to order that Mr. Bartling's hands be freed. To do so, the court ruled, would be to take a positive step to end treatment, and the only precedents for doing so were in cases in which the patients were comatose, brain-dead, or in a chronic vegetative state.

The case was then taken to the California Court of Appeal, which ruled: "If the right of a patient to self-determination as to his own medical treatment is to have any meaning at all, it must be paramount to the interests of the patient's hospitals and doctors. The right of a competent adult patient to refuse medical treatment is a constitutionally guaranteed right which must not be abridged."

The rule came too late for Mr. Bartling. He died twenty-three hours before the court heard his appeal.

1. *Is there any merit to the hospital's position that to remove Mr. Bartling's respirator or to free his hands would be equivalent to assisting suicide? How might Brock's arguments apply to this position?*

2. *On the natural law view, would the request to remove the respirator be, in effect, a request for assistance in committing suicide?*

3. *How can the reasoning in the* Quinlan *case be extended to Mr. Bartling's case?*

4. *Can the arguments offered by Callahan be used to support the view that it would be morally wrong even to untie Mr. Bartling's hands?*

5. *If Mr. Bartling had an implanted feeding tube, would it be morally right to disconnect it at his request? Would the* Cruzan *decision permit it? Would the criteria offered by Lynn and Childress?*

Decision Scenario 4 ••

When two plainclothes detectives arrived at Virginia Crawford's suburban apartment at 6:30 on a Sunday morning to arrest her for murder, she was not terribly surprised to see them.

She cried when they insisted on putting her in handcuffs before transporting her to the jail in the county court building. Yet she had more or less expected to be arrested eventually.

For almost a month, a police investigation had been conducted at Mercy Hospital, where Ms. Crawford worked as a nurse in the intensive-care unit. The entire hospital staff knew about the investigation, and Ms. Crawford herself had been questioned on three occasions by officers conducting the inquiry. At the time, her answers had seemed to be satisfactory to the police, and there was no hint that she was under suspicion. Still, she always believed that eventually they would catch up with her.

The investigation centered on the deaths of four elderly patients during the period February 1979 to March 1980. All of the patients were in the intensive-care unit at the times of their deaths. Each had been diagnosed as suffering from a terminal illness, and the chart notation on each case indicated that they had all suffered irreversible brain damage and were totally without higher brain functions.

The three women and one man were all unmarried and had no immediate family to take an interest in their welfare. All of them were being kept alive by respirators, and their deaths were caused directly by their respirators being turned off. In each instance of death, Ms. Crawford had been the person in charge of the ICU.

After securing the services of an attorney, Ms. Crawford was released on bail, and a time was set for her appearance in court. Through her attorney, Marvin Washington, she made a statement to the media.

"My client has asked me to announce that she fully and freely admits that she was the one who turned off the respirators of the four patients in question at Mercy Hospital. She acted alone and without the knowledge of any other individual. She is prepared to take full responsibility for her actions."

Mr. Washington went on to say that he would request a jury trial for his client. "I am sure," he said, "that no jury will convict Ms. Crawford of murder merely for turning off the life-support systems of people who were already dead."

When asked what he meant by that, Mr. Washington explained. "These patients were no longer people," he said. "Sometime during the course of the treatment, their brains simply stopped functioning in a way that we associate with human life."

Ms. Crawford was present during the reading of her statement, and after a whispered conversation with her attorney, she spoke once for herself. "I consider what I did an act of compassion and humanity," she said. "I consider it altogether moral, and I feel no guilt about it. I did for four people what they would have wanted done, if they had only been in a condition to know."

1. *Does the natural law view offer grounds for removing life-support systems for people who are beyond a reasonable hope of recovery? If so, what are they?*

2. *Why would Gay-Williams's arguments lead us to condemn the actions of Ms. Crawford?*

3. *Can Brock's arguments favoring voluntary active euthanasia be extended to justify Ms. Crawford's actions?*

4. *Might Ms. Crawford be right about the patients being dead according to some concept of death?*

5. *How does the reasoning of the majority in* Cruzan *support the prosecution of Ms. Crawford? Might the minority opinion lend support to Ms. Crawford's actions?*

Decision Scenario 5 ••

Consider the following four cases.

1. Harvey Shick of Tyler, Texas, on June 1, 1983, shot his wife in the head twice with a .22-caliber pistol. Mrs. Marie Shick had suffered from severe arteriosclerosis since the late 1970s and, according to her physician, suffered extreme pain in her lower legs. The couple had

been happily married for forty-five years. Although Mr. Shick was charged with murder, the charges were dismissed by the state district court judge. "I found nothing would be gained in this case by further punishing this man," Judge Donald Carroll said. "This was an act motivated by love," Mr. Shick's attorney said. "He was distressed at the sickness, and additional treatment would have brought only a precarious and burdensome prolonging of life." Mrs. Shick's family supported the action.

2. On September 14, 1984, Mr. Thomas P. Engel, a registered nurse, removed the respirator from Joseph Dohr, a seventy-eight-year-old stroke victim at St. Michael Hospital in Milwaukee. Mr. Engel said that Mr. Dohr's family asked that treatment be stopped. Mr. Dohr's physician said that he had refused the request because he believed that death was imminent.

Mr. Engel described the bedside scene with Mr. Dohr's daughter that had led him to act:

> She was standing there by her father's bed, stroking his arm and cheek and crying and talking to him. He was in a coma, in a steady decline. The only thing keeping him alive was the ventilator breathing for him. "This isn't right," she said. Then she looked across the bed at me, right in my eyes, and she said "If I could do this thing, I would." Now, what would you do?

Mr. Engel was charged with practicing medicine without a license. He pleaded guilty and received a twenty-month suspended sentence. His nursing license was revoked for one year by the state nursing board.

3. On August 8, 1985, seventy-nine-year-old Abel Montigny walked into the intensive-care unit of Worcester Memorial Hospital in Worcester, Massachusetts, and shot his wife in the head. He then shot himself. Both died from the injuries. Mrs. Leona Montigny, seventy-six, had been in the hospital for several months. She suffered from serious stomach and blood disorders and was recovering from surgery. Her illnesses were considered treatable, and she was in no immediate danger of death from them.

4. Roswell Gilbert, a seventy-five-year-old retired engineer, was convicted in Ft. Lauderdale, Florida, on May 9, 1985, for killing his incurably ill seventy-three-year-old wife. The couple had been married fifty-one years. Emily

Gilbert had a debilitating bone disease and Alzheimer's disease; as a consequence, she suffered both severe pain and mental disorientation. According to a witness, on the day of the killing Mrs. Gilbert had said to her husband "I'm in pain. I want to die." Mr. Gilbert said later "Who's that somebody but me? I guess I got cold as ice. I took the gun off the shelf, put a bullet in it and shot her. Then I felt her pulse. I thought, 'Oh, my God, I loused it up.' I put in another bullet and shot her again."

Mr. Gilbert was sentenced to twenty-five years in prison with no chance of parole. As he left the courtroom, his daughter cried out, sobbing, "Daddy, Daddy, I don't want to see my daddy in jail—he'll die in jail."

Mr. Gilbert lost a chance for clemency when two of the members of the Florida Cabinet rejected the governor's recommendation that he be freed while the case was appealed. "The law does not give one person the right to kill another because of illness or age," said Gerald Lewis, one of those who voted against clemency.

In August 1990, Governor Bob Martinez petitioned the cabinet for clemency, citing Gilbert's failing health, and Gilbert was freed on probation. He died on September 4, 1994.

1. *Compare the issues that are raised in these four cases. In what ways are the cases the same? In what ways are they different?*

2. *In which cases, if any, could the action taken be justified by Brock's arguments in favor of voluntary euthanasia?*

3. *In which cases, if any, could the action be justified by the reasoning in the* Cruzan *case?*

4. *Is it likely that the arguments presented by Rachels could be used to justify any of the actions taken?*

5. *Would Callahan condemn the actions in all these cases?*

6. *Would Stoddard's arguments be relevant in any of these circumstances?*

Decision Scenario 6 ••

In 1993, the Netherlands passed a law permitting physicians to assist in the suicide of terminally ill patients. The law requires that the patient's decision to die be informed and irrevocable, and that there be no other solution acceptable to the patient that would improve the situation. (See "The Dutch Experience" in the Introduction for details.)

1. Can the arguments offered by Brock be used to support a public policy of this kind?

2. Are the procedural safeguards adopted in the Netherlands adequate to prevent deliberate homicide? Are they adequate to prevent people who are temporarily depressed or irrational from killing themselves?

3. What dangers does such a policy pose, according to Callahan?

4. Does the right of an individual to refuse life-sustaining medical treatment imply that an individual has a right to terminate his life by active means? If so, does this mean that society has a duty to provide assistance?

5. On what grounds might Elizabeth Bouvia have been permitted to starve herself to death under medical supervision? On what grounds might her request have been refused?

Decision Scenario 7 ••

In March 1991, Dr. Timothy Quill published an article in the *New England Journal of Medicine* in which he described how he had prescribed barbiturates for Patricia Diane Trumbull, a forty-five-year-old woman suffering from leukemia. In prescribing the medication, Dr. Quill also informed Ms. Trumbull, who had been his patient for a long time, how much of the drug would constitute a lethal dose.

Ms. Trumbull later killed herself by taking an overdose of the barbiturate, and Dr. Quill was investigated by a Rochester, New York, grand jury. Although it is illegal in New York to assist someone in committing suicide, the grand jury decided not to indict Dr. Quill on the charge.

Dr. Quill's actions were later reviewed by the three-member New York State Board for Professional Medical Conduct to consider whether he should be charged with professional misconduct. The board arrived at the unanimous decision that "no charge of misconduct was warranted."

The board, in its report, distinguished between Dr. Quill's actions and those of Dr. Jack Kevorkian. The board pointed to Dr. Quill's long-term involvement in caring for Ms. Trumbull and contrasted it with Dr. Kevorkian's lack of any prior involvement with those whom he assisted in killing themselves.

Moreover, the board pointed out that Dr. Quill "did not directly participate in any taking of life" and this too made his actions different from those of Dr. Kevorkian. "One is legal and ethically appropriate, and the other, as reported, is not" the board concluded.

1. How might Stoddard view the situation that Ms. Trumbull was in? Would he consider suicide a legitimate option for her?

2. Would Callahan consider Dr. Quill's action to fall within the scope of a physician's legitimate role?

3. Why might Brock view Dr. Quill's action as justifiable?

4. Would Rachels consider this a case of active euthanasia?

5. Is this a case of assisted suicide? If not, what would be required to make it one?

PART II
RIGHTS

CHAPTER 4
AIDS AND ITS ISSUES

CASE PRESENTATION
The Mysterious Infection of Kimberly Bergalis

In 1987 Kimberly Bergalis traveled from her hometown of Fort Pierce, Florida, to the nearby town of Stuart to keep an appointment with David J. Acer, her dentist. Bergalis had to have her wisdom teeth pulled, and Dr. Acer extracted one that day.

A month later Bergalis developed a rash on her face and a very sore throat. The symptoms eventually disappeared without any treatment, and she had no other medical problems until the spring of 1989, when she was about to graduate from the University of Florida in Gainesville. She was then plagued by fatigue, sore throats, and fits of coughing. White patches appeared inside her mouth. "I thought I was just stressed out," she later told reporter Felicity Barringer.

The first physician she consulted was puzzled by the white patches. He thought the infection might be thrush, but Bergalis was not a diabetic and was not taking any antibiotics. "That's funny," he told her. "Usually you only get thrush when you're a newborn, a diabetic, or on antibiotics. Or if you have AIDS." Over the following summer, Bergalis's health deteriorated. She continued to be fatigued; she lost weight; her hair fell out in clumps. In an effort to find out what was wrong with her, she consulted other physicians and submitted to a number of medical tests. The physicians presented her with a bewildering variety of possible diagnoses: flu, a particular kind of bone cancer, diabetes, hepatitis, and hysteria.

Bergalis denied being sexually active or using IV drugs, and she had never received any blood or blood products by transfusion. Her medical history seemed to rule out the only recognized modes of transmission of the AIDS virus. Hence, none of the physicians who examined her thought it necessary to test her for the presence of HIV, the virus that causes the disease.

A week after the 1989 Thanksgiving vacation with her family, when she had returned to Gainesville, Bergalis was hospitalized with pneumonia. Although the episode was life threatening, the disease was brought under control. Tests were then done that showed she had pneumocystis pneumonia—the variety typical of people with AIDS. Bergalis was finally tested for HIV, and the result was tentatively positive.

In January 1990 a second test confirmed that Kimberly Bergalis had AIDS. She didn't see how it was possible. "I thought maybe the government was wrong," she said. "Maybe you can get it by kissing. That's the only thing that made sense to me, an exchange of saliva."

Bergalis's mother, a nurse, told Kimberly it was essential that she tell the truth to her physicians. Otherwise, they might make the wrong diagnosis and treat her for the wrong disease. Bergalis insisted she was telling the truth.

Bergalis remained puzzled about how she could have become infected with the virus. Then she remembered that her dentist, Dr. Acer, had been canceling a lot of appointments. His staff said he had pneumonia or cancer, but she also recalled hearing the rumor that he had AIDS.

When she suggested to Florida health officials that she might have been infected by Dr. Acer, they told her they were not investigating that possibility. As it turned out, they were investigating her. Health officials asked her about her dates with her boyfriend and inquired in detail about the kinds of bodily contact they had had. They interviewed her friends and asked them about whether her father had ever shown any sexual interest in her.

No one was inclined to believe that Kimberly Bergalis had been infected by the AIDS virus in some previously unknown way. "They want to believe you were using IV drugs," she said later. "They want to believe you were sleeping around."

Then, in July 1990, the Centers for Disease Control released a report concluding that a young woman in Florida had been infected with the AIDS virus by her dentist. The CDC refused to identify her and later referred to her only as "Patient A."

David Acer died in September of AIDS-related cancer, and immediately after his death an open letter to his patients was printed in the *Stuart News*. "I am David J. Acer and I have AIDS," the letter began. It went on to advise his patients to be tested for the virus. Dr Acer was a bisexual who treated an estimated 1,700 patients after becoming infected with the virus.

By the spring of 1991, six hundred patients had been tested, and two more people were identified as likely to have been infected by Dr. Acer. The probability that Dr. Acer was the source of infection in the three cases was based primarily on the similarity of the viral DNA in all four cases. (Eventually about one thousand of Dr. Acer's patients were tested. Ten were HIV-positive, but six patients were found to have strains of the virus almost identical to Dr. Acer's. The last patient, who was only fifteen in 1988 at the likely time of infection, was not identified until 1992—when she was tested as part of her application for military service.)

When Kimberly Bergalis asked Florida officials whether she was the Patient A in the CDC report, they refused to tell her. After weighing the possible impact on her two younger sisters, Bergalis and her family decided to make the matter a public issue to warn others about what might happen to them. Bergalis entered a malpractice suit against Dr. Acer's insurance company.

The suit was settled out of court in January 1991, for one million dollars. Kimberly Bergalis insisted that her interest was not in the money. "It's not going to buy me a cure," she said at the time of the settlement. Her main concern, she claimed, was to make HIV-positive health-care professionals either stop performing invasive procedures or inform patients of the risk they may be taking.

"I'm not asking that we be able to live in a risk-free world," she said in an interview. "I want people to choose their risks. I didn't have a choice to walk out of the office and seek another dentist."

Kimberly Bergalis died of AIDS in 1991. Her testimony before Congress only a short time before she died gave strong impetus to a movement demanding that all health-care workers be tested for HIV and forbidden to practice if the results were positive. The debate continues today, even though Dr. Acer is the only health-care worker infected with the virus who is believed to have transmitted it to his patients. (There have been a few cases of patient-to-patient transmission in hospitals, but they typically have been the result of using unsterile instruments.)

Some sixty health-care workers have revealed that they are HIV-positive, and 19,000 of their patients have been tested. None has been found infected as a result of a medical procedure.

Were Dr. Acer's Patients Truthful?

On June 19, 1994, the CBS news program "Sixty Minutes" questioned whether Kimberly Bergalis and the other five patients were truthful in claiming a lack of risk factors. The program suggested that Dr. Acer was not the source of infection and that the six people had become infected as a result of their own behavior. Kimberly Bergalis, it suggested, might not have been the "innocent victim" she portrayed herself as being.

The program claimed that a court-ordered examination of Bergalis showed evidence of sexual activity and a possible venereal wart, despite her claim that she was a virgin. Moreover, three of the other infected patients were alleged to have had multiple-sex partners and one of the men, a homosexual affair. The sixth person was said to have had a blood transfusion and an extramarital affair.

Responding to some of the claims, investigators said that they knew Bergalis had engaged in nonpenetrating sexual activity, but that the male partners that she identified all tested negative for HIV. The partner of the patient who had the homosexual affair was also negative for the virus. One patient believed her boyfriend might be HIV-positive, but he tested negative. The woman alleged to have had a transfusion never received blood, and her extramarital affair had taken place before the AIDS virus was prevalent. Most important, the strains of virus infecting Dr. Acer and his six patients were so similar that it made it unlikely that they were not related.

Was the Infection Deliberate?

Given the unique and puzzling character of the Bergalis case, some have suggested that Dr. Acer may have deliberately infected some of his patients. Yet, despite investigations of Acer by the Centers for Disease Control and (at the request of Congress) the federal General Accounting Office, no direct evidence has been found to show that Acer, in effect, committed murder. The conclusion has been reached by some as the only reasonable explanation for the spate of infections traceable to Dr. Acer.

A possible motive for deliberate infection emerged when Edward Parsons, a friend of Dr. Acer, revealed to a Florida newspaper that Acer had told him that Americans were ignoring AIDS because it primarily affected homosexuals, drug addicts, and hemophiliacs. "When it starts affecting grandmothers and younger people, then you'll see something done," Parsons quoted Acer as saying. The six patients infected by Dr. Acer included four women and two men, ranging in age from fifteen to sixty-five.

Investigators have not been able to establish any other possibility as likely. The patients had appointments scattered over a long period of time, so it is not probable that they were infected at the same time by unsterile instruments. Dr. Acer's sterilization procedures were no worse than those of other dentists at the time. The youngest patient had no invasive procedure performed, and Acer's staff does not recall that he ever had a cut on his fingers that might have bled into patients' mouths—something not likely to have caused infection in any case. Nor is it likely that he contaminated his instruments by doing dental work on himself. The fact that all six patients were infected with HIV strains that were nearly identical to Dr. Acer's is strong evidence that he was the common source. Four

other HIV-positive patients of Dr. Acer had known behavioral risk factors, and the strains of the virus were different.

The most logical explanation, some charge, is that Dr. Acer, to make a political statement, deliberately injected his own blood into his patients. This would have been something much out of character, according to his friends. His staff does not recall seeing him inject anything into patients that looked like blood. Unfortunately, when he closed his practice in 1989, the year before he died, Dr. Acer destroyed his appointment books and many patient records. They would have been useful to investigators. The infection of Kimberly Bergalis and the other five patients remains a frustrating epidemiological mystery.

SOCIAL CONTEXT: MANDATORY AIDS TESTING AND PREGNANCY

New York State, like other states, tests all newborns to determine if they are infected with HIV, the virus that causes AIDS. The result of the test, however, is not revealed to the parents of the child, even if they ask for it.

In fact, it is *illegal* for physicians or other health professionals to tell parents the result. The tests are performed solely for the purpose of collecting data about the incidence of the virus so that health departments can determine its rate of occurrence and trace its spread.

The reasoning behind not informing the parents is that to do so would violate the mother's right to confidentiality. If the newborn is HIV-positive, the mother is also HIV-positive, because she is the source of the infection. However, the newborn may test positive, yet not be infected with the virus. The test is for antibodies that have passed to the infant through the maternal-fetal circulatory system, and although the infant may have the antibodies at the time of birth, the virus itself may not be present.

Some studies suggest that as many as 75% to 85% of infants that test positive may not be infected. (Whether the child acquires the virus is now thought to be connected with the level of the virus in the mother's blood.) Even if the infant has not acquired the virus from the circulating blood, he or she may become infected at the time of birth through contact with the birth canal or later by ingesting the virus from the mother's milk.

In the United States, about 4 million women give birth each year. About 7,000 of the women are HIV-positive, and roughly 2,000 of their infants will be infected with the virus. The World Health Organization estimates that 5.5 million women are infected with HIV. Mother-to-infant transmission of the virus is a much larger public health problem in Africa, Asia, and Latin America than in the United States and Europe.

Because telling the mother of a newborn that her child is infected with HIV is also to inform her that she is infected, she may be learning something that she has no desire to know. She may prefer to remain ignorant of her own HIV status, and she may not want the father of the child or anyone else to know her status either. The laws governing HIV testing are thus designed to meet the needs of a public health goal (collecting data), while also protecting to the maximum extent possible the mother's right to privacy.

This was the policy that infuriated New York State Assemblywoman Nettie Mayersohn. She considered it reprehensible that hundreds of mothers each year should leave maternity wards not knowing that their babies were infected with HIV. She worried particularly about the babies who would not get treatments. When infants are diagnosed early, initiating therapy can significantly prolong their lives. She found the situation unconscionable.

Mayersohn also dismissed the existing counseling programs as ineffective. They failed to work, in part, because under state law, people seeking to be tested for HIV must be informed that if they test positive, they may suffer discrimination in housing and employment. Many people then decide that they are better off not finding out about their HIV status.

Giving direct expression to her concerns, Mayersohn introduced a mandatory notification bill in the legislature. The bill required, among other provisions, that physicians inform parents of newborns of the results of the required HIV test.

A diverse combination of AIDS groups, gay activists, civil libertarians, and women's organizations strongly opposed Mayersohn's legislative proposal. The argued that the bill would make mothers of newborns the only group subject to mandatory HIV testing. This exception, they claimed, would be the thin tip of a wedge that would eventually crack the wall that provides absolute confidentiality for all who are tested for HIV.

Further, some women, particularly those most at risk for HIV infection, would be likely to stay away from hospitals and clinics to avoid learning their own HIV status. The result would be that the health of these women and their babies would be endangered.

Finally, critics pointed out that because the bill concerned only testing the child at the time of birth, knowing the HIV status would do little good. The test results might not be available for weeks, and during that time, the newborn might become infected through breast milk.

The Mayersohn proposal failed to get the support it needed, but in July 1994 a compromise bill was passed by the assembly. The bill requires that physicians and hospitals offer pregnant women and the mothers of newborns counseling about the benefits of HIV testing. Both the health-care provider and the woman must sign a form stating that the counseling took place.

A new consideration emerged when in November 1994 the *New England Journal of Medicine* published the results of a federal study involving 477 HIV-infected pregnant women. During their pregnancy, half the women were given the drug ZDV (zidovudine), and half were given a placebo. The result was that only 8.3% of the babies born to women taking ZDV were infected with HIV. Of the babies born to women on the placebo, 25.5% were infected. Hence, the drug was effective in lowering the rate of infection in babies born to HIV-positive mothers by about 67%.

While Mayersohn was advocating the testing of newborns and informing parents of the outcome, she was not in a position to argue that knowing the result could bring direct benefit to a child. At most, an infected child would receive earlier treatment, and although the child's life might be prolonged, he or she would still die in the first few years. Because a child is infected in only about one-fourth of the cases in which the mother is HIV-positive, the privacy rights of pregnant women would be compromised for (one might argue) a relatively small gain.

However, the federal study gives the issue of mandatory testing of HIV-positive pregnant women a sharper edge. HIV-positive women can lower the risk of their child being infected only if they agree to take ZDV five times per day during the last six months of pregnancy, and receive it intravenously during delivery. Thus, the availability of a therapy to prevent HIV infection in a high proportion of babies at risk means that the confidentiality rights of pregnant women come into direct conflict with the potential welfare of their infants.

At least three ways of dealing with the problem seem possible. Each one is only briefly examined here.

1. *Provide only prenatal counseling and offer an HIV test.* A woman who is informed by counseling can still insist on not learning her HIV status, and we cannot test her without securing her informed consent. If she refuses to be tested, she will also refuse to follow the course of treatment needed to reduce the chance that her child will be infected with the virus.

In this solution, we acknowledge that the pregnant woman's right to privacy takes precedence over the welfare of her developing child. As a result, we must accept that some babies will be born infected with HIV, even though it could have been avoided.

2. *Require mandatory testing of pregnant women for HIV; then require treatment, if needed.* Mandatory testing is compatible with counseling, but even if a woman does not want to know her HIV status, she still must be tested. If she is HIV-positive, she should be started on a course of treatment with ZDV. If she refuses to take the drug as prescribed, arrangements must be made to guarantee that she does. She might be required to report to a clinic to receive her medications. If she fails to comply, she might be fined, have her living stipend reduced, or even be incarcerated.

In this solution, the justification for violating the autonomy of HIV-positive pregnant women is the need to reduce the chances of their child being born infected with HIV. Thus, the claim is that preventing a child from acquiring an HIV infection offsets the restrictions placed on the autonomy of the pregnant woman.

3. *Require mandatory testing and counseling for HIV, but not mandatory treatment.* Only exceptional circumstances warrant compelling someone to submit to a medical procedure, but testing for HIV is minimally invasive and almost risk free. Information can change people's attitudes and behavior, and even though a woman might not have wanted to know her HIV status, if she learns she is infected with the virus and is told the advantage of ZDV therapy, she will be in a better position to act responsibly.

In this solution, a woman's right not to be treated is recognized as outweighing society's interest in protecting children from HIV infection. However, given the possibility of preventing AIDS in infants, critics claim that the relatively small infringement on autonomy posed by mandatory testing is offset by the potential benefit to infants.

Each of these three positions is open to objections. It seems seriously wrong not to prevent a child from acquiring a fatal disease when this can be done by a relatively small sacrifice. Yet should we legally require that pregnant women make such a sacrifice, even if they choose not to? This is not a standard that we impose on any other group.

Should we even force pregnant women to learn their HIV status, if they don't want to know it? If we do, then we are acting without their consent and violating their privacy. We are forcing them to accept a medical procedure against their wishes. Or, looked at another way, we are forcing them to be altruistic and to act not for themselves, but for the sake of the developing child. Hence, we are imposing on a pregnant woman a burden not imposed on anyone else.

The three ways of dealing with the issue of testing pregnant women for HIV are not the only ones possible. Even so, a solution that will both preserve the autonomy of pregnant women and protect their developing children from HIV infection does not seem possible. As in so many other moral matters, something has to give.

CASE PRESENTATION
Tod Thompson

Tod Thompson opened his sock drawer and took out a round, white enameled snuffbox. A green dragon breathing a jagged tongue of fire was painted on the lid. The box had been given to him almost five years ago by Alan Lauder as a memento of their trip to Cancun. Alan had always bought him a lot of presents; some were just tokens and others expensive, but all were in exquisite taste. In the note accompanying the snuffbox, Alan had said something clever and flattering about the dragon's fiery tongue.

As a matter of principle, Tod had never bought cocaine, but when somebody gave him a little he kept it in the dragon box. Those days now seemed as obscure and fragmentary as scenes from a movie watched in childhood. After Alan got sick, Tod never felt happy enough to risk doing drugs of any kind. He had never minded using them occasionally to intensify his pleasures, but he didn't want to come to depend on them to make life bearable.

After Alan died, he even stopped drinking. He had actually stopped a few months before that. That was now almost two years ago. Alan had been too sick even to eat, and Tod had no wish to drink alone. Now he drank only water and fruit juice, not even wine.

Tod opened the hinged lid of the snuffbox and looked at the blunt purple and gray capsules of Seconal inside. He dumped them into the palm of his hand and counted them, pushing each to one side with a fingertip.

Eight. Including the capsule Ken Hesletine had given him the day before, he had eight. Six was supposed to be enough, but with eight he felt much better. How ghastly it would be to wake up in a hospital feeling very sick and knowing you had failed. If you were going to do it, you should be sure you could pull it off. And he was sure he was going to do it. He had watched Alan, and nothing would make him want to go through that.

Tod put the snuffbox under his socks in the back corner and closed the drawer. He looked up at the mirror hanging above the dresser, and the reflection still shocked him. He couldn't believe how he had changed, and he always seemed to be looking at a stranger.

He was young, really—only twenty-seven. He looked young, but in the way photographs of children in concentration camps made them look young and old simultaneously. His gray eyes were abnormally large as they stared out of deep sockets, and his cheeks were drawn into dark hollows beneath sharp cheekbones. His blond hair was fine and wispy, barely hiding the pale skin of his scalp. His body was shrunken, and his thin shoulders hunched inward like the folded wings of a bat.

He pulled back one side of his shirt collar, exposing an edge of one of the bluish patches that ran across his chest and back and covered his arms and legs—the marks of Kaposi's sarcoma. They had been late in coming, at least compared to what he had heard about what had happened to other people. Maybe the ZDV had helped slow down the process. The drug had appeared too late to do much for Alan, but maybe it had helped him.

He dropped his shirt collar and made himself smile. If he used his imagination, he could still catch a hint of the charm he used to work at developing. When he moved to Dallas from Tyler, his idea was to transfer his credits from Tyler Community College and finish his degree in English.

He would also have to work, though. His parents were barely making it themselves, and he couldn't count on them for support. The job he got with Bluffview Books was full time, but it had enough flexibility to allow him to take classes. That's just what he did for a semester. Then, when he met Alan at a party, they began doing so many things together that finishing his degree stopped being high on his list of priorities. He always planned to go back, but there had seemed plenty of time for that later. Alan was a lawyer, and he wanted Tod to train as a paralegal so they could work together. Tod had preferred the bookstore.

Alan introduced him to a world he never suspected existed. It was a world of glittering parties, long weekends on yachts, quick trips to Mexico, San Francisco, and New York, and above all, abundant and virtually unrestrained sex. Tod found himself the object of much attention, and he liked it. He and Alan had agreed that they wouldn't place any constraints on each other. Paradoxically, that was part of what kept them together.

He still missed Alan many times every day. When Alan first got sick, Tod had been angry and even blamed him for it, as though it were something Alan had done deliberately. He now knew that he had just been afraid then—afraid for Alan and for himself.

But that was long ago. Almost two years—two years that seemed like ten.

Hardly two months after Alan died, Tod got sick. First the night sweats started. He would wake up at three or four in the morning so drenched with sweat he would be freezing and burning up simultaneously. Then the mild but persistent fever had started, and diarrhea had come along with it.

He had put off seeing his doctor for almost a month. He hadn't taken the blood test, because he was sure he would test positive and then he wouldn't be able to deny that something so horrible was going to happen to him. When the symptoms finally started, it was almost a relief in a twisted way. Now he knew the worst and didn't have to fear it anymore.

He finally went to his doctor—to Alan's doctor—when he developed shingles on his legs. The rash was too painful to ignore. By then he had already lost a lot of weight. The diarrhea and the fever seemed to keep him tired. That and the lack of sleep. He was exhausted, but he felt too anxious to sleep. He would wake in the early morning hours while it was still dark and lie in bed and wonder what was going to happen to him.

He always asked for the early shift at the bookstore. Since he couldn't sleep, it was a relief to get up and have a place to go to. Also, few customers came in during the morning hours, and he didn't have to deal with people. Keeping up a normal front was very hard. He started the day by stocking the shelves, and usually he did as much as necessary before getting too exhausted. He was working only half-days now, but he was still tired all the time.

When he first got the diagnosis, he resolved to fight the disease and not give in. He wanted to try everything that people told him to try. He spent six weeks eating a macrobiotic diet, but it seemed to make his diarrhea worse. He tried smuggled doses of Compound Q, but he could tell no difference in what was happening to him. Eventually he simply took ZDV.

It was the only drug he took for half a year. Then, when the first bruiselike Kaposi patch appeared on his leg, his doctor put him on alpha interferon. When he developed a cough and a fever and was found to have pneumonocystis pneumonia, he was given pentamidine spray. And now he was also trying one drug after another to try to control the diarrhea that had become chronic.

He knew he was lucky to be an employee of the bookstore. He was covered by the group Blue Cross policy, and so far it had paid for everything except 20% of his medical bills and medicines. He had tried to get a supplemental policy before Alan died, but he couldn't find a company willing to accept him without a blood test. So far he had been able to pay his part of the bills, but it wouldn't be long before he became so weak he would have to quit his job.

He couldn't ask his parents to help him. They knew the kind of life he had been living, and they didn't approve of it. But that's not why he couldn't turn to them. It was because they themselves had nothing, and he would become another burden for them. Besides, to be honest, he was afraid of their reaction to him. He couldn't stand the idea that they would treat him like a leper, not wanting to touch him or come near him. In sparing them, he was also sparing himself.

When he could no longer work, he knew what would happen, because he had seen it happen to other people. First they moved to a cheaper apartment, if they could find someone willing to rent to them. Then they sold their car. After that, they began to sell whatever furniture, stereo, or video equipment they had. Finally, they were forced to turn to Medicaid and the state welfare agencies for everything—medical care, medicine, rent money, telephone, and even the food they didn't want to eat. Most people grew poorer faster than they grew sicker, and that guaranteed their dying in complete poverty.

He heard the sharp ding of the kitchen timer. The frozen pasta dinner he had put in the oven would be ready now. He would have to get it out before it burned. He picked up his cane from the bed and started to walk away.

Then he turned around and pulled open the drawer once more. He picked up the snuffbox and shook it. The capsules inside rattled reassuringly.

He put the box back inside and closed the drawer.

SOCIAL CONTEXT: DRUG TESTING, AUTONOMY, AND ACCESS TO UNAPPROVED DRUGS

In April 1989, a group of AIDS activists and physicians in private practice agreed to con-

duct a test of the therapeutic effectiveness of a substance called Compound Q. Until that time, drug trials had been the exclusive province of university- and hospital-based physicians and scientists working in cooperation with pharmaceutical companies and the Federal Drug Administration (FDA).

Compound Q, known also as trichosanthic, is a derivative of the root of the Chinese cucumber and had long been used in China to induce abortions and treat tumors. A study done at a San Francisco hospital suggested that the substance would destroy HIV-infected cells in a culture, while leaving normal cells unaffected. Encouraged by this result, a number of people infected with HIV had gone to great lengths and expense to secure Compound Q from China.

Compound Q seemed so promising as an AIDS treatment that Martin Delaney, head of the AIDS-advocacy group Project Inform, decided that it should be tested quickly and made available immediately. The urgent need for action prompted Delaney and his supporters to decide that the complex and time-consuming mechanism for testing a drug and securing approval for its use from the FDA could not be followed. People with AIDS were dying daily, and the need for an effective drug was crucial.

Delaney got in touch with several private physicians in San Francisco, New York, Los Angeles, and Miami and assembled a group willing to administer Compound Q to AIDS patients who wanted it, monitor their clinical signs, and send blood samples to laboratories for analysis.

The immediate problem became obtaining a supply of Compound Q. Delaney turned to James Corti, a registered nurse who over the previous five years had been smuggling in from Mexico various drugs rumored to be effective in treating AIDS. Corti and a friend went to China and obtained 200 doses of Compound Q, then smuggled the drug into the United States.

The Compound Q Trials

Delaney and his associates drew up a set of rules for admitting patients into their program and for administering and evaluating the success of Compound Q. However, the procedures they laid out differed considerably from FDA guidelines. Animal testing was omitted completely. Also, instead of beginning human experimentation by employing low doses of the drug to test for its safety, the Delaney group began administering what they considered likely to be effective therapeutic doses. They then increased doses from that point.

In addition, all patients in the study received the drug. In standard drug testing, a control group would have received either a placebo or, more likely, some other drug with known therapeutic effects. Compound Q would then be compared in effectiveness with the established drug. The initial study began with about thirty patients and nine physicians.

The Compound Q trials were intended to be conducted in complete secrecy. However, when three patients in the study died, the experiment could no longer remain clandestine. Public attention focused on the last of the three, thirty-year-old Scott Sheaffer.

Sheaffer had a compromised immune system, but he had never taken ZDV and seemed stable before taking Compound Q. He then declined rapidly, falling into a coma for three days and regaining consciousness only to die ten days later at the end of August. Physicians at the two hospitals where Sheaffer received treatment were not told he was receiving Compound Q. Whether the drug caused his death has never been established, although some critics of the Delaney group believe it is likely.

The Delaney group's clandestine approach to testing Compound Q was condemned by a number of researchers and AIDS activists. Mark Harrington, speaking for the Aids Coalition to Unleash Power (or Act Up),

said that if advocates for people with AIDS wanted to conduct private studies, they would have to meet the same standards as scientific studies. According to Paul Volberding, a respected AIDS researcher, "What they've done is a real disservice to volunteers in the study and to a drug that might be interesting. It doesn't take a genius to hand out drugs to people without controls, but it takes a certain amount of discipline to ask questions in a rigorous way."

The FDA halted the study of Compound Q, then conducted an investigation. In March 1990, to the surprise of many in the medical and scientific community, the agency announced that it was prepared to allow the trials of Compound Q by Delaney's group to continue, provided certain changes were made in the design of the experiments. Sandoz Pharmaceuticals agreed to supply the group with a synthetic form of Compound Q and awarded it a $250,000 grant to do its work.

The FDA decision attracted immediate criticism from hospital- and university-based AIDS researchers. The decision "grants carte blanche to people to do whatever they want to do," Donald Abrhams at San Francisco General Hospital said. "It opens a Pandora's box, and the only people who are going to be hurt are those we are trying to find an answer for." Paul Meier, a statistician at the University of Chicago, expressed the view that the FDA had been "pushed to do things that are not in the interest of the patient group. . . . For the agency simply to approve a study that was illegally conducted and that caused possibly unnecessary deaths shows a political weakness that is tragic for us all."

Accelerated Approval Plan. The FDA decision signaled an important change in attitude toward drug testing. For more than a decade, critics had charged that the machinery for testing drugs to determine their safety and effectiveness was much too slow in its operation. Some also argued that the standards of being "safe and effective" are not appropriate where fatal diseases are concerned.

Advocates for people with AIDS had repeatedly stressed that AIDS patients need immediate access to any drug that seems at all promising. Accordingly, they were highly critical of federal laws and policies that slowed the testing of potentially useful drugs. In taking this view, the advocates were repeating and reenforcing the complaints of cancer patients, who have often denounced the FDA for its slowness in approving drugs already tested and available in Europe.

This point of view received support in the 1990 recommendations of the Committee to Review Current Procedures for Approval of New Drugs for Cancer and AIDS. The committee suggested that less evidence of the effectiveness of cancer and AIDS drugs should be required before the drugs are given approval for clinical use. The committee also recommended that the FDA drop its requirement that drug companies provide evidence that an experimental drug can "prolong life" in favor of evidence showing that the drug improves the "quality of life."

The committee acknowledged that faster approval of experimental drugs would increase the danger to those using them. However, "Patients with life-threatening diseases who have no alternative therapy are entitled to make this choice."

In 1991, the FDA adopted a "fast track" or accelerated approval plan for drugs. Under the plan, manufacturers have to provide data about a drug's safety, but they do not have to demonstrate its clinical effectiveness. After the drug is licensed for use, its effectiveness is supposed to be monitored, and the drug can be withdrawn if it turns out to be dangerous or therapeutically useless.

However, some researchers, as well as some AIDS activists, are dissatisfied with the way the accelerated approval plan has worked. Critics charge that the effectiveness of the drugs that have been given swift approval has not been determined. The AIDS drugs DDI, d4T, and DDC have been in clinical use for a number of years, but the FDA has yet to say whether they have any therapeutic value. Because the drugs already have been licensed, the pharmaceutical companies have little incentive to spend the large amount of money necessary to conduct the studies necessary to determine their effectiveness.

One member of the AIDS-advocacy group TAG (Treatment Action Group) told reporter Gina Kolata that he was frustrated by the lack of data available on drugs. "We pay huge amounts of money, and we suffer through major toxicities, and we have to take the drug companies' word for it that the drugs work," he said. TAG recommends making use of the FDA's "expanded access" programs as the basis for studies of effectiveness. The provision allows drug companies to make available potentially useful drugs to AIDS patients before applying for a license to sell the drug, and the companies could be required to turn the expanded access programs into controlled clinical trials.

Other AIDS activists are not in agreement with TAG. Martin Delany, the director of Project Inform, thinks that the only problem with the fast-track approval system is that drug companies are not required to do follow-up studies. "Don't punish the current generation of patients to punish drug companies," he says.

Some researchers consider the accelerated approval system a failure and recommend that it be rejected in favor of the older, more scientifically rigorous procedure for determining whether a drug ought to be licensed for clinical use. The new system, in their view, does a disservice to patients. They cannot be assured that the drug they are prescribed will be of any benefit to them. Also, the lack of useful data makes it impossible to compare the effectiveness of one treatment with another, and as a result, progress in developing more effective treatments is not possible.

Complete Freedom of Choice?

For some advocates for people with AIDS or other lethal diseases, the accelerated approval plan and expanded access programs are still too restrictive of patient autonomy. Even with lowered standards for approval and widened access, not every experimental drug is available to anyone who wishes to use it. The fact remains that the government still controls access to drugs and has the power to determine which ones are legally available for use.

The public first became aware that actor Rock Hudson had AIDS when his press representative announced that he was in Paris to seek treatment for the disease. A drug rumored to have some chance of success against AIDS was not legally available in the United States. After treatment, Hudson returned to his home in California where he died a few weeks later.

Every year hundreds, perhaps even thousands, of Americans travel to foreign countries to seek medical treatments that are not available to them at home. They go to clinics in Mexico, West Germany, Switzerland, Brazil, Greece, the Bahamas, and a number of other places. In the past they were almost exclusively cancer patients, but now they include a growing number of AIDS patients. Most have learned that they can reasonably expect to live only a few more weeks or months. Whatever their disease, they all share a sense of desperation. They are trying to save their lives.

Furthermore, drugs they have heard might be helpful simply cannot be obtained legally in the United States. During the last few years, drugs like ribavirin, AL-721, and dextran sulfate thought by some to be useful in treating AIDS have been available only through illegal channels.

Critics ask, Why are Americans required to travel to distant countries and spend large sums of money to get treatments they want? Why are they forced to resort to illegal means to secure access to drugs that might help them? Why should desperate and dying people be forced to make personal and financial sacrifices to gain access to therapies they wish to try?

Responsibilities of the FDA. One answer to these questions lies in the responsibilities assigned to the FDA. It has the task of approving all new drugs and medical devices. Even before a drug is used experimentally in clinical trials, it is supposed to have FDA approval for investigational use. Applications for approval must include data about the use of the drug in test animals. (This is the first requirement the Delaney group circumvented in its testing of Compound Q.) Only after such approval can clinical studies of the drug's safety in specific doses be initiated.

Randomized clinical trials of the drug in patient populations are then conducted, and the significance of the result is established through statistical analysis. In general, an effort is made to design studies that possess the formal features of any good scientific experiment. (These are just the features that the critics claim are missing from the Compound Q study and from all the drugs tested under the accelerated approval system.)

The slow and rigorous process required in the past by the FDA has its advantages. Patients in the United States are provided with a great deal of protection from the harmful effects of new and poorly tested drugs. Perhaps the most dramatic instance of this was the FDA's refusal to approve the drug thalidomide. Even though it was widely prescribed as a tranquilizer in several European countries and some studies of its safety had been done, its effect when taken by pregnant women had not been studied. The tragic outcome was that the children born to women who had taken the drug were severely malformed, blind or deaf, or had seriously defective internal organs. The United States was saved from having a "thalidomide generation" by FDA requirements.

But What about the Terminally Ill?   Under ordinary circumstances, no one wishes to run unknown risks from the effects of a drug. However, people who have been told that they have a terminal disease for which approved therapies are of limited and temporary effectiveness can hardly be said to be in ordinary circumstances.

Should they not be allowed access to whatever drug they might wish to try? Should they not be permitted to experiment on themselves if they choose to do so? Is it not paternalistic to the point of absurdity to attempt to protect people who believe themselves beyond protection and wish only the freedom to attempt to save their lives?

It would be possible to pass laws that would allow anyone diagnosed as having AIDS or any illness expected to be terminal to request treatment of any sort. Thus, anyone who wished to use an untested drug merely rumored to be effective would have the freedom to do so.

Such legislation would promote individual freedom, but it would also have some serious negative consequences. Perhaps the most serious result would be that the integrity and effectiveness of the medical-care system would be severely threatened. The system is supported to a considerable extent by current drug regulations, and if any and all drugs were legalized for even restricted therapeutic use, the way would be opened for the development of various forms of quackery. It is easy to imagine that clinics offering "new miracle drugs" and specializing in the treatment of "hopeless" patients would soon spring up.

The existence of such clinics would have the effect of encouraging patients to place their trust in worthless, but well-publicized, drugs. Patients who might derive benefits from established therapies would be likely to turn away from them in favor of unproved remedies. The very fact of legalization would give an air of legitimacy to virtually any kind of treatment. Those desperately attempting to lengthen their lives might actually shorten them.

No one can deny that placing restrictions on the type of therapy an individual is free to choose can be construed as a form of paternalism. (For a discussion of paternalism, see the General Introduction and Chapter 5.) We legitimately assume that individuals want to protect themselves from therapies judged by ordinary scientific standards as useless and potentially harmful. Thus, we are usually not inclined to regard drug regulations and standards of medical practice as paternalistic. However, from the point of view of someone with AIDS who is desperate enough to try any remedy, such restrictions may be viewed as blatantly paternalistic.

But can we make exceptions for such people without subjecting the rest of the population to unacceptable risks?

INTRODUCTION

The disorder now known as Acquired Immunodeficiency Syndrome, or AIDS, is a focus for a variety of pressing moral and social issues. AIDS faces us constantly with the question of what we should do about such matters as increasing the proportion of medical research funding allocated for AIDS, restricting individual freedom to protect society, balancing the need to protect confidentiality against the need to inform, making it easier for end-stage AIDS patients to die, and testing the effectiveness of AIDS drugs. The infectious, epidemic, and invariably fatal character of AIDS gives these issues an immediacy and urgency with few parallels in the history of medicine.

To understand how the issues connected with AIDS arise, it is helpful to put the disease in a historical and biomedical framework. Hence, we will begin with a sketch of the story of its discovery and the elucidation of its mode of operation, then look at its present social reality. Within that context, a number of moral and social issues will stand out clearly.

Because the ethical issues surrounding the AIDS epidemic are special cases of more general moral issues—confidentiality, distribution of resources, and so on—this chapter will not be structured like others in this book. The emphasis will be more on identifying issues and outlining responses to them, rather than sketching out ways particular moral principles and theories might be applied to them. That will be left to the readings and to the reader.

DISCOVERING THE DISEASE

In the spring of 1981, the federal Centers for Disease Control (CDC) began receiving reports from physicians in New York and Los Angeles that they were seeing patients with an unusual form of pneumonia caused by the protozoan *Pneumocystis carinii*. The patients also showed signs of having damaged immune systems, leaving them prey to opportunistic diseases that included bacterial and viral infections and rare forms of cancer. In fact, the CDC soon learned that a number of the reported cases of the unusual pneumonia, known as PCP, also had developed Kaposi's sarcoma, a rare form of cancer of the skin and internal organs. Until then Kaposi's sarcoma had been found almost exclusively in elderly Jewish and Mediterranean males.

The most striking aspect of the cases was that all the patients were homosexual males. When the CDC checked its records for similar cases in the past, it discovered ones in New York in 1978 and 1979 that also involved homosexual males. A rapid survey of several major cities led to the discovery of almost 100 cases. The almost exclusive occurrence of the disease—whatever it might be—among homosexual men led to the question "What characteristic do male homosexuals have that

might be responsible for the disease they are getting?"

Out of the identified cases, investigators from the CDC intensively interviewed the thirty people known to be alive. The interviews produced information that led to the first hypothesis. Amyl and butyl nitrites, known as "poppers," are stimulants that when inhaled produce a temporary high. They are used almost exclusively by gay men, and more than 90% of those interviewed said that they had used them. This suggested that perhaps the nitrites might damage the immune system in some direct or indirect way. Or perhaps some bad batches of poppers had got on the market, and whatever was in them caused damage. The CDC began experiments with mice, collected samples of the various brands of nitrites, and conducted more interviews about their use.

Meanwhile, additional cases were being reported. The class of those affected grew to include intravenous drug users and Haitian immigrants. The fact that Haiti had a reputation for being a vacation spot for American homosexual men suggested that the disease might have spread from there, but not all the Haitians with the disease were homosexuals. Some intravenous drug users were homosexuals, but by no means all of them. The facts were not falling into any neat and obvious pattern. The names that had been given to the disease, such as "the gay plague" and "gay-related immunological deficiency," or GRID, came to seem quite inappropriate.

Another syndrome that seemed connected with the disease was identified. Called lymphadenopathy, it was characterized by swollen lymph nodes, fever, chills, and night sweats. The diseases that commonly cause such generalized symptoms were all absent. This led physicians and researchers to speculate that the syndrome might be the disease at an early stage.

Other hypotheses were proposed. An early one was the "immune system overload" theory. According to it, the frequency with which gay men engage in sexual activity and the nature of activity expose them to a great variety of foreign substances, and the immune systems of some simply break down from repeated assault. The obvious difficulty with the hypothesis was that such sexual activity had been going on for thousands of years, and there was no particular reason for such immunological assaults suddenly to produce a new disease.

Many researchers favored viewing the disorder as an infectious disease caused by a mutated virus or by an existing virus that was gaining wider circulation. The virus, according to the hypothesis, would in some way attack and destroy the immune system and leave its victims open to the opportunistic infections that people with an intact immune system are not prey to.

The hypothesis gained support when two cases of the disease were diagnosed in hemophiliacs. The only way they could have been exposed was through the injection of the blood factors required to control their hemophilia. Both had received injections of the blood-clotting protein called factor VIII. It is so chemically unstable that it cannot be subjected to the usual purification process of pasteurization without being destroyed. That, plus the fact that a single injection may contain the factor from as many as 2,500 people, means that hemophiliacs are exposed to an unusual extent to blood-borne viruses. It began to look more certain that the mysterious disease was caused by an infectious agent, probably a virus.

BIOMEDICAL ASPECTS OF AIDS

Identifying the Virus

The disease the CDC was sure it had found was given the more neutral name of Acquired Immune Deficiency Syndrome—AIDS—and laboratory work was pursued with speed and vigor. It soon began to reveal

some of the characteristics of AIDS at the biological and molecular level. Researchers discovered that, although AIDS patients may have a normal or elevated level of antibodies in their blood, they lack a normal number of white blood cells known as "helper T-cells" or T-4 lymphocytes that play a crucial role in making antibodies effective. Furthermore, white blood cells known as "suppressor T-cells" or CD-8 lymphocytes (because of the CD-8 receptor on the membrane) that inhibit the antibody system are present in increased numbers. The immune system is thus severely crippled. This was taken as more evidence that a viruslike organism that attacks the immune system might be responsible for the unknown disease.

In the spring of 1984, Robert C. Gallo of the National Cancer Institute and Luc Montagnier of the Pasteur Institute in Paris independently reported the identification of the virus that is the infectious agent causing AIDS. The virus is known as the *human immunodeficiency virus* or HIV.

More Than One Virus

The HIV virus is now recognized as being one of several immunodeficiency viruses. The virus designated as HIV-1 is known to cause AIDS. The virus HIV-2 also causes AIDS, but so far no evidence suggests that anyone has acquired an HIV-2 infection in the United States. For this reason, references here to HIV and the AIDS virus will be to HIV-1.

Many subtypes of HIV-1 have been identified. The one known as "O" includes as many as thirty variants of the virus. They differ from one another, but taken as a group, they are so different from other strains that they were designated *O* for (statistical) *outlier.* O subtypes have been found mostly in Camaroon and the surrounding regions of Africa that have been comparatively little affected by AIDS. (No cases of O-type infections have been diagnosed in the United States, but challenges to screening tests most often used by blood suppliers show that they do not reliably detect the presence of the virus.) The world-wide pandemic is caused by HIV-1.

Historical Origin

Epidemiologists believe AIDS may have originated in central Africa, most likely in Zaire, perhaps as the result of a gene mutation. The early view that the disease came from the AIDS-like disease caused by simian immunodeficiency virus (SIV) that affects the African green monkey is now considered wrong. Current evidence indicates that the similarities among SIV, HIV-1, and HIV-2 might be explained by their having had a common ancestor.

From Africa the disease spread in some way to the Caribbean, was acquired by American homosexuals in Haiti, then began to spread in the United States, probably from New York, then to San Francisco. Recent evidence indicates that the disease appeared several times as early as the late 1950s and 1960s in Britain, the United States, and elsewhere but failed to establish itself within the local population. That did not happen until the 1980s. (The earliest confirmed retrospective diagnosis is that of a British sailor who died of AIDS in 1959.)

Spread of the Disease

The World Health Organization reported (1993 figures) that about 14 million people in the world are infected with HIV. Cases in western Europe number 500,000, and eastern Europe and central Asia each report more than 50,000. South and Southeast Asia now have more than 1.5 million cases, about the same number as Latin America and the Caribbean. North American cases exceed 1 million. The Middle East and North Africa each have more than 75,000 cases, and Australia more than 25,000. Sub-Saharan Africa has in excess of 8 million cases.

The spread of the disease is without a doubt a worldwide phenomenon. As the numbers show, the African continent has been hit particularly hard as AIDS has spread from the cities to the countryside. African nations face a bad situation that is likely to worsen, but other countries are also experiencing an increase in infection. Infection rates in India have tripled since 1992 and risen tenfold in Thailand since 1990. China is thought by some to be in line for a large increase. Sexually transmitted diseases are on the rise there, and HIV infection may follow.

Health officials fear that the virus will break out in an unprepared population before steps can be taken to combat its spread. In four African countries, there was an explosive outbreak of new infections for three or four years, then a stable period during which the infected died and were replaced by the newly infected. In one district in Uganda, AIDS now causes almost half of all deaths and 9 out of 10 deaths of those under the age of thirty-five.

The most recent 1994 estimates put the figure for HIV infection worldwide at 17 million. The number with AIDS is put at 4 million.

AIDS Drugs

After the AIDS virus was identified, additional research soon identified major parts of the mechanism by which it works. The virus is known to be a retrovirus. When it is introduced into the body, it eventually enters helper T-cells, through a particular site (the CD-4 receptor) on the surface and becomes incorporated into the DNA in the cell's nucleus. When the cell is activated in the presence of an infectious agent, the virus reproduces itself and kills the cell, releasing new viruses to infect other cells.

That the virus is inside the cells of the immune system poses a major difficulty in developing a treatment for AIDS, because any drug likely to destroy the virus will also destroy the immune system. Researchers find it a daunting prospect to conceive of a drug that will eliminate immune cells containing the virus while leaving other cells untouched. AIDS itself compromises the immune system, and when the immune system is further weakened or even destroyed by drugs, the body is without defense and even a minor infection can result in severe illness and death.

In September 1986, researchers announced results showing some success in treating AIDS with the drug AZT. (The initials stand for azidothymidine.) The drug is now called zidovudine, or ZDV, and has the trade name Retrovir. ZDV disrupts reverse transcriptase, the biochemical triggering replication, and halts the reproduction of the virus. The drug does not reverse the damage to the immune system caused by the virus, but it slows the progress of the disease.

ZDV has become the standard for judging the effectiveness of all AIDS drugs. Even so, recent studies of the effectiveness of ZDV have shown that it has only limited benefits for a limited time. For reasons not currently known, perhaps because of the development of viral resistance, eventually ZDV stops working and the disease reasserts itself. ZDV may improve the quality of life for those who are HIV-positive, but it is not clear that it extends life or delays the onset of AIDS.

Although several studies show that early treatment with ZDV can delay the onset of symptoms, a three-year, Anglo-French study published in 1993 found that people infected with HIV follow about the same course, whether treated with ZDV or not. The value of ZDV in those who have developed symptoms was not questioned.

Because ZDV and the chemically similar drugs DDI (didanosine), and DDC (zalcitabine), are of only limited effectiveness, the search has continued for other drugs. At the moment, a group of compounds known as *protease inhibitors* is considered most promising. Six of the drugs are now being tested, and about twenty more are under development. The protease inhibitors work by blocking an enzyme (protease) that is necessary for the virus to replicate. Protease slices a long protein chain into fragments that form a functioning virus.

Instead of a single drug, a current treatment strategy is to use several drugs in sequence or combination. One recent study used ZDV, DDC, and Saquinavir (a protease inhibitor). The results showed that the three drugs in combination were more effective than ZDV alone or a two-drug combination in preventing a rise in the level of HIV in patients' blood and in maintaining their immune-cell functioning.

An experimental approach now under development is to use recombinant-DNA techniques and gene therapy to attack the AIDS virus. In one possible approach, an attenuated virus is used to transport a particular gene into infected cells. The gene incorporates itself into the cellular DNA, where it makes an altered version of the *rev* protein. The protein ordinarily functions as part of the system in which the viral messenger RNA (m-RNA) leaves the nucleus and goes to the cytoplasm for replication. The altered version of rev attaches itself to m-RNA, but the combination cannot leave the nucleus. Hence, the virus is prevented from replicating itself.

Because drugs like ZDV interfere with the immune function, people with AIDS can still suffer from a variety of opportunistic infections that must be treated separately. With experience, physicians have become more skilled at treating the diseases that resulted in quick deaths during the early years of the AIDS epidemic. Those with bacterial and fungal infections are treated early and aggressively. The pneumonia that first signaled the outbreak of the epidemic is now treated prophylactically so that its significance as a cause of death has declined. As a result of this more aggressive treatment of secondary infections, AIDS patients are living longer, but they are also beginning to develop various forms of cancer. Devising effective treatment for these patients is seen by AIDS experts as a challenge for the coming years.

Vaccines

When the AIDS virus was identified, it was hoped that a vaccine for it would be developed immediately. AIDS would then become a member of the family of diseases like smallpox and rabies that cannot be effectively treated but can be effectively prevented by vaccination. Unfortunately, HIV has turned out to be a virus that mutates rapidly and exists in many variant forms. Some researchers doubt it will be possible to develop a vaccine that will prevent all forms of the disease. Nevertheless, work is underway, and at least sixteen vaccines are currently being tested in humans, and additional ones are being tested in animals.

In 1994, a federal health advisory committee expressed a lack of confidence in the two most promising vaccines and recommended that the United States not participate in conducting phase-three trials. However, the World Health Organization announced that it would go ahead with trials in some other country. Because Third World nations account for almost 90% of AIDS cases, it is likely that one of them will be the site of the trials.

Wrong Paradigm?

In 1984, Margaret M. Heckler, secretary of the Department of Health and Human Services, made a formal announcement of the discovery of the AIDS virus and predicted that within two years a vaccine would be available to bring the disease under control. Although more than a decade has passed, this has not happened. It has become clear that the AIDS virus poses a greater problem to understanding than was at first imagined, and some prominent researchers are recommending that the scientific community change its approach to dealing with HIV and AIDS.

Unfortunately, the battle against AIDS has not turned out to be like the battle against the polio epidemic, which was essentially won in a relatively short time with the discovery of a vaccine. Some researchers are now saying that we must stop thinking of the polio paradigm as one appropriate for AIDS. Rather, we must think of HIV diseases, including AIDS, in terms of the cancer paradigm.

Cancer is a disease (or group of diseases) that has not responded as well or as quickly as anyone hoped to the great variety of treatment strategies that have been tried against it. Nevertheless, researchers are confident that eventually an understanding of the biology of cancer will lead to effective modes of treatment. The same is no doubt true of AIDS, but, researchers say, we must give up the idea that success is going to happen overnight.

Instead of continuing to emphasize the rapid development and testing of drugs and vaccines, some suggest that efforts be focused on the basic biology of the virus. The drug and vaccine programs lack a solid scientific basis and proceed in a mostly hit-or-miss fashion. So far, despite great effort, there have been an overwhelming number of misses and few hits. Meanwhile, the programs are drawing money away from research that might eventually provide the information needed to develop effective treatments and vaccines. More information about the way the virus behaves is needed if vaccines and therapies are to be designed deliberately.

A recommendation for such a shift in thinking is sure to be a sad and bitter disappointment for those who are HIV-positive or who have AIDS. The recommendation is, after all, an expression of the tacit belief that those infected with the virus cannot expect anything like a cure for AIDS in the near future.

AIDS Transmission and Risks

The way in which the AIDS virus is transmitted is not completely understood. The virus is most concentrated in the blood and semen of those infected, and the introduction of the virus directly into the bloodstream seems the most certain mode of transmission. Thus, IV-drug users who share a syringe with an HIV carrier are at most risk of infection, as are those who receive blood or blood products contaminated with the virus. Health workers who get needle sticks with infected syringes or scalpel cuts during surgery on an HIV patient, or who come into contact with blood containing the virus are at some risk. (The rate of infection from needle sticks is about 1 in 300.)

The virus is also transmitted by sexual relations in which semen comes into contact with mucous membranes. Thus, in the case of male homosexuals or bisexuals, the virus may enter the bloodstream through the lining of the rectum during anal intercourse. In heterosexual intercourse, the vaginal membrane may be the means of entry. Anal sex seems to pose the greatest risk for both men and women, because the rectal membrane is delicate and small tears may allow entry of the virus. Sores or cuts in the mouth may make oral sex a possible mode of infection.

Because of the presence of the virus in semen, transmission seems more likely from male to female than vice versa. (In Zaire, however, infection seems equally likely for men and women.) The mode of transmission of the virus from female to male during intercourse is not clear. An open sore or tear in the skin of the penis may offer a mode of entry. The presence of some other sexually transmitted disease, genital herpes or gonorrhea in particular, increases the likelihood of infection in both males and females. There is no evidence to show that the virus enters the body through the urethra.

Pregnant women who carry the virus may pass it on to the fetus through the maternal-fetal circulatory system. This seems to happen about 25% of the time. If a woman tests HIV-positive and is treated with ZDV, the risk to the newborn drops to about 8.3%.

Individuals at most risk are intravenous-drug users, homosexual or bisexual males, those with multiple-sexual partners, those with a history of sexually transmitted diseases, those receiving blood transfusions or blood products before 1985, and the sexual partners of anyone in one of these categories.

The AIDS virus has been discovered in low concentrations in the saliva and tears of those infected. Kissing in which saliva is exchanged is thought to be a slight risk, but sneezing, coughing, touching, and so on are not considered likely means of transmission. Even food handlers with AIDS are not thought to pose a risk to others.

Outside a host, the AIDS virus seems to be quite fragile, and this means it is unlikely anyone could become infected by using dishes, eating utensils, books, toilet seats, or other articles touched by a carrier. In short, there is strong evidence that AIDS is not spread by means of ordinary social contact in the way that, for example, cold viruses are spread.

Blood Tests

An important development after the discovery of the AIDS virus was a blood test to determine its presence in individuals. ELISA (enzyme-linked immunosorbent assay), the most commonly used test, does not identify the virus directly but detects the presence of antibodies to the virus in a blood sample. The test is good on sensitivity—that is, it rarely fails to detect the presence of the virus. However, it is not as good on specificity; it has many false positives, indicating the virus is present when it is not. For this reason, anyone who tests positive for HIV should have the result confirmed by a test that is more specific. (The usual procedure is to use the ELISA test a second time, then if the results are still positive, the Western blot is used.)

The antibodies to HIV typically develop about four weeks after infection, and the blood test now used cannot detect the presence of the virus before that time. This means an individual may be infected for a four-week period without knowing it and without testing positive for HIV. Some evidence shows that the virus is most infectious before antibodies to it can be detected. Consequently, an individual may transmit the virus to others without being aware of it. (Recent evidence indicates that the immune system responds so well to the virus that ten years or more may pass before AIDS symptoms develop.)

A new test employing blood plasma, the part of blood free of red cells, can confirm the presence of the virus within two weeks of infection. The test works by directly detecting virus particles in the plasma before the immune system responds to the particles as antigens and produces antibodies.

Blood collection agencies routinely screen blood donors for the HIV virus. Yet because of the four-week period between an individual's becoming infected and developing antibodies, the usual test cannot eliminate all potential donors who might be carriers. Using present methods, out of roughly three thousand AIDS cases linked to blood transfusions, fewer than ten have occurred since current screening methods were introduced in 1985. (Blood plasma is also processed in a way that renders the virus harmless.) Public health officials claim that the blood supply is now safer than it has ever been.

The FDA is considering giving its approval to a home test for HIV. In the test, a person pricks a finger, puts some drops of blood on a blotting paper, and mails the paper to a laboratory. In three weeks, the person can call the laboratory, give a special code number, and be given the results. If the results are negative, they may be given by a recording. If they are positive, the person would learn them from a trained counselor, who would provide information about getting appropriate care and practicing safe sex.

Opponents of a home test complain that a telephone conversation is no substitute for counseling. Someone learning bad news may try to commit suicide, and everyone needs emotional support and practical assistance.

Defenders of the test say that many people already learn their HIV status over the telephone from physicians and clinics.

Education and Personal Protection

No genuinely effective treatment for AIDS has been devised. Nor is a vaccine to protect against it available. Accordingly, experts agree, the most practical means to slow the spread of the virus and keep the number of cases from increasing is public education. Thus, people are advised to limit their sexual contacts, avoid anal intercourse, use condoms, avoid using unsterilized syringes, avoid unprotected sexual relations with anyone who might have AIDS, and make an effort to determine the sexual history of a potential sex partner.

Those who think they might have been exposed to the virus should get a blood test, and if it turns out positive, they should get another, more specific, test. Early detection is important, because the treatment of life-threatening secondary diseases like pneumonia is most successful when started early.

In adults, the delay from the time of infection to the development of AIDS is an average of ten years. The number can vary significantly, however.

Current Statistics

Not only do statistics about AIDS change as more information accumulates, but most available statistics are untrustworthy to various degrees. Studies are usually based on small samples, and the samples themselves may be biased by such factors as deceit, denial, and an unwillingness to divulge private information. Also, because of local factors, generalizing to a broader population may often produce misleading results.

Furthermore, in 1993 the Centers for Disease Control introduced a revised set of criteria for AIDS. The definition was broader, and this produced a significant increase in the number of cases. Nevertheless, here is some of what is considered established on the basis of information available as of May 1995:

- About 402,000 cases of AIDS have been reported in the United States. Some 243,000 people have died from the disease. No one has been known to recover.

- About 50,000 Americans are infected with the AIDS virus every year.

- In 1992, 33,566 Americans died of AIDS, an 11.5% increase from 1991. The death rate from AIDS was 11.6 per 100,000 people.

- After the introduction of the new CDC definition of AIDS for the first nine months of 1993, 85,526 cases of AIDS were reported. During the same period in 1992, the number was 35,479. The increase was 148%.

- About 40,000 Americans per year will die of AIDS. The epidemic may be reaching a steady state or even declining, but because of the new redefinition, the death rate for the disease may continue to increase over the next several years.

- Each day in the United States there are about 145 new cases.

- From 800,000 to 1.2 million people in the United States are infected with the virus and may be assumed to be able to pass on the virus to others. (This figure is expected to be lowered when the CDC next meets to review relevant data.)

- The main epidemic has been among gay, white males, but some evidence shows that the incidence of HIV infections is leveling off or declining.

- Using 1993 figures (the latest comparative ones available), gay men accounted for 183,344 of the 334,344 cases reported.

- About one-third of new cases are homosexual males. About another one-third are IV-drug users. The final one-third are infected heterosexually, and most of these are African-American and Hispanic women.

- About 2,000 children are born infected with HIV, and the great majority die within the first few years of life.

- Worldwide, about 17 million people are infected with the AIDS virus. Three million have become infected in the last year.

- Four million have died of AIDS worldwide.

- At the current rate of increase, by the year 2000, the number will reach 30 to 40 million.

ETHICAL AND SOCIAL ISSUES

Confidentiality and Notification

The issue of AIDS and confidentiality is politically volatile throughout the country. Should AIDS tests be offered anonymously? Should physicians be required to report to health agencies the names of patients with AIDS? And most controversial of all, should states and cities adopt notification policies requiring physicians or public health departments to notify the spouses and sex and drug partners of those who test HIV-positive that they have been exposed to the virus?

The controversy over confidentiality involves a tangle of competing interests. On the one hand, individuals who test positive for HIV may not want this fact known to anyone. If it is, then however they acquired the virus, they may be thought to be drug abusers, sexually promiscuous, or, if male, homosexuals or bisexuals. They may fear discrimination or pity or may simply not wish something they consider intensely personal and private to be made public in any degree.

On the other hand, if people who are exposed to the virus without suspecting it are not notified, they may not recognize the need to be tested. Although anyone might choose to be tested, someone knowing of no reason to believe she or he has been put at risk for infection has no reason to seek the test. For example, a wife who does not know her husband is an IV-drug abuser also does not know that she is running a risk of infection when they have sex. If her husband consults a physician and tests positive for HIV, shouldn't the physician notify the wife that she also may be infected with the virus?

The potential conflict between the right to confidentiality of a person with AIDS and the welfare of those he or she may have exposed to the virus is obvious. It would remain potential if everyone testing HIV-positive wished all partners notified or if partners never wished to be notified. However, these logical possibilities never hold in actuality. In fact, a 1988 study concluded that almost 25% of sexually active people tested for the AIDS virus said that even if they tested positive for the virus, they would not inform casual sex partners that they were carriers of the virus. It is not likely that a larger percentage would voluntarily warn sex partners after the fact.

At present no national policy regulates notification, but a number of cities and states have formulated policies. Taken together, these policies do not offer a coherent approach. Almost every conceivable policy has been adopted somewhere, and the degree of enforcement varies as widely as the policies themselves.

Voluntary notification programs permit those who test HIV-positive to authorize health authorities to notify individuals named by those tested. By requiring consent, voluntary programs have the advantage of protecting the privacy and autonomy of those with AIDS.

Yet, the obvious disadvantage is that they may fail to protect the interest of those the person with AIDS has exposed to the virus. The interest of those exposed is totally dependent on decisions made by others. Those at risk may be kept in ignorance of their danger and hence put into a position in which they do not have information relevant to making decisions about their own welfare or that of others. In this respect, their autonomy is violated without their knowledge or consent.

A mandatory notification program seems

the ideal way to protect the welfare of a sex or drug partner of someone who tests HIV-positive. One might reason that violating the confidentiality of the HIV-positive person is warranted by his or her partners' need to know. Although this may be so, an additional consequence of such a policy is that it discourages those who are at highest risk for AIDS from seeking testing.

Few people would be willing to risk such serious consequences as losing their jobs, not being able to find a place to live, or not being able to get insurance if information about their being HIV-positive was deliberately or even accidentally made public. Of course, such possibilities can occur even in the absence of mandatory notification program.

The lack of anonymity in testing is likely to discourage a large group of people from having a test and, hence, from receiving the treatment they may need. In addition, those who are actually infected with the AIDS virus, but ignorant of their condition, may continue to spread the virus to others through sexual contacts.

Considerations such as these have encouraged the development of testing programs that permit anonymity. An individual submitting a blood sample is assigned a number and then can learn the results by using that number. Such a procedure protects the confidentiality of the individual tested and increases the likelihood that high-risk individuals will seek tests and treatment. Of course, the procedure leaves the matter of notifying a partner entirely to individuals tested.

This is not an outcome acceptable to all groups. In 1988, the House of Delegates of the American Medical Association broke with the tradition of presumptive confidentiality and passed a resolution urging physicians, if necessary, to warn the sex partners of patients found to carry the AIDS virus. Physicians should encourage patients to take this step themselves, but if they shirk the responsibility, physicians should issue a warning. The AMA resolution expressed the view that state governments have the primary responsibility for tracing and warning sex partners, just as in the case of other sexually transmitted diseases, and encouraged the adoption of laws to establish notification procedures.

The AMA position is reflected in a general movement by the states to treat AIDS more like any other communicable disease. At least eleven states have laws that require tracing sex partners, and fifteen have quarantine laws that permit authorities to detain people who knowingly spread the disease. At least fifteen also keep lists of people testing HIV-positive, except for those tested anonymously. Those favoring such changes cite the value of early detection and early treatment of those infected with the virus. Both New York and California, which together have some 42% of AIDS cases, oppose this trend. Gay-rights groups, in particular, have spoken against it, citing their fear that violations of confidentiality will lead to discrimination. They also question the value of partner tracing by pointing to the lack of success it has produced in eliminating venereal diseases.

Advocates of more aggressive testing and tracing policies reply that violations of confidentiality have not occurred within the public health system. Hospitals and physicians have been the ones to blame. Furthermore, partner tracing is crucial in protecting unsuspecting people, such as the wife in our example who does not know her husband is an IV-drug user. As a Colorado health commissioner stated, "It's a real women's issue. The individuals least likely to be aware are the female mates of closet bisexual men or secret former intravenous drug users."

Confidentiality, Health Professionals, and Patients

Suppose a physician, dentist, or other health professional has been tested and found to be carrying the HIV virus. Does he or she have a duty to inform patients of that fact?

William H. Behringer was a staff physician at Princeton Medical Center. When he was diagnosed with AIDS he continued to practice there as an ENT (ear-nose-throat) specialist. News of his illness spread, however, and the hospital asked him to give up performing surgery. He refused, and the hospital then required patients to sign consent forms saying that they were aware that Behringer had tested positive for the AIDS virus and that there was "a potential risk of transmission."

Behringer sued the hospital. His lawyers argued that the refusal of patients to sign the forms the hospital required constituted a de facto refusal to allow him to practice surgery. The hospital responded that the consent form was not unreasonable and that it had a duty to protect the interest of patients and itself.

Cases like this raise the issue of resolving the conflict between a patient's need to be informed adequately to assess his own risks and the health-care worker's claim to confidentiality about her own health.

Until the summer of 1990, there was no established case of the transmission of the virus from a health worker to a patient. Then a case involving the infection of the patients of a Florida dentist was documented by the Centers for Disease Control. (See the Bergalis Case Presentation.) Consequently, although the risk of transmission of the virus from a surgeon to a patient is regarded as quite small, it is now viewed as a real possibility. Does even a small risk to the patient require a health worker to disclose relevant but private information?

Behringer, who died of AIDS, believed that he had been infected with the virus when he performed an emergency tracheotomy on an infected patient while not properly masked. The infection may have occurred through contact with the patient's blood and saliva.

Behringer's own infection raises the same moral issue from the other perspective. Should a patient who knows that he is HIV-positive inform health-care workers of that fact? Most people would answer yes to this question, because an infected patient poses the threat of a fatal disease to those who are taking care of him.

One study showed that hospitals do not rely on patients to volunteer such information, even if they possess it. Hospitals regard patients as a potential source of HIV infection, and to protect their staff, many routinely order an HIV test for each admission, even when it is not medically indicated. During the fifteen-month period of the study at the St. Paul-Ramsey Medical Center in St. Paul, Minnesota, 44% of the tests for AIDS had no medical justification. Further, in these and in an additional 44% of tests for which there was justification, the patients' consent was not obtained. In only 10% of the tests was there both consent and a medical reason for the test.

Similar results were found in a study of 560 randomly selected hospitals. Many of the hospitals did not get patients' consent before testing them for AIDS—an illegal practice in many states, including New York, California, and Massachusetts. Further, despite federal guidelines on confidentiality, the test results were included in patients' charts. In 25% of the hospitals, patients who tested negative were never told. Even more surprising, in 2% to 3% of the hospitals, patients who tested positive were not told. Not only does this keep such patients from seeking medical help, but they may unknowingly infect others. (See the Social Context: Mandatory AIDS Testing and Pregnancy for a discussion of the special issues involved in the testing of pregnant women.)

Social Measures in AIDS Prevention

Studies show that the spread of AIDS could be slowed significantly if a federally funded "clean-needle" program was established. During the last fifteen years, AIDS has spread faster among IV-drug users than any other group. During that time, the number of those infected with HIV has more than doubled. Countries that provide addicts with free sterile needles have evidence to prove that such programs are successful in reducing the rate of infection.

Despite this experience, in the United States only a few programs are in place, and some of them even operate in open defiance of the law. New York explicitly rejected a clean-needle program. The only federally funded programs directed to IV-drug users are educational campaigns alerting them to the dangers of using unsterilized needles.

The story is much the same regarding prevention through education. Information about the sexual practices by which the virus is most likely to be transmitted is acknowledged by most public health experts as the only acceptable means currently available to us for bringing the disease under control in the populations now at risk or soon to be at risk.

Public education plays an important role in reaching the population now sexually active. However, to prevent another generation from becoming infected with HIV, the education of teenagers about AIDS prevention is crucial.

This has become a highly contested political issue. Conservative politicians, in particular, object to the detailed discussion of sexual practices required in any effective AIDS prevention program. Some believe that explicit discussions of sex encourage early or illicit sexual activity or think that no form of sex education has a place in the public schools.

Not providing adequate funding for educational programs is likely to have serious health consequences for the nation. As writer Dick Thompson put the issue, "If society is unwilling to expend the energy and resources necessary to teach its young people to avoid AIDS, then the epidemic could grow ever larger and ever more tragic well into the next century."

AIDS Costs and Insurance

The cost of medical care for AIDS treatment in 1993 was nearly $5.5 billion. The cost is expected to rise along with that of all medical care, even if the rate of infection slows. Federal and state programs currently pay 40% of the bill, while private insurance picks up another 40%. The additional 20% is supposed to be paid by the individual. People who have group health insurance and are HIV-positive (or worry that they might be) often try to get supplementary insurance policies to cover this additional amount.

If those who develop AIDS become unable to work or lose their jobs, they may also lose their group health insurance. They must then attempt to get individual coverage. Even if they are fortunate enough to keep their group health or to get an individual policy, if they don't also have a supplemental policy that pays in a timely way, they soon run out of money. In this event, their only resort is quite literally to impoverish themselves by expending their savings and selling their assets until they have a financial worth of less than two thousand dollars. They then become eligible for Medicaid, the federal program for the indigent.

Given these circumstances, there is little wonder that insurance is a major issue generated by the AIDS epidemic. The issues of confidentiality and HIV testing are entwined around the core problem of trying to get enough money to pay for needed drugs, physician visits, and hospitalizations. The cost of medical care for each AIDS patient is about $150,000.

Given the cost of treatment, insurance companies consider it important to determine how likely it is that an applicant will get the disease. Some companies have added a required blood test to the application procedure, while others are forbidden to require such a test by state laws or regulations. In these cases, companies often rely on an applicant's medical and social history to indicate whether he or she is a higher-than-average risk.

Even when companies cannot use a blood test, homosexual-rights groups claim that insurers use questions about AIDS to discriminate against male homosexuals in general.

Further, they point out, such practices are likely to make it difficult for many other unmarried males, who might find it difficult to get insurance.

An indication of this is a memo from Lincoln National advising its underwriters to flag applications "if life style, habits or medical history suggest a person is in one of the AIDS risk groups." The memo suggested using marital status as an indicator of possible homosexuality, particularly among those aged 20 to 49 who live in such cities as New York and Los Angeles. Major insurers like Blue Cross deny they discriminate against people with AIDS. Smaller companies, though, are known to have directed their agents to employ information about an applicant's occupation, address, and domestic arrangements to determine the likelihood that he will develop AIDS.

The insurance industry contends that it should be able to use blood tests to determine whether an applicant is HIV-positive. "If we can't use the test, it will adversely affect our other applicants," an industry spokesperson said. That is, some who are not carriers of the virus will also be refused insurance on the grounds of suspicion alone. A number of states, such as California and Wisconsin, have forbidden the use of a blood test to determine insurability, as have several state regulatory agencies.

The industry does not believe it should be forced to insure individuals without being allowed to determine their HIV status. The industry would stand to increase its profits if it were able to refuse insurance to everyone likely to get AIDS. Critics point out, however, that the very notion of insurance involves spreading the cost of medical care over a large population, thus reducing the amount paid by an individual who needs expensive care. Hence, to allow insurers to eliminate people at risk for AIDS from the insured population is to increase the profit to insurers at the expense of taxpayers, the ones who will have to bear the cost of those who are desperately sick but have no insurance.

Insurers argue that while it is true that insurance involves spreading cost over a population, to be fair to individual buyers, the risk must be similar for all members of the population. Otherwise, buyers with no special medical problems are put into the position of having to pay much more for their insurance than they should. For example, 1987 actuarial figures showed that 200 out of 1,000 thirty-four-year-old AIDS-infected males would die of the disease within seven years, but that only 7.5, in the same category and noninfected, in ordinary health would die of other causes. Carriers of the virus were 26.6 times more likely to die, so ignoring the difference between the two groups meant that those in ordinary health were subsidizing the medical care of those with AIDS.

A national health insurance program would resolve many of the difficulties faced by those who are HIV-positive or who are suspected of being so by private insurance companies.

AIDS and Discrimination

People with AIDS have often been made into the lepers of our time. Some have been unable to rent apartments or renew their leases. Others have lost their jobs and been unable to find another. Some have been refused admission to health-care facilities, and even undertakers have sometimes been unwilling to accept the bodies of those who died of AIDS or have charged higher prices to bury them. In one case, an entire jury refused to hear a case because the defendant had AIDS. In another, because the defendant had AIDS court officers refused to work unless they were permitted to wear masks and heavy rubber gloves during the trial.

In a special form of discrimination, a number of physicians have refused to accept people with AIDS as patients. Some physicians do not want to risk becoming infected themselves, while others do not want to bear the enormous psychological burden that caring for AIDS patients imposes. As a consequence, people with AIDS must often compete to receive treatment from the relatively small number of physicians willing to accept them.

In 1989, the AMA Council on Ethical and Judicial Affairs stated publicly that "A physician may not ethically refuse to treat a patient whose condition is within the physician's current realm of competence" only because the patient is infected with the AIDS virus. Physicians, even those who are AMA members, are not bound in such matters to act in the way the AMA approves.

Discrimination against people with AIDS has also worked in the other direction. Hospitals have sometimes removed HIV-positive physicians from positions in which they come in contact with patients. In addition, a few private physicians have seen their practices dwindle as their patients learned they were HIV-positive or even heard a rumor that they were.

Acting out of fear, various municipalities have passed ordinances of doubtful legality requiring a blood test for applicants for certain jobs, such as restaurant worker or schoolteacher, and making testing positive for HIV grounds for refusing employment. The U.S. armed forces require an HIV blood test for all new recruits and turn down those who test positive. A policy to extend testing to those already enlisted went into effect soon after the policy for recruits was established.

In addition, all people in federal prisons are tested for the virus when they enter an institution or finish their sentences. Some prisoners allege that being infected with the virus is used as grounds to refuse parole. Foreign Service officers and applicants for the Job Corps are also among those required to take a blood test as a condition of employment.

Furthermore, under current immigration law, immigrants, refugees, and even those applying for a visa who are infected with HIV are either not allowed into the country or required to secure a waiver. These restrictions have been condemned by the World Health Organization, the International Committee on AIDS, the Red Cross, and the CDC. Although the law must be changed to alter official policy, strict enforcement of it has been relaxed since 1989.

No one doubts the obligation of government, through its laws and agencies, to protect the welfare of citizens. Protection from infectious disease sometimes requires restricting or abridging the rights of those likely to spread the disease. Thus, those with tuberculosis are not allowed to come into contact with school-children or to hold jobs that may permit the bacillus to be passed on to others. We have many precedents for abridging liberties to keep disease from spreading and to protect the health of individuals.

But, AIDS is not like tuberculosis or any similar disease. AIDS is undeniably an infectious disease, but it is not a highly infectious disease. Although many aspects of its modes of transmission remain obscure, infection apparently requires that a bodily fluid containing the virus come into contact with the bloodstream of a recipient. Infection is not at all a matter of casual contact. Except in extraordinary circumstances, to become infected with AIDS requires engaging in behavior that has high risk of exposing one to the virus.

These are the facts that must be borne in mind when considering controversies over whether a particular policy or practice is warranted by a legitimate concern for safety or whether it is no more than groundless discrimination.

AIDS, Gays, and State Coercion

Richard D. Mohr

Richard D. Mohr emphasizes the independence (autonomy) of the individual as a value threatened by AIDS policies. Mohr claims that, since most cases of AIDS are the result of self-exposure by sexual practices and the use of IV drugs, "direct coercive acts by government" are inappropriate to control the disease. Nor is coercion justifiable because of indirect harm (for example, higher taxes and insurance rates) caused by AIDS.

Coercion is warranted, Mohr says, only when the harm becomes great enough to violate another's rights, and increases in taxes or insurance don't violate rights. Also, Mohr rejects state paternalism, because it "denies independence as a value."

Finally, for Mohr it is justifiable to coerce selected individuals for the sake of public health only to prevent harm to others or to secure a "necessary end" such as the survival of the country. AIDS does not present such a situation.

Alarums and Excursions

Of those dead and dying from AIDS three-quarters are gay men. Government funding for AIDS research was at best sluggish till the disease appeared to the dominant non-gay culture as a threat. That perceived threat has spawned state-mandated discrimination against groups at risk for AIDS in employment and access to services, allegedly on medical grounds but in pointed contradiction to the judgments of the very medical institutions to which society has entrusted the determination of such grounds (the US Department of Health and Human Services, the Centers for Disease Control, and the National Institutes of Health).[1]

Government's disregard for medical opinion and for the lives of gays strongly suggests that prejudicial forces are at work. There is of course noth-

Abridged and reprinted by permission of the author from *Bioethics*, Vol. 1, No. 1, 1987, pp. 35–50.

ing new in this, but the stakes here are high. The armed forces have already established quarantines of those at risk for AIDS on some bases (*The Washington Post,* 19 October 1985, A12; *The Advocate,* #442, 18 March 1986, p. 14). With state-mandated discriminations installed and calls for civilian quarantines circulating, it is clear that the AIDS crisis is going to test the country's mettle. Not since the Supreme Court affirmed the internments of Japanese-Americans in World War II has so live a danger existed to America's traditional commitment to civil liberties. And again the danger is created by hysteria and not a reasoned necessity.

The hysteria, when not simply an expression of old anti-gay prejudices, is based on the presumption that the disease is spread indiscriminately. This presumption permitted Jeane Kirkpatrick to begin a syndicated column by using AIDS as a metaphor for international terrorism—"it can affect anyone"—in the serene belief that her audience, educated America, already thought this about AIDS and might even be ready for extreme measures (*The Washington Post,* 13 October 1985, B8).

Alleged Harms to Others

For public policy purposes, the most important fact about AIDS is not that it is deadly but that it, like hepatitis B, is caused by a blood-transmitted virus. For the disease to spread, body fluids of someone with the virus must *directly enter the bloodstream of another;* "It appears that, in order to infect, this virus must be virtually injected into the blood stream."[2] But not just any bodily fluid will do. Only blood and semen have been implicated in the transmission of the virus (*MMWR* 34: 45, p. 682).

That the virus is blood transmitted means first and foremost that, in countries with reasonable sanitation, groups at risk for the disease are clearly definable—more so than for virtually any other disease known—with 96 per cent of cases having clearly demarcated modes of transmission and cause. And now that blood supplies are screened with a test for antibodies to the AIDS virus, the number of these groups is indeed dropping. Hemophiliacs not already exposed and blood transfusion recipients are now no longer groups at risk. . . .

The July 1985 cover of *Life* informed the nation in three-inch red letters that "NOW NO ONE IS SAFE FROM AIDS." The magazine used as its allegedly compelling example a seemingly typical Pennsylvania family all but one of whose members has the disease. But it turns out that all those members with the disease were indeed in high risk groups. The father was a hemophiliac, his wife had sex with him, and she conveyed the virus to a child in the process of giving birth. No one got the disease either mysteriously or through casual contact. The family example in fact was evidence *against* the article's generic contagion thesis. Equally irresponsible journalists, lobbyists, and elected officials have compared AIDS to air-borne viral disease like influenza and the common cold.

The case for general contagion cannot be made. In consequence government policy which is based on that fear is unwarranted. The extraordinary measures—including the suspension of civil liberties—which government might justifiably take, as in war, to prevent wholesale slaughter simply do not apply here. In particular, quarantining the class of AIDS-exposed persons in order to protect society from indiscriminate harm is unwarranted.

Harm to Self

The disease's mode of contagion assures that those at risk are those whose actions contribute to their risk of infection, chiefly through intimate sexual contact and shared hypodermic needles. In the transmission of AIDS, it is the general feature of self-exposure to contagion that makes direct coercive acts by government—like bathhouse closings—particularly inappropriate as efforts to abate the disease.

If independence—the ability to guide one's life by one's own rights to an extent compatible with a like ability on the part of others—is, as it is, a major value, one cannot respect that value while preventing people from putting themselves at risk through voluntary associations. Voluntary associations are star cases of people acting in accordance with the principle of independence, for mutual consent guarantees that the "compatible extent" proviso of the principle is fulfilled. But the state and even the courts have not been very sensitive to the distinction between one harming oneself and one harming another—nor has the medical establishment.[3] It appears to all of them that a harm is a harm, a disease a disease, however caused or described. The moral difference, however, is enormous. Preventing a person from harming another is required by the principle of independence, but preventing someone from harming himself is incompatible with it. While no further from others, a rather powerful justification is needed if the state is to be warranted in protecting a person from himself.

In the absence of such a justification, the state sometimes tries to split the moral difference and argues that state coercion *may* be used when the harm to others is remote and indirect. Such an argument from indirect harms runs to the effect that state-coerced use of, say, seatbelts and motorcycle helmets is warranted, for helmetless motorcycle crashes and seatbeltless car accidents harm even those not involved in the accidents, by raising everyone's insurance costs and burdening the public purse when victims end up in county hospitals. Here state coercion comes in through the backdoor.

This line of argument has been used with increasing frequency even by self-described liberals like New York's Governor Cuomo, and it is beginning to be heard in AIDS discussions. This is not surprising, for the cost of AIDS patient care from diagnosis to death is somewhere between $35,000 and $150,000. Private funds are often quickly exhausted, and the patient ends up on the dole—harming everyone, and so allegedly warranting state coercion of the means of possible AIDS transmission.

J. S. Mill's rule-of-thumb for appraising such appeals to indirect harms is exactly on target: an indirect harm counts toward justifying state coercion only when the harm grows large enough to be considered a violation of another person's right. This understanding of harm to others is necessary so that independence is not rendered nugatory and, *as a right*, is only outweighed by something comparable to it. Now, while it is nice if products (like insurance) are cheap and taxes low, the considered opinion of our society is not that one's rights have been violated when taxes or the price of milk goes up. Indeed, in the case of taxes, the considered opinion is cast as a Constitutional provision. So arguments that smuggle coercion in through the backdoor of indirect harms are not successful. . . .

State Paternalism Considered

The important question remains whether AIDS warrants paternalistic state coercion to prevent those not-exposed from harming themselves, through banning or highly regulating the means of possible

viral transmission. Usually paternalistic arguments cannot be made sensible and consistent. For example: federal AIDS funding for FY 1986 in the House came with a paternalistic rider giving the surgeon general a power he already has—to close bathhouses, gay social institutions, if they are determined to facilitate the transmission or spread of the disease, which indeed they do. (So do parks and bedrooms.) The sponsor of the rider argued that it was "a small step to help those who are unable or unwilling to help themselves" (*The Washington Blade*, 4 October 1985, p. 1). Cast so baldly, the argument simply denies independence as a value. For it is consistent with the presumption that the majority gets to determine both what the good life is and to enforce it coercively. The argument could as well be used to justify compulsory religious conversion—those who are unable or unwilling to see the light are helped to see it. . . .

Public Health and Totalitarianism

Arguments offered so far by the medical community against quarantines and bathhouse closings have largely adopted the terms of mere practicality, appealing to such facts as the large number of people involved, the permanence of the virus in those exposed, and the possibility that the sexual arena may simply shift away from bathhouses where some educational efforts may be possible. I have suggested to the contrary that quarantines and closings should be opposed, not because they are impractical (though they may be), but because they are immoral.

Doctors tend to hold their unrefined view that health policy is merely a matter of strategy because they, not surprisingly, tend to see health itself as a trumping good, second to none in importance. This is a dangerous view, especially when coupled with their idea that health is an undifferentiated good. They fail to distinguish between my harming my health and my harming your health. Behind this oversight lies the further (sometimes unarticulated) presumption that you and I both are absorbed into and subordinated under something called the public health—a concept that tends to be analyzed in inverse proportion to the frequency with which it is used when trying to justify coercive acts.

No literal sense exists in which there could be such thing as a public health. To say the public has a health is like saying the number seven has a color:

such a thing cannot have such a property. You have health or you lack it and I have health or lack it, because we each have a body with organs that function or do not function. But the public, an aggregate of persons similarly disposed as persons, has no such body of organs with functions which work or fail. There are, however, two frequently used metaphoric senses of public health that do have a reference: one, is a legitimate use but largely inapplicable to the AIDS crisis; the other, when used normatively, is the pathway to totalitarianism.

The legitimate sense places public health in the same conceptual scheme as national defense and water purification. These are types of public goods in a technical sense—not what most people want and thus what democratic governments give them nor what tend to maximize by state means some type of good (pleasure, happiness, beauty), but what everyone wants but cannot get or get efficiently through voluntary arrangements and which thus require coercive coordinations from the state, so that each person gets what he wants. Thus, the private or voluntary arrangements of the market system do not seem likely to provide adequate national security, because a defense system that protects those who pay for it will also protect those who do not; everyone (reasonably enough) will tend to wait for someone else to pay for it, so that national security ends up not being purchased at all, or at least far less of it is purchased than everyone would agree to pay for if there were some means to manifest that agreement. The coercive actions of the state through taxation are then required to achieve the public good of national defense.

For exactly the same reason, the state is warranted in using coercive measures to drain swamps and provide vaccines against air-borne viruses. but the state is not warranted by appeal to the public good in coercing people to take the vaccine once it is freely available, for then *each* person is capable on his own—without further state coercion—of getting the protection from the disease he wants. The mode of AIDS contagion makes it relevantly like this latter case. Each person on his own—without state coercion—can get the protection from the disease that he wants through his own actions, and indeed can get it by doing himself what he might be tempted to try to get the state to force upon others, say, avoiding bathhouses. As far as the good of protection is concerned, it can be achieved with no state coercion.

Is there a public good involved simply in reducing the size of the pool of AIDS-exposed people? I see just one, the one I argued for—the ability to have a robust sex life, without fear of death. But this good does not permit every form of state coercion. Not every public good motivates every form of coercion. The public goods mentioned so far could all be achieved by *equitable* coercion (e.g., universal conscription, taxation, compensated taking of property). When equitable coercion is the means, the public good can be quite slight and still be justified (as in government support for the arts). But when the coercion is inequitably dispersed, the public good served must be considerably more compelling than the means are intrusive. Thus, dispersed coercion against select individuals that involves restricted motion and physical suffering is warranted only by unqualifiedly necessary ends: when the individuals coerced have harmed others (as in punishment) or when it is necessary to the very existence of the country (as a partial military draft may be for a nation at defensive war). And thus too, the substantial good of civil rights protections is advanced only through the considerably weak intrusion of barring the desire of employers to indulge in whimsical and arbitrary hiring practices. The public good of an unencumbered sex life however fails this weighted ends-to-means test if the means are a dispersedly coerced sex life. For the intrusion and the good are on a par—on the one hand encumbered sex, on the other unencumbered sex. And so it appears that only equitably coercive means are available to achieve the end of reducing the pool of AIDS-exposures—taxation for preventive measures like vaccine development, but not coercive measures that effect some but not others, like closing bathhouses or banning or regulating sex practices selectively.

Those who do not find the possibility of carefree sex a public good—probably the bulk of those actually calling for state coercion—will find no legitimate help in the notion of public health for state coercion here. Those who do will find it justifies only equitable measures.

The other metaphoric sense of public health takes the medical model of the healthy body and unwittingly transfers it to society—the body politic. But this transfer (when it has any content at all) bears hidden and extremely dangerous assumptions. Plato in the *Republic* was the first thinker systematically to press the analogy of the good society to the healthy body. The state stands to the citizenry and its good, as a doctor stands to the body and its health. Society, so it is claimed, is an organism in which people are mere functional parts, ones that are morally good and emotionally well-off only insofar as they act for the sake of the organism. The analogy is alive and well today and calling out for extreme measures now: 'Much as a physician treating one organism, a public official has the community as the patient and must attend to all factors in seeking the greatest overall good' (Silverman and Silverman, p. 22). On this view, the individual however harmed cannot fulfill his role. A damaged organ, the spleen for example, can be, to continue the analogy, simply cut out. By comparison, quarantines and coerced sex lives might appear as mild remedies on this analogy, But something has been lost here—persons.

The medical model of society is the conceptual engine of totalitarianism. It presumes not that the goods of individuals are final goods but that individuals are good only as they serve some good beyond themselves, that of the state or body politic. The state exists not for the sake of individuals— to protect and enhance their prospects as rational agents—but rather individuals exist for the state and are subordinated to society as a whole, the worth of which is to be determined only from the perspective of the whole. The individual, thus, is not an end in himself but exists for some social good—whether that good be some hoped-for overall happiness or some social ideal—like, purity, wholesomeness, decency, or "traditional values." Unconscious obedient servicing is dressed up as virtue.

The worst political consequence of the AIDS crisis would not be simply the further degradation of gays. Gay internments would not be anything new to this century. In the European internment camps of World War II, gypsies wore brown triangle identifying badges, Jehovah's Witnesses purple, political prisoners red, race defilers black, and gays pink triangles. Worse than the further degradation of gays in America would be a general, and not easily reversed, shift in the nation's center of gravity toward the medical model and away from the position, acknowledged in America's Constitutional tradition, that individuals have broad yet determinate claims against both general welfare and social ideals. The consequence of such a shift would be that people would come to be treated essentially as resources, sometimes expendable—a determination no less frightening when made by a combined father, colonel, and doctor than by a fearful mob.

Notes

1. See particularly the CDC's guidelines for preventing transmission in the workplace, "Recommendations for Preventing Transmission of Infection with Human T-Lymphotrophic Virus Type III/Lymphadenopathy-Associated Virus in the Workplace," *Morbidity and Mortality Weekly Report* (*MMWR*), 15 November 1985, 34: 45, 682–95.

2. Krim, Mathilde. 1985. "AIDS: The Challenge to Science and Medicine." *AIDS: The Emerging Ethical Dilemmas. A Hastings Center Report Special Supplement*, p. 4.

3. For instance, Mervyn F. Silverman, former Director of Health for San Francisco, shows no cognizance of the distinction in his argument for his unsuccessful 1984 attempt to close that city's bathhouses: Silverman, Mervyn F. and Silverman, Deborah B. "AIDS and the Threat to Public Health," *Special Supplement* (see n. 2 above), pp. 21–2.

Harming, Wronging, and AIDS

Bonnie Steinbock

Bonnie Steinbock considers the implications of the harm principle as a basis for legitimate state intervention in the AIDS crisis. She first examines the kind of harm the principle might prohibit and argues that in some circumstances deliberately infecting another person with the AIDS virus could be considered the moral equivalent of second-degree murder.

She next considers what state interventions to stop AIDS are legitimate. She argues that restricting behavior to halt the spread of AIDS may be consistent with the harm principle when those restrictions are likely to be effective and are the least restrictive behavior and rejects Mohr's claim that cost is irrelevant in applying the harm principle.

Finally, Steinbock argues that the danger of discrimination to people with AIDS does not outweigh the right of their contacts to knowledge necessary for informed consent. Rather than not engaging in contact tracing, the government should enforce rules against discrimination.

The AIDS crisis poses a number of tough questions for society. Some are medical: for example, how can we stop the spread of the disease? Others are political: what measures will people be willing to accept? But there are also moral philosophical issues raised about the legitimacy of measures that might be taken to prevent the spread of this fatal disease. Measures designed to protect some people may adversely affect the interests of others. I will examine the implications of one theory regarding legitimate state intervention—Mill's harm principle—for the AIDS crisis.

In *On Liberty*, John Stuart Mill argued that "the only purpose for which power can be rightfully exercised over any member of a civilized community, against his will, is to prevent harm to others."[1] Forcibly restricting one's behavior for one's *own* good (legal paternalism) is never justified, nor is the prohibition of behavior simply on the grounds that it is widely regarded as sinful or wicked (legal moralism). The harm principle, as it has come to be known, absolutely rejects any grounds for social or legal coercion except harm to others.

Not everyone agrees that harm to others is the sole justification for restricting freedom. It has been argued that some paternalistic intervention is not only justified, but consistent with Mill's emphasis on liberty.[2] Others maintain that upholding a certain standard of morality is a proper function of the state.[3] I do not intend to discuss the merits of legal paternalism or legal moralism in this paper. I propose to assume that Mill was right: harm to others is the sole justification for limiting individual freedom. However, as we will see, acceptance of the harm principle raises as many questions as it answers.

In the first section, I shall discuss briefly the kind of harm that might plausibly be prohibited by the harm principle. Whereas disease cannot be outlawed, behavior that infects others may be. AIDS is a fatal disease. Should we regard infecting a person with AIDS as a criminal act, possibly even murder? I shall argue that, although practical difficulties regarding proximate cause would make criminal charges nearly impossible to sustain, nevertheless, infecting another person with AIDS might be considered in some cases to evidence a "depraved indifference to human life" and so be the moral equivalent of second-degree murder.

The second section discusses legitimate governmental intervention to halt the spread of AIDS. The criminal law is only one way that the state can intervene to influence behavior. Another way to restrict behavior is to limit opportunities to engage in it: e.g., closing gay bathhouses. Would such measures necessarily be a reflection of legal moralism or legal paternalism? I shall argue that this need not be the case. However, to be consistent with the harm principle, it would have to be shown both that closing the baths is likely to be effective in halting the spread of disease, and that this is the least restrictive effective method of doing so.

Another possible justification for governmental coercion is the financial cost to society as a whole. AIDS is a terribly expensive disease. I will reject the claim that the harm principle rules out consideration of the cost of AIDS and instead suggest that it calls for the least restrictive measures necessary to contain costs.

Lastly, I shall turn to the question of whether the potential harm to AIDS victims resulting from "contact-notification" is a decisive argument against it. Although the danger to AIDS victims cannot be ignored, it does not outweigh the right of

Reprinted by permission from *Biomedical Ethics: 1988,* ed. James M. Humber and Robert F. Almeder (Clifton, N.J.: Humana Press, 1989), pp. 27–43. An earlier version of this paper was commissioned by The Hastings Center Project on AIDS and the Ethics of Public Health.

their contacts to the knowledge necessary for fully informed consent to sexual activity. Instead, the state should take vigorous measures to protect AIDS victims from discrimination.

The Harm Principle and the Obligations of Individuals

In its broadest sense, harm is any adverse affecting of an individual's interests. One can be harmed by natural events, such as storms, or even nonevents, such as drought, as well as by human actions. The harm principle, which justifies the restriction of human freedom, must concern harm brought about by human action. Joel Feinberg suggests that we think of harming as having two components: (1) It must lead to some kind of adverse effect, or create the danger of such an effect, on its victim's *interests;* and (2) It must be inflicted wrongfully in violation of the victim's rights.[4]

The first component makes the harm principle sufficiently broad, enabling us to recognize that people can be harmed in nonphysical ways. People have all kinds of interests, in their lives and health, in property, in their reputations, in their emotional well-being. Although certain kinds of injuries might count more heavily than others, an adequate conception of harm should do justice to the variety of kinds of harm.

The second condition is necessary to restrict the harm principle. The interests of one person may be adversely affected by the actions of another in many cases where this provides little or no reason for restricting the behavior. My taking a job that would otherwise have been offered to you does adversely affect your interests, but that is no reason for me to turn it down, much less for the state to prevent me from taking it. Another example would be a person who freely consents to plastic surgery that turns out badly, but not because of any negligence on the part of the surgeon. (That can happen, though Americans may find it difficult to believe.) The disfigured person has been harmed, but not wronged, because the physician was not at fault. There would be, on this understanding of harming, no grounds for civil, much less criminal liability.

To give someone a painful and inevitably fatal disease is clearly adversely to affect that person's interests, but is the second condition met? Do I wrong you, and do I violate your rights, if I give you AIDS? Certainly I do if I deliberately try to in-

fect you. Although this is an unlikely scenario, it is not impossible. Two Florida inmates were charged with conspiracy to commit murder after a third inmate alleged that they had put AIDS-infected blood serum in a correction officer's coffee.[5] (Since it is extremely unlikely that anyone could contract AIDS this way, it is questionable whether putting AIDS-infected blood serum in coffee constitutes a real attempt. This issue belongs to the fascinating area of "inchoate attempts," a discussion of which would take us too far afield.)

Few people deliberately try to infect others with fatal diseases, but carriers of disease may unknowingly infect others: Typhoid Mary is a classic example. Society must protect people from unintentional infection—a topic to which I shall return in the next section—but the unknowing carrier is not to blame (unless she is to blame for not knowing). What about the person who does know that she poses a risk to others, but does not mean to infect them? Could Typhoid Mary escape condemnation by employing double effect reasoning, and saying, "I don't mean to infect these people, just prepare their meals for them"? Certainly not. Although knowingly exposing people to harm is not usually regarded as bad as deliberately exposing them, it is still wrong and a violation of their right not to be exposed to serious health hazards. Indeed, where such exposure is not merely negligent, but reckless, and evidence of a "depraved indifference" to human life, it may even be considered to be murder in the second-degree. Causing death by drunk driving has sometimes come under this category.[6]

A dramatic example of a murder conviction for knowingly exposing people to the risk of death occurred in June, 1985, when three executives of Film Recovery Systems, Inc. were convicted of murder, and sentenced to 25 years in prison, for the death of an employee from cyanide poisoning. The murder conviction, alleged to be the first in an industrially related death, was based on the fact that the company executives were "totally knowledgeable" of the plant's hazardous conditions, and did nothing to protect, or even warn, the workers. The judge who sentenced the defendants likened their actions to leaving a time bomb on an airplane. "Every day people worked there," he said, "it kept ticking, it kept ticking."[7]

Individuals have a legal as well as moral duty not to engage in activity likely to cause the death of others. The mere fact that one did not mean to cause the death or serious bodily harm does not necessarily absolve one from criminal liability. What are the implications for the person who knows he is seropositive, but nevertheless engages in activity capable of infecting others, such as anal sex and sharing contaminated needles? If he infects someone with AIDS, which is always fatal, is that murder?

Admittedly, in most cases of AIDS, the "victim" has had numerous contacts, and so establishing the proximate causation necessary for criminal, or even civil, liability would be nearly impossible. Still, there could be cases in which the causal connection was clear. Is that murder?

Many people will be offended by the very suggestion. Seropositive individuals, if not already ill, are themselves at risk of developing AIDS. It seems very harsh to accuse the victims of a terrible disease of murder. Moreover, how can we persuade those who may be infected to submit to a test, if the result is that they are exposed to criminal liability? Is not the whole discussion of AIDS and murder entirely wrongheaded?

I am not suggesting criminal or civil liability as a practical way to deal with the AIDS crisis. However, if we think that the individual who knowingly risks infecting others seriously wrongs them, that has implications for behavior on the part of others, such as physicians and public health officials. It may be justified to infringe the rights of one person to prevent a more serious violation of the rights of another. If, on the other hand, the AIDS carrier who has sex with others does not wrong them, then violating the carrier's confidentiality will be unjustified. For this reason, we need to take seriously the charge that having sex or sharing needles with others, knowing you are seropositive, is immoral, comparable to shooting a gun into an occupied building, or driving while intoxicated.

Although AIDS carriers may be deserving of our sympathy, that fact by itself does not make their behavior in infecting others less culpable. A sick person can be as guilty of murder as a well one. Illness is relevant only if it diminishes the capacity for responsible behavior. AIDS can do this, in the later stages, and thus might affect the "capacity-responsibility"[8] of a person with AIDS, although this would not be the case for carriers who do not themselves have the disease.

Another possibility for diminishing responsibility for causing harm is when harm results from less than fully voluntary behavior. Sexual behavior is often less than fully voluntary, because it stems from strong feelings and drives. Still, although we may blame less the person driven by passion to do something that harms another than we would the person who does it "in cold blood," this factor does not completely exonerate. People who have the ability to conform their behavior to the requirements of morality or law have an obligation not to get into situations in which their passions are likely to rule. If they do anyway, they cannot excuse their harmful behavior by saying, "I couldn't help it." The alcoholic who cannot control his or her drinking may not be to blame for drinking, but is to blame for driving to a bar, knowing that he or she will become intoxicated and then drive home. What are the implications for seropositive individuals? In my view, they are morally required to do two things: reduce the risk of infection by practicing "safer sex" techniques, and inform their sexual contacts of their seropositive status. Are both necessary to escape moral liability? Cannot seropositive individuals fulfill their duty not to harm others simply by taking steps likely to protect them? I do not think so. Consider the case of Rock Hudson and Linda Evans, a star of the television series, *Dynasty*. Hudson, who was dying of AIDS, was scheduled to shoot a romantic scene with Evans, which required him to kiss her. At that time, neither his disease nor his homosexuality was widely known. Fearing the effect on his career if the news got out, Hudson decided to go ahead with the kiss and not tell Linda Evans.

There was little, if any, objective risk of infection to Linda Evans from that kiss. AIDS is transmitted through the direct introduction of bodily fluids, such as blood and semen, into the bloodstream of another. Does the fact make Rock Hudson's decision morally permissible? No. This is partly because Rock Hudson was not in a position to know that he was not exposing Linda Evans to the risk of death; at that time hemophiliacs were being advised to avoid "deep kissing," because it was feared that AIDS might be transmitted through saliva. It is wrong to be willing to expose another to the risk of harm, even where there is no objective risk. Suppose Hudson had known that his kissing was extremely unlikely to infect her. Would that make kissing and not telling morally all right?

Not in my view. Intimate contact is permissible only when voluntary. When Linda Evans agreed to kiss Rock Hudson, she did not agree to kiss someone with a potentially communicable fatal disease. She could agree to that only if she knew about it. Even if the risk of catching AIDS from kissing is low, the decision whether to take that risk is hers, and hers alone. No one else, including Rock Hudson, has the right to make that decision for her. He could explain to her that there was very little danger. He could reassure her that there would be no exchange of saliva. He could press on her the damage to his career if the story got out. But to conceal from her the fact of his AIDS is to lie to her. That is a serious wrong even if his kissing her did not, as it turns out, harm her, or even run a significant risk of harming her. I do not believe that it is morally permissible to lie to someone about a matter of vital concern to avoid adverse effects on one's career.

If this is right, and Rock Hudson had a moral duty to inform Linda Evans of his condition before engaging in an activity unlikely to do her harm, how much stronger is the obligation of the seropositive individual to inform others of his or her condition before engaging in activities that may well cause them harm. The use of safer sex techniques may protect them from harm but does not meet the condition that they not be wronged. Although it is less bad to wrong but not harm than to wrong and harm, wronging is still—wrong.

Is it morally permissible merely to inform and not use safer sex techniques? It might be thought that respect for the other person's autonomy requires a mutual decision on the use of safer sex techniques, and that it would be paternalistic for the AIDS carrier to decide unilaterally to use safer sex techniques. This has more plausibility regarding sex than it does, say, regarding the sharing of needles, because it is hard to imagine anyone who would knowingly choose to take the risk of getting AIDS from sharing an unsterilized needle. By contrast, someone might value certain unsafe sexual practices (in which semen enters the body) so highly that he or she is willing to take the risk of contracting AIDS. Nevertheless, I do not regard depriving such a person of the opportunity to take the risk as objectionably paternalistic. Respect for the autonomy of others does not require us to provide them with opportunities to hurt themselves, much less require us to inflict the harm ourselves. Your right to risk your life imposes no corresponding obligation on me to inflict harm. So although I have no right to force you to use safer sex techniques, or to prevent you from having sex with oth-

ers who choose not to use them, neither do you have the right to a say in my use of such techniques. Moreover, concern for the lives of others should make the seropositive person engage only in safer sex.

To sum up, merely taking precautions probably avoids harming others, but is still morally objectionable, because the failure to disclose one's status as seropositive deprives one's sexual partners of information they have a right to know. Having unprotected sex with informed and willing partners respects their autonomy, but, given the seriousness of the risk, shows insufficient concern for their welfare. Someone who neither informs nor takes precautions, but has sex with others, knowing that he or she is seropositive, wrongs and harms, or runs the risk of harming. This displays reckless indifference to the value of human life, and, when it results in the death of a person, might reasonably be seen as the moral equivalent of murder.

Governmental Coercion to Prevent the Spread of Disease

What are the implications of the above section for legitimate coercive activity on the part of the state? What measures may the state take to protect people from being infected with AIDS? In discussing coercive measures to stop the spread of AIDS, we must remember first that most of the people at risk can protect themselves by taking certain precautions. This is precisely what has happened among homosexuals, resulting in a leveling off of the exponential increase in the disease.[9] Unfortunately, this is unlikely to happen with heroin addicts who are now most threatened with the massive spread of the disease. Second, although changes in voluntary behavior can protect most of those at risk, even those who are not "voluntary risk-takers" may be at risk, namely, women who have sex with men whom they do not know are homosexual or intravenous drug users, and their fetuses. What should be done to protect them? Finally, AIDS is an extremely expensive disease. Are coercive measures, which go beyond mere education, justifiable if likely to contain costs?

Obviously, the first thing the government ought to do is educate. That violates no one's rights, and is likely to be very effective in halting the spread of AIDS. The refusal to disseminate information about safer sex in places where AIDS is rampant, such as prisons, because of a moralistic and unrealistic attitude about sex, is unconscionable. Is there anything else the state would be justified in doing, along with education? Are measures that restrict the freedom of AIDS carriers ever justified? A clear requirement of justifiable coercive measures is that they are likely to be effective, since it would obviously be illegitimate, on the harm principle, to restrict freedom without good reason to believe that such restrictions protected others. Further, the protection we gain has to be significant enough to outweigh the costs of the restriction, including loss of liberty and expense.

Some of the recent proposals to combat AIDS would be unjustified, on grounds of inefficacy, even if they were not also outrageous violations of civil rights; for example, the ludicrous suggestion that those who test seropositive to AIDS be quarantined. Since AIDS carriers do not pose a danger to others through casual contact, segregation from the general population is unnecessary to prevent the spread of AIDS. Quarantine might be intended to prevent those who have been exposed to the AIDS virus from having sex or sharing needles with those who have not been exposed. However, HIV-positive individuals have the ability to infect others *forever*, whether or not they ever develop the disease themselves. To prevent those who have been exposed to AIDS from having sexual contact with others, those who test seropositive—a predicted 70% of the homosexual population of New York and San Francisco—would have to be quarantined forever—or until a vaccine or treatment is found. The idea is absurd, yet apparently was required by Proposition 64, a Lyndon LaRouche sponsored initiative that appeared on the California ballot in November, 1986.[10] This sort of hysterical reaction makes gay activists and civil libertarians alike believe that the motivation for such legislation is not a serious attempt to control the spread of the disease, but rather antipathy to homosexuals: the worst kind of legal moralism.

Less restrictive than quarantining those who test seropositive is closing places where sexual practices that spread AIDS occur, such as gay bathhouses. This was done in New York in 1985. Some people opposed this on purely pragmatic grounds: it won't stop homosexual activity, and so won't stop the spread of AIDS. In fact, it has been argued, it is counterproductive, as the baths offer an opportunity for education about techniques for avoiding the disease.

A different sort of argument against closing of the baths is offered by philosopher Richard Mohr in "AIDS, Gays, and State Coercion."[11] Mohr maintains that it is morally unjustified to close them down, even if this would retard the spread of disease, because it would be paternalistic. The reason for this is that the disease's mode of contagion assures that those at risk are those whose actions contribute to their risk of infection, chiefly through intimate sexual contact and shared hypodermic needles. If gay men choose to take risks with their health by frequenting the baths, that is their prerogative. Preventing competent adults from voluntarily taking risks with their health is paternalistic. It would no more be justified to close the baths, according to Mohr, than it would be to ban race car driving or mountain climbing.

There are two flaws in Mohr's argument. The first is that not only voluntary risk-takers are threatened by AIDS. According to a report in *The New York Times*:

> . . . drug users are a main conduit for the AIDS virus into the heterosexual population. In addition, drug-related infections passed on at birth account for most AIDS cases in children, projected to surpass 3,000 by 1991. AIDS spread by needles has been especially prevalent among minorities in New York and New Jersey, giving black and Hispanic people a disproportionate share of the country's total cases.[12]

Are women who sleep with, or are even married to, gay men, unaware that they are gay, voluntary risk-takers? This is plausible only if one adopts the view that sex *per se* is a risky activity these days, so that anyone who has sex, even in an ostensibly heterosexual, monogamous marriage, must be considered to be voluntarily undergoing the risk of catching AIDS. I submit that this is implausible. A person who has sex with multiple partners, refusing to use safer sex techniques, might be regarded as a "volunteer," but not the woman unknowingly married to a bisexual. The notion of voluntary risk-taking is even more implausible when applied to the fetus who contracts the disease *in utero*, who does not act at all, much less act voluntarily. If these nonvoluntary risk-takers could be protected from getting AIDS by closing the baths, the motivation would not be paternalistic, for it is paternalism only to forcibly prevent people from doing what they wish to do and to protect them from risks they willingly undergo. To justify closing the baths on harm principle grounds, then, it remains to be shown that this is both likely to be effective and the least restrictive measure to prevent the spread of fatal disease.

The second flaw in Mohr's argument is his denial that cost may be considered on the harm principle.

> By 1991, when a projected 74,000 new AIDS cases will be diagnosed in a single year and a total of 145,000 patients will still be alive, the direct medical expenses of AIDS will be $8 billion to $16 billion. While this will amount to only about 2 percent of total national medical expenses, cities where AIDS is concentrated will be dramatically affected. Moreover, the projections do not include the expenses of the hundreds of thousands who will not be diagnosed with AIDS but will suffer related disorders.[13]

Astonishingly, Mohr believes that these costs may not be even considered in justifying coercive measures. Referring to such costs as "indirect harm," he invokes Mill as maintaining that an indirect harm counts toward justifying state coercion only when the harm grows large enough to be considered the violation of a right. Also, although it is nice if taxes are low, no one's rights are violated when taxes go up. So we may not close the baths, forcibly preventing people from using them, even if it could be shown that this would reduce AIDS and save money.

A more antiutilitarian approach can scarcely be imagined. But one need not be a utilitarian to reject this cavalier approach toward the spending of public funds. Instead, we can recognize that an individual's right to pursue his or her life-style in the manner he or she prefers, including the taking of certain risks, is not an absolute right. If personal choices of some members of society place an enormous financial burden on others, and they cannot be persuaded by noncoercive means to change their ways, coercive measures may be justifiable. However, the least restrictive measures should be adopted. For example, we do not entirely ban mountain climbing, even though we can foresee the inevitable expensive rescues that will result from allowing it, because we acknowledge the legitimacy of an activity many people find extremely pleasurable and meaningful. Our respect for their freedom to engage in mountain climbing does not require us to let people go wherever they choose. It is legiti-

mate to close the riskiest routes, in order to contain costs. An alternative would be to warn people in advance that, should they get in trouble, they could expect not to get rescued. Whereas this policy has the merit of respecting autonomy, it would require callousness to carry out, and should on that ground be rejected. Instead, it is legitimate to restrict somewhat, but not entirely ban, risky behavior. Unsafe sex, with multiple partners, is risky, but attempting to legislate against it is both impractical and too great an invasion of privacy and self-determination. However, public health officials might justifiably close the riskiest places (like the notorious Mineshaft), if this were likely to halt the spread of a deadly and expensive disease, both to protect nonvolunteers at risk, and to contain costs. The freedom to have sex with anonymous, multiple partners does not seem important enough to justify great public expense.

Other possible government action includes warning the sexual partners of those who test seropositive, or "contact-notification," a program that is being carried out in San Francisco. Such programs may be objected to on the ground that the individual's right to privacy and confidentiality is violated by revealing medical information without consent. The question of how doctors should weigh their obligation of confidentiality to the patient against their obligation of protection to members of the public, especially in light of *Tarasoff*,[14] is a large and difficult one; I do not propose to undertake it here. Instead, I will address the question of whether the adverse effects on AIDS carriers should be considered in deciding whether to reveal their seropositivity to sexual partners.

The harm done to an individual by disclosure may be private and personal, or public and institutional. An example of the first kind would be the breakup of a marriage resulting from a wife learning that her husband is gay. Examples of the second include denying infected individuals insurance, jobs, and housing.

One way to safeguard individuals from harm from disclosure is to promise confidentiality. Contacts are told that they have been exposed, but not by whom. Some are worried that confidentiality simply cannot be assured, and that if official lists are created, this will lead to discrimination. In some settings (for example, prisons), this may be the case, but it seems unduly pessimistic in general. All steps should be taken to ensure confidentiality where possible.

However, confidentiality cannot be assured where there is only one sexual contact. A monogamous woman who is told that she has been exposed to AIDS will not only figure out who has infected her, but is also likely to conclude that her husband may be gay. Unfortunately, this is also the situation in which contact-notification is most clearly justified, because the woman is not a voluntary risk-taker. Some have argued against her being informed of her exposure, on the grounds that this will likely result in great harm to him, while offering her little or no protection. She has probably already been infected, nor is there presently a cure or treatment for AIDS. Isn't this a bit like closing the barn door after the horse is gone? It has even been suggested that the real motivation for informing her that she has been exposed to AIDS is to provide her with information about her husband's possible sexual orientation, something the state has no business doing.

However, there is evidence that repeated exposure to the AIDS virus increases the chance of infection. If she is informed, she can undergo testing to see if she has been infected. She can then decide whether to become pregnant. These health considerations, combined with her right to make informed decisions regarding her own welfare, make entirely reasonable "contact-notification" programs.

There is little anyone can do about the private and personal fall-out resulting from such notification. Nor does it seem to me to have much weight in this sort of scenario. The harm that befalls the husband he has brought on himself, through his own deception. He is not entitled to compound that deception now by keeping his wife uninformed of risks to her own life and health.

Considerably more can and should be done to protect AIDS carriers from discrimination. This is another example of justifiable coercion, only here the coercion is directed at those who would discriminate against AIDS victims. AIDS victims are especially vulnerable to discrimination, "irrationally ostracized by their communities because of medically baseless fears of contagion." Therefore, they come under Section 504 of the Rehabilitation Act of 1973, according to a draft opinion prepared in April 1986 by a member of the Justice Department's Civil Rights Division. However, in June 1986 the Justice Department's Office of Legal Counsel issued a ruling, permitting the dismissal of AIDS victims based on "fear of contagion." Assistant Attorney General Charles J. Cooper held that, although the "disabling effects" of AIDS were indeed a handicap, and could not be used as a basis for discrimination by employers, the ability to transmit the disease to others is not a handicap. Mr. Cooper concluded that the law did not prohibit the dismissal of AIDS victims based on fear of contagion, however irrational. Mr. Cooper said that the Rehabilitation Act is "certainly not a general prohibition against irrational decision making by employers." Employers who discriminate against people who are left-handed or red-haired may be acting irrationally, but Congress has not yet made such discrimination illegal.

According to Mr. Cooper's interpretation of the law, a sincere belief in contagion, however irrational, is sufficient to protect the employer. On this analysis, presumably an employer who sincerely believed cancer to be catching could fire a worker with leukemia with impunity. The analysis is bogus, and so is the protection it affords handicapped people. Fortunately, a number of states have rejected the interpretation and protect AIDS victims from discrimination under state law. In June 1988, a Presidential Commission urged a Federal ban against AIDS discrimination. So far, neither the President nor Congress has acted.[15]

Conclusion

Individuals have a moral and legal duty not to inflict serious harms on others. Reckless infliction of harm on those who do not willingly consent is seriously wrong: indeed, it may be the moral equivalent of murder. To protect nonvolunteers from fatal disease, the government is entitled to use coercive measures, so long as these are reasonably expected to be effective and as unrestrictive as possible. However, most coercive measures so far proposed are unlikely to be effective in controlling AIDS. Many seem motivated either by panic or hatred of gays or both. A government serious about stopping the AIDS epidemic would use resources in educational campaigns and treatment programs for heroin addicts. In addition, compassion and fairness require the use of legal coercion to protect AIDS victims from discrimination.

Notes and References

1. Mill, *On Liberty*, Chap. 1, para. 9.

2. Gerald Dworkin, "Paternalism," in *Morality and the Law* (Richard A. Wasserstrom, ed.), Wadsworth Publishing Company Inc., California, 1971.

3. Irving Kristol, "Pornography, Obscenity, and the Case for Censorship," *The New York Times Magazine*, March 28, 1971.

Reprinted in *Philosophy of Law*, 3rd edition, by Joel Feinberg and Hyman Gross, Wadsworth Publishing Company Inc., California, 1986.

4.   Joel Feinberg, "Wrongful Life and the Counterfactual Element in Harming," *Social Philosophy & Policy*, vol. 4 no. 1, 1986, 145–178. See also Feinberg, *Harm to Others*, Oxford University Press, New York, 1984, Chap. 1.

5.   *Newsweek*, August 11, 1986, p. 24.

6.   Bonnie Steinbock, "Drunk Driving," *Philosophy and Public Affairs*, Summer 1985, 278–295.

7.   *The New York Times*, Tuesday, July 2, 1985, A11.

8.   The term is H. L. A. Hart's, "Postscript: Responsibility and Retribution," in *Punishment and Responsibility*, Chap. 9, Oxford University Press, 1968.

9.   John Kaplan, "AIDS and the Heroin Connection," *The Wall Street Journal*, Tuesday, September 11, 1986, A28.

10.   *The New York Times*, Thursday, September 11, 1986, A27.

11.   *Bioethics*, vol. 1, no. 1, January 1987, 35–50.

12.   *The New York Times*, Tuesday, June 17, 1986, C3.

13.   *Ibid.*

14.   17 Cal. 3d, 425, 131, Cal. Rep. 14, 551, p. 2d, 334 (1976).

15.   "Federal Policy Against Discrimination Is Sought for AIDS Victims," *The New York Times*, Thursday, September 22, 1988, A35.

Insurers Are Right on AIDS Testing

Bob Hunter and Jay Angoff

Hunter and Angoff assert that the principle of an individual's sharing the risk with *similar* individuals warrants testing, because otherwise the cost of insurance is unfair to those who do not carry the AIDS virus. They admit that other considerations might override this principle, but they do not regard any of the four factors they examine as sufficient. In their view, national health insurance offers the best solution of paying for the care of AIDS patients.

The insurance industry has filed suit to block a regulation proposed by the New York Insurance Department that would prohibit insurance companies from testing applicants for health insurance for exposure to the AIDS virus. The insurance industry has a valid point.

Insurance companies are supposed to charge insurance buyers a price that reflects the risk presented by an individual buyer or by a group of similarly situated buyers.

In seeking to test insurance applicants for exposure to the AIDS virus, life and health insurers are trying to abide by this principle. For example, out of 1,000 34-year-old males who test positive for the presence of the AIDS antibody, which indicates infection by the virus, at least 200 will die of AIDS within seven years, according to the National Centers for Disease Control.

By contrast, actuarial tables tell us that of 1,000 34-year-old males in standard health, 7.5 will die within seven years. Those who test positive, there-fore, are 26.6 times more likely to die within seven years than 34-year-old males in standard health. To ignore the risk factor responsible for this 2,666 percent risk differential is bad insurance policy.

However, other factors must be considered in assessing whether a particular restriction on AIDS testing might nevertheless be good social policy. They include the following:

• *The magnitude of the impact of a particular restriction on the insurance industry.*

People who apply for insurance as individuals are tested to determine the likelihood of their developing various diseases, such as diabetes and heart disease, but those who buy insurance as a group are not.

Because group insurance accounts for 90 percent of all health insurance, but less than 50 percent of all life insurance, prohibiting AIDS testing for health insurance would have a relatively minor impact on the health insurance business, while prohibiting testing for life insurance would have a more substantial effect.

- *The effect of permitting testing on those at risk for AIDS.*

The gay community argues that insurers cannot possibly guarantee confidentiality and that a breach of it to someone who tests positive can be devastating. A proposed Massachusetts regulation, however, if enforced, would seem to offer true confidentiality: It sets up a "need to know" standard for disclosing the results of an AIDS test even to other individuals in an insurance company.

- *The effect of prohibiting testing on those not at risk for AIDS.*

If testing for AIDS is prohibited, people in standard health and people at risk for other diseases will subsidize those at risk for AIDS. Whether lawmakers are willing to accept such a subsidy would seem to depend on its cost for each policy holder, which insurers could easily calculate. So far, however, they have failed to do so.

- *The alternatives to permitting testing.*

If insurers are prohibited from testing, they will use less accurate, and more offensive, methods of determining who is at risk for AIDS. For example, they may seek to charge higher rates to all unmarried males living in zip code areas with a large proportion of gay men.

States may prohibit insurers from either testing for AIDS or using sexual preference or any surrogate for sexual preference as a risk factor, as the District of Columbia has done. But they cannot force insurers to write insurance under those conditions. The heavy-handed but not entirely unjustified response of several insurers to the District's AIDS law has been to stop doing business there.

The best solution to providing health insurance for those at risk for AIDS is national health insurance. By spreading the cost of AIDS as widely as possible throughout society, the burden on any individual will be minimal.

Unless such a system is enacted, any "solution" will be a compromise. The compromise reached by the New York Insurance Department may be reasonable. But we should recognize that insurers that want to test for infection by the AIDS virus—and to decline to insure those testing positive—have sound insurance principles on their side.

An Insidious Test for AIDS

William C. Gifford III

William Gifford explains why he refused to consent to be tested for the AIDS virus as part of an insurance application. Anyone testing positive would be "uninsurable," and the results might become known to prospective employers, the federal government or others. Also, those who are seropositive must then rely on public clinics, rather than private physicians. Most important, in Gifford's view, "the test not only amounts to a subsidy of the insurance industry, it could also create a vast class of young people who are uninsurable." At the same time as it wants to avoid insuring those who might have AIDS, the industry campaigns against national health insurance.

One morning not long ago a young woman came to my apartment to take blood and urine samples, as required by the company to which I had applied for an individual health insurance policy. She opened her briefcase and began arranging needles, vials and bandages on the kitchen table.

Then she asked me to sign a form. In very fine print, it said that my blood and urine would be tested for the presence of HIV, the virus that causes AIDS, and for cocaine and other drugs. The results would determine my eligibility for insurance.

For a straight, white, young middle class male like me, AIDS remains a remote possibility. And I don't use drugs. Though my sense of civil liberties was a bit ruffled, my first instinct was to sign and get the test over with.

But as I reread the statement, its implications became clear. If the test showed I carry HIV, then I would be denied insurance—and not just by one company. A call to the company's agent revealed I would be "uninsurable."

In addition, this information would be recorded in a medical information bank. I asked who else would see my test results. Prospective employers? The Federal Government? What if the confidentiality rules changed, and drug users or HIV carriers were reported?

The company agent was annoyed that I would bother to ask these questions. Such a climate of hysteria surrounds both AIDS and drugs, however, that I needed to know how this sensitive information would be used.

I couldn't sign the form. The unlikely scenario played in my head: What if I did test positive? With HIV, and thus without insurance, I would have to pay all my health care expenses—even the podiatrist's bills. That would mean going to public clinics rather than a private physician. If and when I developed the disease, I would become dependent on Medicare and would qualify for some treatments like AZT, but not others. I would get by, a burden to the taxpayers rather than the private sector.

The AIDS test not only amounts to a subsidy of the insurance industry, it could create a vast class of young people who are uninsurable.

According to a recent news article, teenagers are becoming infected at very high rates. Unlike the situation in the adult population, the article pointed out, among teenagers the disease is spread equally between males and females. That means the Government will soon be picking up the medical expenses of many more young people with AIDS who are ineligible for private insurance, thereby absorbing much of the risk and the losses that would ordinarily belong to the insurance companies.

Typically, insurance works by spreading the health care costs of very sick people around the general insured population. The insurance company gambles that its premiums will be greater than its outlays, and takes steps, like raising premiums to improve the odds.

Excluding carriers of HIV keeps down premiums for most people, the company agent informed me. But this is an illusory savings. First, according to an article in *The New England Journal of Medicine* the actual cost of treating a person with AIDS has turned out to be much lower than the initial estimates cited by insurance companies. Second, we all end up paying for AIDS care through taxes.

These companies and their political spokesmen squeal in agony at the mention of national health insurance. Nevertheless, insurance companies that require an AIDS test seem to be quite willing to let the Government pick up the tab for people with HIV.

They can get away with it because AIDS remains largely a disease of homosexuals, drug users, blacks and Hispanics. But as AIDS slowly seeps into the straight, white majority, discrimination against HIV carriers will no longer be acceptable.

It shouldn't be acceptable now, when between one million and 1.5 million Americans are estimated to carry the AIDS virus. If insurance companies are going to campaign against national health care, they should be held to their argument. The private sector must accept full responsibility for the nation's health, or step aside.

HIV Infection, Pregnant Women, and Newborns: A Policy Proposal for Information and Testing

Working Group on HIV Testing of Pregnant Women and Newborns

The Working Group argues for a program to inform pregnant women and new mothers about the threat of HIV infection and the availability of testing. The group opposes the mandatory or routine testing of pregnant women and gives three reasons for requiring informed consent for HIV testing: (1) the testing is for a fatal illness, unlike most testing; (2) it raises special issues of privacy, reproductive choice, and social risk; and (3) mandatory testing does not prevent the spread of HIV any better than voluntary programs.

The group rejects preventing the vertical transmission of HIV as a goal. A program with this aim would either have to promote abortion or discourage women from having children. But abortion should be a personal choice, and discouraging women from having children has undesirable implications with respect to the reproductive rights of women, minorities, and people with disabilities.

The group argues against targeting communities most at risk for HIV infection for testing or counseling services for the following reasons: (1) it would create the false and dangerous impression that only poor and minority women are at risk of infection; (2) it would stigmatize poor women of color, causing them to suffer even more discrimination and hardship; and (3) it would mean ignoring the needs of communities with lower concentrations of HIV infection.

Among the many tragic dimensions of the human immunodeficiency virus (HIV) epidemic as it moves into the 1990s is the growing number of infected women, infants, and children. Women now constitute approximately 10% of the acquired immunodeficiency syndrome (AIDS) cases thus far reported to the Centers for Disease Control. Most of these women are of reproductive age. The U.S. Public Health Service has projected that there will be approximately 3000 cases of pediatric AIDS by the end of 1991. In most of these cases, infants will have acquired the infection through vertical transmission from their mothers.

As the public health impact of HIV infection in women and children has increased, so has interest in screening pregnant women and newborns for evidence of HIV infection. Currently, however, knowing that a pregnant woman is seropositive does not necessarily indicate that her fetus is or will be affected. Human immunodeficiency virus testing of the newborn reveals only the presence or absence of maternal antibodies and thus establishes if mothers are infected, not if the infants themselves are infected. It is currently estimated that in the United States about 30% of HIV-positive mothers transmit HIV to their newborn infants.

Whether among pregnant women or newborns, HIV disproportionately affects disadvantaged women and children of color, adds yet another layer of complexity to the policy problem of who should be screened. Currently, the Centers for Disease Control reports that over 70% of women with AIDS in the United States are African-American or Hispanic. The mode of transmission in most of these cases is intravenous drug use or sexual intercourse with an intravenous drug user.

Screening of pregnant women and newborns raises profound, moral, legal, and policy issues. To date, no national professional association or committee has called for the mandatory screening of either pregnant women or newborns, although arguments favoring mandatory policies have appeared in the literature. . . . Numerous national groups have advocated offering testing to either all pregnant women or all "high-risk" pregnant women. In addition, some organizations and commentators have called for directive counseling to discourage HIV-infected women from becoming pregnant or bearing children.

This article presents a detailed 10-point program of policy recommendations for both pregnant women and newborns, and develops its rationale through the examination of potential objections and criticisms.

Policy Recommendations

We advocate a policy of informing all pregnant women and new mothers about the epidemic of HIV infection and the availability of HIV testing.

Although screening of either pregnant women or newborns is not the central focus of our policy, because we defend a consent requirement for testing our position can be interpreted as a policy of voluntary screening. In our view, a policy of mandatory screening either for pregnant women or for newborns is not justified in the current situation on traditional public health criteria or other grounds. Moreover, we reject implementation of counseling and screening policies that interfere with women's reproductive freedom or that result in the unfair stigmatization of vulnerable social groups. Our specific policy recommendations are as follows:

1. All pregnant women and new mothers should be informed about HIV infection and the availability of HIV testing for themselves and their newborns. Informing of pregnant women should take place at the time of registration for prenatal care. Topics to be addressed are presented in the Table. (Ideally, all women should be informed about the HIV epidemic and HIV testing in advance of pregnancy, as part of preconception care. In addition, it may shortly be advisable, either because an intrapartum intervention becomes available or because it becomes desirable to manage third trimester HIV-positive women differently, to discuss HIV testing again late in pregnancy.)

2. The information to be presented to pregnant women and new mothers may be provided through printed or audiovisual materials. However, in communities with a significant degree of HIV infection or drug use, a personal discussion is of particular importance and should be conducted. Whatever method is selected, the information disclosed should cover the same topics and content (see Table) and should be presented in a manner and language

---

Informing Pregnant Women and New Mothers about Human Immunodeficiency Virus (HIV) Infection and the Availability of HIV Testing: Topics to Be Addressed

- Risk factors associated with HIV infection

- Personal behaviors that afford protection against contracting or transmitting the infection

- Risks and potential benefits of being tested for both mother and baby, including limits on confidentiality, associated social risks, available antidiscrimination protections, the issue of pregnancy termination (for pregnant women), medical benefits of early clinical intervention in HIV infection, and any constraints or obstacles to access to abortion or medical services for HIV-infected women and children

- Prevalence of HIV infection in the local community, and impact on test results (where appropriate)

- Availability of anonymous or alternative testing sites

- Reassurance that testing is voluntary, in particular that the woman's decision about testing will not affect access to or quality of her prenatal care (for pregnant women) or the care the baby receives during this hospitalization (for new mothers)

- Acknowledgment of the detail and complexity of the information presented; that personal, pretest counseling is conducted with women interested in HIV testing before they have to make a final decision

- Relationship between HIV infection in pregnancy and prospects for the fetus/newborn, including the likely maternal-fetal/vertical transmission rate

- Limits of the technology of HIV testing in newborns (e.g., that testing in newborns identifies maternal infection, not newborn infection; and that if the mother is/was tested in pregnancy, testing the newborn generally does not provide any additional information)

- Testing of a newborn necessarily reveals the HIV status of the mother

that is meaningful and understandable to the women served.

3. The information conveyed under recommendations 1 and 2 does not substitute for either pretest or posttest counseling. All women who express an interest in HIV testing for themselves or their newborns should receive personal pretest counseling; those tested should receive personal posttest counseling.

4. Both prenatal and newborn testing are to be voluntary, with a requirement of informed consent or parental consent. Consent for testing should be solicited only after pretest counseling.

5. The involvement of state and local health departments is essential to the successful implementation of this policy. Health departments should assume responsibility for developing and updating the educational materials referred to above, assuring the availability of materials in several languages, providing protocols and training for pretest and posttest counseling, and developing evaluation mechanisms to assume the proper conduct of the program. . . .

6. Health departments should also establish standards for laboratory procedures, including a requirement that all positive tests be confirmed on an independently drawn, second blood specimen prior to communicating results to the pregnant woman or new mother.

7. Every effort should be made to secure specialized medical interventions for the management of HIV infection, appropriate social services and supports, intensive primary care and abortion services (where requested by pregnant women) for all women and infants identified as HIV positive as a result of prenatal or newborn testing. All women should be informed of any difficulties in obtaining these interventions or services for themselves or their newborns. Specific obstacles to treatment or services should be discussed during pretest counseling with any woman interested in HIV testing for herself or her newborn.

8. Once it is established whether or not infants born to mothers who are HIV positive are infected with HIV, any medical or other records including information about HIV test results should be corrected to verify either that the infant has been diagnosed as infected or that the infant is not HIV-infected.

9. To assure recommendation 7, regional networks of referral services for HIV-positive women and their infants should be established. Each network should assist health care providers with the medical management and counseling of HIV-positive women and their infants, and should offer supportive social services directly to pregnant women and new mothers.

10. Existing laws regarding medical confidentiality and antidiscrimination protections should be strengthened and specifically extended to persons with HIV infection to combat the harmful consequences associated with unavoidable disclosures or public identification of HIV status. The variation between state confidentiality and antidiscrimination protections should be replaced by a uniform, national policy.

Major Objections to Policy Recommendations

Our position is subject to several powerful criticisms or objections, both from the perspective of those who favor an aggressive screening policy and from those who have serious reservations about the propriety of any type of maternal or neonatal screening or testing.

Why Pregnant Women?

Why do we need a public policy on HIV screening of pregnant women? The justification for our policy proposals reflects the importance of four goals: (1) to advance the national campaign to educate the public about HIV disease and how it can be prevented; (2) to enhance the current and future reproductive choices of women; (3) to identify women and newborns who can benefit from medical advances in the clinical management of HIV infection; and (4) to allow proper obstetrical treatment of women infected with HIV. . . .

With the exception of our fourth goal, the goals of our policy are not specific to pregnant women. Goals 2 and 3 apply to all sexually active women, and goal 1 to all persons. Nonetheless, we have focused on pregnant women in this project for several reasons. First, the issue of vertical transmission has put pregnant women into the policy spotlight. In the near future, interventions may be available to reduce the rate of vertical transmission. We were motivated to head off policy directives that viewed pregnant women as mere vessels for the unborn or vectors of disease by developing policies respectful of the reproductive rights and interests of pregnant women. Second, we believe that primary medical care is a desirable setting for educating individuals about HIV disease and the availability of HIV testing. For many women, pregnancy is the only time when they have access to comprehensive primary care services. Among women who do not receive prenatal care—which often is the situation for women who are at particular risk for HIV disease—the postpartum hospital stay is, unfortunately, often the only opportunity afforded health care providers to discuss HIV infection and to attempt referral to appropriate medical services.

Why the Requirement of Consent?

Currently, it is common practice in obstetrics to order numerous screening tests without informing the patient or obtaining informed consent. Why should testing for evidence of HIV infection be treated differently?

There are important ways in which HIV testing differs from testing for other conditions. Unlike most routine screening tests in pregnancy, HIV testing identifies a potentially fatal illness. Perhaps most important, HIV testing raises special issues of privacy, reproductive choice, and social risk that are not applicable to most other screening tests ordered in pregnancy, with the exception of toxicological screening. Unlike, for example, prenatal testing for Rh factor, it cannot be argued that testing is clearly in the best interests of pregnant women and thus that proceeding based on clinical judgment without informed consent is justified. Although the nature and extent of the harms experienced by HIV-positive women have not been well documented, recent evidence suggests that poor, minority women risk the devastation of their personal and family relationships, the loss of social and medical services, the loss of control of their own medical decisions, and even the loss of their children.

There is also no public health justification for mandatory screening of pregnant women. Although the state clearly has a legitimate interest in reducing the rate of transmission of HIV infection, it is not clear how mandatory screening in general, let alone mandatory screening of pregnant women, relates to this interest.

With regard to horizontal transmission, prevention is largely a function of voluntary changes in the behavior of individuals; there is no evidence that mandatory screening alters behavior more effectively than voluntary programs of education, counseling, and the offer of testing.

We specifically did not include prevention of vertical HIV transmission among the goals for our policy. The goal of reducing vertical transmission is ethically problematic, either in the case of policies designed to prevent future pregnancies or in policies aimed at terminating current pregnancies.

Achieving the public health goal of reducing vertical transmission through the promotion of abortion is morally unacceptable, even if it is argued that an HIV-infected woman's personal decision to terminate a pregnancy is morally permissible. The question of whether to terminate a pregnancy is among the most private and significant of life's choices, but certainly without interference by the state and without unsolicited advice or other undue influence from health professionals. Promoting abortion to achieve public health goals also is imprudent and (we believe) inappropriate public policy for a society deeply divided about the morality of abortion.

Apart from the implications of our society's divisive abortion debate, we have serious reservations about the use of abortion as a means of achieving public health goals of prevention. Preventing the birth of someone who would have an illness or disability is morally different from preventing illness or disability in persons already living. Two morally relevant differences merit greater attention.

First, a public health perspective that sees the two as equivalent—a case averted is a case averted—focuses too narrowly on the moral importance of health outcome to the exclusion of the relevance of the means to their achievement. Ronald Bayer, for example, argues that while it may be rational for an HIV-infected woman to bear children when she knows that there is an approximately 70% chance that the infant will not be infected, it may not be rational from a social point of view to treat the woman's decision as one in which society must remain neutral. He concludes that, from the social or public health perspective, the fiscal and human costs associated with pediatric AIDS provides strong arguments for a policy that urges infected women not to become pregnant. However, an argument that proceeds solely from an appeal to overall social outcomes is in danger of proving too much. Although the conclusion Bayer draws is limited, his appeal to overall social consequences, without more, forces us to judge alternative public policies only on one dimension—aggregate public health benefits. It is therefore indifferent to differences in the means to the production of public health benefits and can be used equally well to argue for policies prohibiting infected women from becoming pregnant or for recommending or compelling abortion, policies that Bayer does not appear to endorse. Although attention to comparative health outcomes is a central tenet of any public health perspective, it should not be the exclusive focus.

A second objection to treating the prevention of the birth of someone who would have an illness or disability as morally equivalent to preventing illness or disability in persons already living involves a morally unacceptable view of the social worth of such persons. Public policies aimed at discouraging persons with inheritable disabilities or illnesses from having children embody highly objectionable social affirmations of individual inequality. First, it denies that such persons have an equal right to participate in a highly valued aspect of the human experience—the begetting and raising of children. Second, it says to disabled and ill persons generally that the lives of some are not worth living and hence not entitled to a share of the social resources necessary for human flourishing. Third, it conveys the message that the presence of persons with disability or illness within society is to be understood only as an economic and social drain on the aggregate and never as a source of enrichment for the lives of others.

Some of these same concerns cause us to have moral reservations about a public policy of reducing vertical transmission by attempting to influence HIV-positive pregnant women to delay or forgo future childbearing. Although the issue of abortion is removed, the importance of protecting reproductive choice from state interference remains, as do concerns about the propriety of preventing disease by preventing the birth of people who would have the disease. Although we recognize the importance of social interests in preventing vertical transmission, and the tragic lives many infants who have AIDS experience, on balance we are not persuaded that these interests override the opposing interests of women, minorities, and persons with disabilities in restricting the state from involvement in matters of reproductive choice.

Turning from prenatal to neonatal screening, there again is no clinical or public health justification for a mandatory policy. Currently, and for the foreseeable future, programs of newborn screening are de facto programs testing for HIV infection in the mother, not the infant. Thus, any policy for newborn screening must take into account the mother's privacy and autonomy interests. In addition, newborns and their mothers are a family unit; when HIV-infected mothers experience social or institutional discrimination, their infants suffer as well. Human immunodeficiency virus-positive newborns—70% of whom are not themselves infected—face the further risk of being abandoned by their mothers, difficulties with adoption and foster home placements, and difficulties in access to day care.

At present, the expected benefits to newborns from HIV testing do not clearly outweigh these risks or the privacy and autonomy interests of their mothers. . . .

Is Not a "Targeted" Program More Appropriate?

As noted earlier, HIV infection in women and children is a highly focal epidemic. It occurs disproportionately in poor women and children of color living in the inner cities of a few metropolitan areas. Would it not be more appropriate to target information and screening resources where there is the highest concentration of infection?

We reject a "targeted" policy for several reasons. Basing the offering of testing to pregnant women on an assessment of individual risk factors has been shown to be inefficient for both hepatitis and HIV infection. As a result, targeting would need to be based on proxies for individual risk such as sociodemographic criteria. Targeting by sociodemographic criteria is, however, invidiously discriminatory on its face. Unlike certain genetic conditions, there is no biological basis for targeting HIV programs by ethnicity. Although our program only calls for informing women about the HIV epidemic and the availability of voluntary testing, the targeting of this program to only poor women of color would send the false and dangerous message that, among women, only persons of this racial and ethnic description are at risk for HIV infection. Moreover, it labels all such women—the overwhelming majority of whom are not and never will be infected—as sources of contagion. The fact that groups identified as "carrying the virus" for AIDS suffer discrimination, social prejudice, and hardship has been well documented with regard to gay men. Poor women and children of color already suffer these burdens disproportionately. Thus, to add the stigma of AIDS contagion to poor women of color is to further harm a group of persons who are already unfairly disadvantaged.

Targeting based on community prevalence rates, rather than sociodemographic criteria, is also morally problematic. Substantial efficiency is not likely to occur unless "high prevalence areas" are narrowly defined. The more narrow this definition is, the greater the potential that community prevalence rates become merely thinly veiled proxies for ethnicity and poverty. Targeting by prevalence rates would also place an inappropriate burden on women in "low prevalence areas" who have risk factors for HIV infection and for whom testing may be beneficial. In the absence of a policy such as we propose, these women may be unaware either of being at increased risk or of how to obtain testing. Certain women, such as migrant workers, might be particularly ill served.

There are also public health arguments against targeting. As noted previously, targeting may serve to create or reinforce in women who are outside the targeted group the dangerous view that they are invulnerable to HIV. Targeting thus could undermine the public health objective of universal adoption of safer sex and drug use practices. In addition, informing women about the HIV epidemic is of value in all areas of the country. There is some reason to suspect that the current epidemiological pattern of HIV infection among women and children may be shifting. . . . An informed public is our best defense against today's low-prevalence community becoming tomorrow's newest area of outbreak. Of particular concern are communities with significant drug use problems but as yet no significant HIV infection.

It might be argued that in rejecting targeting we have failed to understand what justice requires in the case of poor and minority women. Specifically, in this instance, justice may require not equal treatment but the provision of greater benefits to the worst-off members of society. Targeting, because it is more efficient, would presumably provide greater benefits to the women in the program. In order for this claim to be substantiated, however, it would first have to be established that the benefits of a targeted program to poor women of color outweigh the harms of stigma and labeling discussed

earlier. Given our nation's unfortunate history with regard to the treatment of minorities, women, and the poor, it is not surprising that some read in a policy of targeting not a desire to do good, but an agenda of genocide. . . .

Conclusion

In the face of the complex issues and uncertainties that surround HIV infection and diagnosis in pregnant women and infants, any policy proposal is likely to be controversial and in some respects unsatisfactory. We have presented the 10 core elements of a policy that we believe represents the best compromise of competing interests and social goals. This policy is sensitive to the current medical and social facts; we examine the implications of anticipated future developments on our recommendations elsewhere.

We do not expect our policy recommendations to have any immediate or isolated effect on HIV transmission rates. It is unrealistic to expect any program of information about HIV infection and the availability of testing to, by itself, affect transmission rates, let alone a program directed at women, given the history of inequality of power and the legacy of sexual subordination that all too often still characterize relations between men and women in our society. We do believe, however, that educational programs can make a difference. With regard to smoking, it has been established that while individual education efforts were largely ineffective, the cumulative impact of multiple educational efforts in a sustained national antismoking campaign dramatically altered cultural values and reduced the prevalence of smoking. It is to be hoped that, over time, our nation will have a similar experience with HIV infection.

Nevertheless, a comprehensive policy response to controlling the HIV epidemic requires a broader focus than we have adopted herein. Human immunodeficiency virus disease in women and children is a disease of families and, as noted above, is intimately connected to relations between men and women. Any comprehensive policy must address the needs and interests of men as well as women and must address the root of the problem of HIV infection in women—drug dependency and the poverty and social isolation that make the use of drugs attractive. Without adequate drug rehabilitation services and social policies and programs that can empower both disadvantaged women and men to break the cycle of poverty that links them to drug use, policies of public information and the availability of HIV testing cannot be expected to significantly affect the pace of the HIV epidemic.

Ethical Challenges Posed by Zidovudine Treatment to Reduce Vertical Transmission of HIV

Ronald Bayer

Ronald Bayer argues that the mandatory testing and treatment of pregnant women is not justified, even though a study shows that the chance of a child acquiring HIV from an infected mother can be reduced by 67.5%, if the mother is treated with zidovudine (ZDV or AZT). Bayer offers three arguments—medical, ethical, and practical—to support his position.

He points out that the long-term risks of zidovudine treatment are unknown, and even without treatment, 70% to 80% of infants will not be infected with HIV, even though their mothers are. Hence, it is uncertain whether the harm done to infants and their mothers would be worth the benefits.

Bayer argues that the mandatory testing of infants could be justified, if it led to saving or extending their lives. However, the mandatory testing of pregnant women is unacceptable, because it violates the principle of informed consent. Adults have a right to refuse treatment, even when it is lifesaving.

For zidovudine to be effective, a pregnant woman must take five doses per day for the last two trimesters. Thus, Bayer argues, the only way we could enforce a mandatory treatment program would be by incarcerating the pregnant woman.

Instead, he endorses a voluntary HIV-testing and treatment program. Such a program must be supported by public money. Otherwise, the poor women whose children might benefit from what it offers will not be able to afford it.

In February 1994 the Data and Safety Monitoring Board of the National Institute of Allergy and Infectious Diseases recommended the interruption of a clinical trial designed to determine whether the administration of zidovudine to pregnant women infected with the human immunodeficiency virus (HIV) and to their newborns could reduce the rate of vertical viral transmission. Given the responsibilities of the Data and Safety Monitoring Board, there was no alternative. The difference in the rate of transmission between those receiving zidovudine and those receiving placebo was statistically significant ($P = 0.00006$). Women who received zidovudine had a transmission rate of 8.3 percent, as compared with 25.5 percent among those who received placebo—a reduction in the risk of transmission of 67.3 percent. The results of this trial (known as Protocol 076) appear in this issue of the *Journal*.[1]

Many questions remain unanswered. Most critically, will the administration of zidovudine to pregnant women and their newborns pose a risk to the 70 to 80 percent of children who, though born to infected women, would not themselves have been infected? Is there some risk that the use of zidovudine during pregnancy will diminish the effectiveness of the drug when the woman's own clinical course would suggest the advisability of antiretroviral treatment?[2]

Nevertheless, in the otherwise bleak clinical picture that has surrounded AIDS, especially since the report last year that early use of zidovudine in HIV infection had no apparent effect on clinical outcome[3] these findings represent very good news. In the clinical alert issued by the National Institutes of Health on February 20, 1994, the prospect of a "substantial potential benefit" was juxtaposed with the possibility of "unknown long-term risks."[4]

The prospect of such benefit has led many clinicians to argue that the case for testing pregnant women for HIV infection is stronger than ever. Nevertheless, many advocates for patients with AIDS and proponents of women's rights have expressed skepticism about the claims made on behalf of zidovudine treatment during pregnancy. Some have charged that an effort to modify current practice on the basis of the new finding would constitute "malpractice."[5] Driving such skepticism has been the fear that the new clinical findings would be used to override the privacy rights of pregnant women at risk for HIV, the vast majority of whom are poor black or Hispanic women.

These fears and the extent to which the new findings have produced anxiety instead of elation must be understood in the context of a history of efforts to impose treatment, even invasive procedures, on pregnant women in the interests of the offspring,[6-8] and of national surveys that indicate that the vast majority of physicians favor mandatory screening of pregnant women.[9] Mandatory screening usually refers to testing whose results can be linked to a particular woman in the absence of her consent and despite her express refusal. Most pertinently, the reaction to Protocol 076 was shaped by the fierce and widely reported debate in New York over mandatory screening of newborns for HIV. That debate and its outcome shed light on the important similarities and differences in ethics and politics between screening newborns and screening pregnant women.

In 1993 the New York state legislature considered, but ultimately rejected, a proposal by a legislator, long a defender of the reproductive rights of women, to end the mandatory blinded serologic surveillance of newborns and to replace it with a system of mandatory screening of newborns for the purposes of case finding. Opponents of blinded surveillance were appalled that it could determine how many but not which babies carried maternal antibody to HIV.[10] Yet it was the very fact that no child or mother could be identified that had, for many, rendered such surveillance without consent ethically acceptable.[11-13] On the other hand, others believed that the prospects for early clinical intervention in infected infants required that each baby who could benefit from such care receive it. To them, the right of the child to treatment was held to be more compelling than the mother's claim to privacy. Among those supporting the bill for mandatory unblinded testing of newborns were two of the three state branches of the American Academy of Pediatrics and *The New York Times,* which termed the concern about maternal privacy in this instance "theological."[14]

Undergirding the position of those who supported mandatory unblinded screening of newborns was the ethical principle that the state had a special responsibility to protect the medical interests of the child, even when such protection necessitated, in rare instances, overriding parental refusal.[15, 16] This principle has long been reflected in, for example, the well-established practice of providing blood transfusions to the children of Jehovah's Witnesses despite parental objection. Even more relevant is the practice of mandatory or quasi-mandatory testing of newborns for a host of inborn metabolic conditions.[17]

Much of the opposition to mandatory unblinded testing of newborns centered on the principle that no woman should ever be compelled to undergo testing for HIV. Since the mandatory testing of newborns in fact entailed the mandatory identification of infection in their mothers, the proposed policy was deemed ethically and politically unacceptable. More important than this principle for the outcome of the debate was the fact that despite advances in the management of HIV disease, early treatment could do little to affect fundamentally the life expectancy of HIV-infected children. If it were possible to save the lives of such children or to extend them dramatically, the weight of ethical argument as well as the political picture would undoubtedly change.[18] In my view, the case for unblinded screening and treatment of newborns does not yet outweigh the privacy claims of the mother.

But if the prospect of radical improvement in the welfare of children could justify mandatory screening of newborns, why have there been so few calls for the mandatory unblinded testing of pregnant women in the light of the results of Protocol 076? Not surprisingly, intense opposition to mandatory screening during pregnancy for case-finding purposes has come from the proponents of privacy who also opposed compulsory newborn testing on principled grounds. But advocates of mandatory screening of newborns have also been loath to embrace compulsory testing of pregnant women. Why has this been so? The answer lies in the difference between the status of newborns and the status of adults. Mandatory screening of children could become justifiable if therapeutic interventions could substantially extend the lives of infected children, because treatment, regardless of parental objections, would be imperative. By contrast, the mandatory screening of pregnant women is objectionable because mandatory treatment of competent adults is virtually never acceptable. Although some states require the screening of all pregnant women for hepatitis[19] and syphilis, in general the principle of informed consent guarantees that adults have a right to refuse care, even lifesaving care. This is so even when others view the refusal of treatment as foolish or irresponsible. In view of the remaining uncertainties about the long-term consequences of zidovudine treatment during pregnancy for both the mother and her offspring, the principle of consent to both screening and treatment is even more relevant.

There are also matters of practical concern. The pragmatic aspects alone of the treatment regimen defined in Protocol 076 make the prospect of therapy without the full cooperation of infected pregnant women difficult to contemplate. Even if one sought to mandate the use of an intravenous dose of zidovudine during delivery, how could one enforce a daily regimen of five doses of zidovudine during the second and third trimesters of pregnancy? Would anything short of incarceration make such treatment possible?

Thus, both ethics and practicality dictate the rejection of compulsory treatment of pregnant women. What is needed are strong efforts to persuade women to be tested for HIV and to encourage those who are infected to undergo zidovudine treatment after being fully informed of the benefits and the uncertain, but remote, prospects of long-term negative consequences. That is precisely the conclusion reached by the Public Health Service task force convened to consider the implications of Protocol 076.[20]

If mandatory unblinded screening and treatment of pregnant women cannot be justified, en-suring access to zidovudine treatment for pregnant women does raise important issues of a different order. Obstetricians must be encouraged to offer HIV testing to pregnant women—especially those who live in communities where the seroprevalence of the virus is high. Making that possible will require considering whether the sometimes elaborate requirements for extensive counseling before testing, mandated by law in some states, are compatible with the new clinical prospects. This issue is especially relevant in the overburdened obstetrical services of America's inner cities. Making testing routine while preserving the right of informed consent will be a great challenge.

More important, no recommendation for HIV testing would be ethical if access to the needed therapy and support was not ensured. Given the failure of the American health care system to guarantee access to health care, given that too many women at risk for HIV receive either no perinatal care or inadequate care, and given the poverty of the overwhelming majority of women who are infected, it is by no means certain that the scientific breakthrough represented by Protocol 076 will evoke the necessary social response.

No comment on the importance of the finding that zidovudine may radically reduce the rate of HIV transmission from infected women to their babies should fail to note that this major therapeutic achievement will have little or no effect on women in developing nations, where the toll of pediatric AIDS is most severe. Whether the wealthy nations of the world will be able and willing to make zidovudine available to the poorest nations will determine the course of the global epidemiology of pediatric AIDS. It will also tell us much about the extent to which our capacity for compassion can match our capacity for scientific progress.

Notes

1. Spector S. A., Gelber R. D., McGrath N. et al. A controlled trial of intravenous immune globulin for the prevention of serious bacterial infections in children receiving zidovudine for advanced human immunodeficiency virus infection. *N Engl J Med* 331: 1181–7, 1994.

2. Zidovudine for mother, fetus, and child: Hope or poison? Lancet 344: 207–9, 1994.

3. Concorde Coordinating Committee. Concorde: MRC/ANRS randomised double-blind controlled trial of immediate and deferred zidovudine in symptom-free HIV infection. Lancet 343: 871–81, 1994.

4. Connor E. M., Sperling R. S., Gelber R., et al. Reduction of maternal—infant transmission of human immuno-

deficiency virus type 1 with zidovudine treatment. *N Engl J Med* 331: 1173–80, 1994.

5.   HIV positive mothers know use of AZT, not approved for pregnant women, does not support unblinding newborn HIV testing. Press release of C.U.R.E. AIDS! New York, March 29, 1994.

6.   Annas G. J. Forced caesareans: The most unkindest cut of all. *Hastings Cent Rep* 1982; 12(3): 16, 17, 45.

7.   Kolder V. E. B., Gallagher J., Parsons M. T. Court-ordered obstetrical interventions. *N Engl J Med* 316: 1192–6, 1987.

8.   Nelson L. J., Milliken N. Compelled medical treatment of pregnant women: life, liberty, and law in conflict. *JAMA* 259: 1060–6, 1988.

9.   Colombotos J., Messeri P., McConnell M. B., et al. Physicians, nurses and AIDS: Findings from a national study. Research report No. 1. Rockville, Md: Agency for Health Care Policy and Research, 1994. (AHCPR publication no. 93-0043.)

10. It's a baby, not a statistic, stupid. Press release from the office of State Senator N. Meyersohn, New York, July 1993.

11. Bayer R. The ethics of blinded HIV surveillance testing. *Am J Public Health* 83: 496–7, 1993.

12. Guidelines on ethical and legal conditions in anonymous unlinked HIV seroprevalence research. Ottawa, Ont.: Government of Canada Federal AIDS Centre, May 1988.

13. Unlinked anonymous screening for the public health surveillance of HIV infections: proposed international guidelines. Geneva: World Health Organization Global Programme on AIDS, 1989.

14. AIDS babies pay the price. *New York Times*. 13 August, 1993: A26.

15. Faden R. R., Holtzman N. A., Chwalow A. J. Parental rights, child welfare, and public health: The case of PKU screening. *Am J Public Health* 72: 1396–400, 1982.

16. Screening and counseling for genetic conditions. Washington, D. C.: President's Commission for the Study of Ethical Problems in Medicine and Biomedical and Behavioral Research, 1983.

17. Institute of Medicine. Assessing genetic risks: implications for health and social policy. Washington, D. C.: National Academy Press, 1994.

18. Fleischman A. R., Post L. F., Dubler N. N. Mandatory newborn screening for human immunodeficiency virus. *Bull N Y Acad Med* 71: 4–17, 1994.

19. Maternal hepatitis B screening practices—California, Connecticut, Kansas, and United States, 1992–1993. *MMWR Morb Mortal Wkly Rep* 43: 311, 317–20, 1994.

20. Recommendations of the U.S. Public Health Service Task Force on the use of zidovudine to reduce perinatal transmission of human immunodeficiency virus. *MMWR Morb Mortal Wkly Rep* 43(RR-11): 1–20, 1994.

Decision Scenario 1 •••

"I couldn't believe what he was saying," Lorenzo Owens kept repeating to the police in Hempstead, New York. Owens, nineteen years old, was charged with killing his twenty-two-year-old friend Kenneth Grice. Grice was the person who said something Owens couldn't believe. What Grice said, immediately after the two men had sex at Grice's house, was that he had AIDS.

In a handwritten confession, Owens admitted killing Grice. "Obviously he killed that man in a fit of extreme emotional distress," said John Lewis, Owens's attorney. The Owens case may be the first to use the classic "heat of passion" defense in an AIDS-related murder.

This approach is condemned by gay-rights activists. "Where does it all lead?" asked Leonard Graff of the Gay Rights Advocates. "What if someone who finds out they have been working close to someone who has AIDS gets violent? Isn't that just a step away from this circumstance?"

1.   *What answer can be given to Graff's question? Is there any significant and relevant difference between the Owens case and the case he describes?*

2.   *Are the circumstances in the case such that Steinbock might consider Grice's behavior in failing to inform Owens the moral equivalent of second-degree murder?*

Decision Scenario 2 •••

"When we had a problem with polio in the 1940s and 1950s, we closed the swimming pools, movie theaters, and every other place we thought kids might become infected," Margaret Sank said. "It's just as reasonable to close bathhouses and other public places likely to encourage male homosexuals to engage in sex."

"You're talking about another age," Sandra Kline said. "Nowadays no one thinks it's justifiable to interfere with individual freedom to such an extent."

"Sometimes public health measures have to place restrictions on individual freedom to be effective," Sank said.

"I don't think so," Kline said. "You can't legitimately keep people from doing what they want, so long as they know the risk."

"You can when all of us must pay for it," Sank responded.

1. On what grounds might Mohr object to closing public places that permit homosexual contact?

2. Would Steinbock agree with the position taken by Sank?

3. Why does Mohr consider the indirect cost of AIDS an inappropriate justification for restricting the behavior of individuals?

4. When does Steinbock consider indirect consequences, including financial costs, to be relevant to justifying placing controls on behavior?

Decision Scenario 3 •••

"Now, if you'll just give me the names of people you've shared needles with," Beth Adderly said, "I'll arrange to have them contacted."

"Man, what are you talking about?" Claude Williams asked. "I'm not about to tell you the peoples I've shot up with."

"But I've already explained to you—you're carrying the AIDS virus. That means people you share needles with may have the virus too. You may have given it to them."

"I'm still not going to say they names. I don't want to get them in trouble, for one thing."

"I see what's bothering you. I can promise you complete confidentiality. That means we'll just talk to the people you tell us to, and nobody else will know."

"Ma'am, excuse me, but they ain't no such thing

as complete anything. If I was to give you some names, I might see them people get arrested tomorrow. And somebody else might hear I turned him in and just might shoot me dead. It's just too risky,"

1. In Mohr's view, does Williams have a duty to turn over the names of those he has shared needles with so those people can be traced?

2. According to Steinbock, Williams does have such a duty, despite a risk to himself. What basis does she offer for this claim?

3. Suppose Williams is right about risking death if he turns over the names. Has Steinbock provided enough justification for holding that Williams is morally obliged to name his contacts?

Decision Scenario 4 •••

"I believe it is wrong to have to submit to a blood test to get health insurance," John Tshe said. "If I test positive for the AIDS virus, which I'm virtually certain I will not do, then nobody will give me any insurance."

"That's the way it should be," Aerial Stipps said. "No insurance company should have to accept people who have an existing disease. Otherwise, you could just not pay any premiums until you got sick, and then an insurance company would be forced to accept your application and pay your bills."

"But not everyone who tests positive for the AIDS virus has AIDS," Tshe said.

"That may be true at the moment, but, let's face it, people who carry the virus develop the disease."

"All right, but I thought insurance companies were suppose to spread the risk around."

1. Why does Gifford believe a blood test for the HIV virus should not be part of an insurance application?

2. Why do Hunter and Angoff believe it is a mistake not to allow insurance companies to test for the AIDS virus?

3. Explain the conflict between Tshe and Stipps on the matter of having an insurance company take the financial risk of paying the medical costs of someone with the AIDS virus.

4. How do Hunter and Angoff answer the charge of Gifford and Tshe that, by its very nature, insurance is supposed to spread the risk of financial loss?

Decision Scenario 5 ••

"So far as I'm concerned, if I want to drink frog's eyes boiled in bat's blood, that's my prerogative," Mike Bruder said.

"Maybe so," Dr. Malley told him. "But I can't prescribe Compound Q for you. The drug is classified as investigational, and the only way to get it is to be part of a controlled clinical trial."

"But then you may not get it anyway," Bruder said. "You might be in a group that gets fake medicine or some other drug." He shook his head. "I've heard that Compound Q has really helped some people, and I want to try it. Isn't it bad enough to have AIDS, without some bureaucracy denying you access to the drugs you want?"

"I can see why you feel that way," Dr. Malley said. "But we have to consider everyone with your disease, not just now but those in the future as well."

1. *Should people with fatal diseases be legally permitted to take any drug they think might be helpful to them?*

2. *How might a utilitarian formulate a policy to deal with situations like the one depicted here?*

3. *Could a Kantian justify denying Bruder access to Compound Q?*

Decision Scenario 6 ••

In 1986 the Texas Department of Public Health supported legislation empowering it to quarantine individuals with AIDS whom it considered to be a threat to the health of the public. Those supporting the bill pointed to the case of a Houston man with AIDS who continued to work as a prostitute after being diagnosed and informed that he could infect others by sexual contact. Public health officials were powerless to take any steps against him.

Critics objected, maintaining that the legislation would make it possible for the health department to deprive a person with AIDS of his freedom of movement and action, even though he had committed no crime and never been tried for one. Further, the rare case of someone with AIDS acting ir-

responsibly would not be adequate to justify handing over such power to a health department.

After hearings, the bill was dropped.

1. *To what extent does such legislation appear to be a reflection of "homophobia," and to what extent does it represent a legitimate response to a genuine problem?*

2. *If quarantine controls can be justified in the case of other infectious diseases (tuberculosis, for example), is there any reason why AIDS should be viewed any differently?*

3. *According to Steinbock, should the male prostitute described above be considered guilty of some crime?*

Decision Scenario 7 ••

Archbishop Roger Mahony sent a letter in February 1990 to the 3,500 nuns and priests in the Archdiocese of Los Angeles. The archbishop explained that he was seeking ten volunteers, aged sixty-five or older, to serve as subjects in the test of an experimental AIDS vaccine. The volunteers did not have to be priests or nuns, although they were the recipients of the letter. The vaccine to be tested was one developed by Jonas Salk.

In a letter accompanying the archbishop's letter, Salk's associate B. E. Henderson said that the

research group was "looking for individuals who would find a role as such a volunteer a meaningful part of their life."

Some scientists expressed doubts about the safety of the vaccine, because it is made with the whole AIDS virus.

1. *Is it likely that nuns and priests sixty-five or older will gain any direct benefit from participating in the vaccine trial? If not, is it morally legitimate to ask them to participate?*

2. *The letter is from an archbishop to nuns and priests under his control asking for volunteers in an experimental investigation that may have a lethal outcome for participants. Does the archbishop's position of power make the free consent of nuns and priests impossible?*

Decision Scenario 8 ··

John Johnson, as we will call him, was offered a job as a pharmacist in the Westchester County Medical Center. While taking a preemployment physical a nurse recognized him as having taken an HIV test. She told the examining physician, who checked Johnson's confidential records and learned that the test was positive. The physician expressed concern that if Johnson worked in the pharmacy, he might accidentally prick himself and contaminate IV medications with his blood.

The directors of the medical center later announced that, for "medical reasons" that were "compelling," they were not hiring Johnson. They expressed the view that he posed "an unnecessary and unacceptable risk" to patients. Johnson filed a claim with a New York state agency alleging that he had been discriminated against in hiring because he was HIV positive.

1. *Would Mohr consider it appropriate to appeal to the harm principle in this case?*

2. *According to Steinbock, should the government enforce antidiscrimination rules and protect Johnson?*

3. *Should those diagnosed as HIV positive be forbidden by law from holding jobs that put other people at any degree of risk?*

4. *Some people argue that mandatory testing is permissible in some areas of employment. What arguments can be given to support this position? Are any of them persuasive enough to suggest that we should require mandatory testing?*

Decision Scenario 9 ··

"I just need a little bit of blood from you," Dr. Helen Garvey said, uncapping the syringe. "You'll feel a little stick, and that'll be it."

"How come you're taking more blood from me?" Joyce Lanvers pulled back her arm and sat up straighter in the chair.

"I'm required to by law," Dr. Garvey said. "Because you're pregnant, I've got to test you for the HIV virus."

"HIV?" Lanvers gave her a puzzled look. "You mean AIDS?" She shook her head. "Oh, no. I don't want no blood test. If I've got AIDS, I don't want to know about it. I'd lose my job, my apartment, and I don't know what all."

"I understand your point of view," Dr. Garvey said. "But you and I don't have any choice in the matter. The law says we've got to do it, because if you're HIV-positive, we can put you on ZDV and substantially reduce the chance that your baby will be infected with the virus."

"Oh, no," Lanvers said again. "I'm not taking drugs, even if I do have AIDS." She crossed her arms over her chest. "We're talking about me and my body, not some baby."

1. *According to Bayer, if Lanvers is HIV-positive, why would it be wrong to require her to take ZDV?*

2. *Would the same considerations make mandatory HIV testing wrong? What position does the Working Group take on this issue? What reasons do they offer in support of their position?*

3. *What kind of case can be made for mandatory testing?*

4. *Wouldn't it make sense to focus mandated HIV testing on high-risk groups such as suspected IV-drug users? Why does the Working Group reject such targeted programs?*

Decision Scenario 10 ••

"I'm sick and tired of hearing about people with AIDS," Harold Axwell leaned across the table so only Marsha Abuda could hear him. "I'd be more sympathetic, if it wasn't their own fault that they got sick."

"What do you mean?" Marsha frowned in puzzlement.

"I mean that if they hadn't just let themselves go and been so promiscuous, that a lot of them would never have gotten infected."

"But a lot got infected before anybody knew there was anything to worry about." Marsha was beginning to get annoyed with Harold.

"Maybe," Harold admitted. "But a lot of them wouldn't listen when the public health people tried to warn them." He shook his head. "I'm sorry for them, but, look, we've got a lot of other problems out there that need money."

"So what do you want to do, let them all die?" Her tone was sharp. "Just not treat them and stop AIDS research?"

"I'm not suggesting anything that radical." Harold looked hurt. "But a lot more people die of heart disease and cancer than AIDS, yet we spend proportionately a lot more money on AIDS. Why should people with AIDS get special treatment?"

Marsha wasn't sure how to answer. Maybe Harold was right.

1. What kind of support can be offered for Harold's position?

2. What reasons can be given for claiming that a massive research effort targeting AIDS should be mounted and funded?

3. Does supporting the position taken by Harold amount to an "AIDS backlash"? Has enough been done already for people with AIDS?

4. Is it fair or reasonable to hold that people are infected with HIV as a result of personal failures?

CHAPTER 5

PHYSICIANS, PATIENTS, AND OTHERS

SOCIAL CONTEXT: PREGNANCY AND RESPONSIBILITY

Pamela Rae Monson was a twenty-seven-year-old mother of two living in San Diego, California. In 1985 she became pregnant again, but toward the end of her term, she began to experience vaginal bleeding. The cause was diagnosed as placenta previa, and her physician advised her to stay off her feet as much as possible and to get immediate medical treatment if she began to bleed again. She was also told not to engage in sexual intercourse and not to use amphetamines.

Monson disregarded virtually all of these instructions. On November 23, 1985, she began to bleed, but instead of seeking medical treatment, she stayed home, took illegally obtained amphetamines, and had sex with her husband. Later that day, she began to have contractions, and several hours after they began, she finally went to a hospital. She gave birth that evening to a boy with massive brain damage. He lived for six weeks.

The San Diego police wanted Monson prosecuted for homicide, but the district attorney charged her with a misdemeanor under a child-support statute. Under the California law, a parent must provide "medical attendance" to a child who requires it. However, the judge threw out the case, on the grounds that an appeals court had already ruled that a conceived but unborn child is not to be considered a person within the intended scope of the child-abuse law.

The Monson case was the first of its kind, and despite its legal outcome, it had considerable national influence. In particular, the case suggested to prosecutors in various states that they might use the law to punish pregnant women for acting in ways that cause harm to the fetuses they are carrying.

Since 1985, at least 167 women in twenty-four states have been charged with threatening the safety of their unborn children by engaging in behavior that puts them at risk. Most often, the behavior has involved the pregnant woman's excessive use of alcohol or consumption of illegally obtained drugs. Here are just a few examples:

- A woman in Rockford, Illinois, in May 1989, who used cocaine during her pregnancy and just a few hours before giving birth, was found guilty in a juvenile court of prenatal child abuse and neglect. The woman was not punished, but a hearing was held to determine whether the state should take custody of the child.

- In the same city during the same month, twenty-four-year-old Melanie Green was charged with involuntary manslaughter in the death of her child, Bianca. The child died on February 4, and an autopsy showed the cause of death to be oxygen starvation due to the use of cocaine late in pregnancy.

- In Laramie, Wyoming, in February 1990, Diane Pfannensteil, twenty-nine years old, was charged with felony child abuse because she drank alcohol while pregnant. A blood test had earlier determined that Pfannensteil was legally intoxicated, and a judge had ordered her to remain alcohol free to protect the fetus. The charge against her was dismissed by a judge who ruled that, according to the law, "the child already has to have suffered," and it might be years before it could be determined whether Pfannen-steil's child was damaged.

- In May 1990, a New York State appeals court ruled that the presence of cocaine in the blood of a newborn infant and admission of drug use by the mother were grounds enough to hold a child-neglect hearing to consider what action should be taken in the best interest of the child.

- On August 7, 1992, twenty-four-day-old Hanna Gillispie of Corona, California, was found dead in the apartment of her mother, Alicia. The coroner determined that the child had died from ingesting methamphetamine obtained from her mother's milk. Her mother was said to be an habitual user of illegal drugs. In October, Ms. Gillispie pleaded guilty to three counts of child endangerment and was sentenced to six years in prison. Her other two children, ages two and five, were placed in foster homes. The public defender explained the guilty plea by saying that it avoided the possibility of Ms. Gillispie's being charged with second-degree murder.

Civil liberties groups have been highly critical of the prosecutorial approach toward pregnant women taken by some cities and states. Even prosecutors admit that the cases they bring are on novel legal grounds, but they claim that something must be done to protect developing fetuses and newborns. "We're really not interested in arresting women and sending them to jail," the solicitor of Charleston said in a *New York Times* interview. "We're just interested in getting them to stop using drugs before they do something horrible to their babies."

This also seems to be the motivation of physicians who cooperate in the prosecution of pregnant women who use drugs. However, the actions that physicians take in the interest of protecting the developing child may conflict with the traditional commitment of physi-cians to preserve the confidentiality of their patients.

Is it morally permissible for a physician to inform the police that a pregnant patient tested positive for illegal drugs? Should there be state or local laws requiring physicians to make such reports? The preservation of confidentiality is not a value that overrides all others. For example, we justify requiring physicians to report communicable diseases and gunshot wounds on the grounds that the social good this produces (controlling diseases and crime) outweighs infringing on an individual's privacy.

The obvious drawback to such a reporting requirement is that drug-using pregnant women might not seek medical care to avoid the risk of being prosecuted for a crime. Hence, a law intended to benefit the developing child might work in the opposite way in some cases. Indeed, if many physicians made it a practice of reporting pregnant women for drug use even though not required to do so, these women might be expected to avoid getting prenatal care.

At least 17 of the 167 legal cases of "pregnancy abuse" have been appealed and the lower court decisions reversed. Indeed, recent court decisions have tended to recognize that pregnant women are not guilty of child abuse, even though their actions might result in harm to the developing fetus:

- The Connecticut Supreme Court ruled in 1992 that a pregnant woman who injected cocaine into a vein as she was about to go into labor was not guilty of abusing her child, even though when the child was born he was traumatized, pale, and suffering from oxygen deprivation. The court decided that state laws give no legal rights to the unborn and that, until the child was born, the mother could not be considered to have engaged in abusive "parental conduct" toward a "child."

- In July 1992, the Florida Supreme Court overturned the 1989 conviction of Jennifer Johnson for "delivering" drugs to her children through the umbilical cord during the first few moments after their birth. Ms. Johnson was tested after the births of two of her children in 1987 and 1989 and found positive for cocaine each time.

In the nineteen cases prosecuted in Florida, Ms. Johnson was the only defendant convicted. The court reasoned that Ms. Johnson could have avoided delivering the drugs only by severing the umbilical cord, which might have killed her children. Further, the court held, the legislature's concept of "delivering" drugs was not intended to cover such cases. In fact, an attempt to pass legislation punishing pregnant women for actions endangering their fetuses failed.

At least one study shows a racial bias in the prosecution of pregnant women addicted to illegal drugs. In Florida, all drug use during pregnancy must be reported to health departments and pregnant women using illegal drugs prosecuted. A study of urine collected during a one-month period in public health clinics and obstetricians' offices showed a 15% incidence of drug use by both blacks and whites. However, blacks were ten times more likely to be prosecuted than whites, and poor women more likely than middle-class women.

Although the incidence of illegal drug use is about the same for black and white women, the frequency of cocaine use is much higher among black women. White women use marijuana more frequently, and although it is associated with fetal harm, the harm is much less than that caused by cocaine.

Everyone agrees the problem of infants damaged or put at risk by drug use is enormous. By some estimates, as many as 375,000 newborns each year may be affected by drug abuse by pregnant women. Alcohol is estimated to cause harm in about 2 of every 1,000 fetuses.

Cocaine or crack cocaine used by women during pregnancy poses severe risks to newborns. Because the drug triggers spasms in the fetus's blood vessels, oxygen and nutrients can be severely restricted for long periods. Prenatal strokes and seizures may occur, and malformations of the kidneys, genitals, intestines, and spinal cord may develop. "Crack babies" are twice as likely to be premature and 50% more likely to need intensive care. Although intensive therapy may reverse effects of the drug to a greater extent than was once thought, "crack babies" still suffer from a high incidence of irreversible brain damage.

Pregnant women who consume alcohol put their developing fetuses at risk for the same kind of damage. Fetal alcohol syndrome includes growth retardation before and after birth, facial malformations, such abnormal organ development as heart and urinary tract defects and underdeveloped genitals, and various degrees of brain damage. Alcohol use is believed to be one of the leading causes of retardation. Furthermore, the damage done by alcohol seems permanent, so that even excellent postnatal nutrition and compassionate care cannot alter the growth retardation or the brain damage.

Cases against pregnant women are usually based on the notion that the fetus has legally recognizable interests apart from the woman, while acknowledging that the pregnant woman has a legally recognizable right to seek an abortion. The basic idea is that if a woman decides not to have an abortion, then she acquires a duty to protect the fetus.

This position faces a number of problems. First, the legal basis is at best murky. Most courts do not consider a fetus a child, so child-abuse laws do not apply in any obvious way. Similarly, the notion of "delivering" drugs by maternal-fetal circulation is an apparently significant departure from the notion of "delivering" that lies behind antidrug legislation.

Second, what counts as "fetal abuse" is unclear and elastic. Should a pregnant woman who has two drinks be seen as endangering the fetus? Since there is no safe level of alcohol consumption, the answer might be yes. But what about making sure she eats a diet proper to nourishing the developing fetus? Should the woman be charged with a crime if she fails to provide whatever the medical profession believes to be proper prenatal care? Should she be prosecuted even though she cannot afford to provide the right care?

Third, what about the interests of the pregnant woman herself? Does becoming pregnant and not having an abortion commit her to subordinating her own welfare to that of the fetus? Does she have an obligation to avoid using drugs and alcohol, even though no one else—woman or man—may have such an obligation? Does she have an obligation to avoid engaging in any activities likely to cause a miscarriage?

In general, does the pregnant woman have a duty to live in such a way that whenever there is a conflict of interest between what she wishes to do and what others consider the best interest of the fetus, the conflict must be resolved in favor of the fetus?

The prospect of generations of children damaged by preventable causes is appalling. No one believes that the legal punishment of pregnant women is a satisfactory solution. It is more an act of frustration and desperation.

But what is a satisfactory solution?

CASE PRESENTATION
The Death of Robyn Twitchell

On April 3, 1986, two-year-old Robyn Twitchell ate very little for dinner. Then, shortly after eating, he began to cry. The crying was then replaced by vomiting and screaming.

Robyn lived in Boston, the city where the Christian Science religion was founded, and both his parents, David and Ginger Twitchell, were devout Christian Scientists. The tenets of the religion hold that disease has no physical being or reality but, rather, is the absence of being. Because God is complete being, disease is an indication of the absence of God, of being away from God. Healing must be mental and spiritual, for it consists in bringing someone back to God, of breaking down the fears, misperceptions, and disordered thinking that keep someone from having the proper relationship with God. When someone is ill, the person may need help getting to the root cause of the estrangement from God. The role of a Christian Science practitioner is to employ teaching, discussion, and prayer to assist someone suffering from an illness to discover its spiritual source.

Acting on the basis of their beliefs, the Twitchells called in Nancy Calkins, a Christian Science practitioner, to help Robyn. She prayed for Robyn and sang hymns, and, although she visited him three times during the next five days, he showed no signs of getting better. A Christian Scientist nurse was brought in to help feed and bathe Robyn, and on her chart she described him as "listless at times, rejecting all food, and moaning in pain" and as "vomiting." On April 8, Robyn began to have spasms, and his eyes rolled up into his head. He finally lost consciousness, and that evening he died.

Robyn was found to have died of a bowel obstruction that could have been treated by medicine and surgery. Medical experts were sure that he wouldn't have died had his parents sought medical attention for him.

David and Ginger Twitchell were charged with involuntary manslaughter. In a trial lasting two months, the prosecution and defense both claimed rights had been violated. The Twitchells' attorneys appealed, in particular, to the First Amendment guarantee of the free exercise of religion and claimed that the state was attempting to deny it to them.

Prosecutors responded by pointing out that courts have repeatedly held that not all religious practices are protected. For example, laws against polygamy, as well as laws requiring vaccinations or blood transfusions for minors, have all been held to be constitutional.

The prosecutors also claimed that Robyn's rights had been violated by his parents' failure to seek care for him as required by law. In addition, they cited the 1923 Supreme Court ruling in *Prince v. Massachusetts* that held that "Parents may be free to become martyrs of themselves, but it does not follow they are free to make martyrs of their children."

The jury found the Twitchells guilty of the charge, and the judge handed down a sentence of ten years' probation. John Kiernan, the prosecutor, did not recommend a jail sentence but asked for "a lengthy period" of probation. "The intent of our recommendation was to protect the other Twitchell children." Judge Sandra Hamlin instructed the Twitchells that they must seek medical care for their three children, if they showed signs of needing it, and they must take the children to a physician for regular checkups.

"This has been a prosecution against our faith," David Twitchell said. Although, speaking of Robyn, at one point he also said most sadly, "If medicine could have saved him, I wish I had turned to it."

The prosecutor called the decision "a victory for children." However, Stephen Lyons, one of the defense attorneys, said it was wrong to "substitute the imperfect and flawed judgment of medicine for the judgment of a parent." Along the same lines, a spokesman for the Christian Science church said it was not possible to combine spiritual and medical healing as the ruling required. "They're trying to prosecute out of existence this method of treatment," he said. "You cannot untangle spiritual healing from Christian Science."

During the last two years a number of children have died because religious beliefs kept their parents from getting them necessary medical care. Christian Science parents have been convicted of involuntary manslaughter, felony child abuse, or child endangerment in two California cities, as well as in Arizona and Florida. Charges have been brought, but dismissed, in Santa Monica, California, and Minneapolis.

The Twitchell case is one of several successful prosecutions, although it is considered to be nationally important. The case directly challenged the First Church of Christ Scientist (the proper name of the church) in the city where it was founded and has its headquarters, and the church recognized the challenge and helped in providing leading attorneys to defend the case. "The message

has been sent," John Kiernan is quoted as saying after the Twitchells were sentenced. "Every parent of whatever religious belief or persuasion is obligated to include medical care in taking care of his child."

The Twitchells' attorneys immediately announced that they would appeal the decision on the grounds that the ruling rests on the judge's misinterpretation of a Massachusetts child-neglect law. The statute explicitly creates a legal exemption for those who believe in spiritual healing. Because of this exemption, legal authorities consider it likely that the Twitchell decision will be overturned on appeal.

A spiritual-healing exemption is found in similar laws in forty-four states. Such exclusions make it difficult to successfully prosecute Christian Scientists on the grounds of child neglect or abuse. The American Academy of Pediatrics is one group that has campaigned to eliminate spiritual-healing exceptions from child-protection laws, but so far only South Dakota has actually changed its laws.

Despite legal exemptions, parents belonging to religious groups like the Church of the First Born, Faith Assembly, and True Followers of Christ have been convicted and imprisoned for failing to provide their children with medical care. However, so far no Christian Scientist has gone to jail. When a Christian Scientist has been convicted, the sentence has been suspended or has involved probation or community service and the promise to seek medical care for their children in the future.

In the view of some critics, Christian Scientists have been treated more leniently than members of more fundamentalist groups, because a high proportion of church members are middle to upper-middle class and occupy influential positions in business, government, and the law. It has also been suggested that the legal exceptions for spiritual healing in child-protection laws are there because of the social and lobbying power of the Christian Science church and its members.

Some legal observers think that the Twitchell case will spur wider and more intense efforts to eliminate the spiritual-healing exception. Groups representing the rights of children believe such a change is long overdue.

"We're interested not just in the kids who die," said Norman Fost, former head of the bioethics committee of the American Academy of Pediatrics. "What we're concerned about are the hundreds and hundreds more who suffer from inadequate medical treatment.

The Twitchell conviction was overturned on appeal in 1993. The consequence this will have on laws regulating the medical welfare of children remains to be seen.

CASE PRESENTATION
Juan Gonzalez and the Prediction of Dangerousness

In July of 1986, while the Staten Island ferry was making its run across New York harbor, Juan Gonzalez unsheathed a two-foot souvenir sword and began slashing and stabbing the people around him. Shouting incoherently, Gonzalez continued his attack until Edward del Pino, a retired police officer, fired a shot into the air and ordered Gonzalez to drop to the deck. By that time, two people were dead and nine others were wounded.

"The Father, the Son, and the Holy Spirit made me do it," Mr. Gonzalez told the police as he was charged with murder and assault. He was later taken to a hospital for a psychiatric evaluation. Only a few days before, Gonzalez had undergone another evaluation. Police had taken him into custody after he had been reported wandering the streets and making threats like "I'm going to kill! God told me so." At Presbyterian Hospital, psychiatrists had diagnosed his illness as a psychotic paranoid disorder and released him after two days.

After events aboard the ferry, the question asked by the mayor, physicians, and ordinary citizens was, Why was such an obviously dangerous person released? A brief investigation showed that Mr. Gonzalez had responded well to treatment, that no hospital space was available, and that he had been given antipsychotic drugs to take. He had also agreed to report as an outpatient, although he never did.

The Gonzalez case raised in combination two issues that have been the subjects of dispute in recent years—the right of the state to restrict the liberties of mentally ill individuals and the ability of psychiatry to predict dangerous behavior.

For almost thirty years, in response to court decisions, states have moved away from forcibly confining the mentally ill. More effective drugs to control psychoses and the movement to protect the civil rights of the mentally ill are two major factors responsible for this change in legal and social policies. In most states, the grounds for involuntary civil commitment and psychiatric treatment require that an individual be shown to be dangerous to himself or to others or to suffer from a condition that renders him mentally disabled. After a period of time, typically amounting to only a few days, a court hearing is then required to determine whether commitment and treatment may legitimately continue.

Some critics are of the opinion that the movement to keep the majority of mentally ill people out of institutions has gone too far. By some estimates, more than 30% of the homeless people on the streets of larger cities suffer from some kind of psychiatric illness that would warrant their being confined to an institution. The liberty of these people has been protected only by imposing on them a burden of responsibility they are unable to bear.

Furthermore, critics charge, a new standard of involuntary commitment and treatment is needed to prevent incidents like the one on the Staten Island ferry. Those who are judged to pose a *potential*, as well as an immediate, threat to others should be institutionalized and treated. The safety of the public demands no less.

However, the difficulty with adopting such a standard is that it is not possible to make reliable predictions about the dangerousness of an individual. This is a matter on which psychiatric experts are in general agreement. John Monahan, the author of *Predicting Violent Behavior*, points out that "No psychological test has any proven ability, not even the crudest accuracy, in forecasting violence." Furthermore, there is no apparent connection between a particular psychiatric diagnosis and violent behavior. For example, schizophrenics as a group are no more likely to be violent than are other people. Violence is associated with a wide range of both chronic and acute mental problems.

Whether an individual has been violent in the past is something of an indicator of how he is likely to behave in the future. But unless the individual is able to reveal this information and chooses to do so, it is often not known to the psychiatrist who is called upon to make an evaluation. Also, an individual who has "command hallucinations," voices that command him to act in certain ways, may be presumed to be more inclined to violence than others, if the hallucinations have a violent content. (It was the manifestation of command hallucinations that led Mr. Gonzalez to be taken to Presbyterian Hospital for his first psychiatric evaluation.) However, not all who have such hallucinations will admit to them, and a psychiatrist may have little or no objective reason to believe that such a patient may be dangerous.

The dilemma facing the psychiatrist is neatly summed up by Samuel Perry of the Payne-Whitney Clinic. "The decision to hold someone because he is dangerous is psychiatry's Scylla and Charybdis. On one hand, if you hold a patient against his will and there is no good medical reason, you are violating his civil rights. On the other hand, if you fail to keep someone who is disturbed and dangerous, and he harms someone, the victim can sue you for negligence."

INTRODUCTION

Consider the following cases:

1. A state decides to require that all behavioral therapists (that is, all who make use of psychological conditioning techniques to alter behavior patterns) be either licensed psychologists or psychiatrists.

2. A member of the Jehovah's Witnesses religion, which is opposed to the transfusion of blood and blood products, refuses to consent to a needed appendectomy. But when his appendix ruptures and he lapses into unconsciousness, the surgical resident operates and saves his life.

3. A physician decides not to tell the parents of an infant who died shortly after birth that the cause of death was an unpredictable birth defect, because he does not wish to influence their desire to have a child.

4. A janitor employed in an elementary school consults a psychiatrist retained by the school board and tells her that he has on two occasions molested young children; the psychiatrist decides that it is her duty to inform the school board.

5. A six-year-old develops a high fever accompanied by violent vomiting and convulsions while at school The child is rushed to a nearby hospital. The attending physician makes a diagnosis of meningitis and telephones the parents for permission to initiate treatment. Both parents are Christian Scientists, and they insist that no medical treatment be given to her. The physician initiates treatment anyway, and the parents later sue the physician and the hospital.

6. A thirty-year-old woman who is twenty-four-weeks pregnant is involved in an automobile accident that leaves her with a spinal cord injury. Her physician tells her that she would have had a greater chance of recovery had she not been pregnant. She then requests an abortion. The hospital disagrees with her decision and gets a court order forbidding the abortion.

There is perhaps no single moral issue that is present in all these cases. Rather, there is a complex of related issues. Each case involves acting on the behalf of someone else—another individual, the public at large, or a special group. And each action comes into conflict with the autonomy, wishes, or expectations of some person or persons. Even though the issues are related, it is most fruitful to discuss them under separate headings. We will begin with a brief account of autonomy, then turn to a discussion of paternalism and imposed restrictions on autonomy.

AUTONOMY

We are said to act autonomously when our actions are the outcome of our deliberations and choices. To be autonomous is to be self-determining. Hence, autonomy is violated when we are coerced to act by actual force or by explicit and implicit threats or when we act under misapprehension or under the influence of factors that impair our judgment.

We associate autonomy with the status we ascribe to rational agents as persons in the moral sense. Moral theories are committed to the idea that persons are by their nature uniquely qualified to decide what is in their own best interest. This is because they are ends in themselves, not means to some other end. As such, persons have inherent worth, rather than instrumental worth. Others have a duty to recognize this worth and to avoid treating persons as though they were only instruments to be employed to achieve a goal chosen by someone else. To treat someone as if she lacks autonomy is thus to treat her as less than a person.

All the cases above may be viewed as involving violations of the autonomy of the individuals concerned. Consider: (1) laws requiring a license to provide therapy restrict the actions of individuals who do not qualify for a license; (2) the Jehovah's Witness is given blood he does not want; (3) information crucial to decision making is withheld from the parents of the child with the genetic disease, so their future decision cannot be a properly informed one; (4) by breaking confidentiality, the psychiatrist is usurping the prerogative of the janitor to keep secret information that may harm him; (5) by treating the girl with meningitis, the physician is violating the generally recognized right of parents to make decisions concerning their child's welfare; (6) by refusing the woman's request for an abortion, the hospital and the court are forcing her to remain pregnant against her will.

The high value we place on autonomy is based on the realization that without it we can make very little of our lives. In its absence, we become the creatures of others, and our lives assume the forms they choose for us. Without being able to act in ways to shape our own destiny by pursuing our aims and making our own decisions, we are not realizing the potential we have as rational agents. Autonomy permits us the opportunity to make ourselves; even if we are dissatisfied with the result, we have the satisfaction of knowing that the mistakes were our own. We at least acted as rational agents.

One of the traditional problems of social organization is to structure society in such a way that the autonomy of individuals will be preserved and promoted. However, autonomy is not an absolute or unconditional value, but just one among others. For example, few would wish to live in a society in which you could do what you wanted only if you had enough physical power to get your way. Because one person's exercise of autonomy is likely to come into conflict with another's, we are willing to accept some restrictions to preserve as much of our own freedom as possible. We value our own safety, the opportunity to carry out our plans in peace, the lives of other rational beings, and perhaps even their welfare.

Because autonomy is so basic to us, we usually view it as not requiring any justification. However, this predisposition in favor of autonomy means that to violate someone's autonomy, to set aside that person's wishes and render impotent her power of action, requires that we offer a strong justification. Various principles have been proposed to justify conditions under which we are warranted in restricting autonomy.

The one most relevant in discussing the relationships among physicians, patients, and society is the principle of paternalism. The connection of paternalism with the physician-patient relationship and with truth telling and confidentiality in the medical and social context will be discussed in the following section. (For a fuller account of autonomy, as well as the principles invoked to justify restricting its exercise, see Chapter 1. The harm principle is of particular relevance to the topics presented here.)

PATERNALISM

Exactly what paternalism is, is itself a matter of dispute. Roughly speaking, we can say that paternalism consists in acting in a way that is believed to protect or advance the interest of a person, although acting in this way goes against the person's own immediate desires or limits the person's freedom of choice. Oversimplifying, paternalism is the view that "Father knows best." (The word "parentalism" is now often preferred to "paternalism," because of the latter's gender association. See Chapter 1 for the distinction between the weak and strong versions of the principle of paternalism.) Thus, the first three cases presented above are instances of paternalistic behavior.

It is useful to distinguish what we can call "state paternalism" from "personal paternalism." State paternalism, as the name suggests, is the control exerted by a legislature, agency, or other governmental body over particular kinds of practices or procedures. Such control is typically exercised through laws, licensing requirements, technical specifications, and operational guidelines and regulations. (The first case above is an example of state paternalism.)

By contrast, personal paternalism consists in an individual's deciding, on the basis of his own principles or values, that he knows what is best for another person. The individual then acts in a way that deprives the other person of genuine and effective choice. (Cases two and three are examples of this.) Paternalism is personal when it is not a matter of public or semi-public policy but is a result of private, moral decision making.

The line between public and private paternalism is often blurred. For example, suppose a physician on the staff of a hospital believes a pregnant patient should have surgery to improve the chances for the normal development of the fetus. The physician presents his view to the hospital's attorney, and, agreeing with him, the attorney goes to court to request a court order for the surgery. The judge is persuaded and issues the order. Although the order is based on arguments that certain laws are applicable in the case, the order itself is neither a personal decision nor a matter of public policy. The order reflects the judgment of a physician who has succeeded in getting others to agree.

Despite the sometimes blurred distinction between state and personal paternalism, the distinction is useful. Most important, it permits us to separate issues associated with decisions about public policies affecting classes of individuals (for example, people needing medication) from issues associated with decisions by particular people affecting specific individuals (for example, a Dr. Latvia explaining treatment options to a Mr. Zonda).

State Paternalism in Medical and Health Care

At first sight, state paternalism seems wholly unobjectionable in the medical context. We are all certain to feel more confident in consulting a physician when we know that she or he has had to meet the standards for education, competence, and character set by a state licensing board and medical society. We feel relatively sure that we aren't putting ourselves in the hands of an incompetent quack.

Indeed, that we can feel such assurance can be regarded as one of the marks of the social advancement of medicine. As late as the early twentieth century in the United States, the standards for physicians were low, and licensing laws were either nonexistent or poorly enforced. It was possible to qualify as a physician with as little as four months' formal schooling and a two-year apprenticeship.

Rigorous standards and strictly enforced laws have undoubtedly done much to improve medical care in this country. At the very least, they have made it less dangerous to consult a physician. At the same time, however, they have also placed close restrictions on individual freedom of choice. In the nineteenth century, a person could choose among a wide variety of medical viewpoints. That is no longer so today.

We now recognize that some medical viewpoints are simply wrong and, if implemented, may endanger a patient. At the least, people treated by those who espouse such views run the risk of not getting the best kind of medical care available. Unlike people in the nineteenth century, we are confident that we know (within limits) what kinds of medical therapies are effective and what kinds are useless or harmful. The scientific character of contemporary medicine gives us this assurance.

Secure in these beliefs, our society generally endorses paternalism by the state in the regulation of medical practice. We believe it is important to protect sick people from quacks and charlatans, from those who raise false hopes and take advantage of human suffering. We generally accept, then, that the range of choice of health therapy ought to be limited to what we consider to be legitimate and scientific.

This point of view is not one that everyone is pleased to endorse. In particular, those seeking treatment for cancer or for AIDS have sometimes wanted to try drugs rumored to be effective but not approved by the Food and Drug Administration. Such drugs cannot be legally prescribed in the United States, and those wishing to gain access to them must travel to foreign clinics, often at considerable discomfort and expense. (See the Social Context in Chapter 4 for additional discussion of the situation.) Some have claimed that FDA regulations make it impossible for them to choose the therapy they wish and that this is an unwarranted restriction of their rights. It should be enough, they claim, for the government to issue a warning if it thinks one is called for. But after that, people should be free to act as they choose.

The debate about unapproved therapies raises a more general question: To what extent is it legitimate for a government to restrict the actions and choices of its citizens for their own good? It is perhaps not possible to give a wholly satisfactory general answer to this question. People don't object that they are not permitted to drink polluted water from the city water supply or that they are not able to buy candy bars contaminated with insect parts. Yet some do object if they have to drink water that contains fluorides or if they cannot buy candy bars that contain saccharine. But all such limitations result from governmental attempts to protect the health of citizens.

Seeing to the well-being of its citizens certainly must be recognized as one of the legitimate aims of a government. And this aim may easily include seeing to their physical health. State paternalism with respect to health seems, in general, to be justifiable. Yet the laws and regulations through which the paternal concern is expressed are certain to come into conflict with the exercise of individual liberties. Perhaps the only way in which conflicts can be resolved is on an issue-by-issue basis. Later, we will discuss some of the limitations that moral theories place on state paternalism.

It is worth noticing that state paternalism in medical and health-care matters may be more pervasive than it seems at first sight. Laws regulating medical practice, the licensing of physicians and medical personnel, regulations governing the licensing and testing of drugs, and guidelines that must be followed in scientific research are some of the more obvious expressions of paternalism. Less obvious is the fact that government research funds can be expended only in prescribed ways and that only certain approved forms of medical care and therapy will be paid for under government-sponsored health programs. For example, it was a political and social triumph for chiropractors and Christian Science Readers when some of their services were included under Medicare coverage. Thus, government money, as well as laws and regulations, can be used in paternalistic ways.

Personal Paternalism in Medical and Health Care

That patients occupy a dependent role with respect to their physicians seems to be true historically, sociologically, and psychologically. The patient is sick, the physician is well. The patient is in need of the knowledge and skills the physician possesses, but the physician does not need those possessed by the patient. The patient seeks out the physician to ask for help, but the physician does not seek out the patient. The patient is a single individual, while the physician represents the institution of medicine with its hospitals, nurses, technicians, consultants, and so on.

In his dependence on the physician, the patient willingly surrenders some of his autonomy. Explicitly or implicitly, he agrees to allow the physician to make certain decisions for him that he would ordinarily make for himself. The physician tells him what to eat and drink and what to avoid, what medicine he should take and when to take it, how much exercise he should get and what kind it should be. The patient consents to run at least part of his life by "doctor's orders" in the hope that he will regain his health or at least improve his condition.

The physician acquires a great amount of power in this relationship. But she also acquires a great responsibility. It has been recognized at least since the time of Hippocrates that the physician has an obligation to act in the best interest of the patient. The patient is willing to transfer part of his autonomy because he is confident that the physician will act in this way.

If this analysis of the present form of the physician-patient relationship is roughly correct, two questions are appropriate.

First, should the relationship be one in which the patient is so dependent on the paternalism of the physician? Perhaps it would be better if patients did not think of themselves as transferring *any* of their autonomy to physicians. Physicians might better be thought of as people offering advice, rather than as ones issuing orders. Thus, patients, free to accept or reject advice, would retain fully their power to govern their own lives. If this is a desirable goal, it is clear that the present nature of the physician-patient relationship needs to be drastically altered.

The problem with this point of view is that the patient is ordinarily not in a position to judge the advice that is offered. The reason for consulting a physician in the first place is to gain the advantage of her knowledge and judgment. Moreover, courses of medical therapy are often complicated ones involving many interdependent steps. A patient could not expect the best treatment if he insisted on accepting some of the steps and rejecting others. As a practical matter, a patient who expects good medical care must pretty much put himself in the hands of his physician.

For this reason, the second question is perhaps based on a more realistic assessment of the nature of medical care: How much autonomy must be given up by the patient? The power of the physician over the patient cannot be absolute. The patient cannot become the slave or creature of the physician—this is not what a patient consents to when he agrees to place himself under the care of a physician. What, then, are the limits of the paternalism that can be legitimately exercised by the physician?

TRUTH TELLING IN MEDICINE

This question arises most forcefully when physicians deceive patients. When, if ever, is it justifiable for a physician to deceive her or his patient?

The paternalistic answer, of course, is that deception by the physician is justified when it is in the best interest of the patient. Suppose, for example, that a transplant surgeon detects signs of tissue rejection in a patient who has just received a donor kidney. The surgeon is virtually certain that within a week the kidney will have to be surgically removed and the patient transferred to dialysis equipment again. Although in no immediate clinical danger, the patient is suffering from postoperative depression. It is altogether possible that, if the patient is told at this time that the transplant appears to be a failure, his depression will become more severe. This, in turn, might lead to a worsening of the patient's physical condition, perhaps even to a life-threatening extent.

Eventually the patient will have to be told of the need for another operation. But by the time that need arises, his psychological condition may have improved. Is the surgeon justified in avoiding giving a direct and honest answer to the patient when he asks about his condition? In the surgeon's assessment of the situation, the answer is likely to do the patient harm. His duty as a physician, then, seems to require that he deceive the patient, either by lying to him (an act of commission) or by allowing him to believe (an act of omission) that his condition is satisfactory and the transplant was successful.

Yet doesn't the patient have a right to know the truth from his physician? After all, it is his life that is being threatened. Should he not be told how things stand with him so that he will be in a position to make decisions that affect his own future? Is the surgeon not exceeding the bounds of the powers granted to him by the patient? The patient surely had no intention of completely turning over his autonomy to the surgeon.

The issue is one of "truth telling." Does the physician always owe it to the patient to tell the truth? Some writers make a distinction between lying to the patient and merely being nonresponsive or evasive. But is this really a morally relevant distinction? In either case, the truth is being kept from the patient. Both are instances of medical paternalism.

The use of placebos (from the Latin *placebo,* meaning "I shall please") in medical therapy is another issue that raises questions about the legitimate limits of paternalism in medicine. The "placebo effect" is a well-documented psychological phenomenon: even patients who are seriously ill will sometimes show improvement when they are given *any* kind of medication (a sugar pill, for example) or treatment. This can happen even when the medication or treatment is irrelevant to their condition.

The placebo effect can be exploited by physicians for the (apparent) good of their patients. Many patients cannot accept a physician's well-considered judgments. When they come to a physician with a complaint and are told that there is nothing organically wrong with them, that no treatment or medication is called for, they continue to ail. They may then lose confidence in their physician or be less inclined to seek medical advice for more serious complaints.

One way to avoid these consequences is for the physician to prescribe a placebo for the patient. Since the patient (we can assume) suffers from no organic disease condition, he is not in need of any genuine medication. And because of the placebo effect, he may actually find himself relieved of the symptoms that caused him to seek medical help. Moreover, the patient feels satisfied that he has been treated, and his confidence in his physician and in medicine in general remains intact.

Since the placebo effect is not at all likely to be produced if the patient knows he is being given an ineffective medication, the physician cannot be candid about the "treatment" prescribed. She must either be silent, say something indefinite like "I think this might help your condition," or lie. Since the placebo effect is more likely to be achieved if the medication is touted as being amazingly effective against complaints like those of the patient, there is a reason for the physician to lie outright. Because the patient may stand to gain a considerable amount of good from placebo therapy, the physician may think of herself as acting in the best interest of her patient.

Despite its apparent advantages, placebo therapy may be open to two ethical criticisms. First, we can ask whether giving placebos is really in the best interest of a patient. It encourages many patients in their belief that drugs can solve their problems. Patients with vague and general complaints may need some kind of psychological counseling, and giving them placebos merely discourages them from coming to grips with their genuine problems. Also, not all placebos are harmless (see the discussion in the introduction to Chapter 6). Some contain active chemicals that produce side effects (something likely to enhance the placebo effect) so the physician who prescribes placebos may be subjecting her patient to some degree of risk.

Second, by deceiving her patient, the physician is depriving him of the chance to make genuine decisions about his own life. Because the person is not genuinely sick, it does not seem legitimate to regard him as having deputized his physician to act in his behalf or as having transferred any of his power or autonomy to the physician. In Kant's terms, the physician is not acknowledging the patient's status as an autonomous rational agent. She is not according him the dignity that he possesses simply by virtue of being human. (A utilitarian who wished to claim that telling the truth to patients is a policy that will produce the best overall benefits could offer essentially the same criticism.)

Deception is not the only issue raised by the general question of the legitimacy of medical paternalism. Another of some importance is difficult to state precisely, but it has to do with the general attitude of physicians toward their patients. Patients often feel that physicians deal with them in a way that is literally paternalistic—that physicians treat them like children.

The physician, like the magician or shaman, is often seen as a figure of power and mystery, one who controls the forces of nature and, by doing so, relieves suffering and restores health. Some physicians like this role and act in accordance with it. They resent having their authority questioned and fail to treat their patients with dignity and respect.

For example, many physicians call their patients by their first names while expecting patients to refer to them as "Dr. X." In our society, women in particular have been most critical of such condescending attitudes displayed by physicians.

More serious is the fact that many physicians do not make a genuine effort to educate patients about the state of their health, the significance of laboratory findings, or the reasons why medication or other therapy is being prescribed. Patients are not only expected to follow orders, but they are expected to do so blindly.

The issue here is not one of informed consent (which we will discuss in detail in the next chapter). For in informed consent, a patient must give permission for a procedure of a special sort to be performed. Here we are talking only about the ordinary medical situation— someone consults a physician because of a shoulder pain or just to get a yearly checkup.

The amount of time that it takes to help a patient understand his medical condition and the reason for the prescribed therapy is, of course, one reason why physicians do not attempt to provide such information. A busy physician in an office practice might see thirty or forty patients a day, and it is difficult to give each of them the necessary amount of attention. Also, patients without a medical background obviously can find it hard to understand medical explanations—particularly in the ways in which they are often given.

The result, for whatever reasons, is a situation in which physicians make decisions about patients without allowing patients to know the basis for them. Explanations are not given, it is sometimes said, because patients "wouldn't understand" or "might draw the wrong conclusions about their illness" or "might worry needlessly." Patients are thus not only *not* provided information, but they are discouraged from asking questions or revealing their doubts.

The moral questions here concern the responsibility of the physician. Is it ultimately useful for the patients that physicians should play the role of a distant and mysterious figure of power? If so, then it may be that physicians should cultivate the role. Do patients have a right to ask that physicians treat them with the same dignity as physicians treat one another? Should a physician attempt to educate her or his patients about their illnesses? Or is a physician's only real responsibility to provide patients with needed medical treatment?

Furthermore, is it always obvious that the physician knows what will count as the all-around best treatment for a patient? Patients, being human, have values of their own, and they may well not rank their best chance for effective medical treatment above all else. A woman with breast cancer, for example, may wish to avoid having a breast surgically removed (mastectomy) and so prefer another mode of treatment, even though her physician may consider it less effective. Can her physician legitimately withhold from her knowledge of alternative modes of treatment and so allow her no choice? Can he make the decision about treatment himself on the grounds that it is a purely medical matter, one about which the patient has no expert knowledge?

CONFIDENTIALITY

"Whatever I see or hear, professionally or privately, which ought not be divulged, I will keep secret and tell no one," runs one of the pledges in the Hippocratic Oath.

The tradition of medical practice in the West has taken this injunction very seriously. That it has done so is not entirely due to the high moral character of physicians, for the pledge to secrecy also serves an important practical function. Physicians need to have information of an intimate and highly personal sort in order to make diagnoses and prescribe courses of therapy. If physicians were known to reveal such personal information, then patients would be reluctant to cooperate, and the practice of medicine would be adversely affected. Furthermore, because psychological factors play a role in medical therapy, the chances of success in medical treatment are improved when patients can place trust and confidence in their physicians. This aspect of the physician-patient relationship actually forms a part of medical therapy. Of course, this is particularly so of the "talking cures" characteristic of some forms of psychiatry.

A number of states recognize the need for "privileged communication" between physician and patient and have laws to protect physicians from being compelled to testify about their patients in court. Yet physicians are also members of a society, and the society must attempt to protect the general interest. This sometimes places the physician in the middle of a conflict between the interest of the individual and the interest of society.

For example, physicians are often required by law to act in ways that force them to reveal certain information about their patients. The best instance of this is perhaps the legal obligation to report to health departments the names of those patients who are carriers of such communicable diseases as syphilis and tuberculosis. This permits health authorities to warn those with whom the carriers have come into contact and to guard against the spread of the diseases. Thus, the interest of the society is given precedence over physician-patient confidentiality.

Few people would question society's right to demand that physicians violate a patient's confidence when the issue is that of protecting the health of great numbers of people. More open to question are laws that require physicians to report gunshot wounds or other injuries that might be connected with criminal actions. (In some states, before abortion became legal, physicians were required to report cases of attempted abortion.) Furthermore, physicians as citizens have a legal duty to report any information they may have about a crime unless they are protected by a privileged-communication law.

Thus, the physician is placed in a position of conflict. If he acts to protect the patient's confidences, then he runs the risk of acting illegally. If he acts in accordance with the law, then he must violate the confidence of his patients. What needs to be decided from a moral point of view is to what extent the laws that place a physician in such a situation are justified.

The physician who is not in private practice but is employed by a government agency or a business organization also encounters similar conflicts. Her obligations run in two directions: to her patients and to her employer. Should a physician who works for a government agency tell her superiors that an employee has confided in her that he is a drug addict? If she does not, the man may be subject to blackmail or bribery. If she does, then she must violate the patient's confidence. Or what if a psychiatrist retained by a company decides that one of the employees is so psychologically disturbed that she cannot function effectively in her job? Should the psychiatrist inform the employer of this, even if it means going against the wishes of the patient? (Consider also the fourth case cited at the beginning of this Introduction.)

Even more serious problems arise in psychiatry. Suppose that a patient expresses to his psychiatrist feelings of great anger against someone and even announces that he intends to go out and kill that person. What should the psychiatrist do? Is it his obligation to warn the person being threatened? Should he report the threat to the police? This is fundamentally the issue that was dealt with by the California Supreme Court in the case of *Tarasoff* v. *Regents of the University of California*. (See the California Supreme Court decision in this chapter for a discussion.)

The basic question about confidentiality concerns the extent to which we are willing to go to protect it. It is doubtful that anyone would want to assert that confidentiality should be absolutely guaranteed. But, if not, then under what conditions is it better to violate it than to preserve it?

AUTONOMY AND THE INTERESTS OF OTHERS

Patients do not always choose to do as they are advised by their physicians. Some people refuse to take needed medications, change their diets, quit smoking, exercise more, or undergo surgical procedures that promise to improve the quality of their lives, if not lengthen them. Valuing autonomy requires recognizing that people do not always do what is good for them in a medical way, and accepting this as a

consequence. Over the years, the courts have recognized repeatedly and explicitly that the right to refuse or discontinue medical treatment has a basis in the Constitution and in the common law.

Most public and legal attention on the matter of rejecting therapy has focused recently on cases in which terminally ill patients wish to have respirators disconnected or in which the guardians of patients in chronic vegetative states want their nutrition and hydration to be discontinued. The issues have concerned the rights of patients themselves, and in this respect the questions were more or less straightforward.

The matter of refusing treatment becomes more complicated when the interest of someone other than or in addition to the patient is involved. Two sorts of cases, in particular, present difficulties: cases in which parents' beliefs cause them to deny their children necessary medical attention and cases in which a pregnant woman's behaviors result in damage to her fetus.

First is the situation in which parents, acting on the basis of their beliefs, refuse to authorize needed medical treatment for their child. The duty of the physician is to provide the child the best medical care possible. The duty of the parent is to protect and promote the welfare of the child. Ordinarily, in the medical context, these two duties are convergent with respect to the line of action they lead to. The parents ask the physician to "do what is best" for their child, and the physician discusses the options and risks with the parents and secures their consent on behalf of the child. (See the discussion of informed consent in the next chapter.)

However, this convergence of duties leading to agreement about action is dependent on physicians and parents sharing some fundamental beliefs about the nature of disease and the efficacy of medical therapy in controlling it. When these beliefs are not shared, then the outcome is a divergence of opinion about what should be done in the best interest of the child. The actions favored by the physician will be incompatible with the actions favored by the parents.

As in the Case Presentation about Robyn Twitchell and example five above, some parents are adherents of religions like Christian Science that teach that disease has no reality but is a manifestation of incorrect or disordered thinking. People with such beliefs think that the appropriate response to illness is to seek spiritual healing, rather than to employ medical modalities.

What about the children of those with such beliefs? Their parents can legitimately claim that by refusing to seek or accept medical treatment for their children they are doing what they consider best. It is a recognized principle that parents should decide the best interest of their children, except in very special circumstances. We don't think, for example, that a psychotic or clinically depressed parent should be allowed to decide about a child's welfare. Should Christian Scientists and others with similar beliefs be put in the category of incompetent parents and forced to act against their beliefs and seek medical care for their children?

A strong case can be made for answering yes. If mentally competent adults wish to avoid or reject medical treatment for themselves, the principle of autonomy supports a public policy permitting this. However, when the interest of someone who lacks the abilities to deliberate and decide for himself is concerned, it is reasonable to favor a policy that will protect that person from harm. This is particularly so when matters as basic as the person's health and safety are at stake.

Hence, to warrant restricting the generally recognized right of parents to see to the welfare of their children, we can appeal to the harm principle. We might say that, if a parent's action or failure to take action tends to result in harm to a child, then we are justified in restricting his or her freedom to make decisions on behalf of the child. We could then look to

someone else—a court or appointed guardian—to represent the child's best interest.

In general, we consider a legitimate function of the state to be the protection of its citizens. When parents fail to take reasonable steps to secure the welfare of their children, then doing so becomes a matter of interest to the state.

The second kind of case is one that involves an actual or potential conflict between the actions of a pregnant woman and the interest of the fetus she is carrying. This kind of case is illustrated in example six above and discussed in the Social Context section at the beginning of the chapter.

An obvious way of dealing with an alleged conflict between what a pregnant woman wants or does and the interest of her fetus is to deny that conflict is possible. If one holds that the fetus, at every developmental stage, is a part of the woman's body and that she is free to do with her body as she pleases, then there can be no conflict. The woman is simply deciding for herself, and it would be an unjustifiable violation of her autonomy to regulate her actions in ways that those of men or nonpregnant women are not regulated.

However, a number of difficulties are associated with this position. The most significant difficulty is that as a fetus continues to develop it becomes increasingly implausible to hold that it is no different from any other "part" of a woman's body. The problem of when the fetus is a person in the moral sense is one that plagues the abortion dispute (see Chapter 1), and it is no less relevant to this issue.

Furthermore, even if one is not prepared to say that the fetus can claim any serious consideration to life, particularly at the very early stages of pregnancy, it seems prima facie wrong to act as though the fetus (barring miscarriage or abortion) is not going to develop into a child. Suppose a woman knows that she is pregnant and knows that continuing to drink alcohol even moderately is likely to cause the child who will be born to suffer from birth defects. Most people would consider it wrong for her to disregard the consequences of her actions. Once she has decided against (or failed to secure) an abortion, then it seems she must accept the responsibility that goes with carrying a child to term. On even a moderate view, this would imply avoiding behavior she knows will be likely to cause birth defects.

However, another aspect of the question of whether a pregnant woman has any responsibility to protect the welfare of the fetus is to what extent, if any, we are justified in regulating the actions of a pregnant woman. Should a pregnant woman retain her autonomy intact? Or is it legitimate for us to require her, by virtue of being pregnant, to follow a set of rules or laws not applicable to other people?

Once again, the status of the fetus as a person makes such a question hard to answer. Should we regard cases of "fetal neglect" or "fetal abuse" as no different from cases of child neglect or abuse? If the answer is yes, then the pregnant woman is no different from the parent of a minor child. In the same way that the state might order a Christian Science parent to seek medical help for a sick child, we might consider ourselves justified in insisting that a pregnant woman get prenatal care and avoid drugs and alcohol. Just as parents are subject to laws and rules that other people are not, then so are pregnant women.

Assuming this answer is accepted, then the question becomes one of how far we should go in prescribing behavior for a pregnant woman. Should we require a basic minimum, or should we establish an obtainable ideal?

Even the basic questions surrounding the issue of pregnancy and responsibility remain unanswered by our society. We have yet to develop a social policy to reduce the incidence of fetal alcohol syndrome and drug-damaged babies while also protecting the autonomy of pregnant women.

ETHICAL THEORIES: PATERNALISM, TRUTH TELLING, CONFIDENTIALITY

What we have called state paternalism and personal paternalism are compatible with utilitarian ethical theory. But whether they are justifiable is a matter of controversy. If the principle of utility shows that governmental laws, policies, practices, or regulations increase the general happiness, then they are justified. It can be argued that they are justified even if they restrict the individual's freedom of choice or action because for utilitarianism such freedom has no absolute value. Personal paternalism is justified in a similar way. If a physician believes that she can protect her patient from unnecessary suffering or can relieve his pain by keeping him in ignorance, by lying to him, by giving him placebos, or by otherwise deceiving him, then these actions are morally legitimate.

However, John Stuart Mill did not take this view of paternalism. Mill argued that freedom of choice is of such importance that it can be justifiably restricted only when it can be shown that unregulated choice would cause harm to other people. Mill claimed that compelling people to act in certain ways "for their own good" is never legitimate. This position, Mill argued, is one that is justified by the principle of utility. Gerald Dworkin, in the selection included in this chapter, provides an analysis of Mill's position, and there is no need for us to repeat it here. We should note, however, that utilitarianism does not offer a straightforward answer to the question of the legitimacy of paternalism.

What we have said about paternalism also applies more or less to the issue of confidentiality. Generally speaking, if violating confidentiality seems necessary to produce a state of affairs in which happiness is increased, then the violation is justified. This might be the case when, for example, someone's life is in danger or someone is being tried for a serious crime and the testimony of a physician is needed to help establish her innocence. Yet it also might be argued from the point of view of rule utilitarianism that confidentiality is such a basic ingredient in the physician-patient relationship that, in the long run, more good will be produced if confidentiality is never violated.

The Kantian view of paternalism, truth telling, and confidentiality is more clear-cut. Every person is a rational and autonomous agent. As such he or she is entitled to make decisions that affect his or her own life. This means that a person is entitled to receive information relevant to making such decisions and is entitled to the truth, no matter how painful it might be. The use of placebos or any other kind of deception in medicine is morally illegitimate because this would involve denying a person the respect and dignity to which he or she is entitled. The categorical imperative also rules out lying, for the maxim involved in such an action produces a contradiction. (There are special difficulties in applying the categorical imperative that we discussed in the introductory chapter. When these are taken into account, Kant's view is perhaps not quite so straightforward and definite as it first appears.)

It can be argued that Kant's principles also establish that confidentiality should be regarded as absolute. When a person becomes a patient, she does so with the expectation that what she tells her physician will be kept confidential. Thus, in the physician-patient relationship there is an implicit promise. The physician implicitly promises that he will not reveal any information about his patient, either what he has been told or what he has learned for himself. If this analysis is correct, then the physician is under an obligation to preserve confidentiality because keeping promises is an absolute duty, (Here, as in the case of lying, there are difficulties connected with the way in which a maxim is stated. See the introductory chapter for a discussion.)

Ross's principles recognize that everyone has a moral right to be treated as an autonomous agent who is entitled to make decisions affecting his own life. Also, everyone is entitled to make decisions affecting his own life. Also, everyone is entitled to know the truth and to be educated in helpful ways. Similarly, if confidentiality is a form of promise keeping, everyone is entitled to expect that it will be maintained. Thus, paternalism, lying, and violation of confidence are prima facie morally objectionable. But, of course, it is possible to imagine circumstances in which they would be justified. The right course of action that a physician must follow is one that can be determined only on the basis of the physician's knowledge of the patient, the patient's problem, and the general situation. Thus, Ross's principles rule out paternalism, deception, and violations of confidence as general policies, but they do not make them morally illegitimate in an absolute way.

Rawls's theory of social and political morality is compatible with state paternalism of a restricted kind. No laws, practices, or policies can legitimately violate the rights of individuals. At the same time, however, a society, viewing arrangements from the original position, might decide to institute a set of practices that would promote what they agreed to be their interests. If, for example, health is agreed to be an interest, then they might be willing to grant to the state the power to regulate a large range of matters connected with the promotion of health. Establishing standards for physicians would be an example of such regulation. But they might also go so far as to give the state power to decide (on the advice of experts) what medical treatments are legitimate, what drugs are safe and effective to use, what substances should be controlled or prohibited, and so on. So long as the principles of justice are not violated and so long as the society can be regarded as imposing these regulations on itself for the promotion of its own good, then such paternalistic practices are unobjectionable. With respect to personal paternalism, deception, and confidentiality, Rawls's general theory offers no specific answers. But since

Rawls endorses Ross's account of prima facie duties (while rejecting Ross's intuitionism), it seems reasonable to believe that Rawls's view on these matters would be the same as Ross's.

The natural law doctrine of Roman Catholicism suggests that paternalism in both of its forms is legitimate. When the state is organized to bring about such "natural goods" as health, then laws and practices that promote those goods are morally right. Individuals do have a worth in themselves and should be free to direct and organize their own lives. But at the same time, individuals may be ignorant of relevant information, lack the intellectual capacities to determine what is really in their best interest, or be moved by momentary passions and circumstances. For these reasons, the state may act so that people are protected from their own shortcomings, and yet their genuine desires, their "natural ends," are satisfied.

Thus, natural law doctrine concludes that because each individual has an inherent worth, she is entitled to be told the truth in medical situations (and others) and not deceived. But it reasons too that because a physician has superior knowledge, he may often perceive the interest of the patient better than the patient herself. Accordingly, natural law doctrine indicates that, although he should avoid lying, a physician is still under an obligation to act for the best interest of his patient. This may mean allowing the patient to believe something that is not so (as in placebo therapy) or withholding information from the patient. In order for this to be morally legitimate, however, the physician's motive must always be that of advancing the welfare of the patient.

In the matter of confidentiality, the natural law doctrine of Roman Catholicism recognizes that the relationship between physician and patient is one of trust, and a physician has a duty not to betray the confidences of her patients. But the relationship is not sacrosanct and the duty is not absolute. When the physician finds herself in a situation in which a greater wrong will be done if she does not reveal a confidence entrusted to her by a patient, then she has a duty to reveal the confidence. If, for example, the physician possesses knowledge that would save someone from death or unmerited suffering, then it is her duty to make this knowledge available, even if by doing so she violates a patient's trust.

We have been able merely to sketch an outline of possible ways in which our ethical theories might deal with the issues involved in paternalism, truth telling, and confidentiality. Some of the views presented are open to challenge, and none of them has been worked out in a completely useful way. That is one of the tasks that remains to be performed.

No ethical theory would justify, under ordinary circumstances, a pregnant woman's knowingly behaving in a way that would cause birth defects in a child she intends to carry to term. If the woman acts out of ignorance or under various psychological or social pressures, or if she would have to engage in extraordinary sacrifices, there may be reason to excuse her actions, should they result in preventable impairments.

However, it remains to be seen exactly how any moral theory can resolve the issue of to what extent, if any, a pregnant woman is responsible for a fetus she is carrying to term. Relevant to dealing with the problem is the matter of whether the woman intends to carry the fetus to term by choice, whether she has merely neglected to secure an abortion, or whether the unavailability of abortion forces her to remain pregnant. The woman's wishes and circumstances may result in our giving different answers to the basic question.

On the final matter of restricting the autonomy of adults in order to protect the health and safety of their minor children, each ethical theory considered can be interpreted as regarding such restrictions as justified. In terms of each theory, children occupy a special status that must be protected. If a parent acts in ways that cause danger to his child, then the state may legitimately restrict his action. If the parent fails in his basic duty to protect the well-being of his children, the state must assume this function. A state that fails to guarantee protection to a child is open to moral condemnation.

John Stuart Mill, in the final chapter of *On Liberty,* explicitly addresses the issue of whether the state can require parents to act to protect or promote the interest of their children. In accord with his general position that violating the harm principle is the only ground that warrants restricting individual autonomy, Mill observes that, although individuals may do as they choose to themselves, when someone exercises power over someone else the state is "bound to maintain a vigilant control" over that power. However, this is an obligation "almost entirely disregarded in family relations." People tend to treat children as though they were literally a part of themselves, and the state ordinarily does nothing to interfere with the actions of parents. But, Mill observes, such "misapplied notions of liberty are a real obstacle to the fulfillment by the state of its duties."

Education is Mill's example of a parental responsibility that must be enforced by the state. In his view, the state must see to it that families educate children, because to fail to educate a child is to deprive her of "at least the ordinary chance of a desirable existence" and so is "a crime against that being." If the family does not provide the education, then the state must assume the task.

It seems reasonable to believe that a failure to provide a child with needed health care is at least as serious a deprivation as a failure to provide a child an education. Hence, Mill's arguments in *On Liberty* can be employed to support the view that parents should be required to provide needed medical care for dependent children. If the parents fail in their duty, then the state must assume responsibility.

Autonomy, paternalism, truth telling, and confidentiality are bound together in a complicated web of moral issues. We have not identified all the strands of the web, nor have we traced out their connections with one another. We have, however, mentioned enough difficulties to reveal the seriousness of the issues.

Some of the issues are social ones and require that we decide about the moral legitimacy of certain kinds of laws, practices, and policies. Others are matters of personal morality, ones that concern our obligations to society and to other people. Our ethical theories, we can hope, will provide us with the means of arriving at workable and justifiable resolutions of the issues. But before this point is reached, much intellectual effort and ingenuity will have to be invested.

Paternalism

Gerald Dworkin

Gerald Dworkin attempts to show that, even if we place an absolute value on individual choice, a variety of paternalistic policies can still be justified. In consenting to a system of representative government, we understand that it may act to safeguard our interests in certain ways. But, Dworkin asks, what are the "kinds of conditions which make it plausible to suppose that rational men could reach agreement to limit their liberty even when other men's interests are not affected?"

Dworkin suggests that such conditions are satisfied in cases in which there is a "good" such as health involved—one that everybody needs to pursue other goods. Rational people would agree that attaining such a good should be promoted by the government even when individuals don't recognize it as a good at a particular time. There is a sense, Dworkin argues, in which we are not really imposing such a good on people. What we are really saying is that, if everyone knew the facts and assessed them properly, this is what they would choose. Also, we are sometimes influenced by immediate alternatives that look more attractive, or we are careless or depressed and so do not act for what we acknowledge as a good. Thus, we might approve of laws such as ones against cigarette smoking because we know we should not smoke cigarettes.

It is plausible, Dworkin suggests, that rational people would grant to a legislature the right to impose such restrictions on their conduct. But the government has to demonstrate the exact nature of the harmful effects to be avoided. Also, if there is an alternative way of accomplishing the end without restricting liberty, then the society should adopt it.

Neither one person, nor any number of persons, is warranted in saying to another human creature of ripe years, that he shall not do with his life for his own benefit what he chooses to do with it. *Mill*

I do not want to go along with a volunteer basis. I think a fellow should be compelled to become better and not let him use his discretion whether he wants to get smarter, more healthy or more honest. *General Hershey*

I take as my starting point the "one very simple principle" proclaimed by Mill in *On Liberty* . . . "That principle is, that the sole end for which mankind are warranted, individually or collectively, in interfering with the liberty of action of any of their number, is self-protection. That the only purpose for which power can be rightfully exercised over any member of a civilized community, against his will, is to prevent harm to others. He cannot rightfully be compelled to do or forbear because it will be better for him to do so, because it will make him happier, because, in the opinion of others, to do so would be wise, or even right."[1]

This principle is neither "one" nor "very simple." It is at least two principles; one asserting that self-protection or the prevention of harm to others is sometimes a sufficient warrant and the other claiming that the individual's own good is *never* a sufficient warrant for the exercise of compulsion either by the society as a whole or by its individual members. I assume that no one with the possible exception of extreme pacifists or anarchists questions the correctness of the first half of

the principle. This essay is an examination of the negative claim embodied in Mill's principle—the objection to paternalistic interferences with a man's liberty.

I

By paternalism I shall understand roughly the interference with a person's liberty of action justified by reasons referring exclusively to the welfare, good, happiness, needs, interests or values of the person being coerced. One is always well-advised to illustrate one's definitions by examples but it is not easy to find "pure" examples of paternalistic interferences. For almost any piece of legislation is justified by several different kinds of reasons and even if historically a piece of legislation can be shown to have been introduced for purely paternalistic motives, it may be that advocates of the legislation with an anti-paternalistic outlook can find sufficient reasons justifying the legislation without appealing to the reasons which were originally adduced to support it. Thus, for example, it may be that the original legislation requiring motorcyclists to wear safety helmets was introduced for purely paternalistic reasons. But the Rhode Island Supreme Court recently upheld such legislation on the grounds that it was "not persuaded that the legislature is powerless to prohibit individuals from pursuing a course of conduct which could conceivably result in their becoming public charges," thus clearly introducing reasons of a quite different

Reprinted from *The Monist*, LaSalle, IL, Vol. 56, no. 1, with the permission of the author and the publisher. Notes renumbered.

kind. Now I regard this decision as being based on reasoning of a very dubious nature but it illustrates the kind of problem one has in finding examples. The following is a list of the kinds of interferences I have in mind as being paternalistic.

II

1. Laws requiring motorcyclists to wear safety helmets when operating their machines.

2. Laws forbidding persons from swimming at a public beach when lifeguards are not on duty.

3. Laws making suicide a criminal offense.

4. Laws making it illegal for women and children to work at certain types of jobs.

5. Laws regulating certain kinds of sexual conduct, e.g. homosexuality among consenting adults in private.

6. Laws regulating the use of certain drugs which may have harmful consequences to the user but do not lead to anti-social conduct.

7. Laws requiring a license to engage in certain professions with those not receiving a license subject to fine or jail sentence if they do engage in the practice.

8. Laws compelling people to spend a specified fraction of their income on the purchase of retirement annuities. (Social Security)

9. Laws forbidding various forms of gambling (often justified on the grounds that the poor are more likely to throw away their money on such activities than the rich who can afford to).

10. Laws regulating the maximum rates of interest for loans.

11. Laws against duelling.

In addition to laws which attach criminal or civil penalties to certain kinds of action there are laws, rules, regulations, decrees, which make it either difficult or impossible for people to carry out their plans and which are also justified on paternalistic grounds. Examples of this are:

1. Laws regulating the types of contracts which will be upheld as valid by the courts, e.g. (an example of Mill's to which I shall return) no man may make a valid contract for perpetual involuntary servitude.

2. Not allowing as a defense to a charge of murder or assault the consent of the victim.

3. Requiring members of certain religious sects to have compulsory blood transfusions. This is made possible by not allowing the patient to have recourse to civil suits for assault and battery and by means of injunctions.

4. Civil commitment procedures when these are specifically justified on the basis of preventing the person being committed from harming himself. (The D.C. Hospitalization of the Mentally Ill Act provides for involuntary hospitalization of a person who "is mentally ill, and because of that illness, is likely to injure *himself* or others if allowed to remain at liberty." The term injure in this context applies to unintentional as well as intentional injuries.)

5. Putting fluorides in the community water supply.

All of my examples are of existing restrictions on the liberty of individuals. Obviously one can think of interferences which have not yet been imposed. Thus one might ban the sale of cigarettes, or require that people wear safety-belts in automobiles (as opposed to merely having them installed) enforcing this by not allowing motorists to sue for injuries even when caused by other drivers if the motorist was not wearing a seat-belt at the time of the accident. . . .

III

Bearing these examples in mind let me return to a characterization of paternalism. I said earlier that I meant by the term, roughly, interference with a person's liberty for his own good. But as some of the examples show the class of persons whose good is invoiced is not always identical with the class of persons whose freedom is restricted. Thus in the case of professional licensing it is the practitioner who is directly interfered with and it is the would-be patient whose interests are presumably being served. Not allowing the consent of the victim to be a defense to certain types of crime primarily affects the would-be aggressor but it is the interests of the willing victim that we are trying to protect. Sometimes a person may fall into both classes as would be the case if we banned the manufacture and sale of cigarettes and a given manufacturer happened to be a smoker as well.

Thus we may first divide paternalistic interferences into "pure" and "impure" cases. In "pure" paternalism the class of persons whose freedom is restricted is identical with the class of persons whose benefit is intended to be promoted by such restrictions. Examples: the making of suicide a crime, requiring passengers in automobiles to wear seat-belts, requiring a Christian Scientist to receive a blood transfusion. In the case of "impure" paternalism in trying to protect the welfare of a class of persons we find that the only way to do so will involve restricting the freedom of other persons besides those who are benefitted. Now it might be thought that there are no cases of "impure" paternalism since any such case could always be justified on non-paternalistic grounds, i.e. in terms of preventing harm to others. Thus we might ban cigarette manufacturers from continuing to manufacture their product on the grounds that we are preventing them from causing illness to others in the same way that we prevent other manufacturers from releasing pollutants into the atmosphere, thereby causing danger to the members of the community. The difference is, however, that in the former but not the latter case the harm is of such a nature that it could be avoided by those individuals affected if they so chose. The incurring of the harm requires, so to speak, the active co-operation of the victim. It would be mistaken theoretically and hypocritical in practice to assert that our interference in such cases is just like our interference in standard cases of protecting others from harm. At the very least someone interfered with in this way can reply that no one is complaining about his activities. It may be that impure paternalism requires arguments or reasons of a stronger kind in order to be justified since there are persons who are losing a portion of their liberty and they do not even have the solace of having it be done "in their own interest." Of course in some sense, if paternalistic justifications are ever correct then we are protecting others, we are preventing some from injuring others, but it is important to see the differences between this and the standard case.

Paternalism then will always involve limitations on the liberty of some individuals in their own interest but it may also extend to interferences with the liberty of parties whose interests are not in question.

IV

Finally, by way of some more preliminary analysis, I want to distinguish paternalistic interferences with liberty from a related type with which it is often confused. Consider, for example, legislation which forbids employees to work more than, say, 40 hours per week. It is sometimes argued that such legislation is paternalistic for if employees desired such a restriction on their hours of work they could agree among themselves to impose it voluntarily. But because they do not the society imposes its own conception of their best interests upon them by the use of coercion. Hence this is paternalism.

Now it may be that some legislation of this nature is, in fact, paternalistically motivated. I am not denying that. All I want to point out is that there is another possible way of justifying such measures which is not paternalistic in nature. It is not paternalistic because as Mill puts it in a similar context such measures are "required not to overrule the judgment of individuals respecting their own interest, but to give effect to that judgment: they being unable to give effect to it except by concert, which concert again cannot be effectual unless it receives validity and sanction from the law."[2]

The line of reasoning here is a familiar one first found in Hobbes and developed with great sophistication by contemporary economists in the last decade or so. There are restrictions which are in the interests of a class of persons taken collectively but are such that the immediate interest of each individual is furthered by his violating the rule when others adhere to it. In such cases the individuals involved may need the use of compulsion to give effect to their collective judgment of their own interest by guaranteeing each individual compliance by the others. In these cases compulsion is not used to achieve some benefit which is not recognized to be a benefit by those concerned, but rather because it is the only feasible means of achieving some benefit which *is* recognized as such by all concerned. This way of viewing matters provides us with another characterization of paternalism in general. Paternalism might be thought of as the use of coercion to achieve a good which is not recognized as such by those persons for whom the good is intended. Again while this formulation captures the heart of the matter—it is surely what Mill is objecting to in *On Liberty*—the matter is not always quite like that. For example when we force motorcyclists to wear helmets we are trying to promote a good—the protection of the person from injury—which is surely recognized by most of the individuals concerned. It is not that a cyclist doesn't value his bodily integrity; rather, as a supporter of such legislation would put it, he either places, perhaps irrationally, another value or good (freedom from wearing a helmet) above that of physical well-being or, perhaps, while recognizing the danger in the abstract, he either does not fully appreciate it or he underestimates the likelihood of its occurring. But now we are approaching the question of possible justifications of paternalistic measures and the rest of this essay will be devoted to that question.

V

I shall begin for dialectical purposes by discussing Mill's objections to paternalism and then go on to discuss more positive proposals.

An initial feature that strikes one is the absolute nature of Mill's prohibitions against paternalism. It is so unlike the carefully qualified admonitions of Mill and his fellow Utilitarians on other moral issues. He speaks of self-protection as the *sole* end warranting coercion, of the individual's own goals as *never* being a sufficient warrant. . . . The structure of Mill's argument is as follows:

1. Since restraint is an evil the burden of proof is on those who propose such restraint.

2. Since the conduct which is being considered is purely self-regarding, the normal appeal to the protection of the interests of others is not available.

3. Therefore we have to consider whether reasons involving reference to the individual's own good, happiness, welfare, or interests are sufficient to overcome the burden of justification.

4. We either cannot advance the interests of the individual by compulsion, or the attempt to do so involves evil which outweighs the good done.

5. Hence the promotion of the individual's own interests does not provide a sufficient warrant for the use of compulsion.

Clearly the operative premises here is 4 and it is bolstered by claims about the status of the individual as judge and appraiser of his welfare, interests, needs, etc.

With respect to his own feelings and circumstances, the most ordinary man or woman has means of knowledge immeasurably surpassing those that can be possessed by any one else.[3]

He is the man most interested in his own well-being: the interest which any other person, except in cases of strong personal attachment, can have in it, is trifling, compared to that which he himself has.[4]

These claims are used to support the following generalizations concerning the utility of compulsion for paternalistic purposes.

The interferences of society to overrule his judgment and purposes in what only regards himself must be grounded in general presumptions; which may be altogether wrong, and even if right, are as likely as not to be misapplied to individual cases.[5]

But the strongest of all the arguments against the interference of the public with purely personal conduct is that when it does interfere, the odds are that it interferes wrongly and in the wrong place.[6]

All errors which the individual is likely to commit against advice and warning are far outweighed by the evil of allowing others to constrain him to what they deem his good.[7]

Performing the utilitarian calculation by balancing the advantages and disadvantages we find that:

Mankind are greater gainers by suffering each other to live as seems good to themselves, than by compelling each other to live as seems good to the rest.[8]

From which follows the operative premise 4.

. . . [T]his is clearly the main channel of Mill's thought and it is one which has been subjected to vigorous attack from the moment it appeared—most often by fellow Utilitarians. The link that they have usually seized on is, as Fitzjames Stephen put it, the absence of proof that the "mass of adults are so well acquainted with their own interests and so much disposed to pursue them that no compulsion or restraint put upon them by any others for the purpose of promoting their interest can really promote them."[9] . . .

Now it is interesting to note that Mill himself was aware of some of the limitations on the doctrine that the individual is the best judge of his own interests. In his discussion of government intervention in general (even where the intervention does not interfere with liberty but provides alternative institutions to those of the market) after making claims which are parallel to those just discussed, e.g.

> People understand their own business and their own interests better, and care for them more, than the government does, or can be expected to do.[10]

He goes on to an intelligent discussion of the "very large and conspicuous exceptions" to the maxim that:

> Most persons take a juster and more intelligent view of their own interest, and of the means of promoting it that can either be prescribed to them by a general enactment of the legislature, or pointed out in the particular case by a public functionary.[11]

Thus there are things

> of which the utility does not consist in ministering to inclinations, nor in serving the daily uses of life, and the want of which is least felt where the need is greatest. This is peculiarly true of those things which are chiefly useful as tending to raise the character of human beings. The uncultivated cannot be competent judges of cultivation. Those who most need to be made wiser and better, usually desire it least, and, if they desired it, would be incapable of finding the way to it by their own lights.
>
> . . . A second exception to the doctrine that individuals are the best judges of their own interest, is when an individual attempts to decide irrevocably now what will be best for his interest at some future and distant time. The presumption in favor of individual judgment is only legitimate, where the judgment is grounded on actual, and especially on present, personal experience; not where it is formed antecedently to experience, and not suffered to be reversed even after experience has condemned it.[12]

The upshot of these exceptions is that Mill does not declare that there should never be government interference with the economy but rather that

> . . . in every instance, the burden of making out a strong case should be thrown not on those who resist but on those who recommend government interference. Letting alone, in short, should be the general practice: every departure from it, unless required by some great good, is a certain evil.[13]

In short, we get a presumption not an absolute prohibition. The question is why doesn't the argument against paternalism go the same way?

I suggest that the answer lies in seeing that in addition to a purely utilitarian argument Mill uses another as well. . . . A consistent Utilitarian can only argue against paternalism on the grounds that it (as a matter of fact) does not maximize the good. It is always a contingent question that may be refuted by the evidence. But there is also a non-contingent argument which runs through *On Liberty*. When Mill states that "there is a part of the life of every person who has come to years of discretion, within which the individuality of that person ought to rein uncontrolled either by any other person or by the public collectively" he is saying something about what it means to be a person, an autonomous agent. It is because coercing a person for his own good denies this status as an independent entity that Mill objects to it so strongly and in such absolute terms. To be able to choose is a good that is independent of the wisdom of what is chosen. A man's "mode of laying out his existence is the best, not because it is the best in itself, but because it is his own mode."[14]

> It is the privilege and proper condition of a human being, arrived at the maturity of his faculties, to use and interpret experience in his own way.[15]

As further evidence of this line of reasoning in Mill consider the one exception to his prohibition against paternalism.

> In this and most civilised countries, for example, an engagement by which a person should sell himself, or allow himself to be sold, as a slave, would be null and void; neither enforced by law nor by opinion. The ground for thus limiting his power of voluntarily disposing of his own lot in life, is apparent, and is very clearly seen in this extreme case. The reason for not interfering, unless for the sake of others, with a person's voluntary acts, is consideration for his liberty. His voluntary choice is evidence that what he so chooses is desirable, or at least endurable, to him, and his good is on the whole best provided for by allowing him to take his own means of pursuing it. But by selling himself for a slave, he abdicates his liberty; he foregoes any future use of it beyond that single act.
>
> He therefore defeats, in his own case, the very purpose which is the justification of allowing him to dispose of himself. He is no longer free; but is thenceforth in a position which has no longer the presumption in its favour, that would be afforded by his voluntarily remaining in it. The principle of freedom

cannot require that he should be free not to be free. It is not freedom to be allowed to alienate his freedom.[16]

Now leaving aside the fudging on the meaning of freedom in the last line it is clear that part of this argument is incorrect. While it is true that *future* choices of the slave are not reasons for thinking that what he chooses then is desirable for him, what is at issue is limiting his immediate choice; and since this choice is made freely, the individual may be correct in thinking that his interests are best provided for by entering such a contract. But the main consideration for not allowing such a contract is the need to preserve the liberty of the person to make future choices. This gives us a principle—a very narrow one—by which to justify some paternalistic interferences. Paternalism is justified only to preserve a wider range of freedom for the individual in question. How far this principle could be extended, whether it can justify all the cases in which we are inclined upon reflection to think paternalistic measures justified remains to be discussed. What I have tried to show so far is that there are two strains of argument in Mill—one a straight-forward Utilitarian mode of reasoning and one which relies not on the goods which free choice leads to but on the absolute value of the choice itself. The first cannot establish any absolute prohibition but at most a presumption and indeed a fairly weak one given some fairly plausible assumptions about human psychology; the second while a stronger line of argument seems to me to allow on its own grounds a wider range of paternalism than might be suspected. I turn now to a consideration of these matters.

VI

We might begin looking for principles governing the acceptable use of paternalistic power in cases where it is generally agreed that it is legitimate. Even Mill intends his principles to be applicable only to mature individuals, not those in what he calls "non-age." What is it that justifies us in interfering with children? The fact that they lack some of the emotional and cognitive capacities required in order to make fully rational decisions. It is an empirical question to just what extent children have an adequate conception of their own present and future interests but there is not much doubt that there are many deficiencies. For example it is very difficult for a child to defer gratification

for any considerable period of time. Given these deficiencies and given the very real and permanent dangers that may befall the child it becomes not only permissible but even a duty of the parent to restrict the child's freedom in various ways. There is however an important moral limitation on the exercise of such parental power which is provided by the notion of the child eventually coming to see the correctness of his parent's interventions. Parental paternalism may be thought of as a wager by the parent on the child's subsequent recognition of the wisdom of the restrictions. There is an emphasis on what could be called future-oriented consent—on what the child will come to welcome, rather than on what he does welcome.

The essence of this idea has been incorporated by idealist philosophers into various types of "real-will" theory as applied to fully adult persons. Extensions of paternalism are argued for by claiming that in various respects, chronologically mature individuals share the same deficiencies in knowledge, capacity to think rationally, and the ability to carry out decisions that children possess. Hence in interfering with such people we are in effect doing what they would do if they were fully rational. Hence we are not really opposing their will, hence we are not really interfering with their freedom. The dangers of this move have been sufficiently exposed by Berlin in his Two Concepts of Liberty. I see no gain in theoretical clarity nor in practical advantage in trying to pass over the real nature of the interferences with liberty that we impose on others. Still the basic notion of consent is important and seems to me the only acceptable way of trying to delimit an area of justified paternalism.

Let me start by considering a case where the consent is not hypothetical in nature. Under certain conditions it is rational for an individual to agree that others should force him to act in ways in which, at the time of action, the individual may not see as desirable. If, for example, a man knows that he is subject to breaking his resolves when temptation is present, he may ask a friend to refuse to entertain his requests at some later stage.

A classical example is given in the Odyssey when Odysseus commands his men to tie him to the mast and refuse all future orders to be set free, because he knows the power of the Sirens to enchant men with their songs. Here we are on relatively sound ground in later refusing Odysseus' request to be set free. He may even claim to have changed his mind but since it is just such changes that he wishes to guard against we are entitled to ignore them.

A process analogous to this may take place on a social rather than individual basis. An electorate may mandate its representatives to pass legislation which when it comes time to "pay the price" may be unpalatable. I may believe that a tax increase is necessary to halt inflation though I may resent the lower paycheck each month. However in both this case and that of Odysseus the measure to be enforced is specifically requested by the party involved and at some point in time there is genuine consent and agreement on the part of those persons whose liberty is infringed. Such is not the case for the paternalistic measures we have been speaking about. What must be involved here is not consent to specific measures but rather consent to a system of government, run by elected representatives, with an understanding that they may act to safeguard our interests in certain limited ways.

I suggest that since we are all aware of our irrational propensities, deficiencies in cognitive and emotional capacities and avoidable and unavoidable ignorance it is rational and prudent for us to in effect take out "social insurance policies." We may argue for and against proposed paternalistic measures in terms of what fully rational individuals would accept as forms of protection. Now, clearly since the initial agreement is not about specific measures we are dealing with a more-or-less blank check and therefore there have to be carefully defined limits. What I am looking for are certain kinds of conditions which make it plausible to suppose that rational men could reach agreement to limit their liberty even when other men's interests are not affected.

Of course as in any kind of agreement schema there are great difficulties in deciding what rational individuals would or would not accept. Particularly in sensitive areas of personal liberty, there is always a danger of the dispute over agreement and rationality being a disguised version of evaluative and normative disagreement.

Let me suggest types of situations in which it seems plausible to suppose that fully rational individuals would agree to having paternalistic restrictions imposed upon them. It is reasonable to suppose that there are "goods" such as health which any person would want to have in order to pursue his own good—no matter how that good is

conceived. This is an argument that is used in connection with compulsory education for children but it seems to me that it can be extended to other goods which have this character. Then one could agree that the attainment of such goods should be promoted even when not recognized to be such, at the moment, by the individuals concerned.

An immediate difficulty that arises stems from the fact that men are always faced with competing goods and that there may be reasons why even a value such as health—or indeed life—may be overridden by competing values. Thus the problem with the Christian Scientist and blood transfusions. It may be more important for him to reject "impure substances" than to go on living. The difficult problem that must be faced is whether one can give sense to the notion of a person irrationally attaching weights to competing values.

Consider a person who knows the statistical data on the probability of being injured when not wearing seat-belts in an automobile and knows the types and gravity of the various injuries. He also insists that the inconvenience attached to fastening the belt every time he gets in and out of the car outweighs for him the possible risks to himself. I am inclined in this case to think that such a weighing is irrational. Given his life-plans which we are assuming are those of the average person, his interests and commitments already undertaken, I think it is safe to predict that we can find inconsistencies in his calculations at some point. I am assuming that this is not a man who for some conscious or unconscious reasons is trying to injure himself nor is he a man who just likes to "live dangerously." I am assuming that he is like us in all the relevant respects but just puts an enormously high negative value on inconvenience—one which does not seem comprehensible or reasonable.

It is always possible, of course to assimilate this person to creatures like myself. I, also, neglect to fasten my seat-belt and I concede such behavior is not rational but not because I weigh the inconvenience differently from those who fasten the belts. It is just that having made (roughly) the same calculation as everybody else I ignore it in my actions. [Note: a much better case of weakness of the will than those usually given in ethics texts.] A plausible explanation for this deplorable habit is that although I know in some intellectual sense what the probabilities and risks are I do not fully appreciate them in an emotionally genuine manner.

We have two distinct types of situation in which a man acts in a non-rational fashion. In one case he attaches incorrect weights to some of his values; in the other he neglects to act in accordance with his actual preferences and desires. Clearly there is a stronger and more persuasive argument for paternalism in the latter situation. Here we are really not—by assumption—imposing a good on another person. But why may we not extend our interference to what we might call evaluative delusions? After all in the case of cognitive delusions we are prepared, often, to act against the expressed will of the person involved. If a man believes that when he jumps out the window he will float upwards—Robert Nozick's example—would not we detain him, forcibly if necessary? The reply will be that this man doesn't wish to be injured and if we could convince him that he is mistaken as to the consequences of his action he would not wish to perform the action. But part of what is involved in claiming that a man who doesn't fasten his seat-belts is attaching an irrational weight to the inconvenience of fastening them is that if he were to be involved in an accident and severely injured he would look back and admit that the inconvenience wasn't as bad as all that. So there is a sense in which if I could convince him of the consequences of his action he also would not wish to continue his present course of action. Now the notion of consequences being used here is covering a lot of ground. In one case it's being used to indicate what will or can happen as a result of a course of action and in the other it's making a prediction about the future evaluation of the consequences—in the first sense—of a course of action. And whatever the difference between facts and values—whether it be hard and fast or soft and slow—we are genuinely more reluctant to consent to interferences where evaluative differences are the issue. Let me now consider another factor which comes into play in some of these situations which may make an important difference in our willingness to consent to paternalistic restrictions.

Some of the decisions we make are of such a character that they produce changes which are in one or another way irreversible. Situations are created in which it is difficult or impossible to return to anything like the initial stage at which the decision was made. In particular some of these changes will make it impossible to continue to make reasoned choices in the future. I am thinking specifically of decisions which involve taking drugs that are physically or psychologically addictive and those which are destructive of one's mental and physical capacities.

I suggest we think of the imposition of paternalistic interferences in situations of this kind as being a kind of insurance policy which we take out against making decisions which are far-reaching, potentially dangerous and irreversible. . . .

A second class of cases concerns decisions which are made under extreme psychological and sociological pressures. I am not thinking here of the making of the decision as being something one is pressured into—e.g. a good reason for making duelling illegal is that unless this is done many people might have to manifest their courage and integrity in ways in which they would rather not do so—but rather of decisions such as that to commit suicide which are usually made at a point where the individual is not thinking clearly and calmly about the nature of his decision. In addition, of course, this comes under the previous heading of all-too-irrevocable decision. Now there are practical steps which a society could take if it wanted to decrease the possibility of suicide—for example not paying social security benefits to the survivors or as religious institutions do, not allowing such persons to be buried with the same status as natural deaths. I think we may count these as interferences with the liberty of persons to attempt suicide and the question is whether they are justifiable.

Using my argument schema the question is whether rational individuals would consent to such limitations. I see no reason for them to consent to an absolute prohibition but I do think it is reasonable for them to agree to some kind of enforced waiting period. Since we are all aware of the possibility of temporary states, such as great fear or depression, that are inimical to the making of well-informed and rational decisions, it would be prudent for all of us if there were some kind of institutional arrangement whereby we were restrained from making a decision which is (all too) irreversible. What this would be like in practice is difficult to envisage and it may be that if no practical arrangements were feasible then we would have to conclude that there should be no restriction at all on this kind of action. But we might have a "cooling off" period, in much the same way that we now require couples who file for divorce to go through a waiting period. Or, more far-fetched, we might imagine a Suicide Board composed of a psychologist and another member picked by the applicant. The Board would be required to meet and talk with the person proposing to take his life, though its approval would not be required.

A third class of decisions—these classes are not supposed to be disjoint—involves dangers which are either not sufficiently understood or appreciated correctly by the persons involved. Let me illustrate, using the example of cigarette smoking, a number of possible cases.

1. A man may not know the facts—e.g. smoking between 1 and 2 packs a day shortens life expectancy 6.2 years, the costs and pain of the illness caused by smoking, etc.

2. A man may know the facts, wish to stop smoking, but not have the requisite willpower.

3. A man may know the facts but not have them play the correct role in his calculation because, say, he discounts the danger psychologically because it is remote in time and/or inflates the attractiveness of other consequences of his decision which he regards as beneficial.

In case 1 what is called for is education, the posting of warnings, etc. In case 2 there is no theoretical problem. We are not imposing a good on someone who rejects it. We are simply using coercion to enable people to carry out their own goals. (Note: There obviously is a difficulty in that only a subclass of the individuals affected wish to be prevented from doing what they are doing.) In case 3 there is a sense in which we are imposing a good on someone since given his current appraisal of the facts he doesn't wish to be restricted. But in another sense we are not imposing a good since what is being claimed—and what must be shown or at least argued for—is that an accurate accounting on his part would lead him to reject his current course of action. Now we all know that such cases exist, that we are prone to disregard dangers that are only possibilities, that immediate pleasures are often magnified and distorted.

If in addition the dangers are severe and far-reaching we could agree to allowing the state a certain degree of power to intervene in such situations.

The difficulty is in specifying in advance, even vaguely, the class of cases in which intervention will be legitimate.

A related difficulty is that of drawing a line so that it is not the case that all ultra-hazardous activities are ruled out, e.g. mountain-climbing, bullfighting, sports-car racing, etc. There are some risks—even very great ones—which a person is entitled to take with his life.

A good deal depends on the nature of the deprivation—e.g. does it prevent the person from engaging in the activity completely or merely limit his participation—and how important to the nature of the activity is the absence of restriction when this is weighed against the role that the activity plays in the life of the person. In the case of automobile seatbelts, for example, the restriction is trivial in nature, interferes not at all with the use or enjoyment of the activity, and does, I am assuming, considerably reduce a high risk of serious injury. Whereas, for example, making mountain-climbing illegal prevents completely a person engaging in an activity which may play an important role in his life and his conception of the person he is.

In general the easiest cases to handle are those which can be argued about in the terms which Mill thought to be so important—a concern not just for the happiness or welfare, in some broad sense, of the individual but rather a concern for the autonomy and freedom of the person. I suggest that we would be most likely to consent to paternalism in those instances in which it preserves and enhances for the individual his ability to rationally consider and carry out his own decisions.

I have suggested in this essay a number of types of situations in which it seems plausible that rational men would agree to granting the legislative powers of a society the right to impose restrictions on what Mill calls "self-regarding" conduct. However, rational men knowing something about the resources of ignorance, ill-will and stupidity available to the lawmakers of a society—a good case in point is the history of drug legislation in the United States—will be concerned to limit such intervention to a minimum. I suggest in closing two principles designed to achieve this end.

In all cases of paternalistic legislation there must be a heavy and clear burden of proof placed on the authorities to demonstrate the exact nature of the harmful effects (or beneficial consequences) to be avoided (or achieved) and the probability of their occurrence. The burden of proof here is twofold—what lawyers distinguish as the burden of going forward and the burden of persuasion. That the authorities have the burden of going forward means that it is up to them to raise the question and bring forward evidence of the evils to be avoided. Unlike the case of new drugs where the manufacturer must produce some evidence that the drug has been tested and found not harmful, no citizen has to show with respect to self-regarding conduct that it is not harmful or promotes his best interests. In addition the nature and cogency of the evidence for the harmfulness of the course of action must be set at a high level. To paraphrase a formulation of the burden of proof for criminal proceedings—better 10 men ruin themselves than one man be unjustly deprived of liberty.

Finally I suggest a principle of the least restrictive alternative. If there is an alternative way of accomplishing the desired end without restricting liberty then although it may involve great expense, inconvenience, etc. the society must adopt it.

Notes

1. J. S. Mill, *Utilitarianism* and *On Liberty* (Fontana Library Edition, ed. by Mary Warnock, London, 1962), p. 135. All further quotes from Mill are from this edition unless otherwise noted.
2. J. S. Mill, *Principles of Political Economy* (New York: P. F. Collier and Sons, 1900), p. 442.
3. Mill, *Utilitarianism* and *On Liberty*, p. 214.
4. *Ibid.*, p. 206.
5. *Ibid.*, p. 207.
6. *Ibid.*, p. 214.
7. *Ibid.*, p. 207.
8. *Ibid.*, p. 138.
9. J. F. Stephen, *Liberty, Equality, Fraternity* (New York: Henry Holt & Co., n.d.), p. 24.
10. *Ibid.*, p. 33.
11. Mill, *Principles*, II, 458.
12. *Ibid.*, II, 459.
13. *Ibid.*, II, 451.
14. Mill, *Utilitarianism* and *On Liberty*, p. 197.
15. *Ibid.*, p. 186.
16. *Ibid.*, pp. 235–236.

On Telling Patients the Truth

Mack Lipkin

Mack Lipkin provides a defense of the paternalistic practice of withholding information from patients. Lipkin claims it is usually a practical impossibility to tell patients "the whole truth." They usually simply do not possess enough information about how their bodies work to understand the nature of their disease, and their understanding of the terms used by a physician is likely to be quite different from the meaning intended. Besides, some patients do not wish to be told the truth about their illness. Whether it is a matter of telling the truth or of deceiving patients by giving them placebos, the crucial question, according to Lipkin, is "whether the deception was intended to benefit the patient or the doctor."

Should a doctor always tell his patients the truth? In recent years there has been an extraordinary increase in public discussion of the ethical problems involved in this question. But little has been heard from physicians themselves. I believe that gaps in understanding the complex interactions between doctors and patients have led many laymen astray in this debate.

It is easy to make an attractive case for always telling patients the truth. But as L. J. Henderson, the great Harvard physiologist-philosopher of decades ago, commented:

Reprinted by permission from *Newsweek*, 4 June 1979, p. 13.

To speak of telling the truth, the whole truth and nothing but the truth to a patient is absurd. Like absurdity in mathematics, it is absurd simply because it is impossible. . . . The notion that the truth, the whole truth, and nothing but the truth can be conveyed to the patient is a good specimen of that class of fallacies called by Whitehead "the fallacy of misplaced concreteness." It results from neglecting factors that cannot be excluded from the concrete situation and that are of an order of magnitude and relevancy that make it imperative to consider them. Of course, another fallacy is also often involved, the belief that diagnosis and prognosis are more certain than they are. But that is another question.

Words, especially medical terms, inevitably carry different implications for different people. When these words are said in the presence of anxiety-laden illness, there is a strong tendency to hear selectively and with emphases not intended by the doctor. Thus, what the doctor means to convey is obscured.

Indeed, thoughtful physicians know that transmittal of accurate information to patients is often impossible. Patients rarely know how the body functions in health and disease, but instead have inaccurate ideas of what is going on; this hampers the attempts to "tell the truth."

Take cancer, for example. Patients seldom know that while some cancers are rapidly fatal, others never amount to much; some have a cure rate of 99 percent, others less than 1 percent; a cancer may grow rapidly for months and then stop growing for years; may remain localized for years or spread all over the body almost from the beginning; some can be arrested for long periods of time, others not. Thus, one patient thinks of cancer as curable, the next thinks it means certain death.

How many patients understand that "heart trouble" may refer to literally hundreds of different abnormalities ranging in severity from the trivial to the instantly fatal? How many know that the term "arthritis" may refer to dozens of different types of joint involvement? "Arthritis" may raise a vision of the appalling disease that made Aunt Eulalee a helpless invalid until her death years later; the next patient remembers Grandpa grumbling about the damned arthritis as he got up from his chair. Unfortunately but understandably, most people's ideas about the implications of medical terms are based on what they have heard about a few cases.

The news of serious illness drives some patients to irrational and destructive behavior; others handle it sensibly. A distinguished philosopher forestalled my telling him about his cancer by saying, "I want to know the truth. The only thing I couldn't take and wouldn't want to know about is cancer." For two years he had watched his mother die slowly of a painful form of cancer. Several of my physician patients have indicated they would not want to know if they had a fatal illness.

Most patients should be told "the truth" to the extent that they can comprehend it. Indeed, most doctors, like most other people, are uncomfortable with lies. Good physicians, aware that some may be badly damaged by being told more than they want or need to know, can usually ascertain the patient's preference and needs.

Discussions about lying often center about the use of placebos. In medical usage, a "placebo" is a treatment that has no specific physical or chemical action on the condition being treated, but is given to affect symptoms by a psychologic mechanism, rather than a purely physical one. Ethicists believe that placebos necessarily involve a partial or complete deception by the doctor, since the patient is allowed to believe that the treatment has a specific effect. They seem unaware that placebos, far from being inert (except in the rigid pharmacological sense), are among the most powerful agents known to medicine.

Placebos are a form of suggestion, which is a direct or indirect presentation of an idea, followed by an uncritical, i.e., not thought-out, acceptance. Those who have studied suggestion or looked at medical history know its almost unbelievable potency; it is involved to a greater or lesser extent in the treatment of every conscious patient. It can induce or remove almost any kind of feeling or thought. It can strengthen the weak or paralyze the strong; transform sleeping, feeding, or sexual patterns; remove or induce a vast array of symptoms; mimic or abolish the effect of very powerful drugs. It can alter the function of most organs. It can cause illness or a great sense of well-being. It can kill. In fact, doctors often add a measure of suggestion when they prescribe even potent medications for those who also need psychologic support. Like all potent agents, its proper use requires judgment based on experience and skill.

Communication between physician and the apprehensive and often confused patient is delicate and uncertain. Honesty should be evaluated not only in terms of a slavish devotion to language often misinterpreted by the patient, but also in terms of intent. *The crucial question is whether the deception was intended to benefit the patient or the doctor.*

Physicians, like most people, hope to see good results and are disappointed when patients do poorly. Their reputations and their livelihood depend on doing effective work; purely selfish reasons would dictate they do their best for their patients. Most important, all good physicians have a deep sense of responsibility toward those who have entrusted their welfare to them.

As I have explained, it is usually a practical impossibility to tell patients "the whole truth." Moreover, often enough, the ethics of the situation, the true moral responsibility, may demand that the naked facts not be revealed. The now popular complaint that doctors are too authoritarian is misguided more often than not. Some patients who insist on exercising their right to know may be doing themselves a disservice.

Judgment is often difficult and uncertain. Simplistic assertions about telling the truth may not be helpful to patients or physicians in times of trouble.

Lies to the Sick and Dying

Sissela Bok

Sissela Bok reviews three arguments that physicians frequently use to justify not telling the truth to their patients. Bok finds each of them faulty and unpersuasive.

Bok points out that the first of the arguments trades on a confusion between telling "the truth" (that is, everything that is true about a situation) and "truthfulness" (being honest). In effect, the argument asserts that since it is impossible to tell "the truth" to people who are not medical experts, then there is no clear distinction between what is true and what is false. Anything medical said to them is, at best, partially true. When this argument is accepted, Bok claims, the way is open for the physician to decide just how much of "the truth" will be revealed to serve the best interest of the patient.

Are physicians correct in claiming that patients don't want to know the truth? This is an issue that is open to empirical tests. Bok cites studies showing that a large majority of people say they want to be told the truth about themselves, even if they should be diagnosed as having a catastrophic illness.

The last argument examined by Bok holds that information given to a patient might damage the patient (or at least not help the patient); thus, proper health care demands that information not be supplied. This argument also has an empirical aspect and is open to challenge on factual grounds. As Bok observes, the harm associated with the disclosure of bad news and risks is probably greatly overestimated. What is more, very real benefits (such as increased cooperation) are never mentioned.

Bok is not willing to go so far as to say that lying to a patient is never justified. She is primarily concerned with showing that withholding the truth is a serious matter that requires justification in each case.

From *Lying: Moral Choice in Public and Private Life* by Sissela Bok (New York: Pantheon Books, 1978), pp. 221–231, 234–240. Copyright © 1978 by Sissela Bok. Reprinted by permission of Pantheon Books, a division of Random House, Inc. [*Editor's note:* Notes have been renumbered from the original text.]

291

Deception as Therapy

A forty-six-year-old man, coming to a clinic for a routine physical checkup needed for insurance purposes, is diagnosed as having a form of cancer likely to cause him to die within six months. No known cure exists for it. Chemotherapy may prolong life by a few extra months, but will have side effects the physician does not think warranted in this case. In addition, be believes that such therapy should be reserved for patients with a chance for recovery or remission. The patient has no symptoms giving him any reason to believe that he is not perfectly healthy. He expects to take a short vacation in a week.

For the physician, there are now several choices involving truthfulness. Ought he to tell the patient what he has learned, or conceal it? If asked, should he deny it? If he decides to reveal the diagnosis, should he delay doing so until after the patient returns from his vacation? Finally, even if he does reveal the serious nature of the diagnosis, should he mention the possibility of chemotherapy and his reasons for not recommending it in this case? Or should be encourage every last effort to postpone death?

In this particular case, the physician chose to inform the patient of his diagnosis right away. He did not, however, mention the possibility of chemotherapy. A medical student working under him disagreed; several nurses also thought that the patient should have been informed of this possibility. They tried, unsuccessfully, to persuade the physician that this was the patient's right. When persuasion had failed, the student elected to disobey the doctor by informing the patient of the alternative of chemotherapy. After consultation with family members, the patient chose to ask for the treatment.

Doctors confront such choices often and urgently. What they reveal, hold back, or distort will matter profoundly to their patients. Doctors stress with corresponding vehemence their reasons for the distortion or concealment: not to confuse a sick person needlessly, or cause what may well be unnecessary pain or discomfort, as in the case of the cancer patient; not to leave a patient without hope, as in those many cases where the dying are not told the truth about their condition; or to improve the chances of cure, as where unwarranted optimism is expressed about some form of therapy. Doctors use information as part of the therapeutic regimen; it is given out in amounts, in admixtures, and according to timing believed best for patients. Accuracy, by comparison, matters far less.

Lying to patients has, therefore, seemed an especially excusable act. Some would argue that doctors, and *only* doctors, should be granted the right to manipulate the truth in ways so undesirable for politicians, lawyers, and others.[1] Doctors are trained to help patients; their relationship to patients carries special obligations, and they know much more than laymen about what helps and hinders recovery and survival.

Even the most conscientious doctors, then, who hold themselves at a distance from the quacks and the purveyors of false remedies, hesitate to forswear all lying. Lying is usually wrong, they argue, but less so than allowing the truth to harm patients. B. C. Meyer echoes this very common view:

> [O]urs is a profession which traditionally has been guided by a precept that transcends the virtue of uttering truth for truth's sake, and that is, "so far as possible, do no harm."[2]

Truth, for Meyer, may be important, but not when it endangers the health and well-being of patients. This has seemed self-evident to many physicians in the past—so much so that we find very few mentions of veracity in the codes and oaths and writings by physicians through the centuries. This absence is all the more striking as other principles of ethics have been consistently and movingly expressed in the same documents.

The two fundamental principles of doing good and not doing harm—of beneficence and nonmaleficence—are the most immediately relevant to medical practitioners, and the most frequently stressed. To preserve life and good health, to ward off illness, pain, and death—these are the perennial tasks of medicine and nursing. These principles have found powerful expression at all times in the history of medicine. In the Hippocratic Oath physicians promise to:

> use treatment to help the sick . . . but never with a view to injury and wrong-doing.[3]

And a Hindu oath of initiation says:

> Day and night, however thou mayest be engaged, thou shalt endeavor for the relief of patients with all thy heart and soul. Thou shalt not desert or injure the patient even for the sake of thy living.[4]

But there is no similar stress on veracity. It is absent from virtually all oaths, codes, and prayers. The Hippocratic Oath makes no mention of truthfulness to patients about their condition, prognosis, or treatment. Other early codes and prayers are equally silent on the subject. To be sure, they often refer to the confidentiality with which doctors should treat all that patients tell them; but there is no corresponding reference to honesty toward the patient. One of the few who appealed to such a principle was Amattis Lusitanus, a Jewish physician widely known for his skill, who, persecuted, died of the plague in 1568. He published an oath which reads in part:

> If I lie, may I incur the eternal wrath of God
> and of His angel Raphael, and may nothing in
> the medical art succeed for me according to my
> desires.[5]

Later codes continue to avoid the subject. Not even the Declaration of Geneva, adopted in 1948 by the World Medical Association, makes any reference to it. And the Principles of Medical Ethics of the American Medical Association[6] still leave the matter of informing patients up to the physician.

Given such freedom, a physician can decide to tell as much or as little as he wants the patient to know, so long as he breaks no law. In the case of the man mentioned at the beginning of this chapter, some physicians might feel justified in lying for the good of the patient; others might be truthful. Some may conceal alternatives to the treatment they recommend, others not. In each case, they could appeal to the AMA Principles of Ethics. A great many would choose to be able to lie. They would claim that not only can a lie avoid harm for the patient, but that it is also hard to know whether they have been right in the first place in making their pessimistic diagnosis; a "truthful" statement could therefore turn out to hurt patients unnecessarily. The concern for curing and for supporting those who cannot be cured then runs counter to the desire to be completely open. This concern is especially strong where the prognosis is bleak; even more so when patients are so affected by their illness or their medication that they are more dependent than usual, perhaps more easily depressed or irrational.

Physicians know only too well how uncertain a diagnosis or prognosis can be. They know how hard it is to give meaningful and correct answers regarding health and illness. They also know that disclosing their own uncertainty or fears can reduce those benefits that depend upon faith in recovery. They fear, too, that revealing grave risks, no matter how unlikely it is that these will come about, may exercise the pull of the "self-fulfilling prophecy." They dislike being the bearers of uncertain or bad news as much as anyone else. And last, but not least, sitting down to discuss an illness truthfully and sensitively may take much-needed time away from other patients.

These reasons help explain why nurses and physicians and relatives of the sick and dying prefer not to be bound by rules that might limit their ability to suppress, delay, or distort information. This is not to say that they necessarily plan to lie much of the time. They merely want to have the freedom to do so when they believe it wise. And the reluctance to see lying prohibited explains, in turn, the failure of the codes and oaths to come to grips with the problems of truth-telling and lying.

But sharp conflicts are now arising. Doctors no longer work alone with patients. They have to consult with others much more than before; if they choose to lie, the choice may not be met with approval by all who take part in the care of the patient. A nurse expresses the difficulty which results as follows:

> From personal experience I would say that the
> patients who aren't told about their terminal
> illness have so many verbal and mental questions unanswered that many will begin to realize that their illness is more serious than they're
> being told. . . .
> Nurses care for these patients twenty-four
> hours a day compared to a doctor's daily brief
> visit, and it is the nurse many times that the
> patient will relate to, once his underlying fears
> become overwhelming. . . . This is difficult for
> us nurses because being in constant contact
> with patients we can see the events leading up
> to this. The patient continually asks you, "Why
> isn't my pain decreasing?" or "Why isn't the
> radiation treatment easing the pain?" . . . We
> cannot legally give these patients an honest answer as a nurse (and I'm sure I wouldn't want
> to) yet the problem is still not resolved and the
> circle grows larger and larger with the patient
> alone in the middle.[7]

The doctor's choice to lie increasingly involves co-workers in acting a part they find neither humane nor wise. The fact that these problems have not been carefully thought through within the medical profession, nor seriously addressed in medical education, merely serves to intensify the conflicts.[8] Different doctors then respond very differently to patients in exactly similar predicaments. The friction is increased by the fact that relatives often disagree even where those giving medical care to a patient are in accord on how to approach the patient. Here again, because physicians have not worked out to common satisfaction the question of whether relatives have the right to make such requests, the problems are allowed to be haphazardly resolved by each physician as he sees fit.

The Patient's Perspective

The turmoil in the medical profession regarding truth-telling is further augmented by the pressures that patients themselves now bring to bear and by empirical data coming to light. Challenges are growing to the three major arguments for lying to patients: that truthfulness is impossible; that patients do not want bad news; and that truthful information harms them.

The first of these arguments . . . confuses "truth" and "truthfulness" so as to clear the way for occasional lying on grounds supported by the second and third arguments. At this point, we can see more clearly that it is a strategic move intended to discourage the question of truthfulness from carrying much weight in the first place, and thus to leave the choice of what to say and how to say it up to the physician. To claim that "since telling the truth is impossible, there can be no sharp distinction between what is true and what is false"[9] is to try to defeat objections to lying before even discussing them. One need only imagine how such an argument would be received, were it made by a car salesman or a real estate dealer, to see how fallacious it is.

In medicine, however, the argument is supported by a subsidiary point: even if people might ordinarily understand what is spoken to them, patients are often not in a position to do so. This is where paternalism enters in. When we buy cars or houses, the paternalist will argue, we need to have all our wits about us; but when we are ill, we cannot always do so. We need help in making choices, even if help can be given only by keeping us in the dark. And the physician is trained and willing to provide such help.

It is certainly true that some patients cannot make the best choices for themselves when weakened by illness or drugs. But most still can. And even those who are incompetent have a right to have someone—their guardian or spouse perhaps—receive the correct information.

The paternalistic assumption of superiority to patients also carries great dangers for physicians themselves—it risks turning to contempt. The following view was recently expressed in a letter to a medical journal:

> As a radiologist who has been sued, I have reflected earnestly on advice to obtain Informed Consent but have decided to "take the risks without informing the patient" and trust to "God, judge, and jury" rather than evade responsibility through a legal gimmick. . . .
>
> [I]n a general radiologic practice many of our patients are uninformable and we would never get through the day if we had to obtain their consent to every potentially harmful study.
>
> . . . We still have patients with language problems, the uneducated and the unintelligent, the stolid and the stunned who cannot form an Informed Opinion to give an Informed Consent; we have the belligerent and the panicky who do not listen or comprehend. And then there are the Medicare patients who comprise 35 percent of general hospital admissions. The bright ones wearily plead to be left alone. . . . As for the apathetic rest, many of them were kindly described by Richard Bright as not being able to comprehend because "their brains are so poorly oxygenated."[10]

The argument which rejects informing patients because adequate truthful information is impossible in itself or because patients are lacking in understanding must itself be rejected when looked at from the point of view of patients. They know that liberties granted to the most conscientious and altruistic doctors will be exercised also in the "Medicaid Mills"; that the choices thus kept from patients will be exercised by not only competent but incompetent physicians; and that even the best doctors can make choices patients would want to make differently for themselves.

The second argument for deceiving patients refers specifically to giving them news of a frightening or depressing kind. It holds that patients do not, in fact, generally want such information. That they prefer not to have to face up to serious illness and death. On the basis of such a belief, most doctors in a number of surveys stated that they do not, as a rule, inform patients that they have an illness such as cancer.

When studies are made of what patients desire to know, on the other hand, a large majority say that they *would* like to be told of such a diagnosis.[11] All these studies need updating and should be done with larger numbers of patients and nonpatients. But they do show that there is generally a dramatic divergence between physicians and patients on the factual question of whether patients want to know what ails them in cases of serious illness such as cancer. In most of the studies, over 80 percent of the persons asked indicated that they would want to be told.

Sometimes this discrepancy is set aside by doctors who want to retain the view that patients do not want unhappy news. In reality, they claim, the fact that patients say they want it has to be discounted. The more someone asks to know, the more he suffers from fear which will lead to the denial of the information even if it is given. Informing patients is, therefore, useless; they resist and deny having been told what they cannot assimilate. According to this view, empirical studies of what patients say they want are worthless since they do not probe deeply enough to uncover this universal resistance to the contemplation of one's own death.

This view is only partially correct. For some patients, denial is indeed well established in medical experience. A number of patients (estimated at between 15 percent and 25 percent) will give evidence of denial of having been told about their illness, even when they repeatedly ask and are repeatedly informed. And nearly everyone experiences a period of denial at some point in the course of approaching death.[12] Elisabeth Kübler-Ross sees denial as resulting often from premature and abrupt information by a stranger who goes through the process quickly to "get it over with." She holds that denial functions as a buffer after unexpected shocking news, permitting individuals to collect themselves and to mobilize other defenses. She describes prolonged denial in one patient as follows:

> She was convinced that the x-rays were "mixed up"; she asked for reassurance that her pathology report could not possibly be back so soon and that another patient's report must have been marked with her name. When none of this could be confirmed, she quickly asked to leave

the hospital, looking for another physician in the vain hope "to get a better explanation for my troubles." This patient went "shopping around" for many doctors, some of whom gave her reassuring answers, others of whom confirmed the previous suspicion. Whether confirmed or not, she reacted in the same manner, she asked for examination and reexamination. . . .[13]

But to say the denial is universal flies in the face of all evidence. And to take any claim to the contrary as "symptomatic" of deeper denial leaves no room for reasoned discourse. There is no way that such universal denial can be proved true or false. To believe in it is a metaphysical belief about man's condition, not a statement about what patients do and do not want. It is true that we can never completely understand the possibility of our own death, any more than being alive in the first place. But people certainly differ in the degree to which they can approach such knowledge, take it into account in their plans, and make their peace with it.

Montaigne claimed that in order to learn both to live and to die, men have to think about death and be prepared to accept it.[14] To stick one's head in the sand, or to be prevented by lies from trying to discern what is to come, hampers freedom—freedom to consider one's life as a whole, with a beginning, a duration, an end. Some may request to be deceived rather than to see their lives as thus finite; others reject the information which would require them to do so; but most say that they want to know. Their concern for knowing about their condition goes far beyond mere curiosity or the wish to make isolated personal choices in the short time left to them; their stance toward the entire life they have lived, and their ability to give it meaning and completion, are at stake.[15] In lying or withholding the facts which permit such discernment, doctors may reflect their own fears (which, according to one study,[16] are much stronger than those of laymen) of facing questions about the meaning of one's life and the inevitability of death.

Beyond the fundamental deprivation that can result from deception, we are also becoming increasingly aware of all that can befall patients in the course of their illness when information is denied or distorted. Lies place them in a position where they no longer participate in choices concerning their own health, including the choice of whether to be a "patient" in the first place. A terminally ill person who is not informed that his illness is incurable and that he is near death cannot make decisions about the end of his life; about whether or not to enter a hospital, or to have surgery; where and with whom to spend his last days; how to put his affairs in order—these most personal choices cannot be made if he is kept in the dark, or given contradictory hints and clues. . . .

The reason why even doctors who recognize a patient's right to have information might still not provide it brings us to the third argument against telling all patients the truth. It holds that the information given might hurt the patient and the concern for the right to such information is therefore a threat to proper health care. A patient, these doctors argue, may wish to commit suicide after being given discouraging news, or suffer a cardiac arrest, or simply cease to struggle, and thus not grasp the small remaining chance for recovery. And even where the outlook for a patient is very good, the disclosure of a minute risk can shock some patients or cause them to reject needed protection such as a vaccination or antibiotics.

The factual basis for this argument has been challenged from two points of view. The damages associated with the disclosure of sad news or risks are rarer than physicians believe; and the *benefits* which result from being informed are more substantial, even measurably so. Pain is tolerated more easily, recovery from surgery is quicker, and cooperation with therapy is greatly improved. The attitude that "what you don't know won't hurt you" is proving unrealistic; it is what patients do not know but vaguely suspect that causes them corrosive worry.

It is certain that no answers to this question of harm from information are the same for all patients. If we look, first, at the fear expressed by physicians that informing patients of even remote or unlikely risks connected with a drug prescription or operation might shock some and make others refuse the treatment that would have been best for them, it appears to be unfounded for the great majority of patients. Studies show that very few patients respond to being told of such risks by withdrawing their consent to the procedure and that those who do withdraw are the very ones who might well have been upset enough to sue the physician had they not been asked to consent beforehand.[17] It is pos-

sible that on even rarer occasions especially susceptible persons might manifest physical deterioration from shock; some physicians have even asked whether patients who die after giving informed consent to an operation, but before it actually takes place, somehow expire because of the information given to them.[18] While such questions are unanswerable in any one case, they certainly argue in favor of caution, a real concern for the person to whom one is recounting the risks he or she will face, and sensitivity to all signs of distress.

The situation is quite different when persons who are already ill, perhaps already quite weak and discouraged, are told of a very serious prognosis. Physicians fear that such knowledge may cause the patients to commit suicide, or to be frightened or depressed to the point that their illness takes a downward turn. The fear that great numbers of patients will commit suicide appears to be unfounded.[19] And if some do, is that a response so unreasonable, so much against the patient's best interest that physicians ought to make it a reason for concealment or lies? Many societies have allowed suicide in the past; our own has decriminalized it; and some are coming to make distinctions among the many suicides which ought to be prevented if at all possible, and those which ought to be respected.[20]

Another possible response to very bleak news is the triggering of physiological mechanisms which allow death to come more quickly—a form of giving up or of preparing for the inevitable, depending on one's outlook. Lewis Thomas, studying responses in humans and animals, holds it not unlikely that:

> . . . there is a pivotal movement at some stage in the body's reaction to injury or disease, maybe in aging as well, when the organism concedes that it is finished and the time for dying is at hand, and at this moment the events that lead to death are launched, as a coordinated mechanism. Functions are then shut off, in sequence, irreversibly, and, while this is going on, a neural mechanism, held ready for this occasion, is switched on. . . .[21]

Such a response may be appropriate, in which case it makes the moments of dying as peaceful as those who have died and been resuscitated so often testify. But it may also be brought on inappropriately, when the organism could have lived on, perhaps even induced malevolently, by external acts intended to kill. Thomas speculates that some of the deaths resulting from "hexing" are due to such responses. Levi-Strauss describes deaths from exorcism and the casting of spells in ways which suggest that the same process may then be brought on by the community.[22]

It is not inconceivable that unhappy news abruptly conveyed, or a great shock given to someone unable to tolerate it, could also bring on such a "dying response," quite unintended by the speaker. There is every reason to be cautious and to try to know ahead of time how susceptible a patient might be to the accidental triggering—however rare—of such a response. One has to assume, however, that most of those who have survived long enough to be in a situation where their informed consent is asked have a very robust resistance to such accidental triggering of processes leading to death. . . .

Apart from the possible harm from information, we are coming to learn much more about the benefits it can bring patients. People follow instructions more carefully if they know what their disease is and why they are asked to take medications; any benefits from those procedures are therefore much more likely to come about. Similarly, people recover faster from surgery and tolerate pain with less medication if they understand what ails them and what can be done for them.

Respect and Truthfulness

Taken all together, the three arguments defending lies to patients stand on much shakier ground as a counterweight to the right to be informed than is often thought. The common view that many patients cannot understand, do not want, and may be harmed by, knowledge of their condition, and that lying to them is either morally neutral or even to be recommended, must be set aside. Instead, we have to make a more complex comparison. Over against the right of patients to knowledge concerning themselves, the medical and psychological benefits to them from this knowledge, the unnecessary and sometimes harmful treatment to which they can be subjected if ignorant, and the harm to physicians, their profession, and other patients from deceptive practices, we have to set a severely restricted and narrowed paternalistic view—that *some* patients cannot understand, *some*

do not want, and *some* may be harmed by, knowledge of their condition, and that they ought not to have to be treated like everyone else if this is not in their best interest.

Such a view is persuasive. A few patients openly request not to be given bad news. Others give clear signals to that effect, or are demonstrably vulnerable to the shock or anguish such news might call forth. Can one not in such cases infer implied consent to being deceived?

Concealment, evasion, withholding of information may at times be necessary. But if someone contemplates lying to a patient or concealing the truth, the burden of proof must shift. It must rest, here, as with all deception, on those who advocate it in any one instance. They must show why they fear a patient may be harmed or how they know that another cannot cope with the truthful knowledge. A decision to deceive must be seen as a very unusual step, to be talked over with colleagues and others who participate in the care of the patient. Reasons must be set forth and debated, alternatives weighed carefully. At all times, the correct information must go to *someone* closely related to the patient.

The law already permits doctors to withhold information from patients where it would clearly hurt their health. But this privilege has been sharply limited by the courts. Certainly it cannot be interpreted so broadly as to permit a general practice of deceiving patients "for their own good." Nor can it be made to include cases where patients might calmly decide, upon hearing their diagnosis, not to go ahead with the therapy their doctor recommends.[23] Least of all can it justify silence or lies to large numbers of patients merely on grounds that it is not always easy to tell what a patient wants.

For the great majority of patients, on the contrary, the goal must be disclosure, and the atmosphere one of openness. But it would be wrong to assume that patients can therefore be told abruptly about a serious diagnosis—that, so long as openness exists, there are no further requirements of humane concern in such communication. Dr. Cicely Saunders, who runs the well-known St. Christopher's Hospice in England, describes the sensitivity and understanding which are needed:

> Every patient needs an explanation of his
> illness that will be understandable and
> convincing to him if he is to cooperate in his

treatment or be relieved of the burden of unknown fears. This is true whether it is a question of giving a diagnosis in a hopeful situation or of confirming a poor prognosis.

The fact that a patient does not ask does not mean that he has no questions. One visit or talk is rarely enough. It is only by waiting and listening that we can gain an idea of what we should be saying. Silences and gaps are often more revealing than words as we try to learn what a patient is facing as he travels along the constantly changing journey of his illness and his thoughts about it.

. . . So much of the communication will be without words or given indirectly. This is true of all real meeting with people but especially true with those who are facing, knowingly or not, difficult or threatening situations. It is also particularly true of the very ill.

The main argument against a policy of deliberate, invariable denial of unpleasant facts is that it makes such communication extremely difficult, if not impossible. Once the possibility of talking frankly with a patient has been admitted, it does not mean that this will always take place, but the whole atmosphere is changed. We are then free to wait quietly for clues from each patient, seeing them as individuals from whom we can expect intelligence, courage, and individual decisions. They will feel secure enough to give us these clues when they wish.[24]

Above all, truthfulness with those who are suffering does not mean that they should be deprived of all hope: hope that there is a chance of recovery, however small; nor of reassurance that they will not be abandoned when they most need help.

Much needs to be done, however, if the deceptive practices are to be eliminated, and if concealment is to be restricted to the few patients who ask for it or those who can be shown to be harmed by openness. The medical profession has to address this problem.

Notes

1. Plato, *The Republic*, 389 b.

2. B. C. Meyer, "Truth and the Physician," *Bulletin of the New York Academy of Medicine* 45 (1969): 59–71.

3. W. H. S. Jones, trans., *Hippocrates*, Loeb Classical Library (Cambridge, Mass.: Harvard University Press, 1923), p. 164.

4. Reprinted in M. B. Etziony, *The Physician's Creed: An Anthology of Medical Prayers. Oaths and Codes of Ethics* (Springfield, Ill.: Charles C Thomas, 1973), pp. 15–18.

5. See Harry Friedenwald, "The Ethics of the Practice of Medicine from the Jewish Point of View," *Johns Hopkins Hospital Bulletin*, no. 318 (August 1917), pp. 256–61.

6. "Ten Principles of Medical Ethics," *Journal of the American Medical Association* 164 (1957): 1119–20.

7. Mary Barrett, letter, *Boston Globe*, 16 November 1976, p. 1.

8. Though a minority of physicians have struggled to bring them to our attention. See Thomas Percival, *Medical Ethics*, 3d ed. (Oxford: John Henry Parker, 1849), pp. 132–41; Worthington Hooker, *Physician and Patient* (New York: Baker and Scribner, 1849), pp. 357–82; Richard C. Cabot, "Teamwork of Doctor and Patient Through the Annihilation of Lying," in *Social Service and the Art of Healing* (New York: Moffat, Yard & Co., 1909), pp. 116–70; Charles C. Lund, "The Doctor, the Patient, and the Truth," *Annals of Internal Medicine* 24 (1946): 955; Edmund Davies, "The Patient's Right to Know the Truth," *Proceedings of the Royal Society of Medicine* 66 (1973): 533–36.

9. Lawrence Henderson, "Physician and Patient as a Social System," *New England Journal of Medicine* 212 (1955).

10. Nicholas Demy, Letter to the Editor, *Journal of the American Medical Association* 217 (1971): 696–97.

11. For the views of physicians, see Donald Oken, "What to Tell Cancer Patients," *Journal of the American Medical Association* 175 (1961): 1120–28; and tabulations in Robert Veatch, *Death, Dying, and the Biological Revolution* (New Haven and London: Yale University Press, 1976), pp. 229–38. For the view of patients, see Veatch, ibid; Jean Aitken-Swan and E. C. Easson, "Reactions of Cancer Patients on Being Told Their Diagnosis," *British Medical Journal*, 1959, pp. 779–83; Jim McIntosh, "Patients' Awareness and Desire for Information About Diagnosed but Undisclosed Malignant Disease," *The Lancet* 7 (1976): 300–303; William D. Kelly and Stanley R. Friesen, "Do Cancer Patients Want to Be Told?," *Surgery* 27 (1950): 822–26.

12. See Avery Weisman, *On Dying and Denying* (New York: Behavioral Publications, 1972); Elisabeth Kübler-Ross, *On Death and Dying* (New York: The Macmillan Co., 1969); Ernest Becker, *The Denial of Death* (New York: Free Press, 1973); Philippe Ariès, *Western Attitudes Toward Death*, trans. Patricia M. Ranum (Baltimore and London: Johns Hopkins University Press, 1974); and Sigmund Freud, "Negation," *Collected Papers*, ed. James Strachey (London: Hogarth Press, 1950), 5: 181–85.

13. Kübler-Ross, *On Death and Dying*, p. 34.

14. Michel de Montaigne, *Essays*, bk. 1, chap. 20.

15. It is in literature that these questions are most directly raised. Two recent works where they are taken up with striking beauty and simplicity are May Sarton, *As We Are Now* (New York: W. W. Norton & Co., 1973); and Freya Stark, *A Peak in Darien* (London: John Murray, 1976).

16. Herman Feifel *et al.*, "Physicians Consider Death," *Proceedings of the American Psychoanalytical Association*, 1967, pp. 201–2.

17. See Ralph Alfidi, "Informed Consent: A Study of Patient Reaction," *Journal of the American Medical Association* 216 (1971): 1325–29.

18. See Steven R. Kaplan, Richard A. Greenwald, and Arvey I. Rogers, Letter to the Editor, *New England Journal of Medicine* 296 (1977): 1127.

19. Oken, "What to Tell Cancer Patients"; Veatch, *Death, Dying, and the Biological Revolution;* Weisman, *On Dying and Denying.*

20. Norman L. Cantor, "A Patient's Decision to Decline Life-Saving Treatment: Bodily Integrity Versus the Preservation of Life," *Rutgers Law Review* 26: 228–64; Danielle Gourevitch, "Suicide Among the Sick in Classical Antiquity," *Bulletin of the History of Medicine* 18 (1969): 501–18; for bibliography, see Bok, "Voluntary Euthanasia."

21. Lewis Thomas, "A Meliorist View of Disease and Dying," *The Journal of Medicine and Philosophy* 1 (1976); 212–21.

22. Claude Lévi-Strauss, *Structural Anthropology* (New York: Basic Books, 1963), p. 167; see also Eric Cassell, "Permission to Die," in John Behnke and Sissela Bok, eds., *The Dilemmas of Euthanasia* (New York: Doubleday, Anchor Press, 1975), pp. 121–31.

23. See Charles Fried, *Medical Experimentation: Personal Integrity and Social Policy* (Amsterdam and Oxford: North Holland Publishing Co., 1974), pp. 20–24.

24. Cicely M. S. Saunders, "Telling Patients," in S. J. Reiser, W. J. Dyck, A. J. Curran, *Ethics in Medicine* (Cambridge, Mass.: M.I.T. Press, 1977), pp. 238–40.

Confidentiality in Medicine—A Decrepit Concept

Mark Siegler

Mark Siegler calls attention to the impossibility of preserving the confidentiality traditionally associated with the physician-patient relationship. In the modern hospital, a great many people have legitimate access to a patient's chart and so to all medical, social, and financial information the patient has provided. Yet the loss of confidentiality is a threat to good medical care. Confidentiality protects a patient at a time of vulnerability and promotes the trust that is necessary for effective diagnosis and treatment. Siegler concludes by suggesting some possible solutions for preserving confidentiality while meeting the needs of others to know certain things about the patient.

Medical confidentiality, as it has traditionally been understood by patients and doctors, no longer exists. This ancient medical principle, which has been included in every physician's oath and code of ethics since Hippocratic times, has become old, worn-out, and useless; it is a decrepit concept. Efforts to preserve it appear doomed to failure and often give rise to more problems than solutions. Psychiatrists have tacitly acknowledged the impossibility of ensuring the confidentiality of medical records by choosing to establish a separate, more secret record. The following case illustrates how the confidentiality principle is compromised systematically in the course of routine medical care.

A patient of mine with mild chronic obstructive pulmonary disease was transferred from the surgical intensive-care unit to a surgical nursing floor two days after an elective cholecystectomy. On the day of transfer, the patient saw a respiratory therapist writing in his medical chart (the therapist was recording the results of an arterial blood gas analysis) and became concerned about the confidentiality of his hospital records. The patient threatened to leave the hospital prematurely unless I could guarantee that the confidentiality of his hospital record would be respected.

The patient's complaint prompted me to enumerate the number of persons who had both access to his hospital record and a reason to examine it. I was amazed to learn that at least 25 and possibly as many as 100 health professionals and administrative personnel at our university hospital had access

Supported by a grant (OSS-8018097) from the National Science Foundation and by the National Endowment for the Humanities. The views expressed are those of the author and do not necessarily reflect those of the National Science Foundation or the National Endowment for the Humanities.

to the patient's record and that all of them had a legitimate need, indeed a professional responsibility, to open and use that chart. These persons included 6 attending physicians (the primary physician, the surgeon, the pulmonary consultant, and others); 12 house officers (medical, surgical, intensive-care unit, and "covering" house staff); 20 nursing personnel (on three shifts); 6 respiratory therapists; 3 nutritionists; 2 clinical pharmacists; 15 students (from medicine, nursing, respiratory therapy, and clinical pharmacy); 4 unit secretaries; 4 hospital financial officers; and 4 chart reviewers (utilization review, quality assurance review, tissue review, and insurance auditor). It is of interest that this patient's problem was straightforward, and he therefore did not require many other technical and support services that the modern hospital provides. For example, he did not need multiple consultants and fellows, such specialized procedures as dialysis, or social workers, chaplains, physical therapists, occupational therapists, and the like.

Upon completing my survey I reported to the patient that I estimated that at least 75 health professionals and hospital personnel had access to his medical record. I suggested to the patient that these people were all involved in providing or supporting his health-care services. They were, I assured him, working for him. Despite my reassurances the patient was obviously distressed and retorted, "I always believed that medical confidentiality was part of a doctor's code of ethics. Perhaps you should tell me just what you people mean by 'confidentiality'!"

Two Aspects of Medical Confidentiality

Confidentiality and Third-Party Interests

Previous discussions of medical confidentiality usually have focused on the tension between a physician's responsibility to keep information divulged by patients secret and a physician's legal and moral duty, on occasion, to reveal such confidences to third parties, such as families, employers, public health authorities, or police authorities. In all these instances, the central question relates to the stringency of the physician's obligation to maintain patient confidentiality when the health, well-being, and safety of identifiable others or of society in general would be threatened by a failure to reveal information about the patient. The tension in such cases is between the good of the patient and the good of others.

Confidentiality and the Patient's Interest

As the example above illustrates, further challenges to confidentiality arise because the patient's personal interest in maintaining confidentiality comes into conflict with his personal interest in receiving the best possible health care. Modern high-technology health care is available principally in hospitals (often, teaching hospitals), requires many trained and specialized workers (a "health-care team"), and is very costly. The existence of such teams means that information that previously had been held in confidence by an individual physician will now necessarily be disseminated to many members of the team. Furthermore, since health-care teams are expensive and few patients can afford to pay such costs directly, it becomes essential to grant access to the patient's medical record to persons who are responsible for obtaining third-party payment. These persons include chart reviewers, financial officers, insurance auditors, and quality-of-care assessors. Finally, as medicine expands from a narrow, disease-based model to a model that encompasses psychological, social, and economic problems, not only will the size of the health-care team and medical costs increase, but more sensitive information (such as one's personal habits and financial condition) will now be included in the medical record and will no longer be confidential.

The point I wish to establish is that hospital medicine, the rise of health-care teams, the existence of third-party insurance programs, and the expanding limits of medicine all appear to be responses to the wishes of people for better and more comprehensive medical care. But each of these developments necessarily modifies our traditional understanding of medical confidentiality.

The Role of Confidentiality in Medicine

Confidentiality serves a dual purpose in medicine. In the first place, it acknowledges respect for the patient's sense of individuality and privacy. The patient's most personal physical and psychological secrets are kept confidential in order to decrease a sense of shame and vulnerability. Secondly, confidentiality is important in improving the patient's health care—a basic goal of medicine. The promise of confidentiality permits people to trust (i.e., have confidence) that information revealed to a physician in the course of a medical encounter will not be disseminated further. In this way patients are encouraged to communicate honestly and forthrightly with their doctors. This bond of trust between patient and doctor is vitally important both in the diagnostic process (which relies on an accurate history) and subsequently in the treatment phase, which often depends as much on the patient's trust in the physician as it does on medications and surgery. These two important functions of confidentiality are as important now as they were in the past. They will not be supplanted entirely either by improvements in medical technology or by recent changes in relations between some patients and doctors toward a rights-based, consumerist model.

Possible Solutions to the Confidentiality Problem

First of all, in all nonbureaucratic, noninstitutional medical encounters—that is, in the millions of doctor-patient encounters that take place in physicians' offices, where more privacy can be preserved—meticulous care should be taken to guarantee that patients' medical and personal information will be kept confidential.

Secondly, in such settings as hospitals or large-scale group practices, where many persons have opportunities to examine the medical record, we should aim to provide access only to those who have "a need to know." This could be accomplished through such administrative changes as dividing the entire record into several sections—for example, a medical and financial section—and permitting only health professionals access to the medical information.

The approach favored by many psychiatrists—that of keeping a psychiatric record separate from the general medical record—is an understandable strategy but one that is not entirely satisfactory and that should not be generalized. The keeping of separate psychiatric records implies that psychiatry and medicine are different undertakings and thus drives deeper the wedge between them and between physical and psychological illness. Furthermore, it is often vitally important for internists or

surgeons to know that a patient is being seen by a psychiatrist or is taking a particular medication. When separate records are kept, this information may not be available. Finally, if generalized, the practice of keeping a separate psychiatric record could lead to the unacceptable consequence of having a separate record for each type of medical problem.

Patients should be informed about what is meant by "medical confidentiality." We should establish the distinction between information about the patient that generally will be kept confidential regardless of the interest of third parties and information that will be exchanged among members of the health-care team in order to provide care for the patient. Patients should be made aware of the large number of persons in the modern hospital who require access to the medical record in order to serve the patient's medical and financial interests.

Finally, at some point most patients should have an opportunity to review their medical record and to make informed choices about whether their entire record is to be available to everyone or whether certain portions of the record are privileged and should be accessible only to their principal physician or to others designated explicitly by the patient. This approach would rely on traditional informed-consent procedural standards and might permit the patient to balance the personal value of medical confidentiality against the personal value of high-technology, team health care. There is no reason that the same procedure should not be used with psychiatric records instead of the arbitrary system now employed, in which everything related to psychiatry is kept secret.

Afterthought: Confidentiality and Indiscretion

There is one additional aspect of confidentiality that is rarely included in discussions of the subject. I am referring here to the wanton, often inadvertent, but avoidable exchanges of confidential information that occur frequently in hospital rooms, elevators, cafeterias, doctors' offices, and at cocktail parties. Of course, as more people have access to medical information about the patient the potential for this irresponsible abuse of confidentiality increases geometrically.

Such mundane breaches of confidentiality are probably of greater concern to most patients than the broader issue of whether their medical records may be entered into a computerized data bank or whether a respiratory therapist is reviewing the results of an arterial blood gas determination. Somehow, privacy is violated and a sense of shame is heightened when intimate secrets are revealed to people one knows or is close to—friends, neighbors, acquaintances, or hospital roommates—rather than when they are disclosed to an anonymous bureaucrat sitting at a computer terminal in a distant city or to a health professional who is acting in an official capacity.

I suspect that the principles of medical confidentiality, particularly those reflected in most medical codes of ethics, were designed principally to prevent just this sort of embarrassing personal indiscretion rather than to maintain (for social, political, or economic reasons) the absolute secrecy of doctor-patient communications. In this regard, it is worth noting that Percival's Code of Medical Ethics

(1803) includes the following admonition: "Patients should be interrogated concerning their complaint in a tone of voice which cannot be overheard" [Leake, C. D., ed., *Percival's Medical Ethics.* Baltimore: Williams and Wilkins, 1927]. We in the medical profession frequently neglect these simple courtesies.

Conclusion

The principle of medical confidentiality described in medical codes of ethics and still believed in by patients no longer exists. In this respect, it is a decrepit concept. Rather than perpetuate the myth of confidentiality and invest energy vainly to preserve it, the public and the profession would be better served if they devoted their attention to determining which aspects of the original principle of confidentiality are worth retaining. Efforts could then be directed to salvaging those.

Decision in the *Tarasoff* Case

The Supreme Court of California

This ruling of the California Supreme Court has been of particular concern to psychiatrists and psychotherapists. The court ruled that therapists at the student health center of the University of California, Berkeley, were negligent in their duty to warn Tatiana Tarasoff that Prosenjit Poddar, one of their patients, had threatened her life. Although the therapists reported the threat to the police, Tarasoff herself was not warned, and she was murdered by Poddar.

The ruling and dissenting opinions in this case address the issue of balancing the state's interest in protecting its citizens from injury against the interest of patients and therapists in preserving confidentiality. Does a therapist have a duty to warn at all? Should a patient be informed that not everything he tells his therapist will be held in confidence? Is a therapist obliged to seek a court order committing a patient involuntarily to an institution, if the patient poses a threat the therapist deems to be seriously motivated? (See the Juan Gonzalez Case Presentation for an example of how these issues may arise in practice.)

In the majority opinion, Justice Matthew O. Tobriner argues that a therapist whose patient poses a serious danger to someone has a legal obligation to use "reasonable care" to protect the intended victim. This may involve warning the person, but if it is reasonable to believe that a warning is not enough, then the therapist has a duty to seek to have the patient involuntarily institutionalized.

In the dissenting opinion, Justice William P. Clark argues that the law should not interfere with the confidentiality between therapist and patient for three reasons: (1) without the guarantee of confidentiality, those needing treatment may not seek it; (2) violence may increase, because those needing treatment were deterred from getting it; and (3) therapists, to protect their interest, will seek more involuntary commitments, thus violating the rights of their patients and undermining the trust needed for effective treatment.

Poddar was convicted of second-degree murder. The conviction was overturned on appeal, on the grounds that the jury had not been properly instructed. The state decided against a second trial, and Poddar was released on the condition that he return to India. Although Poddar escaped punishment for his actions, the issues of confidentiality raised by the case have yet to be satisfactorily resolved.

Justice Matthew O. Tobriner, Majority Opinion

On October 27, 1969, Prosenjit Poddar killed Tatiana Tarasoff. Plaintiffs, Tatiana's parents, allege that two months earlier Poddar confided his intention to kill Tatiana to Dr. Lawrence Moore, a psychologist employed by the Cowell Memorial Hospital at the University of California at Berkeley. They allege that on Moore's request, the campus police briefly detained Poddar, but released him when he appeared rational. They further claim that Dr. Harvey Powelson, Moore's superior, then directed that no further action be taken to detain Poddar. No one warned plaintiffs of Tatiana's peril. . . .

We shall explain that defendant therapists cannot escape liability merely because Tatiana herself was not their patient. When a therapist determines, or pursuant to the standards of his profession should determine, that his patient presents a serious danger of violence to another, he incurs an obligation to use reasonable care to protect the intended victim against such danger. The discharge of this duty may require the therapist to take one or more of various steps, depending upon the nature of the case. Thus it may call for him to warn the intended victim or others likely to apprise the victim of the danger, to notify the police, or to take whatever other steps are reasonably necessary under the circumstances. . . .

1. Plaintiffs' Complaints.

. . . Plaintiffs' first cause of action, entitled "Failure to Detain a Dangerous Patient," alleges that on August 20, 1969, Poddar was a voluntary outpatient receiving therapy at Cowell Memorial Hospital. Poddar informed Moore, his therapist, that he was going to kill an unnamed girl, readily identifiable as Tatiana, when she returned home from spending the summer in Brazil. Moore, with the concurrence of Dr. Gold, who had initially examined Poddar, and Dr. Yandell, assistant to the director of the department of psychiatry, decided that Poddar should be committed for observation in a mental hospital. Moore orally notified Officers Atkinson and Teel of the campus police that he would request commitment. He then sent a letter to Police Chief William Beall requesting the assistance of the police department in securing Poddar's confinement.

Officers Atkinson, Brownrigg, and Halleran took Poddar into custody, but, satisfied that Poddar was rational, released him on his promise to stay away from Tatiana. Powelson, director of the department of psychiatry at Cowell Memorial Hospital, then asked the police to return Moore's letter, directed that all copies of the letter and notes that Moore had taken as therapist be destroyed, and "ordered no action to place Prosenjit Poddar in 72-hour treatment and evaluation facility."

Plaintiffs' second cause of action, entitled "Failure to Warn On a Dangerous Patient," incorporates the allegations of the first cause of action, but adds the assertion that defendants negligently permitted Poddar to be released from police custody without "notifying the parents of Tatiana Tarasoff that their daughter was in grave danger from Prosenjit Poddar." Poddar persuaded Tatiana's brother to share an apartment with him near Tatiana's residence; shortly after her return from Brazil, Poddar went to her residence and killed her. . . .

2. Plaintiffs Can State a Cause of Action Against Defendant Therapists for Negligent Failure to Protect Tatiana.

The second cause of action can be amended to allege that Tatiana's death proximately resulted from defendants' negligent failure to warn Tatiana or others likely to apprise her of her danger. Plaintiffs contend that as amended, such allegations of negligence and proximate causation, with resulting damages, establish a cause of action. Defendants, however, contend that in the circumstances of the present case they owed no duty of care to Tatiana or her parents and that, in the absence of such duty, they were free to act in careless disregard of Tatiana's life and safety.

. . . In analyzing this issue, we bear in mind that legal duties are not discoverable facts of nature, but merely conclusory expressions that, in cases of a particular type, liability should be imposed for damage done. As stated in *Dillon* v. *Legg* (1968): . . . "The assertion that liability must . . . be denied because defendant bears no 'duty' to plaintiff 'begs the essential question—whether the plaintiff's interests are entitled to legal protection against the defendant's conduct. . . . [Duty] is not sacrosanct in itself, but only an expression of the sum total of those considerations of policy which lead the law to say that the particular plaintiff is entitled to protection.'" . . .

In the landmark case of *Rowland* v. *Christian* (1968), . . . Justice Peters recognized that liability should be imposed "for an injury occasioned to another by his want of ordinary care or skill" as expressed in section 1714 of the Civil Code. Thus, Justice Peters, quoting from *Heaven* v. *Pender* (1883) . . . stated: "'whenever one person is by circumstances placed in such a position with regard to another . . . that if he did not use ordinary care and skill in his own conduct . . . he would cause danger of injury to the person or property of the other, a duty arises to use ordinary care and skill to avoid such danger.'"

. . . We depart from "this fundamental principle" only upon the "balancing of a number of considerations"; major ones "are the foreseeability of harm to the plaintiff, the degree of certainty that the plaintiff suffered injury, the closeness of the connection between the defendant's conduct and the injury suffered, the moral blame attached to the defendant's conduct, the policy of preventing future harm, the extent of the burden to the defendant and consequences to the community of imposing a duty to exercise care with resulting liability for breach, and the availability, cost and prevalence of insurance for the risk involved."

The most important of these considerations in establishing duty is foreseeability. As a general principle, a "defendant owes a duty of care to all persons who are foreseeably endangered by his conduct, with respect to all risks which make the conduct unreasonably dangerous." As we shall explain, however, when the avoidance of foreseeable harm requires a defendant to control the conduct of another person, or to warn of such conduct, the common law has traditionally imposed liability only if the defendant bears some special relationship to the dangerous person or to the potential victim. Since the relationship between a therapist and his patient satisfies this requirement, we need not here decide whether foreseeability alone is sufficient to create a duty to exercise reasonable care to protect a potential victim of another's conduct. . . .

. . . Although plaintiffs' pleadings assert no special relation between Tatiana and defendant therapists, they establish as between Poddar and defendant therapists the special relation that arises between a patient and his doctor or psychotherapist. Such a relationship may support affirmative duties for the benefit of third persons. Thus, for example, a hospital must exercise reasonable care to control the behavior of a patient which may endanger other persons. A doctor must also warn a patient if the patient's condition or medication renders certain conduct, such as driving a car, dangerous to others.

. . . Although the California decisions that recognize this duty have involved cases in which the defendant stood in a special relationship *both* to the victim and to the person whose conduct created the danger, we do not think that the duty should logically be constricted to such situations. Decisions of other jurisdictions hold that the single relationship of a doctor to his patient is sufficient to support the duty to exercise reasonable care to protect others against dangers emanating from the patient's illness. The courts hold that a doctor is liable to persons infected by his patient if he negligently fails to diagnose a contagious disease, . . . or, having diagnosed the illness, fails to warn members of the patient's family.

Since it involved a dangerous mental patient, the decision in *Merchants Nat. Bank & Trust Co. of Fargo* v. *United States* . . . comes closer to the issue. The Veterans Administration arranged for the patient to work on a local farm, but did not inform the farmer of the man's background. The farmer consequently permitted the patient to come and go freely during nonworking hours; the patient borrowed a car, drove to his wife's residence and killed her. Notwithstanding the lack of any "special relationship" between the Veterans Administration and the wife, the court found the Veterans Administration liable for the wrongful death of the wife.

In their summary of the relevant rulings Fleming and Maximov conclude that the "case law should dispel any notion that to impose on the therapists a duty to take precautions for the safety of persons threatened by a patient, where due care so requires, is in any way opposed to contemporary ground rules on the duty relationship. On the contrary, there now seems to be sufficient authority to support the conclusion that by entering into a doctor-patient relationship the therapist becomes sufficiently involved to assume some responsibility for the safety, not only of the patient himself, but also of any third person whom the doctor knows to be threatened by the patient." . . .

Defendants contend, however, that imposition of a duty to exercise reasonable care to protect third persons is unworkable because therapists cannot accurately predict whether or not a patient will resort to violence. In support of this argument amicus representing the American Psychiatric Association and other professional societies cites numerous articles which indicate that therapists, in the present state of the art, are unable reliably to predict violent acts; their forecasts, amicus claims, tend consistently to overpredict violence, and indeed are more often wrong than right. . . .

. . . We recognize the difficulty that a therapist encounters in attempting to forecast whether a patient presents a serious danger of violence. Obviously we do not require that the therapist, in making that determination, render a perfect performance; the therapist need only exercise "that reasonable degree of skill, knowledge, and care

ordinarily possessed and exercised by members of [that professional specialty] under similar circumstances." Within the broad range of reasonable practice and treatment in which professional opinion and judgment may differ, the therapist is free to exercise his or her own best judgment without liability; proof, aided by hindsight, that he or she judged wrongly is insufficient to establish negligence.

In the instant case, however, the pleadings do not raise any question as to failure of defendant therapists to predict that Poddar presented a serious danger of violence. On the contrary, the present complaints allege that defendant therapists did in fact predict that Poddar would kill, but were negligent in failing to warn.

. . . Amicus contends, however, that even when a therapist does in fact predict that a patient poses a serious danger of violence to others, the therapist should be absolved of any responsibility for failing to act to protect the potential victim. In our view, however, once a therapist does in fact determine, or under applicable professional standards reasonably should have determined, that a patient poses a serious danger of violence to others, he bears a duty to exercise reasonable care to protect the foreseeable victim of that danger. While the discharge of this duty of due care will necessarily vary with the facts of each case, in each instance the adequacy of the therapist's conduct must be measured against the traditional negligence standard of the rendition of reasonable care under the circumstances. . . . As explained in Fleming and Maximov, *The Patient or His Victim: The Therapist's Dilemma* (1974): ". . . the ultimate question of resolving the tension between the conflicting interests of patient and potential victim is one of social policy, not professional expertise. . . . In sum, the therapist owes a legal duty not only to his patient, but also to his patient's would-be victim and is subject in both respects to scrutiny by judge and jury." . . .

The risk that unnecessary warnings may be given is a reasonable price to pay for the lives of possible victims that may be saved. We would hesitate to hold that the therapist who is aware that his patient expects to attempt to assassinate the President of the United States would not be obligated to warn the authorities because the therapist cannot predict with accuracy that his patient will commit the crime.

Defendants further argue that free and open communication is essential to psychotherapy; . . .

that "Unless a patient . . . is assured that . . . information [revealed by him] can and will be held in utmost confidence, he will be reluctant to make the full disclosure upon which diagnosis and treatment . . . depends." . . . The giving of a warning, defendants contend, constitutes a breach of trust which entails the relevation of confidential communications.

. . . We recognize the public interest in supporting effective treatment of mental illness and in protecting the rights of patients to privacy, . . . and the consequent public importance of safeguarding the confidential character of psychotherapeutic communication. Against this interest, however, we must weigh the public interest in safety from violent assault. . . .

. . . We realize that the open and confidential character of psychotherapeutic dialogue encourages patients to express threats of violence, few of which are ever executed. Certainly a therapist should not be encouraged routinely to reveal such threats; such disclosures could seriously disrupt the patient's relationship with his therapist and with the persons threatened. To the contrary, the therapist's obligations to his patient require that he not disclose a confidence unless such disclosure is

necessary to avert danger to others, and even then that he do so discreetly, and in a fashion that would preserve the privacy of his patient to the fullest extent compatible with the prevention of the threatened danger.

The revelation of a communication under the above circumstances is not a breach of trust or a violation of professional ethics; as stated in the Principles of Medical Ethics of the American Medical Association (1957), section 9: "A physician may not reveal the confidence entrusted to him in the course of medical attendance . . . *unless he is required to do so by law or unless it becomes necessary in order to protect the welfare of the individual or of the community.*" (Emphasis added.) We conclude that the public policy favoring protection of the confidential character of patient-psychotherapist communications must yield to the extent to which disclosure is essential to avert danger to others. The protective privilege ends where the public peril begins. . . .

For the foregoing reasons, we find that plaintiffs' complaints can be amended to state a cause of action against defendants Moore, Powelson, Gold, and Yandell and against the Regents as their employer, for breath of a duty to exercise reasonable care to protect Tatiana.

Justice William P. Clark, Dissenting Opinion

Until today's majority opinion, both legal and medical authorities have agreed that confidentiality is essential to effectively treat the mentally ill, and that imposing a duty on doctors to disclose patient threats to potential victims would greatly impair treatment. Further, recognizing that effective treatment and society's safety are necessarily intertwined, the Legislature has already decided effective and confidential treatment is preferred over imposition of a duty to warn.

The issue whether effective treatment for the mentally ill should be sacrificed to a system of warnings is, in my opinion, properly one for the Legislature, and we are bound by its judgment. Moreover, even in the absence of clear legislative direction, we must reach the same conclusion because imposing the majority's new duty is certain to result in a net increase in violence. . . .

Overwhelming policy considerations weigh against imposing a duty on psychotherapists to

warn a potential victim against harm. While offering virtually no benefit to society, such a duty will frustrate psychiatric treatment, invade fundamental patient rights and increase violence. . . .

Assurance of confidentiality is important for three reasons.

Deterrence from Treatment

First, without substantial assurance of confidentiality, those requiring treatment will be deterred from seeking assistance. It remains an unfortunate fact in our society that people seeking psychiatric guidance tend to become stigmatized. Apprehension of such stigma—apparently increased by the propensity of people considering treatment to see themselves in the worst possible light—creates a well-recognized reluctance to seek aid. This reluctance is alleviated by the psychiatrist's assurance of confidentiality.

Full Disclosure

Second, the guarantee of confidentiality is essential in eliciting the full disclosure necessary for effective treatment. The psychiatric patient approaches treatment with conscious and unconscious inhibitions against revealing his innermost thoughts. "Every person, however well-motivated, has to overcome resistance to therapeutic exploration. These resistances seek support from every possible source and the possibility of disclosure would easily be employed in the service of resistance." . . . Until a patient can trust his psychiatrist not to violate their confidential relationship, "the unconscious psychological control mechanism of repression will prevent the recall of past experiences." . . .

Successful Treatment

Third, even if the patient fully discloses his thoughts, assurance that the confidential relationship will not be breached is necessary to maintain his trust in his psychiatrist—the very means by which treatment is effected. "[T]he essence of much psychotherapy is the contribution of trust in the external world and ultimately in the self, modelled upon the trusting relationship established during therapy." . . . Patients will be helped only if they can form a trusting relationship with the psychiatrist. . . . All authorities appear to agree that if the trust relationship cannot be developed because of collusive communication between the psychiatrist and others, treatment will be frustrated.

Given the importance of confidentiality to the practice of psychiatry, it becomes clear the duty to warn imposed by the majority will cripple the use and effectiveness of psychiatry. Many people, potentially violent—yet susceptible to treatment—will be deterred from seeking it; those seeking it will be inhibited from making relevations necessary to effective treatment; and, forcing the psychiatrist to violate the patient's trust will destroy the interpersonal relationship by which treatment is effected.

Violence and Civil Commitment

By imposing a duty to warn, the majority contributes to the danger to society of violence by the mentally ill and greatly increases the risk of civil commitment—the total deprivation of liberty—of those who should not be confined. The impairment

of treatment and risk of improper commitment resulting from the new duty to warn will not be limited to a few patients but will extend to a large number of the mentally ill. Although under existing psychiatric procedures only a relatively few receiving treatment will ever present a risk of violence, the number making threats is huge, and it is the latter group—not just the former—whose treatment will be impaired and whose risk of commitment will be increased.

Both the legal and psychiatric communities recognize that the process of determining potential violence in a patient is far from exact, being fraught with complexity and uncertainty. In fact precision has not even been attained in predicting who of those having already committed violent acts will again become violent, a task recognized to be of much simpler proportions. . . .

This predictive uncertainty means that the number of disclosures will necessarily be large. As noted above, psychiatric patients are encouraged to discuss all thoughts of violence, and they often express such thoughts. However, unlike this court, the psychiatrist does not enjoy the benefit of overwhelming hindsight in seeing which few, if any, of his patients will ultimately become violent. Now, confronted by the majority's new duty, the psychiatrist must instantaneously calculate potential violence from each patient on each visit. The difficulties researchers have encountered in accurately predicting violence will be heightened for the practicing psychiatrist dealing for brief periods in his office with heretofore nonviolent patients. And, given the decision not to warn or commit must always be made at the psychiatrist's civil peril, one can expect most doubts will be resolved in favor of the psychiatrist protecting himself.

Neither alternative open to the psychiatrist seeking to protect himself is in the public interest. The warning itself is an impairment of the psychiatrist's ability to treat, depriving many patients of adequate treatment. It is to be expected that after disclosing their threats, a significant number of patients, who would not become violent if treated according to existing practices, will engage in violent conduct as a result of unsuccessful treatment. In short, the majority's duty to warn will not only impair treatment of many who would never become violent but worse, will result in a net increase in violence.

The second alternative open to the psychiatrist

is to commit his patient rather than to warn. Even in the absence of threat of civil liability, the doubts of psychiatrists as to the seriousness of patient threats have led psychiatrists to overcommit to mental institutions. This overcommitment has been authoritatively documented in both legal and psychiatric studies. This practice is so prevalent that it has been estimated that "as many as twenty harmless persons are incarcerated for every one who will commit a violent act." . . .

Given the incentive to commit created by the majority's duty, this already serious situation will be worsened, contrary to Chief Justice Wright's admonition "that liberty is no less precious because forfeited in a civil proceeding than when taken as a consequence of a criminal conviction."

Pregnant Women as Fetal Containers

George J. Annas

George J. Annas uses the Pamela Stewart Monson case to illustrate his argument that to prosecute pregnant women for fetal neglect is to treat women as less important than the fetuses they carry. It deprives women of their status as persons in their own right and relegates them to the role of fetal containers. Annas claims that the child-neglect laws were not written to be applied to fetuses and that applying them in this way has unacceptable consequences. Nor is Annas convinced by the argument that a woman who has "waived" her right to an abortion can be held responsible for fetal neglect.

In Margaret Atwood's *The Handmaid's Tale*, most women are sterile, and the few who retain the capacity to bear children have reproduction as their exclusive function. As one handmaid describes her station: "We are two-legged wombs, that's all; sacred vessels, ambulatory chalices." This future scenario strikes many as unlikely, but a recent criminal indictment directly raises the issue of when it is legally acceptable to treat a pregnant woman as a container, while treating the welfare of the fetus she contains as more significant than hers.

Mrs. Pamela Monson is the subject of what may be the first criminal charge ever brought against a woman for acts and omissions during pregnancy. Criminal charges were filed against her in California in October 1986. The available reports suggest that sometime very late in her pregnancy Mrs. Monson was advised by her physician not to take amphetamines, to stay off her feet, to avoid sexual intercourse, and, because of a placenta previa, to seek immediate medical treatment if she began to hemorrhage.

According to the police, Mrs. Monson noticed some bleeding the morning of November 23, 1985. Nevertheless, she remained at home, took some amphetamines, and had intercourse with her husband. She began bleeding more heavily, and contractions began sometime during the afternoon. It was only later, perhaps, "many hours" later, that she went to the hospital. Her son was born that evening. He had massive brain damage, and died about six weeks thereafter.

Police lieutenant Randy Narramore has said, "We contend that she willfully disobeyed instructions (of the doctor) and as a direct result the child was born brain dead [sic] and later died" (*Washington Post,* October 2, 1986). District Attorney Harry Elias says simply that she "did not follow through on the medical advice she was given" (*New York Times,* October 9, 1986). Police officials wanted Mrs. Monson prosecuted for murder, but the District Attorney has decided to proceed with a prosecution under a California child support statute.

The support statute itself has been amended

From the *Hastings Center Report,* December 1986, pp 13–14. Reprinted by permission of the author.

many times since it was first passed in 1872, and during much of the subsequent time applied only to fathers. The relevant part of the current version reads:

> If a parent of a minor child *willfully omits,* without lawful excuse, *to furnish* necessary clothing, food, shelter or *medical attendance, or other remedial care* for his or her child, he or she is guilty of a misdemeanor punishable by a fine not exceeding two thousand dollars, or by imprisonment [for one year] (emphasis added) (Cal. Penal Code, Sec. 270 [West, 1986]).

A later provision decrees that "a child conceived but not yet born is to be deemed an existing person insofar as this section is concerned."

Use of this statute, instead of a homicide charge, avoids the issue of causation, since violation of the duty itself violates the statute regardless of the consequences to the fetus or child. Thus, for example, a father's failure to provide food for his children would violate the statute, even if the mother was also to provide her children with food from another source. Why the father hasn't been charged in this case is puzzling.

Very few cases have attempted to define the scope of the statute, and the only cases that deal with its application to fetuses were decided during the Depression. These cases hold that a father can fail to provide food, clothing, and shelter to the "unborn child" and that because these needs are "common to all mankind," proof of their "necessity" is not required. In regard to "medical attendance and other remedial care," however, "in a prosecution based on failure to furnish them, it would be incumbent on the prosecution to make affirmative proof of their necessity" (*People v. Yates,* 298 p. 961, 962 [(LA. Sup. 1931]). Such proof would, of course , require medical testimony. Mrs. Monson did provide "medical attendance" by seeking prenatal care and by seeking assistance in childbirth at a hospital.

Fetal Neglect

The District Attorney's use of this provision is an attempt to extend child support statutes to create a crime of "fetal neglect." Does it mean that the pregnant woman must, in effect, live for her fetus? That she must legally "stay off her feet" if walking or working might induce contractions? That she commits a crime if she does not eat only healthy foods; smokes or drinks alcohol; takes any drugs (legal or illegal); has intercourse with her husband?

And how does such a criminal law change the nature of the doctor-patient relationship? It seems evident that, to the police, the doctor's patient was not Mrs. Monson at all, but her fetus. It also seems evident that although the police spoke of "advice" and "instructions," they believed that the physician was giving the fetal container, Mrs. Monson, orders—orders that she *must* follow or face criminal penalties, including jail.

In this case, for example, the doctor had instructed Mrs. Monson not to have intercourse with her husband during the remainder of her pregnancy, because it might induce contractions and a premature delivery. She nonetheless engaged in intercourse. The prosecution alleges that such "disobeying instructions" or "failure to follow through on medical advice" is grounds for criminal action. This strikes me as both silly and dangerous. Silly because medical *advice* should remain *advice:* physicians are neither law makers nor seers.

After the fact prosecutions would not help individual fetuses. Dangerous because medical advice is a vague term that can cover almost anything. Effectively monitoring compliance would require confining pregnant women to an environment in which eating, exercise, drug use, and sexual intercourse could be controlled. This could, of course, be a maximum security country club, but such massive invasions of privacy can only be justified by treating pregnant women during their pregnancy as nonpersons. Like Margaret Atwood's handmaids, they have only one function: to have the healthiest children we can make them have.

Other quandaries arise if we apply child neglect statutes to fetuses. Unlike a child, the fetus is absolutely dependent upon its mother and cannot itself be "treated" without in some way invading the mother. The "fetal protection" policy enunciated by the prosecution seems to assume that like mother and child, mother and fetus are two separate individuals, with separate lights. But treating them separately before birth can only be done by favoring one over the other in disputes. Favoring the fetus radically devalues the pregnant woman and treats her like an inert incubator, or a culture medium for the fetus.

This view makes women unequal citizens, since only they can have children, and relegates them to performing one main function: childbearing. It is one thing for the state to view the fetus as a patient; it is another to assume that the fetus's interests are in opposition to its mother, and to require the mother to be the fetus's servant.

Child neglect covers a wide variety of activities, but generally involves failure to provide necessities like clothing, food, housing, or medical attention to the child. Such laws *do not,* however, require parents to provide optimal clothing, food, housing, or medical attention to their children; and do not even forbid taking risks with children (such as permitting them to engage in dangerous sports) or affirmatively injuring children (corporal punishment to teach them a lesson). None forbid mothers to smoke, take dangerous drugs, or to consume excessive amounts of alcohol, even though these activities may have a negative effect on their children.

While it seems draconian to apply the child neglect standards to the mother's life style during pregnancy, the California statute could be interpreted to apply to fetuses in a way never envisioned by the legislature. Certainly the legislature never intended that women must provide any more "clothing, food or shelter" to their fetuses than they provide for themselves. But what about the terms "medical attendance" and "remedial care"? Historically, medical attendance for the fetus meant medical attendance for the mother. If fetal surgery becomes an accepted procedure sometime in the future, however, "remedial care" may be applicable. Suppose, for example, that instead of the instructions the doctor gave Mrs. Monson, he had diagnosed her fetus as suffering from blocked ureters, and "recommended" surgery on the fetus to attempt to correct the problem. Would her failure to agree to this surgery be tantamount to "fetal neglect" for failure to provide her fetus with "necessary remedial care"?

This carries us into even more problematic waters. If women *must* "consent" to such "care" of their fetuses, they are relegated to the role of containers. Moreover their own rights are made so subordinate that the container may be opened to gain access to the fetus, even when the container may be damaged. (G. J. Annas, "Forced Caesareans: The Most Unkindest Cut of All," *Hastings Center Report,* June 1982, 16–17).

Waiving One's Right to Abortion

Some have argued that it is nonetheless fair to subject pregnant women to fetal neglect statutes because after they waive their right to abortion and decide to have a child, they take on added obligations to the future child, including providing it with such things as "necessary medical attendance." This argument seems misplaced for at least two reasons. First, such a "waiver" never in fact takes place. Women do not appear before judges or even notaries to waive their rights at any time during the pregnancy. Indeed, the vast majority of pregnancies in marriage are planned and welcomed, and viewing all pregnant women as potential aborters seems bizarre. Moreover, insofar as the right to terminate one's pregnancy is constitutionally protected, it remains a woman's legal right to the time of birth, at least when her life or health is at stake.

Second, and more important, women have a constitutional right to bear children if they are physically able to do so. To have a legal rule that there are no restrictions on a woman's decision to have an abortion, but if she elects childbirth instead, then the state will require her to surrender her basic rights of bodily integrity and privacy, creates a state-erected penalty on her exercise of her right to bear a child (D. E. Johnsen, the "Creation of Fetal Rights: Conflicts with Women's Constitutional Rights to Liberty, Privacy and Equal Protection," 95 *Yale Law Journal* 599, 618 [1986]). Such a penalty would (or at least should) be unconstitutional.

Attempts to define fetal neglect and to establish a prenatal police force to protect fetuses from their mothers, are steps backwards in terms of both women's rights and fetal protection. Women's rights will only be fostered when we treat women equally. The best chance the state has to protect fetuses is through actions to enhance the status of all women by fostering reasonable pay for the work they do and equal employment opportunities, and providing a reasonable social safety net, quality prenatal services, and day care programs. It is probably not coincidental that government is trying to blame the pregnant victims of poverty for their problems at the same time it is cutting funds for maternal and child health care and nutrition. If the state really wants to protect fetuses it should do so by improving the welfare of pregnant women—not by oppressing them.

Pregnancy and Prenatal Harm to Offspring

John A. Robertson and Joseph D. Schulman

John A. Robertson and Joseph D. Schulman argue that individuals can be held morally and legally responsible for the harm they cause their children before birth. In the case of pregnant women, the responsibilities and the ways they are enforced must be determined by balancing a child's welfare against the woman's interest in preserving her liberty and bodily integrity.

The most desirable social policy is to inform pregnant women of risks to their unborn child and make needed services (such as drug rehabilitation) available to them. However, if these voluntary measures fail, coercive measures by the state to protect the child's interest may be justified. These may include holding a woman liable to civil and criminal penalties after the birth of a child, prenatal seizure of a woman to prevent her from acting in ways harmful to her developing child, and the forcible treatment of a pregnant woman who has refused therapy medically necessary to protect the interest of the child.

None of this infringes on the right to an abortion, the authors assert, because the duties of a pregnant woman to her unborn child are conditional upon the live birth of the child. We have no duty to see that fetuses are born alive. However, we do have a duty to see that if they are, they show no effects of needless harm as a result of the actions of the pregnant woman or anyone else.

The growing ability to prevent the birth of handicapped infants has raised new issues about the scope of reproductive freedom. For example, recent research in obstetrics and fetal medicine has shown many ways in which behavior during pregnancy can harm babies who would otherwise be born healthy. Most women at risk welcome this knowledge. They avoid risky behavior and accept medical treatments or surgery that will ensure a healthy birth. If a healthy birth is not possible, they may avoid conception or terminate the pregnancy.

Yet not all women benefit from existing knowledge of prenatal risks. Some may not know of the dangers that certain behaviors pose or of the treatment available for congenital conditions. Others may lack access to the prenatal screening and treatment that would prevent handicaps. Sometimes, however, women ignore the knowledge and engage in conduct that causes their children to be born handicapped.

The need for public policies to prevent avoidable prenatal injuries has arisen in several different contexts: prenatal medical or surgical treatment and cesarean section; prenatal abuse of alcohol, heroin and cocaine; exclusion from workplaces posing prenatal hazards to offspring; and prenatal transmission of herpes and syphilis. As more instances of prenatal harm become known, pressure to change the behavior of pregnant women will increase.

Public efforts to modify the behavior of pregnant women are controversial on several grounds. The idea that women could with impunity cause or fail to prevent handicapped births is, of course, troubling. Yet there is no consensus about the seriousness of the problem and the appropriateness of particular remedies. In addition, feminists and others are suspicious of public control of women's bodies during pregnancy for the sake of the unborn child. They view it as a significant intrusion on per-

From John A. Robertson and Joseph D. Schulman, "Pregnancy and Prenatal Harm to Offspring: The Case of Mothers with PKU," *Hastings Center Report,* August 1987, pp. 23–32. Notes and references omitted. Reprinted by permission of the authors and publisher.

sonal liberty with the potential to accord fetuses a legal status that could diminish the right to have an abortion. . . .

Obligations to the Unborn Child

Questions of prenatal obligations to offspring are ethically complex because of the prenatal timing of the harmful conduct and the unborn child's location in the mother's uterus when the harmful conduct occurs. Meeting obligations to the unborn child may require placing limits on the mother's conduct that would not arise if she were not pregnant. Thus the mother's interest in autonomy and bodily integrity must be balanced against her baby's welfare.

Yet it is not unreasonable to regard her as having a moral duty to the baby she is choosing to deliver. All persons have obligations to refrain from harming children after birth. Similarly, they have obligations to refrain from harming children by prenatal actions. There is no reason why the mother who has chosen to go to term should not also have a duty to prevent harm when she may reasonably do so. The timing of the conduct does not affect the duty to avoid causing harm.

Nevertheless, the interests of actual offspring to be free of prenatally caused harm rather than the right of the fetus to complete gestation is at issue. But the offspring's right is contingent on live birth and the mother's decision to continue a pregnancy. Protecting offspring against prenatally caused harm does not diminish the woman's right to terminate pregnancy.

In the PKU case, failure to resume the diet will not prevent the fetus from being born. Rather it will cause a child that could have been born healthy to be born with severe damage. The ethical obligation to future offspring may arise before birth, but it is a duty conditional on the planned and likely possibility of live birth. It is not a duty owed to fetuses to assure that they are born alive.

Thus the tendency of physicians to speak of the fetus as a "patient" should be clarified. The fetus going to term is a "patient" by virtue of the expectation that it will be born alive, and not because physicians have an independent duty to bring all fetuses to term regardless of the mother's wishes.

Prenatal duties owed the planned offspring may arise before viability. The mother's plans, and not the state of fetal development, are determinative. A woman who is undecided or ambivalent about a first-trimester pregnancy may still be morally obligated to act as if she will carry the fetus to term if first-trimester conduct poses serious risk to a baby that is born. Although she is free to terminate the pregnancy later, she is not free to injure offspring prenatally just because she is uncertain about whether to continue the pregnancy.

Ethical analysis must balance the mother's interest in freedom and bodily integrity against the offspring's interest in being born healthy. This balance will vary with the burdens of altering the mother's conduct and the risk of prenatally caused harm to offspring. Depending on the balance of risk, benefits, and burdens, prenatal conduct may be discretionary, advisable, prudent, or even obligatory. . . .

Policy Options: Voluntary Compliance or Compulsion?

Several policy options are available to influence the behavior of women and others during pregnancy, ranging from voluntary compliance to coercive sanctions and seizures.

Relying on voluntary compliance is the most desirable policy, since it raises fewer civil liberties and privacy issues and is more likely to be effective. Most women will welcome such knowledge and act accordingly. If they have not been able to avoid the damaging conduct, many will choose abortion rather than bring the damaged fetus to term. The main need here is to assure that women are adequately informed and have access to treatments that can avoid the harm to offspring.

But women who will not or cannot comply with proper conduct will end up injuring a child who could be born healthy. Should the state go beyond informing and penalize irresponsible maternal behavior during pregnancy by imposing civil or criminal sanctions when actual damage to offspring has occurred? Should it prevent the harm to offspring by incarceration or forced treatment of the pregnant woman? . . .

Coercive Measures: The Noncompliant Mother

Yet some women, even though they are informed of prenatal risks and given access to needed services, may still refuse or be unable to comply with the measures needed to avert harm to their offspring. Given the harm that their behavior will cause offspring and the reasonableness of expecting them to act differently, some persons have proposed that coercive measures, including postbirth sanctions and even prebirth seizures, be employed when education and counseling fail.

However, policies that seek to coerce noncompliant women into adopting the desired behavior are controversial on several grounds. Some of the controversy arises from a failure to distinguish the question of a fetus's right to be born alive from the very different question of the right of offspring who will be born, to be born free of avoidable harm.

However, even when this crucial distinction is made, many people find the notion of sanctions or seizures for conduct during pregnancy to be highly distasteful and an arguably unjustified limitation on personal liberty. They fear that coercive measures would be used without proper justification to restrain a wide range of personal choices by pregnant women. They also foresee a slide down a slippery slope to a state in which every conceivable protective measure is required of pregnant women, including mandatory pregnancy registration and monitoring of the pregnant woman's conduct, leading to seizures and forced treatment if the code of proper prenatal conduct is violated. They view such policies as expressions of hostility toward women and reinforcement of the stereotype of women as vessels of reproduction.

In assessing these claims a distinction must be made between state sanctions applied after the birth of a child severely damaged by culpable prenatal conduct and prebirth seizures that aim to prevent the damage before it occurs. The analysis will show that although coercive sanctions should not be foreclosed as a matter of principle, their role is narrow and should be carefully circumscribed. Only rarely will prebirth seizures ever be justified.

Sanctions after Birth: Civil and Criminal Liability

The law has long recognized that actions or omissions during pregnancy can be as harmful to children as actions or omissions after the child is born. Since the sixteenth century, prenatal actions that cause a child to die after live birth have been prosecuted as homicide. Similarly, under the civil law, damages have been awarded for injuries that occur during pregnancy or before conception when a child is born damaged, who could have been born healthy. Recent developments allowing family members to sue each other now permit such suits by children against parents if the latter have culpably caused the children avoidable injury. Since these duties arise only if the woman chooses to continue a pregnancy that she is legally free to end, penalizing culpable maternal behavior that unreasonably damages offspring does not conflict with *Roe v. Wade*.

In theory a child who is severely retarded as a result of culpable prenatal conduct could sue the mother. However, suits by damaged offspring against mothers will rarely be brought. Thus the threat of civil suit is not likely to deter harmful prenatal conduct.

The state might pursue criminal prosecution for culpable prenatal conduct that causes severe damage to offspring. Although only a few prosecutions for prenatal child abuse have been reported and the applicability of current child abuse and neglect laws to prenatal conduct is uncertain, this avenue may be increasingly pursued as the number of prenatally caused injuries increases.

A highly publicized example of such a prosecution occurred in San Diego when Pamela Stewart, a pregnant woman with placenta previa (a condition in which the placenta blocks part of the cervix, leading to a risk of hemorrhage and oxygen deprivation for the fetus) allegedly ignored her doctor's advice to stop using amphetamines, avoid sex, and go to the hospital when she began bleeding. On the day her child was born she allegedly took amphetamines, had sex with her husband, and delayed going to the hospital for "many hours" after she began bleeding. Her baby was born alive with severe brain damage and died within six weeks in a neonatal intensive care unit.

The district attorney filed misdemeanor charges against the mother under a California statute that penalizes a "parent of a minor child who willfully omits, without lawful excuse, to furnish necessary . . . medical attendance or other remedial care for his or her child. The statute included a provision that "a child conceived but not yet born . . . [is] an existing person" within the meaning of the statute. The father, whose knowledge of the risks to the offspring was less clear, was not prosecuted.

The Stewart case was eventually dismissed on the ground that the statute had not been intended to apply to prenatal acts and omissions. A similar result might occur in other states, since most child abuse and neglect statutes do not explicitly mention prenatal action. However, many state child abuse laws could also reasonably be interpreted to protect born children from prenatal injury, just as homicide statutes have been interpreted. In any event, ambiguities in current statutes could be clarified by legislation specifically directed to prenatal conduct where a live birth is reasonably foreseeable.

Since the state clearly has the constitutional authority to punish mothers (and fathers) for culpable prenatal conduct, the major policy question is whether such statutes are desirable, and whether prosecutions under them should ever be brought for culpably caused prenatal harm. Let us examine this question in the context of a noncompliant PKU woman who gives birth to a severely damaged child as a result of her failure to resume the diet after she has been appropriately notified and counseled of the need to do so.

The argument in favor of prosecution in such cases is that serious child abuse should be punished whether it occurs before or after birth. The mother has substantially harmed another person by avoidable conduct that falls below reasonable community standards, after notice and counseling. The offspring was seriously and willfully harmed. If brain damage caused after birth is punished, then brain damage caused prenatally should also be punished when avoidance of the prenatal harm does not unreasonably risk the mother's life or health. A statute penalizing culpable prenatal conduct is thus desirable "to announce to society that these actions are not to be done and to secure that fewer of them are done."

Yet one would hope that prosecutors would be very careful in their use of such statutes. Uncertainties about the effects of prenatal conduct and the pregnant woman's culpability, and the danger that prosecution will be sought in less clear-cut cases caution against the use of criminal sanctions except in the most egregious cases of harm and culpability. . . .

. . . Each situation must be considered individually, with the certainty and substantiality of the harm to offspring weighed against the burden on the mother of avoiding the harm. Some situations may appear both to be morally obligatory and also rise to levels of egregiousness that justify prosecution. Heavy use of alcohol and cocaine and refusal of minimally intrusive medical treatments could constitute such unreasonable risky behavior that prosecution for prenatal child abuse is justified in particular cases, if maternal culpability is found.

On the other hand, many behaviors that might appear harmful would not justify prosecution as prenatal child abuse. For example, moderate use of alcohol and nicotine do not appear to present a severe enough threat in terms of certainty and substantiality of harm to justify prosecution, even though a prudent person might refrain. If further research establishes a greater certainty of more substantial harm from these drugs, the calculus would change. Similarly, prosecution would rarely be appropriate for conduct that occurs prior to viability because of the difficulty in establishing maternal culpability.

Prosecution for refusing fetal surgery or medical treatment also depends on the burdens and benefits involved. Prenatal treatment would not be morally or legally obligatory where the treatment is experimental, has low efficacy, or imposes unreasonable physical burdens or risks to the woman's life or health. Few kinds of fetal surgery currently have clear enough benefits to be legally mandatory. Yet the risks of future forms of fetal surgery could become so minimal and the benefits to offspring so clear that reasonable persons would consider them to be morally mandatory; refusal would then fit the requirement for criminal prosecution.

The refusal of cesarean section is more difficult to assess because the more certain benefits in particular cases for the baby may be outweighed by the physical burdens required of the mother. However, one could argue that willfull refusal of cesarean section is so irresponsible as to justify prenatal child abuse charges when the child is born with extensive brain damage that the cesarean section would have prevented. But a clear medical need that reasonable persons would not refuse would have to be established.

By now it should be clear that a slide down a slippery slope toward extensive, loosely justified limits on maternal conduct during pregnancy—a fear animating much of the controversy over this issue—is by no means inevitable. Egregious cases of culpable prenatal conduct causing substantial harm and suitable for prosecution can be distinguished from less egregious cases, just as is done with allegations of postnatal child abuse. Fears that obstetricians will become "pregnancy policemen" are no more valid than fears that pediatricians will become "childrearing policemen" under statutes requiring the reporting of postnatal child abuse. Meaningful lines can be drawn here just as they are drawn in myriad other legal situations.

The parallel with postnatal duties is instructive. We cannot ask parents to do more prenatally for their children than we can after birth. Since we do not prosecute for merely imprudent or inadvisable postnatal parental conduct, we should not punish for similar prenatal conduct. Persuasion and voluntary compliance are then the preferred techniques.

Because the pregnant woman may be liable for failing to take medications or to consent to surgery, prosecution for prenatal misconduct may appear to hold the mother to a higher standard before birth than after. But the unborn child's location inside the mother, rather than a more rigorous standard of parental conduct, explains the difference. If the risk to the child were great and the bodily intrusion to the parents minimal, the state might constitutionally hold parents accountable for failing to accept postnatal treatment necessary for their child's well-being.

Finally, it is important to note that legal sanctions to deter harmful prenatal conduct should be used against all persons who culpably injure offspring prenatally, and not solely against pregnant women. For example, harmful conduct by fathers should not be ignored. A father's smoking during his wife's pregnancy should also be subject to sanctions if substantial harm to offspring from passive ingestion of his smoke can be demonstrated. Mr. Stewart should also have been prosecuted if he had culpably engaged in prenatal conduct harmful to the child. Refusing to prosecute culpable fathers for harmful conduct will cast doubt on the legitimacy of prosecuting mothers.

Prebirth Seizures

The most extreme and controversial policy option is incarceration or forced treatment of pregnant women who are unlikely or unwilling to avoid the behavior that is damaging to offspring. From the perspective of the child at risk, this approach is preferable to punishing after the damage occurs, since it prevents the damage altogether.

Direct intervention on the mother, however, is the most troubling option because it involves bodily seizures of varying duration and risk without the woman's consent. The right to be free of seizure and forced bodily intrusions, except for very compelling justification, is a very basic right. It is debatable whether forced treatment in maternal PKU and other situations is compelling and whether such extreme remedies are available under existing law. Few cases would meet the high standards necessary to justify a direct seizure for the benefit of unborn offspring.

In principle, seizures and forced treatment are within state power if a compelling need that outweighs the burdens of the seizure can be shown. While direct bodily seizures are rare in the law, they are not unknown. They occur in civil commitment, prison sentences, capital punishment, the draft, forced treatment of adults for the sake of minor children, and blood tests and surgery to recover evidence of crime. Their validity depends on a sufficient state interest to justify the intrusion on protected personal interests in bodily integrity, liberty, and privacy.

While this standard is purposely high and difficult to meet, there may be rare situations in which prenatal protection of offspring satisfies it because the benefits to offspring clearly outweigh the burdens of the intrusion.

However, prenatal seizures for the benefit of offspring would have to be specifically authorized by statute and accord the woman procedural due process, including judicial review of the need for the seizure. No state has enacted statutes specifically for that purpose, though a few courts have interpreted statutes that protect minor children from neglect as granting the power to order a cesarean section against the mother's wishes. A Baltimore court in 1984 ordered a pregnant drug abuser committed for the last two months of pregnancy. Civil commitment of mentally ill mothers to protect their offspring has also occurred.

What situations would justify seizure or forced treatment of the pregnant woman? The strongest case is when the intrusion or seizure is minimal in length and the harm to be prevented is certain and substantial. Even then, considerable doubt and controversy remain about whether the power should be used. The case for seizure weakens rapidly as the length, risk, and burdens of the seizure increase, and the benefit to the offspring diminishes. . . .

Forcing medical treatment on pregnant women would be justified only in very exceptional cases. The forced treatment could maintain the mother for the sake of her offspring or be administered directly to the fetus. The strongest case for forced treatment is a one-time intervention of minimal risk to the mother, administering a drug, blood, or surgery to avert severe handicap in her offspring. A one-time surgical procedure without high risk and with great benefit, such as Rh transfusion or even an established fetal surgery, could meet these standards in particular cases. . . .

Ordering a cesarean section over the mother's refusal is the most difficult case, since it forces an unwilling person to undergo general anesthesia, abdominal surgery, and the risk of infection and other complications. Yet the benefits to the offspring also appear substantial—avoidance of anoxia and severe brain damage. Several court orders have been granted for cesarean delivery and one has been upheld by the Georgia Supreme Court. Their appropriateness is hotly debated, both because of the degree of intrusion and the likelihood of error in estimating the need. It is widely thought that physicians overuse cesarean section because of malpractice fears and the higher fees it generates. In several cases where physicians have sought to force a cesarean section on an unwilling woman, their predictions proved erroneous. In addition, there is seldom sufficient time for adequate due process and judicial review. . . .

No physician should be required to seek a mandatory cesarean section. Informing the mother of the risks and reporting damaging refusals to child welfare authorities satisfy the physician's duty. The benefit to the few children who would avoid injury seems to be outweighed by the errors likely to occur under forced treatment policies. Sanctions after birth, however, may be imposed for culpable refusals that caused serious damage to offspring.

This discussion of prebirth seizures appears to single out pregnant women for a forced bodily burden that is not placed on fathers or on parents after birth occurs. Yet the situations are very different. The unborn child is inside the mother and at risk because of her voluntary actions or omissions. There are few situations in which fathers during pregnancy or parents after birth create risks to offspring that bodily intrusions on them could avert. Yet the principle that would in exceptional cases allow prebirth seizures of pregnant women would allow postbirth seizures of both parents and prebirth seizures of fathers if the same balance of burdens and benefits arose and specific statutory authorization existed, reflecting the community's conception of parental duties.

For example, the balance of burdens and benefits might justify physical intrusions on a parent for blood and possibly for bone marrow if no other source could save the child's life or prevent substantial harm. A forced kidney donation is more difficult, because the intrusion is greater and dialysis is an alternative. But lesser intrusions could be imposed in rare cases of sufficient cause if statutes specifically authorized such intrusions. Arguably, such a redefinition of parental duties is within the state's authority. . . .

In sum, prebirth seizures may fall within state power in a narrow class of compelling cases, yet rarely if ever should be sought. The likelihood of error in predicting benefit, the difficulty in assuring due process, and the burden of forced treatment and incarceration make such an extreme remedy, except in a few exceptional cases, a dubious avenue to reduction of handicapped births. Given the risks of such an intrusive policy, postbirth sanctions are preferable when coercive measures are deemed justified. . . .

A Tragic Choice

Developments in obstetrics, genetics, fetal medicine, and infectious diseases will continue to provide knowledge and technologies that will enable many handicapped births to be prevented. While most women will welcome this knowledge and gladly act on it, others will not. The ethical, legal, and policy aspects of this situation require a careful balancing of the offspring's welfare and the pregnant woman's interest in liberty and bodily integrity. Each situation has to be examined in light of the burdens and benefits of the prenatal conduct.

. . . The most desirable approach is education, counseling, and assuring access to treatment. Yet ethical and legal traditions do not exclude consideration of punitive measures in very special circumstances. When voluntary measures fail, the interests of children require us to address questions of culpability regarding prenatal conduct that harms offspring.

Decision Scenario 1 ••

"I find it incredible that you plan on allowing your-self to be treated by a chiropractor," Martha Red-path said.

"What's the matter with going to a chiroprac-tor?" Roger Smith asked. "I went to an M.D. and that didn't do any good. I haven't felt really good in years, but he told me there wasn't anything wrong with me."

"Chiropractors are frauds," Martha said. "They work on the basis of a false theory because they claim that all illnesses are caused either di-rectly or indirectly by misalignments of the verte-brae. That is just sheer nonsense."

"Maybe so," said Roger. "But why shouldn't I go if it makes me feel better? I think they help a lot of people."

"Maybe they won't do you any harm. But in gen-eral they're dangerous. They keep a lot of people from getting competent medical treatment, because the people go see a chiropractor instead of a physi-cian. Also, chiropractors often give a lot of X-rays, even though most of them aren't trained to do that, and that means that a great number of people re-ceive massive doses of harmful radiation."

Ralph shook his head. "I don't say that you're wrong. But it seems to me that everybody ought to be free to choose the kind of treatment that he wants to get. If he thinks a chiropractor can do him some good, then he ought to be able to con-sult one."

"Look," Martha said, "I'm as much in favor of individual freedom as you are. But a lot of people just aren't well-enough informed to make good choices about their own medical care. I think that we should have laws that make chiropractic medi-cine illegal. We need to protect people from their own ignorance and from those who take advantage of it."

1. *Using the principles argued for by Dworkin, con-struct an argument in support of Martha's posi-tion.*

2. *Is regulation of the sort advocated by Martha com-patible with Rawls's theory?*

3. *Do such regulations or laws violate the notion of the individual as an autonomous rational agent?*

Decision Scenario 2 ••

"I really don't understand you," Dr. Lowell said. "You definitely have cancer of the bladder. We may be able to remove it all surgically, but even if we can't, chemotherapy or radiation treatments have a good chance of success."

"I want none of those," Patricia Jenkins said. "I believe that a high-fiber diet and pure, filtered water are more likely to help me. I don't want to be cut or poisoned or burned."

"You're crazy," Dr. Lowell said. "That won't do anything."

"I intend to try it. Even if I'm wrong, it's my life."

"I won't let you," said Dr. Lowell. "Anybody who thinks the way you do about cancer is out of touch with reality. That's one of the marks of men-tal illness. And I intend to have you declared men-tally incompetent to make decisions about your own welfare. I shall speak to the psychiatrists on our staff and ask the hospital lawyer to arrange for a sanity hearing."

"That's fascism!"

"Call it anything you like. But my duty as a physician is to give you the best medical care pos-sible. If that means having you declared mentally incompetent, then so be it."

Dr. Lowell picked up the telephone.

1. *State and evaluate the argument Dr. Lowell offers to justify her intended course of action.*

2. *Dr. Lowell claims that it is her duty as a physician to provide Ms. Jenkins with the best medical care possible. If this is so, is it her only duty as a physi-cian? Is there some other duty that conflicts with this one?*

3. *On what grounds might Dr. Lowell be accused of paternalism?*

4. *Suppose that Dr. Lowell is successful in her aims and that Ms. Jenkins has surgery and makes a good recovery. Would such an outcome justify her ac-tions? If not, why not?*

Decision Scenario 3 ••

Angela Carter was diagnosed as having bone cancer when she was thirteen. Over the following years she received a variety of treatments and underwent surgery several times. In one operation, her leg was amputated. By the time she was twenty-seven the cancer had been in remission for three years, and she became pregnant. Twenty-five weeks into the pregnancy, she went for a routine checkup, and her physician discovered a large tumor in a lung. She was told she might have only days to live.

She was admitted to George Washington Hospital, and five days later her condition worsened. Despite the objections of Angela Carter, her family, and even her physician, the hospital decided to attempt to save the developing child. The hospital went to court, and at a hearing staff physicians stated that, despite the fact that the fetus was only twenty-six weeks old, there was a 50–60% chance that it would survive if a caesarean section was performed. Furthermore, they estimated that there was a less than 20% chance that the child would be handicapped. The physicians also testified that the surgery would increase the chances of Angela Carter's death.

The hospital obtained a court order, which was immediately appealed. Because the case demanded a quick resolution, the three judges on appeals court consulted by telephone. The whole process,

hearing and appeal, took less than six hours. During this time, the hospital had ordered Angela prepared for surgery.

The appeals court let the lower court ruling stand, and Angela underwent the court-ordered surgery. The child, a girl, live for only two hours. Angela lived for two days. The surgery was listed as a contributing cause to her death.

1. *On what grounds might Annas object to the court-ordered surgery?*

2. *Is there any reason to view this case any differently than cases involving drug abuse by a pregnant woman? That is, are the issues the same in both kinds of cases?*

3. *Suppose Angela Carter had been further along in her pregnancy so that the chance of her child's survival was virtually certain and that she refused to have a caesarean. Would Robertson and Schulman argue that it would be right to force her to have a caesarean against her will? Are they right?*

4. *Robertson and Schulman claim that while a woman has a right to seek an abortion, if she decides to carry the fetus to term it has a right to have her promote its best interest. Is this position consistent?*

Decision Scenario 4 ••

"You realize that I talked to him for only fifteen or twenty minutes," said Dr. Susan Beck.

"Yeah, but you psychiatrists are supposed to be able to size up a guy just by listening to how he says hello," Dr. Mark Brunetti said.

"Now that I've talked to him, tell me more about him," Beck said.

"I presume you learned his name is T. D. Chang?"

"That was written down for me."

"Fine," said Brunetti. "He's fifty-two years old, a professor of Asian History at Southwestern University. He's married, has two children in college, and has a solid scholarly reputation."

"What was his complaint?" asked Beck.

"About a month ago he began to experience difficult and painful urination. His attending exam-

ined him, found he had an enlarged prostate, and treated with sulfa. No joy. So the attending sent him here. We're doing an X-ray scan and a punch biopsy in the morning."

"And you want me to tell you how I think he'll take it if you tell him you suspect cancer?"

"Right," said Brunetti. "I don't like to scare people unless I have to. My inclination here is just to keep quiet until we know for sure."

"I think he would take it all right. He shows no tendency toward hysteria, and his background reveals him to be a person who functions well under normal conditions of stress."

"Good, then if I have to tell him, I won't worry about it."

"Mark, do you mean you're not going to tell him?"

"That's right. Not until I know for sure. It's a kindness to him. What he doesn't know won't hurt him, and there's no reason to cause him unnecessary anxiety."

"I don't think I agree with that decision," Beck said. "I think a man like Mr. Chang has a right to know as much about his condition as you do."

"That's silly," Brunetti said. "He can't possibly know as much as I do, and he wouldn't know what to make of the information even if I gave it to him. He would probably figure he's going to die in the next hour."

"So you aren't going to tell him what you suspect or why you're doing the biopsy?"

"I'm not that cruel, even if I am a surgeon."

1. Do the arguments presented by Lipkin support Brunetti's views? State the arguments explicitly and, if possible, relate them to this example.

2. Using Bok's line of reasoning, what criticisms might be made of the position taken by Brunetti?

3. Is it reasonable to believe that Mr. Chang might be able to understand and assess the significance of the medical information relevant to the procedures planned?

4. What might an act or rule utilitarian say about this situation?

Decision Scenario 5 ....

Multiple sclerosis is a chronic, progressive, neurological disease with symptoms that include loss of coordination, blurred vision, speech difficulties, and severe fatigue. It is most frequent among young adults. A study at Albert Einstein Medical College revealed that MS patients typically had a very hard time getting an explicit diagnosis and explanation from their physicians. Yet the physicians surveyed reported overwhelmingly that they always or usually tell patients the diagnosis.

The researchers learned that a variety of factors account for this discrepancy. Physicians find many reasons for delay—the patient may be under twenty, emotionally unstable, or apparently incapable of understanding the diagnosis. Also, the patient may not ask specifically, a relative may ask that the patient not be told, the patient may be medically unsophisticated or in the midst of an emotional crisis. Most important, there is no cure or wholly effective therapy for MS, and emotional stress seems to aggravate its symptoms. Telling a patient that she or he has a progressive, incurable disease may do no good and may do harm.

Patients are frequently told that they have "a chronic virus infection," "neuritis," and "inflammation of the nervous system," instead of being told they have MS. This sometimes leads patients to consult several physicians and to undergo expensive and unnecessary diagnostic tests in the attempt to get a diagnosis.

1. Are the physicians who claim they believe in telling MS patients the diagnosis but then don't do so necessarily being hypocritical?

2. What sort of arguments or considerations might Lipkin offer in their defense?

3. In what sort of cases, according to Bok's arguments, would it be justifiable to withhold a diagnosis from a patient?

4. If there is a chance that knowing the diagnosis will make the symptoms of an MS patient worse and if there is no wholly effective therapy for MS, why is it not the duty of a physician to withhold the diagnosis? After all, "Do no harm" is perhaps the most important of the Hippocratic maxims.

Decision Scenario 6 ....

Charles Lofton was a thirty-four-year-old systems analyst who was admitted to Towson Memorial Hospital with a diagnosis of testicular cancer. An intensely private man, Lofton seemed to be as embarrassed by his disease as he was frightened by the impending surgery.

"I want you to guarantee me that an absolute minimum number of people will be told what's wrong with me," he said to Dr. Samuel Shem. "I know the surgeon and the surgical team have to find out, obviously, and maybe three or four nurses, but I would like for that to be all. I don't want people on the staff talking about me."

"I understand how you must feel," Dr. Shem said. "But I have to be honest with you and tell you that a fairly large number of people will have to know about the disease and the surgery."

"How many are you talking about?"

"I don't know for sure. But there are three nursing shifts with eight nurses on each shift. I can't be here all the time so we're talking about the house staff, and that's another two or three people. Then there are some committee reviews involving several people."

"You must be talking about fifty people," Lofton said.

"I wouldn't be surprised."

"Isn't there anything that can be done to protect my privacy?" Lofton asked.

1. *Why is confidentiality important to good medical practice?*

2. *What are some of the more serious threats posed to confidentiality in contemporary medicine?*

3. *Does confidentiality have a different meaning in the current medical setting? That is, does it have to be understood as involving something other than a personal and private relationship with a physician?*

4. *What proposals does Siegler make in order to resolve some of the problems of maintaining a patient's confidentiality?*

5. *If Siegler's proposals were adopted, would confidentiality of the traditional sort be preserved?*

Decision Scenario 7 ••

Jane Montrose told herself that it was just one of the things you had to do if you wanted to get promoted. Talking to eleven department heads might be a bore, but so far they had all been quite nice. And it wasn't even a bad idea. If she were going to be working as an assistant vice-president, she would have to deal with all of these people frequently. It made sense for them to have an opportunity to say whether they would feel comfortable working with her.

"How did you learn so much about computers?" Art Davis asked her.

It was a question people always asked. For some reason, they invariably seemed surprised to learn that a woman was comfortable dealing with the mysteries of data processing.

"I have a degree in computer science," she said. "Besides, I've been working with computers for about eight years now. You get to know their ways."

Davis nodded and smiled at her. She was somewhat surprised that he would ask such a naive question. As head of personnel, he more than anyone knew about her educational background and her work history. She wondered if he wasn't just stalling, making polite conversation until he could ask what really interested him.

"How are you doing with your psychiatrist?" Davis asked.

Jane was totally surprised by the question. She had assumed that only her closest friends knew she had been going to a psychiatrist.

"Fine," she said. "I mean, I've been able to work through a lot of problems that were bothering me."

She didn't really want to talk to Davis about her feelings of depression and lack of self-worth that had been troubling her for the last few years. None of it was any of his business.

"Do you think you'll be able to handle new responsibilities? This is a pretty important job you're being considered for, you know."

"I can handle them. I've always done very well at whatever job I've worked at."

"I know you have," Davis said. "But when we see that an employee has been going to a psychiatrist . . . well, that makes us wonder if that person is really to be trusted with a lot of responsibility. I'm sure you understand."

"I don't really. I don't see what my personal problems have to do with my work, assuming they don't get in the way of my doing it. And they never have."

Davis smiled at her in a way that made her very angry. It was the kind of tolerant but superior smile adults usually reserve for children who are talking about things they don't understand.

"What I want to know," Jane said, "is how you knew about my seeing a psychiatrist. I thought my medical records were all confidential."

"They are, so far as I know. But you did put in an insurance claim for payment, and I have to sign off on all the claims. When I did that, I saw you were getting psychiatric help."

"Are you going to make that public?"

"Not public," Davis said. "But I do feel obliged to mention it to the Executive Planning Group. If they're thinking about promoting you, then that's something they ought to know. I'm surprised you didn't volunteer the information yourself."

"I didn't think it was relevant," Jane said. "I didn't tell them I also suffer from hemorrhoids."

"Well, we'll let them judge whether it's relevant."

1. *Does Davis have an obligation to inform the Executive Planning Group that Jane Montrose is receiving psychiatric treatment?*

2. *In New York, employees of the state government have the right to send medical claims for psychiatric or psychological services directly to the insurance company. Should this be made a legal right for all employees in all states?*

3. *The so-called Privacy Protection Act of 1980 permits federal law-enforcement agencies to secure search warrants and gain access to all private records, except those of the media. Should the act be restricted to exclude medical and mental-health records?*

Decision Scenario 8 ••

In 1992, two pathologists who had participated in performing an autopsy on the body of President John F. Kennedy published an article in *JAMA*, the journal of the American Medical Association, in which they revealed that the president had been almost completely lacking in adrenal glands. He suffered from Addison's disease. The lack of hormones secreted by the glands can produce lethargy, weight loss, loss of appetite, bronzed skin, and low blood pressure. If the disease is not treated by replacing cortisone and related hormones, it leads to a slow-wasting and eventual death. President Kennedy was among the earliest to benefit from hormone replacement therapy.

Kennedy's illness was never publicly disclosed during his lifetime. In 1960, Kennedy described himself as "the healthiest candidate in the country" when he opposed Lyndon Johnson for the Democratic presidential nomination. Johnson had suffered a near-fatal heart attack five years earlier.

Johnson's campaign staff claimed that Kennedy was hiding his hormonal disease, but both Kennedy and his brother Robert, his campaign manager, denied the truth of the allegation. At a news conference on November 10, 1960, Kennedy asserted that he had "never" had Addison's disease. Robert Kennedy issued a statement in which he claimed that John Kennedy "does not now nor has he ever had an ailment described classically as Addison's disease." He admitted that his brother

had mild adrenal insufficiency but made no mention of the cortisone injections that he required.

Robert Kennedy's statement was saved from being completely false only by the fact that Addison's disease "classically described" involves the destruction of the adrenal glands by tuberculosis. The cause in John Kennedy's case was unknown, but he was thirty years old when the first symptoms appeared.

In an editorial accompanying the *JAMA* article, George D. Lundburg raised the question of whether Kennedy would have been elected president if he had publicly acknowledged that for thirteen years he had suffered from "an incurable, potentially fatal, although fully treatable disease and that there were potential serious adverse effects of the treatment." Some of these effects include mood swings and ulcers.

In the view of some political analysts, the disclosure of the information about Kennedy's medical condition during the 1960 presidential campaign against Richard Nixon would most likely have resulted in Nixon's election.

1. *Should a physician be obligated to reveal the medical condition of a patient if the patient is seeking public office, does not reveal the condition himself, and the condition is one that can make a significant difference in the way the patient might perform in office?*

2. *Was it morally legitimate for the authors of the JAMA article to make public information about President Kennedy's disease?*

3. *Describe a case in which a physician's duty to respect the confidentiality of a patient might come into conflict with some other duty.*

Decision Scenario 9 ....

"Sometimes I think that what I really want to do is to kill people and drink their blood."

Dr. Allen Wolfe looked at the young man in the chair across from him. The face was round and soft and innocent looking, like that of a large baby. But the body had the powerful shoulders of a college wrestler. There was no doubt that Hal Crane had the strength to carry out his fantasies.

"Any people in particular?" Dr. Wolfe asked.

"Women. Girls about my age. Maybe their early twenties."

"But no one you're personally acquainted with."

"That's right. Just girls I see walking down the street or getting off a bus. I have a tremendous urge to stick a knife into their stomachs and feel the blood come out on my hands."

"But you've never done anything like that?"

Crane shook his head. "No, but I'm afraid I might."

Dr. Wolfe considered Crane a paranoid schizophrenic with compulsive tendencies, someone who might possibly act out his fantasies. He was a potentially dangerous person.

"Would you be willing to take my advice and put yourself in a hospital under my care for a while?"

"I don't want to do that," Crane said. "I don't want to be locked up like an animal."

"But you don't really want to hurt other people, do you?"

"I guess not," Crane said. "But I haven't done anything yet."

"But you might," Dr. Wolfe said. "I'm afraid you might let yourself go and kill someone."

Crane smiled. "That's just the chance the world will have to take, isn't it? I told you I'm not going to let myself be locked up."

1. *Suppose that you are Dr. Wolfe. To take the legal steps necessary to have Mr. Crane committed against his will requires that you violate confidentiality. What justification might a utilitarian offer for doing this?*

2. *Might a Kantian oppose commitment on the grounds that it would violate Crane's dignity as a person?*

3. *As a physician, how would you justify acting to protect others while going against the wishes of your patient?*

4. *Should a physician be required by law to act to protect the welfare of others?*

5. *How does this case compare to the* Tarasoff *case? What might Justice Tobriner require of Dr. Wolfe in this situation? How does Justice Clark think such situations should be handled?*

Decision Scenario 10 ....

For five years, the hospital of the Medical University of South Carolina followed a controversial policy with respect to pregnant women. Pregnant women admitted to the hospital were asked to sign a consent form agreeing to drug testing, if their physicians decided they needed it. The women who tested positive for cocaine were turned in to local police and were arrested, unless they agreed to take part in a drug rehabilitation program.

Under the hospital policy, forty-two women were turned in. Some agreed to drug treatment,

while others were charged with distributing drugs to minors—their fetuses. (These charges were later dropped.)

Critics of the policy claimed that it focused on poor, black women, who form a large proportion of the hospital's patient population. Furthermore, the policy violated the confidentiality of the physician-patient relationship and the women's right to privacy.

In September 1994, responding to pressure from the federal government, the hospital agreed to change its policy. Had the hospital not complied with federal demands, it stood to lose $18 million of federal research money.

1. How might the line of reasoning taken by Annas be applied to the claim that by signing the consent form for drug testing, the women were tacitly waiving their right to privacy and confidentiality?

2. Under what conditions, according to the position on pregnancy and prenatal harm taken by Robert-son and Schulman, would the hospital's policy be justified?

3. Is there a policy that the hospital might pursue that would prevent prenatal harm, while also avoiding violating the autonomy of the pregnant woman and preserving the confidentiality of the physician-patient relationship?

CHAPTER 6
MEDICAL EXPERIMENTATION AND INFORMED CONSENT

SOCIAL CONTEXT: THE COLD-WAR RADIATION EXPERIMENTS

Amelia Jackson was a cook at Pogue's department store in Cincinnati, in 1966, when she was diagnosed with colon cancer. In October, she was treated with 100 rads of full-body radiation—the equivalent of 7,500 chest X rays. Until the treatment, Ms. Jackson was strong and still working, but after the treatment, she bled and vomited for days and was never again able to care for herself.

Ms. Jackson was treated as part of a program operated by the University of Cincinnati and supported in part by funds from the Pentagon. She was one of several cancer patients in a research program in which people were subjected to radiation in massive doses to determine its biological effects.

The aim of the study, according to researchers, was to develop more effective cancer treatments. However, the military was interested in determining how much radiation military personnel could be subjected to before becoming disoriented and unable to function effectively.

The Cincinnati project was only one of a patchwork of human experiments involving radiation that were carried out with funding from a variety of military and civilian agencies of the U.S. government over a period of at least thirty years. The experiments took place at government laboratories and university hospitals and research centers. Some experiments involved exposing patients to high-energy beams of radiation, while others involved injecting them with such dangerous radioactive substances as plutonium.

The experiments started toward the end of World War II. They were prompted by both scientific curiosity and the practical and military need to know more about the damaging effects of radiation on people. The advent of the Cold War between the United States and the Soviet Union and the real possibility that the political conflict would lead to nuclear war gave a sense of urgency to the research. Little was known about the harmful effects of radiation, and researchers believed that their experiments would not only contribute to understanding, but would provide the basis for more effective medical therapies.

In the late 1940s, Vanderbilt University exposed about eight hundred pregnant women to radiation to determine its effects on fetal development. A follow-up study of the children born to the women showed a higher-than-average rate of cancer.

At the Oak Ridge National Laboratory in Tennessee, patients with leukemia and other forms of cancer were exposed to extremely high levels of radiation from isotopes of cesium and cobalt. Almost two hundred patients, including a six-year-old boy, were subjected to such treatment, until the experiment was ended in 1974 by the Atomic Energy Commission, on the grounds of lack of patient benefit.

From 1963 to 1971, experiments were conducted at Oregon State Prison in which the testicles of sixty-seven inmates were exposed to X rays to determine effects of radiation on sperm production. Prisoners signed consent statements that mentioned some of the risks of the radiation. However, the possibility that the radiation might cause cancer was not mentioned. A similar experiment was conducted on sixty-four inmates at Washington State Prison.

At Columbia University and Montefiore Hospital in New York, during the late 1950s, twelve terminally ill cancer patients were injected with concentrations of radioactive calcium and strontium 85 to measure the rate at which the substances are absorbed by various types of tissues.

At a state residential school in Fernald, Massachusetts, from 1946 to 1956, nineteen mentally retarded teenaged boys were fed radioactive iron and calcium in their breakfast cereal. The aim of the research was to provide information about nutrition and metabolism. In the consent form mailed to parents of the boys, no mention was made of radiation.

The radiation experiments became public only in 1993 when reporters for the *Albuquerque Tribune* tracked down five of the eighteen patients who had been subjects in an experiment conducted from 1945 to 1957, in which patients were injected with plutonium. The work was done at the University of Rochester, Oak Ridge Laboratory, the University of Chicago, and the University of California, San Francisco Hospital. Apparently, some of the patients did not receive information about their treatment and were injected with radioactive materials without first giving consent.

Relying on the Freedom of Information Act, Eileen Welsome, a reporter for the newspaper, attempted to get documents from the Department of Energy concerning the radiation research, including ones containing the names of subjects. However, she was able to secure little information, and Tara O'Toole, Assistant Secretary of Energy for Environment, Health and Safety, expressed reservations about releasing documents containing the names of research subjects. "Does the public's right to know include releasing names?" O'Toole asked. "It is not clear to me that it is part of the ethical obligation of the Government."

Secretary of Energy Hazel R. O'Leary has committed her department to a full investigation of the radiation experiments. A major focus of the inquiry is on whether patients were fully informed about the risks of the treatments they received and whether they gave meaningful consent to them.

In a number of cases, as Ms. O'Leary admits, it appears obvious that experimental subjects were not informed of the risks they faced and did not consent to participate in the research. Evidence suggests that patients were misled about the character of the treatments and that in some cases even the signatures on consent forms were forged. Ms. Jackson's granddaughter claims that although her grandmother was illiterate, she could sign her name, and the signature on the form used by the University of Cincinnati was not hers. The same claim is made by other relatives of subjects in the study.

In at least one instance, a researcher found the radiation experiments to be morally suspect and warned his colleagues against pursuing them. C. E. Newton at the Hanford nuclear weapons plant wrote in an internal memorandum about the work done with prisoners at Washington State Prison: "The experiments do not appear to have been in compliance with the criminal codes of the state of Washington, and there is some question as to whether they were conducted in compliance with Federal laws."

Similarly, in a 1950 memorandum, Joseph G. Hamilton, a radiation biologist, warned his supervisors that the experiments "might have a little of the Buchenwald touch." Hamilton warned that the Atomic Energy Commission would be "subject to considerable criticism."

Some observers claim that work carried out twenty or thirty years ago cannot be judged by the same ethical standards as we would use today. Robert Loeb, speaking for Strong Memorial Hospital, where some of the studies were carried out, puts the point this way: "In the 1940s, what was typical in research involving human subjects was for physicians to tell the patients that they would be involved in a study and not always give full details. That is not the standard today. Many of these studies would be impossible to conduct today."

By contrast, Dr. David S. Egilman, who has investigated instances of research with human subjects conducted by the military and the Atomic Energy Commission, claims that there is adequate evidence to conclude that the researchers and their supporting agencies knew they were conducting immoral experiments. "They called the work, in effect, Nazi-like," he says. "The argument we hear is that these experiments were ethical at the time they were done. It's simply not true."

The initial question about the use of human subjects in radiation experiments conducted under the auspices of what is now the Department of Energy has now expanded to include those conducted by several federal agencies. Currently, it seems as if at least one thousand people were exposed to varying levels of radiation in a variety of experiments conducted over a number of years at various locations. As the investigation proceeds, figures could run much higher.

Records from the Energy Department, Defense Department, Central Intelligence Agency, NASA, and federal health agencies are currently being reviewed to attempt to locate research projects involving radiation and identify the people who were their experimental subjects. Those who were wronged or their relatives may be entitled to compensation.

The Department of Energy and other agencies are continuing their inquiries, and a Congressional subcommittee has been established and charged with investigating the charges that subjects failed to give their informed consent before they were subjected to the risks of high-dose radiation treatments.

After ten years of deliberation, in 1991 the U.S. government issued a set of policy guidelines governing all human research receiving federal support. The guidelines are designed to promote informed consent and guard against abuses of the sort that occurred in the radiation experiments during the Cold War.

Representative David Mann of Ohio, a member of the subcommittee, summed up the views of most current observers: "I believe we have no choice but to conclude that the radiation experiments were simply wrong and that the Government owes a huge apology to the victims, their families, and the nation."

CASE PRESENTATION
The Willowbrook Hepatitis Experiments

The Willowbrook State School in Staten Island, New York, is an institution devoted to housing and caring for mentally retarded children. In 1956 a research group led by Saul Krugman and Joan P. Giles of the New York University School of Medicine initiated a long-range study of viral hepatitis at Willowbrook. The children confined there were made experimental subjects of the study.

Hepatitis is a disease affecting the liver that is now known to be caused by one of two (possibly more) viruses. Although the viruses are distinct, the results they produce are the same. The liver becomes inflamed and increases in size as the invading viruses replicate themselves. Also, part of the tissue of the liver may be destroyed and the liver's normal functions impaired. Often the flow of bile through the ducts is blocked, and bilirubin (the major pigment in bile) is forced into the blood and urine. This produces the symptom of yellowish or jaundiced skin.

The disease is generally relatively mild, although permanent liver damage can be produced. The symptoms are ordinarily flulike—mild fever, tiredness, inability to keep food down. The viruses causing the disease are transmitted orally through contact with the feces and bodily secretions of infected people.

Krugman and Giles were interested in determining the natural history of viral hepatitis—the mode of infection and the course of the disease over time. They also wanted to test the effectiveness of gamma globulin as an agent for inoculating against hepatitis. (Gamma globulin is a protein complex extracted from the blood serum that contains antigens, substances that trigger the production of specific antibodies to counter infectious agents.)

Krugman and Giles considered Willowbrook to be a good choice for investigation because viral hepatitis occurred more or less constantly in the institution. In the jargon of medicine, the disease was endemic. That this was so was recognized in 1949, and it continued to be so as the number of children in the school increased to over 5,000 in 1960. Krugman and Giles claimed that "under the chronic circumstances of multiple and repeated exposure . . . most newly admitted children became infected within the first six to twelve months of residence in the institution."

Over a fourteen-year period, Krugman and Giles collected over 25,000 serum specimens from more than 700 patients. Samples were taken before exposure, during the incubation period of the virus, and for periods after the infection. In an effort to get the kind of precise data they considered most useful, Krugman and Giles decided to deliberately infect some of the incoming children with the strain of the hepatitis virus prevalent at Willowbrook.

They justified their decision in the following way:

> It was inevitable that susceptible children would become infected in the institution. Hepatitis was especially mild in the 3- to 10-year age group at Willowbrook. These studies would be carried out in a special unit with optimum isolation facilities to protect the children from other infectious diseases such as shigellosis [dysentery caused by a bacillus], and parasitic and respiratory infections which are prevalent in the institution.

Most important, Krugman and Giles claimed that being an experimental subject was in the best medical interest of the child, for not only would the child receive special care, but infection with the milder form of hepatitis would provide protection against the more virulent and damaging forms. As they say: "It should be emphasized that the artificial induction of hepatitis implies a 'therapeutic' effect because of the immunity which is conferred."

Krugman and Giles obtained what they considered to be adequate consent from the parents of the children used as subjects. Where they were unable to obtain consent, they did not include the child in the experiment. In the earlier phases of the study, parents were provided with relevant information either by letter or orally, and written consent was secured from them. In the later phases, a group procedure was used:

> First, a psychiatric social worker discusses the project with the parents during a preliminary interview. Those who are interested are invited to attend a group session at the institution to discuss the project in greater detail. These sessions are conducted by the staff responsible for the program, including the physician, supervising nurses, staff attendants, and psychiatric social workers. . . . Parents in groups of six to eight are given a tour of the facilities. The purposes, potential benefits, and potential hazards of the program are discussed with them, and they are encouraged to ask questions. Thus, all parents can hear the response to questions posed by the more articulate members of the group. After leaving this briefing session parents have an opportunity to talk with their private physicians who may call the unit for more information. Approximately two weeks after each visit, the psychiatric social worker contacts the parents for their decision. If the decision is in the affirmative, the consent is signed but parents are informed that signed consent may be withdrawn any time before the beginning of the program. It has been clear that the group method has enabled us to obtain more thorough informed consent. Children who are wards of the state or children without parents have never been included in our studies.

Krugman and Giles point out that their studies have been reviewed and approved by the New York State Department of Mental Hygiene, the New York State Department of Mental Health, the Armed Forces Epidemiological Board, and the human-experimentation committees of the New York University School of Medicine and the Willowbrook School. They also stress that, although they were under no obligation to do so, they chose to meet the World Medical Association's Draft Code on Human Experimentation.

The value of the research conducted by Krugman and Giles has been recognized as significant in furthering a scientific understanding of viral hepatitis and methods for treating it. Yet serious moral doubts have been raised about the nature and conduct of the experiments. In particular, many have questioned the use of retarded children as experimental subjects, some claiming that children should never be experimental subjects in investigations that are not directly therapeutic. Others have raised questions about the ways in which consent was obtained from the parents of the children, suggesting that parents were implicitly blackmailed into giving their consent. The letters to the British medical journal *Lancet* and the selection from Paul Ramsey's *The Patient as Person* presented in this chapter discuss these issues.

SOCIAL CONTEXT: THE ARTIFICIAL HEART— CONSENT TO DISASTER?

On April 4, 1969, Haskell Karp, a forty-seven-year-old printing estimator from Illinois, became the first patient in history to receive an artificial heart. For sixty-three hours the device maintained Karp's blood pressure and circulation; then a transplanted heart was put in its place. Karp died some twenty hours after receiving the transplant.

The surgery was performed at St. Luke's Hospital in Houston by Denton Cooley. Cooley claimed in television interviews after the surgery that he had implanted the artificial device as a desperate measure, because Mr. Karp was dying on the operating table and a donor heart was not available. During the interviews, Cooley made a plea for the donation of a heart to transplant into Mr. Karp.

Almost immediately Cooley's actions became the center of a storm of controversy. In deciding to use the artificial heart, Cooley had consulted no one but his patient. Although a member of the faculty of Baylor University, Cooley had not sought permission from Michael DeBakey, the head of the artificial heart program, nor had he brought the issue before the university's human-subjects committee.

In hearings held before various committees charged with investigating the matter, other charges and criticisms emerged. Most

seriously, Cooley was said to have acted unethically by implanting "an unproved device . . . into a human being for primary experimentation before its safety and effectiveness" had been "proved scientifically in animal experiments." Cooley replied that the device had been tested in seven calves; although all had died, one had lived for forty-four hours. That, Cooley claimed, was enough to justify going forward with using the device in humans. Besides, he said, the device was used because his patient was dying, and no other option was available. The artificial heart was there and ready to use. "Everything came together at once," Cooley said.

Cooley insisted that his experience in heart surgery was the only real grounds for his decision: "Based on this experience, I believe I am qualified to judge what is right and proper for my patients. The permission I receive to do what I do, I receive from my patients. It is not received from a government agency or from one of my seniors."

Critics charged that Cooley had actually engineered the whole episode to seek publicity for himself. DeBakey claimed that Cooley had not made an appeal for a donor heart until after he had performed the operation and gone on television. Furthermore, the situation was not the life-or-death one that Cooley claimed. One surgeon said that Cooley had asked him to participate in the surgery days before it took place. Also, Cooley had planned enough in advance to have the console power source for the heart available and to have movie cameras in place to make a complete record of the operation.

At the end of the inquiry, Cooley was found guilty by the local medical society on eight counts of seeking publicity, but no other disciplinary actions were taken against him. He resigned from Baylor because of his unwillingness to sign National Institutes of Health guidelines on experimental human surgery. He explained that if he did so he would feel that he was giving in to DeBakey, his major critic.

Cooley continued to practice surgery at his Texas Heart Institute, and at medical meetings he was in much demand as a speaker on the Karp operation. Although Karp's widow sued Cooley on the grounds that he had failed to secure a proper consent form for the unprecedented procedure, the courts held that the procedure was primarily therapeutic and not experimental.

The artificial heart program at Baylor was part of a research effort initiated in 1964 by the National Heart, Lung, and Blood Institute of NIH. The head of NIH, James Shannon, had opposed the program on the grounds that not enough was known to make the technology workable and reliable. Michael DeBakey was a strong advocate of the research, however, and convinced Congress that it should be funded. As DeBakey recalled almost fifteen years later: "Jim Shannon was opposed to the concept and NIH's involvement in it, because he thought there wasn't enough basic knowledge and it wasn't scientifically sound. I went over his head to Congress."

The initial aim of the new federal program was to develop a completely implantable artificial heart by 1970, but this goal turned out to be unrealistic. Research then focused on the development of a reliable, externally powered device as a necessary first step.

The controversy around the Cooley affair had subsided before the next major event occurred. In 1982 Barney Clark, a retired dentist, became the first person to receive an implanted artificial heart intended to be permanent. The surgery was performed with federal Food and Drug Administration approval and only after extensive animal testing had taken place. William C. DeVries of the University of Utah Medical Center was the head of the surgical team. Clark received the Jarvik-7 heart, and despite numerous complications he lived for 112 days.

After Barney Clark's, DeVries performed three more permanent implants. An additional implant was made in Sweden so that a total of five were done. Everyone given a permanent implant died. The major problem appeared to be that small blood clots formed on the surface or valves of the artificial heart; when these clots broke off, they blocked blood flow to the brain and caused disabling strokes.

William J. Schroeder lived longer than anyone else with an artificial heart—620 days. However, he suffered three strokes, was often in a coma-like state, and, when aroused, was able to say only a few words. Other medical problems, such as recurrent infections due to the suppression of the immune system, internal bleeding, and respiratory difficulties, affected Mr. Schroeder and all other implant recipients.

The very poor quality of life that the artificial heart provided to patients did not make it a realistic alternative to heart transplants. As DeVries himself remarked, "There is no question that if you have a choice, you have a transplant. Transplants are therapeutic reality and they are good, whereas the artificial heart is still a very highly experimental thing."

DeVries also pointed out that for patients not eligible for transplants because of their age or because they had diseases like pulmonary hypertension, the artificial heart offered the only therapy possible. He mentioned William Schroeder as an example of someone who had a poor quality of life but was at least alive and capable of having experiences that otherwise he would have missed. He was able to enjoy the birth of his grandson, celebrate birthdays, and be present at family gatherings. "We lose track of the fact that he would have been dead" without the artificial heart, DeVries pointed out.

Even at the height of its public acclaim, critics of the artificial heart program charged that the device should not be used as a permanent implant. In their view, even when the surgery was successful and the device functioned properly, the quality of life that it provided was so poor that there was no justification for keeping people alive by such means. The device should be used only as a temporary measure to keep patients alive until a donor heart for transplant could be secured.

Other critics were even more severe in their strictures and argued for a moratorium on the use of the artificial heart. They pointed out that even when the device was used as a temporary bridge to a transplant, results were mixed and a significant number of patients died. Strong evidence suggested that, the longer a patient had an implant, the worse his physical condition became.

Furthermore, the cost of using the artificial heart was staggeringly high. Even when the device was used as a temporary bridge, treatment cost tens of thousands of dollars per patient. If complications developed or if the patient had to remain on the device for an extended period of time, the costs then mounted to hundreds of thousands of dollars. Far more lives could be saved, critics said, by using these resources to prevent heart disease through the funding of programs aimed at improving diet, promoting exercise, or eliminating smoking.

In May 1988, Claude Lenfant, Director of NIH, announced that he was canceling federal funds for research on the artificial heart. "The human body just couldn't seem to tolerate it," he said, citing the many medical problems mentioned by critics. Lenfant did not eliminate money for the support of the left-ventricular assist device or other heart-related technology.

William DeVries, who had now moved to Humana Hospital in Louisville, Kentucky, objected to the cancellation on the grounds that it would halt or interrupt the work of many outstanding researchers who had made long-term commitments to developing the artificial heart. DeVries claimed that he would continue his work without federal funding, although the lack of NIH approval would make it difficult to raise private money.

Others saw the cancellation of federal sup-

port as long overdue. During its twenty-four years, the program consumed $240 million in research funds. Important devices like the intra-aortic balloon pump, blood-flow meters, and oxygenators came from the research program, but in the view of critics the costs were completely out of line with the value.

The artificial heart program has strong defenders who would like to see it revived. Whether it should be remains a serious social question. In addition, while research was in progress, the use of the device was morally controversial in a number of respects. As an experimental therapy, it raised serious questions about consent, participation, and termination. The questions remain genuine, even though the program is no longer supported. In the debate over whether the research program should be reinstituted, the moral questions are particularly relevant. If the research itself is ethically objectionable, this is a powerful—perhaps even decisive—argument against it. We may look to the past to help guide us in the future.

When should an experimental therapy be ended? In the case of the artificial heart, this question is especially relevant, because it may involve turning off the power supply and allowing the patient to die. Barney Clark was given a key to turn off his power source; in principle, he would have been able to terminate the experiment at any time of his choosing. However, because of his stroke and his deteriorated physical condition, very soon after the implant he was not considered mentally competent to make decisions about his own treatment. Decisions involving consent were made by his wife. In practice, Clark's case, as well as the others, suggests that, once a person has agreed to a permanent implant, he is likely to be incapable of exercising any control over the future course of his life.

If this is so, then who should decide when the experiment is to be stopped? Should the patient be allowed to stipulate before the surgery under what conditions he would want the experiment discontinued? Should the physician be allowed to continue the experiment against the wishes of a family member? Furthermore, is turning off an artificial heart no different from turning off a respirator? Or does the certainty of death in the case of the heart make the action different in a morally relevant way? These and others like them are basic questions that were never resolved by researchers in the artificial heart program.

Since the artificial heart was a therapy involving so many risks and uncertainties, it was made available only to those not likely to benefit from established therapies. It was a therapy of last resort. This alone meant that candidates who nominated themselves to become recipients were likely to agree to accept any risks spelled out for them. Dr. DeVries reported that all four of his implant patients "told me in their own way that they didn't care" whether they read the consent form or not. "They were not really interested in listening to the long list of horrors that could happen to them," he said. "They didn't want to hear that they may have a stroke and be unable to use all mental capabilities. Those are issues that they would rather be left unsaid."

In a sense, such people can be regarded as coerced by their own diseases and their own desperation. In such a circumstance, the very notion of informed consent seems to lose the significance ordinarily attached to it. Given that this is so and given the dismal record of outcomes from permanent implant surgery, should we as a society even allow people to agree to become subjects in an experimental therapy that promises so little?

One might argue that the benefits of an artificial heart implant are so meager that individuals ought not be allowed to consent to it. Certainly, then, we should not support the program until enough basic scientific and clinical research has been done to improve the benefits to potential recipients far beyond those of the five people who received the devices. Indeed, perhaps our society should not just refuse to support with federal funds the use of the device; perhaps we should also declare a moratorium on such surgery. Thus, even if DeVries and other researchers secure private funding and find willing and consenting volunteers, perhaps they should not be allowed to implant an artificial heart into their patients.

On the other side, though, how far are we as a society willing to go in refusing to allow individuals to take whatever risks with their own lives that they choose? If an artificial heart offers some additional life, even of poor quality, should we refuse to allow a person to choose this as an option? Further, what if the patient is aware of the consequences but also believes that by participating he is making a contribution to the development of a device that might eventually save the lives of millions?

As DeVries points out, the first twelve dialysis patients died. Presumably he wants us to see that every significant medical advancement typically involves an unavoidable loss of life. Although this may be true, other factors must also be considered. For example, from ancient times until the end of the last century, hundreds of attempts were made to transfuse blood from human to human and from animal to human. Virtually all were disastrous for the recipients, and little or nothing was learned from the attempts. When Karl Landsteiner, building on the work of a number of people, developed blood typing in 1900, successful transfusion became a reality.

Can we say whether someone who consents to receive a heart is contributing to the advancement of medicine and science? That depends upon what stage of research we think the artificial heart has reached. If it is in a pre-Landsteiner phase, then one may be contributing very little. But perhaps even a little is enough.

These are questions to answer about any artificial heart program, past or future.

CASE PRESENTATION
Baby Fae

On October 14, 1984, a baby was born in a community hospital in southern California with a malformation known as hypoplastic left-heart syndrome. In such a condition, the mitral valve or aorta on the left side of the heart is underdeveloped, and essentially only the right side of the heart functions properly. Some 300 to 2,000 infants a year are born with this defect, and most die from it within a few weeks.

The infant, who became known to the public as Baby Fae, was taken to the Loma Linda University Hospital Center. There, on October 26, a surgical team headed by Dr. Leonard Bailey performed a heart transplant; Baby Fae became the first human infant to receive a baboon heart. She died twenty days later.

Baby Fae was not the first human to receive a so-called xenograft, or cross-species transplant. In early 1964, a sixty-eight-year-old man was transplanted with a chimpanzee heart at the University of Mississippi Medical Center. The heart failed after only an hour, and the patient died. Before Baby Fae, three other cross-species transplants had also ended in a quick death.

In the case of Baby Fae, questions about the moral correctness and scientific legitimacy of the transplant were raised immediately. Hospital officials revealed that no effort had been made to find a human donor before implanting the baboon heart, and this led some critics to wonder if research interests were not being given priority over the welfare of the patient. Others questioned whether the parents were adequately informed about alternative corrective surgery, the Norwood procedure, available in Boston and Philadelphia.

Other observers wondered whether the nature of the surgery and its limited value had been properly explained to the parents. Also, some critics raised objections to sacrificing a healthy young animal as part of an experiment not likely to bring any lasting benefit to Baby Fae.

Scientific critics charged that not enough is known about crossing the species barrier to warrant the use of transplant organs at this time. The previous record of failures, with no major advances

in understanding, did not make the prospect of another such transplant reasonable. Furthermore, critics said, chimpanzees and gorillas are genetically more similar to humans than baboons, so the choice of a baboon heart was not a wise one. The only advantage of baboons is that they are easier to breed in captivity. Also, one critic suggested that Dr. Bailey was merely engaged in "wishful thinking" in believing that Baby Fae's immune system would not produce a severe rejection response because of its immaturity.

An autopsy on Baby Fae showed that her death was caused by the incompatibility of her blood with that of the baboon heart. Baby Fae's blood was type O, the baboon's type AB. This resulted in the formation of blood clots and the destruction of kidney function. The heart showed mild signs of rejection.

In an address before a medical conference after Baby Fae's death, Dr. Bailey commented on some of the criticisms. He is reported to have said that it was "an oversight on our part not to search for a human donor from the start." Dr. Bailey also told the conference that he and his team believed that the difference in blood types between Baby Fae and the baboon would be less important than other factors and that the immunosuppressive drugs used to prevent rejection would also solve the problem of blood incompatibility. "We came to regret those assumptions," Dr. Bailey said. The failure to match blood types was "a tactical error that came back to haunt us."

On other occasions Dr. Bailey reiterated his view that, because infant donors are extremely scarce, animal-to-human transplants offer a realistic hope for the future. Before the Baby Fae operation, Dr. Bailey had transplanted organs in more than 150 animals. He indicated that he would use the information obtained from Baby Fae to conduct additional animal experiments before attempting another such transplant.

In March of 1985 the National Institutes of Health released a report of a committee that made a site visit to Loma Linda to review the Baby Fae matter. The committee found that the informed-consent process was generally satisfactory, in that "the parents were given an appropriate and thorough explanation of the alternatives available, the risks and benefits of the procedure and the experimental nature of the transplant." Moreover, consent was obtained in an "atmosphere which allowed the parents an opportunity to carefully consider, without coercion or undue influence, whether to give permission for the transplant."

The committee also pointed out certain flaws in the consent document. First, it "did not include the possibility of searching for a human heart or performing a human heart transplant." Second, the expected benefits of the procedure "appeared to be overstated," because the consent document "stated that 'long-term survival' is an expected possibility with no further explanation." Finally, the document did not explain "whether compensation and medical treatment were available if injury occurred."

The committee did not question the legitimacy of the cross-species transplant. Moreover, it made no mention of the Norwood procedure, except to say that it had been explained to the mother at the community hospital at the birth of the infant. (The consent document described the procedure as a generally unsuccessful "temporizing operation.")

Although the committee was generally critical of the university's Institutional Review Board in "evaluating the entire informed-consent process," it reached the conclusion that "the parents of Baby Fae understood the alternative available as well as the risks and reasonably expected benefits of the transplant."

Officials at Loma Linda University Medical Center promised that before performing another such transplant they would first seek a human infant heart donor.

CASE PRESENTATION
The Detroit Psychosurgery Case

Lafayette Clinic is a research facility in Detroit that is part of the Michigan Department of Mental Health. In 1972, the director of the clinic was Dr. J. S. Gottlieb, a psychiatrist, and its chief of neurology was Dr. Ernst Rodin. Both Rodin and Gottlieb had read the book *Violence and the Brain,* by V. H. Mark and F. R. Ervin, shortly after its publication in 1970. They discussed the work and agreed that some of the techniques it described might be useful in treating patients suffering from uncontrollable sexual and aggressive impulses.

Rodin wrote a description of a research project they might conduct: "Proposal for the Study of the Treatment of Uncontrollable Aggression at Lafayette Clinic." The research was to involve a comparative study of the value of surgical versus drug treatment of aggressive patients. The surgical part of the project proposed implanting depth-electrodes in the brains of twelve subjects to study their brain activity and to attempt to locate areas of electrical abnormality. If such an area was found and if, by brain stimulation, it could be linked to aggressive behavior, then stereotactic surgery would be performed. (Stereotactic surgery involves locating relatively precise areas by using careful

measurements.) The target areas would then be either resectioned (cut out) or destroyed by electro-coagulation. The ultimate aim of the project was said to be to restore patients to a "useful life" in the community.

The proposal, which requested $164,000, was submitted to the State Department of Mental Health. It was approved and included in the Department's legislative budget request. Although the state legislature held two hearings, no questions were raised about the Rodin proposal. The money was made available in July 1972.

Even before the allocation of funds, a search was being conducted for suitable subjects. The candidates were those confined in state institutions under the Michigan "Criminal Sexual Psychopath" law. These were people charged with serious sex crimes who were not prosecuted but confined involuntarily for an indeterminate period of time until considered sufficiently "cured" for release.

One such person, identified for the record only as John Doe, was approached by Dr. E. G. Yudashkin, the director of Ionia State Hospital, where Doe was confined. Yudashkin described the project to Doe and told him he would probably be released within six months or a year whether or not he participated. But he also pointed out that successful treatment in the research project would lead to an even speedier release.

Doe was not interested in the drug part of the research program but thought he might volunteer for the surgical part. Yudashkin and two staff physicians explained to him on three occasions what this might involve. But the knowledge of the physicians on this topic was not extensive, and Doe later testified that they gave him a misleadingly simple account. But, at the time, Doe decided to consent to becoming a subject, and Rodin was informed of this.

Rodin had decided that it was necessary to broaden the population of candidates from which subjects were to be selected. He had gone to Boston and talked with Vernon Mark about the project, and Mark had been critical of the ethical aspects. Rodin wrote in a memo to Gottlieb:

> When I informed Mr. Mark of our project, namely doing amygdalotomies on patients who do not have epilepsy, he became extremely concerned and stated we had no ethical right in so doing. . . . I then retorted that he was misleading us with his previously cited book and he had no right at all from a scientific point of view to state that in the human, aggression is accompanied by seizure discharges in the amygdala, because he is dealing only with patients who have susceptible brains, namely, temporal lobe epilepsy. . . .
>
> He stated categorically that as far as present evidence is concerned, one has no right to make lesions in a "healthy brain" when the individual suffers from rage attacks only.

Rodin discussed this matter with colleagues, and they decided not to do surgery on patients without verifiable organic brain dysfunctions. They expanded the population to be considered to include retarded, epileptic, and self-mutilating patients.

Lafayette Clinic's Human and Animal Experimentation Committee reviewed the project description and procedures and a draft of the informed-consent form. The committee, charged with protecting the rights and welfare of experimental subjects, raised no questions about the moral issues in the project. They approved it in October of 1972.

The project, as approved, required establishing two review committees to supervise patient selection and to protect patients from unethical practices. The three-member Medical Review Committee was to consider the medical condition and history of potential subjects recommended by Rodin. They were to eliminate patients unsuitable from a medical standpoint. After screening, a three-member Human Rights Review Committee was to determine for each patient whether informed consent was adequate and whether any rights were being infringed. After approval by both committees, a patient would then be given a consent form and a detailed explanation of the procedure to be performed on him. Then he and his family would have a week to consider whether they wished to sign the consent form.

None of this procedure was followed in the case of John Doe. Rodin met with John Doe on October 27. They discussed Doe's medical history for an hour, and at the end Doe indicated that he still wanted to participate in the project as a subject. Rodin read him the consent form, which read in part:

> Since conventional treatment efforts over a period of several years have not enabled me to control my outbursts of rage and anti-social behavior, I submit an application to be a subject in a research project which may offer me a form of effective therapy. This therapy is based upon the idea that episodes of anti-social rage and sexuality might be triggered by a disturbance in certain portions of my brain. I understand that in order to be certain that a significant brain disturbance exists, which might relate to my anti-social behavior, an initial operation will have to be performed. This procedure consists of placing fine wires into my brain, which will record the electrical activity from those structures which play a part in anger and sexuality. These electrical waves can then be studied to determine the presence of an abnormality.
>
> In addition electrical stimulation with weak currents passed through these wires will be done in order to find out if one or several points in the brain can trigger my episodes of violence or unlawful sexuality. In other words this stimulation may cause me to want to commit an aggressive or sexual act, but every effort will be made to have a sufficient number of people present to control me. If the brain disturbance is limited to a small area, I understand that the investigators will destroy this part of my brain with an electrical current. If the abnormality comes from a larger part of my

brain, I agree that it should be surgically removed, if the doctors determine that it can be done, without risk of side effects. Should the electrical activity from the parts of my brain into which the wires have been placed reveal that there is no significant abnormality, the wires will simply be withdrawn.

Rodin talked about the meanings of the terms in the form and explained the risks of the surgical procedures.

Later, John Doe was allowed to call his parents. The only explanation they received before signing the consent form was from him. Doe believed that he was agreeing only to implantation of depth-electrodes and not to stereotactic surgery. He thought that additional consent would be required for surgery. He and his parents signed the form.

Eventually, after the signing, both committees were given materials relating to John Doe. The members of the committees were all picked by Rodin. The medical committee never met, but each member considered the materials submitted by Rodin. The Human Rights Committee also examined the materials individually. Thus, neither committee ever met to discuss Doe's case, nor did any member of either committee talk with Doe.

John Doe was the only patient located to participate in the entire research program. Yet by the end of December, all the committee reviews were completed, and plans were made to implant the electrodes in John Doe's brain in early January.

Before this could happen, the process was brought to a halt. A psychiatric resident at Lafayette Clinic was bothered by the secret way in which the project was being run. He expressed these concerns to Gabe Kaimowitz, an attorney for the Michigan Medical Committee for Human Rights. In early January, Kaimowitz filed a petition and complaint with the Wayne County Circuit Court that asked that the State Department of Mental Health be required to "show cause . . . why they should not be enjoined from performing psychosurgery or using chemotherapy on persons involuntarily confined in the state hospital system in order to study 'uncontrollable aggression' or for any other similar purpose." Kaimowitz also asked that a writ of habeas corpus be issued to release John Doe and others from state hospitals because they were not receiving treatment.

Soon afterward, the Department of Mental Health decided to cancel funding for the Rodin

project. But the court decided that the legal issues were not moot and that the case should be heard. On March 23, the court also decided that the Criminal Sexual Psychopath law, under which John Doe had been committed, was unconstitutional. The court ordered him released, and John Doe was freed from Ionia State Hospital after eighteen years of confinement.

The court then heard arguments on the major legal and moral issues of the complaint. For the first time, a court was being asked to given an opinion on the legitimacy of psychosurgery and other experimental treatment methods involving people involuntarily confined to institutions.

On July 10, 1973, the court ruled that an involuntarily detained adult in a facility of the State Department of Mental Health cannot give legally adequate consent to "an innovative or experimental surgical procedure on the brain." The court was careful to point out that its ruling was based upon the state of knowledge about psychosurgery at the time of the decision. Furthermore, the court emphasized that an involuntary mental patient can give adequate consent to accepted neurological procedures. In the court's view, then, the type of neurosurgery proposed for Doe was not of the character to which he could give proper consent.

INTRODUCTION

In 1947, an international tribunal meeting in Nuremberg convicted fifteen German physicians of "war crimes and crimes against humanity." The physicians were charged with taking part in "medical experiments without the subjects' consent." But the language of the charge fails to indicate the cruel and barbaric nature of the experiments. Here are just some of them:

At the Ravensbrueck concentration camp, experiments were conducted to test the effectiveness of the drug sulfanilamide. Cuts were deliberately made on the bodies of people; then the wounds were infected with bacteria. The infection was worsened by forcing wood shavings and ground glass into the cuts. Then sulfanilamide and other drugs were tested for their effectiveness in combatting the infection.

At the Dachau concentration camp, healthy inmates were injected with extracts from the mucous glands of mosquitos to produce malaria. Various drugs were then used to determine their relative effectiveness.

At Buchenwald, numerous healthy people were deliberately infected with the spotted-fever virus merely for the purpose of keeping the virus alive. Over 90% of those infected died as a result.

Also at Buchenwald, various kinds of poisons were secretly administered to a number of inmates to test their efficacy. Either the inmates died or they were killed at once so that autopsies could be performed. Some experimental subjects were shot with poisoned bullets.

At Dachau, to help the German Air Force, investigations were made into the limits of human endurance and existence at very high altitudes. People were placed in sealed chambers, then subjected to very high and very low atmospheric pressures. As the indictment puts it, "Many victims died as a result of these experiments and others suffered grave injury, torture, and ill-treatment."

Seven of the physicians convicted were hanged, and the other eight received long prison terms. From the trial there emerged the Nuremberg Code, a statement of the principles that should be followed in conducting medical research with human subjects. (The principles of the code appear as a selection in this chapter.)

Despite the moral horrors that were revealed at Nuremberg, few people doubt the need for medical experimentation involving human subjects. The extent to which contemporary medicine has become effective in the treatment of disease and illness is due almost entirely to the fact that it has become scientific medicine. This means that contemporary medicine must conduct inquiries in which data are gathered to test hypotheses and general theories related to disease processes and their treatment. Investigations involving nonhuman organisms are essential, but ultimate tests of the correctness and effectiveness of medical treatments must involve human beings as research subjects. Human physiology and psychology are sufficiently different to make animal studies alone inadequate.

The German physicians tried at Nuremberg were charged with conducting experiments without the consent of their subjects. The notion that consent must be given before a person becomes an experimental subject is still considered to be the basic requirement that must be met for an experiment to be morally legitimate. Ordinarily, it is not merely consent—saying yes—but *informed consent* that is demanded. The basic idea is simply that a person decides to participate in research after he or she has been provided with background information relevant to making the decision.

This same notion of informed consent is also considered a requirement that has to be satisfied before a person can legitimately be subjected to medical treatment. Thus, people are asked to agree to submit themselves to such ordinary medical procedures as blood transfusion or to other procedures such as surgical operations or radiation therapy.

The underlying idea of informed consent in both research and treatment is that people have a right to control what is done to their bodies. The notion of informed consent is thus a recognition of an individual's autonomy—of the right to make decisions governing one's own life. This right is recognized both in practice and in the laws of our society. (Quite often, malpractice suits turn on the issue of whether a patient's informed consent was valid.)

In the abstract, informed consent seems a clear and straightforward notion. After all, we all have an intuitive grasp of what it is to make a decision after we have been supplied with information. Yet in practice informed consent has proved to be a slippery and troublesome concept. In this introduction, we will attempt to identify some of the moral and practical difficulties that make the concept controversial and hard to apply. Our focus will be on informed consent in the context of human experimentation. But most of the issues that arise here also arise in connection with giving and securing informed consent for the application of medical therapies. (They also arise in special forms in abortion and euthanasia.) In effect, then, we will be considering the entire topic.

Before starting our discussion of informed consent, it will be useful to have some idea of what takes place in a typical medical experiment. Perhaps the most common type of research involves the testing of new drugs. Let us consider, then, a sketch of what is involved in such testing.

DRUG TESTING

Traditions of medical research and regulations of the U.S. Food and Drug Administration more or less guarantee that the development of new drugs follows a set procedure. The procedure consists of two major parts: preclinical and clinical testing.

When it is thought likely that a chemical substance might be useful, animal experiments are conducted to determine how toxic it is. These tests are also used to estimate the drug's therapeutic index (the ratio of a dose producing toxic effects to a dose producing desired effects). The effects of the substance on particular organs and tissues, as well as on the whole animal, are studied. Efforts are made to determine the drug's potential side effects and hazards (whether, for example, it is carcinogenic).

Clinical testing of the substance occurs in three phases. In phase one, normal human volunteers are used to determine whether the drug produces any toxic effects. If these results are acceptable, then in phase two the drug is administered to a limited number of patients who might be expected to benefit

from it. If the drug produces desirable results and has no serious side effects, then phase three studies are initiated. The drug is administered to a larger number of patients by a larger number of clinical investigators. Such trials usually take place at teaching hospitals or in large public institutions. Successful results achieved in this phase ordinarily lead to the licensing of the drug for general use.

In the clinical part of testing, careful procedures are followed to attempt to exclude bias in the results. Investigators want their tests to be successful and patients want to get well, and either or both of these factors may influence test results. Investigators may perceive a patient as "improved" just because they want or expect him to be. What is more, all medications produce a "placebo effect." That is, when patients are given inactive substances (placebos), they nevertheless often show improvement.

To rule out these kinds of influences, a common procedure followed in drug testing is the "double-blind" test design. In this design, a certain number of patients are given the drug being tested, and the remainder of the test group are given placebos. (In some cases, an established drug may be used instead of or in addition to placebos.) Neither the investigators nor the patients are allowed to know who is receiving the drug and who is not—both are kept "blind." Sometimes a test group is divided so that part receives placebos all of the time, part only some of the time, and part receives genuine medication all of the time.

Often placebos are no more than just sugar pills. Yet, frequently, substances are prepared to produce side effects like those of the drug being tested. If, for example, the drug causes drowsiness, a placebo will be used that produces drowsiness. In this way, investigators will not be able to learn which patients are being given placebos on the basis of irrelevant observations.

The double-blind test design is employed in many kinds of clinical investigation, not just in drug testing. Thus, the testing of new vaccines and therapies often follows the same form. A major variation is the "single-blind" design, in which those who must evaluate the results of some treatment are kept in ignorance of which patients have received it.

THE "INFORMED" PART OF INFORMED CONSENT

At first sight, consent is no more than agreement. A person consents when he or she says "yes" when asked to be a research subject. But legitimate or valid consent cannot be merely saying yes. If people are to be treated as autonomous agents, they must have the opportunity to *decide* whether they wish to become participants in research. Deciding, whatever else it may be, is a process in which we reason about an issue at hand. We consider such matters as the risks to our participation, its possible advantages to ourselves and others, the risks and advantages of other alternatives that are offered to us, and our own values. In short, valid consent requires that we deliberate before we decide.

But genuine deliberation requires both information and understanding. These two requirements are the source of difficulties and controversies. After all, medical research and treatment are highly technical enterprises. They are based on complicated scientific theories that are expressed in a special vocabulary and involve unfamiliar concepts.

For this reason, some physicians and investigators have argued that it is virtually useless to provide patients with relevant scientific information about research and treatment. Patients without the proper scientific background, they argue, simply don't know what to make of the information. Not only do patients find it puzzling, but they find it frightening. Thus, some have suggested, informed consent is at worst a pointless charade and at best a polite fiction. The patient's interest is best served by allowing a physician to make the decision.

This obviously paternalistic point of view (see Chapter 5) implies, in effect, that all patients are incompetent to decide their best interest and that physicians must assume the responsibility of acting for them. An obvious objection to this view is its assumption that, because patients lack a medical background, they cannot be given information in a form they can understand that is at least adequate to allow them to decide how they are to be treated. Thus, it can be argued, proponents of this view confuse the difficulty of communication with the impossibility of communication. It is true that it is often hard to explain technical medical matters to a layperson, but this hardly makes it legitimate to conclude that people should turn over their right to determine what is done to them to physicians. Rather, it imposes on physicians and researchers the obligation to find a way to explain medical matters to their patients.

The information provided to patients must be usable. That is, they must understand enough about the proposed research and treatment in order to deliberate and reach a decision. From the standpoint of the researcher, the problem here is to determine when the patient has an adequate understanding to make informed consent valid. Patients, being people, do not like to appear stupid and say they do not understand an explanation. Also, they may believe they understand an explanation when, as a matter of fact, they do not.

Until recently, very little effort was made to deal with the problem of determining when a patient understands the information provided and is competent to assess it. In the last few years, researchers have investigated situations in which individuals have been asked to consent to become experimental subjects. Drawing upon these data, some writers have attempted to formulate criteria for assessing competency for giving informed consent. The problem is not one that even now admits to an ideal solution, but, with additional empirical investigation and philosophical analysis, the situation may improve even more.

THE "CONSENT" PART OF INFORMED CONSENT

We have talked so far as though the issue of gaining the legitimate agreement of someone to be a research subject involved only providing information to an ordinary person in ordinary circumstances and then allowing the person to decide. But the matter is more complicated than this because often either the person or the circumstances possess special features. These features can call into question the very possibility of valid consent.

It is generally agreed that, in order to be valid, consent must be voluntary. The person must be of his or her "own free will" agree to become a research subject. This means that the person must be capable of acting voluntarily. That is, the person must be *competent*.

This is an obvious and sensible requirement that is accepted by virtually everyone. But the difficulty lies in specifying just what it means to be competent. One answer is that a person is competent if he or she is capable of acting rationally. Since we have some idea of what it is to act rationally, this is a movement in the direction of an answer. The problem with it, however, is that people sometimes decide to act for the sake of moral (or religious) principles in ways that may not seem reasonable. For example, someone may volunteer to be a subject in a potentially hazardous experiment because she believes the experiment holds out the promise of helping countless others. In terms of self-interest alone, such an action would not be reasonable.

At present we do not have adequate criteria that can specify who is competent and who is not. Quite apart from this general theoretical problem is the issue of how children, the mentally retarded, and those suffering from psychiatric illnesses are to be considered with respect to consent. Should no person in any of these groups be considered capable of giving consent? If so, then is it ever legitimate to secure the consent from some third party—from a parent or guardian? One possibility is simply to rule out all research that involves such people as subjects. But this has the undesirable consequence of severely hampering efforts to gain the knowledge that might be of use either to the people themselves or to others with similar medical problems.

The questions we have raised here are still matters very much under dispute. Later we will consider some of the special problems that arise with children and other special groups as research subjects.

The circumstances in which research is done can also call into question the voluntariness of consent. This is particularly so with prisons, nursing homes, and mental hospitals. These are all what the sociologist Erving Goffman calls "total institutions," for within them all aspects of a person's life are connected with the social structure. People have a definite place in the structure and particular social roles. Moreover, there are social forces at work that both pressure and encourage an inmate to do what is expected of him or her.

We will discuss below some of the special problems that arise in research with prisoners. Here we need only to point out that the matter of gaining voluntary consent from inmates in institutions may not be possible at all. If it is possible, then it is necessary to specify the kinds of safeguards that must be followed in order to free them from the pressures that result from the very fact that they are inmates. Those who suffer from psychiatric illnesses may be considered just as capable intellectually of giving consent, but here too safeguards to protect them from the pressures of the institution need to be specified.

To avoid a misimpression, it is also worth pointing out that ordinary patients in hospitals may also be subject to pressures that call into question the voluntariness of the consent that they give. Patients are psychologically predisposed to act in ways that please physicians. Not only do physicians possess a social role that makes them figures of authority, but an ill person feels very dependent on those who may possess the power to make him well.

Thus, he will be inclined to go along with any suggestion or recommendation made by a physician. The ordinary patient, like the inmate in an institution, needs protection from the social and psychological pressures that are exerted by circumstances. Otherwise, the voluntariness of consent will be compromised, and the patient cannot act as a free and autonomous agent.

MEDICAL RESEARCH AND MEDICAL THERAPY

Medical therapy aims at relieving the suffering of people and restoring them to health. It attempts to cure diseases, correct disorders, and bring about normal bodily functioning. Its focus is on the individual patient, and his or her welfare is its primary concern.

Medical research, by contrast, is a scientific enterprise. Its aim is to acquire a better understanding of the chemical and physiological processes that are involved in human functioning. It is concerned with the effectiveness of therapies in ending disease processes and restoring functioning. But this concern is not for the patient as an individual. Rather it is directed toward establishing theories. The hope, of course, is that this theoretical understanding can be used as a basis for treating individuals. But helping a particular patient get well is not a goal of medical research.

The related but distinct aims of medical research and medical therapy are a source of conflict in human experimentation. It is not unusual for a physician to be acting both as a researcher and as a therapist. This means that although she must be concerned with the welfare of her patient, her aims must also include acquiring data that are important to her research project. It is possible, then, that she may quite unconsciously encourage her patients to volunteer to be research subjects, provide them with inadequate information on which to base their decisions, or minimize the risks they are likely to be subject to.

The patient, for his part, may be reluctant to question his physician to acquire more information or to help him understand his role and risks in research. Also, as mentioned above, the patient may feel pressured into volunteering for research, just because he wants to do what his physician expects of him.

Medical research is a large-scale operation in this country and affects a great many people. It has been estimated that 400,000–800,000 people a year are patients in research programs investigating the effectiveness of drugs and other therapies. Since 1980, the number of clinical studies has increased about 30%, from about 3,400 to 4,400. Informed consent is more than an abstract moral issue.

The aims of therapy and the aims of research may also cause moral difficulties for the physician that go beyond the question of consent. This is particularly so in certain kinds of research. Let's look at some of the ethical issues more specifically.

Placebos and Research

As we saw earlier in the description of a typical drug experiment, placebos are considered to be essential in order to determine the true effectiveness of the drug being tested. In practice, this means that during all or some of the time they are being "treated," patients who are also subjects in a research program will not be receiving genuine medication. They are not, then, receiving the best available treatment for their specific condition.

This is one of the risks that a patient needs to know about before consenting to become a research subject. After all, most people become patients in order to be cured, if possible, of their ailments, not to further science or anything of the kind.

The physician-as-therapist will continue to provide medical care to a patient, for under double-blind conditions the physician does not know who is being given placebos and who is not. But the physician-as-researcher will know that a certain number of people will be receiving medication that cannot be expected to help their condition. Thus, the aims of the physician who is also a researcher come into conflict.

This conflict is particularly severe in cases in which it is reasonable to believe (on the basis of animal experimentation, in vitro research, and so on) that an effective disease preventative exists, yet, to satisfy scientific rigor, tests of its effectiveness involve the giving of placebos. This was the case with the development of a polio vaccine by Thomas Weller, John F. Enders, and Frederick C. Robbins in 1960. The initial phase of the clinical testing involved injecting 30,000 children with a substance known to be useless in the prevention of polio—a placebo injection. It was realized, statistically, that some of those children would get the disease and die from it.

Since Weller, Enders, and Robbins believed that they had an effective vaccine, they can hardly be regarded as acting in the best interest of these children. As physicians they were not acting to protect the interest and well-being of the children. They did, of course, succeed in proving the safety and effectiveness of the polio vaccine. The moral question is whether they were justified in failing to provide 30,000 children with a vaccine they believed to be effective, even though it had not been tested on a wide scale with humans. That is, did they correctly resolve the conflict between their roles as researchers and their role as physicians?

Placebos also present physician-researchers with another conflict. As we noticed in the earlier discussion, placebos are not always just "sugar pills." They often contain active ingredients that produce in patients effects that resemble those caused by the medication being tested—nervousness, vomiting, loss of appetite, and so on. This means that a patient receiving a placebo is sometimes not only failing to receive any medication for his illness, but also receiving a medication that may do him some harm. Thus, the physician committed to care for the patient and to relieve his suffering is at odds with the researcher who may be

harming the patient. Do the aims of scientific research and its potential benefits to others justify treating patients in this fashion? Here is another moral question that the physician must face in particular and we must face in general.

We should not leave the topic of the use of placebos without mentioning that it is possible to make use of an experimental design in research that does not require giving placebos to a control group. An investigator can compare the results of two treatment forms: a standard treatment whose effectiveness is known and a new treatment with a possible but not proven effectiveness. This is not as satisfactory scientifically as the other approach because the researcher must do without a control group that has received no genuine treatment. But it does provide a way out of the dilemma of both providing medical care and conducting research.

Therapeutic and Nontherapeutic Research

We have mentioned the conflict that faces the physician who is also an investigator. But the patient who has to decide whether or not to consent to become a research subject is faced with a similar conflict.

Some research holds out the possibility of a direct and immediate advantage to those patients who agree to become subjects. For example, a new drug may, on the basis of limited trials, promise to be more effective in treating an illness than those drugs in standard use. Or a new surgical procedure may turn out to give better results than one that would ordinarily be used. By agreeing to participate in research involving such a drug or procedure, a patient may then have a chance of gaining something more beneficial than he or she would gain otherwise.

Yet the majority of medical research projects do not offer any direct therapeutic advantages to patients who consent to be subjects. The research may eventually benefit many patients, but seldom does it bring direct therapeutic benefits to research participants. Ordinarily, the most that participants can expect to gain is advantages such as having the attention of physicians who are more familiar with their illness than most physicians and receiving close observation and supervision in a research ward.

These are matters that ought to be presented to the patient as information relevant to the decision the patient must make. The patient must then decide whether he or she is willing to become a subject even if there are no special therapeutic advantages to be gained. It is in making this decision that one's moral beliefs can play a role. Some people volunteer to become research subjects without hope of reward because they believe that their action may eventually be of help to others.

Let us now turn to examining some of the problems posed by medical research in dealing with special groups. We will also consider some of the related issues that are involved in fetal research.

Research Involving Children

One of the most controversial areas of all medical experimentation has been that involving children as research subjects. The Willowbrook project discussed in the Case Presentation in this chapter is just one among many investigations that have drawn severe criticism and, quite often, court action.

The obvious question is: Why should children ever be made research subjects? Children clearly lack the physical, psychological, and intellectual maturity of adults. It does not seem that they are as capable as adults of giving informed consent because they can hardly be expected to grasp the nature of research and the possible risks to themselves. Furthermore, because they have not yet developed their capacities, it seems wrong to subject children to risks that might alter, for the worse, the course of their lives. They are in a position of relative dependency, relying upon adults to provide the conditions for their existence and development. It seems almost a betrayal of trust to allow children to be subjected to treatment that is of potential harm to them.

Such considerations help explain why we generally regard research involving children with deep suspicion. It is easy to imagine children being exploited and their lives heedlessly blighted by callous researchers. Some writers have been sufficiently concerned by the possibility of dangers and abuses that they have advocated an end to all research with children as subjects.

But there is another side to the coin. Biologically, children are not just small adults. Their bodies are developing, growing systems. Not only are there anatomical differences; there are also differences in metabolism and biochemistry. For example, some drugs are absorbed and metabolized more quickly in children than in adults, whereas other drugs continue to be active for a longer time. Often some drugs produce different effects when administered to children. Furthermore, just because the bodies of children are still developing, their nutritional needs are different. Findings based on adult subjects cannot simply be extrapolated to children, any more than results based on animal studies can be extrapolated to human beings.

Also, children are prone to certain kinds of diseases (measles, for example) that are either less common in adults or occur in different forms. It is important to know the kinds of therapies that are most successful in the treatment of children afflicted with them. Finally, even familiar surgical procedures cannot be employed in a straightforward way with children. Their developing organ systems are sufficiently different that special pediatric techniques must often be devised.

For many medical purposes, children must be thought of almost as if they were wholly different organisms. Their special biological features set them apart and mark them as subjects requiring special study. To gain the kind of knowledge and understanding required for effective medical treatment of children, it is often impossible to limit research solely to adults.

Failing to conduct research on children raises its own set of ethical issues. If children are excluded from investigations, then the development of pediatric medicine will be severely hindered. In general, this would mean that children would receive medical therapies that are less effective than might be possible. Also, since it is known that children differ significantly from adults in drug reactions, it seems wrong to subject children to the risks of drugs and drug dosages that have been tested only on adults.

Research involving children also seems necessary to avoid causing long-term harm to numerous people. The use of pure oxygen in the environments of prematurely born babies in the early 1940s resulted in blindness and impaired vision in a great number of cases. It was not until a controlled study was done that such damage was traced to the effects of the oxygen. Had the research not been allowed, the chances are very good that the practice would have continued and thousands more infants would have been blinded.

Yet, even if we agree that not all research involving children should be forbidden, we still have to face up to the issues that such research generates. Without attempting to be complete, we can mention the following three issues as among the more prominent.

First, who is to be considered a child? For infants and children in elementary school, this question is not a difficult one. But what about people in their teens? Then the line becomes hard to draw. Indeed, perhaps it is not possible to draw a line at all without being arbitrary. The concern behind the question is with the acquisition of autonomy, of self-direction and responsibility. It is obvious on the basis of ordinary experience that people develop at different rates, and some people at sixteen are more capable of taking charge of their own lives than others are at twenty. Some teenagers are more capable of understanding the nature and hazards of a research project than are many people who are much older.

This suggests that many people who are legally children may be quite capable of giving their informed consent. Of course, many others probably are not, so that decisions about capability would have to rest on an assessment of the individual. Where medical procedures that have a purely therapeutic aim are concerned, an individual who is capable of deciding whether it is in his or her best interest should probably be the one to decide. The issue may be somewhat different when the aim is not therapy. In such cases, a better policy might be to set a lower limit on the age at which consent can be given, and those below that limit should not be permitted to consent to participate in research. The problem is, of course, what should that limit be?

Second, can anyone else consent on behalf of a child? Parents or guardians have a duty to act for the sake of the welfare of a child under their care. In effect, they have a duty to substitute their judgment for that of the child. We generally agree to this because most often we consider the judgment of an adult more mature and informed than a child's. And because the responsibility for care rests with the adult, we customarily recognize that the adult has a right to decide. It is almost as though the adult's autonomy is being shared with the child—almost as though the child were an extension of the adult.

Society and its courts have recognized limits on the power of adults to decide for children. When it seems that the adult is acting in an irresponsible or unreasonable manner, then society steps in to act as a protector of the child's right to be cared for. Thus, courts have ordered that lifesaving procedures or blood transfusions be performed on children even when their parents or guardians have decided against it.

What sort of limits should govern a parent's or guardian's decision to allow a child to become a research subject? Can one person really give informed consent for another? Is it reasonable to believe that, if a parent would allow herself to be the subject of an experiment, then it is also right for her to consent to her child's becoming a subject? Or should something more be required before consent for a child's participation can be considered legitimate?

Third, should children be allowed to be subjects of research that does not offer them a chance of direct therapeutic benefits? Perhaps the "something more" that parents or guardians ought to require before consenting on behalf of a child is the genuine possibility that the research will bring the child direct benefits. This would be in accordance with a parent's duty to seek the welfare of the child. It is also a way of recognizing that the parent's autonomy is not identical with that of the child: one may have the right to take a risk oneself without having the right to impose the risk on someone else.

This seems like a reasonable limitation, and it has been advocated by some writers. Yet there are difficulties with the position. Some research virtually free from risk (coordination tests, for example) might be stopped because of its lack of a "direct therapeutic value." More important, however, much research promising immense long-term benefits would have to be halted. Research frequently involves the withholding of accepted therapies without any guarantee that what is used in their place will be as effective. Sometimes the withholding of accepted treatment is beneficial. Thus, as it turned out, in the research on the incidence of blindness in premature infants in the 1940s, premature infants who were not kept in a pure oxygen environment were better off than those who received ordinary treatment. But no one could know this in advance, and such research as this is, at best, ambiguous as to the promise of direct therapy. Sheer ignorance imposes restrictions. Yet if the experiment had not been done, the standard treatment would have continued with its ordinary course of (statistically) disastrous results.

Here, at least, there was the possibility of better results from the experimental treatment. But in research that involves the substitution of placebos for medications or vaccines known to be effective, it is known in advance that some children will not receive medical care considered to be the best. A child who is a subject in such research is then put in a situation in which he or she is subjected to a definite hazard. The limitation on consent that we are considering would rule out such research. But the consequence of doing this would be to restrict the development of new and potentially more effective medications and treatment techniques. That is, future generations of children would be deprived of at least some possible medical advances.

These, then, are some of the issues that we have to face in arriving at a view of the role of children in research. Perhaps the greatest threat to children, however, has to do with social organization. Children, like prisoners, are often grouped together in institutions (schools, orphanages, detention centers, and so on) and are attractive targets for clinical investigators because they inhabit a limited and relatively controlled environment, can be made to follow orders, and do not ask too many questions that have to be answered. It is a misimpression to see researchers in such situations as "victimizing" children, but at the same time it is clear that careful controls are needed to see that research involving children is legitimate and carried out in a morally satisfactory way.

In response to some of these difficulties, in 1983 the Department of Health and Human Services issued guidelines specifically designed to protect children as research subjects. For children to become subjects, permission must be obtained from parents or guardians, and children must give their "assent." An Institutional Review Board is assigned the responsibility of considering the "ages, maturity, and psychological states" of the children and determining whether they are capable of assenting. (A failure to object cannot be construed as assent.) Children who are wards of the state or of an institution can become subjects only if the research relates to their status as wards or takes place in circumstances in which the majority of subjects are not wards.

Each child must also be supplied with an "advocate" to represent her or his interest.

Research Involving Prisoners

Prisoners are in some respects social outcasts. They have been found guilty of breaking the laws of society and, as a consequence, are removed from it. Stigmatized and isolated, prisoners in the relatively recent past were sometimes thought of as less than human. It seemed only reasonable that such depraved and corrupt creatures should be used as the subjects of experiments that might bring benefits to the members of the society that they wronged. Indeed, it seemed not only reasonable but fitting.

Accordingly, in the early part of this century, tropical medicine expert Richard P. Strong obtained permission from the Governor of the Philippines to inoculate a number of condemned criminals with plague bacillus. The prisoners were not asked for their consent, but they were rewarded by being provided with cigarettes and cigars.

Episodes of this sort were relatively common during the late nineteenth and early twentieth centuries. But as theories about the nature of crime and criminals changed, it became standard practice to use only volunteers and to secure the consent of the prisoners themselves. In the 1940s, for example, the University of Chicago infected over 400 prisoners with malaria in an attempt to discover new drugs to treat and prevent the disease. A committee set up by the Governor of Illinois recommended that potential volunteers be informed of the risks, be permitted to refuse without fear of such reprisals as withdrawal of privileges, and be protected from unnecessary suffering. The committee suggested also that volunteering to be a subject in a medical experiment is a form of good conduct that should be taken into account in deciding whether a prisoner should be paroled or have his sentence reduced.

But the committee also called attention to a problem of great moral significance. They pointed out that, if a prisoner's motive for volunteering is the wish to contribute to human welfare, then a reduction in his sentence would be a reward. But if his motive is to obtain a reduction in sentence, then the possibility of obtaining one is really a form of duress. In this case, the prisoner cannot be regarded as making a free decision.

The issue of duress or "undue influence," as it is called in law, is central to the question of deciding whether, and under what conditions, valid informed consent can be obtained for research involving prisoners. Some ethicists have argued that, to avoid undue influence, prisoners should never be promised any substantial advantages for volunteering to be research subjects. If they volunteer, they should do so for primarily moral or humane reasons.

Others have claimed that becoming research subjects offers prisoners personal advantages that they should not be denied. For example, participation in a research project frees them from the boredom of prison life, gives them an opportunity to increase their feelings of self-worth, and allows them to exercise their autonomy as moral agents. It has been argued, in fact, that prisoners have a *right* to participate in research if the opportunity is offered to them and they wish to do so. To forbid the use of prisoners as research subjects is thus to deny to them, without adequate grounds, a right that all human beings possess. As a denial of their basic autonomy, of their right to take risks and control their own bodies, *not* allowing them to be subjects might constitute a form of cruel and unusual punishment.

By contrast, it can also be argued that prisoners do not deserve to be allowed to exercise such autonomy. Because they have been sentenced for crimes, they should be deprived of the right to volunteer to be research subjects: that right belongs to free citizens. Being deprived of the right to act autonomously is part of their punishment. This is basically the position taken in 1952 by the House of Delegates of the American Medical Association. The

Delegates passed a resolution expressing disapproval of the use as research subjects of people convicted of "murder, rape, arson, kidnapping, treason, and other heinous crimes."

A more worrisome consideration is the question of whether prisoners can be sufficiently free of undue influence or duress to make their consent legitimate. As we mentioned earlier, prisons are total institutions, and the very institutional framework puts pressures on people to do what is desired or expected of them. There need not be, then, promises of rewards (such as reduced sentences) or overt threats (such as withdrawal of ordinary privileges) for coercion to be present. That people may volunteer to relieve boredom is itself an indication that they may be acting under duress. That "good conduct" is a factor in deciding whether to grant parole may function as another source of pressure.

The problem presented by prisoners is fundamentally the same as that presented by inmates in other institutions, such as nursing homes and mental hospitals. In these cases, once it has been determined that potential subjects are mentally competent to give consent, then it must also be decided whether the institutional arrangements allow the consent to be "free and voluntary."

Research Involving the Poor

In the eighteenth century, Princess Caroline of England requested the use of six "charity children" as subjects in the smallpox vaccination experiments she was directing. Then, and until quite recently, charity cases, like prisoners, were regarded by some medical researchers as prime research subjects.

A recent and horrible example of medical research involving the poor is the Tuskegee Syphilis Study that was conducted under the auspices of the U.S. Department of Public Health. From 1932 to 1970, a large but undetermined number of black males suffering from the later stages of syphilis were examined at regular intervals to determine the course their disease was taking. The men in the study were poor and uneducated and believed that they were receiving proper medical care from the state and local public health clinics. As a matter of fact, they were given either no treatment or inadequate treatment, and at least forty of them died as a result of factors connected with their disease. Their consent was never obtained, and the nature of the study, its risks, and the alternatives open to them were never explained. It was known when the study began that those with untreated syphilis have a higher death rate than those whose condition is treated, and although the study was started before the advent of penicillin (which is highly effective against syphilis), other drugs were available but were not used in ways to produce the best results. When penicillin became generally available, it still was not used.

The Tuskegee Study clearly violated the Nuremberg Code, but it was not stopped even after the War Crimes trials. It was reviewed in 1969 by a USPH ad hoc committee, and it was decided that the study should be phased out in 1970. The reasons for ending the study were not moral ones. It was simply believed that there was nothing of much scientific value to be gained by continuing the work. In 1973, a USPH Ad Hoc Advisory Panel, which had been established as a result of public and congressional pressure to review the Tuskegee Study, presented its final report. It condemned the study both on moral grounds and because of its lack of worth and rigor.

No one today argues seriously that disadvantaged people ought to be made subjects of research simply as a result of their social or economic status. The "back wards" in hospitals whose poor patients once served as a source of research subjects have mostly disappeared as a result of such programs as Medicare and Medicaid. Each person is now entitled to his or her own physician and is not merely under the care of the state or of a private charity.

Yet many research projects continue to be based in large public or municipal hospitals. And such hospitals have a higher percentage of disadvantaged people as patients than do private institutions. For this reason, such people are still more likely to become research subjects than are the educated and wealthy. If society continues to accept this state of affairs, special precautions must be taken to see to it that those who volunteer to become research subjects are genuinely informed and free in their decisions.

Research Involving the Terminally Ill

People who have been diagnosed as having a terminal illness characteristically experience overwhelming feelings of despair. Within a few days or weeks, some are able to acknowledge and accept the situation, but others are driven to desperation by the imminent prospect of their death. When they learn that conventional therapies offer little hope of prolonging their lives, they vow to fight their disease by other means. They look for hope in a situation that seems hopeless, and with the encouragement of family and friends, they seek new therapies.

Some turn to quack medicine or suspect remedies, but others seek out clinical trials of new drugs for their diseases. They seek acceptance into trials from the hospitals and medical centers where they are being conducted.

Critics of the policy of accepting terminally ill patients into clinical trials base their objections on the vulnerability of patients. Most often, critics charge, such patients are not sufficiently aware of what they are getting into, nor are they aware of how little personal payoff they may reasonably expect to receive from an experimental therapy.

To be enrolled in a drug trial, patients must satisfy the study's experimental protocol. They must meet diagnostic criteria for having a particular disease or their disease must be at a certain stage in its natural history. Or perhaps the patients must not have received certain treatments, such as radiation, or must not have been taking a particular

drug for several weeks. Perhaps the patients must not have signs of liver damage or kidney disease. Some of the criteria may require that patients be tested. The testing may involve only drawing blood for analysis, but it may also require submitting to painful and potentially harmful surgical procedures to biopsy tissue.

A patient who qualifies for admission into a study may still have a difficult time ahead. If the study is at an institution that is hundreds, even thousands, of miles away, the patient must either move nearer to the institution or travel there regularly. In either case, much expense and inconvenience may be involved.

Critics also charge that patients may have unreasonable expectations about the effectiveness of experimental therapies. Patients may believe, for example, that a drug has at least some record of success, but in fact the therapeutic benefits of the drug may be unknown. Indeed, in the initial stage of drug testing with human subjects, so-called Phase I trials, the aim is not to determine the therapeutic effectiveness of the drug, but to determine such matters as its toxicity, rate of metabolism, or most effective mode of administration.

The chance that a drug under investigation will actually prolong the life of a patient in the final stages of a terminal illness is small. One study reviewed the results of forty-two preliminary reports on drugs used to treat colon cancer and thirty-three on drugs used to treat nonsmall-cell lung cancer, but only one drug was found to have therapeutic effects.

Furthermore, critics charge, patients may not realize the extent to which an experimental drug may turn out to cause unpleasant, painful, or harmful side effects. Patients may suffer nausea, vomiting, chills, fevers, neurological damage, or lowered immunological functioning. Such effects may not even be known to the investigators, and so they cannot inform patients about them at the time consent is sought. The last weeks or months of terminally ill patients may be spent more painfully than if they had simply waited for death, and in fact, patients may even shorten their lives by becoming subjects in a study.

As a sort of final disappointment, critics point out, the study that a dying patient was counting on to give her a last chance at lengthening her life might drop her as a subject. The aim of a clinical trial of a new drug, for example, is to discover such medically important characteristics of the drug as its side effects, what constitutes an effective dosage, and whether the drug has therapeutic benefits. Patients in the study are sources of data, and if a patient who is receiving no therapeutic benefit from a drug turns out to be of no value to the study, then she may be dropped from it. Dying patients may be hit particularly hard by such a rejection.

In the view of critics, the desperation of terminally ill patients makes them too vulnerable to be able to give meaningful consent to participate in experimental trials. Even if they are fairly informed that a drug trial will offer them only a remote possibility of prolonging their lives, they are under such pressure from their illness that, in a sense, they are not free to consent. Patients and their families may be so frightened and emotionally distraught that they hear only what they want to hear about an experimental therapy. They may be unable to grasp that the therapy probably will not benefit them and may even harm them.

Critics of enrolling terminally ill patients in investigations charge that such patients are often treated as though they are only a research resource, a pool from which subjects can be selected for whatever testing needs to be done. That people are dying does not mean that it is justifiable to exploit them, and the only way to avoid this is to exclude them as eligible candidates for research subjects.

No one advocates the exploitation of terminally ill people, but some observers believe that it is morally legitimate to include such patients in clinical trials. The patients themselves may have something to gain. The very act of trying a new drug might make some patients feel better, even if it is only a placebo effect.

Also, patients and their families can feel that they are genuinely doing everything possible to improve the patient's health. Moreover, the drug might be of some therapeutic benefit to the patient, even if the chance of its prolonging the patient's life is remote.

Furthermore, defenders of the policy hold, allowing dying patients to participate in research is to recognize their status as autonomous persons, and to exclude them as candidates for research subjects is to deny them that status.

Finally, defenders claim, in connection with their status as moral agents, dying patients deserve to be given a chance to do something for others. In fact, when dying patients are recruited or seek to enroll in a study, instead of stressing the possible therapeutic benefit they might secure, the experimenter should emphasize the contribution that patients' participation might make to helping others in the future.

To put this last point in perspective, consider the responses of twenty-seven cancer patients enrolled in a Phase I clinical trial who were interviewed by Mark Siegler and his colleagues at the University of Chicago. Eighty-five percent of the patients said they had agreed to participate because they hoped for therapeutic benefits, 11% enrolled at the suggestion of their physicians, and 4% did so at the urging of their families. No one reported enrolling out of a desire to help others.

Research Involving Fetuses

In 1975 legal charges were brought against several physicians in Boston. They had injected antibiotics into living fetuses that were scheduled to be aborted. The aim of the research was to determine by autopsy, after the death of the fetuses, how much of the drug got into the fetal tissues.

Such information is considered to be of prime importance because it increases our knowledge of how to provide medical treatment for a fetus still developing in its mother's womb. It also helps to determine ways in which drugs taken by a pregnant woman may affect a fetus and so points the way toward improved prenatal care.

Other kinds of research involving the fetus also promise to provide important knowledge. Effective vaccines for preventing viral diseases, techniques for treating children with defective immune-system reactions, and hormonal measurements that indicate the status of the developing fetus are just some of the potential advances that are partially dependent on fetal research.

But a number of moral questions arise in connection with such research. Even assuming that a pregnant woman consents to allow the fetus she is carrying to be injected with drugs prior to abortion, is such research ethical? Does the fact that the fetus is going to be aborted alter in any way the moral situation? For example, prior to abortion should the fetus be treated with the same respect and concern for its well-being as a fetus that is not scheduled for abortion?

After the fetus is aborted, if it is viable—if it can live separated from the mother—then we seem to be under an obligation to protect its life. But what if a prenatal experiment threatens its viability? The expectation in abortion is that the fetus will not be viable, but this is not in fact always the case. Does this mean that it is wrong to do anything before abortion to threaten the life of the fetus or reduce its chance for life, even though we do not expect it to live?

These are very difficult questions to answer without first settling the question of whether the fetus is to be considered a person. (See the discussion of this issue in the introduction and selections in Chapter 1.) If the fetus is a person, then it is entitled to the same moral considerations that we extend to other persons. If we decide to take its life, if abortion is considered to be at least sometimes legitimate, then we must be prepared to offer justification. Similarly, if we are to perform experiments on a fetus, even one expected to die,

then we must also be prepared to offer justification. Whether the importance of the research is adequate justification is a matter that currently remains to be settled.

If the fetus is not a person, then the question of fetal experimentation becomes less important morally. Since, however, the fetus may be regarded as a potential person, we may still believe it is necessary to treat it with consideration and respect. The burden of justification may be somewhat less weighty, but it may still be there.

Let us assume that the fetus is aborted and is apparently not viable. Typically, before such a fetus dies, its heart beats and its lungs function. Is it morally permissible to conduct research on the fetus before its death? The knowledge that can be gained, particularly of lung functions, can be used to help save the lives of premature infants, and the fetus is virtually certain of dying, whether or not it is made a subject of research.

After the death of a fetus that is either deliberately or spontaneously aborted, are there any moral restraints on what is done with the remains? It is possible to culture fetal tissues and use them for research purposes. These tissues might, in fact, be commercially grown and distributed by biological supply companies in the way that a variety of animal tissues are now dealt with. Exactly when a fetus can be considered to be dead so that its tissues and organs are available for experimentation, even assuming that one approves of their use in this manner, is itself an unanswered question.

Scientists have been concerned about proposed federal guidelines and state laws regulating fetal research. Most investigators fear that they will be forced to operate under such rigid restrictions that research will be slowed or even prohibited. Nearly everyone agrees, however, that some important moral and social decisions must be made about fetal research. (See Chapter 9.)

Fetal research has to be considered a part of human experimentation. Not only are many fetuses born alive even when deliberately aborted, but they all possess certain human characteristics and potentialities. But who shall give approval to what is done with the fetus? Who is responsible for consent?

It seems peculiar to say that a woman who has decided to have an abortion is also the one who should consent to research involving the aborted fetus. It can be argued that in deciding to have an abortion she has renounced all interest and responsibility with respect to the fetus. Yet, if the fetus does live, we would consider her, at least in part, legally and morally responsible for seeing to its continued well-being.

But if the woman (or the parents) is the one who must give consent for fetal experimentation, are there limits to what she can consent to on behalf of the fetus? With this question we are back where we began. It is obvious that fetal research raises both moral and social issues. We need to decide, then, what is right as a matter of personal conduct and what is right as a matter of social policy. At the moment, issues in each of these areas remain unsettled.

Research Involving Animals

The seventeenth-century philosopher René Descartes doubted whether animals experience pain. They may act *as if* they are in pain, but perhaps they are only complicated pieces of clockwork designed to act that way. Humans feel pain, but then, unlike animals, humans have a "soul" that gives them the capacity to reason, be self-conscious, and experience emotions. The bodies of humans are pieces of machinery, but the mental states that occur within the bodies are not.

If the view of animals represented by Descartes and others in the mechanistic tradition he initiated is correct, we need have no moral concern about the use of animals in research. Animals of whatever species have the status of any other piece of delicate and often expensive lab equipment. They may be used in any way for any purpose.

Here are some of the ways in which animals are used in biomedical research:

- A standard test for determining the toxicity of drugs or chemicals is the "lethal dose-50" (LD-50) test. This is the amount of a substance that, when administered to a group of experimental animals, will kill 50% of them.

- The Draize test, once widely used in the cosmetics industry, involves dripping a chemical substance into the lidless eyes of rabbits to determine its potential to cause eye damage.

- The effects of cigarette smoking were investigated by a series of experiments using beagles with tubes inserted into holes cut into their tracheas so that, when breathing, they were forced to inhale cigarette smoke. The dogs were then "sacrificed" and autopsied to look for significant changes in cells and tissues.

- Surgical procedures are both developed and acquired by using animals as experimental subjects. Surgical residents spend much time in "dog labs" learning to perform standard surgical procedures on live dogs. Limbs may be deliberately broken and organs damaged or destroyed to test the usefulness of surgical repair techniques.

- A traditional medical-school demonstration consisted in exsanguinating (bleeding to death) a dog to illustrate the circulation of the blood. High school and college biology courses sometimes require that students destroy the brains of frogs with long needles (pithing) and then dissect the frogs to learn about physiological processes.

- Chimpanzees and other primates have served as experimental subjects for the study of the induction and treatment of infectious diseases. Perfectly healthy chimps and monkeys have been inoculated with viruses resembling the AIDS virus; then the course of the resulting diseases is studied.

A list of the ways in which animals are used would include virtually all basic biomedical research. The discovery of an "animal model" of a disease typically signals a significant advancement in research. It means that the disease can be studied in ways it cannot be in humans. The assumption is that animals can be subjected to experimental conditions and treatments that humans cannot be subjected to without violating basic moral principles.

Is the assumption that we have no moral obligation toward animals warranted? Certainly the crude "animal machine" view of Descartes has been rejected, and no one is prepared to argue that no nonhuman animal can experience pain.

Exactly what animals have the capacity for suffering is a matter of dispute. Mammals undoubtedly do, and vertebrates in general seem to experience pain, but what about insects, worms, lobsters, and clams? Is the identification of endorphins, naturally occurring substances associated with pain relief in humans, adequate grounds for saying that an organism that produces endorphins must experience pain?

Once it is acknowledged that at least some animals can suffer, most philosophers agree that we have some moral responsibility with respect to them. At the least, some (like Ross) say that, since we have a prima facie duty not to cause unnecessary suffering, we should not inflict needless pain on animals.

This does not necessarily mean that biomedical research should discontinue the use of animals. Strictly construed, it means only that the animals should be treated in a *humane* way. For example, surgical techniques should be practiced only on dogs that have been anesthetized. Understood in this way, the principle raises no objection to humanely conducted animal research, even if its purpose is relatively trivial.

Philosophers like Kant and most of those in the natural law tradition would deny that we have any duties to animals at all. The only proper objects of duty are rational agents; unless we are prepared to argue that animals are rational, we have to refuse them the status of moral persons. We might treat animals humanely because we are magnanimous, but they are not in a position to lay claims against us. Animals have no rights.

Some contemporary philosophers (Tom Regan, in particular) have argued that, although animals are not rational agents, they have preferences. This gives them an autonomy that makes them "moral patients." Like humans, animals possess the right to respectful treatment, and this entails that they not be treated only as a means to some other end. They are ends in themselves, and this intrinsic worth makes it wrong to use them as subjects in research, even when alternatives to animal research are not available.

Contrary to Regan, a number of writers have taken a utilitarian approach to the issue of animal experimentation. Some (like Peter Singer) have argued that, although animals cannot be said to have rights, they have interests. If we recognize that the interests of humans are deserving of equal consideration, then so too are the interests of nonhuman animals. Hence, we can recognize that animals have inherent worth without assigning them rights, but this does not mean that we must treat them exactly as we treat humans.

Most people, whether utilitarians or not, argue that at least some forms of animal experimentation can be justified by the benefits produced. After all, they point out, the understanding of biological processes we have acquired since the time of Aristotle has been heavily dependent on animal experimentation. This understanding has given us insights into the causes and processes of diseases, and, most important, it has put us in a position to invent and test new therapies and modes of prevention.

Without animal experimentation, the identification of the role played by insulin, the development of the polio vaccine, and the perfection of hundreds of major surgical techniques surely would not have been possible. The list could be extended to include virtually every accomplishment of medicine and surgery. Countless millions of human lives have been saved by using the knowledge and understanding gained from animal studies.

Animals, too, have benefited from the theoretical and practical knowledge of research. An understanding of nutritional needs has led to healthier domestic animals, and an understanding of environmental needs has produced a movement to protect and preserve many kinds of wild animals. At the conceptual and scientific levels, veterinary medicine is not really distinct from human medicine. The same sorts of surgical procedures, medicines, and vaccines that benefit the human population also benefit many other species.

However, even from a broadly utilitarian perspective, accepting the general principle that the results justify the practice does not mean that every experiment with animals is warranted. Some experiments might be trivial, unnecessary, or poorly designed. Others might hold no promise of yielding the kind or amount of knowledge sufficient to justify causing the animal subjects to suffer pain and death.

Furthermore, the utilitarian approach supports (as does a rights view like Regan's) looking for an alternative to animal experimentation. If good results can be obtained, for example, by conducting experiments with cell cultures (in vitro), rather than with whole organisms (in vivo), then in vitro experiments are to be preferred. However, if alternatives to animal testing are not available and if the benefits secured promise to outweigh the cost, animal testing may be morally legitimate.

The utilitarian justification faces what some writers see as a major difficulty. It is one posed by the fact that animals like chimpanzees and even dogs and pigs can be shown to possess mental abilities superior to those of humans suffering from severe brain damage and retardation. If experiments on mammals

are justifiable by appealing to the benefits, then why aren't experiments on humans with serious mental impairments equally justified? Indeed, shouldn't we experiment on a human in a chronic vegetative state, rather than on a healthy and alert dog?

The use made of animals in biomedical research is a significant issue, but it is no more than one aspect of the general philosophical question about the status of animals. Do animals have rights? If so, what grounds can be offered for them? Do animals have a right to coexist with humans? Do animals have a right to be free? Is it wrong to eat animals or use products made from their remains? These questions and many others like them are now being given the most careful scrutiny they have received since the last century. How they are answered will do much to shape the character both of medical research and of our society.

Women and Medical Research

Critics have recently charged that medical research has typically failed to include women as experimental subjects, even when women might also stand to benefit from the results. Most strikingly, a study showing the effectiveness of small doses of aspirin in reducing the risk of heart attack included 2,201 subjects—all male. The relevance of the study to women is in doubt, for, although more men than women die of heart disease, after women reach menopause the difference between genders becomes much smaller.

Studies of the therapeutic effectiveness of drugs ordinarily include only males. Although the effects of many drugs are the same for women as for men, this is not always true. Hormonal differences may alter drug reactions, so conclusions based on the reactions of men may be misleading when applied to women.

In the view of critics, the traditionally male-dominated research establishment has been responsible for the current state of affairs.

To change the situation so that both women and men are included in studies would add to their costs. It would introduce gender as a variable, and the study would have to include more subjects in order to get the degree of statistical reliability that could be achieved with fewer subjects of the same gender. However, such studies would have the additional value of yielding results known to be applicable to women.

That this issue is a matter of social fairness is obvious, but its connection with informed consent is less direct. As we mentioned in connection with prisoners, not allowing someone to consent may be viewed as treating that person as having less worth than someone who is allowed to consent. From this perspective, then, women have been denied the opportunity to be full persons in the moral sense. They have not been able to exercise their autonomy in ways permitted to men. Of course, they have also not been permitted to gain benefits that might be associated with the research projects from which they have been excluded.

Summary

There are other areas of medical experimentation that present special forms of moral problems. We have not discussed, for example, research involving military personnel or college and university students. Moreover, we mentioned only a few of the special difficulties presented by the mentally retarded, psychiatric patients, and old people confined to institutions.

We have, however, raised such a multiplicity of questions about consent and human experimentation that it is perhaps worthwhile to attempt to restate some of the basic issues in a general form. Three issues are particularly noteworthy:

1. Who is competent to consent? (Are children? Are mental patients? If a person is not competent, who—if anyone—should have the power to consent for

him or her?) Given that animals have no power to consent, is research involving them legitimate?

2. When is consent voluntary? (Is any institutionalized person in a position to offer free consent? How can even hospitalized patients be made free of pressures to consent?)

3. When are information and understanding adequate for genuine decision making? (Can complicated medical information ever be adequately explained to laypeople? Should we attempt to devise tests for understanding?)

Although we have concentrated on the matter of consent in research, there are other morally relevant matters connected with the character of research that we have not discussed. These often relate to research standards. Among them are the following:

1. Is the research of sufficient scientific and medical worth to justify the human risk involved? Research that involves trivial aims or that is unnecessary (when, for example, it merely serves to confirm what is already well established) cannot be used to justify causing any threat to human well-being.

2. Can the knowledge sought be obtained without human experimentation? Can it be obtained without animal experimentation?

3. Have animal (and other) studies been done to minimize as far as is possible the risk to human subjects? A great deal can be learned about the effects of drugs, for example, by using "animal models," and the knowledge gained can be used to minimize the hazards in human trials. (Ethical issues involving animals in research may also be called into question.)

4. Does the design of the research meet accepted scientific standards? Sloppy research that is scientifically worthless

means that people have been subjected to risks for no legitimate purpose and that animals have been harmed or sacrificed needlessly.

5. Do the investigators have the proper medical or scientific background to conduct the research effectively?

6. Is the research designed to minimize the risks and suffering of the participants? As we noted earlier, it is sometimes possible to test new drugs without using placebos. Thus, people in need of medication are not forced to be without treatment for their condition.

7. Have the aims and the design of the research and the qualifications of the investigators been reviewed by a group or committee competent to judge them? Such "peer review" is intended to assure that only research that is worthwhile and that meets accepted scientific standards is conducted. And although such review groups can fail to do their job properly, as they apparently did in the Tuskegee Syphilis Study, they are still necessary instruments of control.

Most writers on experimentation would agree that these are among the questions that must be answered satisfactorily before research involving human subjects is morally acceptable. Obviously, however, a patient who is asked to give his or her consent is in no position to judge whether the research project meets the standards implied by these questions. For this reason, it is important that there be social policies and practices governing research. Everyone should be confident that a research project is, in general, a legitimate one before having to decide whether to volunteer to become a participant.

Special problems are involved in seeing to it that these questions are properly answered. It is enough for our purposes, however, merely to notice that the character of the research and the manner in which it is to be performed are factors that are relevant to determining the moral legitimacy of experimentation involving human subjects.

ETHICAL THEORIES: MEDICAL RESEARCH AND INFORMED CONSENT

We have clearly raised too many issues in too many areas of experimentation to discuss how each of several ethical theories might apply to them all. We must limit ourselves to considering a few suggestions about the general issues of human experimentation and informed consent.

Utilitarianism's principle of utility tells us, in effect, to choose those actions that will produce the greatest amount of benefit. Utilitarianism must approve human experimentation in general, since there are cases in which the sacrifices of a few bring great benefits to many. We might, for example, design our social policies to make it worthwhile for people to volunteer for experiments with the view that, if people are paid to take risks and are compensated for their suffering or for any damage done to them during the course of a research project, then the society as a whole might benefit.

The principle of utility also tells us to design experiments to minimize suffering and the chance of harm. Also, it forbids us to do research of an unnecessary or trivial kind—research that is not worth its cost in either human or economic resources.

As far as informed consent is concerned, utilitarianism does not seem to require it. If more social good is to be gained by making people research subjects without securing their agreement, then this is morally legitimate. (It is not, of course, necessarily the best procedure to follow. A system of rewards to induce volunteers might be more likely to lead to an increase in general happiness.) Furthermore, the principle of utility suggests that the best research subjects would be "less valuable" members of the society, such as the mentally retarded, the habitual criminal, or the dying. This, again, is not a necessary consequence of utilitarianism, although it is a possible one. If the recognition of rights and dignity would produce a better society in general, then a utilitarian would also say that they must be taken into account in experimentation with human beings.

For utilitarianism, that individual is competent to give consent who is able to balance benefits and risks and then decide what course of action is best for him or her. Thus, if informed consent is taken to be a requirement supported by the principle of utility, those who are mentally ill or retarded or senile have to be excluded from the class of potential experimental subjects. Furthermore, investigators must provide enough relevant information to allow competent people to make a meaningful decision about what is likely to serve their own interests the most.

For Kant, an individual capable of giving consent is one who is rational and autonomous. Kant's principles would thus also rule out as experimental subjects people who are not able to understand experimental procedures, aims, risks, and benefits. People may volunteer for experiments if they expect them to be of therapeutic benefit to themselves, or they may act out of duty and volunteer, thus discharging their imperfect obligation to advance knowledge or to improve human life.

Yet, for Kant, there are limits to the risks that one should take. We have a duty to preserve our lives, so no one should agree to become a subject in an experiment in which the likelihood of death is great. Additionally, no one should subject himself to research in which there is considerable risk that his capacity for rational thought and autonomy will be destroyed. Indeed, Kant's principles appear to require us to regard as morally illegitimate those experiments that seriously threaten the lives or rationality of their subjects. Not only should we not subject ourselves to them, but we should not subject others to them.

Kant's principles also rule out as potential experimental subjects those who are not in a position to act voluntarily, those who cannot exercise their autonomy. This makes it important to determine, from a Kantian point of view, whether children and institutionalized people (including prisoners) can be regarded as free agents capable of moral choice. Also, as in the case of abortion, the status of the fetus must be determined. If the fetus is not a person, then fetal experimentation presents no particular moral problems. But if the fetus is a person, then we must accord it a moral status and act for its sake and not for the sake of knowledge or for others.

Kant's view of people as autonomous rational beings requires that informed consent be obtained for both medical treatment and research. We cannot be forced to accept treatment for "our own good," nor can we be turned into experimental subjects for "the good of others." We must always be treated as ends and never as means only. To be treated in this way requires that others never deliberately deceive us, no matter how good their intentions. In short, we have a right to be told what we are getting into so that we can decide whether we want to go through with it or not.

Ross's theory imposes on researchers prima facie duties to patients that are similar to Kant's requirements. The nature of people as autonomous moral agents requires that their informed consent be obtained. Researchers ought not deceive their subjects, and experiments should be designed in ways in which suffering and the risk of injury or death are minimized.

These are all prima facie duties, of course, and it is possible to imagine situations in which other duties might take precedence over them. In general, however, Ross, like Kant, tells us that human research cannot be based on what is useful; it must be based on what is right. Ross's principles, like Kant's, do not tell us, however, how we are to deal with such special problems as research involving children or prisoners.

As we saw in the introductory chapter, the principle of double effect and the principle of totality, which are based on the natural law theory of morality, have specific applications to experimentation. Because we hold our bodies in trust, we are responsible for assessing the degree of risk to which we might be put if we agree to become research subjects. Thus, others have an obligation to supply us with the information that we need in order to make our decision. If we decide to give our consent, it must be given freely and not be the consequence of deception or coercion.

If available evidence shows that a sick person may gain benefits from participating in an experiment, then the experiment is justified. But if the evidence shows that the benefits may be slight or if the chance of serious injury or death is relatively great, then the experiment is not justified. In general, the likelihood of a person's benefiting from an experiment must exceed the danger of the person's suffering greater losses. The four requirements that govern the application of the principle of double effect determine what is and what is not an allowable experiment. (See the introductory chapter for a discussion of these.)

People can volunteer for experiments from which they expect no direct benefits. The good they seek in doing so is not their own good but the good of others. But there are limits to what they can subject themselves to. A dying patient, for example, cannot be made the subject of a useless or trivial experiment. The probable value of the knowledge to be gained must balance the risk and suffering the patient is subjected to, and there must be no likelihood that the experiment will seriously injure or kill the patient.

These same restrictions also apply to experiments involving healthy people. The principle of totality forbids a healthy person to submit to an experiment that involves the probability of serious injury, impaired health, mutilation, or death.

The status of the fetus is clear in the Roman Catholic version of the natural law theory: the fetus is a person. As such, the fetus is entitled to the same dignity and respect we accord to other persons. Experiments that involve doing it injury or lessening its chances of life are morally prohibited. But not all fetal research is ruled out. That which may be of therapeutic benefit or which does not directly threaten the fetus's well-being is allowable. Furthermore, research involving fetal tissue or remains is permissible, if it is done for a serious and valuable purpose.

From Rawls's point of view, the difficulty with utilitarianism with respect to human experimentation is that the principle of utility would permit the exploitation of some groups (the dying, prisoners, the retarded) for the sake of others. By contrast, Rawls's principles of justice would forbid all experiments that involve violating a liberty to which a person is entitled by virtue of being a member of society. As a result, all experiments that make use of coercion or deception are ruled out. And since a person has a right to decide what risks she is willing to subject herself to, voluntary informed consent is required of all subjects. Society might, as in utilitarianism, decide to reward those who volunteer to become research subjects. As long as this is a possibility open to all, it is not objectionable.

It would never be right, according to Rawls, to take advantage of those in the society who are least well off to benefit those who are better off. In general, inequalities must be arranged so that they bring benefits (ideally) to everyone or at least to those who are most disadvantaged. Research involving direct therapeutic benefits is clearly acceptable (assuming that there is informed consent), but research that takes advantage of the sick, the poor, the retarded, or the institutionalized and does not benefit them is clearly unacceptable. The status of the fetus—whether or not it is a person in the moral sense—is an issue that has to be resolved before we know how to apply Rawls's principles to fetal research.

We have been able to provide only the briefest sketch here of some of the ways in which our moral theories might apply to the issues in human experimentation. The re-marks are not meant to be anything more than suggestive. Clearly, a satisfactory moral theory of human experimentation requires working out the application of principles to problems in detail, as well as resolving such issues as the status of children and fetuses and the capability of institutionalized people to act freely.

Some Ethical Problems in Clinical Investigation

Louis Lasagna

Louis Lasagna discusses some of the issues that face the physician who is in the role of both therapist and researcher. But perhaps the most important aspect of his article is the review of the arguments against informed consent. Lasagna points out that sometimes researchers themselves do not know the risks that may be involved in research, that there are experiments in which information provided to potential subjects can alter the outcome, and that often patients themselves do not wish to be put into a position in which they must make a decision on the basis of information that they are not really competent to evaluate. Taking a basically utilitarian stance, Lasagna suggests that the "greater interest" of society must sometimes be given precedence over the rights of individuals.

One potentially important source of tension in clinical investigation is the fundamental discrepancy in outlook between the clinical investigator and the physician. The two positions are rarely identical. One reads that medical experimentation takes place continually in every doctor's office and that the therapy of disease is an experimental aspect of medicine, but in point of fact, the practice of medicine and the pursuit of a scientific problem are not equivalent.

The physician is primarily concerned with the patient *qua* patient, with getting him well as quickly as possible and with a minimum of discomfort, inconvenience, risk, and cost to the patient. In the practice of his art the doctor has to use any and every measure he considers justified, and he is concerned with what measure (if any) works, not with what contribution (if any) he makes to the body of scientific data.

For the investigator, the primary emphasis is on the research question. This does not mean that he need be callous or lacking in caution; indeed, patients who are in an experiment are likely to be more carefully observed and cared for than if they were not research subjects. (In fact, carefully designed experiments result more often in improved patient care than in exciting new scientific information.) There are good reasons for the preferred status of patients in an experiment. Physicians in a research ward or research institution have usually had the advantage of intensive training, experience, and the intellectual discipline of an academic atmosphere. Further, the patient is, paradoxically, often better served by the restraint observed in the

Reprinted by permission of the publishers from *Human Aspects of Biomedical Innovation,* by Everett Mendelsohn, Judith P. Swazey, and Irene Taviss, eds., Cambridge, Mass.: Harvard University Press, Copyright © 1971 by the President and Fellows of Harvard College.

therapeutic approach of the critical experimentalist. The uncritical use of many therapeutic measures can be less desirable than the wise use of a few well-chosen ones; in medicine two and two sometimes add up to minus four, as the patient finds his medications working at cross purposes and yielding iatrogenic illness to boot. Often in controlled trials, for example, the placebo-treated patients turn out to be the lucky ones, as the new "remedy" proves to be toxic or therapeutically ineffective.

Notwithstanding the admirable qualities of many research-oriented physicians, however, there still remain important differences in orientation between the physician and the investigator which may affect the individual patient to a significant degree and which deserve discussion. Take, for example, the patient with metastatic cancer. Here is a serious disease for which we lack good treatment. There would seem to be no ethical problem in giving a desperately ill patient a new compound which may do some good. Yet the situation is only superficially simple.

The first cancer patients to receive an investigational drug often fail to obtain significant therapeutic benefit, and the dose exploration and tolerability studies involved in such early pharmacologic trials are likely to entail a certain amount of serious risk because of the powerful drugs generally required to treat malignant disease. In such a situation, therefore, the physician might well say "No" to the earliest trial of a new drug in cases where the investigator might say "Yes." If one then moves to a problem such as the treatment of pain or of insomnia, where we have remedies which, while not perfect, are for most purposes excellent and reasonably safe, what is the physician to say? Statistically, there is no doubt that the patient has a better chance of adequate relief if given a standard and accepted drug rather than an untried one, no matter how impressive a case for research can be made from the standpoint of society's long-term needs.

Another difficulty stems from the use of both patients and volunteer subjects in medical research. This practice tends to blur the fundamental distinction between these two kinds of subjects. The volunteer (or the patient who is being studied in a way unrelated to his disease) is truly an experimental subject and usually stands to gain little or nothing medically—at least in the near future—from the experience of being exposed to an investigational

compound. He may run considerable risk. It seems to me that such a volunteer must be handled quite differently from the patient who is also contributing to research goals but who may derive considerable benefit in the immediate future. To the degree that this distinction is blurred, ethical difficulties will be compounded.

It may be useful to consider the currently controversial issue of obtaining "informed consent" from subjects participating in drug investigation. The new Food and Drug Administration (FDA) regulations governing experimentation on human subjects make it clear that except in rare instances informed written consent must be obtained from anyone who is being given an investigational drug.[1] The FDA has spelled out in great detail the kinds of information that must be supplied to subjects of such experiments. It is interesting to contrast this approach with the usual practice of medicine, in which drug administration also plays an important role, and where patients almost certainly suffer more harm (some avoidable, much of it not) from the use of old drugs than experimental subjects suffer from the prescribing of new drugs by experienced investigators. In ordinary practice, consent is usually not informed, and it is almost never written, except for surgical procedures.

In favor of obtaining informed consent in clinical investigation is the reasonable (and generally held) belief that a person should know what is being done to him and what the risks of participation in an experiment may be. Of course, there are also important legal implications in procedures which—in the absence of consent—may be construed as civil or criminal assault on a person's body. There is a strong common law tradition in this regard which goes back at least as far as Justice Cardozo. In addition, unless a physician or committee other than the investigator is making the final decisions, the patient's informed consent represents a check on the motives of the investigator, motives which may be generally admirable but specifically undesirable, or at least questionable, for the individual patient.

What are the arguments *against* informed consent? To begin with, there are instances in which it would seem clearly not in the patient's best interest to discuss matters with full candor. A person dying of terminal cancer who has been given the few weakly effective available drugs, and whose condition is deteriorating, may gain little from an excessively detailed and frank discussion of the situation when a new drug is available which might possibly provide some benefit. Investigational drug use in psychiatric patients poses similar psychic hazards, including the special risk, if the use of drugs is made to look too much like an experiment, of permanently damaging or destroying the patient-doctor relationship.

One may also argue that obtaining informed consent involves the assumption that the investigator knows the risks of giving the drug, of withholding it, and the alternative risks from the use of other, older agents that might be used instead. The language of the FDA regulations does, it seems to me, imply all this. In fact, this information is available only in small measure.[2] One also assumes that the investigator is capable of the exposition required to present this information to the patient and that the patient is capable of grasping the information. One would also like to think that the patient is capable of making a decision in keeping with his own best interests after hearing the information, although a competent adult should, I suppose, have the freedom to make the wrong decision in the hospital or doctor's office no less than in the voting booth. All of these considerations are not, to be sure, so much arguments against informed consent as examples of the difference between the wish and the achievement.

Some important arguments against consent revolve around the possibility of impeding scientific progress if such consent is routinely obtained. (One could, for "scientific progress," substitute "providing benefit to others, including future generations.") There are some trials that will be impossible if a truly candid explanation has to be provided. One prominent investigator has evinced his skepticism about convincing people to participate in a trial that will last for years and in which some individuals are given drugs to lower their blood pressure and others receive placebos. Since it is not clear that all patients with hypertension should receive drugs, it would seem unethical *not* to perform the trial, but there is disagreement as to whether it is ethical to inform the patients of the nature of the trial while they are participating in it. With postpartum patients, we found in one experiment that if women were approached while they are actually having pain and asked to sign a consent form to participate in an experiment in which they might also receive inert preparations, some

80 to 85 percent refused to participate. (In work conducted on patients of this sort without written consent over a decade or so, we have never seen any evidence of serious harm or discontent; indeed, it is reasonably certain that these patients have received closer attention and better medical care than they would otherwise have received.) This would result in such an idiosyncratic selection of the population that we refused to conduct the trial, not only because of the time that would be required to complete it but because of the very real possibility that the results in such a minority of the population might not provide legitimate basis for predicting effects in the majority.

There is also the chance—even if patients consent to participate—that one may destroy the validity of a trial by inducing introspection of various kinds, producing a sort of Heisenberg effect. Some patients, when they know they are in a trial, will try to outwit the investigator by guessing which medications they are receiving. Other patients will be troubled by the nontherapeutic aspects of the experience, so that one may have difficulty in relating the responses to the usual clinical situation. Although investigators quite rightly tend to emphasize the difference between clinical practice and rigorous clinical investigation, it is nevertheless true that those studying new drugs experimentally wish very much to collect data applicable to the use of the drugs in patients treated by "ordinary" doctors in "routine" medical practice.

Finally, there are some experiments which lose their entire point if all the cards are laid on the table. Take, for example, the investigation of the impact of a placebo. Although some patients report benefits from placebos even when they are told they are receiving "sugar pills," the full power of suggestibility and the patient-doctor relationship would almost certainly be affected by a discussion of the experiment with the subjects. This would be the medical equivalent of "bugging" a jury room to study the jurors' deliberations and then showing the jury the hidden microphones.[3]

Are there alternatives to "double-blind" placebo trials? (It is assumed that the obtaining of consent will be more feasible if patients do not have to agree to receive placebos.) One possibility, in drug investigation, is to demonstrate differences between a new drug and a standard drug. If the new one is significantly better, there is no problem. But what if it is significantly worse? This could mean that the drug is ineffective or merely that it is a *less* effective one—an important distinction. Another possibility is the use of dose-response relationships. If such relationships can be shown for new and old drugs in the same experiment, potency estimates can be made which are in no way dependent on the use of placebos. This is quite possible in a situation such as alleviation of postoperative pain, where the challenge is severe, the response to powerful analgesics is reasonably predictable, and placebos are thus rarely needed or used. In postpartum pain, however, dose-response relationships are rather difficult to elaborate, and the same may be true in studies of hypnotic drugs. This phenomenon has important implications for the admission of new drugs to the marketplace. If placebo studies are abandoned, will the FDA accept clinical comparisons where no dose-response relationships are evident? Not to do so may keep an effective drug off the market, but accepting at face value experiments where no difference is demonstrated between doses or drugs will surely result in the occasional admission of ineffective agents to the market.

Is some less formidable and stylized consent approach acceptable? It is apparently not, in regard to investigational drugs, unless one is willing to flaunt the FDA regulations. On the other hand, it may be possible to modify these regulations so as to make the consent provisions more flexible. If one eliminates the *written* aspects of the present informed consent regulations and substitutes verbal discussion (perhaps even placed on tape for the record) it may be possible to avoid some of the threats to experimentation discussed above while at the same time insuring that a certain amount of discussion with the patient has occurred.[4] I believe that the degree of candor utilized in obtaining consent should be related not only to the specific psychological and clinical problems but also to the expected risks of the experiment.

There is also the possibility of monitoring experimentation by use of peer committees or lay-scientific review boards which go over protocols, checking them carefully for flaws of various kinds, including ethical ones. No investigator should be engaged in research that he would be ashamed to have judged by his scientific colleagues or by a responsible group of laymen and scientists. There is at least theoretical advantage to sharing problems of conscience and morality with individuals not directly involved in the research, and of course ample

precedent exists in society for delegation of important decision-making powers to others, although I doubt the legal acceptability of such review as an *alternative* to informed patient consent. It should be remembered, however, that a peer review mechanism may safeguard a subject more efficiently than informed consent; some people will agree to undergo risks that an expert committee would veto on their behalf.

It has been suggested that one way of discouraging unethical research is for editors to prevent the publication of data obtained in unsavory experiments by refusing to accept such manuscripts. Although this is an attractive notion at first glance, one wonders whether in fact important data unethically obtained could or should really be buried in this way. If an unscrupulous investigator were to discover a cure for cancer, would it be ethical to keep this knowledge from being used by others for the benefit of cancer patients, in compulsive adherence to "principle"? Although it is often affirmed that the ends do not justify the means, our society often functions as if they do.

One way of improving the present situation would be to acquaint the public, the regulatory agencies, the governmental granting agencies, and hospital committees with the needs and problems of experimentation. The present FDA regulations on informed consent, for example, quite clearly are the result of a particular climate of opinion. The law is susceptible to change. I heard one distinguished Baltimore judge say recently that the purpose of the law is to harmonize progress with stability. Years ago a property owner possessed the land underneath his feet as far as it went and all of the air directly above his property. With the coming of the airplane, this concept has changed. Similarly, educational facilities once considered "separate but equal" are no longer considered "equal." The law reflects the needs and desires of society as society sees these needs and desires, and it is entirely consistent with history to expect an appropriate legal response from society if it becomes educated to the needs of science and the social benefits of research.[5]

One wonders how many of medicine's greatest advances might have been delayed or prevented by the rigid application of some currently proposed principles to research at large. Even physicians were in a sense intellectually and emotionally unprepared for the earliest triumphs of cardiac surgery. What, then, would have been the layman's reaction to a full exposition of the problems involved in the original Blalock-Taussig shunts? And what of cardiac catheterization? The benefits of this technique have, quite appropriately, won Nobel Prizes for three of the physicians who pioneered in its use, but is it difficult to imagine lay journalists dubbing the early experimentation of these men barbaric and Nazi-like? ("and then, dear readers, these monsters have the temerity to thrust a tube down the length of one's arm into the very chambers of the human heart! The mind of anyone not completely brutalized by prolonged immersion in the bloody charnel houses of Science boggles at the thought"). I doubt, on the other hand, that the public would back—provided they had the facts—legislation like that originally proposed by Senator Thaler in New York State, which would have prohibited pediatric research *of all kinds* in the absence of court orders. Others have already pointed out that such legislation would have rendered impossible the development of the poliomyelitis and other vaccines.

If society is to be educated, there are many items that might be put on the agenda for discussion. The desire to involve the patient in the decision-making process in regard to details of medical care implies that there should be fuller and franker discussion about the use of everything from drugs to surgical techniques. Whether the public wants this is a matter for debate; I personally doubt it. In my own experience as a physician and investigator, not only are patients usually incapable of making the decisions in question (which is not surprising) but they are usually not desirous of making such decisions. In considerable anxiety a lay friend once called me to say that his physician had disclosed to him the controversy over the long-term use of anticoagulants in the management of patients who had recovered from a cardiac infarct. My friend protested that he was in no position to judge whether his wife should receive anticoagulants and that he really would have preferred his physician to make this judgment. In many complex decision-making situations in medicine, the patient is really more in the position of being on an airplane that has defective landing gear, is running out of gas, and whose pilot has to make some sort of landing in one of several alternate places than in the position of a passenger who is asked whether he wishes to board a plane whose pilot indicates that he is about to fly for the first time with his eyes closed and "no hands."

How much should be told to a patient by a surgeon who is requesting permission to perform an established operation, but one he personally is attempting for the first time? How much should be told to a patient about the hazards of a debilitating series of diagnostic abdominal X-rays, which may subject him to days of restricted food and fluid intake, as well as repeated cathartics? How much should be told to individuals exposed to radiation of any kind, for diagnosis or therapy, in view of the evidence in both insects and mammals that *no* amount of radiation is innocent in regard to genetic damage?

There are many other points that require consideration. What special safeguards are required for the study of prisoners? Of children? Of the psychiatrically ill? Of the mentally retarded? Of the dying patient? If an experimental live virus vaccine is to be given to subjects, should consent also be obtained from neighbors or schoolmates who may pick up the virus from the volunteers and come down with the disease? Should the patients in the adjoining beds be asked for permission when a new antibiotic is given to a patient, in view of the ability of antibiotics to disturb the ecology of the normal bacteria resident in the body and cause the development of resistant strains which can then spread to these patients?

Should individuals be recompensed for damage suffered in the course of research, without any attempt to establish blame? The patient or volunteer who is injured by an experimental drug and loses his earning power thereby is entitled to compensation. The children of a patient who dies as the result of unanticipated mischief from a new diagnostic technique under investigation perhaps ought to expect financial remuneration. This implies not that the investigator must shoulder this burden alone but that the burden must be borne somehow. Who, then, shall pay the bill? In seeking an answer to this question, we should perhaps ask, "Who reaps the benefits of research?" While it is true that the investigator will gain when research is successful, and that with new drugs the pharmaceutical industry will profit, in the final analysis the beneficiary is really society as a whole. It would therefore seem incumbent on society to seek means of walking safely the narrow ledge between the twin abysses of hampered research and uncompensated patient injury. Scientists must not be reckless in their research; neither can they operate in an atmosphere of perpetual fear of disabling economic loss (or destroyed reputations) if unavoidable harm is the result of a well-planned experiment. Patients must not seek court settlements capriciously; neither must they silently suffer pain, injury, or death in the course of research. The problem is both subtle and complex and deserves an honest and equitable solution.

What should be society's attitude toward harm to the individual in return for benefits to the population as a whole? Mass chest X-ray surveys to detect treatable tuberculosis or other pulmonary diseases may cause leukemia in a few. Is the benefit worth the risk? Who shall decide? What means should be taken to safeguard the rights and health of individuals approached to participate in such a survey? Should a simple majority decide whether an entire community's water supply should be fluoridated? We have become reconciled to the ability of a governmental agency to expropriate our land or homes in order to build a new school or a new bridge, but it is not traditional to force anyone to participate in research. Yet society frequently tramples on the rights of individuals in the "greater interest." One can object, but can we deny the existence of the phenomenon? Should we have different guidelines for individual sacrifice when health or life is at stake, rather than property?

Finally, a word about the effective implantation of an ethical conscience in the minds of physicians and clinical investigators. The doctor becomes increasingly accustomed to a life which does not allow for leisurely contemplation. He is by trade a non-agnostic. Even when he makes a decision not to treat, for example, he is not suspending judgment but expressing the belief that "no treatment" is better than treatment. He must continually choose between remedies even when he has poor basis for making a choice. The doctor is likely to be propelled increasingly in the direction of quick decisions which at times resemble reflex responses. In this pragmatic, frenetic existence he may quickly absorb the moral atmosphere around him without questioning it. It is my conviction, therefore, that ethical problems must be integrated into the doctor's life at the earliest possible moment. I do not believe that it will be effective to bring up such matters relatively late in the medical career, although the doctor will certainly require constant reinforcement throughout his professional life. The medical student must be made, from the beginning, to consider the ethical aspects of medicine, in regard to *both* practice and research. Many a liver biopsy or laboratory test is now performed in the name of science, with little benefit to the patient. A medical student made emotionally immune to the casual performance of risky procedures by the tacit acceptance of such procedures by his mentors is unlikely to be excessively concerned as a physician or investigator with the subtleties of ethical and moral issues. Some way must be found to incorporate these matters so firmly into his moral fabric that he cannot avoid the ethical implications of his acts. I submit that the successful development of such an ethical conscience, combined with professional skill, will protect the patient or experimental subject much more effectively than any laws or regulations.

I have previously said that for the ethical, experienced investigator no laws are needed and for the unscrupulous incompetent no laws will help, except to allow the injured subjects to obtain compensation or to punish the offending scientists. Between these extremes there still remain many investigators who will unquestionably be constrained in some way by legislation. But it is unlikely that subjects will be *optimally* protected from harm without additional safeguards imposed by the scientific community itself. These safeguards will range all the way from exercise of wisdom and judgment to the invoking of statistical monitoring techniques to halt experiments that were ethical at the outset but cannot ethically be continued.

Some are fond of quoting Claude Bernard when he said, in *An Introduction to the Study of Experimental Medicine*, "The principle of medical and surgical morality, therefore, consists in never performing on man an experiment which might be harmful to him in any event, even though the result might be highly advantageous to science, i.e., to the health of others."[6] This statement is irrelevant to much of clinical investigation, where patients usually are involved in procedures that may be of considerable benefit to them, although they necessarily involve some risk (like almost everything else in the world). One might point out that Claude Bernard also said, "So, among the experiments that may be tried on man, those that can only harm are forbidden, those that are innocent are permissible, and those that may do good are obligatory."[7] The investigator is responsible not only to the patients currently under his care but also to the many that will never be seen by him. Is this responsibility to mankind less noble than that of the physician concerned with the care of the individual patient?

Bernard's statement is—like my own re-marks—full of ambivalence. As J. Bronowski has put it, one of society's major tasks is to reconcile the welfare of man with the welfare of men.[8] In clinical investigation, as in other societal activities, the good of the individual and the good of society are often not identical and sometimes mutually exclusive. I believe it is inevitable that the many will continue to benefit on occasion from the contributions—sometimes involuntary—of the few. The problem is to know when to say "Halt!" There are some societal "gains" that may only be available at an excessively high price. We cannot afford to have the cancer of moral decay that comes from frequent and flagrant disregard of human rights gnawing away at the body of science. We should, therefore, in a very real sense welcome the present and continuing debate on ethics in clinical investigation. That harm has come from exaggerated stories is unquestioned, as is the possibility that additional harm to patients may occur, but I believe that in the long run both the public and science will benefit from a searching analysis of the roots of our ethical conduct.

Notes

1. While the FDA rules apply only to investigational drugs, the issue of consent is relevant to all clinical investigation because of both legal implications and current National Institutes of Health policies on human experimentation which affect the conduct of grantees.

2. It is surrealistic to read, in an editorial in a leading American medical journal, the statement: "How much more important it is to have informed consent, when the potential risk is unknown!"

3. Dinnerstein et al., in an interesting paper, have reviewed some of the literature on the differential effects of drugs in different experimental settings. Their desire to study the effects of drugs "in a completely concealed form, with the subject not even knowing when he has been drugged" and under situations with different "cover stories" would be out of the question if rigid application of this principle of "total disclosure" were made. Albert J. Dinnerstein, Milton Lowenthal, and Bernard Blitz, "The Interaction of Drugs with Placebos in the Control of Pain and Anxiety," *Perspectives in Biology and Medicine*, 10 (1966), 103–117.

4. It is important to remember that there is no *necessary* relation between a consent procedure that satisfies the law and one that safeguards the patient.

5. John Dewey once warned that part of the public protest against experimentation is related to old misunderstandings and dreads about science. He was talking about animal experimentation, but it may be useful to remember his warning to be "on the alert against every revival of the spirit of animosity to discovery and to the application of the fruits of discovery." One does not need to accuse everyone who is concerned about the ethics of clinical investigation of being antiscientific to believe that at least some of the hue and cry can be traced to antiscientism.

6. Claude Bernard, *An Introduction to the Study of Experimental Medicine* (New York: Dover Publications, 1957), p. 101.

7. Ibid., p. 102.

8. J. Bronowski, *Science and Human Values* (London: Hutchinson & Co., 1961), p. 78.

Philosophical Reflections on Experimenting with Human Subjects

Hans Jonas

Hans Jonas argues that, if we justify experiments by considering them a right of society, then we are exposing individuals to dangers for the general good. This, for Jonas, is inherently wrong, and no individual should be forced to surrender himself or herself to a social goal.

Any risk that is taken must be voluntary, but obtaining informed consent, Jonas claims, is not sufficient to justify the experimental use of human beings. Two other conditions must be met: first, subjects must be recruited from those who are most knowledgeable about the circumstances of research and who are intellectually most capable of grasping its purposes and procedures; second, the experiment must be undertaken for an adequate cause. Jonas cautions us that the progress that may come from research is not necessarily worth our efforts or approval, and he reminds us that there are moral values that we ought not to lose in the pursuit of science.

Experimenting with human subjects is going on in many fields of scientific and technological progress. It is designed to replace the overall instruction by natural, occasional experience with the selective information from artificial, systematic experiment which physical science has found so effective in dealing with inanimate nature. Of the new experimentation with man, medical is surely the most legitimate; psychological, the most dubious; biological (still to come), the most dangerous. I have chosen here to deal with the first only, where the case *for* it is strongest and the task of adjudicating conflicting claims hardest. . . .

The Peculiarity of Human Experimentation

Experimentation was originally sanctioned by natural science. There it is performed on inanimate objects, and this raises no moral problems. But as soon as animate, feeling beings became the subjects of experiment, as they do in the life sciences and especially in medical research, this innocence of the search for knowledge is lost and questions of conscience arise. The depth to which moral and religious sensibilities can become aroused over these questions is shown by the vivisection issue. Human experimentation must sharpen the issue as it involves ultimate questions of personal dignity and sacrosanctity. One profound difference between the human experiment and the physical (besides that between animate and inanimate, feeling and unfeeling nature) is this: The physical experiment employs small-scale, artificially devised substitutes for that about which knowledge is to be obtained, and the experimenter extrapolates from these models and simulated conditions to nature at large. Something deputizes for the "real thing"—balls rolling down an inclined plane for sun and planets, electric discharges from a condenser for real lightning, and so on. For the most part, no such substitution is possible in the biological sphere. We must operate on the original itself, the real thing in the fullest sense, and perhaps affect it irreversibly. No simulacrum can take its place. Especially in the human sphere, experimentation loses entirely the advantage of the clear division between vicarious model and true object. Up to a point, animals may fulfill

the proxy role of the classical physical experiment. But in the end man himself must furnish knowledge about himself, and the comfortable separation of noncommittal experiment and definitive action vanishes. An experiment in education affects the lives of its subjects, perhaps a whole generation of schoolchildren. Human experimentation for whatever purpose is always *also* a responsible, nonexperimental, definitive dealing with the subject himself. And not even the noblest purpose abrogates the obligations this involves.

This is the root of the problem with which we are faced: Can both that purpose and this obligation be satisfied? If not, what would be a just compromise? Which side should give way to the other? The question is inherently philosophical as it concerns not merely pragmatic difficulties and their arbitration, but a genuine conflict of values involving principles of a high order. May I put conflict in these terms? On principle, it is felt, human beings *ought* not to be dealt with in that way (the "guinea pig" protest); on the other hand, such dealings are increasingly urged on us by considerations, in turn appealing to principle, that claim to override those objections. Such a claim must be carefully assessed, especially when it is swept along by a mighty tide. Putting the matter thus, we have already made one important assumption rooted in our "Western" cultural tradition: The prohibitive rule is, to that way of thinking, the primary and axiomatic one; the permissive counter-rule, as qualifying the first, is secondary and stands in need of justification. We must justify the infringement of a primary inviolability, which needs no justification itself; and the justification of its infringement must be by values and needs of a dignity commensurate with those to be sacrificed.

Health as a Public Good

The cause invoked [for medical experimentation] is health and, in its more critical aspect, life itself—clearly superlative goods that the physician serves directly by curing and the researcher indirectly by the knowledge gained through his experiments. There is no question about the good served or about the evil fought—disease and premature death. But a good to whom and an evil to whom?

Reprinted by permission of *Daedalus,* Journal of the American Academy of Arts and Sciences, Spring 1969, Boston, Mass. This essay is included, on pp. 105–131, in a 1980 reedition of Jonas's *Philosophical Essays: From Current Creed to Technological Man,* published by the University of Chicago Press.

Here the issue tends to become somewhat clouded. In the attempt to give experimentation the proper dignity (on the problematic view that a value becomes greater by being "social" instead of merely individual), the health in question or the disease in question is somehow predicated on the social whole, as if it were society that, in the persons of its members enjoyed the one and suffered the other. For the purposes of our problem, public interest can then be pitted against private interest, the common good against the individual good. Indeed, I have found health called a national resource, which of course it is, but surely not in the first place.

In trying to resolve some of the complexities and ambiguities lurking in these conceptualizations, I have pondered a particular statement, made in the form of a question, which I found in the *Proceedings* of the earlier *Daedalus* conference: "Can society afford to discard the tissues and organs of the hopelessly unconscious patient when they could be used to restore the otherwise hopelessly ill, but still salvageable individual?" And somewhat later: "A strong case can be made that society can ill afford to discard the tissues and organs of the hopelessly unconscious patient; they are greatly needed for study and experimental trial to help those who can be salvaged."[1] I hasten to add that any suspicion of callousness that the "commodity" language of these statements may suggest is immediately dispelled by the name of the speaker, Dr. Henry K. Beecher, for whose humanity and moral sensibility there can be nothing but admiration. But the use, in all innocence, of this language gives food for thought. Let me, for a moment, take the question literally. "Discarding" implies proprietary rights—nobody can discard what does not belong to him in the first place. Does society then own my body? "Salvaging" implies the same and, moreover, a use-value to the owner. Is the life-extension of certain individuals then a public interest—that is, of the loss or gain involved? And "society" itself—what is it? When does a need, an aim, an obligation become social? Let us reflect on some of these terms.

What Society Can Afford

"Can Society afford . . . ?" Afford what? To let people die intact, thereby withholding something from other people who desperately need it, who in consequence will have to die too? These other, unfortunate people indeed cannot afford not to have a kidney, heart, or other organ of the dying patient, on which they depend for an extension of their lease on life; but does that give them a right to it? And does it oblige society to procure it for them? What is it that *society* can or cannot afford—leaving aside for the moment the question of what it has a *right* to? It surely can afford to lose members through death; more than that, it is built on the balance of death and birth decreed by the order of life. This is too general, of course, for our question, but perhaps it is well to remember. The specific question seems to be whether society can afford to let some people die whose death might be deferred by particular means if these were authorized by society. Again, if it is merely a question of what society can or cannot afford, rather than of what it ought or ought not to do, the answer must be: Of course, it can. If cancer, heart disease, and other organic, noncontagious ills, especially those tending to strike the old more than the young, continue to exact their toll at the normal rate of incidence (including the toll of private anguish and misery), society can go on flourishing in every way.

Here, by contrast, are some examples of what, in sober truth, society cannot afford. It cannot afford to let an epidemic rage unchecked; a persistent excess of deaths over births, but neither—we must add—too great an excess of births over deaths; too low an average life expectancy even if demographically balanced by fertility, but neither too great a longevity with the necessitated correlative dearth of youth in the social body; a debilitating state of general health; and things of this kind. These are plain cases where the whole condition of society is critically affected, and the public interest can make its imperative claims. The Black Death of the Middle Ages was a *public* calamity of the acute kind; the life-sapping ravages of endemic malaria or sleeping sickness in certain areas are a public calamity of the chronic kind. Such situations a society as a whole can truly not "afford," and they may call for extraordinary remedies, including, perhaps, the invasion of private sacrosanctities.

This is not entirely a matter of numbers and numerical ratios. Society, in a subtler sense, cannot "afford" a single miscarriage of justice, a single inequity in the dispensation of its laws, the violation of the rights of even the tiniest minority, because these undermine the moral basis on which society's existence rests. Nor can it, for a similar reason, afford the absence or atrophy in its midst of compassion and of the effort to alleviate suffering—be it widespread or rare—one form of which is the effort to conquer disease of any kind, whether "socially" significant (by reasons of number) or not. And in short, society cannot afford the absence among its members of *virtue*, with its readiness for sacrifice beyond defined duty. Since its presence—that is to say, that of personal idealism—is a matter of grace and not of decree, we have the paradox that society depends for its existence on intangibles of nothing less than a religious order, for which it can hope, but which it cannot enforce. All the more must it protect this most precious capital from abuse.

For what objectives connected with the medico-biological sphere should this reserve be drawn upon—for example, in the form of accepting, soliciting, perhaps even imposing the submission of human subjects to experimentation? We postulate that this must be not just a worthy cause, as any promotion of the health of anybody doubtlessly is, but a cause qualifying for transcendent social sanction. Here one thinks first of those cases critically affecting the whole condition, present and future, of the community we have illustrated. Something equivalent to what in the political sphere is called "clear and present danger" may be invoked and a state of emergency proclaimed, thereby suspending certain otherwise inviolable prohibitions and taboos. We may observe that averting a disaster always carries greater weight than promoting a good. Extraordinary danger excuses extraordinary means. This covers human experimentation, which we would like to count, as far as possible, among the extraordinary rather than the ordinary means of serving the common good under public auspices. Naturally, since foresight and responsibility for the future are of the essence of institutional society, averting disaster extends into long-term prevention, although the lesser urgency will warrant less sweeping licenses.

Society and the Cause of Progress

Much weaker is the case where it is a matter not of saving but of improving society. Much of medical research falls into this category. As stated before, a permanent death rate from heart failure or cancer does not threaten society. So long as certain statistical ratios are maintained, the incidence of disease and of disease-induced mortality is not (in the strict sense) a "social" misfortune. I hasten to

add that it is not therefore less of a human misfortune, and the call for relief issuing with silent eloquence from each victim and all potential victims is of no lesser dignity. But it is misleading to equate the fundamentally human response to it with what is owed to society: it is owed by man to man—and it is thereby owed by society to the individuals as soon as the adequate ministering to these concerns outgrows (as it progressively does) the scope of private spontaneity and is made a public mandate. It is thus that society assumes responsibility for medical care, research, old age, and innumerable other things not originally of the public realm (in the original "social contract"), and they become duties toward "society" (rather than directly toward one's fellow man) by the fact that they are socially operated.

Indeed, we expect from organized society no longer mere protection against harm and the securing of the conditions of our preservation, but active and constant improvement in all the domains of life: the waging of the battle against nature, the enhancement of the human estate—in short, the promotion of progress. This is an expansive goal, one far surpassing the disaster norm of our previous reflections. It lacks the urgency of the latter, but has the nobility of the free, forward thrust. It surely is worth sacrifices. It is not at all a question of what society can afford, but of what it is committed to, beyond all necessity, by our mandate. Its trusteeship has become an established, ongoing, institutionalized business of the body politic. As eager beneficiaries of its gains, we now owe to "society," as its chief agent, our individual contributions toward its *continued pursuit*. I emphasize "continued pursuit." Maintaining the existing level requires no more than the orthodox means of taxation and enforcement of professional standards that raise no problems. The more optional goal of pushing forward is also more exacting. We have this syndrome: Progress is by our choosing an acknowledged interest of society, in which we have a stake in various degrees; science is a necessary instrument of progress; research is a necessary instrument of science; and in medical science experimentation on human subjects is a necessary instrument of research. Therefore, human experimentation has come to be a societal interest.

The destination of research is essentially melioristic. It does not serve the preservation of the existing good from which I profit myself and to which I am obligated. Unless the present state is intolerable, the melioristic goal is in a sense gratuitous, and this not only from the vantage point of the present. Our descendants have a right to be left an unplundered planet; they do not have a right to new miracle cures. We have sinned against them, if by our doing we have destroyed their inheritance—which we are doing at full blast; we have not sinned against them if by the time they come around arthritis has not yet been conquered (unless by sheer neglect). And generally, in the matter of progress, as humanity had no claim on a Newton, a Michelangelo, or a St. Francis to appear, and no right to the blessings of their unscheduled deeds, so progress, with all our methodical labor for it, cannot be budgeted in advance and its fruits received as a due. Its coming-about at all and its turning out for good (of which we can never be sure) must rather be regarded as something akin to grace.

The Melioristic Goal, Medical Research, and Individual Duty

Nowhere is the melioristic goal more inherent than in medicine. To the physician, it is not gratuitous. He is committed to curing and thus to improving the power to cure. Gratuitous we called it (outside disaster conditions) as a *social* goal, but noble at the same time. Both the nobility and the gratuitousness must influence the manner in which self-sacrifice for it is elicited, and even its free offer accepted. Freedom is certainly the first condition to be observed here. The surrender of one's body to medical experimentation is entirely outside the enforceable "social contract."

Or can it be construed to fall within its terms—namely, as repayment for benefits from past experimentation that I have enjoyed myself? But I am indebted for these benefits not to society, but to the past "martyrs" to whom society is indebted itself, and society has no right to call in my personal debt by way of adding new to its own. Moreover, gratitude is not an enforceable social obligation; it anyway does not mean that I must emulate the deed. Most of all, if it was wrong to exact such sacrifice in the first place, it does not become right to exact it again with the plea of the profit it has brought me. If, however, it was not exacted, but entirely free, as it ought to have been, then it should remain so, and its precedence must not be used as a social

pressure on others for doing the same under the sign of duty. . . .

The "Conscription" of Consent

The mere issuing of the appeal, the calling for volunteers, with the moral and social pressures it inevitably generates, amounts even under the most meticulous rules of consent to a sort of *conscripting*. And some soliciting is necessarily involved. . . . And this is why "consent," surely a nonnegotiable minimum requirement, is not the full answer to the problem. Granting then that soliciting and therefore some degree of conscripting are part of the situation, who may conscript and who may be conscripted? Or less harshly expressed: Who should issue appeals and to whom?

The naturally qualified issuer of the appeal is the research scientist himself, collectively the main carrier of the impulse and the only one with the technical competence to judge. But his being very much an interested party (with vested interests, indeed, not purely in the public good, but in the scientific enterprise as such, in "his" project, and even in his career) makes him also suspect. The ineradicable dialectic of this situation—a delicate incompatibility problem—calls for particular controls by the research community and by public authority that we need not discuss. They can mitigate, but not eliminate the problem. We have to live with the ambiguity, the treacherous impurity of everything human.

Self-Recruitment of the Community

To whom should the appeal be addressed? The natural issuer of the call is also the first natural addressee: the physician-researcher himself and the scientific confraternity at large. With such a coincidence—indeed, the noble tradition with which the whole business of human experimentation started—almost all of the associated legal, ethical, and metaphysical problems vanish. If it is full, autonomous identification of the subject with the purpose that is required for the dignifying of his serving as a subject—here it is; if strongest motivation—here it is; if fullest understanding—here it is; if freest decision—here it is; if greatest integration with the person's total, chosen pursuit—here it is. With the fact of self-solicitation the issue of consent in all its insoluble equivocality is bypassed per se. Not even the condition that the particular purpose be truly important and the project reasonably promising, which must hold in any solicitation of others, need be satisfied here. By himself, the scientist is free to obey his obsession, to play his hunch, to wager on chance, to follow the lure of ambition. It is all part of the "divine madness" that somehow animates the ceaseless pressing against frontiers. For the rest of society, which has a deep-seated disposition to look with reverence and awe upon the guardians of the mysteries of life, the profession assumes with this proof of its devotion the role of a self-chosen, consecrated fraternity, not unlike the monastic orders of the past, and this would come nearest to the actual, religious origins of the art of healing. . . .

"Identification" as the Principle of Recruitment in General

If the properties we adduced as the particular qualifications of the members of the scientific fraternity itself are taken as general criteria of selection, then one should look for additional subjects where a maximum of identification, understanding, and spontaneity can be expected—that is, among the most highly motivated, the most highly educated, and the least "captive" members of the community. From this naturally scarce resource, a descending order of permissibility leads to greater abundance and ease of supply, whose use should become proportionately more hesitant as the exculpating criteria are relaxed. An inversion of normal "market" behavior is demanded here—namely, to accept the lowest quotation last (and excused only by the greatest pressure of need); to pay the highest price first.

The ruling principle in our considerations is that the "wrong" of reification can only be made "right" by such authentic identification with the cause that it is the subject's as well as the researcher's cause—whereby his role in its service is not just permitted by him, but *willed*. That sovereign will of his which embraces the end as his own restores his personhood to the otherwise depersonalizing context. To be valid it must be autonomous and informed. The latter condition can, outside the research community, only be fulfilled by degrees; but the higher the degree of understanding regarding the purpose and the technique, the more valid

becomes the endorsement of the will. A margin of mere trust inevitably remains. Ultimately, the appeal for volunteers should seek this free and generous endorsement, the appropriation of the research purpose into the person's own scheme of ends. Thus, the appeal is in truth addressed to the one, mysterious, and sacred source of any such generosity of the will—"devotion," whose forms and objects of commitment are various and may invest different motivations in different individuals. The following, for instance, may be responsive to the "call" we are discussing: compassion with human suffering, zeal for humanity, reverence for the Golden Rule, enthusiasm for progress, homage to the cause of knowledge, even longing for sacrificial justification (do not call that "masochism," please). On all these, I say, it is defensible and right to draw when the research objective is worthy enough; and it is a prime duty of the research community (especially in view of what we called the "margin of trust") to see that this sacred source is never abused for frivolous ends. For a less than adequate cause, not even the freest, unsolicited offer should be accepted.

The Rule of the "Descending Order" and its Counterutility Sense

We have laid down what must seem to be a forbidding rule to the number-hungry research industry. Having faith in the transcendent potential of man, I do not fear that the "source" will ever fail a society that does not destroy it—and only such a one is worthy of the blessings of progress. But "elitistic" the rule is (as is the enterprise of progress itself), and elites are by nature small. The combined attribute of motivation and information, plus the absence of external pressures, tends to be socially so circumscribed that strict adherence to the rule might numerically starve the research process. This is why I spoke of a descending order of permissibility, which is itself permissive, but where the realization that it is a *descending* order is not without pragmatic import. Departing from the august norm, the appeal must needs shift from idealism to docility, from high-mindedness to compliance, from judgment to trust. Consent spreads over the whole spectrum. I will not go into the casuistics of this penumbral area. I merely indicate the principle of the order of preference: The poorer in knowledge, motivation, and freedom of decision (and that, alas, means the more readily available in terms of numbers and possible manipulation), the more sparingly and indeed reluctantly should the reservoir be used, and the more compelling must therefore become the countervailing justification.

Let us note that this is the opposite of a social utility standard, the reverse of the order by "availability and expendability": The most valuable and scarcest, the least expendable elements of the social organism, are to be the first candidates for risk and sacrifice. It is the standard of *noblesse oblige;* and with all its counterutility and seeming "wastefulness," we feel a rightness about it and perhaps even a higher "utility," for the soul of the community lives by this spirit.[2] It is also the opposite of what the day-to-day interests of research clamor for, and for the scientific community to honor it will mean that it will have to fight a strong temptation to go by routine to the readiest sources of supply—the suggestible, the ignorant, the dependent, the "captive" in various senses.[3] I do not believe that heightened resistance here must cripple research, which cannot be permitted; but it may indeed slow it down by the smaller numbers fed into experimentation in consequence. This price—a possibly slower rate of progress—may have to be paid for the preservation of the most precious capital of higher communal life.

Experimentation on Patients

So far we have been speaking on the tacit assumption that the subjects of experimentation are recruited from among the healthy. To the question "Who is conscriptable?" the spontaneous answer is: Least and last of all the sick—the most available of all as they are under treatment and observation anyway. That the afflicted should not be called upon to bear additional burden and risk, that they are society's special trust and the physician's trust in particular—these are elementary responses of our moral sense. Yet the very destination of medical research, the conquest of disease, requires at the crucial stage trial and verification on precisely the sufferers from the disease, and their total exemption would defeat the purpose itself. In acknowledging this inescapable necessity, we enter the most sensitive area of the whole complex, the one most

keenly felt and most searchingly discussed by the practitioners themselves. No wonder, it touches the heart of the doctor-patient relation, putting its most solemn obligations to the test. There is nothing new in what I have to say about the ethics of the doctor-patient relation, but for the purpose of confronting it with the issue of experimentation some of the oldest verities must be recalled.

The Fundamental Privilege of the Sick

In the course of treatment, the physician is obligated to the patient and to no one else. He is not the agent of society, nor of the interests of medical science, nor of the patient's family, nor of his co-sufferers, nor of future sufferers from the same disease. The patient alone counts when he is under the physician's care. By the simple law of bilateral contract (analogous, for example, to the relation of lawyer to client and its "conflict of interest" rule), the physician is bound not to let any other interest interfere with that of the patient in being cured. But manifestly more sublime norms than contractual ones are involved. We may speak of a sacred trust; strictly by its terms, the doctor is, as it were, alone with his patient and God.

There is one normal exception to this—that is, to the doctor's not being the agent of society vis-à-vis the patient, but the trustee of his interests alone: the quarantining of the contagious sick. This is plainly not for the patient's interest, but for that of others threatened by him. (In vaccination, we have a combination of both: protection of the individual and others.) But preventing the patient from causing harm to others is not the same as exploiting him for the advantage of others. And there is, of course, the abnormal exception of collective catastrophe, the analogue to a state of war. The physician who desperately battles a raging epidemic is under a unique dispensation that suspends in a nonspecifiable way some of the structures of normal practice, including possibly those against experimental liberties with his patients. No rules can be devised for the waiving of rules in extremities. And as with the famous shipwreck examples of ethical theory, the less said about it the better. But what is allowable there and may later be passed over in forgiving silence cannot serve as a precedent. We are concerned with non-extreme, non-emergency conditions where the voice of principle can be heard and claims can be adjudicated free from duress. We have conceded that there are such claims, and that if there is to be medical advance at all, not even the superlative privilege of the suffering and the sick can be kept wholly intact from the intrusion of its needs. About this least palatable, most disquieting part of our subject, I have to offer only groping, inconclusive remarks.

The Principle of "Identification" Applied to Patients

On the whole, the same principles would seem to hold here as are found to hold with "normal subjects": motivation, identification, understanding on the part of the subject. But it is clear that these conditions are peculiarly difficult to satisfy with regard to a patient. His physical state, psychic preoccupation, dependent relation to the doctor, the submissive attitude induced by treatment—everything connected with his condition and situation makes the sick person inherently less of a sovereign person than the healthy one. Spontaneity of self-offering was almost to be ruled out; consent is marred by lower resistance or captive circumstance, and so on. In fact, all the factors that make the patient, as a category, particularly accessible and welcome for experimentation at the same time compromise the quality of the responding affirmation that must morally redeem the making use of them. This, in addition to the primacy of the physician's duty, puts a heightened onus on the physician-researcher to limit his undue power to the most important and defensible research objectives and, of course, to keep persuasion at a minimum.

Still, with all the disabilities noted, there is scope among patients for observing the rule of the "descending order of permissibility" that we have laid down for normal subjects, in vexing inversion of the utility order of quantitative abundance and qualitative "expendability." By the principle of this order, those patients who most identify with and are cognizant of the cause of research—members of the medical profession (who after all are sometimes patients themselves)—come first; the highly motivated and educated, also least dependent, among the lay patients come next; and so on down the line. An added consideration here is seriousness of condition, which again operates in inverse proportion.

Here the profession must fight the tempting sophistry that the hopeless case is expendable (because in prospect already expended) and therefore especially usable; and generally the attitude that the poorer the chances of the patient, the more justifiable his recruitment for experimentation (other than for his own benefit). The opposite is true.

Nondisclosure as a Borderline Case

Then there is the case where ignorance of the subject, sometimes even of the experimenter, is of the essence of the experiment (the "double-blind"-control group-placebo syndrome). It is said to be a necessary element of the scientific process. Whatever may be said about its ethics in regard to normal subjects, especially volunteers, it is an outright betrayal of trust in regard to the patient who believes that he is receiving treatment. Only supreme importance of the objective can exonerate it, without making it less of a transgression. The patient is definitely wronged even when not harmed. And ethics apart, the practice of such deception holds the danger of undermining the faith in the *bona fides* of treatment, the beneficial intent of the physician—the very basis of the doctor-patient relationship. In every respect it follows that concealed experiment on patients—that is, experiment under the guise of treatment—should be the rarest exception, at best, if it cannot be wholly avoided.

This has still the merit of a borderline problem. The same is not true of the other case of necessary ignorance of the subject—that of the unconscious patient. Drafting him for nontherapeutic experiments is simply and unqualifiedly impermissible; progress or not, he must never be used, on the inflexible principle that utter helplessness demands utter protection.

When preparing this paper, I filled pages with a casuistics of this harrowing field, but then scrapped most of it, realizing my dilettante status. The shadings are endless, and only the physician-researcher can discern them properly as the cases arise. Into his lap the decision is thrown. The philosophical rule, once it has admitted into itself the idea of a sliding scale, cannot really specify its own application. It can only impress on the practitioner a general maxim or attitude for the exercise of his judgment and conscience in the concrete occasions of his work. In our case, I am afraid, it means making life more difficult for him.

It will also be noted that, somewhat at variance with the emphasis in the literature, I have not dwelt on the element of "risk" and very little on that of "consent." Discussion of the first is beyond the layman's competence; the emphasis on the second has been lessened because of its equivocal character. It is a truism to say that one should strive to minimize the risk and to maximize the consent. The more demanding concept of "identification," which I have used, includes "consent" in its maximal or authentic form, and the assumption of risk is its privilege.

No Experiments on Patients Unrelated to Their Own Disease

Although my ponderings have, on the whole, yielded points of view rather than definite prescriptions, premises rather than conclusions, they have led me to a few unequivocal yeses and nos. The first is the emphatic rule that patients should be experimented upon, if at all, *only* with reference to *their disease*. Never should there be added to the gratuitousness of the experiment as such the gratuitousness of service to an unrelated cause. This follows simply from what we have found to be the only excuse for infracting the special exemption of the sick at all—namely, that the scientific war on disease cannot accomplish its goal without drawing the sufferers from disease into the investigative process. If under this excuse they become subjects of experiment, they do so *because,* and only because, of *their* disease.

This is the fundamental and self-sufficient consideration. That the patient cannot possibly benefit from the unrelated experiment therapeutically, while he might from experiment related to his condition, is also true, but lies beyond the problem area of pure experiment. I am in any case discussing nontherapeutic experimentation only, where *ex hypothesi* the patient does not benefit. Experiment as part of therapy—that is, directed toward helping the subject himself—is a different matter altogether and raises its own problems but hardly philosophical ones. As long as a doctor can say, even if only in his own thought: "There is no known cure for your condition (or: You have responded to none); but there is promise in a new treatment still under investigation, not quite tested yet as to effectiveness

and safety; you will be taking a chance, but all things considered, I judge it in your best interest to let me try it on you"—as long as he can speak thus, he speaks as the patient's physician and may err, but does not transform the patient into a subject of experimentation. Introduction of an untried therapy into the treatment where the tried ones have failed is not "experimentation on the patient."

Generally, and almost needless to say, with all the rules of the book, there is something "experimental" (because tentative) about every individual treatment, beginning with the diagnosis itself; and he would be a poor doctor who would not learn from every case for the benefit of future cases, and a poor member of the profession who would not make any new insights gained from his treatments available to the profession at large. Thus, knowledge may be advanced in the treatment of any patient, and the interest of the medical art and all sufferers from the same affliction as well as the patient himself may be served if something happens to be learned from his case. But his gain to knowledge and future therapy is incidental to the *bona fide* service to the present patient. He has the right to expect that the doctor does nothing to him just in order to learn.

In that case, the doctor's imaginary speech would run, for instance, like this: "There is nothing more I can do for you. But you can do something for me. Speaking no longer as your physician but on behalf of medical science, we could learn a great deal about future cases of this kind if you would permit me to perform certain experiments on you. It is understood that you yourself would not benefit from any knowledge we might gain; but future patients would." This statement would express the purely experimental situation, assumedly here with the subject's concurrence and with all cards on the table. In Alexander Bicker's words: "It is a different situation when the doctor is no longer trying to make [the patient] well, but is trying to find out how to make others well in the future."[4]

But even in the second case, that of the nontherapeutic experiment where the patient does not benefit, at least the patient's own disease is enlisted in the cause of fighting that disease, even if only in others. It is yet another thing to say or think: "Since you are here—in the hospital with its facilities—anyway, under our care and observation anyway, away from your job (or, perhaps, doomed) anyway, we wish to profit from your being available for some other research of great interest we are presently engaged in." From the standpoint of merely medical ethics, which has only to consider risk, consent, and the worth of the objective, there may be no cardinal difference between this case and the last one. I hope that the medical reader will not think I am making too fine a point when I say that from the standpoint of the subject and his dignity there is a cardinal difference that crosses the line between the permissible and the impermissible, and this by the same principle of "Identification" I have been invoking all along. Whatever the rights and wrongs of any experimentation on any patient—in the one case, at least that residue of identification is left him that it is his own affliction by which he can contribute to the conquest of that affliction, his own kind of suffering which he helps to alleviate in others; and so in a sense it is his own cause. It is totally indefensible to rob the unfortunate of this intimacy with the purpose and make his misfortune a convenience for the furtherance of alien concerns.

Conclusion

. . . I wish only to say in conclusion that if some of the practical implications of my reasonings are felt to work out toward a slower rate of progress, this should not cause too great dismay. Let us not forget that progress is an optional goal, not an unconditional commitment, and that its tempo in particular, compulsive as it may become, has nothing sacred about it. Let us also remember that a slower progress in the conquest of disease would not threaten society, grievous as it is to those who have to deplore that their particular disease be not yet conquered, but that society would indeed be threatened by the erosion of those moral values whose loss, possibly caused by too ruthless a pursuit of scientific progress, would make its most dazzling triumphs not worth having. Let us finally remember that it cannot be the aim of progress to abolish the lot of mortality. Of some ill or other, each of us will die. Our mortal condition is upon us with its harshness but also its wisdom—because without it there would not be the eternally renewed promise of the freshness, immediacy, and eagerness of youth; nor would there be for any of us the incentive to number our days and make them count. With all our striving to wrest from our mortality what we can, we should bear its burden with patience and dignity.

Notes

1. *Proceedings of the Conference on the Ethical Aspects of Experimentation on Human Subjects*, November 3–4, 1967 (Boston, Mass.; hereafter called *Proceedings*), pp. 50–51.

2. Socially, everyone is expendable relatively—that is, in different degrees; religiously, no one is expendable absolutely: The "image of God" is in all. If it can be enhanced, then it is not by anyone being expended, but by someone expending himself.

3. This refers to captives of circumstance, not of justice. Prison inmates are, with respect to our problem, in a special class. If we hold to some idea of guilt, and to the supposition that our judicial system is not entirely at fault, they may be held to stand in a special debt to society, and their offer to serve—from whatever motive—may be accepted with a minimum of qualms as a means of reparation.

4. *Proceedings*, p. 33.

Informed (but Uneducated) Consent

F. J. Ingelfinger

F. J. Ingelfinger claims that efforts to secure informed consent from potential patients or subjects are mostly doomed to failure. "The chances are remote," Ingelfinger says, "that the subject really understands what he has consented to—in the sense that the responsible medical investigator understands the goals, nature, and hazards of his study." Nor can the subject be given information that is in any genuine sense complete. In fact, it might even be unethical to present a person with all the contingencies that may be involved in an experiment.

The current procedure, Ingelfinger asserts, is better than ones followed in the past, for then people were not even told that they were going to be research subjects. But, beyond this, the process of obtaining informed consent "is no more than an elaborate ritual that, when the patient is uneducated and uncomprehending, confers no more than the semblance of propriety on human experimentation." The subject's only real protection depends on the person directing the research.

The trouble with informed consent is that it is not educated consent. Let us assume that the experimental subject, whether a patient, a volunteer, or otherwise enlisted, is exposed to a completely honest array of factual detail. He is told of the medical uncertainty that exists and that must be resolved by research endeavors, of the time and discomfort involved, and of the tiny percentage risk of some serious consequences of the test procedure. He is also reassured of his rights and given a formal, quasi-legal statement to read. No exculpatory language is used. With his written signature, the subject then caps the transaction, and whether he sees himself as a heroic martyr for the sake of mankind, or as a reluctant guinea pig dragooned for the benefit of science, or whether, perhaps, he is merely bewildered, he obviously has given his "informed consent." Because established routines have been scrupulously observed, the doctor, the lawyer, and the ethicist are content.

But the chances are remote that the subject really understands what he has consented to—in the sense that the responsible medical investigator understands the goals, nature, and hazards of his study. How can the layman comprehend the importance of his perhaps not receiving, as determined by luck of the draw, the highly touted new treatment that his roommate will get? How can he appreciate the sensation of living for days with a multi-lumen intestinal tube passing through his mouth and pharynx? How can he interpret the information that an intravascular catheter and radiopaque dye injection have an 0.01 per cent probability of leading to a dangerous thrombosis or cardiac arrhythmia? It is moreover quite unlikely that any patient-subject can see himself accurately within the broad context of the situation, to weigh the inconveniences and hazards that he will have to undergo against the improvements that the research project may bring to the management of his disease in general and to his own case in particular. The difficulty that the public has in understanding information that is both medical and stressful is exemplified by [a report that] only half the families given genetic counseling grasped its impact.[1]

Nor can the information given to the experimental subject be in any sense totally complete. It would be impractical and probably unethical for the investigator to present the nearly endless list of all possible contingencies; in fact, he may not himself be aware of every untoward thing that might happen. Extensive detail, moreover, usually enhances the subject's confusion. Epstein and Lasagna showed that comprehension of medical information given to untutored subjects is inversely correlated with the elaborateness of the material presented.[2] The inconsiderate investigator, indeed, conceivably could exploit his authority and knowledge and extract "informed consent" by overwhelming the candidate-subject with information.

Ideally, the subject should give his consent freely, under no duress whatsoever. The facts are that some element of coercion is instrumental in any investigator-subject transaction. Volunteers for experiments will usually be influenced by hopes of obtaining better grades, earlier parole, more substantial egos, or just mundane cash. These pressures, however, are but fractional shadows of those enclosing the patient-subject. Incapacitated and hospitalized because of illness, frightened by strange and impersonal routines, and fearful for his health and perhaps life, he is far from exercising a free power of choice when the person to whom he anchors all his hopes asks, "Say, you wouldn't mind, would you, if you joined some of the other patients on this floor and helped us to carry out some very important research we are doing?" When "informed consent" is obtained, it is not the

Reprinted by permission from the *New England Journal of Medicine* 287, 9 (August 31, 1972): 465–466.
Editor's Note: The notes in this essay have been renumbered.

student, the destitute bum, or the prisoner to whom, by virtue of his condition, the thumb screws of coercion are most relentlessly applied; it is the most used and useful of all experimental subjects, the patient with disease.

When a man or woman agrees to act as an experimental subject, therefore, his or her consent is marked by neither adequate understanding nor total freedom of choice. The conditions of the agreement are a far cry from those visualized as ideal. Jonas would have the subject identify with the investigative endeavor so that he and the researcher would be seeking a common cause: "Ultimately, the appeal for volunteers should seek . . . free and generous endorsement, the appropriation of the research purpose into the person's [i.e., the subject's] own scheme of ends."[3] For Ramsey, "informed consent" should represent a "covenantal bond between consenting man and consenting man [that] makes them . . . joint adventurers in medical care and progress."[4] Clearly, to achieve motivations and attitudes of this lofty type, an educated and understanding, rather than merely informed, consent is necessary.

Although it is unlikely that the goals of Jonas and of Ramsey will ever be achieved, and that human research subjects will spontaneously volunteer rather than be "conscripted,"[3] efforts to promote educated consent are in order. In view of the current emphasis on involving "the community" in such activities as regional planning, operation of clinics, and assignment of priorities, the general public and its political leaders are showing an increased awareness and understanding of medical affairs. But the orientation of this public interest in medicine is chiefly socioeconomic. Little has been done to give the public a basic understanding of medical research and its requirements not only for the people's money but also for their participation. The public, to be sure, is being subjected to a bombardment of sensation-mongering news stories and books that feature "breakthroughs," or that reveal real or alleged exploitations—horror stories of Nazi-type experimentation on abused human minds and bodies. Muckraking is essential to expose malpractices, but unless accompanied by efforts to promote a broader appreciation of medical research and its methods, it merely compounds the difficulties for both the investigator and the subject when "informed consent" is solicited.

The procedure currently approved in the United States for enlisting human experimental subjects has one great virtue: patient-subjects are put on notice that their management is in part at least an experiment. The deceptions of the past are no longer tolerated. Beyond this accomplishment, however, the process of obtaining "informed consent," with all its regulations and conditions, is no more than an elaborate ritual, a device that, when the subject is uneducated and uncomprehending, confers no more than the semblance of propriety on human experimentation. The subject's only real protection, the public as well as the medical profession must recognize, depends on the conscience and compassion of the investigator and his peers.

Notes

1. Leonard, Claire O., et al. Genetic counseling: a consumer's view. *N Engl J Med* 287: 433–449, 1972.
2. Epstein, L. C., Lasagna, L. Obtaining informed consent: form or substance. *Arch Intern Med* 123: 682–688, 1969.
3. Jonas, H. Philosophical reflections on experimenting with human subjects. *Daedalus* 98: 219–247, Spring, 1969.
4. Ramsey, P. The ethics of a cottage industry in an age of community and research medicine. *N Engl J Med* 294: 700–706, 1971.

The Willowbrook Letters: Criticism and Defense

Stephen Goldby, Saul Krugman, M. H. Pappworth, and Geoffrey Edsall

"The Willowbrook Letters," by Stephen Goldby, Saul Krugman, M. H. Pappworth, and Geoffrey Edsall, concern the moral legitimacy of the study of viral hepatitis that was conducted at the Willowbrook School by Krugman and his associates. (See the Case Presentation for more detail.) Goldby charges that the study was "quite unjustifiable" because it was morally wrong to infect children when no benefit to them could result. Krugman defends himself by claiming that his results demonstrated a "therapeutic effect" for the children involved, as well as for others. He presents four reasons for holding that the infecting of the children was justified.

Pappworth claims that Krugman's defense is presented only after the fact, whereas an experiment is ethical or not in its inception. Moreover, he asserts, consent was obtained through the use of coercion. Parents who wished to put their children in the institution were told there was room only in the "hepatitis unit."

In the final letter, Edsall defends the Krugman study. The experiments, he asserts, involved no greater risk to the children involved than they would have run in any case. What is more, the results obtained were of general benefit.

SIR.—You have referred to the work of Krugman and his colleagues at the Willowbrook State School in three editorials. In the first article the work was cited as a notable study of hepatitis and a model for this type of investigation. No comment was made on the rightness of attempting to infect mentally retarded children with hepatitis for experimental purposes, in an institution where the disease was already endemic.

The second editorial again did not remark on the ethics of the study, but the third sounded a note of doubt as to the justification for extending these experiments. The reason given was that some children might have been made more susceptible to serious hepatitis as the result of the administration of previously heated icterogenic material.

I believe that not only this last experiment, but the whole of Krugman's study, is quite unjustifiable, whatever the aims, and however academically or therapeutically important are the results. I am amazed that the work was published and that it has been actively supported editorially by the *Journal of the American Medical Association* and by Ingelfinger in the 1967–68 *Year Book of Medicine*. To my knowledge only the *British Journal of Hospital Medicine* has clearly stated the ethical position on these experiments and shown that it was indefensible to give potentially dangerous infected material to children, particularly those who were mentally retarded, with or without parental consent, when no benefit to the child could conceivably result.

Krugman and Giles have continued to publish the results of their study, and in a recent paper go to some length to describe their method of obtaining parental consent and list a number of influential medical boards and committees that have approved the study. They point out again that, in their opinion, their work conforms to the World Medical Association Draft Code of Ethics on Human Experimentation. They also say that hepatitis is still highly endemic in the school.

This attempted defence is irrelevant to the central issue. Is it right to perform an experiment on a normal or mentally retarded child when no benefit can result to that individual? I think that the answer is no, and that the question of parental consent is irrelevant. In my view the studies of Krugman serve only to show that there is a serious loophole in the Draft Code, which under General Principles and Definitions puts the onus of consent for experimentation on children on the parent or guardian. It is this section that is quoted by Krugman. I would class his work as "experiments conducted solely for the acquisition of knowledge," under which heading the code states that "persons retained in mental hospital or hospitals for mental defectives should not be used for human experiment." Krugman may believe that his experiments were for the benefit of his patients, meaning the individual patients used in the study. If this is his belief he has a difficult case to defend. The duty of a pediatrician in a situation such as exists at Willowbrook State School is to attempt to improve that situation, not to turn it to his advantage for experimental purposes, however lofty the aims.

Every new reference to the work of Krugman

Reprinted by permission of the authors and publisher from *The Lancet*, April 10, May 8, June 5, and July 10, 1971.

and Giles adds to its apparent ethical respectability, and in my view such references should stop, or at least be heavily qualified. The editorial attitude of *The Lancet* to the work should be reviewed and openly stated. The issue is too important to be ignored.

If Krugman and Giles are keen to continue their experiments I suggest that they invite the parents of the children involved to participate. I wonder what the response would be.

Stephen Goldby

SIR.—Dr. Stephen Goldby's critical comments about our Willowbrook studies and our motives for conducting them were published without extending us the courtesy of replying in the same issue of *The Lancet*. Your acceptance of his criticisms without benefit of our response implies a blackout of all comment related to our studies. This decision is unfortunate because our recent studies on active and passive immunisation for the prevention of viral hepatitis, type B, have clearly demonstrated a "therapeutic effect" for the children involved. These studies have provided us with the first indication and hope that it may be possible to control hepatitis in this institution. If this aim can be achieved, it will benefit not only the children, but also their families and the employees who care for them in the school. It is unnecessary to point out the additional benefit to the worldwide populations which have been plagued by an insoluble hepatitis problem for many generations.

Dr. Joan Giles and I have been actively engaged in studies aimed to solve two infectious-disease problems in the Willowbrook State School—measles and viral hepatitis. These studies were investigated in this institution because they represented major health problems for the 5000 or more mentally retarded children who were residents. Uninformed critics have assumed or implied that we came to Willowbrook to "conduct experiments on mentally retarded children."

The results of our Willowbrook studies with the experimental live attenuated measles vaccine developed by Enders and his colleagues are well documented in the medical literature. As early as 1960 we demonstrated the protective effect of this vaccine during the course of an epidemic. Prior to licensure of the vaccine in 1963 epidemics occurred

at two-year intervals in this institution. During the 1960 epidemic there were more than 600 cases of measles and 60 deaths. In the wake of our ongoing measles vaccine programme, measles has been eradicated as a disease in the Willowbrook State School. We have not had a single case of measles since 1963. In this regard the children at the Willowbrook State School have been more fortunate than unimmunised children in Oxford, England, other areas in Great Britain, as well as certain groups of children in the United States and other parts of the world.

The background of our hepatitis studies at Willowbrook has been described in detail in various publications. Viral hepatitis is so prevalent that newly admitted susceptible children become infected within 6 to 12 months after entry in the institution. These children are a source of infection for the personnel who care for them and for their families if they visit with them. We were convinced that the solution of the hepatitis problem in this institution was dependent on the acquisition of new knowledge leading to the development of an effective immunising agent. The achievements with smallpox, diphtheria, poliomyelitis, and more recently measles represent dramatic illustrations of this approach.

It is well known that viral hepatitis in children is milder and more benign than the same disease in adults. Experience has revealed that hepatitis in institutionalised, mentally retarded children is also mild, in contrast with measles, which is a more severe disease when it occurs in institutional epidemics involving the mentally retarded. Our proposal to expose a small number of newly admitted children to the Willowbrook strains of hepatitis virus was justified in our opinion for the following reasons: (1) they were bound to be exposed to the same strains under the natural conditions existing in the institution; (2) they would be admitted to a special, well-equipped, and well-staffed unit where they would be isolated from exposure to other infectious diseases which were prevalent in the institution—namely, shigellosis, parasitic infections, and respiratory infections—thus, their exposure in the hepatitis unit would be associated with less risk than the type of institutional exposure where multiple infections could occur; (3) they were likely to have a subclinical infection followed by immunity to the particular hepatitis virus; and (4) only children with parents who gave informed consent would be included.

The statement by Dr. Goldby accusing us of conducting experiments exclusively for the acquisition of knowledge with no benefit for the children cannot be supported by the true facts.

Saul Krugman

SIR.—The experiments at Willowbrook raise two important issues: What constitutes valid consent, and do ends justify means? English law definitely forbids experimentation on children, even if both parents consent, unless done specifically in the interests of each individual child. Perhaps in the U.S.A. the law is not so clear-cut. According to Beecher, the parents of the children at Willowbrook were informed that, because of overcrowding, the institution was to be closed; but only a week or two later they were told that there would be vacancies in the "hepatitis unit" for children whose parents allowed them to form part of the hepatitis research study. Such consent, ethically if not legally, is invalid because of its element of coercion, some parents being desperately anxious to institutionalise their mentally defective children. Moreover, obtaining consent after talking to parents in groups, as described by Krugman, is extremely unsatisfactory because even a single enthusiast can sway the diffident who do not wish to appear churlish in front of their fellow citizens.

Do ends justify the means? Krugman maintains that any newly admitted children would inevitably have contracted infective hepatitis, which was rife in the hospital. But this ignores the statement by the head of the State Department of Mental Hygiene that, during the major part of the 15 years these experiments have been conducted, a gamma-globulin inoculation programme had already resulted in over an 80 percent reduction of that disease in that hospital. Krugman and Pasamanick claim that subsequent therapeutic effects justify these experiments. This attitude is frequently adopted by experimenters and enthusiastic medical writers who wish us to forget completely how results are obtained but instead enjoy any benefits that may accrue. Immunisation was not the purpose of these Willowbrook experiments but merely a by-product that incidentally proved beneficial to the victims. Any experiment is ethical or not at its inception, and does not become so because it

achieved some measure of success in extending the frontiers of medicine. I particularly object strongly to the views of Willey, ". . . risk being assumed by the subjects of the experimentation balanced against the potential benefit to the subjects *and* [Willey's italics] to society in general." I believe that experimental physicians never have the right to select martyrs for society. Every human being has the right to be treated with decency, and that right must always supersede every consideration of what may benefit mankind, what may advance medical science, what may contribute to public welfare. No doctor is ever justified in placing society or science first and his obligation to patients second. Any claim to act for the good of society should be regarded with distaste because it may be merely a highflown expression to cloak outrageous acts.

M. H. Pappworth

SIR.—I am astonished at the unquestioning way in which *The Lancet* has accepted the intemperate position taken by Dr. Stephen Goldby concerning the experimental studies of Krugman and Giles on hepatitis at the Willowbrook State School. These investigators have repeatedly explained for over a decade that natural hepatitis infection occurs sooner or later in virtually 100% of the patients admitted to Willowbrook, and that it is better for the patient to have a known, timed, controlled infection than an untimed, uncontrolled one. Moreover, the wisdom and human justification of these studies have been repeatedly and carefully examined and verified by a number of very distinguished, able individuals who are respected leaders in the making of such decisions.

The real issue is: Is it not proper and ethical to carry out experiments in children, which would apparently incur no greater risk than the children were likely to run by nature, in which the children generally receive better medical care when artificially infected than if they had been naturally infected, and in which the parents as well as the physician feel that a significant contribution to the future well-being of similar children is likely to result from the studies? It is true, to be sure, that the W.M.A. code says, "Children in institutions and not under the care of relatives should not be the subjects of human experiments." But this unqualified *obiter dictum* may represent merely the well-known inability of committees to think a problem through.

However, it has been thought through by Sir Austin Bradford Hill, who has pointed out the unfortunate effects for these very children that would have re-sulted, were such a code to have been applied over the years.

Geoffrey Edsall

Judgment on Willowbrook

Paul Ramsey

Paul Ramsey reviews the justifications offered for the Willowbrook experiments presented by Krugman. Ramsey observes that there is nothing about hepatitis that requires that research be conducted on children, that no justification except the needs of the experiment is given for withholding gamma globulin from the subjects, and that nothing is said about attempting to control the low-grade epidemic by other means. Furthermore, Ramsey questions the morality of consent secured from the parents of the children. His basic recommendation is that the use of captive populations of children ought to be made legally impossible.

In 1958 and 1959 the *New England Journal of Medicine* reported a series of experiments performed upon patients and new admittees to the Willowbrook State School, a home for retarded children in Staten Island, New York.[1] These experiments were described as "an attempt to control the high prevalence of infectious hepatitis in an institution for mentally defective patients." The experiments were said to be justified because, under conditions of an existing controlled outbreak of hepatitis in the institution, "knowledge obtained from a series of suitable studies could well lead to its control." In actuality, the experiments were designed to duplicate and confirm the efficacy of gamma globulin in immunization against hepatitis, to develop and improve or improve upon that inoculum, and to learn more about infectious hepatitis in general.

The experiments were justified—doubtless, after a great deal of soul searching—for the following reasons: there was a smoldering epidemic throughout the institution and "it was apparent that most of the patients at Willowbrook were naturally exposed to hepatitis virus"; infectious hepatitis is a much milder disease in children; the strain at Willowbrook was especially mild; only the strain or strains of the virus already disseminated at Willowbrook were used; and only those small and incompetent patients whose parents gave consent were used.

The patient population at Willowbrook was 4478, growing at a rate of one patient a day over a three-year span, or from 10 to 15 new admissions per week. In the first trial the existing population was divided into two groups: one group served as uninoculated controls, and the other group was inoculated with 0.01 ml. of gamma globulin per pound of body weight. Then for a second trial new admittees and those left uninoculated before were again divided: one group served as uninoculated controls and the other was inoculated with 0.06 ml. of gamma globulin per pound of body weight. This proved that Stokes et al. had correctly demonstrated that the larger amount would give significant immunity for up to seven or eight months.[2]

Serious ethical questions may be raised about the trials so far described. No mention is made of any attempt to enlist the adult personnel of the institution, numbering nearly 1,000 including nearly 600 attendants on ward duty, and new additions to the staff, in these studies whose excusing reason was that almost everyone was "naturally" exposed to the Willowbrook virus. Nothing requires that major research into the natural history of hepatitis be first undertaken in children. Experiments have been carried out in the military and with prisoners as subjects. There have been fatalities from the experiments; but surely in all these cases the consent of the volunteers was as valid or better than the proxy consent of these children's "representatives." There would have been no question of the understanding consent that might have been given by the adult personnel at Willowbrook, if significant benefits were expected from studying that virus.

Second, nothing is said that would warrant withholding an inoculation of some degree of known efficacy from part of the population, or for withholding in the first trial less than the full amount of gamma globulin that had served to immunize in previous tests, except the need to test, confirm, and improve the inoculum. That, of course, was a desirable goal; but it does not seem possible to warrant withholding gamma globulin for the reason that is often said to justify controlled trials, namely, that one procedure is *as likely* to succeed as the other.

Third, nothing is said about attempts to control or defeat the low-grade epidemic at Willowbrook by more ordinary, if more costly and less experimental, procedures. Nor is anything said about admitting no more patients until this goal had been accomplished. This was not a massive urban hospital whose teeming population would have to be turned out into the streets, with resulting dangers to themselves and to public health, in order to sanitize the place. Instead, between 200 and 250 patients were housed in each of 18 buildings over approximately 400 acres in a semirural setting of fields, woods, and well-kept, spacious lawns. Clearly it would have been possible to secure other accommodation for new admissions away from the infection, while eradicating the infection at Willowbrook building by building. this might have cost money, and it would certainly have required astute detective work to discover the source of the infection. The doctors determined that the new patients likely were not carrying the infection upon admission, and that it did not arise from the procedures and routine inoculations given them at the time of admission. Why not go further in the search for the source of the epidemic? If this had been an orphanage for normal children or a floor of private pa-

tients, instead of a school for mentally defective children, one wonders whether the doctors would so readily have accepted the hepatitis as a "natural" occurrence and even as an opportunity for study.

The next step was to attempt to induce "passive-active immunity" by feeding the virus to patients already protected by gamma globulin. In this attempt to improve the inoculum, permission was obtained from the parents of children from 5 to 10 years of age newly admitted to Willowbrook, who were then isolated from contact with the rest of the institution. All were inoculated with gamma globulin and then divided into two groups: one served as controls while the other group of new patients were fed the Willowbrook virus, obtained from feces, in doses having 50 percent infectivity, i.e., in concentrations estimated to produce hepatitis with jaundice in half the subjects tested. Then twice the 50 percent infectivity was tried. This proved, among other things, that hepatitis has an "alimentary-tract phase" in which it can be transmitted from one person to another while still "inapparent" in the first person. This, doubtless, is exceedingly important information in learning how to control epidemics of infectious hepatitis. The second of the two articles mentioned above describes studies of the incubation period of the virus and of whether pooled serum remained infectious when aged and frozen. Still the small, mentally defective patients who were deliberately fed infectious hepatitis are described as having suffered mildly in most cases: "The liver became enlarged in the majority, occasionally a week or two before the onset of jaundice. Vomiting and anorexia usually lasted only a few days. Most of the children gained weight during the course of hepatitis."

That mild description of what happened to the children who were fed hepatitis (and who continued to be introduced into the unaltered environment of Willowbrook) is itself alarming, since it is now definitely known that cirrhosis of the liver results from infectious hepatitis more frequently than from excessive consumption of alcohol! Now, or in 1958 and 1959, no one knows what may be other serious consequences of contracting infectious hepatitis. Understanding human volunteers were then and are now needed in the study of this disease, although a South American monkey has now successfully been given a form of hepatitis, and can henceforth serve as our ally in its conquest. But not children who cannot consent knowingly. If Peace

Corps workers are regularly given gamma globulin before going abroad as a guard against their contracting hepatitis, and are inoculated at intervals thereafter, it seems that this is the least we should do for mentally defective children before they "go abroad" to Willowbrook or other institutions set up for their care.

Discussions pro and con of the Willowbrook experiments that have come to my attention serve only to reinforce the ethical objections that can be raised against what was done simply from a careful analysis of the original articles reporting the research design and findings. In an address at the 1968 Ross Conference on Pediatric Research, Dr. Saul Krugman raised the question, Should vaccine trials be carried out in adult volunteers before subjecting children to similar tests?[3] He answered this question in the negative. The reason adduced was simply that "a vaccine virus trial may be a more hazardous procedure for adults than for children." Medical researchers, of course, are required to minimize the hazards, but not by moving from consenting to unconsenting subjects. This apology clearly shows that adults and children have become interchangeable in face of the overriding importance of obtaining the research goal. This means that the special moral claims of children for care and protection are forgotten, and especially the claims of children who are most weak and vulnerable. (Krugman's reference to the measles vaccine trials is not to the point.)

The *Medical Tribune* explains that the 16-bed isolation unit set up at Willowbrook served "to protect the study subjects from Willowbrook's other endemic diseases—such as shigellosis, measles, rubella and respiratory and parasitic infections—while exposing them to hepatitis."[4] This presumably compensated for the infection they were given. It is not convincingly shown that the children could by no means, however costly, have been protected from the epidemic of hepatitis. The statement that Willowbrook "had endemic infectious hepatitis and a sufficiently open population so that the disease could never be quieted by exhausting the supply of susceptibles" is at best enigmatic.

Oddly, physicians defending the propriety of the Willowbrook hepatitis project soon began talking like poorly instructed "natural lawyers"! Dr. Louis Lasagna and Dr. Geoffrey Edsall, for example, find these experiments unobjectionable—both, for the reason stated by Edsall: "the children would apparently incur no greater risk than they were likely to run by nature." In any case, Edsall's example of parents consenting with a son 17 years of age for him to go to war, and society's agreements with minors that they can drive cars and hurt themselves were entirely beside the point. Dr. David D. Rutstein adheres to a stricter standard in regard to research on infectious hepatitis: "It is not ethical to use human subjects for the growth of a virus for any purpose."[5]

The latter sweeping verdict may depend on knowledge of the effects of viruses on chromosomal difficulties, mongolism, etc., that was not available to the Willowbrook group when their researches were begun thirteen years ago. If so, this is a telling point against appeal to "no discernible risks" as the sole standard applicable to the use of children in medical experimentation. That would lend support to the proposition that we always know that there are unknown and undiscerned risks in the case of an invasion of the fortress of the body—which then can be consented to by an adult in behalf of a child only if it is in the child's behalf medically.

When asked what she told the parents of the subject-children at Willowbrook, Dr. Joan Giles replied, "I explain that there is no vaccine against infectious hepatitis. . . . I also tell them that we can modify the disease with gamma globulin but we can't provide lasting immunity without letting them get the disease."[6] Obviously vaccines giving "lasting immunity" are not the only kinds of vaccine to be used in caring for patients.

Doubtless the studies at Willowbrook resulted in improvement in the vaccine, to the benefit of present and future patients. In September 1966, "a routine program of GG [gamma globulin] administration to every new patient at Willowbrook" was begun. This cut the incidence of icteric hepatitis 80 to 85 percent. Then follows a significant statement in the *Medical Tribune* article: "A similar reduction in the icteric form of the disease has been accomplished among the employees, who began getting routine GG earlier in the study."[7] Not only did the research team (so far as these reports show) fail to consider and adopt the alternative that new admittees to the staff be asked to become volunteers for an investigation that might improve the vaccine against the strain of infectious hepatitis to which they as well as the children were exposed. Instead, the staff was routinely protected earlier than the inmates were! And, as we have seen, there was evidence from the beginning that gamma globulin provided at least some protection. A "modification" of the disease was still an inoculum, even if this provided no lasting immunization and had to be repeated. It is axiomatic to medical ethics that a known remedy or protection—even if not perfect or even if the best exact administration of it has not been proved—should not be withheld from individual patients. It seems to a layman that from the beginning various trials at immunization of all new admittees might have been made, and controlled observation made of their different degrees of effectiveness against "nature" at Willowbrook. This would doubtless have been a longer way round, namely, the "anecdotal" method of investigative treatment that comes off second best in comparison with controlled trials. Yet this seems to be the alternative dictated by our received medical ethics, and the only one expressive of minimal care of the primary patients themselves.

Finally, except for one episode, the obtaining of parental consent (on the premise that this is ethically valid) seems to have been very well handled. Wards of the state were not used, though by law the administrator at Willowbrook could have signed consent for them. Only new admittees whose parents were available were entered by proxy consent into the project. Explanation was made to groups of these parents, and they were given time to think about it and consult with their own family physicians. Then late in 1964 Willowbrook was closed to all new admissions because of overcrowding. What then happened can most impartially be described in the words of an article defending the Willowbrook project on medical and ethical grounds:

> Parents who applied for their children to get in were sent a form letter over Dr. Hammond's signature saying that there was no space for new admissions and that their name was being put on a waiting list.
>
> But the hepatitis program, occupying its own space in the institution, continued to admit new patients as each new study group began. "Where do you find new admissions except by canvassing the people who have applied for admission?" Dr. Hammond asked.
>
> So a new batch of form letters went out, saying that there were a few vacancies in the hepatitis research unit if the parents cared to consider volunteering their child for that. In some

instances the second form letter apparently was received as closely as a week after the first letter arrived.[8]

Granting—as I do not—the validity of parental consent to research upon children not in their behalf medically, what sort of consent was that? Surely, the duress upon these parents with children so defective as to require institutionalization was far greater than the duress on prisoners given tobacco or paid or promised parole for their cooperation! I grant that the timing of these events was inadvertent. Since, however, ethics is a matter of criticizing institutions and not only of exculpating or making culprits of individual men, the inadvertence does not matter. This is the strongest possible argument for saying that even if parents have the right to consent to submit the children who are directly and continuously in their care to nonbeneficial medical experimentation, this should not be the rule of practice governing institutions set up for their care.

Such use of captive populations of children for purely experimental purposes ought to be made legally impossible. My view is that this should be stopped by legal acknowledgement of the moral invalidity of parental or legal proxy consent for the child to procedures having no relation to a child's own diagnosis or treatment. If this is not done, canons of loyalty require that the rule of practice (by law, or otherwise) be that children in institutions and not directly under the care of parents or relatives should *never* be used in medical investigations having present pain or discomfort and unknown present and future risks to them, and promising future possible benefits only for others.

Notes

1. Robert Ward, Saul Krugman, Joan P. Giles, A. Milton Jacobs, and Oscar Bodansky, "Infectious Hepatitis: Studies of Its Natural History and Prevention," *New England Journal of Medicine* 258, no. 9 (February 27, 1958): 407–16; Saul Krugman, Robert Ward, Joan P. Giles, Oscar Bodansky, and A. Milton Jacobs, "Infectious Hepatitis: Detection of the Virus during the Incubation Period and in Clinically Inapparent Infection," *New England Journal of Medicine* 261, no. 15 (October 8, 1959): 729–34. The following account and unannotated quotations are taken from these articles.

2. J. Stokes, Jr., et al., "Infectious Hepatitis: Length of Protection by Immune Serum Globulin (Gamma Globulin) during Epidemics," *Journal of the American Medical Association* 147 (1951): 714–19. Since the half-life of gamma globulin is three weeks, no one knows exactly why it immunizes for so long a period. The "highly significant protection against hepatitis obtained by the use of gamma globulin," however, had been confirmed as early as 1945 (see Edward B. Grossman, Sloan G. Stewart, and Joseph Stokes, "Post-

Transfusion Hepatitis in Battle Casualties," *Journal of the American Medical Association* 129, no. 15 [December 8, 1945]: 991–94). The inoculation *withheld* in the Willowbrook experiments had, therefore, proved valuable.

3.   Saul Krugman, "Reflections on Pediatric Clinical Investigations," in *Problems of Drug Evaluation in Infants and Children,* Report of the Fifty-eighth Ross Conference on Pediatric Research, Dorado Beach, Puerto Rico, May 5–7, 1968 (Columbus: Ross Laboratories), pp. 41–42.

4.   "Studies with Children Backed on Medical, Ethical Grounds," *Medical Tribune and Medical News* 8, no. 19 (February 20, 1967): 1, 23.

5.   *Daedalus,* Spring 1969, pp. 471–72, 529. See also pp. 458, 470–72. Since it is the proper business of an ethicist to uphold the proposition that only retrogression in civility can result from bad moral reasoning and the use of inept examples, however innocent, it is fair to point out the startling comparison between Edsall's "argument" and the statement of Dr. Karl Brandt, plenipotentiary in charge of all medical activities in the Nazi Reich: "Do you think that one can obtain any worthwhile, fundamental results without a definite toll of lives? The same goes for technological development. You cannot build a great bridge, a gigantic building—you cannot establish a speed record without deaths!" (quoted by Leo Alexander, "War Crimes: Their Social-Psychological Aspects," *American Journal of Psychiatry* 105, no. 3 [September 1948]: 172). Casualties to progress, or injuries accepted in setting speed limits, are morally quite different from death or maiming or even only risks, or unknown risks, directly and deliberately imposed upon an unconsenting human being.

6.   *Medical Tribune,* February 20, 1967, p. 23.

7.   *Medical Tribune,* February 20, 1967, p. 23.

8.   *Medical Tribune,* February 20, 1967, p. 23.

Decision in *Canterbury* v. *Spence*

Circuit Judge Spottswood W. Robinson III

Appeals Judge Spottswood W. Robinson III rules that a physician is under a strict duty to inform a patient of the potential dangers of treatment and that without such disclosure, the patient cannot give informed consent that is legally binding. The physician's duty, Robinson holds, stems from the right of every adult to decide what can be done to his or her own body.

So far as a legal criterion for disclosure is concerned, Robinson rejects the "professional practice" standard in favor of the "reasonable person" standard. According to the first, a physician has failed to inform a patient properly, if he has failed to disclose what physicians in the community would customarily disclose. Robinson rejects this standard on the grounds that (1) it is not clear if there are any standards for disclosure in the medical community, and (2) the duty to disclose information to patients is based on the right of self-determination (autonomy), not medical practice. The law should set a standard for physicians.

Robinson adopts a "reasonable person" standard, holding that a physician has a duty to disclose all the options and risks that a reasonable person would need to make an informed choice. However, Robinson allows physicians two exceptions to adhering to this standard: (1) when a patient is unconscious or otherwise unable to consent or (2) when the disclosure of risks itself poses a serious threat to the patient's health.

Background Note. Back pain led Jerry Canterbury to consult Dr. William T. Spence. Dr. Spence suspected Canterbury had a ruptured disk, and Canterbury agreed to undergo a laminectomy (an excision of the posterior arch of the vertebra) without asking about or being in-formed of the danger of the procedure. While still in the hospital after the surgery, Canterbury tried to get out of bed and walk to the toilet without assistance. He fell to the floor and suffered paralysis from the waist down.

Canterbury eventually recovered some control of

From United States Court of Appeals, *Canterbury* v. *Spence,* 464 Federal Reporter, 2nd Series, 772, 1972. (Notes omitted.)

his lower body, but he had to walk with crutches and suffered from bowel paralysis. Because of incontinence, he was forced to wear a penile clamp. Canterbury sued Dr. Spence for malpractice on the grounds that he had been negligent in performing the laminectomy and had failed to disclose the 1% risk of serious disability associated with the surgery. He also sued Washington Hospital Center for providing him with negligent postoperative care. The U.S. District Court for the District of Columbia rejected Canterbury's claim, and the case went to the U.S. Court of Appeals, which rendered its verdict on May 17, 1972. The decision has become a landmark statement of the legal requirements for informed consent to medical treatment.

Suits charging failure by a physician adequately to disclose the risks and alternatives of proposed treatment are not innovations in American law. They date back a good half-century, and in the last decade they have multiplied rapidly. There is, nonetheless, disagreement among the courts and the commentators on many major questions, and there is no precedent of our own directly in point. For the tools enabling resolution of the issues on this appeal, we are forced to begin at first principles.

Informed Consent

. . . The root premise is the concept, fundamental in American jurisprudence, that "[e]very human being of adult years and sound mind has a right to determine what shall be done with his own body. . . ." True consent to what happens to one's self is the informed exercise of a choice, and that entails an opportunity to evaluate knowledgeably the options available and the risks attendant upon each. The average patient has little or no understanding of the medical arts, and ordinarily has only his physician to whom he can look for enlightenment with which to reach an intelligent decision. From these almost axiomatic considerations springs the need, and in turn the requirement, of a reasonable divulgence by physician to patient to make such a decision possible.

. . . A physician is under a duty to treat his patient skillfully but proficiency in diagnosis and therapy is not the full measure of his responsibility. The cases demonstrate that the physician is under an obligation to communicate specific information to the patient when the exigencies of reasonable care call for it. Due care may require a physician

perceiving symptoms of bodily abnormality to alert the patient to the condition. It may call upon the physician confronting an ailment which does not respond to his ministrations to inform the patient thereof. It may command the physician to instruct the patient as to any limitations to be presently observed for his own welfare, and as to any precautionary therapy he should seek in the future. It may oblige the physician to advise the patient of the need for or desirability of any alternative treatment promising greater benefit than that being pursued. Just as plainly, due care normally demands that the physician warn the patient of any risks to his well-being which contemplated therapy may involve.

. . . The context in which the duty of risk-disclosure arises is invariably the occasion for decision as to whether a particular treatment procedure is to be undertaken. To the physician, whose training enables a self-satisfying evaluation, the answer may seem clear, but it is the prerogative of the patient, not the physician, to determine for himself the direction in which his interests seem to lie. To enable the patient to chart his course understandably, some familiarity with the therapeutic alternatives and their hazards becomes essential.

. . . A reasonable revelation in these respects is not only a necessity but, as we see it, is as much a matter of the physician's duty. It is a duty to warn of the dangers lurking in the proposed treatment, and that is surely a facet of due care. It is, too, a duty to impart information which the patient has every right to expect. The patient's reliance upon the physician is a trust of the kind which traditionally has exacted obligations beyond those associated with arms-length transactions. His dependence upon the physician for information affecting his well-being, in terms of contemplated treatment, is well-nigh abject. . . .

. . . It is well established that the physician must seek and secure his patient's consent before commencing an operation or other course of treatment. It is also clear that the consent, to be efficacious, must be free from imposition upon the patient. It is the settled rule that therapy not authorized by the patient may amount to a tort—a common law battery—by the physician. And it is evident that it is normally impossible to obtain a consent worthy of the name unless the physician first elucidates the options and the perils for the patient's edification. Thus the physician has long borne a duty, on pain of liability for unauthorized treatment, to make adequate disclosure to the patient. The evolution of the obligation to communicate for the patient's benefit as well as the physician's protection has hardly involved an extraordinary restructuring of the law.

Rejection of the Professional Practice Standard

. . . Duty to disclose has gained recognition in a large number of American jurisdictions, but more largely on a different rationale. The majority of courts dealing with the problem have made the duty depend on whether it was the custom of physicians practicing in the community to make the particular disclosure to the patient. If so, the physician may be held liable for an unreasonable and injurious failure to divulge, but there can be no recovery unless the omission forsakes a practice prevalent in the profession. We agree that the physician's noncompliance with a professional custom to reveal, like any other departure from prevailing medical practice, may give rise to liability to the patient. We do not agree that the patient's cause of action is dependent upon the existence and nonperformance of a relevant professional tradition.

. . . There are, in our view, formidable obstacles to acceptance of the notion that the physician's obligation to disclose is either germinated or limited by medical practice. To begin with, the reality of any discernible custom reflecting a professional consensus on communication of option and risk information to patients is open to serious doubt. We sense the danger that what in fact is no custom at all may be taken as an affirmative custom to maintain silence, and that physician-witnesses to the so-called custom may state merely their personal opinions as to what they or others would do under given conditions. . . .

. . . Respect for the patient's right of self-determination on particular therapy demands a standard set by law for physicians rather than one which physicians may or may not impose upon themselves. . . .

. . . Prevailing medical practice, we have maintained, has evidentiary value in determinations as to what the specific criteria measuring challenged professional conduct are and whether they have been met, but does not itself define the standard. . . .

The Duty to Disclose

Once the circumstances give rise to a duty on the physician's part to inform his patient, the next inquiry is the scope of the disclosure the physician is legally obliged to make. The courts have frequently confronted this problem but no uniform standard defining the adequacy of the divulgence emerges from the decisions. Some have said "full" disclosure, a norm we are unwilling to adopt literally. It seems obviously prohibitive and unrealistic to expect physicians to discuss with their patients every risk of proposed treatment—no matter how small or remote—and generally unnecessary from the patient's viewpoint as well. Indeed, the cases speaking in terms of "full" disclosure appear to envision something less than total disclosure, leaving unanswered the question of just how much.

The larger number of courts, as might be expected, have applied tests framed with reference to prevailing fashion within the medical profession. Some have measured the disclosure by "good medical practice," others by what a reasonable practitioner would have bared under the circumstances, and still others by what medical custom in the community would demand. We have explored this rather considerable body of law but are unprepared to follow it. The duty to disclose, we have reasoned, arises from phenomena apart from medical custom and practice. The latter, we think, should no more establish the scope of the duty than its existence. Any definition of scope in terms purely of a professional standard is at odds with the patient's prerogative to decide on projected therapy himself. That prerogative, we have said, is at the very foundation of the duty to disclose, and both the patient's right to know and the physician's correlative obligation to tell him are diluted to the extent that its compass is dictated by the medical profession.

. . . In our view, the patient's right of self-decision shapes the boundaries of the duty to reveal. That right can be effectively exercised only if the patient possesses enough information to enable an intelligent choice. The scope of the physician's communications to the patient, then, must be measured by the patient's need, and that need is the information material to the decision. Thus the test for determining whether a particular peril must be divulged is its materiality to the patient's decision: all risks potentially affecting the decision must be unmasked. And to safeguard the patient's interest in achieving his own determination on treatment, the law must itself set the standard for adequate disclosure.

. . . Optimally for the patient, exposure of a risk would be mandatory whenever the patient would deem it significant to his decision, either singly or in combination with other risks. Such a requirement, however, would summon the physician to second-guess the patient, whose ideas on materiality could hardly be known to the physician. That would make an undue demand upon medical practitioners, whose conduct, like that of others, is to be measured in terms of reasonableness. Consonantly with orthodox negligence doctrine, the physician's liability for nondisclosure is to be determined on the basis of foresight, not hindsight; no less than any other aspect of negligence, the issue on nondisclosure must be approached from the viewpoint of the reasonableness of the physician's divulgence in terms of what he knows or should know to be the patient's informational needs. If, but only if, the fact-finder can say that the physician's communication was unreasonably inadequate is an imposition of liability legally or morally justified.

Of necessity, the content of the disclosure rests in the first instance with the physician. Ordinarily it is only he who is in position to identify particular dangers; always he must make a judgment, in terms of materiality, as to whether and to what extent revelation to the patient is called for. He cannot know with complete exactitude what the patient would consider important to his decision, but on the basis of his medical training and experience he can sense how the average, reasonable patient expectably would react. Indeed, with knowledge of, or ability to learn, his patient's background and current condition, he is in a position superior to that of most others—attorneys, for example—who are called upon to make judgments on pain of liability in damages for unreasonable miscalculation.

. . . From these considerations we derive the breadth of the disclosure of risks legally to be required. The scope of the standard is not subjective as to either the physician or the patient; it remains objective with due regard for the patient's informational needs and with suitable leeway for the physician's situation. In broad outline, we agree that "[a] risk is thus material when a reasonable person, in what the physician knows or should know to be the patient's position, would be likely to attach significance to the risk or cluster of risks in deciding whether or not to forego the proposed therapy."

. . . The topics importantly demanding a communication of information are the inherent and potential hazards of the proposed treatment, the alternatives to that treatment, if any, and the results likely if the patient remains untreated. The factors contributing significance to the dangerousness of a medical technique are, of course, the incidence of injury and the degree of the harm threatened. A very small chance of death or serious disablement may well be significant; a potential disability which dramatically outweighs the potential benefit of the therapy or the detriments of the existing malady may summons discussion with the patient.

. . . There is no bright line separating the significant from the insignificant; the answer in any case must abide a rule of reason. Some dangers—infection, for example—are inherent in any operation; there is no obligation to communicate those of which persons of average sophistication are aware. Even more clearly, the physician bears no responsibility for discussion of hazards the patient has already discovered, or those having no apparent materiality to patients' decision on therapy. The disclosure doctrine, like others marking lines between permissible and impermissible behavior in medical practice, is in essence a requirement of conduct prudent under the circumstances. Whenever non-disclosure of particular risk information is open to debate by reasonable-minded men, the issue is for the finder of the facts.

Two Exceptions

. . . Two exceptions to the general rule of disclosure have been noted by the courts. Each is in the nature of a physician's privilege not to disclose, and the reasoning underlying them is appealing. Each, indeed, is but a recognition that, as important as is the patient's right to know, it is greatly outweighed by the magnitudinous circumstances giving rise to the privilege. The first comes into play when the patient is unconscious or otherwise incapable of consenting, and harm from a failure to treat is imminent and outweighs any harm threatened by the proposed treatment. When a genuine emergency of that sort arises, it is settled that the impracticality of conferring with the patient dispenses with need for it. Even in situations of that character, the physician should, as a current law requires, attempt to secure a relative's consent if possible. But if time is too short to accommodate discussion, obviously the physician should proceed with the treatment.

. . . The second exception obtains when risk-disclosure poses such a threat of detriment to the patient as to become unfeasible or contraindicated from a medical point of view. It is recognized that patients occasionally become so ill or emotionally distraught on disclosure as to foreclose a rational decision, or complicate or hinder the treatment, or perhaps even pose psychological damage to the patient. Where that is so, the cases have generally held that the physician is armed with a privilege to keep the information from the patient, and we think it clear that portents of that type may justify the physician in action he deems medically warranted. The critical inquiry is whether the physician responded to a sound medical judgment that communication of the risk information would present a threat to the patient's well-being.

. . . The physician's privilege to withhold information for therapeutic reasons must be carefully circumscribed, however, for otherwise it might devour the disclosure rule itself. The privilege does not accept the paternalistic notion that the physician may remain silent simply because divulgence might prompt the patient to forego therapy the physician feels the patient really needs. That attitude presumes instability or perversity for even the normal patient, and runs counter to the foundation principle that the patient should and ordinarily can make the choice for himself. Nor does the privilege contemplate operation save where the patient's reaction to risk information, as reasonable foreseen by the physician, is menacing. And even in a situation of that kind, disclosure to a close relative with a view to securing consent to the proposed treatment may be the only alternative open to the physician. . . .

Competency to Give an Informed Consent: A Model for Making Clinical Assessments

James F. Drane

James Drane claims that respect for patients requires securing their informed consent in decisions about their welfare. However, we must not take patients' competence to consent for granted or we may fail in our duty to promote their well-being. We need a standard of competence, but no single standard is workable.

Drane proposes a sliding-scale model consisting of three standards: (1) if a treatment is not dangerous and is in the patient's best interest, the patient need only be *aware* of the general situation and *assent* to it; (2) if a disease is chronic, a diagnosis uncertain, a treatment dangerous, results uncertain, or alternative therapies available, the patient must be able to *understand* the options and *choose* among them (leaving the choice to one's physician is also a possibility); (3) when diagnosis is clear, treatment effective, and death likely to result from refusing treatment, the patient must have "a capacity to appreciate the nature and consequence of the decision." To meet this last standard, a patient must be able to give intelligible reasons for the decision, even if it varies from what most rational people would decide. Drane sees his position as balancing rationality, maximum autonomy, and maximum patient benefit.

In January 1980, as one more indication of the growing importance of medical ethics, a presidential commission was formed and began work on the moral questions posed by the practice of contemporary medicine. After three years of intense work, the commission published a separate volume on 11 different ethical problems in the hope of stimulating thoughtful discussion. Some broad principles were uncovered that apply to any and every bioethical issue, such as the principle of patient respect and its concrete application in the right of informed consent. But there were also recurring perplexities, one of which was competency or, in the language preferred by the commission, the patient's capacity to choose.[1]

Respect for patients means ensuring their participation in decisions affecting their lives. Such participation is a basic form of freedom and stands at the core of Western values. But freedom, participation, and self-determination suppose a capacity for such acts. No one, for example, assumes that an infant has such a capacity and, time and again, doubts arise about the capacity of some older patients. Not to respect a patient's freedom is undoubtedly wrong. But to respect what may be an expression of freedom only in appearance would be a violation of another basic principle of ethical medicine: promotion of the patient's well-being.

Although the commission's report referred many times to competency or capacity to choose, commissioners and staff members privately expressed frustration and disappointment about their conclusions. The commission reports spelled out what are considered to be the components of competency: the possession of a set of values and goals, the ability to communicate and understand information, and the ability to reason and deliberate. In addition, the commission criticized some standards for determining competency that either were too lenient and did not protect a patient sufficiently or were too strict and in effect transferred decision making to the physician. But the commission did not come up with its own standard and left unsettled the question of how to decide whether a particular patient's decision should be respected or overridden because of incompetency. Incompetency is not the only reason for overriding a patient's refusal or setting aside a consent, but it is the most common reason for doing so. Defining incom-

petency or establishing standards of competency is a complex problem because it involves law, ethics, and psychiatry.

Competency Assessment

Competency assessments focus on the patient's mental capacities, specifically, the mental capacities to make an informed medical decision. Does the patient understand what is being proposed? Can the patient come to a decision about treatment based on an adequate understanding? How much understanding and rational decision-making capacity are sufficient for this particular patient to be considered competent? Conversely, how deficient must this patient's decision-making capacity be before he is declared incompetent? A properly performed competency assessment should eliminate two types of error: (1) preventing a competent person from participating in treatment decisions and (2) failing to protect an incompetent person from the harmful effects of a bad decision.

Model for Making the Assessment

The President's commission did not recommend a single standard for determining competency because any one standard is inappropriate for the many different types of medical decisions that people face. What is proposed here is a sliding standard, i.e., the more dangerous the medical decision, the more stringent the standards of competency. The basic idea, following a suggestion of Mark Siegler,[2, 3] is to connect determination of competency to different medical situations (acute or chronic, critical or noncritical), and next to take this idea a step further by specifying three different standards or definitions of what it means to be competent. These standards are then correlated with three different medical situations, each more dangerous than the other. Finally, the sliding standards and different medical situations are correlated with the types of psychiatric abnormalities that ordinarily undermine competency. The interrelationship of

This investigation was supported in part by grant ED 0652-78 from the National Endowment for the Humanities.

all these entities creates a model that can aid the physician faced with a question about a patient's capacity to choose. This model brings together disparate academic disciplines, but its goal is thoroughly pragmatic: to provide a workable guide for clinical decision making.

Standard 1

The first and least stringent standard of competency to give a valid consent applies to those medical decisions that are not dangerous and objectively are in the patient's best interest. If the patient is critically ill because of an acute illness that is life threatening, if there is an effective treatment available that is low in risk, and if few or no alternatives are available, then consent to the treatment is prima facie rational. Even though patients are seriously ill and thereby impaired in both cognitive and conative functioning, they are usually competent to consent to a needed treatment.

The act of consent to such a treatment is considered to be an informed consent as long as the patient is aware of what is going on. *Awareness* in the sense of orientation or being conscious of the general situation satisfies the cognitive requirement of informed consent. *Assent* alone to what is the rational expectation in this medical context satisfies the decisional component. When adult patients go along with needed medical treatment, then a legal presumption of competency holds even though the patients are obviously impaired. To insist on higher standards for capacity to give a valid consent in such a medical setting would amount to requiring surplus mental capacities for a simple task and would result in millions of acutely ill patients being considered incompetent. Such an absurd requirement would produce absurd consequences. Altogether rational and appropriate decisions would be set aside as invalid, and surrogate decision makers would have to be selected to make the same decision. For what purpose? To accomplish what objective? To protect what value? None of the values and objectives meant to be safeguarded by the competency requirement is disregarded or set aside by a lenient standard for this type of decision.

Considering as competent seriously ill patients, even the mentally ill, who are aware and assent to treatment, eliminates the ambiguity and confusion associated with terms such as *virtually competent, marginally competent,* and *competent for*

practical purposes that are used to excuse the commonsense practice of respecting the decisions of patients who would be judged incompetent by a more demanding single standard of decision-making capacity. Refusal by a patient dying of a chronic illness of treatments that are useless and only prolong the dying requires the same modest standard of competency.

Infants, unconscious persons, and the severely retarded would obviously fall short even of this least demanding standard. These persons, and patients who use psychotic defenses that severely compromise reality testing, are the only ones who fail to meet this first definition of decision-making capacity. Children who have reached the age of reason (6 years or older), on the other hand, as well as the senile, the mildly retarded, and the intoxicated, are considered competent.

The law considers 21 and sometimes 18 years to be the age below which persons are presumed incompetent to make binding contracts, including health care decisions. The President's commission, however, endorses a lower age of competency, and so do many authors who write about children and mental retardation. In this model, we are discussing ethical standards, but the physician cannot ignore the law and must obtain consent from the child's legal guardian.

Standard 2

If the illness is chronic rather than acute, or if the treatment is more dangerous or of less definite benefit (or if there are real alternatives to one or another course of action, e.g., death rather than lingering illness), then the risk-benefit balance is tipped differently than in the situation described in the previous section. Consequently, a different standard of competency to consent is required. The patient must be able to *understand* the risks and outcomes of the different options and then be able to *choose* a decision based on this understanding. At this point, competency means capacity to understand the real options and to make an understanding decision, a higher standard than that required for the first type of treatment choice.

Ability to understand is not the same as being able to articulate conceptual or verbal understanding. Some ethicists assume a rationalist epistemology and reduce all understanding to a conceptual or verbal type. Many, in fact, require that patients literally remember what they have been told as a proof of competence. Understanding, however, may be more affective than conceptual. Following an explanation, a patient may grasp what is best for him with strong feelings and convictions, and yet be hard pressed to articulate his understanding/conviction in words.

Competency as capacity for an understanding choice is also reconcilable with a decision to let a trusted physician decide what is the best treatment. Such a choice (waiver) may be made for good reasons and represent a decision in favor of one set of values (safety or anxiety reduction) over another (independence and personal initiative). As such, it can be considered as informed consent and creates no suspicion of incompetency.

Ignorance or inability to understand, however, undermines competency. The same is true of a severe mood disorder or severe shock, which may either impair thought processes or undermine capacity to make an understanding choice. Short-term memory loss, delusion, dementia, and delirium would also render a patient incompetent. On the other hand, mature adolescents, the mildly retarded, and persons with some personality disorders would be competent to make this type of decision.

Standard 3

The most stringent and demanding standard of competency is reserved for those decisions that are very dangerous and fly in the face of both professional and public rationality. When diagnostic uncertainty is minimal, the available treatment is effective, and death is likely to result from treatment refusal, a presumption is established against refusal of consent to treatment. The medical decision now is not a balancing of what are widely recognized as reasonable alternatives. Any decision other than the one to be treated seems to violate basic reasonableness. A decision to refuse treatment, then, is apparently irrational, besides being harmful. Yet, according to this model, such decisions can be respected as long as the patients satisfy the most demanding standard of competency.

Competency in this context requires a capacity to appreciate the nature and consequences of the decision being made. *Appreciation* is a term used to refer to the highest degree of understanding, one that grasps more than just the medical details of the

illness and treatment. To be competent to make apparently irrational and very dangerous choices, the patient must be able to come to a decision based on the medical information and to appreciate the implications of this decision for his life. Competency of this type requires a capacity that is both technical and personal, both cognitive and affective.

Since the patient's decision flies in the face of objective standards of rationality, it must at least be subjectively critical and *rational*. A patient need not conform to what most rational people do to be considered competent, but the competent patient must be able to give reasons for his decision. The patient must be able to show that he has thought through the medical issues and related this information to his personal value system. The patient's personal reasons need not be medically or publicly accepted, but neither can they be purely private, idiosyncratic, or incoherent. Their intelligibility may derive from a set of religious beliefs or from a philosophical view that is shared by only a small minority. This toughest standard of competency does, however, demand a more rationalistic type understanding: one that includes verbalization, argumentation, and consistency.

The higher-level mental capacities required for competency to make this type of decision are impaired by less severe psychiatric abnormality. In fact, much less serious mental affliction suffices to create an assumption of incompetency to refuse a needed and effective treatment. On the other hand, however, not any mental or emotional disturbance would constitute an impairment of decisional capacity. A certain amount of anxiety, for example, goes with any serious decision and cannot make a patient incompetent. Some mild pain would not impair decisional capacity, but severe pain might do so. Even a slight reactive depression may not render a patient incompetent for this type of decision. But intense anxiety associated with mild or severe shock, and/or a mild endogenous depression, would be considered incapacitating. In fact, any mental or emotional disorder that compromises appreciation and rational decision making would make a patient incompetent. For example, persons who are incapable of making the effort required to control destructive behavior (substance abusers and sociopaths), as well as neurotic persons, hysterical persons, and persons who are ambivalent about their choice, would all be incompetent to refuse lifesaving treatment. The same standard applies to consent to experiments not related to one's own illness.

Conclusion

Radical advocates of patient rights and doctrinaire libertarians will worry that this model shifts power back toward physicians who make competency determinations and away from patients whose choices ought to be respected. But only in situation 3 does the physician's power increase, and then only for the patient's welfare. Moreover, this loss in the patient's power never reaches the point where patients' self-determination is set aside. Patients can insist on their decision to refuse a treatment even when the physician knows that the outcome will be certain death, as long as every precaution is taken to ensure that such a decision is not the product of a pathological state.

A balancing of values is the cornerstone of a good competency assessment. Rationality is given its place throughout this model. Maximum autonomy is guaranteed for patients because they can choose to do what is not at all beneficial (a nontherapeutic experiment) or refuse to do what is most beneficial. Maximum benefit is also guaranteed because patients are protected against harmful choices that are more the product of abnormality than of their self-determination. All the values, in fact, on which competency requirements were originally based are guaranteed in this model.

No one proposal will settle the question of which standard or standards of competency are appropriate for medical decisions. More empirical research is required on the issue, and more physicians who have valuable practical experience with complex cases need to be heard from. After much more study and discussion, perhaps the medical profession itself, through its ethics committees, will take a stand on the issue. In the meantime, this proposal is meant to be a contribution to the discussion.

Notes

1. President's Commission for the Study of Ethical Problems in Medicine and Biomedical and Behavioral Research; *Deciding to Forego Life-Sustaining Treatment*. Washington, D.C., U.S. Government Printing Office, 1983.

2. Siegler, M., Goldblatt, A. D.: Clinical intuition: A procedure for balancing the rights of patients and the responsibilities of physicians, in Spicker, S. F., Healey, J. M., Engelhardt, H. T. (eds.): *The Law-Medicine Relation: A Philosophical Exploration*. Dordrecht, The Netherlands, D. Reidel Publishing Co., 1981, pp. 5–29.

3. Jonsen, A. R., Siegler, M., Winslade, W. J.: *Clinical Ethics*. New York: Macmillan Publishing Co., Inc., 1982, pp. 56–85.

Of Mice but Not Men: Problems of the Randomized Clinical Trial

Samuel Hellman and Deborah S. Hellman

Samuel and Deborah Hellman show how randomized clinical trials (RCTs) in medicine may create an ethical dilemma for the physician who is also acting as a scientist. A physician is committed to seeing to the interest of an individual patient, while a scientist may have to sacrifice the interest of present patients to benefit future ones, thus undermining the physician-patient relationship.

The Hellmans reject a utilitarian justification for sacrificing the interest of the individual for the benefit of future patients. They argue that the physician-patient relationship implies that patients have a right to receive a physician's best judgment and care and that physicians have a duty to provide them. The methods typically used in an RCT may require a physician to violate this duty by remaining ignorant of whether a patient is receiving the best therapy available or by continuing to use a therapy after it is believed to be of less worth than an alternative.

The Hellmans conclude by sketching ways in which observer bias and patient selection, problems currently solved by using RCTs, may be achieved without violating the rights inherent in the physician-patient relationship.

As medicine has become increasingly scientific and less accepting of unsupported opinion or proof by anecdote, the randomized controlled clinical trial has become the standard technique for changing diagnostic or therapeutic methods. The use of this technique creates an ethical dilemma.[1,2] Researchers participating in such studies are required to modify their ethical commitments to individual patients and do serious damage to the concept of the physician as a practicing, empathetic professional who is primarily concerned with each patient as an individual. Researchers using a randomized clinical trial can be described as physician-scientists, a term that expresses the tension between the two roles. The physician, by entering into a relationship with an individual patient, assumes certain obligations, including the commitment always to act in the patient's best interests. As Leon Kass has rightly maintained, "the physician must produce unswervingly the virtues of loyalty and fidelity to his patient."[3] Though the ethical requirements of this relationship have been modified by legal obligations to report wounds of a suspicious nature and certain infectious diseases, these obligations in no way conflict with the central ethical obligation to act in the best interests of the patient medically. Instead, certain nonmedical interests of the patient are preempted by other social concerns.

The role of the scientist is quite different. The clinical scientist is concerned with answering questions—i.e., determining the validity of formally constructed hypotheses. Such scientific information, it is presumed, will benefit humanity in general. The clinical scientist's role has been well described by Dr. Anthony Fauci, director of the National Institute of Allergy and Infectious Diseases, who states the goals of the randomized clinical trial in these words: "It's not to deliver therapy. It's to answer a scientific question so that the drug can be available for everybody once you've established safety and efficacy."[4] The demands of such a study can conflict in a number of ways with the

physician's duty to minister to patients. The study may create a false dichotomy in the physician's opinions: according to the premise of the randomized clinical trial, the physician may only know or not know whether a proposed course of treatment represents an improvement; no middle position is permitted. What the physician thinks, suspects, believes, or has a hunch about is assigned to the "not knowing" category, because knowing is defined on the basis of an arbitrary but accepted statistical test performed in a randomized clinical trial. Thus, little credence is given to information gained beforehand in other ways or to information accrued during the trial but without the required statistical degree of assurance that a difference is not due to chance. The randomized clinical trial also prevents the treatment technique from being modified on the basis of the growing knowledge of the physicians during their participation in the trial. Moreover, it limits access to the data as they are collected until specific milestones are achieved. This prevents physicians from profiting not only from their individual experience, but also from the collective experience of the other participants.

The randomized clinical trial requires doctors to act simultaneously as physicians and as scientists. This puts them in a difficult and sometimes untenable ethical position. The conflicting moral demands arising from the use of the randomized clinical trial reflect the classic conflict between rights-based moral theories and utilitarian ones. The first of these, which depend on the moral theory of Immanuel Kant (and seen more recently in neo-Kantian philosophers, such as John Rawls[5]), asserts that human beings, by virtue of their unique capacity for rational thought, are bearers of dignity. As such, they ought not to be treated merely as means to an end; rather, they must always be treated as ends in themselves. Utilitarianism, by contrast, defines what is right as the greatest good for the greatest number—that is, as social utility. This view, articulated by Jeremy Bentham and John

Stuart Mill, requires that pleasures (understood broadly, to include such pleasures as health and well-being) and pains be added together. The morally correct act is the act that produces the most pleasure and the least pain overall.

A classic objection to the utilitarian position is that according to that theory, the distribution of pleasures and pains is of no moral consequence. This element of the theory severely restricts physicians from being utilitarians, or at least from following the theory's dictates. Physicians must care very deeply about the distribution of pain and pleasure, for they have entered into a relationship with one or a number of individual patients. They cannot be indifferent to whether it is these patients or others that suffer for the general benefit of society. Even though society might gain from the suffering of a few, and even though the doctor might believe that such a benefit is worth a given patient's suffering (i.e., that utilitarianism is right in the particular case), the ethical obligation created by the covenant between doctor and patient requires the doctor to see the interests of the individual patient as primary and compelling. In essence, the doctor–patient relationship requires doctors to see their patients as bearers of rights who cannot be merely used for the greater good of humanity.

As Fauci has suggested,[4] the randomized clinical trial routinely asks physicians to sacrifice the interests of their particular patients for the sake of the study and that of the information that it will make available for the benefit of society. This practice is ethically problematic. Consider first the initial formulation of a trial. In particular, consider the case of a disease for which there is no satisfactory therapy—for example, advanced cancer or the acquired immunodeficiency syndrome (AIDS). A new agent that promises more effectiveness is the subject of the study. The control group must be given either an unsatisfactory treatment or a placebo. Even though the therapeutic value of the new agent is unproved, if physicians think that it has promise, are they acting in the best interests of their patients in allowing them to be randomly assigned to the control group? Is persisting in such an assignment consistent with the specific commitments taken on in the doctor–patient relationship? As a result of interactions with patients with AIDS and their advocates, Merigan[6] recently suggested modifications in the design of clinical trials that attempt to deal

with the unsatisfactory treatment given to the control group. The view of such activists has been expressed by Rebecca Pringle Smith of Community Research Initiative in New York: "Even if you have a supply of compliant martyrs, trials must have some ethical validity."[4]

If the physician has no opinion about whether the new treatment is acceptable, then random assignment is ethically acceptable, but such lack of enthusiasm for the new treatment does not augur well for either the patient or the study. Alternatively, the treatment may show promise of beneficial results but also present a risk of undesirable complications. When the physician believes that the severity and likelihood of harm and good are evenly balanced, randomization may be ethically acceptable. If the physician has no preference for either treatment (is in a state of equipoise[7,8]), then randomization is acceptable. If, however, he or she believes that the new treatment may be either more or less successful or more or less toxic, the use of randomization is not consistent with fidelity to the patient.

The argument usually used to justify randomization is that it provides, in essence, a critique of the usefulness of the physician's beliefs and opinions, those that have not yet been validated by a randomized clinical trial. As the argument goes, these not-yet-validated beliefs are as likely to be wrong as right. Although physicians are ethically required to provide their patients with the best available treatment, there simply is no best treatment yet known.

The reply to this argument takes two forms. First, and most important, even if this view of the reliability of a physician's opinions is accurate, the ethical constraints of an individual doctor's relationship with a particular patient require the doctor to provide individual care. Although physicians must take pains to make clear the speculative nature of their views, they cannot withhold these views from the patient. The patient asks from the doctor both knowledge and judgment. The relationship established between them rightfully allows patients to ask for the judgment of their particular physicians, not merely that of the medical profession in general. Second, it may not be true, in fact, that the not-yet-validated beliefs of physicians are as likely to be wrong as right. The greater certainty obtained with a randomized clinical trial is beneficial, but that does not mean that a lesser degree of certainty is without value. Physicians can acquire knowledge through methods other than the randomized clinical trial. Such knowledge, acquired over time and less formally than is required in a randomized clinical trial, may be of great value to a patient.

Even if it is ethically acceptable to begin a study, one often forms an opinion during its course—especially in studies that are impossible to conduct in a truly double-blinded fashion—that makes it ethically problematic to continue. The inability to remain blinded usually occurs in studies of cancer or AIDS, for example, because the therapy is associated by nature with serious side effects. Trials attempt to restrict the physician's access to the data in order to prevent such unblinding. Such restrictions should make physicians eschew the trial, since their ability to act in the patient's best interests will be limited. Even supporters of randomized clinical trials, such as Merigan, agree that interim findings should be presented to patients to ensure that no one receives what seems an inferior treatment.[6] Once physicians have formed a view about the new treatment, can they continue randomization? If random assignment is stopped, the study may be lost and the participation of the previous patients wasted. However, if physicians continue the randomization when they have a definite opinion about the efficacy of the experimental drug, they are not acting in accordance with the requirements of the doctor–patient relationship. Furthermore, as their opinion becomes more firm, stopping the randomization may not be enough. Physicians may be ethically required to treat the patients formerly placed in the control group with the therapy that now seems probably effective. To do so would be faithful to the obligations created by the doctor–patient relationship, but it would destroy the study.

To resolve this dilemma, one might suggest that the patient has abrogated the rights implicit in a doctor–patient relationship by signing an informed-consent form. We argue that such rights cannot be waived or abrogated. They are inalienable. The right to be treated as an individual deserving the physician's best judgment and care, rather than to be used as a means to determine the best treatment for others, is inherent in every person. This right, based on the concept of dignity, cannot be waived. What of altruism, then? Is it not the patient's right to make a sacrifice for the general good? This question must be considered from both positions—that of the patient and that of the physician. Although patients may decide to waive this right, it is not consistent with the role of a physician to ask that they do so. In asking, the doctor acts as a scientist instead. The physician's role here is to propose what he or she believes is best medically for the specific patient, nor to suggest participation in a study from which the patient cannot gain. Because the opportunity to help future patients is of potential value to a patient, some would say physicians should not deny it. Although this point has merit, it offers so many opportunities for abuse that we are extremely uncomfortable about accepting it. The responsibilities of physicians are much clearer; they are to minister to the current patient.

Moreover, even if patients could waive this right, it is questionable whether those with terminal illness would be truly able to give voluntary informed consent. Such patients are extremely dependent on both their physicians and the health care system. Aware of this dependence, physicians must not ask for consent, for in such cases the very asking breaches the doctor–patient relationship. Anxious to please their physicians, patients may have difficulty refusing to participate in the trial the physicians describe. The patients may perceive their refusal as damaging to the relationship, whether or not it is so. Such perceptions of coercion affect the decision. Informed-consent forms are difficult to understand, especially for patients under the stress of serious illness for which there is no satisfactory treatment. The forms are usually lengthy, somewhat legalistic, complicated, and confusing, and they hardly bespeak the compassion expected of the medical profession. It is important to remember that those who have studied the doctor–patient relationship have emphasized its empathetic nature.

> [The] relationship between doctor and patient partakes of a peculiar intimacy. It presupposes on the part of the physician not only knowledge of his fellow men but sympathy. . . . This aspect of the practice of medicine has been designated as the art; yet I wonder whether it should not, most properly, be called the essence.[9]

How is such a view of the relationship consonant with random assignment and informed consent? The Physician's Oath of the World Medical Association affirms the primacy of the deontologic view of patients' rights: "Concern for the interests of the subject must always prevail over the interests of science and society."[10]

Furthermore, a single study is often not considered sufficient. Before a new form of therapy is generally accepted, confirmatory trials must be conducted. How can one conduct such trials ethically unless one is convinced that the first trial was in error? The ethical problems we have discussed are only exacerbated when a completed randomized clinical trial indicates that a given treatment is preferable. Even if the physician believes the initial trial was in error, the physician must indicate to the patient the full results of that trial.

The most common reply to the ethical arguments has been that the alternative is to return to the physician's intuition, to anecdotes, or to both as the basis of medical opinion. We all accept the dangers of such a practice. The argument states that we must therefore accept randomized, controlled clinical trials regardless of their ethical problems because of the great social benefit they make possible, and we salve our conscience with the knowledge that informed consent has been given. This returns us to the conflict between patients' rights and social utility. Some would argue that this tension can be resolved by placing a relative value on each. If the patient's right that is being compromised is not a fundamental right and the social gain is very great, then the study might be justified. When the right is fundamental, however, no amount of social gain, or almost none, will justify its sacrifice. Consider, for example, the experiments on humans done by physicians under the Nazi regime. All would agree that these are unacceptable regardless of the value of the scientific information gained. Some people go so far as to say that no use should be made of the results of those experiments because of the clearly unethical manner in which the data were collected. This extreme example may not seem relevant, but we believe that in its hyperbole it clarifies the fallacy of a utilitarian approach to the physician's relationship with the patient. To consider the utilitarian gain is consistent neither with the physician's role nor with the patient's rights.

It is fallacious to suggest that only the randomized clinical trial can provide valid information or that all information acquired by this technique is valid. Such experimental methods are intended to reduce error and bias and therefore reduce the uncertainty of the result. Uncertainty cannot be eliminated, however. The scientific method is based on increasing probabilities and increasingly refined approximations of truth.[11] Although the randomized clinical trial contributes to these ends, it is neither unique nor perfect. Other techniques may also be useful.[12]

Randomized trials often place physicians in the ethically intolerable position of choosing between the good of the patient and that of society. We urge that such situations be avoided and that other techniques of acquiring clinical information be adopted. For example, concerning trials of treatments for AIDS, Byar et al.[13] have said that "some traditional approaches to the clinical-trials process may be unnecessarily rigid and unsuitable for this disease." In this case, AIDS is not what is so different; rather, the difference is in the presence of AIDS activists, articulate spokespersons for the ethical problems created by the application of the randomized clinical trial to terminal illnesses. Such arguments are equally applicable to advanced cancer and other serious illnesses. Byar et al. agree that there are even circumstances in which uncontrolled clinical trials may be justified: when there is no effective treatment to use as a control, when the prognosis is uniformly poor, and when there is a reasonable expectation of benefit without excessive toxicity. These conditions are usually found in clinical trials of advanced cancer.

The purpose of the randomized clinical trial is to avoid the problems of observer bias and patient selection. It seems to us that techniques might be developed to deal with these issues in other ways. Randomized clinical trials deal with them in a cumbersome and heavy-handed manner, by requiring large numbers of patients in the hope that random assignment will balance the heterogeneous distribution of patients into the different groups. By observing known characteristics of patients, such as age and sex, and distributing them equally between groups, it is thought that unknown factors important in determining outcomes will also be distributed equally. Surely, other techniques can be developed to deal with both observer bias and patient selection. Prospective studies without randomization, but with the evaluation of patients by uninvolved third parties, should remove observer bias. Similar methods have been suggested by Royall.[12] Prospective matched-pair analysis, in which patients are treated in a manner consistent with their physician's views, ought to help ensure equivalence between the groups and thus mitigate the effect of patient selection, at least with regard to known co-variates. With regard to unknown covariates, the security would rest, as in randomized trials, in the enrollment of large numbers of patients and in confirmatory studies. This method would not pose ethical difficulties, since patients would receive the treatment recommended by their physician. They would be included in the study by independent ob-servers matching patients with respect to known characteristics, a process that would not affect pa-tient care and that could be performed indepen-dently any number of times.

This brief discussion of alternatives to random-ized clinical trials is sketchy and incomplete. We wish only to point out that there may be satisfac-tory alternatives, not to describe and evaluate them completely. Even if randomized clinical trials were much better than any alternative, however, the eth-ical dilemmas they present may put their use at variance with the primary obligations of the physi-cian. In this regard, Angell cautions, "If this com-mitment to the patient is attenuated, even for so good a cause as benefits to future patients, the im-plicit assumptions of the doctor–patient relation-ship are violated."[14] The risk of such attenuation by the randomized trial is great. The AIDS activists have brought this dramatically to the attention of the academic medical community. Techniques ap-propriate to the laboratory may not be applicable to humans. We must develop and use alternative methods for acquiring clinical knowledge.

Notes

1. Hellman S. Randomized clinical trials and the doctor–patient relationship: an ethical dilemma. *Cancer Clin Trials* 1979: 2: 189–93.

2. *Idem.* A doctor's dilemma: the doctor–patient relationship in clinical investigation. In: Proceedings of the Fourth Na-tional Conference on Human Values and Cancer. New York, March 15–17, 1984. New York: American Cancer Society, 1984: 144–6.

3. Kass LR. Toward a more natural science: biology and human affairs. New York: Free Press, 1985: 196.

4. Palca J. AIDS drug trials enter new age. *Science* 1989: 246: 19–21.

5. Rawls J. A theory of justice. Cambridge, Mass.: Belknap Press of Harvard University Press, 1971: 183–92, 446–52.

6. Merigan TC. You *can* teach an old dog new tricks—how AIDS trials are pioneering new strategies. *N Engl J Med* 1990: 323: 1341–3.

7. Freedman B. Equipoise and the ethics of clinical research. *N Engl J Med* 1987: 317: 141–5.

8. Singer PA, Lantos JD, Whitington PF, Broelsch CE, Siegler M. Equipoise and the ethics of segmental liver transplanta-tion. *Clin Res* 1988: 36: 539–45.

9. Longcope WT. Methods and medicine. Bull Johns Hopkins Hosp 1932: 50: 4–20.

10. Report on medical ethics. *World Med Assoc Bull* 1949: 1: 109, 111.

11. Popper K. The problem of induction. In: Miller D, ed. *Popper selections*. Princeton, N.J.: Princeton University Press, 1985: 101–17.

12. Royall RM. Ethics and statistics in randomized clinical trials. *Stat Sci* 1991: 6(1): 52–62.

13. Byar DP, Schoenfeld DA, Green SB, et al. Design considera-tions for AIDS trials. *N Engl J Med* 1990: 323: 1343–8.

14. Angell M. Patients' preferences in randomized clinical trials. *N Engl J Med* 1984: 310: 1385–7.

Clinical Trials: Are They Ethical?

Eugene Passamani

Eugene Passamani argues that randomized clinical trials (RCTs) are the most reli-able means of evaluating new therapies. Without RCTs, chance and bias may af-fect our conclusions.

Passamani rejects the argument that the physician-patient relationship de-mands that physicians recommend the "best" therapy for patients, no matter how poor the data on which the recommendation is based. He acknowledges that RCTs pose ethical problems for physician-researchers, but he believes the difficulties can be overcome by employing three procedural safeguards.

First, all participants must give their informed consent. They must be told about the goals of the research and its potential benefits and risks. Moreover, they must be informed about alternatives to their participation, and they must be per-mitted to withdraw from the trial at any time they choose.

Second, for an RCT to be legitimate, a state of clinical *equipoise* must exist. Competent physicians must be genuinely uncertain about which of the alternative therapies in the trial is superior and content to allow their patients to be treated with any of them.

Finally, the clinical trial must be designed as a critical test of the therapeutic alternatives.

Properly carried out, Passamani holds, RCTs protect physicians and patients from therapies that are ineffective or toxic.

Biomedical research leads to better understanding of biology and ultimately to improved health. Physicians have for millenniums attempted to understand disease, to use this knowledge to cure or palliate, and to relieve attendant suffering. Improving strategies for prevention and treatment remains an ethical imperative for medicine. Until very recently, progress depended largely on a process of carefully observing groups of patients given a new and promising therapy; outcome was then compared with that previously observed in groups undergoing a standard treatment. Outcome in a series of case patients as compared with that in nonrandomized controls can be used to assess the treatment of disorders in which therapeutic effects are dramatic and the pathophysiologic features are relatively uncomplicated, such as vitamin deficiency or some infectious diseases. Observational methods are not very useful, however, in the detection of small treatment effects in disorders in which there is substantial variability in expected outcome and imperfect knowledge of complicated pathophysiologic features (many vascular disorders and most cancers, for example). The effect of a treatment cannot easily be extracted from variations in disease severity and the effects of concomitant treatments. Clinical trials have thus become a preferred means of evaluating an ever increasing flow of innovative diagnostic and therapeutic maneuvers. The randomized, double-blind clinical trial is a powerful technique because of the efficiency and credibility associated with treatment comparisons involving randomized concurrent controls.

The modern era of randomized trials began in the early 1950s with the evaluation of streptomycin in patients with tuberculosis.[1] Since that time trial techniques and methods have continuously been refined.[2] In addition, the ethical aspects of these experiments in patients have been actively discussed.[3-7]

In what follows I argue that randomized trials are in fact the most scientifically sound and ethically correct means of evaluating new therapies. There is potential conflict between the roles of physician and physician-scientist, and for this reason society has created mechanisms to ensure that the interests of individual patients are served should they elect to participate in a clinical trial.[6]

Clinical Research

The history of medicine is richly endowed with therapies that were widely used and then shown to be ineffective or frankly toxic. Relatively recent examples of such therapeutic maneuvers include gastric freezing for peptic ulcer disease, radiation therapy for acne, MER-29 (triparanol) for cholesterol reduction, and thalidomide for sedation in pregnant women. The 19th century was even more gruesome, with purging and bloodletting. The reasons for this march of folly are many and include, perhaps most importantly, the lack of complete understanding of human biology and pathophysiology, the use of observational methods coupled with the failure to appreciate substantial variability between patients in their response to illness and to therapy, and the shared desire of physicians and their patients for cure or palliation.

Chance or bias can result in the selection of patients for innovative treatment who are either the least diseased or the most severely affected. Depending on the case mix, a treatment that has no effect can appear to be effective or toxic when historical controls are used. With the improvement in diagnostic accuracy and the understanding of disease that has occurred with the passage of time,

Reprinted by permission of *The New England Journal of Medicine,* May 30, 1991, Vol. 324, no. 22, pp. 1589–1591. © 1991 Massachusetts Medical Society.

today's patients are identified earlier in the natural history of their disease. Recently selected case series therefore often have patients who are less ill and an outcome that is considerably better than that of past case series, even without changes in treatment.

Randomization tends to produce treatment and control groups that are evenly balanced in both known and unrecognized prognostic factors, which permits a more accurate estimate of treatment effect in groups of patients assigned to experimental and standard therapies. A number of independent randomized trials with congruent results are powerful evidence indeed.

A physician's daily practice includes an array of preventive, diagnostic, and therapeutic maneuvers, some of which have been established by a plausible biologic mechanism and substantial evidence from randomized clinical trials (e.g., the use of beta-blockers, thrombolytic therapy, and aspirin in patients with myocardial infarction).[8] It is unlikely that our distant descendants in medicine will discover that we late-20th-century physicians were wrong in these matters. However, new therapeutic maneuvers that have not undergone rigorous assessment may well turn out to be ineffective or toxic. Every therapy adopted by common consent on the basis of observational studies and plausible mechanism, but without the benefit of randomized studies, may be categorized by future physicians as useless or worse. Physicians are aware of the fragility of the evidence supporting many common therapies, and this is why properly performed randomized clinical trials have profound effects on medical practice. The scientific importance of randomized, controlled trials is in safeguarding current and future patients from our therapeutic passions. Most physicians recognize this fact.

Like any human activity, experimentation involving patients can be performed in an unethical and even criminal fashion. Nazi war crimes led to substantial efforts to curb abuse, beginning with the Nuremberg Code and the Helsinki Declaration and culminating in the promulgation of clearly articulated regulations in the United States and elsewhere.[4-6] There are abuses more subtle than those of the Gestapo and the SS. Involving patients in experiments that are poorly conceived and poorly executed is unethical. Patients who participate in such research may incur risk without the hope of contributing to a body of knowledge that will benefit them or others in the future. The regulations governing human experimentation are very important, as is continuing discussion and debate to improve the scientific and ethical aspects of this effort.

Several general features must be part of properly designed trials. The first is informed consent, which involves explicitly informing a potential participant of the goals of the research, its potential benefits and risks, the alternatives to participating, and the right to withdraw from the trial at any time. Whether informed consent is required in all trials has been debated.[9] I believe that patients must always be aware that they are part of an experiment. Second, a state of clinical equipoise must exist. Clinical equipoise means that on the basis of the available data, a community of competent physicians would be content to have their patients pursue any of the treatment strategies being tested in a randomized trial, since none of them have been clearly established as preferable.[7] The chief purpose of a data-monitoring committee is to stop the trial if the accumulating data destroy the state of clinical equipoise—that is, indicate efficacy or suggest toxicity. Finally, the trial must be designed as a critical test of the therapeutic alternatives being assessed. The question must be clearly articulated, with carefully defined measures of outcome; with realistic estimates of sample size, including probable event rates in the control group and a postulated and plausible reduction in the event rates in the treatment group; with Type I and II errors specified; and with subgroup hypotheses clearly stated if appropriate. The trial must have a good chance of settling an open question.[2] [A Type I error consists in deciding that therapy A is better than therapy B, when, in fact, both are of equal worth (i.e., a true null hypothesis is rejected). A Type II error consists in deciding that the treatments are equally good, when A is actually better than B (i.e., a false null hypothesis is accepted).—ed.]

Ethical Dimensions of Properly Constituted Trials

Experimentation in the clinic by means of randomized, controlled clinical trials has been periodically attacked as violating the covenant between doctor and patient.[10-12] Critics have charged that physicians engaged in clinical trials sacrifice the interests of the patient they ask to participate to the good of all similarly affected patients in the future. The argument is that physicians have a personal obligation to use their best judgment and recommend the "best" therapy, no matter how tentative or inconclusive the data on which that judgment is based. Physicians must play their hunches. According to this argument, randomized clinical trials may be useful in seeking the truth, but carefully designed, legitimate trials are unethical and perhaps even criminal because they prevent individual physicians from playing their hunches about individual patients. Therefore, it is argued, physicians should not participate in such trials.

It is surely unethical for physicians to engage knowingly in an activity that will result in inferior therapy for their patients. It is also important that the community of physicians be clear in distinguishing between established therapies and those that are promising but unproved. It is this gulf between proved therapies and possibly effective therapies (all the rest) that defines the ethical and unethical uses of randomized clinical trials. Proved therapies involve a consensus of the competent medical community that the data in hand justify using a treatment in a given disorder. It is this consensus that defines an ethical boundary. The physician-investigator who asks a patient to participate in a randomized, controlled trial represents this competent medical community in asserting that the community is unpersuaded by existing data that an innovative treatment is superior to standard therapy. Arguments that a physician who believes that such a treatment *might* be useful commits an unethical act by randomizing patients are simply wrong. Given the history of promising but discarded therapies, hunches about potential effectiveness are not the ideal currency of the patient–doctor interchange.

Lest readers conclude that modern hunches are more accurate than older ones, I have selected an example from the current cardiovascular literature that reveals the problems inherent in relying on hunches to the exclusion of carefully done experiments.

The Cardiac Arrhythmia Suppression Trial

Sudden death occurs in approximately 300,000 persons in the United States each year and is thus a problem worthy of our best efforts. In the vast majority of cases the mechanism is ventricular fibrillation superimposed on a scarred or ischemic myocardium. It had been observed that the ventricular extrasystoles seen on the ambulatory electrocardiographic recordings of survivors of myocardial infarction were independently and reproducibly associated with an increased incidence of subsequent mortality.[13,14] It had been established that a variety of antiarrhythmic drugs can suppress ventricular extrasystoles. Accordingly, physicians had the hunch that suppressing ventricular extrasystoles in the survivors of myocardial infarction would reduce the incidence of ventricular fibrillation and sudden death.

The Cardiac Arrhythmia Suppression Trial (CAST) investigators decided to test this hypothesis in a randomized, controlled trial. They sought survivors of myocardial infarction who had frequent extrasystoles on electrocardiographic recordings. The trial design included a run-in period during which one of three active drugs was administered and its effect on extrasystoles noted. Those in whom arrhythmias were suppressed were randomly assigned to active drug or placebo. The trial had to be stopped prematurely because of an unacceptable incidence of sudden death in the treatment group.[15] During an average follow-up of 10 months, 56 of 730 patients (7.7 percent) assigned to active drug and 22 of 725 patient (3.0 percent) assigned to placebo died. Clinical equipoise was destroyed by this striking effect. It is quite unlikely that observational (nonrandomized) methods would have detected this presumably toxic effect.

The CAST trial was a major advance in the treatment of patients with coronary disease and ventricular arrhythmia. It clearly revealed that the hunches of many physicians were incorrect. The trial's results are applicable not only to future patients with coronary disease and ventricular arrhythmia but also to the patients who participated in the study. By randomizing, investigators ensured that half the participants received the better therapy—in this case placebo—and, contrary to intuition, most of them ultimately received the better therapy after the trial ended prematurely and drugs were withdrawn.

To summarize, randomized clinical trials are an important element in the spectrum of biomedical research. Not all questions can or should be addressed by this technique; feasibility, cost, and the relative importance of the issues to be addressed are weighed by investigators before they elect to proceed. Properly carried out, with informed consent, clinical equipoise, and a design adequate to answer the question posed, randomized clinical trials protect physicians and their patients from therapies that are ineffective or toxic. Physicians and their patients must be clear about the vast gulf separating promising and proved therapies. The only reliable way to make this distinction in the face of incomplete information about pathophysiology and treatment mechanism is to experiment, and this will increasingly involve randomized trials. The alternative—a retreat to older methods—is unacceptable.

Physicians regularly apply therapies tested in groups of patients to an individual patient. The likelihood of success in an individual patient depends on the degree of certainty evident in the group and the scientific strength of the methods used. We owe patients involved in the assessment of new therapies the best that science and ethics can deliver. Today, for most unproved treatments, that is a properly performed randomized clinical trial.

Notes

1. Streptomycin in Tuberculosis Trials Committee, Medical Research Council. Streptomycin treatment of pulmonary tuberculosis: a Medical Research Council investigation. *BMJ* 1948: 2: 769–82.

2. Friedman LM, Furberg CD, DeMets, DL. *Fundamentals of clinical trials.* Boston: John Wright/PSG, 1981.

3. Beecher HK. Ethics and clinical research. *N Engl J Med* 1966: 274: 1354–60.

4. Appendix II (The Nuremberg Code). In: Beauchamp TL, Childress JF. *Principles of biomedical ethics.* New York: Oxford University Press, 1979: 287–9.

5. Appendix II (The World Medical Association Declaration of Helsinki). In: Beauchamp TL, Childress JF. *Principles of biomedical ethics.* New York: Oxford University Press, 1979: 289–93.

6. The National Commission for the Protection of Human Subjects of Biomedical and Behavioral Research. The Belmont report: ethical principles and guidelines for the protection of human subjects of research. Washington, D.C.: Government Printing Office, 1978. (DHEW publication no. (05) 78–0012.)

7. Freedman B. Equipoise and the ethics of clinical research. *N Engl J Med* 1987: 317: 141–5.

8. Yusuf S, Wittes J, Friedman L. Overview of results of randomized clinical trials in heart disease. I. Treatments following myocardial infarction. *JAMA* 1988: 260: 2088–93.

9. Brahams D. Randomized trials and informed consent. *Lancet* 1988: 1033–4.

10. Burkhardt R, Kienle G. Controlled clinical trials and medical ethics. *Lancet* 1978: 2: 1356–9.

11. Marquis D. Leaving therapy to chance. *Hastings Cent Rep* 1983: 13(4): 40–7.

12. Gifford F. The conflict between randomized clinical trials and the therapeutic obligation. *J Med Philos* 1986: 11: 347–66.

13. Ruberman W, Weinblatt E, Goldberg JD, Frank CW, Shapiro S. Ventricular premature beats and mortality after myocardial infarction. *N Engl J Med* 1977: 297: 750–7.

14. Lown B. Sudden cardiac death: the major challenge confronting contemporary cardiology. *Am J Cardiol* 1979: 43: 313–28.

15. The Cardiac Arrhythmia Suppression Trial (CAST) investigators. Preliminary report: effect of encainide and flecainide on mortality in a randomized trial of arrhythmia suppression after myocardial infarction. *N Engl J Med* 1989: 321: 406–12.

Animal Experimentation

Peter Singer

Peter Singer argues that the vast majority of animal experiments cannot be justified. They exact an extraordinary cost in animal suffering, while producing little or no knowledge—and that can usually be obtained in other ways.

Singer provides multiple examples of painful, pointless experiments leading to the death of animal subjects. He argues that our willingness to tolerate such experiments can be explained only by our "speciesism"—the notion that the interests of nonhuman animals need not be considered. Speciesism, Singer holds, is analogous to racism and is just as indefensible.

Singer argues that the fundamental issue in determining how we may treat animals is whether they suffer and that the pains of animals and humans deserve equal consideration. Many animals are more intelligent than severely retarded or infant humans, so that if lack of intelligence would justify painful animal experiments, it would also justify the same experiments on retarded and infant humans. Because it is immoral to subject humans to such experiments, we have good reason to believe it is also wrong to subject animals to them.

Singer holds that researchers should be required to demonstrate that the benefits of their research will outweigh the suffering of the animals involved. He recommends that ethics committees, with members representing the welfare of animals, be established to oversee experiments.

There has been opposition to experimenting on animals for a long time. This opposition has made little headway because experimenters, backed by commercial firms that profit by supplying laboratory animals and equipment, have been able to convince legislators and the public that opposition comes from uniformed fanatics who consider the interests of animals more important than the interests of human beings. But to be opposed to what is going on now it is not necessary to insist that all animal experiments stop immediately. All we need to say is that experiments serving no direct and urgent purpose should stop immediately, and in the remaining fields of research, we should, whenever possible, seek to replace experiments that involve animals with alternative methods that do not. . . .

. . . Professor [Harry] Harlow, who worked at the Primate Research Center in Madison, Wisconsin, was for many years editor of a leading psychology journal, and until his death a few years ago was held in high esteem by his colleagues in psychological research. His work has been cited approvingly in many basic textbooks of psychology, read by millions of students taking introductory psychology courses over the last twenty years. The line of research he began has been continued after his death by his associates and former students.

In a 1965 paper, Harlow describes his work as follows:

> For the past ten years we have studied the effects of partial social isolation by raising monkeys from birth onwards in bare wire cages. . . . These monkeys suffer total maternal deprivation. . . . More recently we have initiated a series of studies on the effects of total social isolation by rearing monkeys from a few hours after birth until 3, 6, or 12 months of age in [a] stainless steel chamber. During the prescribed sentence in this apparatus the monkey has no contact with any animal, human or sub-human.

These studies, Harlow continues, found that

> sufficiently severe and enduring early isolation reduces these animals to a social-emotional level in which the primary social responsiveness is fear.

In another article Harlow and his former student and associate Stephen Suomi described how they were trying to induce psychopathology in infant monkeys by a technique that appeared not to be working. They were then visited by John Bowlby, a British psychiatrist. According to Harlow's account, Bowlby listened to the story of their troubles and then toured the Wisconsin laboratory. After he had seen the monkeys individually housed in bare wire cages he asked, "Why are you trying to produce psychopathology in monkeys? You already have more psychopathological monkeys in the laboratory than have ever been seen on the face of the earth."

Bowlby, incidentally, was a leading researcher on the consequences of maternal deprivation, but his research was conducted with children, primarily war orphans, refugees, and institutionalized children. As far back as 1951, before Harlow even began his research on nonhuman primates, Bowlby concluded:

> The evidence has been reviewed. It is submitted that evidence is now such that it leaves no room for doubt regarding the general proposition that the prolonged deprivation of the young child of maternal care may have grave and far-reaching effects on his character and so on the whole of his future life.

This did not deter Harlow and his colleagues from devising and carrying out their monkey experiments.

In the same article in which they tell of Bowlby's visit, Harlow and Suomi describe how they had the "fascinating idea" of inducing depression by "allowing baby monkeys to attach to cloth surrogate mothers who could become monsters":

> The first of these monsters was a cloth monkey mother who, upon schedule or demand, would eject high-pressure compressed air. It would blow the animal's skin practically off its body. What did the baby monkey do? It simply clung tighter and tighter to the mother, because a frightened infant clings to its mother at all costs. We did not achieve any psychopathology.
>
> However, we did not give up. We built another surrogate monster mother that would rock so violently that the baby's head and teeth would rattle. All the baby did was cling tighter and tighter to the surrogate. The third monster we built had an embedded wire frame within its body which would spring forward and eject the infant from its ventral surface. The infant would subsequently pick itself off the floor, wait for the frame to return into the cloth body, and then cling again to the surrogate. Finally, we built our porcupine mother. On command, this mother would eject sharp brass spikes over all of the ventral surface of its body. Although the infants were distressed by these pointed rebuffs, they simply waited until the spikes receded and then returned and clung to the mother.

These results, the experimenters remark, were not so surprising, since the only recourse of an injured child is to cling to its mother. . . .

Harlow is now dead, but his students and admirers have spread across the United States and continue to perform experiments in a similar vein. . . .

Since Harlow began his maternal deprivation experiments some thirty years ago, over 250 such experiments have been conducted in the United States. These experiments subjected over seven thousand animals to procedures that induced distress, despair, anxiety, general psychological devastation, and death. . . .

An equally sad tale of futility is that of experiments designed to produce what is known as "learned helplessness"—supposedly a model of depression in human beings. In 1953 R. Solomon, L. Kamin, and L. Wynne, experimenters at Harvard University, placed forty dogs in a device called a "shuttlebox," which consists of a box divided into two compartments, separated by a barrier. Initially the barrier was set at the height of the dog's back. Hundreds of intense electric shocks were delivered to the dogs' feet through a grid floor. At first the dogs could escape the shock if they learned to jump the barrier into the other compartment. In an attempt to "discourage" one dog from jumping, the experimenters forced the dog to jump one hundred times onto a grid floor in the other compartment that also delivered a shock to the dog's feet. They said that as the dog jumped he gave a "sharp anticipatory yip which turned into a yelp when he landed on the electrified grid." They then blocked the passage between the compartments with a piece of plate glass and tested the dog again. The dog "jumped forward and smashed his head against the glass." The dogs began by showing symptoms such as "defecation, urination, yelping and shrieking, trembling, attacking the apparatus, and so on; but after ten or twelve days of trials dogs who were prevented from escaping shock ceased to resist. The experimenters reported themselves "impressed" by this, and concluded that a combination of the plate glass barrier and foot shock was "very effective" in eliminating jumping by dogs.

This study showed that it was possible to induce a state of hopelessness and despair by repeated administration of severe inescapable shock. Such "learned helplessness" studies were further refined in the 1960s. One prominent experimenter was Martin Seligman of the University of Pennsylvania. He electrically shocked dogs through a steel grid with such intensity and persistence that the dogs stopped trying to escape and "learned" to be helpless. In one study, written with colleagues Steven Maier and James Geer, Seligman describes his work as follows:

> When a normal, naive dog receives escape/avoidance training in a shuttlebox, the following behavior typically occurs: at the onset of electric shock the dog runs frantically about, defecating, urinating, and howling until it scrambles over the barrier and so escapes from shock. On the next trial the dog, running and howling, crosses the barrier more quickly, and so on, until efficient avoidance emerges.

Seligman altered this pattern by strapping dogs in harnesses and giving them shocks from which they had no means of escape. When the dogs were then placed in the original shuttlebox situation from which escape was possible, he found that such a dog reacts initially to shock in the shuttlebox in the same manner as the naive dog. However in dramatic contrast to the naive dog it soon stops running and remains silent until shock terminates. The dog does not cross the barrier and escape from shock. Rather it seems to "give up" and passively "accept" the shock. On succeeding trials the dog continues to fail to make escape movements and thus takes 50 seconds of severe, pulsating shock on each trial. . . . A dog previously exposed to inescapable shock . . . may take unlimited shock without escaping or avoiding at all. . . .

Electric shock has also been used to produce aggressive behavior in animals. In one study at the University of Iowa, Richard Viken and John Knutson divided 160 rats into groups and "trained" them in a stainless steel cage with an electrified floor. Pairs of rats were given electric shocks until they learned to fight by striking out at the other rat while facing each other in an upright position or by biting. It took an average of thirty training trials before the rats learned to do this immediately on the first shock. The researchers then placed the shock-trained rats in the cage of untrained rats and recorded their behavior. After one day, all the rats were killed, shaved, and examined for wounds. The experimenters concluded that their "results were not useful in understanding the offensive or defensive nature of the shock-induced response. . . ."

. . . When experiments can be brought under the heading "medical" we are inclined to think that any suffering they involve must be justifiable because the research is contributing to the alleviation of suffering. But . . . the testing of therapeutic drugs is less likely to be motivated by the desire for maximum good to all than by the desire for maximum profit. The broad label "medical research" can also be used to cover research that is motivated by a general intellectual curiosity. Such curiosity may be acceptable as part of a basic search for knowledge when it involves no suffering, but should not be tolerated if it causes pain. Very often, too, basic medical research has been going on for decades and much of it, in the long run, turns out to have been quite pointless. As an illustration, consider the following series of experiments stretching back nearly a century, on the effects of heat on animals:

In 1880 H. C. Wood placed a number of animals in boxes with glass lids and placed the boxes on a brick pavement on a hot day. He used rabbits, pigeons, and cats. His observations on a rabbit are typical. At a temperature of 109.5 degrees Fahrenheit the rabbit jumps and "kicks hind legs with great fury." The rabbit then has a convulsive attack. At 112 degrees Fahrenheit the animal lies on its side slobbering. At 120 degrees Fahrenheit it is gasping and squealing weakly. Soon after it dies.

In 1881 a report appeared in *The Lancet* on dogs and rabbits whose temperatures had been raised to 113 degrees Fahrenheit. It was found that death could be prevented by cool air currents, and the results were said to indicate "the importance of keeping down the temperature in those cases in which it exhibits a tendency to rise to [an] extreme height."

In 1927 W. W. Hall and E. G. Wakefield of the U.S. Naval Medical School placed ten dogs in a hot humid chamber to produce experimental heatstroke. The animals first showed restlessness, breathing difficulties, swelling and congestion of the eyes, and thirst. Some had convulsions. Some died early in the experiment. Those who did not had severe diarrhea and died after removal from the chamber.

In 1954 at Yale University School of Medicine, M. Lennox, W. Sibley, and H. Zimmerman placed thirty-two kittens in a "radiant-heating" chamber. The kittens were "subjected to a total of 49 heating periods. . . . Struggling was common, particularly as the temperature rose." Convulsions occurred on nine occasions: "Repeated convulsions were the rule." As many as thirty convulsions occurred in rapid sequence. Five kittens died during convulsions, and six without convulsions. The other kittens were killed by the experimenters for autopsies. The experimenters reported: "The findings in artificially induced fever in kittens conform to the clinical and EEG findings in human beings and previous clinical findings in kittens. . . ."

In 1969 S. Michaelson, a veterinarian at the University of Rochester, exposed dogs and rabbits to heat-producing microwaves until their temperatures reached the critical level of 107 degrees Fahrenheit or greater. He observed that dogs start panting shortly after microwave exposure begins. Most "display increased activity varying from restlessness to extreme agitation." Near the point of death, weakness and prostration occur. In the case of rabbits "within 5 minutes, desperate attempts are made to escape the cage," and the rabbits die within forty minutes. Michaelson concluded that an increase in heat from microwaves produces damage "indistinguishable from fever in general. . . ."

In 1984 experimenters working for the Federal Aviation Administration, stating that "animals occasionally die from heat stress encountered during shipping in the nation's transportation systems," subjected ten beagles to experimental heat. The dogs were isolated in chambers, fitted with muzzles, and exposed to 95 degrees Fahrenheit combined with high humidity. They were given no food or water, and were kept in these conditions for twenty-four hours. The behavior of the dogs was observed; it included "deliberate agitated activity such as pawing at the crate walls, continuous circling, tossing of the head to shed the muzzle, rubbing the muzzle back and forth on the floor of the crate, and aggressive acts on the sensor guards." Some of the dogs died in the chambers. When the survivors were removed, some vomited blood, and all were weak and exhausted. The experimenters refer to "subsequent experiments on more than 100 beagles. . . ."

Here we have cited a series of experiments going back into the nineteenth century—and I have had space sufficient to include only a fraction of the published literature. The experiments obviously caused great suffering; and the major finding seems to be the advice that heatstroke victims should be cooled. . . . Similar series of experiments are to be found in many other fields of medicine. In the New York City offices of United Action for Animals there are filing cabinets full of photocopies of experiments reported in the journals. Each thick file contains reports on numerous experiments, often fifty or more, and the labels on the files tell their own story: "Acceleration," "Aggression," "Asphyxiation," "Blinding," "Burning," "Centrifuge," "Compression," "Concussion," "Crowding," "Crushing," "Decompression," "Drug Tests," "Experimental Neurosis," "Freezing," "Heating," "Hemorrhage," "Hindleg Beating," "Immobilization," "Isolation," "Multiple Injuries," "Prey Killing," "Protein Deprivation," "Punishment," "Radiation," "Starvation," "Shock," "Spinal Cord Injuries," "Stress," "Thirst," and many more. While some of the experiments may have led to advances in medical knowledge, the value of this knowledge is often questionable, and in some cases the knowledge might have been gained in other ways. Many of the experiments appear to be trivial or misconceived, and some of them were not even designed to yield important benefits. . . .

When are experiments on animals justifiable? Upon learning of the nature of many of the experiments carried out, some people react by saying that all experiments on animals should be prohibited immediately. But if we make our demands as absolute as this, the experimenters have a ready reply: Would we be prepared to let thousands of humans die if they could be saved by a single experiment on a single animal?

This question is, of course, purely hypothetical. There has never been and never could be a single experiment that saved thousands of lives. The way to reply to this hypothetical question is to pose another. Would the experimenters be prepared to carry out their experiment on a human orphan under six months old if that were the only way to save thousands of lives?

If the experimenters would not be prepared to use a human infant then their readiness to use non-human animals reveals an unjustifiable form of discrimination on the basis of species, since adult apes, monkeys, dogs, cats, rats, and other animals are more aware of what is happening to them, more self-directing, and, so far as we can tell, at least as sensitive to pain as a human infant. (I have specified that the human infant be an orphan, to avoid the complications of the feelings of parents. Specifying the case in this way is, if anything, overgenerous to those defending the use of nonhuman animals in experiments, since mammals intended for experimental use are usually separated from their mothers at an early age, when the separation causes distress for both mother and young.)

So far as we know, human infants possess no morally relevant characteristic to a higher degree than adult nonhuman animals, unless we are to count the infants' potential as a characteristic that makes it wrong to experiment on them. Whether this characteristic should count is controversial—if we count it, we shall have to condemn abortion along with experiments on infants, since the potential of the infant and the fetus is the same. To avoid the complexities of this issue, however, we can alter our original question a little and assume that the infant is one with irreversible brain damage so severe as to rule out any mental development beyond the level of a six-month-old infant. There are, unfortunately, many such human beings, locked away in special wards throughout the country, some of them long since abandoned by their parents and other relatives, and, sadly, sometimes unloved by anyone else. Despite their mental deficiencies, the anatomy and physiology of these infants are in nearly all respects identical with those of normal humans. If, therefore, we were to force-feed them with large quantities of floor polish or drip concentrated solutions of cosmetics into their eyes, we would have a much more reliable indication of the safety of these products for humans than we now get by attempting to extrapolate the results of tests on a variety of other species. The LD50 tests, the Draize eye tests, the radiation experiments, the heatstroke experiments, and many others . . . could have told us more about human reactions to the experimental situation if they had been carried out on severely brain-damaged humans instead of dogs or rabbits.

So whenever experimenters claim that their experiments are important enough to justify the use of animals, we should ask them whether they would be prepared to use a brain-damaged human being at a similar mental level to the animals they are planning to use. I cannot imagine that anyone would seriously propose carrying out the experiments described in this chapter on brain-damaged human beings. Occasionally it has become known that medical experiments have been performed on human beings without their consent; one case did concern institutionalized intellectually disabled children, who were given hepatitis. When such harmful experiments on human beings become known, they usually lead to an outcry against the experimenters, and rightly so. They are, very often, a further example of the arrogance of the research worker who justifies everything on the grounds of increasing knowledge. But if the experimenter claims that the experiment is important enough to justify inflicting suffering on animals, why is it not important enough to justify inflicting suffering on humans at the same mental level? What difference is there between the two? Only that one is a member of our species and the other is not? But to appeal to that difference is to reveal a bias no more defensible than racism or any other form of arbitrary discrimination.

The analogy between speciesism and racism applies in practice as well as in theory in the area of experimentation. Blatant speciesism leads to painful experiments on other species, defended on the grounds of their contribution to knowledge and possible usefulness for our species. Blatant racism has led to painful experiments on other races, defended on the grounds of their contribution to knowledge and possible usefulness for the experimenting race. Under the Nazi regime in Germany, nearly two hundred doctors, some of them eminent in the world of medicine, took part in experiments on Jews and Russian and Polish prisoners. Thousands of other physicians knew of these experiments, some of which were the subject of lectures at medical academies. Yet the records show that the doctors sat through verbal reports by doctors on how horrible injuries were inflicted on these "lesser races," and then proceeded to discuss the medical lessons to be learned from them, without anyone making even a mild protest about the nature of the experiments. The parallels between this attitude and that of experimenters today toward animals are striking. Then, as now, subjects were frozen, heated, and put in decompression chambers. Then, as now, these events were written up in dispassionate scientific jargon. The following paragraph is taken from a report by a Nazi scientist of an experiment on a human being, placed in a decompression chamber:

> After five minutes spasms appeared; between the sixth and tenth minute respiration increased in frequency, the TP [test person] losing consciousness. From the eleventh to the thirtieth minute respiration slowed down to three inhalations per minute, only to cease entirely at the end of that period. . . . About half an hour after breathing ceased, an autopsy was begun.

Decompression chamber experimentation did not stop with the defeat of the Nazis. It shifted to nonhuman animals. At the University of Newcastle on Tyne, in England, for instance, scientists used pigs. The pigs were subjected to up to eighty-one periods of decompression over a period of nine months. All suffered attacks of decompression sickness, and some died from these attacks. The example illustrates only too well what the great Jewish writer Isaac Bashevis Singer has written: "In their behavior towards creatures, all men [are] Nazis. . . ."

We have still not answered the question of when an experiment might be justifiable. It will not do to say "Never!" Putting morality in such black-and-white terms is appealing, because it eliminates the need to think about particular cases; but in extreme circumstances, such absolutist answers always break down. Torturing a human being is almost always wrong, but it is not absolutely wrong. If torture were the only way in which we could discover the location of a nuclear bomb hidden in a New York City basement and timed to go off within the hour, then torture would be justifiable. Similarly, if a single experiment could cure a disease like leukemia, that experiment would be justifiable. But in actual life the benefits are always more remote, and more often than not they are nonexistent. So how do we decide when an experiment is justifiable?

We have seen that experimenters reveal a bias in favor of their own species whenever they carry out experiments on nonhumans for purposes that they would not think justified them in using human beings, even brain-damaged ones. This principle gives us a guide toward an answer to our question. Since a speciesist bias, like a racist bias, is unjustifiable, an experiment cannot be justified unless the experiment is so important that the use of a brain-damaged human would also be justifiable.

This is not an absolutist principle. I do not believe that it could never be justifiable to experiment on a brain-damaged human. If it really were possible to save several lives by an experiment that would take just one life, and there were no other way those lives could be saved, it would be right to do the experiment. But this would be an extremely rare case. Certainly none of the experiments described in this chapter could pass this test. Admittedly, as with any dividing line, there would be a gray area where it was difficult to decide if an experiment could be justified. But we need not get distracted by such considerations now. As this chapter has shown, we are in the midst of an emergency in which appalling suffering is being inflicted on millions of animals for purposes that on any impartial view are obviously inadequate to justify the suffering. When we have ceased to carry out all those experiments, then there will be time enough to discuss what to do about the remaining ones which are claimed to be essential to save lives or prevent greater suffering. . . .

. . . In the United States, where experimenters can do virtually as they please with animals, one way of making progress might be to ask those who use this argument to defend the need for animal ex-

periments whether they would be prepared to accept the verdict of an ethics committee that, like those in many other countries, includes animal welfare representatives and is entitled to weigh the costs to the animals against the possible benefits of the research. If the answer is no, the defense of animal experimentation by reference to the need to cure major diseases has been proved to be simply a deceitful distraction that serves to mislead the public about what the experimenters want: permission to do whatever they like with animals. For otherwise why would the experimenter not be prepared to leave the decision on carrying out the experiment to an ethics committee, which would surely be as keen to see major diseases ended as the rest of the community? If the answer is yes, the experimenter should be asked to sign a statement asking for the creation of such an ethics committee.

Suppose that we were able to go beyond minimal reforms of the sort that already exist in the more enlightened nations. Suppose we could reach a point at which the interests of animals really were given equal consideration with the similar interests of human beings. That would mean the end of the vast industry of animal experimentation as we know it today. Around the world, cages would empty and laboratories would close down. It should not be thought, though, that medical research would grind to a halt or that a flood of untested products would come on to the market. So far as new products are concerned it is true, as I have already said, that we would have to make do with fewer of them, using ingredients already known to be safe. That does not seem to be any great loss. But for testing really essential products, as well as for other kinds of research, alternative methods not requiring animals can and would be found. . . .

The defenders of animal experimentation are fond of telling us that animal experimentation has greatly increased our life expectancy. In the midst of the debate over reform of the British law on animal experimentation, for example, the Association of the British Pharmaceutical Industry ran a full-page advertisement in the *Guardian* under the headline "They say life begins at forty. Not so long ago, that's about when it ended." The advertisement went on to say that it is now considered to be a tragedy if a man dies in his forties, whereas in the nineteenth century it was commonplace to attend the funeral of a man in his forties, for the average life expectancy was only forty-two. The advertisement stated that "it is thanks largely to the breakthroughs that have been made through research which requires animals that most of us are able to live into our seventies."

Such claims are simply false. In fact, this particular advertisement was so blatantly misleading that a specialist in community medicine, Dr. David St. George, wrote to *The Lancet* saying "the advertisement is good teaching material, since it illustrates two major errors in the interpretation of statistics." He also referred to Thomas McKeown's influential book *The Role of Medicine*, published in 1976, which set off a debate about the relative contributions of social and environmental changes, as compared with medical intervention, in improvements in mortality since the mid-nineteenth century; and he added:

> This debate has been resolved, and it is now widely accepted that medical interventions had only a marginal effect on population mortality and mainly at a very late stage, after death rates had already fallen strikingly.

J. B. and S. M. McKinley reached a similar conclusion in a study of the decline of ten major infectious diseases in the United States. They showed that in every case except poliomyelitis the death rate had already fallen dramatically (presumably because of improved sanitation and diet) before any new form of medical treatment was introduced. Concentrating on the 40 percent fall in crude mortality in the United States between 1910 and 1984, they estimated "conservatively" that

perhaps 3.5 percent of the fall in the overall death rate can be explained through medical interventions for the major infectious diseases. Indeed, given that it is precisely for these diseases that medicine claims most success in lowering mortality, 3.5 percent probably represents a reasonable upper-limit estimate of the total contribution of medical measures to the decline in infectious disease mortality in the United States.

Remember that this 3.5 percent is a figure for all medical intervention. The contribution of animal experimentation itself can be, at most, only a fraction of this tiny contribution to the decline in mortality. . . .

Finally, it is important to realize that the major health problems of the world largely continue to exist, not because we do not know how to prevent disease and keep people healthy, but because no one is putting enough effort and money into doing what we already know how to do. The diseases that ravage Asia, Africa, Latin America, and the pockets of poverty in the industrialized West are diseases that, by and large, we know how to cure. They have been eliminated in communities that have adequate nutrition, sanitation, and health care. It has been estimated that 250,000 children die each week around the world, and that one quarter of these deaths are by dehydration caused by diarrhea. A simple treatment, already known and needing no animal experimentation, could prevent the deaths of these children. Those who are genuinely concerned about improving health care would probably make a more effective contribution to human health if they left the laboratories and saw to it that our existing stock of medical knowledge reached those who need it most.

The Case for the Use of Animals in Biomedical Research

Carl Cohen

Carl Cohen rejects arguments by those who favor severely curbing or eliminating animal experimentation, then defends the position that we have a strong duty to conduct such experiments to alleviate human suffering and extend human lives.

Animals have no rights, Cohen claims. To have a right is to have a moral claim against others. This means having the capacity to recognize conflicts between one's self-interest and what is right and being able to restrain one's self-interest when appropriate. Animals lack these capacities. Hence, they are not the sort of beings who *can* possess rights, and lacking rights, their interests may be sacrificed for the welfare of others.

Cohen rejects Peter Singer's argument that the pleasures and pains of animals deserve consideration equal to those of humans in calculating the overall benefits of animal experiments, because holding otherwise is "speciesism." Singer's analogy with racism and sexism does not hold, Cohen claims, because animals lack autonomy and membership in the moral community. Indeed, speciesism is "essential to right conduct," because those who fail to make the relevant distinctions between humans and nonhumans will fail to recognize their moral duties.

In his conclusion, Cohen claims that a proper analysis of animal experimentation shows that, contrary to Singer, instead of having a duty to decrease the use of animal experimentation, we have a duty to increase it.

Using animals as research subjects in medical investigations is widely condemned on two grounds: first, because it wrongly violates the *rights* of animals,[1] and second, because it wrongly imposes on sentient creatures much avoidable *suffering*.[2] Neither of these arguments is sound. The first relies on a mistaken understanding of rights; the second relies on a mistaken calculation of consequences. Both deserve definitive dismissal.

Why Animals Have No Rights

A right, properly understood, is a claim, or potential claim, that one party may exercise against another. The target against whom such a claim may be registered can be a single person, a group, a community, or (perhaps) all humankind. The content of rights claims also varies greatly: repayment of loans, nondiscrimination by employers, noninterference by the state, and so on. To comprehend any genuine right fully, therefore, we must know *who* holds the right, *against whom* it is held, and *to what* it is a right.

Alternative sources of rights add complexity. Some rights are grounded in constitution and law (e.g., the right of an accused to trial by jury); some rights are moral but give no legal claims (e.g., my right to your keeping the promise you gave me); and some rights (e.g., against theft or assault) are rooted both in morals and in law.

The differing targets, contents, and sources of rights, and their inevitable conflict, together weave

a tangled web. Notwithstanding all such complications, this much is clear about rights in general: they are in every case claims, or potential claims, within a community of moral agents. Rights arise, and can be intelligibly defended, only among beings who actually do, or can, make moral claims against one another. Whatever else rights may be, therefore, they are necessarily human; their possessors are persons, human beings.

The attributes of human beings from which this moral capability arises have been described variously by philosophers, both ancient and modern: the inner consciousness of a free will (Saint Augustine[3]); the grasp, by human reason, of the binding character of moral law (Saint Thomas[4]); the self-conscious participation of human beings in an objective ethical order (Hegel[5]); human membership in an organic moral community (Bradley[6]); the development of the human self through the consciousness of other moral selves (Mead[7]); and the underivative, intuitive cognition of the rightness of an action (Prichard[8]). Most influential has been Immanuel Kant's emphasis on the universal human possession of a uniquely moral will and the autonomy its use entails.[9] Humans confront choices that are purely moral; humans—but certainly not dogs or mice—lay down moral laws, for others and for themselves. Human beings are self-legislative, morally *auto-nomous.*

Animals (that is, nonhuman animals, the ordinary sense of that word) lack this capacity for free moral judgment. They are not beings of a kind ca-

Reprinted by permission of *The New England Journal of Medicine,* Oct. 2, 1986, Vol. 315, no. 14, pp. 865–870. © 1986 Massachusetts Medical Society.

pable of exercising or responding to moral claims. Animals therefore have no rights, and they can have none. This is the core of the argument about the alleged rights of animals. The holders of rights must have the capacity to comprehend rules of duty, governing all including themselves. In applying such rules, the holders of rights must recognize possible conflicts between what is in their own interest and what is just. Only in a community of beings capable of self-restricting moral judgments can the concept of a right be correctly invoked.

Humans have such moral capacities. They are in this sense self-legislative, are members of communities governed by moral rules, and do possess rights. Animals do not have such moral capacities. They are not morally self-legislative, cannot possibly be members of a truly moral community, and therefore cannot possess rights. In conducting research on animal subjects, therefore, we do not violate their rights, because they have none to violate.

To animate life, even in its simplest forms, we give a certain natural reverence. But the possession of rights presupposes a moral status not attained by the vast majority of living things. We must not infer, therefore, that a live being has, simply in being alive, a "right" to its life. The assertion that all animals, only because they are alive and have interests, also possess the "right to life" [10] is an abuse of that phrase, and wholly without warrant.

It does not follow from this, however, that we are morally free to do anything we please to animals. Certainly not. In our dealings with animals, as in our dealings with other human beings, we have obligations that do not arise from claims against us based on rights. Rights entail obligations, but many of the things one ought to do are in no way tied to another's entitlement. Rights and obligations are not reciprocals of one another, and it is a serious mistake to suppose that they are.

Illustrations are helpful. Obligations may arise from internal commitments made: physicians have obligations to their patients not grounded merely in their patients' rights. Teachers have such obligations to their students, shepherds to their dogs, and cowboys to their horses. Obligations may arise from differences of status: adults owe special care when playing with young children, and children owe special care when playing with young pets. Obligations may arise from special relationships: the payment of my son's college tuition is something to which he may have no right, although it

may be my obligation to bear the burden if I reasonably can; my dog has no right to daily exercise and veterinary care, but I do have the obligation to provide these things for her. Obligations may arise from particular acts or circumstances: one may be obliged to another for a special kindness done, or obliged to put an animal out of its misery in view of its condition—although neither the human benefactor nor the dying animal may have had a claim of right.

Plainly, the grounds of our obligations to humans and to animals are manifold and cannot be formulated simply. Some hold that there is a general obligation to do no gratuitous harm to sentient creatures (the principle of nonmaleficence); some hold that there is a general obligation to do good to sentient creatures when that is reasonably within one's power (the principle of beneficence). In our dealings with animals, few will deny that we are at least obliged to act humanely—that is, to treat them with the decency and concern that we owe, as sensitive human beings, to other sentient creatures. To treat animals humanely, however, is not to treat them as humans or as the holders of rights.

A common objection, which deserves a response, may be paraphrased as follows:

> If having rights requires being able to make moral claims, to grasp and apply moral laws, then many humans—the brain-damaged, the comatose, the senile—who plainly lack those capacities must be without rights. But that is absurd. This proves [the critic concludes] that rights do not depend on the presence of moral capacities. [1, 10]

This objection fails; it mistakenly treats an essential feature of humanity as though it were a screen for sorting humans. The capacity for moral judgment that distinguishes humans from animals is not a test to be administered to human beings one by one. Persons who are unable, because of some disability, to perform the full moral functions natural to human beings are certainly not for that reason ejected from the moral community. The issue is one of kind. Humans are of such a kind that they may be the subject of experiments only with their voluntary consent. The choices they make freely must be respected. Animals are of such a kind that it is impossible for them, in principle, to give or withhold voluntary consent or to make a moral choice. What humans retain when disabled, animals have never had.

A second objection, also often made, may be paraphrased as follows:

> Capacities will not succeed in distinguishing humans from the other animals. Animals also reason; animals also communicate with one another; animals also care passionately for their young; animals also exhibit desires and preferences.[11, 12] Features of moral relevance—rationality, interdependence, and love—are not exhibited uniquely by human beings. Therefore [this critic concludes], there can be no solid moral distinction between humans and other animals.[10]

This criticism misses the central point. It is not the ability to communicate or to reason, or dependence on one another, or care for the young, or the exhibition of preference, or any such behavior that marks the critical divide. Analogies between human families and those of monkeys, or between human communities and those of wolves, and the like, are entirely beside the point. Patterns of conduct are not at issue. Animals do indeed exhibit remarkable behavior at times. Conditioning, fear, instinct, and intelligence all contribute to species survival. Membership in a community of moral agents nevertheless remains impossible for them. Actors subject to moral judgment must be capable of grasping the generality of an ethical premise in a practical syllogism. Humans act immorally often enough, but only they—never wolves or monkeys—can discern, by applying some moral rule to the facts of a case, that a given act ought or ought not to be performed. The moral restraints imposed by humans on themselves are thus highly abstract and are often in conflict with the self-interest of the agent. Communal behavior among animals, even when most intelligent and most endearing, does not approach autonomous morality in this fundamental sense.

Genuinely moral acts have an internal as well as an external dimension. Thus, in law, an act can be criminal only when the guilty deed, the actus reus, is done with a guilty mind, mens rea. No animal can ever commit a crime; bringing animals to criminal trial is the mark of primitive ignorance. The claims of moral right are similarly inapplicable to them. Does a lion have a right to eat a baby zebra? Does a baby zebra have a right not to be eaten? Such questions, mistakenly invoking the concept of right where it does not belong, do not make good sense.

Those who condemn biomedical research because it violates "animal rights" commit the same blunder.

In Defense of "Speciesism"

Abandoning reliance on animal rights, some critics resort instead to animal sentience—their feelings of pain and distress. We ought to desist from the imposition of pain insofar as we can. Since all or nearly all experimentation on animals does impose pain and could be readily forgone, say these critics, it should be stopped. The ends sought may be worthy, but those ends do not justify imposing agonies on humans, and by animals the agonies are felt no less. The laboratory use of animals (these critics conclude) must therefore be ended—or at least very sharply curtailed.

Argument of this variety is essentially utilitarian, often expressly so[13]; it is based on the calculation of the net product, in pains and pleasures, resulting from experiments on animals. Jeremy Bentham, comparing horses and dogs with other sentient creatures, is thus commonly quoted: "The question is not, Can they reason? nor Can they talk? but, Can they suffer?"[14]

Animals certainly can suffer and surely ought not to be made to suffer needlessly. But in inferring, from these uncontroversial premises, that biomedical research causing animals distress is largely (or wholly) wrong, the critic commits two serious errors.

The first error is the assumption, often explicitly defended, that all sentient animals have equal moral standing. Between a dog and a human being, according to this view, there is no moral difference; hence the pains suffered by dogs must be weighed no differently from the pains suffered by humans. To deny such equality, according to this critic, is to give unjust preference to one species over another; it is "speciesism." The most influential statement of this moral equality of species was made by Peter Singer:

> The racist violates the principle of equality by giving greater weight to the interests of members of his own race when there is a clash between their interests and the interests of those of another race. The sexist violates the principle of equality by favoring the interests of his own sex. Similarly the speciesist allows the interests of his own species to override the

greater interests of members of other species. The pattern is identical in each case.[2]

This argument is worse than unsound; it is atrocious. It draws an offensive moral conclusion from a deliberately devised verbal parallelism that is utterly specious. Racism has no rational ground whatever. Differing degrees of respect or concern for humans for no other reason than that they are members of different races is an injustice totally without foundation in the nature of the races themselves. Racists, even if acting on the basis of mistaken factual beliefs, do grave moral wrong precisely because there is no morally relevant distinction among the races. The supposition of such differences has led to outright horror. The same is true of the sexes, neither sex being entitled by right to greater respect or concern than the other. No dispute here.

Between species of animate life, however—between (for example) humans on the one hand and cats or rats on the other—the morally relevant differences are enormous, and almost universally appreciated. Humans engage in moral reflection; humans are morally autonomous; humans are members of moral communities, recognizing just claims against their own interest. Human beings do have rights; theirs is a moral status very different from that of cats or rats.

I am a speciesist. Speciesism is not merely plausible; it is essential for right conduct, because those who will not make the morally relevant distinctions among species are almost certain, in consequence, to misapprehend their true obligations. The analogy between speciesism and racism is insidious. Every sensitive moral judgment requires that the differing natures of the beings to whom obligations are owed be considered. If all forms of animate life—or vertebrate animal life?—must be treated equally, and if therefore in evaluating a research program the pains of a rodent count equally with the pains of a human, we are forced to conclude (1) that neither humans nor rodents possess rights, or (2) that rodents possess all the rights that humans possess. Both alternatives are absurd. Yet one or the other must be swallowed if the moral equality of all species is to be defended.

Humans owe to other humans a degree of moral regard that cannot be owed to animals. Some humans take on the obligation to support and heal others, both humans and animals, as a principal duty in their lives; the fulfillment of that duty may require the sacrifice of many animals. If biomedical investigators abandon the effective pursuit of their professional objectives because they are convinced that they may not do to animals what the service of humans requires, they will fail, objectively, to do their duty. Refusing to recognize the moral differences among species is a sure path to calamity. (The largest animal rights group in the country is People for the Ethical Treatment of Animals; its codirector, Ingrid Newkirk, calls research using animal subjects, "fascism" and "supremacism." "Animal liberationists do not separate out the *human* animal," she says, "so there is no rational basis for saying that a human being has special rights. A rat is a pig is a dog is a boy. They're all mammals."[15])

Those who claim to base their objection to the use of animals in biomedical research on their reckoning of the net pleasures and pains produced make a second error, equally grave. Even if it were true—as it is surely not—that the pains of all animate beings must be counted equally, a cogent utilitarian calculation requires that we weigh all the consequences of the use, and of the nonuse, of animals in laboratory research. Critics relying (however mistakenly) on animal rights may claim to ignore the beneficial results of such research, rights being trump cards to which interest and advantage must give way. But an argument that is explicitly framed in terms of interest and benefit for all over the long run must attend also to the disadvantageous consequences of not using animals in research, and to all the achievements attained and attainable only through their use. The sum of the benefits of their use is utterly beyond quantification. The elimination of horrible disease, the increase of longevity, the avoidance of great pain, the saving of lives, and the improvement of the quality of lives (for humans and for animals) achieved through research using animals is so incalculably great that the argument of these critics, systematically pursued, establishes not their conclusion but its reverse: to refrain from using animals in biomedical research is, on utilitarian grounds, morally wrong.

When balancing the pleasures and pains resulting from the use of animals in research, we must not fail to place on the scales the terrible pains that would have resulted, would be suffered now, and would long continue had animals not been used. Every disease eliminated, every vaccine developed, every method of pain relief devised, every surgical procedure invented, every prosthetic device implanted—indeed, virtually every modern medical therapy is due, in part or in whole, to experimentation using animals. Nor may we ignore, in the balancing process, the predictable gains in human (and animal) well-being that are probably achievable in the future but that will not be achieved if the decision is made now to desist from such research or to curtail it.

Medical investigators are seldom insensitive to the distress their work may cause animal subjects. Opponents of research using animals are frequently insensitive to the cruelty of the results of the restrictions they would impose.[2] Untold numbers of human beings—real persons, although not now identifiable—would suffer grievously as the consequence of this well-meaning but shortsighted tenderness. If the morally relevant differences between humans and animals are borne in mind, and if all relevant considerations are weighed, the calculation of long-term consequences must give overwhelming support for biomedical research using animals.

Concluding Remarks

Substitution

The humane treatment of animals requires that we desist from experimenting on them if we can accomplish the same result using alternative methods—in vitro experimentation, computer simulation, or others. Critics of some experiments using animals rightly make this point.

It would be a serious error to suppose, however, that alternative techniques could soon be used in most research now using live animal subjects. No other methods now on the horizon—or perhaps ever to be available—can fully replace the testing of a drug, a procedure, or a vaccine, in live organisms. The flood of new medical possibilities being opened by the successes of recombinant DNA technology will turn to a trickle if testing on live animals is forbidden. When initial trials entail great risks, there may be no forward movement whatever without the use of live animal subjects. In seeking knowledge that may prove critical in later clinical applications, the unavailability of animals for inquiry may spell complete stymie. In the United

States, federal regulations require the testing of new drugs and other products on animals, for efficacy and safety, before human beings are exposed to them.[16, 17] We would not want it otherwise.

Every advance in medicine—every new drug, new operation, new therapy of any kind—must sooner or later be tried on a living being for the first time. That trial, controlled or uncontrolled, will be an experiment. The subject of that experiment, if it is not an animal, will be a human being. Prohibiting the use of live animals in biomedical research, therefore, or sharply restricting it, must result either in the blockage of much valuable research or in the replacement of animal subjects with human subjects. These are the consequences—unacceptable to most reasonable persons—of not using animals in research.

Reduction

Should we not at least reduce the use of animals in biomedical research? No, we should increase it, to avoid when feasible the use of humans as experimental subjects. Medical investigations putting human subjects at some risk are numerous and greatly varied. The risks run in such experiments are usually unavoidable, and (thanks to earlier experiments on animals) most such risks are minimal or moderate. But some experimental risks are substantial.

When an experimental protocol that entails substantial risk to humans comes before an institutional review board, what response is appropriate? The investigation, we may suppose, is promising and deserves support, so long as its human subjects are protected against unnecessary dangers. May not the investigators be fairly asked, Have you done all that you can to eliminate risk to humans by the extensive testing of that drug, that procedure, or that device on animals? To achieve maximal safety for humans we are right to require thorough experimentation on animal subjects before humans are involved.

Opportunities to increase human safety in this way are commonly missed; trials in which risks may be shifted from humans to animals are often not devised, sometimes not even considered. Why? For the investigator, the use of animals as subjects is often more expensive, in money and time, than the use of human subjects. Access to suitable human subjects is often quick and convenient, whereas access to appropriate animal subjects may be awkward, costly, and burdened with red tape. Physician-investigators have often had more experience working with human beings and know precisely where the needed pool of subjects is to be found and how they may be enlisted. Animals, and the procedures for their use, are often less familiar to these investigators. Moreover, the use of animals in place of humans is now more likely to be the target of zealous protests from without. The upshot is that humans are sometimes subjected to risks that animals could have borne, and should have borne, in their place. To maximize the protection of human subjects, I conclude, the wide and imaginative use of live animal subjects should be encouraged rather than discouraged. This enlargement in the use of animals is our obligation.

Consistency

Finally, inconsistency between the profession and the practice of many who oppose research using animals deserves comment. This frankly ad hominem observation aims chiefly to show that a coherent position rejecting the use of animals in medical research imposes costs so high as to be intolerable even to the critics themselves.

One cannot coherently object to the killing of animals in biomedical investigations while continuing to eat them. Anesthetics and thoughtful animal husbandry render the level of actual animal distress in the laboratory generally lower than that in the abattoir. So long as death and discomfort do not substantially differ in the two contexts, the consistent objector must not only refrain from all eating of animals but also protest as vehemently against others eating them as against others experimenting on them. No less vigorously must the critic object to the wearing of animal hides in coats and shoes, to employment in any industrial enterprise that uses animal parts, and to any commercial development that will cause death or distress to animals.

Killing animals to meet human needs for food, clothing, and shelter is judged entirely reasonable by most persons. The ubiquity of these uses and the virtual universality of moral support for them confront the opponent of research using animals with an inescapable difficulty. How can the many common uses of animals be judged morally worthy, while their use in scientific investigation is judged unworthy?

The number of animals used in research is but the tiniest fraction of the total used to satisfy assorted human appetites. That these appetites, often base and satisfiable in other ways, morally justify the far larger consumption of animals, whereas the quest for improved human health and understanding cannot justify the far smaller, is wholly implausible. Aside from the numbers of animals involved, the distinction in terms of worthiness of use, drawn with regard to any single animal, is not defensible. A given sheep is surely not more justifiably used to put lamb chops on the supermarket counter than to serve in testing a new contraceptive or a new prosthetic device. The needless killing of animals is wrong; if the common killing of them for our food or convenience is right, the less common but more humane uses of animals in the service of medical science are certainly not less right.

Scrupulous vegetarianism, in matters of food, clothing, shelter, commerce, and recreation, and in all other spheres, is the only fully coherent position the critic may adopt. At great human cost, the lives of fish and crustaceans must also be protected, with equal vigor, if speciesism has been forsworn. A very few consistent critics adopt this position. It is the reductio ad absurdum of the rejection of moral distinctions between animals and human beings.

Opposition to the use of animals in research is based on arguments of two different kinds—those relying on the alleged rights of animals and those relying on the consequences for animals. I have argued that arguments of both kinds must fail. We surely do have obligations to animals, but they have, and can have, no rights against us on which research can infringe. In calculating the consequences of animal research, we must weigh all the long-term benefits of the results achieved—to animals and to humans—and in that calculation we must not assume the moral equality of all animate species.

Notes

1. Regan T. *The case for animal rights.* Berkeley, Calif.: University of California Press, 1983.
2. Singer P. *Animal liberation.* New York: Avon Books, 1977.
3. St. Augustine. *Confessions. Book Seven.* 397 A.D. New York: Pocketbooks, 1957: 104–26.
4. St. Thomas Aquinas. *Summa theologica. 1273 A.D. Philosophic texts.* New York: Oxford University Press, 1960: 353–66.
5. Hegel GWF. *Philosophy of right.* 1821. London: Oxford University Press, 1952: 105–10.
6. Bradley FH. Why should I be moral? 1876. In: Melden, AI, ed. *Ethical theories.* New York: Prentice-Hall, 1950: 345–59.

7. Mead GH. The genesis of the self and social control. 1925. In: Reck AJ, ed. *Selected writings*. Indianapolis: Bobbs-Merrill, 1964: 264–93.

8. Prichard HA. Does moral philosophy rest on a mistake? 1912. In: Cellars W, Hospers J, eds. *Readings in ethical theory*. New York: Appleton-Century-Crofts, 1952: 149–63.

9. Kant I. *Fundamental principles of the metaphysic of morals*. 1785. New York: Liberal Arts Press, 1949.

10. Rollin BE. *Animal rights and human morality*. New York: Prometheus Books, 1981.

11. Hoff C. Immoral and moral uses of animals. *N Engl J Med* 1980; 302: 115–8.

12. Jamieson D. Killing persons and other beings. In: Miller HB, Williams WH, eds. *Ethics and animals*. Clifton, N.J.: Humana Press, 1983: 135–46.

13. Singer P. Ten years of animal liberation. *New York Review of Books*. 1985; 31: 46–52.

14. Bentham J. *Introduction to the principles of morals and legislation*. London: Athlone Press, 1970.

15. McCabe K. Who will live, who will die? *Washingtonian Magazine*. August 1986: 115.

16. U.S. Code of Federal Regulations. Title 21, Sect. 505(i). Food, drug, and cosmetic regulations.

17. U.S. Code of Federal Regulations. Title 16, Sect. 1500.40–2. Consumer product regulations.

Principles of the Nuremberg Code

1. The voluntary consent of the human subject is absolutely essential.

2. The experiment should be such as to yield fruitful results for the good of society, unprocurable by other methods or means of study, and not random and unnecessary in nature.

3. The experiment should be so designed and based on the results of animal experimentation and a knowledge of the natural history of the disease or other problem under study that the anticipated results will justify the performance of the experiment.

4. The experiment should be so conducted as to avoid all unnecessary physical and mental suffering and injury.

5. No experiment should be conducted where there is an a priori reason to believe that death or disabling injury will occur; except, perhaps, in those experiments where the experimental physicians also serve as subjects.

6. The degree of risk to be taken should never exceed that determined by the humanitarian importance of the problem to be solved by the experiment.

7. Proper preparations should be made and adequate facilities provided to protect the experimental subject against even remote possibilities of injury, disability, or death.

8. The experiment should be conducted only by scientifically qualified persons. The highest degree of skill and care should be required through all stages of the experiment of those who conduct or engage in the experiment.

9. During the course of the experiment the human subject should be at liberty to bring the experiment to an end if he has reached the physical or mental state where continuation of the experiment seems to him to be impossible.

10. During the course of the experiment the scientist in charge must be prepared to terminate the experiment at any stage, if he has probable cause to believe, in the exercise of good faith, superior skill and careful judgment required of him that a continuation of the experiment is likely to result in injury, disability, or death to the experimental subject.

Decision Scenario 1 ··

In October 1993, fifteen-year-old Benito Agrela stopped taking FK506, a toxic drug that suppresses the immune response. Agrela was taking the drug to prevent the rejection of his second liver transplant.

In June, the Florida Department of Health learned that he was no longer taking his medicine and forcibly removed him from his parents' home. Agrela was confined to the transplant floor of a Miami hospital for four days, but he refused to give blood or to cooperate in any examination other than a basic physical.

Agrela had been born with an enlarged liver, and at the age of eight he had his first transplant. After a few years, the donor organ failed, and a second transplant was necessary. However, Agrela did not have an easy time with the result. The drug's side effects left him feeling weak and constantly ill, and finally he decided that he did not want to continue to take the medication. He wanted only to die in peace.

Judge Arthur Birken of Broward County Circuit Court ruled that Agrela could stop taking his medication and return to his family's home to live out the remainder of his life. Judge Birken reached his decision after a long visit with Agrela and listening to four hours of testimony from his physicians.

"I should have the right to make my own decisions," Agrela said as he left the hospital after the judge's ruling. "I know the consequences, I know the problems."

Benito Agrela died shortly before 5 A.M. on Saturday, August 21. "He went in a very good way," his sister said. "He didn't complain of any pain."

1. *Benito Agrela was only fifteen. Should a minor ever be allowed to decide whether to reject a lifesaving therapy?*

2. *Do the criteria suggested by Drane offer guidelines helpful in deciding whether a minor is capable of giving informed consent?*

Decision Scenario 2

You are an agent of the Ethics Committee of the National Association of Physicians. You have been sent to Laural, Mississippi, to look into the experimental work of Dr. Joseph Camwell at the Laural State Hospital.

"Our basic concern," Dr. Camwell tells you, "was to test the effectiveness of a hormone-based substance in controlling conception by the regulation of ovulation."

"A birth-control pill."

"Exactly," says Dr. Camwell. "We ran a double-blind test with HB-4, the test substance, and a sucrose-based compound flavored and shaped to be phenomenologically indistinguishable from the tablets of HB-4."

"So that neither the experimenter nor the subjects knew who was getting HB-4 and who was getting the sugar pills. But who were your test subjects?"

"Patients who presented themselves at our state-sponsored outpatient clinic and requested contraceptive medication formed our candidate population. We drew from them subjects with a good medical history and no present major illnesses, who seemed reliable enough to take their medications on schedule."

"What were the racial percentages?"

"We didn't consider that to be a relevant factor in the experiment. It just happened that about 90% of our subjects were black, although race was not a criterion for selection."

"Did you secure from these women their informed consent to be subjects in this experiment?"

"Of course," Dr. Camwell says. "I personally explained to each of them that they were going to participate in an experiment but that it wouldn't hurt them any. I told them they would be given birth-control pills that we were testing for effectiveness. 'You might get pregnant while you're taking these pills,' I said."

"But you didn't tell them that at least half of them would be receiving sugar pills that would do absolutely nothing to prevent pregnancy?"

"I think that I warned them sufficiently," says Dr. Camwell. "I told them they might get pregnant. None of these women is able to understand medical sophistications. If I tried to tell them about the experiment, they wouldn't understand me. They knew they might get pregnant, and I figured that was enough."

"Did they all agree to participate?"

"Every last person we approached agreed to participate," Dr. Camwell says. "People always want to help out doctors, and they'll do it if you just put it to them in the right way. I never have any trouble getting subjects for my work."

1. *Would you recommend to the Ethics Committee that Dr. Camwell's consent procedures be condemned? If so, on what grounds?*

2. *Camwell apparently endorses Ingelfinger's view that informed consent is impossible. Evaluate this claim.*

3. *What sort of information would have to be provided to the potential subjects to satisfy the principles of informed consent argued for by Passamani?*

4. *How does Drane's "sliding-scale" model of consent apply to such cases?*

5. *On what grounds would Hellman and Hellman condemn this clinical trial?*

Decision Scenario 3 ....

"In effect," said Dr. Sanchez, "the drug is a powerful tranquilizer. We are not sure how it works, but we know that it has a great calming effect on people diagnosed as schizophrenics. It's much like thorazine, which you may have heard of."

"Does it have any side effects?" Monica Jones asked.

"If taken over a period of a couple of weeks, it produces a palsied condition—muscular tremors, difficulty in walking and in controlling the face muscles, and so on. These don't seem to be permanent."

"That's in schizophrenics," Monica said.

"That's right. We don't know the likely effects in other people. Perhaps you will notice no change whatsoever, and perhaps you will never develop the muscular tremors. But perhaps you'll develop them sooner or more severely. That's part of what we need to find out."

"I'm not in danger of death, then?"

"Not to any great extent. That is, all medication has associated with it some risk. But we don't believe the risk here to be great. There is some possibility of long-term nerve or brain damage. We simply don't know the risks here."

"And you need so-called normal people like me to act as subjects so that you can compare the effects of the drug on us with its effects on schizophrenics?"

"Exactly right," said Dr. Sanchez. "But I should tell you that you may not get the drug. None of us involved in the experiment as patients or experimenters will know who is getting the tranquilizer and who is getting a placebo."

"So maybe I'm not running any risk at all," said Monica.

"Maybe not. But your participation is still important. This drug may do much to relieve the symptoms of a great number of schizophrenics."

"Now, if I understand correctly," said Monica Jones, "I will be paid for my participation."

"That's right. You will be paid a flat fee for participation—half at the beginning of the study and the rest at the end. I want you to be clear on one thing, however. You must waive your right to claim compensation due to any injury or ill effects you may suffer as a result of the medication."

"I understand that. I've got to take a risk. I'm not too happy about that, but I can't get a job and I need the money so I can go back to school next semester."

"Fine," said Dr. Sanchez. "I have the consent forms right here."

1. *Is a society in which risking one's health for financial gain one compatible with Rawls's principles of justice?*

2. *Do Kant's principles allow one to take such a risk?*

3. *Does the natural law doctrine of Catholicism?*

4. *Would the view of human experimentation advocated by Jonas regard such an experiment as legitimate? Would the view of Lasagna?*

5. *Do you think it is possible for Sanchez to give Jones good reasons for participating that do not involve some form of pressure or duress?*

Decision Scenario 4 ....

The drug DES, diethylstilbestrol, was once believed to be effective in preventing miscarriages. But in 1971 sufficient evidence was available to establish a link between DES and vaginal cancer and cervical cell abnormalities in the daughters of women given the drug. About one million women were given DES in the first trimester of pregnancy, and over 120 daughters of these women have been shown to have cancer. Sons, apparently, do not develop cancer, but the group shows a higher-than-average proportion of genital abnormalities and sterility.

In late 1951 and early 1952, women receiving prenatal care at the University of Chicago's Lying-In Hospital were given unmarked tablets of DES as part of a study conducted by Dr. William Dieckmann. One of those receiving the tablets was Ms. Patsy T. Mink, who later became an assistant secretary of state.

"I remember quite clearly the doctor giving me those pills and telling me they were vitamins," Ms. Mink says.

Ms. Mink's daughter Gwendolyn was born in the hospital in 1952. Ms. Mink was not notified that she had been given DES until twenty-four years later. She rushed her daughter to a medical examination, and it was discovered that Gwendolyn had abnormal cell changes in the cervix—a condition known as adenosis and thought to be a precursor of cancer.

Ms. Mink is outraged by the experiment in which she was an unwitting subject. She feels that she was not given the drug for a legitimate medical reason and that she was deceived by her doctor. "There's no way we could know," she says. "If they had given me a choice, if they had said, 'We think you are a risk case and this drug may help you,' that's different. That's the choice we should have been presented with. But I wasn't a risk case, and I wasn't told anything."

1. *Did those who gave her DES act immorally? After all, at the time she was given the drug there was no reason to believe that it might have harmful effects.*

2. *If Ms. Mink's informed consent had been obtained, the outcome would have been exactly the same because she could not have been warned of dangers that no one knew existed. Doesn't this show that the whole notion of informed consent is pointless and that one simply must trust in the integrity and best judgment of a physician, as Ingelfinger suggests?*

3. *Explain the way in which the "reasonable person" standard in* Canterbury v. Spence *might be applied to this situation.*

Decision Scenario 5

"You realize," Dr. Thorne said, "that you may not be in the group that receives medication? You may be in the placebo group for at least part of the time."

"Right," Ms. Ross said. "You're just going to give me some medicine."

"And do you understand the aims of the experiment?"

"You want to help me get better," Ms. Ross suggested hesitantly.

"We hope you get better, of course. But that's not what we're trying to accomplish here. We're trying to find out if this particular medication will help other people in your condition if we can treat them earlier than we were able to treat you."

"You want to help people," Ms. Ross said.

"That's right. Now, do you understand that we may not be helping you in this experiment?"

"But you're going to try?"

"Not exactly. I mean, we aren't going to try to harm you. But we aren't necessarily going to be giving you the preferred treatment for your complaint either. Do you know the difference between research and therapy?"

"Research is when you're trying to find something out. You're searching around."

"That's right. And we're asking you to be part of a research effort. As I told you, there are some risks. Besides the possibility of not getting treatment that you need, the drug may produce some limited hepatic portal damage. We're not sure how much."

"I think I understand," Ms. Ross said.

"I hope so," said Dr. Thorne. "Now I understand that you are freely volunteering to participate in this research."

"Yes, sir. Mrs. Woolerd, she told me if I volunteered I'd get a letter put in my file and I could get early release."

"Mrs. Woolerd told you the Review Board would take your volunteering into account when they considered whether you should be put on work-release."

"Yes, sir. And I'm awfully anxious to get out of here. I've got two children staying with my aunt, and I need to get out of this place as quick as I can."

"I understand. We can't promise you release, of course. But your participation will look good on your record. Now I have some papers here I want you to sign."

1. *Discuss some of the difficulties involved in explaining research procedures to nonexperts and determining whether they are aware of the nature and risks of their participation.*

2. *What reasons are there for believing that Ms. Ross does not understand what she is volunteering for?*

3. *Also, discuss the problems involved in securing free and voluntary consent from a person involuntarily confined to an institution (a prisoner, for example).*

4. *Would the concept of equipoise in this case be the same for Hellman and Hellman and Passamani?*

5. *Is experimentation in this case justified on Passa-mani's criteria? On what grounds might Hellman and Hellman object to a clinical trial of this kind?*

6. *Which, if any, of Drane's three standards seems rel-evant in this case?*

Decision Scenario 6 ··

The ad in the newspapers was simple and uninfor-mative:

> Subjects (male and female) wanted to partici-pate in scientific study. Must be 21 or over. $2.00 per hour.

Karen Barty wrote down the address. She could use the money, and in 1962 $2.00 an hour wasn't bad pay for what was sure to be very little work. Besides, the hours were probably flexible, and she could fit the time into her class schedule.

The next Tuesday morning at ten o'clock, Karen and nine other people reported to Room 711 of the Basic Sciences Building in the Western Med-ical Center. A man who introduced himself as Dr. Carlo Raphael explained what would be required of them as research subjects.

"First of all, you must all sign consent forms," he said. "These state that you are voluntary partici-pants in this study and that for your assistance you will receive a financial reward. If you are not will-ing to sign the forms, then we cannot accept you as a subject."

He interrupted himself to pass out badly mimeographed sheets of paper that had "Voluntary Consent of Research Subjects" printed at the top. Karen signed hers at once, without bothering to read it. The others in her group, she noticed, did the same thing.

"Very good," Dr. Raphael said, after collect-ing the forms. "We are going to ask that you pro-vide us with the answers to a series of questions. Some of you may think of these as 'tests,' but I want to assure you that they are not tests in the way you ordinarily think of them. You can neither pass nor fail. Just give us your immediate and truthful responses."

With the help of two assistants, Dr. Raphael distributed test booklets with coded answer sheets tucked inside. Everyone was then supplied with a black IBM pencil with soft, black lead.

Karen listened, half bored, as Dr. Raphael ex-plained how the answer sheets were to be filled in. She had heard the same kind of explanation a dozen times before, but she guessed that the same thing always had to be said as part of the test proce-dure. Despite herself, she felt a twinge of anxiety. It was all well and good to say these weren't tests they were taking, but they were enough like every other test she had taken to make her adrenalin flow.

At noon, they handed in their test booklets and took a break for lunch. When they reported back, it was to another room in the same building. It was not a classroom this time but a lounge. Steel-framed chairs and sofas covered in gray and orange plastic were set about the room, and the floor was covered with beige carpet, its industrial finish looking flat and somewhat dirty.

A long table at the front was draped with white crepe paper, and pitchers of water surrounded by glasses were set at one end. At the opposite end, a red cafeteria tray with small paper cups was watched over by a woman Karen hadn't seen before.

The cups looked like the sort that are usually filled with nuts or hard candies. When Karen got close enough, she saw that each cup contained only what looked like a single cube of sugar.

That's what it tasted like when Karen got hers. Dr. Raphael lined up the ten subjects, and as each one reached the table, the woman handed over one of the cups.

"Let the cube dissolve in your mouth," Dr. Raphael told them. "Then have some water, if you like, but don't eat or drink anything else. Then you may just sit around in this room and talk to each other."

It was pretty disgusting, just eating plain sugar. But within twenty minutes, Karen knew that it wasn't just plain sugar. She was sitting on one of the sofas talking to another woman about an English group called the Beatles. The woman had never heard of them, and Karen spelled the name for her.

But as she started to spell it, she suddenly found it very hard to concentrate. She knew where she was and what she was doing, but the woman in front of her began to look strange. She seemed to be surrounded by a halo of brightly colored light. The features of her face lost their outlines and became twisted and distorted.

In a few minutes, Karen gave up trying to talk. Somewhere at the back of her mind, she felt fear and confusion. But what was happening to her wasn't unpleasant. It was interesting, really, and she surrendered herself to the fantastic images that seemed to take over her mind without her being able to control them.

Somewhere in that time, Karen fell asleep or at least she thought she did. She vaguely remembered one of Dr. Raphael's assistants holding her by the arm and leading her back to the classroom. She tried to talk to him, but she wasn't sure what she said. When she was handed another test booklet, she was surprised to find how easy it was to fill out the answer sheet. This time there was no anxiety at all.

By five o'clock that afternoon, Karen was herself again. It was not until seventeen years later that she realized she had been an unwitting participant in a research project sponsored by the army to determine psychological effects of LSD.

1. *What kind of information would Karen Barty have had to be given to satisfy Passamani's principles of informed consent?*

2. *On what grounds would Jonas disapprove of the way in which Karen was employed as a subject?*

3. *This was clearly a case of nontherapeutic research. Can a case be made for it on utilitarian grounds?*

4. *Would the principles enunciated in* Canterbury v. Spence *provide Karen with any grounds for claiming compensation if in years after the research she suffers from effects that may reasonably be attributed to her participation as a subject?*

5. *Suppose that Dr. Raphael had fully informed the group about the nature and aims of the research and warned them about potential dangers. Given that very little was known in 1962 about the possible effects of LSD, would any person be justified in risking life or health by participating in the experiment?*

Decision Scenario 7 ·······································

Paul Cox was tried for murder in Westchester County, New York, in June 1994. According to the prosecutor, on New Year's Eve in 1988, Cox entered the house in Larchmont where he had grown up and killed Shanta Chervu and her husband Lakshman Chervu, strangers who had bought the house in 1974.

The police had no suspects in the case until they were tipped off that Cox had revealed at an Alcoholics Anonymous meeting that, although his memories were unclear, he might have killed the couple during an alcoholic blackout. He might have been so confused that he thought his parents still lived in the house and that he was attacking them.

Although a number of Cox's AA associates heard him make such statements, two years passed before one of them, acting through an intermediary, reported his revelations to the police. Charges were filed against Cox, and when he was brought to trial, seven members of Alcoholics Anonymous were subpoenaed by the prosecution to testify against him.

Members of Alcoholics Anonymous or similar self-help groups have no legal duty to report any information about crimes that they might hear dur-

ing their meetings. Nor must therapists report to the police the knowledge of someone's past criminal behavior acquired during therapy. Indeed, therapists may be sued by their patients or clients for violating a confidence, even one that is grounds for criminal prosecution. However, some states require that therapists report cases of child abuse or violence against a spouse or the elderly.

Licensed therapists and physicians enjoy limited protection from being subpoenaed to give evidence against a patient. The same holds for certain others. For example, confessions made to pastors may be privileged. (But if the person making the incriminating statement is of a different faith or did not make the statement in the context of religious practice, the pastor may be compelled to give evidence against him.) Similarly, some states do not require spouses to testify against one another, but at least twenty states do.

Some observers in the Cox case expressed the view that he would never have been brought to trial had someone not broken the confidentiality practiced by Alcoholics Anonymous. Also, there would never have been a legal case against him, had the seven fellow members not been forced to testify.

Representatives of self-help groups viewed the Cox case as evidence that groups like Alcoholics Anonymous need laws granting them the privilege of maintaining the confidentiality of conversations that take place under their auspices. Otherwise, advocates point out, the aims of such organizations cannot be achieved. Achieving them depends on members being able to speak freely without fear that their secrets will be revealed to outsiders or that what they say may later be used as evidence against them in court.

Cox's first trial ended in a mistrial when one juror would not accept the others' verdict of first-degree murder. In a 1994 retrial, the jury convicted Cox of manslaughter.

1. *On what grounds can a law requiring therapist-patient confidentiality be justified?*

2. *Would the same grounds justify a law requiring confidentiality among the members of a self-help group?*

3. *"It is more important to protect the privacy of individuals than to bring criminals to justice." What defense can be made for this claim?*

Decision Scenario 8 ••

In April of 1979, a suit was filed in Illinois by the Cook County Public Guardian against the Illinois Department of Mental Health. The suit alleged that during the 1950s and 1960s between 25 and 100 patients underwent "unauthorized and secret" surgery at a state mental health center.

The suit charged that the patients, without their consent, were subjected to experimental surgery to remove their adrenal glands. A memo from a psychiatrist was cited that described the health center as "virtually a human dog lab."

A spokesman for the mental health department publicly denied the charges in the suit. He claimed that an internal investigation showed that consent from the patients had been obtained and each had been informed of the possible risks and of the short- and long-term effects.

Moreover, the surgery was said to have a therapeutic aim, as well as an experimental one. A theory at the time suggested that the removal of the adrenal gland might correct a hormonal imbalance that some research psychiatrists believed to be a cause of schizophrenia. Furthermore, it was claimed that only four schizophrenic patients were involved.

As a matter of fact, the surgery did not lead to improvement in any of the patients, and the theory suggesting that it might is no longer held. Those who had their adrenal glands removed required injections of cortisone for the rest of their lives to compensate for the loss of natural secretions from the gland.

1. *Suppose that the charge made by the Public Guardian is correct. What utilitarian argument might be offered to support the use of mental patients as subjects in the experimental surgery?*

2. *Clearly, the only proper candidates for an experimental procedure aimed at treating schizophrenia are people who are schizophrenic. Is it reasonable to believe that people who suffer from psychosis are capable of giving informed consent?*

3. *If the reasonable person standard of* Canterbury v. Spence *does not apply in this case, what other standard would be appropriate?*

4. *Is it possible to argue that the principle of autonomy requires that patients diagnosed as psychotic ought to be allowed to consent to any procedure that may help their condition? If not, why not?*

5. *How relevant to the moral issue of consent is the nonmoral question of the degree of confirmation of a theory that is the basis of an experimental procedure with a therapeutic aim?*

Decision Scenario 9 ••

At six A.M. on Wednesday, March 6, 1985, Dr. Kevin Cheng of Phoenix got a call from cardiac surgeon Dr. Cecil Vaughn. "Is your heart ready to be implanted?" Dr. Vaughn asked.

Dr. Cheng thought the question was about implanting the artificial heart he had invented into a calf, an experiment he and Dr. Vaughn had done once before and were planning to do again. When he learned that the intended recipient was a human, he hesitated. "Wait a minute," Dr. Cheng said. "It's designed for a calf and not ready for a human yet."

"Think about it, decide, and I'll call back in ten minutes," Dr. Vaughn told him.

The heart was needed because Thomas Creighton, a thirty-three-year-old automobile mechanic and divorced father of two, had rejected the heart he had received from an accident victim. Dr. Jack Copeland and the transplant team at University Medical Center in Tucson immediately began a search for another donor heart, and Mr. Creighton was placed on the heart-lung machine. Dr. Copeland had also called Utah and requested that the Jarvik-7 heart be flown in.

"I knelt and prayed," Dr. Cheng recalled later. When Dr. Vaughn called him back, he said "The pump is sterile and ready to go."

Around noon of the same day, Dr. Vaughn implanted the device in Mr. Creighton. Mr. Creighton's physicians had decided that it would be dangerous to leave him on the heart-lung machine any longer, and the Jarvik-7 heart had not yet arrived. The Phoenix heart maintained Mr. Creighton's circulation until a donor heart was located.

At eleven that night, the device was turned off, and Mr. Creighton was put back on the heart-lung machine. At three A.M. on Thursday, Dr. Copeland transplanted the second donor heart. However, despite all efforts, Mr. Creighton died the following day. The Phoenix heart had nothing to do with causing his death.

However, in deciding to use the Phoenix heart, Dr. Vaughn and Dr. Copeland had apparently violated FDA regulations by employing a device that had not been approved for experimental use in humans. They and their defenders justified their action by claiming that their use of the device was an emergency measure. They were not performing an experiment with Mr. Creighton, but attempting to save his life. The only other option was just to let him die. "We had nothing to lose" by using the heart, Dr. Copeland said.

1. *Would the line of reasoning taken by Dr. Copeland lead to the conclusion that anything at all can be done to a patient, if it can be justified as an effort to save the patient's life?*

2. *What response can be given to the charge that Mr. Creighton's condition was not a true medical emergency, because transplant rejection is one of the anticipated risks of that kind of surgery?*

3. *Although Mr. Creighton gave consent to the original surgery, he was in no condition to give consent to the use of the artificial heart. (Consent was given by his mother and sister.) Because of the risks known to be associated with artificial hearts (strokes and consequent brain damage, for example), the fact that he consented to a heart transplant does not mean that he would have consented to even the temporary use of an artificial heart. As far as he knew, the matter would never arise. Does this mean that Mr. Creighton was illegitimately denied the opportunity to decide what sort of risks he was willing to take?*

Decision Scenario 10 ••

The first human heart was transplanted in 1967 in South Africa by Dr. Christian Barnard. However, this was not the first heart transplant on a human being. In January of 1964, Dr. James D. Hardy of the University of Mississippi transplanted a chimpanzee heart into Boyd Rush.

Boyd Rush was a deaf-mute who was brought to the University of Mississippi Medical Center unconscious and on the verge of dying. A stepsister, the only relative who could be located, signed a consent form permitting, if necessary, "the insertion of a suitable heart transplant." The form made no reference to the sort of heart that might be employed. Mr. Rush lived for two hours after the transplant.

Dr. Hardy justified the use of the chimpanzee heart on the ground that it was impossible to obtain a human heart. Also, he was encouraged to think the transplant might be successful because of the limited success obtained by Dr. Keith Reentsma in transplanting chimpanzee kidneys into a man dying of glomerulonephritis. The kidney recipient lived for two months.

Dr. Leonard Bailey, the surgeon who transplanted the baboon heart into the child known as Baby Fae, expressed his view of Dr. Hardy in an interview: "He's an idol of mine because he followed through and did what he should have done . . . he took a gamble to try to save a human life."

1. *Evaluate the quality of the consent that was secured for transplant surgery in this case.*

2. *Suppose that Mr. Rush's stepsister did know that it was possible that a chimpanzee heart might be used. Should anyone be permitted to give consent to such a transplant on behalf of someone else?*

3. *If the only way to save the life of Mr. Rush was to transplant a chimpanzee heart, was the surgery justified?*

4. *Suppose the transplant could have been expected to postpone Mr. Rush's death for only a relatively short time. Would Singer regard the sacrifice of a baboon justified? Would Cohen?*

5. *Evaluate the criticism that Dr. Hardy was doing no more than performing a medical experiment in which Mr. Rush was the unknowing and unconsenting subject.*

Decision Scenario 11 ••

In 1988 cardiologist William O'Neill decided he would have to go to Germany to do a clinical test on a device to clean out clogged arteries. Several years previously, researchers at the Centers for Disease Control planned to test the effectiveness of giving vitamin supplements to pregnant women to prevent spina bifida in their children. The National Institute for Child Health and Development objected to the plan to withhold vitamins from the control group. The researchers found Chinese collaborators who arranged for the clinical studies to be done.

Some clinical researchers are of the opinion that such cases are widespread and increasing in number. In general, they claim, more and more often researchers and drug companies are choosing to test medical devices, therapies, and drugs in foreign countries. As a result, some researchers fear that the American reputation for innovative, cutting-edge clinical research is being eroded. If the process continues, the United States will eventually lose its well-established and respected tradition of clinical research, and the trained researchers the tradition produces will disappear. Furthermore, Americans will no longer be able to count on being among the first to receive the most effective medical treatments.

Two reasons are frequently mentioned as causing this switch in testing to foreign countries. First, the Federal Drug Administration and other federal agencies require so many levels of approval and so much paperwork that efforts to mount clinical trials are discouraged. Second, overzealous advocates of patients' rights have both complicated the approval process and made it difficult to recruit test subjects.

Speaking of informed-consent forms to test a new clot-dissolving drug used during a heart attack, one British researcher said: "The American documents were three pages of legalistic junk. That's not the sort of thing you want to push under someone's nose as he's having a heart attack, terrified with chest pain, on morphine. You want to tell him about the trial, but you want to be humane." Furthermore, critics of testing have made people so suspicious of medical experimentation that they refuse to participate when asked. By contrast, patients in other countries are more trusting and give their consent more readily.

The situation has been encouraged by an FDA decision to accept data from some foreign trials. The aim of the policy change was to make effective drugs more quickly available in the United States, but a consequence has been to encourage researchers to avoid problems at home by going abroad.

1. *Do we have an obligation to make sure that clinical trials in other countries involve the free and informed consent of participants? How might a Kantian answer this question? Do we have a prima facie duty to protect research subjects everywhere?*

2. *Suppose that in a scientifically well-designed trial a drug to prevent strokes was found to be amazingly effective, but we learn that the trial was conducted in a Third-World country and that none of the patients in the study were aware of their status as experimental subjects. Should we refuse to use the drug until the same studies were repeated with subjects who were informed and consenting participants?*

3. *Is there a possibility that the FDA policy of accepting data from foreign studies will encourage the exploitation of people in countries with practices offering less protection to patients than those in the United States? If so, then should the FDA policy be reversed in order to discourage such exploitation?*

4. *Might a utilitarian find the reasons mentioned for shifting testing to foreign countries relevant grounds for weakening current laws designed to protect research subjects?*

Decision Scenario 12 ···

During the two years he had worked for the Bioplus Foundation, Dennis Quade had been in many labs. Before he could renew the funding of a grant, he was required to make an on-site inspection of the facilities and review the work of the investigators. Now he was sitting in a small, chilly conference room about to watch a videotape of a phase of the work done at Carolyn Sing's lab.

Sing herself was sitting at the table with him, and she leaned forward and pushed the play button. "The experimental subjects we used are baboons," she told him. "We think they possess facial and cranial similarities sufficiently similar to humans to make them the best animal models."

Dennis nodded, then watched the monitor in complete silence. He was appalled by what he saw. An adult animal, apparently limp from anesthesia, was strapped to a stainless-steel table. Its head was fitted into a viselike device and several clamps tightened to hold it immobile. The upper-left side of the baboon's head had been shaved and the area painted with a faintly purple antiseptic solution. A dark circle had been drawn in the center of the painted area.

The white-coated arms of an assistant appeared in the tight focus of the picture. The assistant was holding a device that looked like an oversized electric drill. A long, transparent plastic sleeve stuck out from the chuck-end of the device, and through it Dennis could see a round, stainless-steel plate. A calibrated dial was visible on the side of the device, but Dennis couldn't read the marks.

"That's an impact hammer," Dr. Sing said. "We thought at first we were going to be able to use one off the shelf, but we had to modify one. That's an item we didn't anticipate in our initial budget."

The assistant centered the plastic tube over the spot marked on the baboon's head and pulled the trigger of the impact hammer. The motion of the steel plate was too swift for Dennis to see, but he saw the results. The animal's body jerked in spasm, and a froth of blood, brain tissue, and bone fragments welled up from the purple spot.

Dennis Quade turned away from the monitor, unable to stand the images any longer.

"Through induced head trauma studies, we have been able to learn an enormous amount," Carolyn Sing said. "Not only do we know more about what happens to brain tissue during the first few minutes after trauma, but we've used that knowledge to develop some new management techniques that may save literally tens of thousands of people from permanent brain damage."

Dennis Quade nodded.

1. *Would Peter Singer oppose such experiments? Suppose it is true that brain damage from head trauma may be reduced or eliminated in thousands of people. Would this make a difference to Singer?*

2. *If you knew that the information gained from the study described would prevent your child from suffering from brain damage, should this count in your decision about whether such an experiment is justifiable?*

3. *Is there any reason to suppose that a human life (of any sort) is worth more than an animal life (of any sort)? On what moral grounds, if any, might one object to using patients in a chronic vegetative state as experimental subjects in the study?*

4. *Would Cohen find the experiment described morally justified? What features does the experiment have that might lead him to approve it? What importance does he attach to animal suffering in an experimental context?*

PART III
CONTROLS

CHAPTER 7
GENETICS:
INTERVENTION, CONTROL, AND RESEARCH

SOCIAL CONTEXT: THE HUMAN GENOME PROJECT

The 46 human chromosomes contain an estimated 100,000 genes. This complete set of genes is known as the *human genome*. Metaphorically, the genome is the total set of blueprints for assembling a human being stored in the nucleus of each cell. At present, less than 2,000 genes have been located or "mapped" on the DNA strands, and only about 600 genes have been sequenced—that is, the precise order of their base pairs determined.

In 1985, Robert Sinsheimer began promoting the idea that the entire human genome should be mapped and its genes sequenced. Since the genome is believed to consist of some three billion base pairs, the genome project would be on a scale unprecedented in the biological sciences. It would compare with efforts of physical scientists to develop the atomic bomb during World War II and with the launching of the manned space project in the 1960s.

The size of the genome project made many scientists skeptical about supporting it. Many believed it would drain money away from smaller projects of immediate value in favor of one with only distant and uncertain value. Also, some feared the genome project would turn out to be too much like the space project, emphasizing the solution to engineering problems more than the advancement of basic science.

Attitudes changed in 1988 when the National Research Council endorsed the genome project and outlined a gradual approach of coordinated research that would protect the interest of the basic sciences. When James Watson agreed to be director of the project, most critics dropped their opposition, and many became enthusiastic participants. Watson headed the project with great success until he resigned in 1993, when the position was taken over by Francis S. Collins.

Mapping and sequencing the human genome is expected to take fifteen to twenty years and cost between $3 and $5 billion. In 1989, Congress approved $31 million to initiate the program, but the project is currently being supported at about $165 million per year, and most biological and medical scientists view the money as well and wisely spent.

The genome project in the United States is divided among nine different centers at both national laboratories and universities, and hundreds of scientists are participating in the research and contributing to the final product. France is the other recognized world leader in genomics, and the national research effort there is in Paris at the Centre d'Etude du Polymorphisme Humain (CEPH).

The payoff of the genome project is now considered by most biological and medical researchers to be of inestimable worth. The information has already provided us with a better understanding of the patterns and processes of human evolution and clarified our degree of genetic relatedness with other organisms. Further, the connections between genes and humans has become clearer, even though this is an area of inquiry still at an early stage of development.

Most important, the detailed genetic information the project is supplying has given us a much improved understanding of the relationships between certain genes and particular diseases. This information may eventually permit us to develop gene therapy to such a degree that genetic diseases can be wholly eliminated or their results effectively controlled.

The genome project has advanced much more rapidly toward its goal than even its most avid supporters ever thought possible. In 1993, Daniel Cohen, the head of CEPH, assembling data from some 129 researchers, published a complete map of human chromosomes. The map is sketchy, but it is four times more detailed than the first chromosomal-linkage map published in 1987. The map makes it ten times quicker to locate a particular gene than by using earlier linkage maps. Since the Cohen map a number of other maps, based on increasingly more complete data, have been published.

The rapidity with which the genes responsible for a large number of human diseases have been identified has been astounding. A sampling from a list of about nine hundred gives some idea of how successful researchers have been in locating actual genes or gene markers for diseases:

Colon cancer. For the familial form of colon cancer, a marker was found on the upper end of chromosome 2 for a "repair" gene that corrects minor errors in cellular DNA. In its mutant form, the gene seems to function by triggering hundreds of thousands of mutations in other genes. One in 200 people has the gene; 65% of the carriers are liable to develop cancer. The familial form accounts for about 15% of all colon tumors. (A blood test is expected to be available soon.)

Amyotrophic lateral sclerosis. The familial form of ALS (Lou Gehrig's Disease) results from a mutation of a gene on chromosome 21 that codes for the enzyme superoxide dismutase, which plays a role in eliminating free radicals. If the free radicals are not controlled, it is believed that they may damage motor neurons, which will then lead to muscle degeneration. The familial form of the disease accounts for only about 10% of cases, but those with a family history of the disease can now be screened for the defective gene.

Type II (adult onset) diabetes. A still unidentified gene on chromosome 7 codes for glucokinase, an enzyme that stimulates the pancreas to produce insulin. At least twenty-three mutated forms of the gene may cause the disease by coding for a faulty enzyme that apparently fails to trigger insulin production. A screening test for the mutated genes could be available before long.

Alzheimer's disease. The gene ApoE on chromosome 19 codes for a protein that transports cholesterol. People who have both alleles for the form of the protein known as E4 have eight times the risk of developing Alzheimer's; those with one allele have two to three times the risk. The gene could account for as many as half of those with the disease, although the causal role of E4 in producing it is not yet known.

X-linked SCID. Severe combined immunodeficiency diseases (SCID) is caused by a defective gene passed from mothers to sons on the X chromosome. The normal gene codes for part of the receptor of interleukin-2, which serves in the cytokine messenger system that keeps the T-cells of the immune system functioning. Newborns with the mutated gene have few or no T-cells, and even a mild infection is life threatening. The disease occurs in only 1 in every 100,000 births.

(The cells used in the study were from "David," who died in Houston after he was removed from the sterile environment where he had spent almost twelve years of his life and given a bone marrow transplant. Because of the publicity surrounding him, SCIDS is known popularly as "the Bubble Boy disease.")

Familial breast cancer susceptibility. Mutations in the gene BRCA1, located on chromosome 17, were identified in 1994 as being responsible for the susceptibility to breast cancer and ovarian cancer in a group of families with multiple incidence of the diseases. A "frame-shift mutation" apparently causes the translation of codons to start in the wrong place, producing a nonsense protein. A second gene, BRCA2, located on chromosome 13, also seems to cause susceptibility, and the two genes may explain most hereditary breast cancers.

To the surprise of researchers, no evidence suggests that the BRCA1 or BRCA2 gene plays a role in the 90% to 95% of "sporadic" breast cancers—that is, ones not due to inherited susceptibility. The possibility that mutations in other genes are responsible is currently under investigation.

This list could be multiplied to include spinocerebellar ataxia (a degenerative disease linked to a gene on chromosome 6), Huntington's disease (see the Case Presentation: Huntington's Disease in this chapter), Lorenzo's disease (adrenoleukodystrophy, or ALD, which involves the degeneration of the myelin sheath around nerves), Canavan disease (a rare and fatal brain disorder affecting mostly Ashkenazi Jews and similar to ALD), achondroplastic dwarfism, (the gene, FGR3, causes about one-third of the cases of dwarfism), and cystic fibrosis (in which mucous accumulates in the lungs and pancreas and the gene, discovered on chromosome 7, is known to exist in hundreds of mutant forms).

The Human Genome Project's aim of mapping, identifying, and sequencing all the genes in the human body is far from being achieved. Yet researchers have come so far so fast that it is now reasonable to believe that eventually we will have something like a complete understanding of our genetic makeup. That understanding will provide us with scientific, medical, social, and ethical opportunities and challenges as staggering in their complexity as the human genome itself.

Genetic Screening and Discrimination

The discovery of new genes may be expected to be followed by the development of new screening tests. Indeed, for the diseases previously mentioned, tests either already exist or may be expected soon. Given the increasing sophistication of biotechnology, tests that are now complex and expensive will probably become relatively simple and cheap. This leads some thinkers to worry that our newly acquired understanding of parts of the human genome may result in opening the way for new forms of genetic discrimination—ones based on genetic predisposition.

As discussed, researchers are well on the way to identifying an entire catalogue of

DNA Tests Currently Available

Disease	Description	Incidence	Approximate Cost
Adult polycystic kidney disease	Multiple kidney growths	1 in 1,000	$350
Alpha-1-Antitrypsin deficiency	Can cause hepatitis, cirrhosis of the liver, emphysema	1 in 1,000	$350
Familial adenomatous polyposis	Colon polyps by age 35, often leading to cancer	1 in 5,000	$1,000
Hemophilia	Blood fails to clot properly	1 in 10,000	$250 to $350
Huntington's disease	Lethal neurological deterioration	1 in 10,000	$250 to $350
Myotonic dystrophy (a form of muscular dystrophy)	Progressive degeneration of muscles	1 in 8,000	$250

genes and their associated diseases. The concept of a genetic disease is not a clear-cut one. Rarely is it the case that if a person had a certain gene, she will invariably have a certain disease. (Single-gene illnesses, like sickle-cell disease, account for only about 2% of genetic disorders.) Diseases result from a multiplicity of conditions such as the particular form of a gene (many genes have scores and even hundreds of mutated forms), the presence or absence of other genes, and the presence or absence of specific environmental factors.

Information about a genetic predisposition to a particular disease can be beneficial to individuals. It can alert them to the need to seek medical surveillance so that they can receive appropriate therapy for the disease, should it develop, at the earliest time. Further, it can make them aware of the need to avoid environmental factors that may trigger the disease. For example, those with the gene for xeroderma pigmentosum are extremely sensitive to ultraviolet radiation, and exposure to it is likely to lead to a form of melanoma that is usually incurable. However, if those with the gene avoid prolonged exposure to sunlight, they have a good chance of avoiding developing melanoma.

As straightforward as the benefits of genetic screening for disease predisposition may seem, they are entangled with thorny issues of public policy and business practices. Consider another example. The enzyme AHH (amyl hydrocarbon hydroxylase) acts to break down hydrocarbons in smoke and other industrial pollutants. About 10% of the population possess variant forms of the genes that produce the enzyme, and their bodies produce it in an excessive amount. The excess enzyme reacts with hydrocarbons and turns them into carcinogenic substances. People with the variant genes are thus some twenty-six times more likely to get lung cancer from breathing air polluted with hydrocarbons.

Such information offers the opportunity for individuals who are screened and found to be particularly susceptible to a certain environmental pollutant or manufacturing substance to avoid contact with that agent. For example, people who are prone to develop an acute form of anemia after exposure to naphthalene should avoid jobs in which that chemical is employed.

In principle, susceptible workers could be assigned to jobs that would allow them to avoid being exposed to the chemicals particularly harmful to them. With such an end in view, in 1982 some 59% of large companies surveyed indicated that they either had a genetic screening program or intended to institute one. Their motivation was partly based on economic self-interest; the costs of damage suits and insurance premiums could be lowered by keeping susceptible workers out of danger.

By 1986, most plans to screen workers had been abandoned by corporations that had initially favored them. This was mostly in response to criticisms from civil-rights groups, women's organizations, and labor unions. The critics pointed out that the results of genetic screening could be used to discriminate against the hiring of entire classes of workers. Because African Americans are more susceptible to environmentally induced anemia, they would be effectively shut out of jobs in which the risk to them was greater than to other workers.

Similarly, because fetuses are likely to be affected by a number of chemicals used in manufacturing, pregnant women would not be hired for a wide variety of jobs. Indeed, the possibility that a woman might be or might become pregnant might result in the exclusion of women as a group.

The possibility of genetic screening in connection with employment presents us with a number of dilemmas of a moral and social kind. We wish to promote equal opportunity for workers, yet we also wish to protect their health and safety. If those genetically predisposed to certain diseases are allowed to compete for jobs that place them at risk, then we are not seeing to their health and safety. Yet if we see to their health, we are not allowing

them equal opportunity. Similarly, we wish to promote individual freedom in the society, but at what point do we decide that an individual is taking an unacceptable risk? If we allow someone to risk her health, are we willing to bear the social cost associated with her falling ill?

A worker found to be susceptible to a common manufacturing chemical would be at a clear disadvantage in attempting to get a job and might claim that an employer who required him to take a screening test as a condition of employment was violating his right to privacy. Yet should employers be allowed no protection from the added costs of damage suits and higher insurance premiums caused by a higher rate of illness among susceptible workers?

Quite apart from the issues of employment, individuals who are screened for whatever reason and found to be at risk for the development of some genetic disease may find they can get only very expensive health insurance, if they can get it at all. Insurance companies, for their part, may decide to make genetic screening for probabilities of known disorders a condition of insurability. Are individuals entitled to keep such information about themselves private? Are insurers entitled to know what risk they are taking before insuring an applicant?

In addition to issues connected with employment and insurance, genetic screening opens up the possibility of identifying a class of people that may become regarded as socially undesirable. Being predisposed to a genetic disease may become a stigma in a society that prizes health. Genetic carriers might be shunned as marriage partners and might find it difficult to make their way into positions of social power and influence. Regarded as genetic pariahs, they might come to be outcasts in their own society, stigmatized by their biological inheritance.

These are merely some of the difficulties that are raised by the new possibilities of screening for genetic predisposition to diseases. The promise of being able to prevent the occurrence of disease in many individuals is a genuine one, but we have yet to make an adequate effort to resolve the social and moral issues that fulfilling the promise presents. Until we resolve them, a powerful technology will remain underutilized.

Should Children Be Informed?

Researchers attempting to identify the gene that predisposes women to breast cancer conducted their work among families with a high incidence of the disease. During the course of their work, they learned which females in the family had to be carriers of the BRCA1 gene and so had an 85% chance of developing the disease. The question they faced was, Should they inform the women that they or their children were at such risk?

Some researchers decided that they would not volunteer any information and would provide it only to women eighteen or older who asked for it. They refused to divulge any information about children, even when pressed to do so by their parents, because being predisposed to breast cancer is not a condition for which there is a treatment. Also, these researchers reasoned, if a child knew she was predisposed to breast cancer, she might be inclined to think of herself as sick and her breasts as likely to kill her.

Some critics of screening have argued that children should not be included in screening tests, except when there is some direct benefit for them. The acquisition of knowledge is not in itself a justification for screening children, the critics hold, nor is the usefulness of the knowledge in the treatment of others. Screening tests and the results they yield have the potential to damage or destroy a child's self-esteem, causing emotional harm, or altering the way in which the family views the child. In some instances, upon learning that a child is likely to develop a disease, some families have distanced themselves from the child, even to the point of placing the child in a foster home. When the child herself receives no benefit, the threat of such outcomes makes the test unjustifiable.

At least one survey shows, however, that parents often believe that children should be aware of their risks for developing a particular disease. Some 61% of parents visiting prenatal testing clinics said that they should be permitted to have their children tested for Alzheimer's, and 47% said that parents should inform the children of the results.

However, another survey of families with members already diagnosed with genetic diseases shows a different result. Survey participants seemed to feel strongly that parents should have their children tested for a disease only when it is a treatable or preventable one. When the disease is neither, as is the case with Alzheimer's, the screening should not be done.

The issue may be complicated in some cases by the recent discovery that a disease that is mild or even asymptomatic in a parent may be much worse in an offspring. This was discovered to be the case with myotonic muscular dystrophy, the most common form of the disease. A segment of DNA on chromosome 19 appears to repeat itself with increasing frequency over generations. Hence, someone who does not have any clinical sign of the disease may pass on the gene to a child, who will develop a devastating form of the disease. It might be argued that if a parent knows that a child is at high risk for developing a life-threatening disease, the parent has a duty to inform the child, although perhaps only after the child has reached a certain level of maturity.

The questions of whether children should be tested and who should decide when and how much they should know are issues that are likely to become more pressing as the number of tests for disease-causing genes increases.

CASE PRESENTATION
Gene Therapy

In 1980, Dr. Martin J. Cline of UCLA treated two patients suffering from an incurable blood disorder called beta-zero thalassemia with an entirely new therapeutic technique. The disease is one in which the gene for beta globulin, one of the constituents of the hemoglobin in red blood cells, is either missing or unexpressed. Those with the disease usually die very early, and frequently they suffer from anemia, cirrhosis of the liver, and serious heart problems because of the inability of their blood to transport sufficient oxygen to their tissues.

The aim of Dr. Cline's treatment was to provide the patients with the gene required to produce normal hemoglobin. The technique he employed, call *transformation*, is one that had been developed through research with animals. The basic idea behind the technique is simple. Copies of a normal gene are inserted into the cells of a patient who lacks the gene or who possesses it only in a malfunctioning form. The DNA of the cells is induced to incorporate the new gene so that, when the cells reproduce themselves, copies of the new gene are made along with copies of the other genes encoded by the cellular DNA. In this way, the patient acquires a population of normal cells. The problem that was caused by the missing or defective gene is thus corrected.

The technique as applied by Cline in this particular situation depended on the chemical properties of DNA and on the fact that cells take in calcium from their environment. Under proper conditions, the cells will take up DNA fragments, which include new genes, along with the calcium. Cells in the bone marrow (stem cells) are among those responsible for the production of red blood cells.

Accordingly, Cline and his associates took bone marrow from the patients and added the appropriate DNA segments to a cell culture of that material. The hope was that the DNA would be incorporated into the genetic code of the cells and that the cells would be transformed. Afterward, the treated cells would then multiply, and their copies would include the new genes. The patients would thus be supplied with the cells necessary to produce beta globulin.

The plan was not successful. Transformation is a very ineffective process, and very few cells in a culture actually incorporate the foreign DNA. Perhaps the material injected into the patients did not contain enough transformed cells to make a difference. Or perhaps the transformed cells did not multiply sufficiently or otherwise perform as expected. In any case, the patients were not helped by the attempt at therapy, although there was no indication they were harmed, either.

Cline was reprimanded by the National Institutes of Health for engaging in medical experiments without securing the approval of the appropriate UCLA committees. In his own view, the experiments were both scientifically and morally justifiable.

The techniques developed in recombinant-DNA research are crucial to the procedures of gene therapy. It must be possible to identify the defective gene and manipulate the cell's DNA so that a new DNA segment containing a functioning gene is included in it. Furthermore, these tasks must be accomplished without damaging the cell or destroying its ability to reproduce normally.

Although Cline used transformation, the more common technique in animal research is to employ a genetically engineered retrovirus to introduce the new gene into the cellular DNA. Unmodified retroviruses frequently cause diseases in humans, such as AIDS and certain forms of cancer. Consequently, one of the aims of recent gene-therapy research has been to modify retroviruses so that they will insert a desired gene into the DNA of a human cell, without causing a dangerous infection. (See the Introduction for more information about recombinant DNA.)

Gene therapy has now developed to the point that it can claim, within limits, to constitute a successful mode of treatment for some diseases. Most important, new steps forward are being taken rapidly and techniques developed to deal with a wide range of diseases. Cline's experiments may have been haphazard and crude, but the amazing success of recent experimental treatments demonstrate that the idea behind them was fundamentally correct.

On September 14, 1990, at the National Institutes of Health in Bethesda, Maryland, a four-year-old girl became the first patient under an approved protocol to be treated by gene therapy. The child, whose parents asked that her identity not be made public, lacked the gene for producing adenosine deaminase (ADA), an enzyme required to keep immune cells alive and functioning.

Her life expectancy was low because without ADA she would almost certainly develop cancers and opportunistic infections that cannot be effectively controlled by conventional treatments. The aim of the therapy was to provide her with cells that would boost her immune system by increasing the production of essential antibodies. During the following months, she received four injections of altered cells.

The treatment, under the direction of W. French Anderson, R. Michael Blaese, and Kenneth Culver, involved taking blood from the patient, isolating the T-cells, and then growing a massive number of them. These cells were then infected with a weakened retrovirus into which a copy of the human gene for ADA had been spliced. The cells were then injected into the patient in a blood transfusion.

The idea behind the therapy was for the ADA gene to migrate to the cellular DNA, switch on, and begin producing ADA. If the cells then produced enough of the enzyme, the child's immune system would not be destroyed. Because most T-cells live for only weeks or months, the process had to be repeated at regular intervals.

The girl's parents, from a Cleveland suburb, later revealed their daughter's identity. She is Ashanthi Desilva, and more than five years later, she is alive and doing well. Soon after her treatment, on January 30, 1991, nine-year-old Cynthia Cutshall, became the second person to receive gene therapy.

Laboratory tests showed that both children's immune systems were functioning effectively. But, the need to replace short-lived T-cells meant that Ashanthi and Cynthia had to continue to receive regular injections of altered cells. However, Anderson and his collaborators had always hoped to find the way around this need, and the break came when an NIH group developed a procedure for isolating stem cells from the bone marrow. If enough stem cells could be obtained and genetically al-

tered, then when injected back into the patient, the cells might produce enough T-cells for an adequately functioning immune system.

In May 1993, Cynthia's stem cells were harvested, exposed to the retrovirus containing the normal ADA gene, and reinjected. She tolerated the procedure with no apparent ill effects, and later that year, essentially the same procedure was repeated with Ashanthi. If the immune systems of both continue to function within the normal range, the therapy can be said to have produced a cure for ADA.

The promise gene therapy holds for those who suffer from a variety of genetic disorders is enormous. Experimental clinical protocols for the treatment of a wide range of relatively common diseases such as cystic fibrosis, hemophilia, phenylketonuria, sickle-cell anemia, hypercholesterolemia, AIDS, cardiovascular disease, cancer, lupus erythematous, and blood-clotting either have already been initiated or are under review.

In one proposed cancer treatment, researchers will make trillions of copies of the gene that codes for the antigen HLA-B7, then inject them directly into the tumors of those suffering from melanoma. The DNA is expected to enter the cells of the tumor, insert itself in the cellular DNA, then trigger the production of HLA-B7. The antigen will then extrude from the cell, causing the cell to be attacked by killer T-cells. Animal experiments suggest that the immune system will attack not only tumor cells with the antigen markers, but those around it.

James Wilson, at the University of Michigan, initiated procedures in the summer of 1992 to treat people with hypercholesterolemia, a disease in which the excess production of cholesterol often leads to heart attacks and early death. The procedure involved removing part of a patient's liver, then culturing the cells and inserting into them a gene that produces the low-density lipoprotein receptor. The receptor plays an important role in removing cholesterol from the blood. The treated cells were then to be injected into the patient's liver, where it was expected that they would attach themselves to the liver's capillaries and start producing the protein of the receptor. Six months after the experimental study was started, the results were so satisfactory that Wilson sought federal approval to include more patients in the study.

A group from Boston recently initiated a study that will employ gene therapy for the treatment of a form of cardiovascular disease in which clogged arteries in the leg reduce circulation and cause intractable pain and unhealing ulcers. Some thirty to forty thousand people per year are diagnosed with such severe leg-artery atherosclerosis. The plan is to treat such people with the gene that codes for vascular endothelial growth factor (vegf), a protein that stimulates the growth of collateral blood vessels. If the proposed therapy is successful, it should be possible for patients to avoid the usual treatment by angioplasty or bypass surgery or, in some cases, amputation.

In April 1993, a twenty-three-year-old man became the first patient to receive human gene therapy for the treatment of cystic fibrosis. An altered form of the adenovirus was used to transport into his lungs the gene that codes for cystic fibrosis transmembrane conductance regulator. The regulator controls the flow of chloride through body cells. Cystic fibrosis patients lack the regulator gene, and as a result, they suffer severe salt imbalances that cause abnormal mucous excretions in the lungs and pancreas. If the gene functions properly, it may be possible to offer the 30,000 Americans who suffer from cystic fibrosis a cure for the disease.

Several experiments are underway utilizing gene therapy to treat AIDS. In one of them, a few CD4 cells, the principle target of the HIV virus, will be taken from an AIDS patient, and a molecule called a "hairpin ribozyme" spliced into their DNA. The ribozyme slices up RNA, and because HIV depends on RNA for replication, cells with altered DNA should prevent the virus from reproducing. If enough altered CD4 cells were present in an HIV-positive individual, the level of infection might be lowered.

Paralleling the development of gene therapy are other treatment strategies that are based on the technology of recombinant DNA. One of the most promising is the use of drugs to alter the function of genes that are not behaving normally. The drugs in effect "turn on" a malfunctioning gene so that it plays the role it is supposed to. Some promising results in the treatment of thalassemia and sickle-cell anemia have been reported.

Another technique involves transplanting cells into the brain, and it has been used experimentally in the treatment of Parkinson's disease. (See Chapter 9 for a fuller discussion.) The disease appears to result from the destruction of brain cells in the substantia nigra and the consequent reduction in dopamine production. Dopamine is a neurotransmitter involved in the movement of voluntary muscles. Its absence results in loss of control and shaky, involuntary movements. Researchers in Sweden in 1990 reported success in transplanting cells from fetal tissue into the substantia nigra of the brain. Other recent work also supports the idea that transplant therapy for diseases such as Parkinson's and Alzheimer's will be effective in the not-too-distant future.

The gene therapy in humans currently under development is somatic-cell therapy, where modifications take place in the body cells of patients, not in the sex cells. This means that even if the therapy can eliminate the disease produced in an individual who has inherited a defective gene, the therapy will do nothing to alter the probability that a child of that person will inherit the same defective gene. To change this circumstance, germ-line cells would have to be altered. That is, the defective gene in an ovum or sperm cell would have to be replaced.

If this were possible, then certain genetic diseases could be eliminated from families. Germ-line therapy would make it unnecessary to perform somatic-cell therapy for each generation of affected individuals. As appealing as this prospect is, at the present germ-line therapy has many more technical difficulties associated with it than does somatic-cell therapy. Uniformly encouraging results have not so far been produced in animal research, and even somatic-cell therapy in humans remains a distant prospect.

Most of the moral issues discussed in connection with gene therapy have centered around germ-line therapy. It holds out the prospect of genetically engineering sex cells to produce offspring with virtually any set of characteristics desired. This possibility has led many critics to warn that "genetic surgery" may be leading us into a sort of "Brave New World" in which we practice eugenics and manufacture our children to order. (See the Introduction for a fuller discussion.) However, any dangers posed by germ-line therapy are far from immediate.

Somatic-cell therapy continues to be an experimental treatment. However, it's likely to become an established form of treatment within the next two to five years. It will for some time remain an experimental treatment, and as such it raises the same sorts of moral questions typical of any experimental procedure—questions of informed consent, benefit, and risk.

CASE PRESENTATION
Huntington's Disease: Genetic Testing and Ethical Dilemmas

Huntington's disease is a particularly cruel and frightening genetic disorder. It has no effective treatment and is invariably fatal. Furthermore, each child of an affected parent has a 50% chance of developing the disease.

The disease typically makes its appearance between the ages of thirty-five and forty-five in men and women who have shown no previous symptoms. The signs of its onset may be quite subtle— a certain clumsiness in performing small tasks, a slight slurring of speech, a few facial twitches. But the disease is progressive. Over time the small, subtle signs develop into massive physical and mental changes. Walking becomes jerky and unsteady, the face contorts into wild grimaces, the hands repeatedly clench and relax, and the whole body writhes with involuntary muscle spasms. The victim eventually loses the power of speech, becomes disoriented, and gives way to irrational emotional outbursts. Before mental deterioration becomes too advanced, HD victims often kill themselves out of sheer hopelessness and despair. Death may occur naturally from fifteen to twenty years after the beginning of the symptoms. Usually, it results from massive infection and malnutrition—because as the disease progresses, the victim loses the ability to swallow normally.

In the United States, at any given time, some 30,000 people are diagnosed as having the disease. It has been estimated that as many as 150,000 more may have the gene responsible for the disease. The incidence of the disease is only 1 in 10,000, but for the child of a victim of the disease, the chances are 1 out of 2.

The gene causing the disease was identified in 1993 after ten years of intensive research carried out in six laboratories in the United States, England, and Wales. Following the leads provided by genetic markers for the disease, the gene was finally located near the tip of chromosome 4. When researchers sequenced the nucleotides making up the gene, they discovered that the mutation was a trinucleotide repeat. In healthy individuals, the nucleotides CAG are repeated 11 to 34 times, whereas in individuals with HD, the repetitions typically range from 37 to 86. Some evidence suggests that higher numbers of repetitions are associated with earlier onset.

When the HD gene was identified, it was expected that this would have almost immediate consequences for the development of an effective treatment. This has not turned out to be the case because the mechanism of the gene's action is not yet understood. Furthermore, the gene was expected to be found functioning only in the brain, but in fact radioactive tagging has shown that the gene operates in virtually every tissue of the body, including the colon, liver, pancreas, and testes. The protein the gene codes for is believed to be toxic to neuronal development, but the protein itself has not yet been isolated.

Before the HD gene was identified or a marker for it discovered, the disease was known to be transmitted from generation to generation in a hereditary pattern, indicating that it is caused by a single gene. However, since the disease makes its appearance relatively late in life, an unsuspecting victim may already have passed on the gene to a child before he or she shows any sign of the disease. In the absence of a genetic test to detect the presence of the gene, the individual could not know whether he or she was a carrier of the gene.

In 1983, a major step toward the development of such a test was announced by James F. Gusella and his group at Massachusetts General Hospital. The team did not locate the gene itself, but discovered a "genetic marker" indicating its presence. They began by studying the DNA taken from members of a large American family with a history of

Huntington's disease, then employed recombinant-DNA techniques to attempt to locate DNA segments that might be associated with the HD gene.

The techniques involved using proteins known as *restriction enzymes*. A particular enzyme, when mixed with a single strand of DNA, cuts the strand at specific locations known as *recognition sites*. After the DNA strand has been cut up by restriction enzymes, short sections of radioactive, single-stranded DNA are added to serve as probes. The probes bind to particular segments of the DNA. Because the probes are radioactive, the segments to which they are attached can be identified on photographic film.

The various fragments of DNA produced by the restriction enzymes and identified by probes form a pattern that is typical of individuals. A mutation of a normal gene may change the point at which an enzyme makes a cut. This produces a DNA fragment that is not the usual length and alters the pattern of that person. Thus, if the pattern of someone who does not have the disease is compared with the pattern of a family member who does, the fragments that include the faulty gene can be identified, even when the gene itself is unknown. The abnormal pattern serves as a *marker* for the presence of the gene.

Gusella's group faced the problem of finding a marker consistently inherited by those with Huntington's disease but not by those free of the disease. This meant identifying perhaps as many as eight hundred markers and determining whether one could serve as the marker for the HD gene. Incredibly, the team identified a good candidate on its twelfth try. It was a marker found in all members of the family they were studying. Those with the disease had the same form of the marker, while those free of the disease had some other form.

Gusella and other researchers were supported in their work by the Hereditary Disease Foundation. The organization was founded by Milton Wexler after his wife was diagnosed with Huntington's. Wexler hoped that a treatment for the disease could be found that might benefit his daughters, Nancy and Alice, who stood a 50–50 chance of developing the disease. Nancy Wexler soon became an active participant in research activities aimed at discovering a genetic marker.

In collaboration with the Hereditary Disease Foundation, plans were made to test Gusella's candidate marker in a large population. It was known that a large family with a high incidence of HD lived along the shores of Lake Maracaibo in Venezuela. Nancy Wexler led a team to this remote location to collect family history and to obtain blood and skin samples for analysis. The lake-dwelling family included some 100 people with the disease and 1,100 children with the risk of developing it.

Analysis of the samples showed that those with the disease also carried the same form of the marker as their American counterparts. Gusella estimated that the odds were 100 million to 1 that the marker was linked to the HD gene. Subsequent work by Susan Naylor indicated that the marker was on chromosome 4. When the gene itself was identified in 1993, this turned out to be correct.

Once the location of the gene for Huntington's disease was known, a genetic test for its presence was quickly developed. However, the availability of the test raises a number of serious ethical and social questions. The basic question people with a family history that puts them at risk for developing the disease must ask is whether they should have the test.

A study conducted in Wales in the 1970s revealed that more than half of those whose parents or relatives were victims of Huntington's disease would not want to have a test that would tell them whether they had the HD gene, even if such a test were available. Considering that the disease is virtually untreatable and invariably fatal, this is not a surprise finding.

Nancy Wexler confided to a reporter that she and her sister had assumed that once a test for determining whether they were carrying the HD gene was available, they would take it. However, when they met with their father to work out the details for a test based on a genetic marker, he suddenly said, "What are we doing here? Are we sure we want to do this?" The sisters "had a visceral understanding that either one of us could get bad news and that it would certainly destroy my father."

But do those who are at risk have obligations to others? Because a test is available, is it fair to a potential marriage partner to marry without finding out whether one is a carrier of the HD gene and informing the potential partner of the result? Perhaps he or she may be willing to take the chance that the offspring of an HD parent will not have the disease. Even so, because of the tremendous burden the disease places on the other spouse, the possibility of being tested for the presence of the gene deserves serious consideration.

The decision about whether to have children can also be affected by the knowledge that one partner is a carrier of the HD gene so that there is a 50% chance that any child will also develop the disease. Should a potential carrier of the gene impose on the other partner the risk of having a child who will inherit the gene? Should such a risk be imposed on a potential child? The genetic test can determine whether an individual carries the gene. If he or she does, then the couple has knowledge of the relevant facts that will put them in a position to make a decision about having a child.

The test now in use can also be employed in conjunction with amniocentesis to determine whether a developing fetus carries the HD gene. Possessing such information may add a particular difficulty to making an abortion decision for some. A child born with the HD gene will inevitably develop the disease but may not do so for three, four, or even five or more decades. Is the fact that the child will eventually succumb to the disease reason enough to make an abortion morally obligatory? On the other hand, should the parents even have the fetus tested, if they are not prepared to have it aborted in the event of a positive test for the HD gene?

One disadvantage of the direct testing of the fetus for the presence of the HD gene is that if the fetus is found to have the gene, then the parent with the family history of the disease will know that she or he has the gene also. To avoid this consequence, a so-called nondisclosing prenatal test can be performed. The test employs a gene-probe method to determine how a segment of fetal chromosome 4 compares with segments from grandparents. If the segment resembles that of a healthy grandparent, the child is not likely to have the gene. If it matches that of the grandparent with the disease, there is a 1 in 2 chance that the child possesses the gene.

This is the same as the risk for a mother or father with one parent who developed the disease. Hence, the potential parent has learned nothing new about his or her own chances of having the gene, and it is this that makes the test nondisclosing. However, if the potential parents do not plan to abort the fetus if they learn that it has a 50–50 chance of possessing the HD gene, there is no reason to perform the test.

The advent of a standard, inexpensive test for the HD gene raises various other moral and social issues. For example, insurance companies may refuse to provide life or health insurance to those from families with Huntington's disease, unless they prove that they are not carriers of the gene. Employers may refuse to provide health benefits to family members unless they are tested and found to lack the gene. Adoption agencies have requested that infants available for adoption be tested to assure potential adopting families that the children are not at risk for HD. As Nancy Wexler put the point, "In our culture, people assume that knowledge is always good. . . . But our experience with Huntington's has shown that some things may be better left unknown."

Informing someone that he or she carries the gene also has problems associated with it. Such news can be devastating, both to the person and to the person's family. About 10% to 12% of HD victims kill themselves, and 30% of those at risk say that this is what they will do if they learn they have the disease. Thus, the mere act of conveying the information that someone will later develop the signs of a fatal disease can itself constitute a threat to life. Nancy Wexler has refused to disclose publicly whether she has been tested for the HD gene. "I don't want to influence anyone's decision," she says.

In the best of worlds, an effective means of preventing the onset of Huntington's disease or treating it effectively would be available. Then the moral and social issues associated with a genetic test for it would disappear without having to be resolved. Regrettably, that world still lies in the future.

INTRODUCTION

The two great triumphs of nineteenth-century biology were Darwin's formulation of the theory of organic evolution and Mendel's statement of the laws of transmission genetics. One of the twentieth century's outstanding accomplishments has been the development of an understanding of the molecular structures and processes that are involved in genetic inheritance. All three great achievements give rise to moral and social issues of considerable complexity. The theories are abstract, but the problems they generate are concrete and immediate.

Major problems are associated with our increased knowledge of inheritance and genetic change. One class of problems concerns the use we make of the knowledge we possess in dealing with individuals. We know a great deal about the ways in which genetic diseases are transmitted and about the sorts of errors that can occur in human development. We have the means to make reliable predictions about the chances of the occurrence of a disease in a particular case, and we have the medical technology to detect some disorders before birth.

To what extent should we employ this knowledge? One possibility is that we might use it to detect, treat, or prevent genetic disorders. Thus, we might require that everyone submit to screening and counseling before having children. Or we might require that children be tested either prenatally or immediately after birth. We might recommend or require selective abortions. In this way, it might be possible to bring many genetic diseases under control in much the same way that we have brought contagious diseases under control.

Requiring screening and testing suggests another possibility, one that involves taking a broader view of human genetics. Eliminating genetic disease might simply become part of a much more ambitious plan for deliberately improving the entire species. Shall we attempt to control human evolution by formulating policies and practices designed to alter the genetic composition of the human population? Shall we make use of "gene surgery" and recombinant DNA technology to shape physical and mental attributes of our species? That is, shall we practice some form of eugenics?

Another class of problems has to do with the wider social and environmental consequences of genetic research and technology. Research in molecular genetics that is concerned with recombinant DNA has already re-

vealed to us ways in which the machinery of cells can be altered in beneficial ways. We are able to make bacteria synthesize such important biological products as human insulin, and we are able to alter bacteria to serve as vaccines against some diseases. In effect, recombinant-DNA technology produces life forms that have never existed before. Should biotech industries be allowed to patent such forms, in exactly the same way as new inventions are patented? Or do organisms belong to us all?

Also, what are we to say about the deliberate release of genetically altered organisms into the environment? Is the threat that such organisms pose greater than the benefits they are likely to produce? We have already witnessed the great damage that can be done by pesticides and chemical pollution. Is there any way that we can avoid the potential damage that might be caused by genetically engineered organisms?

In the following three sections, we shall focus attention on the issues that are raised by the actual and potential use of genetic information. Our topics are these: genetic intervention (screening, counseling, and prenatal diagnosis), eugenics, and genetic research (therapy, technology, and biohazards).

GENETIC INTERVENTION: SCREENING, COUNSELING, AND DIAGNOSIS

Our genes play a major role in making us what we are. Biological programs of genetic information work amazingly well to produce normal, healthy individuals. But sometimes things can go wrong, and when they do, the results can be tragic.

Almost 2,000 human diseases have been identified as involving genetic factors. Some of the diseases are quite rare, whereas others are relatively common. Some are invariably fatal, whereas others are comparatively minor. Some respond well to treatment, whereas others do not.

The use of genetic information in predicting and diagnosing diseases has significantly increased during the last two decades. New scientific information, new medical techniques, and new social programs have all contributed to this increase.

Three approaches in particular have been adopted by the medical community as means of acquiring and employing genetic information related to diseases: genetic screening, genetic counseling, and prenatal genetic diagnosis. Each approach has been the source of significant ethical and social issues, but before examining the approaches and the problems they present, we need to consider what is usually meant in talking about genetic disease.

Genetic Disease

The concept of a "genetic" disease is far from being clear. Generally speaking, a genetic disease is one in which genes or the ways in which they are expressed are causally responsible for particular biochemical, cellular, or physiological defects. Rather than rely upon such a general definition, it is more useful for the purpose of understanding genetic diagnosis to consider some of the ways in which genes may play a role in producing diseases.

Gene Defects.   The program of information that is coded into DNA (the genetic material) may in some way be abnormal because of the occurrence of a mutation at some time or other. (That is, a particular gene may have been lost or damaged, or a new gene added.) Consequently, when the DNA blueprint is "read" and its instructions followed, the child that develops will have defects.

For example, a number of diseases (such as PKU and Tauri's disease) are the result of so-called "inborn errors of metabolism." The diseases are produced by the lack of a particular enzyme necessary for ordinary metabolic functioning. In each case, the genetic information required in coding for the production of

the enzyme is simply not present. The gene for the enzyme is missing.

A missing or defective gene may be due to a new mutation, but more often the condition has been inherited. It has been transmitted to the offspring through the genetic material contributed by its parents. Because defective genes can be passed on in this way, the diseases that they produce are themselves described as heritable. (Thus, PKU is a genetically transmissible disease.) The diseases follow regular patterns through generations, and tracing out those patterns has been one of the great accomplishments of modern biology and medicine.

Developmental Defects.   The biological development of a human being from a fertilized egg to a newborn child is an immensely complicated process. It involves an interplay between both genetic and environmental factors, and the possibility of the occurrence of errors is quite real.

Mistakes that result as part of the developmental process are ordinarily called "congenital." Such defects are not in the original blueprint (genes) but result either from genetic damage or from the reading of the blueprint. When either happens, the manufacture and assembly of materials required for normal fetal development are affected.

Radiation, drugs, chemicals, and nutritional deficiencies can all cause changes in an otherwise normal process. Also, biological disease agents, such as certain viruses, may intervene in development. They may alter the machinery of the cells, interfere with the formation of tissues, and defeat the carefully programmed processes that lead to a normal child.

Finally, factors internal to fetal development may also alter the process and lead to defects. The most common form of Down syndrome, for example, is known to be caused by a failure of chromosomes to separate normally. (However, the cause of this failure is at present unknown.) The result is a child that has failed to develop properly and displays physical anomalies and some degree of mental retardation.

Defects that occur during the developmental process are not themselves the results of inheritance, and they cannot be passed on to the next generation.

Genetic Carriers. Some diseases are produced only when an individual inherits both genes (alleles) for the disease from his or her parents. The parents themselves possess only one gene for the disease and generally show none of its symptoms. However, sometimes a parent may have symptoms of the same kind as are associated with the disease, although to a much lesser degree of severity.

In the metabolic disease PKU, for example, individuals who have inherited only one of the genes (that is, the offspring are heterozygous, rather than homozygous) may show a greater-than-normal level of phenylalanine in their blood. Such people are somewhat deficient in the enzyme required to metabolize this substance. The level of the substance may not be high enough to have caused any damage to them. Yet they are carriers of a gene that, when passed on with the same gene from the other parent, can cause the disease PKU in their offspring. (As we will see later, the same is also true for those who are carriers of sickle-cell trait.) The individual who receives both genes for PKU obviously has the disease, but what about the parents? Clearly, the point at which a condition becomes a disease is often a matter of degree.

Genetic Predisposition. It has been suggested that virtually every disease involves a genetic component in some way or other. Whether or not this is true, there is good evidence that hypertension, heart disease, various forms of cancer, and differential responses to environmental agents (such as sunlight, molds, or chemical pollutants) run in families,

and it has been established in a number of cases that the genetic makeup of particular individuals may predispose them to specific diseases.

At present, it is not generally possible to say just what genetic factor might be partly responsible for a particular disease, just what role it plays, or through what mechanism it expresses itself. It is important to keep in mind that predispositions are not themselves diseases. At best, they can be regarded only as causal conditions that, in conjunction with other conditions, can produce disease.

The action of genes in disease processes is much more complicated than we have been able to discuss here. Nevertheless, our general categories are adequate to allow us to talk about the use made of information in genetic diagnosis.

Genetic Screening

In 1962 Dr. Robert Guthrie of the State University of New York developed an automated procedure for testing the blood of newborn children for the disease PKU. Although a diagnostic for PKU had been available since 1934, it was time consuming and labor intensive. The Guthrie test made it practical to diagnose a large number of infants at a relatively low price.

PKU (phenylketonuria) is a serious metabolic disorder. Infants affected are deficient in the enzyme phenylalanine hydroxylase. Since the enzyme is necessary to convert the amino acid phenylalanine into tyrosine, as part of the normal metabolic process, a deficiency of the enzyme leads to a high concentration of phenylalanine in the infant's blood. The almost invariable result is severe mental retardation.

However, if the high level of phenylalanine in an infant's blood is detected very early, the infant can be put on a diet that is very low in that particular amino acid. Keeping children on the diet until they are around the age of six significantly reduces the severity of the retardation that is otherwise inescapable.

The availability of the Guthrie test and the prospects of saving newborn children from irreparable damage encouraged state legislatures to pass mandatory screening laws. Massachusetts passed the first such law in 1963, and by 1967 similar legislation had been adopted by forty-one states.

The term "genetic screening" is sometimes used to refer to any activity having to do with locating or advising people with genetically connected diseases. In our discussion, we will restrict the term's application and use it to refer only to public health programs that survey or test target populations with the aim of detecting individuals who are at risk of disease for genetic reasons.

The Massachusetts PKU law pointed the way for the development of public screening programs. PKU was the first disease tested for, but before long others were added to the list. For example, New York state law requires that an infant be tested for seven diseases. A number of public health programs now screen particular populations for such conditions as sickle-cell anemia, sickle-cell trait, metabolic disorders, hypothyroidism, and chromosome anomalies.

Although genetic screening is relatively new as a social program, the concept is historically connected with public health measures for the detection of communicable diseases like tuberculosis and syphilis. If an individual with such a disease is identified, then he or she can receive treatment. Furthermore, the diseased individual can be prevented from spreading the disease to other members of the population.

Similarly, it is possible to think of diseases with a genetic basis resembling contagious diseases. Individuals are affected, and they can pass on the disease. But with genetic diseases the potential spread is not horizontal through the population, but vertical through the generations.

In terms of this model, public health measures similar to the ones that continue to be so effective in the control of contagious diseases might be used to help bring genetic diseases under control. When screening locates an individual with a genetic disorder, then steps can be taken to ensure that he or she receives appropriate therapy. Furthermore, when carriers of genes that produce diseases are identified, then they can be warned about their chances of having children that are genetically defective. Thus, at least a limited amount of control over the spread of genetic disease can be exercised, and the suffering of at least some individuals can be reduced or eliminated.

The justification of laws mandating screening programs can be sought in the power and responsibility of government to see to the welfare of its citizens. Here again, the public health measures employed to control contagion might be looked to as a model. We do not permit the parents of a child to decide on their own whether the child should be vaccinated against smallpox. We believe that the society, operating through its government, has a duty to protect the child. Similarly, it can be argued that the society owes it to the child with PKU to see to it that the condition is discovered as quickly as possible so that appropriate treatment can be instituted.

Critics of screening programs have not been convinced that the contagious-disease model is at all appropriate in dealing with genetic diseases. Because the way in which genetic diseases are spread is so different, only a very small part of the population can be said to suffer any risk at all. By contrast, an epidemic of smallpox may threaten millions of people. Furthermore, some genetic screening programs do not have follow-up or counseling services attached to them, so often nothing is done that benefits the participants. By being told that they are the carriers of a genetic disease, people may be more harmed than helped by the programs.

In general, there are serious questions about whether the benefits of screening programs are sufficient to outweigh the liabilities. In particular, are screening programs so worthwhile that they justify the denial of individual choice entailed by required participation?

These issues and others related to them are easier to appreciate when they are considered in the context of particular kinds of screening programs. We will discuss briefly two programs that have been both important and controversial.

PKU Screening. As we pointed out earlier, screening for PKU was the first mass testing program to be mandated by state laws. It is generally agreed that it has also been the most successful program.

PKU is a relatively rare disease. It accounts for only about 0.8% of mentally retarded people who are institutionalized, and among the infants screened during a year in a state like Massachusetts, only three or four cases of PKU may be discovered. (The incidence is 5.4 per 100,000 infants.) Given this relatively low incidence of the disease, some critics have argued that the abrogation of the freedom of choice required by a mandatory program does not make the results worthwhile.

This is particularly true, they suggest, because of the difficulties with the testing procedure itself. The level of phenylalanine in the blood may fluctuate so that not all infants with a higher-than-normal level at the time of the test actually have PKU. If they are put on the restricted diet, then they may suffer consequences from the diet that are harmful to their health. Thus, in attempting to protect the health of some infants, a mandatory program may unintentionally injure the health of other infants.

Tests more refined than the Guthrie one are possible. However, their use increases considerably the cost of the screening program, even if they are employed only when the Guthrie test is positive for PKU. In social terms, then, the financial cost of preventing a few cases of PKU may be much greater than allowing the cases to remain undetected and untreated.

Furthermore, there are additional hidden social costs. Female infants who are successfully treated for PKU may grow into adults and have children of their own. Their children run a very high risk of being born with brain damage. The reason for this is not genetic but developmental. The uterine environment of PKU mothers is one high in phenylalanine, and in high concentrations it causes damage to the infant. Thus, one generation may be saved from mental retardation by screening only to cause mental retardation in the next.

Sickle-Cell. Sickle-cell disease is a group of genetic disorders involving the hemoglobin in red blood cells. Because of faulty hemoglobin, the cells assume a characteristic sickle shape and do not transport oxygen as well as normal red cells. They are also fragile and break apart more frequently. The result is anemia and, often, the blocking of blood vessels by fragments of ruptured cells. The pain can be excruciating, and infections in tissues that have broken down because of oxygen deprivation can be life threatening.

The disease occurs only in those who have inherited both alleles for the disease from their parents. (That is, the gene for the disease is recessive, and those who are homozygous for the gene are the ones who develop the disease.) Those with only one allele for the disease (that is, are heterozygous) are said to have sickle-cell trait. Sickle-cell disease may develop at infancy, or it may manifest itself later in life in painful and debilitating symptoms. Those with sickle-cell trait rarely show any of the more serious clinical symptoms.

In the United States, the disease is most common among African Americans, but it is also found among those of Mediterranean, Caribbean, and Central and South American ancestry. The trait is carried by about 7% to 9% of African Americans (2.5 million people), and the disease occurs in about 0.3% of the population. Many people with the disease are not severely affected and can live relatively normal lives. However, the disease may also be fatal, and at the present there is no cure for it. There is, however, a means of diagnosing it prenatally.

In 1970, a relatively inexpensive and accurate test for sickle-cell hemoglobin was developed, making it possible to identify the carriers of sickle-cell trait. This technological development combined with political pressures generated by rising consciousness among African Americans led to the passage of various state laws mandating sickle-cell screening. During 1971 and 1972, twelve states enacted sickle-cell legislation.

The results were socially disastrous. Some laws required African Americans who applied for a marriage license to undergo screening. Because the only way to reduce the incidence of the disease is for two carriers to avoid having children, many African Americans charged that the mandatory screening laws were a manifestation of a plan for genocide.

Medical reports that carriers of sickle-cell trait sometimes suffer from the pain and disability of sickling crises served as a new basis of discrimination. Some employers and insurance companies began to require tests of African American employees, and as a result some job possibilities were closed off to people with sickle-cell trait.

In 1972, Congress passed the National Sickle-Cell Anemia Control Act. In order to qualify for federal grants under the act, states were required to make sickle-cell screening voluntary, provide genetic counseling, and take steps to protect the confidentiality of participants. The most significant impact of the act was to force states to modify their laws to bring them into conformity with the act's requirements. In response, thirty-four states with sickle-cell screening laws now require universal screening.

The National Genetic Diseases Act, passed in 1976 and funded annually since then, provides testing and counseling for the diagnosis and treatment of a number of genetic diseases. The act further strengthens the commitment to voluntary participation and to guarantees of confidentiality.

The lesson learned from the public controversy over the first sickle-cell screening programs is that genetic information can be used in ways that are harmful to the interests of individuals. Furthermore, the information can be used as a basis for systematic discrimination.

In April 1993, an expert panel assembled by the Agency for Health Care and Policy (a part of the Public Health Service) recommended that all newborns, regardless of race, be screened for sickle-cell. In making its recommendations, the panel stressed that sickle-cell is not uniquely a disease of African Americans and that the general belief that it is can result in failing to see to it that people of non-African origin receive appropriate treatment.

Furthermore, the panel claimed, targeted screening of high-risk groups is not adequate to identify all infants with sickle-cell disease because it is not always possible to know an individual's racial heritage. Targeted screening, according to one study, may miss as many as 20% of cases.

What the panel did not point out was that one advantage of universal screening is that it permits individuals needing treatment to be identified without stigmatizing them just by requiring screening. However, whether having the disease or the trait becomes a social stigma is not a matter that can be resolved by an expert panel. It is something that must be dealt with by law, social policy, and public education.

Genetic Counseling

Much is known about the ways in which a number of genetic diseases are inherited. Ones like PKU, sickle-cell, and Tay-Sachs follow the laws of Mendelian transmission genetics. Accordingly, given the appropriate information, it is often possible to determine how likely it is that a particular couple will have a child with a certain disease.

Suppose, for example, that an African American couple is concerned about the possibility of having a child with sickle-cell disease. They will be tested to discover whether either or both of them are carriers of sickle-cell trait.

Sickle-cell disease occurs only when two recessive genes are both present—one inherited from the mother, one from the father. If only one of the parents is a carrier of the trait (is heterozygous), then no child will have the disease. However, if both parents are carriers of the trait, then the chances are one out of four that their child will have the disease. (This is determined simply by considering which combinations of the two genes belonging to each parent will produce a combination that is a homozygous recessive. The combination of Ss and Ss will produce ss in only 25% of the possible cases.)

Such information can be used to explain to potential parents the risks they might run in having children. But, as the case of sickle-cell disease illustrates quite well, it is often very difficult for individuals to know what to do with such information.

Is a 25% risk of having a child with sickle-cell disease sufficiently high that a couple ought to decide to have no children at all? Since the prenatal test for the disease is not easily available to everyone, this question is one that is best considered in advance of a pregnancy. If the couple is opposed to abortion, the question becomes especially crucial. Answering it is made more difficult by the fact that sickle-cell disease varies greatly in severity. A child with the disease may be virtually normal, or doomed to a short life filled with suffering. No one can say in advance of its birth which possibility is more likely.

It is generally agreed that the question of whether to have a child when a serious risk is involved is a decision that must be made by the couple. The counselor may provide information about the risk, and—just as important—the counselor may provide information about medical therapies that are available for a child born with a hereditary disease.

In diseases in which prenatal diagnosis is possible, the option of abortion may be open to potential parents. Here, too, the object of counseling is to see to it that the couple is educated in ways relevant to their needs.

Prenatal Genetic Diagnosis

A variety of new technological developments now make it possible to secure a great amount of information about the developing fetus while it is still in the uterus. Ultrasound, radiography, and fiber optics allow examination of soft-tissue and skeletal development. Anatomical abnormalities can be detected early enough to permit an abortion to be safely performed, if that is the decision of the woman carrying the fetus.

Yet the most common methods of prenatal diagnosis are amniocentesis and chorionic villus sampling (CVS), which involve direct cell studies. In amniocentesis, the amnion (the membrane surrounding the fetus) is punctured with a needle and some of the amniotic fluid is removed for study. The procedure cannot be usefully performed until fourteen to sixteen weeks into the pregnancy. Until that time, there is an inadequate amount of fluid. The risk to the woman and to the fetus from the procedure is relatively small, usually less than 1%. (The risk that the procedure will result in a miscarriage is about 1 in 200.)

Chorionic villus sampling involves retrieving hairlike villi cells from the developing placenta. The advantage of the test is that it can be employed six to ten weeks after conception. Although the procedure is as safe as amniocentesis, a 1994 study by the Centers for Disease Control found that infants whose mothers had undergone CVS from 1988 to 1992 had a 0.03% risk of missing or undeveloped fingers or toes. The normal risk is 0.05%. A later study questioned this finding and found reason to believe that the risk of fetal damage is greater than normal.

Amniocentesis came into wide use only in the early 1960s. At first, it was mostly restricted to testing fetuses in cases in which there was a risk of Rh incompatibility. When the mother lacks a group of blood proteins called the Rh (or Rhesus) factor, and the fetus has it, the immune system of the mother may produce antibodies against the fetus. The result for the fetus may be anemia, brain damage, and even death.

It was soon realized that additional information about the fetus could be gained from further analysis of the amniotic fluid and the fetal cells in it. The fluid can be chemically assayed, and the cells can be grown in cultures for study. An examination of the chromosomes from the cells will show whether there are any known abnormalities that are likely to cause serious physical or mental defects. Some metabolic disorders (such as Tay-Sachs disease) can be detected by chemical analysis of the amniotic fluid. However, some of the more common ones, such as PKU, cannot be diagnosed in this way. The presence or absence of the Y chromosome will also show the sex of the fetus. (Only males have a Y chromosome, so it is impossible to examine the chromosomes without discovering the sex of the fetus.)

Amniocentesis and CVS do have some hazards attached to them. Accordingly, it is not at all regarded as a routine procedure to be performed in every pregnancy. There must be some indication that the fetus is at risk from a genetic or developmental disorder. One indication is the age of the mother. Down syndrome is much more likely to occur in fetuses conceived in women over the age of thirty-five. Since the syndrome is produced by a chromosome abnormality, an examination of the chromosomes in the cells of the fetus can reveal the defect. (See the Introduction in Chapter 2 for a fuller discussion.)

A new test for Down syndrome employs a blood sample taken from the pregnant woman. The sample is examined for the presence of three fetal proteins. About sixteen to eighteen weeks after gestation, fetuses with the syndrome are known to produce abnormally small quantities of estriol and alpha fetoprotein and abnormally large amounts of chorionic gonadotropin. The levels of the proteins, plus such factors as the woman's age, can be used to determine the statistical probability of a child with the syndrome.

Genetic screening can also provide an indication of a need to perform amniocentesis. For example, Tay-Sachs disease is a metabolic disorder that occurs ten times as often among Jews originating in central and eastern Europe (the Ashkenazi) as in the general population. (The disease is invariably fatal and follows a sad course. An apparently normal child progressively develops blindness and brain damage, then dies at an early age.) Carriers of the Tay-Sachs gene can be identified by a blood test, and couples who are both carriers of the trait run a 25% risk of having a child with the disease. In such a case, there would be a good reason to perform amniocentesis.

Until recently, there was no way to use amniocentesis to determine whether a fetus was affected with a neural tube defect. (See Chapter 2 for a discussion of such defects as spina bifida.) The situation has now changed quite dramatically. The cause of neural tube defects is unknown, and they occur in about 1 out of every 500 births in the United States. They follow no known family patterns, have no known genetic basis, and cannot be predicted by genetic screening. They are also considered to be among the worst of all birth defects.

However, a test is available to indicate the presence of a neural tube defect in a developing fetus. In 1972, David H. Brock of Edinburgh discovered that there is an unusually large amount of the substance alpha fetoprotein (AFP) in the amniotic fluid taken from women who give birth to children with neural tube defects.

The blood test is not wholly reliable. Because the level of AFP varies in all women, the test produces many false positives. Also, women with twins or triplets have a level of AFP that is higher than that of women carrying a single fetus. Consequently, the blood test must be supplemented by ultrasound examination to determine whether only one fetus is present. If so, then amniocentesis is performed to get a more accurate measurement of the AFP present.

A recent controversy has developed as pregnant women younger than thirty-five with no particular risk factors in their background have increasingly sought prenatal screening. The women argue that even though their risk of having a child with a detectable genetic abnormality is small, the financial and emotional consequences of raising an impaired child are so serious that they should be allowed to take advantage of the technology available to minimize even the slight risk.

Opponents of this view point out that the risk of a miscarriage from a diagnostic procedure is around 1 in 200 while the risk of a woman below the age of forty having an impaired child is about 1 in 192. Hence, the chance of losing a normal child to miscarriage is greater than the chance of having an impaired child. Further, amniocentesis costs from $1000 to $2500 to perform, and the money spent on such unnecessary screening procedures contributes to the general rise in health-care costs.

Such replies are not found convincing by those advocating access to prenatal testing. Some see the issue as one of the right of a person to make choices affecting her body and her life. For some, the distress caused by a miscarriage is much less than that they would experience by having to raise an impaired child, but in any case, women should be the ones to decide what risks and burdens they are willing to bear. Such decisions should not be made unilaterally by physicians, hospitals, and health-policy planners.

Advocates of access to prenatal testing argue that, as far as increasing the cost of health care is concerned, when the costs of raising an impaired child are considered, the money spent on testing is insignificant. It costs about $100,000 to support a Down syndrome child during just the first year of life, and expenditures in the millions may be required to meet the needs of a severely impaired person over a lifetime. In addition, the potential emotional burden of the parents and other family members must be taken into account, even though they cannot be assigned a dollar cost.

Some women want the added feeling of control that prenatal screening can provide. The test can give them information that will put them in a position to make a decision about abortion, depending on the test results, or will provide them the peace of mind that comes from knowing that their pregnancy is proceeding with only a very small likelihood that the developing child suffers from a serious impairment. The general attitude is that the technology to secure relevant information exists, and it should be available to anyone who wants to make use of it.

Selective Abortion

In most cases in which prenatal diagnosis indicates that the fetus suffers from a genetic disorder or developmental defect, the only means of avoiding the birth of an impaired child is abortion.

Because those who go through the tests required to determine the condition of the fetus are concerned with having a child, abortion performed under such circumstances is called *selective*. That is, the woman decides to have an abortion to avoid producing a child with birth impairments, not just to avoid having a child.

Those who oppose abortion in principle (see Chapter 1) also oppose selective abortion. In the view of some, the fact that a child will be born impaired is in no way a justification for terminating the life of the fetus.

Those who are prepared to endorse abortion at all typically approve of selective abortion as an acceptable way of avoiding suffering. In their view, it is better that the potential person that is the fetus not become an actual person, full of pain, disease, and disability.

At this time, there is some hope that the painful decision between having an abortion or giving birth to an impaired child may someday be avoided. For example, C. Thomas Caskey has been working on a procedure for screening ova to determine whether a woman heterozygous for a disease has produced an ovum that contains the abnormal allele. The technique involves examining the first polar body, a group of cells containing half the genetic material that is dropped off the ovum during cell division.

Also, in the last few years, techniques of fetal surgery have been employed to correct certain abnormal physical conditions. Repairs to the heart, the insertion of shunts to drain off excess brain fluids, and the placement of tubes to inflate collapsed lungs are some of the intrauterine surgical procedures now being performed. It is believed that it may be possible to expose the fetus within the uterus, perform surgery, then close up the amnion again. This would make possible more extensive surgery for a greater variety of conditions.

The present hope is that as new surgical techniques for the treatment of fetuses are perfected and expanded, the need to rely on abortion to avoid the birth of impaired children will significantly decline. Of course, surgery cannot, even in principle, provide a remedy for a large number of hereditary disorders. Surgery can do nothing for a child with Tay-Sachs disease or PKU.

Helplessness in this regard is matched by another hope. Perhaps in future years pharmaceutical and biochemical therapies will be available to employ in cases involving missing enzymes. Or perhaps "gene surgery" will make it possible to insert the proper gene for manufacturing a needed biochemical into the DNA of the cells of a fetus.

Hopeful though we may be, the painful present reality is that for most children born with genetic diseases or defects very little can be done. Selective abortion continues to be the primary means to avoid the birth of a child known to be genetically or developmentally impaired.

Difficulties with Genetic Intervention

Genetic screening, counseling, and prenatal diagnosis present bright possibilities for those who believe in the importance of exercising control through rational planning and decision making. The prospect of avoiding the birth of children with crippling impairments is seen by them as one of the triumphs of contemporary medicine.

Furthermore, the additional prospect of wholly eliminating some genetic diseases by counseling and control holds the promise of an even better future. For example, if people who are carriers of diseases caused by a dominant gene (such as Huntington's) produced no children with the disease, the disease would soon disappear entirely. The gene causing the disease would simply not be passed on to the next generation.

A vision of a world without the misery caused by genetic defects is a motivating factor among those who are strong advocates of programs of genetic intervention. (See the section on eugenics in this chapter for more details.) The vision must have its appeal to all who are moved by compassion in the face of suffering. Yet whether or not one shares this vision and is prepared to use it as a basis for social action, there are serious ethical questions about genetic intervention that must be faced.

We have already mentioned some of the issues in connection with particular programs and procedures. We can now add some more general questions to that list, but it should be kept in mind that our discussion cannot be complete. The moral and social issues connected with genetic intervention are woven into a complicated fabric of personal and social considerations. We can merely sketch the main outline of the pattern.

1. Is there a right to have children who are likely to be impaired? Suppose that a woman is informed, after an alphafeto-protein (AFP) test and amniocentesis, that the child she is carrying will be born with a neural tube defect. Does she have the right to refuse an abortion and have the child anyway?

    Those who are opposed to all abortion on the grounds of natural law would favor the woman's having the child. By contrast, a utilitarian might well argue that the decision would be wrong. The amount of suffering the potential child might be expected to undergo outweighs any parental loss. For different reasons, a Kantian might endorse this same point of view. Even if we assume the fetus is a person, a Kantian might argue that we are obliged to prevent its suffering. (For more details of these and similar arguments, see Chapters 1 and 2.)

    Suppose we decide that a woman does have a right to have a child that is almost certain to be impaired. If so, then is the society obligated to bear the expense of caring for such a child? On the natural law view, the answer is almost certainly yes. The child, impaired or not, is a human person and, as such, is entitled to the support and protection of the society. If we agree that the impaired child is a person, then he or she is also a disadvantaged person. Thus, an argument based on Rawls's principles of justice would support the view that the child is entitled to social support. (Again, see Chapter 2 for more detail.)

2. Is society justified in requiring that people submit to genetic screening, counseling, and prenatal diagnosis? Children born with genetic diseases and defects require the expenditure of large amounts of public funds. Mandatory diagnosis need not be coupled with mandatory abortion or abstention from bearing chil-dren. (A related question is whether society ought to make available genetic testing to all who wish it, regardless of their ability to pay.)

    On utilitarian grounds, it might be argued that society has a legitimate interest in seeing to it that, no matter what people ultimately decide, they should at least have the information about the likelihood that they will produce an impaired child.

    If this view is adopted, then a number of specific medically related questions become relevant. For example, who should be screened? It is impractical and unnecessary to screen everyone. Why should we screen schoolchildren or prisoners, those who are sterile, or those past the age of childbearing?

    This is closely connected with a second question: What should people be screened for? Should everyone be screened for Tay-Sachs disease, even though it is the Jewish population that is most at risk? Should everyone be screened for sickle-cell trait, even though it is primarily the African American population that is at risk?

    Those who accept the contagious-disease model of genetic screening frequently defend it on the utilitarian grounds that screening promotes the general social welfare. However, one might argue that screening can also be justified on deontological grounds. It could be claimed that we owe it to developing fetuses, regarded as persons, to see to it that they receive the opportunity for the most effective treatment. For example, it might be said that we have an obligation to provide a PKU child with the immediate therapy required to save him or her from severe mental retardation. The restriction of the autonomy of individuals by requiring screening might be regarded as justified by this obligation. If screening is voluntary, then the welfare of the child is made to depend on ignorance and accidental opportunity.

3. Do physicians have an obligation to inform their patients who are prospective parents about the kinds of genetic tests that are available? A study of one population of women screened for Tay-Sachs disease showed that none had sought testing on the recommendation of her physician.

If the autonomy of the individual is to be preserved, then it seems clear that it is the duty of a physician to inform patients about genetic testing. A physician who disapproves of abortion might be reluctant to inform patients about tests that might encourage them to seek an abortion. Nevertheless, to the extent that abortion is a moral decision, it is a decision properly made by the individual, not by someone acting paternalistically in her behalf.

The duty of a physician to inform patients about the possibility of genetic tests seems quite straightforward. Yet the issue becomes more complicated in light of the next question about truth telling.

4. Do patients have a right to be informed of all of the results of a genetic test? Ethical theories that are based on respect for the autonomy of the individual (such as Kant's and Ross's) suggest that patients are entitled to know what has been learned from the tests.

But what if the test reveals that the fetus has only a quite minor genetically transmissible disease? Should the physician run the risk of the patient's deciding to have an abortion merely because she is committed to the ideal of a "perfect" baby? Is such a decision really one for the physician to make?

Furthermore, what about the matter of sex determination? Screening tests that involve chromosome examination also reveal the sex of the fetus. Are prospective parents entitled to know this information? When abortion is elective, it is quite possible for the woman to decide to have an abortion to avoid giving birth to a child of a particular sex.

It might be argued on both utilitarian and deontological grounds that the sex of the fetus is information that is not relevant to the health of the fetus. Accordingly, the physician is under no obligation to reveal the sex of the fetus. Indeed, the physician may be under an obligation *not* to reveal the sex of the fetus in order to avoid the possibility of its destruction for a basically trivial reason. But, again, is this really a decision for the physician?

5. Should public funds be used to pay for genetic tests when an individual is unable to pay? This is a question that holders of various ethical theories may not be prepared to answer in a simple yes-or-no fashion. Those who oppose abortion on natural law grounds might advocate providing funds only for genetic screening and counseling. That is, they might favor providing prospective parents with information that they might then use to decide whether to refrain from having children. Yet opponents of abortion might be against spending public money on tests that might encourage the use of abortion to prevent the birth of a defective child.

The views of Rawls and of utilitarianism might well support the use of public funds for genetic testing as part of a more general program of providing for health-care needs. Whether genetic testing programs are funded and what the level of funding might be would then depend on judgments about their expected value in comparison with other health-care programs.

A present ethical and social difficulty is caused by the fact that federal funds may be employed to pay for genetic screening and testing, yet federal money cannot legally be used to pay for abortions. Consequently, it is possible for a woman to discover that she is carrying a fetus with a serious genetic disease, wish to have an abortion, yet lack the financial means to pay for it.

Issues about the confidentiality of test results, informed consent, the use of genetic testing to gather epidemiological information, and a variety of other matters might be mentioned here in connection with genetic intervention. Those that have been discussed are sufficient to indicate that the difficulties presented by genetic intervention are at least as numerous as the benefits it promises.

EUGENICS

Like other organisms, we are the products of millions of years of evolutionary development. This process has taken place through the operation of natural selection on randomly produced genetic mutations. Individual organisms are successful in an evolutionary sense when they contribute a number of genes to the gene pool of their species proportionately greater than the number contributed by others. Most often, this means that the evolutionarily successful individuals are those with the largest number of offspring. These are the individuals favored by natural selection. That is, they possess the genes for certain properties that are favored by existing environmental factors. (This favoring of properties is natural selection.) The genes of "favored" individuals will occur with greater frequency than the genes of others in the next generation. If the same environmental factors continue to operate, these genes will spread through the entire population.

Thanks to Darwin and the evolutionary biologists who have come after him, we now have a sound understanding of the evolutionary process and the mechanisms by which it operates. This understanding puts us in a position to intervene in the process. That is, we no longer have to consider ourselves subject to the blind working of natural selection. If we choose to do so, we can modify the course of human evolution. As the evolutionary biologist Theodosius Dobzhansky expressed the point: "Evolution need no longer be a destiny imposed from without; it may conceivably be controlled by man, in accordance with his wisdom and values."

Those who advocate eugenics accept just this point of view. They favor social policies and practices that, over time, offer the possibility of increasing the number of genes in the human population responsible for producing or improving traits (for example, intelligence) that we value.

The aim of increasing the number of favorable genes in the human population is called *positive eugenics*. By contrast, *negative eugenics* aims at decreasing the number of undesirable or harmful genes. Those who advocate negative eugenics are generally most interested in eliminating or reducing the number of those genes that are responsible for various kinds of birth defects and genetic diseases.

Both positive and negative eugenics require instituting some sort of control over human reproduction. Several kinds of policies and procedures have been advocated, and we will discuss a few of the possibilities.

Genetic Intervention

The discussion in the preceding section of genetic screening, counseling, and prenatal genetic diagnosis makes it unnecessary to repeat here information about the possibilities and procedures we currently possess for predicting and diagnosing genetic diseases. It is enough to recall that, given information about the genetic makeup and background of potential parents, a number of genetic diseases can be predicted with a certain degree of probability as likely to occur in a child of such parents. This is true of such diseases as PKU, sickle-cell anemia, hemophilia, Huntington's disease, and Tay-Sachs disease.

When genetic information is not adequate to serve as a basis for a reliable prediction, then information about the developing fetus can often be obtained by employing one of several procedures of prenatal diagnosis. Even when genetic information is adequate for a statistical prediction, whether the fetus has a certain disease can be determined by prenatal testing. Thus, in addition to the disorders named above, prenatal tests can be performed for such other defects as neural tube anomalies and Down syndrome.

A proponent of negative eugenics might advocate that a screening process for all or some currently detectable genetic diseases be required by law. When the probability of the occurrence of a disease is high (whatever figure that might be taken to be), then the potential parents might be encouraged to have no children. Indeed, the law might *require* that such a couple abstain from having children and prescribe a penalty for going against the decision of the screening board. If those carrying the genes for some genetic diseases could be prevented from having children, then over time the incidence of the diseases in the population would decrease. In some cases when the disease is the result of a dominant gene (as it is in Huntington's disease), the disease would eventually disappear.

When the disease is a kind that can be detected only after a child is conceived, then if the results of a prenatal diagnosis show that the developing fetus has a heritable disease, an abortion might be encouraged. Short of a law requiring abortion, a variety of social policies might be adopted to make abortion an attractive option. (For example, the cost of an abortion might be paid for by government funds, or women choosing abortion might be financially rewarded.) The aborting of a fetus found to have a transmissible genetic disease

would not only prevent the birth of an impaired infant, but it would also eliminate a potential carrier of the genes responsible for the disease.

Similarly, the sterilization of people identified as having genes that are responsible for certain kinds of physical or mental impairments would prevent them from passing on these defective genes. In this way, the number of such genes in the population would be proportionately reduced.

Currently, there are no state or federal laws that make it a crime for couples who are genetically a bad risk to have children. Yet a tendency toward more genetic regulation may be developing. As we mentioned earlier, several states now require screening of newborn infants in order to detect the presence of certain genetic diseases that respond well to early treatment. Also, genetic screening programs are frequently offered in communities to encourage people to seek information about particular diseases.

At present, genetic screening (for adults) and genetic counseling are voluntary. They aim at providing information and then leave reproductive decisions up to the individuals concerned. Most often, they are directed toward the immediate goal of decreasing the number of children suffering from birth defects and genetic diseases. Yet genetic screening and counseling might also be viewed as a part of negative eugenics. To the extent that they discourage the birth of children carrying deleterious genes, they also discourage the spread of those genes in the human population.

Obviously, screening programs and genetic counseling might also be used to promote *positive* eugenics. Individuals possessing genes for traits that society values might be encouraged to have large numbers of children. In this way, genes for traits that are considered worthwhile would increase in relative frequency within the population.

There are no programs of positive eugenics. Yet it is easy to imagine a variety of social and economic incentives (for example, government bonuses) that might be introduced as part of a plan to promote the spread of certain genes by rewarding favored groups of people for having children.

Use of Desirable Germ Cells

Artificial insemination by the use of stored sperm is already a reality. The implantation of a donor ovum in the wall of the uterus is also possible, and we have developed a biotechnology that permits the long-term storage of ova. Thus, a man or woman might choose to have a child by selecting stored germ cells contributed by individuals possessing traits that they admire. Sperm banks and ova banks would then provide a way for the human population to improve itself—that is, to increase the number of genes for desirable traits in the population. (See Chapter 8.)

Difficulties with Eugenics

Critics have been quick to point out that the proposals we have discussed suffer from serious drawbacks. First, negative eugenics is not likely to make much of a change in the species as a whole. Most hereditary diseases are genetically recessive and so occur only when both parents possess the same defective gene. Even though a particular couple might be counseled (or required) not to have children, the gene will still be widespread in the population among people we would consider wholly normal. For a similar reason, sterilization would have few long-range effects. Also, there is the uncomfortable fact that geneticists have estimated that, on the average, everyone carries recessive genes for five genetic defects or diseases. Genetic counseling may help individuals, but negative eugenics does not promise much for the population as a whole.

Positive eugenics can promise little more. It is difficult to imagine that we would all agree on what traits we would like to see increased in the human species. But even if we could, it is not clear that we would be able to increase them in any simple way. For one thing, we have little understanding of the genetic basis of traits such as "intelligence," "honesty," "musical ability," and so on. It is clear, however, that there is not just a single gene for them, and the chances are that they are the result of a complicated interplay between genetic endowment and social and environmental factors. Consequently, the task of increasing their frequency is quite different from that of, say, increasing the frequency of short-horned cattle. Furthermore, the desirable traits may well be accompanied by less desirable traits, and we may not be able to increase the first without also increasing the second.

Quite apart from biological objections, eugenics also raises questions of a moral kind. Have we indeed become the "business manager of evolution," as Julian Huxley once claimed? If so, then do we have a responsibility to future generations to improve the human race? Would this responsibility justify our requiring genetic screening? Would it justify our establishing a program of positive eugenics? Affirmative answers to these questions may generate conflicts with notions of individual dignity and self-determination.

Of the ethical theories we have discussed, it seems likely that only utilitarianism might be construed as favoring a program of positive eugenics. The possibility of increasing the frequency of desirable traits in the human species might, in terms of the principle of utility, justify present restrictions on reproduction. It is not clear that this is so, however. The goal of an improved society or human race might well be regarded as too distant and uncertain to warrant the imposition of restrictions that would increase current human unhappiness.

As far as negative eugenics is concerned, the principle of utility could certainly be appealed to in order to justify social policies that would discourage or prohibit parents who are serious genetic risks from having children. The aim here need not be the remote one of improving the human population but the more immediate one of preventing the increase in sorrows and pains that would be caused by an impaired child.

Natural law doctrines of Roman Catholicism forbid abortion (see the Introduction in Chapter 1 and the introductory chapter) and sterilization. Thus, these means of practicing negative eugenics are ruled out. Also, the natural law view that reproduction is a natural function of sexual intercourse seems, at least prima facie, to rule out negative eugenics as a deliberate policy altogether. It could be argued, however, that voluntary abstinence from sexual intercourse or some other acceptable form of birth control would be a legitimate means of practicing negative eugenics.

Ross's prima facie duty of causing no harm might be invoked to justify negative eugenics. If there is good reason to believe that a child is going to suffer from a genetic disease, then we may have a duty to prevent the child from being born. Similarly, Rawls's theory might permit a policy that would require the practice of some form of negative eugenics for the benefit of its immediate effects of preventing suffering and sparing all the cost of supporting those with genetic diseases.

It is difficult to determine what sort of answer to the question of negative eugenics might be offered in terms of Kant's ethical principles. Laws regulating conception or forced abortion or sterilization might well be considered to violate the dignity and autonomy of individuals. Yet moral agents as rational decision makers require information on which to base their decisions. Thus, programs of genetic screening and counseling might be considered to be legitimate.

GENETIC RESEARCH, THERAPY, AND TECHNOLOGY

By replacing natural selection with artificial selection that is directly under our control, we can, over time, alter the genetic composition of populations of organisms. This has been done for thousands of years by animal and plant breeders, and our improved understanding of genetics allows us to do it today with more effectiveness and certainty of results. Yet such alterations require long periods of time. Molecular genetics holds out the possibility of immediate changes. Bacteria continue to be the major organisms of research, but genetic technology is already being applied to plants and animals. The same technology is now on the verge of being applied to humans.

Recombinant DNA

The information required for genetic inheritance is coded in the two intertwined strands of DNA (deoxyribonucleic acid) found in plant and animal cells—the double helix. The strands are made up of four kinds of chemical units called nucleotides, and the genetic message is determined by the particular sequence of nucleotides. Three nucleotides in sequence form a triplet codon. Each codon directs the synthesis of a particular amino acid and determines the place that it will occupy in making up a protein molecule. Since virtually all properties of organisms (enzymes, organs, eye color, and so on) depend on proteins, the processes directed by DNA are fundamental.

Alterations in the nucleotide sequence in DNA occur naturally as mutations—random changes introduced as "copying errors" when DNA replicates (reproduces) itself. These alterations result in changes in the properties of organisms since the properties are under the control of DNA. Much research in current molecular genetics is directed toward bringing about desired changes by deliberately manipulating the nucleotide sequences in DNA. The major steps toward this goal have involved the development of techniques for recombining DNA from different sources.

The recombinant process begins by taking proteins known as restriction enzymes from bacteria and mixing them with DNA that has been removed from cells. These enzymes cut open the DNA strands at particular nucleotide locations. DNA nucleotide sequences from another source can then be added, and certain of these will attach to the cut ends. Thus, DNA from distinct sources can be recombined to form a single molecule.

This recombinant DNA can then be made to enter a host cell. The organism almost universally employed as a host is the one-celled bacterium *E. coli* that inhabits the human intestine by the billions. In addition to the DNA that makes up the chromosome of the cell, *E. coli* also possesses small circular strands of DNA known as plasmids. The DNA of a plasmid can be recombined with the DNA of a foreign source and returned to the cell. There the plasmid will start replicating again. It will make copies of the original nucleotides *plus* copies of the added segments. Thus, a strain of bacteria can be produced that will make limitless numbers of copies of the foreign DNA.

The obvious question is, what benefits might this recombinant technique produce? It might lead to the understanding and control of the molecular processes involved in such diseases as cancer, diabetes, hemophilia. It might provide more effective treatment for metabolic diseases like PKU and Tay-Sachs.

From the more commercial standpoint, recombinant-DNA technology might lead to the development of new breeds of plants that are able to utilize nitrogen from the air and thus require no fertilizer. Specially engineered bacteria might be used to clean up the environment by breaking down currently nonbiodegradable compounds like DDT and Agent Orange. Other bacteria might be used to convert petroleum into other useful chemical compounds, including plastics.

The most immediate benefits of recombinant DNA are likely to be the use of modified bacteria as chemical factories to produce biological materials of medical importance. In addition, the transplanting of human genes into nonhuman embryos promises to lead to an understanding of the ways in which genes can be made to reproduce themselves and be passed on to succeeding generations.

Just a glance at a few of the many recent research developments is enough to gain an appreciation of the powerful potential of genetic technology:

- Hypopituitary dwarfism is a condition caused by a deficiency in growth hormone. The hormone itself consists of molecules that are too large and structurally complex to synthesize in the laboratory. In 1979 researchers in California employed recombinant-DNA technology to induce bacteria to produce the hormone. It is now available in quantities large enough to be used in medical therapy.

- In 1982 Dr. John D. Baxter and his associates developed a bacterial strain capable of producing endorphin. Because endorphin is a natural opiate, the hope is that it can be used as an effective substitute for such addictive drugs as morphine.

- Modified bacteria now produce human insulin in quantities large enough to meet the need of diabetics who are allergic to swine or bovine insulin.

- Genetically engineered bacteria have also been used to produce a vaccine against hepatitis B and against a strain of genital herpes. The clotting factor employed in the treatment of hemophilia has been similarly produced.

- In 1985 the Cetus Corporation was awarded the first patent for an altered form of the protein interleukin-2. Il-2 activates the immune system and shows promise in the treatment of some forms of cancer. It occurs naturally but in very small amounts; thus, it was not possible to test its effectiveness until it was produced in quantity by genetically altered bacteria.

- Researchers have inserted human genes into plants and induced the plants to produce large quantities of medically significant proteins. Antibodies, serum albumin, enkephalins, hormones, and growth factors are among those currently produced.

- Substances occurring in the human body in minute amounts that can be important as drugs when available are now being produced in large quantities by genetic engineering. For example, tissue plasminogen activator, which is produced in blood vessels, dissolves blood clots and is a useful drug in the treatment of heart attacks. Also, blood factor-8, a clotting agent, may improve the lives and health of hemophiliacs by reducing their chances of viral infection from donated blood.

Gene Therapy

The rapid advancement in genetic knowledge during the last few years makes it seem likely to most experts that the use of recombinant-DNA techniques as part of a program of medical therapy is now virtually at hand. Therapy in which a needed gene is inserted has already been employed in an experimental way. (See the Case Presentation for more details.)

The ability to alter the basic machinery of life to correct its malfunctioning is surely the most powerful form of therapy imaginable. The immediate prospects for gene therapy are most likely to involve the relatively modest, but very dramatic, task of splicing into the DNA of body cells a gene that controls the production of a specific substance. Diseases such as PKU that are caused by the absence of a particular enzyme might then be corrected by inducing the patient's cells to manufacture that enzyme. Some genetic diseases involve dozens or even hundreds of genes, and often the mechanism by which the genes produce the disease is not understood. Consequently, it is likely to be a long while before most genetic

diseases can be treated by gene therapy. However, the treatment of single-gene disorders is a most promising possibility.

Few special moral or social issues are raised by the use of gene therapy as long as the cells modified are somatic (body) sells. However, the issues change significantly with the prospect of modifying human germ-line (sex) cells. Somatic-cell changes cannot be inherited, but germ-line cell changes can be. This possibility holds out the benign prospect of eliminating forever a number of sex-linked diseases. However, it also points toward the more frightening outcome of "engineering" human beings to produce people who meet our predetermined specification. We will discuss this possibility further below. Here it is relevant only to note that the technology that would be required to alter the sex cells of human beings does not exist at present.

Biohazards

The issues connected with gene therapy and screening may be overshadowed in significance by questions concerning dangers inherent in the development of genetic technology and in the release of its products into the natural environment.

The question of whether recombinant-DNA research ought to be halted is no longer a serious social issue. However, this has not always been so. In 1974 a group of scientists active in such research issued a report recommending that scientists be asked to suspend work voluntarily on recombinant experiments involving tumor viruses, increased drug resistance in harmful bacteria, and increased toxicity in bacteria. The discussion that ensued resulted in the formulation of guidelines by the National Institutes of Health to regulate research.

The major concern initially was that recombinant techniques might be employed to produce essentially new organisms that would threaten human health. Suppose that the nucleotide sequence for manufacturing a lethal toxin were combined with the DNA of *E. coli.* This currently harmless inhabitant of the intestine might be transformed into a deadly organism that would threaten the existence of the entire human population. Or perhaps a nucleotide sequence that transforms normal cells into cancerous ones might trigger an epidemic of cancer. Without a thorough knowledge of the molecular mechanisms involved, little could be done to halt the outbreak. Indeed it is not even clear what would happen if an insulin-producing strain of bacteria spread through the human population.

These and similar dangers prompted some critics to call for an end to all genetic-engineering research. However, almost two decades of recombinant-DNA research have passed without the occurrence of any biological catastrophes. Most observers regard this as sufficient proof of the essential safety of the research. Yet, in the view of others, the fact that no catastrophes have yet occurred must not be allowed to give us a false sense of security. Almost no one advocates that the research be abandoned, but several molecular geneticists have argued that the very fact that we still do not know enough to estimate the risks involved with a high degree of certainty is a good reason for continuing to control it severely.

The release of genetically altered organisms into the environment still remains a focus of concern, more so than does research itself. In 1988 health officials in Argentina concluded that several farm workers had become infected with a genetically altered vaccinia virus containing a gene from the rabies virus. The modified virus was experimentally injected into cattle to stimulate the production of antibodies against rabies.

Although American experts expressed skepticism about the possibility of the altered virus affecting humans, critics pointed out that the incident indicates the ways in which researchers are beginning to turn to overseas

trials to escape having to comply with protective regulation. Also, a number of other incidents show how easy it is to skirt the complex regulatory process that is supposed to provide protection from the products of genetically altered organisms.

The concern of critics is based on the possibility that such organisms may multiply, mutate, and cause unforeseeable damage. Most animal viruses do not infect people, but an altered virus may. Also, it almost certainly could spread to other animals, both domestic and wild. The virus might act in ways that would cause disease in other animals or make them more susceptible to numerous diseases.

In response to a variety of incidents, the Environmental Protection Agency has tightened standards governing environmental testing of genetically altered organisms. Very few critics are calling for abandoning the use of such organisms, for they hold too much promise as vaccines, growth enhancers, and pesticides. However, within the scientific community there is a widespread attitude of caution and a demand for rigorous testing.

Quite apart from the possible hazards associated with genetic engineering, many people continue to be uneasy about the direction of research. A number of biotechnological possibilities are on the horizon, some of which might have far-reaching consequences. As we discussed earlier, gene surgery offers more possibilities than just medical therapy. If undesirable DNA segments can be sliced out of the genetic code and replaced with others, then this would permit the "engineering" of human beings to an extent and to a degree of precision never before imagined. The eugenic dream of producing people to match an ideal model would be a reality. What would happen then to such traditional and moral values as autonomy, diversity, and the inherent worth of the individual?

The same techniques employed to manufacture the ideal person might also be used to design others to fit special needs. It is not difficult to imagine using genetic surgery to engineer a subhuman race to serve as a slave class for the society. The scenarios of cautionary science fiction might be acted out in our own future.

In addition, the biological technique of asexual reproduction known as *cloning* might be employed to produce individuals that are exact genetic copies of the DNA donor. A step toward making the cloning of humans a practical reality was taken in 1993 when Jerry Hall and Robert Stillman took seventeen fertilized (but defective) human eggs, separated the blastomeres and coated them with artificial zona pellucida, and placed them in nutrient solutions. The outcome was the production of forty-eight new embryos, all of which were genetically identical.

The process used by Hall and Stillman was, technically speaking, not really cloning, which would have required taking tissue from a completely developed organism, extracting the DNA, then growing an embryo from it. Even so, the process of "twinning" that was employed shows that it would take very little more technically to employ the techniques of in vitro fertilization to produce a number of genetically identical individuals. Or someone might use the technology to have several children that are all copies of one another. If the embryos were stored, some of these might be born years apart.

Consider one last possibility. Virtually new organisms might be produced by splicing together DNA from two or more sources. Thus, the world might be faced with creatures of an unknown and unpredictable nature that are not the product of the natural processes of evolution.

It is little wonder that molecular biologists have become concerned about the nature and direction of their research. As Robert Sinsheimer of the California Institute of Technology says, "Biologists have become, without wanting it, custodians of great and terrible power." Such power in the hands of a tyrannical government could be used with irresistible effectiveness to control its subjects. Societies might create a race of semihuman slaves or armies of genetically engineered soldiers. The possibilities are both fantastic and unlimited.

Difficulties with Genetic Research, Therapy, and Technology

The risks involved in gene therapy are not unique ones. In most respects, they exactly parallel those involved in any new medical treatment. Accordingly, it seems reasonable to believe that the same standards of safety and the same consideration for the welfare of the patient that are relevant to the use of other forms of therapy should be regarded as relevant to gene therapy.

The principles of Kant and Ross would suggest that the autonomy of the individual be respected and preserved. In particular, the individual ought not to be viewed as an experimental case for testing out a procedure that may later prove helpful. If the person is well enough to be adequately informed and to give consent, and there is no alternative therapy likely to be effective, it would be morally legitimate for the patient to be given the opportunity to benefit from the therapy. However, if the hazards are great or if they are completely unknown, then it is doubtful whether the patient would be justified in risking his or her life.

By contrast, on utilitarian principles, if the outcome of gene therapy can be reasonably expected to produce more benefit than harm, then the use of the therapy might be considered justifiable. If we assume that a person is likely to die anyway, then that in itself might be enough to warrant the use of the therapy. In addition, since each case treated is likely to contribute to increased understanding and to benefit others, this tends to support the use of gene therapy, even in cases in which it is of doubtful help to the individual. (See Chapter 6 for a fuller discussion.)

Genetic research and its associated technology present issues that are much greater in scope than those raised by gene therapy. They are issues that require us to decide what sort of society we want to live in.

Very few responsible people currently believe that we should call a halt to research in molecular genetics and forgo the increase in power and understanding that it is likely to bring. However, the possibilities of genetic engineering include ones that are frightening and threatening, ones that could wholly alter our society and destroy some of our most cherished values. These are the possibilities that require that we make decisions about whether or to what extent we want to see them realized.

The natural law view of ethics would not, in general, support any policy of restricting scientific inquiry in the area of molecular genetics. For on this view there is a natural inclination (and hence a natural duty) to seek knowledge. Yet certain types of experiments and gene engineering would be ruled out. Those that aim at altering human beings or creating new species from mixed DNA are most likely to be considered to violate the natural order. On the Roman Catholic view, such a violation of nature would run counter to God's plan and purpose and so be immoral.

The principle of utility might be invoked to justify limiting, directing, or even ending research in molecular genetics. If research or its results are more likely to bring about more harm than benefit, then regulation would be called for. Yet if the promise of relieving misery or increasing well-being is great, then some risk that we might also acquire dangerous knowledge in the process might be acceptable. On the utilitarian view, knowledge may be recognized as a good, but it is only one good among others. Possessing the knowledge to alter human beings in accordance with a eugenic ideal or to create new species means that we have to make a decision about whether doing so would result in an overall benefit. That judgment will then be reflected in our social policies and practices. Such an analysis also seems to be consistent with Rawls's principles. There is not, for Rawls, an absolute right to seek knowledge, nor is there any obligation to employ knowledge that is available. Restriction might well be imposed on scientific research and on the technological possibilities it presents if the good of society seems to demand it.

Genetics and Reproductive Risk: Can Having Children Be Immoral?

Laura M. Purdy

Laura M. Purdy argues that it can sometimes be immoral to have children when we know (or should know) that our offspring may have a genetic disease. Purdy supports this claim by arguing for three interconnected theses: (1) we have a duty to provide every child with a normal opportunity for a good life; (2) we do not harm possible children by preventing them from existing; and (3) the duty to provide a normal opportunity for a good life takes precedence over a potential parent's right to reproduce.

Purdy maintains that this duty not to reproduce when there is a high likelihood of passing on a debilitating genetic disease applies most strictly to those who are unwilling to have prenatal testing and selective abortions. If a couple is willing to have the potential child tested for the presence of the genetic disease and to abort if that test is positive, Purdy argues it is permissible for them to attempt to conceive genetically related offspring. But for those who are unwilling to have selective abortions, Purdy maintains there is a strong moral duty for them not to conceive children in some cases.

Is it morally permissible for me to have children?[1] A decision to procreate is surely one of the most significant decisions a person can make. So it would seem that it ought not to be made without some moral soul-searching.

There are many reasons why one might hesitate to bring children into this world if one is concerned about their welfare. Some are rather general, like the deteriorating environment or the prospect of poverty. Others have a narrower focus, like continuing civil war in Ireland, or the lack of essential social support for childrearing persons in the United States. Still others may be relevant only to individuals at risk of passing harmful diseases to their offspring.

There are many causes of misery in this world, and most of them are unrelated to genetic disease. In the general scheme of things, human misery is most efficiently reduced by concentrating on noxious social and political arrangements. Nonetheless, we shouldn't ignore preventable harm just because it is confined to a relatively small corner of life. So the question arises: can it be wrong to have a child because of genetic risk factors?[2]

Unsurprisingly, most of the debate about this issue has focused on prenatal screening and abortion: much useful information about a given fetus can be made available by recourse to prenatal testing. This fact has meant that moral questions about reproduction have become entwined with abortion politics, to the detriment of both. The abortion connection has made it especially difficult to think about whether it is wrong to prevent a child from coming into being since doing so might involve what many people see as wrongful killing; yet there is no necessary link between the two.

Clearly, the existence of genetically compromised children can be prevented not only by aborting already existing fetuses but also by preventing conception in the first place. Worse yet, many discussions simply assume a particular view of abortion, without any recognition of other possible positions and the difference they make in how people understand the issues. For example, those who object to aborting fetuses with genetic problems often argue that doing so would undermine our conviction that all humans are in some important sense equal.[3] However, this position rests on the assumption that conception marks the point at which humans are endowed with a right to life. So aborting fetuses with genetic problems looks morally the same as killing "imperfect" people without their consent.

This position raises two separate issues. One pertains to the legitimacy of different views on abortion. Despite the conviction of many abortion activists to the contrary, I believe that ethically respectable views can be found on different sides of the debate, including one that sees fetuses as developing humans without any serious moral claim on continued life. There is no space here to address the details, and doing so would be once again to fall into the trap of letting the abortion question swallow up all others. Fortunately, this issue need not be resolved here. However, opponents of abortion need to face the fact that many thoughtful individuals do not *see* fetuses as moral persons. It follows that their reasoning process and hence the implications of their decisions are radically different from those envisioned by opponents of prenatal screening and abortion. So where the latter see genetic abortion as murdering people who just don't measure up, the former see it as a way to prevent the development of persons who are more likely to live miserable lives. This is consistent with a world view that values persons equally and holds that each deserves high quality life. Some of those who object to genetic abortion appear to be oblivious to these psychological and logical facts. It follows that the nightmare scenarios they paint for us are beside the point: many people simply do not share the assumptions that make them plausible.

How are these points relevant to my discussion? My primary concern here is to argue that conception can sometimes be morally wrong on grounds of genetic risk, although this judgment will not apply to those who accept the moral legitimacy of abortion and are willing to employ prenatal screening and selective abortion. If my case is solid, then those who oppose abortion must be especially careful not to conceive in certain cases, as they are, of course, free to follow their conscience about abortion. Those like myself who do not see abortion as murder have more ways to prevent birth.

Huntington's Disease

There is always some possibility that reproduction will result in a child with a serious disease or handicap. Genetic counselors can help individuals determine whether they are at unusual risk and, as the Human Genome Project rolls on, their knowledge will increase by quantum leaps. As this knowledge becomes available, I believe we ought to use it to determine whether possible children are at risk *before* they are conceived.

I want in this paper to defend the thesis that it is morally wrong to reproduce when we know there is a high risk of transmitting a serious disease or defect. This thesis holds that some reproductive acts are wrong, and my argument puts the burden of proof on those who disagree with it to show why its conclusions can be overridden. Hence it denies that people should be free to reproduce mindless of the consequences.[4] However, as moral argument, it should be taken as a proposal for further debate and discussion. It is not, by itself, an argument in favor of legal prohibitions of reproduction.[5]

There is a huge range of genetic diseases. Some are quickly lethal; others kill more slowly, if at all. Some are mainly physical, some mainly mental; others impair both kinds of function. Some interfere tremendously with normal functioning, others less. Some are painful, some are not. There seems to be considerable agreement that rapidly lethal diseases, especially those, like Tay-Sachs, accompanied by painful deterioration, should be prevented even at the cost of abortion. Conversely, there seems to be substantial agreement that relatively trivial problems, especially cosmetic ones, would not be legitimate grounds for abortion.[6] In short, there are cases ranging from low risk of mild disease or disability to high risk of serious disease or disability. Although it is difficult to decide where the duty to refrain from procreation becomes compelling, I believe that there are some clear cases. I have chosen to focus on Huntington's disease to illustrate the kinds of concrete issues such decisions entail. However, the arguments presented here are also relevant to many other genetic diseases.[7]

The symptoms of Huntington's disease usually begin between the ages of thirty and fifty. It happens this way:

> Onset is insidious. Personality changes (obstinacy, moodiness, lack of initiative) frequently antedate or accompany the involuntary choreic movements. These usually appear first in the face, neck, and arms, and are jerky, irregular, and stretching in character. Contractions of the facial muscles result in grimaces, those of the respiratory muscles, lips, and tongue lead to hesitating, explosive speech. Irregular movements of the trunk are present; the gait is shuffling and dancing. Tendon reflexes are increased. . . . Some patients display a fatuous euphoria; others are spiteful, irascible, destructive, and violent. Paranoid reactions are common. Poverty of thought and impairment of attention, memory, and judgment occur. As the disease progresses, walking becomes impossible, swallowing difficult, and dementia profound. Suicide is not uncommon.[8]

The illness lasts about fifteen years, terminating in death.

Huntington's disease is an autosomal dominant disease, meaning that it is caused by a single defective gene located on a non-sex chromosome. It is passed from one generation to the next via affected individuals. Each child of such an affected person has a fifty percent risk of inheriting the gene and thus of eventually developing the disease, even if he or she was born before the parent's disease was evident.[9]

Until recently, Huntington's disease was especially problematic because most affected individuals did not know whether they had the gene for the disease until well into their childbearing years. So they had to decide about childbearing before knowing whether they could transmit the disease or not. If, in time, they did not develop symptoms of the disease, then their children could know they were not at risk for the disease. If unfortunately they did develop symptoms, then each of their children could know there was a fifty percent chance that they, too, had inherited the gene. In both cases, the children faced a period of prolonged anxiety as to whether they would develop the disease. Then, in the 1980s, thanks in part to an energetic campaign by Nancy Wexler, a genetic marker was found that, in certain circumstances, could tell people with a relatively high degree of probability whether or not they had the gene for the disease.[10] Finally, in March 1993, the defective gene itself was discovered.[11] Now individuals can find out whether they carry the gene for the disease, and prenatal screening can tell us whether a given fetus has inherited it. These technological developments change the moral scene substantially.

How serious are the risks involved in Huntington's disease? Geneticists often think a ten percent risk is high.[12] But risk assessment also depends on what is at stake: the worse the possible outcome the more undesirable an otherwise small risk seems. In medicine, as elsewhere, people may regard the same result quite differently. But for devastating diseases like Huntington's this part of the judgment should be unproblematic: no one wants a loved one to suffer in this way.[13]

There may still be considerable disagreement about the acceptability of a given risk. So it would be difficult in many circumstances to say how we should respond to a particular risk. Nevertheless, there are good grounds for a conservative approach, for it is reasonable to take special precautions to avoid very bad consequences, even if the risk is small. But the possible consequences here *are* very bad: a child who may inherit Huntington's disease has a much greater than average chance of being subjected to severe and prolonged suffering. And it is one thing to risk one's own welfare, but quite another to do so for others and without their consent.

Is this judgment about Huntington's disease really defensible? People appear to have quite different opinions. Optimists argue that a child born into a family afflicted with Huntington's disease has a reasonable chance of living a satisfactory life. After all, even children born of an afflicted parent still have a fifty percent chance of escaping the disease. And even if afflicted themselves, such people will probably enjoy some thirty years of healthy life before symptoms appear. It is also possible, although not at all likely, that some might not mind the symptoms caused by the disease. Optimists can point to diseased persons who have lived fruitful lives, as well as those who seem genuinely glad to be alive. One is Rick Donohue, a sufferer from the Joseph family disease. "You know, if my mom hadn't had me, I wouldn't be here for the life I have had. So there is a good possibility I will have chil-

dren."[14] Optimists therefore conclude that it would be a shame if these persons had not lived.

Pessimists concede some of these facts, but take a less sanguine view of them. They think a fifty percent risk of serious disease like Huntington's appallingly high. They suspect that many children born into afflicted families are liable to spend their youth in dreadful anticipation and fear of the disease. They point out that Rick Donohue is still young, and has not experienced the full horror of his sickness. It is also well-known that some young persons have such a dilated sense of time that they can hardly envision themselves at thirty or forty, so the prospect of pain at that age is unreal to them.[15]

More empirical research on the psychology and life history of sufferers and potential sufferers is clearly needed to decide whether optimists or pessimists have a more accurate picture of the experiences of individuals at risk. But given that some will surely realize pessimists' worst fears, it seems unfair to conclude that the pleasures of those who deal with the situation simply cancel out the suffering of those others when that suffering could be avoided altogether.

I think that these points indicate that the morality of procreation in situations like this demands further investigation. I propose to do this by looking first at the position of the possible child, then at that of the potential parent.

Possible Children and Potential Parents

The first task in treating the problem from the child's point of view is to find a way of referring to possible future offspring without seeming to confer some sort of morally significant existence upon them. I will follow the convention of calling children who might be born in the future but who are not now conceived "possible" children, offspring, individuals, or persons.

Now, what claims about children or possible children are relevant to the morality of childbearing in the circumstances being considered? Of primary importance is the judgment that we ought to try to provide every child with something like a minimally satisfying life. I am not altogether sure how best to formulate this standard but I want clearly to reject the view that it is morally permissible to conceive individuals so long as we do not expect them to be so miserable that they wish they were dead.[16] I believe that this kind of moral minimalism is thoroughly unsatisfactory and that not many people would really want to live in a world where it was the prevailing standard. Its lure is that it puts few demands on us, but its price is the scant attention it pays to human well-being.

How might the judgment that we have a duty to try to provide a minimally satisfying life for our children be justified? It could, I think, be derived fairly straightforwardly from either utilitarian or contractarian theories of justice, although there is no space here for discussion of the details. The net result of such analysis would be the conclusion that neglecting this duty would create unnecessary unhappiness or unfair disadvantage for some persons.

Of course, this line of reasoning confronts us with the need to spell out what is meant by "minimally satisfying" and what a standard based on this concept would require of us. Conceptions of a minimally satisfying life vary tremendously among societies and also within them. *De Rigeur* in some circles are private music lessons and trips to Europe, while in others providing eight years of schooling is major accomplishment. But there is no need to consider this complication at length here since we are concerned only with health as a prerequisite for a minimally satisfying life. Thus, as we draw out what such a standard might require of us, it seems reasonable to retreat to the more limited claim that parents should try to ensure something like normal health for their children. It might be thought that even this moderate claim is unsatisfactory since in some places debilitating conditions are the norm, but one could circumvent this objection by saying that parents ought to try to provide for their children health normal for that culture, even though it may be inadequate if measured by some outside standard.[17] This conservative position would still justify efforts to avoid the birth of children at risk for Huntington's disease and other serious genetic diseases in virtually all societies.[18]

This view is reinforced by the following considerations. Given that possible children do not presently exist as actual individuals, they do not have a right to be brought into existence, and hence no one is maltreated by measures to avoid the conception of a possible person. Therefore, the conservative course that avoids the conception of those who would not be expected to enjoy a minimally satisfying life is at present the only fair course of action. The alternative is a laissez-faire approach which brings into existence the lucky, but only at the expense of the unlucky. Notice that attempting to avoid the creation of the unlucky does not necessarily lead to *fewer* people being brought into being; the question boils down to taking steps to bring those with better prospects into existence, instead of those with worse ones.

I have so far argued that if people with Huntington's disease are unlikely to live minimally satisfying lives, then those who might pass it on should not have genetically related children. This is consonant with the principle the greater the danger of serious problems, the stronger the duty to avoid them. But this principle is in conflict with what people think of as the right to reproduce. How might one decide which should take precedence?

Expecting people to forego having genetically related children might seem to demand too great a sacrifice of them. But before reaching that conclusion we need to ask what is really at stake. One reason for wanting children is to experience family life, including love, companionship, watching kids grow, sharing their pains and triumphs, and helping to form members of the next generation. Other reasons emphasize the validation of parents as individuals within a continuous family line, children as a source of immortality, or perhaps even the gratification of producing partial replicas of oneself. Children may also be desired in an effort to prove that one is an adult, to try to cement a marriage or to benefit parents economically.

Are there alternative ways of satisfying these desires? Adoption or new reproductive technologies can fulfill many of them without passing on known genetic defects. Replacements for sperm have been available for many years via artificial insemination by donor. More recently, egg donation, sometimes in combination with contract pregnancy,[19] has been used to provide eggs for women who prefer not to use their own. Eventually it may be possible to clone individual humans, although that now seems a long way off. All of these approaches to avoiding the use of particular genetic material are controversial and have generated much debate. I believe that tenable moral versions of each do exist.[20]

None of these methods permits people to extend both genetic lines, or realize the desire for immortality or for children who resemble both parents; nor is it clear that such alternatives will necessarily succeed in proving that one is an adult, cementing a marriage, or providing economic benefits. Yet, many people feel these desires strongly. Now, I am sympathetic to William James's dictum regarding desires: "Take any demand, however slight, which any creature, however weak, may make. Ought it not, for its own sole sake be satisfied? If not, prove why not."[21] Thus a world where more desires are satisfied is generally better than one where fewer are. However, not all desires can be legitimately satisfied since, as James suggests, there may be good reasons—such as the conflict of duty and desire—why some should be overruled.

Fortunately, further scrutiny of the situation reveals that there are good reasons why people should attempt—with appropriate social support—to talk themselves out of the desires in question or to consider novel ways of fulfilling them. Wanting to see the genetic line continued is not particularly rational when it brings a sinister legacy of illness and death. The desire for immortality cannot really be satisfied anyway, and people need to face the fact that what really matters is how they behave in their own lifetime. And finally, the desire for children who physically resemble one is understandable, but basically narcissistic, and its fulfillment cannot be guaranteed even by normal reproduction. There are other ways of proving one is an adult, and other ways of cementing marriages—children don't necessarily do either. Children, especially prematurely ill children, may not provide the expected economic benefits anyway. Nongenetically related children may also provide benefits similar to those that would have been provided by genetically related ones, and expected economic benefit is, in many cases, a morally questionable reason for having children.

Before the advent of reliable genetic testing, the options of people in Huntington's families were cruelly limited. On the one hand, they could have children, but at the risk of eventual crippling illness and death for them. On the other, they could refrain from childbearing, sparing their possible children from significant risk of inheriting this disease, perhaps frustrating intense desires to procreate—only to discover, in some cases, that their sacrifice was unnecessary because they did not develop the disease. Or they could attempt to adopt or try new reproductive approaches.

Reliable genetic testing has opened up new possibilities. Those at risk who wish to have children can get tested. If they test positive, they know their possible children are at risk. Those who are opposed to abortion must be especially careful to avoid conception if they are to behave responsibly.

Those not opposed to abortion can responsibly conceive children, but only if they are willing to test each fetus and abort those who carry the gene. If individuals at risk test negative, they are home free.

What about those who cannot face the test for themselves? They can do prenatal testing and abort fetuses who carry the defective gene. A clearly positive test also implies that the parent is affected, although negative tests do not rule out that possibility. Prenatal testing can thus bring knowledge that enables one to avoid passing the disease to others, but only, in some cases, at the cost of coming to know with certainty that one will indeed develop the disease. This situation raises with peculiar force the question of whether parental responsibility requires people to get tested.

Some people think that we should recognize a right "not to know." It seems to me that such a right could be defended only where ignorance does not put others at serious risk. So if people are prepared to forego genetically related children, they need not get tested. But if they want genetically related children then they must do whatever is necessary to ensure that affected babies are the result. There is, after all, something inconsistent about the claim that one has a right to be shielded from the truth, even if the price is to risk inflicting on one's children the same dread disease one cannot even face in oneself.

In sum, until we can be assured that Huntington's disease does not prevent people from living a minimally satisfying life, individuals at risk for the disease have a moral duty to try not to bring affected babies into this world. There are now enough options available so that this duty needn't frustrate their reasonable desires. Society has a corresponding duty to facilitate moral behavior on the part of individuals. Such support ranges from the narrow and concrete (like making sure that medical testing and counseling is available to all) to the more general social environment that guarantees that all pregnancies are voluntary, that pronatalism is eradicated, and that women are treated with respect regardless of the reproductive options they choose.

Notes

1. This paper is loosely based on "Genetic Diseases: Can Having Children Be Immoral?" originally published in *Genetics Now*, ed. John L Buckley (Washington, DC: University Press of America, 1978) and subsequently anthologized in a number of medical ethics texts. Thanks to Thomas Mappes and David DeGrazia for their helpful suggestions about updating the paper.

2. I focus on genetic considerations, although with the advent of AIDS the scope of the general question here could be expanded. There are two reasons for sticking to this relatively narrow formulation. One is that dealing with a smaller chunk of the problem may help us think more clearly, while realizing that some conclusions may nonetheless be relevant to the larger problem. The other is the peculiar capacity of some genetic problems to affect ever more individuals in the future.

3. For example, see Leon Kass, "Implications of Prenatal Diagnosis for the Human Right to Live," *Ethical Issues in Human Genetics*, eds. Bruce Hilton et al. (New York: Plenum Press, 1973).

4. This is, of course, a very broad thesis. I defend an even broader version in "Loving Future People," *Reproduction, Ethics and the Law*, ed. Joan Callahan (Bloomington: Indiana University Press, forthcoming).

5. Why would we want to resist legal enforcement of every moral conclusion? First, legal action has many costs, costs not necessarily worth paying in particular cases. Second, legal enforcement would tend to take the matter in question out of the realm of debate and treat it as settled. But in many cases, especially where mores or technology are rapidly evolving, we don't want that to happen. Third, legal enforcement would undermine individual freedom and decision-making capacity. In some cases, the ends envisioned are important enough to warrant putting up with these disadvantages, but that remains to be shown in each case.

6. Those who do not see fetuses as moral persons with a right to life may nonetheless hold that abortion is justifiable in these cases. I argue at some length elsewhere that lesser defects can cause great suffering. Once we are clear that there is nothing discriminatory about failing to conceive particular possible individuals, it makes sense, other things being equal, to avoid the prospect of such pain if we can. Naturally, other things rarely are equal. In the first place, many problems go undiscovered until a baby is born. Secondly, there are often substantial costs associated with screening programs. Thirdly, although women should be encouraged to consider the moral dimensions of routine pregnancy, we do not want it to be so fraught with tension that it becomes a miserable experience. (See "Loving Future People.")

7. It should be noted that failing to conceive a single individual can affect many lives: in 1916, nine hundred and sixty-two cases could be traced from six seventeenth-century arrivals in America. See Gordon Rattray Taylor, *The Biological Time Bomb* (New York, 1968), p. 176.

8. *The Merck Manual* (Rathway, N. J.: Merck, 1972), pp. 1363, 1346. We now know that the age of onset and severity of the disease is related to the number of abnormal replications of the glutamine code on the abnormal gene. See Andrew Revkin, "Hunting Down Huntington's," *Discover*, December 1993, p. 108.

9. Hymie Gordon, "Genetic Counseling," *JAMA*, Vol. 217, n. 9 (August 30, 1971), p. 1346.

10. See Revkin, "Hunting Down Huntington's," pp. 99–108.

11. "Gene for Huntington's Disease Discovered," *Human Genome News*, Vol. 5, n. 1 (May, 1993), p. 5.

12. Charles Smith, Susan Holloway, and Alan E. H. Emery, "Individuals at Risk in Families—Genetic Disease," *Journal of Medical Genetics*, Vol. 8 (1971), p. 453.

13. To try to separate the issue of the gravity of the disease from the existence of a given individual, compare this situation with how we would assess a parent who neglected to vaccinate an existing child against a hypothetical viral version of Huntington's.

14. *The New York Times*, September 30, 1975, p. 1, col. 6. The Joseph family disease is similar to Huntington's disease except that the symptoms start appearing in the twenties. Rick Donohue was in his early twenties at the time he made this statement.

15. I have talked to college students who believe that they will have lived fully and be ready to die at those ages. It is astonishing how one's perspective changes over time, and how ages that one once associated with senility and physical collapse come to seem the prime of human life.

16. The view I am rejecting has been forcefully articulated by Derek Parfit, *Reasons and Persons* (Oxford: Oxford University Press, 1984). For more discussion, see "Loving Future People."

17. I have some qualms about this response since I fear that some human groups are so badly off that it might still be wrong for them to procreate, even if that would mean great changes in their cultures. But this is a complicated issue that needs its own investigation.

18. Again, a troubling exception might be the isolated Venezuelan group Nancy Wexler found where, because of inbreeding, a large portion of the population is affected by Huntington's. See Revkin, "Hunting Down Huntington's."

19. Or surrogacy, as it has been popularly known. I think that "contract pregnancy" is more accurate and more respectful of women. Eggs can be provided either by a woman who also gestates the fetus or by a third party.

20. The most powerful objections to new reproductive technologies and arrangements concern possible bad consequences for women. However, I do not think that the arguments against them on these grounds have yet shown the dangers to be as great as some believe. So although it is perhaps true that new reproductive technologies and arrangements shouldn't be used lightly, avoiding the conceptions discussed here is well worth the risk. For a series of viewpoints on this issue, including my own "Another Look at Contract Pregnancy," see Helen B. Holmes, *Issues in Reproductive Technology I: An Anthology* (New York: Garland Press, 1992).

21. *Essays in Pragmatism*, ed. A. Castell (New York: 1948), p. 73.

Implications of Prenatal Diagnosis for the Human Right to Life

Leon R. Kass

Leon R. Kass expresses concern that the practice of "genetic abortion" will strongly affect our attitudes toward all who are "defective" or abnormal. Those who escape the net of selective abortion might receive less care and might even come to think of themselves as second-class specimens. Furthermore, on Kass's view, genetic abortion might encourage us to accept the general principle that defectives of any kind ought not to be born. This, in turn, would threaten our commitment to the basic moral principle that each person, despite any physical or mental handicap, is the inherent equal of every other person.

Kass presents six criteria that he suggests ought to be satisfied to justify the abortion of a fetus for genetic reasons. In the remainder of his paper, he focuses on the question raised by the last criterion: According to what standards should we judge a fetus with genetic abnormalities unfit to live? As candidates for such standards, Kass examines the concepts of social good, family good, and the "healthy and sound" fetus. He finds difficulty with all, and in the end he professes himself unable to provide a satisfactory justification for genetic abortion. Kass's difficulty with the "healthy and sound" fetus as a standard puts his general position in conflict with that taken by Purdy. What Purdy regards as a relatively clear-cut criterion, Kass views as a relatively vague and arbitrary social standard.

I wish to focus on the special ethical issues raised by the abortion of "defective" fetuses (so-called "abortion for fetal indications"). I shall consider only the cleanest cases, those cases where well-characterized genetic diseases are diagnosed with a high degree of certainty by means of amniocentesis, in order to sidestep the added moral dilemmas posed when the diagnosis is suspected or possible, but unconfirmed. However, many of the questions I shall discuss could also be raised about cases where genetic analysis gives only a statistical prediction about the genotype of the fetus, and also about cases where the defect has an infectious or chemical rather than a genetic cause (e.g., rubella, thalidomide). . . .

. . . Precisely because the quality of the fetus is central to the decision to abort, the practice of genetic abortion has implications which go beyond those raised by abortion in general. What may be at stake here is the belief in the radical moral equality of all human beings, the belief that all human beings possess equally and independent of merit certain fundamental rights, one among which is, of course, the right to life.

To be sure, the belief that fundamental human rights belong equally to all human beings has been but an ideal, never realized, often ignored, sometimes shamelessly. Yet it has been perhaps the most powerful moral idea at work in the world for at least two centuries. It is this idea and ideal that animates most of the current political and social criticism around the globe. It is ironic that we should acquire the power to detect and eliminate the genetically unequal at a time when we have finally succeeded in removing much of the stigma and disgrace previously attached to victims of congenital illness, in providing them with improved care and support, and in preventing, by means of education, feelings of guilt on the part of their parents. One might even wonder whether the development of amniocentesis and prenatal diagnosis may represent a backlash against these same humanitarian and egalitarian tendencies in the practice of medicine, which, by helping to sustain to the age of reproduction persons with genetic disease has itself contributed to the increasing incidence of genetic disease, and with it, to increased pressures for genetic screening, genetic counseling, and genetic abortion.

No doubt our humanitarian and egalitarian principles and practices have caused us some new difficulties, but if we mean to weaken or turn our backs on them, we should do so consciously and thoughtfully. If, as I believe, the idea and practice of genetic abortion points in that direction, we should

Reprinted from *Ethical Issues in Human Genetics: Genetic Counseling and the Use of Genetic Knowledge,* edited by Bruce Hilton, Daniel Callahan, Maureen Harris, Peter Condliffe, and Burton Berkeley (New York: Plenum Press, 1973), pp. 186–199. A revised version of this essay ("Perfect Babies: Prenatal Diagnosis and the Equal Right to Life") appears in Dr. Kass's book, *Toward a More Natural Science: Biology and Human Affairs* (New York: The Free Press, 1985). Notes omitted.

make ourselves aware of it. And if, as I believe, the way in which genetic abortion is described, discussed, and justified is perhaps of even greater consequence than its practice for our notions of human rights and of their equal possession by all human beings, we should pay special attention to questions of language and in particular, to the question of justification. Before turning full attention to these matters, two points should be clarified.

First, my question "What decision, and why?" is to be distinguished from the question "Who decides, and why?" There is a tendency to blur this distinction and to discuss only the latter, and with it, the underlying question of private freedom versus public good. I will say nothing about this, since I am more interested in exploring what constitutes "good," both public and private. Accordingly, I would emphasize that the moral question—What decision, and why?—does not disappear simply because the decision is left in the hands of each pregnant woman. It is the moral question she faces. I would add that the moral health of the community and of each of its members is as likely to be affected by the aggregate of purely private and voluntary decisions on genetic abortions as by a uniform policy imposed by statute. We physicians and scientists especially should refuse to finesse the moral question of genetic abortion and its implications and to take refuge behind the issue, "Who decides?" For it is we who are responsible for choosing to develop the technology of prenatal diagnosis, for informing and promoting this technology among the public, and for the actual counseling of patients.

Second, I wish to distinguish my discussion of what ought to be done from a descriptive account of what in fact is being done, and especially from a consideration of what I myself might do, faced with the difficult decision. I cannot know with certainty what I would think, feel, do, or want done, faced with the knowledge that my wife was carrying a child branded with Down syndrome or Tay-Sachs disease. But an understanding of the issues is not advanced by personal anecdote or confession, We all know that what we and others actually do is often done out of weakness, rather than conviction. It is all-too-human to make an exception in one's own case (consider, e.g., the extra car, the "extra" child, income tax, the draft, the flight from the cities). For what it is worth, I confess to feeling more than a little sympathy with parents who choose abortions for severe genetic defect. Nevertheless, as I shall indicate later, in seeking for reasons to justify this practice, I can find none that are in themselves fully satisfactory and none that do not simultaneously justify the killing of "defective" infants, children and adults. I am mindful that my arguments will fall far from the middle of the stream, yet I hope that the oarsmen of the flagship will pause and row more slowly, while we all consider whither we are going.

Genetic Abortion and the Living Defective

The practice of abortion of the genetically defective will no doubt affect our view of and our behavior toward those abnormals who escape the net of detection and abortion. A child with Down syndrome or with hemophilia or with muscular dystrophy born at a time when most of his (potential) fellow sufferers were destroyed prenatally is liable to be looked upon by the community as one unfit to be alive, as a second-class (or even lower) human type. He may be seen as a person who need not have been, and who would not have been, if only someone had gotten to him in time.

The parents of such children are also likely to treat them differently, especially if the mother would have wished but failed to get an amniocentesis because of ignorance, poverty, or distance from the testing station, or if the prenatal diagnosis was in error. In such cases, parents are especially likely to resent the child. They may be disinclined to give it the kind of care they might have before the advent of amniocentesis and genetic abortion, rationalizing that a second-class specimen is not entitled to first-class treatment. If pressed to do so, say by physicians, the parents might refuse, and the courts may become involved. This has already begun to happen.

In Maryland, parents of a child with Down syndrome refused permission to have the child operated on for an intestinal obstruction present at birth. The physicians and the hospital sought an injunction to require the parents to allow surgery. The judge ruled in favor of the parents, despite what I understand to be the weight of precedent to the contrary, on the grounds that the child was Mongoloid, that is, had the child been "normal," the decision would have gone the other way. Although the decision was not appealed to and hence not affirmed by a higher court, we can see through the prism of this case the possibility that the new powers of human genetics will strip the blindfold from the lady of justice and will make official the dangerous doctrine that some men are more equal than others.

The abnormal child may also feel resentful. A child with Down syndrome or Tay-Sachs disease will probably never know or care, but what about the child with hemophilia or with Turner's syndrome? In the past decade, with medical knowledge and power over the prenatal child increasing and with parental authority over the postnatal child decreasing, we have seen the appearance of a new type of legal action, suits for wrongful life. Children have brought suit against their parents (and others) seeking to recover damages for physical and social handicaps inextricably tied to their birth (e.g., congenital deformities, congenital syphilis, illegitimacy). In some of the American cases, the courts have recognized the justice of the child's claim (that he was injured due to parental negligence), although they have so far refused to award damages, due to policy considerations. In other countries, e.g., in Germany, judgments with compensation have gone for the plaintiffs. With the spread of amniocentesis and genetic abortion, we can only expect such cases to increase. And here it will be the soft-hearted rather than the hard-hearted judges who will establish the doctrine of second-class human beings, out of compassion for the mutants who escaped the traps set out for them.

It may be argued that I am dealing with a problem which, even if it is real, will affect very few people. It may be suggested that very few will escape the traps once we have set them properly and widely, once people are informed about amniocentesis, once the power to detect prenatally grows to its full capacity, and once our "superstitious" opposition to abortion dies out or is extirpated. But in order even to come close to this vision of success, amniocentesis will have to become part of every pregnancy—either by making it mandatory, like the test for syphilis, or by making it "routine medical practice," like the Pap smear. Leaving aside the other problems with universal amniocentesis, we would expect that the problem for the few who escape is likely to be even worse precisely because they will be few.

The point, however, should be generalized. How will we come to view and act toward the many "abnormals" that will remain among us—the retarded, the crippled, the senile, the deformed, and the true mutants—once we embark on a program to root out genetic abnormality? For it must be remembered that we shall always have abnormals—some who escape detection or whose disease is undetectable *in utero*, others a result of new mutations, birth injuries, accidents, maltreatment, or disease—who will require our care and protection. The existence of "defectives" cannot be fully prevented, not even by totalitarian breeding and weeding programs. Is it not likely that our principle with respect to these people will change from "We try harder" to "Why accept second best?" The idea of "the unwanted because abnormal child" may become a self-fulfilling prophecy, whose consequences may be worse than those of the abnormality itself.

Genetic and Other Defectives

The mention of other abnormals points to a second danger of the practice of genetic abortion. Genetic abortion may come to be seen not so much as the prevention of genetic disease, but as the prevention of birth of defective or abnormal children—and, in a way, understandably so. For in the case of what other diseases does preventive medicine consist in the elimination of the patient-at-risk? Moreover, the very language used to discuss genetic disease leads us to the easy but wrong conclusion that the afflicted fetus or person is rather than has a disease. True, one is partly defined by his genotype, but only partly. A person is more than his disease. And yet we slide easily from the language of possession to the language of identity, from "He has hemophilia" to "He is a hemophiliac," from "She has diabetes" through "She is diabetic" to "She is a diabetic," from "The fetus has Down syndrome" to "The fetus is a Down's." This way of speaking supports the belief that it is defective persons (or potential persons) that are being eliminated, rather than diseases.

If this is so, then it becomes simply accidental that the defect has a genetic cause. Surely, it is only because of the high regard for medicine and science, and for the accuracy of genetic diagnosis, that genotypic defectives are likely to be the first to go. But once the principle, "Defectives should not be born," is established, grounds other than cytological and biochemical may very well be sought. Even ignoring racialists and others equally misguided—of course, they cannot be ignored—we should know that there are social scientists, for example, who believe that one can predict with a high degree of accuracy how a child will turn out from a careful, systematic study of the socio-economic and psycho-dynamic environment into which he is born and in which he grows up. They might press for the prevention of socio-psychological disease, even of "criminality," by means of prenatal environmental diagnosis and abortion. I have heard a rumor that a crude, unscientific form of eliminating potential "phenotypic defectives" is already being practiced in some cities, in that submission to abortion is allegedly being made a condition for the receipt of welfare payments. "Defectives should not be born" is a principle without limits. We can ill-afford to have it established.

Up to this point, I have been discussing the possible implications of the practice of genetic abortion for our belief in and adherence to the idea that, at least in fundamental human matters such as life and liberty, all men are to be considered as equals, that for these matters we should ignore as irrelevant the real qualitative differences amongst men, however important these differences may be for other purposes. Those who are concerned about abortion fear that the permissible time of eliminating the unwanted will be moved forward along the time continuum, against newborns, infants, and children. Similarly, I suggest that we should be concerned lest the attack on gross genetic inequality in fetuses be advanced along the continuum of quality and into the later stages of life.

I am not engaged in predicting the future; I am not saying that amniocentesis and genetic abortion will lead down the road to Nazi Germany. Rather, I am suggesting that the principles underlying genetic abortion simultaneously justify many further steps down that road. . . .

Perhaps I have exaggerated the dangers; perhaps we will not abandon our inexplicable preference for generous humanitarianism over consistency. But we should indeed be cautious and move slowly as we give serious consideration to the question "What price the perfect baby?"

Standards for Justifying Genetic Abortion

. . . According to what standards can and should we judge a fetus with genetic abnormalities unfit to live, i.e., abortable? It seems to me that there are at least three dominant standards to which we are likely to repair.

The first is societal good. The needs and interest of society are often invoked to justify the practices of prenatal diagnosis and abortion of the genetically abnormal. The argument, full blown, runs something like this. Society has an interest in the genetic fitness of its members. It is foolish for society to squander its precious resources ministering to and caring for the unfit, especially for those who will never become "productive," or who will never in any way "benefit" society. Therefore, the interests of society are best served by the elimination of the genetically defective prior to their birth.

The societal standard is all-too-often reduced to its lowest common denominator: money. Thus one physician, claiming that he has "made a cost-benefit analysis of Tay-Sachs disease," notes that "the total cost of carrier detection, prenatal diagnosis and termination of at-risk pregnancies for all Jewish individuals in the United States under 30 who will marry is $5,730,281. If the program is set up to screen only one married partner, the cost is $3,122,695. The hospital costs for the 990 cases of Tay-Sachs disease these individuals would produce over a thirty-year period in the United States is $34,650,000. Another physician, apparently less interested or able to make such a precise audit has written: "Cost-benefit analyses have been made for the total prospective detection and monitoring of Tay-Sachs disease, cystic fibrosis (when prenatal detection becomes available for cystic fibrosis) and other disorders, and in most cases, the expenditures for hospitalization and medical care far exceed the cost of prenatal detection in properly selected risk populations, followed by selective abortion." Yet a third physician has calculated that the costs to the state of caring for children with Down syndrome is more than three times that of detecting and aborting them. (These authors all acknowledge the additional non-societal "costs" of personal suffering, but insofar as they consider society, the costs are purely economic.)

There are many questions that can be raised about this approach. First, there are questions about the accuracy of the calculations. Not all the costs have been reckoned. The aborted defective child will be "replaced" by a "normal" child. In keeping the ledger, the "costs" to society of his care and maintenance cannot be ignored—costs of educating him, or removing his wastes and pollutions, not to mention the "costs" in non-replaceable natural resources that he consumes. Who is a greater drain on society's precious resources, the average inmate of a home for the retarded or the average graduate of Harvard College? I am not sure we know or can even find out. Then there are the costs of training the physician, and genetic counselors, equipping their laboratories, supporting their research, and sending them and us to conferences to worry about what they are doing. An accurate economic analysis seems to me to be impossible, even in principle. And even if it were possible, one could fall back on the words of that ordinary language philosopher, Andy Capp, who, when his wife said that she was getting really worried about the cost of living, replied: "Sweet'eart, name me one person who wants t'stop livin' on account of the cost."

A second defect of the economic analysis is that there are matters of social importance that are not reducible to financial costs, and others that may not be quantifiable at all. How does one quantitate the costs of real and potential social conflict, either between children and parents, or between the community and the "deviants" who refuse amniocentesis and continue to bear abnormal children? Can one measure the effect on racial tensions of attempting to screen for and prevent the birth of children homozygous (or heterozygous) for sickle cell anemia? What numbers does one attach to any decreased willingness or ability to take care of the less fortunate, or to cope with difficult problems? And what about the "costs" of rising expectations? Will we become increasingly dissatisfied with anything short of the "optimum baby?" How does one quantify anxiety? humiliation? guilt? Finally, might not the medical profession pay an unmeasurable price if genetic abortion and other revolutionary activities bring about changes in medical ethics and medical practice that lead to the further erosion of trust in the physician?

An appeal to social worthiness or usefulness is a less vulgar form of the standard of societal good. It is true that great social contributions are unlikely to be forthcoming from persons who suffer from most serious genetic diseases, especially since many of them die in childhood. Yet consider the following remarks of Pearl Buck (1968) on the subject of being a mother of a child retarded from phenylketonuria:

> "My child's life has not been meaningless. She has indeed brought comfort and practical help to many people who are parents of retarded children or are themselves handicapped. True, she has done it through me, yet without her I would not have had the means of learning how to accept the inevitable sorrow, and how to make that acceptance useful to others. Would I be so heartless as to say that it has been worthwhile for my child to be born retarded? Certainly not, but I am saying that even though gravely retarded it has been worthwhile for her to have lived.
>
> "It can be summed up, perhaps, by saying that in this world, where cruelty prevails in so many aspects of our life, I would not add the weight of choice to kill rather than to let live. A retarded child, a handicapped person, brings its own gift to life, even to the life of normal human beings. That gift is comprehended in the lessons of patience, understanding, and mercy, lessons which we all need to receive and to practice with one another, whatever we are."

The standard of potential social worthiness is little better in deciding about abortion in particular cases than is the standard of economic cost. To drive the point home, each of us might consider retrospectively whether he would have been willing to stand trial for his life while a fetus, pleading only his worth to society as he now can evaluate it. How many of us are not socially "defective" and with none of the excuses possible for a child with phenylketonuria? If there is to be human life at all, potential social worthiness cannot be its entitlement.

Finally, we should take note of the ambiguities in the very notion of societal good. Some use the term "society" to mean their own particular political community, others to mean the whole human race, and still others speak as if they mean both simultaneously, following that all-too-human belief that what is good for me and mine is good for mankind. Who knows what is genetically best for mankind, even with respect to Down syndrome? I would submit that the genetic heritage of the human species is largely in the care of persons who do not live along the amniocentesis frontier. If we in the industrialized West wish to be really serious about the genetic future of the species, we would concentrate our attack on mutagenesis, and especially on our large contribution to the pool of environmental mutagens.

But even the more narrow use of society is ambiguous. Do we mean our "society" as it is today? Or do we mean our "society" as it ought to be? If the former, our standards will be ephemeral, for ours is a faddish "society." (By far the most worrisome feature of the changing attitudes on abortion is the suddenness with which they changed.) Any such socially determined standards are likely to provide too precarious a foundation for decisions about genetic abortion, let alone for our notions of human rights. If we mean the latter, then we have transcended the societal standard, since the "good society" is not to be found in "society" itself, nor is it likely to be discovered by taking a vote. In sum, societal good as a standard for justifying genetic abortion seems to be unsatisfactory. It is hard to define in general, difficult to apply clearly to particular cases, susceptible to overreaching and abuse (hence, very dangerous), and not sufficient unto itself if considerations of the good community are held to be automatically implied.

A second major alternative is the standard of parental or familial good. Here the argument of justification might run as follows. Parents have a right to determine, according to their own wishes and based upon their own notions of what is good for them, the qualitative as well as the quantitative character of their families. If they believe that the birth of a seriously deformed child will be the cause of great sorrow and suffering to themselves and to their other children and a drain on their time and resources, then they may ethically decide to prevent the birth of such a child, even by abortion.

This argument I would expect to be more attractive to most people than the argument appealing to the good of society. For one thing, we are more likely to trust a person's conception of what is good for him than his notion of what is good for society. Also, the number of persons involved is small, making it seem less impossible to weigh all the relevant factors in determining the good of the family. Most powerfully, one can see and appreciate the possible harm done to healthy children if the parents are obliged to devote most of their energies to caring for the afflicted child.

Yet there are ambiguities and difficulties perhaps as great as with the standard of societal good. In first place, it is not entirely clear what would be good for the other children. In a strong family, the experience with a suffering and dying child might help the healthy siblings learn to face and cope with adversity. Some have even speculated that the lack of experience with death and serious illness in our affluent young people is an important element in their difficulty in trying to find a way of life and

in responding patiently yet steadily to the serious problems of our society (Cassell, 1969). I suspect that one cannot generalize. In some children and in some families, experience with suffering may be strengthening, and in others, disabling. My point here is that the matter is uncertain, and that parents deciding on this basis are as likely as not to be mistaken.

The family or parental standard, like the societal standard, is unavoidably elastic because "suffering" does not come in discontinuous units, and because parental wishes and desires know no limits. Both are utterly subjective, relative, and notoriously subject to change. Some parents claim that they could not tolerate having to raise a child of the undesired sex; I know of one case where the woman in the delivery room, on being informed that her child was a son, told the physician that she did not even wish to see it and that he should get rid of it. We may judge her attitude to be pathological, but even pathological suffering is suffering. Would such suffering justify aborting her normal male fetus?

Or take the converse case of two parents, who for their own very peculiar reasons, wish to have an abnormal child, say a child who will suffer from the same disease as grandfather or a child whose arrested development would preclude the threat of adolescent rebellion and separation. Are these acceptable grounds for the abortion of "normals"?

Granted, such cases will be rare. But they serve to show the dangers inherent in talking about the parental right to determine, according to their wishes, the quality of their children. Indeed, the whole idea of parental rights with respect to children strikes me as problematic. It suggests that children are like property, that they exist for the parents. One need only look around to see some of the results of this notion of parenthood. The language of duties to children would be more in keeping with the heavy responsibility we bear in affirming the continuity of life with life and in trying to transmit what wisdom we have acquired to the next generation. Our children are not our children. Hopefully, reflection on these matters could lead to a greater appreciation of why it is people do and should have children. No better consequence can be hoped for from the advent of amniocentesis and other technologies for controlling human reproduction.

If one speaks of familial good in terms of parental duty, one could argue that parents have an obligation to do what they can to insure that their children are born healthy and sound. But this formulation transcends the limitation of parental wishes and desires. As in the case of the good society, the idea of "healthy and sound" requires an objective standard, a standard in reality. Hard as it may be to uncover it, this is what we are seeking. Nature as a standard is the third alternative.

The justification according to the natural standard might run like this. As a result of our knowledge of genetic diseases, we know that persons afflicted with certain diseases will never be capable of living the full life of a human being. Just as a no-necked giraffe could never live a giraffe's life, or a needle-less porcupine would not attain true "porcupine-hood," so a child or fetus with Tay-Sachs disease or Down syndrome, for example, will never truly be human. They will never be able to care for themselves, nor have they even the potential for developing the distinctively human capacities for thought or self-consciousness. Nature herself has aborted many similar cases, and has provided for the early death of many who happen to get born. There is no reason to keep them alive; instead, we should prevent their birth by contraception or sterilization if possible, and abortion if necessary.

The advantages of this approach are clear. The standards are objective and in the fetus itself, thus avoiding the relativity and ambiguity in societal and parental good. The standard can be easily generalized to cover all such cases and will be resistant to the shifting sands of public opinion.

This standard, I would suggest, is the one which most physicians and genetic counselors appeal to in their heart of hearts, no matter what they say or do about letting the parents choose. Why else would they have developed genetic counseling and amniocentesis? Indeed, the notions of disease, of abnormal, of defective, make no sense at all in the absence of a natural norm of health. This norm is the foundation of the art of the physician and of the inquiry of the health scientist. Yet, as Motulsky and others [1971] . . . have pointed out, the standard is elusive. Ironically, we are gaining increasing power to manipulate and control our own nature at a time in which we are increasingly confused about what is normal, healthy, and fit.

Although possibly acceptable in principle, the natural standard runs into problems in application when attempts are made to fix the boundary between potentially human and potentially not hu-

man. Professor Lejeune (1970) has clearly demonstrated the difficulty, if not the impossibility, of setting clear molecular, cytological, or developmental signposts for this boundary. Attempts to induce signposts by considering the phenotypes of the worst cases is equally difficult. Which features would we take to be the most relevant in, say, Tay-Sachs disease, Lesch-Nyhan syndrome, Cri du chat, Down syndrome? Certainly, severe mental retardation. But how "severe" is "severe"? As . . . I argued earlier, mental retardation admits of degree. It too is relative. Moreover it is not clear that certain other defects and deformities might not equally foreclose the possibility of a truly or fully human life. What about blindness or deafness? Quadriplegia? Aphasia? Several of these in combination? Not only does each kind of defect admit of a continuous scale of severity, but it also merges with other defects on a continuous scale of defectiveness. Where on this scale is the line to drawn: after mental retardation? blindness? muscular dystrophy? cystic fibrosis? hemophilia? diabetes? galactosemia? Turner's syndrome? XYY? club foot? Moreover, the identical two continuous scales—kind and severity—are found also among the living. In fact, it is the natural standard which may be the most dangerous one in that it leads most directly to the idea that there are second-class human beings and sub-human human beings.

But the story is not complete. The very idea of nature is ambiguous. According to one view, the one I have been using, nature points to or implies a peak, a perfection. According to this view, human rights depend upon attaining the status of humanness. The fetus is only potential; it has no rights, according to this view. But all kinds of people fall short of the norm: children, idiots, some adults. This understanding of nature has been used to justify not only abortion and infanticide, but also slavery.

There is another notion of nature, less splendid, more humane and, though less able to sustain a notion of health, more acceptable to the findings of modern science. Animal nature is characterized by impulses of self-preservation and by the capacity to feel pleasure and to suffer pain. Man and other animals are alike on this understanding of nature. And the right to life is ascribed to all such self-preserving and suffering creatures. Yet on this understanding of nature, the fetus—even a defective fetus—is not potential, but actual. The right to life belongs to him. But for this reason, this understanding of nature does not provide and may even deny what it is we are seeking, namely, a justification for genetic abortion, adequate unto itself, which does not simultaneously justify infanticide, homicide and enslavement of the genetically abnormal.

There is a third understanding of nature, akin to the second, nature as sacrosanct, nature as created by a Creator. Indeed, to speak about this reminds us that there is a fourth possible standard for judgments about genetic abortion: the religious standard. I shall leave the discussion of this standard to those who are able to speak of it in better faith.

Now that I am at the end, the reader can better share my sense of frustration. I have failed to provide myself with a satisfactory intellectual and moral justification for the practice of genetic abortion. Perhaps others more able than I can supply one. Perhaps the pragmatists can persuade me that we should abandon the search for principled justification, that if we just trust people's situational decisions or their gut reactions, everything will turn out

fine. Maybe they are right. But we should not forget the sage observation of Bertrand Russell: "Pragmatism is like a warm bath that heats up so imperceptibly that you don't know when to scream." I would add that before we submerge ourselves irrevocably in amniotic fluid, we take note of the connection to our own baths, into which we have started the hot water running.

References

Buck, P. S. (1968). Foreword to *The Terrible Choice: The Abortion Dilemma*. New York: Bantam Books, pp.ix–xi.

Cassell, E. (1969). "Death and the Physician," Commentary (June), pp. 73–79.

Lejeune, J. (1970). *American Journal of Human Genetics*, 22, p. 121.

Lincoln, A. (1854). In *The Collected Works of Abraham Lincoln*, R. P. Basler, editor. New Brunswick, N.J.: Rutgers University Press, Vol. II, p. 222.

Motulsky, A. G., G. R. Fraser, and J. Felsenstein (1971). In Symposium on Intrauterine Diagnosis, D. Bergsma, editor. *Birth Defects: Original Article Series*, Vol. 7, No. 5.

Neel, J. (1972). In *Early Diagnosis of Human Genetic Defects: Scientific and Ethical Considerations*, M. Harris, editor. Washington, D.C.: U.S. Government Printing Office, pp. 366–380.

Social and Ethical Issues in the Human Genome Project

Daniel J. Kevles

Daniel Kevles claims that the fear that the Human Genome Project will lead to eugenics programs is out of proportion to the real danger. He admits that the knowledge gained by the project has the potential to be abused, but he argues that the anti-eugenic constituencies in contemporary democracies are powerful enough to prevent the reintroduction of eugenics into social policy.

Kevles holds that a more pressing concern than eugenics is the way in which the information generated by the project may be used. Of particular concern is what private insurers may do with the data. When little is known about who will suffer from a disabling disease, risks and premiums are spread evenly throughout the insured population. But as our ability to predict who will develop such diseases increases, this raises questions about the distribution of costs. Should we make disease suffers pay their own costs or should we pass on part of their costs to the healthy? Should we allow insurers to test individuals to determine their susceptibility to diseases? These are the sort of questions raised by the Human Genome Project that require immediate and practical answers.

Reprinted by permission of the author. From *National Forum*, the Phi Kappa Phi Journal, Spring 1993, Volume LXXIII, Number 2, pp. 18–21.

In the late 1980s, the United States government inaugurated the Human Genome Project, an unprecedented effort in biology that will transform our capacities to predict what we may become and may enable us to improve or to prevent our genetic fates, medically or otherwise. The project's immediate purpose is to obtain all the particulars about the human genome—that is, the complete details of the encyclopedia of genetic information that is housed in every human cell. In these details lie the keys to what make us human instead of, say, chimpanzees, to what defines our physical and mental possibilities and limits as a species.

The human genome has been estimated to contain between 50,000 and 100,000 genes, which are spread through twenty-four different chromosomes—the two sex chromosomes, X and Y, and the twenty-two others. The genes themselves are material entities, double-helical strands of deoxyribonucleic acid (DNA). The two strands of the helix are joined at regular intervals by a union of one of two pairs of chemicals—adenine with thymine or cytosine with guanine. Called "base pairs," these rungs across the double helix can occur in any sequential order. The order in which they do occur defines the genetic code, the hereditary information that the helix contains.

The genome project has two fundamental aims. The first is to construct a map of the human genome, which means to determine on which chromosome each human gene resides and to specify where on the chromosome it is located. The second is to obtain the sequencee—that is, the order of occurrence—of all the base pairs in human DNA. The number of all the base pairs has been estimated at around 3 billion.

The mapping and sequencing of the human genome will not be completed until at least a decade from now, probably longer, but the knowledge that is acquired as they proceed will undoubtedly revolutionize understanding of human development, including the development of characteristics both normal and abnormal (such as disease). However, expectations of such a revolution have been accompanied by apprehensions of misuse, especially the type of misuse of biology that occurred early in the century with eugenics.

The basic idea of eugenics was to improve the human stock by increasing the number of allegedly desirable human beings (called "positive eugenics) and getting rid of allegedly undesirable people (called "negative" eugenics). In the United States,

eugenics led to, among other things, the enactment of sterilization laws in many states, including California, which by 1929 had sterilized almost twice as many people—some 6,250—as had all other states of the union combined. In Nazi Germany, the eugenics movement prompted the sterilization of several hundred thousand people and helped lead to the death camps.

Some commentators have warned that the human genome project may spark a revival of state programs to intervene in reproductive behavior by fostering sterilization, voluntary or otherwise, to keep "bad" genes from being transmitted in the population. Economics could easily prompt the development of such negative eugenics programs. As health care becomes a public responsibility, funded through taxes, and as the cost escalates, taxpayers may ultimately rebel against paying for the care of those whom genes doom to severe disease or disability. Governments and institutions may come to feel pressure, in the interest of keeping public-health costs down, to encourage, or even to compel, people not to bring genetically disadvantaged children into the world. For example, national health policy might declare that a first child with a genetic disease will be covered but not any subsequent ones similarly afflicted. In recent years, several governments have developed crude eugenics policies. For instance, in 1988, China's Gansu Province adopted a eugenics law that would—so the authorities said—improve "population quality" by banning the marriage of mentally retarded people unless they first submitted to sterilization.

However, reproductive freedom is much more easily curtailed in dictatorships than in democracies, and contemporary political democracies contain powerful anti-eugenics constituencies. Most geneticists, and the public at large, are aware of the barbarities and cruelties of past state-sponsored eugenics and tend to oppose such programs. And although prejudice continues against people living with a variety of disabilities and diseases, today such people are politically empowered to a degree that they were not in the early twentieth century, They may not have enough power to counter all quasi-eugenic threats to themselves, but they are politically positioned, with allies in the media, the medical profession, and elsewhere—including the Roman Catholic Church, which in 1930 denounced eugenics in a Papal encyclical—to block or at least to hinder eugenics proposals that might affect them.

In the future, the advance of human genetics

and biotechnology may make some kind of positive eugenics possible, giving parents opportunities to have babies superior in some sense to those they might blindly conceive. However, genetic enhancement would inevitably involve manipulating human embryos, and for better or for worse, human-embryo research is prohibited by the U.S. government and powerfully opposed by virtually all the major western democracies, especially in heavily Roman Catholic ones. A broad spectrum of lay and religious opinion on both sides of the Atlantic agrees with the European Parliament's 1989 declaration that genetic analysis "must on no account be used for the scientifically dubious and politically unacceptable purpose of 'positively improving' the population's gene pool" and with the parliament's call for "an absolute ban on all experiments designed to reorganize on an arbitrary basis the genetic makeup of humans."

In any event, human genetic improvement is not likely to yield to human effort for some time to come. While the Human Genome Project will undoubtedly speed the process of identifying genes for physical and medically related traits, it is unlikely that it will soon reveal how genes contribute to the formation of those qualities—particularly talent, creativity, behavior, appearance—that the world so much wants and admires. The idea that genetic knowledge will soon permit us to engineer "Einsteins" or even enhance general intelligence is simply preposterous.

The prospect and possibilities of human genetic engineering remain tantalizing, of course, even if they are still the stuff of science fiction. However, the near-term ethical challenges of the Human Genome Project do not lie in private forays in human genetic improvement or in state-mandated programs of eugenics but in what the project will produce in abundance: genetic information. How will we control, diffuse, and use that information within the context of a market economy? The prospects are deeply troubling.

Many individuals and families already seek genetic information. Yet acquiring certain information may have wrenching ripple effects. A test on one family member may reveal, for example, that other family members such as siblings have a disease gene—that for Huntington's disease, say—for which there is no treatment, let alone cure. Genetic counseling may help a couple make important reproductive decisions, but genetic testing after conception may just show that the fetus has lost the roll of the genetic dice. The pregnant couple is then confronted with the only therapeutic choice available at the moment—to abort or not to abort a child that is usually wanted. Uncertainty can compound the problem. For example, the test for whether an individual is a carrier of the recessive cystic fibrosis gene was originally only 75 percent reliable—that is, it detected the gene in only three out of four people who carry it. So it revealed only 56 percent (that's 75 percent of 75 percent) of the couples who are truly at risk for bearing a child with the disease. It missed 44 percent of such couples. Even if couples are provided with good counseling about the meaning of such tests—a considerable and costly task—most will face anxiety about how to act on the results.

As technology allows us to pinpoint an increasing number of genetic diseases, more and more people will be drawn into the testing network. Many people may not wish to obtain their genetic profiles, particularly if they are at risk for an inheritable disease for which no treatment is known, but commercial and medical interests may pressure them to be tested anyway. Benjamin S. Wilford and Norman Fost, physicians and medical ethicists on the faculty at the University of Wisconsin Medical School, have estimated that the potential market for genetic carrier screening and prenatal testing is enormous, eventually including 2.8 million people who will get themselves tested each year to learn whether they are carriers of the recessive genes for cystic fibrosis, sickle cell anemia, hemophilia, and muscular dystrophy. Wilford and Fost predict that screening could become a billion-dollar industry, with tests for, among others, the 8 million Americans who may be carriers of the cystic fibrosis gene alone. Still, genetic testing, prenatal or otherwise, can also reveal to individuals that either they or their newly-conceived children are safe from some specific genetic doom, and in that sense it can be liberating. "After twenty-eight years of not knowing, it's like being released from prison," said a young woman who was tested and found to be without the gene for Huntington's. "To have hope for the future . . . to be able to see my grandchildren."

The torrents of new human genetic information will undoubtedly pose challenges across a broad spectrum of socioeconomic values and practices. Employers and medical or life insurers might seek to learn the genetic profiles of prospective employees or clients. Employers might wish to identify workers likely to contract disorders that allegedly affect job performance or whose onset could be brought about by features of the workplace. Both employers and insurers might wish to identify people who are likely to fall victim to diseases that result in costly medical or disability payouts. The employers could use the information to assign susceptible people to risk-free duties or environments. They might also use it to deny them jobs, just as medical or life insurers might exploit it to exclude them from coverage. Whatever the purpose, genetic identification would brand people with what an American union official has called a lifelong "genetic scarlet letter" or what some Europeans term a "genetic passport."

A good deal of evidence suggests that we are right to worry about the use of genetic information. Around 1970, a fear spread that people with a sickle cell trait—those who possess one of the recessive genes for the disease—might suffer the sickling of their red blood cells in the reduced oxygen environment of high altitudes. Such people, a disproportionately large number of whom are black, were prohibited from entering the Air Force Academy, restricted to ground jobs by several major commercial air carriers, and often charged higher premiums by insurance companies. Recently, a couple whose first child suffers from cystic fibrosis became pregnant and sought to have their fetus diagnosed prenatally for the disease. Their medical insurer agreed to pay for the test so long as the mother would abort the second child if the results were positive; otherwise, the company would cancel the family health plan. (The company relented, but only when threatened with a lawsuit.)

A good deal of the genetic discrimination so far appears to have been arbitrary, callous, and, especially in the employment area, a product of ignorance—for example, taking the presence of a single recessive disease gene as evidence that the applicant is vulnerable to specific conditions in a workplace. A recent survey conducted by several members of the Harvard Medical School faculty turned up some thirty instances of genetic discrimination. People with inherited biochemical disorders were denied insurance even though they had been successfully treated and were not ill. An auto insurer refused to cover a man with a genetically based neuromuscular disorder who suffered no disability, and an employer declined to hire a woman after she revealed that she had the same disorder. Paul Billings, a medical geneticist now at the University of California, Berkeley, and one of the survey authors, noted that the study was not designed to determine whether these agencies "have active policies of genetic discrimination," but he added that the findings "suggest that such polices exist."

A number of commentators have argued that employers and insurers ought to be prohibited from nosing into anybody's genomic passport. In September 1991 the California state legislature passed a bill banning employers, health-service agencies, and disability insurers from withholding jobs or protection simply because a person is a carrier of a single gene associate with disability. However, insurers could sidestep such a prohibition by setting high common rates and offering discounts to clients with healthy genetic profiles, which such clients would, of course, submit voluntarily. Insurers have a natural interest in information that bears on risk. To them, rate discrimination based on genuine knowledge of risk is neither arbitrary nor illegitimate; it is sound business practice.

The prevailing view in the industry, which has become increasingly well informed about genetic disease, is clear in a June 1989 report entitled "The Potential Role of Genetic Testing in Risk Classification" that was largely prepared by Robert Pokorski and circulated by the American Council of Life Insurance. "If insurers were unable to use genetic tests during the underwriting process 'risks should only be classified on the basis of factors that people can control'," Pokorski wrote, "then equity would give way to equality (equal premiums regardless of risk) and private insurance as it is known today might well cease to exist."

Industry representatives believe that equality would have a negative effect not only on insurance providers but also on many of the people they cover. If a client has a high genetic medical risk that is not reflected in his or her premiums, then that person would receive a high payout at low cost to himself or herself but high cost to the company. The problem would be compounded if such a person hides the risk from the company—and buys a large amount of insurance. In either case, the company would have to pass its increased costs along to other policyholders, which is to say that high-risk policyholders would be taxing low-risk ones.

To keep that from happening, insurance companies want to know as much about their clients, genetically and otherwise, as their clients know about themselves. They may also decide to go further and to require genetic testing of clients so that they can tailor rates to risk. The industry rightly, and somewhat ruefully, expects consumers to resist. "It seems unavoidable that there will be lots of legal battles as this technology unfolds," says Rob Bier, the managing director of communications for the American Council of Life Insurance. "The insurance industry actually wishes genetic testing had never been developed."

The legal battles could grow more heated as the Human Genome Project accumulates more data. As we come to a detailed understanding of the relationship between genetics and disease, companies will be able to determine an individual's risk to the point, perhaps, where risk becomes certainty and lifetime medical costs can be exactly calculated. In that case, medical insurance premiums will amount to payment for lifetime medical care on the layaway plan.

Alternatively, the more we learn about the human genome, the more it will become obvious that everyone is susceptible to some kind of genetic disease or disability. Everyone carries some genetic load and is likely to fall ill in one way or another. Of course, the cost and severity of the illnesses will vary, but if everyone is aware of his or her genetic jeopardy, we may well see more interest in a rating system that expresses what the Europeans call solidarity. In Europe, according to G. W. de Wit, a professor of insurance economics at Erasmus University in the Netherlands, if, for example, parents with a genetically diseased fetus choose to have the child, "all medical expenses for that child will be borne by the insurer. It seems fully justified to have the other policyholders contribute [solidarity]," he adds, "because otherwise the free choice of the parents is jeopardized." De Wit doubts that European medical insurers will demand genetic information from clients.

To suggest that providing care or coverage for a genetically based disease or disorder is unacceptably costly is to cast a shadow over people who suffer from it. Already those who would abort a newly conceived child with such an affliction have been attacked as stigmatizing the living who have the ailment. Protests have come from individuals and families with such diseases as cystic fibrosis and sickle cell anemia and especially from the handicapped and their advocates. Barbara Faye Waxman, an activist for the disabled who herself has a neuromuscular impairment, has criticized her fellow workers in a Los Angeles Planned Parenthood clinic for displaying "a strong eugenics mentality that exhibited disdain, discomfort, and ignorance toward disabled babies."

In the European Parliament, the Committee on Legal Affairs has warned against seeing the birth of handicapped children "only as an avoidable technical error," pointing out that selective abortion of the handicapped "not only undermines our ability to accept the disabled but also makes no significant impact on the problem of disability." In the United States, some advocates for the disabled have joined the antiabortion movement. But it seems to make little sense to try to preserve the dignity of one group by limiting the reproductive freedom of another. It would make a good deal more sense to recognize that values of social decency compel us to live with conflicting practices—endorsing the use of genetic information in personal reproductive choices while upholding the rights and dignity of the diseased and disabled.

The fears that the genome project will foster a drive to produce "superbabies" or to callously eliminate the unfit are grossly exaggerated. They also divert attention from the scientific and social issues that the project actually does raise—particularly how human genetic information should be used by geneticists, the media, insurers, employers, and government. There should be no need, as Congressman Bob Wise of West Virginia noted in 1991 at a House subcommittee hearing on the issue, "to create a new genetic underclass."

Germ-Line Gene Therapy and the Medical Imperative

Ronald Munson and Lawrence H. Davis

Ronald Munson and Lawrence Davis point out that although germ-line gene therapy has the potential to eliminate hundreds of genetic diseases, critics claim that it is morally unacceptable. The authors examine three objections: (1) germ-line therapy violates the rights of future persons to an unaltered genetic inheritance; (2) eliminating or adding genetic traits will produce conflicts between individuals and society and exacerbate social and economic inequalities; (3) tampering with the basic structure of humans is "playing God" and may produce results we are not competent to predict or control.

Munson and Davis maintain that none of the objections justifies prohibiting germ-line gene therapy. Moreover, they argue that medicine has a "therapeutic imperative" that imposes on it a prima facie obligation to pursue therapies that promise to promote human health effectively. Because germ-line gene therapy holds such a promise, medicine has a prima facie obligation to pursue it.

. . . Gene therapy refers to the use of recombinant DNA techniques to treat diseases involving missing or impaired genes. It is still in the experimental stages with only a handful of patients at the National Institutes of Health currently undergoing the therapy. Within this decade, however, two types of gene therapy—gene augmentation and gene modification—are likely to become established modes of treatment (see Verma 1990). Gene augmentation, in which a normal copy of a gene is inserted into a cell to direct the synthesis of a protein that would normally be produced by the missing or defective gene, is the only approach so far attempted in humans. Gene modification, in which an impaired gene is corrected by splicing in a gene at a specific location in the cellular DNA but not otherwise altering the cell's genome, has been demonstrated in several mammalian species. Gene surgery, which involves excising an impaired gene and replacing it with a normal copy, remains a distant—although real—possibility.

Although even the experimental use of gene therapy is recent, its possibilities have been discussed extensively for more than a decade, and critics have raised a number of objections to it or some aspects of it (President's Commission 1982; OTA 1984; Nichols 1988; Walters 1991). NIH committees overseeing the research and many other observers now approve of somatic cell therapy as long as safeguards needed in any experimental procedure are followed and protocols pass appropriate review. No similar consensus has been reached, however, regarding the application of gene therapy to cells in the germ line—ova, sperm, and cells that give rise to them. This is partly because of the enormous technical difficulties facing germ-line gene therapy. But it is also because germ-line gene therapy strikes many as involving especially difficult moral issues. In this paper we examine the most important of these. We argue that none presents an insurmountable moral obstacle to germ-line gene therapy. To the contrary, we will argue that medicine has a positive duty to proceed with its development.

The Limits and Possibilities of Somatic Cell and Germ-Line Therapy

Gene therapy is likely to have the most impact in treating diseases caused by single gene defects, especially autosomal recessive disorders (Nichols 1988; Anderson 1990; Holtzman 1989). This accounts for many conditions, including sickle-cell disease, Tay-Sachs disease, phenylketonuria, and cystic fibrosis. The hundreds of diseases caused by chromosomal disorders (e.g., Down Syndrome) or by an interaction between genes and the environment during fetal development (e.g., neural tube defects) are not obvious prospects. But the estimated 4,000 monogenic diseases cause 7 percent of neonatal deaths, affect 1 percent of newborns, and are responsible for almost 10 percent of childhood deaths. About half of these diseases cause early death, and almost three-quarters of the rest produce severe impairments that make ordinary life virtually impossible (Nichols 1988, p. 9)

The thrust of efforts to find ways to treat these diseases so far has involved somatic cell therapy. Hence, even if the therapy can treat or eliminate

From *Kennedy Institute of Ethics Journal* Vol. 2, No. 2, 137–158, June 1992. Reprinted by permission of the Johns Hopkins University Press.

a disease from an individual who has inherited a faulty gene, it will do nothing to alter the probability that the person's offspring will inherit the same defective gene. For example, someone with Huntington's disease has a 50–50 chance of passing on the gene causing the disease. Even if somatic cell therapy could eliminate the way the gene is expressed, the 50–50 chance of passing it on would remain.

Alteration of germ-line cells might change this. For dominant conditions, the aim would be to remove the defective gene from a person's gametes (ova or sperm cells) or their precursors, and replace it with one that would function normally. For recessive conditions, it might suffice to insert a gene that would function normally. Or instead of this "gametocyte therapy," the cells of an already-conceived pre-embryo might be similarly treated. ("pre-embryo transformation"). Success of either of these forms of germ-line gene therapy would mean that neither the individuals resulting from treated gametes or pre-embryo, nor their progeny, would inherit the disorder (Fowler et al. 1989).

If germ-line gene therapy were possible, practical, and widely employed, hundreds of genetic diseases might be eliminated from families. In each case, it would be possible for the disease to occur again through mutation, but the risk would be no greater than in the population at large, and the total number of cases needing somatic cell or other therapy would be greatly reduced. Horrible diseases like Lesch-Nyhan, PKU, and Tay-Sachs would simply disappear as a nightmarish heritage in certain family lines. . . . We would reach the goal described over a decade ago by Joseph Fletcher:

> The ultimate goal of [gene therapy] is not to ameliorate the ills of patients prenatally or postnatally, but to start people off healthy and free of disease through the practice of medicine preconceptively. . . . It aims to control people's initial genetic design and constitution—their genotypes—by gene surgery and by genetic design. (1974, p. 56)

. . .

Moral Objections to Germ-Line Gene Therapy

Against Fletcher's vision, some argue that there is a morally relevant distinction between somatic and germ-line therapy, and that germ-line therapy is a morally unacceptable means of achieving the goal of eradicating genetic disease.

But what wrong can be alleged about germ-line therapy? Its distinguishing feature is its impact on future generations. (In some cases, somatic cell therapy can also have an effect on future generations, but this is not the aim of the treatment—see Lappé 1991, pp. 623f., 627, 629f.) Somehow, this feature has led to a widespread feeling that the procedure is morally questionable. However, the moral doubts are often only hinted at in a rhetorical fashion and are not carefully articulated. Part of what we want to do here is to state those doubts as clearly and persuasively as we can so that we can lay them to rest definitively.

We think all the doubts about germ-line therapy express the single basic worry that it is illegitimate "tampering." The three lines of objection that have played important roles in the public debate see this as tampering with the rights of individuals, with the social order, and with the order of nature itself. We will present and examine each of these in turn, emphasizing the third. In no case will we find an insurmountable moral barrier to the development and use of germ-line therapy.

1. Germ-Line Therapy and Individual Rights

The Parliamentary Assembly of the Council of Europe (1982b) refers to a person's right to a genome that has not been "tampered" with:

> [The Assembly r]ecommends that the Committee of Ministers: . . . provide for explicit recognition in the European Convention on Human Rights of the right to a genetic inheritance which has not been artificially interfered with, except in accordance with certain principles which are recognized as being fully compatible with respect for human rights (as, for example, in the field of therapeutic applications). . . .

The basis for this alleged right is none too clear, even if we do not question (as many would) the very idea of a right possessed by as-yet-unconceived individuals. Prior to the passage quoted, the recommendation invokes the "rights to life and to human dignity protected by Articles 2 and 3 of the European Convention on Human Rights," and claims that these "imply" the right to a pristine genetic inheritance. We fail to see the "implication." For philosophers like Kant, human dignity is equated with our dignity as rational beings, and not with the whole of our biological nature as homo sapiens. Thus as rational beings, we are ends in ourselves, and have a right not to be treated as mere means to the ends of others (Kant [1785] 1959, p. 47). This may entail that others ought not to interfere (unjustifiably) with our pursuit of our own legitimate ends. It does not entail that others ought not to have interfered with our chances to have been conceived, say, with genes for hazel eye color. . . .

Another possible basis mentioned by Mauron and Thévoz (1991) is Hans Jonas's view that we have "an ontological responsibility toward the preservation of the 'image of man.'" We reject this view, although we cannot discuss it here. We conclude then that the alleged right to an untouched genome has no basis and in fact there is no such right. . . .

Less dramatically, germ-line therapy involves "tampering" with a person's body, so it may easily infringe on several genuine and important individual rights. Yet all forms of gene therapy—indeed, all forms of therapy—can be viewed as doing this. For example, procedures like coronary-artery bypass surgery could violate a person's autonomy and right not to be subjected to harm or to the risk of harm. We offer protection against such violation and legitimate the "tampering" by requiring the individual's "informed consent." Perhaps this would suffice for germ-line therapy as well.

A critic might object that this is a bad analogy because germ-line therapy can affect the descendants of the recipient, too. As many writers have emphasized, this feature makes it impossible to secure the informed consent of all the individuals affected (see, for example, Fletcher 1983; Lappé 1991).

This is undeniably true. However we are aware of no persuasive reasons for thinking that non-existent potential progeny or member of future generations have (as yet) any autonomy that could be tampered with. So there is nothing to protect by requiring their "informed consent." Thus, we see no point in lamenting the impossibility of our obtaining it.

We are less certain about whether those in this group of potential offspring and descendants have the right not to be harmed or subjected to risk of harm. But we are certain that insofar as they have such rights—or, more simply, insofar as we are obligated not to subject them to harm or (extra) risk of harm—neither the rights not the obligations are absolute.

Some may claim that even if these rights and obligations are not absolute, they still are strong enough so that in practice, germ-line gene therapy would rarely if ever be permissible. This seems implied by the "Declaration of Inuyama" adopted by the Council for International Organizations of Medical Sciences (CIOMS 1991): "There would have to be confidence that, when treatment affecting future generations is undertaken, descendants of those so treated would still agree with the decision generations later."

Similarly, Berger and Gert (1991, p. 679) would limit germ-line therapy to "cases in which the benefits to the person receiving the initial treatment is [sic] so great that it outweighs the risks not only for him but also for all of his descendants" since "the genetic make-up of an unlimited number of people" is affected. We cannot confidently predict what the conditions of life or people's values will be generations from now, so we cannot confidently predict our remote descendant's agreement with our decisions, nor can we judge precisely about benefits and risks to infinitely many of our descendants, so germ-line gene therapy would rarely if ever meet the requirements set by these statements.

But these statements are too strong. The first seems unduly influenced by the idea of informed consent, which we have already argued is irrelevant in this context. And the second views our actions as more momentous than they probably are. We should bear in mind that a remote future generation may be able to reverse a genetic change we introduce that turns out disadvantageous (Moseley 1991, p. 644). And as several authors have pointed out, we regularly make decisions that we know will affect future generations—including the very decision to have children—without acknowledging requirements as strong as these (Moseley 1991, pp. 642f.; Lappé 1991, p. 631; and cf. Zimmerman 1991, p. 597). It is implausible that this practice is wrong, even if we have not been as responsible as we should be in our actions (including reproduction) affecting future generations. . . . Whatever exactly the rights of offspring and descendants, the promise of good enough consequences—say, the eradication of Lesch-Nyhan disease—could outweigh a sufficiently uncertain threat of harm and justify "tampering" with those rights.

If germ-line therapy involves illegitimate tampering, it is not illegitimate tampering with the rights of those directly affected or their descendants.

2. Germ-Line Therapy and Conflicts of Interest

H. J. J. Leenen (1988, p. 79) has pointed out another area of concern. The introduction of germ-line therapy as an option could lead to clashes between parental autonomy and the interests of present society or groups within society. For example, suppose a woman refused to agree to a demand by society or an insurance company that to become a parent she must have germ-line therapy to prevent her offspring from inheriting her gene for Huntington's disease. Should she be forced to submit?

Fletcher and Anderson (1992) ask about clashes of a different sort: "Can genetic diagnosis and therapy be equitably distributed, so as not primarily to benefit elites? Will germ-line therapy invest too-radical power in the hands of few?" Similarly, Zimmerman (1991, pp. 606–7) cites fears that germ-line therapy will lead to the development of nontherapeutic "enhancement" procedures, so that parents having the means will use it to guarantee themselves above-average children "[T]he distribution of desirable biological traits among different socioeconomic and ethnic groups would become badly skewed, resulting de facto in exacerbated social and economic inequality" (Zimmerman 1991, p. 607; see also Anderson 1989).

Concerns like these suggest that germ-line therapy threatens to open a Pandora's box of new moral conflicts and dilemmas, and therefore some people would avoid it. Even making it available, would be a kind of "tampering" with the social order. But the problems are no different in kind from conflicts and dilemmas we already face. For example, should we require those with Huntington's disease in their family history to be tested for the gene and allow them to reproduce only when the result is negative (Purdy 1988)? Or, to take a different kind of case, should we legally require a pregnant woman to act in ways that will not subject the fetus to greater than normal risks? Doing so would mean, at the least, that she should not smoke, consume alcohol, or use nonprescribed drugs (Mathieu 1991), and might also mean she should eat a proper diet and exercise regularly.

The examples could be multiplied, but these two are enough to show that Pandora's box is already open. Similarly, we should remember that problems of fair distribution of scarce resources are hardly unprecedented. We already have the kind of social and moral difficulties in our society to which germ-line therapy would give rise. Introduction of the therapy, then, would not be an illegitimate "tampering" with the social order.

3. Germ-Line Therapy as "Playing God"

The novel feature of germ-line therapy is that by it we modify the very genetic structure that as-yet-unconceived individuals are to have. This seems both more serious and potentially more sinister than any other medical therapies or public health measures. An individual's genetic structure, after all, determines the kind of being an individual will be, apart from and prior to the influence of both the biological and social environment. It determines whether the creature that develops is a bird or a beaver, a horse or a human. Hence, changing the genetic makeup of germ cells is tampering with the very order of nature. In the popular phrase, it is "playing God."

As rhetorically effective as this phrase may be in encouraging a negative attitude toward germ-line therapy, it is not at all clear just what is wrong with "playing God" in this particular way. Three attempts to explain are worth considering. (See also the President's Commission's 1982 report, *Splicing Life*, pp. 53–60.)

a. Germ-Line Therapy as a Prelude to Eugenics. Some argue that what begins as genetic "tampering" aimed at obliterating disease will lead to positive eugenics—"tampering" aimed at improving our children and the whole of humanity. As our understanding of the genetic basis of socially desirable traits like musical talent, mathematical insight, and athletic skill increases, we will be able to engineer human beings to meet our specifications. But trying to do this would be wrong (apart from the questions of fair distribution already mentioned) because, as Paul Ramsey (1970, p. 124) puts it, "Man [is not] wise enough to make himself a successful self-modifying system or wise enough to begin doctoring the species." (See also Anderson 1989.)

At least two problems weaken the force of this objection. First, the objection is only to genetic modification in the service of positive eugenics. Even if Ramsey is right about our lacking the wisdom to turn ourselves into a "self-modifying system," it does not follow that there is anything intrinsically wrong with employing germ-line therapy to eliminate diseases. And as for the worry that negative eugenics will lead to positive eugenics, we may note that the potential for practicing positive eugenics has been with us at least since the time we recognized that there is a connection between the traits of offspring and those their parents. We have resisted virtually all efforts and proposals to make use of selective breeding to shape the human species to satisfy an articulated ideal (Ludmerer 1972). Perhaps our experience with attempts at eugenics fits the description that Mauron and Thévoz give of the whole history of bioethical issues:

> [T]he slippery slope really looks more like a ramshackle staircase: once in a while, we trip down a few steps. This makes us wake up, take stock of ethical shortcomings and climb up the stairs by appropriate measures such as societal regulation. (1991, p. 658)

While it is true that germ-line engineering offers an easier and more effective way to exert control over the human gene pool, we have no reason to suppose that just because we possessed the technology we would employ it. It is simply not true that as a society we have always done whatever it is possible to do. . . .

. . . Our second problem for Ramsey, then, is that it is not obvious that we lack the wisdom to "doctor" ourselves in the manner indicated. In truth, we do not know yet whether we have it or not. After we have had experience modifying the genome of other organisms and predicting the outcome, when we have learned the possible drawbacks and the chances of success in modifications performed on humans, then perhaps we can judge our wisdom. We can imagine ways of making ourselves better than we are now, but the unanswered questions concern how much and what kinds of risk we will be willing to take and what sort of price we will be willing to pay to improve ourselves. These questions cannot be answered usefully in a vacuum. (For other discussion of the acceptability of positive eugenics, see Mauron and Thévoz 1991, pp. 651–52.)

b. Germ-Line Therapy and Unpredictable Losses.   Even if gene therapy remains confined to therapeutic applications, some raise the question "whether something important may be lost as disease genes are eliminated" (Cavalieri 1983, p. 473). On one interpretation, this worry is illustrated by the following sort of case. Suppose we are successful in eliminating sickle-cell disease from the human population by removing the disease causing gene and substituting a gene producing normal red blood cells. As it happens, those with sickle-cell trait (i.e., those who are heterozygous for the gene) are more resistant to falciparum malaria. Hence, if we eliminated the gene, we would also be eliminating potential benefits its possession bestows.

The objection takes it for granted that eliminating this potential benefit would be obviously wrong. Yet what it fails to consider is that, since we know about the connection between sickle-cell disease and resistance to malaria, we might decide that eliminating a lethal disease like sickle-cell is worth the loss of a relative immunity to malaria. This would be a reasonable decision, especially since we have effective ways of controlling and treating malaria, but lack adequate treatments for sickle-cell disease.

However, a critic might ask, "How many other connections might there be between diseases and important biological capacities that we don't even realize we have but would be lost forever if we rushed to eradicate the diseases by germ-line therapy?" It would be better not to "tamper" with something whose full significance we cannot hope to appreciate in advance.

Critics who invoke the hazard of an unforeseen disaster cannot be satisfied completely. No one can guarantee that an unexpected hazard might not result from germ-line gene therapy. However, we are not totally ignorant of the nature of genes and of the evolutionary process, and there is no reason to fear that germ-line therapy is more likely to produce an unanticipated disaster than is somatic cell therapy or any other use of recombinant DNA technology. These matters must be assessed in individual cases on the basis of acquired knowledge and experience. When the potential benefits of germ-line therapy are considered, rejecting its use on the basis of potential but unknown hazards is not justifiable.

c. Germ-Line Therapy as Threatening "Humanity."   The previous question about "whether something important may be lost" by the use of germ-line therapy refers to specific biological capacities. However, the question may be understood as having to do with the impossible-to-specify cluster of capacities and features that make us human. Thus, germ-line therapy might be said to be wrong because "tampering" with our humanity is wrong.

As we observed in our discussion of eugenics, germ-line gene therapy is unlikely to compromise the humanity of its products. "Humanity" may be understood just as membership in our biological species, or it may be interpreted as something more subtle, perhaps as our distinctive kind of consciousness or capacities to think and feel. Either way, it is unreasonable to think that the possession of the defective genes that would be eliminated by germ-line therapy—or the absence of genes that would be added—is essential to being human.

Even straightforward examples of nontherapeutic enhancement would not endanger the humanity of its products (cf. Anderson 1989, p. 685). By operating on a person's gametocytes so that her or his descendants would be prone to low cholesterol levels or unusual musical talent, we would not render these descendants nonhuman. Even if such a procedure tended to have genetic effects beyond those specifically planned and desired this would not alter matters. After all, mutations have been occurring throughout human history without compromising the humanity of those in whom they occurred. The human species, like any other, is not a fixed Platonic idea, but an ever-changing population of genes.

Nonetheless, the human species might change. First, it is possible that over many generations genetic changes, some introduced by gene therapy and some occurring by mutation, might accumulate in the gene pool of the human population. Alone, each change might be relatively unimportant, yet the total impact might be that the population embodying these changes is no longer human. In biological terms, phyletic evolution would have occurred. A second possibility is that genetic intervention, by accident or design, might produce immediate and wholesale changes in the progeny of some individuals.

Leon Kass evidently has the first possibility in mind:

> It may . . . mark the end of *human* life as we and all other humans have known it. It is possible that the non-human life which may take our place will be superior, but I think it most unlikely and certainly not demonstrable. In either case, we are ourselves human beings; therefore, we have a proprietary interest in our survival, and our survival *as human beings*. (1972, p. 61)

We can call this the homo superior objection to germ-line gene therapy.

H. J. J. Leenen is concerned with a variant of the second possibility, which we can call the cyborg objection:

> In my opinion . . . the science of genetics with human cells has to remain within human boundaries. . . . the creation of animal-human creatures and of plant-human combinations is inadmissible. This is not to say that the same holds for hybrids, which cannot develop. When scientists transgress the boundaries of what is human, they place themselves outside human society. (1988, p. 75)

Each of these authors views the production of nonhumans from humans with evident dismay. What is striking in these passages is that neither gives a cogent explanation why he feels this way, or why the feeling is justified.

Leenen perhaps is thinking of cyborgs, the monsters of ancient mythology or modern science fiction. Bringing such creatures into existence would be a great evil—to others, to the unhappy creatures themselves, or to both. But that is because these creatures are depicted as subhuman, and/or active enemies of humans. If animal- or plant-human combinations remain favorably disposed toward their human ancestors, and are superior to those ancestors, why should the scientists who originally produce them be considered "outside human society"? (cf. President's Commission (1982, pp. 57–60), which also considers "hybrids," and assumes they would be inferior to us.) Suppose for example that through genetic modification our offspring and their descendants were equipped with chlorophyll-bearing patches on their skin and the capacity for photosynthesis. The resulting partial or complete independence of the usual food chain might be a good thing on the whole, even if we had to classify them all as nonhuman.

Kass's position is that even if our nonhuman descendants are superior to us, their existence would be contrary to our "proprietary interest" in our "survival as human beings." He claims the existence of this interest is a consequence simply of the fact that we are human. But this claim is a blatant nonsequitur. From the fact that we are human, it does not follow that we have an interest in our survival as humans, nor that we have any interest in survival at all. Compare: we (the authors) are Missourians and Americans. We have some interest in our survival as Americans, but none to speak of in our survival as Missourians. Of course Kass is speaking of collective survival. But we have no strong feeling about the survival of Missouri, nor of our descendants (or anyone else's) as Missourians. We do care about the survival of the United States, but we could accept its replacement by something "superior," to use Kass's term. By the same token, we would accept our descendants being citizens of this replacement.

In short, for Kass's argument to work, he needs a premise articulating just what it is about being human that he thinks gives us all a "proprietary interest" in survival as such. This he has conspicuously failed to supply.

Perhaps the thought underlying the objections of Kass, Leenen, and others to tampering with our humanity is something like this. We are Americans and Missourians contingently but humans necessarily. To have a sense of self-worth, then, we need to feel that being human is a good thing to be, that a life lived within the limits of what is humanly possible is [potentially] a good kind of life to lead. There may be "superior" things actual or possible, but there is nothing unsatisfactory about being human. If our offspring will ultimately be nonhuman, then something of value which we exemplify will cease to be. If we choose to bring it about that our offspring are nonhuman, then we seem to be rendering a final negative judgment on our humanity. Tampering with the genetic structure that makes us human is wrong, then, because it conflicts with our sense of our own value.

In reply to this argument, it may be denied that a sense of self-worth requires such an attitude towards one's humanity. Nonetheless such attitudes are common, and may often play the role described. One further example may be the view of Hans Ruh as presented by Mauron and Thévoz (1991, p. 656), "that we ought to transmit to future generations . . . the capability to live a genuinely human life (with its ups and downs)." What is wrong with transmitting the capability to live a superior kind of life, with more "ups" and fewer "downs"?

We concede that people like Leenen and Kass, on our analysis of their position, do have a legitimate concern. But we insist that this attachment to our humanity cannot be adequate grounds for opposition to germ-line gene therapy. First, both of the scenarios described whereby nonhumans would result from the procedure are exceedingly remote. Especially if applications of the techniques are limited to the therapeutic for the foreseeable future, the "end of human life as we know it" that worries Kass could not be a serious threat for thousands of years, if ever (cf. OTA 1984, p. 32). Nor is there any reason to think a clearly nonhuman being

could or would be produced deliberately by even the most enthusiastic advocates of positive eugenics. The bare conceivability of these disasters surely does not warrant refusing to develop the techniques for eliminating genetic diseases. Second, if we imagine future circumstances in which the end of humanity because of these techniques was an immediate threat, we might find that alternatives were worse. Being remembered by whatever nonhumans succeed us may be better than simple extinction without a trace. In any case, this sort of concern need affect our values and present day practical reasoning no more than speculation about the ultimate "cosmic crunch" or heat death of the universe.

This completes our examination of reasons for thinking it wrong to tamper with our genetic structure by performing germ-line gene therapy. We have found no cogent objection. The claim that "we are not wise enough" is at best premature. The worry that something of great value depends on the genes that we would remove is without foundation. The concern that germ-line gene therapy, or nontherapeutic use of the techniques employed in it, may pose a threat to our humanity or our feelings about our humanity, cannot be taken seriously as offsetting the value of eliminating genetic diseases.

In sum, all three objections are open to the same counterobjection: It may be wrong for us not to tamper with our genetic structure. Faced with the reality of genetic diseases, how can we justify not developing and employing a promising remedy? Are we wise enough to see a compelling reason for not doing so? Can we be sure that we will never face even worse dangers, against which skill in manipulating genes in germ-line cells would be our only protection? Conceivably, a day might come when our very survival as humans would depend on our ability to use complex techniques for which germ-line gene therapy is only the beginning. Why are the objections any more plausible than this counterobjection? (Mauron and Thévoz (1991, p. 660) point out that if we had foresworn recombinant DNA research since the Berg Moratorium, we would know less about AIDS today than we do; perhaps we would not even have been able to identify the HIV virus as the agent of AIDS.)

The objections take for granted that by tampering with our genetic natures, we are likely to cause more trouble than we prevent. What evidence supports this rather than its exact opposite? Occasionally, mention is made of the "wisdom of evolution" (see, for example, Cavalieri 1983, p. 472; President's Commission 1982, p. 62). But even if some "wisdom" can be found in the mechanism by which natural selection has left us susceptible to genetic diseases, it cannot be supposed that this "wisdom" is a reliable guide for us (cf. President's Commission 1982, pp. 62–63).

A more likely support for the objections is the common belief that our genetic nature is the design of a good and wise Being. His wisdom can be relied upon; if our design permits genetic diseases, there must be a good reason, which we cannot expect to fathom. Moreover, common belief also suggests that He has a right and an interest in our survival as humans which would be violated if we engineered our eventual replacement by another species. On this analysis, all the objections reduce to the claim: Germ-line gene therapy is wrong because it is tampering with His handiwork.

None of the objectors cited express themselves in these terms, and none would, not even the ones who share the belief in a good and wise Designer of humanity. The parallel to "If God wanted us to fly He would have given us wings" is too obvious and unanswerable. This sort of theological appeal cannot be correct, whether or not God exists. But we have seen that the objections as actually expressed do not work either. Germ-line gene therapy cannot be branded as illegitimate "tampering" with the order of nature.

Medicine and the Therapeutic Imperative

We wish now to go beyond the moral legitimacy of this therapy and argue—still on the assumptions noted—that medicine itself has a prima facie duty to pursue and employ germ-line gene therapy. Sometimes, a certain course of action is morally right, although no one has an obligation to take it. For example, it would be right for physicians to work one day a month without fees in community clinics, but they have no moral duty to do so, either individually or collectively. However, in contrast, we want to claim that members of the medical professions would be collectively derelict if research aimed at the therapeutic use of germ-line gene therapy were neglected without good reason.

We should stress that our claim is only for the existence of a collective obligation, a duty falling on medicine as an enterprise. Very likely, if we are right and our assumptions are correct, then this collective obligation will entail some individual obligations on specific person or groups of persons. But without a detailed examination of the structure, membership, and existing practices of the medical enterprise, these individual obligations cannot be determined. For a somewhat parallel example, suppose it were argued that the American people had a collective obligation to provide shelter for its homeless; exactly which members of the "American people" had precisely which specific obligations toward this end would be a matter for a wholly different argument, depending on the structure and existing practices of our governmental and other bodies, and many other factors. We shall not attempt this "wholly different argument" for the case of medicine, and so shall not say how the collective obligation differentially affects physicians, medical researchers, public health officials, and others affiliated with the medical enterprise. Our interest is rather in the prima facie duty itself, and its basis in the nature of medicine.

Many assume unreflectively that medicine is a science, and many also think that science is "value-neutral" in some sense. These views may lead one to conclude that "medicine" cannot have any duty at all, prima facie or actual. At most, individual physicians or researchers have obligations to heal or develop therapies because of general moral principles, such as beneficence. (The arguments of Zimmerman (1991, p. 591) and Fletcher and Anderson (1992) may be read this way.) We believe that medicine itself has an obligation.

We escape the reasoning of the preceding paragraph by denying that medicine is a science. (For a detailed defense of this position, see Munson 1981.) We begin our argument by contrasting medicine with science in the respect most relevant here, the idea of what it is most concerned with. . . .

Medicine, like science, pursues knowledge, but not in a disinterested way. Indeed, it is antithetical to the character of medicine as an enterprise to seek knowledge as an inherent or self-justifying good. Medicine's concern with knowledge is unequivocally instrumental or conditional. Medicine is joined so closely with science in inquiry and experiment, because it is by means of scientific understanding that medicine can most effectively secure its end of promoting human health.

Not all aspects of medicine involve the basic theories and concepts of the natural sciences. Clinical medicine, in particular, involves complicated human interactions, and part of the "art" of medicine involves "taking care" of patients without the guidance of established theories and proven rules. Nevertheless, science is one of contemporary medicine's major means of working to promote the welfare of patients as a population.

An enterprise is successful when it achieves its aims. Loosely speaking, science does its job when it provides persuasive reasons for accepting empirical theories about the nature and character of the world. The success of medicine cannot be judged by any comparable epistemic criterion. Rather, the basic standard of evaluation must be practical or instrumental success with respect to its specific aim.

In seeking to meet health needs, medicine can be described as a quest for control over the factors affecting health. Understanding (knowledge) is important to medicine because it leads to control. Yet where understanding is lacking, medicine will seek control by relying on low-level empirical rules validated by practical success.

A consequence of medicine's aim of meeting health needs is that medicine possesses a therapeutic obligation imposed by its own character. That is, basic to medicine as an enterprise is the prima facie duty to treat those who are ill in ways that will help them achieve the degree of health of which they are capable.

Treatment by drugs or surgery, diet or exercise, is one way in which medicine exercises control over disease, but the therapeutic obligation can also be regarded as involving an obligation to prevent the occurrence of disease. Although the success of a treatment might be most dramatic, preventing a disease altogether might be seen as the most effective form of control. Medicine aims at promoting human health by exercising control over disease, and since elimination is the most effective form of control, elimination of disease is the ultimate aim of medicine.

The eradication of smallpox from the world's population exemplifies the realization of this aim in a particular instance. The elimination of the disease was announced by the World Health Organization in 1979, and certainly the disappearance of the disease is to be preferred over all forms of therapy, no matter how effective. To our knowledge, no one argued that it would be morally wrong to eradicate smallpox through vaccination and other public health measures.

What is true of infectious diseases like smallpox is, of course, also true of genetic diseases. Somatic cell therapy promises to become a valuable means of controlling them and minimizing the suffering they cause. Once again, however, complete control would go beyond prevention or effective treatment in individual cases.

Germ-line gene therapy offers us the chance to rid ourselves completely (except for new mutations) of many serious genetic diseases for which there is no effective treatment. Given medicine's aim of seeing to the health of people and its instrumental character, it is this ideal that medicine is obligated to pursue. Social circumstances (such as a lack of resources to conduct research) and unavoidable difficulties (such as not being able to solve the technical problems of safely and effectively altering sex cells) may make the road leading to germ-line gene therapy a long one. Nevertheless, the prima facie duty to pursue this ideal remains.

Conclusion

The more than 4,000 genetic diseases involving a defect in a single gene cause thousands of deaths, an incalculable amount of suffering, and staggering economic costs. We have shown that the objections most often raised to germ-line gene therapy are not so persuasive as to stand in the way of using it to treat diseases. And we have shown that the character of medicine imposes on medical professionals a prima facie duty to pursue the development and use of germ-line gene therapy.

The diseases are so serious and the promise of the therapy so great, that it would be wrong to give in to the objections that have been raised to gene therapy. If they are allowed to prevail, then the social and scientific support needed to realize the therapeutic possibilities of gene therapy may never materialize. This outcome would be as wrong and almost as serious as if we had failed to develop and use antibiotics or vaccines.

We thank Robert Cook-Deegan and LeRoy Walters for extremely valuable comments on an earlier version of this paper. Ronald Munson gratefully acknowledges the support of a University of Missouri-St. Louis Faculty Research Fellowship.

References

Anderson, W. French. 1989. Human Gene Therapy: Why Draw a Line? *The Journal of Medicine and Philosophy* 14: 681–93.

———. 1990. Genetics and Human Malleability. *Hastings Center Report* 20 (1): 21–24.

Berger, Edward M., and Gert, Bernard M. 1991. Genetic Disorders and the Ethical Status of Germ-line Gene Therapy. *The Journal of Medicine and Philosophy* 16: 667–83.

Cavalieri, Liebe F. 1983. Testimony at a Hearing before the Sub-committee and Oversight Committee on Science and Technology, U.S. House of Representatives, 16–18 November 1982. In *Human Genetic Engineering*, Committee Print No. 170, pp. 470–76. Washington, DC: U.S. Government Printing Office.

CIOMS [Council for International Organizations of Medical Sciences]. 1991. *Human Genome Mapping, Genetic Screening and Gene Therapy: Ethical Issues.* Proceedings of the XXIVth CIOMS Conference: Human Genome Mapping, Genetic Screening and Therapy, ed. Z. Bankowski and A, M. Capron. Geneva.

Council of Europe, Parliamentary Assembly. 1982a. Report on genetic engineering presented by the Legal Affairs Committee, J. P. Elmquist rapporteur. Document 4832 of the 33rd Ordinary Session, 18 January. Strasbourg, France.

———. 1982b. Recommendation 934 "On Genetic Engineering." Strasbourg, France.

Fletcher, John C. 1983. Moral Problems and Ethical Issues in Prospective Human Gene Therapy. *Virginia Law Review* 69: 538–40.

Fletcher, John C., and Anderson, W. French. 1992. Germ-Line Gene Therapy: A New Stage of Debate. *Law, Medicine, and Health Care* 20 (1–2). forthcoming.

Fletcher, Joseph. 1974. The Ethics of Genetic Control. New York: Doubleday.

Fowler, Gregory; Juengst, Eric T.; and Zimmerman, Burke K. 1989. Germ-line Gene Therapy and the Clinical Ethos of Medical Genetics. *Theoretical Medicine* 10: 151–65.

Holtzman, Neil A. 1989. *Proceed with Caution.* Baltimore, MD: The Johns Hopkins University Press.

Kant, Immanuel. [1785] 1959. *Foundations of the Metaphysics of Morals.* Trans. Lewis White Beck. Indianapolis: The Bobbs Merrill Company, Inc.

Kass, Leon. 1972. New Beginnings in Life. In *The New Genetics,* ed. Michael Hamilton, pp. 15–63. Grand Rapids, MI: Eerdmans.

Lappé, Marc. 1991. Ethical Issues in Manipulating The Human Germ Line. *The Journal of Medicine and Philosophy* 16: 621–39.

Leenen, H. J. J. 1988. Genetic Manipulation with Human Beings. *Medicine and Law* 7: 71–79.

Ludmerer, Kenneth M. 1972. *Genetics and American Society: A Historical Appraisal.* Baltimore, MD: The Johns Hopkins University Press.

Mathieu, Deborah. 1991. *Preventing Prenatal Harm: Should the State Intervene?* Dordrecht, Holland: Kluwer Academic Publishers.

Mauron, Alex, and Thévoz, Jean-Marie. 1991. Germ-line Engineering: A Few European Voices. *The Journal of Medicine and Philosophy* 16: 649–66.

Moseley, Ray. 1991. Commentary: Maintaining the Somatic/Germ-line Distinction: Some Ethical, Drawbacks. *The Journal of Medicine and Philosophy* 16: 641–47.

Munson, Ronald. 1981. Why Medicine Cannot Be a Science. *The Journal of Medicine and Philosophy* 6: 183–208.

Nichols, Eve K. 1988. Human Gene Therapy. Cambridge, MA: Harvard University Press.

OTA. 1984. *Human Gene Therapy—A Background Paper.* Washington, DC: Office of Technology Assessment.

President's Commission for the Study of Ethical Problems in Medicine and Biomedical and Behavioral Research. 1982. *Splicing Life: A Report on the Social and Ethical Issues of Genetic Engineering with Human Beings.* Washington, DC: U.S. Government Printing Office.

Purdy, L. M. 1988. Genetic Diseases: Can Having Children Be Immoral? In *Intervention and Reflection: Basic Issues in Medical Ethics,* ed. Ronald Munson, pp. 364–71. Belmont, CA: Wadsworth Publishing Co.

Ramsey, Paul. 1970. *Fabricated Man.* New Haven: Yale University Press.

Walters, LeRoy. 1991. Human Gene Therapy: Ethics and Public Policy. *Human Gene Therapy* 2: 115–22.

Verma, Inder M. 1990. Gene Therapy. *Scientific American* 172: 68–72.

Zimmerman, Burke K. 1991. Human Germ-line Therapy: The Case for Its Development and Use. *The Journal of Medicine and Philosophy* 16: 593–612.

Decision Scenario 1 ••

In 1983, a group of Orthodox Jews in New York and Israel initiated a screening program with the aim of eliminating from their community diseases transmitted as recessive genes. The group called itself Dor Yeshorim, "the generation of the righteous."

Because Orthodox Jews do not approve of abortion in most instances, the program does not employ prenatal testing. Instead, high-school students are given a blood test to determine if they carry the genes for Tay-Sachs, cystic fibrosis, or Gaucher's disease. Each student is given a six-digit identification number, and if two students consider dating, they are encouraged to call a hotline. They are told either that they are "compatible" or that they each carry a recessive gene for one of the three diseases. Couples who are carriers are offered genetic counseling.

During 1993, 8,000 people were tested, and eighty-seven couples who were considering marriage decided against it, after they learned that they were both carriers of recessive genes. The test costs twenty-five dollars, and the program is supported in part by funds from the Department of Health and Human Services. Some view the Dor Yeshorim program as a model that might be followed by other groups or by society in general.

The tests were initially only for Tay-Sachs, but over time the other two diseases were added.

Current plans are to continue to add tests for other diseases. However, some critics regard it as a mistake to have moved from testing for almost invariably lethal, untreatable diseases like Tay-Sachs to testing for cystic fibrosis. Individuals may feel pressured into being tested, and those who are carriers of one or more disease-predisposing genes may become unmarriageable, social outcasts. Considering that genes for most diseases manifest themselves in various degrees of severity, many individuals may suffer social rejection for inadequate reasons.

For example, Gaucher's disease, which involves an enzyme defect producing anemia and an enlarged liver and spleen, manifests itself only after age forty-five in half the diagnosed cases. Further, although the disease may be fatal, it often is not, and the symptoms can be treated.

1. *Is the Dor Yeshorim screening program a form of eugenics? If so, does this make it unacceptable?*

2. *Is the program a good model for a national screening program? If not, why not?*

3. *Is it reasonable to screen for nonlethal, genetic diseases?*

4. *What are the dangers inherent in any screening program?*

5. *Would Purdy's arguments tend to support a mandatory screening program? Explain your position.*

Decision Scenario 2 ··

Sara Straus was frightened. She sat in the counselor's office with her hands folded in her lap, trying to look calm.

"Mrs. Straus," the counselor said, "I have the results back on your AFP test. I'm sorry to tell you that the level of alpha protein in your blood is quite high."

"What does that mean?" Mrs. Straus asked.

"It means," said the counselor, "that your chances of having a baby with what we call neural tube defect are quite high. Your child might be born with an open spine or with part of its brain missing."

"Oh, my God. Is there anything I can do?"

The counselor shook her head. "If you mean can you do anything to make the baby normal, the answer is no. The test is about 90% accurate. The only reasonable course is to have an abortion and begin another child when you feel ready."

"But I don't believe in abortion," said Mrs. Straus.

"There's no way we can force you to have one. But, according to the law, if you have been informed of the chances of a defect and do not have an abortion, then you and your husband must accept full financial responsibility for the care of the impaired child."

"How much would that cost?"

"Probably around $100,000 a year."

"We can't afford that," said Mrs. Straus. "Nobody could afford to pay money like that."

"I'm just telling you the law," said the counselor.

"What if we have the child and then can't pay?"

"The law requires that you and your husband declare yourselves bankrupt. The child will then be placed in a public institution, and a fixed percentage of your future earnings will go to pay for its upkeep. Even after its death you must continue to pay until the accumulated costs to the state have been repaid."

"That's unfair," said Mrs. Straus. "We're being forced to go against what we think is right."

1. *At this time, there is no such law as that mentioned by the counselor. Should there be such a law? After all, don't we generally believe that people should accept responsibility for their actions and decisions?*

2. *Is it ever right for society to force people to act in ways they consider to be morally wrong?*

3. *Does Kass's position take into account the social costs that may result from discouraging abortion for genetic or developmental reasons?*

4. *Should screening programs be voluntary and advisory, or should they be backed up by laws that aim to protect society by requiring that individuals act in certain ways as a result of the screening?*

5. *Following Purdy's line of argument, might one claim that, when there is a reason to believe that a child may suffer from a serious genetic disease, the parents have a duty to undergo genetic screening?*

Decision Scenario 3 ••

"I'm sorry I wasn't able to bring you better news," Dr. Valery Mendez said. "I hope our first consultation helped prepare you for it."

Timothy Schwartz shook his head. "We gambled and lost," he said. "We can't say we didn't know what we were doing."

"That doesn't make it much easier," Judith Schwartz said. "When you said we were both Tay-Sachs carriers, I thought 'Well, it won't happen to us.' But I was wrong."

"The odds were in our favor," Mr. Schwartz said. I still think we did the right thing."

"Maybe we shouldn't even have had ourselves tested," Mrs. Schwartz said. "Then we wouldn't even know we've got a problem."

"But we'd have one anyway," her husband said. "Ignorance is bliss only when it's folly to be wise. Now we at least know what we're up against."

"What about this new test?" Mrs. Schwartz asked. "Can we really trust the results?"

"I'm afraid so," said Dr. Mendez. "The fetal cells taken during amniocentesis were cultured, and the chromosome study showed that the child you're carrying will have Tay-Sachs."

"What do you recommend?" Mr. Schwartz asked.

"It's not for me to recommend. I can give you some information—tell you the options—but you've got to make your own decision."

"Is abortion the only solution?" Mrs. Schwartz asked.

"If you call it a solution," Mr. Schwartz said.

"The disease is almost invariably fatal," Dr. Mendez said. "And there is really no effective treatment for it. A lot of people think there may be in the future, but that doesn't help right now."

"So what does it involve?" Mr. Schwartz asked.

"At first your child will seem quite normal, but that's only because it takes time for a particular chemical to build up in the brain. After the first year or so, the child will start to show signs of deterioration. He'll start losing his sight. Then, as brain damage progresses, he'll lose control over his muscles, and eventually he will die.

"And we just have to stand by and watch that happen?" Mrs. Schwartz asked.

"Nothing can be done to stop it," Dr. Mendez said. "It's a terrible and sad disease."

"We certainly do want to have a child," Mr. Schwartz said. "But we don't want to have one that is going to suffer all his life. I don't think I could stand that."

1. How persuasive is Kass's argument that genetic abortion constitutes a threat to the principle that all persons are of equal value in this case?

2. Can Purdy's argument that every child deserves a normal opportunity for a good life be used to justify requiring abortion in a case such as this?

3. Kass contends that none of the three standards he examines can allow us to justify selective abortion. State and evaluate his arguments.

4. How unfavorably must the odds be against having a normal child before (according to Purdy) parents have a duty not to reproduce? In what way is the seriousness of the disease at issue relevant to the odds?

Decision Scenario 4 ••

"The concept behind the bill is very simple, Senator," said Mrs. Laude. "We want to improve the human race, and we know exactly how to do it. The principles of genetics can be used to guide changes in the population."

"You mean," said the Senator, "you can make people smarter?"

"Not as individuals. But we can increase the level of intelligence in society. We can do this by seeing to it that intelligent people have more children than the less intelligent. Over time, the statistical balance will shift toward intelligence."

"And does your draft of the bill make that possible?"

"By a system of financial incentives and disincentives," said Mrs. Laude. "Those above a certain level of intelligence will be offered a yearly stipend to pay part of the expenses for each of their children. Those below that level will receive nothing, and, having to bear the full cost themselves, they are likely to limit the number of children they have. We will also make use of genetic counseling programs to encourage or discourage children, whatever is appropriate in each case."

"These genetic counseling programs will be government run and supported?" the Senator asked.

"That's right. The law will require that everyone be screened and classified before his or her fifteenth birthday."

"Is intelligence all that you'll screen for?"

"It's the only positive trait we will try to increase. We will also screen against genetic diseases, like Tay-Sachs and sickle-cell anemia."

"This will be very controversial, you know," said the Senator.

"We know," Mrs. Laude said. "It will take a person of courage to introduce such a bill into the Senate. But we think it's the most important piece of legislation imaginable. The improvement of our society and of the whole human race will be the end result."

1. *What problems and dangers are inherent in Mrs. Laude's proposal for a program of positive and negative eugenics?*

2. *What can be said in defense of such a program?*

3. *Would a utilitarian be likely to favor such a program?*

4. *Could such a program be defended as compatible with Rawls's principles of justice?*

5. *In what way might germ-line gene therapy be used to reach some of the goals mentioned by Mrs. Laude? Would Munson and Davis consider the eugenic possibilities of germ-line gene therapy a good reason to prohibit its use?*

Decision Scenario 5 ••

"I don't know what your problem is," Harold Lucas said. "We have the opportunity to eliminate sickle cell forever. This is a disease that has caused suffering and death to untold generations of human beings, yet you seem to want to keep it around. What possible reasons could you have?"

"I'm not sure you'll understand," Amy Lamont said. "I'm not in favor of sickle cell. It's a horrible disease, and I have nothing but sympathy for those who have the disease or carry the trait."

"So, let's slice out the defective gene that produces the abnormal hemoglobin and splice in one that does the job right," Lucas said. "We can use somatic-cell therapy to treat those who have the disease now, but let's look to the future. Let's use cell-line therapy to modify the sex cell of the carriers and just get rid of the disease."

Amy Lamont shook her head. "It sounds humane, but it's not so easy as that," she said. "To do that means modifying human beings, and if we start doing that, I don't know when we would stop. We might do anything at all with them."

"You're afraid of some kind of wild eugenics scheme?"

"That's one problem I have," Amy Lamont said. "It's something deeper than that, though. I just don't like the idea of tampering with human life and human destiny. To change ourselves deliberately is, I think, to make us something less than human.

"If I understand you correctly, I couldn't disagree with you more," Harold Lucas said.

1. *Rephrase Amy Lamont's arguments so they are in an explicit form.*

2. *Possessing sickle-cell trait has been found to offer protection from a particular form of malaria. Is this an adequate reason for not eliminating the gene from the human gene pool, if we were able to do so?*

3. *Do Munson and Davis share Lamont's point of view as far as eugenic enhancement is concerned?*

4. *Do Munson and Davis endorse Lamont's objection that germ-line therapy would be wrong because it alters the human genome?*

Decision Scenario 6 ••

"The screening program is for the *benefit* of our employees," Carl Larski said. "Amchem production involves radiologic agents and potentially harmful chemical substances. It is absolute madness not to monitor people for overexposure to radiation. I'm sure you agree with that. And it's ridiculous to expose women who are pregnant to a radiation hazard, because that could cause serious impairments in the child. Of course, sometimes women are pregnant for a while before they realize it, so it makes sense to keep all women of childbearing age away from radiation."

Susan Spencer shook her head to show that she disagreed. "You're using company policy to make decisions that people ought to make for themselves," she said. "If a woman wants to take a risk, she should be allowed to. After all, radiation can make men sterile, as well as causing them direct harm. Amchem's practices are inherently discriminatory. And they don't stop with radiation, and they don't stop with women. The company excludes African Americans from jobs that put them into contact with naphthalene."

"That's correct," Larski said. "That's because they are much more likely to develop a serious form of anemia than most other workers. And we also keep women away from most of the chemicals we work with. We're concerned about them, of course, but no more so than we are concerned about the men who work with them. We are, once again, worried about the effects on their children."

"Mostly you are worried about insurance claims and lawsuits."

"That's a factor," Larski admitted. "If some people are more prone to develop serious illnesses than others and we can detect it in advance, then we have a corporate duty to keep them out of harm's way. It's true the we help control our insurance cost by doing that, but we also help people avoid getting ill."

"We are impressed with Amchem's humane concerns," Spencer said. "But the Committee Against Screening is much more interested in protecting the individual's right to seek employment of her or his choice. Also, CAS believes that the data used to exclude people from jobs may also be used to exclude them from other benefits. For example, insurance companies are likely to refuse health insurance to someone who runs a greater than average risk of developing a serious disease. The result is that people are penalized because of their genetic makeup, and that's an accident of birth. Our society has a duty to protect individuals from just that sort of discrimination, and CAS intends to do all it can to make sure that society lives up to that duty."

"That's very eloquent," Larski said. "But you're trying to force equality where none exists. People are different, and the society can't alter that fact."

1. *Is it a legitimate function of society to protect individuals from hazards in the workplace? Is there a limit to steps that can be taken to provide protection?*

2. *Suppose that certain jobs present greater hazards to women and African Americans that to others. Would it be wrong to exclude these groups from the jobs? Are all forms of discrimination that are not directly related to job performance unjustifiable?*

3. *"We value individual autonomy, and it may seem enough to warn people of the hazards they may face in accepting a particular job. However, the need to earn a living may force some to accept jobs that put them at a greater-than-average risk. Consequently, it is misleading to think that we are preserving autonomy by allowing individuals to decide for themselves whether they wish to accept a job that is more than normally hazardous to them. Economic necessity makes a mockery out of the notion that people are free to choose." Evaluate this argument.*

Decision Scenario 7 ••

"The trick," said Martin Anders, "is to make use of the virus as part of our production system."

"How's that?" Hilda Presti asked.

"The DNA of the virus contains a segment of

DNA that we introduced into it. When the virus attacks a bacterial cell, it injects the DNA into it. The viral DNA then takes over the cell machinery enough to get the cell to make copies of the DNA and get it to synthesize the proteins coded for by the DNA segment we spliced in."

"That means that, if the proteins are something that are useful—like a hormone—then you've got a chemical factory working to produce it."

"That's the idea," Anders said. "We can harness the power of literally billions of bacteria to make what we want."

"Isn't that dangerous, though?" Presti asked. "Isn't it at least possible that the viruses might contain some DNA segments that would make the bacteria resistant to antibiotics?"

"That's the sort of Andromeda Strain scenario people used to worry about in the seventies, but we realize today that that's just not something that's going to happen."

"Can you really be sure of that?" Presti asked.

"Reasonably certain," Anders said. "Nothing serious has happened so far. Besides, we've taken a lot of steps to avoid the danger. Even when genetically altered bacteria are released directly into the environment or when altered viruses have been used as vaccines, everything reasonable has been done to make them safe. The bacteria are harmless ones, and the viruses are always weakened strains."

"Probably you're right," Presti said. "But the risks seem to me genuine. Why can't we do without genetically altered organisms? What is there to be gained?"

"The most immediate gain is that we can exploit an entirely new form of technology. We can grow better crops, manufacture better and more effective drugs. There is really no end to what we might be able to do in the future."

"If there is one," Presti said.

1. *What are the potential dangers of genetically altered organisms? What are the potential benefits?*

2. *Why do some scientists believe that the so-called Andromeda Strain scenario is not one that we need to take seriously?*

3. *What considerations suggest that we ought to proceed with caution in exploiting the promises of genetic engineering?*

CHAPTER 8

REPRODUCTIVE CONTROL: IN VITRO FERTILIZATION, ARTIFICIAL INSEMINATION, AND SURROGATE PREGNANCY

CASE PRESENTATION
Louise Brown: The First "Test-Tube Baby"

Under other circumstances, the birth announcement might have been perfectly ordinary, the sort that appears in newspapers every day: *Born to John and Lesley Brown: a baby girl, Louise, 5 lbs. 12 ozs., 11:47 P.M., July 25, 1978, Oldham General Hospital (Oldham, England).*

But the birth of Louise Brown was far from being an ordinary event, and the announcement of its occurrence appeared in headlines throughout the world. For the first time in history, a child was born who was conceived outside the mother's body under controlled laboratory conditions.

Louise Brown was the world's first "test-tube baby."

For John and Lesley Brown, the birth of Louise was a truly marvelous event. "She's so small, so beautiful, so perfect," her mother told a reporter. "It was like a dream. I couldn't believe it," her father said.

The joy of the Browns was understandable, for, from the time of their marriage in 1969, they had both very much wanted to have a child. Then they discovered that Mrs. Brown was unable to conceive because of blocked Fallopian tubes—the ova would not descend so fertilization could not occur. In 1970, she underwent an operation in an attempt to correct the condition, but the procedure was unsuccessful.

The Browns decided they would adopt a child, since they couldn't have one of their own. After two years on a waiting list, they gave up that plan. But the idea of having their own child was rekindled when a nurse familiar with the work of embryologist Robert Edwards and gynecologist Patrick Steptoe referred the Browns to them.

For the previous twelve years, Steptoe and Edwards had been working on the medical and biochemical techniques required for embryo transfer. Steptoe developed techniques for removing a ripened ovum from a woman's ovaries, then reimplanting it in the uterus after it has been fertilized. Edwards improved the chemical solutions needed to keep ova functioning and healthy outside the body and perfected a method of external fertilization with sperm.

Using their techniques, Steptoe and Edwards had successfully produced a pregnancy in one of their patients in 1975, but it had resulted in a miscarriage. They continued to refine their procedures and were confident that their techniques could produce a normal pregnancy that would result in a healthy baby.

They considered Lesley Brown an excellent candidate for an embryo transfer. She was in excellent general health, at thirty-one she was not too old for pregnancy, and she was highly fertile. In 1976, Steptoe did an exploratory operation and found that Mrs. Brown's Fallopian tubes were not functional and could not be surgically repaired. He removed them so that he would have clear access to the ovaries.

In November of 1977, Mrs. Brown was given injections of a hormone to increase the maturation rate of her egg cells. Then, in a small private hospital in Oldham, Dr. Steptoe performed a minor surgical procedure. Using a laparoscope to guide him—a tube with a built-in eyepiece and light source that is inserted through a tiny slit in the abdomen—he extracted an ovum with a suction needle from a ripened follicle.

The ovum was then placed in a small glass vessel containing biochemical nutrients and sperm that had been secured from John Brown. Once the egg was fertilized, it was transferred to another nutrient solution. More than fifty hours later, the ovum had reached the eight-cell stage of division. Guided by their previous experience and research, Steptoe and Edwards had decided that it was at this stage that an ovum should be returned to the womb. Although in normal human development the ovum has divided to produce sixty-four or more cells before it completes its descent down the Fallopian tube and becomes attached to the uterine wall, they had learned that attachment is possible at an earlier stage. The stupendous difficulties in creating and maintaining the proper biochemical environment for a multiplying cell made it reasonable to reduce the time outside the body as much as possible.

Mrs. Brown had been given another series of hormone injections to prepare her uterus. Two and a half days after the ovum was removed, the fertilized egg—an embryo—was reimplanted. Using a laparoscope and a hollow plastic tube (a cannula), Dr. Steptoe introduced the small sphere of cells into Mrs. Brown's uterus. It successfully attached itself to the uterine wall.

Mrs. Brown's pregnancy proceeded normally. But, because of the special nature of her case, seven weeks before the baby was due she entered the Oldham Hospital maternity ward so that she could be continuously monitored. About a week before the birth was expected, the baby was delivered by Caesarean section. Mrs. Brown had developed toxemia, a condition associated with high blood pressure that can lead to stillbirth.

The baby was normal, and all concerned were jubilant. "The last time I saw the baby it was just eight cells in a test tube," Dr. Edwards said. "It was beautiful then, and it's still beautiful now." After the delivery, Dr. Steptoe said "She came out crying her head off, a beautiful normal baby."

Mr. Brown almost missed the great event, because no one on the hospital staff had bothered to tell him that his wife was scheduled for the operation. Only when he had been gone for about two hours and called back to talk to his wife did he find out what was about to happen.

He rushed back and waited anxiously until a nurse came out and told him "You're the father of a wonderful little girl." As he later told a reporter, "Almost before I knew it, there I was holding our daughter in my arms."

Like many ordinary fathers, he ran down the halls of the hospital telling people he passed "It's a girl! I've got a baby daughter."

To calm down, he went outside and stood in the rain. It was there that a reporter from a London newspaper captured Mr. Brown's view of the event. "The man who deserves all the praise is Dr. Steptoe," he said. "What a man to be able to do such a wonderful thing."

SOCIAL CONTEXT: MOTHERHOOD AFTER MENOPAUSE

On Christmas Day, 1993, a fifty-nine-year-old British woman, identified only as Jennifer F., gave birth to twins. This highly unusual event was not an accident of nature, but the result of deliberate planning and technological manipulation.

Jennifer F. was married and highly successful in business, but even though she was a millionaire, there came a time when she realized that she regretted not having a child of her own. By then she had undergone menopause, making it impossible for her to conceive a child. Refusing to surrender her dream, Jennifer F. visited a National Health Service fertility clinic in London and requested a procedure in which a donor egg would be fertilized in vitro with her husband's sperm and the resulting embryo implanted in her uterus. Physicians at the clinic declined to perform the procedure on the grounds that she was too old to cope with the physical and emotional stress required to be a mother.

Determined that she would do everything possible to have a child, Jennifer F. then went to the clinic operated by Severino Antinori in Rome. Antinori agreed to accept her as a patient and performed the in vitro fertilization and embryo transfer procedure.

Antinori and his clinic have been at the center of the controversy over postmenopausal pregnancies. He claims that he has assisted more than fifty women over the age of fifty to become pregnant. Indeed, three days after Jennifer F.'s twins were born, another of Antinori's patients, Rossana Dalla Corte, a sixty-three-year-old Italian woman, revealed that she was pregnant and would give birth in June.

Like Jennifer F., Dalla Corte had a serious reason for seeking extraordinary means to make it possible for her to have a child. She and her sixty-five-year-old husband had lost their only child, an eighteen-year-old son, in a motorcycle accident three years earlier.

Although both Jennifer F. and Dalla Corte attracted much media attention, other postmenopausal women had earlier become pregnant and borne children. In 1993 Geraldine Wesoloski, fifty-three, gave birth to a baby who was both her child and her grandchild. She was the gestational surrogate for her son, Mark, and his wife, Susan. As a result of an accident, Susan had undergone a hysterectomy, but she and Mark were able to provide the embryo that was implanted.

A year earlier, Mary Shearing, also fifty-three, gave birth to twin girls. She was implanted with embryos produced by the use of donated eggs and sperm from her thirty-two-year-old husband. Even though Mary Shearing was no longer ovulating, she and her husband had decided to have a child of their own.

It has been technologically possible for a postmenopausal woman to become pregnant with donor eggs since 1987, but relatively few pregnancies have occurred. Partly this may be the result of the policies of in-vitro fertilization clinics. Most clinics in the United States will not accept as patients women past their early forties on the grounds that such pregnancies have a low success rate. Given the scarcity of donor eggs, some fertility specialists argue, they ought to be reserved for younger women, who are more likely to have successful pregnancies.

In the case of Jennifer F., the decision of the fertility clinic was supported by the British Secretary of Health, Virginia Bottomly. "Women do not have a right to have a child," she said in an interview. "There are deep ethical considerations, and the child's welfare must be considered. A child has a right to a suitable home." Critics of Jennifer F. generally agreed that older women should not be given access to the fertility procedures offered by the National Health Service.

The French government proposed a legal ban on postmenopausal pregnancies. Health Minister, Philippe Douste-Blazy, described such pregnancies as "immoral" and urged women not to be so "egoistic" as to try to have a child late in life. He said that the child's welfare should be paramount. "What will happen when he is fifteen or twenty, and his mother is eighty or eighty-five?" The debate in both France and Britain was complicated by controversy over a report that a black woman wanted to become the gestational surrogate for an ovum obtained from a white woman.

Critics of barring access by postmenopausal women to fertility procedures generally raise three objections. First, the women themselves may have their health damaged by undergoing the rigors of pregnancy. Second, the success rate is even lower than that for in vitro procedures involving younger women, and thus the younger women have a greater claim on the scarce resources. Third, it is best for a child to have physically and mentally active parents.

Defenders of giving access to fertility services to older women argue that it is pure gender bias to deny them the possibility of having a child. Men often father children well into their old age and are often admired for doing so. Charlie Chaplin was seventy-three when he had his last child, and Senator Strom Thurmond had four children during his sixties and seventies. Also, just because a woman is relatively young does not mean she will be a better mother. On the contrary, it seems likely that an older woman with more psychological and financial security will be a better parent than many young women. Besides, younger women do not have to prove they will be good mothers before they are allowed to have children, so why should older women? Finally, while it is true that pregnancy poses more health risks for older women, careful medical monitoring can significantly reduce the chances that either the mother or the developing child will be harmed. Babies born to older women using eggs obtained from younger women do just as well as babies born to younger women.

The number of women past menopause wishing to become pregnant is never expected to become great. Even so, the conflict between those who argue that older women are entitled to access to fertility services and those who argue that older women should be denied access can be expected to continue over the next few years. Eventually, after a number of children have been born to older mothers, some relevant questions of fact may be resolved, and this may make it easier to resolve the ethical and policy questions.

CASE PRESENTATION
The Orphaned Embryos of Mario and Elsa Rios

In 1983 Mario and Elsa Rios died in a plane crash. Their deaths left others to face some unique moral and legal issues.

The Los Angeles couple had been trying to have a child. Ova from Mrs. Rios and sperm from an anonymous donor were combined, and the embryos that developed were frozen and stored at the Queen Victoria Medical Center in Melbourne, Australia. The aim of freezing the embryos was to allow other attempts at pregnancy without subjecting Mrs. Rios to additional surgery.

A scholarly committee that was asked to study the question of what should be done with the embryos recommended that they be destroyed. However, the Parliament of the State of Victoria rejected the recommendation and passed a bill with an amendment that required the embryos to be put up for adoption and implanted in surrogate mothers. (The amendment was intended to cover only the Rioses' embryos, not to establish a general policy. In the future, couples participating in in vitro fertilization programs will be required to indicate what should be done with frozen embryos in the event of death or separation.)

The Rios estate was valued at about one million dollars, and what claim, if any, the embryos might have on it is a complicating factor. According to Victoria law, the embryo implants would be considered the children only of their surrogate/ adoptive parents. California courts have disqualified such children from making any claims on the Rios estate on the basis of a state law requiring that a beneficiary be born or in utero at the time of parental death.

Almost a decade after the embryos were frozen, they remain submerged in a tank of liquid nitrogen, unimplanted and controversial. Their chance of survival if thawed is estimated by researchers to be less than 5%.

CASE PRESENTATION
Embryos in Court: The Davis Case

The subject of the dispute between Mary Sue Davis and her estranged husband, Junior Davis, was seven embryos lying frozen in liquid nitrogen in the Fertility Center of East Tennessee.

Junior Davis did not want Mary Sue Davis to use the embryos to bear their child after their divorce. Mary Sue Davis wished to be free to do just that. In her view, the embryos were already living children, while for Junior Davis they were not alive in any significant way. For him, the only issue was the legal one of settling a joint property dispute, and he had no wish to be forced into fatherhood against his wishes. That was why he sued his estranged wife to gain recognition of what he considered to be his right to exercise a veto power over the use of the embryos.

The Davises had met when both were in the army and stationed in Germany. They married in 1979 and, after their military discharge, moved to Maryville, Tennessee. Mrs. Davis got a job as a service representative for a boat dealer, and Mr. Davis found work as a refrigeration technician. They tried to start a family, but luck was not with them. Mrs. Davis suffered through five ectopic pregnancies. The last resulted in the rupturing and scarring of one Fallopian tube and the tying off of the other for medical reasons.

Convinced that normal conception was impossible, in October of 1988 the couple entered an in vitro fertilization program in Knoxville. Originally nine ova were retrieved and fertilized with Mr. Davis's sperm. An attempt was made to implant two of the embryos, but it was unsuccessful. The plan was to try again at a more propitious time in Mrs. Davis's reproductive cycle, and the remaining seven embryos were frozen. Unfortunately, for reasons the Davises have not made public, their marriage began to break down, and on February 24, 1989, Junior Davis filed for divorce.

Junior Davis also filed suit to exercise joint control over the frozen embryos. During the trial, Mary Sue Davis took the position that the embryos were the product of her years of suffering through surgery, tests, and injections and represented her best chance to have a child. "I consider [the embryos] life," Mrs. Davis said. "To me it would be killing them if you destroyed them." In her view, the case involved the issues of custody of children and a woman's right to decide whether to bring a pregnancy to term. Her lawyer argued that the frozen embryos should be regarded as "preborn children."

In contrast with Mary Sue Davis's position, Junior Davis testified that he would feel "raped of my reproductive rights" if his wife were allowed to use the embryos to produce a child. He also op-

posed their donation for use by someone else. He insisted that he did not wish to be a father and that he had the right to make that decision. His attorney argued that the embryos were "mere tissue" and that they should be kept frozen indefinitely.

Testimony by fertility experts put Mary Sue Davis's chances of bearing a child with the implanted embryos at about 10%. Testimony also supported the view that the embryos would probably cease to be viable after two years.

Circuit Judge W. Dale Young rendered his decision on September 21, 1989. He ruled that "The temporary custody of the seven human embryos is vested in Mrs. Davis for the purpose of implantation." Furthermore, "Human embryos are not property. Human life begins at conception. Mr. and Mrs. Davis have produced human beings, in vitro, to be known as their child or children.

The judge's decision was explicitly based on the notion that the embryos already have the status of children. According to the decision, "It is in the manifest interest of the child or children that they be available for implantation. It serves the best interest of the child or children for their mother, Mrs. Davis, to be permitted the opportunity to bring them to term through implantation." Furthermore, Judge Young held, "To allow the seven human embryos to remain so preserved for a period exceeding two years is tantamount to the destruction of these human beings."

Judge Young declared that, if Mrs. Davis had a baby after implantation of the embryos, he would then decide the issues of child custody, support, and visitation rights.

Mr. Davis announced that he would appeal the ruling, and Mary Sue Davis said she would make no attempt to implant the ova until the appeal was heard. Soon afterward she married again, and in May 1990, without explaining her reasons, she said she didn't want to use the embryos. However, she wanted to be free to donate them to some childless couple who might be able to benefit from them. Junior Davis said he was totally against this. In September 1990 the Appeals Court granted joint custody of the embryos to Junior Davis and Mary Sue Davis Stowe.

In 1992, the Tennessee Supreme Court decided that the embryos "are not, strictly speaking, either 'persons' or 'property,' but occupy an interim category that entitles them to special respect because of their potential for human life." On this basis, the court refused to assign the embryos an independent legal status, holding that the only rights involved were those of the donors of the eggs and the sperm. Those rights revolve around the concept of "procreational autonomy," which is composed of the right to procreate and the right to avoid procreation. Hence, Junior Davis could not be forced to procreate against his wishes.

Mary Sue Davis Stowe, the court decided, had ways of having a child other than being implanted with the embryos, including adoption. As a result, her wishes could not automatically outweigh the interest of her ex-husband in not having a child.

Junior Davis had argued that as an orphan himself, he could not stand the idea that the embryos might be donated and implanted. If a child were born, he would be forced to remain ignorant of the fate of his own offspring. Citing this consideration, the court decided that his ex-wife could not donate the embryos. "Donation, if a child came of it, would rob him twice, in that his procreational autonomy would be defeated and his relationship with his offspring would be prohibited."

Junior Davis was described by his lawyer as grateful for the court's decision. Mary Sue Davis Stowe said through her lawyer that the decision would mean that "seven unique potential children" would be denied the opportunity to live and grow.

CASE PRESENTATION
Baby M: Surrogate Pregnancy in Court

On March 30, 1986, Dr. Elizabeth Stern, a professor of pediatrics, and her husband, William, accepted from Mary Beth Whitehead a baby who had been born four days earlier. The child's biological mother was Mrs. Whitehead, but she had been engaged by the Sterns as a surrogate mother. Even so, it was not until almost exactly a year later that the Sterns were able to claim legal custody of the child.

The Sterns, working through the Infertility Center of New York, had first met with Mrs. Whitehead and her husband, Richard, in January of 1985. Mrs. Whitehead, who already had a son and a daughter, had indicated her willingness to become a surrogate mother by signing up at the Infertility Center. "What brought her there was empathy with childless couples who were infertile," her attorney later stated. Her own sister had been unable to conceive.

According to court testimony, the Sterns considered Mrs. Whitehead a "perfect person" to bear a child for them. Mr. Stern said that it was "compelling" for him to have children, for he had no relatives "anywhere in the world." He and his wife planned to have children, but they put off attempts to conceive until his wife completed her medical residency in 1981. However, in 1979 she was diagnosed as having an eye condition indicating that she probably had multiple sclerosis. When she learned that the symptoms of the disease might be worsened by pregnancy and that she might become temporarily or even permanently paralyzed, the

Sterns "decided the risk wasn't worth it." It was this decision that led them to the Infertility Center and to Mary Beth Whitehead.

The Sterns agreed to pay Mrs. Whitehead $10,000 to be artificially inseminated with Mr. Stern's sperm and to bear a child. Mrs. Whitehead would then turn the child over to the Sterns, and Dr. Stern would be allowed to adopt the child legally. The agreement was drawn up by a lawyer specializing in surrogacy arrangements. Mr. Stern later testified that Mrs. Whitehead seemed perfectly pleased with the agreement and expressed no interest in keeping the baby she was to bear. "She said she would not come to our doorstep," he said. "All she wanted from us was a photograph each year and a little letter on what transpired that year."

The baby was born on March 27, 1986. According to Dr. Stern, the first indication that Mrs. Whitehead might not keep the agreement was her statement to the Sterns in the hospital two days after the baby's birth. "She said she didn't know if 'I can go through with it,'" Dr. Stern testified. Although Mrs. Whitehead did turn the baby over to the Sterns on March 30, she called a few hours later. "She said she didn't know if she could live any more," Dr. Stern said. She called again the next morning and asked to see the baby, and she and her sister arrived at the Sterns' house before noon.

According to Dr. Stern, Mrs. Whitehead told her that she "woke up screaming in the middle of the night" because the baby was gone, that her husband was threatening to leave her, and that she had "considered taking a bottle of Valium." Dr. Stern quoted Mrs. Whitehead as saying, "I just want her for a week, and I'll be out of your lives forever." The Sterns allowed Mrs. Whitehead to take the baby home with her.

Mrs. Whitehead then refused to return the baby voluntarily and took the infant with her to the home of her parents in Florida. The Sterns obtained a court order, and on July 31 the child was seized from Mrs. Whitehead. The Sterns were granted temporary custody. Then Mr. Stern, as the father of the child, and Mrs. Whitehead, as the mother, each sought permanent custody from the Superior Court of the State of New Jersey.

The seven-week trial attracted considerable attention, for the legal issues were virtually without precedent. Mrs. Whitehead was the first to challenge the legal legitimacy of a surrogate agreement in a U.S. court. She argued that the agreement was "against public policy" and violated New Jersey prohibitions against selling babies. In contrast, Mr. Stern was the first to seek a legal decision to uphold the "specific performance" of the terms of a surrogate contract. In particular, he argued that Mrs. Whitehead should be ordered to uphold her agreement and to surrender her parental rights and permit his wife to become the baby's legal mother. In addition to the contractual issues, the judge had to deal with the "best interest" of the child as required by New Jersey child-custody law. In addition to being a vague concept, the "best interest" standard had never been applied in a surrogacy case.

On March 31, 1987, Judge Harvey R. Sorkow announced his decision. He upheld the legality of the surrogate-mother agreement between the Sterns and Mrs. Whitehead and dismissed all arguments that the contract violated public policy or prohibitions against selling babies. Immediately after he read his decision, Judge Sorkow summoned Elizabeth Stern into his chambers and allowed her to sign documents permitting her to adopt the baby she and her husband called Melissa. The court deci-

sion effectively stripped Mary Beth Whitehead of all parental rights concerning this same baby, the one she called Sara.

The Baby M story did not stop with Judge Sorkow's decision. Mrs. Whitehead's attorney appealed the ruling to the New Jersey Supreme Court, and on February 3, 1988, the seven members of the court, in a unanimous decision, reversed Judge Sorkow's ruling on the surrogacy agreement. The court held that the agreement violated the state's adoption laws, because it involved a payment for a child. "This is the sale of a child, or at the very least, the sale of a mother's right to her child." Chief Justice Wilentz wrote. The agreement "guarantees the separation of a child from its mother . . . ; it takes the child from the mother regardless of her wishes and her maternal fitness . . . ; and it accomplishes all of its goals through the use of money." The court held that surrogacy agreements might be acceptable if they involved no payment and if a surrogate mother voluntarily surrendered her parental rights. In the present case, though, the court regarded paying for surrogacy "illegal, perhaps criminal, and potentially degrading to women."

The court let stand the award of custody to the Sterns, because "Their household and their personalities promise a much more likely foundation for Melissa to grow and thrive." Mary Beth Whitehead, having divorced her husband three months earlier, was romantically involved with a man named Dean Gould and was pregnant at the time of the court decision.

Despite awarding custody to the Sterns, the court set aside the adoption agreement signed by Elizabeth Stern. Mary Beth Whitehead remained a legal parent of Baby M, and the court ordered a lower court hearing to consider visitation rights for the mother.

The immediate future of the child known to the court and to the public as Baby M was settled. Neither the Sterns nor Mary Beth Whitehead had won exactly what they had sought, but neither had they lost all.

CASE PRESENTATION
The Unclaimed Infant

In January 1983, Judy Stiver of Lansing, Michigan, gave birth to a child nine months after she was

artificially inseminated with sperm from Alexander Malahoff of Queens, New York. Mr. Malahoff had agreed to pay Mrs. Stiver $10,000 for her services as a surrogate mother.

Mrs. Stiver had a long and difficult labor, and trouble started as soon as the child was born. The child, a boy, was microcephalic and suffered from a severe infection. Mr. Malahoff, as the presumed father, refused to authorize the treatment necessary to sustain the life of the infant. However, the hospital obtained a court order, and the infant was successfully treated.

Before Mrs. Stiver and her husband could cash the check given to her by Mr. Malahoff, Mr. Malahoff informed them that there was a problem. The baby's blood type was O-positive, while Mr. Malahoff's was AB-positive. Thus, the child could not be his, and he refused to accept responsibility for it. Before that time, according to Mr. Stiver, Mr. Malahoff had accepted the baby's impairment, had the child baptized, and planned to place him in an institution.

"We don't feel the baby is ours," Mr. Stiver said. "We feel no maternal or paternal relationship. We feel sorry for it, but we don't want it." Mrs. Stiver reported that she felt "some affection" for the baby but "there is no bond."

Mrs. Stiver said that she had a thorough medical examination to guarantee that she was not pregnant before she was inseminated with Mr. Malahoff's sperm. She and her husband then avoided sexual intercourse for thirty days. Mr. Malahoff, who had separated from his wife, sued the Stivers for $30,000, alleging that they violated the terms of the contract by having intercourse during the insemination period. The Stivers sued the physician who performed the insemination, and several suits and countersuits are still in litigation.

The child, who was named Christopher, is a patient at the Beekman Center for Therapy. According to Mrs. Stiver, "They say he has the capabilities of a two- to four-month old, and he probably won't get much beyond that."

The case of Christopher Stiver prompted the introduction of legislation in Michigan to protect the interests of children born through various fertility techniques, including surrogate pregnancy, and to establish legal rights and responsibilities of contractual parents. New Jersey and Washington, two states in which legislation directly addresses the issues of surrogacy, require that the contractual father be recognized as the legal father.

CASE PRESENTATION
The Calvert Case: Gestational Surrogacy

Disease forced Crispina Calvert of Orange County, California, to have a hysterectomy, but only her uterus was removed by surgery, not her ovaries. She and her husband, Mark, wanted a child of their own, but without a uterus Crispina would not be able to bear it. For a fee of $10,000 they arranged with Anna Johnson to act as a surrogate.

Unlike the more common form of surrogate pregnancy, Johnson would have no genetic investment in the child. The ovum that would be fertilized would not be hers. Mary Beth Whitehead, the surrogate in the controversial Baby M case, had received artificial insemination. Thus, she made as much genetic contribution to the child as did the biological father.

Johnson, however, would be the gestational surrogate. In a standard in vitro fertilization process, ova were extracted from Crispina Calvert and mixed with sperm from Mark. A fertilized ovum

was implanted in Anna Johnson's uterus, and a fetus began to develop.

Johnson's pregnancy proceeded along a normal course, but in her seventh month she announced that she had changed her mind about giving up the child. She filed suit against the Calverts to seek custody of the unborn child. "Just because you donate a sperm and an egg doesn't make you a parent," said Johnson's attorney. "Anna is not a machine, an incubator."

"That child is biologically Chris and Mark's," said the Calverts' lawyer. "That contract is valid."

Johnson was not the first woman to serve as a gestational surrogate. No official records are kept, but the Center for Surrogate Parenting in Beverly Hills estimates that about 80 such births have occurred since 1987. This compares to some 2,000 surrogate pregnancies during the same period. According to the Center's figures, probably around

4,000 surrogate births have occurred since the late 1970s.

Critics of genetic surrogate pregnancy are equally critical of gestational surrogate pregnancy. Both methods, some claim, exploit women, particularly poor women. Further, in gestational pregnancy the surrogate is the one who must run the risks and suffer the discomforts and dangers of pregnancy. She has a certain biological claim to be the mother, because it was her body that produced the child according to the genetic information.

Defenders of surrogate pregnancy respond to the first criticism by denying that surrogates are exploited. They enter freely into a contract to serve as a surrogate for pay, just as anyone might agree to perform any other form of service for pay. Pregnancy has hazards and leaves its marks on the body, but so do many other paid occupations. As far as gestational surrogacy is concerned, defenders say, since the surrogate makes no genetic contribution to the developing child, in no reasonable way can she be regarded as the child's parent.

The Ethics Committee of the American Fertility Society has endorsed a policy opposing surrogate pregnancy "for non-medical reasons." The apparent aim of the policy is to permit the use of gestational surrogate pregnancy in cases like that of Mrs. Calvert, while condemning it when its motivation is mere convenience or an unwillingness to be pregnant. When a woman is fertile but, because of diabetes, uncontrollable hypertension, or some other life-threatening disorder, is unable to bear the burden of pregnancy, then gestational surrogacy would be a legitimate medical option.

The child carried by Anna Johnson, a boy, was born on September 19, and for a while, under a court order, Johnson and the Calverts shared visitation rights. Then, in October, 1990, a California Superior Court denied to Anna Johnson the parental right she had sought. Justice R. N. Parslow awarded complete custody of the child to the Calverts and terminated Johnson's visitation rights.

"I decline to split the child emotionally between two mothers," the judge said. He said Johnson had nurtured and fed the fetus in the way a foster parent might take care of a child, but she was still a "genetic stranger" to the boy and could not claim parenthood because of surrogacy.

Justice Parslow found the contract between the Calverts and Johnson to be valid, and he expressed doubt about Johnson's contention that she had "bonded" with the fetus she was carrying. "There is substantial evidence in the record that Anna Johnson never bonded with the child till she filed her lawsuit, if then," he said. While the trial was in progress, Johnson had been accused of planning to sue the Calverts from the beginning to attempt to make the case famous so she could make money from book and movie rights.

Justice Parslow also urged the California Legislature to establish legal guidelines to deal with surrogacy cases. He suggested a process in which all parties undergo psychological evaluation and agree at the beginning that the surrogate mother will have no custody rights. He also suggested that a surrogate be required to have had previous successful experience with childbirth and that surrogacy be used only in cases in which the genetic mother is unable to give birth.

"I see no problem with someone getting paid for her pain and suffering," he said. "There is nothing wrong with getting paid for nine months of what I understand is a lot of misery and a lot of bad days. They are not selling a baby; they are selling pain and suffering."

The Calverts were overjoyed by the decision.

INTRODUCTION

"Oh, brave new world that has such people in it!" exclaims Miranda in Shakespeare's *The Tempest*.

It is a phrase from this line that provided Aldous Huxley with the title for his dystopian novel *Brave New World*. A dystopia is the opposite of a utopia, and the future society depicted by Huxley is one that we are invited to view with shock and disapproval.

In this society, "pregnancy" is a dirty word, sex is purely recreational, and children are produced according to explicit genetic standards in the artificial wombs of state "hatcheries." Furthermore, an individual's genetic endowment determines the social position and obligations that he or she has within the society. Of course, everyone is conditioned to believe that the role he finds himself in is the best one to have.

In significant ways, that future is now. The new and still-developing medical technologies of human reproduction have now reached a stage in which the technical innovations imagined by Huxley in 1932 to make such a society possible are well within the limits of feasibility.

We have no state hatcheries and no artificial uteruses. But we do have sperm banks and surrogate mothers. We have it within our power to remove an ovum from a woman's body, fertilize it, then return it so that it may develop into a child. By relatively simple surgical procedures, we can end forever the reproductive potentialities of otherwise fertile men or women.

The new technology associated with human reproduction is so powerful that it differs only in degree from that of Huxley's dystopian world. What we have yet to do is to employ the technology as part of a deliberate social policy to restructure our world along the lines imagined by Huxley.

Yet the potentiality is there. Perhaps more than anything else, it is the bleak vision of such a mechanistic and dehumanized future that has motivated much of the criticism of current reproductive technology. The "brave new world" of Huxley is one in which traditional values associated with reproduction and family life, values based on individual autonomy, have been replaced by values of a purely social kind. In such a society, it is the good of the society or of the species, not the good of individuals, that is the touchstone of justification.

The possible loss of personal values is a legitimate and serious concern. The technologies of human reproduction are sometimes viewed as machines that may be employed to pave the road leading to a world of bleakness and loss. Yet it is important to remember that those same technologies also promise to enhance the lives of those presently living and to prevent potential suffering and despair.

Some women who are unable to bear children may now find it possible to do so through the use of in vitro fertilization techniques. Artificial insemination offers a means of impregnation when biological dysfunction makes the normal means impossible. Further, those women who would be at risk from becoming pregnant may now be protected by choosing surgical sterilization.

These are all potentialities that have become actualities; in vitro fertilization, artificial insemination, and sterilization are all procedures currently being performed. In the view of some, these procedures merely mark a beginning, and the possibilities inherent in reproductive technology still remain relatively unrealized. If we wish, we can employ the technology to change the very fabric and pattern of our society.

Should we do that? Or will the use of the technology necessarily promote the development of a dystopia? One way of thinking about these general questions is to turn once more to Huxley.

It is frequently overlooked that in 1962 Huxley published a utopian novel entitled *Island*. Like the society in *Brave New World*, Huxley's ideal society also relies upon the principles of science, but in the ideal society they are used to promote autonomy and personal development.

Island portrays a society on the island of Pala that for over a hundred years has developed itself in accordance with the principles of reason and science. Living is communal, sexual repression is nonexistent, children are cared for by both their biological parents and other adults, drugs are used to enhance perceptual awareness, and social obligations are assigned on the basis of personal interest and ability.

More to the present point, the society makes use of reproductive technology to achieve its ends. It practices contraception, eugenics, and artificial insemination. Negative eugenics to eliminate genetic diseases is considered only rational. But more than this, by the use of "DF" and "AI" (Deep Freeze and Artificial Insemination), sperm from donors with superior genetic endowments is available for the use of couples who wish to improve their chances of having a child with special talents or with higher-than-usual intelligence.

Huxley's ideal society is not above criticism, even from those who are sympathetic toward the values he endorses. Yet *Brave New World* is such a powerful cautionary tale of what might happen if science were pressed into the service of repressive political goals that it makes it difficult to imagine other possible futures in which some of the same technology plays a more benign role. Since *Island* is an attempt to present such an alternative future, in thinking about the possibilities inherent in reproductive technology, fairness demands that we also consider Palinese society and not restrict our attention to the world of soma and state hatcheries.

IN VITRO FERTILIZATION

The birth of Louise Brown in 1978 (see the Case Presentation) was treated as a major media event. Photographs, television coverage, interviews, and news stories presented the world with minute details of the lives of the people involved and with close accounts of the technical procedures that led to Louise's conception.

Despite the unprecedented character of the event, few people seemed surprised by it. The idea of a "test-tube baby" was one already familiar from fiction and folklore. Medieval alchemists were thought capable of generating life in their retorts, and hundreds of science fiction stories depicted a future in which the creation of life in the laboratory was an ordinary occurrence. In some ways, then, the birth of Louise Brown was seen as merely a matter of science and medicine catching up with imagination. (Indeed, they didn't quite catch up, for the "test tube" contained sperm and an egg, not just a mixture of chemicals.)

Although it is doubtful whether the public appreciated the magnitude of the achievement that resulted in the birth of Louise Brown, it was one of considerable significance. The first embryo transfer was performed in rabbits in 1890, but it was not until the role of hormones in reproduction, the nutritional requirements of developing cells, and the reproductive process itself were better understood that it became possible to consider seriously the idea of fertilizing an egg outside the mother's body and then returning it for ordinary development.

In vitro is a Latin phrase that means "in glass," and in embryology, it is used in contrast with *in utero,* or "in the uterus." Ordinary human fertilization takes place in utero (strictly speaking, in the Fallopian tubes) when a sperm cell unites with an ovum. In vitro fertilization, then, is fertilization that is artificially performed outside the woman's body—in a test tube, so to speak.

The ovum that produced Louise Brown was fertilized in vitro. But the entire process involved *embryo transfer.* That is, an ovum had to be taken from her mother's body. Then, after it was fertilized and had become an embryo, it was returned for in utero development.

Robert Edwards and Patrick Steptoe were responsible for developing and performing the techniques of in vitro fertilization and embryo transfer that led to the birth of Louise Brown. Basically, they followed a four-step process that, allowing for technical improvements, is still employed.

1. The patient is given a reproductive hormone to cause ova to ripen. A few hours before ovulation is expected, a small incision is made in the abdomen just below the navel. A laparoscope is inserted through the incision, and the ovaries are examined directly. When mature eggs are found, the thin walls of the ovarian follicle are punctured and the contents are removed by a vacuum aspirator (a hollow suction needle). Several eggs may be removed.

2. The eggs are transferred to a nutrient solution that is biochemically similar to

that found in the Fallopian tubes. Sperm is added to the solution, and when a single sperm cell penetrates the ovum, the ovum is fertilized.

3. The fertilized egg is transferred to another nutrient solution where, after about a day, it begins to undergo cell division. When the zygote reaches the eight-cell stage, it is ready to be returned to the uterus. The patient is given injections of hormones to prepare her uterus to receive it.

4. The small ball of cells is placed in the uterus through the cervix (the opening that leads to the vagina) by means of a hollow plastic tube called a *cannula*. The zygote continues to divide, and somewhere between the thirty-two- and sixty-four-cell stage, it attaches to the uterine wall.

If the attachment is successful, from this point on, development should proceed as if fertilization had taken place in the ordinary fashion.

On December 28, 1981, Elizabeth Jordan Carr was born at Norfolk General Hospital, Norfolk, Virginia. She has the distinction of being the first baby conceived in vitro born in the United States. Like Louise Brown, she also weighed 5 pounds, 12 ounces, was born ahead of schedule, and was perfectly healthy.

As of 1991, some twenty-three thousand births have resulted from using the methods of reproductive technology. In the United States alone, nearly three hundred clinics currently perform the procedure. Success rates vary, but in the best programs, the chance of a woman becoming pregnant is about 23% to 25%, roughly the same odds as those of a normal, healthy couple attempting conception during the woman's regular monthly cycle. (Ways of calculating rates of success vary. The American Fertility Society estimates that the success rate for couples who produce healthy eggs, sperm, and embryos is only 15.2%. During the 1970s and early 1980s, the success rate was hardly more than 5%.) Each fertilization and transplantation attempt costs around ten

thousand dollars, and in most cases, such expenses are not covered by insurance.

The technical procedures are still fundamentally the same as those pioneered by Steptoe and Edwards. However, numerous modifications and extensions have been introduced. One of the more important ones is the development of a nonsurgical procedure for securing ova. After hormones are used to stimulate the ovarian follicles, ultrasound is employed to locate the follicles, and a hollow needle is inserted through the vaginal wall and into a follicle. Fluid is withdrawn, and egg cells are identified under the microscope. The egg cells are then fertilized with the sperm, cultured, and reimplanted.

An additional modification is to attempt to implant two, three, or even more fertilized ova at a time. This increases the chances that at least one of them will attach to the uterine wall and develop normally. The procedure also increases the chances of multiple births, and clinics that use this technique have patients that produce a higher than average percentage of twins and triplets.

A variation of in vitro techniques is gamete intrafallopian transfer, or GIFT. It involves inserting both ova and sperm into the Fallopian tubes. If fertilization takes place, it does so inside the woman's body. Some regard this as being more "natural" than in vitro fertilization. (The second most common technique is ZIFT—zygote intrafallopian transfer. After fertilization in vitro, zygotes are placed into a woman's Fallopian tubes.)

Intravaginal culture (IVC) is another attempt at naturalness. Ova are placed in a tube to which sperm cells are added, and the tube is then inserted into the vagina and kept next to the cervix by a diaphragm. Normal sexual intercourse can take place with the tube in place. Two days later, the tube is removed, the contents decanted, and fertilized ova transferred into the uterus.

Another important development is the perfection of techniques for freezing embryos. Evidence to date indicates that embryos can be stored in a frozen condition and then unfrozen and implanted without any damage to the chromosomes. The advantage of the procedure is that it eliminates the need for a woman to undergo the surgery and the lengthy and uncomfortable process required to secure additional ova. If a woman fails to become pregnant at a first attempt, an embryo saved from the initial fertilization can be employed in another effort. Furthermore, the technique makes it possible to delay an embryo transplant until the potential mother has reached the most favorable time in her menstrual cycle.

This advance in reproductive technology also has brought problems with it. During one year about twenty-five thousand embryos are frozen at fertility clinics. Not all the embryos are implanted, and this raises what many consider to be the serious question of what should be done with them. Those who store them are usually reluctant to have them destroyed. But what if the couple storing their embryos get divorced? What if both die? (See the Case Presentations in this chapter.) Would it be morally acceptable for an adult offspring of the couple to be implanted with the embryo stored by her parents? At present there are no national regulations or guidelines for dealing with frozen embryos. Fertility centers set their own policies. Sometimes the embryos are destroyed or used in research. In some cases, they are kept frozen indefinitely, as long as someone pays for the cost.

By virtue of being first, Louise Brown continues to be a symbol of what it is possible to achieve by means of the techniques developed by Steptoe and Edwards. But by now she has quietly taken her place among the ranks of the thousands of others whose conception occurred in a glass bottle.

Gestational Surrogates and Donor Ova

This is perhaps the most dramatic possibility opened up by in vitro fertilization and embryo transfer. A woman whose uterus has been removed, making her incapable of normal pregnancy, can contribute an ovum that, after being fertilized in vitro, is implanted in the uterus of a second woman whose uterus has been prepared to receive it. The "host" or gestational surrogate mother then carries the baby to term.

In a similar procedure, when a woman is incapable of producing ova, as the result either of disease, injury, or normal aging, a donor ovum may be fertilized in vitro then implanted in her uterus, and she then carries the child to term. Thus, postmenopausal women or many women once considered hopelessly barren may now become pregnant and give birth to a baby, even though they are genetically unrelated to the child.

Gestational surrogacy is a relatively new practice, and it opens up a number of possibilities that may have significant social consequences. That women past the natural age of childbearing can now become mothers is a stunning possibility that has already given rise to ethical and policy questions. (For a discussion, see Social Context: Motherhood after Menopause.)

Second, women using the services of a gestational surrogate do so at present because they are unable to bear children themselves. However, it is only a short step from being unable to bear children to being *unwilling* to bear children.

Thus, it is easy to imagine that some women might choose to free themselves from the rigors of pregnancy by hiring a gestational surrogate. The employer would be the source of the ovum, which would then be fertilized in vitro and implanted as an embryo in the uterus of the surrogate. Women who could afford to do so could have their own genetic children without ever having to be pregnant.

Although a few have advocated using "genetically superior" women as a source of ova and "less superior" women as gestational surrogates, it is unlikely that such a program will ever be endorsed by society. (See the Introduction in Chapter 10 for the difficulties in determining genetic "superiority.") Nevertheless, such practices are entirely possible, and it is likely that they will continue to excite discussion.

The possibilities inherent in in vitro fertilization and embryo transfer mentioned here as sources of immediate or future benefits are all currently employed or easily implemented. By contrast, the development of "baby factories" or "hatcheries" similar to those described in *Brave New World* are technologically unlikely, judged in terms of current science and medicine. Machines would have to serve the function now served by the uterus, and designing such machines would require knowing enough about the needs of the developing fetus to reproduce that function. At the present, it is not possible even to state all the problems that would have to be solved.

Benefits

The processes involved in in vitro fertilization and its technical variations are complicated and require a great amount of skill and knowledge. An obvious question to ask about the whole assisted-fertility process is, What is to be gained by it? That is, what are the benefits of such a technically difficult and expensive medical procedure?

The most direct and perhaps the most persuasive answer is that assisted fertility makes it possible for many couples to conceive children who would not otherwise be able to do so. For those couples, this is a decisive consideration. Research shows that about 10% of married couples in the United States are infertile—that is, they have attempted to conceive a child for a year or longer without success. Infertility affects almost 5 million women and an estimated 4 million men. In 1993, more than 1 million people sought professional help in conceiving a child. About $2 billion per year is spent on fertility-related medical services.

In vitro fertilization is not a solution to all problems of fertility, but it is the only solution possible in a large number of cases. Figures show that as many as 45% of all cases of female infertility are caused by abnormal or obstructed Fallopian tubes. Although normal ova are produced, they cannot move down the tubes to be fertilized. In some cases, tissue blocking the tubes may be removed, or the tubes reconstructed. In other cases, however, the tubes may be impossible to repair or may be entirely absent. (Only 40% to 50% of infertile women can be helped through surgery.) This means that the only way in which these women can expect to have a child of their own is by means of in vitro fertilization. (This is also true, of course, when the woman has no uterus or is postmenopausal and must rely on a donated ovum.) Thus, the procedure offers a realistic possibility of becoming parents to many people who once had no hope at all of having a child.

A second, and quite ironic, benefit of research into improving in vitro fertilization and embryo transfer is that it may lead to better and more effective contraceptives. This almost paradoxical result is due to the fact that the sort of knowledge required to make fertilization and reimplantation of the embryo successful is also knowledge that can be employed to prevent pregnancy. For example, a knowledge of the biochemical mechanism by which a sperm penetrates an ovum and renders the ovum impenetrable to all other sperm cells can be turned in the direction either of promoting fertilization or of preventing it. Similarly, understanding how the embryo attaches itself to the wall of the uterus may lead to methods for either decreasing or increasing the likelihood of an embryo becoming attached.

Third, reproductive research with animals can be employed to determine the ways in which various environmental toxins and drugs affect the developing fetus. At present, research groups are exposing fertilized monkey ova to chemicals, then reimplanting them. The aim is to discover the means by which specific chemicals alter development and result in defective offspring.

Such information is of obvious value. If we are to be successful in eliminating or reducing human birth defects that are caused by chemical agents, then we must know what the chemicals do. Only in such ways can safe levels of exposure be determined and steps taken to avoid or prevent the presence of environmental toxins and harmful ingredients in drugs.

Fourth, in vitro techniques may make it possible to "repair" genes in the future. The way the genetic code in the DNA of a fertilized egg directs the development of the egg into a baby is far from understood. Nonetheless, fragments of the total picture are now emerging. The technology of recombinant DNA (see the introduction to Chapter 7) has made it possible to isolate single genes and to identify their products. It is a long way from this stage to being able, for example, to outline all of the steps by which the heart develops. Yet such work is promising enough to fuel the hope that we will eventually understand the way in which DNA controls the entire developmental process.

This kind of detailed knowledge may make it possible to locate defects in genes that, when uncorrected, lead to faulty development of the fetus. At present, to avoid the birth of a child with birth defects associated with damaged or missing genes, abortion is the only recourse. Additional knowledge might allow faulty genes to be replaced or repaired. Thus, developmental failures like Down syndrome and spina bifida or heritable genetic defects like Tay-Sachs disease might be treated at the level of the genes. An entirely new chapter of fetal medicine would then be opened.

These are just four of the more direct advantages associated with in vitro fertilization. Other possibilities inherent in the procedure might make up a substantial list.

Criticisms of Current IVF Practices

While admitting the present and potential values of reproductive technology, many critics think that it has been oversold. Despite their hopes, the majority of women who must rely on IVF (in vitro fertilization) do not become pregnant. Also, women are not always properly informed about their chances of becoming pregnant. A particular clinic may have a general success rate of 25%, but for a woman in her early forties, the rate may be only a 1% to 2% chance per month of trying. (Only about half of the people who seek assistance overcome their infertility.)

Critics also point out that the expense of trying to become pregnant can be quite high. Each attempt costs about ten thousand dollars, and three to four attempts are not unusual. Further, the procedures involve anxiety and discomfort. The risk of injury and infection from surgery is not great, but it is real. In addition, the safety of the fertility drugs used to trigger ovulation and to prepare the uterus for implantation is questionable. One study suggests that the drugs are linked with a twofold to threefold increase in ovarian cancer among those who take them. Also, there is a possibility that the high hormone levels in the blood that the drugs produce may increase a woman's risk of breast cancer.

An increase in the use of "donated" eggs raises serious issues about donors. All are young women, many are college students, and most are significantly motivated to contribute their eggs for money. The typical fee is around two thousand dollars, and some women contribute two or more times. Sperm donors (see further on) usually receive only about fifty dollars, but egg donors must spend more time, experience discomfort, and run risks to their own health. They must agree to be injected with drugs to stimulate their ovaries (which may produce nausea) and have frequent blood tests and ultrasound scans to determine when the ova are ready. They must then be anesthetized and the eggs retrieved from the follicles.

Donated ova are a scarce commodity, and some fertility clinics and programs make an effort to recruit donors so that ova will be available for their clients. Some critics regard the situation as one in which young women in need lack the protection of the law and risk being exploited by those in a financial position to offer them money. As matters stand, only the moral principles of those who recruit donors regulate the practice.

Ethical and Social Difficulties

Several aspects of in vitro fertilization and the way in which it is being employed are regarded by some people as troublesome. Very briefly, we will consider just five.

1. The ova that are removed for fertilization are not all used. Although they may all be mixed with sperm and several may be fertilized, only a single fertilized ovum is selected for implantation. They others are simply discarded.

    For those who believe that human life begins at the moment of conception, the destruction of fertilized ova may be viewed as tantamount to abortion. Thus, for some people, the destruction may be regarded as destroying innocent human life.

    Others, who are not prepared to ascribe personhood to a fertilized ovum, may still be troubled by its pointless destruction. They may believe that its potential to develop, under certain conditions, into a human being at least requires that it be treated with concern and respect. Those who subscribe to such a view might well argue that the only legitimate form of in vitro fertilization is one in which the effort is made to fertilize only a single ovum. A failure in fertilization would then be similar to the failure that occurs naturally, and what would be eliminated would be the necessity of destroying fertilized eggs that cannot be implanted.

2. At present, when human in vitro fertilization is a relatively new procedure, it is impossible to assess the risks to the fetus and to the person it may become. A fetus that is conceived from an ovum that is removed to an alien environment and sustained by a nutrient solution that may not contain some necessary ingredients for development may well be at much greater risk than a fetus conceived in the ordinary way. Not only may the child be more likely to suffer defects evident at birth, but it may suffer some defects that will not show up until years later. (Mrs. Brown is rumored to have signed an agreement stating that she would submit to an abortion if there were signs that the fetus she was carrying was not developing normally.)

    Experience has taken the teeth out of this objection. The rate of birth defects in children born of in vitro fertilization is about 3%, virtually the same as that of ordinary births. So far there is no evidence that children conceived in vitro differ in any way from other children.

3. In vitro fertilization may encourage the development of eugenic ideas about improving the species. Rather than having children of their own, would-be parents might be motivated to seek out ova (and sperm) from people who possess physical and intellectual characteristics that are particularly admired. Thus, even without an organized plan of social eugenics (see Chapter 7), individuals might be tempted to follow their own eugenic notions.

4. Similarly, would-be parents might be inclined to exercise the potential for control over the sex of their offspring. Only males contain both an X and a Y chromosome, and their presence is detectable in the cells of the developing embryo. Determination of the sex of the embryo would allow the potential parents to decide whether they wish to have a male or female child. Consequently, a potential human being (the developing fetus)

might be destroyed for what is basically a trivial reason.

5. In vitro fertilization is likely to promote a social climate in which having children becomes severed from the family. The procedure places emphasis on the mechanics of fertilization and, in doing so, minimizes the significance of the shared love and commitments of the parents of a child conceived by normal intercourse. Furthermore, the procedure offers the opportunity for an unmarried woman to have a child without having anything at all to do with the biological father of the child.

Obviously, these difficulties are not ones likely to be considered equally serious by everyone. Those who do not believe that life begins at conception will hardly be troubled by the discarding of unimplanted embryos. Additional research and experience will no doubt reduce whatever risks there may be to a fetus conceived in vitro. Sex choice is possible now by the use of amniocentesis, so it is not a problem unique to in vitro fertilization, and the same is true of the implementation of eugenic ideas.

Finally, whether in vitro procedures actually lead to a weakening of the values associated with the family is partly an empirical question that only additional use of the method will show. Even if childbearing does become severed from current family structure, it still must be shown that this is itself something of which we ought to disapprove. It is clearly not impossible that alternative social structures for childbearing and childrearing might be superior to ones currently dominant in Western culture.

CLONING

Cloning involves producing individuals that are exact genetic copies of the donor from whom the DNA was obtained. Some animal cells have been cloned for more than five decades, but a step toward making the cloning of human cells a practical reality was taken only in 1993. Jerry Hall and Robert Stillman took 17 two-to-eight-cell human embryos, separated the blastomeres (the individual cells) and coated them with artificial zona pellucida (the protective coat surrounding egg cells), and placed them in various nutrient solutions. The outcome was the production of forty-eight new embryos from the original ones. The cells continue to divide, but development stopped after six days, partly because the embryos were abnormal. The original ones were deliberately chosen because they were defective. The work was purely experimental, and it was never intended that the embryos would be implanted.

The immediate advantage of the techniques developed by Hall and Stillman (as well as many others) is expected to be to increase the supply of implantable embryos for couples with fertility problems. If a couple's embryos, produced by in vitro fertilization, could be cloned into several embryos, they could be used in repeated implantation attempts. Thus, the woman would not have to undergo repetitions of the unpleasant, expensive, and somewhat risky procedures involved in triggering ovulation, then retrieving ova for in vitro fertilization. Regarded from this point of view, for some couples, the techniques promise to make having a child easier, cheaper, and less time-consuming.

The process used by Hall and Stillman was, strictly speaking, not actually cloning, which requires taking a somatic cell from a developed organism, extracting the DNA, then growing an embryo from it. Even so, the process of "twinning" that they employed showed that it would take very little more technically to employ the techniques of assisted reproduction and produce a number of genetically identical humans.

Such techniques, when combined with the freezing of embryos, open up a number of surprising and controversial social possibilities. Here are a few:

1. The production of several clones would make a market in embryos possible. If a child had already been born and could be shown to have desirable qualities, the couple who had produced the embryos might sell them at high prices. It would be then possible for someone to have a child literally "just like" the one with the desirable qualities.

2. Parents could have a family in which all their children are clones—that is, exact genetic copies of one another. The oldest child and the youngest would have the same genetic endowment. If several gestational mothers were employed, it would be possible to produce a dozen or more genetically identical children who would all be the same age.

3. A couple might have a child, while also freezing an embryo clone as a spare. If the child should die, then a genetic twin could be grown from the embryo. The clone would be as much like the lost child as genetics makes possible.

4. If embryo clones were frozen and stored, they could be implanted in a gestational mother years apart. Thus, one identical twin might be sixty, while the other is only six.

5. Clones of an individual might be stored so that if the person needed something like a bone marrow or kidney transplant, the clone could be implanted in a gestational surrogate and allowed to develop. The issue match from the clone would be perfect, and the problem of rejection would not arise.

6. Using a stored embryo, a woman would be able to give birth to her own genetic twin. She would be both mother and sister to the child. In a variant of this, a woman might have a child who is a clone of her husband. Thus, the man would be both father and sibling of the child.

The general issue raised by these possibilities is, In what circumstances is the cloning of humans legitimate? Some uses of cloning may be acceptable, involving nothing more than a reconstrual of our idea of what a family should be. However, other uses may result in such a cheapening or commercialization of human life as to be undesirable options.

None of the possibilities is likely to be realized in the immediate future. But each of them generates a variety of specific moral questions that are worth considering before the possibilities become too pressing.

ARTIFICIAL INSEMINATION

In 1909, an unusual letter appeared in the professional journal *Medical World*. A. D. Hard, the author of the letter, claimed that when he was a student at Jefferson Medical College in Philadelphia, a wealthy businessman and his wife consulted a physician on the faculty about their inability to conceive a child.

A detailed examination of each of the spouses showed that the man was incapable of producing sperm. The case was presented for discussion in a class of which Hard was a member. According to Hard, the class suggested that semen should be taken from the "best-looking member of the class" and used to inseminate the wife.

The letter claimed that this was done while the woman was anesthetized and that neither the husband nor the wife was told about the process. The patient became pregnant and gave birth to a son. The husband was then told how the pregnancy was produced, and, although he was pleased with the result, he asked that his wife not be informed.

The event described by Hard took place in 1884, and there is reason to believe that Hard was "the best-looking member of the class."

The Philadelphia case is generally acknowledged to be the first recorded instance of artificial insemination of donor sperm in a human patient. However, the process of artificial insemination itself has a much longer history. Arab horsemen in the fourteenth century apparently inseminated mares with semen-soaked sponges, and in the eighteenth century the Italian physiologist Spallansani documented experiments in which he fertilized dogs, reptiles, and frogs.

The first recorded case of the artificial insemination of a human being occurred in 1790, when the English physician John Hunter used semen obtained from a husband to inseminate his wife. Sporadic uses of the technique continued to occur in England, France, and the United States, and during the early part of the present century, they became more and more frequent. At present, probably more than 2,000 children a year are born in this country who were conceived by artificial insemination.

Artificial insemination has become generally recognized as a legitimate medical procedure. The process is employed by hospitals, fertility clinics, and physicians who specialize in problems involving conception. Before looking at some of the ethical and legal issues involved in artificial insemination, it is useful to consider some relevant factual information about the process.

The Artificial Insemination Procedure

Artificial insemination is a relatively simple procedure. It is initiated when the woman's body temperature indicates that ovulation is to take place in one or two days. It is then repeated one or two more times until her body temperature shows that ovulation is completed. Typically, three inseminations are performed during a monthly cycle.

In the insemination, the patient is usually placed in a position so that her hips are raised. A semen specimen, collected earlier through masturbation or taken from a sperm bank, is placed in a syringe attached to a narrow tube or catheter. The catheter is gently inserted into the cervical canal, and the semen is slowly injected into the uterus. The patient then stays in her position for fifteen or twenty minutes to increase the chances that the sperm will fertilize an ovum.

The overall success rate of artificial insemination is about 85%. Success on the first attempt is quite rare, and the highest rate occurs in the third month. In unusual cases, efforts may be made every month for as long as six months or a year. Such efforts are continued, however, only when a detailed examination shows that the woman is not suffering from some unrecognized problem preventing her from becoming pregnant.

When sperm taken from donors is used, the rate of congenital abnormalities is a little lower than that for the general population. There seems to be no evidence to support the fear that manipulating the sperm causes any harm. (Many physicians prefer to employ fresh, rather than frozen, sperm to minimize the amount of environmental change the sperm is subjected to. Other physicians claim that frozen sperm is to be preferred, for it provides a means of screening out defective cells or chromosome abnormalities.)

Reasons for Seeking Artificial Insemination

Artificial insemination may be sought for a variety of reasons. When a couple is involved, the reasons are almost always associated with physiological or physical factors that make it impossible for the couple to conceive a child in the usual sexual way.

About 10% of all married couples are infertile, and 40% of those cases are due to factors involving the male. In some instances, the male may be unable to produce any sperm at all (a condition called asospermia), or the number of sperm the male produces may be too low to make impregnation of the female likely (a condition called oligospermia). In other cases, adequate numbers of sperm cells may be produced, but they may not function normally. They may not be sufficient motile to make their way past the vaginal canal and through the opening to the uterus. Hence, their chances of reaching and penetrating an ovum are slight. Finally, the male may suffer from a neurological condition that makes ejaculation impossible or from a disease (such as diabetes) that renders him impotent.

If the female cannot ovulate, or if her Fallopian tubes are blocked so that ova cannot descend, then artificial insemination can accomplish nothing. (See the section above on in vitro fertilization.) Yet there are factors affecting the female that artificial insemination can be helpful in overcoming. For example, if the female has a vaginal environment that is biochemically inhospitable to sperm, the artificial insemination may be successful. Because the sperm need not pass through the vagina, they have a better chance of surviving. Also, if the female has a small cervix (the opening to the uterus) or if her uterus is in an abnormal position, then artificial insemination may be used to deliver the sperm to an advantageous position for fertilization, a position they otherwise might not reach.

A couple might also seek artificial insemination for genetic reasons. Both may be carriers of a recessive gene for a genetic disorder (Tay-Sachs disease, for example) or the male may be the carrier of a dominant gene for a genetic disorder (Huntington's disease, for example). In either case, the couple may not want to run the statistical risk of their child's being born with a genetic disease. To avoid the possibility, they may choose to make use of artificial insemination with sperm secured from a donor.

The traditional recipient of artificial insemination is a married woman who, in consultation with her husband, has decided to have a child. Some physiological or physical difficulty in conceiving leads them to turn to artificial insemination.

But the traditional recipient is no longer the only recipient. Those seeking to have the procedure performed now include single women who wish to have a child but do not wish to have it fathered in the usual fashion. Some estimates place the number of such women at 150 a year. The percentages of such inseminations may increase in the future if the notion of being a single parent continues to be met with acceptance or approval within our society. The increase may be quite rapid if the attitudes of physicians, in particular, change. At present, single women who wish to become mothers are likely to be discouraged, and some physicians will not accept them as candidates for artificial insemination.

Types of Artificial Insemination

Artificial insemination can be divided into types in accordance with the source of the sperm employed in the procedure.

Artificial insemination (homologous) uses sperm obtained from the male partner. The name of the process is usually abbreviated as AIH, and the H is frequently taken to stand for "husband." While it is true that the male of a couple is most frequently the woman's husband, legal marriage is not necessary for AIH. The male need only be, in some sense, the functional equivalent of a husband.

Artificial insemination (heterologous) uses sperm from a sperm donor. For this reason, the process is usually referred to by the abbreviation AID. The use of semen obtained from a donor is the most frequent of AI procedures, and it is the one that gives rise to most of the social and legal issues surrounding the practice.

Artificial insemination (confused) employs a mixture of sperm from the male partner and sperm obtained from a donor. CAI, as it is commonly called, has no particular biological advantage, but it does offer a couple a degree of psychological support. Because they cannot be sure that it was not sperm from the male partner that resulted in conception, they may be more inclined to accept the child as the product of their union. The role of the third-party sperm donor is thus psychologically minimized.

Sperm Donors

Sperm donors are typically selected from medical-student and hospital-staff volunteers. An effort is made to employ as donors people in excellent health with a high level of intellectual ability. Their family histories are reviewed to reduce the possibility of transmitting a genetic disorder, and their blood type is checked to determine its compatibility with that of the AID recipient.

Such general physical features of the donor as body type, hair and eye color, and complexion are matched in a rough way with those of the potential parents. To be a donor, an individual must also be known to be fertile. This means that he must already be a biological parent or that he must fall within the normal range in several semen analyses.

Donors are typically paid for their services. What is more, their identity is kept secret from the recipient and her husband. A coding system is ordinarily used both to preserve the anonymity of the donor and to ensure that the same donor is used in all inseminations.

Sperm contributed by a donor might be employed in an insemination within one or three hours after the semen is obtained. As mentioned earlier, some physicians prefer to use freshly obtained sperm in the procedure. But sperm may also be maintained in a frozen condition and, after being restored to the proper temperature, used in the same way as fresh sperm. Sperm banks are no more than freezers containing racks of coded plastic tubes holding donated sperm.

The semen stored in sperm banks is not necessarily that of anonymous donors. For a variety of reasons, individuals may wish to have their sperm preserved and pay a fee to a sperm-bank operator for this service. For example, a man planning a vasectomy or one expecting to become sterile because of a progressive disease may store his sperm in the event that he may later want to father a child.

Issues in Artificial Insemination

Artificial insemination presents a great variety of moral, legal, and social issues. The truth is, most of those issues have not been addressed in a thorough fashion. Legal scholars have explored some of the consequences that AI has for traditional legal doctrines of paternity, legitimacy, and inheritance. They have also made recommendations for formulating new laws (or reformulating old ones) to take into account the reality of the practice of AI.

Others who have written about AI have mostly focused on its potential for altering the relationship between husbands and wives and for producing undesirable social changes. Many of the objections to in vitro fertilization have also been offered to artificial insemination. For example, it has been argued that AI will take the love out of sexual procreation and make it a purely mechanical process, that AI will promote the practice of eugenics and so denigrate the worth of babies that fall short of some ideal, and that AI is just another step down the road toward the society of *Brave New World*.

While such issues are of great importance, they have usually been discussed in such a general fashion that specific ethical questions about the use of artificial insemination as a medical procedure have rarely been raised. As a result, those questions have not been subjected to the dialectical process of argument and criticism that is important in helping us arrive at reasoned opinions.

Some of the issues that need close attention from philosophers concern individual rights and responsibilities. For example, does a man who has served as a sperm donor have any special moral responsibilities? He certainly must have some responsibilities. For example, it would be wrong for him to lie about any genetic diseases in his family history. But does he have any responsibilities to the child that is produced by AI employing his sperm? If donating sperm is no different from donating blood, then perhaps he does not. But is such a comparison apt?

Can a child born as a result of AI legitimately demand to know the name of his biological father? We need not assume that mere curiosity might motivate such a request. Someone might need to know his family background in order to determine how likely it is that a potential child might have a genetic disorder. After all, it is unreasonable to assume that a donor is fully informed about his own biological background. Perhaps the current practice of maintaining the anonymity of sperm donors is not one that can stand critical scrutiny.

Should a woman be allowed to order sperm donated by someone who approximates her concept of an ideal person? Should she be able to request a donor from a certain ethnic group, with particular eye and hair color, certain minimum or maximum height, physical attractiveness, with evidence of intelligence, and so on? At present, the physician who performs the procedure also makes the choice of the donor. But why should the physician be granted the right to make the selection? One might argue that allowing the physician to exercise such a power violates the autonomy of the AI recipient.

A number of other ethical questions are easily raised about AI: Does any woman (married or single, of any age) have the right to demand AI? Should a physician make AID available to a married women even if her husband is opposed?

Other questions concerning the proper procedures to follow in the practice of AI are also of considerable significance. For example, how thoroughly must sperm donors be screened for genetic defects? What standards of quality must sperm as a biological material be required to satisfy? What physical, educational, or general social traits (if any) should individual donors possess? Should records be maintained and shared through an established network to prevent the marriage or mating of individuals born from AID with the same biological father?

At present, these questions have been answered only by individual physicians or clinics, if at all. There are no general medical or legal policies that govern the practice of AI. Even if present practices are adequate, most people would agree that there is a need to develop uniform policies to regulate AI.

Obviously, we have touched upon only a few of the ethical and social issues that the practice of artificial insemination generates. Indeed, at the moment, it is not wholly clear even what the more significant issues may be. In this area of medical ethics, in particular, philosophers still have a great deal of work to do.

SURROGATE PREGNANCY

We have already discussed gestational surrogacy in connection with in vitro fertilization. A gestational surrogate is a "host mother," a woman who is implanted with an embryo produced by in vitro fertilization of the ovum of another woman. Terms in this area are still in flux, and gestational surrogates are sometimes called *surrogate mothers*.

However, surrogate mothers in the more usual sense are women who agree to become pregnant by means of artificial insemination with sperm from a male of a married couple. The surrogate mother carries the baby to term, then turns the baby over to the couple for adoption. Surrogate mothers are typically sought by couples who wish to have a child with whom they have a genetic link and who have been unsuccessful in conceiving one themselves.

Various legal complications surround surrogate pregnancy, and at least eighteen states have passed laws regulating surrogacy arrangements. When surrogacy arrangements are allowed, a major problem is to find a way to pay women who agree to be surrogate mothers. Adoption laws forbid the selling of children or even the payment of money to one of the parents in connection with adoption. The child must be freely surrendered. Since a child born to a surrogate mother is, in the absence of laws to the contrary, legally her child, the child must be adopted by the couple securing her services. How then can the surrogate mother be paid?

Some women have simply volunteered to be surrogate mothers so that the issue of payment would not arise. In general, however, the difficulty has been resolved by paying the mother to compensate her for the loss of her time and her inconvenience. Technically, then, the surrogate mother is not being paid for conceiving and bearing a child, nor is she being paid for the child who is handed over for adoption. Hence, laws against selling a child are not violated, and the surrogate is paid from ten to twenty-five thousand dollars.

A second problem is finding a way to permit surrogacy, while avoiding turning it into a commercial operation resembling the breeding of horses or show dogs. Surrogacy is often arranged by an attorney acting as a broker on behalf of a couple who want a child. The attorney finds the surrogate and draws up a contract between her and the couple wishing to employ her services. (The contract can include such items as a prorated fee if the surrogate miscarries or a requirement that the surrogate have an abortion if prenatal tests reveal a fetal abnormality.) Of course, the surrogate must agree to relinquish her maternal rights and not stand in the way of adoption by the contracting couple. For arranging the surrogacy, as well as for drawing up the contract, the broker receives a fee of fifteen to twenty thousand dollars.

In the view of some critics, despite the claim that a surrogate is being paid for her time and inconvenience, surrogacy arrangements are no more than "baby selling." To avoid this appearance, New York State passed a law with the aim of removing the profit motive from surrogacy arrangements and making them completely noncommercial. The state kept it legal for a woman to become a surrogate, but made it illegal to pay a broker to handle the arrangements. Further, the state made it illegal to pay a surrogate for anything more than her medical expenses. A contract agreeing to pay a fee to a broker or to a woman acting as a surrogate would have no legal standing in court.

Four to five thousand babies have been born in the United States through surrogacy arrangements. About 40% of them have been born in New York. Consequently, the New York law may affect the practice of using surrogates. Rather than decrease the number of surrogacy arrangements, however, the law will probably only encourage "underground" and illegal arrangements.

Some of the same reasons offered to justify in vitro fertilization can also be offered for surrogate pregnancy. Fundamentally, couples who wish to have a child of their own but are unable to do so because of some uncorrectable medical difficulty experienced by the woman view surrogate pregnancy as the only hope remaining to them. Some rule out adoption because of the relative shortage of available infants, and some simply want there to be a genetic connection between them and the child. Many people are quite desperate to have a child of their own.

Some critics have charged that surrogate pregnancy is no more than a specialized form of prostitution. A woman, in effect, rents out her body for a period of time and is paid for doing so. Such a criticism rests on the assumption that prostitution is morally wrong, and this is a claim that at least some would deny is correct. Furthermore, the criticism fails to take into account the differences in aims. Some surrogate mothers have volunteered their services with no expectation of monetary reward, and some women have agreed to be surrogate mothers at the request of their sister, friend, daughter, or son. Even those who are paid mention that part of their motivation is to help those couples who so desperately want a child. Far from condemning surrogate mothers as acting immorally, it is perhaps possible to view at least some of them as acting in a morally heroic way by contributing to the good of others through their actions.

Perhaps the most serious objection to surrogate mothers is that they are likely to be recruited from the ranks of those most in need of money. Women of upper- and middle-income groups are not likely to serve as surrogate mothers. Women with low-paying jobs or no jobs at all are obviously the prime candidates for recruiters. It might be charged, then, that women who become surrogate mothers are being exploited by those who have money enough to pay for their services.

However, merely paying someone in need of money to do something does not constitute exploitation. To make such a charge stick, it would be necessary to show that women who become surrogate mothers are under a great deal of social and economic pressure and have no other realistic options. Furthermore, it could be argued that, within limits, individuals have a right to do with their bodies as they choose. If a woman freely decides to earn money by serving as a surrogate mother, then we have no more reason to object to her decision than we would have to object to a man's decision to earn money by working as a construction laborer.

There is good reason to believe that, as the population ages and women with careers postpone having children, the employment of surrogate mothers is likely to increase. The practice is now well established, but the ethical and social issues are far from being resolved to the general satisfaction of our society.

ETHICAL THEORIES AND REPRODUCTIVE CONTROL

One of the themes of Mary Shelley's famous novel *Frankenstein* is that it is both wrong and dangerous to tamper with the natural forces of life. It is wrong because it disturbs the natural order of things, and it is dangerous because

it unleashes forces beyond human control. The "monster" that is animated by Dr. Victor Frankenstein stands as a warning and reproach to all who seek to impose their will on the world through the powers of scientific technology.

The fundamental ethical question about the technology of human reproductive control is whether it ought to be employed at all. Is it simply wrong for us to use our knowledge of human biology to exercise power over the processes of human reproduction?

The natural law view, as represented by currently accepted doctrines of the Roman Catholic Church, suggests that all the techniques for controlling human reproduction that we have discussed here are fundamentally wrong.

Children may ordinarily be expected as a result of sexual union within marriage. However, if no measures are wrongfully taken to frustrate the possibility of their birth (contraception, for example), then a married couple has no obligation to attempt to conceive children by means such as artificial insemination or in vitro fertilization.

Indeed, those processes themselves are inherently objectionable. Artificial insemination requires male masturbation, which is prima facie wrong, since it is an act that can be considered to be unnatural, given the natural end of sex. Furthermore, AI, even when semen from the husband is used, tends to destroy the values inherent in the married state. It makes conception a mechanical act.

In vitro fertilization is open to the same objections. In addition, the process itself involves the destruction of fertilized ova. On the view that human conception takes place at the moment of fertilization, this means that the discarding of unimplanted embryos amounts to the destruction of human life.

On the utilitarian view, no reproductive technology is in itself objectionable. The question that has to be answered is whether the use of any particular procedure, in general or in a certain case, is likely to lead to more good than not. In general, it is reasonable to believe that a utilitarian would be likely to approve of the three sorts of procedures we have discussed here.

However, it is worth mentioning that a rule utilitarian might well oppose any or all of the procedures. If there is strong evidence to support the view that the use of reproductive technology will lead to a society in which the welfare of its members will not be served, then a rule utilitarian would be on firm ground in arguing that reproductive technology ought to be abandoned.

According to Ross's ethical theory, we have prima facie duties of beneficence. That is, we have an obligation to assist others in bettering their lives. This suggests that the use of reproductive technology may be justified as a means to promote the well-being of others. For example, if a couple desires to have a child but is unable to conceive one, then either in vitro fertilization procedures or artificial insemina-

tion might be employed to help them satisfy their shared desire.

Kantian principles do not seem to supply grounds for objecting either to in vitro fertilization or to artificial insemination as inherently wrong. However, the maxim involved in each action must always be one that satisfies the categorical imperative. Consequently, some instances of in vitro fertilization and artificial insemination would no doubt be morally wrong.

The technology of reproduction is a reality of ordinary life. So far it has made our society into neither a dystopia nor a utopia. It is just one set of tools among the many others that science and medicine have forged.

Yet the tools are powerful ones, and we should beware of allowing familiarity to produce indifference. The moral and social issues raised by reproductive technology are just as real as the technology. So far we have not treated some of them with the seriousness that they deserve.

Instruction on Respect for Human Life in Its Origin and on the Dignity of Procreation: Replies to Certain Questions of the Day

Congregation for the Doctrine of the Faith

This "Instruction" was issued on February 22, 1987. It was approved and ordered published by Pope John Paul II and thus may be taken as representing the official position of the Roman Catholic Church on the issues addressed.

The document takes the position that a number of current or potential practices connected with reproductive technology are morally illegitimate. Included are the following:

- Prenatal diagnosis by amniocentesis or ultrasound for the purpose of identifying impaired fetuses so that abortion can be performed;
- Therapeutic intervention that may cause a risk to a fetus disproportionate to a potential benefit;
- Experimentation on a living embryo that is not directly therapeutic;
- Keeping alive human embryos for experimental or commercial purposes;

- Destroying human embryos produced by in vitro techniques for the purpose of either research or procreation;

- Cross-species fertilization involving human and animal gametes;

- The gestation of a human embryo in an animal uterus or an artificial uterus;

- The use of human genetic material in procedures like cloning, parthenogenesis, and twin fission (the splitting of gametes);

- Attempts to manipulate genetic material for the purpose of sex selection or to promote desirable characteristics;

- Artificial insemination involving unmarried individuals or the artificial insemination of an unmarried woman or a widow, even if the sperm is that of her deceased husband;

- Acquiring sperm by means of masturbation;

- Surrogate motherhood.

Some techniques and practices, according to the document, are morally legitimate. Included are the following:

- Medical intervention to remove the causes of infertility;

- The prescription of drugs to promote fertility;

- Prenatal diagnosis with the aim of promoting the welfare of the fetus;

- Prenatal therapeutic intervention (including genetic manipulation) with the aim of healing the developing embryo or fetus;

- Prenatal research that is limited to monitoring or observing the embryo.

The document also makes a number of specific recommendations to governments to establish laws and policies governing reproductive technologies. It asks that civil laws be passed to prohibit the donation of sperm or ova between unmarried people. Laws should "expressly forbid" the use of living embryos for experimentation and protect them from mutilation and destruction. Further, legislation should prohibit "embryo banks, postmortem insemination and 'surrogate motherhood.'"

Some Roman Catholic theologians disagreed sharply with parts of the document. "The document argues that a child can be born only from a sexual act," Richard A. McCormick pointed out. "The most that can be argued is that a child should be born within a marriage from a loving act. Sexual intercourse is not the only loving act." Some suggested that individuals would make up their own minds on the issues, quite apart from the Vatican position. The significance of the document to non-Catholics is that the positions taken and the arguments for them are likely to affect the character of the discussion about reproductive technology and have an impact on legislation that will place restraints on research and practices many currently consider legitimate.

Notes and references are omitted in this excerpt.

Part 1: Respect for Human Embryos

Careful reflection on this teaching of the Magisterium and on the evidence of reason . . . enables us to respond to the numerous moral problems posed by technical interventions upon the human being in the first phases of his life and upon the processes of his conception.

1. What Respect Is Due to the Human Embryo, Taking into Account His Nature and Identity?

The human being must be respected—as a person—from the very first instant of his existence.

The implementation of procedures of artificial fertilization has made possible various interventions upon embryos and human fetuses. The aims pursued are of various kinds: diagnostic and therapeutic, scientific and commercial. From all of this, serious problems arise. Can one speak of a right to experimentation upon human embryos for the purpose of scientific research? What norms or laws should be worked out with regard to this matter? The response to these problems presupposes a detailed reflection on the nature and specific identity—the word "status" is used—of the human embryo itself. . . .

This Congregation is aware of the current debates concerning the beginning of human life, concerning the individuality of the human being and concerning the identity of the human person. The Congregation recalls the teachings found in the Declaration on Procured Abortion: "From the time that the ovum is fertilized, a new life is begun which is neither that of the father nor of the mother: it is rather the life of a new human being with his own growth. It would never be made human if it were not human already. To this perpetual evidence . . . modern genetic science brings valuable confirmation. It has demonstrated that, from the first instant, the programme is fixed as to what this living being will be: a man, this individual-man with his characteristic aspects already well determined. Right from fertilization is begun the adventure of a human life, and each of its great capacities requires time . . . to find its place and to be in a position to act." This teaching remains valid and is further confirmed, if confirmation were needed, by recent findings of human biological science which recognize that in the zygote* resulting from fertilization the biological identity of a new human individual is already constituted. . . .

Thus the fruit of human generation, from the first moment of its existence, that is to say from the moment the zygote has formed, demands the unconditional respect that is morally due to the human being in his bodily and spiritual totality. The human being is to be respected and treated as a person from the moment of conception; and therefore from that same moment his rights as a person must be recognized, among which in the first place is the inviolable right of every innocent human being to life.

The doctrinal reminder provides the fundamental criterion for the solution of the various problems posed by the development of the biomedical sciences in this field: since the embryo must be treated as a person, it must also be defended in its integrity, tended and cared for, to the extent possible, in the same way as any other human being as far as medical assistance is concerned.

2. Is Prenatal Diagnosis Morally Licit?

If prenatal diagnosis respects the life and integrity of the embryo and the human fetus and is directed towards its safeguarding or healing as an individual, then the answer is affirmative.

For prenatal diagnosis makes it possible to know the condition of the embryo and of the fetus when still in the mother's womb. It permits, or makes it possible to anticipate earlier and more effectively, certain therapeutic, medical or surgical procedures.

Such diagnosis is permissible, with the consent of the parents after they have been adequately informed, if the methods employed safeguard the life and integrity of the embryo and the mother, without subjecting them to disproportionate risks. But this diagnosis is gravely opposed to the moral law when it is done with the thought of possibly inducing an abortion depending upon the results: a diagnosis which shows the existence of a malformation or a hereditary illness must not be the equivalent of a death-sentence. Thus a woman would be committing a gravely illicit act if she were to request such a diagnosis with the deliberate intention of having an abortion should the results confirm the existence of a malformation or abnormality. The

*The zygote is the cell produced when the nuclei of the two gametes have fused.

spouse or relatives or anyone else would similarly be acting in a manner contrary to the moral law if they were to counsel or impose such a diagnostic procedure on the expectant mother with the same intention of possibly proceeding to an abortion. So too the specialist would be guilty of illicit collaboration if, in conducting the diagnosis and in communicating its results, he were deliberately to contribute to establishing or favoring a link between prenatal diagnosis and abortion.

In conclusion, any directive or program of the civil and health authorities or of scientific organizations which in any way were to favor a link between prenatal diagnosis and abortion, or which were to go as far as directly to induce expectant mothers to submit to prenatal diagnosis planned for the purpose of eliminating fetuses which are affected by malformations or which are carriers of hereditary illness, is to be condemned as a violation of the unborn child's right to life and as an abuse of the prior rights and duties of the spouses.

3. Are Therapeutic Procedures Carried Out on the Human Embryo Licit?

As with all medical interventions on patients, *one must uphold as licit procedures carried out on the human embryo which respect the life and integrity of the embryo and do not involve disproportionate risks for it but are directed towards its healing, the improvement of its condition of health, or its individual survival.*

Whatever the type of medical, surgical or other therapy, the free and informed consent of the parents is required, according to the deontological rules, followed in the case of children. The application of this moral principle may call for delicate and particular precautions in the case of embryonic or fetal life. . . .

4. How Is One to Evaluate Morally Research and Experimentation on Human Embryos and Fetuses?

Medical research must refrain from operations on live embryos, unless there is a moral certainty of not causing harm to the life or integrity of the unborn child and the mother, and on condition that the parents have given their free and informed consent to the procedure. It follows that all research, even when limited to the simple observation of the embryo, would become illicit were it to involve risk to the embryo's physical integrity or life by reason of the methods used or the effects induced.

As regards experimentation, and presupposing the general distinction between experimentation for purposes which are not directly therapeutic and experimentation which is clearly therapeutic for the subject himself, in the case in point one must also distinguish between experimentation carried out on embryos which are still alive and experimentation carried out on embryos which are dead. *If the embryos are living, whether viable or not, they must be respected just like any other human person; experimentation on embryos which is not directly therapeutic is illicit.*

No objective, even though noble in itself, such as a foreseeable advantage to science, to other human beings or to society, can in any way justify experimentation on living human embryos or fetuses, whether viable or not, either inside or outside the mother's womb. The informed consent ordinarily required for clinical experimentation on adults cannot be granted by the parents, who may not freely dispose of the physical integrity or life of the unborn child. Moreover, experimentation on embryos and fetuses always involves risk, and indeed in most cases it involves the certain expectation of harm to their physical integrity or even their death. . . .

In the case of experimentation that is clearly therapeutic, namely, when it is a matter of experimental forms of therapy used for the benefit of the embryo itself in a final attempt to save its life, and in the absence of other reliable forms of therapy, recourse to drugs or procedures not yet fully tested can be licit. . . .

5. How Is One to Evaluate Morally the Use for Research Purposes of Embryos Obtained by Fertilization "In Vitro"?

Human embryos obtained in vitro are human beings and subjects with rights: their dignity and right to life must be respected from the first moment of their existence. *It is immoral to produce human embryos destined to be exploited as disposable "biological material."*

In the usual practice of in vitro fertilization, not all of the embryos are transferred to the woman's body; some are destroyed. Just as the Church condemns induced abortion, so she also forbids acts against the life of these human beings. *It is a duty to condemn the particular gravity of the voluntary destruction of human embryos obtained "in vitro" for the sole purpose of research, either by means of artificial insemination or by means of "twin fission."* By acting in this way the researcher usurps the place of God; and, even though he may be unaware of this, he sets himself up as the master of the destiny of others inasmuch as he arbitrarily chooses whom he will allow to live and whom he will send to death and kills defenseless human beings.

Methods of observation or experimentation which damage or impose grave and disproportionate risks upon embryos obtained in vitro are morally illicit for the same reasons. Every human being is to be respected for himself, and cannot be reduced in worth to a pure and simple instrument for the advantage of others. *It is therefore not in conformity with the moral law deliberately to expose to death human embryos obtained "in vitro."* In consequence of the fact that they have been produced in vitro, those embryos which are not transferred into the body of the mother and are called "spare" are exposed to an absurd fate, with no possibility of their being offered safe means of survival which can be licitly pursued.

6. What Judgment Should Be Made on Other Procedures of Manipulating Embryos Connected with the "Techniques of Human Reproduction"?

Techniques of fertilization in vitro can open the way to other forms of biological and genetic manipulation of human embryos, such as attempts or plans for fertilization between human and animal gametes and the gestation of human embryos in the uterus of animals, or the hypothesis or project of constructing artificial uteruses for the human embryos. *These procedures are contrary to the human dignity proper to the embryo, and at the same time they are contrary to the right of every person to be conceived and to be born within marriage and from marriage. Also, attempts or hypotheses for obtaining a human being without any connection with sexuality through "twin fission," cloning or parthenogenesis are to be considered contrary to the moral law, since they are in opposition to the dignity both of human procreation and of the conjugal union.*

The *freezing of embryos,* even when carried out in order to preserve the life of an embryo—cryopreservation—*constitutes an offense against the respect due to human beings* by exposing them to grave risks of death or harm to their physical integrity and depriving them, at least temporarily, of maternal shelter and gestation, thus placing them in a situation in which further offenses and manipulation are possible.

Certain attempts to influence chromosomic or genetic inheritance are not therapeutic but are aimed at producing human beings selected according to sex or other predetermined qualities. These manipulations are contrary to the personal dignity of the human being and his or her integrity and identity. Therefore in no way can they be justified on the grounds of possible beneficial consequences for future humanity. Every person must be respected for himself: in this consists the dignity and right of every human being from his or her beginning.

Part II: Interventions upon Human Procreation

By "artificial procreation" or "artificial fertilization" are understood here the different technical procedures directed towards obtaining a human conception in a manner other than the sexual union of man and woman. This Instruction deals with fertilization of an ovum in a test-tube (in vitro fertilization) and artificial insemination through transfer into the woman's genital tracts of previously collected sperm.

A preliminary point for the moral evaluation of such technical procedures is constituted by the consideration of the circumstances and consequences which those procedures involve in relation to the respect due the human embryo. Development of the practice of in vitro fertilization has required innumerable fertilizations and destructions of human embryos. Even today, the usual practice presupposes a hyper-ovulation on the part of the woman: a number of ova are withdrawn, fertilized and then cultivated in vitro for some days. Usually not all are transferred into the genital tracts of the woman; some embryos, generally called "spare," are destroyed or frozen. On occasion, some of the implanted embryos are sacrificed for various eugenic, economic or psychological reasons. Such deliberate destruction of human beings or their utilization for different purposes to the detriment of their integrity and life is contrary to the doctrine on procured abortion already recalled.

The connection between in vitro fertilization and the voluntary destruction of human embryos occurs too often. This is significant: through these procedures, with apparently contrary purposes, life and death are subjected to the decision of man, who thus sets himself up as the giver of life and death by decree. This dynamic of violence and domination may remain unnoticed by those very individuals who, in wishing to utilize this procedure, become subject to it themselves. The facts recorded and the cold logic which links them must be taken into consideration for a moral judgment on IVF and ET (in vitro fertilization and embryo transfer): the abortion-mentality which has made this procedure possible, thus leads, whether one wants it or not, to man's domination over the life and death of his fellow human beings and can lead to a system of radical eugenics.

Nevertheless, such abuses do not exempt one from a further and thorough ethical study of the techniques of artificial procreation considered in themselves, abstracting as far as possible from the destruction of embryos produced in vitro.

The present Instruction will therefore take into consideration in the first place the problems posed by heterologous artificial fertilization (II, 1–3),* and subsequently those linked with homologous artificial fertilization (II, 4–6).†

Before formulating an ethical judgment on each of these procedures, the principles and values which determine the moral evaluation of each of them will be considered.

---

*By the term heterologous artificial fertilization or procreation, the Instruction means techniques used to obtain a human conception artificially by the use of gametes coming from at least one donor other than the spouses who are joined in marriage. Such techniques can be of two types:

a. Heterologous IVF and ET: the technique used to obtain a human conception through the meeting in vitro of gametes taken from at least one donor other than the two spouses joined in marriage.

b. Heterologous artificial insemination: the technique used to obtain a human conception through the transfer into the genital tracts of the woman of the sperm previously collected from a donor other than the husband.

†By artificial homologous fertilization or procreation, the Instruction means the technique used to obtain a human conception using the gametes of the two spouses joined in marriage. Homologous artificial fertilization can be carried out by two different methods:

a. Homologous IVF and ET: the technique used to obtain a human conception through the meeting in vitro of the gametes of the spouses joined in marriage.

b. Homologous artificial insemination: the technique used to obtain a human conception through the transfer into the genital tracts of a married woman of the sperm previously collected from her husband.

A. Heterologous Artificial Fertilization

1. Why Must Human Procreation Take Place in Marriage?   *Every human being is always to be accepted as a gift and blessing of God. However, from the moral point of view a truly responsible procreation vis-a-vis the unborn child must be the fruit of marriage.*

For human procreation has specific characteristics by virtue of the personal dignity of the parents and of the children: the procreation of a new person, whereby the man and the woman collaborate with the power of the Creator, must be the fruit and the sign of the mutual self-giving of the spouses, of their love and of their fidelity. *The fidelity of the spouses in the unity of marriage involves reciprocal respect of their right to become a father and a mother only through each other.*

The child has the right to be conceived, carried in the womb, brought into the world and brought up within marriage: it is through the secure and recognized relationship to his own parents that the child can discover his own identity and achieve his own proper human development.

The parents find in their child a confirmation and completion of their reciprocal self-giving: the child is the living image of their love, the permanent sign of their conjugal union, the living and indissoluble concrete expression of their paternity and maternity.

By reason of the vocation and social responsibilities of the person, the good of the children and of the parents contributes to the good of civil society; the vitality and stability of society require that children come into the world within a family and that the family be firmly based on marriage.

The tradition of the Church and anthropological reflection recognize in marriage and in its indissoluble unity the only setting worthy of truly responsible procreation.

2. Does Heterologous Artificial Fertilization Conform to the Dignity of the Couple and to the Truth of Marriage?   Through IVF and ET and heterologous artificial insemination, human conception is achieved through the fusion of gametes of at least one donor other than the spouses who are united in marriage. *Heterologous artificial fertilization is contrary to the unity of marriage, to the dignity of the spouses, to the vocation proper to parents, and to the child's right to be conceived and brought into the world in marriage and from marriage.* . . .

These reasons lead to a negative moral judgment concerning heterologous artificial fertilization: consequently fertilization of a married woman with the sperm of a donor different from her husband and fertilization with the husband's sperm of an ovum not coming from his wife are morally illicit. Furthermore, the artificial fertilization of a woman who is unmarried or a widow, whoever the donor may be, cannot be morally justified.

The desire to have a child and the love between spouses who long to obviate a sterility which cannot be overcome in any other way constitute understandable motivations; but subjectively good intentions do not render heterologous artificial fertilization conformable to the objective and inalienable properties of marriage or respectful of the rights of the child and of the spouses.

3. Is "Surrogate"* Motherhood Morally Licit?

No, for the same reasons which lead one to reject heterologous artificial fertilization: for it is contrary to the unity of marriage and to the dignity of the procreation of the human person.

Surrogate motherhood represents an objective failure to meet the obligations of maternal love, of conjugal fidelity and of responsible motherhood; it offends the dignity and the right of the child to be conceived, carried in the womb, brought into the world and brought up by his own parents; it sets up, to the detriment of families, a division between the physical, psychological and moral elements which constitute those families.

B. Homologous Artificial Fertilization

Since heterologous artificial fertilization has been declared unacceptable, the question arises of how to evaluate morally the process of homologous artificial fertilization: IVF and ET and artificial in-

*By "surrogate mother" the Instruction means:

a. the woman who carries in pregnancy an embryo implanted in her uterus and who is genetically a stranger to the embryo because it has been obtained through the union of the gametes of "donors." She carries the pregnancy with a pledge to surrender the baby once it is born to the party who commissioned or made the agreement for the pregnancy.

b. the woman who carries in pregnancy an embryo to whose procreation she has contributed the donation of her own ovum, fertilized through insemination with the sperm of a man other than her husband. She carries the pregnancy with a pledge to surrender the child once it is born to the party who commissioned or made the agreement for the pregnancy.

semination between husband and wife. First a question of principle must be clarified.

4. What Connection Is Required from the Moral Point of View between Procreation and the Conjugal Act?

... In reality, the origin of a human person is the result of an act of giving. The one conceived must be the fruit of his parents' love. He cannot be desired or conceived as the production of an intervention of medical or biological techniques; that would be equivalent to reducing him to an object of scientific technology. No one may subject the coming of a child into the world to conditions of technical efficiency which are to be evaluated according to standards of control and dominion.

The moral relevance of the link between the meanings of the conjugal act and between the goods of marriage, as well as the unity of the human being and the dignity of his origin, demand that the procreation of a human person be brought about as the fruit of the conjugal act specific to the love between spouses. The link between procreation and the conjugal act is thus shown to be of great importance on the anthropological and moral planes, and it throws light on the positions of the Magisterium with regard to homologous artificial fertilization.

5. Is Homologous "In Vitro" Fertilization Morally Licit?

The answer to this question is strictly dependent on the principles just mentioned. Certainly one cannot ignore the legitimate aspirations of sterile couples. For some, recourse to homologous IVF and ET appears to be the only way of fulfilling their sincere desire for a child. The question is asked whether the totality of conjugal life in such situations is not sufficient to insure the dignity proper to human procreation. It is acknowledged that IVF and ET certainly cannot supply for the absence of sexual relations and cannot be preferred to the specific acts of conjugal union, given the risks involved for the child and the difficulties of the procedure. But it is asked whether, when there is no other way of overcoming the sterility which is a source of suffering, homologous in vitro fertilization may not constitute an aid, if not a form of therapy, whereby its moral licitness could be admitted.

The desire for a child—or at the very least an openness to the transmission of life—is a necessary prerequisite from the moral point of view for responsible human procreation. But this good intention is not sufficient for making a positive moral evaluation of in vitro fertilization between spouses. The process of IVF and ET must be judged in itself and cannot borrow its definitive moral quality from the totality of conjugal life of which it becomes part nor from the conjugal acts which may precede or follow it.

It has already been recalled that, in the circumstances in which it is regularly practiced, IVF and ET involves the destruction of human beings, which is something contrary to the doctrine on the illicitness of abortion previously mentioned. But even in a situation in which every precaution were taken to avoid the death of human embryos, homologous IVF and ET dissociates from the conjugal act the actions which are directed to human fertilization. For this reason the very nature of homologous IVF and ET also must be taken into account, even abstracting from the link with procured abortion.

Homologous IVF and ET is brought about outside the bodies of the couple through actions of third parties whose competence and technical activity determine the success of the procedure. Such fertilization entrusts the life and identity of the embryo into the power of doctors and biologists and establishes the domination of technology over the origin and destiny of the human person. Such a relationship of domination is in itself contrary to the dignity and equality that must be common to parents and children.

Conception in vitro is the result of the technical action which presides over fertilization. *Such fertilization is neither in fact achieved or positively willed as the expression and fruit of specific acts of the conjugal union. In homologous IVF and ET, therefore, even if it is considered in the context of "de facto" existing sexual relations, the generation of the human person is objectively deprived of its proper perfection: namely, that of being the result and fruit of a conjugal act* in which the spouses can become "cooperators with God for giving life to a new person." . . .

Certainly, homologous IVF and ET fertilization is not marked by all that ethical negativity found in extra-conjugal procreation; the family and marriage continue to constitute the setting for the birth and upbringing of the children. Nevertheless, in conformity with the traditional doctrine relating to the goods of marriage and the dignity of the person, *the*

Church remain opposed from the moral point of view to homologous "in vitro" fertilization. Such fertilization is in itself illicit and in opposition to the dignity of procreation and of the conjugal union, even when everything is done to avoid the death of the human embryo.

Although the manner in which human conception is achieved with IVF and ET cannot be approved, every child which comes into the world must in any case be accepted as a living gift of the divine Goodness and must be brought up with love.

6. How Is Homologous Artificial Insemination to Be Evaluated from the Moral Point of View? *Homologous artificial insemination within marriage cannot be admitted except for those cases in which the technical means is not a substitute for the conjugal act but serves to facilitate and to help so that the act attains its natural purpose.*

The teaching of the Magisterium on this point has already been stated. This teaching is not just an expression of particular historical circumstances but is based on the Church's doctrine concerning the connection between the conjugal union and procreation and on a consideration of the personal nature of the conjugal act and of a human procreation. "In its natural structure, the conjugal act is a personal action, a simultaneous and immediate cooperation on the part of the husband and wife, which by the very nature of the agents and the proper nature of the act is the expression of the mutual gift which, according to the words of Scripture, brings about union 'in one flesh.'" Thus moral conscience "does not necessarily proscribe the use of certain artificial means destined solely either to the facilitating of the natural act or to insuring that the natural act normally performed achieves its proper end." If the technical means facilitates the conjugal act or helps it to reach its natural objectives, it can be morally acceptable. If, on the other hand, the procedure were to replace the conjugal act, it is morally illicit.

Artificial insemination as a substitute for the conjugal act is prohibited by reason of the voluntarily achieved dissociation of the two meanings of the conjugal act. Masturbation, through which the sperm is normally obtained, is another sign of this dissociation: even when it is done for the purpose of procreation, the act remains deprived of its unitive meaning: "It lacks the sexual relationship called for by the moral order, namely the relationship which realizes 'the full sense of mutual self-giving and human procreation in the context of true love.'" . . .

8. The Suffering Caused by Infertility in Marriage. *The suffering of spouses who cannot have children or who are afraid of bringing a handicapped child into the world is a suffering that everyone must understand and properly evaluate.*

On the part of the spouses, the desire for a child is natural: it expresses the vocation to fatherhood and motherhood inscribed in conjugal love. This desire can be even stronger if the couple is affected by sterility which appears incurable. Nevertheless, marriage does not confer upon the spouses the right to have a child, but only the right to perform those natural acts which are per se ordered to procreation.

A true and proper right to a child would be contrary to the child's dignity and nature. The child is not an object to which one has a right, nor can be considered as an object of ownership: rather, a child is a gift, "the supreme gift" and the most gratuitous gift of marriage, and is a living testimony of the mutual giving of his parents. For this reason, the child has the right, as already mentioned, to be the fruit of the specific act of the conjugal love of his parents; and he also has the right to be respected as a person from the moment of his conception.

Nevertheless, whatever its cause or prognosis, sterility is certainly a difficult trial. The community of believers is called to shed light upon and support the suffering of those who are unable to fulfill their legitimate aspiration to motherhood and fatherhood. Spouses who find themselves in this sad situation are called to find in it an opportunity for sharing in a particular way in the Lord's Cross, the source of spiritual fruitfulness. Sterile couples must not forget that "even when procreation is not possible, conjugal life does not for this reason lose its value. Physical sterility in fact can be for spouses the occasion for other important services to the life of the human person, for example, adoption, various forms of educational work, and assistance to other families and to poor or handicapped children."

Many researchers are engaged in the fight against sterility. While fully safeguarding the dignity of human procreation, some have achieved results which previously seemed unattainable. Scientists therefore are to be encouraged to continue their research with the aim of preventing the causes of sterility and of being able to remedy them so that sterile couples will be able to procreate in full respect for their own personal dignity and that of the child to be born. . . .

Creating Embryos _____

Peter Singer

_____

Peter Singer begins by showing that the "standard argument" used to support ascribing a right to life to an embryo fails to be convincing. The premise "Every human being has a right to life" is acceptable only if we appeal to specific mental qualities; yet doing so raises questions about the premise "A human embryo is a human being," for the embryo lacks just these qualities. The standard argument employs "human" equivocally, and Singer finds attempts to rescue the argument unpersuasive.

In his "positive approach," Singer argues that the minimum characteristic that gives an embryo claim to consideration is "the capacity to feel pain or pleasure." At this stage, like many nonhuman animals, the embryo is "conscious but not self-conscious," and we must rigorously control research. Before then, with parental consent, there is no moral objection to discarding early embryos.

The Moral Status of the Embryo

The Standard Argument

The standard argument in favor of attributing a right to life to the embryo goes like this:

> Every human being has a right to life.
> A human embryo is a human being.
> Therefore the embryo has a right to life.

To avoid questions about capital punishment, or killing in self-defense, it can be stipulated that the term "innocent" is assumed whenever we are talking of human beings and their rights.

The standard argument has a standard response. The standard response is to accept the first premise, that all human beings have a right to life, but to deny the second premise, that the human embryo is a human being. This standard response, however, runs into difficulties, because the embryo is clearly a being of some sort, and it can't possibly be of any other species than *Homo sapiens*. So it seems to follow that it must be a human being. Attempts to say that it only becomes a human being at viability, or at birth, are not entirely convincing. Viability is so closely tied to the state of development of neonatal intensive care that it is hardly the kind of thing that can determine when a being gets a right to live. As for birth, those who draw the line there must explain why an infant born premature at 26 weeks should have a right to life, whereas a fetus of 32 weeks, more developed in every respect, should not. Can location relative to the cervix really make so much difference to one's right to life?

Questioning the First Premise

So the standard argument for attributing a right to life to the embryo can withstand the standard response. It is not easy to mount a direct challenge to the claim that the embryo is a human being. What the standard argument cannot withstand, however, is a more critical examination of its first premise: the premise that every human being has a right to life. At first glance, this seems the stronger premise. Do we really want to deny that every (innocent) human being has a right to life? Are we about to condone murder? No wonder it is at the second premise that most of the fire has been directed. But the first premise is surprisingly vulnerable. Its vulnerability becomes apparent as soon as

we cease to take "Every human being has a right to life" as some kind of unquestionable moral axiom, and instead inquire into the moral basis for our particular objection to killing human beings.

By "our particular objection to killing human beings" I mean the objection we have to killing human beings, over and above any objections we may have to killing other living beings, such as pigs and cows and dogs and cats, and even trees and lettuces. Why is it that we think killing human beings is so much more serious than killing these other beings?

The obvious answer is that human beings are different from other animals, and the greater seriousness of killing them is a result of these differences. But which of the many differences between humans and other animals justify such a distinction? Again, the obvious response is that the morally relevant differences are those based on our superior mental powers—our self-awareness, our rationality, our moral sense, our autonomy, or some combination of these. They are the kinds of thing, we are inclined to say, which make us "truly human." To be more precise, they are the kinds of thing which make us *persons*.

That the particular objection to killing human beings rests on such qualities is very plausible. To take the most extreme of the differences between living things, consider a person who is enjoying life, is part of a network of relationships with other people, is looking forward to what tomorrow may bring, and freely choosing the course her or his life will take for the years to come. Now think about a lettuce, which, we can safely assume, knows and feels nothing at all. One would have to be quite mad, or morally blind, or warped, not to see that killing the person is far more serious than killing the lettuce.

We shall postpone, for the present, asking just which of the mental qualities make the difference in the moral seriousness between the killing of a person and the killing of a lettuce. For our immediate purposes, all we need to note is that the plausibility of the assertion that human beings have a right to life depends on the fact that human beings generally possess mental qualities which other living beings do not possess. So should we accept the premise that every human being has a right to life? We may do so, but *only* if we bear in mind that by "human being" here we refer to those beings who have the mental qualities that generally distinguish members of our species from members of other species.

Two Senses of "Human"

If this is the sense in which we can accept the first premise, however, what of the second premise? It is immediately clear that in the sense of the term "human being" which is required to make the first premise acceptable, the second premise is false. The embryo, especially the early embryo, is obviously not a being with the mental qualities which generally distinguish members of our species from members of other species. The early embryo has no brain, no nervous system. It is reasonable to assume that, so far as its mental life goes, it has no more awareness than a lettuce.

It is still true that the human embryo is a member of the species *Homo sapiens*. That is, as we saw, why it is difficult to deny that the human embryo is a human being. But we can now see that this is not the sense of "human being" we need to make the standard argument work. A valid argument cannot equivocate on the meanings of the central terms it uses. If the first premise is true when "human" means "a being with certain mental qualities" and the second premise is true when "human" means "member of the species *Homo sapiens*," the argument is based on a slide between the two meanings and is invalid.

Speciesism

Can the argument be rescued? It obviously cannot be rescued by claiming that the embryo is a being with the requisite mental qualities. That *might* be arguable for some later stage of the development of the embryo or fetus, but it is impossible to make out the claim for the early embryo. If the second premise cannot be reconciled with the first in this way, can the first perhaps be defended in a form which makes it compatible with the second? Can it be argued that human beings have a right to life, not because of any moral qualities they may possess, but because they—and not pigs, cows, dogs, or lettuces—are members of the species *Homo sapiens*?

This is a desperate move. Those who make it find themselves having to defend the claim that species membership is *in itself* morally relevant to the wrongness of killing a being. But why should

species membership in itself be morally crucial? If we are considering whether it is wrong to destroy something, surely we must look at its actual characteristics, not just the species to which it belongs. If ET and similar visitors from other planets turn out to be sensitive, thinking, planning beings, who get homesick just like we do, would it be acceptable to kill them simply because they are not members of our species? Should you be in any doubt, ask yourself the same kind of question, but with "race" substituted for "species." If we reject the claim that membership of a particular race is *in itself* morally relevant to the wrongness of killing a being, it is not easy to see how we could accept the same claim when based on species membership. Remember that the fact that other races, like our own, can feel, think, and plan for the future is not relevant to this question, for we are considering the simple fact of membership of the particular group—whether race or species—as the *sole* basis for distinguishing between the wrongness of killing those who belong to *our* group, and those who are of some *other* group. As long as we keep this in mind, I am sure that we will conclude that neither race nor species can, *in itself*, provide any justifiable basis for such a distinction.

So the standard argument fails. It fails not because of the standard response that the embryo is not a human being, but because the sense in which the embryo is a human being is not the sense in which we should accept that every human being has a right to life.

The Argument from Potential

At this point in the discussion, those who wish to defend the embryo's right to life often switch ground. We should not, they say, base our views of the status of the embryo on the mental qualities it *actually has while an embryo;* we must, rather, consider what it has the potential to *become.*

Indeed, we do need to consider the moral relevance of the embryo's potential. But this argument is not as easy to grasp as it may appear. If we attempt to set it out in an argument of standard form, as we did with the previous argument, we get

> Every potential human being has a right to life.
> The embryo is a potential human being.
> Therefore the embryo has a right to life.

There is no equivocation in this argument, and its second premise is undoubtedly true. The problem is with the first premise. The claim that every potential human being has a right to life is by no means self-evidently true. We would need to be given good grounds for accepting it. What grounds could there be?

One might try to argue that since full-fledged human beings (those with at least some of the mental qualities I have been discussing) have a right to life, anything with the potential to become a full-fledged human being must also have a right to life. But there is no general rule that a potential X has the rights of an X. If there were, Prince Charles, who is a potential King of England, would now have the rights of a King of England. But he does not.

Another possible argument might go like this: there is nothing of greater moral significance than a thinking, choosing rational being. We value such beings above almost everything else. Therefore anything which can give rise to such a being has value because of what it can become.

What is this argument asserting? It suggests that the destruction of an embryo is wrong because it means that a person who might have existed will now not exist; and since we value people, the destruction of the embryo has caused us to lose something of value. But this proves too much. For destroying an embryo is not the only way of ensuring that a person who might have existed will not exist. If a couple decide, after their second, or third, or fourth child, that their family is complete, it is also the case that a person who might have existed—in fact, several people who might have existed—will not exist. Since some people who oppose abortion also oppose the use of contraceptives, it is worth pointing out that this is true whether the couple use contraceptives, or simply abstain from sexual intercourse during the woman's fertile periods (though admittedly the latter method gives the possible people a greater chance of existence). Yet those who condemn the destruction of embryos do not condemn with equal weight the use of contraceptives, and they generally do not condemn at all the use of sexual abstinence to limit the size of one's family. So it seems that the basis for their objection to the destruction of the embryo cannot be that a person who might have existed will now not exist.

Another example, more relevant to the question of embryo research, suggests the same conclusion. Suppose that a scientist has obtained two ripe eggs from two women, let us call them Jan and Maria. They are hoping to have their eggs fertilized with their husbands' sperm and transferred to their wombs. Jan had her laparoscopy first, her egg was put into a petri dish, and her husband's sperm added to it some hours ago. On checking it, the scientist finds that fertilization has taken place. In the case of Maria's eggs the sperm has only just been added to the dish, so fertilization cannot yet have taken place, but the laboratory has a 90 percent success rate for achieving fertilization in these circumstances, and the scientist is reasonably confident that fertilization will take place within the next few hours. Some would say that to destroy Jan's embryo would be gravely wrong, but to destroy the egg and sperm from Maria and her husband would not be wrong at all, or would be much less seriously wrong. In terms of preventing a possible person from existing, however, the difference is only that there is a slightly higher probability of a person resulting from what is in Jan's petri dish than there is of a person resulting from what is in Maria's petri dish. If the difference in the wrongness of disposing of the contents of the two dishes is greater than this slightly higher probability would justify, it cannot be preventing the existence of a possible future person that makes such disposal wrong. To borrow a phrase from the Oxford philosopher Jonathan Glover, if it is cake we are after, it doesn't make much difference whether we throw away the ingredients separately, or after they are mixed together (7).

Uniqueness

At this point some will say that it is wrong to destroy an embryo because the embryo already contains the unique genetic basis for a particular person. When a couple abstain from intercourse, or the scientist washes out the petri dish before fertilization has taken place, the genetic constitution of the person who might have existed has yet to be determined. This is true, of course, but does it matter? *All* human beings are genetically determinate, and all, except identical siblings, are genetically unique. Imagine that instead of just dropping lots of sperm into a petri dish containing a ripe egg, we carried out a program of artificial reproduction by singling out just *one* sperm and placing it with the egg. Then, once the sperm had been singled out and placed with the egg, the genetic constitution of the person who could develop from the egg-and-sperm would also have been uniquely determined. Suppose now that after the egg and sperm have been placed together, but before fertilization has taken place, the woman is found to have a medical condition which makes pregnancy inadvisable. Freezing is not available, and there are no patients interested in a donated embryo. Would it be wrong to throw out the egg and sperm at this stage? If you do not think that it would be wrong to dispose of the egg and the sperm in *this* situation (and worse than it would be if the usual procedure, involving millions of sperm, had been used) then you cannot be attributing much moral significance to the existence of a genetically unique entity.

I have pursued the will-o-wisp of potential for a long time—not just today, but over the past five years in which I have been working on this topic. I can understand the view that fertilization is one step in the development of a person and that if potentiality is a matter of degree, the embryo is a degree closer to being a person than a collection of egg and sperm in a petri dish before fertilization has taken place. What I still cannot find is any basis for the view that this difference of degree makes an enormous difference in the moral status of what we have before us.

A Positive Approach

We have now seen the inadequacy of attempts to argue that the early embryo has a right to life. It remains only to say something positive about when in its development the embryo may acquire rights.

The answer must depend on the actual characteristics of the embryo. The minimal characteristic which is needed to give the embryo a claim to consideration is sentience, or the capacity to feel pain or pleasure. Until the embryo reaches that point, there is nothing we can do to the embryo which causes harm to *it*. We can, of course, damage it in such a way as to cause harm to the person it will become, if it lives, but if it never becomes a person, the embryo has not been harmed, because its total lack of awareness means that it can have no interest in becoming a person.

Once an embryo may be capable of feeling pain, there is a clear case for very strict controls over the experimentation which can be done with it. At this point the embryo ranks, morally, with other creatures who are conscious but not self-conscious. Many nonhuman animals come into this category, and in my view they have often been unjustifiably made to suffer in scientific research. We should have stringent controls over research to ensure that this cannot happen to embryos, just as we should have stringent controls to ensure that it cannot happen to animals.

Practical Implications of the Moral Status of Embryos

The conclusion to draw from this is that as long as the parents give their consent, there is no ethical objection to discarding a very early embryo. If the early embryo can be used for significant research, so much the better. What is crucial is that the embryo not be kept beyond the point at which it has formed a brain and a nervous system, and might be capable of suffering. Two government committees—the Warnock Committee in Britain (8) and the Waller Committee in Victoria, Australia (9)—have recently recommended that research on embryos should be allowed, but only up to 14 days after fertilization. This is the period at which the so-called "primitive streak," the first indication of the development of a nervous system, begins to form, and up to this stage there is certainly no possibility of the embryo feeling anything at all. In fact, the 14-day limit is unnecessarily conservative. A limit of, say, 28 days would still be very much on the safe side of the best estimates of when the embryo may be able to feel pain; but such a limit would, in contrast to the 14-day limit, allow research on embryos at the stage at which some of the more specialized cells have begun to form. As we saw earlier, this research would, according to Robert Edwards, have the potential to cure such terrible diseases as sickle cell anemia and leukemia (2).

As for freezing the embryo with a view to later implantation, the question here is essentially one of risk. If freezing carries no special risk of abnormality, there seems to be nothing objectionable about it. With embryo freezing, this appears to be the case. The ethical objections some people have to freezing embryos has led to the suggestions that it would be better to freeze eggs (8); for this and other reasons there has been a considerable research effort directed at freezing eggs. Human eggs are more difficult to freeze than human embryos, and until recently it had not proved possible to freeze them in a manner which allowed fertilization after thawing. In December 1985, however, an IVF team at Flinders University, in Adelaide, South Australia, announced that it had succeeded in obtaining a pregnancy from an egg which had been frozen and thawed before being fertilized (10). The technique used involved stripping away a protective outer layer from the egg, so that it would take up a chemical which would protect it during the freezing process. This technique does overcome the ethical problems some find in freezing embryos, but it does so at the cost of introducing a new potential cause of risk to the offspring, the risk that the chemicals absorbed by the egg may have some harmful effect (11). Whether or not this risk proves to be a real one, from the point of view of ethics, one may doubt whether the risk is worth running, if the primary reason for running it is to avoid objections, which we have now seen to be ill-founded, to the freezing of embryos. . . .

Notes

1.   Singer, P., Wells, D. *Making babies.* New York: Scribner's 1985.

2.   Edwards, R. G. Paper presented at the Fourth World Congress on IVF. Melbourne, Australia, Nov. 22, 1985.

3.   Abstract. Proceedings of the Fifth Scientific Meeting of the Fertility Society of Australia, Adelaide, Dec. 2–6, 1986.

4.   Rowland, R. Reproductive technologies: the final solution to the woman question? In: Arditti, R., Klein, R. D., Minden, S., eds., *Test-tube women: what future for motherhood?* London: Pandora, 1984.

5.   Firestone, S. *The dialectic of sex.* New York: Bantam, 1971.

6.   Breeze, N. Who is going to rock the petri dish? In: Arditti, R., Klein, R. D., Minden, S., eds., *Test-tube women: what future for motherhood?* London: Pandora, 1984.

7.   Glover, J. *Causing death and saving lives.* Harmondsworth, England: Penguin, 1977.

8.   Warnock, M. (Chairperson). Report on the Committee of Inquiry into Human Fertilisation and Embryology. London: Her Majesty's Stationery Office, 1984, p. 66.

9.   Waller, L. (Chairman). Victorian Government Committee to Consider the Social, Ethical and Legal Issues Arising from In Vitro Fertilization. Report on the disposition of embryos produced by in vitro fertilization. Melbourne: Victorian Government Printer, 1984, p. 47.

10.   *The Australian,* Dec. 19, 1985.

11.   Trounson, A. Paper presented at the Fourth World Congress on IVF, Melbourne, Australia, Nov. 22, 1985.

Surrogate Motherhood as Prenatal Adoption

Bonnie Steinbock

Bonnie Steinbock reviews the Baby M case and maintains that the court decision was inconsistent in considering the best interest of the child. This aim of legislation, she claims, should be to minimize potential harms and prevent cases like that of Baby M from happening again. This can be so only if surrogacy is not intrinsically wrong.

This leads Steinbock to examine three lines of argument and attempt to show that neither paternalism of the sort outlined by Gerald Dworkin (see Chapter 5) nor such considerations as threats of exploitation, loss of dignity, or harm to the child are adequate to show that surrogacy is inherently objectionable. In Steinbock's view, regulating surrogacy—and protecting liberty—is preferable to prohibiting it.

The recent case of "Baby M" has brought surrogate motherhood to the forefront of American attention. Ultimately, whether we permit or prohibit surrogacy depends on what we take to be good reasons for preventing people from acting as they wish. A growing number of people want to be, or hire, surrogates; are there legitimate reasons to prevent them? Apart from its intrinsic interest, the issue of surrogate motherhood provides us with an opportunity to examine different justifications for limiting individual freedom.

In the first section, I examine the Baby M case, and the lessons it offers. In the second section, I examine claims that surrogacy is ethically unaccept-

From "Surrogate Motherhood as Prenatal Adoption," by Bonnie Steinbock, *Law, Medicine and Health Care,* Vol. 16, No. 1 (Spring/Summer 1988), 44–50.

able because exploitive, inconsistent with human dignity, or harmful to the children born of such arrangements. I conclude that these reasons justify restrictions on surrogate contracts, rather than an outright ban.

I. Baby M

Mary Beth Whitehead, a married mother of two, agreed to be inseminated with the sperm of William Stern, and to give up the child to him for a fee of $10,000. The baby (whom Mrs. Whitehead named Sara, and the Sterns named Melissa) was born on March 27, 1986. Three days later, Mrs. Whitehead took her home from the hospital, and turned her over to the Sterns.

Then Mrs. Whitehead changed her mind. She went to the Sterns' home, distraught, and pleaded to have the baby temporarily. Afraid that she would kill herself, the Sterns agreed. The next week, Mrs. Whitehead informed the Sterns that she had decided to keep the child, and threatened to leave the country if court action was taken.

At that point, the situation deteriorated into a cross between the Keystone Kops and Nazi storm troopers. Accompanied by five policemen, the Sterns went to the Whitehead residence armed with a court order giving them temporary custody of the child. Mrs. Whitehead managed to slip the baby out of a window to her husband, and the following morning the Whiteheads fled with the child to Florida, where Mrs. Whitehead's parents lived. During the next three months, the Whiteheads lived in roughly twenty different hotels, motels, and homes to avoid apprehension. From time to time, Mrs. Whitehead telephone Mr. Stern to discuss the matter: He taped these conversations on advice of counsel. Mrs. Whitehead threatened to kill herself, to kill the child, and falsely to accuse Mr. Stern of sexually molesting her older daughter.

At the end of July 1986, while Mrs. Whitehead was hospitalized with a kidney infection, Florida police raided her mother's home, knocking her down, and seized the child. Baby M was placed in the custody of Mr. Stern, and the Whiteheads returned to New Jersey, where they attempted to regain custody. After a long and emotional court battle, Judge Harvey R. Sorkow ruled on March 31, 1987, that the surrogate contract was valid, and that specific performance was justified in the best interests of the child. Immediately after reading his

decision, he called the Sterns into his chambers so that Mr. Stern's wife, Dr. Elizabeth Stern, could legally adopt the child.

This outcome was unexpected and unprecedented. Most commentators had thought that a court would be unlikely to order a reluctant surrogate to give up an infant merely on the basis of a contract. Indeed, if Mrs. Whitehead had never surrendered the child to the Sterns, but had simply taken her home and kept her there, the outcome undoubtedly would have been different. It is also likely that Mrs. Whitehead's failure to obey the initial custody order angered Judge Sorkow, and affected his decision.

The decision was appealed to the New Jersey Supreme Court, which issued its decision on February 3, 1988. Writing for a unanimous court, Chief Justice Wilentz reversed the lower court's ruling that the surrogacy contract was valid. The court held that a surrogacy contract which provides money for the surrogate mother, and which includes her irrevocable agreement to surrender her child at birth, is invalid and unenforceable. Since the contract was invalid, Mrs. Whitehead did not relinquish, nor were there any other grounds for terminating, her parental rights. Therefore, the adoption of Baby M by Mrs. Stern was improperly granted, and Mrs. Whitehead remains the child's legal mother.

The Court further held that the issue of custody is determined solely by the child's best interests, and it agreed with the lower court that it was in Melissa's best interests to remain with the Sterns. However, Mrs. Whitehead, as Baby M's legal as well as natural mother, is entitled to have her own interest in visitation considered. The determination of what kind of visitation rights should be granted to her, and under what conditions, was remanded to the trial court.

The distressing details of this case have led many people to reject surrogacy altogether. Do we really want police officers wrenching infants from their mothers' arms, and prolonged custody battles when surrogates find they are unable to surrender their children, as agreed? Advocates of surrogacy say that to reject the practice wholesale, because of one unfortunate instance, is an example of a "hard case" making bad policy. Opponents reply that it is entirely reasonable to focus on the worst potential outcomes when deciding public policy. Everyone can agree on at least one thing: This particular case seems to have been mismanaged from start to finish, and could serve as a manual of how not to arrange a surrogate birth.

First, it is now clear that Mary Beth Whitehead was not a suitable candidate for surrogate motherhood. Her ambivalence about giving up the child was recognized early on, although this information was not passed on to the Sterns.[1] Second, she had contact with the baby after birth, which is usually avoid in "successful" cases. Typically, the adoptive mother is actively involved in the pregnancy, often serving as the pregnant woman's coach in labor. At birth, the baby is given to the adoptive, not the biological, mother. The joy of the adoptive parents in holding their child serves both to promote their bonding, and to lessen the pain of separation of the biological mother.

At Mrs. Whitehead's request, no one at the hospital was aware of the surrogacy arrangement. She and her husband appeared as the proud parents of "Sara Elizabeth Whitehead," the name on her birth certificate. Mrs. Whitehead held her baby, nursed her, and took her home from the hospital—just as she would have done in a normal pregnancy and birth. Not surprisingly, she thought of Sara as her child, and she fought with every weapon at her disposal, honorable and dishonorable, to prevent her being taken away. She can hardly be blamed for doing so.[2]

Why did Dr. Stern, who supposedly had a very good relation with Mrs. Whitehead before the birth, not act as her labor coach? One possibility is that Mrs. Whitehead, ambivalent about giving up her baby, did not want Dr. Stern involved. At her request, the Sterns' visits to the hospital to see the newborn baby were unobtrusive. It is also possible that Dr. Stern was ambivalent about having a child. The original idea of hiring a surrogate was not hers, but her husband's. It was Mr. Stern who felt a "compelling" need to have a child related to him by blood, having lost all his relatives to the Nazis.

Furthermore, Dr. Stern was not infertile, as was stated in the surrogacy agreement. Rather, in 1979 she was diagnosed by two eye specialists as suffering from optic neuritis, which meant that she "probably" had multiple sclerosis. (This was confirmed by all four experts who testified.) Normal conception was ruled out by the Sterns in late 1982, when a medical colleague told Dr. Stern that his wife, a victim of multiple sclerosis, had suffered a temporary paralysis during pregnancy. "We decided the risk wasn't worth it," Mr. Stern said.[3]

Mrs. Whitehead's lawyer, Harold J. Cassidy, dismissed the suggestion that Dr. Stern's "mildest case" of multiple sclerosis determined their decision to seek a surrogate. He noted that she was not even treated for multiple sclerosis until after the Baby M dispute had started. "It's almost as though it's an afterthought," he said.[4]

Judge Sorkow deemed the decision to avoid conception "medically reasonable and understandable." The Supreme Court did not go so far, noting that "her anxiety appears to have exceeded the actual risk, which current medical authorities assess as minimal."[5] Nonetheless the court acknowledged that her anxiety, including fears that pregnancy might precipitate blindness and paraplegia, was "quite real." Certainly, even a woman who wants a child very much, may reasonably wish to avoid becoming blind and paralyzed as a result of pregnancy. Yet is it believable that a woman who really wanted a child would decide against pregnancy *solely* on the basis of *someone else's* medical experience? Would she not consult at least one specialist on her *own* medical condition before deciding it wasn't worth the risk? The conclusion that she was at best ambivalent about bearing a child seems irresistible.

This possibility conjures up many people's worst fears about surrogacy: That prosperous women, who do not want to interrupt their careers, will use poor and educationally disadvantaged women to bear their children. I will return shortly to the question of whether this is exploitive. The issue here is psychological: What kind of mother is Dr. Stern likely to be? If she is unwilling to undergo pregnancy, with its discomforts, inconveniences, and risks, will she be willing to make the considerable sacrifices which good parenting requires? Mrs. Whitehead's ability to be a good mother was repeatedly questioned during the trail. She was portrayed as immature, untruthful, hysterical, overly identified with her children, and prone to smothering their independence. Even if all this is true—and I think that Mrs. Whitehead's inadequacies were exaggerated—Dr. Stern may not be such a prize either. The choice for Baby M may have been between a highly strung, emotional, over-involved mother, and a remote, detached, even cold one.

The assessment of Mrs. Whitehead's ability to be a good mother was biased by the middle-class prejudices of the judge and mental health officials who testified. Mrs. Whitehead left school at 15, and is not conversant with the latest theories on child rearing: She made the egregious error of giving Sara teddy bears to play with, instead of the more "age-appropriate," expert-approved pans and spoons. She proved to be a total failure at patty-cake. If this is evidence of parental inadequacy, we're all in danger of losing our children.

The Supreme Court felt that Mrs. Whitehead was "rather harshly judged" and acknowledged the possibility that the trial court was wrong in its initial award of custody. Nevertheless, it affirmed Judge Sorkow's decision to allow the Sterns to retain custody, as being in Melissa's best interests. George Annas disagrees with the "best interests" approach. He points out that Judge Sorkow awarded temporary custody of Baby M to the Sterns in May 1986 without giving the Whiteheads notice or an opportunity to obtain legal representation. That was a serious wrong and injustice to the Whiteheads. To allow the Sterns to keep the child compounds the original unfairness: ". . . justice requires that reasonable consideration be given to returning Baby M to the permanent custody of the Whiteheads."[6]

But a child is not a possession, to be returned to the rightful owner. It is not fairness to all parties that should determine a child's fate, but what is best for her. As Chief Justice Wilentz rightly stated, "The child's interests comes first: We will not punish it for judicial errors, assuming any were made."[7]

Subsequent events have substantiated the claim that giving custody to the Sterns was in Melissa's best interests. After losing custody, Mrs. Whitehead, whose husband had undergone a vasectomy, became pregnant by another man. She divorced her husband and married Dean R. Gould last November. These developments indicate that the Whiteheads were not able to offer a stable home, although the argument can be made that their marriage might have survived, but for the strains introduced by the court battle, and the loss of Baby M. But even if Judge Sorkow had no reason to prefer the Sterns to the Whiteheads back in May 1986, he was still right to give the Sterns custody in March 1987. To take her away then, at nearly eighteen months of age, from the only parents she had ever known, would have been disruptive, cruel, and unfair to her.

Annas's preference for a just solution is premised partly on his belief that there is no "best interest" solution to this "tragic custody case." I take it that he means that however custody is resolved, Baby M is the loser. Either way, she will be deprived of one parent. However, a best interests solution is not a perfect solution. It is simply the solution which is on balance best for the child, given the realities of the situation. Applying this standard, Judge Sorkow was right to give the Sterns custody, and the Supreme Court was right to uphold the decision.

The best interests argument is based on the assumption that Mr. Stern has at least a *prima facie* claim to Baby M. We certainly would not consider allowing a stranger who kidnapped a baby, and managed to elude the police for a year, to retain custody on the grounds that he was providing a good home to a child who had known no other parent. However, the Baby M case is not analogous. First, Mr. Stern is Baby M's biological father and, as such, has at least some claim to raise her, which no non-parental kidnapper has. Second, Mary Beth Whitehead agreed to give him their baby. Unlike the miller's daughter in *Rumpelstiltskin*, the fairy tale to which the Baby M case is sometimes compared, she was not forced into the agreement. Because both Mary Beth Whitehead and Mr. Stern have *prima facie* claims to Baby M, the decision as to who should raise her should be based on her present best interests. Therefore we must, regretfully, tolerate the injustice to Mrs. Whitehead, and try to avoid such problems in the future.

It is unfortunate that the Court did not decide the issue of visitation on the same basis as custody. By declaring Mrs. Whitehead Gould the legal mother, and maintaining that she is entitled to visitation, the Court has prolonged the fight over Baby M. It is hard to see how this can be in her best interests. This is no ordinary divorce case, where the child has a relation with both parents which it is desirable to maintain. As Mr. Stern said at the start of the court hearing to determine visitation, "Melissa has a right to grow and be happy and not be torn between two parents."[8]

The court's decision was well-meaning but internally inconsistent. Out of concern for the best interests of the child, it granted the Sterns custody. At the same time, by holding Mrs. Whitehead Gould to be the legal mother, with visitation rights, it precluded precisely what is most in Melissa's interest, a resolution of the situation. Further, the decision leaves open the distressing possibility that a Baby M situation could happen again. Legislative efforts should be directed toward ensuring that this worsecase scenario never occurs.

II. Should Surrogacy Be Prohibited?

On June 27, 1988, Michigan became the first state to outlaw commercial contracts for women to bear children for others. Yet making a practice illegal does not necessarily make it go away: Witness black market adoption. The legitimate concerns which support a ban on surrogacy might be better served by careful regulation. However, some practices, such as slavery, are ethically unacceptable, regardless of how carefully regulated they are. Let us consider the arguments that surrogacy is intrinsically unacceptable.

A. Paternalistic Arguments

These arguments against surrogacy take the form of protecting a potential surrogate from a choice she may later regret. As an argument for banning surrogacy, as opposed to providing safeguards to ensure that contracts are freely and knowledgeably undertaken, this is a form of paternalism.

At one time, the characterization of a prohibition as paternalistic was a sufficient reason to reject it. The pendulum has swung back, and many people are willing to accept at least some paternalistic restrictions on freedom. Gerald Dworkin points out that even Mill made one exception to his otherwise absolute rejection of paternalism: He thought that no one should be allowed to sell himself into slavery, because to do so would be to destroy his future autonomy.

This provides a narrow principle to justify some paternalistic interventions. To preserve freedom in the long run, we give up the freedom to make certain choices, those which have results which are "far-reaching, potentially dangerous and irreversible."[9] An example would be a ban on the sale of crack. Virtually everyone who uses crack becomes addicted and, once addicted, a slave to its use. We reasonably and willingly give up our freedom to buy the drug, to protect our ability to make free decisions in the future.

Can a Dworkinian argument be made to rule out surrogacy agreements? Admittedly, the decision to give up a child is permanent, and may have disastrous effects on the surrogate mother. However, many decisions may have long-term, disastrous effects (e.g., postponing childbirth for a career, having an abortion, giving a child up for adoption). Clearly we do not want the state to make decisions for us in all these matters. Dworkin's argument is rightly restricted to paternalistic interferences which protect the individual's autonomy or ability to make decisions in the future. Surrogacy does not involve giving up one's autonomy, which distinguishes it from both the crack and selling-oneself-into-slavery examples. Respect for individual freedom requires us to permit people to make choices which they may later regret.

B. Moral Objections

Four main moral objections to surrogacy were outlined in the Warnock Report.[10]

1. It is inconsistent with human dignity that a woman should use her uterus for financial profit.
2. To deliberately become pregnant with the intention of giving up the child distorts the relationship between mother and child.
3. Surrogacy is degrading because it amounts to child-selling.
4. Since there are some risks attached to pregnancy, no woman ought to be asked to undertake pregnancy for another in order to earn money.

We must all agree that a practice which exploits people or violates human dignity is immoral. However, it is not clear that surrogacy is guilty on either count.

1. Exploitation.   The mere fact that pregnancy is *risky* does not make surrogate agreements exploitive, and therefore morally wrong. People often do risky things for money; why should the line be drawn at undergoing pregnancy? The usual response is to compare surrogacy and kidney-selling. The selling of organs is prohibited because of the potential for coercion and exploitation. But why should kidney-selling be viewed as intrinsically coercive? A possible explanation is that no one would do it, unless driven by poverty. The choice is both forced and dangerous, and hence coercive.

The situation is quite different in the case of the race car driver or stuntman. We do not think that they are *forced* to perform risky activities for money: They freely choose to do so. Unlike selling one's kidneys, these are activities which we can understand (intellectually, anyway) someone choosing to do. Movie stuntmen, for example, often enjoy their work, and derive satisfaction from doing it well. Of course they "do it for the money," in the sense that they would not do it without compensation; few people are willing to work "for free." The element of coercion is missing, however, because they enjoy the job, despite the risks, and could do something else if they chose.

The same is apparently true of most surrogates. "They choose the surrogate role primarily because the fee provides a better economic opportunity than alternative occupations, but also because they enjoy being pregnant and the respect and attention that it draws."[11] Some may derive a feeling of self-worth from an act they regard as highly altruistic: Providing a couple with a child they could not otherwise have. If these motives are present, it is far from clear that the surrogate is being exploited. Indeed, it seems objectionably paternalistic to insist that she is.

2. Human Dignity. It may be argued that even if womb-leasing is not necessarily exploitive, it should still be rejected as inconsistent with human dignity. But why? As John Harris points out, hair, blood and other tissue is often donated or sold; what is so special about the uterus?[12]

Human dignity is more plausibly invoked in the strongest argument against surrogacy, namely, that it is the sale of a child. Children are not property, nor can they be bought or sold. It could be argued that surrogacy is wrong because it is analogous to slavery, and so is inconsistent with human dignity.

However, there are important differences between slavery and a surrogate agreement. The child born of a surrogate is not treated cruelly or deprived of freedom or resold; none of the things which make slavery so awful are part of surrogacy. Still, it may be thought that simply putting a market value on a child is wrong. Human life has intrinsic value; it is literally priceless. Arrangements which ignore this violate our deepest notions of the value of human life. It is profoundly disturbing to hear the boyfriend of a surrogate say, quite candidly in a television documentary on surrogacy, "We're in it for the money."

Judge Sorkow accepted the premise that producing a child for money denigrates human dignity, but he denied that this happens in a surrogate agreement. Mrs. Whitehead was not paid for the surrender of the child to the father: She was paid for her willingness to be impregnated and carry Mr. Stern's child to term. The child, once born, is his biological child. "He cannot purchase what is already his."

This is misleading, and not merely because Baby M is as much Mrs. Whitehead's child as Mr. Stern's. It is misleading because it glosses over the fact that the surrender of the child was part—indeed, the whole point—of the agreement. If the surrogate were paid merely for being willing to be impregnated and carrying the child to term, then she would fulfill the contract upon giving birth. She could take the money *and* the child. Mr. Stern did not agree to pay Mrs. Whitehead merely to *have* his child, but to provide him with a child. The New Jersey Supreme Court held that this violated New Jersey's laws prohibiting the payment or acceptance of money in connection with adoption.

One way to remove the taint of baby-selling would be to limit payment to medical expenses associated with the birth or incurred by the surrogate during pregnancy (as is allowed in many jurisdictions, including New Jersey, in ordinary adoptions). Surrogacy could be seen, not as baby-selling, but as a form of adoption. Nowhere did the Supreme Court find any legal prohibition against surrogacy when there is no payment, and when the surrogate has the right to change her mind and keep the child. However, this solution effectively prohibits surrogacy, since few women would become surrogates solely for self-fulfillment or reasons of altruism.

The question, then, is whether we can reconcile paying the surrogate, beyond her medical expenses, with the idea of surrogacy as prenatal adoption. We can do this by separating the terms of the agreement, which include surrendering the infant at birth to the biological father, from the justification for payment. The payment should be seen as compensation for the risks, sacrifice, and discomfort the surrogate undergoes during pregnancy. This means that if, through no fault on the part of the surrogate, the baby is stillborn, she should still be paid in full, since she has kept her part of the bargain. (By contrast, in the Stern-Whitehead agreement, Mrs. Whitehead was to receive only $1,000 for a stillbirth.) If, on the other hand, the surrogate changes her mind and decides to keep the child, she would break the agreement, and would not be entitled to any fee, or compensation for expenses incurred during pregnancy.

C. The Right of Privacy

Most commentators who invoke the right of privacy do so in support of surrogacy. However, George Annas makes the novel argument that the right to rear a child you have borne is also a privacy right, which cannot be prospectively waived. He says:

> [Judge Sorkow] grudgingly concedes that [Mrs. Whitehead] could not prospectively give up her right to have an abortion during pregnancy. . . . This would be an intolerable restriction on her liberty and under *Roe* v. *Wade,* the state has no constitutional authority to enforce a contract that prohibits her from terminating her pregnancy.
>
> But why isn't the same logic applicable to the right to rear a child you have given birth to? Her constitutional rights to rear the child she has given birth to are even stronger since they involve even more intimately, and over a lifetime, her privacy rights to reproduce and rear a child in a family setting.[13]

Absent a compelling state interest (such as protecting a child from unfit parents), it certainly would be an intolerable invasion of privacy for the state to take children from their parents. But Baby M has two parents, both of whom now want her. It is not clear why only people who can give birth (i.e., women) should enjoy the right to rear their children.

Moreover, we do allow women to give their children up for adoption after birth. The state enforces those agreements, even if the natural mother, after the prescribed waiting period, changes her mind. Why should the right to rear a child be unwaivable before, but not after birth? Why should the state have the constitutional authority to uphold postnatal, but not prenatal, adoption agreements? It is not clear why birth should affect the waivability of this right, or have the constitutional significance which Annas attributes to it.

Nevertheless, there are sound moral and policy, if not constitutional, reasons to provide a postnatal waiting period in surrogate agreements. As the Baby M case makes painfully clear, the surrogate may underestimate the bond created by gestation, and the emotional trauma caused by relinquishing the baby. Compassion requires that we acknowledge these feelings, and not deprive a woman of the baby she has carried because, before conception, she underestimated the strength of her feelings for it. Providing a waiting period, as in ordinary postnatal adoptions, will help protect women from making irrevocable mistakes, without banning the practice.

Some may object that this gives too little protection to the prospective adoptive parents. They cannot be sure that the baby is theirs until the waiting period is over. While this is hard on them, a similar burden is placed on other adoptive parents. If the absence of a guarantee serves to discourage people from entering surrogacy agreements, that is not necessarily a bad thing, given all the risks inherent in such contracts. In addition, this requirement would make stricter screening and counselling of surrogates essential, a desirable side effect.

D. Harm to Others

Paternalistic and moral objections to surrogacy do not seem to justify an outright ban. What about the effect on the offspring of such contracts? We do not yet have solid data on the effects of being a "surrogate child." Any claim that surrogacy creates psychological problems in the children is purely speculative. But what if we did discover that such children have deep feelings of worthlessness from learning that their natural mothers deliberately created them with the intention of giving them away? Might we ban surrogacy as posing an unacceptable risk of psychological harm to the resulting children?

Feelings of worthlessness are harmful. They can prevent people from living happy, fulfilling lives. However, a surrogate child, even one whose life is miserable because of these feelings, cannot claim to have been harmed by the surrogate agreement. Without the agreement, the child would never have existed. Unless she is willing to say that her life is not worth living because of these feelings, that she would be better off never having been born, she cannot claim to have been harmed by being born of a surrogate mother.

Children can be *wronged* by being brought into existence, even if they are not, strictly speaking, *harmed.* They are wronged if they are deprived of the minimally decent existence to which all citizens are entitled. We owe it to our children to see that they are not born with such serious impairments that their most basic interests will be doomed in advance. If being born to a surrogate is a handicap of this magnitude, comparable to being born blind or deaf or severely mentally retarded, then surrogacy can be seen as wronging the offspring. This would be a strong reason against permitting such contracts. However, it does not seem likely. Probably the problems arising from surrogacy will be like those faced by adopted children and children whose parents divorce. Such problems are not trivial, but neither are they so serious that the child's very existence can be seen as wrongful.

If surrogate children are neither harmed nor wronged by surrogacy, it may seem that the argument for banning surrogacy on grounds of its harmfulness to the offspring evaporates. After all, if the children themselves have no cause for complaint, how can anyone else claim to reject it on their behalf? Yet it seems extremely counter-intuitive to suggest that the risk of emotional damage to the children born of such arrangements is not even relevant to our deliberations. It seems quite reasonable and proper—even morally obligatory—for policymakers to think about the possible detrimental effects of new reproductive technologies, and to reject those likely to create physically or emotionally damaged people. The explanation for this must involve the idea that it is wrong to bring people into the world in a harmful condition, even if they are not, strictly speaking, harmed by having been brought into existence. Should evidence emerge that surrogacy produces children with serious psychological problems, that would be a strong reason for banning the practice.

There is some evidence on the effect of surrogacy on the other children of the surrogate mother. One woman reported that her daughter, now 17, who was 11 at the time of the surrogate birth, ". . . is still having problems with what I did, and as a result she is still angry with me." She explains, "Nobody told me that a child could bond with a baby while you're still pregnant. I didn't realize then that all the times she listened to his heartbeat and felt his legs kick that she was becoming attached to him."[14]

A less sentimental explanation is possible. It seems likely that her daughter, seeing one child given away, was fearful that the same might be done to her. We can expect anxiety and resentment on the part of children whose mothers give away a brother or sister. The psychological harm to these children is clearly relevant to a determination of whether surrogacy is contrary to public policy. At the same time, it should be remembered that many things, including divorce, remarriage, and even moving to a new neighborhood, create anxiety and resentment in children. We should not use the effect on children as an excuse for banning a practice we find bizarre or offensive.

Conclusion

There are many reasons to be extremely cautious of surrogacy. I cannot imagine becoming a surrogate, nor would I advise anyone else to enter into a contract so fraught with peril. But the fact that a practice is risky, foolish, or even morally distasteful is not sufficient reason to outlaw it. It would be better for the state to regulate the practice, and minimize the potential for harm, without infringing on the liberty of citizens.

Notes

1. Had the Sterns been informed of the psychologist's concerns as to Mrs. Whitehead's suitability to be a surrogate, they might have ended the arrangement, costing the Infertility Center its fee. As Chief Justice Wilentz said, "It is apparent that the profit motive got the better of the Infertility Center." In the matter of Baby M, Supreme Court of New Jersey, A-39, at 45.

2. "[W]e think it is expecting something well beyond normal human capabilities to suggest that this mother should have parted with her newly born infant without a struggle. . . . We . . . cannot conceive of any other case where a perfectly fit mother was expected to surrender her newly born infant, perhaps forever, and was then told she was a bad mother because she did not." *Id.* at 79.

3. Father recalls surrogate was "perfect." *New York Times,* January 6, 1987, B2.

4. *Id.*

5. In the matter of Baby M, *supra* note 1 at 8.

6. Annas, G. J.: Baby M: babies (and justice) for sale. *Hastings Center Report* 17 (3): 15, 1987.

7. In the matter of Baby M, *supra* note 1, at 75.

8. Anger and Anguish at Baby M Visitation Hearing, *New York Times,* March 29, 1988, 17.

9. Dworkin, G.: Paternalism. In Wasserstrom, R. A., ed.: *Morality and the Law.* Belmont, Calif., Wadsworth, 1971; reprinted in Feinberg, J., Gross, H., eds., *Philosophy of Law,* 3rd ed. Wadsworth, 1986, p. 265.

10. Warnock, M., chair: *Report of the committee of inquiry into human fertilisation and embryology.* London: Her Majesty's Stationery Office, 1984.

11. Robertson, J. A.: Surrogate mothers: not so novel after all. *Hastings Center Report* 13 (5): 29, 1983. Citing Parker, P.: Surrogate mother's motivations: initial findings. *American Journal of Psychiatry* (140): 1, 1983.

12. Harris, J.: *The Value of Life.* London: Routledge & Kegan Paul, 1985, 144.

13. Annas, *supra* note 6.

14. Baby M case stirs feelings of surrogate mothers. *New York Times,* March 2, 1987, B1.

The Right to Lesbian Parenthood

Gillian Hanscombe

Gillian Hanscombe sees the possibility of becoming a single parent as a major advantage of reproductive technology. She argues that homosexual parents are entitled to the same treatment from physicians and institutions as heterosexual ones. The objection that lesbian women should not be allowed to reproduce by artificial insemination is not one that can be supported by relevant evidence, Hanscombe claims. No studies have demonstrated that lesbian mothering is any different from heterosexual mothering or that children of lesbian mothers "fall victim to negative psychosexual developmental influences." She mentions instances of what she considers to be groundless prejudice against lesbian women by the medical establishment.

Anyone daring to address the subject of human rights faces both an appalling responsibility and being accused of an unnatural arrogance of utterance. I accept these risks not because I think myself expert on the subject of human rights, but because my experience is that human rights in the domain of parenthood are so very often denied existence.

I refer to a large minority in our population, that of lesbian women and gay men. Even at the most conservative estimate—which is that at least 1 in 20 adult people are homosexual—a group comprising 5 per cent—we are dealing with a group larger than the 4 per cent ethnic minorities group which already receives, as indeed it deserves to do, special attention. Lesbian women and gay men have to date, in all matters of social policy, been traditionally regarded as a deviant group.

It is the case, nonetheless, that the pathologising of this group is increasingly questioned, not only by members of the gay community themselves, but also by the agencies of our institutional life: that is, by medical practitioners, by teachers and social workers, and by working parties of religious and/or political orientation.

I am the co-author of a book about lesbian mothers.[1] It is written for the general public, rather than for specialists, but is nevertheless the only book to date on the subject which I know of. It records the experiences of a selected group of lesbian mothers—selected to range over the varieties of social existence these parents and their children experience—from divorced women to single women who have deliberately chosen to conceive their children by artificial insemination by donor (AID).

The question asked by many heterosexual professionals who are charged with the theory or practice of social policy, is whether lesbian women, for example, should be (a) allowed, and (b) aided, to become mothers.

Objections to lesbian women being *allowed* to reproduce can only be social, since no physiological studies seeking to find physical differences between lesbian and non-lesbian women have ever succeeded in demonstrating such a difference.

Social objections fall into two categories: (a) the extent to which the psychopathology of the lesbian mother is assumed or demonstrated to deviate negatively from the norm. No studies to date have demonstrated that lesbian mothering is either significantly different from heterosexual mothering or that the lesbian mother is psychologically inadequately equipped to mother;[2] (b) the extent to which the children of lesbian mothers are assumed to fall victim to negative psychosexual developmental influences. No study to date has succeeded in demonstrating such a phenomenon.[3]

There remains social objections issuing from prejudice, which in turn issues from ignorance. Since the medical profession forms a professional

Reprinted by permission of *Journal of Medical Ethics*, 1983, vol. 9, 133–135.

part of our social policy-making institutional life, it is required that medical practitioners do not form judgments based on ignorance. A mere assumption that because, historically, lesbian women have been pathologised this somehow proves that they are "not normal" (and that in a negative sense) is, of course, unacceptable.

A good way of thinking about this is to begin with what is known about female sexuality. In the first place, it is clear that women, unlike men, are able to separate their sexual practice from their reproductive practice. It is possible, that is, for a woman (a) to become sexually aroused and reach orgasm without any possibility that she will become pregnant and (b) for a woman to be inseminated—either naturally or artificially—and become pregnant whether or not, at the same time, she experiences any sexual pleasure. Whatever might be thought, therefore, about lesbian sexual practice, it is clear that lesbian women are able to conceive and bear children in the same way as non-lesbian women do.

Hence, attempting not to allow them to do so would be highly problematic, even apart from the massive dilemma—were such a decision taken—of not being able to enforce the sanction. Contrary to popular prejudice, it is the case that lesbian women, like other women, are quite capable of engaging in sexual intercourse with a man and, like other women, often solely for the reason that they intend to become pregnant.

Prejudice is not only rife within what are called the "helping professions," it is rife, too, in the courts. Lesbian mothers in dispute with husbands almost all lose custody of their children solely on the grounds of their lesbianism.[4] Because of this, as well as for many other reasons, young women in the last decade have turned increasingly to the alternative of AID. They have found, by and large, that medical practitioners are not willing to provide AID for them, again solely on the grounds of their lesbianism. They have decided, increasingly, in response to this attitude, to conduct AID by themselves, with the assistance of sympathetic men. This is neither technically difficult nor is it illegal. Many AID daughters and sons of lesbian women are now in our nurseries and schools.

There are over two million lesbian mothers in the United States. Calculations for Britain are well-nigh impossible, owing to the professional non-recognition of the existence of the group, together with the mothers' reticence in the face of prejudice. They are rightly anxious to conceal their sexuality since, like nearly all mothers, they love their children and will not willingly give them up, either to the courts or to any other social agency.

We might consider one case in particular. A lesbian woman, of middle-class background and professional standing in her own right, decided that she wanted to become a mother. It was, for her, a natural fulfillment of her womanhood, just as it is for millions of other women.

She became pregnant, deliberately, but unfortunately suffered a miscarriage, accompanied by much distress and depression. The usual practice of the hospital treating her was that, following the customary D & C, the patient should report to her own general practitioner. This she did, some six weeks later, wanting very much to know whether there were any clinical reasons why she might suffer further miscarriages. She asked the GP whether the hospital had sent her report.

"Yes, why?" came the reply.

"I want to know whether there is anything wrong with me which explains why I lost the baby," the woman explained.

"Why do you want to know?" persisted the GP.

"Because if there isn't, I want to become pregnant again," said the woman. "It was so dreadful losing the baby that I wouldn't knowingly go through it again. But if I can have a normal, full-term pregnancy, I want to try."

"But you can't have a baby," replied the GP, appalled; "you're not married!"

"What's that got to do with it?" asked the woman. And so ensued an embarrassing session of moralistic instruction from the GP to the silent woman. Her question remained unanswered.

She asked a friend who was a GP in a different area to write to the hospital for the information. This was done. There was no clinical reason for the miscarriage and the woman was pronounced normal and healthy.

The woman became pregnant again. But instead of feeling she could be cared for by her GP, she felt forced to opt for ante-natal care in the impersonal atmosphere of the hospital, where hundreds of women attended the clinic and where the same practitioner hardly ever appeared twice. At each visit, she was seen by different staff, which was comfortless but which at least ensured minimal questioning.

When she was nearly three months pregnant, the sister-in-charge said she must see the social worker. It was "hospital policy." But only, of course, for the unmarried. The woman felt angry and hurt, but didn't want to be accused of "making trouble." The social worker was sympathetic. "Just for the record, do you want your baby?" she asked. "Just for the record," the woman replied, "I planned my baby."

After delivery, she and her baby were not placed in an ordinary ward, but in one where mothers with handicapped babies were placed, together with mothers who had not had normal deliveries. In addition, she was "strongly advised" to stay for the full period, rather than go home after 48 hours. And yet both she and her baby were fit and healthy.

This mother keeps away from the "helping professionals." She is not open with her present GP, her child's school or the para-medical services, either about the circumstances of her child's birth or about her own sexuality. When she is offered contraception during her cervical smear tests, she simply declines it, not daring to explain that she is one of thousands of lesbian women who don't need it.

This woman is a proud and independent mother.[5] And her story is only one among scores. There is the mother who was refused AID by her local medical services and who then answered an advertisement in a lonely hearts column in order to find a man who would make her pregnant. She chartered her ovulation cycle, and when she was fertile, dated the man, who only and clearly wanted casual sex. Her "experiment" worked and she bore a healthy child. There is the mother who came home from work one day to find a weeping partner who had to tell her that both her children—a son aged nine and a daughter aged seven—had been taken into care, because someone had told the social worker that the two women were lesbians.[6]

Hardly any histories of lesbian mothers and their children are on the record. But they are amongst us and they deserve the same care from professional careers as do other mothers and their children.

There are, too, gay men who parent and there are lesbian women and gay men who, though not biological parents themselves, are necessarily involved in childcare by virtue of their partners' parenthood. And there are men who donate semen for the insemination of women who take on themselves the responsibility of conception in order to exercise their rights to reproduce and bring up children. None of the considered and intricate planning undertaken by all these people is mentioned in the vast literature about the family, either in professional or popular publications. Hardly any of this material finds its way into discussions and seminars about family policy, about education, about poverty and so on.

In addition, cruel and heartless lobbying from powerful religious and political quarters—aimed against the human rights of adult homosexual women and men—is ongoing, despite its lack of scientific objectivity. Such pressure is also richly funded. The onus is therefore on the rational, well-informed and compassionate professionals in our caring institutions to consider how they will respond to those of our number born to homosexual parents. Removing the right to reproduce is both immoral and impractical. Neglecting the need of parents for normal support is both discriminatory and cruel. Removing their children from the natural custody of their parents—merely on grounds of the parents' sexuality—is a monstrous interference, with consequences for the children which are no better than the fate of children who are unwanted by their natural mothers. What is needed is education, not legislation.

There are no data—scientific, psychological, or social—which could support the thesis that homosexual people should not have the right to reproduce and to bring up their children. There are only differing opinions and prejudices, which are not capable of sustaining the rigorous intellectual analysis upon which any given body of knowledge must rest. Hitler didn't like homosexuals. Or the handicapped. Or Jews. His answer was to attempt to exterminate them. Our cruelties are not so extreme. What we do is simply to ignore groups of people whose existence troubles us.

I submit, humbly but confidently, that using an argument to exclude adult people from parenthood which is based solely on the definition of an individual's sexual practice, is untenable and uncivilised. Adult people have in their gift the right to dispose of their own reproductive potential as they themselves think suitable. And the rest of us share, all of us, in the responsibility to care for all those committed to parenting and for the children for whom they care.

References and Notes

1. Hanscombe, G. E., Forster, J. *Rocking the cradle*. London: Peter Owen, 1981 and Sheba Feminist Publishers, 1982.

2. Green, R. Sexual identity of 37 children raised by homosexual or transexual parents. *American Journal of Psychiatry* 1978; 6: 692–697.

3. See project comparing the psychosexual development of lesbians' children with that of single non-lesbians' children, undertaken by Michael Rutter, Susan Golombok and Ann

Spencer, of the Institute of Psychiatry in London. Not all the data is yet published—to my present knowledge—but see reference (1) 85–87.

4. In February of this year the Court of Appeal ruled in favour of a lesbian mother retaining custody of her two daughters. The case made newspaper headlines, not least because such rulings have been so rare.

5. Identity and details withheld.

6. Identities and details withheld.

Is Women's Labor a Commodity?

Elizabeth S. Anderson

Elizabeth S. Anderson argues that commercial surrogacy should not be allowed. The practice of paying women to be surrogate mothers involves a "commodification" of both children and women. It treats women and their children as things to be used, instead of as persons deserving respect. Hence, surrogacy contracts should be unenforceable and those who arrange them should be subject to criminal penalties.

Anderson holds that the introduction of market values and norms into a situation previously based on respect, consideration, and unconditional love has the effect of harming children and degrading and exploiting women. The values of the market contribute to a tendency to view children as property. When this happens, they are no longer valued unconditionally (as is the case with parental love), but are valued only because they possess characteristics with a market value.

Market values require that surrogate mothers repress whatever parental love they may feel for their children. Hence, the feelings of women are manipulated, degraded, and denied legitimacy. Further, women are exploited by having the personal feelings that incline them to become surrogates turned into something that can be marketed as part of a commercial enterprise.

In the past few years the practice of commercial surrogate motherhood has gained notoriety as a method for acquiring children. A commercial surrogate mother is anyone who is paid money to bear a child for other people and terminate her parental rights, so that the others may raise the child as exclusively their own. The growth of commercial surrogacy has raised with new urgency a class of concerns regarding the proper scope of the market. Some critics have objected to commercial surrogacy on the ground that it improperly treats children and women's reproductive capacities as commodities.[1] The prospect of reducing children to consumer durables and women to baby factories surely inspires revulsion. But are there good reasons behind the revulsion? And is this an accurate description of what commercial surrogacy implies? This article offers a theory about what things are properly regarded as commodities which supports the claim that commercial surrogacy constitutes an

From *Philosophy & Public Affairs* 19, no. 1, (Winter 1990), pp. 71–87, 91–92. Copyright © 1990 by Princeton University Press. Reprinted by permission of Princeton University Press.

unconscionable commodification of children and of women's reproductive capacities.

What Is a Commodity?

The modern market can be characterized in terms of the legal and social norms by which it governs the production, exchange, and enjoyment of commodities. To say that something is properly regarded as a commodity is to claim that the norms of the market are appropriate for regulating its production, exchange, and enjoyment. To the extent that moral principles or ethical ideals preclude the application of market norms to a good, we may say that the good is not a (proper) commodity.

Why should we object to the application of a market norm to the production or distribution of a good? One reason may be that to produce or distribute the good in accordance with the norm is to *fail to value it in an appropriate way.* Consider, for example, a standard Kantian argument against slavery, or the commodification of persons. Slaves are treated in accordance with the market norm that owners may use commodities to satisfy their own interests without regard for the interests of the commodities themselves. To treat a person without regard for her interests is to fail to respect her. But slaves are persons who may not be merely used in this fashion, since as rational beings they possess a dignity which commands respect. In Kantian theory, the problem with slavery is that it treats beings worthy of *respect* as if they were worthy merely of *use.* "Respect" and "use" in this context denote what we may call different *modes of valuation....*

These considerations support a general account of the sorts of things which are appropriately regarded as commodities. Commodities are those things which are properly treated in accordance with the norms of the modern market. We can question the application of market norms to the production, distribution, and enjoyment of a good by appealing to ethical ideals which support arguments that the good should be valued in some other way than use. Arguments of the latter sort claim that to allow certain market norms to govern our treatment of a thing expresses a mode of valuation not worthy of it. If the thing is to be valued appropriately, its production, exchange, and enjoyment must be removed from market norms and embedded in a different set of social relationships.

The Case of Commercial Surrogacy

Let us now consider the practice of commercial surrogate motherhood in the light of this theory of commodities. Surrogate motherhood as a commercial enterprise is based upon contracts involving three parties: the intended father, the broker, and the surrogate mother. The intended father agrees to pay a lawyer to find a suitable surrogate mother and make the requisite medical and legal arrangements for the conception and birth of the child, and for the transfer of legal custody to himself.[2] The surrogate mother agrees to become impregnated with the intended father's sperm, to carry the resulting child to term, and to relinquish her parental rights to it, transferring custody to the father in return for a fee and medical expenses. Both she and her husband (if she has one) agree not to form a parent-child bond with her child and to do everything necessary to effect the transfer of the child to the intended father. At current market prices, the lawyer arranging the contract can expect to gross $15,000 from the contract, while the surrogate mother can expect a $10,000 fee.[3]

The practice of commercial surrogacy has been defended on four main grounds. First, given the shortage of children available for adoption and the difficulty of qualifying as adoptive parents, it may represent the only hope for some people to be able to raise a family. Commercial surrogacy should be accepted as an effective means for realizing this highly significant good. Second, two fundamental human rights support commercial surrogacy: the right to procreate and freedom of contract. Fully informed autonomous adults should have the right to make whatever arrangements they wish for the use of their bodies and the reproduction of children, so long as the children themselves are not harmed. Third, the labor of the surrogate mother is said to be a labor of love. Her altruistic acts should be permitted and encouraged.[4] Finally, it is argued that commercial surrogacy is no different in its ethical implications from many already accepted practices which separate genetic, gestational, and social parenting, such as artificial insemination by donor, adoption, wet-nursing, and day care. Consistency demands that society accept this new practice as well.[5]

In opposition to these claims, I shall argue that commercial surrogacy does raise new ethical issues, since it represents an invasion of the market into a new sphere of conduct, that of specifically women's labor—that is, the labor of carrying children to term in pregnancy. When women's labor is treated as a commodity, the women who perform it are degraded. Furthermore, commercial surrogacy degrades children by reducing their status to that of commodities. Let us consider each of the goods of concern in surrogate motherhood—the child, and women's reproductive labor—to see how the commercialization of parenthood affects people's regard for them.

Children as Commodities

The most fundamental calling of parents to their children is to love them. Children are to be loved and cherished by their parents, not to be used or manipulated by them for merely personal advantage. Parental love can be understood as a passionate, unconditional commitment to nurture one's child, providing it with the care, affection, and guidance it needs to develop its capacities to maturity. This understanding of the way parents should value their children informs our interpretation of parental rights over their children. Parents' rights over their children are trusts, which they must always exercise for the sake of the child. This is not to deny that parents have their own aspirations in raising children. But the child's interests beyond subsistence are not definable independently of the flourishing of the family, which is the object of specifically parental aspirations. The proper exercise of parental rights includes those acts which promote their shared life as a family, which realize the shared interests of the parents and the child.

The norms of parental love carry implications for the ways other people should treat the relationship between parents and their children. If children are to be loved by their parents, then others should not attempt to compromise the integrity of parental love or work to suppress the emotions supporting the bond between parents and their children. If the rights to children should be understood as trusts, then if those rights are lost or relinquished, the duty of those in charge of transferring custody to others is to consult the best interests of the child.

Commercial surrogacy substitutes market norms for some of the norms of parental love. Most importantly, it requires us to understand parental rights no longer as trusts but as things more like

property rights—that is, rights of use and disposal over the things owned. For in this practice the natural mother deliberately conceives a child with the intention of giving it up for material advantage. Her renunciation of parental responsibilities is not done for the child's sake, nor for the sake of fulfilling an interest she shares with the child, but typically for her own sake (and possibly, if "altruism" is a motive, for the intended parents' sakes). She and the couple who pay her to give up her parental rights over her child thus treat her rights as a kind of property right. They thereby treat the child itself as a kind of commodity, which may be properly bought and sold.

Commercial surrogacy insinuates the norms of commerce into the parental relationship in other ways. Whereas parental love is not supposed to be conditioned upon the child having particular characteristics, consumer demand is properly responsive to the characteristics of commodities. So the surrogate industry provides opportunities to adoptive couples to specify the height, I.Q., race, and other attributes of the surrogate mother, in the expectation that these traits will be passed on to the child.[6] Since no industry assigns agents to look after the "interests" of its commodities, no one represents the child's interests in the surrogate industry. The surrogate agency promotes the adoptive parents' interests and not the child's interests where matters of custody are concerned. Finally, as the agent of the adoptive parents, the broker has the task of policing the surrogate (natural) mother's relationship to her child, using persuasion, money, and the threat of a lawsuit to weaken and destroy whatever parental love she may develop for her child.[7]

All of these substitutions of market norms for parental norms representing ways of treating children as commodities which are degrading to them. Degradation occurs when something is treated in accordance with a lower mode of valuation than is proper to it. We value things not just "more" or "less," but in qualitatively higher and lower ways. To love or respect someone is to value her in a higher way than one would if one merely used her. Children are properly loved by their parents and respected by others. Since children are valued as mere use-objects by the mother and the surrogate agency when they are sold to others, and by the adoptive parents when they seek to conform the child's genetic makeup to their own wishes, commercial surrogacy degrades children insofar as it treats them as commodities.[8]

One might argue that since the child is most likely to enter a loving home, no harm comes to it from permitting the natural mother to treat it as property. So the purchase and sale of infants is unobjectionable, at least from the point of view of children's interests.[9] But the sale of an infant has an expressive significance which this argument fails to recognize. By engaging in the transfer of children by sale, all of the parties to the surrogate contract express a set of attitudes toward children which undermine the norms of parental love. They all agree in treating the ties between a natural mother and her children as properly loosened by a monetary incentive. Would it be any wonder if a child born of a surrogacy agreement feared resale by parents who have such an attitude? And a child who knew how anxious her parents were that she have the "right" genetic makeup might fear that her parent's love was contingent upon her expression of these characteristics.[10]

The unsold children of surrogate mothers are also harmed by commercial surrogacy. The children of some surrogate mothers have reported their fears that they may be sold like their half-brother or half-sister, and express a sense of loss at being deprived of a sibling.[11] Furthermore, the widespread acceptance of commercial surrogacy would psychologically threaten all children. For it would change the way children are valued by people (parents and surrogate brokers)—from being loved by their parents and respected by others, to being sometimes used as objects of commercial profit-making.[12]

Proponents of commercial surrogacy have denied that the surrogate industry engages in the sale of children. For it is impossible to sell to someone what is already his own, and the child is already the father's own natural offspring. The payment to the surrogate mother is not for her child, but for her services in carrying it to term.[13] The claim that the parties to the surrogate contract treat children as commodities, however, is based on the way they treat the *mother's* rights over her child. It is irrelevant that the natural father also has some rights over the child; what he pays for is exclusive rights to it. He would not pay her for the "service" of carrying the child to term if she refused to relinquish her parental rights to it. That the mother regards only her labor and not her child as requiring compensation is also irrelevant. No one would argue

that the baker does not treat his bread as property just because he sees the income from its sale as compensation for his labor and expenses and not for the bread itself, which he doesn't care to keep.[14]

Defenders of commercial surrogacy have also claimed that it does not differ substantially from other already accepted parental practices. In the institutions of adoption and artificial insemination by donor (AID), it is claimed, we already grant parents the right to dispose of their children.[15] But these practices differ in significant respects from commercial surrogacy. The purpose of adoption is to provide a means for placing children in families when their parents cannot or will not discharge their parental responsibilities. It is not a sphere for the existence of a supposed parental right to dispose of one's children for profit. Even AID does not sanction the sale of fully formed human beings. The semen donor sells only a product of his body, not his child, and does not initiate the act of conception.

Two developments might seem to undermine the claim that commercial surrogacy constitutes a degrading commerce in children. The first is technological: the prospect of transplanting a human embryo into the womb of a genetically unrelated woman. If commercial surrogacy used women only as gestational mothers and not as genetic mothers, and if it was thought that only genetic and not gestational parents could properly claim that a child was "theirs," then the child born of a surrogate mother would not be hers to sell in the first place. The second is a legal development: the establishment of the proposed "consent-intent" definition of parenthood.[16] This would declare the legal parents of a child to be whoever consented to a procedure which leads to its birth, with the intent of assuming parental responsibilities for it. This rule would define away the problem of commerce in children by depriving the surrogate mother of any legal claim to her child at all, even if it was hers both genetically and gestationally.[17]

There are good reasons, however, not to undermine the place of genetic and gestational ties in these ways. Consider first the place of genetic ties. By upholding a system of involuntary (genetic) ties of obligation among people, even when the adults among them prefer to divide their rights and obligations in other ways, we help to secure children's interests in having an assured place in the world, which is more firm than the wills of their parents. Unlike the consent-intent rule, the principle of respecting genetic ties does not make the obligation to care for those whom one has created (intentionally or not) contingent upon an arbitrary desire to do so. It thus provides children with a set of pre-existing social sanctions which give them a more secure place in the world. The genetic principle also places children in a far wider network of associations and obligations than the consent-intent rule sanctions. It supports the roles of grandparents and other relatives in the nurturing of children, and provides children with a possible focus of stability and an additional source of claims to care if their parents cannot sustain a well-functioning household.

In the next section I will defend the claims of gestational ties to children. To deny these claims, as commercial surrogacy does, is to deny the significance of reproductive labor to the mother who undergoes it and thereby to dehumanize and degrade the mother herself. Commercial surrogacy would be a corrupt practice even if it did not involve commerce in children.

Women's Labor as a Commodity

Commercial surrogacy attempts to transform what is specifically women's labor—the work of bringing forth children into the world—into a commodity. It does so by replacing the parental norms which usually govern the practice of gestating children with the economic norms which govern ordinary production processes. The application of commercial norms to women's labor reduces the surrogate mothers from persons worthy of respect and consideration to objects of mere use.

Respect and consideration are two distinct modes of valuation whose norms are violated by the practices of the surrogate industry. To respect a person is to treat her in accordance with principles she rationally accepts—principles consistent with the protection of her autonomy and her rational interests. To treat a person with consideration is to respond with sensitivity to her and to her emotional relations with others, refraining from manipulating or denigrating these for one's own purposes. . . .

The application of economic norms to the sphere of women's labor violates women's claims to respect and consideration in three ways. First, by requiring the surrogate mother to repress whatever parental love she feels for the child, these norms convert women's labor into a form of alienated la-

bor. Second, by manipulating and denying legitimacy to the surrogate mother's evolving perspective on her own pregnancy, the norms of the market degrade her. Third, by taking advantage of the surrogate mother's noncommercial motivations without offering anything but what the norms of commerce demand in return, these norms leave her open to exploitation. The fact that these problems arise in the attempt to commercialize the labor of bearing children shows that women's labor is not properly regarded as a commodity.

The key to understanding these problems is the normal role of the emotions in noncommercialized pregnancies. Pregnancy is not simply a biological process but also a social practice. Many social expectations and considerations surround women's gestational labor, marking it off as an occasion for the parents to prepare themselves to welcome a new life into their family. For example, obstetricians use ultrasound not simply for diagnostic purposes but also to encourage maternal bonding with the fetus.[18] We can all recognize that it is good, although by no means inevitable, for loving bonds to be established between the mother and her child during this period.

In contrast with these practices, the surrogate industry follows the putting-out system of manufacturing. It provides some of the raw materials of production (the father's sperm) to the surrogate mother, who then engages in production of the child. Although her labor is subject to periodic supervision by her doctors and by the surrogate agency, the agency does not have physical control over the product of her labor as firms using the factory system do. Hence, as in all putting-out systems, the surrogate industry faces the problem of extracting the final product from the mother. This problem is exacerbated by the fact that the social norms surrounding pregnancy are designed to encourage parental love for the child. The surrogate industry addresses this problem by requiring the mother to engage in a form of emotional labor.[19] In the surrogate contract, she agrees not to form or to attempt to form a parent-child relationship with her offspring.[20] Her labor is alienated, because she must divert it from the end which the social practices of pregnancy rightly promote—an emotional bond with her child. The surrogate contract thus replaces a norm of parenthood, that during pregnancy one create a loving attachment to one's child, with a norm of commercial production, that the producer shall not form any special emotional ties to her product. . . .

Commercial surrogacy is also a degrading practice. The surrogate mother, like all persons, has an independent evaluative perspective on her activities and relationships. The realization of her dignity demands that the other parties to the contract acknowledge rather than evade the claims which her independent perspective makes upon them. But the surrogate industry has an interest in suppressing, manipulating, and trivializing her perspective, for there is an ever-present danger that she will see her involvement in her pregnancy from the perspective of a parent rather than from the perspective of a contract laborer.

How does this suppression and trivialization take place? The commercial promoters of surrogacy commonly describe the surrogate mothers as inanimate objects: mere "hatcheries," "plumbing," or "rented property"—things without emotions which could make claims on others.[21] They also refuse to acknowledge any responsibility for the consequences of the mother's emotional labor. Should she suffer psychologically from being forced to give up her child, the father is not liable to pay for therapy after her pregnancy, although he is liable for all other medical expenses following her pregnancy.[22]

The treatment and interpretation of surrogate mothers' grief raises the deepest problems of degradation. Most surrogate mothers experience grief upon giving up their children—in 10 percent of cases, seriously enough to require therapy.[23] Their grief is not compensated by the $10,000 fee they receive. Grief is not an intelligible response to a successful deal, but rather reflects the subject's judgment that she has suffered a grave and personal loss. Since not all cases of grief resolve themselves into cases of regret, it may be that some surrogate mothers do not regard their grief, in retrospect, as reflecting an authentic judgment on their part. But in the circumstances of emotional manipulation which pervade the surrogate industry, it is difficult to determine which interpretation of her grief more truly reflects the perspective of the surrogate mother. By insinuating a trivializing interpretation of her emotional responses to the prospect of losing her child, the surrogate agency may be able to manipulate her into accepting her fate without too much fuss, and may even succeed in substituting its interpretation of her emotions for

her own. Since she has already signed a contract to perform emotional labor—to express or repress emotions which are dictated by the interests of the surrogate industry—this might not be a difficult task.[24] A considerate treatment of the mothers' grief, on the other hand, would take the evaluative basis of their grief seriously.

Some defenders of commercial surrogacy demand that the provision for terminating the surrogate mother's parental rights in her child be legally enforceable, so that peace of mind for the adoptive parents can be secured.[25] But the surrogate industry makes no corresponding provision for securing the peace of mind of the surrogate. She is expected to assume the risk of a transformation of her ethical and emotional perspective on herself and her child with the same impersonal detachment with which a futures trader assumes the risk of a fluctuation in the price of pork bellies. By applying the market norms of enforcing contracts to the surrogate mother's case, commercial surrogacy treats a moral transformation as if it were merely an economic change.[26]

The manipulation of the surrogate mother's emotions which is inherent in the surrogate parenting contract also leaves women open to grave forms of exploitation. A kind of exploitation occurs when one party to a transaction is oriented toward the exchange of "gift" values, while the other party operates in accordance with the norms of the market exchange of commodities. Gift values, which include love, gratitude, and appreciation of others, cannot be bought or obtained through piecemeal calculations of individual advantage. Their exchange requires a repudiation of a self-interested attitude, a willingness to give gifts to others without demanding some specific equivalent good in return each time one gives. The surrogate mother often operates according to the norms of gift relationships. The surrogate agency, on the other hand, follows market norms. Its job is to get the best deal for its clients and itself, while leaving the surrogate mother to look after her own interests as best as she can. The situation puts the surrogate agencies in a position to manipulate the surrogate mothers' emotions to gain favorable terms for themselves. For example, agencies screen prospective surrogate mothers for submissiveness, and emphasize to them the importance of the motives of generosity and love. When applicants question some of the terms of the contract, the broker sometimes intimidates them by questioning their character and morality: if they were really generous and loving they would not be so solicitous about their own interests.[27] . . .

Many surrogate mothers see pregnancy as a way to feel "adequate," "appreciated," or "special." In other words, these women feel inadequate, unappreciated, or unadmired when they are not pregnant.[28] Lacking the power to achieve some worthwhile status in their own right, they must subordinate themselves to others' definitions of their proper place (as baby factories) in order to get from them the appreciation they need to attain a sense of self-worth. But the sense of self-worth one can attain under such circumstances is precarious and ultimately self-defeating. For example, those who seek gratitude on the part of the adoptive parents and some opportunity to share the joys of seeing their children grow discover all too often that the adoptive parents want nothing to do with them.[29] For while the surrogate mother sees in the arrangement some basis for establishing the personal ties she needs to sustain her emotionally, the adoptive couple sees it as an impersonal commercial contract, one of whose main advantages to them is that all ties between them and the surrogate are ended once the terms of the contract are fulfilled.[30] To them, her presence is a threat to marital unity and a competing object for the child's affections.

These considerations should lead us to question the model of altruism which is held up to women by the surrogacy industry. It is a strange form of altruism which demands such radical self-effacement, alienation from those whom one benefits, and the subordination of one's body, health, and emotional life to the independently defined interests of others.[31]

The primary distortions which arise from treating women's labor as a commodity—the surrogate mother's alienation from loved ones, her degradation, and her exploitation—stem from a common source. This is the failure to acknowledge and treat appropriately the surrogate mother's emotional engagement with her labor. Her labor is alienated, because she must suppress her emotional ties with her own child, and may be manipulated into reinterpreting these ties in a trivializing way. She is degraded, because her independent ethical perspective is denied, or demoted to the status of a cash sum. She is exploited, because her emotional needs and vulnerabilities are not treated as characteristics which call for consideration, but as factors which may be manipulated to encourage her to make a grave self-sacrifice to the broker's and adoptive couple's advantage. These considerations provide strong grounds for sustaining the claims of women's labor to its "product," the child. The attempt to redefine parenthood so as to strip women of parental claims to the children they bear does violence to their emotional engagement with the project of bringing children into the world.

Commercial Surrogacy, Freedom, and the Law

In the light of these ethical objections to commercial surrogacy, what position should the law take on the practice? At the very least, surrogate contracts should not be enforceable. Surrogate mothers should not be forced to relinquish their children if they have formed emotional bonds with them. Any other treatment of women's ties to the children they bear is degrading.

But I think these arguments support the stronger conclusion that commercial surrogate contracts should be illegal, and that surrogate agencies who arrange such contracts should be subject to criminal penalties. Commercial surrogacy constitutes a degrading and harmful traffic in children, violates the dignity of women, and subjects both children and women to a serious risk of exploitation. . . .

If commercial surrogate contracts were prohibited, this would be no cause for infertile couples to lose hope for raising a family. The option of adoption is still available, and every attempt should be made to open up opportunities for adoption to couples who do not meet standard requirements—for example, because of age. While there is a shortage of healthy white infants available for adoption, there is no shortage of children of other races, mixed-race children, and older and handicapped children who desperately need to be adopted. Leaders of the surrogate industry have proclaimed that commercial surrogacy may replace adoption as the method of choice for infertile couples who wish to raise families. But we should be wary of the racist and eugenic motivations which make some people rally to the surrogate industry at the expense of children who already exist and need homes.

The case of commercial surrogacy raises deep questions about the proper scope of the market in modern industrial societies. I have argued that there are principled grounds for rejecting the substitution of market norms for parental norms to govern the ways women bring children into the world. Such substitutions express ways of valuing mothers and children which reflect an inferior conception of human flourishing. When market norms are applied to the ways we allocate and understand parental rights and responsibilities, children are reduced from subjects of love to objects of use. When market norms are applied to the ways we treat and understand women's reproductive labor, women are reduced from subjects of respect and consideration to objects of use. If we are to retain the capacity to value children and women in ways consistent with a rich conception of human flourishing, we must resist the encroachment of the market upon the sphere of reproductive labor. Women's labor is *not* a commodity.

Notes

The author thanks David Anderson, Steven Darwall, Ezekiel Emanuel, Daniel Hausman, Don Herzog, Robert Nozick, Richard Pildes, John Rawls, Michael Sandel, Thomas Scanlon, and Howard Wial for helpful comments and criticisms.

1. See, for example, Gena Corea, *The Mother Machine* (New York: Harper and Row, 1985), pp. 216, 219; Angela Holder, "Surrogate Motherhood: Babies for Fun and Profit," *Case and Comment* 90 (1985): 3–11; and Margaret Jane Radin, "Market Inalienability," *Harvard Law Review* 100 (June 1987): 1849–1937.

2. State laws against selling babies prevent the intended father's wife (if he has one) from being a party to the contract.

3. See Katie Marie Brophy, "A Surrogate Mother Contract to Bear a Child," *Journal of Family Law* 20 (1981–82): 263–91, and Noel Keane, "The Surrogate Parenting Contract," *Adelphia Law Journal* 2 (1983): 45–53, for examples and explanations of surrogate parenting contracts.

4. Mary Warnock, *A Question of Life* (Oxford: Blackwell, 1985), p. 45. This book reprints the Warnock Report on Human Fertilization and Embryology, which was commissioned by the British government for the purpose of recommending legislation concerning surrogacy and other issues. Although the Warnock Report mentions the promotion of altruism as one defense of surrogacy, it strongly condemns the practice overall.

5. John Robertson, "Surrogate Mothers: Not So Novel after All," *Hastings Center Report*. October 1983, pp. 28–34; John Harris, *The Value of Life* (Boston: Routledge and Kegan Paul, 1985).

6. See "No Other Hope for Having a Child," *Time,* 19 January 1987, pp. 50–51. Radin argues that women's traits are also commodified in this practice. See "Market Inalienability," pp. 1932–35.

7. Here I discuss the surrogate industry as it actually exists today. I will consider possible modifications of commercial surrogacy in the final section below.

8. Robert Nozick has objected that my claims about parental love appear to be culture-bound. Do not parents in the Third World, who rely on children to provide for the family subsistence, regard their children as economic goods? In promoting the livelihood of their families, however, such children need not be treated in accordance with market norms—that is, as commodities. In particular, such children usually remain a part of their families and hence can still be loved by their parents. But insofar as children are treated according to the norms of modern capitalists markets, this treatment is deplorable wherever it takes place.

9. See Elizabeth Landes and Richard Posner, "The Economics of the Baby Shortage," *Journal of Legal Studies* 7 (1978): 323–48, and Richard Posner, "The Regulation of the Market in Adoptions," *Boston University Law Review* 67 (1987): 59–72.

10. Of course, where children are concerned, it is irrelevant whether these fears are reasonable. One of the greatest fears of children is separation from their parents. Adopted children are already known to suffer from separation anxiety more acutely than children who remain with their natural mothers, for they feel that their original mothers did not love them. In adoption, the fact that the child would be even worse off if the mother did not give up justifies her severing of ties and can help to rationalize this event to the child. But in the case of commercial surrogacy, the severing of ties is done not for the child's sake, but for the parents' sakes. In the adoption case there are explanations for the mother's action which may quell the child's doubts about being loved which are unavailable in the case of surrogacy.

11. Kay Longcope, "Surrogacy: Two Professionals on Each Side of Issue Give Their Arguments for Prohibition and Regulation," *Boston Globe*, 23 March 1987, pp. 18–19; and Iver Peterson, "Baby M Case: Surrogate Mothers Vent Feelings," *New York Times*, 2 March 1987, pp. B1, B4.

12. Herbert Krimmel, "The Case against Surrogate Parenting," *Hastings Center Report*, October 1983, pp. 35–37.

13. Judge Sorkow made this argument in ruling on the famous case of Baby M. See *In Re Baby M*, 217 N.J. Super 313. Reprinted in *Family Law Reporter* 13 (1987): 2001–30. Chief Justice Wilentz of the New Jersey Supreme Court overruled Sorkow's judgment. See *In the Matter of Baby M*, 109 N.J. 396, 537 A.2d 1227 (1988).

14. Sallyann Payton has observed that the law does not permit the sale of parental rights, only their relinquishment or forced termination by the state, and these acts are subject to court review for the sake of the child's best interests. But this legal technicality does not change the moral implications of the analogy with baby-selling. The mother is still paid to do what she can to relinquish her parental rights and to transfer custody of the child to the father. Whether or not the courts occasionally prevent this from happening, the actions of the parties express a commercial orientation to children which is degrading and harmful to them. The New Jersey Supreme Court ruled that surrogacy contracts are void precisely because they assign custody without regard to the child's best interests. See *In the Matter of Baby M*, p. 1246.

15. Robertson, "Surrogate Mothers: Not So Novel After All," p. 32; Harris, *The Value of Life*, pp. 144–45.

16. See Philip Parker, "Surrogate Motherhood: The Interaction of Litigation, Legislation and Psychiatry," *International Journal of Law and Psychiatry* 5 (1982): 341–54.

17. The consent-intent rule would not, however, change the fact that commercial surrogacy replaces parental norms with market norms. For the rule itself embodies the market norm which acknowledges only voluntary, contractual relations among people as having moral force. Whereas familial love invites children into a network of unwilled relationships broader than those they have with their parents, the willed contract creates an exclusive relationship between the parents and the child only.

18. I am indebted to Dr. Ezekiel Emanuel for this point.

19. One engages in emotional labor when one is paid to express or repress certain emotions. On the concept of emotional labor and its consequences for workers, see Arlie Hochschild, *The Managed Heart* (Berkeley and Los Angeles: University of California Press, 1983).

20. Noel Keane and Dennis Breo, *The Surrogate Mother* (New York: Everest House, 1981), p. 291; Brophy, "A Surrogate Mother Contract," p. 267. The surrogate's husband is also required to agree to this clause of the contract.

21. Corea, *The Mother Machine*, p. 222.

22. Keane and Breo, *The Surrogate Mother*, p. 292.

23. Kay Longcope, "Standing Up for Mary Beth," *Boston Globe*, 5 March 1987, p. 83; Daniel Goleman, "Motivations of Surrogate Mothers," *New York Times*, 20 January 1987, p. C1; Robertson, "Surrogate Mothers: No So Novel after All," pp. 30, 34 n. 8. Neither the surrogate mothers themselves nor psychiatrists have been able to predict which women will experience such grief.

24. See Hochschild, *The Managed Heart*, for an important empirical study of the dynamics of commercialized emotional labor.

25. Keane and Breo, *The Surrogate Mother*, pp. 236–37.

26. For one account of how a surrogate mother who came to regret her decision viewed her own moral transformation, see Elizabeth Kane: *Birth Mother: The Story of America's First Legal Surrogate Mother* (San Diego: Harcourt Brace Jovanovich, 1988). I argue below that the implications of commodifying women's labor are not significantly changed even if the contract is unenforceable.

27. Susan Ince, "Inside the Surrogate Industry," in *Test-Tube Women*, ed. Rita Ardith, Ranate Duelli Klein, and Shelley Minden (Boston: Pandora Press, 1984), p. 110.

28. The surrogate broker Noel Keane is remarkably open about reporting the desperate emotional insecurities which shape the lives of so many surrogate mothers, while displaying little sensitivity to the implications of his taking advantage of these motivations to make his business a financial success. See especially Keane and Breo, *The Surrogate Mother*, pp. 247ff.

29. See, for example, the story of the surrogate mother Nancy Barrass in Anne Fleming, "Our Fascination with Baby M," *New York Times Magazine*, 29 March 1987, p. 38.

30. For evidence of these disparate perspectives, see Peterson, "Baby M Case: Surrogate Mothers Vent Feelings," p. B4.

31. The surrogate mother is required to obey all doctor's orders made in the interests of the child's health (See Brophy, "A Surrogate Mother Contract"; Keane, "The Surrogate Parenting Contract"; and Ince, "Inside the Surrogate Industry.") These orders could include forcing her to give up her job, travel plans, and recreational activities. The doctor could confine her to bed, and order her to submit to surgery and take drugs. One can hardly exercise an autonomous choice over one's health if one could be held in breach of contract and liable for $35,000 damages for making a decision contrary to the wishes of one's doctor.

Entitled to the Embryo?

Susan Jacoby

Susan Jacoby points out that cloning embryos to assist couples with reproduction opens up the possibility that unused embryos might be sold. Jacoby argues that infertility is merely a misfortune and that cloning for the purpose of treating it is not morally justified. Indeed, Jacoby finds no moral justification for cloning and sees selling embryos as a social threat to be averted. As she concludes, "No one has the right to jeopardize the precious uniqueness of all members of the human race in order to assuage individual heartbreak and gratify individual desires."

I once interviewed a woman who was enraged because her health insurance company, after paying for two unsuccessful attempts at in vitro fertilization, had refused to reimburse her for further infertility treatments. "They're depriving me of my right to become a mother," she said, "and I'm going to sue them."

But where is it written that our society owes everyone the "right" to become a parent, regardless of the financial or ethical cost? The woman's comment offers yet another example of the pervasive, bloated sense of entitlement that forms a crucial, largely unexamined backdrop to the debate over the ethics of cloning human embryos.

The ethical controversy erupted last week after scientists at George Washington University Medical Center announced that they had developed a cloning procedure that would help infertile couples conceive artificially by providing them with identical extra embryos. But this "breakthrough" also creates a real possibility that unused embryos could be sold to other couples.

The debate pits the so-called right of people to control their own embryos—and to have children in any way they desire—against society's need to protect itself from those who would cheerfully clone and sell endless multiples of human beings as long as there was a profit to be made.

Almost no one has questioned the notion of parenthood as a right and infertility as a violation of that right—and a disaster that must be fought with all the high-tech tools of modern medicine. To say that infertility is not a tragedy but a disappointment, albeit a grievous one, is to commit sacrilege.

If infertility is indeed a tragedy, it would be churlish to prohibit cloning. But when infertility is viewed simply as one misfortune on a scale of sorrows—less horrible, say, than mind-destroying diseases or mass starvation—the ethical balance looks quite different.

Because I consider infertility a sorrow rather than a tragedy, I cannot conceive of any ethical justification for cloning humans. I am far more concerned about the potential social consequences of merchants' peddling "desirable" embryos (no doubt white and proved Harvard material) than about the personal disappointment experienced by couples who cannot easily produce children.

To take this position is to risk accusations of being a Luddite. Any scientific advance can, of course, be misused, but the real question is whether the possible benefit outweighs the possible risk. Gene therapy also raises grave ethical questions, but the risks are worth taking because such experiments hold out the possibility of correcting lethal genetic defects. Embryo-cloning, by contrast, will surely be used not only to remedy infertility but to enable affluent Americans to get what they want when they want it.

I am 48 and deeply regret having no children. Yet I am perfectly aware that the career-oriented decisions made in my 20's and early 30's are largely responsible for my childless state. Cloning would certainly get someone like me off the hook. If such a procedure had been available back in the 70's, my then-husband and I could have stored away a number of identical future babies. (Cloning would be much more efficient than storing non-identical embryos, because conception would have to be accomplished only once.)

Now that I'm older and ready to be a parent, I could take my bundles of joy off the freezer shelf. Because I no longer have a uterus, I'd have to rent another woman for the pregnancy. And the baby wouldn't have a father, because my ex-husband died some years after our divorce. But why worry? I'd have exactly what I want exactly when it suited me.

An unlikely scenario? In an era of rights run wild, anything is not only possible but likely. Twenty years ago, who would have believed that we would witness court battles between surrogate mothers and well-off couples determined to do anything to reproduce at least one partner's precious genes?

It is past time for our society to call a halt to the "me first" expansion of rights. No one has the right to jeopardize the precious uniqueness of all members of the human race in order to assuage individual heartbreak and gratify individual desires.

Decision Scenario 1 ••

"I'm sorry we can't help you," Patricia Spring said. "But what you want is simply against our policy."

Charles Blendon and Carla Neuman didn't try to hide their disappointment. The San Diego Reproductive Clinic had been their last hope. They very badly wanted to have a child, but Carla's Fallopian tubes had been surgically removed as part of a successful effort to treat precancerous growths.

"In fact," Patricia Spring said, "you don't meet at least two of our criteria."

"We can afford to pay," Charles Blendon said.

"That's not it. First of all, Carla is thirty-eight, and we set thirty-five as the upper limit. And second, you two are not married, and we require that the donor and the patient be husband and wife."

"Who makes those rules?" Carla Neuman asked. "It seems to me that if we want to have a child, then that's our business and nobody else's."

"The Clinic makes the rules," Patricia Spring said. "You see, there is some greater risk of birth defects in women who are over the age of thirty-five. There are sound medical reasons for our criteria."

"But what if we're willing to take the risk?" Charles Blendon asked.

"You can't take a risk that is likely to affect an unborn child."

"But I'm willing to have tests," Carla Neuman said. "And neither of us is against abortion. If there is something wrong with the fetus, then I'll have an abortion."

"And just what sort of medical basis is there for the marriage requirement?" Charles Blendon asked. "It seems to me that the Clinic is just imposing its own moral standards on Carla and me."

"Look," Patricia Spring said, "I know you're both upset and disappointed. I sympathize with you. But the Clinic operates in a community, and our criteria reflect both good medical judgment and the standards of the community."

"Does the Clinic receive any public money?" Carla Neuman asked.

"We have some research grants."

"Then it seems to me that we have grounds for a suit," Carla said. "The Clinic is discriminating against us because we aren't married, and it's denying us the right to take a risk we're willing to take."

"I can only tell you what our criteria are," Patricia Spring said. "I can't arrange for you to be accepted as a patient here, and there's nothing you or I can do about it."

"That remains to be seen," Charles Blendon said.

1. Is the Clinic justified in setting an age limit on the women it will accept as patients? If so, why?

2. How might a rule utilitarian justify the Clinic's requirement that a couple be married in order for the woman to be accepted as a patient?

3. Does the fact that the Clinic receives public funds provide any reason to believe that its services should be open to everyone?

4. On what grounds might the Vatican "Instruction" and Anderson object to the very existence of such a clinic? Is such a clinic consistent with Steinbock's views?

Decision Scenario 2 ••

In January of 1985, the British High Court took custody of a five-day-old girl, the first child known to be born in Britain to a woman paid to be a surrogate mother.

An American couple, known only as "Mr. and Mrs. A," were reported to have paid about $7,500 to a twenty-eight-year-old woman who allowed herself to be artificially inseminated with sperm from Mr. A. The woman, Kim Cotton, was prevented from turning the child over to Mr. and Mrs. A by a court order issued because of the uncertainty over the legal status of a surrogate mother.

The court permitted "interested parties, including the natural father" to apply for custody of the child. Mr. A applied, and judge Sir John Latey ruled that the couple could take the baby girl out of the country, because they could offer her the chance of "a very good upbringing."

1. Are there any moral reasons that might have made the court hesitate before turning over the child to her biological father? For example, could it be persuasively argued that Kim Cotton was, in effect, selling her baby to Mr. and Mrs. A?

2. Kim Cotton agreed to be a surrogate mother for the sake of the money. Is surrogate pregnancy a practice that tends to exploit the poor? Or is it a legitimate way to earn money by providing a needed service? How might Steinbock respond to these questions?

3. Is serving as a surrogate mother essentially the same as prostitution? If it is not, then what are the relevant differences?

4. On what grounds do the Vatican "Instruction" and Anderson oppose the practice of surrogate pregnancy? How persuasive are the arguments?

Decision Scenario 3 ••

Dr. Charles Davis quickly scanned the data sheet on his desk, then looked at the woman seated across from him. Her name was Nancy Callahan. She was twenty-five years old and worked as a print conservator at an art museum.

"I see that you aren't married," Dr. Davis said.

"That's right," Nancy Callahan said. "That's basically the reason I'm here." When Dr. Davis looked puzzled, she added, "I still want to have a child."

Dr. Davis nodded and thought for a moment. Nancy Callahan was the first unmarried person to come to the Bayside Fertility Clinic to request AID. As the legal owner and operator of the Clinic, as well as the Chief of Medical Services, Dr. Davis was the one ultimately responsible for the Clinic's policies.

"I hope you understand that I have to ask you some personal questions," Dr. Davis said. "Of course."

"You're not engaged or planning to get married?"

"No. At least not at the moment. I don't want to rule out the possibility that I will want to get married someday."

"Don't you know anybody you would want to have a child with in the ordinary sexual way?"

"I might be able to find someone," Nancy Callahan said. "But you see, I don't want to get involved with anybody right now. I'm ready to be a mother, but I'm not ready to get into the kind of situation that having a child in what you call 'the ordinary sexual way' would require."

"I see."

"I hope you do. This is something I really want to do. I think I'll be a good mother. I want a child very much, and I can afford to support one."

"It's just somewhat unusual," Dr. Davis said.

"But it's not illegal, is it?"

"No," Dr. Davis said. "It's not illegal."

"So what's the problem? I'm healthy. I'm financially sound and mentally stable, and I'm both able and eager to accept the responsibility of being a mother."

"It's just that at the moment the policy of our Clinic requires that patients be married and that both husbands and wives agree to the insemination procedure."

"But there's nothing magical about a policy," Nancy Callahan said. "It can be changed for good reasons, can't it?"

"Perhaps so," said Dr. Davis.

1. *Suppose that Ms. Callahan is a lesbian. Should this be a relevant consideration in deciding whether she should receive AID? Why, according to Hanscombe, should it not be?*

2. *What utilitarian argument can be advanced in favor of the Clinic's policy?*

3. *Does the Vatican's natural law view support such a policy?*

4. *How might it be argued that respect for Ms. Callahan's autonomy makes it wrong to deny her the service she requests, while providing it to a married woman? Is Steinbock's position consistent with the Clinic's policy?*

Decision Scenario 4 ••

"My husband and I have talked over the matter in great detail," Marge Gower said. "We don't care about the sex of the child, but we know exactly the kinds of features we want to try for."

"Mrs. Gower," Dr. Louise Singh said. "You've got to understand that we're not running a mail-order-catalogue business for babies."

"I'm not trying to order a *baby*. I just want to tell you what I'm looking for in a sperm donor. I want somebody who is at least six feet tall, muscular—not fat—has light-colored hair and is very

good looking. Also, I want some proof that he has a good sense of humor and is intelligent. He has to have at least a college degree. I'll leave all the rest to you. I mean, things about health."

"Thank you," said Dr. Singh. "But I really don't think I can go along with that."

"I don't see why not. If I were going to have a child in the usual way and I were deliberately going to get pregnant, I would certainly choose somebody like I described."

"But you aren't doing it in the usual way.

You're going to be using donor semen."

"But who is going to choose the donor? You are, aren't you?"

"I plan to. I'll select somebody from our list of applicants who resembles you and your husband in a general way."

"I don't see why you should have that kind of power," Mrs. Gower said. "It's going to be my baby. I think I have the right to say what the father should be like."

"That's against Reproductive Medicine's policy."

"Well, that's too bad. Just tell me who to talk to to get the policy changed. I'm going to have a baby like my husband and I want. As long as I have to have artificial insemination, I want to get the most out of it."

1. *On what grounds might a utilitarian support the claim that Dr. Singh ought to be wholly responsible for choosing the sperm donor?*

2. *On what grounds might a utilitarian support the claim that Mrs. Gower and her husband ought to be able to select the features that a sperm donor should have?*

3. *Would it be better for the potential recipient of artificial insemination if the sperm donor were known personally to her and her husband? What are some of the problems caused by anonymity?*

4. *Might the choice of a sperm donor by the physician be regarded as an unacceptable form of paternalism? (See the discussion of paternalism in Chapter 5.)*

5. *Consider the issue involved here from the standpoint of the potential sperm donor. Should a sperm donor have some control over the use of his sperm in artificial insemination? Mrs. Gower argues that since the child will be hers, she should be the one who specifies what traits the donor should have. Since, biologically speaking, the child will equally be the offspring of the sperm donor, should he be able to specify the traits the sperm recipient should have?*

Decision Scenario 5 ••

"I'm going to sell my sperm for the simple reason that I need the money," John Lolton said. "It's no big deal."

"I think it is," Mary Cooper said. "You seem to think it's like selling your blood, but it isn't. If somebody is transfused with your blood, that's an end to things. But if a woman is inseminated with your sperm, a child may result."

"I don't have any responsibilities for what people do with my sperm," Lolton replied. "It's just a product."

"Not so," Cooper said. "It's a product all right, but if it's used in artificial insemination, that means that you're the father of a child. And if you're the father of a child, that means you have to be willing to accept responsibility for that child."

"That is absolute nonsense," Lolton said.

1. *If sperm is just a product, is Lolton correct in saying that he has no responsibilities for its use?*

2. *State as explicitly as possible Cooper's argument that a sperm donor is responsible for any child resulting from AI using his donated sperm.*

3. *We expect biological parents to take responsibility for their offspring. Can a departure from this standard be justified when the child is born as a result of donated sperm or egg?*

4. *According to the Vatican "Instruction," are there instances in which AI is morally licit? What is the moral status of a child conceived by AI?*

5. *Ova as well as sperm may be donated. Although women get paid more, on what grounds might one argue that they are exploited while men are not?*

Decision Scenario 6 ••

"I'm curious," Lois Ramer said. "What happens to the eggs you take from me that get fertilized but not implanted?"

"We destroy them," Dr. Martha Herman said.

"Oh," Lois Ramer said, sounding surprised. "I guess I never really thought about it before, but maybe I shouldn't be doing this."

"Why is that?"

"Because I believe life begins at conception. And I guess that means I think that the fertilized eggs that you destroy are human beings with the same rights I have."

"If you genuinely believe that," Dr. Herman said, "then you really shouldn't be having this procedure."

1. *What position does the Vatican "Instruction" take on the question of the status of an egg that is fertilized for the purpose of implantation, but then not used?*

2. *If every egg fertilized was implanted, would this make the procedure of embryo transfer morally legitimate according to the Vatican "Instruction"?*

3. *Does the Vatican's position on these matters rely on what Singer calls the "standard argument"? State Singer's version of the argument, and explain why he considers it unpersuasive.*

4. *Why does Singer believe the destruction of early embryos is morally legitimate? When does he consider it morally wrong to destroy an embryo?*

Decision Scenario 7 ··

"I'm going to have to be blunt about it," Dr. Carl McKensie said. "You are fifty-five, and that's far too old to have a child."

"You're not trying to tell me it's impossible, are you?" Kisha Clare asked. "I've read that you can used donated eggs and donated sperm to fertilize them outside the body, then implant them and have a normal pregnancy. I'm sure it's expensive, but Tom and I have got enough money, and I want to have a baby."

"Oh, it's possible," McKensie admitted. "But it's a bad idea, because you'll be too old to take care of a child properly. When he starts first grade, you'll be sixty-two, and when he graduates from high school, you'll be seventy-four—if you're still alive." McKensie shook his head. "You should have thought of having a child earlier."

"I had a career to work on and a lot of personal problems." Clare frowned, remembering the long hours in the office and about how relieved she was when her husband finally left her. "I can be a better mother now than I could have been when I was thirty or even forty. I'm financially secure, I'm happy with myself, and I really want a child." She shook her head. "Statistically, I'm going to live for about another twenty-five years, and that's enough to raise a child."

"But is it fair to a child to be raised by an old person?"

"Grandparents raise children all the time." Clare glared at McKensie. "And men have children whenever they want to, no matter how old they are. They don't have to get permission from some doctor."

"But an older man can have children only if he has some younger woman as a partner." McKensie glared back at Clare. "That way the child has one younger parent."

"I think you're discriminating against me," Clare said in a flat voice.

"I am." McKensie nodded his head. "But it's justifiable. There are compelling reasons why an older, postmenopausal woman, even if she has the money, should not be allowed to become a mother, just because she wants to. It's unfair to society, to younger women with fertility problems, and to the child."

1. *Should the interest of the child be taken into account in deciding whether to prohibit pregnancy by postmenopausal women? If so, does this mean we should take into account the interest of the child when older men are involved? What about when alcoholics or the unemployed are involved?*

2. *Restate Dr. McKensie's argument in an explicit form. Explain how one might support the claim that it would be unfair to society, younger women, and the child to permit older women to become mothers.*

Decision Scenario 8 ···

"I want to make this a straightforward business proposition." Sam Witt looked across the table at

Susan Becker. "Dorla and I think that Carolyn is a fine little girl. She's healthy and strong, she's pretty, and smart as a whip."

"Thank you for saying all those nice things about my daughter." Becker frowned in puzzlement. "But what does Carolyn have to do with a business proposition?"

"This is a delicate matter." Witt glanced down at his coffee cup, then looked up again. "I don't want to get too personal, but I know that you and Joe had some problems having a kid."

"That's no secret." Becker shook her head. "I've got scarred tubes, so we had to use in vitro fertilization. The embryo was cloned into six copies so if the first try didn't work, we could do it again." She smiled. "But the first try did work."

"So you've still got five embryos on ice." Witt leaned toward her. "That's what I was talking about. Dorla and I want to buy one of them, and we're prepared to pay you and Joe fifteen thousand dollars for it."

"Fifteen thousand dollars." Becker sat up straight, her eyes opened wide. "But why? Why not have your own child?"

"We could, but like I said, Dorla and I really like everything we see in Carolyn. We're not so sure how things would turn out with our own kid, given our genetic backgrounds. There's a lot of depression on my side, and the women in Dorla's family have a high incidence of breast cancer." Witt shrugged. "Let's just say we want a daughter, but we also want some insurance to go along with her."

"She would be just like Carolyn," Becker said in a distracted voice. "But we could sure use the money."

1. If it is morally acceptable to create, and freeze human embryos, is there any reason why it would be morally objectionable to sell them?

2. Might Anderson's objection to surrogacy as involving the "commodification" of children apply to this kind of case as well?

3. On what grounds does Jacoby claim that it would be legitimate to restrict the sale of embryos? Are the reasons offered persuasive?

4. What social difficulties might arise for a child in this particular case? Would the difficulties be so severe as to make the sale of embryos in such cases morally wrong?

PART IV

RESOURCES

CHAPTER 9

ACQUIRING AND ALLOCATING SCARCE MEDICAL RESOURCES

SOCIAL CONTEXT: DISTRIBUTING TRANSPLANT ORGANS

Organ transplantation is perhaps the most dramatic example of how the high technology of contemporary medicine can save the lives of thousands of people who only a decade earlier would have died untimely deaths.

However, behind the wonder and drama of transplant surgery lies the troubling fact that allocation decisions must be made. Daily, physicians, surgeons, and committees are put in the position of making judgments that will offer an opportunity for some, while destroying the last vestige of hope for others.

Replacing damaged, diseased, or defective organs by surgically transplanting donor organs has become increasingly common during the last fifteen years. Although transplanting kidneys began as early as the 1950s, the list of organs now transplanted with a significant degree of success has been expanded to include corneas, bone marrow, bone and skin grafts, livers, lungs, pancreases, intestines, and hearts.

Worldwide, over 100,000 kidney transplants have been performed, and about 93% of the organs are still functioning one year later. (Some recipients are still alive after thirty years or more.) Pancreas transplants are almost as successful, with an 89% survival rate. Thomas Starzl and his team successfully transplanted the first liver in 1967, and now some 6,000 transplants have been done. The success rate is about 75%. Also in 1967, Christian Barnard transplanted a human heart, and since then, almost 8,000 more transplants have been performed. More than 82% of the procedures are considered successful. Lung transplants, though still a relatively new procedure, have a 54% success rate. New techniques of management and the development of drugs to suppress part of the immune response promise to make possible even more transplants in the future. (See the Introduction for more details.)

Costs

A major social and moral difficulty of transplant surgery is that it is extremely expensive. For example, a kidney transplant may cost about $60,000, a heart transplant about $125,000, and a liver transplant in the range of $200,000 to $300,000. Questions have been raised in recent years about what restrictions, if any, should be placed on access to transplants. Should society deny them to everyone, pay for all who need them but cannot afford them, or pay for only some who cannot pay? (For a discussion of some of these issues, see Chapter 10.)

Availability

The second major problem, after cost, is the availability of donor organs. The increase in the number of transplant operations performed during the last twenty-five years has resulted in a condition of chronic scarcity for most organs. For example, in the five-year period 1981 to 1985, the demand for livers increased by a factor of 35, and the demand for hearts by a factor of 22. Unlike corneas or bones, kidneys, hearts, and livers are always in short supply because there is no way in which they can be preserved in usable condition for more than a few hours.

This chronic shortage means that at any given time, some thirty-five thousand people in the United States are waiting for organ transplants. In 1993, thirty-six thousand people needed a kidney, but twenty-six thousand were forced to wait until one became available for transplant. Three thousand were left waiting for hearts and about the same number for livers. Thousands of people are currently in need of kidneys, livers, pancreases, lungs, and hearts, and many of these people are likely to die before appropriate organs become available. Those in need of a kidney or pancreas can rely on dialysis and insulin injections to treat their diseases, but those in need of a liver or heart have almost no alternative treatment. Artificial livers remain experimental, and ventricular-assist devices can help only some heart patients. For those waiting for livers, lungs, or hearts, the lack of a suitable transplant organ spells almost certain death.

Given the currently limited supply of organs, we face two key questions today: How can the supply be increased? How are those who will actually receive organs to be selected from the pool of candidates?

Increasing Supply.   The obvious answer to the first question is that the supply of organs can be increased by increasing donations. The overwhelming majority of organs that could be used for transplant are not salvaged from the recently dead. According to one estimate, only about 15% of available organs are retrieved. Most people are simply buried with all their organs. This is true even though virtually every state has enacted some form of the Uniform Anatomical Gift Act. The act is the model for the legal basis of organ donation cards, which are printed on the back of driver's licenses in many states. State laws based on the act spell out a person's right to donate all or part of his body and to designate a person or institution as a recipient.

Even with the support of the law, physicians and hospital administrators have been reluctant to intrude on a family's grief by asking that a deceased patient's organs be donated for use as transplants. Even if a patient has signed an organ donation card, the permission of the immediate family is required, in most cases, before the organs can be removed. In 1991, a federal appeals court ruled in favor of an Ohio woman who argued that the coroner who had removed her husband's corneas during an autopsy and donated them to the Cincinnati Eye Bank had violated her property rights. Her property interest in her husband's body was found to be protected under the due process clause of the Fourteenth Amendment.

In an attempt to overcome the reluctance of physicians to request organ donations, a 1987 federal law requires that hospitals receiving Medicare or Medicaid payments (97% of the nation's 6,800 hospitals) identify patients who could become organ donors at death. The law also requires that hospitals discuss organ donations with the families of such patients and inform them of their legal power to authorize donations. Before the law, only about four thousand people per year donated their organs, and if organs could be retrieved after brain death, this alone would increase the number of donors to twenty thousand. However, because of difficulties in administering the law, including the reluctance by physicians to approach worried or bereaved families, the law has not led to a dramatic increase in the supply of transplant organs.

An approach recently devised at the University of Pittsburgh involves acting on the requests of patients (or their representatives) to remove their organs when their hearts stop beating, even though they may not yet be brain-dead. (See Chapter 3 for a discussion of criteria for determining death.) Hence, someone on a respirator may want to be weaned off the machine, and she asks that her organs be used for transplant, in case the withdrawal results in her death. The respirator is removed in an operating room, and two minutes after a patient's heart has stopped beating, the transplant organs are removed. Most of the patients have been severely brain damaged but are not brain-dead, and permission has been obtained from their families.

Critics of the practice have raised questions about the use of cessation of heartbeat as a proper criterion for death. Some have also wondered if the practice does not put pressure on mentally competent, but seriously ill, patients to give up the struggle for their lives by volunteering to become organ donors. Similarly, critics have charged, by providing a rationalization, the practice may make it too easy for the parents or other representatives of comatose patients on life support to decide to withdraw support and end the person's life.

A second innovative approach employed by some hospitals associated with the Regional Organ Bank of Illinois involves injecting a preservative solution into the kidneys of patients who die in an emergency room or who have died on the way. The kidneys are not removed from the body, but by preserving them in this way, physicians gain additional time to seek permission from the families.

Critics of the Illinois practice claim that it borders on desecration and denies dignity to individuals whose dead bodies are subjected to an invasive procedure without their prior consent. Furthermore, critics say, we have no generally accepted ideas about what it is legitimate to do to a newly dead body to provide benefit to others. Defenders of the practice say that it gives families time to recover from the shock of learning about the death of a loved one and allows them to make a more considered decision. In this respect, the practice is more humane than asking a family for permission to take an organ from a loved one right at the time they learn of the loved one's death.

These practices are seen as providing a way to fill the gap between the number of transplant organs that could be obtained from brain-dead individuals and the number of organs needed by those awaiting transplant. Some ten to twelve thousand people are declared brain-dead every year, yet nearly thirty-two thousand people are on the waiting list for transplants.

Selling Organs.   Another possibility for increasing the organ supply is to permit organs to be offered for sale on the open market. Before death, an individual might arrange payment for the posthumous use of one or more of his organs. Or after the individual's death, his survivors might sell his organs to those in need of them. In a variation of this proposal, donors or their families might receive certain forms of tax credits, or a donor might be legally guaranteed that if a family member or friend required a transplant organ, then that person would be given priority in the distribution. Under either plan, there would be a strong incentive to make organs available for transplant.

The public reaction to any plan for marketing organs has been strongly negative. People generally regard the prospect of individuals in need of transplants bidding against one another in an "organ auction" as ghoulish and morally repugnant, and this attitude extends to all forms of the market approach. In 1984, the National Organ Transplantation Act made the sale of organs for transplant illegal in the United States. At least twenty other countries, including Canada, Britain, and most of Europe, have similar laws.

A third possibility would be to allow living individuals to sell their nonvital organs to those in need of transplants. Taking hearts and livers from living people would be illegal as it would involve homicide by the surgeon who removed them. However, kidneys occur in pairs, and we already permit individuals to donate one of their kidneys to a family member—indeed, we celebrate those who do. It is only a short step from the heroic act of giving away a kidney to the commercial act of selling one.

Kidney donors must undergo surgery that involves incurring a 12-inch incision, the removal of a rib, and three to six weeks of recuperation. Donors face odds of 1 in 20,000 of dying from surgical complications, but the risk of dying as a result of having only one kidney is extremely small. People with one kidney are slightly more likely to develop high blood pressure than those with two.

Allowing the sale of an organ would be in keeping with the generally acknowledged principle that people ought to be free to do as they wish with their own bodies. We already permit the sale of blood, plasma, bone marrow, ova, and sperm. However, the decisive disadvantage to allowing such transactions as a matter of social policy is that it would be the poor who would be most likely to suffer from it.

It is all too easy to imagine a mother wishing to improve the lives and opportunities of her children deciding to sell a kidney to help make that possible. That the economically advantaged should thrive by literally exploiting the bodies of the poor seems morally repulsive to most people. (The 1984 Organ Transplant Act was in direct response to the operations of the International Kidney Exchange, which was established in Virginia for the purpose of selling kidneys from living donors. The donors were predominantly indigent.) It is no answer to object that someone should be permitted to do as he wishes with his body to provide for

the welfare of his family. If selling a kidney and putting his own life and health at risk is the only option open to someone with that aim, this in itself constitutes a prima facie case for major social reform.

"Everyone Makes a Fee, Except for the Donor." Despite strong public sentiment against selling organs, a telephone poll conducted in 1991 by the United Network for Organ Sharing and the National Kidney Foundation showed that 48% of the people interviewed favored some form of "donor compensation." Under the Transplant Act, there can be none.

The law does permit payments associated with removing, preserving, transporting, and storing human organs. As a result, a large industry has developed around organ transplants. Sixty-nine procurement organizations, operating in federally defined geographical regions, collect organs from donors and transport them to the almost three hundred hospitals with transplant facilities.

For its services, a procurement agency may be paid about twenty-five thousand dollars. This includes ambulance trips to pick up and deliver the organ, fees to the hospital for the use of the operating room where the organ is removed, costs of tissue matching and blood testing, and overhead expenses for the agency and its personnel.

In addition, costs involved in a transplant may include fees paid to local surgeons to prepare the patient for organ removal and fees paid to a surgical team coming into town to remove the organ. Such fees typically amount to several thousand dollars.

Hospitals pay for the organs they receive, but they pass on their costs and more. In 1991 hospitals charged, as a rough average, sixteen thousand dollars for a kidney or a heart and twenty-one thousand dollars for a liver. According to one study, hospitals may mark up the cost of an organ by as much as 200% to cover costs that patients are unable to pay or that exceed the amount the government will reimburse. A donor of several organs can produce considerable income for the transplanting hospital.

Some critics of current transplant practices have pointed out that everyone makes a fee from donated organs except for the donor. Matters show little sign of changing. A representative of the National Kidney Foundation proposed to a congressional committee that the law be changed to allow a relatively small amount of money (perhaps two thousand dollars) to be given to the families of organ donors as a contribution to burial expenses. However, the recommendation was not acted on.

Given current transplant practices, it is understandable why some donor families can become bitter. When Judy Sutton's daughter Susan killed herself, Mrs. Sutton donated Susan's heart and liver and so helped save the lives of two people. Mrs. Sutton then had to borrow the money to pay for Susan's funeral. "Susan gave life even in death," Mrs. Sutton told a reporter. "It's wrong that doctors make so much money off donors. Very wrong."

Presumed Consent.   A final possibility that has been widely discussed as a means of increasing the number of organs available for transplant is the adoption of a policy of "presumed consent." That is, a state or federal law would allow hospitals to take it for granted that a recently deceased person has tacitly consented to having any needed organs removed, unless the person had indicated otherwise or unless the family objects. The burden of securing consent would be removed from physicians and hospitals, but the burden of denying consent would be imposed on individuals or their families. To withdraw consent would require a positive action.

A policy of presumed consent has been adopted by several European countries. Critics of the policy point out that this has not, in general, done much to reduce the shortage of transplant organs in those countries. Although legally empowered to remove or-

gans without a family's permission, physicians continue to be reluctant to do so. It is doubtful that a policy of presumed consent would be any more successful in this country. Also, if families are to be given the opportunity to deny consent, they must be notified of the death of the patient, and in many cases this would involve not only complicated practical arrangements, but also considerable loss of time. Thus, it is doubtful that presumed consent would do a great deal to increase the number of usable transplant organs.

Voluntary Donation.   In the view of many observers, the present system of organ procurement by voluntary donation is the best system. It appeals to the best in people, rather than to greed and self-interest, it avoids exploiting the poor, and it is efficient. Families who donate organs can gain some satisfaction from knowing that the death of a loved one brought some benefit to others.

One modification of the present system would be to eliminate rules that require that a living kidney donor belong to the same family as the recipient. This would allow those who wish to act in a generous, admirable fashion to directly benefit a friend, a coworker, or a complete stranger. The problem of securing enough kidneys to meet the needs of those waiting for a transplant would be at least partially solved.

Many believe that even without any fundamental alterations in the system it is still possible to increase the number of available organs. As one observer commented, there is no shortage of donors, just a shortage of askers. If so, then the current U.S. policy of requiring that the next of kin be asked to donate organs holds the best promise of relieving the chronic shortage.

Organ Distribution

Whatever the future may promise, the fact remains that at present there is a limited supply of transplant organs, and the demand far exceeds the supply. Thus, the key question to-day is, "How are organs to be distributed when they become available?" There are currently no national policies or procedures for answering this question. Typically, such decisions are made in accordance with policies adopted by particular regional or hospital-based transplant programs.

In a characteristic instance, a member of a hospital staff notifies someone in a transplant program of a potential donor, often a patient recently declared brain-dead. Someone from the program then approaches the family to secure consent. If consent is granted, the organs are removed and arrangements made to transplant them as soon as possible. Patients who are judged to be most in need medically and who have a good (not necessarily perfect) tissue match with the donor organ are chosen as the recipients.

Medical need is not the only factor considered in all instances. Decisions are also based on the patient's general medical condition, how much he might be expected to benefit from the transplant, his age, his ability to pay for the operation, whether he has a family that will assist him during recovery, and whether he belongs to the constituency that the hospital is committed to serving. In addition, other factors, such as the individual's "social worth" (education, occupation, accomplishments), may be taken into account.

Guidelines for Distribution. Some of these factors, particularly the patient's social worth and ability to pay, have been strongly criticized as morally irrelevant to deciding who is to receive a transplant organ. A good example of an effort to formulate acceptable guidelines for making such decisions about allocating transplant organs is the Massachusetts Task Force on Organ Transplantation. The group issued a unanimous report that included the following recommendations:

1. Transplant surgery should be provided "to those who can benefit most from it in terms of probability of living for a significant period of time with a reasonable prospect for rehabilitation."

2. Decisions should not be based on "social worth" criteria.

3. Age may be considered as a factor in the selection process, but only to the extent that age is relevant to life expectancy and prospects for rehabilitation. Age must not be the only factor considered.

4. If not enough organs are available for all those who might benefit from them, final selections should be made by some random process (for example a lottery or first-come, first-served basis).

5. Transplants should be provided to residents of New England on the basis of need, regardless of their ability to pay, as long as this does not adversely affect health-care services with a higher priority. Those who are not residents of New England should be accepted as transplant candidates only after they have demonstrated their ability to pay for the procedure.

A presidential commission in 1986 proposed that a national network of organ procurement and matching be established, one that would include all private, nonprofit agencies that currently undertake this work. It also recommended that a transplant program be funded so that no American in need of a heart, liver, or kidney transplant would be kept from receiving one because of an inability to pay.

The Reagan administration did not endorse the recommendations. It expressed the view that it would be more appropriate for the private sector, rather than the federal government, to accept the responsibilities associated with organ transplantation. Even so, under legislation that took effect in 1987, private procurement agencies are now tied into a single national network. For many people, however, the inability to pay for an organ transplant still remains an unbreachable barrier to receiving one.

CASE PRESENTATION

The Ayalas' Solution: Having a Child to Save a Life

Anissa Ayala was fifteen years old in 1988 when she was diagnosed with chronic myelogenous leukemia. She received radiation and chemotherapy treatments to destroy diseased bone marrow and blood cells, but the usual outcome of such treatments is that the bone marrow is left unable to produce an adequate number of normal blood cells.

Anissa's parents, Mary and Andy Ayala, were informed that without a bone marrow transplant of stem cells her survival chances were virtually zero, while with a transplant she would have a 70–80% chance.

Tests showed that neither the Ayalas nor their nineteen-year-old son, Airon, had bone marrow that was sufficiently compatible for them to be donors for Anissa. They turned to a public registry to assist them and during the next two years searched for a donor. The odds of a match between two nonrelated people is only one in 20,000, and as time passed and no one was found, the Ayalas began to feel increasingly desperate. Anissa's health had stabilized, yet that condition couldn't be counted on to last forever.

The Ayalas decided that the only way they could do more to help save their daughter's life was to try to have another child. Anissa's physician tried to discourage them, pointing out that the odds were only one in four that the child would have the right tissue type to be a stem-cell donor. Furthermore, the possibility that they could conceive another child was doubtful. Andy Ayala was 45 and had had a vasectomy performed sixteen years earlier. Mary Ayala was 42, well past the period of highest fertility. Nevertheless, the Ayalas decided to go ahead with their plan, and as the first step Andy Ayala had surgery to repair the vasectomy.

Against all the odds, Mary Ayala became pregnant.

When it became known that the Ayalas planned to have a child because their daughter needed compatible bone marrow, they became the subjects of intense media attention and received much harsh criticism. Some said that they were treating the baby they expected to have as a means only and not as a person of unique worth. One commentator described their actions as "outrageous."

Others said they were taking a step down the path that would lead to conceiving children merely as a source of tissue and organs.

A few opposed this outpouring of criticism by pointing out that people decide to have children for many and complex reasons and sometimes for no reason at all. No one observed that a reason for having a child need not determine how one regards the child. Also, those who condemned the Ayalas often emphasized the "child-as-an-organ bank" notion but never mentioned the relative safety of a bone marrow transplant.

The Ayalas themselves reported that they were hurt by the criticisms. Mary Ayala said she had wanted a third child for a number of years but had been unable to get her husband to agree. Andy Ayala admitted that he would not have wanted another child had Anissa not become ill, but he said he also had in mind the comfort a child would bring to the family should Anissa die. The whole family said they would want and love the child, whether or not its bone marrow was a good match.

In February 1990 the Ayalas found they had beat the odds once more. Tests of the developing fetus showed that the stem cells were nearly identical with Anissa's. During an interview after the results were known, Anissa Ayala said "A lot of people think 'How can you do this? How can you be having this baby for your daughter?' But she's my baby sister and we're going to love her for who she is, not for what she can give me."

Then, on April 6, in a suburban Los Angeles hospital, more than a week before the predicted date, Mary Ayala gave birth to a healthy six-pound baby girl. The Ayalas named her Marissa Eve.

Anissa's physician, pediatric oncologist Patricia Konrad, collected and froze blood from the baby's umbilical cord. Umbilical blood contains a high concentration of stem cells, and she wanted the blood available should Anissa need it before Marissa was old enough to be a donor.

When Marissa Eve was fourteen months old and had reached an adequate weight, she was given general anesthesia and marrow was extracted from her hipbone. After preparation, it was injected into one of Anissa's veins. The procedure was successful, and the stem cells migrated to Anissa's marrow and began to multiply. Anissa's own bone marrow began to produce normal blood cells.

In 1993 Anissa married Bryan Espinosa, and Marissa Eve was the flower girl at the wedding. The radiation treatments destroyed Anissa's chances of having a child, but she claims that the bond between her and Marissa Eve is especially close. "Marissa is more than a sister to me," Anissa told reporter Anni Griffiths Belt. "She's almost like my child too."

"I was struck by the extraordinary bond between the sisters," Belt said. "The fact is, neither one would be alive today without the other."

SOCIAL CONTEXT: FETAL-CELL IMPLANTS

Parkinson's disease often begins with tremors and a mild stiffening of the limbs that is followed by a gradual but progressive loss of muscle control. Although remaining intellectually lucid, people with the disease are often unable to walk, use the toilet, wash, or even eat without assistance.

Their behavior also has a peculiar and disturbing off/on aspect. Someone may be walking or talking when, without the least warning, he freezes during the action. Some find this feature of the disease so disconcerting that they become recluses, fearful of freezing in mid-motion in public or in a dangerous place. Over 1.5 million people, most of them over sixty, are estimated to suffer from the disease.

The disease is causally connected with the dying off of cells in a darkly pigmented part of the brain called the *substantia nigra*. These cells produce dopamine, a neurotransmitter essential in conveying impulses to brain cells that control muscle movements. A major therapeutic advance in the treatment of parkinsonism occurred with the introduction of the drug L-dopa. L-dopa is a biochemical precursor of dopamine, and when the body converts the drug to dopamine, people often make an amazing recovery from the effects of the disease. Unfortunately, within a few years L-dopa ceases to be effective, and the old problems of rigidity, "freezing," and general loss of muscle control return.

In 1987, Ignacio Madrazo reported in Mexico that he had successfully transplanted cells from the adrenal cortex of two Parkinson patients into the caudate nucleus area of their brains. The adrenal gland is known to produce dopamine, and Madrazo described his patients as making substantial functional recoveries that he expected to continue over the long term. (Five years previously, Swedish researchers performed a similar operation but reported that their patients made only slight and transitory improvements.) Madrozo's results were never reported in a scientific journal, and although efforts were made to repeat the work he reported, no one was successful. Thus, early hopes for adrenal-cell transplants as an effective treatment for parkinsonism were disappointed.

Then in February 1990, matters began to look hopeful again. Olle Lindvall of University Hospital in Lund, Sweden, reported in *Science* that he and his research team had implanted fetal brain cells into the brain of a forty-nine-year-old man with severe Parkinson's disease. The cells were injected into the left putamen, an area known to be the site of numerous dopamine pathways.

The man's symptoms were significantly relieved. Previously, even with medication, he had spent more than half his time in a frozen "off" position, but within three months after the implant, he had only one or two brief "off" periods each day. (The man's course was followed from eleven months before the surgery, and it was still being followed at the time of publication five months afterward.) Most important, brain-imaging methods indicated that the fetal cells were continuing to function and to produce dopamine.

Lindvall's team had been working on the

problem since 1979, and the team's reputation, experimental procedures, and data convinced most of the biomedical community that their results were reliable. Other researchers indicated that they had experiments underway that were likely to confirm Lindvall's results.

The Swedish procedure involved taking neural tissue from four fetuses eight to nine weeks old. Fetal brain tissue offers the possibility of a better biological match than cells even from an individual's own adrenal gland. Further, neural fetal tissue seems to be unlikely to provoke an autoimmune response and cause graft-host rejection. Treating parkinsonism with fetal-cell implants is an exciting therapeutic possibility that may benefit hundreds of thousands of sufferers. Furthermore, the treatment points the way toward the development of other therapies involving fetal tissues.

Fetal liver cells may be used to generate new bone marrow to treat those suffering from leukemia, sickle-cell anemia, thalassemia, aplastic anemia, or radiation sickness. (Robert Gale employed fetal liver cells to treat some victims of the Chernobyl disaster, although without success.) Alzheimer's disease, Huntington's disease, and spinal-cord injuries may all yield to treatments involving fetal neural cells. Fetal heart tissue may be used to replace damaged heart muscle, and the bodies of the more than 2 million insulin-dependent (Type-I) diabetics may someday be able to produce their own insulin, if implants of islet cells from fetal pancreatic tissue should be successful.

The potential therapeutic marvels promised by fetal cells hold out the only hope for literally millions of people suffering from a wide range of diseases. However, fetal-cell implants and their use in research and therapy have also produced serious moral and social issues we have yet to resolve.

The most vexed issue is that of induced abortion as the source of fetal tissue. Opponents of elective abortion argue that research and therapy using fetal tissue both condone and encourage abortion. According to a National Right to Life Committee official, John C. Wilke, the medical use of fetal tissue will "offer an additional rationalization to those who defend the killings."

Also, both opponents and advocates of elective abortion express concern over the possibility that some women might deliberately conceive a child, then have an abortion for the sole purpose of obtaining the fetal tissue. The tissue could then either be used to help some member of the woman's family or sold as a commodity. Although a 1988 amendment to the National Organ Transplant Act prohibits the sale of fetal organs and tissue, the success of fetal-cell therapy could lead to a repeal. Some have suggested that fetal tissue, like blood, bone marrow, and sperm, can be considered a renewable resource. The potential for a fetal-tissue market exists, and some have speculated that the current law may only encourage the establishment of an off-shore source of supply. People will seek out illegal sources of supplies of fetal tissue in much the same way they seek illegal sources of drugs they believe are crucial to their survival.

Kate Michaelman of the National Abortion Rights Action League sees "a potential for the abuse of women in this whole thing." The idea that women might be put under pressure by social expectations or by their friends, husbands, or families to have an abortion to provide fetal tissue needed to treat an ailing relative is not farfetched. Further, if there were a market in fetal tissue, women might be under similar pressure to produce a fetus to secure money needed to support themselves or their families. (It should be kept in mind, though, that even in the absence of pressure, a woman might choose to sell or donate fetal tissue for a variety of reasons.)

While the Catholic Church condemns induced abortion, it condones the use of fetal tissue, particularly that secured by spontaneous abortion, within certain limits. The "fetal organ donor" must be treated with the same respect as any other organ donor, and it is necessary to be certain that the donor is dead. This requirement presents a difficulty, however, for the standards for fetal brain death are far from clear.

Almost 1.5 million abortions are performed each year, and most fetal tissue used in research is obtained from those performed during the first four months of pregnancy. Although the matter is in dispute, some researchers regard tissue from eight- to nine-week-old fetuses to be preferable, while some claim older tissue is better. In either case, social and economic pressure on a woman to delay an abortion may start to build, and the best interest of the woman may be compromised by the need for mature fetal tissue. Instead of using a drug like RU-486 to inhibit the implantation of a fertilized ovum or instead of having an early abortion, a woman might carry the fetus until a time dictated by needs other than her own health.

The possibility of using only spontaneously aborted fetuses is dimmed by the fact that up to 60% show chromosomal abnormalities or other defects that might affect the tissue recipient.

One way of addressing the abortion objection to the use of fetal tissue is to employ cells from a single fetus, grow them in cultures, then harvest them as needed. This would eliminate the need for a large number of mature fetuses and make the research and treatment more independent of abortion.

Another possibility is to use the techniques of molecular biology to clone cells taken from an individual patient. If the cells can be made to multiply in sufficient quantity, then the patient can be treated with his own cells. The problem of an immune reaction would be eliminated, and cell therapy would be severed from abortion.

Because fetal cells are now available and not dependent on technological development, people suffering from Parkinson's disease and other disorders that might be helped by fetal-cell implants are understandably not eager to see research in this area delayed. For a great number, the development of a future technology that will disconnect cell therapy and abortion will come too late to help.

In 1987, the Department of Health and Human Services suspended the support of research projects using fetal tissue obtained through induced abortions. After two reviews of the issues, a special panel of the National Institutes of Health decided in 1988 that the use of fetal tissue for research and treatment can be morally legitimate. The panel separated the question of elective abortion from that of the use of fetal tissue and took no position on the moral status of abortion. The panel also recommended that women not be permitted to donate fetal tissue for the treatment of their friends or family.

In April 1989, NIH, following most of the recommendations of its panel, issued guidelines for the use of fetal tissue in research and experimental therapy. However, the ban on the use of such tissue initiated during the Reagan administration was continued by the Bush administration, and federal funds could not be used for human fetal-tissue implants. In addition, at least seven states passed laws forbidding the use of fetal tissue obtained from induced abortions.

Many researchers objected to these restrictions. Some claimed that the restrictions were immoral because they seriously impeded the development of effective treatments for devastating diseases. Others used funds from private foundations to continue their research.

Despite objections from the research community, the ban on federal financing of studies using cells from aborted fetuses remained in effect until it was lifted by President Clinton in one of his first official acts. In January 1994, the National Institute of Neurological Disorders announced grants of $4.5 million to three institutions to study the effects of fetal-cell implants in Parkinson's patients.

One of the grants was awarded to researchers at the University of Colorado, in Denver. During the ban, the researchers, operating on private financing, injected fetal brain cells into sixteen patients with Parkinson's disease. The outcome was that about one-third of the patients improved significantly, one-third improved some, and one-third showed no measurable improvement. The new, federally financed study will be a double-blind therapeutic trial.

Patients with diseases that might be relieved by fetal-cell therapy, as well as their families, are eager to see it developed as rapidly as possible. Some are angered by what they see as an unjustified delay in federal research funding.

CASE PRESENTATION
Policy Decision and the Neonatal Unit

Jake Hanna (as we will call him) stood by the admitting desk in the emergency room of Commerce County Hospital and couldn't believe what was happening. It was like being trapped in a nightmare.

Less than ten miles away, his wife Christine lay in a recovery room at Valley View Hospital. She had just given birth to their first child and was still groggy from the anesthesia.

Martha, as they had already decided to name their daughter before her birth, had been premature. She was almost six weeks early, and both Jake and Chris had been surprised when Chris began to experience labor pains. At first they didn't know what the pains were; then they decided that, to be safe, they had better get Chris to the hospital Chris's obstetrician had told them to go to. They were lucky to have gotten to Valley View in time, because the birth was a difficult one, and Chris had needed help and reassurance.

In another respect, they hadn't been so lucky. Valley View was a small private hospital with restricted facilities. It had an emergency room but no intensive-care or neonatal units.

And Martha needed help. She was small and underdeveloped. Her heart sounds were weak and slightly irregular, she was having difficulty breathing, and her blood chemistry was unbalanced and showed inadequate kidney function. If she was to have a good chance at living, she needed special treatment and continuous monitoring.

"You need to get her into a special facility," Dr. Birk told Jake. "We're doing all we can for her here, but that's not very much. We aren't even set up to do dialysis. We simply don't have the equipment or

the personnel to provide her with the kind of care she needs."

"Where could she go?" Jake asked.

"Commerce County Hospital—it's the only place in the area with a neonatal setup."

"Can you make the arrangements?"

"I'm sorry, I can't. They won't take referrals anymore. Somebody on their staff has to do the admitting. I think they're trying to cut back on their program."

"Can I get her in?"

"I'm not sure," Dr. Birk said. "But she needs to be there. They may take her as a walk-in. So you're going to have to go in person and take the baby with you. Do you have a friend or family member here?"

"Chris's mother is with her. But isn't it dangerous to move the baby?"

"Not really. She's in a stable condition, and if you take her you'll save a lot of time. She needs help as fast as she can get it."

With Martha wrapped in a gray hospital blanket and held by Chris's mother, Jake drove the ten miles to Commerce County Hospital and double-parked at the emergency entrance. He literally ran through the wide doors.

He explained to the clerk at the admitting desk that Dr. Birk had said that the baby needed to be in a neonatal unit at once. The clerk said that he had no authority to make that kind of admission and told Jake to sit down while he paged Dr. Donna Chavez, the director of the unit.

The wait seemed interminable to Jake, but in less than ten minutes Dr. Chavez appeared in the emergency room. Jake walked over to her, and while they stood by the admitting desk with a dozen people waiting for their names to be called, he explained the problem once again.

When Jake had finished, Dr. Chavez shook her head. "We can't admit the child," she said. "I'm sorry, but we just can't do it."

"Why not?" Jake asked. "Don't you have room or something?"

"That's not the problem. We actually have enough space."

"Then what is it?"

"This is going to be hard for you to understand," Dr. Chavez said. "But the hospital has adopted a new policy. At no time can we have more than twenty patients in the neonatal unit, and that's the number we have now. The problem is with costs."

"But I'm willing to pay, and I have insurance."

"It's not particular costs, Mr. Hanna. It's the cost of the whole unit, and Commerce has just decided to cut back on its size. That's why they've imposed a twenty-infant limit."

"But what about my child?" Jake asked. "She needs help, and she needs it right now."

"I'm very, very sorry," Dr. Chavez said. "If the decision were mine alone, I would admit her at once. But as things are, I simply have to follow the hospital's policy guidelines."

"So you refuse to take her?"

"I must. I don't have any real choice in the matter."

"What am I supposed to do? Just let her die?"

"I suggest you take the child back to Valley View. They will do everything they can, and with luck things will work out for her. I certainly hope so."

Jake thought he had never had a nightmare as bad as this. He had never before felt so helpless, so powerless. There was no way he could force them to admit Martha, and there was nothing he could do for her himself. It surprised him that he didn't feel particularly angry at Dr. Chavez or at the hospital. He was simply too numb to feel much of anything.

Jake said nothing more to Dr. Chavez. He want out to the car and drove back to Valley View. Mrs. Williams cried all the way back, and Jake wished that he could.

Inside the emergency room at Valley View, a nurse took the baby from Mrs. Williams. They took Martha to a small treatment room and gave her oxygen to help her breathing.

Jake and Mrs. Williams sat in the waiting area. They agreed that there was no need to tell Chris anything yet. She was asleep and no purpose would be served by waking her.

Three hours later, a doctor Jake had never seen before came to tell him that Martha was dead.

CASE PRESENTATION
Selection Committee for Dialysis

In 1966 Brattle, Texas, proper had a population of about 10,000 people. In Brattle County there were 20,000 more people who lived on isolated farms deep within the pine forests, or in crossroads towns with a filling station, a feed store, one or two white frame churches, and maybe twenty or twenty-five houses.

Brattle was the marketing town and county seat, the place all the farmers, their wives, and children went to on Saturday afternoon. It was also the medical center because it had the only hospitals in the county. One of them, Conklin Clinic, was hardly more than a group of doctors' offices. But Crane Memorial Hospital was quite a different sort of place. Occupying a relatively new three-story brick building in downtown Brattle, the hospital offered new equipment, a well-trained staff, and high-quality medical care.

This was mostly due to the efforts of Dr. J. B. Crane, Jr. The hospital was dedicated to the memory of his father, a man who practiced medicine in Brattle County for almost fifty years. Before Crane became a memorial hospital, it was Crane Clinic. But J. B. Crane, Jr., after returning from The Johns Hopkins Medical School, was determined to expand the clinic and transform it into a modern hospital. The need was there, and private investors were easy to find. Only a year after his father's death, Dr. Crane was able to offer Brattle County a genuine hospital.

It was only natural that, when the County Commissioner decided that Brattle County should have a dialysis machine, he would turn to Dr. Crane's hospital. The machine was bought with county funds, but Crane Memorial Hospital would operate it under a contract agreement. The hospital was guaranteed against loss by the county, but the hospital was also not permitted to make a profit on dialysis. Furthermore, although access to the machine was not restricted to county residents, residents were to be given priority.

Dr. Crane was not pleased with this stipulation. "I don't like to have medical decisions influenced by political considerations," he told the Commissioner. "If a guy comes in and needs dialysis, I don't want to tell him that he can't have it because somebody else who doesn't need it as much is on the machine and that person is a county resident."

"I don't know what to tell you," the Commissioner said. "It was county tax money that paid for the machine, and the County Council decided that the people who supplied the money ought to get top priority."

"What about the kind of case that I mentioned?" Dr. Crane asked. "What about somebody who could wait for dialysis who is a resident as opposed to somebody who needs it immediately who's not a resident?"

"We'll just leave that sort of case to your discretion," the Commissioner said. "People around here have confidence in you and your doctors. If you say they can wait, then they can wait. I know you won't let them down. Of course, if somebody died while some outsider was on the machine . . . Well, that would be embarrassing for all of us, I guess."

Dr. Crane was pleased to have the dialysis machine in his hospital. Not only was it the only one in Brattle County, but none of the neighboring counties had even one. Only the big hospitals in places like Dallas, Houston, and San Antonio had the machines. It put Crane Memorial up in the top rank.

Dr. Crane was totally unprepared for the problem when it came. He hadn't known there were so many people with chronic renal disease in Brattle County. But when news spread that there was a kidney machine available at Crane Memorial Hospital, twenty-three people applied for the dialysis program. Some were Dr. Crane's own patients or patients of his associates on the hospital staff. But a number of them were ones referred to the hospital by other physicians in Brattle and surrounding towns. Two of them were from neighboring Lopez County.

Working at a maximum, the machine could accommodate fourteen patients. But the staff decided that maximum operation would be likely to lead to dangerous equipment malfunctions and breakdowns. They settled on ten as the number of patients that should be admitted to the program.

Dr. Crane and his staff interviewed each of the program's applicants, reviewed their medical history, and got a thorough medical workup on each. They persuaded two of the patients to continue to commute to Houston, where they were already in dialysis. In four cases, renal disease had already progressed to the point that the staff decided that the patients could not benefit sufficiently from the program to make them good medical risks. In one other case, a patient suffering intestinal cancer and in generally poor health was rejected as a candidate. Two people were not in genuine need of dialysis but could be best treated by a program of medication.

That left fourteen candidates for the ten positions. Thirteen were from Brattle County and one from Lopez County.

"This is not a medical problem," Dr. Crane told the Commissioner. "And I'm not going to take the responsibility of deciding which people to condemn to death and which to give an extra chance at life."

"What do you want me to do?" the Commissioner asked. "I wouldn't object if you made the decision. I mean, you wouldn't have to tell everybody about it. You could just decide."

"That's something I won't do," Dr. Crane said. "All of this has to be open and aboveboard. It's got to be fair. If I decide, then everybody will think I am favoring my own patients or just taking the people who can pay the most money."

"I see what you mean. If I appoint a selection committee, will you serve on it?"

"I will. As long as my vote is the same as everybody else's."

"That's what I'll do, then," the Commissioner said.

The Brattle County Renal Dialysis Selection Committee was appointed and operating within the week. In addition to Dr. Crane, it was made up of three people chosen by the Commissioner.

Amy Langford, a Brattle housewife in her middle fifties whose husband owned the largest automobile and truck agency in Brattle County, was one member. Reverend David Johnson was another member. He was the only African American on the committee and the pastor of the largest predominantly African American church in Brattle. The last member was Jacob Sims, owner of a hardware store in the nearby town of Silsbee. He was the only member of the committee not from the town of Brattle.

"Now I'm inclined to favor this fellow," said Mr. Sims at the Selection Committee's first meeting. "He's twenty-four years old, he's married, and he has a child two years old."

"You're talking about James Nelson?" Mrs. Langford asked. "I had some trouble with him. I've heard that he used to drink a lot before he got sick, and from the looks of his record he's had a hard time keeping a job."

"That's hard to say," said Reverend Johnson. "He works as a pulp-wood hauler, and people who do that change jobs a lot. You just have to go where the work is."

"That's right," said Mr. Sims. "One thing, though. I can't find any indication of his church membership. He says he's a Methodist, but I don't see where he's told us what his church is."

"I don't either," said Mrs. Langford." And he's not a member of the Masons or the Lions Club or any other sort of civic group. I wouldn't say he's made much of a contribution to this community."

"That's right," said Reverend Johnson. "But let's don't forget that he's got a wife and baby depending on him. That child is going to need a father."

"I think he is a good psychological candidate," said Dr. Crane. "That is, I think if he starts the program he'll stick to it. I've talked with his wife, and I know she'll encourage him."

"We should notice that he's a high school drop-out," Mrs. Langford said. "I don't think we can ever expect him to make much of a contribution to this town or to the county."

"Do you want to vote on this case?" asked Mr. Sims, the chairman of the committee.

"Let's talk about all of them, then go back and vote," Reverend Johnson suggested.

Everyone around the table nodded in agreement. The files were arranged by date of application, and Mr. Sims picked up the next one from the stack in front of him.

"Alva Algers," he said. "He's a fifty-three-year old lawyer with three grown children. His wife is still alive, and he's still married to her. He's Secretary of the Layman's Board of the Brattle Episcopal Church, a member of the Rotary Club and the Elks. He used to be a scoutmaster."

"From the practical point of view," said Dr. Crane, "he would be a good candidate. He's intelligent and educated and understands what's involved in dialysis."

"I think he's definitely the sort of person we want to help," said Mrs. Langford. "He's the kind of person that makes this a better town. I'm definitely in favor of him."

"I am too," said Reverend Johnson. "Even if he does go to the wrong church."

"I'm not so sure," said Mr. Sims. "I don't think fifty-three is old—I'd better not, because I'm fifty-two myself. Still, his children are grown; he's led a good life. I'm not sure I wouldn't give the edge to some younger fellow."

"How can you say that?" Mrs. Langford said. "He's got a lot of good years left. He's a person of good character who might still do a lot for other people. He's not like that Nelson, who's not going to do any good for anybody except himself."

"I guess I'm not convinced that lawyers and members of the Rotary Club do a lot more good for the community than drivers of pulp-wood trucks," Mr. Sims said.

"Perhaps we ought to go on to the next candidate," Reverend Johnson said.

"We have Mrs. Holly Holton, a forty-three-year-old housewife from Mineral Springs," Mr. Sims said.

"That's in Lopez County, isn't it?" Mrs. Langford asked. "I think we can just reject her right off. She didn't pay the taxes that bought the machine, and our county doesn't have any responsibility for her."

"That's right," said Reverend Johnson.

Mr. Sims agreed, and Dr. Crane raised no objection.

"Now," said Mr. Sims, "here's Alton Conway. I believe he's our only African American candidate."

"I know him well," said Reverend Johnson "He owns a dry-cleaning business, and people in the black community think very highly of him."

"I'm in favor of him," Mrs. Langford said. "He's married and seems quite settled and respectable."

"I wouldn't want us to take him just because he's black," Reverend Johnson said. "But I think he's got a lot in his favor."

"Well," said Mr. Sims, "unless Dr. Crane wants to add anything, let's go on to Nora Bainridge. She's a thirty-year-old divorced woman whose eight-year-old boy lives with his father over in Louisiana. She's a waitress at the Pep Cafe."

"She is a very vital woman," said Dr. Crane. "She's had a lot of trouble in her life, but I think she's a real fighter."

"I don't believe she's much of a churchgoer," said Reverend Johnson. "At least she doesn't give us a pastor's name."

"That's right," said Mrs. Langford. "And I just wonder what kind of morals a woman like her has. I mean, being divorced and working as a waitress and all."

"I don't believe we're trying to award sainthood here," said Mr. Sims.

"But surely moral character is relevant," said Mrs. Langford.

"I don't know anything against her moral character," said Mr. Sims. "Do you?"

"I'm only guessing," said Mrs. Langford. "But I wouldn't say that a woman of her background and apparent character is somebody we ought to give top priority to."

"I don't want to be the one to cast the first stone," said Reverend Johnson. "But I wouldn't put her at the top of our list either."

"I think we had better be careful not to discriminate against people who are poor and uneducated," said Dr. Crane.

"I agree," said Mrs. Langford. "But surely we have to take account of a person's worth."

"Can you tell us how we can measure a person's worth?" asked Mr. Sims.

"I believe I can," Mrs. Langford said. "Does the person have a steady job? Is he or she somebody we would be proud to know? Is he a churchgoer? Does he or she do things for other people? We can see what kind of education the person has had, and consider whether he is somebody we would like to have around."

"I guess that's some of it, all right," said Mr. Sims. "But I don't like to rely on things like education, money, and public service. A lot of people just

haven't had a decent chance in this world. Maybe they were born poor or have had a lot of bad luck. I'm beginning to think that we ought to make our choices just by drawing lots."

"I can't approve of that," said Reverend Johnson. "That seems like a form of gambling to me. We ought to choose the good over the wicked, reward those who have led a virtuous life."

"I agree," Mrs. Langford said. "Choosing by drawing straws or something like that would mean we are just too cowardly to make decisions. We would be shirking our responsibility. Clearly, some people are more deserving than others, and we ought to have the courage to say so."

"All right," said Mr. Sims. "I guess we'd better get on with it, then. Simon Gootz is a forty-eight-year-old baker. He's got a wife and four children. Owns his own bakery—probably all of us have been there. He's Jewish."

"I'm not sure he's the sort of person who can stick to the required diet and go through the dialysis program," Dr. Crane said.

"I'll bet his wife and children would be a good incentive," said Mrs. Langford.

"There's not a Jewish church in town," said Reverend Johnson. "So of course we can't expect him to be a regular churchgoer."

"He's an immigrant," said Mr. Sims. "I don't believe he has any education to speak of, but he did start that bakery and build it up from nothing. I think that says a lot about his character."

"I think we can agree he's good candidate," said Mrs. Langford.

"Let's just take one more before we break for dinner," Mr. Sims said. "Rebecca Scarborough. She's a sixty-three-year-old widow. Her children are all grown and living somewhere else."

"She's my patient," Dr. Crane said. "She's a tough and resourceful old woman. I believe she can follow orders and stand up to the rigors of the program, and her health in general is good."

Reverend Johnson said, "I just wonder if we shouldn't put a lady like her pretty far down on our list. She's lived a long life already, and she hasn't got anybody depending on her."

"I'm against that," Mrs. Langford said. "Everybody knows Mrs. Scarborough. Her family has been in this town for ages. She's one of our most substantial citizens. People would be scandalized if we didn't select her."

"Of course, I'm not from Brattle," said Mr. Sims. "And maybe that's an advantage here, because I don't see that she's got much in her favor except being from an old family."

"I think that's worth something," said Mrs. Langford.

"I'm not sure it's enough, though," said Reverend Johnson.

After dinner at the Crane Memorial Hospital cafeteria, the Selection Committee met again to discuss the seven remaining candidates. It was past ten o'clock before their final decisions were made. James Nelson, the pulp-wood truck driver, Holly Holton, the housewife from Mineral Springs, and Nora Bainridge, the waitress, were all rejected as candidates. Mrs. Scarborough was rejected also. The lawyer, Alva Algers, the dry cleaner, Alton Conway, and the baker, Simon Gootz, were selected to participate in the dialysis program. Others selected were a retired secondary schoolteacher, an assembly-line worker at the Rigid Box Company, a Brattle County Sheriff's Department patrolman, and a twenty-seven-year-old woman file clerk in the office of the Texas Western Insurance Company.

Dr. Crane was glad that the choices were made so that the program could begin operation. But he was not pleased with the selection method and resolved to talk to his own staff and with the County Commissioner about devising some other kind of selection procedure.

Without giving any reasons, Mr. Sims sent a letter to the County Commissioner resigning from the Renal Dialysis Selection Committee.

Mrs. Langford and Reverend Johnson also sent letters to the Commissioner. They thanked him for appointing them to the committee and indicated their willingness to continue to serve.

INTRODUCTION

TRANSPLANTS, KIDNEYS, MACHINES

The story of Robin Cook's novel *Coma* takes place in a large Boston hospital at the present time. What sets the novel apart from dozens of others with similar settings and characters is the fact that the plot hinges on the operations of a large-scale black market in transplant organs. For enormous fees, the criminals running the operation will supply corneas, kidneys, or hearts to those who can pay.

Cook claims that the inspiration for his novel came from an advertisement in a California newspaper. The anonymous ad offered to sell for $5,000 any organ that a reader wanted to buy. Thus, Cook's novel seems to be a book rooted firmly in the world we know today and not just a leap into the speculative realms of science fiction.

Organ transplants have attracted a considerable amount of attention in the last few years. Not only are transplants dramatic, often offering last-minute salvation from an almost certain death, but the very possibility of organ transplants is bright with promise. We can easily imagine a future in which any injured or diseased organ can be replaced almost as easily as the parts on a car. The present state of biomedical technology makes this more than a distant dream, although not a current reality.

The basic problem with organ transplants is the phenomenon of tissue rejection by the immune system. Alien proteins trigger the body's defense mechanisms. In the past, the proteins in the transplanted tissues were matched as carefully as possible with those of the recipient; then powerful immunosuppressive drugs were used in an effort to allow the host body to accommodate itself to the foreign tissue. These drugs left the body open to infections that it could normally cope with without much difficulty.

Use of the drug cyclosporine dramatically improved the success of organ transplants when it was first used a decade ago. Cyclosporine selectively inhibits only part of the immune system and leaves enough of the system sufficiently functional to fight off most of the infections that were once fatal to large numbers of transplant recipients. Also, although tissue matching is still important, particularly for kidneys, the matches do not have to be as close as before. Now 90% to 96% of transplanted kidneys function after one year; in the 1970s only about 50% did. Since 1970, the one-year survival rate for children with liver transplants has increased from 38% to more than 75%, and there is good reason to believe that if children survive for as long as one year, they have a genuine chance to live a normal life. About 82% of heart transplant recipients now live for at least one year, a major increase from the 20% of the 1970s. Lung and heart–lung transplants have a success rate of about 54%.

Some new drugs promise to be even more effective than cyclosporine in controlling rejection. One of the drugs, K-506, was approved by the FDA in 1994, and some data suggest that up to 8% more adult liver-transplant patients and 15% more pediatric patients survive with the drug than with cyclosporine. Although the drug was approved only for liver transplants, some studies of patients receiving it for transplanted kidneys, bone marrow, and intestines indicate that it may also be more effective than cyclosporine in such cases.

Because of the relatively high rate of success in organ transplants, the need for organs (kidneys in particular) is always greater than the supply. (The black-market operation in Cook's novel is not wholly unrealistic.) In such a situation, where scarcity and need conflict, it is frequently necessary to decide who among the candidates for a transplant will receive an available organ. Relatively objective considerations such as the "goodness" of tissue matching, the size of the organ, and the general medical condition of the candidates may rule out some individuals. But it does happen that choices have to be made.

Who should make such choices? Should they be made by a physician, following his or her own intuitions? Should they be made by a committee or board? If so, who should be on the committee? Should a patient have a representative to speak for his or her interest— someone to "make a case" for receiving the transplant organ?

Should the decision be made in accordance with a set of explicit criteria? If so, then what criteria are appropriate? Are matters such as age, race, sex, and place of residence irrelevant? Should the character and accomplishments of the candidates be given any weight? Should people be judged by their estimated "worth to the community"? Should the fact that someone is a parent be given any weight?

What if one is a smoker, an alcoholic, or obese? Are these to be considered "medical" or "behavioral" risk factors that may legitimately be employed to eliminate someone as a candidate for a transplant? Or, on the other hand, are these aspects of people's chosen "life-style" that cannot be used as a basis for denying them an organ needed to save their lives?

These are just some of the questions relevant to the general issue of deciding how to allocate medical goods in situations in which the available supply is surpassed by a present need. Transplant organs are an example of one type of goods. In the future, assuming an improvement in transplant technology, the allocation of organs will no doubt become an even more frequent problem than at present. It is, of course, already a serious moral problem. (See Social Context: Distributing Transplant Organs.)

It was not organ transplants that first called public attention to the issue of resource allocation. This occurred most dramatically in the early 1960s when the Artificial Kidney Center in Seattle, Washington, initiated an effective large-scale treatment program for people with renal diseases. Normal kidneys filter waste products from the blood that have accumulated as a result of ordinary cellular metabolism—salt, urea, creatinine, potassium, uric acid, and other substances. These waste products are sent from the kidneys to the bladder, where they are then secreted as urine. Kidney failure, which can result from one of a number of diseases, allows waste products to build up in the blood. This can cause high blood pressure and even heart failure, tissue edema (swelling), and muscular seizure. If unremedied, the condition results in death.

When renal failure occurs, hemodialysis is a way of cleansing the blood of waste products by passing it through a cellophane-like tube immersed in a chemical bath. The impurities in the blood pass through the membrane and into the chemical bath by osmosis, and the purified blood is then returned to the patient's body.

At the beginning of the Seattle program, there were many more candidates for dialysis than there were units ("kidney machines") to accommodate them. As a response to this situation, the Kidney Center set up a committee to select patients who would receive treatment. (See the Case Presentation for an account of how such a committee might work.) In effect, the committee was offering to some a better chance for life than they would have without access to dialysis equipment.

As other centers and hospitals established renal units, they faced the same painful decisions that Seattle did. Almost always there were many more patients needing hemodialysis than there was equipment available to treat them. It was partly in response to this situation that Section 299-1 of Public Law 92-603 was passed by Congress in 1972. Those with end-stage renal disease who require hemodialysis or kidney transplants are now guaranteed treatment under Medicare.

More than 195,000 patients are now receiving dialysis paid for by Medicare. Present costs are over $8 billion per year, and the patient load is expected to increase by about 40,000 per year. By the end of the century, some 350,000 patients are predicted to be enrolled in the program, at a cost of more than $10 billion.

Although the average cost of each treatment session dropped from $150 in 1973 to $115 in 1993, many more groups of patients now have dialysis than were treated earlier. In particular, the treatment population now includes many more elderly and diabetic people than was envisioned when the dialysis program was established.

Quite apart from the cost, which is about four times higher than originally expected, dialysis continues to present moral difficulties. Resources are still finite so that at a given time (although with less frequency now than even a short wile ago) more patients may both need and want dialysis than can be accommodated. Hence, the need to make choices among patients is still present, and this brings with it all the problems that we have discussed.

In addition, because more dialysis equipment is available and is financially available to virtually everyone, physicians face a serious difficulty. Even if a physician believes that a patient is not likely to gain benefits from dialysis sufficient to justify the expense, should she recommend the patient for dialysis anyway? Not to do so may mean almost certain death for the patient in the near future, yet the social cost (measured in terms of the cost of equipment and its operation, hospital facilities, and the time of physicians, nurses, and technicians) may be immense. It can be $100,000 or more per year for a single person.

Nor does dialysis solve all problems for patients with terminal kidney diseases. Although time spent on the machine varies, some patients spend five hours, three days per week, attached to the machine. Medical and psychological problems are typical even when the process works at its most efficient. Prolonged dialysis can produce neurological disorders, severe headaches, gastrointestinal bleeding, and bone diseases. Psychological and physical stress is always present, and particularly before dialysis treatments, severe depression is common. One study showed that 5% of dialysis patients take their own lives, and "passive suicide," resulting from dropping out of treatment programs, is the third most common cause of death among older dialysis patients. (The overall death rate for those on dialysis is about 25% per year. The worst outlook is for diabetics starting dialysis at age 55 or older. After one year, only 18% are still alive.) For these reasons, strong motivation, psychological stability, age, and a generally sound physical condition are factors considered important in deciding whether to admit a person to dialysis.

The characteristics required to make someone a "successful" dialysis patient are to some extent "middle-class virtues." A patient must not only be motivated to save his life, but he must also understand the need for the dialysis, be capable of adhering to a strict diet, show up for scheduled dialysis sessions, and so on. As a consequence, where decisions about whether to admit a patient to dialysis are based on estimates of the likelihood of the patient's doing what is required, members of the white middle class have a definite edge over others. Selection criteria that are apparently objective may actually involve hidden class or racial bias.

Various ways of dealing with both the costs and the personal problems presented by dialysis are currently under discussion. In the view of some, increasing the number of kidney transplants would do the most to improve the lives of patients and to reduce the cost of the kidney program. (This would have the result of increasing even more the demand for transplant organs. See the Social Context: Distributing Transplant Organs for a discussion of proposals for doing this.) Others have pressed for training more patients to perform home dialysis, which is substantially cheaper than dialysis performed in clinics or hospitals. However, those who are elderly, live alone, or lack adequate facilities are not likely to be able to use and maintain the complicated equipment involved. Other things being equal, should such people be given priority for transplants?

Some critics have questioned the legitimacy of the dialysis program and pointed to it as an example of social injustice. While it is true that thousands of people have benefited from the program, why should kidney disease be treated differently from other diseases? Why should the treatment of kidney disease alone be federally funded? Why shouldn't the society also pay for the treatment of those afflicted with cancer or neurological disorders?

Perhaps only the development of a new national health-care policy will render this criticism irrelevant.

The problems of transplants and dialysis involve decisions that affect individuals in a direct and immediate way. For example, either a person is accepted into a dialysis program or he is not. As we will see in the next chapter, there are a number of broader social issues connected with providing and distributing medical resources. But our concern here is with the sort of decision making that involves the welfare of particular people in specific situations. The situations are ones in which there is not enough of what is needed to go around. The basic question, of course, is who shall get it and who shall go without?

Any commodity or service that can be in short supply relative to the need for it raises the issue of fair and justifiable distribution. Decisions that control the supply itself, that determine, for example, what proportion of the federal budget will be spent on medical care, are generally referred to as *macroallocation* decisions. These are the large-scale decisions that do not involve individuals in a direct way. Similarly, deciding what proportion of the money allocated to health care should be spent on dialysis is another example of a macroallocation decision.

By contrast, *microallocation* decisions are ones that directly impinge on individuals. Thus, when one donor heart is available and six people in need of a transplant make a claim on it, the decision as to who gets the heart is a microallocation decision. In Chapter 10, in discussing the claim to health care, we will focus more on macroallocation, but in this chapter we will be concerned mostly with microallocation. (The distinction between macroallocation and microallocation is often less clear than the explanation here suggests. After all, there are many levels of decision making in the distribution of resources, and the terms "macro" and "micro" are relative ones.)

Although the examples we have considered have been restricted to transplant organs and dialysis machines, the question of fair distribution can be raised just as appropriately about cardiac resuscitation teams, microsurgical teams, space in burn units or intensive-care wards, hospital beds, drugs and vaccines, medical-evacuation helicopters, operating rooms, physicians' time, and all other medical goods and services that are in limited supply with respect to the demand for them.

Earlier, in connection with transplants, we considered some of the more specific questions that have to be asked about distribution. The questions generally fall into two categories: Who shall decide? What criteria or standards should be employed in making the allocation decision? These are the questions that must be answered whenever there is scarcity relative to needs and wants.

ETHICAL THEORIES AND THE ALLOCATION OF MEDICAL RESOURCES

An analogy that is frequently used in the discussion of the distribution of limited medical resources compares such a situation to the plight of a group of people adrift in a lifeboat. If some of the group are sacrificed, then the others will have a much better chance of surviving. But who should be sacrificed?

One answer to this question is that no one should be. Simply by virtue of being human, each person in the lifeboat has an equal worth. An action that involved sacrificing anyone for the good of the others in the boat would not be morally defensible. This suggests that the only right course of action would be simply to do nothing.

This point of view is one that may be regarded as compatible with Kant's ethical principles. Because each individual may be considered to have inherent value, considerations such as talent, intelligence, age, social worth, and so on are morally irrelevant. Accordingly, there seem to be no grounds for distinguishing those who are to be sacrificed from those who may be saved. In the medical context, this would mean that when there are not enough goods and services to go around, then no one should receive them.

This is not a result that is dictated by Kant's principles, however. One might also ar-

gue that the fact that every person is equal to every other in dignity and worth does not require the sacrifice of all. A random procedure—such as drawing straws—might be used to determine who is to have an increased chance of survival. In such a case, each person is being treated as having equal value, and the person who loses might be regarded as exercising autonomy by sacrificing himself or herself.

The maxim underlying the sacrifice would, apparently, be one that would meet the test of the categorical imperative. Any rational person might be expected to sacrifice himself in such a situation and under the conditions in which the decision was made. In the case of medical resources, a random procedure would seem to be a morally legitimate procedure.

The natural law view and Ross's would seem to support a similar line of argument. Although we all have a duty, on these views, to preserve our lives, this does not mean that we do not sometimes have to risk them. Just such a risk might be involved in agreeing to abide by the outcome of a random procedure to decide who will be sacrificed and who saved.

Utilitarianism does not dictate a specific answer to the question of who, if anyone, should be saved. It does differ radically in one respect, however, from those moral views that ascribe an intrinsic value to each human life. The principle of utility suggests that we ought to take into account the consequences of sacrificing some people rather than others. Who, for example, is more likely to make a contribution to the general welfare of the society, an accountant or a nurse? This approach opens the way to considering the "social worth" of people and makes morally relevant such characteristics as education, occupation, age, record of accomplishment, and so on.

To take this approach would require working out a set of criteria to assign value to various properties of people. Those to be sacrificed would be those whose point total put them at the low end of the ranking. Here, then, a typical "calculus of utilities" would be relied on to solve the decision problem. The decision problem about the allocation of medical resources would follow exactly the same pattern.

This approach is not one required by the principle of utility, however, Someone might argue that a policy formulated along those lines would have so many harmful social consequences that some other solution would be preferable. Thus, a utilitarian might argue that a better policy would be one based on some random process. In connection with medical goods and services, a "first-come, first-served" approach might be superior. (This is a possible option for rule utilitarianism. It could be argued that an act utilitarian would be forced to adopt the first approach.)

Rawls's principles of justice seem clearly to rule out distributing medical resources on the criterion of "social worth." Where special benefits are to be obtained, those benefits must be of value to all and open to all. It is compatible with Rawls's view, of course, that there should be no special medical resources. But if there are, and they must be distributed under conditions of scarcity, then some genuinely fair procedure, such as random selection, must be the procedure used.

No ethical theory that we have considered gives a straightforward answer to the question of who shall make the selection. Where a procedure is random or first-come, first-served, the decision-making process requires only establishing the right kind of social arrangements to implement the policy. Only when social worth must be judged and considered as a relevant factor in decision making does the procedure assume importance. (This is assuming that medical decisions about appropriateness—decisions that establish a class of candidates for the limited resources—have already been made.)

A utilitarian answer as to who shall make the allocation decision might be that the decision should be made by those who are in a good position to judge the likelihood of an individual's contributing to the welfare of the society as a whole. Since physicians are not uniquely qualified to make such judgments, leaving decisions to an individual physician or a committee of physicians would not be the best approach. A better one would probably be to rely on a committee composed of a variety of people representative of the society.

There are many more questions of a moral kind connected with the allocation of scarce resources than we have mentioned here. We have not, for example, considered whether an individual should be allowed to make a case for receiving resources. Nor have we examined any of the problems with employing specific criteria for selection (such as requiring that a person be a resident of a certain community or state). We have, however, touched upon enough of the basic issues that it should be easy to see how other appropriate questions might be asked.

The Allocation of Exotic Medical Lifesaving Therapy

Nicholas Rescher

Nicholas Rescher makes a useful distinction between two kinds of criteria: criteria of inclusion (for the selection of candidates) and criteria of comparison (for section of recipients). Rescher argues that three areas need to be considered in establishing a class of candidates: (1) constituency (Is the person a member of the community the institution is designed to serve?); (2) progress of science (Can new knowledge be gained from the case?); and (3) success (Is the treatment of the person likely to be effective?).

Five factors, Rescher claims, ought to be considered in deciding upon recipients of the goods or services: (1) the likelihood of successful treatment compared with others in the group; (2) the life expectancy of the person; (3) the person's family role, (4) the potential of the person in making future contributions; and (5) the person's record of services or contributions.

Rescher argues that it is necessary to have a rational selection system, but he admits that the exact manner in which a system takes into account relevant factors cannot be fixed and exact. In his view, which is basically a utilitarian one, an acceptable selection system might be one that makes use of point ratings of the factors mentioned above. This would establish a smaller group, but as a final step, he suggests, the best procedure might well be to make use of a chance factor (such as a lottery) to choose recipients.

I. The Problem

Technological progress has in recent years transformed the limits of the possible in medical therapy. However, the elevated state of sophistication of modern medical technology has brought the economists' classic problem of scarcity in its wake as an unfortunate side product. The enormously sophisticated and complex equipment and the highly trained teams of experts requisite for its utilization are scarce resources in relation to potential demand. The administrators of the great medical institutions that preside over these scarce resources thus come to be faced increasingly with the awesome choice: *Whose life to save?*

A (somewhat hypothetical) paradigm example of this problem may be sketched within the following set of definitive assumptions: We suppose that persons in some particular medically morbid condition are "mortally afflicted": It is virtually certain that they will die within a short time period (say ninety days). We assume that some very complex course of treatment (e.g., a heart transplant) represents a substantial probability of life prolongation for persons in this mortally afflicted condition. We assume that the facilities available in terms of human resources, mechanical instrumentalities, and requisite materials (e.g., hearts in the case of heart transplant) make it possible to give a certain treatment—this "exotic (medical) lifesaving therapy," or ELT for short—to a certain, relativity small number of people. And finally we assume that a substantially greater pool of people in the mortally afflicted condition is at hand. The problem then may be formulated as follows: How is one to select within the pool of afflicted patients the ones to be given the ELT treatment in question; how to select those "whose lives are to be saved"? Faced with many candidates for an ELT process that can be made available to only a few, doctors and medical administrators confront the decision of who is to be given a chance at survival and who is, in effect, to be condemned to die.

As has already been implied, the "heroic" variety of spare-part surgery can pretty well be assimilated to this paradigm. One can foresee the time when heart transplantation, for example, will have become pretty much a routine medical procedure, albeit on a very limited basis, since a cardiac surgeon with the technical competence to transplant hearts can operate at best a rather small number of times each week and the elaborate facilities for such operations will most probably exist on a modest scale. Moreover, in "spare-part" surgery there is always the problem of availability of the "spare parts" themselves. A report in one British newspaper gives the following picture: "Of the 150,000 who die of heart disease each year [in the U.K.], Mr. Donald Longmore, research surgeon at the National Heart Hospital [in London] estimated that 22,000 might be eligible for heart surgery. Another 30,000 would need heart and lung transplants. But there are probably only between 7,000 and 14,000 potential donors a year." Envisaging this situation in which at the very most something like one in four heart-malfunction victims can be saved, we clearly confront a problem in ELT allocation.

A perhaps even more drastic case in point is

Reprinted from *Ethics* 79 (April 1969), by permission of The University of Chicago Press and the author. © The University of Chicago Press. (*Notes omitted.*)

afforded by long-term haemodialysis, an ongoing process by which a complex device—an "artificial kidney machine"—is used periodically in cases of chronic renal failure to substitute for a nonfunctional kidney in "cleaning" potential poisons from the blood. Only a few major institutions have chronic haemodialysis units, whose complex operation is an extremely expensive proposition. For the present and foreseeable future the situation is that "the number of places available for chronic haemodialysis is hopelessly inadequate."

The traditional medical ethos has insulated the physician against facing the very existence of this problem. When swearing the Hippocratic Oath, he commits himself to work for the benefit of the sick in "whatsoever house I enter." In taking this stance, the physician substantially renounces the explicit choice of saving certain lives rather than others. Of course, doctors have always in fact had to face such choices on the battlefield or in times of disaster, but there the issue had to be resolved hurriedly, under pressure, and in circumstances in which the very nature of the case effectively precluded calm deliberation by the decision maker as well as criticism by others. In sharp contrast, however, cases of the type we have postulated in the present discussion arise predictably, and represent choices to be made deliberately and "in cold blood."

It is, to begin with, appropriate to remark that this problem is not fundamentally a medical problem. For when there are sufficiently many afflicted candidates for ELT then—so we may assume—there will also be more than enough for whom the purely medical grounds for ELT allocation are decisively strong in any individual case, and just about equally strong throughout the group. But in this circumstance a selection of some afflicted patients over and against others cannot *ex hypothesi* be made on the basis of purely medical considerations.

The selection problem, as we have said, is in substantial measure not a medical one. It is a problem *for* medical men, which must somehow be solved by them, but that does not make it a medical issue—any more than the problem of hospital building is a medical issue. As a problem it belongs to the category of philosophical problems—specifically a problem of moral philosophy or ethics. Structurally, it bears a substantial kinship with those issues in this field that revolve about the notorious whom-to-save-on-the-lifeboat and whom-to-throw-to-the-wolves-pursuing-the-sled questions. But whereas questions of this just-indicated sort are

artificial, hypothetical, and farfetched, the ELT issue poses a genuine policy question for the responsible administrators in medical institutions, indeed a question that threatens to become commonplace in the foreseeable future.

Now what the medical administrator needs to have, and what the philosopher is presumably *ex officio* in a position to help in providing, is a body of *rational guidelines* for making choices in these literally life-or-death situations. This is an issue in which many interested parties have a substantial stake, including the responsible decision maker who wants to satisfy his conscience that he is acting in a reasonable way. Moreover, the family and associates of the man who is turned away—to say nothing of the man himself—have the right to an acceptable explanation. And indeed even the general public wants to know that what is being done is fitting and proper. All of these interested parties are entitled to insist that a reasonable code of operating principles provides a defensible rationale for making the life-and-death choices involved in ELT.

II. The Two Types of Criteria

Two distinguishable types of criteria are bound up in the issue of making ELT choices. We shall call these *Criteria of Inclusion* and *Criteria of Comparison*, respectively. The distinction at issue here requires some explanation. We can think of the selection as being made by a two-stage process: (1) the selection from among all possible candidates (by a suitable screening process) of a group to be taken under serious consideration as candidates for therapy, and then (2) the actual singling out, within this group, of the particular individuals to whom therapy is to be given. Thus the first process narrows down the range of comparative choices by eliminating *en bloc* whole categories of potential candidates. The second process calls for a more refined case-by-case comparison of those candidates that remain. By means of the first set of criteria one forms a selection group; by means of the second set, an actual selection is made within this group.

Thus what we shall call a "selection system" for the choice of patients to receive therapy of the ELT type will consist of criteria of these two kinds. Such a system will be acceptable only when the reasonableness of its component criteria can be established.

III. Essential Features of an Acceptable ELT Selection System

To qualify as reasonable, an ELT selection must meet two important "regulative" requirements: it must be *simple* enough to be readily intelligible, and it must be *plausible,* that is, patently reasonable in a way that can be apprehended easily and without involving ramified subtleties. Those medical administrators responsible for ELT choices must follow a modus operandi that virtually all the people involved can readily understand to be acceptable (at a reasonable level of generality, at any rate). Appearances are critically important here. It is not enough that the choice be made in a *justifiable* way; it must be possible for people—*plain* people— to "see" (i.e., understand without elaborate teaching or indoctrination) that *it is justified,* insofar as any mode of procedure can be justified in cases of this sort.

One "constitutive" requirement is obviously an essential feature of a reasonable selection system: all of its component criteria—those of inclusion and those of comparison alike—must be reasonable in the sense of being *rationally defensible.* The ramifications of this requirement call for detailed consideration. But one of its aspects should be noted without further ado: it must be *fair*—it must treat relevantly like cases alike, leaving no room for "influence" or favoritism, etc.

IV. The Basic Screening Stage: Criteria of Inclusion (and Exclusion)

Three sorts of considerations are prominent among the plausible criteria of inclusion/exclusion at the basic screening stage: the constituency factor, the progress-of-science factor, and the prospect-of-success factor.

A. The Constituency Factor

It is a "fact of life" that ELT can be available only in the institutional setting of a hospital or medical institute or the like. Such institutions generally have normal clientele boundaries. A veterans' hospital will not concern itself primarily with treating non-veterans, a children's hospital cannot be expected to accommodate the "senior citizen," an army hospital can regard college professors as outside its sphere. Sometimes the boundaries are geographic—a state hospital may admit only residents of a certain state. (There are, of course, indefensible constituency principles—say race or religion, party membership, or ability to pay; and there are cases of borderline legitimacy, e.g., sex.) A medical institution is justified in considering for ELT only persons within its own constituency, provided this constituency is constituted upon a defensible basis. Thus the haemodialysis selection committee in Seattle "agreed to consider only those applications who were residents of the state of Washington. They justified this stand on the grounds that since the basic research . . . had been done at . . . a state-supported institution—the people whose taxes had paid for the research should be its first beneficiaries."

While thus insisting that constituency considerations represent a valid and legitimate factor in ELT selection, I do feel there is much to be said for minimizing their role in life-or-death cases. Indeed a refusal to recognize them at all is a significant part of medical tradition, going back to the very oath of Hippocrates. They represent a departure from the ideal arising with the institutionalization of medicine, moving it away from its original status as an art practiced by an individual practitioner.

B. The Progress-of-Science Factor

The needs of medical research can provide a second valid principle of inclusion. The research interests of the medical staff in relation to the specific nature of the cases at issue is a significant consideration. It may be important for the progress of medical science—and thus of potential benefit to many persons in the future—to determine how effective the ELT at issue is with diabetics or persons over sixty or with a negative RH factor. Considerations of this sort represent another type of legitimate factor in ELT selection. A very definitely *borderline* case under this head would revolve around the question of a patient's willingness to pay, not in monetary terms, but in offering himself as an experimental subject, say by contracting to return at designated times for a series of tests substantially unrelated to his own health, but yielding data of importance to medical knowledge in general.

C. The Prospect-of-Success Factor

It may be that while the ELT at issue is not without *some* effectiveness in general, it has been established to be highly effective only with patients in certain specific categories (e.g., females under forty of a specific blood type). This difference in effectiveness—in the absolute or in the probability of success—is (we assume) so marked as to constitute virtually a difference in kind rather than in degree. In this case, it would be perfectly legitimate to adopt the general rule of making the ELT at issue available only or primarily to persons in this substantial-promise-of-success category. (It is on grounds of this sort that young children and persons over fifty are generally ruled out as candidates for haemodialysis.)

We have maintained that the three factors of constituency, progress of science, and prospect of success represent legitimate criteria of inclusion for ELT selection. But it remains to examine the considerations which legitimate them. The legitimating factors are in the final analysis practical or pragmatic in nature. From the practical angle it is advantageous—indeed to some extent necessary that the arrangements governing medical institutions should embody certain constituency principles. It makes good pragmatic and utilitarian sense that progress-of-science considerations should be operative here. And, finally, the practical aspect is reinforced by a whole host of other considerations—including moral ones—in supporting the prospect-of-success criterion. The workings of each of these factors are of course conditioned by the ever-present element of limited availability. They are operative only in this context, that is, prospect of success is a legitimate consideration at all only because we are dealing with a situation of scarcity.

V. The Final Selection Stage: Criteria of Selection

Five sorts of elements must, as we see it, figure primarily among the plausible criteria of selection that are to be brought to bear in further screening the group constituted after application of the criteria of inclusion: the relative-likelihood-of-success factor, the life-expectancy factor, the family role factor, the potential-contributions factor, and the services-rendered factor. The first two represent the *biomedical* aspect, the second three the *social* aspect.

A. The Relative-Likelihood-of-Success Factor

It is clear that the relative likelihood of success is a legitimate and appropriate factor in making a selection within the group of qualified patients that

are to receive ELT. This is obviously one of the considerations that must count very significantly in a reasonable selection procedure.

The present criterion is of course closely related to item C of the preceding section. There we were concerned with prospect-of-success considerations categorically and *en bloc*. Here at present they come into play in a particularized case-by-case comparison among individuals. If the therapy at issue is not a once-and-for-all proposition and requires ongoing treatment, cognate considerations must be brought in. Thus, for example, in the case of a chronic ELT procedure such as haemodialysis it would clearly make sense to give priority to patients with a potentially reversible condition (who would thus need treatment for only a fraction of their remaining lives).

B. The Life-Expectancy Factor

Even if the ELT is "successful" in the patient's case he may, considering his age and/or other aspects of his general medical condition, look forward to only a very short probable future life. This is obviously another factor that must be taken into account.

C. The Family Role Factor

A person's life is a thing of importance not only to himself but to others—friends, associates, neighbors, colleagues, etc. But his (or her) relationship to his immediate family is a thing of unique intimacy and significance. The nature of his relationship to his wife, children, and parents, and the issue of their financial and psychological dependence upon him, are obviously matters that deserve to be given weight in the ELT selection process. Other things being anything like equal, the mother of minor children must take priority over the middle-aged bachelor.

D. The Potential Future-Contributions Factor (Prospective Service)

In "choosing to save" one life rather than another, "the society," through the mediation of the particular medical institution in question—which should certainly look upon itself as a trustee for the social interest—is clearly warranted in considering the likely pattern of future *services to be rendered* by the patient (adequate recovery assumed), considering his age, talent, training, and past record of performance. In its allocations of ELT, society "invests" a scarce resource in one person as against another and is thus entitled to look to the probable prospective "return" on its investment.

It may well be that a thoroughly egalitarian society is reluctant to put someone's social contribution into the scale in situations of the sort at issue. One popular article states that "the most difficult standard would be the candidate's value to society," and goes on to quote someone who said: "You can't just pick a brilliant painter over a laborer. The average citizen would be quickly eliminated." But what if it were not a brilliant painter but a brilliant surgeon or medical researcher that was at issue? One wonders if the author of the *obiter dictum* that one "can't just pick" would still feel equally sure of his ground. In any case, the fact that the standard is difficult to apply is certainly no reason for not attempting to apply it. The problem of ELT selection is inevitably burdened with difficult standards.

Some might feel that in assessing a patient's value to society one should ask not only who if permitted to continue living can make the greatest contribution to society in some creative or constructive way, but also who by dying would leave behind the greatest burden on society in assuming the discharge of their residual responsibilities. Certainly the philosophical utilitarian would give equal weight to both these considerations. Just here is where I would part ways with orthodox utilitarianism. For—though this is not the place to do so—I should be prepared to argue that a civilized society has an obligation to promote the furtherance of positive achievements in cultural and related areas even if this means the assumption of certain added burdens.

E. The Past Services-Rendered Factor (Retrospective Service)

A person's services to another person or group have always been taken to constitute a valid basis for a claim upon this person or group—of course a moral and not necessarily a legal claim. Society's obligation for the recognition and reward of services rendered—an obligation whose discharge is also very possibly conductive to self-interest in the long run—is thus another factor to be taken into account. This should be viewed as a morally necessary correlative of the previously considered factor of *prospective* service. It would be morally indefensible of society in effect to say: "Never mind about services you rendered yesterday—it is only the services to be rendered tomorrow that will count with

us today." We live in very future-oriented times, constantly preoccupied in a distinctly utilitarian way with future satisfactions. And this disinclines us to give much recognition to past services. But parity considerations of the sort just adduced indicate that such recognition should be given *on grounds of equity*. No doubt a justification for giving weight to services rendered can also be attempted along utilitarian lines. ("The reward of past services rendered spurs people on to greater future efforts and is thus socially advantageous in the long-run future.") In saying that past services should be counted "on grounds of equity"—rather than "on grounds of utility"—I take the view that even if this utilitarian defense could somehow be shown to be fallacious, I should still be prepared to maintain the propriety of taking services rendered into account. The position does not rest on a utilitarian basis and so would not collapse with the removal of such a basis.

As we have said, these five factors fall into three groups: the biomedical factors *A* and *B*, the familial factor *C*, and the social factors *D* and *E*. With items *A* and *B* the need for a detailed analysis of the medical considerations comes to the fore. The age of the patient, his medical history, his physical and psychological condition, his specific disease, etc., will all need to be taken into exact account. These biomedical factors represent technical issues: they call for the physicians' expert judgment and the medical statisticians' hard data. And they are ethically uncontroversial factors—their legitimacy and appropriateness are evident from the very nature of the case.

Greater problems arise with the familial aid social factors. They involve intangibles that are difficult to judge. How is one to develop subcriteria for weighing the relative social contributions of (say) an architect or a librarian or a mother of young children? And they involve highly problematic issues. (For example, should good moral character be rated a plus and bad a minus in judging services rendered?) And there is something strikingly unpleasant in grappling with issues of this sort for people brought up in times greatly inclined towards maxims of the type "Judge not!" and "Live and let live!" All the same, in the situation that concerns us here such distasteful problems must be faced, since a failure to choose to save some is tantamount to sentencing all. Unpleasant choices are intrinsic to the problem of ELT selection; they are of the very essence of the matter.

But is reference to all these factors indeed inevitable? The justification for taking account of the medical factors is pretty obvious. But why should the social aspect of services rendered and to be rendered be taken into account at all? The answer is that they must be taken into account not from the *medical* but from the *ethical* point of view. Despite disagreement on many fundamental issues, moral philosophers of the present day are pretty well in consensus that the justification of human actions is to be sought largely and primarily—if not exclusively—in the principles of utility and of justice. But utility requires reference of services to be rendered and justice calls for a recognition of services that have been rendered. Moral considerations would thus demand recognition of these two factors. (This, of course, still leaves open the question of whether the point of view provides a valid basis of action: Why base one's actions upon moral principles—or, to put it bluntly—Why be moral? The present paper is, however, hardly the place to grapple with so fundamental an issue, which has been canvassed in the literature of philosophical ethics since Plato.)

VI. More Than Medical Issues Are Involved

An active controversy has of late sprung up in medical circles over the question of whether nonphysician laymen should be given a role in ELT selection (in the specific context of chronic haemodialysis). One physician writes: "I think that the assessment of the candidates should be made by a senior doctor on the [dialysis] unit, but I am sure that it would be helpful to him—both in sharing responsibility and in avoiding personal pressure—if a small unnamed group of people [presumably including laymen] officially made the final decision. I visualize the doctor bringing the data to the group, explaining the points in relation to each case, and obtaining their approval of his order of priority."

Essentially this procedure of a selection committee of laymen has for some years been in use in one of the most publicized chronic dialysis units, that of the Swedish Hospital of Seattle, Washington. Many physicians are apparently reluctant to see the choice of allocation of medical therapy pass out of strictly medical hands. Thus in a recent symposium

on the "Selection of Patients for Haemodialysis," Dr. Ralph Shakman writes: "Who is to implement the selection? In my opinion it must ultimately be the responsibility of the consultants in charge of the renal units . . . I can see no reason for delegating this responsibility to lay persons. Surely the latter would be better employed if they could be persuaded to devote their time and energy to raise more and more money for us to spend on our patients." Other contributors to this symposium strike much the same note. Dr. F. M. Parsons writes: "In an attempt to overcome . . . difficulties in selection some have advocated introducing certain specified lay people into the discussions. Is it wise? I doubt whether a committee of this type can adjudicate as satisfactorily as two medical colleagues, particularly as successful therapy involves close cooperation between doctor and patient." And Dr. M. A. Wilson writes in the same symposium: "The suggestion has been made that lay panels should select individuals for dialysis from among a group who are medically suitable. Though this would relieve the doctor-in-charge of a heavy load of responsibility, it would place the burden on those who have no personal knowledge and have to base their judgments on medical or social reports. I do not believe this would result in better decisions for the group or improve the doctor-patient relationship in individual cases."

But no amount of flag waving about the doctor's facing up to his responsibility—or prostrations before the idol of the doctor-patient relationship and reluctance to admit laymen into the sacred precincts of the conference chambers of medical consultations—can obscure the essential fact that ELT selection is not a wholly medical problem. When there are more than enough places in an ELT program to accommodate all who need it, then it will clearly be a medical question to decide who does have the need and which among these would successfully respond. But when an admitted gross insufficiency of places exists, when there are ten or fifty or one hundred highly eligible candidates for each place in the program, then it is unrealistic to take the view that purely medical criteria can furnish a sufficient basis for selection. The question of ELT selection becomes serious as a phenomenon of scale—because, as more candidates present themselves, strictly medical factors are increasingly less adequate as a selection criterion precisely because by numerical category-crowding there will be more and more cases whose "status is much the same" so far as purely medical considerations go.

The ELT selection problem clearly poses issues that transcend the medical sphere because—in the nature of the case—many residual issues remain to be dealt with once *all* of the medical questions have been faced. Because of this there is good reason why laymen as well as physicians should be involved in the selection process. Once the medical considerations have been brought to bear, fundamental social issues remain to be resolved. The instrumentalities of ELT have been created through the social investment of scarce resources, and the interests of the society deserve to play a role in their utilization. As representatives of their social interests, lay opinions should function to complement and supplement medical views once the proper arena of medical considerations is left behind. Those physicians who have urged the presence of lay members on selection panels can, from this point of view, be recognized as having seen the issue in proper perspective

One physician has argued against lay representation on selection panels for haemodialysis as follows: "If the doctor advises dialysis and the lay panel refuses, the patient will regard this as a death sentence passed by an anonymous court from which he has no right of appeal." But this drawback is not specific to the use of a lay panel. Rather, it is a feature inherent in every *selection* procedure, regardless of whether the selection is done by the head doctor of the unit, by a panel of physicians, etc. No matter who does the selecting among patients recommended for dialysis, the feelings of the patient who has been rejected (and knows it) can be expected to be much the same, provided that he recognizes the actual nature of the choice (and is not deceived by the possibly convenient but ultimately poisonous fiction that because the selection was made by physicians it was made entirely on medical grounds).

In summary, then, the question of ELT selection would appear to be one that is in its very nature heavily laden with issues of medical research, practice, and administration. But it will not be a question that can be resolved on solely medical grounds. Strictly social issues of justice and utility will invariably arise in this area—questions going outside the medical area in whose resolution medical laymen can and should play a substantial role.

VII. The Inherent Imperfection (Non-Optimality) of Any Selection System

Our discussion to this point of the design of a selection system for ELT has left a gap that is a very fundamental and serious omission. We have argued that five factors must be taken into substantial and explicit account:

A. *Relative likelihood of success.* Is the chance of the treatment's being "successful" to be rated as high, good, average, etc.?

B. *Expectancy of future life.* Assuming the "success" of the treatment, how much longer does the patient stand a good chance (75 per cent or better) of living—considering his age and general condition?

C. *Family role.* To what extent does the patient have responsibilities to others in his immediate family?

D. *Social contributions to be rendered.* Are the patient's past services to his society outstanding, substantial, average, etc.?

E. *Social contributions to be rendered.* Considering his age, talents, training, and past record of performance, is there a substantial probability that the patient will—*adequate recovery being assured*—render in the future services to his society that can be characterized as outstanding, substantial, average, etc.?

This list is clearly insufficient for the construction of a reasonable selection system, since that would require not only *that these factors be taken into account* (somehow or other), but—going beyond this—would specify *a specific set of procedures for taking account of them.* The specific procedures that would constitute such a system would have to take account of the interrelationship of these factors (e.g., *B* and *E*), and to set out exact guidelines as to the relevant weight that is to be given to each of them. This is something our discussion has not as yet considered.

In fact, I should want to maintain that there is no such thing here as a single rationally superior selection system. The position of affairs seems to me to be something like this: (1) It is necessary (for reasons already canvassed) to have a system, and to have a system that is rationally defensible, and

(2) to be rationally defensible, this system must take the factors *A–E* into substantial and explicit account. But (3) the exact manner in which a rationally defensible system takes account of these factors cannot be fixed in any one specific way on the basis of general considerations. Any of the variety of ways that give *A–E* "their due" will be acceptable and viable. One cannot hope to find within this range of workable systems some one that is optimal in relation to the alternatives. There is no one system that does "the (uniquely) best"—only a variety of systems that do "as well as one can expect to do" in cases of this sort.

The situation is structurally very much akin to that of rules of partition of an estate among the relations of a decedent. It is important *that there be* such rules. And it is reasonable that spouse, children, parents, siblings, etc., be taken account of in these rules. But the question of the exact method of division—say that when the decedent has neither living spouse nor living children then his estate is to be divided, dividing 60 per cent between parents, 40 per cent between siblings versus dividing 90 per cent between parents, 10 per cent between siblings—cannot be settled on the basis of any general abstract considerations of reasonableness. Within broad limits, *a variety* of resolutions are all perfectly acceptable—so that no one procedure can justifiably be regarded as "the (uniquely) best" because it is superior to all others.

VIII. A Possible Basis for a Reasonable Selection System

Having said that there is no such thing as *the optimal* selection system for ELT, I want now to sketch out the broad features of what I would regard as *one acceptable* system.

The basis for the system would be a point rating. The scoring here at issue would give roughly equal weight to the medical considerations (*A* and *B*) in comparison with the extramedical considerations (*C* = family role, *D* = services rendered, and *E* = services to be rendered), also giving roughly equal weight to the three items involved here (*C, D,* and *E*). The result of such a scoring procedure would provide the essential starting point of our ELT selection mechanism. I deliberately say "starting point" because it seems to me that one should not follow the results of this scoring in an *automatic*

way. I would propose that the actual selection should only be guided but not actually be dictated by this scoring procedure, along lines now to be explained.

IX. The Desirability of Introducing an Element of Chance

The detailed procedure I would propose—not of course as optimal (for reasons we have seen), but as eminently acceptable—would combine the scoring procedure just discussed with an element of chance. The resulting selection system would function as follows:

1. First the criteria of inclusion of Section IV above would be applied to constitute a *first phase selection group*—which (we shall suppose) is substantially larger than the number *n* of persons who can actually be accommodated with ELT.

2. Next the criteria of selection of Section V are brought to bear via a scoring procedure of the type described in Section VIII. On this basis a *second phase selection group* is constituted which is only *somewhat* larger—say by a third or a half—than the critical number *n* at issue.

3. If this second phase selection group is relatively homogeneous as regards rating by the scoring procedure—that is, if there are no really major disparities within this group (as would be likely if the initial group was significantly larger than *n*)—then the final selection is made by *random* selection of *n* persons from within this group.

This introduction of the element of chance—in what could be dramatized as a "lottery of life and death"—must be justified. The fact is that such a procedure would bring with it three substantial advantages.

First, as we have argued above (in Section VII), any acceptable selection system is inherently nonoptimal. The introduction of the element of chance prevents the results that life-and-death choices are made by the automatic application of an admittedly imperfect selection method.

Second, a recourse to chance would doubtless make matters easier for the rejected patient and those who have a specific interest in him. It would surely be quite hard for them to accept his exclusion by relatively mechanical application of objective criteria in whose implementation subjective judgment is involved. But the circumstances of life have conditioned us to accept the workings of chance and to tolerate the element of luck (good or bad): human life is an inherently contingent process. Nobody, after all, has an absolute right to ELT—but most of us would feel that we have "every bit as much right" to it as anyone else in significantly similar circumstances. The introduction of the element of chance assures a like handling of like cases over the widest possible area that seems reasonable in the circumstances.

Third (and perhaps least), such a recourse to random selection does much to relieve the administrators of the selection system of the awesome burden of ultimate and absolute responsibility.

These three considerations would seem to build up a substantial case for introducing the element of chance into the mechanism of the system for ELT selection in a way limited and circumscribed by other weightier considerations, along some such lines as those set forth above.

It should be recognized that this injection of *man-made* chance supplements the element of *natural* chance that is present inevitably and in any case (apart from the role of chance in singling out certain persons as victims for the affliction at issue). As F. M. Parsons has observed: "any vacancies [in an ELT program—specifically haemodialysis] will be filled immediately by the first suitable patients, even though their claims for therapy may subsequently prove less than those of other patients refused later." Life is a chancy business and even the most rational of human arrangements can cover this over to a very limited extent at best.

The Prostitute, the Playboy, and the Poet: Rationing Schemes for Organ Transplantation

George J. Annas

George Annas takes a position on transplant selection that introduces a modification of the first-come, first-served principle. He reviews four approaches to rationing scarce medical resources—market, selection committee, lottery, and customary—and finds each has disadvantages so serious as to make them all unacceptable. An acceptable approach, he suggests, is one that combines efficiency, fairness, and a respect for the value of life. Because candidates should both want a transplant and be able to derive significant benefits from one, the first phase of selection should involve a screening process that is based exclusively on medical criteria that are objective and as free as possible of judgments about social worth.

Since selection might still have to be made from this pool of candidates, it might be done by social-worth criteria or by lottery. However, social-worth criteria seem arbitrary, and a lottery would be unfair to those who are in more immediate need of a transplant—ones who might die quickly without it. After reviewing the relevant considerations, a committee operating at this stage might allow those in immediate need of a transplant to be moved to the head of a waiting list. To those not in immediate need, organs would be distributed in a first-come, first-served fashion. Although absolute equality is not embodied in this process, the procedure is sufficiently flexible to recognize that some may have needs that are greater (more immediate) than others.

In the public debate about the availability of heart and liver transplants, the issue of rationing on a massive scale has been credibly raised for the first time in United States medical care. In an era of scarce resources, the eventual arrival of such a discussion was, of course, inevitable.[1] Unless we decide to ban heart and liver transplantation, or make them available to everyone, some rationing scheme must be used to choose among potential transplant candidates. The debate has existed throughout the history of medical ethics. Traditionally it has been stated as a choice between saving one of two patients, both of whom require the immediate assistance of the only available physician to survive.

National attention was focused on decisions regarding the rationing of kidney dialysis machines when they were first used on a limited basis in the late 1960s. As one commentator described the debate within the medical profession:

> "Shall machines or organs go to the sickest, or to the ones with most promise of recovery; on a first-come, first-served basis; to the most 'valuable' patient (based on wealth, education, position, what?); to the one with the most dependents; to women and children first; to those who can pay; to whom? Or should lots be cast, impersonally and uncritically?"[2]

In Seattle, Washington, an anonymous screening committee was set up to pick who among competing candidates would receive the life-saving technology. One lay member of the screening committee is quoted as saying:

> "The choices were hard . . . I remember voting against a young woman who was a known prostitute. I found I couldn't vote for her, rather than another candidate, a young wife and mother. I also voted against a young man who, until he learned he had renal failure, had been a ne'er do-well, a real playboy. He promised he would reform his character, go back to school, and so on, if only he were selected for treatment. But I felt I'd lived long enough to know that a person like that won't really do what he was promising at the time."[3]

When the biases and selection criteria of the committee were made public, there was a general negative reaction against this type of arbitrary device. Two experts reacted to the "numbing accounts of how close to the surface lie the prejudices and mindless cliches that pollute the committee's deliberations," by concluding that the committee was "measuring persons in accordance with its own middle-class values." The committee process, they noted, ruled out "creative nonconformists" and made the Pacific Northwest "no place for a Henry David Thoreau with bad kidneys."[4]

To avoid having to make such explicit, arbitrary, "social worth" determinations, the Congress, in 1972, enacted legislation that provided federal funds for virtually all kidney dialysis and kidney transplantation procedures in the United States.[5] This decision, however, simply served to postpone the time when identical decisions will have to be made about candidates for heart and liver transplantation in a society that does not provide sufficient financial and medical resources to provide all "suitable" candidates with the operation.

There are four major approaches to rationing scarce medical resources: the market approach; the selection committee approach; the lottery approach; and the "customary" approach.[1]

The Market Approach

The market approach would provide an organ to everyone who could pay for it with their own funds or private insurance. It puts a very high value on individual rights, and a very low value on equality and fairness. It has properly been criticized on a number of bases, including that the transplant technologies have been developed and are supported with public funds, that medical resources used for transplantation will not be available for higher priority care, and that financial success alone is an insufficient justification for demanding a medical procedure. Most telling is its complete lack of concern for fairness and equity.[6]

A "bake sale" or charity approach that requires the less financially fortunate to make public appeals for funding is demeaning to the individuals involved, and to society as a whole. Rationing by financial ability says we do not believe in equality, but believe that a price can and should be placed on human life and that it should be paid by the individual whose life is at stake. Neither belief is

Reprinted by permission of the author and *The American Journal of Public Health,* Vol. 75, no. 2, 1985, pp. 187–189.

tolerable in a society in which income is inequitably distributed.

The Committee Selection Process

The Seattle Selection Committee is a model of the committee process. Ethics Committees set up in some hospitals to decide whether or not certain handicapped newborn infants should be given medical care may represent another.[7] These committees have developed because it was seen as unworkable or unwise to explicitly set forth the criteria on which selection decisions would be made. But only two results are possible, as Professor Guido Calabresi has pointed out: either a pattern of decision-making will develop or it will not. If a pattern does develop (e.g., in Seattle, the imposition of middle-class values), then it can be articulated and those decision "rules" codified and used directly, without resort to the committee. If a pattern does not develop, the committee is vulnerable to the charge that it is acting arbitrarily, or dishonestly, and therefore cannot be permitted to continue to make such important decisions.[1]

In the end, public designation of a committee to make selection decisions on vague criteria will fail because it too closely involves the state and all members of society in explicitly preferring specific individuals over others, and in devaluing the interests those others have in living. It thus directly undermines, as surely as the market system does, society's view of equality and the value of human life.

The Lottery Approach

The lottery approach is the ultimate equalizer which puts equality ahead of every other value. This makes it extremely attractive, since all comers have an equal chance at selection regardless of race, color, creed, or financial status. On the other hand, it offends our notions of efficiency and fairness since it makes *no* distinctions among such things as the strength of the desires of the candidates, their potential survival, and their quality of life. In this sense it is a mindless method of trying to solve society's dilemma which is caused by its unwillingness or inability to spend enough resources to make a lottery unnecessary. By making this macro spending decision evident to all, it also undermines society's view of the pricelessness of human life. A first-come, first-served system is a type of natural lottery since referral to a transplant program is generally random in time. Nonetheless, higher income groups have quicker access to referral networks and thus have an inherent advantage over the poor in a strict first-come, first-served system.[8,9]

The Customary Approach

Society has traditionally attempted to avoid explicitly recognizing that we are making a choice not to save individual lives because it is too expensive to do so. As long as such decisions are not explicitly acknowledged, they can be tolerated by society. For example, until recently there was said to be a general understanding among general practitioners in Britain that individuals over age 55 suffering from end-stage kidney disease not be referred for dialysis or transplant. In 1984, however, this unwritten practice became highly publicized, with figures that showed a rate of new cases of end-stage kidney disease treated in Britain at 40 per million (versus the US figure of 80 per million) resulting in 1500–3000 "unnecessary deaths" annually.[10] This has, predictably, led to movements to enlarge the National Health Service budget to expand dialysis services to meet this need, a more socially acceptable solution than permitting the now publicly recognized situation to continue.

In the U.S., the customary approach permits individual physicians to select their patients on the basis of medical criteria or clinical suitability. This, however, contains much hidden social worth criteria. For example, one criterion, common in the transplant literature, requires an individual to have sufficient family support for successful aftercare. This discriminates against individuals without families and those who have become alienated from their families. The criterion may be relevant, but it is hardly medical.

Similar observations can be made about medical criteria that include IQ, mental illness, criminal records, employment, indigency, alcoholism, drug addiction, or geographical location. Age is perhaps more difficult, since it may be impressionistically related to outcome. But it is not medically logical to assume that an individual who is 49 years old is necessarily a better medical candidate for a transplant than one who is 50 years old. Unless specific examination of the characteristics of older persons that make them less desirable candidates is undertaken, such a cut off is arbitrary, and thus devalues the lives of older citizens. The same can be said of blanket exclusions of alcoholics and drug addicts.

In short, the customary approach has one great advantage for society and one great disadvantage: it gives us the illusion that we do not have to make choices; but the cost is mass deception, and when this deception is uncovered, we must deal with it either by universal entitlement or by choosing another method of patient selection.

A Combination of Approaches

A socially acceptable approach must be fair, efficient, and reflective of important social values. The most important values at stake in organ transplantation are fairness itself, equity in the sense of equality, and the value of life. To promote efficiency, it is important that no one receive a transplant unless they want one and are likely to obtain significant benefit from it in the sense of years of life at a reasonable level of functioning.

Accordingly, it is appropriate for there to be an initial screening process that is based *exclusively* on medical criteria designed to measure the probability of a successful transplant, i.e., one in which the patient survives for at least a number of years and is rehabilitated. There is room in medical criteria for social worth judgments, but there is probably no way to avoid this completely. For example, it has been noted that "in many respects social and medical criteria are inextricably intertwined" and that therefore medical criteria might "exclude the poor and disadvantaged because health and socioeconomic status are highly interdependent."[11] Roger Evans gives an example. In the End Stage Renal Disease Program, "those of lower socioeconomic status are likely to have multiple comorbid health conditions such as diabetes, hepatitis, and hypertension" making them both less desirable candidates and more expensive to treat.[11]

To prevent the gulf between the haves and have nots from widening, we must make every reasonable attempt to develop medical criteria that are objective and independent of social worth categories. One minimal way to approach this is to require that medical screening be reviewed and approved by an ethics committee with significant public representation, filed with a public agency,

and made readily available to the public for comment. In the event that more than one hospital in a state or region is offering a particular transplant service, it would be most fair and efficient for the individual hospitals to perform the initial medical screening themselves (based on the uniform, objective criteria), but to have all subsequent nonmedical selection done by a method approved by a single selection committee composed of representatives of all hospitals engaged in a particular transplant procedure, as well as significant representation of the public at large.

As this implies, after the medical screening is performed, there may be more acceptable candidates in the "pool" than there are organs or surgical teams to go around. Selection among waiting candidates will then be necessary. This situation occurs now in kidney transplantation, but since the organ matching is much more sophisticated than in hearts and livers (permitting much more precise matching of organ and recipient), and since dialysis permits individuals to wait almost indefinitely for an organ without risking death, the situations are not close enough to permit use of the same matching criteria. On the other hand, to the extent that organs are specifically tissue- and size-matched and fairly distributed to the best matched candidate, the organ distribution system itself will resemble a natural lottery.

When a pool of acceptable candidates is developed, a decision about who gets the next available, suitable organ must be made. We must choose between using a conscious, value-laden, social worth selection criterion (including a committee to make the actual choice), or some type of random device. In view of the unacceptability and arbitrariness of social worth criteria being applied, implicitly or explicitly, by committee, this method is neither viable nor proper. On the other hand, strict adherence to a lottery might create a situation where an individual who has only a one-in-four chance of living five years with a transplant (but who could survive another six months without one) would get an organ before an individual who could survive as long or longer, but who will die within days or hours if he or she is not immediately transplanted. Accordingly, the most reasonable approach seems to be to allocate organs on a first-come, first-served basis to members of the pool but permit individuals to "jump" the queue if the second level selection committee believes they are in immediate danger of death (but still have a reasonable prospect for long-term survival with a transplant) and the person who would otherwise get the organ can survive long enough to be reasonably assured that he or she will be able to get another organ.

The first-come, first-served method of basic selection (after a medical screen) seems the preferred method because it most closely approximates the randomness of a straight lottery without the obviousness of making equity the only promoted value. Some unfairness is introduced by the fact that the more wealthy and medically astute will likely get into the pool first, and thus be ahead in line, but this advantage should decrease sharply as public awareness of the system grows. The possibility of unfairness is also inherent in permitting individuals to jump the queue, but some flexibility needs to be retained in the system to permit it to respond to reasonable contingencies.

We will have to face the fact that should the resources devoted to organ transplantation be limited (as they are now and are likely to be in the future), at some point it is likely that significant numbers of individuals will die in the pool waiting for a transplant. Three things can be done to avoid this: 1) medical criteria can be made stricter, perhaps by adding a more rigorous notion of "quality" of life to longevity and prospects for rehabilitation; 2) resources devoted to transplantation and organ procurement can be increased; or 3) individuals can be persuaded not to attempt to join the pool.

Of these three options, only the third has the promise of both conserving resources and promoting autonomy. While most persons medically eligible for a transplant would probably want one, some would not—at least if they understood all that was involved, including the need for a lifetime commitment to daily immunosuppression medications, and periodic medical monitoring for rejection symptoms. Accordingly, it makes public policy sense to publicize the risks and side effects of transplantation, and to require careful explanations of the procedure be given to prospective patients *before* they undergo medical screening. It is likely that by the time patients come to the transplant center they have made up their minds and would do almost anything to get the transplant. Nonetheless, if there are patients who, when confronted with all the facts, would voluntarily elect not to proceed, we

enhance both their own freedom and the efficiency and cost-effectiveness of the transplantation system by screening them out as early as possible.

Conclusion

Choices among patients that seem to condemn some to death and give others an opportunity to survive will always be tragic. Society has developed a number of mechanisms to make such decisions more acceptable by camouflaging them. In an era of scarce resources and conscious cost containment, such mechanisms will become public, and they will be usable only if they are fair and efficient. If they are not so perceived, we will shift from one mechanism to another in an effort to continue the illusion that tragic choices really don't have to be made, and that we can simultaneously move toward equity of access, quality of services, and cost containment without any challenges to our values. Along with the prostitute, the playboy, and the poet, we all need to be involved in the development of an access model to extreme and expensive medical technologies with which we can live.

Notes

1. Calabresi G, Bobbitt P: *Tragic Choices.* New York: Norton, 1978.

2. Fletcher J: Our shameful waste of human tissue. In: Cutler DR (ed): *The Religious Situation,* Boston: Beacon Press, 1969; 223–252.

3. Quoted in Fox R, Swazey J: *The Courage to Fail.*, Chicago: Univ of Chicago Press, 1974; 232.

4. Sanders & Dukeminier: Medical advance and legal lag: hemodialysis and kidney transplantation. *UCLA L Rev* 1968; 15: 357.

5. Rettig RA: The policy debate on patient care financing for victims of end stage renal disease. *Law & Contemporary Problems* 1976; 40: 196.

6. President's Commission for the Study of Ethical Problems in Medicine: *Securing Access to Health Care.* US Govt Printing Office, 1983; 25.

7. Annas GJ: Ethics committees on neonatal care: substantive protection or procedural diversion? *Am J Public Health* 1984; 74: 843–845.

8. Bayer R: Justice and health care in an era of cost containment: allocating scarce medical resources. *Soc Responsibility* 1984; 9: 37–52.

9. Annas GJ: Allocation of artificial hearts in the year 2002: *Minerva v National Health Agency. Am J Law Med* 1977; 3: 59–76.

10. Commentary: UK's poor record in treatment of renal failure. *Lancet,* July 7, 1984; 53.

11. Evans R: Health care technology and the inevitability of resource allocation and rationing decisions, Part 11. *JAMA* 1983; 249: 2208, 2217.

Take My Kidney, Please

Michael Kinsley

Michael Kinsley examines the issue of whether we should permit the sale of transplant organs. How far, he asks, are we willing to pursue the logic of capitalism? Kinsley shows that, in the final analysis, when we react with horror to the spectacle of a man forced to sell a kidney to pay for his daughter's operation, we are actually reacting to the injustices of life.

Even Margaret Thatcher's devotion to the free market has some limits, it seems. Reacting to newspaper reports that poor Turkish peasants are being paid to go to London and give up a kidney for transplant, the British Prime Minister said that "the sale of kidneys or any organs of the body is utterly repugnant." Emergency legislation is now being prepared for swift approval by Parliament to make sure that capitalism does not perform its celebrated magic in the market for human organs.

Commercial trade in human kidneys does seem grotesque. But it's a bit hard to say why. After all, the moral logic of capitalism does not stop at the epidermis. That logic holds, in a nutshell, that if an exchange is voluntary, it leaves both parties better off. In one case, a Turk sold a kidney for £2,500 ($4,400) because he needed money for an operation for his daughter. Capitalism in action: one person had $4,400 and wanted a kidney, another person had a spare kidney and wanted $4,400, so they did a deal. What's more, it seems like an advantageous deal all around. The buyer avoided a lifetime of dialysis. The seller provided crucial help to his child, at minimum risk to himself. (According to the *Economist*, the chance of a kidney donor's dying as a result of the loss is 1 in 5,000.)

Nevertheless, the conclusion that such trade is abhorrent is not even controversial. Almost everyone agrees. Is almost everyone right? This question of how far we are willing to push the logic of capitalism will be thrust in our faces increasingly in coming years. Medical advances are making it possible to buy things that were previously unobtainable at any price. (The Baby M. "womb renting"

case is another example.) Meanwhile, the communications and transportation revolutions are breaking down international borders, making new commercial relations possible between the comfortably rich and the desperately poor. On what basis do we say to a would-be kidney seller, "Sorry, this is one deal you just can't make?"

One widely accepted category of forbidden deals involves health and safety regulations: automobile standards, bans on food additives, etc. Although we quarrel about particular instances, only libertarian cranks reject in principle the idea that government sometimes should protect people from themselves. But it is no more dangerous to sell one of your kidneys than it is to give one away to a close relative—a transaction we not only allow but admire. On health grounds alone, you can't ban the sale without banning the gift as well. Furthermore, the sale of a kidney is not necessarily a foolish decision that society ought to protect you from. To pay for a daughter's operation, it seems the opposite.

But maybe there are some things money just shouldn't be allowed to buy, sensibly or otherwise. Socialist philosopher Michael Walzer added flesh to this ancient skeleton of sentiment in his 1983 book, *Spheres of Justice*. Walzer argued that a just society is not necessarily one with complete financial equality—a hopeless and even destructive goal—but one in which the influence of money is not allowed to dominate all aspects of life. By outlawing organ sales, you are indeed keeping the insidious influence of money from leaching into a new sphere and are thereby reducing the power of the rich. Trouble is, you are also reducing opportunity for the poor.

The grim trade in living people's kidneys would not be necessary if more people would voluntarily offer their kidneys (and other organs) when they die. Another socialist philosopher, Richard Titmuss, wrote a famous book two decades ago called *The Gift Relationship,* extolling the virtues of donated blood over purchased blood and, by extension, the superiority of sharing over commerce. Whatever you may think of Titmuss's larger point, the appeal of the blood-donor system as a small testament to our shared humanity is undeniable. Perhaps we should do more to encourage organ donation at death for the same reason. On the other hand, however cozy and egalitarian it might seem, a system that supplied all the kidneys we need through voluntary donation would be no special favor to our Turkish friend, who would be left with no sale and no $4,400. Why not at least let his heirs sell his kidneys when he dies? A commercial market in cadaver organs would wipe out the sale of live people's parts a lot more expeditiously than trying to encourage donations.

The logic of capitalism assumes knowledgeable, reasonably intelligent people on both sides of the transaction. Is this where the kidney trade falls short? At $4,400, the poor Turk was probably underpaid for his kidney. But in an open, legal market with protections against exploitation, he might have got more. At some price, the deal would make sense for almost anyone. I have no sentimental attachment to my kidneys. Out of prudence, I'd like to hang on to one of them, but the other is available. My price is $2 million.

Of course, I make this offer safe in the knowledge that there will always be some poor Turk ready to undercut me. So maybe, because of who the sellers inevitably will be, the sale of kidneys is by its very nature exploitation. A father shouldn't have to sacrifice a kidney to get a necessary operation for his daughter. Unfortunately, banning the kidney sale won't solve the problem of paying for the operation. Nor can the world yet afford expensive operations for everyone who needs one. And leaving aside the melodrama of the daughter's operation, we don't stop people from doing things to support their families—working in coal mines, for example—that reduce their life expectancies more than would the loss of a kidney. In fact, there are places in the Third World where even $4,400 can do more for a person's own life expectancy than a spare kidney.

The horror of kidney sales, in short, is a sentimental reaction to the injustice of life—injustice that the transaction highlights but does not increase. This is not a complaint. In fact, it may even be the best reason for a ban on such transactions. That kind of sentiment ought to be encouraged.

Organs for Sale? Propriety, Property, and the Price of Progress

Leon R. Kass

Leon Kass objects to the sale of transplant organs, while supporting the notion of organ donation. Kass argues that neither property rights nor principles of liberty can justify organ donation without also justifying organ sales—if one is free to donate, then one is free to sell. But selling organs, Kass argues, promotes the "commodification of humanity itself." If permitted, organ selling would be another breech in the barriers of imagination and custom protecting humanity. It would be a big step toward transforming humans from beings to be respected into mere things to be used.

Reprinted with permission of the author and *The Public Interest,* no. 107 (Spring 1992), pp. 72, 76–82, 84–85. Copyright 1992, National Affairs, Inc.

Culture and the Body

. . . Most of our attitudes regarding invasions of the body and treatment of corpses are carried less by maxims and arguments, more by sentiments and repugnances. They are transmitted inadvertently and indirectly, rarely through formal instruction. For this reason, they are held by some to be suspect, mere sentiments, atavisms tied to superstitions of a bygone age. Some even argue that these repugnances are based mainly on strangeness and unfamiliarity: the strange repels *because* it is unfamiliar. On this view, our squeamishness about dismemberment of corpses is akin to our horror at eating brains or mice. Time and exposure will cure us of these revulsions, especially when there are—as with organ transplantation—such enormous benefits to be won.

These views are, I believe, mistaken. To be sure, as an empirical matter, we can probably get used to many things that once repelled us—organ swapping among them. As Raskolnikov put it, and he should know, "Man gets used to everything—the beast." But I am certain that the repugnances that protect the dignity and integrity of the body are not based solely on strangeness. And they are certainly not irrational. On the contrary, they may just be—like the human body they seek to protect—the very embodiment of reason . . .

II. Property

The most common objections to permitting the sale of body parts, especially from live donors, have to do with matters of equity, exploitation of the poor and the unemployed, and the dangers of abuse—not excluding theft and even murder to obtain valuable commodities. People deplore the degrading sale, a sale made in desperation, especially when the seller is selling something so precious as a part of his own body. Others deplore the rich man's purchase, and would group life-giving organs with other most basic goods that should not be available to the rich when the poor can't afford them (like allowing people to purchase substitutes for themselves in the military draft). . . .

I certainly sympathize with these objections and concerns. As I read about the young healthy Indian men and women selling their kidneys to wealthy Saudis and Kuwaitis, I can only deplore the socioeconomic system that reduces people to such a level of desperation. And yet, at the same time, when I read the personal accounts of some who have sold, I am hard-pressed simply to condemn these individuals for electing apparently the only non-criminal way open to them to provide for a decent life for their families. As several commentators have noted, the sale of organs—like prostitution or surrogate motherhood or baby-selling—provides a double-bind for the poor. Proscription keeps them out of the economic mainstream, whereas permission threatens to accentuate their social alienation through the disapproval usually connected with trafficking in these matters.

Torn between sympathy and disgust, some observers would have it both ways: they would permit sale, but ban advertising and criminalize brokering (i.e., legalize prostitutes, prosecute pimps), presumably to eliminate coercive pressure from unscrupulous middlemen. But none of these analysts, it seems to me, has faced the question squarely. For if there were nothing fundamentally wrong with trading organs in the first place, why should it bother us that some people will make their living at it? The objection in the name of exploitation and inequity—however important for determining policy—seems to betray deeper objections, unacknowledged, to the thing itself. . . .

True, some things freely giveable ought not to be marketed because they cannot be sold: love and friendship are prime examples. So, too, are acts of generosity: it is one thing for me to offer in kindness to take the ugly duckling to the dance, it is quite another for her father to pay me to do so. But part of the reason love and generous deeds cannot be sold is that, strictly speaking, they cannot even be *given*—or, rather, they cannot be given *away*. One "gives" one's love to another or even one's body to one's beloved, one does not donate it; and when friendship is "given" it is still retained by its "owner." But the case with organs seems to be different: obviously material, they are freely alienable, they can be given and given away, and, therefore, they can be sold, and without diminishing the unquestioned good their transfer does for the recipient—why, then, should they not be for sale, of course, only by their proper "owner"? Why should not the owner-donor get something for his organs? We come at last to the question of the body as property.

Whose Body?

. . . What kind of *property* is my body? Is it mine or is it me? Can it—or much of it—be alienated, like my other property, like my car or even my dog? And on what basis do I claim property *rights* in my body? Is it really "my own"? Have I labored to produce it? Less than did my mother, and yet it is not hers. Do I claim it on merit? Doubtful: I had it even before I could be said to be deserving. Do I hold it as a gift—whether or not there be a giver? How does one possess and use a gift? Are there limits on my right to dispose of it as I wish—especially if I do not know the answer to these questions? Can one sell—or even give away—that which is not clearly one's own?

The word property comes originally from the Latin adjective *proprius* (the root also of "proper"—fit or apt or suitable—and, thus, also of "propriety"), *proprius* meaning "one's own, special, particular, peculiar." Property is both that which is one's own, and also the right—indeed, the exclusive right—to its possession, use, or disposal. And while there might seem to be nothing that is more "my own" than my own body, common sense finally rejects the view that my body is, strictly speaking, my property. For we do and should distinguish among that which is *me*, that which is *mine*, and that which is mine as *my property*. My body is me; my daughters are mine (and so are my opinions, deeds, and speeches); my car is my property. Only the last can clearly be alienated and sold at will.

Philosophical reflection, deepening common sense, would seem to support this view, yet not without introducing new perplexities. If we turn to John Locke, the great teacher on property, the right of property traces home in fact to the body:

> Though the earth and all creatures be common to all men, yet every man has a property in his own person; this nobody has a right to but himself. The labour of his body and the work of his hands we may say are properly his.

The right to the fruits of one's labor seems, for Locke, to follow from the property each man has in his own person. But unlike the rights in the fruits of his labor, the rights in one's person are for Locke surely inalienable (like one's inalienable right to liberty, which also cannot be transferred to another, say, by selling oneself into slavery). The property in my own person seems to function rather to limit intrusions and claims possibly made upon me by others; it functions to exclude me—and every other human being—from the commons available to all men for appropriation and use. Thus, though the right to property stems from the my-own-ness

(rather than the in-commons-ness) of my body and its labor, the body itself cannot be, for Locke, property like any other. It is, like property, exclusively mine to use; but it is, unlike property, not mine to dispose of. . . .

Yet here we are in trouble. The living body as a whole is surely not alienable, but parts of it definitely are. I may give blood, bone marrow, skin, a kidney, parts of my liver, and other organs without ceasing to be me, as the by-and-large self-same embodied being I am. It matters not to my totality or identity if the kidney I surrendered was taken because it was diseased or because I gave it for donation. . . .

The analysis of the notion of the body as property produces only confusion—one suspects because there is confusion in the heart of the idea of property itself, as well as deep mystery in the nature of personal identity. Most of the discussion would seem to support the common-sense and common-law teaching that *there is no property in a body*—not in my own body, not in my own corpse, and surely not in the corpse of my deceased ancestor. . . .

Yet if my body is not my property; if I have no property right in my body—and here, philosophically and morally, the matter is surely dubious at best—by what *right* do I give parts of it away? And, if it be by right of property, how can one then object—in principle—to sale?

Liberty and Its Limits

. . . Let us shift our attention from the vexed question of ownership to the principle of freedom. It was, you will recall, something like the principle of freedom—voluntary and freely given donation—that was used to justify the gift of organs, overcoming the presumption against mutilation . . .

Our society has perceived a social need for organs. We have chosen to meet that need not by direct social decision and appropriation, but, indirectly, through permitting and encouraging voluntary giving. It is, as I have argued, generosity—that is, more the "giving" than the "voluntariness"—that provides the moral ground; yet being liberals and not totalitarians, we put the legal weight on freedom—and hope people will use it generously. As a result, it looks as if, to facilitate and to justify the practice of organ donation, we have enshrined something like the notions of property rights and free contract in the body, notions that usually include the possibility of buying and selling. This is slippery business. Once the principle of private right and autonomy is taken as the standard, it will prove difficult—if not impossible—to hold the line between donation and sale. (It will even prove impossible, philosophically, to argue against voluntary servitude, bestiality, and other abominations.) Moreover, the burden of proof will fall squarely on those who want to set limits on what people may freely do with their bodies or for what purposes they may buy and sell body parts. It will, in short, be hard to prevent buying and selling human flesh not only for transplantation, but for, say, use in luxury nouvelle cuisine, once we allow markets for transplantation on libertarian grounds. We see here, in the prism of this case, the limits and, hence, the ultimate insufficiency of rights and the liberal principle.

Astute students of liberalism have long observed that our system of ordered liberties presupposes a certain kind of society—of at least minimal decency, and with strong enough familial and religious institutions to cultivate the sorts of men and women who can live civilly and responsibly with one another, while enjoying their private rights. We wonder whether freedom of contract regarding the body, leading to its being bought and sold, will continue to make corrosive inroads upon the kind of people we want to be and need to be if the uses of our freedom are not to lead to our willing dehumanization. We have, over the years, moved the care for life and death from the churches to the hospitals, and the disposition of mortal remains from the clergy to the family and now to the individual himself—and perhaps, in the markets of the future, to the insurance companies or the state or to enterprising brokers who will give new meaning to insider trading. No matter how many lives are saved, is this good for how we are to live?

Commodification

The idea of commodification of human flesh repels us, quite properly I would say, because we sense that the human body especially belongs in that category of things that defy or resist commensuration—like love or friendship or life itself. To claim that these things are "priceless" is not to insist that they are of infinite worth or that one cannot calculate (albeit very roughly, and then only with aid of very crude simplifying assumptions) how much it costs to sustain or support them. Rather it is to claim that the bulk of their meaning and their hu-

man worth do not lend themselves to quantitative measures; for this reason, we hold them to be incommensurable, not only morally but factually.

Against this view, it can surely be argued that the entire system of market exchange rests on our arbitrary but successful attempts to commensurate the (factually) incommensurable. The genius of money is precisely that it solves by convention the problem of natural incommensurability, say between oranges and widgets, or between manual labor and the thinking time of economists. The possibility of civilization altogether rests on this conventional means of exchange, as the ancient Greeks noted by deriving the name for money, *nomisma*, from the root *nomos*, meaning "convention"—that which has been settled by human agreement—and showing how this fundamental convention made possible commerce, leisure, and the establishment of gentler views of justice.

Yet the purpose of instituting such a conventional measure was to facilitate the satisfaction of *natural* human needs and the desires for well-being and, eventually, to encourage the full flowering of human possibility. Some notion of need or perceived human good provided always the latent non-conventional standard behind the nomismatic convention—tacitly, to be sure. And there's the rub: In due course, the standard behind money, being hidden, eventually becomes forgotten, and the counters of worth become taken for worth itself.

Truth to tell, commodification by conventional commensuration always risks the homogenization of worth, and even the homogenization of things, all under the aspect of quantity. In many transactions, we do not mind or suffer or even notice. Yet the human soul finally rebels against the principle, whenever it strikes closest to home. Consider, for example, why there is such widespread dislike of the pawnbroker. It is not only that he profits from our misfortunes and sees the shame of our having to part with heirlooms and other items said (inadequately) to have "sentimental value." It is especially because he will not and cannot appreciation their human and personal worth and pays us only their market price. How much more will we object to those who would commodify our very being?

We surpass all defensible limits of such conventional commodification when we contemplate making the convention-maker—the human being—just another one of the commensurables. The end comes to be treated as mere means. Selling our bodies, we come perilously close to selling out our souls. There is even a danger in contemplating such a prospect—for if we come to think about ourselves like pork bellies, pork bellies we will become. . . .

III. The Price of Progress

The arguments I have offered are not easy to make. I am all too well aware that they can be countered, that their appeal is largely to certain hard-to-articulate intuitions and sensibilities that I at least believe belong intimately to the human experience of our own humanity. Precious though they might be, they do not exhaust the human picture, far from it. And perhaps, in the present case, they should give way to rational calculation, market mechanisms, and even naked commodification of human flesh—all in the service of saving life at lowest cost. Perhaps this is not the right place to draw a line or to make a stand.

Consider, then, a slightly more progressive and enterprising proposal, one anticipated by my colleague, Willard Gaylin, in an essay, "Harvesting the Dead," written in 1974. Mindful of all the possible uses of newly dead—or perhaps not-quite-dead—bodies, kept in their borderline condition by continuous artificial respiration and assisted circulation, intact, warm, pink, recognizably you or me, but brain dead, Gaylin imagines the multiple medically beneficial uses to which the bioemporium of such "neomorts" could be put: the neomorts could, for example, allow physicians-in-training to practice pelvic examinations and tracheal intubations without shame or fear of doing damage; they could serve as unharmable subjects for medical experimentation and drug testing, provide indefinite supplies of blood, marrow, and skin, serve as factories to manufacture hormones and antibodies, or, eventually, be dismembered for transplantable spare parts. Since the newly dead body really is such a precious resource, why not really put it to full and limitless use?

Gaylin's scenario is not so far-fetched. Proposals to undertake precisely such body-farming have been seriously discussed among medical scientists in private. The technology for maintaining neomorts is already available. Indeed, in the past few years, a publicly traded corporation has opened a national chain of large, specialized nursing homes—or should we rather call them nurseries?—for the care and feeding solely of persons in persistent vegetative state or ventilator-dependent irreversible coma. Roughly ten establishments, each

housing several hundred of such beings, already exist. All that would be required to turn them into Gaylin's bioemporia would be a slight revision in the definition of death (already proposed for other reasons)—to shift from death of the whole brain to death of the cortex and the higher centers—plus the will not to let these valuable resources go to waste. (The company's stock, by the way, has more than quadrupled in the last year alone; perhaps someone is already preparing plans for mergers and manufacture.) Repulsive? You bet. Useful? Without doubt. Shall we go forward into this brave new world?

Forward we are going, without anyone even asking the question. In the twenty-five years since I began thinking about these matters, our society has overcome longstanding taboos and repugnances to accept test-tube fertilization, commercial sperm-banking, surrogate motherhood, abortion on demand, exploitation of fetal tissue, patenting of living human tissue, gender-change surgery, liposuction and body shops, the widespread shuttling of human parts, assisted-suicide practiced by doctors, and the deliberate generation of human beings to serve as transplant donors—not to speak about massive changes in the culture regarding shame, privacy, and exposure. Perhaps more worrisome than the changes themselves is the coarsening of sensibilities and attitudes, and the irreversible effects on our imaginations and the way we come to conceive of ourselves. For there is a sad irony in our biomedical project, accurately anticipated in Aldous Huxley's *Brave New World:* We expend enormous energy and vast sums of money to preserve and prolong bodily life, but in the process our embodied life is stripped of its gravity and much of its dignity. This is, in a word, progress as tragedy.

In the transplanting of human organs, we have made a start on a road that leads imperceptibly but surely toward a destination that none of us wants to reach. A divination of this fact produced reluctance at the start. Yet the first step, overcoming reluctance, was defensible on benevolent and rational grounds: save life using organs no longer useful to their owners and otherwise lost to worms.

Now, embarked on the journey, we cannot go back. Yet we are increasingly troubled by the growing awareness that there is neither a natural nor a rational place to stop. Precedent justifies extension, so does rational calculation: We are in a warm bath that warms up so imperceptibly that we don't know when to scream.

Alcoholics and Liver Transplantation

Carl Cohen, Martin Benjamin, and the Ethics and Social Impact Committee of the Transplant and Health Policy Center, Ann Arbor, Michigan

Carl Cohen, Martin Benjamin, and their associates examine the moral and medical arguments for excluding alcoholics as candidates for liver transplants and conclude that neither kind of argument justifies a categorical exclusion.

The moral argument holds that alcoholics are morally blameworthy for their condition. Thus, when resources are scarce, it is preferable to favor an equally sick nonblameworthy person over a blameworthy one. The authors maintain that if this argument were sound, it would require physicians to examine the moral character of all patients before allocating scarce resources. But this is not feasible, and such a policy could not be administered fairly by the medical profession.

The medical argument holds that because of their bad habits, alcoholics have a lower success rate with transplants. Hence, scarce organs should go to others more likely to benefit. The authors agree that the likelihood of someone following a treatment regimen should be considered, but they maintain that the consideration must be given case by case.

We permit transplants in cases where the prognosis is the same or worse, and the categorical exclusion of alcoholics is unfair. We cannot justify discrimination on the grounds of alleged self-abuse, "unless we are prepared to develop a detailed calculus of just deserts for health care based on good conduct."

Alcoholic cirrhosis of the liver—severe scarring due to the heavy use of alcohol—is by far the major cause of end-stage liver disease.[1] For persons so afflicted, life may depend on receiving a new, transplanted liver. The number of alcoholics in the United States needing new livers is great, but the supply of available livers for transplantation is small. *Should those whose end-stage liver disease was caused by alcohol abuse be categorically excluded from candidacy for liver transplantation?* This question, partly medical and partly moral, must now be confronted forthrightly. Many lives are at stake.

Reasons of two kinds underlie a widespread unwillingness to transplant livers into alcoholics: First, there is a common conviction—explicit or tacit—that alcoholics are morally blameworthy, their condition the result of their own misconduct, and that such blameworthiness disqualifies alcoholics in unavoidable competition for organs with others equally sick but blameless. Second, there is a common belief that because of their habits, alcoholics will not exhibit satisfactory survival rates after transplantation, and that, therefore, good stewardship of a scarce lifesaving resource requires that alcoholics not be considered for liver transplantation. We examine both of these arguments.

The Moral Argument

A widespread condemnation of drunkenness and a revulsion for drunks lie at the heart of this public policy issue. Alcoholic cirrhosis—unlike other causes of end-stage liver disease—is brought on by a person's conduct, by heavy drinking. Yet if the dispute here were only about whether to treat someone who is seriously ill because of personal conduct, we would not say—as we do not in cases of other serious diseases resulting from personal conduct—that such conduct disqualifies a person

From *JAMA*, March 13, 1991, vol. 265, pp. 1299–1301. Copyright 1991, American Medical Association.

from receiving desperately needed medical attention. Accident victims injured because they were not wearing seat belts are treated without hesitation; reformed smokers who become coronary bypass candidates partly because they disregarded their physicians' advice about tobacco, diet, and exercise are not turned away because of their bad habits. But new livers are a scarce resource, and transplanting a liver into an alcoholic may, therefore, result in death for a competing candidate whose liver disease was wholly beyond his or her control. Thus we seem driven, in this case unlike in others, to reflect on the weight given to the patient's personal conduct. And heavy drinking—unlike smoking, or overeating, or failing to wear a seat belt—is widely regarded as morally wrong.

Many contend that alcoholism is not a moral failing but a disease. Some authorities have recently reaffirmed this position, asserting that alcoholism is "best regarded as a chronic disease."[2] But this claim cannot be firmly established and is far from universally believed. Whether alcoholism is indeed a disease, or a moral failing, or both, remains a disputed matter surrounded by intense controversy.[3-9]

Even if it is true that alcoholics suffer from a somatic disorder, many people will argue that this disorder results in deadly liver disease only when coupled with a weakness of will—a weakness for which part of the blame must fall on the alcoholic. This consideration underlies the conviction that the alcoholic needing a transplanted liver, unlike a nonalcoholic competing for the same liver, is at least partly responsible for his or her need. Therefore, some conclude, the alcoholic's personal failing is rightly considered in deciding upon his or her entitlement to this very scarce resource.

Is this argument sound? We think it is not. Whether alcoholism is a moral failing, in whole or in part, remains uncertain. But even if we suppose that it is, it does not follow that we are justified in categorically denying liver transplants to those alcoholics suffering from endstage cirrhosis. We could rightly preclude alcoholics from transplantation only if we assume that qualification for a new organ requires some level of moral virtue or is canceled by some level of moral vice. But there is absolutely no agreement—and there is likely to be none—about what constitutes moral virtue and vice and what rewards and penalties they deserve. The assumption that undergirds the moral argument for precluding alcoholics is thus unaccept-

able. Moreover, even if we could agree (which, in fact, we cannot) upon the kind of misconduct we would be looking for, the fair weighting of such a consideration would entail highly intrusive investigations into patients' moral habits—investigations universally thought repugnant. Moral evaluation is wisely and rightly excluded from all deliberations of who should be treated and how.

Indeed, we do exclude it. We do not seek to determine whether a particular transplant candidate is an abusive parent or a dutiful daughter, whether candidates cheat on their income taxes or their spouses, or whether potential recipients pay their parking tickets or routinely lie when they think it is in their best interests. We refrain from considering such judgments for several good reasons: (1) We have genuine and well-grounded doubts about comparative degrees of voluntariness and, therefore, *cannot pass judgment fairly*. (2) Even if we could assess degrees of voluntariness reliably, we *cannot know what penalties different degrees of misconduct deserve*. (3) *Judgments of this kind could not be made consistently in our medical system*—and a fundamental requirement of a fair system in allocating scarce resources is that it treat all in need of certain goods on the same standard, without unfair discrimination by group.

If alcoholics should be penalized because of their moral fault, then all others who are equally at fault in causing their own medical needs should be similarly penalized. To accomplish this, we would have to make vigorous and sustained efforts to find out whose conduct has been morally weak or sinful and to what degree. That inquiry, as a condition for medical care or for the receipt of goods in short supply, we certainly will not and should not undertake.

The unfairness of such moral judgments is compounded by other accidental factors that render moral assessment especially difficult in connection with alcoholism and liver disease. Some drinkers have a greater predisposition for alcohol abuse than others. And for some who drink to excess, the predisposition to cirrhosis is also greater; many grossly intemperate drinkers do not suffer grievously from liver disease. On the other hand, alcohol consumption that might be considered moderate for some may cause serious liver disease in others. It turns out, in fact, that the disastrous consequences of even low levels of alcohol consumption may be much more common in women than in men.[10] Therefore, penalizing cirrhotics by denying them transplant candidacy would have the effect of holding some groups arbitrarily to a higher standard than others and would probably hold women to a higher standard of conduct than men.

Moral judgments that eliminate alcoholics from candidacy thus prove unfair and unacceptable. The alleged (but disputed) moral misconduct of alcoholics with end-stage liver disease does not justify categorically excluding them as candidates for liver transplantation.

Medical Argument

Reluctance to use available livers in treating alcoholics is due in some part to the conviction that, because alcoholics would do poorly after transplant as a result of their bad habits, good stewardship of organs in short supply requires that alcoholics be excluded from consideration.

This argument also fails, for two reasons: First, it fails because the premise—that the outcome for alcoholics will invariably be poor relative to other groups—is at least doubtful and probably false. Second, it fails because, even if the premise were true, it could serve as a good reason to exclude alcoholics only if it were an equally good reason to exclude other groups having a prognosis equally bad or worse. But equally low survival rates have not excluded other groups; fairness therefore requires that this group not be categorically excluded either.

In fact, the data regarding the post-transplant histories of alcoholics are not yet reliable. Evidence gathered in 1984 indicated that the 1-year survival rate for patients with alcoholic cirrhosis was well below the survival rate for other recipients of liver transplants, excluding those with cancer.[11] But a 1988 report, with a larger (but still small) sample number, shows remarkably good results in alcoholics receiving transplants: 1-year survival is 73.2%—and of 35 carefully selected (and possibly nonrepresentative) alcoholics who received transplants and lived 6 months or longer, only two relapsed into alcohol abuse.[12] Liver transplantation, it would appear, can be a very sobering experience. Whether this group continues to do as well as a comparable group of non-alcoholic liver recipients remains uncertain. But the data, although not supporting the broad inclusion of alcoholics, do suggest that medical considerations do not now justify categorically excluding alcoholics from liver transplantation.

A history of alcoholism is of great concern when considering liver transplantation, not only because of the impact of alcohol abuse upon the entire system of the recipient, but also because the life of an alcoholic tends to be beset by general disorder. Returning to heavy drinking could ruin a new liver, although probably not for years. But relapse into heavy drinking would quite likely entail the inability to maintain the routine of multiple medication, daily or twice-daily, essential for immunosuppression and survival. As a class, alcoholic cirrhotics may therefore prove to have substantially lower survival rates after receiving transplants. All such matters should be weighed, of course. But none of them gives any solid reason to exclude alcoholics from consideration categorically.

Moreover, even if survival rates for alcoholics selected were much lower than normal—a supposition now in substantial doubt—what could fairly be concluded from such data? Do we exclude from transplant candidacy members of other groups known to have low survival rates? In fact we do not. Other things being equal, we may prefer not to transplant organs in short supply into patients afflicted, say, with liver cell cancer, knowing that such cancer recurs not long after a new liver is implanted.[13,14] Yet in some individual cases we do it. Similarly, some transplant recipients have other malignant neoplasms or other conditions that suggest low survival probability. Such matters are weighed in selecting recipients, but they are insufficient grounds to categorically exclude an entire group. This shows that the argument for excluding alcoholics based on survival probability rates alone is simply not just.

The Arguments Distinguished

In fact, the exclusion of alcoholics from transplant candidacy probably results from an intermingling, perhaps at times a confusion, of the moral and medical arguments. But if the moral argument indeed does not apply, no combination of it with probable survival rates can make it applicable. Survival data, carefully collected and analyzed, deserve to be weighed in selecting candidates. These data do not come close to precluding alcoholics from consideration. Judgments of blameworthiness, which ought to be excluded generally, certainly should be excluded when weighing the impact of those survival rates. Some people with a strong antipathy to alcohol abuse and abusers may, without realizing it, be relying on assumed unfavorable data to support a fixed moral judgment. The arguments must be untangled. Actual results with transplanted alcoholics must be considered without regard to moral antipathies.

The upshot is inescapable: there are no good grounds at present—moral or medical—to disqualify a patient with end-stage liver disease from consideration for liver transplantation simply because of a history of heavy drinking.

Screening and Selection of Liver Transplant Candidates

In the initial evaluation of candidates for any form of transplantation, the central questions are whether patients (1) are sick enough to need a new organ and (2) enjoy a high enough probability of benefiting from this limited resource. At this stage the criteria should be noncomparative.[15,16] Even the initial screening of patients must, however, be done individually and with great care.

The screening process for those suffering from alcoholic cirrhosis must be especially rigorous—not for moral reasons, but because of factors affecting survival, which are themselves influenced by a history of heavy drinking—and even more by its resumption. Responsible stewardship of scarce organs requires that the screening for candidacy take into consideration the manifold impact of heavy drinking on long-term transplant success. Cardiovascular problems brought on by alcoholism and other systematic contraindications must be looked for. Psychiatric and social evaluation is also in order, to determine whether patients understand and have come to terms with their condition and whether they have the social support essential for continuing immunosuppression and follow-up care.

Precisely which factors should be weighed in this screening process have not been firmly established. Some physicians have proposed a specified period of alcohol abstinence as an "objective" criterion for selection—but the data supporting such a

criterion are far from conclusive, and the use of this criterion to exclude a prospective recipient is at present medically and morally arbitrary.[17,18]

Indeed, one important consequence of overcoming the strong presumption against considering alcoholics for liver transplantation is the research opportunity it presents and the encouragement it gives to the quest for more reliable predictors of medical success. As that search continues, some defensible guidelines for case-by-case determination have been devised, based on factors associated with sustained recovery from alcoholism and other considerations related to liver transplantation success in general. Such guidelines appropriately include (1) refined diagnosis by those trained in the treatment of alcoholism, (2) acknowledgment by the patient of a serious drinking problem, (3) social and familial stability, and (4) other factors experimentally associated with long-term sobriety.[19]

The experimental use of guidelines like these, and their gradual refinement over time, may lead to more reliable and more generally applicable predictors. But those more refined predictors will never be developed until prejudices against considering alcoholics for liver transplantation are overcome.

Patients who are sick because of alleged self-abuse ought not be grouped for discriminatory treatment—unless we are prepared to develop a detailed calculus of just deserts for health care based on good conduct. Lack of sympathy for those who bring serious disease upon themselves is understandable, but the temptation to institutionalize that emotional response must be tempered by our inability to apply such considerations justly and by our duty *not* to apply them unjustly. In the end, some patients with alcoholic cirrhosis may be judged, after careful evaluation, as good risks for a liver transplant.

Objection and Reply

Providing alcoholics with transplants may present a special "political" problem for transplant centers. The public perception of alcoholics is generally negative. The already low rate of organ donation, it may be argued, will fall even lower when it becomes known that donated organs are going to alcoholics. Financial support from legislatures may also suffer. One can imagine the effect on transplantation if the public were to learn that the liver of a teenager killed by a drunken driver had been transplanted into an alcoholic patient. If selecting even a few alcoholics as transplant candidates reduces the number of lives saved overall, might that not be good reason to preclude alcoholics categorically?

No. The fear is understandable, but excluding alcoholics cannot be rationally defended on that basis. Irresponsible conduct attributable to alcohol abuse should not be defended. No excuses should be made for the deplorable consequences of drunken behavior, from highway slaughter to familial neglect and abuse. But alcoholism must be distinguished from those consequences; not all alcoholics are morally irresponsible, vicious, or neglectful drunks. If there is a general failure to make this distinction, we must strive to overcome that failure, not pander to it.

Public confidence in medical practice in general, and in organ transplantation in particular, depends on the scientific validity and moral integrity of the policies adopted. Sound policies will prove publicly defensible. Shaping present health care policy on the basis of distorted public perceptions or prejudices will, in the long run, do more harm than good to the process and to the reputation of all concerned.

Approximately one in every 10 Americans is a heavy drinker, and approximately one family in every three has at least one member at risk for alcoholic cirrhosis.[3] The care of alcoholics and the just treatment of them when their lives are at stake are matters a democratic policy may therefore be expected to act on with concern and reasonable judgment over the long run. The allocation of organs in short supply does present vexing moral problems: if thoughtless or shallow moralizing would cause some to respond very negatively to transplanting livers into alcoholic cirrhotics, that cannot serve as good reason to make such moralizing the measure of public policy.

We have argued that there is now no good reason, either moral or medical, to preclude alcoholics categorically from consideration for liver transplantation. We further conclude that it would therefore be unjust to implement that categorical preclusion simply because others might respond negatively if we do not.

Notes

1. Consensus conference on liver transplantation. NIH. *JAMA.* 1983; 250: 2961–2964.

2. Klerman F. L. Treatment of alcoholism. *N Engl J Med.* 1989: 320: 394–396.

3. Vaillant G. E. *The Natural History of Alcoholism.* Cambridge. Mass: Harvard University Press; 1983.

4. Jellinek E. M. *The Disease Concept of Alcoholism.* New Haven Conn: College and University Press: 1960.

5. Rose R. M. and Barret J. E., eds. *Alcoholism: Origins and Outcome.* New York, NY: Raven Press: 1988.

6. *Alcohol and Health: Sixth Special Report to the Congress.* Washington, DC: US Dept of Health and Human Services: 1987. DHHS publication ADM 87-1519.

7. Fingarette H. Alcoholism: the mythical disease. *Public Interest.* 1988; 91: 3–22.

8. Madsen W. Thin thinking about heavy drinking. *Public Interest.* 1989; 95: 112–118.

9. Fingarette H. A rejoinder to Madsen. *Public Interest.* 1989; 95: 118–21.

10. Berglund M. Mortality in alcoholics related to clinical state at first admission: a study of 537 deaths. *Acta Psychiatr Scand.* 1984: 70: 407–416.

11. Scharschmidt B. F. Human liver transplantation: analysis of data on 540 patients from four centers. *Hepatology.* 1984: 4: 95–111.

12. Starzl T. E., Van Thiel D., and Tzakis A. G. et al. Orthotopic liver transplantation for alcoholic cirrhosis. *JAMA,* 1988: 260: 2542–2544.

13. Gordon R. D., Iwatsuki S., and Tazkis A. G. et al. The Denver-Pittsburgh Liver Transplant Series. In: Terasaki P. I. ed. *Clinical Transplants.* Los Angeles, Calif: UCLA Tissue-Typing Laboratory: 1987: 43–49.

14. Gordon R. D., Iwatsuki S., and Esquivel C. O. Liver transplantation. In: Cerilli G. I. ed. *Organ Transplantation and Replacement.* Philadelphia, PA: J. B. Lippincott: 1988: 511–534.

15. Childress J. F. Who shall live when not all can live? *Soundings.* 1970: 53: 339–362.

16. Starzl T. E., Gordon R. D., and Tzakis S. et al. Equitable allocation of extrarenal organs: with special reference to the liver. *Transplant Proc.* 1988: 20: 131–138.

17. Schenker S., Perkins H. S., and Sorrell M. F. Should patients with end-stage alcoholic liver disease have a new liver? *Hepatology.* 1990: 11: 314–319.

18. *Allen v. Mansour A.* US District Court for the Eastern District of Michigan. Southern Division. 1986: 86–73429.

19. Beresford T. P., Turcotte J. G., and Merion R. et al. A rational approach to liver transplantation for the alcoholic patient. *Psychosomatics* 1990: 31: 241–254.

Rights, Symbolism, and Public Policy in Fetal Tissue Transplants

John A. Robertson

John Robertson examines some moral objections raised by opponents of fetal tissue transplants. To those who charge that fetal tissue transplants encourage or abet abortion, he argues that the decision to end an unwanted pregnancy is a separate issue; the use of fetal tissue from such cases does not entail approval of abortion any more than the use of an organ from a homicide victim entails approval of homicide.

Also, in Robertson's view, whether it is legitimate to abort (or conceive and abort) a fetus to obtain material for transplant is more morally complex than usually recognized and in some circumstances "may be more justified than previously thought."

As to recruiting unrelated donors of fetal tissue, Robertson sees the possibility of becoming a donor as within the range of a woman's autonomy. The fear that women will become "tissue farms" is wholly unfounded.

Fetal tissue transplants hold great hope for many patients. Extensive work with animal models has shown that human fetal brain cells transplanted into the substantia nigra of monkeys with oxogenously produced Parkinson's disease have restored their function. Physicians expect similar results in humans, to the benefit of thousands of patients.[1] Experimental evidence is also strong that fetal islet cell transplants will restore normal insulin function in diabetics.[2] And fetal thymus and liver transplants may have utility for blood and immune system disorders.

Clarifying the Issues

As with many issues in bioethics, careful analysis will help elucidate the normative conflict, showing both areas of agreement and irreducible conflict. An essential distinction in the fetal tissue controversy is between procuring tissue from family planning abortions and procuring tissue from abortions performed expressly to provide tissue for transplant. Although opponents of fetal tissue transplants have often conflated the two, tissue from family planning abortions may be used without implying approval of abortions to produce tissue. Indeed, with ample tissue available from family planning abortions, the latter scenario may never occur.

A second important distinction is that between retrieving tissue for transplant from dead and from live fetuses. Only the use of tissue from dead fetuses is at issue. Researchers are not proposing to maintain nonviable fetuses ex utero to procure tissue, or to take tissue from them before they are dead, practices that current regulations and law prohibit.[3] . . .

Tissue from Family Planning Abortions

Fetal tissue transplant research for Parkinson's disease, diabetes, and other disorders will use tissue retrieved from the one and a half million abortions performed annually in the United States to end unwanted pregnancies. Nearly 80 percent of induced abortions are performed between the sixth and eleventh weeks of gestation, at which time neural and other tissue is sufficiently developed to be retrieved and transplanted.[4] Abortions performed at fourteen to sixteen weeks provide pancreatic tissue used in diabetes research, but it may prove possible to use pancreases retrieved earlier.[5]

No need now or in the foreseeable future exists to have a family member conceive and abort to produce fetal tissue. The neural tissue to be transplanted in Parkinson's disease lacks antigenicity, thus obviating the need for a close match between donor and recipient. Fetal pancreas is more antigenic, but processing can reduce this, also making family connection less important.

The key question is whether women who abort to end unwanted pregnancies may donate the aborted fetuses for use in medical research or therapy by persons who have no connection with or influence on the decision to terminate the pregnancy. One's views on abortion need not determine one's answer to this question, because the abortion and subsequent transplant use are clearly separated. But some opposed to abortion object that transplanting fetal tissue involves complicity in an immoral act and will legitimate and even encourage abortion. Analysis of these concerns will show that they are insufficient to justify a public policy that bans or refuses to fund research or therapy with fetal tissue from induced abortion.

Complicity in Abortion

Even proponents of the complicity argument recognize that not all situations of subsequent benefit make one morally complicitous in a prior evil act. For example, James Burtchaell claims that complicity occurs not merely from partaking of benefit but only when one enters into a "supportive alliance" with the underlying evil that makes the benefit possible. He distinguishes "a neutral or even an opponent and an ally" of the underlying evil by "the way in which one does or does not hold oneself apart from the enterprise and its purposes."[6]

On this analysis, a researcher using fetal tissue from an elective abortion is not necessarily an accomplice with the abortionist and woman choosing abortion. The researcher and recipient have no role in the abortion process. They will not have requested it, and may have no knowledge of who performed the abortion or where it occurred since a third-party intermediary will procure the tissue.

They may be morally opposed to abortion, and surely are not compromised because they choose to salvage some good from an abortion that will occur regardless of their research or therapeutic goals.

A useful analogy is transplant of organs and tissue from homicide victims. Families of murder victims are often asked to donate organs and bodies for research, therapy, and education. If they consent, organ procurement agencies retrieve the organs and distribute them to recipients. No one would seriously argue that the surgeon who transplants the victim's kidneys, heart, liver, or corneas, or the recipient of the organs, becomes an accomplice in the homicide that made the organs available, even if aware of the source. Nor is the medical student who uses the cadaver of a murder victim to study anatomy.

If organs from murder victims may be used without complicity in the murder that makes the organs available, then fetal remains could also be used without complicity in the abortion. Burtchaell's approach to the problem of complicity assumes that researchers necessarily applaud the underlying act of abortion. But one may benefit from another's evil act without applauding or approving of that evil. X may disapprove of Y's murder of Z, even though X gains an inheritance or a promotion as a result. Indeed, one might even question Burtchaell's assumption that X becomes an accomplice in Y's prior act if he subsequently applauds it. Applauding Y's murder of Z might be insensitive or callous. But that alone would not make one morally responsible for, complicitous in, the murder that has already occurred. In any event, the willingness to derive benefit from another's wrongful death does not create complicity in that death because the beneficiary played no role in causing it.

The complicity argument against use of aborted fetuses often draws an analogy to a perceived reluctance to use the results of unethical medical research carried out by the Nazis. Burtchaell and others have claimed that it would make us retroactively accomplices in the Nazi horrors to use the results of their unethical and lethal research.[7] This ignores, however, the clear separation between the perpetrator and beneficiary of the immoral act that breaks the chain of moral complicity for that act.

Thus one could rely on Nazi-generated data while decrying the horrendous acts of Nazi doctors that produced the data. Nor would it necessarily dishonor those unfortunate victims. Indeed, it could reasonably be viewed as retrospectively honoring them by saving others. The Jewish doctors who made systematic studies of starvation in the Warsaw ghetto to reap some good from the evil being done to their brethren were not accomplices in that evil, nor are doctors and patients who now benefit from their studies.[8]

If the complicity claim is doubtful when the underlying immorality of the act is clear, as with Nazi-produced data or transplants from murder victims, it is considerably weakened when the act making the benefit possible is legal and its immorality vigorously debated, as is the case with abortion. Even persons opposed to abortion might agree that perceptions of complicity should not determine public policy on fetal tissue transplants.

Legitimizing, Entrenching, and Encouraging Abortion

A second objection is that salvaging tissue for transplant from aborted fetuses will make abortion more morally offensive and more easily tolerated both by individual pregnant women and by society, and perhaps transform it into a morally positive act. This will encourage abortions that would not otherwise occur, and dilute support for reversing the legal acceptability of abortion, in effect creating complicity in future abortions.[9]

But the feared impact on abortion practices and attitudes is highly speculative, particularly at a time when few fetal transplants have occurred. The main motivation for abortion is the desire to avoid the burdens of an unwanted pregnancy. The fact that fetal remains may be donated for transplant will continue to be of little significance in the total array of factors that lead a woman to abort a pregnancy.

Having decided to abort, a woman may feel better if she then donates the fetal remains. But this does not show that tissue donation will lead to a termination decision that would not otherwise have occurred, particularly if the decision to abort is made before the opportunity to donate the remains is offered. Perhaps a few more abortions will occur because of the general knowledge that tissue can be donated for transplant, but it is highly unlikely that donation—as opposed to contraceptive practices and sex education—will contribute significantly to the rate of abortion.[10]

Nor does the use of fetal remains for transplant mean that a public otherwise ready to outlaw abortion would refrain form doing so. Legal acceptance of abortion flows from the wide disagreement that exists over early fetal status. If a majority agreed that fetuses should be respected as persons despite the burdens placed on pregnant women, such possible secondary benefits of induced abortion as fetal tissue transplants would not prevent a change in the legality of abortion.

Indeed, one could make the same argument against organ transplants from homicide, suicide, and accident victims. The willingness to use their organs might be seen to encourage or legitimate such deaths, or at least make it harder to enact lower speed limits, seatbelt, gun control, and drunk driving laws to prevent them. After all, the need to prevent murder, suicide, and fatal accidents becomes less pressing if some good to others might come from use of victims' organs for transplant. In either case, the connection is too tenuous and speculative to ban organ or fetal tissue transplants.

In sum, fetal tissue transplants are practically and morally separate from decisions to end unwanted pregnancy. Given that abortion is legal and occurring on a large scale, the willingness to use resulting tissue for transplant neither creates complicity in past abortions nor appears significantly to encourage more future abortions. Such ethical concerns and speculations are not sufficient, given the possible good to others, to justify banning use of fetal tissue for research or therapy.

Aborting to Obtain Tissue for Transplant

Central to the argument for transplanting fetal tissue from family planning abortions has been the assumption that the abortion occurs independently of the need for tissue, and that permitting such transplants does not also entail pregnancy and abortion to produce fetal tissue.

But successful tissue transplants may create the need to abort to produce fetal tissue in two future situations. One situation would arise if histocompatability between the fetus and recipient were necessary for effective fetal transplants. Female relatives, spouses, or even unrelated persons might then seek to conceive to provide properly matched fetal tissue for transplant.

The second situation would arise if fetal transplants were so successful that demand far out-stripped supply, such as might occur if the treatment were advantageous to most patients with Parkinson's disease and diabetes, or if the number of surgical family planning abortions decreased. Pressure on supply might also occur if tissue from several aborted fetuses were needed to produce one viable transplant.

The hypothetical possibility of such situations is not a sufficient reason to ban all tissue transplants from family planning abortions. But should such abortions be banned if the imagined situations occurred? Most commentators assume that conception and abortion for tissue procurement is so clearly unethical that the prospect hardly merits discussion.[11] Accordingly, they would ban all tissue transplants from related persons and deny the donor the right to designate the recipient of a fetal tissue transplant.

Analysis will show, however, that the question is more ethically complicated than generally assumed, and should not be the driving force in setting policy for tissue transplants from family planning abortions.

A Hypothetical Situation

Consider first the situation where a woman pregnant with her husband's child learns that tissue from her fetus could cure severe neurologic disease in herself or a close relative, such as her husband, child, parent, father or mother-in-law, sibling, or brother or sister-in-law. May she ethically abort the pregnancy to obtain tissue for transplant to the relative? Or may a woman not yet pregnant conceive a fetus that she will then abort to provide tissue for transplant to herself or to her relative?

To focus analysis on fetal welfare, assume in each case that no other viable tissue source exists, and that the advanced state of neurologic disease has become a major tragedy for the patient and family. The woman has broached the question of abortion to obtain tissue without any direct pressure or inducements from the family or others. Her husband accepts an abortion for transplant purposes if she is willing, but exerts no pressure on her to abort.

The woman is already pregnant. If the woman is already pregnant, the question is whether a first trimester fetus that would otherwise have been carried to term may be sacrificed to procure tissue for transplant to the woman herself or to a sick family member. The answer depends on the value placed on early fetuses and on the acceptable reasons for abortion. One may distinguish between fetuses that have developed the neurologic and cognitive capacity for sentience and interests in themselves, and those so neurologically immature that they cannot experience harm.[12] While aborting fetuses at that earlier stage prevents them from achieving their potential, it does not harm or wrong them, since they are insufficiently developed to experience harm.[13]

Although aborting the fetus at that early stage does not wrong the fetus, it may impose symbolic costs measurable in terms of the reduced respect for human life generally that a willingness to abort early fetuses connotes. Still the abortion may be ethically acceptable if the good sought sufficiently outweighs the symbolic devaluation of life that occurs when fetuses that cannot be harmed in their own right are aborted. Many persons find that the burdens of unwanted pregnancy outweigh the symbolic devaluation of human life. Others would require a more compelling reason for abortion, such as protecting the mother's life or health, avoiding the birth of a handicapped child, or avoiding the burdens of a pregnancy due to rape or incest.

By comparison, abortion to obtain tissue to save one's own life or the life of a close relative seems equally, if not more compelling. If abortion in the case of an unwanted pregnancy is deemed permissible, surely abortion to obtain tissue to save another person's life is. Indeed, aborting to obtain tissue would seem as compelling as the most stringent reasons for permitting abortion. In fact, many would find this motive more compelling than the desire to end an unwanted pregnancy.

Of course, aborting a wanted pregnancy to prevent severe neurologic disease in oneself or a close relative will hardly be done joyfully, and will place the mother in an excruciating dilemma. A fetus that could be carried to term will have to be sacrificed to save a parent, spouse, sibling, or child who already exists. Such a tragic choice will induce fear and trembling, and engender loss or grief whatever the decision. Yet one cannot say that the choice to abort is ethically impermissible. There is no sound ethical basis for prohibiting *this* sacrifice of the fetus when its sacrifice to end an unwanted pregnancy or pursue other goals is permitted.

Public attitudes toward a woman aborting an otherwise wanted pregnancy to benefit a family member would most likely reflect attitudes toward abortion generally. Those who are against abortion in all circumstances will object to abortions done to treat severe neurologic disease in the mother or in a family member. Similarly, persons who accept family planning abortions should have no objection to abortion to procure tissue for transplant, since fetal status is no more compelling and the interest of the woman in controlling her body and reproductive capacity is similar.

Since neither group forms a majority, however, persons who object to family planning abortions but accept abortions necessary to protect the mother's health, in cases of rape or incest, or to prevent the birth of a handicapped child will determine whether a majority of people approve.[14] It is conceivable that many persons in this swing group would find abortion to produce tissue for transplant to a family member to be acceptable. The benefit of alleviating severe neurologic disease is arguably as great as the benefits in the cases they accept as justifiable abortion, and more compelling than abortions done for family planning purposes.

Conceiving and aborting for transplant purposes. What is the objection, then, when a woman not yet pregnant seeks to conceive in order to abort and provide tissue for transplant?

In terms of fetal welfare, no greater harm occurs to the fetus conceived expressly to be aborted, as long as the abortion occurs at a stage at which the fetus is insufficiently developed to experience harm, such as during the first trimester. Of course, such deliberate creation may have greater symbolic significance, because it denotes a willingness to use fetuses as a means or object to serve other ends. However, aborting when already pregnant to procure tissue for transplant (or aborting for the more customary reasons) also denotes a willingness to use the fetus as a means to other ends.

As long as abortion of an existing pregnancy for transplant purposes is ethically accepted, conceiving in order to abort and procure tissue for transplant should also be ethically acceptable when necessary to alleviate great suffering in others.[15] People could reasonably find that the additional symbolic devaluation is negligible, or in any case, insufficient to outweigh the substantial gain to transplant recipients that deliberate creation provides.

Many people, no doubt, will resist this conclusion, even if they accept abortion to procure tissue when the woman is already pregnant. Whether rational or not, they assign moral or symbolic significance to deliberate creation, and are less ready to sanction such a practice. Others who accept abortion for tissue procurement when the woman is already pregnant will find an insufficient difference in deliberate creation to outweigh the resulting good. Public acceptability of such a practice thus depends on how the swing group that views abortion as acceptable only for very stringent reasons views the fact of deliberate creation for the purpose of abortion. If it would accept abortion to produce tissue when the pregnancy is unplanned, it might accept conception to produce fetal tissue as well.

In sum, deliberate creation of fetuses to be aborted for tissue procurement is more ethically complex, and more defensible, than its current widespread dismissal would suggest. Such a practice is, of course, not in itself desirable, but in a specific situation of strong personal or familial need may be more justified than previously thought. In any case, the fear that fetal tissue transplants will lead to abortions performed solely to obtain tissue for transplant should not prevent use of tissue from abortions not performed for that purpose.

Recruiting Unrelated Fetal Tissue Donors

The strongest case for conception and abortion to produce fetal tissue—if the need arose—is to save oneself or a close relative from death or serious harm. But many patients in need would lack a female relative willing to donate. May unrelated women be recruited for this purpose?

If the hypothetical need arose, a strong case for unrelated fetal tissue donors can be made. If a relative may provide tissue, why not a stranger who chooses to do so altruistically? At this point concerns about fetal status become less important, and the focus shifts toward the welfare of the donor. But the physical effects of pregnancy and abortion to produce fetal tissue are roughly comparable to the effects of kidney or bone marrow donation, though somewhat less since general anesthesia will not be involved. While few unrelated persons now act as kidney donors, there is a national registry for unrelated bone marrow donors. Even if fetal tissue donation were psychologically more complicated, the risks to the woman would appear to be within the boundaries of autonomous choice.

Some persons might object that this will turn women into "fetal tissue farms," thus denigrating their inherent worth as persons. This charge would also be made against any living donor, whether of kidney, bone marrow, blood, sperm, or egg. Insofar as persons donate body parts, they may be viewed as mere tissue or organ producers. Indeed, women who bear children are always in danger of being viewed as "breeders." But such views oversimplify the complex emotional reality of organ and tissue donation and of human reproduction. The risk of misperception does not justify barring women from freely choosing to be fetal tissue donors.

Special attention should be given to consent procedures that will protect the woman from being coerced or unduly pressured by prospective recipients and their families, just as occurs with living related kidney and marrow donors. Waiting periods, consent advisors and monitors, and other devices to guarantee free, informed consent are clearly justified.[16]

Notes

The author gratefully acknowledges the helpful comments of Richard Markovits, Douglas Laycock, Michael Sharlot, Alan Fine, Albert R. Jonsen, George J. Annas, Arthur L. Caplan, Pat Cain, and Jean Love on a much longer version of this article.

1. Alan Fine, "The Ethics of Fetal Tissue Transplants," *Hastings Center Report* 18: 3 (June 1988), 5–8.

2. Kevin Lafferty, statement to the Fetal Transplantation Research Panel, National Institutes of Health, September 15, 1988.

3. 45 CFR 46.209; John A. Robertson, "Relaxing the Death Standard for Pediatric Organ Donations," in *Organ Substitution Technology:* Ethical, Legal, and Public Policy Issues (Boulder, CO: Westview Press, 1988), 69–77.

4. Stanley K. Henshaw *et al.* "A Portrait of American Women Who Obtain Abortions," *Family Planning Perspectives* 17: 2 (1985), 90–96.

5. Lafferty, "Statement."

6. James Burtchaell, "Case Study: University Policy on Experimental Use of Aborted Fetal Tissue," *IRB: A Review of Human Subjects Research* 10: 4 (July/August 1988), 7–11.

7. Burtchaell, "Case Study," 10; Phillip Shabecott, "Head of E.P.A. Bars Nazi Data in Study on Gas," *New York Times,* March 23, 1988, 1.

8. Leonard Tushnet, *The Uses of Adversity: Studies of Starvation in the Warsaw Ghetto* (New York: Thomas Yoseloff, 1966); "Minnesota Scientist Plans to Publish a Nazi Study," *New York Times,* May 12, 1988, 9.

9. Tamar Lewin, "Medical Use of Fetal Tissue Spurs New Abortion Debate," *New York Times,* Aug. 16, 1987, A1.

10. John A. Robertson, "Fetal Tissue Transplants," *Washington University Law Quarterly* 66: 3 (November 1988) (forthcoming).

11. Mary B. Mahowald, Jerry Silver, and Robert A. Ratcheson, "The Ethical Options in Transplanting Fetal Tissue," *Hastings Center Report* 17: 2 (February 1987), 9–15; Mark Danis, "Fetal Tissue Transplants: Restricting Recipient Designation," *Hastings Law Journal* 39: 5 (July 1988), 1079–1107.

12. Clifford Grobstein, *Science and the Unborn* (New York: Basic Books, 1988).

13. John A. Robertson, "Gestational Burdens and Fetal Status: A Defense of *Roe v. Wade.*" *American Journal of Law and Medicine* 13: 2/3 (1988), 189–212; John Bigelow and Robert Pargetter, "Morality, Potential Persons, and Abortion," *American Philosophical Quarterly* 25 (1988), 173–81.

14. See, for example, "America's Abortion Dilemma," *Newsweek,* January 14, 1985, 22–26.

15. John A. Robertson, "Embryos, Families, and Procreative Liberty: The Legal Structure of the New Reproduction," *Southern California Law Review* 59 (1986), 939–1041.

16. John A. Robertson, "Taking Consent Seriously: IRB Interventions in the Consent Process," *IRB: A Review of Human Subjects Research* 4: 5 (May 1982), 1–5.

Decision Scenario 1 ••

"What do you mean, you don't know who he is?" asked Dr. Bridewell, the head of the Oakbrook Hospital Renal Unit.

"He was unconscious when the police brought him to the ER. We started the IV, stopped his bleeding, and patched him up. But he still hasn't recovered consciousness. The police think it was a hit-and-run driver." Dr. Kathy McDowell spoke in a precise, matter-of-fact voice. Dr. Bridewell always frightened her, but she was determined not to show it.

"He didn't have any identification?"

"That's right. They think that either the driver robbed him or somebody else who came along did. Anyway, he was wearing jeans and a sweatshirt, nothing that gives any clue as to his background. There is one thing we do know definitely."

"What's that?" asked Dr. Bridewell.

"Both of his kidneys were hopelessly damaged, but his general physical condition is good. We think he's a good candidate for a transplant."

"Then you know we've got a guy whose brain waves we're waiting to flatten out?"

"Dr. Liebsbaum told me."

"He ought to keep his mouth shut," Dr. Bridewell said. "Oh, don't take that seriously. I'm just upset because this faces us with a big problem. We're only going to have one kidney to transplant. The other one's shot."

"That's all we want," said McDowell.

Bridewell ignored her. "You did a tissue check?" he asked.

"It's close enough."

"Too bad. What I mean is that I've got another candidate. Now we have to decide which of the two gets the kidney."

"Who's the other candidate?"

"A Mrs. Benson. She's a woman in her early sixties who's active in local affairs. She was on the school board. Her husband's a rich lawyer, and both of them move in high social circles. She does a lot of work now with a foundation that's supposed to help minority children in school. She also happens to be a pretty good candidate physically for a transplant."

"So you'll choose her over my patient?" McDowell felt herself getting angry.

"I didn't say that. How old is this guy?"

"I would estimate that he's in his early or middle thirties. He seems to be in good physical condition."

"But we don't know anything about him," said Dr. Bridewell. "He might just be a drifter passing through town. He's probably not a member of the community that this hospital is supposed to serve, the one that pays bills and makes donations."

"Not that we know of," Dr. McDowell admitted. "But he might be. He might be a person of great value. Maybe he's even a physician."

"But we don't know for sure, do we?" said Dr. Bridewell.

1. *Suppose you are Dr. Bridewell and have to decide between the unknown man and Mrs. Benson. On what grounds might you make your decision?*

2. *In the absence of any information about "social worth" and "family role," is it possible to apply Rescher's criteria in this case?*

3. *Does Annas's position suggest that the best way to solve the problem is just by tossing a coin?*

4. *Suppose the unknown patient regains consciousness and reveals that he is a state senator, the father of a two-year-old child, and a writer of detective novels. Might this information alter the way in which the decision would be made according to Annas? Might it alter the outcome of a decision based on the use of Rescher's criteria?*

Decision Scenario 2 ●●

Colin Benton, a British citizen, died in the summer of 1988 of renal disease after a kidney transplant failed. Benton's widow later revealed that the donor kidney has been obtained from a Turkish citizen who traveled to London for the surgery. The kidney donor was paid the equivalent of around $4,400. When asked why he had sold the organ, the man explained that he needed the money to pay for medical treatment for his daughter. It was this case that led the British Parliament to outlaw organ sales.

1. *Suppose that we own our own bodies, then on what grounds might Kass consider selling one of our kidneys wrong?*

2. *What view of selling an organ might be taken by a natural law theorist? For such a theorist, is there a moral distinction between donating a kidney out of benevolence and selling one for financial gain?*

3. *If a father has no other way to raise money for surgery necessary to preserve the life of his child, would it be morally permissible for him to sell a kidney? Should we hold him morally blameworthy if, given the opportunity, he refused to do so?*

4. *Is selling one's kidney different in any morally relevant way from selling one's labor under potentially hazardous conditions (e.g., mining coal)?*

Decision Scenario 3 ●●●

Valdez Regional Hospital is the primary medical facility for the residents of Valdez County, Arizona. Its intensive-care unit is the only one available in the entire county, and the closest comparable unit is eighty-five miles away in Somora County.

The Valdez ICU is a twelve-bed facility and,

from the statistical point of view, it is generally adequate to serve the needs of its patient population. That is, the cost of adding extra equipment and staff to increase the size of the facility is much greater than its actual use would justify.

Valdez's ICU policy, which is similar to policies of hospitals everywhere, requires that the staff make the effort to keep at least one of the twelve beds free for use in a genuine emergency.

On a bright, clear afternoon one day after Christmas, sixty-eight-year-old Harry Aveni was brought to the emergency room of Valdez after he had collapsed on the patio of his house. Mr. Aveni had been brought to the emergency room twice before. Both were episodes of congestive heart failure, and this third occasion was no different. Mr. Aveni had broken his diet during the holidays and consumed an unaccustomed amount of salt.

Mr. Aveni responded well to emergency treatment. The fluid surrounding his heart was withdrawn, a glycoside medication was administered, and his condition seemed to stabilize. Then, that evening, there was a sudden onset of fibrillation—his heart started beating erratically. Again, Mr. Aveni responded well to treatment, and after emergency defibrillation his condition again stabilized.

"He needs to be put into the ICU," Dr. Ellen Gracian said. "We can't care for him sufficiently on the wards, because he's got to have constant monitoring."

"I don't think Dr. Franklin is going to want to admit him," the nurse said. "There's only one bed left."

Dr. Gracian immediately left the floor and went to the ICU director's office. She explained what she wanted and waited while he seemed to be thinking it over.

"I don't think I can admit him," Dr. Franklin said. "Here we have an elderly gentleman who has now gone through three episodes of congestive failure and also seems to have something wrong to cause the fibrillation. He didn't stick to his diet, and

in general his days are likely to be in the rather small numbers."

"But if he doesn't have intensive care, the numbers may be even smaller," Dr. Gracian said.

"That's no doubt true. But as things are, we've got eleven people who need to stay right where they are for God knows how long, and we've got just one bed at our disposal."

"But that's all I need, just one bed."

"I understand that," said Dr. Franklin. "But let's suppose we install your patient in the ICU and fifteen minutes after we put him there an eighteen-year-old accident victim is brought in. She's going to have to have emergency treatment, then close and constant monitoring, or she's likely to die."

"But you don't know that somebody like that is going to come in," Dr. Gracian said. "And Mr. Aveni is here right now and is in need right now."

"I'm sorry," said Dr. Franklin. "But the chances are very good that somebody is going to need that bed, somebody we can do more for than we can do for your patient. Somebody who's got a better chance to live a longer and more normal life."

"I see," Dr. Gracian said. "But I thought we were in the business of saving lives."

"We are. But we can't save them all, and that's where the problems come in."

1. What argument can be made from the point of view of an act utilitarian to support Dr. Franklin's decision?

2. Is the fact that Mr. Aveni broke his diet and so is, in some sense, responsible for being in immediate need relevant to deciding whether he should be admitted to the ICU?

3. Would any of the criteria presented by Rescher lead to the selection of Mr. Aveni over an eighteen-year-old accident victim?

4. Would Annas's recognition of immediate need as a justification for selection in transplants also justify granting intensive care to Mr. Aveni?

Decision Scenario 4 ••

The microsurgical team at Benton Public Hospital consisted of twenty-three people. Five were surgeons, three were anesthesiologists, three were internists, two were radiologists, and the remain-

ing members were various sorts of nurses and technicians.

Early Tuesday afternoon on a date late in March, the members of the team that had to be sterile were scrubbing while the others were preparing to start operating on Mr. Hammond Cox. Mr. Cox was a fifty-nine-year-old unmarried African American who worked as a janitor in a large apartment building. While performing his duties, Mr. Cox had caught his hand in the mechanism of a commercial trash compactor. The bones of his wrist had been crushed and the blood vessels severed.

The head of the team, Dr. Herbert Lagorio, believed that it was possible to restore at least partial functioning to Mr. Cox's hand. Otherwise, the hand would have to be amputated.

Mr. Cox had been drunk when the accident happened. When the police ambulance brought him to the emergency room, he was still so drunk that a decision was made to delay surgery for almost an hour to give him a chance to burn up some of the alcohol he had consumed. As it was, administering anesthesia to Mr. Cox would incur a greater-than-average risk. Furthermore, blood tests had shown that Mr. Cox already suffered from some degree of liver damage. In both short- and long-range terms, Mr. Cox was not a terribly good surgical risk.

Dr. Lagorio was already scrubbed when Dr. Carol Levine, a resident in emergency medicine, had him paged.

"This had better be important," he told her. "I've got a guy prepped and waiting."

"I know you do," Dr. Levine said. "But there's something you ought to know about before you start."

"Tell me quickly."

"They just brought in a thirty-five-year-old white female with a totally severed right hand. She's a biology professor at Columbia and was working late in her lab when some maniac looking for drugs came in and attacked her with a cleaver."

"What shape is the hand in?"

"Excellent. The campus cops were there within minutes, and there was ice in the lab. One of the cops had the good sense to put the hand in a plastic bag and bring it with her."

"Is she in good general health?"

"It seems excellent," Dr. Levine said.

"This is a real problem."

"You can't do two cases at once?"

"No way. We need everybody we've got to do one."

"How about sending her someplace else?"

"No place else is set up to do what has to be done," Dr. Lagorio said.

"So what are you going to do?"

"That's what I've got to decide," Dr. Lagorio said.

1. Does a "first-come, first-served" criterion like that defended by Annas require that Mr. Cox receive the surgery?

2. Does a "social-value" criterion require that the biology professor receive the surgery?

3. Can the chance of a successful outcome in each case be used as a criterion without violating the notion that all people are of equal inherent worth?

4. Should the fact that Mr. Cox's injury is the consequence of his own negligence be considered in determining to whom Dr. Lagorio ought to devote his attentions? How are Cohen and Benjamin likely to stand on this question?

5. In your view, who should have the potential benefits of the surgery? Give reasons to support your view.

Decision Scenario 5 •••

"Your baby's pituitary gland is not fully developed," Dr. Robert Amatin said.

Clarissa Austin nodded to show that she understood that at least something was wrong with her child. She had already made up her mind to do whatever she had to do to see to it that her baby was all right.

"That means he's not getting enough of a hormone—a chemical—produced there," Dr. Amatin went on. "He won't undergo the normal course of development without that chemical."

"Can you give it to him?"

Dr. Amatin avoided answering the question directly. "A transplant is the best hope," he said. "If we can surgically remove the malformed pituitary and attach a new one, then the baby has a very good chance of being normal."

"I'll be happy to give my permission, if that's what you're waiting for," Clarissa said.

"It's not that simple," Dr. Amatin said. He looked uncomfortable. "It really comes down to a matter of money."

"I don't have much money," Clarissa said. "You know my bills are being paid by Medicaid."

"I know that, and the government won't pay for transplant organs."

"How much does it cost?"

"I've got a family right now that says it wants $5,000 for the pituitary of their baby. She just died this morning."

"I can't get money like that," Clarissa said.

"I can ask them to come up and talk to you. Maybe they would take less, or maybe you could work out some kind of deferred payment with them."

"What if I can't?"

Dr. Amatin shook his head. "I can't arrange for a transplant without an organ, and I suspect they will just try to find somebody else to sell it to."

"That don't seem fair," Clarissa said. "Just because I haven't got the money, my little baby is going to have to be some kind of cripple and maybe die."

1. Does the possibility of such situations demonstrate that the present policy of relying on donated organs is a superior one?

2. If organs are sold on the open market, are such situations inevitable?

3. What other organ procurement policy, besides voluntary donation and organ sales, might be worth considering as a means to increase the number of transplant organs available?

4. Is Ms. Austin correct in saying that it would be unfair for her child not to have the organ because she cannot afford to pay the asking price? After all, surely it is not unfair for her child not to have, say, a silver drinking cup because she cannot afford to pay the asking price.

5. On what grounds does Annas object to the market approach? What position might Kinsley take?

Decision Scenario 6 ••

Jean-Pierre Bosze, twelve years old, had leukemia. The disease was under control for a while, but then Jean-Pierre had a relapse. His father was told that his son's only hope was to have a bone marrow transplant, but neither the boy's father nor his mother was a suitable match. Bosze's twenty-two-year-old son from a previous marriage also failed to be a match, and his thirteen-month-old daughter by another woman was too young to be a donor.

In desperation, Tamas Bosze turned to his other children, Jimmy and Allison Curran, three-year-old twins by yet another woman. The chance of a tissue match between them and their half-brother would be much greater than the 1-in-20,000 chance offered by an unrelated individual.

However, the mother of the twins, Nancy Curran, from whom Tamas Bosze was estranged, refused to permit the children to be tested. Curran explained that she did not want the twins to suffer the pain of having the marrow extracted or to be subjected to the risk involved. General anesthesia carries a risk of death in 1 in 10,000 cases and of complications in about 1 in 300 cases.

Bosze's paternity had been established in a suit by Curran seeking child support. The blood tests showed that the twins matched Jean-Pierre in two of the six factors considered basic for compatibility. "Strangers are calling up to offer bone marrow and blood, and she won't help," Bosze said. He decided to file suit to force Curran to allow the twins to be tested.

"I don't feel that I'm killing this boy," Curran said. "I could be killing my own children if I let this happen."

On September 28, 1990, the Illinois Supreme Court ruled that the mother of the twins could not be compelled to permit them to be tested as potential bone marrow donors for Jean-Pierre. Jean-Pierre Bosze died early in 1991.

1. *The court offered no reasons for its decision. What grounds might be offered?*

2. *Might a utilitarian argue that the twins should be tested, because the slight risk it poses to them is offset by the potentially great advantage to Jean-Pierre?*

3. *Would putting the twins at any risk to provide benefit to someone else violate the Kantian notion that it is wrong to treat persons as a means only?*

4. *What reasons might be presented in favor of a national policy of testing that would make virtually every citizen a potential organ donor? What might be said in criticism of such a policy?*

Decision Scenario 7 ••

"My client asked me not to tell you his name, but he did want me to be perfectly explicit about everything else," Consuelo Cortez said. "He's married and has two children, but he also suffers from Parkinson's disease. His doctors think that a transplant of fetal cells has a good chance of stopping or at least slowing the progress of his disease."

"He wants me to get pregnant," Alice Williams said, cutting into the other woman's explanation.

"Well, yes," Cortez said. "He wants you to get pregnant and then have an abortion at a time the doctors think best. My client will then become owner of the fetal tissue, and it will be used to treat him."

"Who does he want me to become pregnant with?"

"That's entirely up to you. I think you should work this out with your husband. If he doesn't want to make you pregnant, then artificial insemination is always a possibility."

"Twenty thousand and expenses?" Williams asked.

"Five thousand when you get pregnant, and the rest of the money when my client receives the tissue."

"But would I be doing something wrong?" Williams asked.

1. *Apart from the issue of abortion, is there anything inherently wrong in selling fetal tissue?*

2. *If the tissue were going to be donated to someone in need, would this change the moral character of the act?*

3. *Suppose that abortion was not involved and the tissue in question was from miscarriages. Would it be wrong to sell this tissue?*

4. *Why does Robertson think that the issue of conception with the aim of having an abortion to obtain fetal tissue is more morally complicated than is usually recognized?*

5. *If Williams is already pregnant and planning to have an abortion, would it necessarily be wrong, according to Robertson, to employ the fetal tissue in a medical treatment? How does he answer the charge that to do so would be to encourage abortion and contribute to its entrenchment as a social practice?*

Decision Scenario 8 ••

Dr. Sarah Brandywine hurried into Dr. Kline's inner office. Dr. Kline was transplant coordinator at Midwestern General Hospital, and he was expecting her. She had called him for an appointment as soon as she had realized the dimension of the problem with Mr. Wardell.

"So tell me about Mr. Wardell," Dr. Kline said, nodding toward the chair beside his desk.

"He's a fifty-one-year-old man who came to the hospital two days ago because he was fright-ened by the jaundice and ascites he developed over the course of the last week," Dr. Brandywine said. "He had been experiencing fatigue and loss of appetite several weeks prior to the jaundice. His liver is swollen and lumpy."

"Sounds like cirrhosis," Dr. Kline said. "I'm sure you did liver function tests, but what about a biopsy?"

"We did both yesterday, and I called you right after the final results. There's so much scarring that

Mr. Wardell has little liver function left." She shook her head. "I want to put him on the transplant list."

"He's within the age guidelines." Dr. Kline nodded. "What's the cause of his disease?"

"It's alcohol-induced."

"No way." Dr. Kline shook his head. "No livers for alcoholics. No ifs, ands, or buts about it."

"This is a man with two kids." Dr. Brandywine tried to keep her voice level. "One's twelve, and the other is eight. Their mother died two years ago, and their dad is all they've got left."

"Oh, God, the kids make it particularly sad." Dr. Kline's face took on a pained expression. "But look, thirty thousand people a year die from alcoholic cirrhosis, and we can't treat them all."

"I know we can't, but can't we treat some?" Dr. Brandywine leaned forward. "Is being an alcoholic enough for an automatic turndown?"

"I'm afraid so." Dr. Kline nodded. "These are people who created their own problem. There are far from being enough livers to go around, so it's only fair for us to put folks with problems not of their own making on the list and to leave others off."

"But, look, this guy's got two kids depending on him." Sarah squeezed her hands into fists. "If I can get him into a rehab program, can we promise him the chance at a liver then?" She quickly added. "Not a guaranteed liver, but just a chance at one."

"I'm sorry to say it, but the answer's still no." Dr. Kline paused. "I'm not saying alcoholics can't be reformed, but I am saying they're bad risks. If we give a transplant to somebody whose liver was destroyed by biliary cirrhosis, we're likely to get a good, long-term survival. But if we transplant somebody who's been drinking for the last ten or twenty years, we're not likely to get good, long-term results. The guy may promise to stop drinking, and maybe he'll do it for a while. But chances are good that, within a few years, he's going to be back in the hospital with liver failure again, and alcohol is going to be the cause."

"I admit the numbers are against me." Dr. Brandywine inhaled deeply, then let her breath out in a long whoosh. "There's nothing I can say to convince you?"

"We can't afford to risk wasting a liver," Dr. Kline said. "That's what I've got to convince you of." He shook his head. "It breaks my heart to think about Mr. Wardell's children, but we've got children who need livers too. I've got to think about them, and I've got to think about the parents with cirrhosis who aren't alcoholics."

1. State explicitly the two arguments against liver transplants for alcoholics that Dr. Kline invokes.

2. Why should so-called life-style factors be considered relevant in making transplant decisions? By the same reasoning, shouldn't we deny heart transplants to people who, through overeating and lack of exercise, have allowed themselves to become fat? Why should alcoholics be held to a higher standard than others needing transplants?

3. How would Cohen, Benjamin et al. respond to Dr. Kline's argument? What might Dr. Kline say in response to their criticisms?

4. If you were responsible for determining whether there would be a categorical exclusion of alcoholics from receiving liver transplants, what would you decide? How would you justify that decision?

CHAPTER 10

THE CLAIM TO HEALTH CARE [

SOCIAL CONTEXT: THE UNRESOLVED CRISIS IN HEALTH CARE

A crisis exists in a social institution when there are factors present that tend to destroy the institution or render it ineffective in achieving its goals. Two major factors have led observers to say that the American health-care system is in a state of crisis: the increasing cost to the society of health care and the failure to deliver health care to those who need it.

Despite the widespread expectation in 1994 that either the "Clinton plan" or some other legislative proposal would deal with the crisis and drastically alter the way American health care is funded and utilized, this did not happen. The crisis remains unresolved. We will briefly examine each major factor constitutive of the situation, then consider some solutions that have been offered.

Cost of Health Care

In 1950 the United States spent about the same amount on health care as on national defense. Around half that amount was spent on education. Now education and defense spending are about equal, while the costs of health care takes more of the gross domestic product than the other two added together.

Looking at the same point from another perspective, in 1960 health spending in the United States amounted to some $27 billion. In 1970 it rose to $75 billion, and in 1983 it increased to $356 billion. By 1994, spending had climbed to an estimated $1 trillion. This represents an expenditure of over $3,000 per capita, compared to the 1960 figure of $145. As a per-

cent of the gross domestic product, the cost of health care has virtually tripled, from 5.3% to about 15%.

The steadily increasing cost of health care to the nation is reflected in increasing costs to patients. In a 1994 survey of 1,623 households, 1 in 5 families reported difficulty in paying medical bills. To the surprise of the researchers, nearly three-quarters of those families were insured. A 1993 report from the Henry J. Kaiser Family foundation reported that Americans had an average of $909 in medical expenses not covered by medical insurance. This was so, even though the average adult spent $86 per month on medical insurance premiums, for an annual expenditure of over $2,000. Six percent of the adult population spent over $3,600 a year on health insurance, and 11 percent spent more than $2,000 on medical care, over and above insurance premiums.

Thirty percent of those who have to pay bills for home care or nursing homes are out-of-pocket more than three thousand dollars per year. Only 1 in 5 Americans contribute nothing toward health insurance.

Federal health spending has also risen sharply. Money spent caring for the elderly and handicapped under Medicare and for the very poor under Medicaid rose from $128 billion in 1988 to $200 billion in 1992. State spending for its share of Medicaid went up 22% in 1991 and 33% in 1992. According to some reports, states in 1994 are spending more for medical care than for education.

Even though the United States spends considerably more on health care than any other country, the expenditure does not clearly yield the results that might be expected. The life expectancy (using a 1992 base) in Japan is

78.6 years, even though Japan spends (using 1991 figures) 6.8% of its GDP on health care. Life expectancy in Greece, which spends only 4.8% of GDP on medical care, is 77.3 years. The United States spends (1992) 13.3% of its GDP on health care, yet when ranked in terms of life expectancy, it ranks near the bottom of the list of industrialized nations.

Analysts see the spiraling costs of health care as threatening the economic welfare of the country. The over three thousand dollars per person the United States spends on health costs is not matched by other industrialized nations. Japan spends hardly more than half this amount, and Great Britain about one-third. Because the United States spends such a large percentage of its GDP on health care, the costs of U.S. goods will be comparatively higher than those of other exporting nations. (Health-care expenditures contribute about 10% to the cost of a car.) Consequently, the United States will not be as effective a competitor in world trade and will be faced with an ever more serious balance of payments problem and with the loss of even more domestic industries.

Various explanations have been given for the rising costs of health care. Economists point out that in medicine a surplus of services does not drive the price down. Instead, it seems to drive up demand. The availability of laboratories, high-technology equipment, hospital beds, and a variety of medical services increases the probability that they will be used. As economist Dick Davidson put the point, "We pay for medical care on a piece-work basis." Hence, "there is an incentive for more medical encounters."

Apart from the way the health-care system operates, other factors having to do with a changing population and the state of medicine itself are no doubt responsible to some extent for increasing costs. Here are three of them:

- As children born during the baby boom of the 1940s have reached adulthood, the median age of the population has increased. An aging population requires more medical care and more expensive medical care than a population with a lower median age.

- Advancements in medical technology now make it possible to provide a greater number of services to hospitalized patients. Hence, more people are likely to be hospitalized in order to receive the services.

- Improvements in medicine and surgery now make it possible to provide therapies for diseases that once would not have been treated. The availability of such treatments means increasing the hospital population, and the success of such treatments means that more people will be alive who can benefit from additional care. The success of medicine creates the need for more medicine.

Such considerations as these have persuaded nearly everyone concerned about national health-care needs and policies that the current state of affairs needs to be changed. A common (though by no means universal) belief is that if the American health-care system is not substantially altered, it will become so economically unrealistic that it will collapse. The result then is likely to be the emergence of a three-tier system in which the rich get the care they need, the middle class the care they can afford and the poor the care we are willing to give them.

The Need for Health Care

- Trinidad Estrada is twenty-nine years old and has three children. She has a full-time job making burritos in a restaurant. The job requires her to stand all day, and she needs foot surgery that will cost one thousand dollars. She has neither insurance nor the cash to pay for it. She can get the surgery she needs only if she quits her job, goes on welfare, and qualifies for Medicaid.

- Rick Reckoway works hard as an electrician and was careful to get medical insurance for his family. When his son was born with heart and respiratory problems, Reckoway believed that he would be able to pay the medical bills. Yet he found that his insurance had a cap of $100,000, and to pay for his son's treatment, he had to go into debt for $700,000.

- Bob Hughes spent years as a manager with overseas companies, but after he lost his last job, he returned to Houston. He wanted to get health insurance for himself and his wife, but he was unable to afford the $568-monthly premiums quoted to him. "I don't want a dole from the government," Mr. Hughes said. "Just a little help, a little protection until I get reemployed."

- Laura Bright is a twenty-six-year-old actress who lives in New York and supports herself by waiting on tables. "I'm honestly thinking of giving up acting in search of a career with benefits," she told a reporter. "It's a sad thing."

Despite the great economic investment in health care, the U.S. medical system has a great many shortcomings. Some studies show that more than 10% of the population receive no care at all and that more than 4 million people in need of care do not get it.

Although efforts over the past two decades have improved access to health care for low-income and minority groups, a significant portion of this population is still not receiving needed care. The situation continues to grow worse. The tightening of federal and state regulations determining eligibility for Medicaid and Medicare has led to a sharp decline in the percentage of poor people receiving benefits.

Furthermore, the number of people without medical insurance has reached 39 million, up from 29 million in 1979. Because people leave and enter the insurance rolls, some analysts estimate that as many as 50 to 60 million people are uninsured for at least some of the time during the year. Half those without insurance are children or are families with children, and children themselves make up about 20% of the uninsured.

Recent studies show that when uninsured people are admitted to hospitals, they are discharged earlier and receive fewer diagnostic and therapeutic procedures than those who have insurance. Some see results of this kind as evidence that the United States has already moved to at least a two-tier medical system in which the poor are provided with second-class care, while those able to pay receive the best care available.

It is a mistake to think of the uninsured as homeless drifters. According to 1992 figures, 52.4% have full-time, year-round jobs, while 7.8% work part-time year round. Only 15.6% do not work at least some during the year. In half of uninsured households, one person works full-time, and in another third, a person works part time or part of the year. Working families with low to moderate income make up the largest group of the uninsured. The extremely poor are covered by Medicaid, but those who earn above the Medicaid limit must finance their own health care.

Why are millions of Americans lacking coverage to pay the expenses that accompany serious illness or injury? The situation is partly due to the loss of jobs in industries that provided insurance coverage for their workers and to the rise in part-time jobs in companies that offer no health insurance. Another major cause has been the increase in insurance costs. For group plans, benefits have been cut back and rates increased. The cost of family coverage under an average group-rate plan went from $235 per month in 1988 to $436 per month in 1992.

Those forced to buy their own insurance have faced a steadily rising increase of about 20% per year. High administrative costs and a lack of bargaining power also means that individuals must pay much higher premiums. It is small wonder, then, that the self-employed or the unemployed (like Bob Hughes) are forced to go without medical insurance.

The "working poor" (like Trinidad Estrada) often find they make too much money to be eligible for the stringent requirements of Medicaid, yet they make too little money to buy health insurance after they have paid for food and housing.

The increased number of people with AIDS or with chronic diseases who are rejected by insurance companies has also contributed to the number of uninsured. Also, insurance companies have been accused of blacklisting groups of workers and denying them coverage. Bartenders, dentists, AIDS workers, gas-station attendants, and oil drillers are a few of the more than forty occupational groups sometimes declared uninsurable.

In the 1980s, not only did more Americans start losing insurance than signing up for it, but millions of others had their coverage reduced. They became underinsured for all but relatively uncomplicated medical needs. We saw earlier that in a large survey, 1 in 5 people reported that they had difficulty paying their medical bills, and that three-quarters of them had medical insurance. Those faced with medical catastrophes (as Rick Reckoway was) often find themselves forced to go deeply into debt or even to declare bankruptcy.

Furthermore, studies show that the underinsured often delay seeking medical treatment. The result is often that a disease that could have been treated effectively and inexpensively at an early stage can only be treated with greater expense and less effectiveness.

The fear of being in medical need and not being able to get care has become a specter haunting many Americans. Many keep unwanted jobs, rather than take others or start businesses of their own, primarily because they fear losing health insurance for themselves and their families. Laura Bright no doubt represents thousands who make decisions about their careers significantly on the basis of their need to be sure that they will be cared for if they become sick or injured.

The failure of the current medical system to guarantee an adequate level of health care (a "decent minimum," as often phrased) to everyone in the society in need of it was a major force behind the recent effort by President Clinton to establish a national health plan that would provide universal coverage. Although the Clinton plan met with legislative defeat, few doubt that we need some sort of plan. The current system is not working properly. We now live with a system offering two kinds of medicine—one for the rich and one for the poor. And it too often happens that the medicine for the poor is none at all.

Proposed Solutions

The intense national debate about health care in 1994 produced a number of proposals for radically reforming the ways in which medical care is financed and delivered. All the proposals addressed the conjoined issues of increasing costs and the need to provide greater access to health care, but the proposals differed significantly in advocating ways in which costs might be controlled and in recommending how and to what extent access might be provided.

Managed Competition.   People in a geographical region would be clustered into state based pools or "health alliances." The pools would include the uninsured, people now paying for their own insurance, and those working for small companies. Companies with many employees would, in effect, constitute their own health alliance.

The health alliances (and large companies) would bargain with the representatives of various health plans (including those operated by private, for-profit insurance companies) to obtain a standard set of basic benefits for reasonable rates.

The plan would offer universal care, and everyone would have access to the same basic insurance. However, group members would be offered the choice of several plans. People without resources would have no option but to choose one of the basic plans. Tax incentives would encourage all members to choose lower-cost plans, but if members could pay extra, they would get extra coverage or privileges (for example, consulting a physician who is not in the health plan).

Physicians, hospitals, and insurers would join together to form provider groups. The provider groups would offer health plans to the health alliances. Most plans would probably be like those now offered by health maintenance organizations (HMOs), in which for a set yearly fee the HMO undertakes to provide all needed medical care. The provider groups would compete with one another to offer plans to attract the most patients. The plans would be judged in terms of price and quality. Hence, the mechanism of competition should keep prices as low as possible, while providing as much quality as possible.

The role of government would be to supervise the process, guarantee the quality of care, and make sure that the poor are enrolled in alliances.

The managed-care plan could be financed in a variety of ways. The way it was proposed by President Clinton, it would be paid for by a combination of taxes, employee premiums, and an "employer mandate" (that is, a premium paid by employers). Small businesses and poor individuals would be subsidized by the government.

Advantages. Managed care offers universal coverage, portability of insurance (people can move from one health alliance to another without losing insurance), accessibility (everyone has access to the medical system), and comprehensiveness (coverage for medically necessary conditions). In addition, managed care makes the promise of controlling costs, while also providing high quality medical care.

Criticisms. Most people are happy with the present system of medical care, and man-

aged care would force them into a new and untried system. The HMO-type plans would require people to choose physicians from an approved list, and people would be forced to deal with a "gatekeeper" to gain access to specialists.

Provider groups, forced to lower prices in response to competition, may reduce the quality of care they give to patients. Even with government oversight, the pressure on investor-owned groups to make a profit is likely to lead to undertreatment, undertesting, and a delay in referring patients to needed specialists.

The awkward structure of a health alliance–provider group system would only add to the already high costs of paperwork. The almost 25% of health costs now spent on administration could be better spent on improving care. If private investors (insurance companies) were removed from the system, savings would be even greater.

The system is completely untried, and as a result, it is not clear that the savings from implementing it would be as great as they need to be to control health costs. Also, from a practical perspective, how would the system handle rural areas, where there can be no competition because there are few physicians? What could be done about plans that attract a disproportionately large number of older or sicker patients?

These criticisms are not necessarily unanswerable. They are some of the questions raised about the managed-competition health plan proposed by President Clinton and rejected by the Congress.

Single-Payer Plan. All citizens and legal residents would be automatically enrolled in a program of national health insurance established by the federal government and administered by the states. Everyone would be provided with a basic minimum of medical care, and would be able to choose their own physicians. Private insurance premiums could be replaced by a combination of taxes that would include payroll taxes on employers and a tax on employee's income. Private insurers would offer policies for benefits not covered in the basic-services packages.

Advantages. The single-payer plan offers universal coverage, portability of insurance, accessibility, and comprehensiveness. It offers the possibility of controlling costs, while providing high-quality medical care. It cuts down on overhead expenses, preserves people's freedom to choose physicians, and breaks the control that the insurance industry has on American medical care. The emphasis on primary care and prevention would not only save money, but also lead to a general improvement in the health of the nation.

The single-payer system is the simplest and most direct way of providing for universal coverage. Further, it has a proven track record in Canada, and a very similar system has been successful in Hawaii. (See the two Case Presentations.)

Criticisms. The change is too radical to be accepted by Americans, and it involves the government too deeply in health care. There is no reason to believe that the system will control costs adequately, and it is likely to lead to long delays in treatment and even a rationing system. The emphasis on primary care would eventually result in slowing the advance in American medical technology.

Managed Care. Managed care is the name given to medical care that is provided in such a way that costs are controlled by restricting access to the more expensive forms of testing and treatment. Typically, patients are limited to seeing specific physicians and being admitted to particular hospitals. In principle, emphasis is placed on preventive care, and patients receive only the testing and therapies that they genuinely require.

In the last twenty years, businesses have steadily moved away from group health insurance paying fees-for-service toward managed care. The earliest and most popular form of managed care is the health maintenance organization. An HMO is a medical plan in which a fixed annual fee is paid to an organized group of physicians and hospitals ("health-care providers"). The group then undertakes to supply the individual with most kinds of needed medical services, at no additional charge.

Enrollment in HMOs has soared from 12.5 million in 1983 to 45.2 million in 1993. The HMO is popular with business because it permits the chance to reduce medical costs to a company by negotiating fees with the provider group. The provider group agrees to supply medical care in accordance with specific rules. These rules are designed to avoid unnecessary tests and procedures, because the profit of the provider group is determined by the money remaining after the expenses of patients have been paid.

Patients are penalized for going "out of network" to other physicians and hospitals, and physicians must follow strict rules in approving or denying care. Often, there is a personal financial incentive for the physician not to refer a patient to a specialist. In every case, the primary-care physician serves as a "gatekeeper," controlling the patient's access to specialized testing and care.

Better patient care is claimed to result from HMOs because they encourage patients to consult a physician at the beginning of an illness, rather than waiting until it grows serious. This is advantageous both to the patient and the HMO, which can avoid spending a larger part of its budget treating the patient's more serious condition.

The managed-care concept is applied in various forms. Some HMOs have actual physical locations, while others are "HMOs without walls." Preferred provider operations (PPOs) have the advantage of allowing individuals to choose their physicians from a list of those who have entered into the arrangement. In this way, a major complaint against HMOs—that the individual is required to receive care from a group and has no physician of his own—is avoided.

In the view of many analysts, managed care offers the best approach to providing universal coverage. As an approach to medical care, it is compatible with a number of plans for providing care—including the two previously discussed.

Advantages. Managed care can reduce health-care costs for particular groups by restricting access to secondary and tertiary health care. Further, by emphasizing preventive care and keeping out-of-pocket expenses low, people are encouraged to consult physicians more often. The outcomes of treatment rules are typically researched, with the result that a rational basis for decisions can be established. Surveys show that people in managed-care groups are generally pleased with the care they receive.

Criticisms. Economists question whether managed care provides overall savings on health care. Contracts that are negotiated with providers may be so low that they result in physicians and hospitals shifting some of the cost of a managed-care patient to patients with more insurance benefits.

Both managers and physicians have an incentive to encourage physicians to provide less-than-optimal care to maximize profits. Patients may be dissatisfied with the care they receive and yet not be able to do much about it. For example, an HMO may refuse to pay for the long-term use of an expensive drug to treat an enlarged prostate, but be willing to pay for prostate surgery. The choice is not left up to the patient. Acting as gatekeepers, physicians (often, in practice, their staff) are empowered to turn down requests for medical services or consultations.

Disability-rights groups have asserted strongly that the disabled should have access to the best specialists, even if they are not part of the network. Also, anecdotal evidence suggests that many individuals, accustomed to taking charge of their own medical care, become highly dissatisfied with managed care.

Physicians have often been critical of managed care. Some have felt that the rules imposed on them by the managers of particular plans do not allow them to practice medicine in the best way. Even when they do not disagree with the rules, some say that they find the rules irksome, narrow, and demeaning.

Physicians have also complained of being excluded from membership in managed-care organizations. If the physicians do not follow the rules, they may be dropped from a group without recourse. Or if they are in an area dominated by managed-care groups, they might wish to join one or more of the groups, yet be turned down. This could be financially and professionally disastrous for them.

Incremental Solutions. The debates over health care in 1994 left many people pessimistic about the possibility of a wholesale change in American health care. Neither the political nor the public will to make the change seemed present. Others became convinced that there was no need to make wholesale changes and that the problems of increasing costs and access to care could be solved merely by altering some aspects of the current system.

The American Medical Association, with a membership of 42% of licensed physicians in the United States, abandoned its ambitious plan for health-care reform that would include universal coverage and recommended that the nation "search for ways to expand access to care with an incremental reform approach." Executive Vice-President James Todd said, "Our goal of universal coverage has not changed, it's just that we need to find ways of getting there in an incremental fashion."

The following are among the numerous proposals being discussed for patching up the present system of health care:

1. *Subsidies.* To deal with the uninsured and the underinsured, provide direct government subsidies to pay for the cost of their insurance. Critics fear that such a program would encourage employers to reduce even further the insurance cover-

age they provide their workers. Why should a business pay for a high level of benefits, if the government will make up the difference between the cost of care covered by insurance and the cost billed to the patient?

2. *Standard benefits.* Insurers should be required to offer a minimal level of benefits. In this way, those who are underinsured would be covered. Critics see such a step as an unwarranted interference with market forces.

3. *Insurance regulations.* Insurers should be required to cover people with preexisting conditions. They should also be required to make insurance portable, so that people can take their coverage with them when they change jobs or become unemployed.

4. *Community rating.* Insurers currently charge different rates to different segments of the population. The rates are based on the expected frequency of diseases in the various segments. Thus, the old pay higher rates than the young. Community rating would even out premiums to reflect the average cost of insuring the whole community.

Critics claim that this would unfairly penalize young people and lead many of them to drop their insurance. Indeed, something like this happened in 1993 when New York State ended rate variation based on age. Rates went down for people in their sixties, while rising for the young and healthy. A half million younger people canceled their insurance. The result was that the premiums of those remaining sharply increased because those left in the pool were, on the average, sicker than before.

5. *State experiments.* Several states have already attempted innovative health-care plans for their citizens. However, the development of some types of plans is inhibited by federal regulations affecting Medicare, Medicaid, and other programs. Setting aside these regulations would allow states to experiment with a variety of approaches.

Critics point out that having a variety of state health-care programs will make it difficult for companies that do business across the country to operate. They will be faced with a patchwork of laws and regulations. Furthermore, state programs may become so entrenched that they stand in the way of eventually achieving a needed national reform.

Faced with the failure of complete health reform, yet recognizing the nagging persistence of a host of problems, almost every analyst and politician is willing to endorse at least some small-scale changes. The attitude of most is summed up in health economist Uwe Reinhardt's statement about incremental change: "It's like fixing a car, and in some ways this car is going to get worse, but it will still carry you some miles."

The crisis in health care has not abated, yet the system has not collapsed either. Significant reform probably lies in the future, but meanwhile, we must deal with today.

CASE PRESENTATION
Drawing the Line in Oregon: Rationing Health Care

A new law took effect in Oregon in June 1988: No longer would the state pay for heart, liver, pancreas, or bone marrow transplants for the poor.

States typically pay from 25% to 40% of the $100,000 to $200,000 cost of a transplant under the Medicaid program for the poor, and the federal government pays the rest. However, no one is eligible for federal funds until the state has agreed to pay its share. Oregon decided to use the $1.1 million it annually spent on organ transplants to increase the funding for prenatal care, a program it believed would provide more health benefits.

A consequence of this decision was immediately obvious. Oregon residents began seeing posters with photographs of children needing organ transplants. The children's parents, unable to get support from the state and unable to pay the bills themselves, were desperately trying to keep their children alive by raising enough money from donations to meet the enormous costs of transplants.

Coby Howard, a seven-year-old boy, was the first to appear on a poster. He needed $100,000 for a bone marrow transplant, but before the last $30,000 could be raised he died.

Donna Arnason and her fourteen-year-old son were luckier. Through their "Save a Mom" campaign, they were able to raise all of the $100,000 she needed for a liver transplant.

At least five states have followed Oregon's initial lead in eliminating or restricting payments for transplants. So individuals who are poor and live in the wrong state cannot get organ transplants for themselves or their children. However, even in states that pay a share of transplant costs, people who lack the proper kind of insurance, do not qualify for Medicaid, or are unable to afford the cost may also not be able to secure most organ transplants.

Oregon is also setting the lead in another and even more far-reaching respect. The transplant issue convinced some in the Oregon legislature that it made little sense to consider the relative value of the money spent on transplants without going on to consider the relative value of other medical services. As a result, Oregon has become the first state to develop and implement a plan for rationing health care for the poor.

Oregon's problems in financing and distributing health care are not significantly different from those in other states. The legislature's decision to address the rationing question was influenced to a considerable extent by the public discussion of health-care issues promoted by a group called Oregon Health Decisions. The organization was founded in 1981 by psychiatrist Ralph Crawshaw to provide a forum for addressing the moral and economic issues in health care. The group's 1984 report, "Society Must Decide," played a major role in shaping the views of both citizens and legisla-

tors on matters of fairness in health care. The legislature's efforts to address issues of fairness in allotting state-funded medical services led to a program of assigning relative values to govern their distribution.

According to the Oregon plan, the legislature must decide who is eligible for Medicaid assistance and how much money it is going to allocate as the state contribution to the program. The money must then be spent according to a list of priorities drawn up by the Oregon Medicaid Priority Executive Group.

This group developed a formula to rank each procedure covered by Medicaid based on three factors: the cost of the procedure, the number of people who might be helped by it, and how long a patient would be healthy after treatment. In effect, the group asked, "How much health are we buying per dollar spent?" Medical procedures that provided a poor return on money invested were ranked lowest on the list.

The ranking system the group devised makes 10 the highest priority and 1 the lowest. A number of medical services may be ranked at the same level, so the demands for services at a given rank must be met before services at the next lowest rank are provided. In effect, then, a line was drawn below which no services could be provided. Hence, although procedures like liver transplants were still on the list, since they were ranked 3, the chances were good that no money would be available to fund them.

Here is a selection from the original 1988 list. It is divided into the four main headings of Medicare funding:

1. Reproductive Services
    Rank 10. genetic counseling, prenatal services, termination of pregnancy; amniocentesis; laboratory studies; ultrasound; labor and delivery services; high-risk pregnancy services; postpartum care
    Rank 3. infertility counseling and workup services

2. Health Promotion and Disease Prevention
    Rank 10. immunizations; nutritional supplements; providing food to hungry people whose poor nutrition makes them a significant health risk, with priority given to children and the elderly
    Rank 7. periodic screening (e.g., Pap smears and mammograms); prevention and educa-

tion programs in: sexually transmitted diseases and teen parents; quitting smoking and alcohol and drug abuse; safety, suicide prevention, physical and sexual abuse; eating disorders

3. Chronic Disease Management

Rank 10. procedures, therapies, or interventions that can restore patients with chronic diseases to near-full or manageable levels of function and independence (e.g., cataract surgery, lens implants, or corneal transplants)

Rank 9. interventions that would maintain patients in the most appropriate environment: therapy and clinical management; education and training for primary care givers; provision of appropriate support services (e.g., respite care)

4. Acute Illnesses and Episodic Treatment

Rank 10. diagnosis and treatment of acute illnesses: emergency and trauma care; anesthesia and surgery; diagnostic and therapeutic radiology; diagnostic lab and pathology studies; medications; admissions for psychiatric emergencies

Rank 9. preventive dentistry for children; restorative dental care for adults where necessary for nutrition; occupational therapy and speech therapy with predictable return of functions; eye exams and eyeglasses for children and the elderly every two years; hearing exams and aids for children and elderly every three years

Rank 8. hip replacement for intractable pain or absence of mobility; restorative dentistry for children's permanent teeth; routine dental care for the elderly; necessary reconstructive surgery

Rank 7. rehabilitation for improvement of function

Rank 6. therapy for alcohol and drug abuse

Rank 5. eye exams and glasses for nonelderly adults every two years; hearing exams and hearing aids every three

Rank 4. routine dental care for adults

Rank 3. organ transplantation

The list gives priority to prenatal care, disease prevention, and the treatment of acute and chronic diseases. It gives low priority to dental procedures, plastic surgery, and infertility treatments. Age alone was not considered a reason to restrict access to a service, although the treatment of diseases and conditions affecting mostly the elderly are ranked much lower than those affecting younger people or women of childbearing age.

In February 1991, the Oregon Health Services Commission, responding to intense criticism, significantly revised its original rationing plan and produced a new ranked list. Conditions receiving the highest benefit on the revised list are infectious diseases (for example, pneumonia and tuberculosis) and acute disorders (for example, peritonitis, appendicitis, ectopic pregnancy).

Those given the lowest rank in the revision are superficial wounds; benign conditions (for example, kidney cysts); and disorders that are relatively unaffected by any sort of treatment (like chronic pancreatitis, terminal HIV disease, and anencephaly). Organ transplants were moved from near the bottom of the list to around the middle.

The new list uses the same cost-benefit formula, but the final version was also based on polls, interviews with Oregon citizens, and item-by-item votes by the eleven members of the commission. "We realized that the initial formula did not take into account what people were telling us in public hearings and polls," one member said. Although the same principles were followed, common-sense judgment was used to modify the results of the formula, and many consider the new list to come much closer to capturing popular sentiment than the original one did.

Preventive care and treatable life-threatening diseases affecting many people remain at the top of the list. Minor diseases, rare diseases, incurable, fatal diseases, and treatments of marginal value continue to be ranked much lower. The list ranks 688 medical procedures and services, and Oregon Medicaid will pay for the top 568.

John Kitzhaber, a physician who was president of the Oregon senate, was a sponsor of the 1988 law that eliminated Medicaid payments for most transplants. He has also been one of the strongest proponents of the rationing plan, and partly on this basis, he was elected governor in 1994. "Although we prefer not to recognize it, we do ration health care in this country," he says. "But that rationing is enormously inequitable and not based on any consistent social policy or sound clinical criteria."

Officials in Oregon say their concern is not only to find a rational and just way of distributing medical resources to the poor, but to develop a model for health-care rationing that could be adopted by the federal government and insurance companies as ways of bringing health-care costs under control. Under Oregon's present Medicaid system, almost all medical services are available, but access is limited to only the poorest segment of the population. Under the rationing scheme, officials estimate that Oregon can provide Medicaid assistance to an additional 120,000 citizens who are below the poverty line.

Rationing systems have had several other advocates in recent years. Notably, Daniel Callahan in his book *Setting Limits* has argued for an age-based rationing of health-care costs. As our population ages, Callahan points out, it will produce an increasing demand for very expensive medical services, such as coronary-artery-bypass surgery, and organ transplants. The costs of caring for older people may rise to over $200 billion by the end of the century.

Furthermore, when long-term care is needed in nursing homes or similar facilities, the money spent to care for the elderly reduces the amount available to Medicaid to spend for other purposes. This reduction leads to a tightening of the eligibility requirements. Hence, large numbers of people who are young and poor are denied the medical care they need. Rationing care to the elderly, although providing different forms of care, would make available funds that could be used to care for younger people in need.

According to Callahan, the strain on the health-care system is also the result of our commitment to the development and use of high-technology devices and surgical procedures. He advocates that we more carefully review the social and economic consequences of medical technology before we attempt to develop it or make it available.

Not everyone sees rationing health care and placing limits on the development of medical technology as responses that are either necessary or desirable. A number of economists, in opposition to Callahan, say that a reduction in costs should be enough to postpone, if not eliminate, the need for rationing. For example, Alain Enthoven points to the large numbers of inappropriate medical procedures (as many as one-third of coronary-artery-bypass procedures) and unnecessary hospitalizations (as many as one-fourth) as evidence that health-care costs could be reduced by as much as one-third.

Others claim that discouraging the develop-

ment of high-technology care will, in the long run, work to the detriment of all. The use of medical-imaging devices like CT-scanners and MRIs has eliminated the need for much of the expensive exploratory surgery of the past, made diagnoses more reliable, and so, in general, led to more appropriate and effective treatments. Those who initially opposed buying imaging devices for hospitals can now be shown to have been advocating a false economy. The technology of the future may turn out to be an even better bargain.

Finally, with respect to rationing plans like the one in Oregon, critics point out that the plans are inherently unfair. The rationing is not to everyone in the society but just to the poor, to those who must depend on Medicaid for their medical care.

Alameda County, California, which includes Oakland, felt itself so threatened by medical costs connected with AIDS and the problems of the urban poor that when it learned of the Oregon rationing plan, it began to develop one of its own. "Decision making by default masks the reality of the choices that have to be made," the head of the county health department said.

After almost a year of meetings and discussions, a commission set up to devise a list of priorities similar to Oregon's turned in a report that declared the entire procedure "immoral." According to the report, the health-care needs of the poor people in Alameda County are so severe that no list could be established. All forms of care were essential.

Americans have mixed feelings about providing access to medical care. They want every sick or suffering person to have access to every treatment that will help, but they don't want to pay for it. This ambivalent attitude is borne out by statistical surveys. According to a Harris poll, 91% of Americans agreed with the statement that "everybody should have the right to get the best possible health care—as good as the treatment a millionaire gets." Similarly, in a survey by the Public Agenda Foundation, a strong majority said they would support a federal plan to provide catastrophic health coverage for everyone, even if it costs $10 billion per year. However, when people were asked if they would be willing to pay $125 per year more in taxes to support this universal coverage, 90% said they would not.

In August 1993, the Oregon legislature approved legislation to implement the rationing plan as part of a five-year experiment. The legislature also approved a ten-cent increase in the taxes on cigarettes to help raise the $65 million needed to cover the initial stage of the plan. The plan is expected to require an additional $400 million over four years.

As an additional part of the attempt to expand health care, the Oregon legislature agreed to impose a new law on businesses with twenty-six or more employees in March 1997, and all businesses in January 1998, requiring them to provide all full-time workers with health care. Some observers consider this step as offering a model more likely to be adopted in the rest of the nation than the rationing scheme.

In 1993, Oregon received the federal waiver it needed to allow it to deviate from some of the requirements of the Medicaid system. The rationing plan finally went into effect on February 1, 1994.

Discussions of rationing health care are just now beginning in earnest. In the years ahead, the issues are likely to provoke public and political debates as serious and acrimonious as those surrounding abortion. Should the poor quietly accept a state of affairs in which their children go without liver transplants, while the children of the rich and the middle class have their lives prolonged? Do we want our society to be one in which a poor child must beg to raise money to pay for the only surgery that may save his life?

Suzan McGee, Coby Howard's aunt, remembers his final days with anger and regret. "In his last few weeks, the family spent every minute trying to raise funds," she said. "We are bitter that we had to market Coby Howard so that the public would want to save his life."

CASE PRESENTATION
Employer-Mandated Health Insurance: The Hawaiian Example

Hawaii's Prepaid Health Care Act was passed in 1974 and took effect in 1975. The act requires all employers, no matter their size, to provide health-insurance coverage for their workers. Part-time employees working less than twenty hours per week are the only ones who need not be included in the coverage.

Workers can be compelled to pay a share of the insurance premium up to 50% of its cost or 1.5% of their wages, whichever figure is lower. Some employers require that their workers contribute to the cost of their insurance up to the legal maximum, while others pay the entire premium as a job benefit. Also, although employers are not required to do so, most companies pay part of all of the costs of health insurance for their workers' families.

As a result of the act and its influence, about 96% of the 1.2 million Hawaiians have health coverage—a figure unrivaled by any other state. (Before 1975, 17% of Hawaiians had no health insurance.) Unemployed and seasonal workers are covered by state medical subsidies. The coverage required includes physician and hospital bills, but it need not include the costs of prescription medications, vision care, or dental care.

Hawaii's twenty years of experience with virtually universal health-care coverage for its citizens has produced generally satisfying results. Most important, by placing emphasis on primary and preventive care, the Hawaiian system has improved the overall health of the state's people. For example, despite the high rate of breast cancer in Hawaii, the early detection of tumors, which is the direct result of including mammography in health coverage, has permitted the state to achieve the lowest rate of mortality from the disease.

General measurements of health that focus on a variety of determinants also confirm the success of Hawaii's approach. The American Public Health Association rated the overall health of Hawaiians as better than that of people in any other state. The Center for Disease Control put Hawaii either at or near the top of the list of states in lowering infant mortality, increasing longevity, and lowering rates of premature death from cancer, lung disease, and heart disease.

Hawaii's almost-universal coverage of its citizens has also had consequences for controlling increases in health-care costs. Insurance premiums in Hawaii are 30% lower than the cost for comparable coverage on the mainland. Indeed, insurance cost is about the only commodity that is cheaper in Hawaii than in other parts of the United States. Part of the control of costs may be the result of the Hawaiian system's emphasis on preventive measures and the detection of diseases at early stages when the cost of treatment may be both cheaper and more effective.

Commercial, for-profit insurers chose to stay out of the Hawaiian market, rather than give up their freedom to decide which applicants they were willing to accept. As a result, the competition for customers mostly has been between Hawaii Medical Service Association (the Blue Cross organization with about 50% of the market) and the Kaiser-Permanente HMO (with about 20%). Competition between them has helped keep prices down, while also encouraging primary and preventive care. The larger insurers have also done much to control cost by exerting pressure on physicians and hospitals to keep rates low.

Another cost-saving aspect of the Hawaiian plan is that the pool of workers covered by a given insurance plan is not drawn from a single workplace but from the entire population. By spreading the risk in a large pool, the cost per person of paying for even an expensive medical service is kept low.

Most of the 17% of people who lacked health insurance before 1975 worked for small factories, shops, or restaurants. Most large businesses already provided their employees with insurance coverage. The Prepaid Health Care Act had a more direct effect on small businesses because for the first time they were required to pay a large portion of the insurance premium for their workers. Nevertheless, this did not force companies out of business. Nor did it result in an increase in unemployment. Most businesses in Hawaii have simply come to accept the requirements of the act as one more item in the cost of doing business.

Indeed, despite the fact that the insurance that businesses must provide is mandated, businesses, in general, express approval of the requirement. The state's economy is mostly run by small businesses, with more than 90% of businesses employing fifty or fewer people. In a U.S. Chamber of Commerce survey of its members (who are typi-

cally in small businesses), Hawaii was the only state in which a majority of members favored compulsory health insurance. Many small businesses that pay the whole premium see insurance coverage as an inducement to help them keep valued workers.

Large businesses in Hawaii also express general approval of mandated insurance. The president of Hawaiian Electric put the point this way: "Probably speaking for most big businesses, we support the idea of the Prepaid Health Care Act. As a company we are very much focused on the preventive end. In the long run, it will save us money."

But businesses have not been happy with every aspect of mandated care. In particular, they have been concerned about whether the state government would keep costs that businesses must pay within reasonable limits. Grounds for this concern arose most dramatically when the state legislature decided to add benefits to workers' insurance and found themselves unable to do so without engaging in some creative lawmaking.

Federal laws make it impossible for the state to raise the level of workers' contributions to health-care premiums that was set when the law was passed in 1974. Because the legislature could not require employees to pay more, they changed the state's insurance laws to require that all health insurers and HMOs add mental health and drug and alcohol treatment, mammograms, well-baby care, and in vitro fertilization to their coverage. The result of this maneuver was to pass on the cost of the benefits to businesses. This provoked resentment in many in business, because it seemed that there was no limit on what sort of coverage the legislature might decide to force them to pay for.

Hawaii's transition to its present system was made easier by a number of factors. The population is small, the climate is healthful, and because of the large number of workers in unions, the state has a long tradition of generous medical coverage for employees. Also, Hawaii has an historically low rate of unemployment so insurers have had little need to shift costs incurred by the uninsured to the insured. Further, Hawaii has always had a much larger number of primary care physicians than specialists. This encourages the sort of preventive care that produces an above-average number of office visits, yet also results in lower rates of surgery and hospitalization.

Hawaii has maintained the relatively high proportion of primary-care physicians to specialists, but similar ratios are not found in most other states. This alone would make it difficult for them to switch to a system in which primary-care physicians play the predominant role. Also, Hawaii's geographical isolation makes it difficult for businesses dissatisfied with the health-care plan to relocate. On the mainland, it is a relatively simple matter to move a business across a state line to avoid the demands of a state-based, health-care system.

Whether an employer-mandated insurance plan similar to the one that has been successful in Hawaii would be successful in other states or in the country as a whole remains very much a matter of dispute. At the very least, however, Hawaii stands as an example of how a mandated plan operates and provides us with an opportunity to examine its strengths and limits.

CASE PRESENTATION
The Canadian System as a Model for the United States?

The United States remains the only nation in the industrialized, Western world in which parents worry about being able to pay for the medical care needed by their child, workers worry about losing their medical coverage by changing jobs, people without jobs worry about paying for medical insurance, and husbands and wives worry about going bankrupt to pay for the long-term care needed by an ailing spouse.

A Single-Payer System?

During the course of debate in recent years, some critics have pointed to these failings of the present health-care system and recommended that it be replaced by a so-called *single-payer* system. Under such a system, universal coverage would be provided to all citizens, regardless of their ability to pay, and the single-payer would be the federal government.

"Socialized medicine" was the phrase once used to condemn all single-payer systems. The phrase was a label suggesting something like political heresy. How could a capitalist society adopt a plan exempting medical care from the rules of the market economy? Medical care, like house painting, was a service one could purchase from a provider for an agreed upon fee. The physician-provider, like the painter-provider, was an independent economic agent, and to suggest otherwise would be to recommend the practice of socialism.

Of course, those unable to pay a physician's fee would have to do without the service. A charitable organization or benevolent physician might provide treatment for some truly in need. This

wasn't something to be counted on, and in neither case was need a basis for demanding the service. Clearly, just as you couldn't expect a painter to paint your house without pay, so you couldn't expect a physician to provide you with medical care for nothing. Nor did anyone expect the government to pick up the bill. The role of the government in a market economy is not to provide some citizens with free goods, whether it is painting their houses or providing them with medical care.

Changing Attitudes. For decades this view dominated public discussions about national health programs. Critics of a proposed program hardly had to do more than apply the label "socialized medicine" to bring discussion to a close. Then attitudes began to change for a complex of reasons, including the spiraling cost of health care, the increasing power and value of medical intervention, and the growing number of citizens needing care but lacking insurance.

The introduction of the Medicare program in 1965 provided care to millions of people, many of whom would have received no medical assistance at all. Medicare also helped change the thinking of many people. They came to realize that a social-insurance plan like Medicare was not "socialized medicine" and that a plan for universal medical care might be offered along the same lines.

Other factors have also encouraged many to look with favor on the introduction of a single-payer plan. The steady increase in the number of citizens lacking health insurance and unable to pay for even basic medical care is the most dramatic.

The number of people in this predicament is estimated at 39 to 40 million, and the number has been growing at a rate of 1 million per year.

Even people with medical insurance are willing to consider other ways of supporting health care, for they do not feel secure. Most are aware, either from news accounts or experience, that their coverage may not be adequate to pay for their medical needs and that they may be forced to do without care or go into debt to pay for it. People also fear that their policies might be canceled because their medical expenses are too high or their insurer sees them as too much of a risk. Some fail even to get needed medical attention out of fear that their insurer will cancel their policy. The loss of insurance because of a change in jobs or unemployment is also feared. Those who suffer from a "preexisting condition," such as diabetes, may find it impossible to buy insurance or, if they can, to afford the extraordinarily high premiums that are likely.

Factors such as these may have been responsible for prompting 60% of the respondents in a survey to say that "fundamental changes are needed to make the American health-care system work better." In another survey, 75% said they were in favor of abandoning the private fee-for-service medical system in favor of some form of government-backed national health system.

Many proponents of a single-payer system consider the Canadian system a model for what the American health-care system should become. At least at first sight, Canada and the United States seem much alike in relevant respects. They are both democracies with partially regulated, free-market economies. Furthermore, both have a central, federal government, as well as a number of independent provincial or state governments. These similarities suggest that the Canadian experience with its health-care system might provide detailed guidance for reforming the United States system.

The Canadian Health-Care System

Canada established universal health insurance coverage in 1971. It did not nationalize hospitals or make physicians government employees, as did Great Britain. Rather, it eliminated most forms of private medical insurance and enrolled citizens in a government plan administered by the ten provinces. The plan is paid for by a variety of federal and provincial taxes. The system is not "socialized medicine." It is, rather, a form of tax-based insurance and does not differ in principle from the United States' Social Security or Medicare.

In addition to physician services, diagnostic testing, hospitalization, and surgery, the plan provides for long-term care, prescription drugs for those over 65, and mental-health care. Benefits vary slightly among provinces, and private insurance is used only to bridge the gaps in provincial coverage.

Principles of the Health Act.   The details of insurance coverage are decided by each province, but every plan adopted must conform to the five principles spelled out in the Canadian Health Act:

1. *Universality.*   Every citizen is covered.

2. *Portability.*   People can move to another province, change jobs, or be unemployed and retain their coverage.

3. *Accessibility.*   Everyone has access to physicians, hospitals, and other elements of the health-care system.

4. *Comprehensiveness.*   Medically necessary treatments must be covered.

5. *Public administration.*   The system is publicly operated and publicly accountable.

The first four of these principles are often mentioned as ones that should guide reform of the United States' system. However, suggestions that the fifth one be adopted have occasioned much controversy.

Canadian Citizens as Patients.   Every Canadian citizen is guaranteed access to a physician, and she may see any primary-care physician she chooses. If hospitalization, testing, or surgery is necessary, then the government insurance plan will pay for it without any direct cost to the patient.

Patients do not receive bills, fill out claim forms, make copayments, or wait for reimbursement. Instead, they need only show their identification card to receive medical services. Their physician bills the insurance plan of the province, and payment is made within two to four weeks. Paperwork is kept at a minimum, and this helps lower administrative costs.

Popularity and Effectiveness of the Program. The medical system is highly popular with Canadian citizens. In one survey, 7 out of 10 said they receive good or excellent care, and 9 out of 10 said the health-care system "is one of the things that makes Canada the best country in the world in which to live." Only 3% of Canadians in another poll said that they would "prefer a health-care system like that in the United States."

Various objective measures of health care show that the Canadian system has been successful. The infant mortality rate of 7.1 per 1,000 live births is superior to the U.S. rate of 8.9. The Canadian life-expectancy is 77.2 years (from 1992), while life-expectancy in the United States is 75.2 years.

Cost control also has been successful under the plan. In 1991, Canada spent about 9.2% of its national income for medical care; the United States spent 12.3%. In 1971, the year Canadian Medicare became universal, the proportions were 7.3% and 7.4%, respectively. This suggests that the Canadians were able to provide both universal coverage and high-quality care, while successfully controlling costs.

Canadian Physicians. Canadian physicians, like U.S. physicians, practice in their own offices and provide care for the patients who choose to consult them. The significant difference is that Canadian physicians must charge for their services according to a fee schedule. The schedule is negotiated by the Ministry of Health and the Provincial Medical Association.

Canadian physicians were initially bitterly opposed to the universal health-care system. Many now approve of it, though, for it has turned out to have aspects they like. Although they cannot charge as much as physicians in the United States, they need not contend with the paperwork burden. Nor do they have to argue with insurance representatives who challenge their judgment about a needed medical service.

Physicians' fees in the United States are 2.4 times that of Canadian fees. However, Canadian physicians have incomes equal to two-thirds that of U.S. physicians. The reason the incomes are not lower is that Canadian physicians see more patients.

Canada has 100 primary-care or family physi-cians per 100,000 people. The United States has 20. Even when pediatricians, gynecologists, internists, and family and general practitioners are considered, only 30% of physicians in the United States offer primary care to their patients.

Provincial plans encourage patients to seek a referral to a specialist from a general practitioner. If a specialist sees a patient without a referral, the specialist can bill only for the same amount as a general practitioner would charge. (As sometimes happens, the specialist calls the general practitioner only after the patient has seen her.)

The preponderance of Canadian physicians committed to primary care means that it is possible to emphasize disease prevention. In the long run, this may help prevent the need for costly treatments. Furthermore, primary-care physicians are not as likely to order expensive diagnostic testing as are specialists.

Coverage and Costs. Canada spends $1,915 per capita (all dollars are U.S.) on health care. For that amount of money, it covers, for the entire population of the country, hospitalization, physician visits, rehabilitation therapy, most dental work, prescription drugs for the poor and those over sixty-five, and most laboratory tests. In comparison, the United States spends $2,867 per capita. The United States has no coverage standards for insurance, so many people who are insured have uneven coverage. In addition, the 17% of the population that is uninsured receives little or no health care.

Drawbacks of the System: How Serious Are They? The Canadian system has aspects that can be viewed as negative. One of the ways in which costs are kept down is to restrict investment in high-cost medical technology. The United States has 1,500 cardiac catheterization labs (166 people per unit), while Canada has 31 (816 people per unit). Canada has 12 magnetic resonance imagers (2,108 people per unit), while the United States has 1,375 (182 people per unit). Similarly, Canada has increased the number of general practitioners and pediatricians, but it has cut back the number of people in medical specialties. Canada has only 11 heart surgery units, while the United States has 793.

The strength of the Canadian system is its emphasis on basic care and prevention. Its weakness is the restricted access it permits to specialized care, equipment, and procedures. Patients may have to wait from three to six months for heart surgery, a hip replacement, or a bed in a cancer unit. Care is not explicitly rationed, but it is organized so that those with a greater need are given higher priorities.

In fairness, the restrictions on care may not be as serious as critics sometimes claim. Government statistics show that 96% of Canadians receive medical care within seven days of requesting it. Hundreds of therapeutic and diagnostic procedures—general surgery, endoscopy, thyroid function tests, x rays, ultrasound, amniocentesis, EKGs, and so on—are performed regularly and with little or no waiting.

Canadian physicians are definitely more sparing in the use of MRIs and other high technology, and patients must wait longer to receive whatever benefits it offers than in the United States. The only other option, defenders of the system say, is to waste resources by unnecessarily duplicating equipment. By not taking this path, Canada has avoided the dizzying cost increases that plague the United States.

The most impressive difference in comparing the Canadian health-care system with that of the United States is administrative costs. While Canada spends about 12% of its health-care money on administration, the United States spends almost 25%.

A Canadian System for the United States?

Would the single-payer Canadian system work in the United States? Some observers who know both systems well express doubts. According to economist Victor Fuchs, "There is reason to doubt that the quality of our civil services is up to the quality of the Canadian civil services. There is also reason to question whether the organization and degree of discipline in the [medical] profession is as strong as in Canada. We are very much individualists, and that includes physicians."

Similar doubts have been expressed by David Woods, who sees the different systems of health care as expressions of "national character." "Canada's system is a centralized public enterprise, cautious and based upon ingrained notions (or delusions) of egalitarianism. America's system is decentralized, market-driven, entrepreneurial, and with 37 [now 39] million citizens uninsured by it, certainly unequal in terms of access."

Further, access to specialized care and technology is highly restricted in the Canadian system, something Americans would find particularly galling. Also, Canadians have indicated a greater willingness to pay much higher taxes, both explicit and hidden, to guarantee universal access than have Americans.

Finally, John Iglehart, in a study of the Canadian system published in the *New England Journal of Medicine*, suggests that all is not as well with the system as may seem from the outside: "Canada's Health Insurance Program resembles a pressure cooker that is building up steam on a hot stove. The federal government is reducing its financial commitment, the supply of physicians is increasing, and the physical plants of many Canadian hospitals—particularly the teaching institutions—are nearing obsolescence."

Despite these doubts and criticisms, many continue to believe that a single-payer system, with attributes of the Canadian system, would solve a significant number of the problems that plague the present system:

1. The money now spent on private insurance, with its high administrative costs and spotty coverage for individuals, when combined with Medicaid and Medicare funds, could be used to extend basic coverage to all citizens. The problems of what to do about the uninsured and the underinsured would disappear.

2. People would no longer have to worry about having their policies canceled, exceeding the limits of their coverage, or being uninsurable because of a preexisting medical condition.

3. Universal access would encourage individuals to get medical help early, and rapid intervention would lead to cost savings from prevention and early detection and treatment.

4. The single payer would be able to negotiate with physicians, hospitals, laboratories, and pharmaceutical companies to hold down prices.

The big financial losers in a single-payer system are private health insurance companies. The role they play is reduced to that of offering policies covering treatments not included in the single-payer plan. To a lesser extent, physicians, hospitals, and suppliers also stand to lose more financially in the change to a single-payer system. However, erosions in income due to HMOs and other forms of managed care have already taken place in all sectors of the health economy.

What physicians might expect to gain from a switch to a single-payer system is a freedom from some of the more rigid and time-consuming utilization review processes of managed care. In this respect, physicians might expect to regain some of the autonomy that some claim has been declining steadily as third-party payers have taken a more active role in determining what procedures and treatments they are willing to pay for.

What remains unanswered is the basic question of whether the virtues of the Canadian single-payer system could be reproduced in the United States and whether the United States would be satisfied with a system that, for many people, is more restrictive than the one they are accustomed to.

Nevertheless, the Canadian system is one that the United States ought to consider carefully, with an eye to altering its own system, if not forsaking it. As T. R. Marmor and John Godfrey observe, "Canada is the country closest to ours in wealth, geography, ethnic diversity and patterns of medical practice. If we cannot learn from Canada, we cannot learn from any country."

INTRODUCTION

It has been estimated that it was not until the middle 1930s that the intervention of a physician in the treatment of an illness was likely to affect the outcome in a substantial way. The change was brought about by the discovery and development of antibiotic agents such as penicillin and sulfa drugs. They made it possible, for the first time, both to control infection and to provide specific remedies for a variety of diseases. Additional advances in treatment modalities, procedures, and technology have helped establish contemporary medicine as an effective enterprise.

Before these dramatic changes occurred, there was little reason for anyone to be particularly concerned with the question of the distribution of medical care within society. The situation in the United States has altered significantly, and a number of writers have recently argued that everyone ought to be guaranteed at least some form of medical care. In part this is a reflection of the increased effectiveness of contemporary medicine, but it is also no doubt due to a growing awareness of the serious difficulties faced by disadvantaged groups within society.

In the last chapter we discussed one aspect of the problem of the distribution of medical resources—that of allocating limited resources among competing individuals in a particular situation. Here we need to call attention to some of the broader social issues. These are ones that transcend moral decisions about particular people and raise questions about the basic aims and obligations of society.

A great number of observers believe that the United States is currently faced with a health-care crisis. Some of the reasons supporting this belief, as well as some proposed solutions, are outlined in the Social Context parts of this chapter, and we need not repeat them here. But one element of the crisis is often said to be the lack of any program to provide health care for everyone in the society. That there should be people forced to do without needed health care for primarily financial reasons has seemed to some a morally intolerable state of affairs.

This point of view has frequently been based on the claim that everyone has a *right* to health care. Thus, it has been argued, society has a duty to provide that care; if it does not, then it is sanctioning a situation that is inherently wrong. To remedy the situation requires redesigning the health-care system and present practices to see to it that all who need and want health care have access to it.

The language of "rights" is very slippery. To understand and evaluate arguments that involve claiming (or denying) rights to health care, it is important to understand the nature of the claim. The word "rights" is used in several distinct ways, and a failure to be clear about the use in any given case leads only to unproductive confusion.

The following distinctions may help capture some of the more important sorts of things that people have in mind when they talk about rights.

CLAIM-RIGHTS, LEGAL RIGHTS, AND STATUTORY RIGHTS

Suppose I own a copy of the book *Anne of Green Gables.* If so, then I may be said to have a right to do with the book whatever I choose. Other people may be said to have a duty to recognize my right in appropriate ways. Thus, if I want to read the book, burn it, or sell it, others have a duty not to interfere with me. If I lend the book to someone, then he or she has a duty to return it.

It is generally agreed in the philosophy of law that a claim-right to something serves as a ground for other people's duties. A claim-right, then, always entails a duty or duties on the part of someone else.

Generally speaking, *legal rights* are claim-rights. Someone has a legal right when someone else has a definable duty, and legal remedies are available when the duty is not performed. Either the person can be forced to perform the duty, or damages of some sort can be collected for failure to perform. If I pay someone to put a new roof on my house by a certain date, she has contracted a duty to perform the work we have agreed to. If the task is not performed, then I can turn to the legal system for enforcement or damages.

Statutory rights are claim-rights that are explicitly recognized in legal statutes or laws. They impose duties on certain classes of people under specified conditions. A hospital contractor, for example, has a duty to meet certain building codes. If he fails to meet them, he is liable to legal penalties. But not all legal rights are necessarily statutory rights. Such considerations as "customary and estab-lished practices" may sometimes implicitly involve a legally enforceable claim-right.

MORAL RIGHTS

Generally speaking, a *moral right* is one that is stated in or derived from the principles of a moral theory. More specifically, to say that someone has a moral right to certain goods or manner of treatment is to say that others have a moral duty to see to it that she receives what she has a right to. A moral right is a certain kind of claim-right. Here, though, the source of justification for the right and for the corresponding duty lies in moral principles and not in the laws or practices of a society.

According to Ross, for example, people have a duty to treat other people benevolently. This is a duty that is not recognized by our legal system. We may, if we wish, treat others in a harsh and unsympathetic manner and in doing so violate no law.

Of course, many rights and duties that are based upon the principles of moral theories are also embodied in our laws. Thus, to take Ross again as an example, we have a prima facie duty not to injure or kill anyone. This duty, along with its correlative right to be free from injury or death at the hands of another, is reflected in the body of statutory law and common law that deals with bodily harm done to others and with killing.

The relationship between ethical theories and the laws of a society is complicated and controversial. The fundamental question is always the extent to which laws should reflect or be based upon an ethical theory. In a society such as ours, it does not seem proper that an ethical theory accepted by only a part of the people should determine the laws that govern us all. It is for this reason that some object to laws regulating sexual activity, pornography, and abortion. These are considered best regarded as a part of personal morality.

At the same time, however, it seems that we must rely upon ethical theories as a basis for evaluating laws. Unless we are prepared to say that what is legal is, in itself, what is right, we must recognize the possibility of laws that are bad or unjust. But what makes a law bad? A possible answer is that a law is bad when it violates a right derived from the principles of an ethical theory. Similarly, both laws and social practices may be criticized for failing to recognize a moral right. A moral theory, then, can serve as a basis for a demand for the reform of laws and practices.

Clearly there is no sharp line separating the moral and the legal. Indeed, virtually all of the moral theories we discussed in the introductory chapter have been used by philosophers and other thinkers as the basis for principles applying to society as a whole. Within such frameworks as utilitarianism, natural law theory, and Rawls's theory of a just society, legal and social institutions are assigned roles and functions in accordance with more general moral principles.

POLITICAL RIGHTS

Not everyone attempts to justify claims to rights by referring such claims directly to a moral theory. Efforts are frequently made to provide justification by relying upon principles or commitments that are generally acknowledged as basic to our society. (Of course, to answer how these are justified may force us to invoke moral principles.) Our society, for example, is committed to individual autonomy and equality, among other values. It is by reference to commitments of this sort that we evaluate proposals and criticize practices.

From this point of view, to recognize health care as a right is to acknowledge it as a *political* right. This means showing that it is required by our political commitments or principles. Of course, this may also mean resolving any conflicts that may arise from other rights that also seem to be demanded by our principles. But this is a familiar state of affairs. We

are all aware that the constitutional guarantee of freedom of speech, for example, is not absolute and unconditional. It can conflict with other rights or basic commitments, and we look to the courts to provide us with guidelines to resolve the conflicts.

With the distinctions that we have discussed in mind, let us return now to the question of a general right to health care. What can those who make such a claim be asserting?

Obviously everyone in our society is free to seek health care and, when the proper arrangements are made, to receive it. That is, health care is a service available in society, and people may avail themselves of it. At the same time, however, no physician or hospital has a duty to provide health care that is sought. The freedom to seek does not imply that others have a duty to provide what we seek.

There is not in our society a legally recognized claim-right to health care. Even if I am sick, no one has a legal duty to see to it that I receive treatment for my illness. (A few states, such as New York, do impose legal duties on physicians and hospitals to treat people faced with life-threatening emergencies. Even this is not generally the case, however.) I may request care, or I may attempt to persuade a physician that it is his or her moral duty to provide me with care. But I have no legal right to health care, and, if someone refuses to provide it, I cannot seek a legal remedy.

Of course, I may contract with a physician, clinic, or hospital for care, either in general or for a certain ailment. If I do this, then the other party acquires a legally enforceable duty to provide me the kind of care that we agreed upon. In this respect, contracting for health care is not relevantly different from contracting for a new roof on my house.

Those who assert that health care is a right cannot be regarded as merely making the obviously false claim that there is a legal right to care. Their claim, rather, must be interpreted as one of a moral or political sort. They might be taken as asserting something like

"Everyone in the society *ought* to be entitled to health care, regardless of his or her financial condition."

Anyone making such a claim must be prepared to justify it by offering reasons and evidence in support of it. The ultimate source of the justification is most likely to be the principles of a moral theory. For example, Kant's principle that every person is of inherent and equal worth might be used to support the claim that every person has an equal right to medical care, simply by virtue of being a person.

Justification might also be offered in terms of principles that express the aims and commitments of the society. A society that endorses justice and equality, it might be argued, must be prepared to offer health care to all if it offers it to anyone.

However justification is offered, it is clear that to claim that health care is a right is to go beyond merely expressing an attitude. It is to say more than something like "Everyone would like to have health care" or "Everyone needs health care." It is true that the language of "rights" is frequently used in a rhetorical way to encourage us to recognize the wants and needs of people—or even other organisms, such as animals and trees. This is a perfectly legitimate way of talking. But, at bottom, to urge that something be considered a right is to make a claim requiring justification in terms of some set of legal, social, or moral principles.

Why not recognize health care for all as a right? Certainly virtually everyone would admit that in the abstract it would be a good thing. If this is so, then why should anyone wish to oppose it? Briefly stated, arguments against a right to health care are most frequently of two kinds.

First, those who subscribe to a position sometimes called "medical individualism" argue that to recognize a right to health care would have the consequence of violating the rights of physicians and other medical practitioners. Physicians, they claim, would be required to employ their intelligence, knowledge, and skills in a way dictated by society. Thus, physicians would be deprived of their autonomy and, in a very real sense, made slaves of the state.

Second, some writers have pointed out that, while it is possible to admit health care to the status of a right, we must also recognize that health care is just one social good among others. Education, transportation, housing, legal assistance, and so on are other goods that are also sought and needed by members of our society. It is impossible to admit all of these (and perhaps others) to the status of rights, for the society simply cannot afford to pay for them.

The first line of argument, medical individualism, fails to recognize that the health-care situation is perhaps best regarded as one in which there is a *conflict* of rights (between patients and providers) and not just one in which the rights of physicians are being restricted.

The second line of argument does not necessarily lead to the conclusion that we should not recognize a right to health care. It does serve to warn us that we must be very careful to specify just what sort of right—if any—we want to support. Do we want to claim, for example, that everyone has a right to a certain *minimum* of health care? Or do we want to claim that everyone has a right to *equal* health care (whatever anyone can get, everyone can demand)?

Furthermore, this line of argument warns us that we have to make decisions about what we, as a society, are willing to pay for. Would we, for example, be willing to give up all public support for education in order to use the money for health care? Probably not. But we might be willing to reduce the level of support for education in order to increase that for health care. Whatever we decide, we have to face up to the problem of distributing our limited resources. This is an issue that is obviously closely connected with what sort of right to health care (or, really, the right to what sort of health care) we are prepared to endorse.

None of the selections in this chapter attempt to provide detailed answers to the multitude of questions that swarm around the issues of a public health-care policy. Yet each of them calls attention to some of the fundamental issues of rights, values, and social goals that must be resolved before any practical policy can be accepted as legitimate. If we are to recognize a right to health care, then we must be clear about exactly what is involved in recognizing such a right. Are we prepared to offer only a "decent minimum"? Does justice require that we make available to all whatever is available to any? Are we prepared to restrict the wants of some people in order to satisfy the basic needs of all people?

The issues discussed in this chapter are of more than academic interest, and they concern more than just a handful of patients and physicians. How they are resolved will affect us all, both directly and indirectly, through the character of our society.

An Ethical Framework for Access to Health Care

President's Commission for the Study of Ethical Problems in Medicine

The commission claims that the role played by health care in enabling people to live full and satisfying lives gives it a special importance. The crucial role of health care explains why it ought to be accessible in an equitable fashion to everyone in the society. After reviewing various meanings of "equitable access," the commission concludes that fairness is satisfied if everyone has access to "an adequate level of care."

The commission stops short of endorsing a "right" to health care. It holds, rather, that society has a moral obligation to provide everyone with access to adequate care. The government, as one social institution among others, is not solely or even primarily responsible for providing the access. It might be achieved by a pluralistic approach that relies on both the private and public sectors. Ultimately, though, it is the government that has a duty to see to it that society's moral obligation to provide care is satisfied.

. . . Most Americans believe that because health care is special, access to it raises special ethical concerns. In part, this is because good health is by definition important to well-being. Health care can relieve pain and suffering, restore functioning, and prevent death; it can enhance good health and improve an individual's opportunity to pursue a life plan; and it can provide valuable information about a person's overall health. Beyond its practical importance, the involvement of health care with the most significant and awesome events of life—birth, illness, and death—adds a symbolic aspect to health

From President's Commission for the Study of Ethical Problems in Medicine and Biomedical and Behavioral Research, Securing Access to Health Care, Vol. 1 (1983), pp. 11–12, 16–21, 22–23, 30–132, 34–37. Notes and references omitted.

care: it is special because it signifies not only mutual empathy and caring but the mysterious aspects of curing and healing.

Furthermore, while people have some ability—through choice of life-style and through preventive measures—to influence their health status, many health problems are beyond their control and are therefore undeserved. Besides the burdens of genetics, environment, and chance, individuals become ill because of things they do or fail to do—but it is often difficult for an individual to choose to do otherwise or even to know with enough specificity and confidence what he or she ought to do to remain healthy. Finally, the incidence and severity of ill health is distributed very unevenly among people. Basic needs for housing and food are predictable, but even the most hardworking and prudent person may suddenly be faced with overwhelming needs for health care. Together, these considerations lend weight to the belief that health care is different from most other goods and services. In a society concerned not only with fairness and equality of opportunity but also with the redemptive powers of science, there is a felt obligation to ensure that some level of health services is available to all.

There are many ambiguities, however, about the nature of this societal obligation. What share of health costs should individuals be expected to bear, and what responsibility do they have to use health resources prudently? Is it society's responsibility to ensure that every person receives care or services of as high quality and as great extent as any other individual? Does it require that everyone share opportunities to receive all available care or care of any possible benefit? If not, what level of care is "enough"? And does society's obligation include a responsibility to ensure both that care is available and that its costs will not unduly burden the patient?

The resolution of such issues is made more difficult by the spectre of rising health care costs and expenditures. . . . Although the finitude of national resources demands that trade-offs be made between health care and other social goods, there is little agreement about which choices are most acceptable from an ethical standpoint. In this chapter, the Commission attempts to lay an ethical foundation for evaluating both current patterns of access to health care and the policies designed to address remaining problems in the distribution of health care resources. . . .

The Special Importance of Health Care

Although the importance of health care may, at first blush, appear obvious, this assumption is often based on instinct rather than reasoning. Yet it is possible to step back and examine those properties of health care that lead to the ethical conclusion that it ought to be distributed equitably.

Well-Being

Ethical concern about the distribution of health care derives from the special importance of health care in promoting personal well-being by preventing or relieving pain, suffering, and disability and by avoiding loss of life. The fundamental importance of the latter is obvious: pain and suffering are also experiences that people have strong desires to avoid, both because of the intrinsic quality of the experience and because of their effects on the capacity to pursue and achieve other goals and purposes. Similarly, untreated disability can prevent people from leading rewarding and fully active lives.

Health, insofar as it is the absence of pain, suffering, or serious disability, is what has been called a primary good, that is, there is no need to know what a particular person's other ends, preferences, and values are in order to know that health is good for that individual. It generally helps people carry out their life plans, whatever they may happen to be. This is not to say that everyone defines good health in the same way or assigns the same weight or importance to different aspects of being healthy, or to health in comparison with the other goods of life. Yet though people may differ over each of these matters, their disagreement takes place within a framework of basic agreement on the importance of health. Likewise, people differ in their beliefs about the value of health and medical care and their use of it as a means of achieving good health, as well as in their attitudes toward the various benefits and risks of different treatments.

Opportunity

Health care can also broaden a person's range of opportunities, that is, the array of life plans that is reasonable to pursue within the conditions obtaining in society. In the United States equality of opportunity is a widely accepted value that is reflected throughout public policy. The effects that meeting (or failing to meet) people's health needs have on the distribution of opportunity in a society become apparent if diseases are thought of as adverse departures from a normal level of functioning. In this view, health care is that which people need to maintain or restore normal functioning or to compensate for inability to function normally. Health is thus comparable in importance to education in determining the opportunities available to people to pursue different life plans.

Information

The special importance of health care stems in part from its ability to relieve worry and to enable patients to adjust to their situation by supplying reliable information about their health. Most people do not understand the true nature of a health problem when it first develops. Health professionals can then perform the worthwhile function of informing people about their conditions and about the expected prognoses with or without various treatments. Though information sometimes creates concern, often it reassures patients either by ruling out a feared disease or by revealing the self-limiting nature of a condition and, thus, the lack of need for further treatment. Although health care in many situations may thus not be necessary for good physical health, a great deal of relief from unnecessary concern—and even avoidance of pointless or potentially harmful steps—is achieved by health care in the form of expert information provided to worried patients. Even when a prognosis is unfavorable and health professionals have little treatment to offer, accurate information can help patients plan how to cope with their situation.

The Interpersonal Significance of Illness, Birth, and Death

It is no accident that religious organizations have played a major role in the care of the sick and dying and in the process of birth. Since all human beings are vulnerable to disease and all die, health care has a special interpersonal significance: it expresses and nurtures bonds of empathy and compassion. The depth of a society's concern about health care can be seen as a measure of its sense of solidarity in the face of suffering and death. Moreover, health care takes on special meaning because of its role in the beginning of a human being's life as well as the end. In spite of all the advances in the scientific understanding of birth, disease, and death, these profound and universal experiences remain shared mysteries that touch the spiritual side of human nature. For these reasons a society's commitment to health care reflects some of its most basic attitudes about what it is to be a member of the human community.

The Concept of Equitable Access to Health Care

The special nature of health care helps to explain why it ought to be accessible, in a fair fashion, to all. But if this ethical conclusion is to provide a basis for evaluating current patterns of access to health care and proposed health policies, the meaning of fairness or equity in this context must be clarified. The concept of equitable access needs definition in its two main aspects: the level of care that ought to be available to all and the extent to which burdens can be imposed on those who obtain these services.

Access to What?

"Equitable access" could be interpreted in a number of ways: equality of access, access to whatever an individual needs or would benefit from, or access to an adequate level of care.

Equity as Equality. It has been suggested that equity is achieved either when everyone is assured of receiving an equal quantity of health care dollars or when people enjoy equal health. The most common characterization of equity as equality, however, is as providing everyone with the same level of health care. In this view, it follows that if a given level of care is available to one individual it must be available to all. If the initial standard is set high, by reference to the highest level of care presently received, an enormous drain would result on the resources needed to provide other goods. Alternatively, if the standard is set low in order to avoid an excessive use of resources, some beneficial services would have to be withheld from people who wished to purchase them. In other words, no one would be allowed access to more services or services of higher quality than those available to everyone else, even if he or she were willing to pay for those services from his or her personal resources.

As long as significant inequalities in income and wealth persist, inequalities in the use of health care can be expected beyond those created by differences in need. Given people with the same pattern of preferences and equal health care needs, those with greater financial resources will purchase more health care. Conversely, given equal financial resources, the different patterns of health care preferences that typically exist in any population will result in a different use of health services by people with equal health care needs. Trying to prevent such inequalities would require interfering with people's liberty to use their income to purchase an important good like health care while leaving them free to use it for frivolous or inessential ends. Prohibiting people with higher incomes or stronger preferences for health care from purchasing more care than everyone else gets would not be feasible, and would probably result in a black market for health care.

Equity as Access Solely According to Benefit or Need. Interpreting equitable access to mean that everyone must receive all health care that is of any benefit to them also has unacceptable implications. Unless health is the only good or resources are unlimited, it would be irrational for a society—as for an individual—to make a commitment to provide whatever health care might be beneficial regardless of cost. Although health care is of special importance, it is surely not all that is important to people. Pushed to an extreme, this criterion might swallow up all of society's resources, since there is virtually no end to the funds that could be devoted to possibly beneficial care for diseases and disabilities and to their prevention.

Equitable access to health care must take into account not only the benefits of care but also the cost in comparison with other goods and services to which those resources might be allocated. Society will reasonably devote some resources to health care but reserve most resources for other goals. This, in turn, will mean that some health services (even of a lifesaving sort) will not be developed or employed because they would produce too few benefits in relation to their costs and to the other ways the resources for them might be used.

It might be argued that the notion of "need" provides a way to limit access to only that care that confers especially important benefits. In this view, equity as access according to need would place less severe demands on social resources than equity according to benefit would. There are, however, difficulties with the notion of need in this context. On the one hand, medical need is often not narrowly defined but refers to any condition for which medical treatment might be effective. Thus "equity as access according to need" collapses into "access according to whatever is of benefit."

On the other hand, "need" could be even more expansive in scope than "benefit." Philosophical and economic writings do not provide any clear distinction between "needs" and "wants" or "preferences." Since the term means different things to different people, "access according to need" could become "access to any health service a person wants." Conversely, need could be interpreted very narrowly to encompass only a very minimal level of services—for example, those "necessary to prevent death."

Equity as an Adequate Level of Health Care. Although neither "everything needed" nor "everything beneficial" nor "everything that anyone else is getting" are defensible ways of understanding equitable access, the special nature of health care dictates that everyone have access to *some* level of care: enough care to achieve sufficient welfare, opportunity, information, and evidence of interpersonal concern to facilitate a reasonably full and satisfying life. That level can be termed "an adequate level of health care." The difficulty of sharpening this amorphous notion into a workable foundation for health policy is a major problem in the United States today. This concept is not new; it is implicit in the public debate over health policy and has manifested itself in the history of public policy in this country. In this chapter, the Commission attempts to demonstrate the value of the concept, to clarify its content and to apply it to the problems facing health policymakers.

Understanding equitable access to health care to mean that everyone should be able to secure an adequate level of care has several strengths. Because an adequate level of care may be less than "all beneficial care" and because it does not require that all needs be satisfied, it acknowledges the need for setting priorities within health care and signals a clear recognition that society's resources are limited and that there are other goods besides health. Thus, interpreting equity as access to adequate care does not generate an open-ended obligation. One of the chief dangers of interpretations of equity that require virtually unlimited resources for health care is that they encourage the view that equitable access is an impossible ideal. Defining equity as an adequate level of care for all avoids an impossible commitment of resources without falling into the opposite error of abandoning the enterprise of seeking to ensure that health care is in fact available for everyone.

In addition, since providing an adequate level of care is a limited moral requirement, this definition also avoids the unacceptable restriction on individual liberty entailed by the view that equity requires equality. Provided that an adequate level is available to all, those who prefer to use their resources to obtain care that exceeds that level do not offend any ethical principle in doing so. Finally, the concept of adequacy, as the Commission understands it, is society-relative. The content of adequate care will depend upon the overall resources available in a given society, and can take into account a consensus of expectations about what is adequate in a particular society at a particular time in its historical development. This permits the definition of adequacy to be altered as societal resources and expectations change.

With What Burdens?

It is not enough to focus on the care that individuals receive; attention must be paid to the burdens they must bear in order to obtain it—waiting and travel time, the cost and availability of transport, the financial cost of the care itself. Equity requires not only that adequate care be available to all, but also that these burdens not be excessive.

If individuals must travel unreasonably long distances, wait for unreasonably long hours, or spend most of their financial resources to obtain care, some will be deterred from obtaining adequate care, with adverse effects on their health and well-being. Others may bear the burdens, but only at the expense of their ability to meet other important needs. If one of the main reasons for providing

adequate care is that health care increases welfare and opportunity, then a system that required large numbers of individuals to forego food, shelter, or educational advancement in order to obtain care would be self-defeating and irrational.

The concept of acceptable burdens in obtaining care, as opposed to excessive ones, parallels in some respects the concept of adequacy. Just as equity does not require equal access, neither must the burdens of obtaining adequate care be equal for all persons. What is crucial is that the variations in burdens fall within an acceptable range. As in determining an adequate level of care, there is no simple formula for ascertaining when the burdens of obtaining care fall within such a range. Yet some guidelines can be formulated. To illustrate, since a given financial outlay represents a greater sacrifice to a poor person than to a rich person, "excessive" must be understood in relation to income. Obviously everyone cannot live the same distance from a health care facility, and some individuals choose to locate in remote and sparsely populated areas. Concern about an inequitable burden would be appropriate, however, when identifiable groups must travel a great distance or long time to receive care—though people may appropriately be expected to travel farther to get specialized care, for example, than to obtain primary or emergency care. . . .

A Societal Obligation

Society has a moral obligation to ensure that everyone has access to adequate care without being subject to excessive burdens. In speaking of a societal obligation the Commission makes reference to society in the broadest sense—the collective American community. The community is made up of individuals, who are in turn members of many other, overlapping groups, both public and private: local, state, regional, and national units; professional and workplace organizations; religious, educational, and charitable organizations; and family, kinship, and ethnic groups. All these entities play a role in discharging societal obligations.

The Commission believes it is important to distinguish between society, in this inclusive sense, and government as one institution among others in society. Thus the recognition of a collective or societal obligation does not imply that government should be the only or even the primary institution involved in the complex enterprise of making health care available. It is the Commission's view that the societal obligation to ensure equitable access for everyone may best be fulfilled in this country by a pluralistic approach that relies upon the coordinated contributions of actions by both the private and public sectors.

Securing equitable access is a societal rather than a merely private or individual responsibility for several reasons. First, while health is of special importance for human beings, health care—especially scientific health care—is a social product requiring the skills and efforts of many individuals; it is not something that individuals can provide for themselves solely through their own efforts. Second, because the need for health care is both unevenly distributed among persons and highly unpredictable and because the cost of securing care may be great, few individuals could secure adequate care without relying on some social mechanism for sharing the costs. Third, if persons generally deserved their health conditions or if the need for health care were fully within the individual's control, the fact that some lack adequate care would not be viewed as an inequity. But differences in health status, and hence differences in health care needs, are largely undeserved because they are, for the most part, not within the individual's control. . . .

In light of the special importance of health care, the largely undeserved character of differences in health status, and the uneven distribution and unpredictability of health care needs, society has a moral obligation to ensure adequate care for all. Saying that the obligation is societal (rather than merely individual) stops short, however, of identifying who has the ultimate responsibility for ensuring that the obligation is successfully met.

Who Should Ensure That Society's Obligation Is Met?

. . .

A Role for Government

The extent of governmental involvement in securing equitable access to care depends on the extent to which the market and private charity achieve this objective. . . . Although it is clear that—even for those with adequate resources—the purchase of health care differs from other market trans-

actions, the market (which includes private health insurance) is capable of providing many people with an adequate level of health care. However, when the market and charity do not enable individuals to obtain adequate care or cause them to endure excessive burdens in doing so, then the responsibility to ensure that these people have equitable access to health care resides with the local, state, and Federal governments.

Locating Responsibility. Although it is appropriate that all levels of government be involved in seeing that equitable access to health care is achieved, the *ultimate* responsibility for ensuring that this obligation is met rests with the Federal government. The Commission believes it is extremely important to distinguish between the view that the Federal government ought to provide care and the view that the Federal government is ultimately responsible for seeing that there is equitable access to care. It is the latter view that the Commission endorses. It is not the purpose of this Report to assign the precise division of labor between public and private provision of health care. Rather, the Commission has attempted here only to locate the ultimate responsibility for ensuring that equitable access is attained.

A view that has gained wide acceptance in this country is that the government has a major responsibility for making sure that certain basic social goods, such as health care and economic security for the elderly, are available to all. Over the past half-century, public policy and public opinion have increasingly reflected the belief that the Federal government is the logical mechanism for ensuring that society's obligation to make these goods available is met. In the case of health care, this stance is supported by several considerations. First, the obligation in question is society-wide, not limited to particular states or localities; it is an obligation of all to achieve equity for all. Second, government responsibility at the national level is needed to secure reliable resources. Third, only the Federal government can ultimately guarantee that the burdens of providing resources are distributed fairly across the whole of society. Fourth, meeting society's obligation to provide equitable access requires an "overview" of efforts. Unless the ultimate responsibility has been clearly fixed for determining whether the standard of equitable access is being met, there is no reason to believe it will be achieved.

The Limitations of Relying upon the Government. Although the Commission recognizes the necessity of government involvement in ensuring equity of access, it believes that such activity must be carefully crafted and implemented in order to achieve its intended purpose. Public concern about the inability of the market and of private charity to secure access to health care for all has led to extensive government involvement in the financing and delivery of health care. This involvement has come about largely as a result of ad hoc responses to specific problems; the result has been a patchwork of public initiatives at the local, state, and Federal level. These efforts have done much to make health care more widely available to all citizens, but, as discussed in Chapters Two and Three, they have not achieved equity of access.

To a large extent, this is the result of a lack of consensus about the nature of the goal and the proper role of government in pursuing it. But to some degree, it may also be the product of the nature of government activity. In some instances, government programs (of all types, not just health-related) have not been designed well enough to achieve the purposes intended or have been subverted to serve purposes explicitly not intended.

In the case of health care, it is extremely difficult to devise public strategies that, on the one hand, do not encourage the misuse of health services and, on the other hand, are not so restrictive as to unnecessarily or arbitrarily limit available care. There is a growing concern, for example, that government assistance in the form of tax exemptions for the purchase of employment-related health insurance has led to the overuse of many services of only very marginal benefit. Similarly, government programs that pay for health care directly (such as Medicaid) have been subject to fraud and abuse by both beneficiaries and providers. Alternatively, efforts to avoid misuse and abuse have at times caused local, state, and Federal programs to suffer from excessive bureaucracy, red tape, inflexibility, and unreasonable interference in individual choice. Also, as with private charity, government programs have not always avoided the unfortunate effects on the human spirit of "discretionary benevolence," especially in those programs requiring income or means tests.

It is also possible that as the government role in health care increases, the private sector's role will decrease in unforeseen and undesired ways. For example, government efforts to ensure access to nursing home care might lead to a lessening of support from family, friends, and other private sources for people who could be cared for in their homes. Although these kinds of problems do not inevitably accompany governmental involvement, they do occur and their presence provides evidence of the need for thoughtful and careful structuring of any government enterprise.

A Right to Health Care?

Often the issue of equitable access to health care is framed in the language of rights. Some who view health care from the perspective of distributive justice argue that the considerations discussed in this chapter show not only that society has a moral obligation to provide equitable access, but also that every individual has a moral right to such access. The Commission has chosen not to develop the case for achieving equitable access through the assertion of a right to health care. Instead it has sought to frame the issues in terms of the special nature of health care and of society's moral obligation to achieve equity, without taking a position on whether the term "obligation" should be read as entailing a moral right. The Commission reaches this conclusion for several reasons: first, such a right is not legally or Constitutionally recognized at the present time; second, it is not a logical corollary of an ethical obligation of the type the Commission has enunciated; and third, it is not necessary as a foundation for appropriate governmental actions to secure adequate health care for all. . . .

Moral Obligations and Rights. The relationship between the concept of a moral right and that of a moral obligation is complex. To say that a person has a moral right to something is always to say that it is that person's due, that is, he or she is morally entitled to it. In contrast, the term "obligation" is used in two different senses. All moral rights imply corresponding obligations, but, depending on the sense of the term that is being used, moral obligations may or may not imply corresponding rights. In the broad sense, to say that society has a moral obligation to do something is to say that it ought morally to do that thing and that failure to do it makes society liable to serious moral criticism. This does not, however, mean that there is a corresponding right. For example, a person may have a moral obligation to help those in need, even though the needy cannot, strictly speaking, demand that person's aid as something they are due.

The government's responsibility for seeing that the obligation to achieve equity is met is independent of the existence of a corresponding moral right to health care. There are many forms of government involvement, such as enforcement of traffic rules or taxation to support national defense, to protect the environment, or to promote biomedical research, that do not presuppose corresponding moral rights but that are nonetheless legitimate and almost universally recognized as such. In a democracy, at least, the people may assign to government the responsibility for seeing that important collective obligations are met, provided that doing so does not violate important moral rights.

As long as the debate over the ethical assessment of patterns of access to health care is carried on simply by the assertion and refutation of a "right to health care," the debate will be incapable of guiding policy. At the very least, the nature of the right must be made clear and competing accounts of it compared and evaluated. Moreover, if claims of rights are to guide policy they must be supported by sound ethical reasoning and the connections between various rights must be systematically developed, especially where rights are potentially in conflict with one another. At present, however, there is a great deal of dispute among competing theories of rights, with most theories being so abstract and inadequately developed that their implications for health care are not obvious. Rather than attempt to adjudicate among competing theories of rights, the Commission has chosen to concentrate on what it believes to be the more important part of the question: what is the nature of the societal obligation, which exists whether or not people can claim a corresponding right to health care, and how should this societal obligation be fulfilled?

Meeting the Societal Obligation
How Much Care Is Enough?

Before the concept of an adequate level of care can be used as a tool to evaluate patterns of access

and efforts to improve equity, it must be fleshed out. Since there is no objective formula for doing this, reasonable people can disagree about whether particular patterns and policies meet the demands of adequacy. The Commission does not attempt to spell out in detail what adequate care should include. Rather it frames the terms in which those who discuss or critique health care issues can consider ethics as well as economics, medical science, and other dimensions.

Characteristics of Adequacy. First, the Commission considers it clear that health care can only be judged adequate in relation to an individual's health condition. To begin with a list of techniques or procedures, for example, is not sensible: A CT scan for an accident victim with a serious head injury might be the best way to make a diagnosis essential for the appropriate treatment of that patient; a CT scan for a person with headaches might not be considered essential for adequate care. To focus only on the technique, therefore, rather than on the individual's health and the impact the procedure will have on that individual's welfare and opportunity, would lead to inappropriate policy.

Disagreement will arise about whether the care of some health conditions falls within the demands of adequacy. Most people will agree, however, that some conditions should not be included in the societal obligation to ensure access to adequate care. A relatively uncontroversial example would be changing the shape of a functioning, normal nose or retarding the normal effects of aging (through cosmetic surgery). By the same token, there are some conditions, such as pregnancy, for which care would be regarded as an important component of adequacy. In determining adequacy, it is important to consider how people's welfare, opportunities, and requirements for information and interpersonal caring are affected by their health condition.

Any assessment of adequacy must consider also the types, amounts, and quality of care necessary to respond to each health condition. It is important to emphasize that these questions are implicitly comparative: the standard of adequacy for a condition must reflect the fact that resources used for it will not be available to respond to other conditions. Consequently, the level of care deemed adequate should reflect a reasoned judgment not only about the impact of the condition on the welfare and opportunity of the individual but also about the efficacy and the cost of the care itself in relation to other conditions and the efficacy and cost of the care that is available for them. Since individual cases differ so much, the health care professional and patient must be flexible. Thus adequacy, even in relation to a particular health condition, generally refers to a range of options.

The Relationship of Costs and Benefits. The level of care that is available will be determined by the level of resources devoted to producing it. Such allocation should reflect the benefits and costs of the care provided. It should be emphasized that these "benefits," as well as their "costs," should be interpreted broadly, and not restricted only to effects easily quantifiable in monetary terms. Personal benefits include improvements in individuals' functioning and in their quality of life, and the reassurance from worry and the provision of information that are a product of health care. Broader social benefits should be included as well, such as strengthening the sense of community and the belief that no one in serious need of health care will be left without it. Similarly, costs are not merely the funds spent for a treatment but include other less tangible and quantifiable adverse consequences, such as diverting funds away from other socially desirable endeavors including education, welfare, and other social services.

There is no objectively correct value that these various costs and benefits have or that can be discovered by the tools of cost/benefit analysis. Still, such an analysis, as a recent report of the Office of Technology Assessment noted, "can be very helpful to decisionmakers because the process of analysis gives structure to the problem, allows an open consideration of all relevant effects of a decision, and forces the explicit treatment of key assumptions. But the valuation of the various effects of alternative treatments for different conditions rests on people's values and goals, about which individuals will reasonably disagree. In a democracy, the appropriate values to be assigned to the consequences of policies must ultimately be determined by people expressing their values through social and political processes as well as in the marketplace.

Approximating Adequacy. The intention of the Commission is to provide a frame of reference for policymakers, not to resolve these complex questions. Nevertheless, it is possible to raise some of the specific issues that should be considered in determining what constitutes adequate care. It is important, for example, to gather accurate information about and compare the costs and effects, both favorable and unfavorable, of various treatment or management options. The options that better serve the goals that make health care of special importance should be assigned higher value. As already noted, the assessment of costs must take two factors into account: the cost of a proposed option in relation to alternative forms of care that would achieve the same goal of enhancing the welfare and opportunities of the patient, and the cost of each proposed option in terms of foregone opportunities to apply the same resources to social goals other than that of ensuring equitable access.

Furthermore, a reasonable specification of adequate care must reflect an assessment of the relative importance of many different characteristics of a given form of care for a particular condition. Sometimes the problem is posed as: What *amounts* of care and what *quality* of care? Such a formulation reduces a complex problem to only two dimensions, implying that all care can readily be ranked as better or worse. Because two alternative forms of care may vary along a number of dimensions, there may be no consensus among reasonable and informed individuals about which form is of higher overall quality. It is worth bearing in mind that adequacy does not mean the highest possible level of quality or strictly equal quality any more than it requires equal amounts of care; of course, adequacy does require that everyone receive care that meets standards of sound medical practice.

Any combination of arrangements for achieving adequacy will presumably include some health care delivery settings that mainly serve certain groups, such as the poor or those covered by public programs. The fact that patients receive care in different settings or from different providers does not itself show that some are receiving inadequate care. The Commission believes that there is no moral objection to such a system so long as all receive care that is adequate in amount and quality and all patients are treated with concern and respect. . . .

Autonomy, Equality and a Just Health Care System _____

Kai Nielsen

Kai Nielsen claims that autonomy requires a society in which equality is also a fundamental value. A society of equals is committed to an equality of conditions, so everyone is equally entitled to have basic needs met. Where the life of everyone matters equally, everyone should receive the same quality of medical treatment, regardless of the ability to pay. Hence, two or three-tier systems are unjustified.

To achieve equality, Nielsen argues, medicine must be taken out of the private sector. If physicians were put on salaries in a government-operated system, this would remove the profit motive and allow them to practice better medicine. The result would be "a health care system befitting an autonomy-respecting democracy committed to the democratic and egalitarian belief that the life of everyone matters equally."

I

Autonomy and equality are both fundamental values in our firmament of values, and they are frequently thought to be in conflict. Indeed the standard liberal view is that we must make difficult and often morally ambiguous trade-offs between them.[1] I shall argue that this common view is mistaken and that autonomy cannot be widespread or secure in a society which is not egalitarian: where, that is, equality is not also a very fundamental value which has an operative role within the society.[2] I shall further argue that, given human needs and a commitment to an autonomy respecting egalitarianism, a very different health care system would come into being than that which exists at present in the United States.

I shall first turn to a discussion of autonomy and equality and then, in terms of those conceptions, to a conception of justice. In modernizing societies of Western Europe, a perfectly just society will be a society of equals and in such societies there will be a belief held across the political spectrum in what has been called *moral* equality. That is to say, when viewed with the impartiality required by morality, the life of everyone matters and matters equally.[3] Individuals will, of course, and rightly so, have their local attachments but they will acknowledge that justice requires that the social institutions of the society should be such that they work on the premise that the life of everyone matters and matters equally. Some privileged elite or other group cannot be given special treatment simply because they are that group. Moreover, for there to be a society of equals there must be a rough equality of condition in the society. Power must be sufficiently equally shared for it to be securely the case that no group or class or gender can dominate others through the social structures either by means of their frequently thoroughly unacknowledged latent functions or more explicitly and manifestly by institutional arrangements sanctioned by law or custom. Roughly equal material resources or power are not things which are desirable in themselves, but they are essential instrumentalities for the very possibility of equal well-being and for as many people as possible having as thorough and as complete a control over their own lives as is compatible with this being true for everyone alike. Liberty cannot flourish without something approaching this equality of condition, and people without autonomous lives will surely live impoverished lives. These are mere commonplaces. In fine, a commitment to achieving equality of condition, far from undermining liberty and autonomy, is essential for their extensive flourishing.

If we genuinely believe in moral equality, we will want to see come into existence a world in

From *International Journal of Applied Ethics*, vol. 4, Spring 1989, pp. 39–44. Reprinted by permission of the publisher.

which all people capable of self-direction have, and have as nearly as is feasible equally, control over their own lives and can, as far as the institutional arrangements for it obtaining are concerned, all live flourishing lives where their needs and desires as individuals are met as fully as possible and as fully and extensively as is compatible with that possibility being open to everyone alike. The thing is to provide institutional arrangements that are conducive to that.

People, we need to remind ourselves, plainly have different capacities and sensibilities. However, even in the extreme case of people for whom little in the way of human flourishing is possible, their needs and desires, as far as possible, should still also be satisfied in the way I have just described. Everyone in this respect at least has equal moral standing. No preference or pride of place should be given to those capable, in varying degrees, of rational self-direction. The more rational, or, for that matter, the more loveable, among us should not be given preference. No one should. Our needs should determine what is to be done.

People committed to achieving and sustaining a society of equals will seek to bring into stable existence conditions such that it would be possible for everyone, if they were personally capable of it, to enjoy an equally worthwhile and satisfying life or at least a life in which, for all of them, their needs, starting with and giving priority to their more urgent needs, were met and met as equally and as fully as possible, even where their needs are not entirely the same needs. This, at least, is the heuristic, though we might, to gain something more nearly feasible, have to scale down talk of meeting needs to providing conditions propitious for the equal satisfaction for everyone of their *basic* needs. Believers in equality want to see a world in which everyone, as far as this is possible, have equal whole life prospects. This requires an equal consideration of their needs and interests and a refusal to just override anyone's interests: to just regard anyone's interests as something which comes to naught, which can simply be set aside as expendable. Minimally, an egalitarian must believe that taking the moral point of view requires that each person's good is afforded equal consideration. Moreover, this is not just a bit of egalitarian ideology but is a deeply embedded considered judgment in modern Western culture capable of being put into wide reflective equilibrium.[4]

II

What is a need, how do we identify needs and what are our really basic needs, needs that are presumptively universal? Do these basic needs in most circumstances at least trump our other needs and our reflective considered preferences?

Let us start this examination by asking if we can come up with a list of universal needs correctly ascribable to all human beings in all cultures. In doing this we should, as David Braybrooke has, distinguish *adventitious* and *course-of-life* needs.[5] Moreover, it is the latter that it is essential to focus on. Adventitious needs, like the need for a really good fly rod or computer, come and go with particular projects. Course-of-life needs, such as the need for exercise, sleep or food, are such that every human being may be expected to have them all at least at some stage of life.

Still, we need to step back a bit and ask: how do we determine what is a need, course-of-life need or otherwise? We need a relational formula to spot needs. We say, where we are speaking of needs, B needs x in order to y, as in Janet needs milk or some other form of calcium in order to protect her bone structure. With course-of-life needs the relation comes out platitudinously as in "People need food and water in order to live" or "People need exercise in order to function normally or well." This, in the very identification of the need, refers to human flourishing or to human well-being, thereby giving to understand that they are basic needs. Perhaps it is better to say instead that this is to specify in part what it is for something to be a basic need. Be that as it may, there are these basic needs we *must* have to live well. If this is really so, then, where they are things we as individuals can have without jeopardy to others, no further question arises, or can arise, about the desirability of satisfying them. They are just things that in such circumstances ought to be met in our lives if they can. The satisfying of such needs is an unequivocally good thing. The questions "Does Janet need to live?" and "Does Sven need to function well?" are at best otiose.

In this context David Braybrooke has quite properly remarked that being "essential to living or to functioning normally may be taken as a criterion for being a basic need. Questions about whether needs are genuine, or well-founded, come to an end of the line when the needs have been connected with life or health."[6] Certainly to flourish we must have these things and in some instances they must be met at least to a certain extent even to survive. This being so, we can quite properly call them basic needs. Where these needs do not clash or the satisfying them by one person does not conflict with the satisfying of the equally basic needs of another no question about justifying the meeting of them arises.

By linking the identification of needs with what we must have to function well and linking course-of-life and basic needs with what all people, or at least almost all people, must have to function well, a list of basic needs can readily be set out. I shall give such a list, though surely the list is incomplete. However, what will be added is the same sort of thing similarly identified. First there are needs connected closely to our physical functioning, namely the need for food and water, the need for excretion, for exercise, for rest (including sleep), for a life supporting relation to the environment, and the need for whatever is indispensable to preserve the body intact. Similarly there are basic needs connected with our function as social beings. We have needs for companionship, education, social acceptance and recognition, for sexual activity, freedom from harassment, freedom from domination, for some meaningful work, for recreation and relaxation and the like.[7]

The list, as I remarked initially, is surely incomplete. But it does catch many of the basic things which are in fact necessary for us to live or to function well. Now an autonomy respecting egalitarian society with an interest in the well-being of its citizens—something moral beings could hardly be without—would (trivially) be a society of equals, and as a society of equals it would be committed to (a) *moral* equality and (b) an equality of *condition* which would, under conditions of moderate abundance, in turn expect the equality of condition to be rough and to be principally understood (cashed in) in terms of providing the conditions (as far as that is possible) for meeting the needs (including most centrally the basic needs) of everyone and meeting them equally, as far as either of these things is feasible.

III

What kind of health care system would such an autonomy respecting egalitarian society have under conditions of moderate abundance such as we find in Canada and the United States?

The following are health care needs which are also basic needs: being healthy and having conditions treated which impede one's functioning well or which adversely affect one's well-being or cause suffering. These are plainly things we need. Where societies have the economic and technical capacity to do so, as these societies plainly do, without undermining other equally urgent or more urgent needs, these health needs, as basic needs, must be met, and the right to have such medical care is a right for everyone in the society regardless of her capacity to pay. This just follows from a commitment to *moral* equality and to an equality of condition. Where we have the belief, a belief which is very basic in non-fascistic modernizing societies, that each person's good is to be given equal consideration, it is hard not to go in that way, given a plausible conception of needs and reasonable list of needs based on that conception.[8] If there is the need for some particular regime of care and the society has the resources to meet that need, without undermining structures protecting other at least equally urgent needs, then, *ceteris paribus,* the society, if it is a decent society, must do so. The commitment to more equality—the commitment to the belief that the life of each person matters and matters equally—entails, given a few plausible empirical premises, that each person's health needs will be the object of an equal regard. Each has an equal claim, *prima facie,* to have her needs satisfied where this is possible. That does not, of course, mean that people should all be treated alike in the sense of their all getting the same thing. Not everyone needs flu shots, braces, a dialysis machine, a psychiatrist, or a triple bypass. What should be equal is that each person's health needs should be the object of equal societal concern since each person's good should be given equal consideration.[9] This does not mean that equal energy should be directed to Hans's rash as to Frank's cancer. Here one person's need for a cure is much greater than the other, and the greater need clearly takes precedence. Both should be met where possible, but where they both cannot then the greater need has pride of place. But what should not count in the treatment of Hans and Frank is that Hans is wealthy or prestigious or creative and Frank is not. Everyone should have their health needs met where possible. Moreover, where the need is the same, they should have (where possible), and where other at least equally urgent needs are not thereby undermined, the same quality treatment. No differentiation should be made between them on the basis of their ability to pay or on the basis of their being (one more so than the other) important people. There should, in short, where this is possible, be open and free medical treatment of the same quality and extent available to everyone in the society. And no two- or three-tier system should be allowed to obtain, and treatment should only vary (subject to the above qualification) on the basis of variable needs and unavoidable differences in different places in supply and personnel, e.g., differences between town and country. Furthermore, these latter differences should be remedied where technically and economically feasible. The underlying aim should be to meet the health care needs of everyone and meet them, in the sense explicated, equally: everybody's needs here should be met as fully as possible; different treatment is only justified where the need is different or where both needs cannot be met. Special treatment for one person rather than another is only justified where, as I remarked, both needs cannot be met or cannot as adequately be met. Constrained by ought implies can; where these circumstances obtain, priority should be given to the greater need that can feasibly be met. A moral system or a social policy, plainly, cannot be reasonably asked to do the impossible. But my account does not ask that.

To have such a health care system would, I think, involve taking medicine out of the private sector altogether including, of course, out of private entrepreneurship where the governing rationale has to be profit and where supply and demand rules the roost. Instead there must be a health care system firmly in the public sector (publicly owned and controlled) where the rationale of the system is to meet as efficiently and as fully as possible the health care needs of everyone in the society in question. The health care system should not be viewed as a business anymore than a university should be viewed as a business—compare a university and a large hospital—but as a set of institutions and practices designed to meet urgent human needs.

I do not mean that we should ignore costs of efficiency. The state-run railroad system in Switzerland, to argue by analogy, is very efficient. The state cannot, of course, ignore costs in running it. But the aim is not to make a profit. The aim is to produce the most rapid, safe, efficient and comfortable service meeting traveller's needs within the parameters of the overall socio-economic priorities of the state and the society. Moreover, since the state in question is a democracy, if its citizens do not like the policies of the government here (or elsewhere) they can replace it with a government with different priorities and policies. Indeed the option is there (probably never to be exercised) to shift the railroad into the private sector.

Governments, understandably, worry with aging populations about mounting health care costs. This is slightly ludicrous in the United States, given its military and space exploration budgets, but is also a reality in Canada and even in Iceland where there is no military or space budget at all. There should, of course, be concern about containing health costs, but this can be done effectively with a state-run system. Modern societies need systems of socialized medicine, something that obtains in almost all civilized modernizing societies. The United States and South Africa are, I believe, the only exceptions. But, as is evident from my own country (Canada), socialized health care systems often need altering, and their costs need monitoring. As a cost-cutting and as an efficiency measure that would at the same time improve health care, doctors, like university professors and government bureaucrats, should be put on salaries and they should work in medical units. They should, I hasten to add, have good salaries but salaries all the same; the last vestiges of petty entrepreneurship should be taken from the medical profession. This measure would save the state-run health care system a considerable amount of money, would improve the quality of medical care with greater cooperation and consultation resulting from economies of scale and a more extensive division of labor with larger and better equipped medical units. (There would also be less duplication of equipment.) The overall quality of care would also improve with a better balance between health care in the country and in the large cities, with doctors being systematically and rationally deployed throughout the society. In such a system doctors, no more than university professors or state bureaucrats, could not just set up a practice anywhere. They would no more be free to do this than university professors or state bureaucrats. In the altered system there would be no cultural space for it. Placing doctors on salary, though not at a piece work rate, would also result in its being the case that the financial need to see as many patients as possible as quickly as possible would be removed. This would plainly enhance the quality of medical care. It would also be the case that a different sort of person would go into the medical profession. People would go into it more frequently because they were actually interested in medicine and less frequently because this is a rather good way (though hardly the best way) of building a stock portfolio.

There should also be a rethinking of the respective roles of nurses (in all their variety), paramedics and doctors. Much more of the routine work done in medicine—taking the trout fly out of my ear for example—can be done by nurses or paramedics. Doctors, with their more extensive training, could be freed up for other more demanding tasks worthy of their expertise. This would require somewhat different training for all of these different medical personnel and a rethinking of the authority structure in the health care system. But doing this in a reasonable way would improve the teamwork in hospitals, make morale all around a lot better, improve medical treatment and save a very considerable amount of money. (It is no secret that the relations between doctors and nurses are not good.) Finally, a far greater emphasis should be placed on preventative medicine than is done now. This, if really extensively done, utilizing the considerable educational and fiscal powers of the state, would result in very considerable health care savings and a very much healthier and perhaps even happier population. (Whether with the states we actually have we are likely to get anything like that is—to understate it—questionable. I wouldn't hold my breath in the United States. Still, Finland and Sweden are very different places from the United States and South Africa.)

IV

It is moves of this *general* sort that an egalitarian and autonomy loving society under conditions of moderate scarcity should implement. (I say "general sort" for I am more likely to be wrong about some of the specifics than about the general thrust of my argument.) It would, if in place, limit the freedom of some people, including some doctors and some patients, to do what they want to do. That is obvious enough. But any society, any society at all, as long as it had norms (legal and otherwise) will limit freedom in some way.[10] There is no living in society without some limitation on the freedom to do some things. Indeed a society without norms and thus without any limitation on freedom is a contradiction in terms. Such a mass of people wouldn't be a society. They, without norms,

would just be a mass of people. (If these are "grammatical remarks," make the most of them.) In our societies I am not free to go for a spin in your car without your permission, to practice law or medicine without a license, to marry your wife while she is still your wife and the like. Many restrictions on our liberties, because they are so common, so widely accepted and thought by most of us to be so reasonable, hardly *seem* like restrictions on our liberty. But they are all the same. No doubt some members of the medical profession would feel quite reined in if the measures I propose were adopted. (These measures are not part of conventional wisdom.) But the restrictions on the freedom of the medical profession and on patients I am proposing would make for both a greater liberty all around, everything considered, and, as well, for greater well-being in the society. Sometimes we have to restrict certain liberties in order to enhance the overall system of liberty. Not speaking out of turn in parliamentary debate is a familiar example. Many people who now have a rather limited access to medical treatment would come to have it and have it in a more adequate way with such a socialized system in place. Often we have to choose between a greater or lesser liberty in a society, and, at least under conditions of abundance, the answer almost always should be "Choose the greater liberty." If we really prize human autonomy, if, that is, we want a world in which as many people as possible have as full as is possible control over their own lives, then we will be egalitarians. Our very egalitarianism will commit us to something like the health care system I described, but so will the realization that, without reasonable health on the part of the population, autonomy can hardly flourish or be very extensive. Without the kind of equitability and increased coverage in health care that goes with a properly administered socialized medicine, the number of healthy people will be far less than could otherwise feasibly be the case. With that being the case, autonomy and well-being as well will be neither as extensive nor as thorough as it could otherwise be. Autonomy, like everything else, has its material conditions. And to will the end is to will the necessary means to the end.

To take—to sum up—what since the Enlightenment has come to be seen as the moral point of view, and to take morality seriously, is to take it as axiomatic that each person's good be give equal consideration.[11] I have argued that (a) where that is accepted, and (b) where we are tolerably clear about the facts (including facts about human needs), and (c) where we live under conditions of moderate abundance, a health care system bearing at least a family resemblance to the one I have gestured at will be put in place. It is a health care system befitting an autonomy respecting democracy committed to the democratic and egalitarian belief that the life of everyone matters and matters equally.

Notes

1. Isaiah Berlin, "On the Pursuit of the Ideal," *The New York Review of Books* XXXV (March 1987), pp. 11–18. See also his "Equality" in his *Concepts and Categories* (Oxford, England: Oxford University Press, 1980), pp. 81–102. I have criticized that latter paper in my "Formulating Egalitarianism: Animadversions on Berlin," *Philosophia* 13: 3–4 (October 1983), pp. 299–315.

2. For three defenses of such a view see Kai Nielsen, *Equality and Liberty* (Totowa, New Jersey: Rowman and Allanheld, 1985), Richard Norman, *Free and Equal* (Oxford, England: Oxford University Press, 1987), and John Baker, *Arguing for Equality* (London: Verso Press, 1987).

3. Will Kymlicka, "Rawls on Teleology and Deontology," *Philosophy and Public Affairs* 17: 3 (Summer 1988), pp. 173–190 and John Rawls, "The Priority of Right and Ideas of the Good," *Philosophy and Public Affairs* 17: 4 (Fall 1988), pp. 251–276.

4. Kai Nielsen, "Searching for an Emancipatory Perspective: Wide Reflective Equilibrium and the Hermeneutical Circle" in Evan Simpson (ed.), *Anti-Foundationalism and Practical Reasoning* (Edmonton, Alberta: Academic Printing and Publishing, 1987), pp. 143–164 and Kai Nielsen, "In Defense of Wide Reflective Equilibrium" in Douglas Odegard (ed.) *Ethics and Justification* (Edmonton, Alberta: Academic Printing and Publishing, 1988) pp. 19–37.

5. David Braybrooke, *Meeting Needs* (Princeton, New Jersey: Princeton University Press, 1987), p. 29.

6. Ibid., p. 31.

7. Ibid., p. 37.

8. Will Kymlicka, op cit, p. 190.

9. Ibid.

10. Ralf Dahrendorf, *Essays in the Theory of Society* (Stanford, California: Stanford University Press, 1968), pp. 151–78 and G. A. Cohen, "The Structure of Proletarian Unfreedom," *Philosophy and Public Affairs* 12 (1983), pp. 2–33.

11. Will Kymlicka, op cit, p. 190.

The Case for a Single-Payer Approach

Jim McDermott

Jim McDermott argues in favor of a single-payer system in which the major difference between it and the current one is that the federal government would become the insurer and institute a budget to control costs. The traditional physician-patient relationship will be preserved; people can still choose physicians and physicians can act for patients and not have to justify treatment choices to a third party.

McDermott believes that before any single-payer system is likely to be accepted, we must get rid of the idea that government cannot do anything competently. Actually, some problems are so large and far-reaching that only governments can solve them. National defense, NIH-funded research, and NASA are cases of effective administration of activities that could not be carried out as well by private enterprise or state governments.

McDermott argues against managed competition. Because such a system has never been tried, its long-term effectiveness is uncertain. Also, by using a patchwork of private and governmental insurance, managed competition would leave many people uninsured and continue the high costs of administration.

From *JAMA*, March 9, 1994—vol. 271, no. 10, pp. 782–784.

Throughout history, the medical profession has struggled in its conflict between belief and science. In the late 18th century, this struggle was exemplified by a religious adherence to Dr. Benjamin Rush's theory that bleeding patients would restore health. The result of this mistaken belief—as opposed to proven hypothesis—was that George Washington is historically thought to have been bled to death therapeutically.

Two hundred years later, American medicine is still locked in its ambivalence between science and belief. But in 1993, the issue is health care system reform. In the debate emerging from the presentation of President Clinton's plan, the challenge for our profession will be whether it can move beyond time-honored mantras to examine objectively and scientifically the options with which it is presented.

The Need for Change

Few would dispute the need for change. American physicians are the most dissatisfied and frustrated in the industrialized world.[1] Approximately 15% of our people have no health insurance at any one time, and at least 57 million nonelderly Americans lack health insurance for some part of the year.[2,3] This does not even include the underinsured and those on Medicaid whose coverage cannot begin to provide them with access that is consistent with good health care.[4] One hundred thousand additional people lose their health insurance every month.[5] Health care costs rise at 11% annually, further guaranteeing that more will become uninsured as employers become unable to bear the burden.[6] In a misguided attempt to control costs, insurance companies require physicians to spend extraordinary amounts of time defending their treatment decisions.

There is very little that individual physicians can do to remedy this situation. They have no power to affect systemic dynamics, they have little information on which to relate individual practice to that of others, and delivery decisions have largely been taken out of the physician's hands.

So the questions become how do we change general cost trends, how do we provide physicians the data they need to make prudent decisions, and how do we put control of the delivery system back in the hands of the caregivers? How do we bring about reform that provides universal access to care,

controls costs, and recaptures the personalization of health care essential to illness prevention and healing?

Lessons Learned

Based on evidence from most of the industrialized world, the answer lies in providing health care through a single-payer system.[7] Single-payer health system reform severs the link between employment and health insurance. A single-payer system is essentially a financing mechanism that preserves the primary foundation of the American health care delivery system—the physician-patient relationship. The single payer—the government—provides the insurance for health care for all Americans, and the states negotiate the fees of health care providers. The health care delivery system remains primarily in private hands with free choice of provider. The government manages the rate of growth of price increases. This is the system that exists in varying forms in every society in the Western world, one that has brought health standards that are superior or equal to ours by most morbidity and mortality measurements, and one that has left its physicians and patients content.[8]

In single-payer systems throughout the world, patients choose their own practitioners, and physicians do not have to justify individual treatment decisions to insurance companies or their government or seek permission in advance to perform procedures. This is the system that has been proven to actually work to control costs, guarantee access, assure quality, and command loyalty by both patients and physicians.

Germans spend 57% of U.S. health care expenditures per capita on health care and on the first day of unification between East Germany and West Germany, every East German was included in the West German health care system without a moment's transition.[9] Canada spends 68% of U.S. health spending per capita. Australia spends 51% of U.S. spending. And all these systems have unrestricted free choice of provider. Interference in physician treatment decisions on a case-by-case basis is unheard of in these countries.

The single-payer system has been demonstrated to reduce administrative costs to less then 2%, instead of the 14% (range 5% to 40%) we experience in the United States at the hands of private insurance companies.[5,10] Overall, Americans spend at least 20% of their health care dollars on insurance company, physician, and hospital administrative costs.[11] Indeed, administrative cost is the fastest-growing sector of the American health care economy.[12] Medicare, on the other hand, our own single-payer system for elderly and disabled Americans, expends 2.1% on administrative costs.[4]

We have had virtually uncontrolled insurance free enterprise in the American health care delivery system since World War II, and it has brought us to our current dilemma. Health care cost inflation of 11% annually completely refutes the notion that competition between insurance companies will reduce costs.[5]

We can no longer ignore the implications of the fact that inability to pay medical bills is the leading cause of personal bankruptcy in the United States[5] or that out-of-pocket medical costs now consume more than 10% of average household income.[2] And most Americans know that the termination of their health insurance is but one pink slip away. On the other hand, our trading partners through single-payer systems have preserved freedom of choice of provider, enhanced quality, controlled costs, and provided unquestioned security of health insurance coverage.[12] To deny this reality is to argue for leeches in the face of penicillin.

That is why earlier this year I introduced the American Health Security Act, HR 1200, in the House of Representatives. It is based on proven systems. And because it is based on experience, it provides solutions that are based on the lessons learned from years of experiments in many other countries resulting in their current health systems.

American Single-Payer System

The American Health Security Act establishes a single-payer system that is federally financed, administered at the state and local level, and privately delivered. This means that physicians are not employees of the government or any insurance company—the private delivery system remains intact. Patients have unfettered free choice of provider. Access to providers (and providers to patients) is not limited by the insurance plan with which they are affiliated. This not only enables patients to choose the best provider for them, it also assures continuity of care, a critical element in quality enhancement, because patients are not required to lose their physician every time they need to change

insurance plans because of changes in their economic situation. The financial imperatives to change insurance plans and therefore physicians with every variation in the patient's personal situation is a fundamental flaw in both the president's and the pure managed competition approaches. In a single-payer system, a patient is never impelled to leave his or her personal caregiver.

Key provisions of HR 1200 include universal coverage, cost containment through global budgets, a reformulation of quality review mechanisms to explicitly eliminate insurer interference in the physician-patient relationship, creation of a uniform database, promotion of primary care practice including general internal medicine and general pediatrics, and provision of the financing of insurance from the federal government. These key provisions operate to maintain stability in the delivery of care, to focus on the physician-patient relationship as the centerpiece of the health care system, and to provide total security to the patient in the form of uninterrupted insurance coverage that requires no changes in plans as circumstances change.

Under HR 1200, the premium for health insurance is collected by the government in a separate health security trust fund. Health care expenditures are based on a national budget based on the preceding year's national health care expenditures plus growth in gross domestic product and population. That money is then distributed to state health security funds according to population and health status. The states contribute approximately 14% of the budget.

The providers and the single payer negotiate the payment rate for services. The negotiation process itself anticipates that providers bring bargaining power to the table, as in Germany—bargaining power that is much greater than the negotiating posture physicians traditionally have had with insurance companies. Certainly, the bargaining position of providers will be much stronger with a government accountable for the public good than with the monopsony market power of insurance companies under any managed competition proposal. Competition is based on quality, not cost, which will lead inevitably to a minimalist approach to care.[11]

As long as they stay within the budget, providers and states are basically unconstrained in how they negotiate reimbursement, with one exception. We face a critical shortage of primary care in this country, where specialists outnumber our primary care providers 7:3.[1] If we do not address this issue forcefully by training more primary care physicians and then rewarding them, we will continue to confront both the health care problems created by insufficient primary care and the cost problems associated with excess specialty-oriented care.

To reverse this trend, HR 1200 requires states to weight reimbursement to favor primary care providers so that direct incentives are created to enter primary care and stay there. In addition, funding of graduate medical education is directly tied to the state's ability to produce primary care residencies in a 1:1 ratio with specialty residencies.

Quality

Compounding the failure to recognize the primary care crisis in this country is the inattention to quality-of-care issues. Yet the way we currently review quality and control utilization is as flawed as our existing financing system.

The HR 1200 bill scraps the existing system of case-by-case utilization review and substitutes a system of outlier identification. Based on practice profiles rather than individual cases, providers whose pattern of practice is consistently outside the norms of their peers are identified and their practice methods reviewed. This enables the profession to look at the practices of individuals who pose systematic quality problems and to reeducate them. It enables physicians to deviate from routine practices in individual cases without the concern that a particular case will trigger a review. It provides an opportunity to reach providers who are isolated from their peer community and might never be discovered in random case-by-case reviews.

Because HR 1200 strives to return the health care delivery system to the caregivers, precertification of procedures is explicitly prohibited. Rather, practice guidelines are developed based on outcomes data and research. The bill establishes a national clinical database to contain raw patient data based on patient charts rather than billing information. The database would be established by the year 2000 based on the use of uniform software. Patient identity would be shielded from nonproviders and access restricted. Other privacy protection mechanisms are included. With this database, valid outcomes research can be performed and systematized, and physicians will have much more information on which to base treatment decisions.

Most evidence suggests, and HR 1200 assumes, that physicians respond to information.[13] The best way then to change practice patterns is not to regulate physicians, but to provide the data on what actually works.

In addition to enhancing our clinical research capacity, the database will enable broad-based epidemiological studies to be undertaken. Through it, we can track the course of the growing tuberculosis epidemic and evaluate the methods to contain it as well as monitor the incidence and origins of other diseases. It should become an important tool in the conduct of basic research.

Myths

The goals of health system reform outlined above will not be attainable unless we cast out the myths that make this struggle for reform unnecessarily difficult. The notion that government cannot do anything competently must be fairly examined. We must recognize that there are problems whose scope and impact are so large that solving them simply requires government coordination. Maintaining private financing to coordinate health care makes no more sense than privately financing our national defense, and defense is a smaller part of our economy than our heath care expenditures.[14]

For example, the vigor of American biomedical research is largely a result of federal funding of research administered by the National Institutes of Health and conducted by private institutions. It provides a perfect illustration of the effectiveness of federal financing of privately conducted projects as seen in our major private research institutions. The funding of the National Aeronautics and Space Administration provides another excellent example of how federally coordinated programs have resulted in great private gain, such as the sharing of space technology to achieve the sophistication of the hospital intensive care unit.

From an operational standpoint, the potential for the government to bring real benefits is persuasive. The administrative cost of Medicare programs is just 2.1%[4] compared with the private rate of 14%.[5] Our publicly financed pension system, Social Security, has never missed a payment in its 60-year history. Its trust fund runs with a consistent surplus.

Nor are physician livelihoods threatened by a single-payer system. A Congressional Budget Office study demonstrated that if a single-payer system similar to Medicare had been in effect in 1991, we would have reimbursed health care providers $21 billion more than we did then and still reduced national health expenditures by $14 billion.[15] It is important to realize that the administrative savings achieved by eliminating insurance companies stays in the system and is converted to payment to providers for delivering more care.

What, in fact, happens to provider incomes in a single-payer system? Certainly the rate of growth is controlled—but the baseline does not change. Second, there will be changes in how the money flows to different specialty groups within medicine. It appears likely that the rate of increases in fees for internists and pediatricians, for example, is going to be greater than for cardiac surgeons. But that scenario will likely occur whether you have a single-payer system or not. Physicians in single-payer countries that retain the private delivery system prosper.[16]

In return for negotiated fee schedules, physicians are guaranteed that they will be paid 100% of the fee for every patient within 60 days of bill submission, paperwork is completely eliminated (Canadian physicians submit one diskette to their provincial governments monthly, which constitutes their entire non-chart-related administrative burden), financial anxiety and discussion is eliminated from the physician-patient relationship, and insurance companies are not second-guessing individual treatment decisions.

The Options

The alternative to single-payer health care reform is President Clinton's plan, a more regulated version of managed competition to attempt to achieve universal coverage and cost containment. Costs will be controlled by herding patients into plans dominated by health maintenance organizations that compete primarily on the basis of cost, not quality. Insurance companies are placed directly in charge of the delivery system, as evidenced by the fact that cost containment is based on unifying the delivery system and the insurance system through health maintenance organizations and enforced through capping insurance premiums and taxing higher cost plans, presumably fee-for-service-plans.[17] Most physicians will become contractees of insurance companies.

While there is a great deal of rhetoric about patient choice being based on quality, all the incentives in the president's proposal are financial. To the extent that quality improves with plans above the average premium plan, consumers can select quality only to the extent that they can pay for it with out-of-pocket, after-tax resources beyond what their employer contributes to their health coverage. Quality enforcement is left to the insurance plans whose reporting to patients is based on average results. There are no mechanisms for identification of specific provider quality problems for improving that provider's performance.

Enforcement of quality is essentially relegated to the patient who must evaluate quality report cards and choose plans accordingly to the extent the average premium permits. Since these sorts of quality assessments are extremely complicated for skilled professionals, it is difficult to imagine how the average patient is supposed to be able to distill this information. In effect, this aspect of the president's plan merely passes the buck to the people it is supposed to be protecting.

The only statement that can be made with certainty about the president's approach is that its applicability to the entire spectrum of any nation's health care delivery system has never been observed.[11] Its continuation of the patchwork of private-public insurance is destined to maintain large cracks that will leave many Americans still uninsured, assure high administrative expense,[12] and further establish the control of insurance companies over the delivery system.

Indeed, examined objectively, it is mystifying why the medical profession would prefer private financing. The expectation that physicians can have higher fees will certainly be defeated by the reality of fees set by insurance companies, which must be low enough to assure large insurance company profit margins. And there is at least as much reason to expect that needed care will be denied to subsidize executive skyboxes at the nation's stadiums as there is to believe that insurance companies will preside over better preventive care and improved health care delivery to rural areas. Insurance companies simply have no mandate to protect the public good.

Ultimately, a single-payer system and HR1200 offer the solution that is most conducive to physician and patient satisfaction and to good medical practice. It is the only system that has actually worked to remove financial anxiety and coverage concerns from the physician-patient relationship. It is the only system that has in fact reduced administrative cost to its necessary minimum, thereby reducing physician overhead and freeing more resources for actual delivery of care. It is the only system that in fact operates without insurer interference in individual treatment decisions and restores the physician's role in the delivery system.

There are three major options controlling the health system reform debate. We can continue the current system, but the data show conclusively that it has failed by most major criteria and will only get worse. We can adopt managed competition in its regulatory form, which is completely untested but contains incentives that adversely affect quality and will institutionally remove physician control of the delivery system. Or we can adopt a plan that not only can be supported by objective data, but which has the potential for providing the best environment in which to practice medicine. For scientists, for clinicians, a single-payer system can prove to be the cure we have all been seeking.

Notes

1. Levinsky N. Recruiting for primary care. *N Engl J Med.* 1993; 328: 656–660.

2. *Half of Us, Families Priced Out of Health Protection.* Washington, DC: Families USA; April 1993.

3. Swartz K. Dynamics of people without health insurance: don't let the numbers fool you. *JAMA.* 1994; 271: 64–66.

4. Ford M. *Medicaid: Financing, Trends, and the President's FY 1993 Budget Proposals.* Washington, DC: Congressional Research Service; 1992. CSR report for Congress 92-168 EPW.

5. Iglehart J. The American health care system: private insurance. *N Engl J Med.* 1992; 326: 1716.

6. *Managed Competition and Its Potential to Reduce Health Spending: A CBO Study.* Washington, DC: Congressional Budget Office; May 1993.

7. Glaser W. A. The United States needs a health system like other countries. *JAMA.* 1993; 270: 980–984.

8. Shikles J. *Canadian Health Insurance: Lessons for the United States.* Washington, DC: General Accounting Office; 1991. GAO report GAO/HRD-91-90.

9. Schieber J, Poullier J-P. and Greenwald L. U.S. health expenditure performance: an international comparison and data update. *Health Care Financing Rev.* 1992; 13: 1–15.

10. Blendon R. J., Edwards J. N. and Hyams A. L. Making the critical choices. *JAMA.* 1992: 267: 2509–2530.

11. Angell M. How much will health care reform cost? *N Engl J Med.* 1993: 328: 1778–1779.

12. Himmelstein D. and Woolhandler S. The deteriorating administrative efficiency of the U.S. health care system. *N Engl J Med.* 1991: 324: 1253–1258.

13. Merlis M. *Controlling Health Care Costs.* Washington, DC: Congressional Research Service; January 26, 1990. CRS report for Congress 90-64 EPW.

14. *Economic Indicators Report.* Washington, DC: Joint Economic Committee of Congress; June 2, 1993.

15. Rich S. Single payer health care savings seen: CBO reports system could cut $14 billion. *Washington Post.* May 9, 1993; section A:5.

16. Fuchs B. and Sokolovsky J. *The Canadian Health Care System.* Washington, DC: Congressional Research Service; February 20, 1990. CRS report for Congress 90-95 EPW.

17. *The President's Draft Proposal for Health Care Reform.* Washington, DC: Office of the President; September 7, 1993.

It Is Time for Universal Access, Not Universal Insurance

James S. Todd

James Todd argues against a federal single-payer system of universal health insurance. Such a system would create a bureaucracy that would focus on cost control, instead of patient care, and Americans would not easily accept the inevitable long waits and limits on choice. Our current pluralistic system, Todd claims, works well in general, and it would be dangerous to replace it completely.

Rather than providing universal insurance, Todd favors guaranteeing universal access to medical care. We should "define a basic level of health care to which everyone is entitled, supported by multiple funding systems." Medicaid could be expanded to include everyone below the poverty line, and the uninsured could be provided with health-care vouchers. Our challenge is "to improve the greatest health care system in the world, not destroy it."

An editorial by Relman proclaims, "Universal Health Insurance: Its Time Has Come."[1] Other recent *Journal* articles recommend various consumer-choice health care systems,[2,3] and the report of the National Leadership Commission on Health Care proposes what is essentially a national health insurance scheme.[4] I submit, instead, that the idea whose time has come is universal access to care—not through universal insurance that is funded from a central source or tightly controlled by forces other than medical need, but through a pluralistic delivery system.

Universal health insurance is not a good idea. To control goods or services through a single agency—especially when the driving force is economic—would fly in the face of the American way of doing things. We have tried central controls, and the results have been less than first-rate. Surely, for instance, we would not want to trust health care to a monolithic and monumentally ineffective monster like the postal service. Lost letters are one thing; lost lives are another.

What about the argument that we need government intervention to take care of those who are unable to care for themselves? Micromanagement in the health care system has become very much worse under the federal programs that exist today. And certainly our national experience with welfare and public housing has shown that a central bureaucracy fails miserably in addressing the heart of human need.

Rather than support such unworkable, soulless programs, I propose universal access through a pluralistic funding mechanism. Those who can take care of themselves should do so; those who need help should receive it according to their need; and we should define a basic level of health care to which everyone is entitled, supported by multiple funding systems. Those who want special procedures (such as cosmetic surgery, the lack of which will cause no harm) or the ambience and comfort of "Cadillac care" should pay for them out of their own pockets.

The American Medical Association has made a series of proposals[5] whose implementation would not only increase access to health care but also go a long way toward providing appropriate, effective care in the proper setting. The proposals would expand eligibility and coverage under Medicaid to everyone below the poverty line and would create state risk pools with assistance, by means of vouchers, for uninsured people who are above the poverty line. The undergirding premise is to each according to his or her need and from each according to his or her means. When did this become undemocratic?

I am suggesting a pluralistic system because pluralism has made this country great in all respects—in large part because it offers built-in checks and balances that do not exist in monolithic systems of government. Turning the funding of health care over to the federal government, or any single entity, cannot seem a particularly reassuring or realistic idea to anyone. And dare we create a tax program that might or might not be used appropriately? Why do we keep getting bogged down in discussions of universal health insurance, ignoring the opportunity to do something really dramatic and humane?

Perhaps it is because so many countries now have such plans. But a look at universal health insurance programs in other countries inspires little confidence that a similar system here would solve the problem of access to care. The United States is unique, and our pluralistic approach is unique. There is no reason to think that an imported system would be successful here or that American citizens would accept its implicit restrictions.

Furthermore, no country has a system without major flaws. In many cases, the flaws would be particularly unacceptable to American consumers. For instance, despite recent favorable analyses of the Canadian experience,[6,7] the temporal rationing that occurs in that system—forcing patients to wait months or even years for what in this country are common medical procedures—is not the American way. Consider that in Vancouver there is a wait of two to four years for corneal transplantation, and up to three months for a psychiatric, neurosurgical, or routine orthopedic opinion.[8] Americans will not stand for temporal rationing or priorities by triage.

The problem with existing universal health insurance plans is that they focus primarily on paying for care. If cost is the only focus, it is easy to devise a plan that will at least function. Any budget can be controlled by making sure there is only one source of funds and then turning the spigot on and off according to what is available from that source. And this is essentially what has happened in every country with universal health insurance. Indeed, it is happening in this country, as the health care system continues to have a disproportionate role in the reduction of a federal budget deficit it did not create.

Other countries ignore appropriateness and effectiveness; they ignore the many complex elements of high-quality care that we in America demand; and they largely ignore the citizen's right to free choice, a concept we hold very dear. Americans will not stand for closing the spigot as long as there is a genuine need for care. In 1989 it is unrealistic to expect health care expenditures to level off, much less to decrease, in the absence of economic rationing. Instead, the level of health care activity will continue to grow as a result of various factors, including an aging population, increased demand (fostered in part by more consumer awareness of health issues), and the simple fact that medicine can do more for people now than ever before.

The American health care system at its best is universally acknowledged to be the best in the world, yet clearly that is not enough. Although we do need to address the enormous problems that exist in American health care, any plan that seeks to revamp completely a system that is working as well as ours is a dangerous proposition. We must not kill the can-do spirit that has fostered what is best in American medicine—the breakthrough research, technological advances, and widespread availability of life-enhancing procedures. It would be tragic to jeopardize the best of this best-in-the-world system just because there are problems with it. These can be addressed in an evolutionary and equitable fashion if we have the resolve to do so.

What is the siren song of foreign programs? It is unrealistic to think we can import systems from different cultures—or try to revolutionize a system that has produced some of the greatest technology and physicians in the world—and expect success. Our political and economic climate is unique, and our pluralistic tradition is unique as well. Health care expenditures cannot be controlled by controlling the reimbursement of physicians or capping economic resources at some magic number, usually related to the gross national product.

Ignoring the demands or expectations of its patients dooms any monolithic system before it starts. To control health expenditures solely on the basis of economic targets does violence to all involved. Cost, access, and quality are interrelated; manipulating one has an astounding impact on the others.

So, we ought not to be talking about a universal health insurance scheme, but rather about universal access—access to needed care, on a timely basis, with controls on quality and use that have been accepted by everyone involved. The key principle of effective access and limited cost is the rationalization of care. In this age of high-technology medicine and miracle drugs, we must realize that we can no longer do everything for everybody just because it is possible.

Rather, we should develop a system in which decisions about what we do, when, where, and to whom are based on reasonable expectations of the benefits involved and on sound medical principles communicated clearly to patients and their families.

Our only salvation lies in developing a greater sense of restraint and responsibility, ignoring the quick fix and the revolutionary brainchild of those who would control costs at the expense of patients and progress. What other countries have done is irrelevant to our problems. No country has reached a comfortable accommodation with its current system.

So universal access, not universal insurance, is an idea whose time has long since come. And if all of us—the health care community and our patients (those who do pay as well as those who should)—assume our rightful responsibilities, the idea can become a reality. We ought to be smart enough to devise in the United States a system of universal access at a cost that we can afford and in keeping with the principles of freedom we hold dear. This is the challenge before us; to improve the greatest health care system in the world, not to destroy it.

Notes

1. Relman, A. S. Universal health insurance: its time has come. *N. Engl J Med* 1989; 320: 117–118.

2. Enthoven A. C. and Kronick R. A consumer-choice health plan for the 1990s; universal health insurance in a system designed to promote quality and economy. *N. Engl J Med* 1989; 320: 29–37, 94–101.

3. Himmelstein D. U., and Woolhandler S. Writing Committee of the Working Group on Program Design. A national

health program for the United States: a physicians' proposal. *N Engl J Med* 1989; 320: 102–108.

4. For the health of a nation. Washington, D.C.: National Leadership commission on Health Care, 1989.

5. Health policy agenda for the American People Ad Hoc Committee on Medicaid. American Medical Association Board of Trustees report UU, A-88. Presented at the Annual Meeting of the American Medical Association, Chicago, June 26–30, 1988.

6. Evans R. G., Lomas J., Barer M. L., et al. Controlling health expenditures—the Canadian reality. *N Engl J Med* 1989; 320 571–577.

7. Relman A. S. American medicine at the crossroads: signs from Canada. *N Engl J Med* 1989; 320: 590–591.

8. Comment on the AARP study: the Canadian health care system: a special report on Quebec and Ontario. Chicago: Center for Health Policy Research, American Medical Association, 1988: 2.

Aging and the Ends of Medicine

Daniel Callahan

Daniel Callahan claims that the goal of medicine in the care of the elderly should be to improve the quality of life, not to extend it. Callahan argues that allocating medical resources on the basis of need is neither feasible nor sensible and that we must take age into account. Once people have reached the end of a "natural life span," government should provide them with the means of alleviating their suffering, but not with the means of extending their lives.

Eventually, Callahan holds, our society must confront the fact that we must ration health care and make a choice between the young and the elderly. If we focus our resources on extending the lives of the young and improving the quality of life of the elderly, then we will benefit both.

In October of 1986, Dr. Thomas Starzl of the Presbyterian-University Hospital in Pittsburgh successfully transplanted a liver into a 76-year-old woman. The typical cost of such an operation is over $200,000. He thereby accelerated the extension to the elderly of the most expensive and most demanding form of high-technology medicine. Not long after that, Congress brought organ transplantation under Medicare coverage, thus guaranteeing an even greater extension of this form of life-saving care to older age groups.

This is, on the face of it, the kind of medical progress we have long grown to hail, a triumph of medical technology and a new-found benefit to be provided by an established entitlement program. But now an oddity. At the same time those events were taking place, a parallel government campaign for cost containment was under way, with a special targeting of health care to the aged under the medicare program.

It was not hard to understand why. In 1980, the 11% of the population over age 65 consumed some 29% of the total American health care expenditures of $219.4 billion. By 1986, the percentage of consumption by the elderly had increased to 31% and total expenditures to $450 billion. Medicare costs are projected to rise from $75 billion in 1986 to $114 billion in the year 2000, and in real not inflated dollars.

There is every incentive for politicians, for those who care for the aged, and for those of us on the way to becoming old to avert our eyes from figures of that kind. We have tried as a society to see if we can simply muddle our way through. That, however, is no longer sufficient. The time has come, I am convinced, for a full and open reconsideration

From *Annals of the New York Academy of Sciences,* vol. 530 (15 June 1988), pp. 125–132. Reprinted by permission of the author and the publisher.

of our future direction. We can not for much longer continue on our present course. Even if we could find a way to radically increase the proportion of our health care dollar going to the elderly, it is not clear that that would be a good social investment.

Is it sensible, in the face of a rapidly increasing burden of health care costs for the elderly, to press forward with new and expensive ways of extending their lives? Is it possible to even hope to control costs while, simultaneously, supporting the innovative research that generates ever-new ways to spend money? These are now unavoidable questions. Medicare costs rise at an extraordinary pace, fueled by an ever-increasing number and proportion of the elderly. The fastest-growing age group in the United States are those over the age of 85, increasing at a rate of about 10% every two years. By the year 2040, it has been projected that the elderly will represent 21% of the population and consume 45% of all health care expenditures. Could costs of that magnitude be borne?

Yet even as this intimidating trend reveals itself, anyone who works closely with the elderly recognizes that the present Medicare and Medicaid programs are grossly inadequate in meeting the real and full needs of the elderly. They fail, most notably, in providing decent long-term care and medical care that does not constitute a heavy out-of-pocket drain. Members of minority groups, and single or widowed women, are particularly disadvantaged. How will it be possible, then, to keep pace with the growing number of elderly in even providing present levels of care, much less in ridding the system of its present inadequacies and inequalities—and, at the same time, furiously adding expensive new technologies?

The straight answer is that it will not be possible to do all of those things and that, worse still, it may be harmful to even try. It may be harmful because of the economic burdens it will impose on younger age groups, and because of the skewing of national social priorities too heavily toward health care that it is coming to require. But it may also be harmful because it suggests to both the young and the old that the key to a happy old age is good health care. That may not be true.

It is not pleasant to raise possibilities of that kind. The struggle against what Dr. Robert Butler aptly and brilliantly called "ageism" in 1968 has been a difficult one. It has meant trying to persuade the public that not all the elderly are sick and senile.

It has meant trying to convince Congress and state legislators to provide more help for the old. It has meant trying to educate the elderly themselves to look upon their old age as a time of new, open possibilities. That campaign has met with only partial success. Despite great progress, the elderly are still subject to discrimination and stereotyping. The struggle against ageism is hardly over.

Three major concerns have, nonetheless, surfaced over the past few years. They are symptoms that a new era has arrived. The first is that an increasingly large share of health care is going to the elderly in comparison with benefits for children. The federal government, for instance, spends six times as much on health care for those over 65 as for those under 18. As the demographer Samuel Preston observed in a provocative 1984 presidential address to the Population Association of America:

> There is surely something to be said for a system in which things get better as we pass through life rather than worse. The great leveling off of age curves of psychological distress, suicide and income in the past two decades might simply reflect the fact that we have decided in some fundamental sense that we don't want to face futures that become continually bleaker. But let's be clear that the transfers from the working-age population to the elderly are also transfers away from children, since the working ages bear far more responsibility for childrearing than do the elderly.[1]

Preston's address had an immediate impact. The mainline aging advocacy groups responded with pained indignation, accusing Preston of fomenting a war between the generations. But led by Dave Durenberger, Republican Senator from Minnesota, it also stimulated the formation of Americans for Generational Equity (AGE), an organization created to promote debate on the burden to future generations, but particularly the Baby Boom generation, of "our major social insurance programs."[2] These two developments signalled the outburst of a struggle over what has come to be called "Intergenerational equity" that is only now gaining momentum.

The second concern is that the elderly dying consume a disproportionate share of health care costs. Stanford economist Victor Fuchs has noted:

> At present, the United States spends about 1 percent of the gross national product on health care for elderly persons who are in their

last year of life. . . . One of the biggest challenges facing policy makers for the rest of this century will be how to strike an appropriate balance between care of the [elderly] dying and health services for the rest of the population.[3]

The third concern is summed up in an observation by Jerome L. Avorn, M.D., of the Harvard Medical School:

> With the exception of the birth-control pill, each of the medical-technology interventions developed since the 1950s has its most widespread impact on people who are past their fifties—the further past their fifties, the greater the impact.[4]

Many of these interventions were not intended for the elderly, Kidney dialysis, for example, was originally developed for those between the age of 15 and 45. Now some 30% of its recipients are over 65.

These three concerns have not gone unchallenged. They have, on the contrary, been strongly resisted, as has the more general assertion that some form of rationing of health care for the elderly might become necessary. To the charge that the elderly receive a disproportionate share of resources, the response has been that what helps the elderly helps every other age group. It both relieves the young of the burden of care for elderly parents they would otherwise have to bear and, since they too will eventually become old, promises them similar care when they come to need it. There is no guarantee, moreover, that any cutback in health care for the elderly would result in a transfer of the savings directly to the young. Our system is not that rational or that organized. And why, others ask, should we contemplate restricting care for the elderly when we wastefully spend hundreds of millions of dollars on an inflated defense budget?

The charge that the elderly dying receive a large share of funds hardly proves that it is an unjust or unreasonable amount. They are, after all, the most in need. As some important studies have shown, moreover, it is exceedingly difficult to know that someone is dying; the most expensive patients, it turns out, are those who are expected to live but who actually die. That most new technologies benefit the old more than the young is perfectly sensible: most of the killer diseases of the young have now been conquered.

These are reasonable responses. It would no doubt be possible to ignore the symptoms that the raising of such concerns represents, and to put off

for at least a few more years any full confrontation with the overpowering tide of elderly now on the way. There is little incentive for politicians to think about, much less talk about, limits of any kind on health care for the aged; it is a politically hazardous topic. Perhaps also, as Dean Guido Calabresi of the Yale Law School and his colleague Philip Bobbitt observed in their thoughtful 1978 book *Tragic Choices*, when we are forced to make painful allocation choices, "Evasion, disguise, temporizing . . . [and] averting our eyes enables us to save some lives even when we will not save all."[5]

Yet however slight the incentives to take on this highly troubling issue, I believe it is inevitable that we must. Already rationing of health care under Medicare is a fact of life, though rarely labeled as such. The requirement that Medicare recipients pay the first $500 of the costs of hospital care, that there is a cutoff of reimbursement of care beyond 60 days, and a failure to cover long-term care, are nothing other than allocation and cost-saving devices. As sensitive as it is to the votes of the elderly, the Reagan administration only grudgingly agreed to support catastrophic health care costs of the elderly (a benefit that will not, in any event, help many of the aged.). It is bound to be far more resistant to long-term care coverage, as will any administration.

But there are other reasons than economics to think about health care for the elderly. The coming economic crisis provides a much-needed opportunity to ask some deeper questions. Just what is it that we want medicine to do for us as we age? Earlier cultures believed that aging should be accepted, and that it should be in part a time of preparation for death. Our culture seems increasingly to reject that view, preferring instead, it often seems, to think of aging as hardly more than another disease, to be fought and rejected. Which view is correct? To ask that question is only to note that disturbing puzzles about the ends of medicine and the ends of aging lie behind the more immediate financing worries. Without some kind of answer to them, there is no hope of finding a reasonable, and possibly even a humane, solution to the growing problem of health care for the elderly.

Let me put my own view directly. The future goal of medicine in the care of the aged should be that of improving the quality of their life, not in seeking ways to extend that life. In its longstanding ambition to forestall death, medicine has in the care of the aged reached its last frontier. That is hardly because death is absent elsewhere—children and young adults obviously still die of maladies that are open to potential cure—but because the largest number of deaths (some 70%) now occur among those over the age of 65, with the highest proportion in those over 85. If death is ever to be humbled, that is where the essentially endless work remains to be done. But however tempting that challenge, medicine should now restrain its ambition at that frontier. To do otherwise will, I believe, be to court harm to the needs of other age groups and to the old themselves.

Yet to ask medicine to restrain itself in the face of aging and death is to ask more than it, or the public that sustains it, is likely to find agreeable. Only a fresh understanding of the ends and meaning of aging, encompassing two conditions, are likely to make that a plausible stance. The first is that we—both young and old—need to understand that it is possible to live out a meaningful old age that is limited in time, one that does not require a compulsive effort to turn to medicine for more life to make it bearable. The second condition is that, as a culture, we need a more supportive context for aging and death, one that cherishes and respects the elderly while at the same time recognizing that their primary orientation should be to the young and the generations to come, not to their own age group. It will be no less necessary to recognize that in the passing of the generations lies the constant reinvigoration of biological life.

Neither of these conditions will be easy to realize. Our culture has, for one thing, worked hard to redefine old age as a time of liberation, not decline. The terms "modern maturity" or "prime time" have, after all, come to connote a time of travel, new ventures in education and self-discovery, the ever-accessible tennis court or golf course, and delightfully periodic but gratefully brief visits from well-behaved grandchildren.

This is, to be sure, an idealized picture. Its attraction lies not in its literal truth but as a widely-accepted utopian reference point. It projects the vision of an old age to which more and more believe they can aspire and which its proponents think an affluent country can afford if it so chooses. That it requires a medicine that is singleminded in its aggressiveness against the infirmities of old age is of a piece with its hopes. But as we have come to discover, the costs of that kind of war are prohibitive.

No matter how much is spent the ultimate problem will still remain: people age and die. Worse still, by pretending that old age can be turned into a kind of endless middle age, we rob it of meaning and significance for the elderly themselves. It is a way of saying that old age can be acceptable only to the extent that it can mimic the vitality of the younger years.

There is a plausible alternative: that of a fresh vision of what it means to live a decently long and adequate life, what might be called a natural life span. Earlier generations accepted the idea that there was a natural life span—the biblical norm of three score years and ten captures that notion (even though, in fact, that was a much longer life span than was then typically the case). It is an idea well worth reconsidering, and would provide us with a meaningful and realizable goal. Modern medicine and biology have done much, however, to wean us away from that kind of thinking. They have insinuated the belief that the average life span is not a natural fact at all, but instead one that is strictly dependent upon the state of medical knowledge and skill. And there is much to that belief as a statistical fact: the average life expectancy continues to increase, with no end in sight.

But that is not what I think we ought to mean by a natural life span. We need a notion of a full life that is based on some deeper understanding of human need and sensible possibility, not the latest state of medical technology or medical possibility. We should instead think of a natural life span as the achievement of a life long enough to accomplish for the most part those opportunities that life typically affords people and which we ordinarily take to be the prime benefits of enjoying a life at all— that of loving and living, of raising a family, of finding and carrying out work that is satisfying, of reading and thinking, and of cherishing our friends and families.

If we envisioned a natural life span that way, then we could begin to intensify the devising of ways to get people to that stage of life, and to work to make certain they do so in good health and social dignity. People will differ on what they might count as a natural life span; determining its appropriate range for social policy purposes would need extended thought and debate. My own view is that it can now be achieved by the late 70s or early 80s.

That many of the elderly discover new interests and new facets of themselves late in life—my mother took up painting in her seventies and was selling her paintings up until her death at 86—does not mean that we should necessarily encourage a kind of medicine that would make that the norm. Nor does it mean that we should base social and welfare policy on possibilities of that kind. A more reasonable approach is to ask how medicine can help most people live out a decently long life, and how that life can be enhanced along the way.

A longer life does not guarantee a better life—there is no inherent connection between the two. No matter how long medicine enabled people to live, death at any time—at age 90, or 100, or 110—would frustrate some possibility, some as-yet-unrealized goal. There is sadness in that realization, but not tragedy. An easily preventable death of a young child is an outrage. The death from an incurable disease of someone in the prime of young adulthood is a tragedy. But death at an old age, after a long and full life, is simply sad, a part of life itself.

As it confronts aging, medicine should have as its specific goal that of averting premature death, understood as death prior to a natural life span, and the relief of suffering thereafter. It should pursue those goals in order that the elderly can finish out their years with as little needless pain as possible, and with as much vigor as can be generated in contributing to the welfare of younger age groups and to the community of which they are a part. Above all, the elderly need to have a sense of the meaning and significance of their stage in life, one that is not dependent for its human value on economic productivity or physical vigor.

What would a medicine oriented toward the relief of suffering rather than the deliberate extension of life be like? We do not yet have a clear and ready answer to that question, so long-standing, central, and persistent has been the struggle against death as part of the self-conception of medicine. But the Hospice movement is providing us with much helpful evidence. It knows how to distinguish between the relief of suffering and the extension of life. A greater control by the elderly over their dying—and particularly a more readily respected and enforceable right to deny aggressive life-extending treatment—is a long-sought, minimally necessary goal.

What does this have to do with the rising cost of health care for the elderly? Everything. The indefinite extension of life combined with a never-satisfied improvement in the health of the elderly is a recipe for monomania and limitless spending. It fails to put health in its proper place as only one among many human goods. It fails to accept aging and death as part of the human condition. It fails to present to younger generations a model of wise stewardship.

How might we devise a plan to limit health care for the aged under public entitlement programs that is fair, humane, and sensitive to their special requirements and dignity? Let me suggest three principles to undergird a quest for limits. First, government has a duty, based on our collective social obligations to each other, to help people live out a natural life span, but not actively to help medically extend life beyond that point. Second, government is obliged to develop under its research subsidies, and pay for, under its entitlement programs, only that kind and degree of life-extending technology necessary for medicine to achieve and serve the end of a natural life span. The question is not whether a technology is available that can save the life of someone who has lived out a natural life span, but whether there is an obligation for society to provide them with that technology. I think not. Third, beyond the point of natural life span, government should provide only the means necessary for the relief of suffering, not life-extending technology. By proposing that we use age as a specific criterion for the limitation of life-extending care, I am challenging one of the most revered norms of contemporary geriatrics: that medical need and not age should be the standard of care. Yet the use of age as a principle for the allocation of resources can be perfectly valid, both a necessary and legitimate basis for providing health care to the elderly. There is not likely to be any better or less arbitrary criterion for the limiting of resources in the face of the open-ended possibilities of medical advancement in therapy for the aged.

Medical "need," in particular, can no longer work as an allocation principle. It is too elastic a concept, too much a function of the state of medical art. A person of 100 dying from congestive heart failure "needs" a heart transplant no less than someone who is 30. Are we to treat both needs as equal? That is not economically feasible or, I would argue, a sensible way to allocate scarce resources. But it would be required by a strict need-based standard.

Age is also a legitimate basis for allocation because it is a meaningful and universal category. It can be understood at the level of common sense. It is concrete enough to be employed for policy purposes. It can also, most importantly, be of value to the aged themselves if combined with an ideal of old age that focuses on its quality rather than its indefinite extension.

I have become impressed with the philosophy underlying the British health care system and the way it meets the needs of the old and the chronically ill. It has, to begin with, a tacit allocation policy. It emphasizes improving the quality of life through primary care medicine and well-subsidized home care and institutional programs for the elderly rather than through life-extending acute care medicine. The well-known difficulty in getting dialysis after 55 is matched by like restrictions on access to open heart surgery, intensive care units, and other forms of expensive technology. An undergirding skepticism toward technology makes that a viable option. That attitude, together with a powerful drive for equity, "explains," as two commentators have noted, "why most British put a higher value on primary care for the population as a whole than on an abundance of sophisticated technology for the few who may benefit from it."[6]

That the British spend a significantly smaller proportion of their GNP (6.2%) on health care than Americans (10.8%) for an almost identical outcome in health status is itself a good advertisement for its priorities. Life expectancies are, for men, 70.0 years in the U.S. and 70.4 years in Great Britain; and, for women, 77.8 in the U.S. and 76.7 in Great Britain. There is, of course, a great difference in the ethos of the U.S. and Britain, and our individualism and love of technology stand in the way of a quick shift of priorities.

Yet our present American expectations about aging and death, it turns out, may not be all that reassuring. How many of us are really so certain that high-technology American medicine promises us all that much better an aging and death, even if some features appear improved and the process begins later than in earlier times? Between the widespread fear of death in an impersonal ICU, cozened about with machines and invaded by tubes, on the one hand, or wasting away in the back ward of a nursing home, on the other, not many of us seem comforted.

Once we have reflected on those fears, it is not impossible that most people could be persuaded that a different, more limited set of expectations for health care could be made tolerable. That would be all the more possible if there was a greater assurance than at present that one could live out a full life span, that one's chronic illnesses would be better supported, and that long-term care and home care would be given a more powerful societal backing than is now the case. Though they would face a denial of life-extending medical care beyond a certain age, the old would not necessarily fear their aging any more than they now do. They would, on the contrary, know that a better balance had been struck between making our later years as good as possible rather than simply trying to add more years.

This direction would not immediately bring down the costs of care of the elderly; it would add new costs. But it would set in place the beginning of a new understanding of old age, one that would admit of eventual stabilization limits. The time has come to admit we can not go on much longer on the present course of open-ended health care for the elderly. Neither confident assertions about American affluence, nor tinkering with entitlement provisions and cost-containment strategies will work for more than a few more years. It is time for the dream that old age can be an infinite and open frontier to end, and for the unflagging, but self-deceptive, optimism that we can do anything we want with our economic system be put aside.

The elderly will not be served by a belief that only a lack of resources, or better financing mechanisms, or political power, stand between them and the limitations of their bodies. The good of younger age groups will not be served by inspiring in them a desire to live to an old age that will simply extend the vitality of youth indefinitely, as if old age is nothing but a sign that medicine has failed in its mission. The future of our society will not be served by allowing expenditures on health care for the elderly endlessly and uncontrollably to escalate, fueled by a false altruism that thinks anything less is to deny the elderly their dignity. Nor will it be served by that pervasive kind of self-serving that urges the young to support such a crusade because they will eventually benefit from it also.

We require instead an understanding of the process of aging and death that looks to our obligation to the young and to the future, that recognizes the necessity of limits and the acceptance of decline and death, and that values the old for their age and not for their continuing youthful vitality. In the name of accepting the elderly and repudiating discrimination against them, we have mainly succeeded in pretending that, with enough will and money, the unpleasant part of old age can be abolished. In the name of medical progress we have carried out a relentless war against death and decline, failing to ask in any probing way if that will give us a better society for all age groups.

The proper question is not whether we are succeeding in giving a longer life to the aged. It is whether we are making of old age a decent and honorable time of life. Neither a longer lifetime nor more life-extending technology are the way to that goal. The elderly themselves ask for greater financial security, for as much self-determination and independence as possible, for a decent quality of life and not just more life, and for a respected place in society.

The best way to achieve those goals is not simply to say more money and better programs are needed, however much they have their important place. We would do better to begin with a sense of limits, of the meaning of the human life cycle, and of the necessary coming and going of the generations. From that kind of a starting point, we could devise a new understanding of old age.

Notes

1. Preston, S. H. 1984. Children and the elderly: divergent paths for America's dependents. *Demography* 21: 491–495.

2. Americans for Generational Equity. Case Statement. May 1986.

3. Fuchs, V. R. 1984. Though much is taken: reflections on aging, health, and medical care. *Milbank Mem. Fund Q.* 62: 464–465.

4. Avorn, J. L. 1986. Medicine, health, and geriatric transformation. *Daedalus* 115: 211–225.

5. Calabresi, G. & P. Bobbitt. 1978. *Tragic Choices*. W. W. Norton. New York, NY.

6. Miller, F. H. & G. A. H. Miller. 1986. The painful prescription: a procrustean perspective. *N. Engl. J. Med.* 314: 1385.

Decision Scenario 1 ••

The Cashier's Office of Archway Memorial Hospital is, even for the wealthy and best educated, a place of frustration. Bills are presented in the form of long computer printouts, covered with unfamiliar names referring to supplies, medical treatment, and diagnostic tests. Associated with each item is a price that seems absurdly high.

For someone without any form of medical insurance, being faced with such a bill can be more than confusing—it can be frightening. And that is just the situation that Marvin Baldesi found himself in.

"Your age makes you ineligible for Medicare," said Ms. Kearney, the Archway billing officer. "And you say you aren't covered by Blue Cross or a private insurance plan."

"That's right," said Mr. Baldesi. "I own my own business. My wife and me, we run a small upholstery shop. We decided we couldn't afford to keep up our insurance."

"Normally we wouldn't have admitted you," said Ms. Kearney. "It's only because you came in as an acute emergency that you were allowed to run up such a bill."

Mr. Baldesi looked down to keep from meeting Ms. Kearney's eyes. He felt embarrassed. He had always paid his bills, and now this woman didn't bother to disguise the fact that she saw him as a deadbeat.

"I don't guess you have any money in savings?" Ms Kearney asked.

"About fifty dollars. Just enough to keep the account open."

"Then it looks to me like you've only got two choices," Ms. Kearney said. "You've got to borrow the money or you've got to declare yourself bankrupt. If you do that, then you'll be eligible for Medicaid payments, and the hospital may be able to collect from the government. I'm not sure of the legal process."

"But the bill is almost fifty thousand dollars," Mr. Baldesi said. "I can't borrow money like that. My family and friends don't have it, and no bank would loan it to me without collateral."

"Then you'll just have to get a lawyer and get yourself declared bankrupt."

"But if I do that, I'll lose my business. My credit will be ruined, and I won't be able to get the materials I need from suppliers. Isn't there any other way?"

"I don't know of any," said Ms. Kearney. "But that's not really my problem. All I know is that Archway has to be paid. You received our services, and we have to have the money for them."

1. *Is Mr. Baldesi's predicament possible in the United States today? If the plan proposed by Jim McDermott were implemented, would it eliminate such cases? How would Archway Hospital get paid?*

2. *How might the health-care proposal outlined by Todd apply to such a case?*

3. *Archway (through Ms. Kearney) is asserting its claim as an agent in a market economy. Why does Nielsen regard market considerations as inappropriate in determining the distribution of health care? Would Nielsen's position on this case differ in any respect from the position taken by the President's Commission?*

4. *Suppose Mr. Baldesi's illness is connected with his failure to give up smoking and drinking, even though advised to do so by his physician. Would this lead you to view his situation any differently?*

Decision Scenario 2 ••

"There's more than one way to get to Rome," Dr. Kenton said. "And we've got a couple of options to offer you."

"I'll take anything that will make the pain stay away," Mr. Czahz said.

"We can do a surgical procedure that we call a coronary-artery bypass. In your case, there are two arteries involved so it would be a double bypass."

"This is not something experimental, is it?"

"No, it's a well-established procedure with a pretty good safety record. Now something like 80% of the people who have the bypass get rid of their angina pains."

"I don't much like the idea of being cut, but I'd do most anything to stop those chest pains."

"Let me tell you the other option. We can treat you medically instead of surgically. That is, we can try you on some drugs and see how you do, put you on a diet, and keep a close watch on you. Now people we treat this way do a little bit better in terms of living longer than those treated surgically do. That's a little misleading, though, because those who have surgery usually have worse cases of the disease."

"What about the angina pains?" Mr. Czahz asked.

"There's the problem. Medical treatment can do something about the pains, but it's really not as effective as surgery."

"So I'll take the surgery."

"Aren't you on health stamps?" Dr. Kenton asked.

"That's right."

"We've got a problem then. You see, health stamps won't cover the cost of bypass surgery. It's an optional procedure under the HHS guidelines, and they won't kick in the extra money to pay for it."

"So I have to make up the difference myself?"

"That's right," Dr. Kenton said. "You're going to have to come up with about two thousand in cash."

"Dr. Kenton, there's no way I can do that."

"Okay, then. I just wanted you to know what the possibilities were. We can put you on a treatment program, and I'm sure you'll do just fine."

"But what about the angina pain?"

"We'll do what we can," Dr. Kenton said.

1. *A health-stamp (or voucher) program suggested by Todd might operate by granting a fixed amount of money to each person below a certain income level. This would permit someone to shop around for the best health care bargain he or she could afford. What might be the advantages and disadvantages of such a program?*

2. *Would such a program be likely to provide the sort of equal access to health care argued for by Nielsen?*

3. *Would such a program be likely to guarantee the decent minimum of health care argued for by the President's Commission and Buchanan?*

4. *Is a two-tiered health-care system compatible with the single-payer system supported by McDermott?*

Decision Scenario 3 ....

When the pain began, Alan Warfard was certain he was having a heart attack. The pain lasted more than an hour, and when it was finally over he was weak and exhausted. He knew there was something seriously wrong with him, and as soon as he was able he called his next-door neighbor and asked her to drive him to Southwest Hospital.

"You have no insurance coverage, except for Medicare?" the man at the admitting desk asked Mr. Warfard. "No private insurance at all?"

"Just Medicare," Mr. Warfard said.

"Can you show us any financial records, such as savings-account passbooks, to establish that you are able to pay your charges here?"

I live on my Social Security check, and I don't have a savings account."

"Do you have any relatives who would be willing to sign a statement assuming financial responsibility for your treatment here?"

"I'm afraid not," Mr. Warfard said. "But I don't see what the problem is. I told you—I'm covered by Medicare. Isn't that enough?"

The admitting clerk shook his head. "I'm afraid it's not. We don't know what your treatment is likely to cost, and we don't know whether Medicare would pay for all of it. You know, they pay only a certain amount, and you might run up bills above that. This is a private hospital, and I'm afraid that, without your being able to guarantee that you can pay us, I can't admit you for treatment."

"But I'm sick," Mr. Warfard said. "What am I supposed to do, just go home and die?"

"That's not really our concern," the clerk said. "But I suggest you see if you can get yourself admitted to a public hospital. Taking care of people like you is their responsibility."

The phrase "people like you" stung Mr. Warfard's pride. After all those years of paying his taxes and being a good citizen, how could he be dismissed so easily?

1. *The problem of underinsurance is not confined to those who receive Medicare. Is a situation such as this consistent with the recommendations of the President's Commission to guarantee a decent minimum of health care to all citizens? Would it be a permissible aspect of a voucher system such as Todd proposes?*

2. *Do private, for-profit hospitals pose particular difficulties for public hospitals and the public financing of health care?*

3. *How might it be argued that health care is such a special commodity that it should not be bought and sold on the open market the way that other goods are?*

4. *When cost control is at issue, why might Nielsen think that Canadian physicians are in a better position to act for the sake of patients, even under constraints, than their American counterparts?*

Decision Scenario 4 ....

"Let me see if I understand you correctly," Mrs. Burgone said. "I need a liver transplant, but I'm not allowed to have such an operation?"

"That's correct," Dr. Popp said. "The National Health policy stipulates that transplant surgery cannot be performed on patients over the age of seventy."

Mrs. Burgone shook her head. "But I don't expect National Health to pay for it. I'm able to pay for it myself."

"That doesn't matter. It's a matter of social policy, not medicine. The idea is that we can't afford, as a society, to do everything for every patient. You might be able to pay for such an operation, but not

everybody can. Then society would have to pay for those who can't afford it, and society can't afford to do that. Consequently, to be fair, the operation is denied to everyone above the age of seventy."

"That doesn't seem fair to me," Mrs. Burgone said. "How can it be fair to condemn someone to pain and a greater risk of death when a way of changing this is available?"

"I didn't make the policy," Dr. Popp said.

1. *According to Nielsen, the standard for determining who shall receive medical care is need alone. Moreover, his commitment to the principle of moral equality forbids allowing some persons to receive*

needed medical care denied to others. Unless we are willing to finance potentially unlimited medical care for all persons, we would be required to restrict access. Would the policy described above be a legitimate restriction on access?

2. *Is this sort of system consistent with the position taken by the President's Commission?*

3. *How would the position proposed by Todd handle such situations? And how would he justify the unequal treatment that results?*

4. *Why might Callahan argue in support of the position explained by Dr. Popp? Has Mrs. Burgone lived out what Callahan would call a "natural life span?"*

Decision Scenario 5 ••

"Let me explain it to you, Mr. Faust," Charles Young said. "Although your wife is covered by Medicare, we cannot pay for the care she is receiving in the nursing home. As an Alzheimer's patient, she is receiving what we consider to be 'custodial' care, and that is explicitly excluded from Medicare coverage. Do you have any private insurance?"

"Yes, I do. But you're telling me exactly the same thing I heard from my insurance company. My policy doesn't cover long-term, chronic, or custodial care."

"I'm sorry to hear that," Charles Young said. "That means that you will have to pay the total cost of the care yourself."

"Where can I get that kind of money?" Mr. Faust said. "A nursing home will cost me thirty or forty thousand dollars a year. If I sell our house and use all our savings, I could pay for maybe a year, but then I wouldn't have anything to live on myself. Where could I live? How could I eat?"

"I understand. But the only alternative is to divest yourself of your assets so that you cannot be held legally responsible for paying for your wife's care. Then you and she can both get assistance under the Medicaid program."

"Then I have to literally bankrupt myself and become a pauper before I can get any help?"

"I'm sorry to say that's true."

1. *Should a national health-care program pay for the custodial care that is required by patients with Alzheimer's and similar diseases?*

2. *Should family members (adult children or grandchildren) be required by law to help pay the health-care expenses of other family members?*

3. *What reasons might Callahan offer in support of funding for "custodial care"?*

4. *Should people with incomes adequate to cover the cost of their health care or to buy private insurance be ineligible to participate in a national health-insurance plan?*

5. *We expect people to pay for the goods and services that they receive. Since Mrs. Faust is receiving goods and services in getting custodial care, why is it unfair to expect her husband to pay for them?*

Decision Scenario 6 ••

"I've decided to do something that may cause me a lot of trouble," Dr. Miles Toliver said.

Alan Burford took a sip of his drink and sat back in his chair. He had known Miles for a long time and knew he could be counted on to see most things in a novel way. Sometimes Miles could be annoying but he always made you think.

"I'm not going to accept women as patients anymore," Toliver said. "I don't like dealing with

them, and there's nothing that says I have to. From now on, I'm restricting my practice to men only."

"I don't think you can do that," Burford said. "I suspect that involves civil rights violations of some sort. You know, discriminating on the basis of race or sex or something like that."

"Then I'll get a lawyer and show that the government can't force me to treat women without violating my own rights."

"I don't follow you."

"Look at it this way," Toliver said. "My medical knowledge and skills belong to me. I acquired them through the exercise of my own mind, and I have a constitutional right to privacy and freedom of expression. Therefore, I have a right to exercise my knowledge and skills in the way I see fit. Therefore, if I don't want to treat women, then I don't have to."

"That's an argument I've never heard," Burford said.

"The government can't force me to do what I don't want to do without violating my rights and being despotic."

"I suspect you'll have to prove that in court."

"I'm prepared to," Toliver said.

1. *State explicitly (and more fully if it seems necessary) the argument presented by Dr. Toliver.*

2. *Toliver's argument might be construed as one supporting what is sometimes called "medical individualism." What sort of arguments might be offered against such a position? Is medical individualism consistent with any of the positions taken by the authors in this section?*

NOTES AND REFERENCES FOR INTRODUCTIONS, CASES, AND SCENARIOS

Moral Principles, Ethical Theories, and Medical Decisions: An Introduction

I learned much about medical ethics and about presenting it to a general audience from those who have gone before me. I have benefitted from the example (among others) of Samuel Gorovitz et al., eds., *Moral Problems in Medicine* (Englewood Cliffs, N.J.: Prentice-Hall 1976), Robert Hunt and John Arras, eds., *Ethical Issues in Modern Medicine* (Palo Alto, Calif.: Mayfield, 1977), and Richard W. Wertz, ed., *Readings on Ethical and Social Issues in Biomedicine* (Englewood Cliffs, N.J.: Prentice-Hall, 1973). All three have informative introductions, but the one by Hunt and Arras I found most helpful and most philosophically interesting.

My discussion of ethical theories is generally indebted to Richard B. Brandt, *Ethical Theory* (Englewood Cliffs, N.J.: Prentice Hall, 1959) and William K. Frankena, *Ethics*, 2nd ed. (Englewood Cliffs, N.J.: Prentice-Hall 1973). My treatment of utilitarianism owes much to the excellent introductory essay by Paul Taylor in his *Problems of Moral Philosophy* (Belmont, Calif.: Dickenson, 1971), pp. 137–151. Mill's statement of the principle of utility is from *Utilitarianism* (Indianapolis: Bobbs-Merrill, 1971), p. 18; the second quotation is from p. 24. In the discussion of act and rule utilitarianism and their attendant difficulties, I am indebted to Michael D. Bayles and Kenneth Henley's introduction in their *Right Conduct* (New York: Random House, 1983), pp. 86–94, and to Carl Wellman, *Morals and Ethics* (New York: Scott, Foresman, 1975), pp. 39–42, 47–50. The quotation from Wellman is on p. 49.

The statements of Kant's categorical imperative are more paraphrases than literal translations. They are from his *Groundwork of the Metaphysics of Morals*, translated by H. J. Paton (New York: Harper & Row, 1964). Other translations and editions are easily available. Some of the criticisms of Kant are based on those of Brandt (*Ethical Theory*, pp. 27–35) and Frankena (*Ethics*, pp. 30–33).

The quotation from Ross is from his *The Right and the Good* (New York: Oxford University Press, 1930), p. 24. The prima facie duties are found on pp. 21–22 and the "rules" for resolving conflict on pp. 41–42. My exposition is indebted, in part, to G. J. Warnock, *Contemporary Moral Philosophy* (New York: St. Martin's Press, 1967) and to Fred Feldman, *Introductory Ethics* (Englewood Cliffs, N. J.: Prentice-Hall, 1978), pp. 149–160.

Rawls's theory is presented in *A Theory of Justice* (Cambridge, Mass.: Harvard University Press, 1971). The principles are quoted from p. 203; "natural duties" are discussed on pp. 340–350. My statement of the theory is indebted to Norman Daniels's introduction to his anthology *Reading Rawls* (New York: Basic Books, 1976). The first criticism is one made by Thomas Nagel, "Rawls on Justice" (Daniels, pp. 1–16) and Ronald Dworkin, "The Original Position" (Daniels, pp. 16–53). The second criticism is urged by R. M. Hare, "Rawls's Theory of Justice" (Daniels, pp. 81–108) and David Lyons, "Nature and Soundness of the Contract and Coherence Arguments" (Daniels, pp. 141–169). A relatively easy entrance into Rawls's theory is provided by the general reviews of the book that are listed in the Bibliography.

For Aquinas's view on "man," see his *Summa Theologica*, Part II (First Part), vol. 6, translated by Fathers of the English Dominican Province (London: Burns Oates and Washbourne, 1914). For his views on natural law and law in general, see vol. 8, "Treatise on Law." For an interpretation of Aquinas, see Frederick Copleston, *A History of Philosophy*, vol. 2, part 2 (New York: Doubleday, 1962), pp. 126–131, to which my account is indebted. For the presentation of the current Catholic natural law view I am indebted to Charles J. McFadden, *Medical Ethics*, 6th ed. (Philadelphia: F. A. Davis, 1967). The doctrine of double effect is treated on pp. 121–155; euthanasia, extraordinary means, and medical experimentation, pp. 239–270. The quotations from the Directives are from the appendix in McFadden: abortion, p. 441, euthanasia, p. 442.

My discussion of moral principles is indebted to Tom. L. Beauchamp and James F. Childress, *Principles of Biomedical Ethics* (New York: Oxford University Press, 1979), pp. 56–201, and to Beauchamp's and LeRoy Walters's introduction in *Contemporary Issues in Bioethics*, 2d ed. (Belmont, Calif.: Wadsworth, 1982), pp. 26–32. The discussion of liberty-limiting principles is based on Joel Feinberg, *Social Philosophy* (Englewood Cliffs, N.J.: Prentice-Hall, 1973), pp. 20–33, as is the discussion of principles of justice, pp. 98–119.

Chapter 1: Abortion

The Case Presentation is a fictionalized treatment based on the case of an unnamed minor in the United Press International story "Court Orders Abortion for Rape Victim, 12" (Oklahoma City, 29 September 1981).

The Social Context on abortion draws information about the Pennsylvania case (*Casey*) and the U.S. Supreme Court decision from *New York Times* (22 January 1992; 23 April 1992; 30 June 1992; 13 May 1993; 30 January 1994). Information about the *Webster* case is from *Newsweek* (1 May 1989; 17 July 1989) and *Time* (1 May 1989). Response to the *Webster* decision is based on Linda Greenhouse, "Supreme Court Upholds Sharp State Limits on Abortion," *New York Times* (4 July 1990) and E. Dionne, "On Both Sides, Advocates Predict a 50-State Battle" in the same issue. The account of the killing of David Gunn and the turn toward violence is based on *New York Times* (12, 13, 14 March 1993; 20 August 1993; 20 September 1993). The killing of John Britton and James Barrett, with a related story, is reported in *New York Times* (30 July 1994). For more information about both Hill and Britton, see *New York Times* (31 July 1994; 2 August 1994); Hill's conviction and sentencing are reported in 3 November 1994 and 7 December 1994. More reports about making abortion providers targets are found in *New York Times* (24 November 1991; 29 April 1992; 13, 31 March 1993). Difficulty in getting access to abortion is covered in *New York Times* (5 January 1992, 15 March 1992). The actions of militant groups are discussed in *New York Times* (8, 10, 12, 13 August 1991; 17 October 1991; 2, 20, 21, 22, 23, 25 April 1992; 2 May 1992; 3 July 1992; 14 January 1993; 25 January 1994; 11 June 1994) and *Time* (21 October 1991, 19 July 1993). The Court ruling on access to clinics and its background is reported in

New York Times (25 January 1994, 1 July 1994). The Clinton order ending some abortion restrictions is reported in *New York Times* (25 January 1993) and *Time* (1 February 1993). The administration's policy is discussed in *New York Times* (17, 24 January 1993; 29 March 1993).

Information on fetal development is found in Arthur J. Vender, J. H. Sherman, and D. S. Luciano, *Human Physiology*, Chapter 15 (New York: McGraw-Hill, 1970).

The Finkbine Case Retrospective is based on Allen F. Guttmacher, *The Case for Legalized Abortion* (Berkeley, Calif.: Diablo Press, 1977), pp. 15–17. The Bishop Decision Scenario is based on a case reported in the *New York Times* (11 April 1982). The procedure described was developed at Mount Sinai Medical Center by Drs. Thomas Kerenyi and Usha Chitkara.

The Social Context on RU-486 is based on *New York Times* stories: (28 October 1994; 28 March 1994; 18 February 1994; 2, 20 April 1993; 27 July 1990; 22 June 1990; 18 November 1993; 23 February 1992; 13 October 1993; 23 September 1989; 26, 27, 29, 30 October 1988; 22 February 1988). It also draws from *Newsweek* (22 November 1993); *Time* (14 July 1993; 4 June 1994; 4 October 1992; 7 November 1988); and Steven Greenhouse, "A Fierce Battle," *New York Times Magazine* (12 February 1989). For an account of the seizure of RU-486 by U.S. customs, see *New York Times* (2, 17 July 1992). More background material can be found in *New York Times* (15 November 1992; 15, 16, 17, 23 July 1992; 6 April 1990; 15 June 1988; 9 March 1990; 14 February 1990; 6 April 1990; 11 May 1990; 30 June 1990).

Chapter 2: Treating or Terminating

Much of the information in the Social Context on premature infants is based on the following series of articles from *New York Times*: Elisabeth Rosenthal, "As More Tiny Infants Live, Choices and Burdens Grow" (29 September 1991); Gina Kolata, "Parents of Tiny Infants Find Care Choices Are Not Theirs" (30 September 1991); and Jane E. Brody, "A Quality of Life Determined by a Baby's Size." See also David Harvey, R. W. I. Cooke, and G. A. Levitt, *The Baby Under 1000g* (London: Wright, 1989) and Jane E. Brody, "Steroid Therapy Is Saving Lives of Premature Babies," *New York Times* (9 March 1994). For the functioning of a hospital ethics committee and the struggle of parents to make a decision about life-sustaining treatment for their child, see Lisa Belkin, *First, Do No Harm* (New York: Simon and Schuster, 1993). For an account of efforts at treating birth disorders before birth, see Gina Kolata, *The Baby Doctors* (New York: Delacorte Press, 1990).

Details of the Baby K case are to be found in Linda Greenhouse, "Court Order to Treat Baby Prompts a Debate on Ethics," *New York Times* (19 February 1994). The Gregory Messenger Decision Scenario is based on information from Suzan Chira, "Medical and Legal Quandary in Father's Letting Baby Die," *New York Times* (3 August 1994).

"The Baby Doe Cases" is based on George J. Annas, "Disconnecting the Baby Doe Hotline," *Hastings Center Report* 13 (June 1983): 14–16 and "Baby Doe Redux," *Hastings Center Report* 13 (October 1983): 26–27; Bonnie Steinbock, "Baby Jane Doe in the Courts," *Hastings Center Report* 14 (February 1984): 13–19; Thomas H. Murray, "The Final Anticlimactic Rule on Baby Doe," *Hastings Center Report* 15 (June 1985): 5–9; and *Time* (14 November 1983); 107. Also, see the following articles from the *New York Times*: Marcia Chambers, "U.S. Suing for L.I. Records of Baby in Surgery Dispute" (3 November 1983) and "Letting Panels Decide the Fate of Defective Infants" (15 January 1984); Harold M. Schmeck, Jr., "Life, Death and the Rights of Handicapped Babies" (18 June 1985); Stuart Taylor, Jr., "High Court Upsets U.S. Intervention on Infants' Lives" (10 June 1986); and Andrew H. Malcolm, "Ruling on Baby Doe: Impact Limited" (11 June 1986).

The Baby Owens Case is based on an actual case presented in James M. Gustafson, "Mongolism, Parental Desires, and the Right to Life," *Perspectives in Biology and Medicine* 16 (1973): 529–557 and in Milton D. Heifetz and Charles Mangel, *The Right to Die* (New York: G. P. Putnam's, 1975), pp. 59–60. For a discussion of the medical and biological aspects of birth defects, see E. P. Volpe, *Human Heredity and Birth Defects* (New York: Pegasus, 1971). The R. S. Duff and A. G. M. Campbell article referred to is "Moral and Ethical Dilemmas in the Special-Care Nursery," *New England Journal of Medicine* 289 (1973): 75–78.

The Juli Decision Scenario is based on a case reported in B. D. Colen, *Karen Ann Quinlan: Dying in the Age of Eternal Life* (New York: Nash, 1976), pp. 130–137. The Susan Roth Decision Scenario is based on a case reported in Richard Trubo, *An Act of Mercy* (Los Angeles: Nash, 1973), pp. 149–150.

The Irene Towers Decision Scenario is based on a Chicago case reported by the Associated Press (18 May 1981). The Dr. Daniel McKay Decision Scenario is based on material from E. R. Shipp, "Mistrial in Killing of Malformed Baby Leaves Town Uncertain about Law," *New York Times* (18 February 1985). The AMA policy decision is reported in Andrew H. Malcom, "Reassessing Care of the Dying," *New York Times* (16 March 1986). The Bartling case is based on the *New York Times* (28 December 1984) and George J. Annas, "Prisoner in the ICU: The Tragedy of William Bartling," *Hastings Center Report* 14 (December 1984): 28–29. The Virginia Crawford Decision Scenario is based on a Baltimore case reported by United Press International (25 February 1979). The facts in the Shick case are from a United Press International story (8 February 1983); the Dohr-Engel case was reported in *New York Times* (20 March 1985); the Montigny case was reported by the Associated Press (8 August 1985); and the Gilbert case was reported by *New York Times* (9 August 1985) and the Associated Press (26 August 1985). The original policy endorsed by the Netherlands Supreme Court was outlined in a *New York Times* story (27 November 1984).

Chapter 3: Euthanasia

The Social Context on Kevorkian and assisted suicide draws material from *Time* (31 May 1993; *New York Times*, David Margolick, "Jurors Acquit Dr. Kevorkian in Suicide Case" (3 May 1994); "Michigan Panel Narrowly Backs Suicide" (5 March 1994); Larence K. Altman, "A How-to Book on Suicide Surges to the Top of the Best-Seller List" (August 1991); and Jane Gross, "Voters Turn Down Legal Euthanasia" (7 November 1991). See also Robert I. Misbin, ed. *Euthanasia*, Part I: Euthanasia in the United States: Physicians' Responses," (Fredrick, Md.: University Publishing Group, 1992), pp. 9–55.

On the Oregon measure, see Associated Press, "Voters in Oregon Allow Doctors to Help the Terminally Ill" (10 November 1994) and "Suicide Plan Would Permit Prescription for Lethal Drugs" (15 October 1994). For more background, see Timothy Egan, "Suicide Law Placing Oregon On Several Uncharted Paths," *New York Times* (20 November 1994). For criticism, see Robert A. Burt, "Death Made Too Easy," *New York Times* (16 November 1994).

The most detailed account of the Karen Quinlan case is Joseph and Julia Quinlan with Phyllis Battelle, *Karen Ann Quinlan* (New York: Doubleday, 1977). The facts in the Case Presentation are mostly from Phyllis Battelle, "The Story of Karen Quinlan," *Ladies' Home Journal* 93 (September 1976): 69–76, 172–180. Direct quotations are from Battelle. I have also drawn from B. D. Colen, *Karen Ann Quinlan: Dying in the Age of Eternal Life* (New York: Nash, 1976) and *In the Matter of Karen Quinlan: The Complete Legal Briefs, Court Proceedings, and Decisions* (Arlington, VA.: University Publications of America, 1975).

The Elizabeth Bouvia Case Presentation draws heavily upon George J. Annas, "When Suicide Prevention Becomes Brutality," *Hastings Center Report* 14 (April 1984): 20–21, 46. Additional information is from a United Press International article (2 November 1983); an Associated Press article (23 May 1985); and Robert Lindsy, "Ruling Is Upheld in Suicide Appeal," *New York Times* (20 January 1983). More recent events are reported in the following *New York Times* articles: Marcia Chambers "Woman Who Fought to Die Is Back in Court" (9 February 1986); "Winner of Right to Starve Faces New Fight at Hospital" (20 April 1986); and "Quadriplegic Obtains Court Help on Morphine" (24 April 1986).

No philosophical or legal analysis has so far been made of the J. K. Collums case. The facts and quotations in the Case Presentation are from the account by William K. Stevens, *New York Times* (9 December 1981). The facts and quotations about the punishment hearing are from a United Press International (UPI) news story (5 February 1982). Information about the sentencing is also from a UPI story (5 March 1982). The Timothy Quill Decision Scenario is based on "State Won't Press Case on Doctor in Suicide," *New York Times* (17 August 1991).

The Social Context on the Cruzan case draws from: *Time* (11 December 1989; 19 March 1990; 9 July 1990); *Newsweek*, Marcia Angell, "The Right to Die in Dignity" (23 July 1990); *New York Times* (17 November 1988; 29 July 1988; 25 July 1989; 19 January 1990; 26, 27 June 1990; 23 July 1990).

The discussion on euthanasia in the Netherlands is based on the following articles from *New York Times*: Tom Kuntz, "Helping a Man Kill Himself as Shown on Dutch TV" (includes partial transcript of dialogue during the process) (14 November 1994); Marliese Simons, "Dutch Move to Enact Law Making Euthanasia Easier" and "Dutch

Parliament Approves Law Permitting Euthanasia" (9, 10 February 1993); and F. X. Klines, "Dutch Quietly in Lead in Euthanasia Requestions" (31 October 1986). The California proposal is discussed in *New York Times* (18 May 1988). See also Maurice A. M. de Wachter, "Euthanasia in the Netherlands," *Hastings Center Report* (April 1992): 23–33 and Robert I. Misbin, ed. *Euthanasia*, "Part II: Euthanasia in the Netherlands," (Fredrick, Md.: University Publishing Group, 1992), pp. 55–107. Information about and the criticisms of the California Natural Death Act are from Karen Lebacqz, "On 'Natural Death,'" *Hastings Center Report* 7 (1977): 14. An excellent discussion of the history and practice of euthanasia and of euthanasia legislation is O. Ruth Russell, *Freedom to Die: Moral and Legal Aspects of Euthanasia* (New York: Dell, 1976).

Chapter 4: AIDS

On the Kimberly Bergalis case, see Lawrence K. Altman's articles in *New York Times*: "AIDS Mystery That Won't Go Away" (5 July 1994) and "AIDS and a Dentist's Secrets" (6 June 1993). Also, see Gina Kolata, "The Face That Haunts," *New York Times* (10 July 1994); Associated Press, "Sixth Patient of Dentist in Florida Has the AIDS Virus" (6 May 1993); and "Man Infected with HIV by Florida Dentist Dies" (28 July 1993).

The Social Context on pregnancy and testing is based on the following *New York Times* articles: Kevin Sack, "Deal Made in Albany on Required HIV Counseling" (3 July 1994) and "Lawmakers Drawing Battle Lines over Disclosures of Newborn HIV" (26 June 1994); Editorial, "AIDS Babies Deserve Testing" (27 June 1994); Lawrence K. Altman, "High HIV Levels Said to Raise Newborn's Risk" (17 August 1994); and Gina Kolata, "Debate on Infant AIDS vs. Mother's Rights" (3 November 1994).

The Social Context on autonomy and drug testing draws from Gina Kolata's articles in *New York Times*: "Group Conducts Secret AIDS Drug Tests" (28 June 1989); Critics Fault Secret Effort to Test AIDS Drug" (21 September 1989); "Unorthodox Trials of AIDS Drug Are Allowed by FDA to Go On" (9 March 1990); and "Debate Reopens on AIDS Drug Access" (12 September 1994). For the panel recommendation, see Robert Pear, "Faster Approval of AIDS Drugs Is Urged," *New York Times* (15 April 1990); on yet another panel, see Philip J. Hilts, "Panel Is Created to Speed Effort on AIDS Drugs," *New York Times* (1 December 1993). See also Daniel E. Hoth, Jr. et al., "Current Status of HIV Therapy: Antiretroviral Agent," in Lawrence Corey, ed., *AIDS: Problems and Prospects* (New York: Norton, 1993), pp. 51–71 and "Is AZT a False Hope," *Time* (12 April 1993): 25. On prediction, see Lawrence K. Altman, "New Blood Test Forecasts Progression from HIV Infection to AIDS," *New York Times* (1 February 1994).

On AIDS and gene therapy, see Gena Kolata, "Genetic Attacks Readied on AIDS," *New York Times* (31 May 1994) and R. Lipkin, "High-Tech Gene Therapy to Target AIDS," *Science News* (18 September 1993): 182.

The Tod Thompson case is wholly fictional, but it is based on first-person accounts of a number of people with AIDS. The issue of AIDS and suicide is reported by Seth Mydans, "AIDS patients' Silent Companion Is Often Suicide," *New York Times* (25 February 1990). The basic account of the AIDS struggle from the point of view of the homosexual community is Randy Shilts's, *And the Band Played On* (New York: Viking-Penguin, 1987).

On biomedical aspects of AIDS and the social-political situation, see Steve Connor and Sharon Kingman, *The Search for the Virus,* 2d ed. (New York: Penguin Books, 1989). I am also indebted to the following *New York Times* articles: Andrew Pollack, "Meeting Lays Bare the Abyss Between AIDS and Its Cure" (12 August 1994); "Japan Opens AIDS Forum; Note of Gloom" (8 August 1994); Gina Kolata, "Scientists Say Research on AIDS Needs Redirection" (12 May 1994); Lawrence K. Altman, "At AIDS Talks, Science Faces a Daunting Maze" (6 June 1993); and Erik Eckholm, "AIDS Fatally Steady in the U.S., Accelerates Worldwide" (28 June 1992). See also Associated Press, "Full-Blown AIDS Cases Estimated at 4 Million" (2 July 1994) and "Americans Living Longer, But AIDS Limits the Gain" (16 December 1994).

Information about anonymous testing is found in *New York Times* (9 July 1989). The Behringer case is discussed in J. F. Sullivan, "Should a Hospital Inform Patients If One of Its Surgeons Has AIDS?" *New York Times* (12 December 1989). The study of how many would warn partners is reported in an Associated Press story, Chicago (8 January 1988). The study of testing without consent is reported in *New York Times* (8 January 1988), and the second study in 16 February 1990. The issues surrounding privacy and testing are thoroughly laid out in Mar-

tin Gunderson, D. J. Mayo, and F. S. Rhame, *AIDS: Testing and Privacy* (Salt Lake City: University of Utah Press, 1989). The insurance problems are discussed in W. C. Gifford III, "An Insidious Test for AIDS," *New York Times* (14 December 1989) and Bob Hunter and Jay Angoff, "Insurers Are Right on AIDS Testing" (18 September 1987). Policies concerning testing in the military and in immigration are reported in *New York Times* (9 June 1987; 13 December 1988; 18 June 1988; and 28 February 1990). In the decision scenarios, the solicitation of volunteers was reported by the Associated Press (12 March 1990); the "Johnson" case in *New York Times* (4 March 1988); and the Owens case in P. S. Gutis, "AIDS Cited in Killing of Sex Partner," *New York Times* (4 March 1987).

Chapter 5: Physicians, Patients, and Others

The Social Context on pregnancy and prosecution is based on: Martha Field, "Controlling the Woman to Protect the Fetus," *Law Medicine and Health Care* 2 (1989): 114–129 for the Monson and similar cases; *New York Times* (15 January 1986; 30 August 1988) for effects of alcohol and other drugs; (4 May 1989; 9 May 1989) for the Illinois cases; (2 February 1990) for the Wyoming case; (30 May 1990) for the New York court ruling; (18 August 1992) for the Connecticut Supreme Court ruling; (19 July 1990) for racial bias; (28 October 1992) for the Gillespie case; (24 July 1992) for the Florida Supreme Court decision; *Time* (19 September 1988) for statistics about crack babies and hospital experiences in California and South Carolina. For an account of therapeutic approaches with crack-cocaine babies, see Joseph Treaster, "For Children of Cocaine, Fresh Reasons for Hope," *New York Times* (16 February 1993). The factual account of the Carter case is based on the Field article already mentioned, pp. 117–118.

The Twitchell Case Presentation draws substantially from David Margolic, "Death and Faith, Law and Christian Science," *New York Times* (6 August 1990). Other sources were *New York Times* (3, 6 July 1990) and "Convicted of Relying on Prayer," *Time* (16 July 1990). The overturn of the conviction was reported on CNN in November 1994. The Decision Scenario dealing with the health of President Kennedy is based on Lawrence K. Altman, "Disturbing Issue of Kennedy's Secret Illness," *New York*

Times (6 October 1992). The Medical University of South Carolina Decision Scenario is based on information from the Associated Press report, "Hospital Bows to U.S. Pressure" (7 September 1994). The Cox case is based on Jan Hoffman, "Murder Case Damages Faith in Confidentiality of Therapy," *New York Times* (15 June 1994). The quotations and facts in the Gonzalez Case Presentation are from Daniel Goleman, "Emergency Room Struggle: Deciding Who Is Dangerous," *New York Times* (13 July 1986) and Frank Trippett, "The Madman on the Ferry," *Time* (21 July 1986); 28.

For an account of the physician-patient relationship and the development of licensing procedures for physicians in the United States, see John Duffy, *The Healers: The Rise of the Medical Establishment* (New York: McGraw-Hill, 1977). Duffy also deals with American medical quackery, but the classic works in this area are James Harvey Young, *The Toadstool Millionaires: A Social History of Patent Medicines in America Before Federal Regulation* (Princeton, N.J.: Princeton University Press, 1961) and *The Medical Messiahs* (Princeton, N.J.: Princeton University Press, 1971). An influential sociological account of the nature of the doctor-patient relationship as a social role is Talcott Parsons, "Illness and the Role of the Physician: A Sociological Perspective," in Clyde Kluckhohn and H. A. Murray, eds., *Personality in Nature, Society, and Culture* (New York: Knopf, 1961). The multiple sclerosis study is reported in *Hastings Center Report* 13 (June 1983): 2–3. The Korin Decision Scenario is based on information in Dudley Clendinen, "Therapist's Notes Issue in Fraud Case," *New York Times* (17 March 1985).

Chapter 6: Medical Experimentation and Informed Consent

The Social Context on radiation research is in part based on the following from the *New York Times*: Keith Schneider, "Nuclear Scientists Irradiated People in Secret Research" (17 December 1993); "1950 Memo Shows Worry over Radiation Tests" (28 December 1993); "Signatures in Experiment Called Forgery" (12 April 1994); and John H. Cushman, Jr., "Study Sought on All Testing on Humans" (10 January 1994). The account of research on terminally ill patients is from Gina Kolata, "When the Dying Enroll in Studies: A Debate over False Hopes," *New York Times* (29 January 1994).

For information about foreign testing, see Elisabeth Rosenthal, "For More Drugs, First Test Is Abroad," *New York Times* (7 August 1990) and Warren E. Leary, "U.S. Ethics Are Questioned by Critics of Vaccine Test in Italy and Sweden," *New York Times* (13 March 1994). The Benito Agrela Decision Scenario is based on "Behind a Fifteen-Year-Old's Decision to Forgo Medical Treatment," Associated Press (12 June 1994) and "Youth Who Receives a Liver Transplant Drug Dies," Associated Press (21 August 1994).

The Artificial Heart Case Presentation draws from the following sources: for a discussion of the Cooley controversy, see Thomas Thompson, *Hearts* (New York: Fawcett, 1971), pp. 227–235; for current criticisms, see Philip M. Boffey, "Artificial Heart: Should It Be Scaled Back?" *New York Times* (3 December 1985); and for questions about terminating the experiment and DeVries's responses, see L. K. Altman, "The Ongoing Ordeal of a 'Human Experiment,'" *New York Times* (14 May 1985). The quotations from Lenfant and DeVries are from Malcolm Browne, "U.S. Halts Funds to Develop Artificial Hearts for Humans," *New York Times* (13 May 1988). For a negative response, see P. M. Boffey, "Panel Appeals for Funds in Artificial Heart Work," *New York Times* (19 May 1988).

The Baby Fae Case Presentation is based on information from the following: *New York Times* stories: L. K. Altman, "Learning from Baby Fae," (18 November 1984); Philip M. Boffey, "Medicine Under Scrutiny" (20 November 1984); Sandra Blakeslee, "Baboon Implant in Baby Fae Assailed" (20 December 1985); and Erik Eckholm, "Baby Death Laid to Wrong Blood" (17 October 1985). The NIH report is summarized in the Associated Press story "Baby Fae's Survival Chances Overstated, U.S. Report Says" (14 March 1985), and in "NIH Approves the Consent for Baby Fae, or Does It?" *Hastings Center Report* 15 (April 1985): 2.

The Detroit Psychosurgery Case Presentation is based on the opinion of the Wayne County Circuit Court (references cited in the selection. The quotation from the consent form is from the notes of the opinion.) But it is most indebted to the excellent account by Ronald S. Gass, *"Kaimowitz v. Department of Mental Health,"* in W. M. Gaylin and J. S. Meister, eds., *Operating on the Mind* (New York: Basic Books, 1975), pp. 73–87. The full opinion is reprinted as an appendix to the book.

The details of the experiments in the Willow-brook Case Presentation are taken from Saul Krugman and Joan P. Giles, "Viral Hepatitis: New Light on an Old Disease," *JAMA*, 212 (1970): 1019–1021.

The description of Nazi medical experiments is from the indictment in *United States vs. Karl Brandt*, part of which is reprinted in *Hastings Center Report*, "Special Supplement: Biomedical Ethics and the Shadow of Nazism" (6 August 1976): 5. The description of drug testing is based on the account by Ross J. Baldessarini, *Chemotherapy in Psychiatry* (Cambridge, Mass.: Harvard University Press, 1977), pp. 4–11.

The paternalistic view, that physicians must decide because patients can never understand, is expressed in Eugene G. Laforet, "The Fiction of Informed Consent," *Journal of the American Medical Association* 235 (12 April 1976): 1579–1585. Problems with placebos are discussed in Sissela Bok, "The Ethics of Giving Placebos," *Scientific American* 231 (November 1974): 17–23. The discussion of research and children is indebted to Jean D. Lockhart, "Pediatric Drug Testing," *Hastings Center Report* 7 (June 1977): 8–10. Prisoners and research is discussed at length in Jessica Mitford, *Kind and Usual Punishment* (New York: Knopf, 1973). The historical cases of research on the poor are from M. H. Pappworth, *Human Guinea Pigs* (Boston: Beacon Press, 1961), pp. 61–62. The details of the Tuskegee case are from the "Final Report of the Tuskegee Syphilis Study Ad Hoc Advisory Panel," U.S. Public Health Service (Washington, D.C., 1973), part of which is reprinted in S. J. Reiser et al., *Ethics in Medicine* (Cambridge, Mass.: MIT Press, 1977), pp. 316–321. I am indebted to the letter by Jay Katz, in particular. In the discussion of fetal experimentation, I am indebted to "Individual Risks vs. Societal Benefits: The Fetus," a forum appearing in *Experiments and Research with Humans: Values in Conflict* (Washington, D.C.: National Academy of Sciences, 1975), pp. 59–90. HHS regulations on using children as research subjects were published in the Federal Register (8 March 1983). They are summarized in "Finally, Final Rules on Children Who Become Research Subjects," *Hastings Center Report* 13 (August 1983): 2–3.

The Phoenix Heart Decision Scenario draws information and quotations from the following articles in the *New York Times:* Lawrence K. Altman, "Anguish, Hope, a Moment of Fame" (19 March 1985) and Irvin Molotsky, "F.D.A. Ponders Action

on Unsanctioned Implant" (8 March 1985). The questions reflect the doubts expressed by George J. Annas, in "The Phoenix Heart: What We Have to Lose," *Hastings Center Report* 15 (June 1985): 15–16.

The Boyd Rush Decision Scenario is drawn from information cited in George J. Annas, "Baby Fae: The 'Anything Goes' School of Human Experimentation," *Hastings Center Report* 15 (February 1985): 15–17. The case of Ms. Mink presented in the scenario is based on a report in *Time* (9 May 1977); 44 and on Marlene Cimons's article in the *Los Angeles Times* (16 May 1977). The quotations are from these sources. A report on the charges of "guinea-pig" surgery involving mental patients in Chicago is found in *New York Times* (19 April 1979). Additional information is from *Time* (23 April 1979).

Chapter 7: Genetics: Intervention, Control, and Research

The Social Context: The Human Genome Project is indebted to Leon Jaroff's excellent "The Gene Hunt," *Time* (20 March 1989): 22–67. Also, *Science* (30 September 1994) is wholly devoted to the HGP; see in particular, B. M. Knoppers and Ruth Chadwick, "The Human Genome Project: Under an International Ethical Microscope," (235–236). For a readable presentation of the research involved in the search for disease-causing genes, see Jerry E. Bishop and Michael Waldhoz, *Genome* (New York: Simon and Schuster/Touchstone, 1991). For a more patient-centered approach, see Lois Wingerson, *Mapping Our Genes: The Genome Project and the Future of Medicine* (New York: Dutton, 1990). For a survey of identified genes, see "The Year in Genes," *Discover* (January 1994): 19. On genetic disorders that worsen over generations, see Anastasia Toufexis, "The Generational Saga of the Vicious Gene," *Time* (17 February 1992): 72 and Gina Kolata, "Discovery Upsets Geneticists' Ideas on Inherited Ills," *New York Times* (6 February 1992). On breast cancer, see Rachel Nowa, "Breast Cancer Gene Offers Surprises," *Science* (23 September 1994): 1796—1799; Gregory Cowley, "Family Matters: Hunt for a Breast Cancer Gene," *Newsweek* (6 December 1993): 46–52; and Kenneth Offit, "Hostage to Our Genes?" *New York Times* (22 September 1994).

On cystic fibrosis, see Andrew Purvis, "Laying Siege to a Deadly Gene," *Time* (24 February 1992) and Natalie Angier, "Researchers Trace Primary Cause of Cystic Fibrosis to the Stone Age," *New York Times* (1 June 1994). The account of the discovery of the cystic fibrosis gene is based on Sandra Blakeslee, "Discovery May Help Cystic Fibrosis Victims," *New York Times* (24 August 1989). See the Associated Press stories "Gene Defect for a Type of Dwarfism Is Found" (31 July 1994, on Canavan disease); "Researchers Find Key to Rare Brain Disorder" (4 October 1993); "Gene Linked for First Time to High Blood Pressure" (7 October 1992); "Gene Linked to Diabetes Found" (12 January 1993); and "Genetic Defect Linked to Alzheimer's" (23 October 1992). See E. Pennisi, "Free-Radical Scavenger Gene Tied to ALS," *Science News* (6 March 1993). See the following *New York Times* stories: Tim Hilchey, "Researchers Find Genetic Defect That Causes Rare Immune Disease" [namely, severe-combined-immunodeficiency disease] (9 April 1993) and Natalie Angier, "Gene Is Found That Causes Rare Type of Hypertension" (16 January 1992). For a discussion of issues of genetic discrimination, see *Science News* (21 January 1989): 40–42; Gina Kolata, "Nightmare or the Dream of a New Era in Genetics," *New York Times* (7 December 1993); Sharon Begley, "When DNA Isn't Destiny," *Newsweek* (6 December 1993): 53–55; and George J. Annas, "Who's Afraid of the Human Genome?" *Hastings Center Report* (July/August 1989), 19–21. The Spring 1993 issue of *National Forum* is devoted exclusively to the Human Genome Project.

The contrary views on the relative safety of CVS are reported in the Associated Press, "Early Down Syndrome Test Is Found to Be Safe" (23 October 1994). Guidelines on sickle-cell are in Warren E. Leary, "Sickle-Cell Screen Urged for All Newborns," *New York Times* (28 April 1993); on treatments, see Leary's "Intractable Pain of Sickle Cell Begins to Yield," *New York Times* (7 June 1994). The discussion of ethical issues about screening and children is based on Gina Kolata's, "Should Children Be Told If Genes Predict Illness?" *New York Times* (26 September 1994). For an account of screening and its relationship to legal and social issues, see George Annas and B. Coyne, "Fitness for Birth and Reproduction: Legal Implications of Genetic Screening," *Family Law Quarterly* 9 (Fall 1975): 463–490 and Marc Lappe, "The Predictive Powers of the New Genetics," *Hastings Center Report* 14 (October 1984): 18–21. A review of some diagnostic possibilities is offered by Harold M. Schmeck, Jr., "Fetal Tests Can Now Find Many More Genetic Flaws," *New York Times* (11 March 1986). A critical look at Tay-Sachs screening is offered in Madeleine

J. Goodman and Lenn E. Goodman, "The Overselling of Genetic Anxiety," *Hastings Center Report* 12 (October 1982): 20–27.

The Huntington's Disease Case Presentation relies heavily on Gina Kolata, "Closing in on a Killer Gene, *Discover* (March 1984): 83–87. See also Lawrence K. Altman, "Researchers Report Genetic Test Detects Huntington's Disease," *New York Times* (9 November 1983) and Albert Rosenfeld, "At Risk for Huntington's Disease," *Hastings Center Report* 14 (June 1984): 5–8. Nancy Wexler's views on genetic testing are quoted from Mary Murray, "Nancy Wexler," *New York Times Magazine* (13 February 1993): 28–31. For a profile of Wexler see *Time* (10 February 1992). On more recent developments, see the following *New York Times* articles: Sandra Blakeslee, "Unusual Clues Help in Long Fight to Solve Huntington's Disease" (27 October 1992) and Natalie Angier, "Action of Gene in Huntington's Is Proving a Tough Puzzle" (2 November 1993).

The Gene Therapy Case Presentation draws information from Eve K. Nicholas, *Human Gene Therapy* (Cambridge, Mass.: Harvard University Press, 1988). The plan to initiate ADA gene therapy is described in Natalie Angier, "Gene Implant Therapy," *New York Times* (8 March 1990), and her account of the first case is in "Girl, 4, Becomes First Human to Receive Engineered Genes," (15 September 1990). Biographical details of Ashanthi Desilva and additional treatments are reported in Larry Thompson, "The First Kids with New Genes," *Time* (7 June 1993): 50–53. The first case, as well as plans for future ones, is discussed in W. French Anderson, "Human Gene Therapy," *Science* (8 May 1992): 808–813. The entire issue of the journal is devoted to "Molecular Advances in Genetic Disease." See also in *Science News*: K. A. Fackelman, "Gene Therapy Corrects Mouse Lupus" (19 March 1994): 180; "Gene Therapy Ameliorates Clotting Disorder" (2 December 1993): 215; "Gene Courier Targets Skin-tumor Cells" (4 December 1993): 372; C. Ezell, "Gene Therapy for Rare Cholesterol Disorder (12 October 1991): 229; and E. Pennisi, "Gene Therapy Seeks to Mend Cystic Fibrosis" (20 March 1993): 183. See also the following from *New York Times*: Natalie Angier, "Doctors Have Success in Treating Blood Disease with Gene Injections" (28 July 1991); "A New Gene Therapy to Fight Cholesterol Is Being Prepared" (29 October 1991); "Gene Therapy for Cystic Fibrosis May Be Possible (10 January 1992); "With Direct Injections, Gene Therapy Takes a Step into a New Age" (14 April 1992); "Gene Therapy Begins for Fatal Lung Disease" (30 April 1993); "Gene Experiment to Reverse Inherited Disease Is Working" (1 April 1994); Sandra Blakeslee, "Treatment for 'Bubble Boy Disease'" (18 May 1993); and Gina Kolata, "Big Gain in Gene Therapy Is Seen for Treatment of Cystic Fibrosis" (15 October 1993) and "Gene Therapy Is Approved for Cardiovascular Study" (14 September 1994). Additional background information is drawn from the following *New York Times* articles: Harold M. Schmeck, "Activity of Genes Reported Altered in Treating Man" (9 December 1982); Walter Sullivan, "Transplanting Cells into Brain Offers Promise as Therapy" (11 September 1984); and Harold M. Schmeck, "Hereditary Disease: Therapies Are Closer" (28 January 1986). I am also indebted to the Fletcher article reprinted here and to Clifford Grobstein and Michael Flower, "Gene Therapy: Proceed with Caution" *Hastings Center Report* 14 (April 1984): 13–17.

Other information relevant to the topic is drawn from these *New York Times* articles: Walter Sullivan, "Transplanting Cells into Brain Offers Promise as Therapy" (11 September 1984) and Harold M. Schmeck, Jr., "U.S. Sets Guidelines on Using Gene Transplants in Humans" (23 September 1985).

A general survey of screening and the ethical problems it poses is presented by Tabitha M. Powledge, "Genetic Screening," in Warren T. Reich, ed., *Encyclopedia of Bioethics*, vol. 2 (New York: Free Press, 1978), pp. 567–573. The account of the experiences and problems (social and scientific) in PKU screening is found in National Academy of Sciences, *Genetic Screening: Programs, Principles, and Research* (Washington, D.C.: National Academy of Sciences, 1975). For an account of alpha-fetoprotein screening, see Barbara Gastel et al., eds., *Maternal Serum Alpha Fetoprotein: Issues in the Prenatal Screening and Diagnosis of Neural Tube Defects* (U.S. Department of Health and Human Services Publication HE 20.2: M41, 1981). For a discussion of social problems caused by PKU laws and sickle-cell screening, see Philip Reilly, "There's Another Side to Genetic Screening," *Prism* (January 1976): 55–57.

Genetic screening and the problems it poses for rights is considered by Susan West, "Genetic Testing on the Job," *Science* 82 (September 1982): 16. See also Philip M. Boffey, "Rapid Advances Point to the Mapping of All Human Genes," *New York Times*

(15 July 1986) and Morton Hunt, "The Total Gene Screen," *New York Times Magazine* (19 January 1986).

Chapter 8: Reproductive Control: In Vitro Fertilization, Artificial Insemination, and Surrogate Pregnancy

Louise Brown has apparently grown into a well-adjusted teenager. See Carol Lawson, "Celebrated Birth Aside, Teen Has a Typical Life," *New York Times* (2 October 1993). The Louise Brown Case Presentation is based on *Newsweek* (7 August 1978); *Time* (7 August 1978); and *U.S. News and World Report* (7 August 1978). For a discussion of the techniques and issues of in vitro fertilization, see R. G. Edwards, "Fertilization of Human Eggs In Vitro: Morals, Ethics, and the Law," *Quarterly Review of Biology* 49 (March 1974): 3–26. The technique of retrieving undeveloped ova is described in Larry Thompson, "Fertility with Less Fuss," *Time* (14 November 1994): 79.

"Motherhood after Menopause" draws on facts about postmenopausal pregnancy and the controversy surrounding it from Margaret Carlson, "Old Enough to Be Your Mother," *Time* (10 January 1994): 41; Associated Press, "California Woman, 53, Gives Birth to Twins" (11 November 1992); and the following from *New York Times*: Gina Kolata, "When Grandmother Is the Mother, Until Birth" (5 August 1991); Lindsey Gruson, "A Mother's Gift: Bearing Her Grandchild" (16 February 1993); William F. Schmidt, "Birth to a 59-Year-Old Generates an Ethical Controversy in Britain" (29 December 1993); Susan Chira, "Of a Certain Age, and in a Family Way" (2 January 1994); Linda Wolfe, "And Baby Makes 3, Even If You're Gray" (4 January 1994); and Alan Riding, "French Government Proposes Ban On Pregnancies after Menopause" (5 January 1994).

Information on the Davis case is from UPI stories (21 September 1989); *New York Times* (22 April 1989, 8 August 1989); Ronald Smothers, "Court Gives Ex-Husband Rights on Use of Embryos" (2 June 1992) and "Doctor's Act on Embryos Sends Case Back to Court" (4 June 1992); and AP stories (26 May 1990, 13 September 1990). Information about the Baby M case is drawn from *New York Times* articles (4, 5, 6, 10, 26, 27 January 1987; 2, 3, 9, 10, 11, 17 February 1987; 5, 9, 10, 31 March 1987; 2 April 1987). Additional information about the Rios case is from James Lieber, "The Case of the Frozen

Embryos," *The Saturday Evening Post* (October, 1989): pp. 50–53. The Calvert case is based on materials from Carol Lawson, "Couple's Own Embryos Used in Birth Surrogacy," *New York Times* (12 August 1990); Seth Mydans, "Surrogate Loses Custody Bid in Case Defining Motherhood," *New York Times* (22 October 1990); and *Time* (22 August 1990).

The Unclaimed Infant Case Presentation employs facts and quotations from the Associated Press story "Surrogate Infant Left Unclaimed" (22 January 1983) and from Iver Peterson, "Legal Snarl Developing Around Case of a Baby Born to Surrogate Mother," *New York Times* (7 February 1983). Additional information about the Stiver case is from "In Brief," *Hastings Center Report* (April 86): 2. The Rios Case Presentation is based on information from the Associated Press story "Australians Reject an Effort to Destroy Frozen Embryos" (23 October 1984).

For information about assisted fertility techniques, fertility clinics, and patient accounts, see *New York Times*: Gina Kolata, "Reproductive Revolution Is Jostling Old Views," (11 January 1993) and Glenn Kramon, "Infertility Chain: The Good and Bad in Medicine" (19 June 1992). See also Benedict Carey, "Sperm, Inc.," *In Health* (July/August 1991): 52–56; Philip Elmer-Dewitt, "Making Babies," *Time* (30 September 1991): 56–63; Ellen Hopkins, "Tales from the Baby Factory," *New York Times Magazine* (15 March 1992): 40 ff.; and Anne Taylor Fleming, "Sperm in a Jar," *New York Times Magazine* (12 June 1994): 52–55. The account of the debate about the selling of ova is based on Gina Kolata, "Young Women Offer to Sell Their Eggs to Infertile Couples," *New York Times* (10 November 1991). On transplanting ovaries from aborted fetuses, see the same Gina Kolata, *New York Times*, "Fetal Ovary Transplant Is Envisioned" (6 January 1994). For problems over embryos, see Gina Kolata, "Frozen Embryos: Few Rules in a Rapidly Growing Field," *New York Times* (5 June 1992). On one of the "natural" approaches to IVF, see Claude Ranoux et al., "A New In Vitro Fertilization Technique," *Fertility and Sterility 49* (1988): 654 ff. On the technique of sperm injection into ova, see Gina Kolata, "New Pregnancy Hope: A Single Sperm Injected," *New York Times* (11 August 1993).

The account of the Hall and Stillman cloning experiments is based on Geoffrey Cowley, "Clone Hype," *Newsweek* (8 November 1993): 60–64; David Gelman, "How Will the Clone Feel," same issue, (65–66); Philip Elmer-Dewitt, "Cloning: Where Do We Draw the Line?" *Time* (8 November 1993): 65–70; and K. A. Fackelman, "Cloning Human Embryos," *Science News* (5 February 1994): 92–95. See also Gina Kolata, "Cloning Human Embryos: Debate Erupts over Ethics," *New York Times* (26 October 1993). A more technical account is given in Rebecca Kolberg, "Human Embryo Cloning Reported," *Science* (29 October 1993).

Information about sterility and the moratorium on in vitro research that slowed U.S. research is found in Michael Gold, "The Baby Makers," *Science 85* (April 1985): 26–38. See also Susan Abramowitz, "A Stalemate on Test Tube Baby Research," *Hastings Center Report 14* (February 1984): 5–9. For a general survey of all the issues in reproductive technology from a feminist perspective, see Gena Corea, *The Mother Machine* (New York: Harper & Row, 1985).

The historical background on artificial insemination is presented in R. Snowden and G. D. Mitchell, *The Artificial Family* (London: Allen and Unwin, 1981). The technical aspects of the process and the statistics mentioned are discussed in Ronald P. Goldstein, "Artificial Insemination by Donor: Status and Problems," in Aubrey Milunsky and George J. Annas, eds., *Genetics and the Law* (New York: Plenum Press, 1976), pp. 197–202. For general objections to artificial insemination and other forms of reproductive technology, see Paul Ramsey, *Fabricated Man* (New Haven, Conn.: Yale University Press, 1970), Chapter 3.

The New York law regulating surrogacy is summarized in Lisa Belkin, "Childless Couples Hang on to Last Hope, Despite Laws," *New York Times* (28 July 1992); see also the letters on 27 June 1992. for a case in Cincinnati of a surrogate suing the lawyer who made the arrangements, see Tamar Lewin, "Mother Able to Sue for Surrogacy Negligence in Arrangements," *New York Times* (20 September 1992). Background information surrounding surrogate mothers can be found in Nadine Brozan, "Surrogate Mothers: Problems and Goals," *New York Times* (27 February 1984). The nonsurgical technique of ova recovery is discussed in Walter Sullivan, "Clinic Offers Aid for Fertilization," *New York Times* (30 January 1986).

For a general review of most of the issues in the Motherhood Social Context, see "Making

Babies: The New Science of Conception," *Time* (10 September 1984): 46–56. The legal issues in reproductive technology are well reviewed by George Annas in, "Surrogate Embryo Transfer" and "Redefining Parenthood and Protecting Embryos," *Hastings Center Report* 14 (June 1984): 25–26 and 14 (October 1984): 50–52, respectively. The Kim Cotton case is reported in the Associated Press story "Surrogate Mother's Child in English Court Custody" (9 January 1985). Information about the Vatican Instruction and reaction to it is from *New York Times* (10, 11 March 1987).

Chapter 9: Acquiring and Allocating Scarce Medical Resources

For the current status of transplants, see "Improving Transplant Success," *American Health* (September 1994): 8; "Can Pigs Solve the Transplant Crisis," *American Health* (June 1994): 9; and Mark Caldwell, "The Transplant Self," *Discover* (April 1992). See also the following *New York Times* articles: Gina Kolata, "Doctors Are Questioning the Use of Waiting Lists for Receiving Organs" (20 May 1993); Elisabeth Rosenthal, "Parents Find Solace in Donating Organs" (1 May 1993); Sandra Blakeslee, "New Technique in Lab Prevents Rejection of Organ Transplants" (10 March 1992) and "High Doses of Drugs Forestall Heart Transplants" (28 October 1992); and Gina Kolata, "Ethicists Debating a New Definition of Death" (29 April 1992). See also from the Associated Press, "Artificial Liver Used After Removal of Organ" (18 May 1993); "Mandatory Organ Donation Sought by Ethics Group" (22 December 1992); "Mouse Study May Lead to Transplant Advances" (7 August 1992); "Success Rate Listed for Organ Transplant" (20 September 1992); and "Pig Liver Transplant for Dying Patient Is Defended" (13 October 1992), and from Reuters, "Artificial Liver Shows Promise in British Study" (15 November 1994).

Additional background information on transplants and problems of allocation can be found in Susan Jacoby, "Lifesavers: The Drive for More Organ Donations," *New York Magazine* (18 July 1983): 39–43; Donald Sullivan, "New York to Require That Hospitals Seek Donation of Organs," *New York Times* (14 August 1985); and H. Tristram Engelhardt, Jr., "Allocating Scarce Medical Resources and the Availability of Organ Transplantation," *New England Journal of Medicine* 311 (5 July 1984): 66–71.

The debate about means of increasing the supply is rehearsed in the following *Hastings Center Report* articles: Arthur L. Caplan, "Organ Transplants: The Costs of Success" 13 (December 1983): 23–32; George J. Annas, "Life, Liberty, and the Pursuit of Organ Sales" 14 (February 1984): 22–23; Alfred M. Sadler, Jr., and B. L. Sadler, "A Community of Givers, Not Takers" 14 (October 1984): 6–9; and Arthur L. Caplan, "Organ Procurement: It's Not in the Cards" 14 (October 1984): 9–12 and "In Minn. and Mass., No Transplants for the Sickest" 15 (April 1985): 2–3.

On selling organs, see the following articles from *New York Times*: Peter S. Young, "Moving to Compensate Families in Human Organ Market" (8 July 1994); Sanjoy Hazarka, "India Debates Ethics of Buying Transplant Kidneys" (17 August 1992); and Chris Hedges, "Egypt's Doctors Impose Kidney Transplant Curbs" (23 January 1992) and "Egypt's Desperate Trade" (22 September 1991). See also, "Trading Flesh Around the Globe," *Time* (17 June): 61.

The facts and opinions in the Ayala case are presented in Lance Morrow, "When One Body Can Save Another," *Time* (7 June 1991) 54–58; the Associated Press story, "Mom, 43, Having Baby to Save Daughter's Life" (17 February 1990); Irene Chang, "Bone Marrow Baby Is Born to the Ayalas," *Los Angeles Times* (6 April 1990); and Rebecca Norris, "Made in Heaven," *American Health* (October 1994): 100. The marriage of Anissa is reported in Rebecca Norris, "Made in Heaven," *American Health* (October 1994): 100.

The developing story of fetal-cell implants and the public debate told in the Fetal-Cell Social Context is drawn, in part, from J. Eric Ahlskog, "Cerebral Transplantation for Parkinson's Disease: Current Progress and Future Prospects," *Mayo Clinic Proceedings* 68 (1993): 578–591; Associated Press, "Fetal Tissue Study Approved, the First Since the Ban Was Lifted" (4 January 1994); "Fetal Tissue Grafts Reverse Parkinson's," *Science News* (28 November 1992): 372; and the following *New York Times* articles: Warren Leary, "Call to Regulate Transplant Tissue" (15 August 1993), Gwen Ifill, "House Aproves Fetal Tissues in Federally Funded Research" (26 June 1991); Walter Sullivan, "Transplanting Cells into Brain Offers Promise as Therapy" (11 September 1984); Tamar Lewin, "Medical Uses of Fetal Tissue Spurs New Abortion Debate (16 August 1987); Warren Leary, "Panel Supports

Research Use of Fetal Tissues" (17 September 1988) and "Panel Says Use of Fetal Tissue 'Is Acceptable Public Policy'" (21 October 1988); Tamar Lewin, "Reagan Signs Bill to Bar Sale of Fetal Organs and Tissues" (6 November 1988); William Regelson, "A Wise Fetal Tissue Policy" (14 November 1988); and Gina Kolata, "Fetal Tissue Implant Said to Be Aiding a Parkinson Patient" (2 February 1990). See also Howard Wolinsky, "Transplants from the Unborn," *American Health* (April 1988): 47–49.

The Policy Decision Case Presentation is based on a real incident. See the St. Louis *Post-Dispatch* (5 July 1981) for an account of the policy at Tampa General Hospital.

There is no Brattle County, Texas, and the Case Presentation is wholly fictional. It does represent, however, the problem that was faced by some dialysis centers when programs were just starting. For a fine account of the workings of a real committee (the one at Swedish Hospital, Seattle, Washington, in 1961), see Shana Alexander, "They Decide Who Lives, Who Dies." The piece first appeared in *Life* magazine in 1962.

On dialysis and kidney transplants, see from *New York Times*: Lawrence K. Altman, "With Dialysis, Outlook Grim as People Age" (5 January 1994); Gina Kolata, "Unrelated Kidney Donors Win Growing Acceptance by Hospitals" (30 June 1993); and Elisabeth Rosenthal, "Method of Matching Donor Kidney Gains" (3 September 1993), and from Associated Press, "A Bleak U.S. Report on Kidney Failure Patients" (3 November 1993).

The story of cyclosporine is presented in Carol Bolotin, "Drug as Hero," *Science* 85 (June 1985): 68–71. For an account of how dialysis takes place and of what it is like from a personal point of view, see Lee Foster, "Man and Machine: Life Without Kidneys," *Hastings Center Report* 6 (June 1976): 5–8. The lifeboat analogy is discussed by Paul Ramsey in *The Patient as Person* (New Haven, Conn.: Yale University Press, 1970). The classic sociological study on dialysis and transplants is Renee C. Fox, "A Sociological Perspective on Organ Transplantation and Hemodialysis," *New Dimensions in Legal and Ethical Concepts for Human Research, Annals of the New York Academy of Sciences* 169 (1970): 406–428. See also the relevant chapters in Paul Ramsey, *The Patient as Person* (New Haven, Conn.: Yale University Press, 1970).

For the Sepulveda case, see Bruce Lambert, "Jesse Sepulveda Is Dead at Seven," *New York Times*

(18 July 1993). For the Bosze case, see Isabel Wilkerson, "Search for Marrow Donor Questions Nature of Altruism and Child Rights," *New York Times* (30 July 1990) and "Setback for Boy Needing Marrow," Associated Press (28 September 1990). For the Benton case, see Terry Trucco, "Sales of Kidneys Prompt New Laws and Debate," *New York Times* (1 August 1990).

Chapter 10: Claim to Health Care

Information about Oregon's rationing efforts is drawn from Ira Mothner, "Drawing the Line," *American Health* (July/August 1989); John Elson, "Rationing Medical Care," *Time* (27 March 1989); Mary Cantwell, "The Death Dilemma," *New York Times* (14 February 1990); Jane Gross, "What Medical Care the Poor Can Have: Lists Are Drawn Up," *New York Times* (27 March 1990); Timothy Egan, "Controversial Oregon Health Plan Delayed," *San Francisco Chronicle* (31 July 1990); L. A. Chung, "Alameda County Admits Health Rationing Failed," *San Francisco Chronicle* (2 August 1989); L. A. Chung, "Rationing Health Care—Oregon Lists Priorities," *San Francisco Chronicle* (4 April 1989), which contains the list of ratings; "Health Care Overhaul Is Approved in Oregon," *New York Times* (6 August 1993); and "Health Plan Originator Wins in Oregon," Associated Press (18 May 1994).

The Hawaiian Example Case Presentation is drawn from Timothy Egan, "Hawaii Shows It Can Offer Health Insurance for All," *New York Times* (23 July 1991) and Adam Clymer, "Hawaii Is a Health Care Lab As Employers Buy Insurance," *New York Times* (4 May 1994).

The Canadian Case Presentation is based on the following *New York Times* pieces: Milt Freudenhen, "Debating Canadian Health Model" (29 June 1989); David Woods, "Health Care Canadian Style: Americans Beware" (4 July 1989); H. M. Lerner, "Don't Look to Canada's Health System" (3 February 1990); Letters by Mark Warren and Janey Joy: Shanke K. Cobb; and I. S. Tummon under the title "Canada's Health Care Succeeds Where Ours Doesn't" (26 February 1990); Theodore R. Marmor and John Godfrey, "Canada's Medical System Is a Model. That's a Fact" (23 July 1992); Clyde H. Farnsworth, "In Canada, Elderly Praise Their Health Care," (6 July 1993); and Robin Toner, "In Health Care Debate, Canada Plan Still Lives" (4 May 1993). Other materials used were Anthony Schmitz, "Health Assurance," *In Health* (January/

February 1991): 39–47 and *Consumer Reports* (September 1992): 579–592. For a detailed comparison of the U.S. system with those in Canada and Germany, see Donald Drake, Susan Fitzgerald, and Mark Jaffe, *Hard Choices: Health Care At What Cost?* (Kansas City: Andrews and McMeel, 1993).

The materials on health-care costs and proposals are drawn from the following articles in *New York Times*: Erik Eckholm, "Frayed Nerves of People Without Health Coverage" (11 July 1994) [the three cases of the uninsured are from this source] and "On Managed Competition: Primer on Health-Care Idea" (1 May 1993); Robert Pear, "Doctors Alter Position on Health Legislation" (11 December 1994), "$1 Trillion in Health Costs Is Predicted" (29 December 1993), "New Health Plan Stresses Medicare for the Uninsured" (1 March 1994), "Second Thoughts on Health Data" (9 May 1994), "AMA and Insurers Clash Over Restrictions on Doctors" (24 May 1994), "Tough Decision on Health Care If Employers Won't Pay the Bill" (9 July 1994), "Health Care Debate to Shift to Federal Employee Plan" (7 September 1994), "Once in Forefront, HMOs Lose Their Luster in Health Debate" (23 August 1994); Milt Freudenheim, "Doctors Are Sparring with Insurers over Right to Join Health Networks" (12 July 1994) and "To Economists, Managed Care Is No Cure at All" (6 September 1994); Robin Toner, "Posturing and Principle: Tactics in the 11th Hour" (19 July 1994); and Adam Clymer, "With Health Overhaul Dead, a Search for Minor Repairs" (28 August 1994). See also Christopher Byron, "Supermarket Medicine," *New York* (17 January 1994): 14–15; Jeanne Kassler, "Managed Care or Chaos? A Doctor's Report on How HMOs Really Work." *New York* (23 August 1993): 45–50 and "Wasted Health Dollars," *Consumer Reports* (July 1992): 435–448.

For a discussion of the current health system and proposals for change, see Michael D. Reagan, *Curing the Crisis: Options for America's Health Care* (Boulder: Westview Press, 1992). For a clear presentation of philosophical issues, see Charles J. Dougherty, *American Health Care: Realities, Rights, and Reforms* (New York: Oxford University Press, 1988).

The discussion of rights in the Introduction is indebted to Joel Feinberg, "The Nature and Value of Rights," *Journal of Value Inquiry* 4 (1970): 243–257.

BIBLIOGRAPHY

The number of books and articles dealing with medical ethics is staggering, and it is growing larger at a rapid rate. The materials listed here are no more than a sample of those currently available. Thus, this bibliography is best thought of as a guide to further reading. The general and special bibliographies listed below—some book-length works—will provide guides for those who are looking for comprehensiveness.

I have tried to select works with substantial philosophical content. Thus, with a few exceptions, I have not listed publications that are primarily medical, biological, sociological, or otherwise scientific. Furthermore, I have not attempted to duplicate the references given in the selections or in the chapter introductions, and for the most part I have restricted this bibliography to works that have appeared in the last five to ten years.

General Works and Anthologies

American Hospital Association. *Values in Conflict: Resolving Issues in Health Care.* 2d ed. Chicago: American Hospital Association, 1994.

American Medical Association Council on Ethical and Judicial Affairs. *Current Opinions of the Judicial Council.* Chicago: AMA, 1991.

———. *1992 Code of Medical Ethics: Annotated Current Opinions of the Council on Ethical and Judicial Affairs of the American Medical Association.* Chicago: AMA, 1992.

———. *Code of Medical Ethics.* Chicago: AMA, 1994.

Annas, George J. *Standard of Care: The Law of American Bioethics.* New York: Oxford University Press, 1993.

Arras, John and Bonnie Steinbach. *Ethical Issues in Modern Medicine.* 4th ed. Palo Alto: Calif.: Mayfield, 1994.

Augenstein, Leroy. *Come, Let Us Play God.* New York: Harper & Row, 1969.

Bandman, Elsie and Bertram Bandman, eds. *Bioethics and Human Rights: A Reader for Health Professionals.* Boston: Little, Brown, 1978.

Beauchamp, Tom and Leroy Walters. *Contemporary Issues in Bioethics.* 4th ed. Belmont, Calif.: Wadsworth, 1994.

Bishop, Laura J. and Mary Carrington Coutts. *Religious Perspectives on Bioethics,* scope note 25. Washington, D.C.: National Reference Center for Bioethics Literature, 1994.

Blank, Robert H. and Andrea L. Bonnicksen, eds. *Emerging Issues in Biomedical Policy: An Annual Review, vol. 2.* New York: Columbia University Press, 1993.

———. *Medicine Unbound: The Human Body and the Limits of Medical Intervention.* New York: Columbia University Press, 1994.

Brock, Dan W. *Life and Death: Philosophical Essays in Biomedical Ethics.* New York: Cambridge University Press, 1993.

Callahan, Daniel. "Ethics Committees and Social Issues: Potentials and Pitfalls." *Cambridge Quarterly of Healthcare Ethics* 1, (1) (Winter 1992): 5–10.

Camenisch, Paul F., ed. *Religious Methods and Resources in Bioethics.* Boston: Kluwer Academic Publishers, 1994.

Chadwick, Ruth and Win Tadd. *Ethics and Nursing Practice: A Case Study Approach.* London: Macmillan, 1992.

Chapman, Carleton B. "The Importance of Being Ethical." *Perspectives in Biology and Medicine* 24 (Spring 1981): 422–439.

Charlesworth, Max. *Bioethics in a Liberal Society.* New York: Cambridge University Press, 1993.

Copp, David and David Zimmerman, eds. *Morality, Reason and Truth: New Essays on the Foundations of Ethics.* Totowa, N.J.: Rowman and Allanheld, 1984.

Council on Ethical and Judicial Affairs. "Gender Discrimination in the Medical Profession." *Women's Health Issues* 4 (1) (1994): 1–11.

Curran, William J. "The Proper and Improper Concerns of Medical Law and Ethics." *New England Journal of Medicine* 259 (4 November 1976): 1057–1058.

Curtin, Leah and M. Josephine Flaherty. *Nursing Ethics: Theories and Pragmatics.* Bowie, Md.: Robert J. Brady, 1982.

Duncan, A. S. et al., eds. *Dictionary of Medical Ethics.* London: Darton, Longman, and Todd, 1975.

Emanuel, Ezekiel J. *The Ends of Human Life: Medical Ethics in a Liberal Polity.* Cambridge: Harvard University Press, 1991.

Engelhardt, H. Tristram. *The Foundations of Bioethics.* New York: Oxford University Press, 1986.

Engelhardt, H. Tristram, Jr. *Bioethics and Secular Humanism: The Search for a Common Morality.* Philadelphia: Trinity Press, 1991.

Engelhardt, H. Tristram, Jr. and Daniel Callahan, eds. *Science, Ethics and Medicine.* Hastings-on-Hudson, N.Y.: Institute of Society, Ethics and the Life Sciences, 1976.

Flack, Harley E. and Edmund D. Pellegrino, eds. *African-American Perspectives on Biomedical Ethics.* Washington, D.C.: Georgetown University Press, 1992.

Fletcher, Joseph. *Morals and Medicine.* Boston: Beacon Press, 1954. A classic book stating the "situation ethics" view of euthanasia, truth telling, contraception, and so on.

Francoeur, Robert T. *Biomedical Ethics: A Guide to Decision Making.* New York: Wiley, 1983.

Fulford, K. W. M., Grant Gillett, and Janet Martin Soskice, eds. *Medicine and Moral Reasoning.* New York: Cambridge University Press, 1994.

Giles, James E. *Medical Ethics: A Patient-Centered Approach.* Cambridge: Schenkman, 1983.

Glover, Jonathan. *Causing Death and Saving Lives.* New York: Penguin Books, 1977.

Hunt, Geoffrey, ed. *Ethical Issues in Nursing.* New York: Routledge, 1994.

Jonsen, Albert R. *The New Medicine & The Old Ethics.* Cambridge, Mass.: Harvard University Press, 1990.

Levine, Carol, ed. *Taking Sides: Clashing Views on Controversial Bioethical Issues,* 5th ed. Guilford, Conn.: Dushkin Publishing Group, 1993.

Lockwood, Michael, ed. *Moral Dilemmas in Modern Medicine.* Oxford: Oxford University Press, 1985.

Mabie, Margot J. *Bioethics and the New Medical Technology.* New York: Atheneum, 1993.

Macklin, Ruth. "Women's Health: An Ethical Perspective." *Journal of Law, Medicine & Ethics* 21 (1) (Spring 1993): 23–29.

Mappes, Thomas A. and Jane S. Zembaty, eds. *Biomedical Ethics.* 3d ed. New York: McGraw-Hill, 1991.

O'Neill, Terry, ed. *Biomedical Ethics: Opposing Viewpoints.* San Diego, Calif.: Greenhaven Press, 1994.

Pellegrino, Edmund D. and David C. Thomasma. *The Virtues in Medical Practice.* New York: Oxford University Press, 1993.

Pellegrino, Edmund D., Robert M. Veatch, and John P. Langan, eds. *Ethics, Trust, and the Professions: Philosophical and Cultural Aspects.* Washington, D.C.: Georgetown University Press, 1991.

Post, Stephen G. *Inquiries in Bioethics.* Washington, D.C.: Georgetown University Press, 1993.

President's Commission for the Study of Ethical Problems in Medicine and Biomedical and Behavioral Research. *Summing Up.* Washington, D.C.: President's Commission, 1983.

Rachels, James. "Can Ethics Provide Answers?" *Hastings Center Report* 10 (1980): 32–40.

———. *The Elements of Moral Philosophy.* Philadelphia: Temple University Press, 1986.

Ramsey, Paul. *The Patient as Person.* New Haven, Conn.: Yale University Press, 1970. A classic work by a Christian theologian that presents influential views on experimentation, transplantation, allocation of resources, and so on.

———. *Ethics at the Edges of Life: Medical and Legal Intersections.* New Haven, Conn.: Yale University Press, 1978.

Reich, W. T., ed. *Encyclopedia of Bioethics.* New York: Macmillan, 1978. A wide-ranging collection of articles by many scholars. Good for a quick survey of major issues.

Scales-Trent, Judy. "Women of Color and Health: Issues of Gender, Community, and Power." *Stanford Law Review* 43 (6) (1993): 1357–1368.

Shannon, Thomas A., ed. *Twelve Problems in Health Care Ethics.* Lewiston, N.Y.: Edwin Mellen Press, 1985.

———. *Bioethics: Basic Writings on the Key Ethical Questions That Surround the Major, Modern Biological Possibilities and Problems.* 4th ed. Mahwah, N.J.: Paulist Press, 1993.

Shannon, Thomas A. and Jo Ann Manfra, eds. *Bioethics.* New York: Paulist Press, 1981.

———. *Law and Bioethics.* Ramsey, N.J.: Paulist Press, 1982.

Shelp, Earl E., ed. *Virtue and Medicine: Explorations in the Character of Medicine.* Boston: D. Reidel, 1985.

Sherwin, Susan. *No Longer Patient: Feminist Ethics & Health Care.* Philadelphia: Temple University Press, 1992.

U.S. Congress, Office of Technology Assessment. *Biomedical Ethics in U.S. Public Policy—Background Paper,* OTA-BP-BBS-105. Washington, D.C.: U.S. Government Printing Office, June 1993.

Vaux, Kenneth. *Biomedical Ethics: Morality for the New Medicine.* New York: Harper & Row, 1974.

Veatch, Robert M. *Death, Dying, and the Biological Revolution.* New Haven, Conn.: Yale University Press, 1976. Deals with dying patients, euthanasia, birth defects, defining death, and transplant organs. Contains much information.

———. *Case Studies in Medical Ethics.* Cambridge, Mass.: Harvard University Press, 1977.

———. *A Theory of Medical Ethics.* New York: Basic Books, 1981.

Williams, Bernard. *Ethics and the Limits of Philosophy.* Cambridge, Mass.: Harvard University Press, 1985.

Williams, Granville. *The Sanctity of Life and the Criminal Law.* New York: Knopf, 1957.

Zaner, Richard M. *Troubled Voices: Stories of Ethics and Illness.* Cleveland, Ohio: Pilgrim Press, 1993.

Moral Principles, Ethical Theories, and Medical Decisions: An Introduction

A. General Works on Ethics

Beauchamp, Tom L. and Terry Pinkard, eds. *Ethics and Public Policy: An Introduction to Ethics.* Englewood Cliffs, N.J.: Prentice-Hall, 1983.

Brandt, Richard B. *Ethical Theory.* Englewood Cliffs, N.J.: Prentice-Hall, 1959.

Ewing, A. C. *Ethics.* New York: Free Press, 1965.

Feinberg, Joel. *Doing and Deserving: Essays in the Theory of Responsibility.* Princeton, N.J.: Princeton University Press, 1970.

———. *Social Philosophy.* Englewood Cliffs, N.J.: Prentice-Hall, 1973.

———. *Rights, Justice, and the Bounds of Liberty.* Princeton, N.J.: Princeton University Press, 1980.

Frankena, William K. *Ethics.* 2d ed. Englewood Cliffs, N.J.: Prentice-Hall, 1973.

Gert, Bernard. *The Moral Rules.* New York: Harper & Row, 1970.

Ladd, John. *Ethical Relativism.* Belmont, Calif.: Wadsworth, 1973.

MacIntyre, Alasdair. *After Virtue.* Notre Dame, Ind.: University of Notre Dame Press, 1981.

Rachels, James. *Understanding Moral Philosophy.* Encino, Calif.: Dickenson, 1976. A short, readable introduction.

Taylor, Paul W., ed. *The Moral Judgment: Readings in Contemporary Meta-Ethics.* Englewood Cliffs, N.J.: Prentice-Hall, 1963.

———, **ed.** *Problems of Moral Philosophy.* Belmont, Calif.: Dickenson, 1971. Clear and sophisticated introduction.

Warnock, Geoffrey James. *Contemporary Moral Philosophy.* New York: St. Martin's Press, 1967.

Wellman, Carl. *Morals and Ethics.* New York: Scott, Foresman, 1975.

White, Alan R. *Rights.* Oxford: Clarendon Press, 1984.

Williams, Bernard. *Morality: An Introduction to Ethics.* New York: Harper & Row, 1972.

B. Utilitarianism

Bayles, Michael D., ed. *Contemporary Utilitarianism.* New York: Doubleday, 1968.

Bentham, Jeremy. *A Fragment on Government and an Introduction to the Principles of Morals and Legislation.* Edited by Wilfried Harrison. Oxford: Blackwell, 1967.

Hodgson, D. H. *Consequences of Utilitarianism: A Study in Normative Ethics and Legal Theory.* Oxford: Clarendon Press, 1967.

Lyons, David. *Forms and Limits of Utilitarianism.* New York: Oxford University Press, 1965.

———. *In the Interest of the Governed: A Study in Bentham's Philosophy of Utility and Law.* Oxford: Oxford University Press, 1973.

Mill, John Stuart. *Utilitarianism: With Critical Essays.* Edited by Samuel Gorovitz. Indianapolis: Bobbs-Merrill, 1971.

Quinton, A. M. *Utilitarian Ethics.* New York: St. Martin's Press, 1973.

Regan, Donald H. *Utilitarianism and Co-operation.* New York: Oxford University Press, 1980.

Scheffler, Samuel, ed. *Consequentialism and Its Critics.* Oxford: Oxford University Press, 1988.

Sen, Amartya and Bernard Williams, eds. *Utilitarianism and Beyond.* New York: Cambridge University Press, 1982.

Sheng, C. L. *A New Approach to Utilitarianism: A Unified Utilitarian Theory and Its Application to Distributive Justice.* Boston: Kluwer, 1991.

Smart, J. J. C. and Bernard Williams. *Utilitarianism: For and Against.* New York: Cambridge University Press, 1973.

C. Kant

Beck, L. W. *Studies in the Philosophy of Kant.* Indianapolis: Bobbs-Merrill, 1965.

Kant, Immanuel. *Lectures on Ethics.* New York: Harper & Row, 1963.

————. *Foundations of the Metaphysics of Morals: Text and Critical Essays.* Edited by Robert P. Wolff. New York: Bobbs-Merrill, 1969.

Paton, H. J. *The Categorical Imperative: A Study of Kant's Moral Philosophy.* New York: Harper & Row, 1967.

Singer, Marcus G. *Generalization in Ethics: An Essay in the Logic of Ethics with the Rudiments of a System of Moral Philosophy.* New York: Atheneum, 1971.

Wolff, R. P., ed. *Kant: A Collection of Critical Essays.* Garden City, N.Y.: Doubleday, 1967.

D. Ross

Ross, W. D. *The Right and the Good.* Oxford: Clarendon Press, 1930. (For evaluations of Ross, see relevant sections of Frankena, Brandt, Ewing, Rachels, and Taylor listed in (**A**).)

————. *Foundations of Ethics.* Oxford: Oxford University Press, 1963. A reissue of the 1939 edition.

E. Rawls

Barry, Brian. *The Liberal Theory of Justice.* New York: Oxford University Press, 1974. An exposition and criticism of Rawls.

Chen, Marshall. "The Social Contract Explained and Defended." *New York Book Review* (16 July 1972): 1.

Daniels, Norman, ed. *Reading Rawls.* New York: Basic Books, 1976. This volume has a helpful introduction and contains some of the more important critical articles.

F. Aquinas and Natural Law

Copleston, F. C. *Aquinas.* Baltimore: Penguin Books, 1965.

Gilson, Etienne. *The Philosophy of St. Thomas Aquinas.* 3d ed. Translated by Edward Bullough. St. Louis: Herder, 1937.

Kelly, Gerald. *Medico-Moral Problems.* St. Louis: Catholic Hospital Association, 1958.

McFadden, Charles J. *Medical Ethics.* 6th ed. Philadelphia: F. A. Davis, 1967.

O'Connor, D. J. *Aquinas and Natural Law.* New York: St. Martin's Press, 1969.

Pegis, Anton, ed. *Basic Writings of St. Thomas Aquinas.* New York: Random House, 1945.

Tuck, Richard. *Natural Rights Theories: Their Origin and Development.* New York: Cambridge University Press, 1980.

G. Feminist Ethics

Baier, Annette. "What Do Women Want in a Moral Theory?" *Nous* 19 (1985): 53–56.

Blustein, Jeffrey. *Care and Commitment: Taking the Personal Point of View.* New York: Oxford University Press, 1991.

Carse, Alisa. "The Voice of Care: Implications for Bioethical Education." *Journal of Medicine and Philosophy* 16 (1991): 5–28.

Gilligan, Carol. *In a Different Voice.* Cambridge, Mass.: Harvard University Press, 1982.

Holmes, Helen Bequaert and Laura M. Purdy, eds. *Feminist Perspectives in Medical Ethics.* Bloomington, Ind.: Indiana University Press, 1992.

Journal of Clinical Ethics 3 (1992). Special issue: See Hilde L. Nelson, "Against Caring"; Nel Noddings, "In Defense of Caring"; and Toni M. Vezeau, "Caring: From Philosophical Concerns to Practice."

Noddings, Nel. *Caring: A Feminine Approach to Ethics and Moral Education.* Berkeley: University of California Press, 1984.

Sherwin, Susan. *No Longer Patient: Feminist Ethics and Health Care.* Philadelphia: Temple University Press, 1992.

Bibliographies

The Aged and Allocation of Health Care Resources (1990); *A Right to Health Care* (1992). Bibliographies available from the National Reference Center for Bioethics Literature. Kennedy Institute of Ethics, Georgetown University. Washington, D.C., 20057. Beginning 1991, all except revised bibliographies are published in the *Kennedy Institute of Ethics Journal.*

American Nurses' Association. *Ethics References for Nurses.* Kansas City, Mo.: American Nurses' Association, 1982.

American Nurses' Association, Committee on Ethics. *Ethics in Nursing: References and Resources.* Kansas City, Mo.: American Nurses' Association, 1979.

Arizona State University Center for the Study of Law, Science and Technology. "The Human Genome Project: Bibliography of Ethical, Social, Legal, and Scientific Aspects." *Jurimetrics Journal* 32 (1992): 223–311.

Basic Resources in Bioethics (1991); *Teaching Ethics in the Health Care Setting, Part I: Survey of the Literature* (1991); *Teaching Ethics in the Health Care Setting, Part II: Sample Syllabus* (1991). Bibliographies available from the National Reference Center for Bioethics Literature, Kennedy Institute of Ethics, Georgetown University, Washington, D.C. 20057. Published in the *Kennedy Institute of Ethics Journal,* beginning in 1991.

Goldstein, Doris Mueller. *Bioethics: A Guide to Information Sources.* Detroit: Gale Research Company, 1982.

Leatt, Peggy et al. *Perspectives on Physician Involvement in Resource Allocation and Utilization Management: An Annotated Bibliography* Toronto: University of Toronto, 1991.

Lineback, Richard H., ed. *Philosopher's Index.* Vols. 1–27. Bowling Green, Ohio: Philosophy Documentation Center, Bowling Green State University.

Musgrove, Michèle, comp. *Artificial Insemination Bibliography.* Ottawa: Royal Commission on New Reproductive Technologies, 1992.

Walter, LeRoy and Tamar Joy Kahn, eds. *Bibliography of Bioethics,* vol. 20. Washington, D.C.: Kennedy Institute of Ethics, 1994.

Computer Databases

AIDSLINE, National Library of Medicine, indexes over 3,000 journals in the clinical, research, epidemiology, and social policy literature of the disease.

BIOETHICSLINE, National Library of Medicine, covers relevant literature in medicine law, religion, philosophy, and the social sciences.

ETHICS INDEX, American Theological Library Association, a CD-ROM resource of information on ethical issues.

FACTS ON FILE contains the full text of the weekly printed reference publication of the same name. Topics include news concerning abortion (specifically) and medicine in general.

MEDLINE, National Library of Medicine, contains summaries of articles in clinical and research medicine and related areas. Includes articles on ethics, economics, and society as related to medicine, and over 250,000 records are added each year.

PHILOSOPHER'S INDEX provides indexes and abstracts from journals and books in philosophy and related fields. The journals are indexed from 1940, and the file contains more than 140,000 items.

Part I: Termination

Chapter 1: Abortion

Altman, Andrew. "Abortion and the Indigent." *Journal of Social Philosophy* 11 (1980): 5–9. Favors the Supreme Court decision that states need not fund abortions.

Annas, George J. "The Supreme Court, Liberty, and Abortion." *NEJM* 327 (9) (27 August 1992): 651–654.

Brandt, R. B. "The Morality of Abortion." *Monist* 56 (1972): 503–526.

Brock, Dan W. "Taking Human Life." *Ethics* 95 (1985): 851–865.

Brody, Baruch. "Thomson on Abortion." *Philosophy and Public Affairs* 1 (1972): 335–340.

———. *Abortion and the Sanctity of Human Life.* Cambridge, Mass.: MIT Press, 1975. Brody's several papers are embodied here.

Callahan, Daniel. *Abortion: Law, Choice and Morality.* New York: Macmillan, 1970.

———. "The Abortion Debate: Can This Chronic Public Illness Be Cured?" *Clinical Obstetrics and Gynecology* 35(4) (December 1992): 783–791.

Callahan, Sidney. "Abortion and the Sexual Agenda." *Commonweal* 113(8) (25 April 1986): 232–238.

Callahan, Sidney and Daniel Callahan, eds. *Abortion: Understanding Differences.* New York: Plenum Press, 1984.

Camenisch, Paul F. "Abortion: For the Fetus's Own Sake?" *Hastings Center Report* 6 (1976): 38–41.

———. "Abortion Analogies and the Emergence of Value." *Journal of Religious Ethics* 4 (1976): 131–158.

Chervenak, Frank A. et al. "When Is Termination of Pregnancy During the Third Trimester Morally Justifiable?" *New England Journal of Medicine* 310 (23 February 1984): 501–504.

Cohen, Marshall et al., eds. *The Rights and Wrongs of Abortion.* Princeton, N.J.: Princeton University Press, 1974.

Connery, John R. *Abortion: The Development of the Roman Catholic Perspective.* Chicago: Loyola University Press, 1977.

Council on Ethical and Judicial Affairs, American Medical Association. "Mandatory Parental Consent to Abortion." *JAMA* 269(1) (6 January 1993): 82–86.

Cudd, Ann E. "Sensationalized Philosophy: A Reply to Marquis's 'Why Abortion Is Immoral.'" *Journal of Philosophy* 87 (1990): 262–264.

Daniels, Charles B. "Abortion and Potential." *Dialogue* 18 (June 1979): 220–223.

Davis, Michael. "Fetuses, Famous Violinists, and the Right to Continued Aid." *Philosophical Quarterly* 33 (1983): 259–278.

Davis, Nancy. "Abortion and Self-Defense." *Philosophy & Public Affairs* 13 (1984): 175–207.

Devine, Philip E. *The Ethics of Homicide.* Ithaca, N.Y.: Cornell University Press, 1978.

Dickens, Bernard M. "Abortion and Distortion of Justice in the Law." *Law, Medicine and Health Care* 17 (1989): 395–406.

Dore, Clement. "Abortion, Some Slippery Slope Arguments and Identity over Time." *Philosophical Studies* 55 (1989): 279–291.

Drucker, Dan. *Abortion Decisions of the Supreme Court, 1973 through 1989: A Comprehensive Review with Historical Commentary.* Jefferson, N.C.: McFarland, 1990.

Dworkin, Ronald. *Life's Dominion: An Argument about Abortion, Euthanasia, and Individual Freedom.* New York: Alfred A. Knopf, 1993.

Engelhardt, H. Tristram. "The Ontology of Abortion." *Ethics* 84 (April 1974): 217–234.

English, Jane. "Abortion and the Concept of a Person." *Canadian Journal of Philosophy* 5 (October 1975): 233–243.

Feinberg, Joel. "Is There a Right to Be Born?" In **James Rachels, ed.** *Understanding Moral Philosophy.* Belmont, Calif.: Dickenson, 1976.

———. "Abortion." In **Tom Regan, ed.** *Matters of Life and Death.* New York: Random House, 1980, pp. 183–217.

———, **ed.** *The Problem of Abortion.* 2d ed. Belmont, Calif.: Wadsworth, 1984.

Finnis, John, Judith Thomson, Michael Tooley, and Roger Wertheimer. *The Rights and Wrongs of Abortion.* Princeton, N.J.: Princeton University Press, 1974. A collection of influential articles.

Fleming, Lorette. "The Moral Status of the Fetus: A Reappraisal." *Bioethics* 1 (January 1987): 15–34.

Fletcher, Joseph. "Four Indicators of Humanhood—the Enquiry Matures." *Hastings Center Report* 4 (December 1974): 4–7.

Foot, Phillippa. "The Problem of Abortion and the Doctrine of Double Effect." *Oxford Review* 5 (1967): 5–15.

Gertler, Gary B. "Brain Birth: A Proposal for Defining When a Fetus Is Entitled to Human Life Status." *Southern California Law Review* 59(5) (July 1986): 1061–1078.

Goldberg, Susan. "Medical Choices During Pregnancy: Whose Decision Is It, Anyway?" *Rutgers Law Review* 41 (1989): 591–623.

Goldenring, John. "The Brain-Life Theory: Towards a Consistent Biological Definition of Humaneness." *Journal of Medical Ethics* 11 (December 1985): 194–204.

Goldman, Alan H. "Abortion and the Right to Life." *Personalist* 60 (October 1979): 402–406.

Gordon, Robert M. "The Abortion Issue." In **Eugene Freeman, ed.** *The Abdication of Philosophy: Essays in Honor of Paul A. Schilpp.* Chicago: Open Court, 1974, pp. 267–277.

Granfield, David. *The Abortion Decision.* New York: Doubleday, 1971. A Catholic point of view.

Grobstein, Clifford. "The Early Development of Human Embryos." *Journal of Medicine and Philosophy* 10 (August 1985): 213–236.

Hare, R. M. "Abortion and the Golden Rule." *Philosophy and Public Affairs* 4 (1975): 201–222.

Harris, C. E. "Aborting Abnormal Fetuses: The Parental Perspective." *Journal of Applied Philosophy* 8(1) (1991): 57–68.

Hursthouse, Rosalind. "Virtue Theory and Abortion." *Philosophy & Public Affairs* 20 (1991): 223–246.

Jordan, James M. "Incubating for the State: The Precarious Autonomy of Persistently Vegetative and Brain-Dead Pregnant Women." *Georgia Law Review* 22 (1988): 1103–1165.

King, Patricia A. "The Juridical Status of the Fetus: A Proposal for Legal Protection of the Unborn." *Michigan Law Review* 77 (1979): 1647–1687.

Kluge, Eike-Henner W. "When Cesarean Section Operations Imposed by a Court Are Justified." *Journal of Medical Ethics* 14 (1988): 206–211.

Loewy, Arnold H. "Why *Roe* v. *Wade* Should Be Overruled." *North Carolina Law Review* 67 (1989): 939–948.

Macklin, Ruth. "Antiprogestin Drugs: Ethical Issues." *Law, Medicine and Health Care* (1992): 215–219.

Mahowald, Mary B. "Is There Life After *Roe* v. *Wade?*" *Hastings Center Report* 19 (1989): 22–29.

Marquis, Donald. "Why Abortion Is Immoral." *Journal of Philosophy* 86 (1989): 183–202.

Mathieu, Deborah. *Preventing Prenatal Harm: Should the State Intervene?* Boston: Kluwer Academic, 1991.

Noonan, John T. *A Private Choice: Abortion in America in the Seventies.* New York: Free Press, 1979.

Parness, Jeffrey. "Crimes Against the Unborn: Protecting and Respecting the Potentiality of Human Life." *Harvard Journal on Legislation* 22(1) (Winter 1985): 97–172.

Petchesky, Rosalind Pollack. *Abortion and Woman's Choice: The State, Sexuality, and Reproductive Freedom.* New York: Longman, 1984.

Regan, Tom, ed. *Matters of Life and Death.* 3d ed. New York: Random House, 1992.

Rhoden, Nancy K. "A Compromise on Abortion." *Hastings Center Report* 19 (1989): 32–37.

Rorty, Amelie O. "Persons, Policies, and Bodies." *International Philosophical Quarterly* 13 (March 1973): 63–80.

Ryan, Kenneth J. "Abortion or Motherhood, Suicide and Madness." *American Journal of Obstetrics and Gynecology* 166 (1992): 1029–1036.

Sher, George. "Hare, Abortion and the Golden Rule." *Philosophy and Public Affairs* 6 (Winter 1977): 185–190.

Solomon, Renee I. "Future Fear: Prenatal Duties Imposed by Private Parties." *American Journal of Law and Medicine* 17 (1991): 411–434.

Steinbock, Bonnie. *Life before Birth: The Moral and Legal Status of Embryos and Fetuses.* New York: Oxford University Press, 1992.

Sumner, L. W. *Abortion and Moral Theory.* Princeton, N.J.: Princeton University Press, 1981.

Talmage, R. S. "Utilitarianism and the Morality of Killing." *Philosophy* 47 (1972): 55–63.

Tauer, Carol. "Personhood and Human Embryos and Fetuses." *Journal of Medicine and Philosophy* 10 (August 1985): 253–266.

Thomson, Judith Jarvis. "Rights and Deaths." *Philosophy and Public Affairs* 2 (1973): 146–159.

Tooley, Michael. *Abortion and Infanticide.* New York: Oxford University Press, 1983.

Tribe, Laurence H. *Abortion: The Clash of Absolutes.* New York: Norton, 1990.

Warren, Mary Anne. "Do Potential People Have Moral Rights?" *Canadian Journal of Philosophy* 7 (June 1977): 275–289.

Wasserstrom, Richard. "The Status of the Fetus." *Hastings Center Report* 5 (June 1975): 18–22.

Wertheimer, Roger. "Understanding the Abortion Argument." *Philosophy and Public Affairs* 1 (1971): 67–95. A clear statement of issues.

Wing, Kenneth R. "Speech, Privacy, and the Power of the Purse:

Lessons from the Abortion 'Gag Rule' Case." *Journal of Health Politics, Policy and Law* 17 (1992): 163–175.

Chapter 2: Treating or Terminating: The Problem of Impaired Infants

Abrams, Natalie. "Defective Newborns: A Framework for a Case Analysis." *Westminister Institute Review* 2 (Winter 1983): 3–7.

American Academy of Pediatrics, ed. "Selected Readings on Infant Care Review Committees and Bioethical Issues in the Care of Seriously Ill and Disabled Newborns." May 1984.

Anspach, Renée R. *Deciding Who Lives: Fateful Choices in the Intensive-Care Nursery.* Berkeley and Los Angeles: University of California Press, 1993.

Caplan, Arthur L., Robert H. Blank, and Janna C. Merrick, eds. *Compelled Compassion: Government Intervention in the Treatment of Critically Ill Newborns.* Totowa, N.J.: Humana Press, 1992.

Drane, James F. "The Defective Child: Ethical Guidelines for Painful Dilemmas." *Journal of Obstetric Gynecologic and Neo-Natal Nursing* 13 (January/February 1984): 42–48.

Duff, R. S. and A. G. M. Campbell. "Moral and Ethical Dilemmas in the Special Care Nursery." *New England Journal of Medicine* 289 (1973): 890–894.

Engelhardt, H. T. "Euthanasia and Children: The Inquiry of Continued Existence." *Journal of Pediatrics* 83 (1973): 170–171.

Fleischman, Alan R. "Parental Responsibility and the Infant Bioethics Committee." *Hastings Center Report* 20 (March/April 1990): 31–32.

Fletcher, John C. "Attitudes toward Defective Newborns." *Hastings Center Studies* 2 (1974): 21–32.

———. "Abortion, Euthanasia, and Care of Defective Newborns." *New England Journal of Medicine* 292 (1975): 75–78.

———. "Choices for Life or Death in the Case of Defective Newborns." *Social Responsibility: Journalism, Law, Medicine.* Program on Society and the Professions: Studies in Applied Ethics. Lexington, Va.: Washington and Lee University, 1975, pp. 62–78.

Gostin, Larry. "A Moment in Human Development: Legal Protection, Ethical Standards and Social Policy on the Selective Non-Treatment of Handicapped Neonates." *American Journal of Law & Medicine* 11(1) (1985): 31–78.

Hastings Center Research Project on the Care of Imperiled Newborns. "Imperiled Newborns: A Report." *Hastings Center Report* 17 (December 1987): 5–32.

Jonsen, A. R. et al. "Critical Issues in Newborn Intensive Care: A Conference Report and Policy Proposal." *Pediatrics* 55 (1975): 756–768.

——— and Michael J. Garland, eds. *Ethics of Newborn Intensive Care.* Berkeley: University of California, Institute of Governmental Studies, 1976.

King, Nancy M. P. "Transparency in Neonatal Intensive Care." *Hastings Center Report* 22 (May/June 1992): 18–25.

Kohl, Marvin, ed. *Infanticide and the Value of Life.* Buffalo, N.Y.: Prometheus Books, 1978. See in particular papers by Richard Brandt and R. S. Duff.

Kuhse, Helga and Peter Singer. *Should the Baby Live? The Problem of Handicapped Newborns.* New York: Oxford University Press, 1985.

Lund, Nelson. "Infanticide, Physicians, and the Law: The 'Baby Doe' Amendments to the Child Abuse Prevention and Treatment Act." *American Journal of Law and Medicine* 11(1) (1985): 1–30.

Lyon, Jeff. *Playing God in the Nursery.* New York: W. W. Norton, 1985.

Magnet, Joseph E. and Eike-Henner W. Kluge. *Withholding Treatment from Defective Newborn Children.* Cowansville, Quebec: Brown Legal Publications, 1985.

Murray, Thomas H. and Arthur L. Caplan, eds. *Which Babies Shall Live? Humanistic Dimensions of the Care of Imperiled Newborns.* Clifton, N.J.: Humana Press, 1985.

Newman, Stephan A. "Baby Doe, Congress and the States: Challenging the Federal Treatment Standard for Impaired Infants." *American Journal of Law and Medicine* 15 (1989): 1–60.

Rhoden, Nancy K. "The New Neonatal Dilemma: Live Births from Late Abortions." *Georgetown Law Journal* 72 (June 1984): 1451–1509.

———. "Treatment Dilemmas for Imperiled Newborns: Why Quality of Life Counts." *Southern California Law Review* 58(6) (September 1985): 1283–1347.

——— **and John D. Arras.** "Withholding Treatment from Baby Doe: From Discrimination to Child Abuse." *Milbank Memorial Fund Quarterly/Health and Society* 63(1) (1985).

Shelp, Earl E. *Born to Die? Deciding the Fate of Critically Ill Newborns.* New York: Free Press, 1986.

Walters, James W. "Proximate Personhood as a Standard for Making Difficult Treatment Decisions: Imperiled Newborns as a Case Study." *Bioethics* 6(1) (1992): 12–22.

Weir, Robert. *Selective Nontreatment of Handicapped Newborns.* New York: Oxford University Press, 1984.

Chapter 3: Euthanasia

American Academy of Pediatrics. "Guidelines on Forgoing Life-Sustaining Medical Treatment." *Pediatrics* 93(3) (1994): 532–536.

American Geriatrics Society. Public Policy Committee. "Voluntary Active Euthanasia." *Journal of the American Geriatrics Society* 39 (August 1991).

American Medical Association. Council on Ethical and Judicial Affairs. "Decisions Near the End of Life." *JAMA* 267 (1992): 2229–2233.

American Medical Association, Council on Ethical and Judicial Affairs. "Guidelines for the Appropriate Use of Do-Not-Resuscitate Orders." *JAMA* 265(14) (10 April 1991): 1868–1871.

Annas, George J. "The Health Care Proxy and the Living Will." *New England Journal of Medicine* 324 (1991): 1210–1213.

Arras, John D. "Beyond *Cruzan:* Individual Rights, Family Autonomy and the Persistent Vegetative State." *Journal of the American Geriatric Society* 39(10) (October 1991): 1018–1024.

Battin, Margaret Pabst. "Voluntary Euthanasia and the Risks of Abuse: Can We Learn Anything from the Netherlands?" *Law, Medicine & Health Care* 20 (Spring/Summer, 1992): 135.

———. *The Least Worst Death: Essays in Bioethics on the End of Life.* New York: Oxford University Press, 1994.

Beauchamp, Tom L. "A Reply to Rachels on Active and Passive Euthanasia." In **Wade L. Robinson and Michael S. Pritchard, eds.** *Medical Responsibility.* Clifton, N.J.: Humana Press, 1979, pp. 182–195. See also Rachels.

———. "The Moral Justification for Withholding Heroic Procedures." In **Noral K. Bell, ed.** *Who Decides? Conflicts of Rights in Health Care.* Clifton, N.J.: Humana Press, 1982.

———. "Suicide." In **Tom Regan, ed.** *Matters of Life and Death.* 3d ed. New York: Random House, 1992.

——— **and S. Perlin, eds.** *Ethical Issues in Death and Dying.* Englewood Cliffs, N.J.: Prentice-Hall, 1978.

Beresford, Larry. "Hospice and the End of Life Debate." *California Hospice Report* 9(2) (Summer 1991): 1–10.

Bernat, James L., Bernard Gert, and R. Peter Mogielnicki. "Patient Refusal of Hydration and Nutrition: An Alternative to Physician-Assisted Suicide or Voluntary Active Euthanasia." *Archives of Internal Medicine* 153(24) (1993): 2723–2728.

Brock, Dan. "Trumping Advance Directives." *Hastings Center Report* 21 (September/October 1991).

Brody, Howard. "Assisted Death: A Compassionate Response to a Medical Failure." *New England Journal of Medicine* 327(19) (5 November 1992): 1384–1388.

———. "Causing, Intending, and Assisting Death." *Journal of Clinical Ethics* 4(2) (Summer 1993): 112–117.

Callahan, Daniel. "Medical Futility, Medical Necessity: The Problem-Without-a-Name." *Hastings Center Report* 21 (July/August 1991): 30–35.

———. *The Troubled Dream of Life: Living with Mortality.* New York: Simon and Schuster, 1993.

Campbell, Courtney S. et al. "Cruzan: Clear and Convincing?" *Hastings Center Report* 20 (September/October 1990): 5–11. Introduction and six responses to the decision.

———. "Religious Ethics and Active Euthanasia in a Pluralistic Society." *Kennedy Institute of Ethics Journal* 2(3) (1992): 253–277.

Cantor, Norman L. *Advance Directives and the Pursuit of Death with Dignity.* Bloomington: Indiana University Press, 1993.

Capron, Alexander M., guest ed. "Medical Decision-Making and the 'Right to Die' after *Cruzan.*" *Law, Medicine & Health Care* 19 (1–2) (Spring/Summer 1991): 5–104.

Cohen, Cynthia B. and Peter J. Cohen. "Do-Not-Resuscitate Orders in the Operating Room." *NEJM* 325(26) (26 December 1991): 1879–1882.

Colen, B. D. *The Essential Guide to a Living Will: How to Protect Your Right to Refuse Medical Treatment.* New York: Prentice-Hall, 1991.

Eisendrath, Stuart and Albert R. Jonsen. "The Living Will." *Journal of the American Medical Association* 249 (15 April 1983): 2054–2058.

Emanuel, Ezekiel J. and Linda L. Emanuel. "Proxy Decision Making for Incompetent Patients: An Ethical and Empirical Analysis." *JAMA* 267 (1992): 2067–2071.

Evans, Andrew L. and Baruch A. Brody. "The Do-Not-Resuscitate Order in Teaching Hospitals." *Journal of the American Medical Association* 253 (19 April 1985): 2236–2239.

Feinberg, Joel. "Voluntary Euthanasia and the Inalienable Right to Life." *Philosophy and Public Affairs* 7 (Winter 1978): 93–123.

Glick, Henry R. *The Right to Die: Policy Innovation and Its Consequences.* New York: Columbia University Press, 1992.

Gostin, Lawrence O. "Drawing a Line between Killing and Letting Die: The Law, and Law Reform, on Medically Assisted Dying." *Journal of Law, Medicine & Ethics* 21(1) (Spring 1993): 94–101.

Hare, R. M. "Euthanasia: A Christian View." *Proceedings of the Center for Philosophic Exchange* 2 (1975): 43–52.

Hill, T. Patrick. "Freedom from Pain: A Matter of Rights:" *Cancer Investigation* 12(4) (1994): 438–443.

Jecker, Nancy S. "Giving Death a Hand: When the Dying and the Doctor Stand in a Special Relationship." *Journal of American Geriatric Society* 39(8) (August 1991): 831–835.

———. "Physician-Assisted Death in the Netherlands and the United States: Ethical and Cultural Aspects of Health Policy Development." *Journal of the American Geriatrics Society* 42(6) (1994): 672–687.

———. **ed.** *Aging & Ethics: Philosophical Problems in Gerontology.* Clifton, N.J.: Humana Press, 1991.

Kamisar, Yale. "Some Non-Religious Views against Proposed 'Mercy-Killing' Legislation." *Minnesota Law Review* 42 (1958): 969–1042.

Kelly, Gerald. "The Duty of Using Artificial Means of Preserving Life." *Theological Studies* 11 (1950): 203–220.

Lachs, John. "When Abstract Moralizing Runs Amok." *Journal of Clinical Ethics* 5(1) (1994): 10–12.

Menzel, Paul T. "Are Killing and Letting Die Morally Different in Medical Contexts?" *Journal of Medicine and Philosophy* 4 (September 1979): 269–293.

Miles, Steven H., Peter A. Singer, and Mark Siegler. "Conflicts Between Patients' Wishes to Forgo Treatment and the Policies of Health Care Facilities." *New England Journal of Medicine* 321 (1989): 48–50.

Misbin, Robert I. "Physicians' Aid in Dying." *NEJM* 325(18) (31 October 1991): 1307–1311.

New York State Task Force on Life and the Law. *When Death Is Sought: Assisted Suicide and Euthanasia in the Medical Context.* New York: New York State Task Force on Life and the Law, 1994.

O'Connell, Laurence J., Ronald E. Cranford, T. Patrick Hill, and Roberta Springer Loewy, commentators. "The United States Bishops' Committee Statement on Nutrition and Hydration." *Bioethics* 2(3) (Summer 1993): 341–352.

Orentlicher, David. "The Illusion of Patient Choice in End-of-Life Decisions." *JAMA* 267 (1992): 2101–2104.

President's Commission for the Study of Ethical Problems in Medicine and Biomedical and Behavioral Research. *Deciding to Forego Life Sustaining Treatment.* Washington, D.C.: President's Commission, 1983.

Pugliese, Julia. "Don't Ask—Don't Tell: The Secret Practice of Physician-Assisted Suicide." *Hastings Law Journal* 44(6) (1993): 1291–1330.

Quill, Timothy E. *Death and Dignity: Making Choices and Taking Charge.* New York: W. W. Norton, 1993.

———, **Christine K. Cassel, and Diane E. Meier.** "Death and Dignity: A Case of Individualized Decision Making." *NEJM* 324(10) (7 March 1991): 691–694.

———. "Care of the Hopelessly Ill: Proposed Clinical Criteria for Physician-Assisted Suicide." *New England Journal of Medicine* 327(19) (5 November 1992): 1380–1384.

Rachels, James. "Euthanasia, Killing, and Letting Die." In **Wade L. Robinson and Michael S. Pritchard, eds.** *Medical Responsibility.* Clifton, N.J.: Humana Press, 1979, pp. 153–169. See also Beauchamp.

———. "Killing and Starving to Death." *Philosophy* 54 (1979): 159–171.

———. *The End of Life: Euthanasia and Morality.* New York: Oxford University Press, 1986.

Ramsey, Paul. "The Two-Step Fantastic: The Continuing Case of Brother Fox." *Theological Studies* 42 (March 1981): 122–134.

Reichenbach, Bruce R. "Euthanasia and the Active-Passive Distinction." *Bioethics* 1 (January 1987): 51–73.

Robertson, John A. "Cruzan and the Constitutional Status of Non-treatment Decisions for Incompetent Patients." *Georgia Law Review* 25 (1991): 1139–1202.

———. "Second Thoughts on Living Wills." *Hastings Center Report* 21 (November/December 1991): 6–9.

Singer, Peter A. et al. "Advance Directives: Are They an Advance?" *Canadian Medical Association Journal* 146 (1992): 127–134.

Society for the Right to Die. *Refusal of Treatment Legislation, 1991: A State by State Compilation of Enacted and Model Statutes.* New York: The Society, March 1991.

Solomon, Mildred Z. et al. "Decisions Near the End of Life: Professional Views on Life-Sustaining Treatments." *American Journal of Public Health* 83(1) (January 1993): 14–23.

Sullivan, Mark D. and Stuart J. Youngner. "Depression, Competence, and the Right to Refuse Lifesaving Medical Treatment." *American Journal of Psychiatry* 151(7) (1994): 971–977.

Sullivan, Thomas D. "Active and Passive Euthanasia: An Impertinent Distinction?" *Human Life Review* 3 (Summer 1977): 40–47.

Veatch, Robert M. "An Ethical Framework for Terminal Care Decisions: A New Classification of Patients." *Journal of the American Geriatrics Society* 32 (September 1984): 665–669.

———. "Forgoing Life-Sustaining Treatment: Limits to the Consensus." *Kennedy Institute of Ethics Journal* 3(1) (March 1993): 1–19.

Weir, Robert F., ed. *Ethical Issues in Death and Dying.* New York: Columbia University Press, 1977.

Weir, Robert F. and Larry Gostin. "Decisions to Abate Life-Sustaining Treatment for Non-Autonomous Patients: Ethical Standards and Legal Liability for Physicians after *Cruzan.*" *Journal of the American Medical Association* 264 (1990): 1846–1853.

Williams, Glanville. "Mercy-Killing Legislation—A Rejoinder." *Minnesota Law Review* 43 (1958): 1–12.

Williams, Phillip. *The Living Will and the Durable Power of Attorney for Health Care Book* (with forms). Oak Park, Ill.: The P. Gaines Co., 1991.

Winslade, William J. and Judith Wilson Ross. *Choosing Life or Death: A Guide for Patients, Families, and Professionals.* New York: Free Press, 1986.

Part II: Rights

Chapter 4: AIDS and Its Issues

AIDS: From the Beginning. Chicago: American Medical Association, 1986.

AIDS: Public Health and Civil Liberties. *The Hastings Center Report* 16 (December 1986): 1–36. Special supplement.

Allen, James R. et al. "AIDS: The Responsibilities of Health Professionals" [special supplement]. *Hastings Center Report* 18 (April/May 1988), S1–S32.

Almond, Brenda, ed. *AIDS: A Moral Issue—The Ethical, Legal and Social Aspects.* New York: St. Martin's Press, 1990.

Altman, Dennis. *AIDS in the Mind of America.* Garden City, N.Y.: Doubleday, 1986.

American Council of Life Insurance. "White Paper: The Acquired Immunodeficiency Syndrome and HTLV-III Testing." *AIDS & Public Policy Journal* 2 (1987): 32–41.

Angell, Marcia. "A Dual Approach to the AIDS Epidemic." *New England Journal of Medicine* 324(21) (23 May 1991): 1498–1500.

Bayer, Ronald. *Private Acts, Social Consequences: AIDS and the Politics of Public Health.* New York: Free Press, 1989.

———. "AIDS Prevention and Cultural Sensitivity: Are They Compatible?" *American Journal of Public Health* 84(6) (1994): 895–898.

———, **C. Levine, and S. M. Wolf.** "HIV Antibody Screening: An Ethical Framework for Evaluating Proposed Programs." In **P. O'Malley, ed.** *The AIDS Epidemic.* Boston: Beacon Press, 1989.

——— **and Kathleen E. Toomey.** "HIV Prevention and the Two Faces of Partner Notification." *Health Law and Ethics* 82(8) (August 1992): 1158–1164.

Black, David. *The Plague Years: A Chronicle of AIDS, the Epidemic of Our Times.* New York: Simon & Schuster, 1986.

Blaine, Jack H. "AIDS: Regulatory Issues for Life and Health Insurers." *AIDS & Public Policy Journal* 2 (1987): 2–10.

Blendon, Robert J., Karen Donelan, and Richard A. Knox. "Public Opinion and AIDS: Lessons for the Second Decade." *JAMA* 267 (1992): 981–986.

Brandt, Allen M. "The Syphilis Epidemic and Its Relationship to AIDS." *Science* 239 (1988): 375–380.

Brennan, Troyen A. "The Challenge of AIDS." In his *Just Doctoring: Medical Ethics in the Liberal State.* Berkeley, CA: University of California Press, 1991, pp. 147–174, 264–268.

————."Transmission of the Human Immunodeficiency Virus in the Health Care Setting—Time for Action." *New England Journal of Medicine* 324 (1991): 1504–1509.

Cahill, Kevin M., ed. *The AIDS Epidemic.* New York: St. Martin's Press, 1983.

Cameron, Miriam E. *Living with AIDS: Experiencing Ethical Problems.* Newbury Park, CA: Sage Publications, 1993.

Childress, James F. "An Ethical Framework for Assessing Policies to Screen for Antibodies to HIV." *AIDS & Public Policy Journal* 2 (1987): 28–31.

Cohen, Elliot D. and Michael Davis, eds. *AIDS: Crisis in Professional Ethics.* Philadelphia: Temple University Press, 1994.

Cooper, Ellen R. "AIDS in Children: An Overview of the Medical, Epidemiological, and Public Health Problems." In P. O'Malley, ed. *The AIDS Epidemic.* Boston: Beacon Press, 1989.

Daniels, Norman. "Insurability and the HIV Epidemic: Ethical Issues in Underwriting." *Milbank Quarterly* 68 (1990): 497–525.

————. "HIV-Infected Professionals, Patient Rights, and the 'Switching Dilemma.'" *JAMA* 267(10) (11 March 1992): 1368–1371.

Dickens, Bernard M. "Legal Rights and Duties in the AIDS Epidemic." *Science* 239 (1988): 580–587.

————. "Confidentiality and the Duty to Warn." In **Lawrence O. Gostin, ed.** *AIDS and the Health Care System.* New Haven: Yale University Press, 1990, pp. 98–112, 259–261.

Dixon, John. *Catastrophic Rights: Experimental Drugs & AIDS.* Vancouver: New Star Books, 1990.

Erin, Charles A. and John Harris. "AIDS: Ethics, Justice, and Social Policy." *Journal of Applied Philosophy* 10(2) (1993): 165–173.

Faden, Ruth R. et al. "Reproductive Preferences of Pregnant Women under Shifting Probabilities of Vertical HIV Transmission." *Women's Health Issues* 3(4) (1993): 216–222.

————, **Gail Geller, and Madison Powers, eds.** *AIDS, Women and the Next Generation: Toward a Morally Acceptable Public Policy for HIV Testing of Pregnant Women and Newborns.* New York: Oxford University Press, 1991.

Fernando, M. Daniel. *AIDS and Intravenous Drug Use: The Influence of Morality, Politics, Social Science, and Race in the Making of a Tragedy.* Westport, Conn.: Praeger, 1993.

Fleck, Leonard and Marcia Angell. "Please Don't Tell!" [case study]. *Hastings Center Report* 21 (November/December 1991): 39–40.

Fox, Daniel M. "The Cost of AIDS from Conjecture to Research." *AIDS & Public Policy Journal* 2 (1987): 25–27.

Freedman, Benjamin. "Violating Confidentiality to Warn of a Risk of HIV Infection: Ethical Work in Progress." *Theoretical Medicine* 12 (1991): 309–323.

Gallagher, Thomas A., ed. "Twenty-third Annual Symposium: AIDS: At the Limits of the Law." *Villanova Law Review* 34(5) (September 1989).

Gostin, Lawrence O. "The AIDS Litigation Project: A National Review of Court and Human Rights Commission Decisions." *Journal of the American Medical Association* 263(14, 15), Part 1 (11 April 1990): 1961–1974; Part 2 (18 April 1990): 2086–2093.

————. "The HIV-Infected Health Care Professional: Public Policy, Discrimination, and Patient Safety." *Law, Medicine & Health Care* 18(4) (Winter 1990): 303–310.

————, **William J. Curran, and Mary E. Clark.** "The Case Against Compulsory Casefinding in Controlling AIDS—Testing, Screening, and Reporting." *American Journal of Law and Medicine* 12 (1987): 17–53.

————, **ed.** *AIDS and the Health Care System.* New Haven, Conn.: Yale University Press, 1990.

Graubard, Stephen R., ed. *Living with AIDS.* Cambridge, Mass.: MIT Press, 1990.

Gray, Alec. "The AIDS Epidemic: A Prism Distorting Social and Legal Principles." In P. O'Malley, ed. *The AIDS Epidemic.* Boston: Beacon Press, 1989.

Grodin, Michael A., P. V. Kaminow, and R. Sassower. "Ethical Issues in AIDS Research." In P. O'Malley, ed. *The AIDS Epidemic.* Boston: Beacon Press, 1989.

Hastings Center. *AIDS: An Epidemic of Ethical Puzzles.* Brookfield, Vt.: Dartmouth, 1991.

Holder, Angela R. "Is This a Job for the IRB? The Case of the ELISA Assay." *IRB: A Review of Human Subjects Research* 7 (November/December 1985): 7–8.

Humber, James M. and Robert F. Almeder. *AIDS and Ethics.* Biomedical Ethics Reviews 1988. Clifton, N.J.: Humana Press, 1989.

Hummel, Robert F. "AIDS, Public Policy, and Insurance." *AIDS & Public Policy Journal* 2 (1987): 1.

———— **et al., eds.** *AIDS: Impact on Public Policy.* New York: Plenum Press, 1986.

Institute of Medicine, Committee for the Oversight of AIDS Activities. *Confronting AIDS: Update 1988.* Washington, D.C.: National Academy Press, 1988.

Institute of Medicine of the National Academy of Science. *Mobilizing Against AIDS.* Cambridge, Mass.: Harvard University Press, 1986.

Iuculano, Russel P. "D.C. Act 6–170: The Five-Year Ban on Risk-Based Pricing for AIDS." *AIDS & Public Policy Journal* 2 (1987): 15–18.

Jonsen, Albert R. and Jeff Stryker, eds. *The Social Impact of AIDS in the United States.* Washington, D.C.: National Academy Press, 1993.

Juengst, Eric T. and Barbara A. Koenig, eds. *The Meaning of AIDS: Implications for Medical Science, Clinical Practice, and Public Health Policy.* New York: Praeger, 1989.

Kass, Nancy E., Ruth R. Faden, Robin Fox, et al. "Homosexual and Bisexual Men's Perceptions of Discrimination in Health Services." *American Journal of Public Health* 82 (1992): 1277–1279.

Kulstad, Ruth, ed. *AIDS: Papers from Science 1982–1985.* Washington, D.C.: American Association for the Advancement of Science, 1986.

Landesman, Sheldon H., Harold M. Ginzberg, and Stanley H. Weiss. "Special Report: The AIDS Epidemic." *New England Journal of Medicine* 312(8) (21 February 1985): 521–525.

Law, Medicine, and Health Care 15 (Summer 1987). Special issue on "AIDS: Law and Policy."

Levine, Carol and Ronald Bayer. "The Ethics of Screening for Early Intervention in HIV Disease." *American Journal of Public Health* 79(12) (December 1989): 1661–1667.

Lo, Bernard. "Ethical Dilemmas in HIV Infection: What Have We Learned?" *Law, Medicine and Health Care* 20 (1992): 92–103.

———— **and Robert Steinbrook.** "Health Care Workers Infected with the Human Immunodeficiency Virus: The Next Steps." *JAMA* 267(8) (26 February 1992): 1100–1105.

Loewy, Erich H., ed. "Ethical and Communal Issues in AIDS": [topical issue]. *Theoretical Medicine* 11 (1990): 173–226.

McKenzie, Nancy F., ed. *The AIDS Reader: Social, Political, Ethical Issues.* New York: Meridian, 1991.

Miller, David et al. "HTLV-III: Should Testing Ever Be Routine?" *British Medical Journal* 292 (5 April 1986): 941–943.

Miller, Heather G., Charles F. Turner, and Lincoln E. Moses, eds. *AIDS: The Second Decade.* Washington, D.C.: National Academy Press, 1990.

Mohr, Richard D. "AIDS: What to Do—And What Not to Do." *Report from the Center for Philosophy and Public Policy* 5 (1985): 6–9.

———. *Gays/Justice: A Study of Ethics, Society, and Law.* New York: Columbia University Press, 1988.

Murphy, Timothy F. "No Time for an AIDS Backlash." *Hastings Center Report* 21 (March/April 1991): 7–11.

National Commission on AIDS. *America Living with AIDS.* Washington, D.C.: National Commission on AIDS, 1991.

National Research Council, Commission on Behavioral and Social Sciences and Education, Committee on AIDS Research and the Behavioral, Social, and Statistical Sciences. *AIDS: Sexual Behavior and Intravenous Drug Use.* Edited by Charles F. Turner, Heather G. Miller, and Lincoln E. Moses. Washington, D.C.: National Academy Press, 1989.

National Research Council. Panel on Monitoring the Social Impact of the AIDS Epidemic. *The Social Impact of AIDS in the United States.* Washington, D.C.: National Academy Press, 1993.

Nelkin, Dorothy, David P. Willis, and Scott V. Parris, eds. *A Disease of Society: Cultural and Institutional Responses to AIDS.* New York: Cambridge University Press, 1991.

Nicholas, Eve K. Institute of Medicine, National Academy of Sciences. *Mobilizing against AIDS.* Newly revised and enlarged ed. Cambridge: Harvard University Press, 1989.

Nichols, Chris D. "AIDS—A New Reason to Regulate Homosexuality?" *Journal of Contemporary Law* 11 (1984): 315–343.

Oppenheimer, Gerald M. and Robert A. Padgug. "AIDS and Health Insurance: Social and Ethical Issues." *AIDS & Public Policy Journal* 2 (1987): 11–14.

Overall, Christine and William P. Zion, eds. "AIDS: The Risk to Insurers, the Threat to Equity." *Hastings Center Report* 16 (October 1986): 18–22.

———. *Perspectives on AIDS: Ethical and Social Issues.* New York: Oxford University Press, 1991.

Pascal, Anthony et al. "State Policies and the Financing of Acquired Immunodeficiency Syndrome." *Health Care Financing Review* 11(1) (Fall 1989): 91–104.

Pierce, Christine and Donald Van DeVeer, eds. *AIDS: Ethics and Public Policy.* Belmont, Calif.: Wadsworth, 1988.

Reamer, Frederic G., ed. *AIDS & Ethics.* New York: Columbia University Press, 1991.

Scherzer, Mark. "AIDS and Insurance: The Case Against HIV Antibody Testing." *AIDS & Public Policy Journal* 2 (1987): 19–24.

Shilts, Randy. *And the Band Played On.* New York: Penguin, 1988.

Sieghart, Paul. *AIDS & Human Rights: A UK Perspective.* London: British Medical Association Foundation for AIDS, 1989.

"Special Section: AIDS—Responding to the Crisis." *Health Progress* (May 1986): 29–56.

Sprintz, Heather. "The Criminalization of Perinatal AIDS Transmission." *Health Matrix* 3(2) (1994): 495–537.

United States. "Americans with Disabilities Act of 1990" (Public Law No. 101–336). [*United States*] *Statutes at Large* 104, pp. 327 ff.

United States, National Commission on AIDS. *America Living with AIDS.* Washington, D.C.: U.S. Government Printing Office, 1991.

United States, National Commission on AIDS. *AIDS: An Expanding Tragedy—The Final Report of the National Commission on AIDS.* Washington, D.C.: U.S. Government Printing Office, 1993.

Walters, LeRoy. "Ethical Issues in the Prevention and Treatment of HIV Infection and AIDS." *Science* 239 (5 February 1988): 597–603.

Winston, Morton and Sheldon H. Landesman. "AIDS and a Duty to Protect." *Hastings Center Report* 17 (February 1987): 22–23.

Chapter 5: Physicians, Patients, and Others

Angell, Marcia. "The Doctor as Double Agent." *Kennedy Institute of Ethics Journal* 3(3) (1993): 279–286.

Annas, George J. "Confidentiality and the Duty to Warn." *Hastings Center Report* 6 (December 1976): 6–8.

———. "Informed Consent, Cancer, and Truth in Prognosis." *NEJM* 330(3) (1994): 223–225.

——— **and Joan E. Densberger.** "Competence to Refuse Medical Treatment: Autonomy vs. Paternalism." *The University of Toledo Law Review* 15 (Winter 1984): 561–596.

Appelbaum, Paul S. et al. "Confidentiality: An Empirical Test of the Utilitarian Perspective." *Bulletin of the American Academy of Psychiatry Law* 12(2) (1984): 109–116.

———. "Researchers' Access to Patient Records: An Analysis of the Ethical Problems." *Clinical Research* 32 (October 1984): 399–403.

Beck, James C., ed. *Confidentiality Versus the Duty to Protect: Foreseeable Harm in the Practice of Psychiatry.* Washington, D.C.: American Psychiatry Press, Inc., 1990.

Blank, Robert H. *Fetal Protection in the Workplace: Women's Rights, Business Interests, and the Unborn.* New York: Columbia University Press, 1993.

Bok, Sissela. *Lying: Moral Choice in Public and Private Life.* New York: Pantheon Books, 1978.

Burnum, John F. "Secrets about Patients." *New England Journal of Medicine* 324 (18 April 1991): 1130–1133.

Childress, James F. *Who Should Decide? Paternalism in Health Care.* New York: Oxford University Press, 1982.

Coleman, Lee. *The Reign of Error.* Boston: Beacon Press, 1984.

"Compulsory Medical Treatment: The State's Interest Re-evaluated." *Minnesota Law Review* 51 (1966): 293–305.

"The Confidentiality of Health Records." *Psychiatric Opinion* 12 (January 1975). Entire issue on confidentiality and society.

Friedland, Bernard. "Physician-Patient Confidentiality: Time to Re-examine a Venerable Concept in Light of Contemporary Society and Advances in Medicine." *Journal of Legal Medicine* 15(2) (1994): 249–277.

Gaylin, Willard and Daniel Callahan. "The Psychiatrist as Double Agent." *Hastings Center Report* 4 (February 1974): 11–14.

Gewirth, Alan. "Human Rights and the Prevention of Cancer." *American Philosophical Quarterly* 17 (April 1980): 117–125.

Gillon, Raanan. "Telling the Truth and Medical Ethics." *British Medical Journal* 291 (30 November 1985): 1556–1557.

Gordis, Leon and Ellen Gold. "Privacy, Confidentiality, and the Use of Medical Records in Research." *Science* 207 (11 January 1980).

Grossman, M. "Confidentiality in Medical Practice." *Annual Review of Medicine* 28 (1977): 43–55.

Group for the Advancement of Psychiatry, Committee on Government Policy. *Forced into Treatment: The Role of Coercion in Clinical Practice.* Washington, D.C.: American Psychiatric Press, 1994.

Gurevitz, Howard. "Tarasoff: Protective Privilege Versus Public Peril." *American Journal of Psychiatry* 134 (March 1977): 289–292.

Havard, John. "Medical Confidence." *Journal of Medical Ethics* 11 (March 1985): 8–11.

Horn, Sheila E. "What's in a Name?" *Journal of Medical Humanities and Bioethics* 6 (Fall/Winter 1985): 99–108.

Jackson, Jennifer. "Telling the Truth." *Journal of Medical Ethics* (1991): 5–9.

Kessler, David A. "Communicating with Patients about Their Medications." *NEJM* 325(23) (5 December 1991): 1650–1652.

Kleinig, John. *Paternalism*. Totowa, N.J.: Rowman and Allanheld, 1984.

Kottow, Michael H. "Medical Confidentiality: An Intransigent and Absolute Obligation." *Journal of Medical Ethics* 12 (1986): 117–122.

Lasagna, Louis. "The Boston State Hospital Case (Rogers v. Okin): A Legal, Ethical and Medical Morass." *Perspectives in Biology and Medicine* 25 (Spring 1982): 382–403.

Lomasky, Loren E. and Michael Detlefsen. "Medical Paternalism Reconsidered." *Pacific Philosophical Quarterly* 62 (1981): 95–98.

Macklin, Ruth. *Enemies of Patients*. New York: Oxford University Press, 1993.

Mahowald, Mary B. "Against Paternalism: A Developmental View." *Philosophy Research Archives* 6(1386) (1980).

Novack, Dennis, Barbara J. Detering, Robert Arnold et al. "Physicians' Attitudes Toward Using Deception to Resolve Difficult Ethical Problems." *JAMA* 261 (26 May 1989): 2980–2985.

Pellegrino, Edmund. "Patient and Physician Autonomy: Conflicting Rights and Obligations in the Physician-Patient Relationship." *Journal of Contemporary Health Law and Policy* 10(47) (1994): 47–68.

Schoeman, Ferdinand D. ed. *Philosophical Dimensions of Privacy: An Anthology*. New York: Cambridge University Press, 1984.

Schöne-Seifert, Bettina and James F. Childress. "How Much Should the Patient Know and Decide?" *CA—A Cancer Journal for Clinicians* 36 (1986): 85–94.

Siminoff, L. A., J. H. Fetting, and M. D. Abeloff. "Doctor–Patient Communication about Breast Cancer Adjuvant Therapy." *Journal of Clinical Oncology* 7 (1989): 1192–1200.

Standard, Samuel and Helmuth Nathan, eds. *Should the Patient Know the Truth?* New York: Springer, 1955.

Thomson, Judith J. "The Right to Privacy." *Philosophy and Public Affairs* 4 (1975): 295–314.

Turkington, Richard C., George B. Trubow, and Anita L. Allen, eds. *Privacy: Cases and Materials*. Houston: John Marshall Publishing Co., 1992.

United Hospital Fund of New York. *The Tuberculosis Revival: Individual Rights and Societal Obligation in a Time of AIDS: A Special Report*. New York: United Hospital Fund, 1992.

U.S. Congress. House Committee on the Judiciary, Subcommittee on Civil and Constitutional Rights. *Unauthorized Access to Individual Medical Records*. Washington, D.C.: Government Printing Office, 1986.

Van de Veer, Donald. "Paternalism and Subsequent Consent." *Canadian Journal of Philosophy* 9 (1979): 631–642.

———. "Autonomy Respecting Paternalism." *Social Theory Practice* 6 (Summer 1980): 187–208.

———. "The Contractual Argument for Withholding Medical Information." *Philosophy and Public Affairs* 9 (Winter 1980): 198–205.

———. *Paternalistic Intervention: The Moral Bounds of Benevolence*. Princeton, N.J.: Princeton University Press, 1986.

Wangenstein, O. H. "Should Patients Be Told They Have Cancer?" *Surgery* 27 (1950): 944–947.

Weir, Robert. "Truthtelling in Medicine." *Perspectives in Biology and Medicine* 24 (Autumn 1980): 95–112.

Wolf, Susan M. "Quality Assessment of Ethics in Health Care: The Accountability Revolution." *American Journal of Law & Medicine* 20(1, 2) (1994): 105–128.

Chapter 6: Medical Experimentation and Informed Consent

Angell, Marcia. "Patient Preferences in Randomized Clinical Trials." *New England Journal of Medicine* 310 (24 May 1984): 1385–1387.

Annas, George J. *The Rights of Hospital Patients*. New York: Avon Books, 1975.

———. *Informed Consent to Human Experimentation: The Subject's Dilemma*. Cambridge, Mass.: Ballinger, 1977.

———. "Report on the National Commission: Good as Gold." *Bioethics Quarterly* 2 (Summer 1980): 84–93. On the protection of human subjects.

Annas, George J. and Michael A. Grodin, eds. *The Nazi Doctors and the Nuremberg Code: Human Rights in Human Experimentation*. New York: Oxford University Press, 1992.

Appelbaum, Paul and Thomas Grisso. "Assessing Patients' Capacities to Consent to Treatment." *New England Journal of Medicine* 319 (22 December 1988): 1635–1638.

Appelbaum, Paul S., Charles W. Lidz, and Alan Meisel. *Informed Consent: Legal Theory and Clinical Practice*. New York: Oxford University Press, 1987.

Beauchamp, Tom L. and Ruth R. Faden. "Decision-Making and Informed Consent: A Study of the Impact of Disclosed Information." *Social Indicators Research* 7 (1980): 313–336. An empirical and normative study.

Beecher, H. K. "Experimentation in Man." *JAMA* 169 (1959): 461–478.

———. "Ethics and Clinical Research." *New England Journal of Medicine* 274 (1966): 1354–1360.

———. *Research and the Individual: Human Studies*. Boston: Little, Brown, 1970.

Bok, Sissela. "Informed Consent in Tests of Patient Reliability." *JAMA* 267 (26 February 1992): 1118–1119.

Buchanan, Allen E. and Dan W. Brock. *Deciding for Others: The Ethics of Surrogate Decision Making*. Cambridge: Cambridge University Press, 1989.

Caplan, Arthur L., ed. *When Medicine Went Mad: Bioethics and the Holocaust*. Totowa, N.J.: Humana Press, 1992.

Curran, William J. "The Tuskegee Syphilis Study." *New England Journal of Medicine* 289 (4 October 1973): 730–731.

———. "Informed Consent in Malpractice Cases: A Turn Toward Reality." *New England Journal of Medicine* 314 (13 February 1986): 429–431.

Drane, James F. "Competence to Give Informed Consent: A Model for Making Clinical Assessments." *JAMA* 2(7) (17 August 1984): 925–927.

Emanuel, Ezekiel J. and Linda L. Emanuel. "Proxy Decision Making for Incompetent Patients: An Ethical and Empirical Analysis." *JAMA* 267(15) (15 April 1992): 2067–2071.

Faden, Ruth R. and Tom L. Beauchamp. *A History and Theory of Informed Consent*. New York: Oxford University Press, 1986.

Freedman, Benjamin. "Equipoise and the Ethics of Clinical Research." *New England Journal of Medicine* 317 (16 July 1987): 141–145.

Fried, Charles. *Medical Experimentation: Personal Integrity and Social Policy*. New York: American Elsevier, 1974.

Gaylin, Willard and Ruth Macklin, eds. *Who Speaks for the Child: The Problems of Proxy Consent*. New York: Plenum Press, 1982.

Gunderson, Martin. "Justifying a Principle of Informed Consent: A Case Study in Autonomy-based Ethics." *Public Affairs Quarterly* 4 (1990): 240–265.

"Inclusion of Women in Clinical Research." *Academic Medicine* 69(9) (1994): 693–715.

Journal of Medicine and Philosophy 11 (1986). Special issue on "Ethical Issues in the Use of Clinical Controls."

Katz, Jay. *Experimentation with Human Beings.* New York: Russell Sage Foundation, 1972.

———. "Informed Consent—A Fairy Tale? Law's Vision." *University of Pittsburgh Law Review* 39 (1977): 137–174.

———. *The Silent World of Doctor and Patient.* New York: Free Press, 1984.

———. "Duty and Caring in the Age of Informed Consent and Medical Science: Unlocking Peabody's Secret." *Humane Medicine* 8(3) (July 1992): 187–197.

———. "Informed Consent: Must It Remain a Fairy Tale?" *Journal of Contemporary Health Law and Policy* 10(69) (1994): 69–91.

Kidd, Alexander M. "Limits of the Right of a Person to Consent to Experimentation on Himself." *Science* 117 (1953): 211–212.

Kushner, Thomasine Kimbrough and Raymond Belliotti. "Baby Fae: A Beastly Business." *Journal of Medical Ethics* 11 (December 1985): 178–183.

Levine, Robert J. *Ethics and Regulation of Human Research.* 2d ed. Baltimore: Urban & Schwarzenberg, 1986.

Lipsett, Mortimer B. "On the Nature and Ethics of Phase I Clinical Trials of Cancer Chemotherapies." *JAMA* 248 (27 August 1982): 941–942.

Macklin, Ruth. "Consent, Coercion, and Conflicts of Rights." *Perspectives in Biology and Medicine* 20 (Spring 1977): 360–371.

———. "Some Problems in Gaining Informed Consent from Psychiatric Patients." *Emory Law Journal* 31(2) (Spring 1982): 345–374.

——— and Susan Sherwin. "Experimenting on Human Subjects: Philosophical Perspectives." *Case-Western Reserve Law Review* 25 (1975): 434–471. A good review of issues with respect to Mill, Kant, and Rawls. Part of a symposium on human experimentation.

Margolis, Joseph. "Conceptual Aspects of a Patient's Bill of Rights." *Journal of Value Inquiry* 11 (Summer 1977): 126–135.

Marquis, Donald. "An Argument That All Prerandomized Clinical Trials Are Unethical." *Journal of Medicine and Philosophy* 11 (1986).

Mastroianni, Anna C., Ruth Faden, and Daniel Federman, eds. *Women and Health Research: Ethical and Legal Issues of Including Women in Clinical Studies,* vols. 1 and 2. Washington, D.C.: National Academy Press, 1994.

McCormick, Richard A. "Proxy Consent in the Experimentation Situation." *Perspectives in Biology and Medicine* 18 (Autumn 1974): 2–20.

———. "A Reply to Paul Ramsey—Experimentation in Children: Sharing in Sociality." *Hastings Center Report* 6 (December 1976): 41–46.

McNeill, Paul M. *The Ethics and Politics of Human Experimentation.* New York: Cambridge University Press, 1993.

Merz, Jon F. "On a Decision-Making Paradigm of Medical Informed Consent." *Journal of Legal Medicine* 14(2) (June 1993): 231–264.

Merz, Jon F. and Baruch Fischoff. "Informed Consent Does Not Mean Rational Consent." *Journal of Legal Medicine* 11 (1990): 321–350.

Miller, Bruce. "Experimentation on Human Subjects: The Ethics of Random Clinical Trials." In Donald VanDeVeer and Tom Regan, eds., *Health Care Ethics.* Philadelphia: Temple University Press, 1987.

Mistichelli, Judith. *Baby Fae: Ethical Issues Surrounding Cross-Species Organ Transplantation.* Scope Note #5. Washington, D.C.: Kennedy Institute of Ethics, 1985.

Morrissey, James M., Adele D. Hoffmann, and Jeffrey C. Thrope. *Consent and Confidentiality in the Health Care of Children and Adolescents: A Legal Guide.* New York: Free Press, 1986.

Murphy, Jeffrie G. "Total Institution and the Possibility of Consent to Organic Therapies." *Human Rights* 5 (Fall 1975): 25–45.

———. "Therapy and the Problem of Autonomous Consent." *International Journal of Law and Psychiatry* 2 (1979): 415–430.

Nicholson, Richard H., ed. *Medical Research with Children: Ethics, Law, and Practice.* Oxford: Oxford University Press, 1986.

Office for Protection from Research Risks. *Protecting Human Research Subjects: Institutional Review Board Guidebook.* Pittsburgh: U.S. Government Printing Office, Superintendent of Documents, 1993.

President's Commission for the Study of Ethical Problems in Medicine and Biomedical and Behavioral Research. *Protecting Human Subjects: First Biennial Report on the Adequacy and Uniformity of Federal Rules and Policies, and Their Implementation, for the Protection of Human Subjects in Biomedical and Behavioral Research.* Washington, D.C.: President's Commission, 1981.

———. *Making Health Care Decisions: Empirical Studies of Informed Consent.* Volume Two: Appendices. Washington, D.C.: President's Commission, 1982.

———. *Making Health Care Decisions: The Ethical and Legal Implications of Informed Consent in the Patient-Practitioner Relationship.* Washington, D.C.: President's Commission, 1982.

———. *Implementing Human Research Regulations.* Washington, D.C.: President's Commission, 1983.

Ramsey, Paul. "The Ethics of a Cottage Industry in an Age of Community and Research Medicine." *New England Journal of Medicine* 284 (1971): 700–706.

———. "The Enforcement of Morals: Nontherapeutic Research on Children." *Hastings Center Report* 6 (1975): 21–30.

———. *The Ethics of Fetal Research.* New Haven, Conn.: Yale University Press, 1975.

———. "A Reply to Richard McCormick—The Enforcement of Morals: Nontherapeutic Research on Children." *Hastings Center Report* 6 (August 1976): 21–30.

———. "Children as Research Subjects—A Reply." *Hastings Center Report* 7 (April 1977): 40–41.

Swazey, Judith P., Judith C. Watkins, and Renee Fox. "Assessing the Artificial Heart: The Clinical Moratorium Revisited." *International Journal of Technology Assessment in Health Care* 2 (July 1986): 387–410.

Veatch, Robert M. "'Experimental' Pregnancy." *Hastings Center Report* 1 (1971): 2–3. About the Goldzieher experiment, in which placebos were used instead of contraceptive pills.

———. "Human Experimentation: The Crucial Choices Ahead." *Prism* 2 (1974): 58 ff.

———. *The Patient as Partner: A Theory of Human-Experimentation Ethics.* Bloomington, Ind.: Indiana University Press, 1987. Chaps. 3 and 12.

Weisbard, Alan J. "Informed Consent: The Law's Uneasy Compromise with Ethical Theory." *Nebraska Law Review* 65(4) (1986): 749–767.

Animal Experimentation

Bateson, Patrick. "When to Experiment on Animals." *New Scientist* 109 (February 1986): 30–32.

Fox, Michael Allen. *The Case for Animal Experimentation: An Evolutionary and Ethical Perspective.* Berkeley: University of California Press, 1986.

Frey, R. G. "Animal Parts, Human Wholes: On the Use of Animals as a Source of Organs for Human Transplants." In James M. Humber and Robert F. Almeder, eds. *Biomedical Ethics Reviews: 1987.* Clifton, N.J.: Humana Press, 1987, pp. 89–107.

Gallup, Gordon and Susan D. Suarez. "Alternatives to the Use of Animals in Psychological Research." *American Psychologist* 40 (October 1985): 1104–1111.

Great Britain. *The Animals (Scientific Procedures) Act*, 1986.

Hargrove, Eugene C., ed. *The Animal Rights/Environmental Ethics Debate: The Environmental Perspective.* Albany, N.Y.: State University of New York Press, 1992.

Jamieson, Dale and Tom Regan. "On the Ethics of the Use of Animals in Science." In **Tom Regan and Donald VanDeVeer, eds.** *And Justice for All.* Totowa, N.J.: Rowman and Allanheld, 1982, pp. 169–196.

Kuhse, Helga. "Interests." *Journal of Medical Ethics* 11 (September 1985): 146–149.

Leader, Robert W. and Dennis Stark. "The Importance of Animals in Biomedical Research." *Perspectives in Biology and Medicine* 30(4) (Summer 1987): 470–485.

McCarthy, Charles R. "Improved Standards for Laboratory Animals?" *Kennedy Institute of Ethics Journal* 3(3) (1993): 293–302.

Paton, William. *Man & Mouse: Animals in Medical Research.* New York: Oxford University Press, 1984.

Rowan, Andrew N. *Of Mice, Models, and Men: A Critical Evaluation of Animal Research.* Albany, N.Y.: State University of New York Press, 1984.

Ryder, Richard. *Victims of Science: The Use of Animals in Research.* Rev. ed. London: Anti-Vivisection Society, 1983.

Singer, Peter. *Animal Liberation.* 2d ed. New York: New York Review (Random House), 1990.

———, ed. *In Defense of Animals.* New York: Blackwell, 1985.

Tannenbaum, Jerry and Andrew N. Rowan. "Rethinking the Morality of Animal Research." *Hastings Center Report* 15 (October 1985): 32–43.

Part III: Controls

Chapter 7: Genetics: Intervention, Control, and Research

AAAS-ABA National Conference of Lawyers and Scientists and AAAS Committee on Scientific Freedom and Responsibility. *The Genome, Ethics, and the Law: Issues in Genetic Testing.* Washington, D.C.: American Association for the Advancement of Science, 1992.

American Medical Association, Council on Ethical and Judicial Affairs. "Use of Genetic Testing by Employers." *JAMA* 226 (1991): 1827–1830.

———. "Ethical Issues Related to Prenatal Genetic Testing." *Archives of Family Medicine* 3 (1994): 633–642.

Anderson, W. French. "Human Gene Therapy: Why Draw a Line?" *Journal of Medicine and Philosophy* 14 (1989): 681–693.

———. "Genetic Engineering and Our Humanness." *Human Gene Therapy* 5 (1994): 755–759.

Andrews, Lori B. et al. "Genetics and the Law." *Emory Law Journal* 39 (1990): 619–853. Symposium.

Annas, George J. "Privacy Rules for DNA Databanks: Protecting Coded 'Future Diaries.'" *JAMA* 270(19) (1993): 2346–2350.

——— and Sherman Elias, eds. *Gene Mapping: Using Law and Ethics as Guides.* New York: Oxford University Press, 1992.

Bankowski, Zbigniew and Alexander Morgan Capron, eds. Council for International Organizations of Medical Sciences. *Genetics, Ethics, and Human Values: Human Genome Mapping, Genetic Screening and Gene Therapy.* Geneva: Council for International Organizations of Medical Sciences, 1990.

Bartels, Dianne M., Bonnie S. LeRoy, and Arthur L. Caplan, eds. *Prescribing Our Future: Ethical Challenges in Genetic Counseling.* New York: Aldine De Gruyter, 1993.

Billings, Paul R., ed. *DNA on Trial: Genetic Identification and Criminal Justice.* Plainview, N.Y.: Cold Spring Harbor Laboratory Press, 1992.

Bonnicksen, Andrea L. "National and International Approaches to Human Germ-Line Gene Therapy." *Politics and the Life Sciences* 13(1) (1994): 39–49.

Boyle, Philip J. et al. "Genetic Grammar: 'Health,' 'Illness,' and the Human Genome Project." *Hastings Center Report* 22 (Supplement, July/August 1992): S1–S20.

Capron, Alexander. "Reflections on Issues Posed by Recombinant DNA Molecule Technology." *Annals of the American Academy of Sciences* 265 (1976): 71–81. Entire issue is devoted to genetic issues.

———. *Genetic Counseling: Facts, Values and Norms.* New York: Alan R. Liss, 1979.

Carmen, Ira H. *Cloning and the Constitution: An Inquiry into Governmental Policymaking and Genetic Experimentation.* Madison: University of Wisconsin Press, 1986.

Collins, Francis S. "Medical and Ethical Consequences of the Human Genome Project." *Journal of Clinical Ethics* 2 (1991): 260–267.

Committee on Assessing Genetic Risks, Division of Health Sciences Policy, Institute of Medicine. *Assessing Genetic Risks: Implications for Health and Social Policy.* Washington, D.C.: National Academy Press, 1994.

Cook-Deegan, Robert M. *The Gene Wars: Science, Politics, and the Human Genome.* New York: W. W. Norton, 1993.

Culliton, Barbara. "Gene Therapy: Research in Public." *Science* 227 (February 1985): 493–496.

Daedalus 90 (1961). "Evolution and Man's Progress." See in particular the articles by Muller and Crow.

Davis, Bernard D. "Prospects for Genetic Intervention in Man." *Science* 170 (1970): 1279–1283.

———. *Storm over Biology: Essays on Science, Sentiment, and Public Policy.* Buffalo, N.Y.: Prometheus Books, 1986.

DeGrazia, David. "The Ethical Justification for Minimal Paternalism in the Use of the Predictive Test for Huntington's Disease." *Journal of Clinical Ethics* 2 (1991): 219–228.

Draper, Elaine. *Risky Business: Genetic Testing and Exclusionary Practices in the Hazardous Workplace.* New York: Cambridge University Press, 1991.

Duster, Troy. *Backdoor to Eugenics.* New York: Routledge, Chapman and Hall, 1990.

Fletcher, John C. "Moral and Ethical Problems of PreNatal Diagnosis." *Clinical Genetics* 8 (1975): 251–257.

———. "Ethics and Amniocentesis for Fetal Sex Identification." *Hasting Center Report* 10 (1980): 15–17.

———. "Ethical Issues in Genetic Screening and Antenatal Diagnosis." *Clinical Obstetrics and Gynecology* 24 (December 1981): 1151–1168.

———. "Moral Problems and Ethical Issues in Prospective Human Gene Therapy." *Virginia Law Review* 69(3) (April 1983): 515–546.

———. "Ethics and Trends in Applied Human Genetics." *Birth Defects* 19(5) (1983): 143–158.

———. "Ethical Issues in and Beyond Prospective Clinical Trials of Human Gene Therapy." *Journal of Medicine and Philosophy* 10 (August 1985): 293–309.

——— and W. French Anderson. "Germ-Line Gene Therapy: A New Stage of Debate." *Law, Medicine and Health Care* 20 (1992): 26–39.

Fletcher, Joseph. "Ethical Aspects of Genetic Controls." *New England Journal of Medicine* 285 (1971): 776–783.

Fowler, Gregory, Eric T. Juengst and Burke K. Zimmerman. "Germ-Line Gene Therapy and the Clinical Ethos of Medical Genetics." *Theoretical Medicine* 10 (1989): 151–165.

Friedman, Theodore. "Progress toward Human Gene Therapy." *Science* 244 (1989): 1275–1281.

Garver, Kenneth L. and Bettylee Garver. "The Human Genome Project and Eugenic Concerns." *American Journal of Human Genetics* 54(1) (1994): 148–158.

Gostin, Larry J. "The Human Genome Initiative and the Impact of Genetic Testing and Screening Technologies." *American Journal of Law & Medicine* 17(1–2) (1991): 1–208.

Gustafson, James M. "A Christian Perspective on Genetic Engineering." *Human Gene Therapy* 5 (1994): 747–754.

Harris, John. *Wonderwoman and Superman: The Ethics of Human Biotechnology*. New York: Oxford University Press, 1992.

Hilton, Bruce et al., eds. *Ethical Issues in Human Genetics: Genetic Counseling and the Use of Genetic Knowledge*. New York: Plenum Press, 1973.

Holtzman, Neil A. *Proceed with Caution: Predicting Genetic Risks in the Recombinant DNA Era*. Baltimore: Johns Hopkins University Press, 1989.

"The Human Genome Project." *National Forum* 73(2) (Spring 1993): 2–42.

Jackson, David A. and Stephen P. Stich, eds. *The Recombinant DNA Debate*. Englewood Cliffs, N.J.: Prentice-Hall, 1979.

Juengst, Eric T., ed. "Human Germ-Line Engineering." *Journal of Medicine and Philosophy* 16 (1991): 587–694. Topical issue.

Karjala, Dennis S. "A Legal Research Agenda for the Human Genome Initiative." *Jurimetrics Journal* 32 (1992): 121–222.

Kevles, Daniel J. and Leroy Hood, eds. *The Code of Codes: Scientific and Social Issues in the Human Genome Project*. Cambridge, Mass.: Harvard University Press, 1992.

Kolata, Gina B. "Prenatal Diagnosis of Neural Tube Defects." *Science* 209 (12 September 1980): 1216–1218.

Krimsky, Sheldon. *Biotechnics and Society: The Rise of Industrial Genetics*. Westport, Conn.: Praeger, 1991.

Lappé, Marc. *Broken Code: The Exploitation of DNA*. San Francisco: Sierra Club Books, 1984.

——— et al. "Ethical and Social Issues in Screening for Genetic Disease." *New England Journal of Medicine* 286 (1972): 1129–1132. Problems and guidelines in social programs.

———. "Moral Obligations and the Fallacies of Genetic Control." *Theological Studies* 33 (1972): 411–427.

———. *Genetics Politics: The Limits of Biological Control*. New York: Simon & Schuster, 1979.

——— and Robert S. Morrison, eds. "Ethical and Scientific Issues Posed by Human Uses of Molecular Genetics." *Annals of the New York Academy of Sciences* 265 (1976): 1–208.

——— and Peter Steinfels. "Choosing the Sex of Our Children." *Hastings Center Report* 4 (1974): 1–4.

Lederberg, Joshua. "Experimental Genetics and Human Evolution." *American Naturalist* 100 (1966): 519–531.

———. "Orthobiosis: The Perfection of Man." In **Nicholas Rescher**, ed. *The Place of Value in a World of Facts*. New York: Wiley, 1970.

———. "DNA Splicing: Will Fear Rob Us of Its Benefits?" *Prism* 2 (November 1975): 33–37.

Lee, Thomas F. *The Human Genome Project: Cracking the Genetic Code of Life*. New York: Plenum Press, 1991.

Lewontin, Richard. "The Dream of the Human Genome: Doubts about the Human Genome Project." *New York Review of Books* 39 (28 May 1992): 31–40.

Lippman, Abby. "Prenatal Genetic Testing and Screening: Constructing Needs and Reinforcing Inequities." *American Journal of Law and Medicine* 17 (1991): 15–50.

Ludmerer, Kenneth M. *Genetics and American Society*. Baltimore: Johns Hopkins University Press, 1972. A history of the eugenics movement.

Man and Medicine 2 (Winter 1977): 78–132. Special issue on recombinant DNA.

McCarrick, Pat Milmoe. *Genetic Testing and Genetic Screening*. Scope Note 22. Washington, D.C.: National Reference Center for Bioethics Literature, Kennedy Institute of Ethics, 1993.

McCormick, Richard. "Genetic Medicine: Notes on the Moral Literature. " *Theological Studies* 33 (September 1972): 531–532.

———. "Genetic Technology and Our Common Future." *America* 152(16) (27 April 1985): 337–342.

Miringoff, Marque-Luisa. *The Social Costs of Genetic Welfare*. New Brunswick, N.J.: Rutgers University Press, 1991.

Muller, H. J. "The Guidance of Human Evolution." *Perspectives in Biology and Medicine* 3 (1959): 1–43.

———. "What Genetic Course Will Man Steer?" In **J. F. Crow and J. V. Neel**, eds. *Proceedings of the Third International Congress of Human Genetics*. Baltimore: Johns Hopkins University Press, 1967.

National Academy of Sciences, Committee on DNA Technology in Forensic Science. *DNA Technology in Forensic Science*. Washington, D.C.: National Academy Press, 1992.

National Research Council. *Mapping and Sequencing the Human Genome*. Washington, D.C.: National Academy Press, 1988.

Natowicz, Marvin R., Jane K. Alper, and Joseph S. Alper. "Genetic Discrimination and the Law." *American Journal of Human Genetics* 50 (1992): 465–475.

Nelkin, Dorothy and Laurence Tancredi. *Dangerous Diagnostics: The Social Power of Biological Information*. New York: Basic Books, 1989.

Nichols, Eve K. *Human Gene Therapy*. Cambridge, Mass.: Harvard University Press, 1988.

NIH/DOE Working Group on Ethical, Legal, and Social Implications of Human Genome Research. *Genetic Information and Health Insurance*. Washington, D.C.: National Institute of Health, National Center for Human Genome Research, 1993.

Pollack, Robert. *Signs of Life: The Language and Meanings of DNA*. New York: Houghton Mifflin, 1994.

President's Commission for the Study of Ethical Problems in Medicine and Biomedical and Behavioral Research. *Splicing Life: The Social and Ethical Issues of Genetic Engineering with Human Beings*. Washington, D.C.: President's Commission, 1982.

———. *Screening and Counseling for Genetic Conditions: The Ethical, Social, and Legal Implications of Genetic Screening, Counseling, and Education Programs*. Washington, D.C.: President's Commission, 1983.

Proctor, Robert N. *Racial Hygiene: Medicine under the Nazis*. Cambridge, Mass.: Harvard University Press, 1988.

Ramsey, Paul. *Fabricated Man: The Ethics of Genetic Control*. New Haven, Conn.: Yale University Press, 1970.

———. "Genetic Engineering." *Bulletin of the Atomic Scientists* 29 (December 1972): 14–17.

Reilly, Philip R. *The Surgical Solution: A History of Involuntary Sterilization in the United States*. Baltimore: Johns Hopkins University Press, 1991.

Resnik, David. "Debunking the Slippery Slope Argument against Human Germ-Line Gene Therapy." *Journal of Medicine and Philosophy* 19(1) (1994): 23–40.

Robertson, John A. "Ethical and Legal Issues in Preimplantation Genetic Screening." *Fertility and Sterility* 57 (1992): 1–11.

Sinsheimer, Robert. "Troubled Dawn for Genetic Engineering." *New Scientist* 68 (1975): 148–151. An excellent review of problems.

———. "An Evolutionary Perspective for Genetic Engineering." *New Scientist* 73 (20 January 1977): 150–152.

Smith, J. David and K. Ray Nelson. *The Sterilization of Carrie Buck.* Far Hills, N.J.: New Horizon Press, 1989.

Sorenson, James R., Judith P. Swazey, and Norman A. Scotch. *Reproductive Pasts, Reproductive Futures: Genetic Counseling and Its Effectiveness.* New York: Alan R. Liss, 1982.

Southern California Law Review **51** (September 1978): 969–1573. "Biotechnology and the Law: Recombinant DNA and the Control of Scientific Research." Special issue.

Suzuki, David and Peter Knudtson. *Genethics: The Clash between the New Genetics and Human Values.* Revised and updated edition. Cambridge, Mass.: Harvard University Press, 1990.

Sylvester, Edward J. and Lynn C. Klotz. *The Gene Age: Genetic Engineering and the Next Industrial Revolution.* New York: Scribner's, 1983.

United States Congress, Office of Technology Assessment. *Genetic Witness: Forensic Uses of DNA Tests.* Washington, D.C.: U.S. Government Printing Office, July 1990.

United States Congress, Office of Technology Assessment. *Genetic Monitoring and Screening in the Workplace.* Washington, D.C.: U.S. Government Printing Office, October 1990.

United States Congress, Office of Technology Assessment. *Cystic Fibrosis and DNA Tests: Implications of Carrier Screening.* Washington, D.C.: U.S. Government Printing Office, August 1992.

Walters, LeRoy. "Human Gene Therapy: Ethics and Public Policy." *Human Gene Therapy* 2 (1991): 115–122.

Watson, James D. "Moving toward Clonal Man: Is That What We Want?" *Atlantic Monthly* 227 (1971): 50–53.

Weir, Robert F., Susan C. Lawrence, and Evan Fales, eds. *Genes and Human Self-Knowledge: Historical and Philosophical Reflections on Modern Genetics.* Iowa City: University of Iowa Press, 1994.

White, Gladys B. "Human Growth Hormone: The Dilemma of Expanded Use in Children." *Kennedy Institute of Ethics Journal* 3(4) (1993): 401–409.

Wilfond, Benjamn S. and Kathleen Nolan. "National Policy Development for the Clinical Application of Genetic Diagnostic Technologies: Lessons from Cystic Fibrosis." *JAMA* 270 (24) (1993): 2948–2954.

Wilkie, Tom. *Perilous Knowledge: The Human Genome Project and Its Implications.* London: Faber and Faber, 1993.

Wivel, Nelson A. and LeRoy Walters. "Germ-line Gene Modification and Disease Prevention: Some Medical and Ethical Perspectives." *Science* 262 (1993): 533–538.

Chapter 8: Reproductive Control: In Vitro Fertilization, Artificial Insemination and Surrogate Pregnancy

Allen, Anita L. "Surrogacy, Slavery, and the Ownership of Life." *Harvard Journal of Law and Public Policy* 13 (1990): 139–149.

Alpern, Kenneth D. *The Ethics of Reproductive Technology.* New York: Oxford University Press, 1992.

American College of Obstetricians and Gynecologists, Committee on Ethics. "Ethical Issues in Surrogate Motherhood." *Women's Health Issues* 1 (1991): 129–134, 135–160.

American Fertility Society, Ethics Committee. "Ethical Considerations of the New Reproductive Technologies." *Fertility and Sterility* 53 (Supplement 2, 1990): 1S–109S.

Andrews, Lori B. "Control and Compensation: Laws Governing Extracorporeal Generative Materials." *Journal of Medicine and Philosophy* 14 (1989): 541–560.

Annas, George J. "The Baby Broker Boom." *Hastings Center Report* 16 (June 1986): 30–31.

———. "Crazy Making: Embryos and Gestational Mothers." *Hastings Center Report* 21 (January/February 1991): 35–38.

———. "Using Genes to Define Motherhood—The California Solution." *New England Journal of Medicine* 326 (1992): 417–420.

——— **and Sherman Elias.** "In Vitro Fertilization and Embryo Transfer: Medicolegal Aspects of a New Technique to Create a Family." *Family Law Quarterly* 17(2) (Summer 1983): 199–223.

Arneson, Richard J. "Commodification and Commercial Surrogacy." *Philosophy and Public Affairs* 21 (1992): 132–164.

Bartels, Diane M. et al., eds. *Beyond Baby M: Ethical Issues in New Reproductive Techniques.* Clifton N.J.: Humana Press, 1990.

Blank, Robert H. *Regulating Reproduction.* New York: Columbia University Press, 1990.

Cahill, Lisa Sowle. "Moral Traditions, Ethical Language, and Reproductive Technologies." *Journal of Medicine and Philosophy* 14 (1989): 497–522.

California, Court of Appeal, Fourth District, Division 3. Anna J. v. Mark C. *California Reporter* 286 Cal. Rptr. 369 (1991).

California Supreme Court, Anna Johnson v. Mark Calvert. *Pacific Reporter,* 2d Series, 851. P 2d 776–801 (1993).

Capron, Alexander M. "Whose Child Is This?" *Hastings Center Report* 21 (November/December 1991): 37–38.

———. "Parenthood and Frozen Embryos: More Than Property and Privacy." *Hastings Center Report* 22 (September/October 1992): 32–33.

Cohen, Cynthia B., ed. Special Issue: Ethics and the Cloning of Human Embryos. *Kennedy Institute of Ethics Journal* 4(3) (1994).

Corea, Gena. *The Mother Machine: Reproductive Technologies from Artificial Insemination to Artificial Wombs.* New York: Harper & Row, 1985.

———. *Man-Made Women: How New Reproductive Technologies Affect Women.* Bloomington: Indiana University Press, 1987.

Dawson, Karen and Peter Singer. "Should Fertile People Have Access to In Vitro Fertilization?" *British Medical Journal* 300 (1990): 167–170.

Eaton, Thomas A. "Comparative Responses to Surrogate Motherhood." *Nebraska Law Review* 65(4) (1986): 686–727.

Field, Martha A. *Surrogate Motherhood.* Cambridge, Mass.: Harvard University Press, 1988.

Glover, Jonathan et al. *Ethics of New Reproductive Technologies: The Glover Report to the European Commission.* DeKalb: Northern Illinois University Press, 1989.

Gostin, Larry O., ed. *Surrogate Motherhood: Politics and Privacy.* Bloomington: Indiana University Press, 1990.

Henry, Vickie L. "A Tale of Three Women: A Survey of the Rights and Responsibilities of Unmarried Women Who Conceive by Alternative Insemination and a Model for Legislative Reform." *American Journal of Law & Medicine* 19(3) (1993): 285–311.

Hull, Richard T., ed. *Ethical Issues in the New Reproductive Technologies.* Belmont, Calif.: Wadsworth, 1990.

Klein, Renate D. "IVF Research: A Question of Feminist Ethics." *Issues in Reproductive and Genetic Engineering* 3 (1990): 243–251.

McCullough, Laurence B. and Frank A. Chervenak. *Ethics in Obstetrics and Gynecology*. New York: Oxford University Press, 1994.

New Jersey, Supreme Court. *In the Matter of Baby M. Atlantic Reporter* 537 A.2d 1227 (1988).

Overall, Christine. *Ethics and Human Reproduction: A Feminist Analysis*. Boston: Allen & Unwin, 1987.

———, ed. *The Future of Human Reproduction*. Toronto: The Women's Press, 1989.

Pellegrino, Edmund D., John Collins Harvey, and John P. Langan, eds. *Gift of Life. Catholic Scholars Respond to the Vatican Instruction*. Washington, D.C.: Georgetown University Press, 1990.

Ramsey, Paul. "Shall We Reproduce?" *JAMA* 220 (5 June 1972): 1346–1350.

Raymond, Janice G. *Women as Wombs: Reproductive Technologies and the Battle over Women's Freedom*. New York: HarperCollins, 1993.

Robertson, John A. *Autonomy and Ambivalence: Reproductive Technology and the Limits of Procreative Liberty*. Princeton: Princeton University Press, 1994.

———. *Children of Choice: Freedom and the New Reproductive Technologies*. Princeton, N.J.: Princeton University Press, 1994.

Rothenberg, Karen H. "Gestational Surrogacy and the Health Care Provider: Put Part of the 'IVF Genie' Back in the Bottle." *Law, Medicine and Health Care* 18 (1990): 345–352.

Rothman, Barbara Katz. "Not All That Glitters Is Gold." *Hastings Center Report* 22 (Supplement; July/August 1992): S11–S15.

Rowland, Robyn. *Living Laboratories: Women and Reproductive Technology*. Bloomington: Indiana University Press, 1992.

Royal Commission on New Reproductive Technologies. *Proceed with Care: Final Report of the Royal Commission on New Reproductive Technologies*. Ottowa, Ontario: Canada Communications Group-Publishing, 1993.

Ryan, Maura A. "The Argument for Unlimited Procreative Liberty: A Feminist Critique." *Hastings Center Report* 20 (July/August 1990): 6–12.

Satz, Debra. "Markets in Women's Reproductive Labor." *Philosophy and Public Affairs* 21 (1992): 107–131.

Shannon, Thomas A. *Surrogate Motherhood: The Ethics of Using Human Beings*. New York: Crossroad, 1989.

Singer, Peter and Deane Wells. *Making Babies: The New Science and Ethics of Conception*. New York: Scribner's, 1985.

Steinbock, Bonnie. *Life Before Birth: The Moral and Legal Status of Embryos and Fetuses*. New York: Oxford University Press, 1992.

Tennessee, Supreme Court. Davis v. Davis. *Southwestern Reporter*, SW.2d 842, 588–604 (1992).

United States, Congress, Office of Technology Assessment. *Infertility: Medical and Social Choices*. Washington, D.C.: U.S. Government Printing Office. May, 1988.

Walters, LeRoy. "Ethics and New Reproductive Technologies: An International Review of Committee Statements." *Hastings Center Report* 17 (Supplement; June 1987): 3–9.

Warnock, Mary, and United Kingdom, Department of Health and Social Security. Committee of Inquiry into Human Fertilisation and Embryology. *A Question of Life: The Warnock Report on Human Fertilisation and Embryology*. New York: Basil Blackwell, 1985.

Warnock, Mary. "Ethical Challenges in Embryo Manipulation." *British Medical Journal* 304 (18 April 1992): 1045–1049.

Wikler, Daniel and Norma J. Wikler. "Turkey-Baster Babies: The Demedicalization of Artificial Insemination." *Milbank Quarterly* 69(1) (1991): 5–40.

Part IV: Resources

Chapter 9: Acquiring and Allocating Scarce Medical Resources

American Medical Association, Council on Ethical and Judicial Affairs. "Strategies for Cadaveric Organ Procurement, Mandated Choice and Presumed Consent." *JAMA* 272(10) (1994): 809–812.

American Medical Association Judicial Council. "Ethical Guidelines for Organ Transplantation." *JAMA* 25 (1968): 341–342.

Beecher, Henry K. "Scarce Resources and Medical Advancement." In Paul Freund, ed. *Experimentation with Human Subjects*. New York: George Braziller, 1970.

Campbell, Courtney S. "The Selling of Organs, the Sharing of Self." *Second Opinion* 19(2) (1993): 69–79.

Caplan, Arthur L. "Assume Nothing: The Current State of Cadaver Organ and Tissue Donation in the United States." *Journal of Transplant Coordination* 1 (1991): 78–83.

———. *If I Were a Rich Man Could I Buy a Pancreas? and Other Essays on the Ethics of Health Care*. Bloomington: Indiana University Press, 1992.

———. "Must I Be My Brother's Keeper? Ethical Issues in the Use of Living Donors as Sources of Liver and Other Solid Organs." *Transplantation Proceedings* 25(2) (April 1993): 1997–2000.

Childress, James F. "Ethics, Public Policy, and Human Fetal Tissue Transplantation Research." *Kennedy Institute of Ethics Journal* 1(2) (June 1991): 93–121.

Cohen, Cynthia B. and Albert R. Jonsen, for The National Advisory Board on Ethics in Reproduction. "The Future of the Fetal Tissue Bank." *Science* 262(5140) (1993): 1663–1665.

Daniels, Norman. "Cost-Effectiveness and Patient Welfare." In Marc Basson, ed. *Rights and Responsibilities in Medicine*. New York: Alan R. Liss, 1981, pp. 159–170.

———. "Am I My Parents' Keeper?" *Midwest Studies in Philosophy* VII (1982): 517–540.

Dougherty, Charles J. "The Right to Health Care: First Aid in the Emergency Room." *Public Law Forum* 4(1) (1984): 101–128.

———. "A Proposal for Ethical Organ Donation." *Health Affairs* 5(3) (Fall 1986): 105–110.

Engelhardt, H. Tristram, Jr., "Shattuck Lecture: Allocating Scarce Medical Resources and the Availability of Organ Transplantation: Some Moral Presuppositions." *New England Journal of Medicine* 331(1) (5 July 1984): 66–71.

Evans, Roger W. "Health Care Technology and the Inevitability of Resource Allocation and Rationing Decisions." Parts I and II. *JAMA* 249 (15 and 16) (15 and 22/29 April 1983): 2047–2053, 2208–2219.

Fox, R. C. and J. P. Swazey. *The Courage to Fail: A Social View of Organ Transplants and Dialysis*. Chicago: University of Chicago Press, 1974.

Fox, Renée C. and Judith P. Swazey. *Spare Parts: Organ Replacement in American Society*. New York: Oxford University Press, 1992.

Gaston, Robert S. et al. "Racial Equity in Renal Transplantation: The Disparate Impact of HLA-Based Allocation." *JAMA* 270(11) (1993): 1352–1356.

Gerrand, Nicole. "Creating Embryos for Research." *Journal of Applied Philosophy* 10(2) (1993): 175–187.

———. "The Notion of Gift-Giving and Organ Donation." *Bioethics* 8(2) (1994): 127–150.

Hanink, J. G. "On the Survival Lottery." *Philosophy* 51 (1976): 223–225. Criticism of John Harris's "The Survival Lottery."

Harris, John. "The Survival Lottery." *Philosophy* 50 (1975): 81–87. Argues that perfection of transplants would make it right to sacrifice a healthy person chosen by lottery to save lives of several people needing organs.

Harrison, Michael R. "Organ Procurement for Children: The Anencephalic Fetus as Donor." *Lancet* 2 (December 1986): 1383–1386.

——— **and Gilbert Meilander.** "The Anencephalic Newborn as Organ Donor." *Hastings Center Report* 16 (April 1986): 21–23.

Jecker, Nancy S. and Alfred O. Berg. "Allocating Medical Resources in Rural America: Alternative Perceptions of Justice." *Social Science and Medicine* 34(5) (1992): 467–474.

Kass, Leon R. "Organs for Sale? Propriety, Property, and the Price of Progress," *Public Interest* 107 (Spring 1992): 65–86.

Nelson, James Lindemann. "The Rights and Responsibilities of Potential Organ Donors: A Communitarian Approach." Position Paper for the Communitarian Network and for *The Responsive Community: Rights and Responsibilities*, 1992.

"New Medical Technologies: Economic, Ethical, and Political Considerations for Policy." *Journal of Social Issues* 49(2) (1993): 1–211.

Peters, David A. "Protecting Autonomy in Organ Procurement Procedures: Some Overlooked Issues." *Milbank Memorial Fund Quarterly* 64(2) (1986): 241–270.

Rhoads, Steven E. "How Much Should We Spend to Save a Life?" *Public Interest* 51 (Spring 1978): 74–92.

———. "The Sale of Human Body Parts." *Michigan Law Review* 72 (1974): 1182–1264.

———. "Scarce Medical Resources." *Columbia Law Review* 69 (1969): 620–692.

Robertson, John A. "Extracorporeal Embryos and the Abortion Debate." *Journal of Contemporary Health Law and Policy* 2 (Spring 1986): 53–70.

———. "Supply and Distribution of Hearts for Transplantation: Legal, Ethical, and Policy Issues." *Circulation* 75 (January 1987): 77–87.

Ross, Lainie Friedman. "Justice for Children: The Child as Organ Donor." *Bioethics* 8(2) (1994): 105–126.

Sanner, Margareta. "Attitudes toward Organ Donation and Transplantation: A Model for Understanding Reactions to Medical Procedures after Death." *Social Science and Medicine* 38(8) (1994): 1141–1152.

Schiffer, R. M. and Benjamin Freedman. "Case Studies in Bioethics: The Last Bed in the ICU." *Hastings Center Report* 7 (December 1977): 21–22.

Ubel, Peter A. et al. "Rationing Failure: The Ethical Lessons of the Retransplantation of Scarce Vital Organs." *JAMA* 270(20) (1993): 2469–2474.

U.S. Department of Health and Human Services, Task Force on Organ Transplantation. *Report of the Task Force on Organ Transplantation: Issues and Recommendations.* Washington, D.C.: DHHS, 1986.

Veatch, Robert M. "Research on 'Big Ticket' Items: Ethical Implications for Equitable Access." *Journal of Law, Medicine, & Ethics* 22(2) (1994): 148–151.

Winslow, Gerald R. *Triage and Justice: The Ethics of Rationing Life-Saving Medical Resources.* Berkeley: University of California Press, 1982.

Youngner, Stuart J. et al. "Psychosocial and Ethical Implications of Organ Retrieval." *New England Journal of Medicine* 313(5) (1 August 1985): 321–324.

Chapter 10: The Claim to Health Care

Barry, Robert L. and Gerard V. Bradley, eds. *Set No Limits: A Rebuttal to Daniel Callahan's Proposal to Limit Health Care for the Elderly.* Urbana: University of Illinois Press, 1991.

Battin, Margaret P. "Age Rationing and the Just Distribution of Health Care: Is There a Duty to Die?" *Ethics* 97 (January 1987): 317–340.

Bayer, Ronald, Arthur Caplan, and Norman Daniels, eds. *In Search of Equity: Health Needs and the Health Care System.* New York: Plenum Press, 1983.

Bayles, Michael D. "National Health Insurance and Non-Covered Services." *Journal of Health Politics, Policy and Law* 2 (Fall 1977): 335–348.

Binstock, Robert H. and Stephen G. Post, eds. *Too Old for Health Care? Controversies in Medicine, Law, Economics, and Ethics.* Baltimore: Johns Hopkins University Press, 1991, pp. 92–119.

Blank, Robert. *Rationing Medicine.* New York: Columbia University Press, 1988.

Bole, Thomas J. and William B. Bondeson, eds. *Rights to Health Care.* Boston: Kluwer Academic Publishers, 1991.

Brock, Dan W. "Justice, Health Care, and the Elderly." *Philosophy & Public Affairs* 18 (1989): 297–312.

Brock, Dan W. and Norman Daniels. "Ethical Foundations of the Clinton Administration's Proposed Health Care System." *JAMA* 271(15) (1994): 1189–1196.

Buchanan, Allen. "Health-Care Delivery and Resource Allocation." In **Robert M. Veatch, ed.** *Medical Ethics.* Boston: Jones and Bartlett, 1989, pp. 291–327.

Byrne, Peter, ed. *Health, Rights and Resources: King's College Studies 1987–1988.* London: Oxford University Press, 1988.

Califano, Joseph A., Jr. *America's Health Care Revolution: Who Lives? Who Dies? Who Pays?* New York: Random House, 1986.

Callahan, Daniel. "How Much Is Enough? A National Perspective." *Alabama Journal of Medical Sciences* 17 (January 1980): 76–80.

———. "Adequate Health Care and an Aging Society: Are They Morally Compatible?" *Daedalus* (Winter 1986): 247–267.

———. *Setting Limits: Medical Goals in an Aging Society.* New York: Simon & Schuster, 1987.

——— **and Bruce Jennings, eds.** *Ethics, the Social Sciences, and Policy Analysis.* New York: Plenum Press, 1983.

———. *What Kind of Life: The Limits of Medical Progress.* New York: Simon & Schuster, 1990.

———. "Rationing Medical Progress: The Way to Affordable Health Care." *New England Journal of Medicine* 322 (21 June 1990): 1810–1813.

———. "Reforming the Health Care System for Children and the Elderly to Balance Cure and Care." *Academic Medicine* 67(4) (April 1992): 219–222.

———. "Symbols, Rationality, and Justice: Rationing Health Care." *American Journal of Law and Medicine* 18(1–2) (1992): 1–13.

———. "What Is a Reasonable Demand on Health Care Resources? Designing a Basic Package of Benefits." *Journal of Contemporary Health Law and Policy* 8(1) (Spring 1992): 1–12.

Capron, Alexander Morgan. "Oregon's Disability: Principles or Politics?" *Hastings Center Report* 22 (November/December 1992): 18–20.

Catholic Health Association. *With Justice for All? The Ethics of Healthcare Rationing.* St. Louis: CHA, 1991.

Chapman, Audrey R., ed. *Health Care Reform: A Human Rights Approach.* Washington, D.C.: Georgetown University Press, 1994.

Childress, James F. *Priorities in Biomedical Ethics.* Philadelphia: Westminster Press, 1981.

Churchill, Larry M. *Rationing Health Care in America: Perceptions and Principles of Justice.* Notre Dame, Ind.: University of Notre Dame Press, 1987.

———. *Self-Interest and Universal Health Care: Why Well-Insured Americans Should Support Coverage for Everyone.* Cambridge, Mass.: Harvard University Press, 1994.

Daniels, Norman. *Just Health Care.* New York: Cambridge University Press, 1985.

———. *Am I My Parents' Keeper? An Essay on Justice Between the Young and the Old.* New York: Oxford University Press, 1988.

———. "Cost Containment and Justice." *Mount Sinai Journal of Medicine* 56 (1989): 180–184.

———. "Insurability and the HIV Epidemic: Ethical Issues in Underwriting." *Milbank Quarterly* 68 (1990): 497–525.

———. "Liberalism and Medical Ethics." *Responsive Community* 3(3) (Summer 1993): 45–48.

Dougherty, Charles J. "Setting Health Care Priorities: Oregon's Next Steps." *Hastings Center Report* 21 (May/June 1991): S1–S10.

Eddy, David M. "Rationing by Patient Choice." *JAMA* 265 (2 January 1991): 105–108.

———. "The Individual vs. Society: Resolving the Conflict." *JAMA* 265 (8 May 1991): 2399–2401, 2405–2406.

———. "What's Going On in Oregon?" *JAMA* 266 (17 July 1991): 417–420.

———. "Will Controlling Costs Require Rationing Services?" *JAMA* 272(4) (1994): 324–328.

Emanuel, Ezekiel J. and Allan S. Brett. "Managed Competition and the Patient-Physician Relationship." *New England Journal of Medicine* 329(12) (1993): 879–882.

Emanuel, Ezekiel J. and Linda L. Emanuel. "The Economics of Dying: The Illusion of Cost Savings at the End of Life." *NEJM* 330(8) (1994): 540–544.

Epstein, Arnold M. "Changes in the Delivery of Care under Comprehensive Health Care Reform." *NEJM* 329(22) (1993): 1672–1676.

Fleck, Leonard M. "Justice, HMOs, and the Invisible Rationing of Health Care Resources." *Bioethics* 4 (1990): 97–120.

Fried, Charles. "Rights and Health Care—Beyond Equity and Efficiency." *New England Journal of Medicine* 293 (31 July 1975): 241–245.

———. "Equality and Rights in Medical Care." *Hastings Center Report* 6 (February 1976): 29–34.

Fuchs, Victor R. *The Future of Health Policy.* Cambridge, Mass.: Harvard University Press, 1993.

Garland, Michael J. "Justice, Politics, and Community: Expanding Access and Rationing Health Services in Oregon." *Law, Medicine and Health Care* 20 (1992): 67–81.

Green, Ronald M. "The Priority of Health Care." *Journal of Medicine and Philosophy* 8 (1983): 373–380.

Hadorn, David C. "The Problem of Discrimination in Health Care Priority Setting." *JAMA* 268 (16 September 1992): 1454–1459.

Health Affairs 10 (1991). Special issue on "Rationing." See essays by Daniel M. Fox, Amitai Etzioni, and Daniel Callahan.

Hackler, Chris, ed. *Health Care for an Aging Population.* New York: State University of New York Press, 1994.

"Health Care Policy in America." *National Forum* 73(3) (Summer 1993): 2–48.

Hiatt, Howard H. "Protecting the Medical Commons: Who Is Responsible?" *New England Journal of Medicine* 293 (31 July 1975): 235–241.

———. *America's Health in the Balance: Choice or Chance?* New York: Harper & Row, 1987.

Iglehart, John K., ed. "Special Issue: HMO's." *Health Affairs* 5(1) (Spring 1986).

Jecker, Nancy S. "Age-Based Rationing and Women." *JAMA* 266(21) (4 December 1991): 3012–3015.

———. "Can an Employer-Based Health Insurance System Be Just?" *Journal of Health Politics, Policy and Law* 18(3) (1993): 657–673.

Jennings, Bruce, Daniel Callahan, and Arthur Caplan. "Ethical Challenges of Chronic Illness." *Hastings Center Report* 18 (March 1988): S1–S16.

Journal of the American Geriatrics Society 40 (1992). Special issue on "Ethics and Rationing."

Journal of Medicine and Philosophy 4 (1979). Special issue on "The Right to Health Care."

Journal of Medicine and Philosophy 13 (1988). Special issue on "Justice Between Generations and Health Care for the Elderly."

Kamm, Frances M. *Morality, Mortality. Vol. 1. Death and Whom to Save From It.* New York: Oxford University Press, 1993.

Lamm, Richard D. "Infinite Needs—Finite Resources: The Future of Healthcare." *Cambridge Quarterly of Healthcare Ethics* 3(1) (1994): 83–98.

La Puma, John. "Quality-Adjusted Life Years: Ethical Implications and the Oregon Plan." *Issues in Law and Medicine* (1992): 429–441.

"Managed Competition: Health Reform American Style?" *Health Affairs* (Supplement; 1993): 7–299.

McBride, David. "Black America: From Community Health Care to Crisis Medicine." *Journal of Health Politics, Policy and Law* 18(2) (Summer 1993): 319–337.

Mechanic, David. *The Growth of Bureaucratic Medicine: An Inquiry into the Dynamics of Patient Behavior and the Organization of Medical Care.* New York: Wiley, 1976.

———. "Rationing Health Care: Public Policy and the Medical Marketplace." *Hastings Center Report* 6 (1976): 34–37.

———. "Approaches to Controlling the Costs of Medical Care: Short-Range Alternatives." *New England Journal of Medicine* 298 (2 February 1978): 249–254.

———. *From Advocacy to Allocation: The Evolving American Health Care System.* New York: Free Press, 1986.

———. "Mental Health Services in the Context of Health Insurance Reform." *Milbank Quarterly* 71(3) (1993): 349–364.

———. "Managed Care: Rhetoric and Realities." *Inquiry* 31 (1994): 124–128.

———. "Trust and Informed Consent to Rationing." *Milbank Quarterly* 72(2) (1994): 217–223.

Menzel, Paul. *Medical Costs, Moral Choices.* New Haven, Conn.: Yale University Press, 1983.

———. *Strong Medicine: The Ethical Rationing of Health Care.* New York: Oxford University Press, 1990.

———. "At Law—Oregon's Denial: Disabilities and Quality of Life." *Hastings Center Report* 22 (November/December 1992): 21–25.

———. "Equality, Autonomy, and Efficiency: What Health Care System Should We Have?" *Journal of Medicine & Philosophy* 17 (1992): 33–57.

———. "Some Ethical Costs of Rationing." *Law, Medicine and Health Care* 20 (1992): 57–66.

Nelson, Robert M. and Theresa Drought. "Justice and the Moral Acceptability of Rationing Medical Care: The Oregon Experiment." *Journal of Medicine and Philosophy* 17 (1992): 97–117.

Omenn, Gilbert S. and Douglas A. Conrad. "Implications of DRGs for Clinicians." *New England Journal of Medicine* 311 (15 November 1984): 1314–1317.

Outka, Gene. "Social Justice and Equal Access to Health Care." *Journal of Religious Ethics* 2 (1974): 11–32.

Pellegrino, Edmund D. "Rationing Health Care: The Ethics of Medical Gatekeeping." *Journal of Contemporary Health Law and Policy* 2 (Spring 1986): 23–45.

President's Commission for the Study of Ethical Problems in Medicine and Biomedical and Behavioral Research. *Securing Access to Health Care: The Differences in the Availability of Health Services.* Washington, D.C.: President's Commission, 1982.

Raffel, Marshall W., ed. *Comparative Health Systems: Descriptive Analyses of Fourteen National Health Systems.* University Park: Pennsylvania State University Press, 1984.

Randall, Vernellia R. "Racist Health Care: Reforming an Unjust Health Care System to Meet the Needs of African-Americans." *Health Matrix* 3(127) (1993): 127–194.

Reinhardt, Uwe E. "An American Paradox." *Health Progress* (November 1986).

Reiser, Stanley J. "Consumer Competence and the Reform of Health Care." *JAMA* 267(11) (18 March 1992): 1511–1515.

Relman, Arnold S. "The Trouble with Rationing." *New England Journal of Medicine* 323 (27 September 1990): 911–913.

Russell, Louise B. "Some of the Tough Decisions Required by a National Health Plan." *Science* 246 (17 November 1989): 892–896.

Sass, Hans-Martin, and Robert U. Massey, eds. *Health Care Systems: Moral Conflicts in European and American Public Policy.* Boston: Kluwer Academic, 1988.

Shelp, Earl, ed. *Justice and Health Care.* Boston: D. Reidel, 1981.

Smeeding, Timothy M., ed. *Should Medical Care Be Rationed by Age?* Totowa, N.J.: Rowman and Littlefield, 1987.

Steinbrook, Robert and Bernard Lo. "The Oregon Medicaid Demonstration Project—Will It Provide Adequate Medical Care?" *NEJM* 326(5) (30 January 1992): 340–344.